GOVERNMENT ASSISTANCE ALMANAC
★2006-2007★

GOVERNMENT ASSISTANCE ALMANAC
★ 2006-2007 ★

The Guide to Federal Domestic Financial and Other Programs

Covering Grants, Loans, Insurance, Personal Payments and Benefits, Subsidies, Fellowships, Scholarships, Traineeships, Technical Information, Advisory Services, Investigation of Complaints, Sales and Donations of Federal Property — with Funding Summaries, over 4,000 Program Headquarters and Field Office Addresses and Phone Numbers, an Agency Index, and a Comprehensive Master Index

★ **TWENTIETH EDITION** ★

by J. Robert Dumouchel

Omnigraphics

615 Griswold Street, Detroit, MI 48226
Phone (800) 234-1340 • Fax (800) 875-1340 • www.omnigraphics.com

GOVERNMENT ASSISTANCE ALMANAC 2006–07:
The Guide to Federal Domestic Financial and Other Programs Covering Grants, Loans, Insurance, Personal Payments and Benefits, Subsidies, Fellowships, Scholarships, Traineeships, Technical Information, Advisory Services, Investigation of Complaints, Sales and Donations of Federal Property — with Funding Summaries, Over 4,000 Program Headquarters and Field Office Addresses and Phone Numbers, and a Comprehensive Master Index

by J. Robert Dumouchel

Co-published and distributed by:

Omnigraphics, Inc.
Ford Building
Detroit, Michigan 48226

Co-published by:

Foggy Bottom Publications
P.O. Box N-7776
Nassau, Bahamas

All rights reserved. No part of this book may be reproduced or transmitted in any form or by any means, electronic or mechanical, including photocopying, recording, or by any information storage and retrieval system, without written permission from the author and the publisher, except for the inclusion of brief quotations in a review.

Copyright © 2006 by J. Robert Dumouchel
Printed in the United States of America

The Library of Congress has assigned the following International Standard Serial Number:

ISSN 0883-8690

Library of Congress card number: **86-658073**

International Standard Book Number:

ISBN 0-7808-0701-4

CONTENTS

Abbreviations Used in This Book ix

PART I. Obtaining Federal Assistance

What This Book Gives You 1
Timeliness of the Information 3
Domestic Assistance Program Totals 1984-2006 (table) 4
Types of Federal Assistance Available 4
Resources for the Resourceful 8
Who May Obtain Federal Assistance? 10
Organization of the Federal Programs in This Book 12
Red Tape—Should You Hire a Consultant? 13
Obtaining Federal Assistance—How to Use Part II 15
   Step One: Use the Master Index 15
   Step Two: "Read" a Federal Program 17
   Step Three: Ask the Right Questions 24
   Step Four: Complete Your Homework 26
Finding More Information 26

PART II. Program Information

(*Note: the organization and sequence of the described programs are explained on page 12. For an* alphabetical listing *of administrative units and sub-units consult the* **AGENCY INDEX** *beginning on page 871.*)

DEPARTMENT OF AGRICULTURE 31
DEPARTMENT OF COMMERCE 109
DEPARTMENT OF DEFENSE 143
DEPARTMENT OF HOUSING AND URBAN
   DEVELOPMENT 158
DEPARTMENT OF THE INTERIOR 200
DEPARTMENT OF JUSTICE 247
DEPARTMENT OF LABOR 286
DEPARTMENT OF STATE 305
DEPARTMENT OF TRANSPORTATION 316
DEPARTMENT OF THE TREASURY 335
APPALACHIAN REGIONAL COMMISSION 337
OFFICE OF PERSONNEL MANAGEMENT 339

COMMISSION ON CIVIL RIGHTS	341
EQUAL EMPLOYMENT OPPORTUNITY COMMISSION	342
FEDERAL COMMUNICATIONS COMMISSION	345
FEDERAL MARITIME COMMISSION	345
FEDERAL MEDIATION AND CONCILIATION SERVICE	346
FEDERAL TRADE COMMISSION	346
GENERAL SERVICES ADMINISTRATION	347
GOVERNMENT PRINTING OFFICE	349
LIBRARY OF CONGRESS	350
NATIONAL AERONAUTICS AND SPACE ADMINISTRATION	351
NATIONAL CREDIT UNION ADMINISTRATION	352
NATIONAL FOUNDATION ON THE ARTS AND THE HUMANITIES	353
NATIONAL LABOR RELATIONS BOARD	362
NATIONAL SCIENCE FOUNDATION	363
RAILROAD RETIREMENT BOARD	367
SECURITIES AND EXCHANGE COMMISSION	368
SMALL BUSINESS ADMINISTRATION	369
DEPARTMENT OF VETERANS AFFAIRS	378
ENVIRONMENTAL PROTECTION AGENCY	393
NATIONAL GALLERY OF ART	432
OVERSEAS PRIVATE INVESTMENT CORPORATION	432
COMMODITY FUTURES TRADING COMMISSION	433
DEPARTMENT OF ENERGY	434
DEPARTMENT OF EDUCATION	443
HARRY S TRUMAN SCHOLARSHIP FOUNDATION	495
CHRISTOPHER COLUMBUS FELLOWSHIP FOUNDATION	496
BARRY M. GOLDWATER SCHOLARSHIP FELLOWSHIP FOUNDATION	496
WOODROW WILSON INTERNATIONAL CENTER FOR SCHOLARS	497
MORRIS K. UDALL SCHOLARSHIP AND EXCELLENCE IN NATIONAL ENVIRONMENTAL POLICY FOUNDATION	497
JAMES MADISON MEMORIAL FELLOWSHIP FOUNDATION	498
SMITHSONIAN INSITUTION	499
PENSION BENEFIT GUARANTY CORPORATION	500

ARCHITECTURAL AND TRANSPORTATION
    BARRIERS COMPLIANCE BOARD............... 500
NATIONAL ARCHIVES AND RECORDS
    ADMINISTRATION.............................. 501
DENALI COMMISSION 502
DELTA REGIONAL AUTHORITY 502
JAPAN-U.S. FRIENDSHIP COMMISSION 504
ELECTIONS ASSISTANCE COMMISSION 504
UNITED STATES INSTITUTE OF PEACE 505
DEPARTMENT OF HEALTH AND HUMAN SERVICES .. 506
CORPORATION FOR NATIONAL AND COMMUNITY
    SERVICE... 644
SOCIAL SECURITY ADMINISTRATION 648
DEPARTMENT OF HOMELAND SECURITY 652
UNITED STATES AGENCY FOR INTERNATIONAL
    DEVELOPMENT 680

PART III. Program Funding Levels—Summary Tables 687

    Table 1. Estimated Outlays/Credits for All Domestic
    Assistance Programs, by Administrative Entity
    (FY 03, 04, 05, 06)................................ 689
    Table 2. Summary of Estimated Outlays/Credits, by
    Federal Department or Agency (FY 03, 04, 05, 06) 725
    Table 3. The Fifty Largest Domestic Assistance Programs
    in FY 2005, by Funds Outlayed and/or Credited 729
    Table 4. The Fifty Smallest Domestic Assistance Programs
    in FY 2005, by Funds Outlayed and/or Credited 730

PART IV. Field Office Contacts 731

AGENCY INDEX 871

MASTER INDEX 881

DISCLAIMER/INVITATION

We have attempted to compile and present the information in this book accurately and in the most helpful form possible. The information is intended to provide basic guidance concerning programs and benefits available from the federal agencies cited.

Federal program policies, regulations, funding levels, addresses, and phone numbers tend to change. There could be unintentional errors in the information, caused by changes in government programs or organization, inaccuracies in the source material, omissions, or typographical or other inadvertent mistakes. A great deal of care was taken to avoid such errors.

The information in this publication was compiled from the sources cited and from other sources considered reliable. While every possible effort has been made to ensure reliability, the publisher and the editor will not assume liability for damages caused by inaccuracies in the data, and make no warranty, express or implied, on the accuracy of the information contained herein.

Users of *GOVERNMENT ASSISTANCE ALMANAC* are invited to send their observations about the book, its form, and their experience in referring to the information, to the editor at the address below. Suggestions for improvements in any aspect of the book will be especially appreciated.

> J. Robert Dumouchel, Editor
> GOVERNMENT ASSISTANCE ALMANAC
> c/o Omnigraphics, Inc.
> Ford Building
> Detroit, MI 48226

Abbreviations Used in This Book

ACF	Administration for Children and Families (HHS)
ADA	Americans with Disabilities Act
ADAA	Anti-Drug Abuse Act of 1988
AFDC	Aid to Families with Dependent Children
AIDS	acquired immunodeficiency syndrome
AMS	Agricultural Marketing Service (USDA)
AOA	Administration on Aging (HHS)
ARDA	Appalachian Regional Development Act of 1965
ARDRA	Appalachian Regional Development Reform Act of 1998
ARS	Agricultural Research Service (USDA)
ATEDPA	Anti-Terrorism and Effective Death Penalty Act of 1996
ATELS	Apprenticeship, Training, Employer and Labor Service (DOL)
ATF	Bureau of Alcohol, Tobacco and Firearms (DOJ)
AREERA	Agricultural Research, Extension, and Education Reform Act of 1998
BAT	Bureau of Apprenticeship and Training (DOL) *(Note: BAT functions now are in OATELS)*
BEA	Bureau of Export Administration (USDC) *(Note: BEA is now Bureau of Industry and Security*
BECA	Bureau of Educational and Cultural Affairs (Department of State)
BIA	Bureau of Indian Affairs (DOI)
BJA	Bureau of Justice Assistance (DOJ)
BLM	Bureau of Land Management (DOI)
BLS	Bureau of Labor Statistics (DOI)
BPRM	Bureau of Population, Refugees, and Migration (Department of State)
C of C	chamber of commerce
CAA	Clean Air Act
CARE	Comprehensive AIDS Resources Emergency
CBRNE	chemical, biological, radiological, nuclear, and explosive (devices)
CCC	Commodity Credit Corporation (USDA)
CDAPCA	Comprehensive Drug Abuse Prevention and Control Act of 1970

CDBG	Community Development Block Grant
CDCP	Centers for Disease Control and Prevention (HHS)
CDCU	Community Development Credit Union
CDPVTEA	Carl D. Perkins Vocational and Technical Education Act of 1998
CEPP	Chemical Emergency Preparedness and Prevention
CERCLA	Comprehensive Environmental Response, Compensation and Liability Act ("Superfund")
CERT	Council of Energy Resource Tribes
CFDA	Catalog of Federal Domestic Assistance
CFRDA	Consolidated Farm and Rural Development Act
CJAA	Children's Justice and Assistance Act of 1986
CMHS	Center for Mental Health Services (SAMHSA-DHS)
CMS	Centers for Medicare and Medicaid Services (HHS) *(formerly, HCFA)*
CNCS	Corporation for National and Community Service
COATES	Community Opportunities, Accountability, Training, and Educational Services Act of 1998
CODIS	Combined DNA Index System
COPS	Community Oriented Policing Services
CPD	Community Planning and Development (HUD)
CRA	Civil Rights Act of 1964
CRIPA	Civil Rights of Institutionalized Persons Act
CRP	Conservation Reserve Program
CRS	Community Relations Service (DOJ)
CSAP	Center for Substance Abuse Prevention (SAHMSA-HHS)
CSAT	Center for Substance Abuse Treatment (SAHMSA-HHS)
CSBG	Community Services Block Grant
CSREES	Cooperative State Research, Education and Extension Service (USDA)
CWA	Clean Water Act
DC	District of Columbia
DEA	Drug Enforcement Administration (DOJ)
DHS	Department of Homeland Security
DIC	dependency and indemnity compensation
DOD	Department of Defense
DOE	Department of Energy
DOED	Department of Education
DOI	Department of the Interior
DOJ	Department of Justice

DOL	Department of Labor
DOT	Department of Transportation
DVA	Department of Veterans Affairs
EBS	Emergency Broadcast System
EBSA	Employee Benefits Security Administration (DOL)
ECOA	Equal Credit Opportunity Act
EDA	Economic Development Administration (USDC)
EEOC	Equal Employment Opportunity Commission
EFN	exceptional financial need
EHS	environmental health center
EIS	environmental impact statement
ELOA	Early Learning Opportunities Act of 2001
EMI	Emergency Management Institute (FEMA-DHS)
EMS	emergency medical services
EOC	emergency operating center
EPA	Environmental Protection Agency
ERDDIA	Educational Research, Development, Dissemination, and Improvement Act of 1994
ESA	Economics and Statistics Administration (USDA)
ESEA	Elementary and Secondary Education Act of 1965
ESL	English as a second language
EST.	estimate
ETA	Employment and Training Administration (DOL)
FAA	Federal Aviation Administration (DOT)
FACE	Freedom of Access to Clinic Entrances Act
FACTA	Food, Agriculture, Conservation, and Trade Act of 1990
FAIRA	Federal Agriculture Improvement and Reform Act of 1996
FAS	Foreign Agricultural Service (USDA)
FCA	Flood Control Act
FCC	Federal Communications Commission
FCIC	Federal Crop Insurance Corporation (USDA)
FDA	Food and Drug Administration (HHS)
FEMA	Federal Emergency Management Agency (DHS)
FFB	Federal Financing Bank
FFP	federal financial participation
FHA	Federal Housing Administration (HUD)
FHAP	Fair Housing Assistance Program
FHIP	Fair Housing Initiatives Program
FHWA	Federal Highway Administration (DOT)

FIFRA	Federal Insecticide, Fungicide, and Rodenticide Act
FIP	Forestry Incentives Program
FLAS	foreign language and area studies
FMCS	Federal Mediation and Conciliation Service
FMCSA	Federal Motor Carrier Safety Administration (DOT)
FmHA	Farmers Home Administration (USDA)
	(Note: FmHA functions now are within FSA and RHS)
FNS	Food and Nutrition Service (USDA)
FRA	Fund for Rural America
FS	Forest Service (USDA)
FSRIA	Farm Security and Rural Investment Act of 2002
FSA	Farm Service Agency (USDA)
FTA	Federal Transit Administration (DOT)
FTC	Federal Trade Commission
FTZ	foreign trade zone
FY	Fiscal Year *(Federal fiscal year: October 1 through September 30)*
FWS	U.S. Fish and Wildlife Service (DOI)
GAA	Government Assistance Almanac
GPO	U.S. Government Printing Office
GSA	General Services Administration
HBCU	Historically Black College and University
HCFA	Health Care Financing Administration (HHS)
	(Note: HCFA functions now are within CMS)
HEA	Higher Education Act of 1965
HEAL	Health Education Assistance Loan
HHS	Department of Health and Human Services
HIP	Housing Improvement Program (BIA)
HIV	human immunodeficiency virus
HMO	health maintenance organization
HOPE	Housing Opportunities for People Everywhere
HPEPA	Health Professions Education Partnership Act of 1998
HQ	headquarters
HRSA	Health Resources and Services Administration (HHS)
HSA	health system agency
HUD	Department of Housing and Urban Development
IBDC	Indian business development center

ICE	Immigration and Customs Enforcement (DHS) (*formerly*, INS)
IDEA	Individuals with Disabilities Education Act
IHE	institution of higher education
IHS	Indian Health Service (DHS)
IMLS	Institute of Museum and Library Services
INS	Immigration and Naturalization Service (DHS) (*Now, ICE*)
IRS	Internal Revenue Service
ISDEAA	Indian Self-Determination and Education Assistance Act
ITA	International Trade Administration (USDC)
JJDPA	Juvenile Justice and Delinquency Prevention Act
JTPA	Job Training Partnership Act of 1982
LC	Library of Congress
LEA	local education agency
LSCA	Library Services and Construction Act
MARC	minority access to research careers
MB&IA	minority business and industry association
MBDA	Minority Business Development Agency (USDC)
MBDC	minority business development center
MBE	minority business enterprise
MECEA	Mutual Educational and Cultural Exchange Act of 1961
MFB	marine and freshwater biology
MIA	missing in action
MIP	mortgage insurance premium
MMA	Medicare Modernization Act (i.e., Medicare Prescription Drug, Improvement and Modernization Act of 2003)
MMA	Merchant Marine Act
MPRSA	Marine Protection, Research, and Sanctuaries Act
MRA	Migration and Refugee Assistance Act of 1962
MSA	Metropolitan Statistical Area
MSLA	Museum and Library Services Act of 1996
MVHAA	McKinney-Vento Homeless Assistance Act
N.A.	not available, or not applicable
NAFSA	National Association of Foreign Student Advising Associations

NAHASDA	Native American Housing Assistance and Self-Determination Act of 1996
NARETPA	National Agricultural Research, Extension, and Teaching Policy Act of 1977
NASA	National Aeronautics and Space Administration
NASS	National Agricultural Statistics Service (USDA)
NBS	National Bureau of Standards (USDC) (*Note: as of 1988, NBS became NIST*)
NBSOA	National Bureau of Standards Organic Act
NCIC	National Crime Information Center
NCRR	National Center for Research Resources (HHS)
NCSA	National Community Service Act
NCSCI	National Center for Standards and Certification Information
NCUA	National Credit Union Administration
NEA	National Endowment for the Arts
NEH	National Endowment for the Humanities
NEIC	National Energy Information Center
NESDIS	National Environmental Satellite, Data, and Information Service
NFAHA	National Foundation on the Arts and Humanities Act of 1965
NFIP	National Flood Insurance Program
NHA	National Housing Act of 1934
NHSC	National Health Service Corps (HHS)
NIAAA	National Institute on Alcohol and Abuse and Alcoholism (HHS)
NIDA	National Institute on Drug Abuse (HHS)
NIEHS	National Institute of Environmental Health Sciences (HHS)
NIH	National Institutes of Health (HHS)
NIMH	National Institute of Mental Health (HHS)
NINDS	National Institute of Neurological Disorders and Stroke (HHS)
NIOSH	National Institute for Occupational Safety and Health (HHS)
NIS	New Independent States (of the former Soviet Union)
NIST	National Institute for Standards and Technology (USDC)
NLRB	National Labor Relations Board
NMFS	National Marine Fisheries Service (USDC)
NOAA	National Oceanic and Atmospheric Administration (USDC)
NOS	National Ocean Service (USDC)

NPS	National Park Service (DOI)
NRC	Nuclear Regulatory Commission
NRCS	Natural Resources Conservation Service (USDA)
NRSA	National Research Service Award
NSA	National Security Agency (DOD)
NSEP	National Security Education Program
NSF	National Science Foundation
NSFA	National Science Foundation Act of 1950
NSRDS	National Standard Reference Data System
NTIA	National Telecommunications and Information Administration (USDC)
NTIS	National Technical Information Service (USDC)
NWS	National Weather Service (NOAA-USDC)
OAA	Older Americans Act of 1965
OAR	Office of Air and Radiation (EPA)
OATELS	Office of Apprenticeship, Training, Employer and Labor Service (DOL)
OCCSSA	Omnibus Crime Control and Safe Streets Act
OCSE	Office of Child Support Enforcement
OEA	Office of Export Administration (USDC)
OECA	Office of Enforcement and Compliance Assurance (EPA)
OEERE	Office of Energy Efficiency and Renewable Energy (DOE)
OERI	Office of Educational Research and Improvement (DOED)
OESE	Office of Elementary and Secondary Education (DOED)
OFCCP	Office of Federal Contract Compliance Programs
OFHEO	Office of Fair Housing and Equal Opportunity (HUD)
OFSA	Office of Federal Student Aid (DOED)
OJJDP	Office of Juvenile Justice and Delinquency Prevention (DOJ)
OJP	Office of Justice Programs (DOJ)
OMB	Office of Management and Budget
OPDR	Office of Policy Development and Research (HUD)
OPE	Office of Postsecondary Education (DOED)
OPIC	Overseas Private Investment Corporation
OPM	Office of Personnel Management
OPPPTS	Office of Pollution Prevention, Pesticides, and Toxic Substances (EPA)
OS	Office of the Secretary
OSERS	Office of Special Education and Rehabilitative Services (DOED)

OSHA	Occupational Safety and Health Administration (DOL)
OSTI	Office of Scientific and Technical Information (USDC)
OSWER	Office of Solid Waste and Emergency Response (EPA)
OTAA	Office of Trade Adjustment Assistance
OVAE	Office of Vocational and Adult Education (DOED)
OW	Office of Water (EPA)
OWOW	Office of Wetlands, Oceans, and Watersheds (EPA)
PACA	Perishable Agricultural Commodities Act
PD&R	Office of Policy Development and Research (HUD)
PHPEPA	Public Health Professions Education Partnership Act of 1998
PHS	Public Health Service (HHS)
PHSA	Public Health Service Act
PIK	payment-in-kind
PL	Public Law
PR	Puerto Rico
PRM	Population, Refugees, and Migration *(Bureau of)* (Department of State)
PRNS	projects of regional and national significance
PRWORA	Personal Responsibility and Work Opportunity Reconciliation Act of 1996
PWBA	Pension and Welfare Benefits Administration (DOL) *(Note: PWBA is now EBSA)*
PWEDA	Public Works and Economic Development Act of 1965
R&D	research and development
RBCS	Rural Business-Cooperative Service (USDA)
RC&D	resource conservation and development
RCRA	Resource Conservation and Recovery Act
REA	Rural Electrification Act of 1936
REA	Rural Electrification Administration (USDA) *(Note: REA functions now are within RUS)*
REACH	Racial and Ethnic Approaches to Community Health
RHA	River and Harbor Act
RHS	Rural Housing Service (USDA)
RLUIPA	Religious Land Use and Institutionalized Persons Act
RMA	Research and Marketing Act of 1946
RMA	Risk Management Agency (USDA)
RSVP	Retired and Senior Volunteer Program
RUS	Rural Utilities Service (USDA)

SAMHSA	Substance Abuse and Mental Health Services Administration (HHS)
SARA	Superfund Amendments and Reauthorization Act
SBA	Small Business Administration
SBIC	Small Business Investment Center
SBIR	small business innovation research
SBIRPRA	Small Business Innovation Research Program Reauthorization Act of 1992
SBMHAA	Stewart B. McKinney Homeless Assistance Act of 1987
SBRDEA	Small Business Research and Development Enhancement Act of 1992
SCORE	Service Corps of Retired Executives (SBA)
SCS	Soil Conservation Service (USDA) *(Note: SCS functions now are within NRCS)*
SDWA	Safe Drinking Water Act
SEA	state education agency
SEOG	supplemental educational opportunity grant
SEPA	Science Education Partnership Award
SERCA	Special Emphasis Research Center Award
SESA	state employment security agency
SIG	shared instrumentation grant
SMSA	Standard Metropolitan Statistical Area
SPRANS	special projects of regional and national significance
SRM	Standard Reference Materials
SRO	single room occupancy
SSA	Social Security Act of 1935
SSA	Social Security Administration
SSBG	Social Services Block Grant
SSBIC	Specialized Small Business Investment Center
SSI	Supplemental Security Income
STORET	storage and retrieval
STTR	Small Business Technology Transfer
SWDA	Solid Waste Disposal Act
TANF	Temporary Assistance to Needy Families
TDD	telecommunications devices for the deaf
TDHE	Tribally-Designated Housing Authority
TERO	Tribal Employment Rights Office
TRIO	three—i.e., not an abbreviation *(Per DOED, when the "TRIO" programs began in the Division of Student Services, Office of Postsecondary Education, three*

xviii ABBREVIATIONS

	programs were established; the original nomenclature has remained.)
TSA	Transportation Security Administration (DHS)
TSCA	Toxic Substances Control Act
TVA	Tennessee Valley Authority *(Note: TVA programs were deleted from the CFDA in 2001)*
USAID	United States Agency for International Development
USAPA	U.S.A. Patriot Act of 2001 *(officially,* Uniting and Strengthening America by Providing Appropriate Tools Required to Intercept and Obstruct Terrorism Act of 2001)
U.S.C.	United States Code
USCG	U.S. Coast Guard (DHS)
USDA	U.S. Department of Agriculture
USDC	U.S. Department of Commerce
USDOD	U.S. Department of Defense
USFS	U.S. Forest Service (USDA)
USGPO	U.S. Government Printing Office
USGS	U.S. Geological Survey (DOI)
USIA	U.S. Information Agency *(Note: USIA no longer exists; its functions now are in BECA)*
USIP	U.S. Institute of Peace
USIS	U.S. Information Service
VA	Veterans Administration *(Note: as of 1989, VA became DVA)*
VAWA	Violence Against Women Act of 2000
VCCLEA	Violent Crime Control and Law Enforcement Act
VI	Virgin Islands (U.S.)
VISTA	Volunteers in Service to America
VOCA	Victims of Crime Act
VTVPA	Victims of Trafficking and Violence Prevention Act of 2000
WIA	Workforce Investment Act of 1998
WIC	Women, Infants, and Children
WIN	Work Incentive Program
WMD	weapons of mass destruction *(including nuclear, biological, chemical, and explosive)*

PART I

Obtaining Federal Assistance

What This Book Gives You

GOVERNMENT ASSISTANCE ALMANAC has two purposes: (1) to provide information enabling users to identify *all domestic programs offering financial or nonfinancial assistance available from federal agencies*; (2) to help users reach the point of obtaining assistance.

This twentieth annual edition describes 1,636 federal programs as the government approaches its Fiscal Year 2007, 90 of which were added during the last year. The information presented is based on data in the *Catalog of Federal Domestic Assistance* ("CFDA"), maintained by the General Services Administration pursuant to federal statute.

The *ALMANAC* reduces the information in the CFDA's approximately 2,500 pages to the essentials needed by most persons seeking federal assistance. Modifications in the presentation of the information, especially the *ALMANAC*'s indexes, enable users to identify available programs and their features more efficiently.

PART I provides *basic guidance on using this book* to identify and obtain available assistance. The guidelines are intended for newcomers to federal programs; more experienced users of similar information may find some helpful reminders.

PART II outlines *domestic financial and other assistance programs available per the CFDA as of February 1, 2006*. For each program the following is provided:

- federal program number and title; popular title when applicable;
- types of assistance available;
- description of objectives, permitted uses of funds, and project examples when they clarify program purposes; enacting legislation is noted to help define program purposes;

1

- eligibility factors concerning both applicants and beneficiaries;
- range and average amounts awarded through programs providing financial assistance;
- summary of recent activity;
- mailing address, phone number, and web site for program headquarters, and other referrals when applicable; generic e-mail addresses appearing in the CFDA.

PART III provides tables showing *funding levels for all programs and administering agencies* for the last *four fiscal years*. To our knowledge such comprehensive tables showing allocations specifically for federal domestic programs are exclusive to the *ALMANAC*. Table 1 also serves as a *listing of the programs in the numerical sequence* in which they appear in PART II. The *fifty largest and smallest programs* also are identified.

PART IV provides *addresses and phone numbers for more than 3,000 field offices*, organized to correspond with the program numbers within their purview. This system was established specifically for users of the *ALMANAC*; like the tables, this system exists nowhere else.

The **AGENCY INDEX** provides an *alphabetical listing of federal administrative units and sub-units,* including the program numbers within their purview. (The CFDA does not provide an alphabetical listing.) While administrative units also are incorporated within the MASTER INDEX, the AGENCY INDEX may expedite user searches specifically for these entities.

ALMANAC users will find the **MASTER INDEX** unique and exhaustive, particularly its subject headings, references, and cross-references. This index identifies all available federal domestic assistance programs. It also includes: administrative units and cross-references to sub-units; official and popular program titles; abbreviated program, agency, and other titles and terms; many enabling laws and their section and title numbers; and, general program references not found in other indexes of government assistance. The format enables users to distinguish programs providing financial assistance from those that do not, through the use of italicized program numbers. The copyright for *GOVERNMENT ASSISTANCE ALMANAC* makes its index an exclusive feature.

The list of **Abbreviations Used in This Book** preceding this section does not appear in the CFDA.

By definition, "domestic programs" do not necessarily include assistance available through ongoing government activities—e.g., operation of federal facilities and services, public information activities, enforcement of many federal laws and regulations, or products or services obtained through contractors, etc. The section entitled "Types of Federal Assistance Available," beginning on page 4, explains what assistance is and is not covered.

Encountering the information in this book for the first time, some will be surprised by the scope of available federal assistance, which may seem very broad or rather meager in many areas. The assistance is available subject to program eligibility criteria, discussed under "Who May Obtain Federal Assistance?"

Timeliness of the Information

The nineteenth edition of the *ALMANAC* (2004-05), based on CFDA-2004, identified 1,613 federal programs. During the last year 90 programs were added and 67 were deleted, producing the present total of 1,636 as of February 1, 2006; this twentieth edition incorporates the new programs, as well as program changes as of the CFDA-2005 released by GSA in August 2005 in its "on-line" version.

Federal programs rarely are terminated unless similar assistance is available through another program; this book helps identify those other programs. The accompanying table shows an almost steady increase in the total number of domestic programs since the mid-1980s.

Currently some 60 departments, commissions, agencies, bureaus, and other federal entities administer the assistance programs. They manage the programs either through their main offices, through 175 "administrative sub-units," or through approximately 3,000 field offices.

Regarding the reliability of addresses and phone numbers, generally, ten to twelve percent of phone numbers and five to seven percent of office addresses change in the course of a year, based on federal directories studied. It can reasonably be expected that few changes in program contact information will be encountered.

Changes are inevitable in program application requirements, governmental organization, and addresses and phone numbers. Keeping abreast of all changes would require a daily compilation, such as is

DOMESTIC ASSISTANCE PROGRAM TOTALS
1984 THROUGH 2006

(Per GOVERNMENT ASSISTANCE ALMANAC, 1st-20th editions.)

GAA 1985-86	—	989 programs in 1984
		1,013 programs in 1985
GAA 1988	—	1,025 programs in 1987
		1,052 programs in 1988
GAA 1989-90	—	1,117 programs in 1989
GAA 1990-91	—	1,157 programs in 1990
GAA 1991-92	—	1,183 programs in 1991
GAA 1992-93	—	1,246 programs in 1992
GAA 1993-94	—	1,288 programs in 1993
GAA 1994-95	—	1,335 programs in 1994
GAA 1995-96	—	1,370 programs in 1995
GAA 1996-97	—	1,392 programs in 1996
GAA 1997-98	—	1,327 programs in 1997
GAA 1998-99	—	1,368 programs in 1998
GAA 1999-00	—	1,386 programs in 1999
GAA 2000-01	—	1,424 programs in 2000
GAA 2001-02	—	1,454 programs in 2001
GAA 2002-03	—	1,479 programs in 2002
GAA 2003-04	—	1,499 programs in 2003
GAA 2004-05	—	1,557 programs in 2004
GAA 2005-06	—	1,613 programs in 2005
GAA 2006-07	—	1,636 programs in 2006

provided in the *Federal Register*. However, most substantive program changes affect the details of regulations, seldom affecting the factors included in the *ALMANAC*'s program entries; in pursuing programs with federal officials, inquirers will be advised of major changes.

Types of Federal Assistance Available

Fifteen types of federal domestic assistance are available through existing programs, providing financial or nonfinancial resources.

Programs that provide *financial assistance* are classified as:

Direct loans—offering the loan of federal funds for a specific term, with or without interest, with repayment expected. Example: FSA's "Emergency Loans" program provides USDA loans directly to farmers and others (see **10.404**).

Direct payments/specified use—providing funds for a specified purpose, with no repayment expected. Example: "Payments for Essential Air Services" to air carriers by DOT (see **20.901**).

Direct payments/unrestricted use—providing federal funds for use at will by the recipient, with no repayment expected. Example: "Social Security—Retirement Insurance," administered by SSA (see **96.002**). Programs in this classification may be known as "entitlements."

Formula grants—through which federal funds are distributed to states or other recipients according to a formula (often based on population), for continuing activities not confined to a specific project. No repayment is expected. Example: DOED's "Adult Education—State Grant Program" (see **84.002**). Programs in this classification also may be known as "entitlements."

Guaranteed/insured loans—offering private or public lending institutions a guarantee or insurance against loan defaults, covering all or a portion of the amount borrowed. Example: HUD's "Mortgage Insurance—Homes" program (see **14.117**).

Insurance—assuring reimbursement for losses under specified conditions. Insurance coverage may be provided directly by a federal agency or through a private company, depending on specific program provisions. Example: "Foreign Investment Insurance," administered by OPIC (see **70.003**). Some programs also provide for federal payment of a portion of insurance premiums. Example: USDA's "Crop Insurance" program (see **10.450**).

Project grants—awarding federal funds for specific projects, services, products, or other activities such as scholarships, construction, research, planning, technical assistance. Some project grants cover cooperative agreement arrangements with state governments or other organizations to assist the federal granting agency in the performance of a certain function. No repayment is expected. Project grants do not necessarily cover 100 percent of project costs. Example: NSF's "Geosciences" program (see **47.050**).

The classifications of programs providing *nonfinancial assistance* are:

Advisory services/counseling—through which federal specialists provide consultation, advice, or other assistance—delivered through conferences, workshops, personal contacts, or published information. Example: USDA-NRCS's "Soil and Water Conservation" program (see **10.902**).

Federal employment—offering jobs with the federal government through the activities of OPM in recruiting and hiring civilian personnel. Example: "Federal Summer Employment" (see **27.006**). Note that only OPM programs provide federal employment as structured programs; the ongoing recruitment activities of other federal agencies are not classified as "domestic programs."

Investigation of complaints—through which federal agencies examine or investigate claims of violations of federal laws, policies, or regulatory procedures. The claim must originate outside the federal government. Example: "Shipping—Investigation of Complaints," conducted by the Federal Maritime Commission (see **33.001**).

Sale, exchange, or donation of property and goods—featuring the transfer of federally-owned real estate or personal property, commodities, and other goods including equipment, food, drugs, or supplies. Example: "Disposal of Federal Surplus Real Property," administered by GSA **(39.002)**.

Specialized services—providing federal personnel to perform certain services for communities, individuals, or others. Example: "Planning Assistance to States," administered by the DOD-Corps of Engineers **(12.110)**. *(Note that several Corps of Engineers programs provide specialized services involving construction activities; however, these programs are not classified as providing financial assistance, and a portion of total costs for such projects usually must be matched locally.)*

Technical information—through which technical information is prepared, published, and distributed—often through clearinghouses, libraries, centers, or through electronic media. Example: USDC-NIST's "Standard Reference Materials" (see **11.604**).

Training—offering federal agency instruction to persons not employed by the federal government. Example: DHS-FEMA's "Emergency Management Institute (EMI)—Resident Educational Program" (see **97.028**).

Use of property, facilities, and equipment—providing for the temporary use of or access to federally-owned resources, with or without charge to the user. Example: "National Gallery of Art Extension Service" (see **68.001**).

Not included as a classification, but reflected in the list and included, are "block grants" which may be used for a range of related activities. Block grants usually are awarded as "formula grants" or "project grants." Their permitted uses generally are more flexible than other types of programs. Such programs are cited in the index under the subject heading "Block grant programs."

Many programs offer more than one type of assistance; for example, the second program listed in PART II, **10.025**, offers project grants as well as specialized services, advisory services/counseling, technical information, and training.

The following types of government activities are not defined as domestic programs; they are *not included*:

- *Procurement contracts* for the purchase of goods and services by the federal government. For instance, basic DOD contracting activities do not meet the definition of domestic programs; however, DOD administers several programs classified as providing "domestic assistance." Programs offering assistance to firms wanting to do business with the federal government through its procurement contracts *are included*.

- *U.S. government foreign activities* without a direct benefit in the domestic economy. For instance, most Department of State activities are not classified as domestic programs; however, the state department also administers several domestic programs; and, the federal government sponsors several programs pertaining to importing and exporting—which *are included*.

- *Employee recruitment programs* of individual federal departments and agencies.

- *Programs benefiting only current or retired military personnel or federal employees.* However, all DVA benefit programs *are included*—although many DVA programs are not classified as providing financial assistance.

- *Ongoing public information services* of federal entities.

- *Basic domestic functions of the federal government* such as operation and maintenance of services and facilities, collection of taxes, enforcement of federal laws and regulations, judicial processes, etc.

- *Smithsonian Institution programs*, several of which formerly were classified as "domestic programs" (and were included in early *ALMANAC* editions), but are no longer listed in the CFDA.

Also not included are various tax incentives offered through the Internal Revenue Code, which are not classified as federal programs. These include so-called tax shelters, tax credits, writeoffs, and the like. Such government benefits to private taxpayers have stimulated activity in the domestic economy in recent years. Their features are the subject of other books dealing with taxes, finance, investment, etc.

Frequently, however, such "non-programs" relate directly to certain structured domestic programs which *are included* in this book. Examples: program **15.904**, "Historic Preservation Fund Grants-in-Aid," can be used to obtain accelerated depreciation of the value of improvements for tax purposes; program **20.812**, "Construction Reserve Fund," relating to merchant vessels, offers tax incentives to participants.

Resources for the Resourceful

GOVERNMENT ASSISTANCE ALMANAC may reveal previously unknown resources available to various types of users—farmers, students, small businesses, investors, entrepreneurs, homemakers, scientists, the elderly, parents, journalists, civic and social organizations, health professionals, guidance counselors, scholars, state and municipal governments, educators, artists and arts sponsors, members of minority groups, veterans and their dependents, community improvement groups, researchers, and others including those interested in the needs of the foregoing groups, as well as persons planning to enter those fields. They may find programs that offer technical information, services, training, or other types of assistance that they did not know existed.

The simplest assistance programs are those meeting a single purpose. For instance, someone seeking resources for an elderly person whose home needs repairs will find that the index cites a number of programs that could provide help. Selecting the most appropriate of the available programs is a matter of finding the programs in the index, carefully reading the program entries in PART II, and pursuing the most promising. The section entitled "Obtaining Federal Assistance: How to Use PART II," beginning on page 15, provides guidance along these lines.

Frequently, assistance will be found for elderly persons with several needs. For instance, in addition to programs providing loan or grant funds to repair property, subsidies are available to help pay fuel bills—even the cost of air conditioning under certain conditions. Also available are programs through which older persons might obtain part-time employment, or meals, or help with home management tasks; dependents of deceased veterans may be entitled to pensions, health care, and burial expenses and grave markers for the deceased veteran.

Seeking federal assistance becomes more challenging when two or more programs are combined to meet more complex needs. For instance, someone interested in obtaining mortgage insurance on a loan covering a multi-unit housing structure in an older declining area through **14.123** may decide to also pursue the rental subsidies available to tenants through **14.871**.

Resourcefulness often is the key to obtaining federal assistance. The successful outcome of use of available assistance is illustrated across the country, in virtually all fields—from child care to environmental enhancement to job creation to the performing arts to scientific research.

Often, those who have successfully applied public resources are eager to show what they did and how they went about it. Their experience could save prospective applicants countless hours of trial and error. Federal officials also may provide guidance in learning how to use federal programs effectively; their perspective can be unique, an important resource to tap.

The challenge may increase when federal assistance is channeled through a state, municipal, or private organization. The next section, "Who May Obtain Federal Assistance?" addresses the situation. In such instances, the application *process* is usually similar to making federal office contacts. However, the competition for funds help could be stiffer.

The award process could be more complicated, requiring a good deal of groundwork at the community level to obtain the assistance. An applicant's resourcefulness usually pays off, just as with federal contacts.

Who May Obtain Federal Assistance?

Eligibility depends on the specific program.

Assistance through many programs is available to the general public—e.g., use of the national libraries, technical information, and similar facilities and services.

Some programs, because of laws or regulations governing their administration, offer assistance only to certain categories of *applicants*—e.g., farmers, states, small businesses, native Americans. Only specified categories of prospective recipients may *apply.*

Other programs may directly *benefit* only certain industries—e.g., shipbuilding or agriculture, or certain population groups such as the elderly, or teenagers, or immigrants from specific countries.

Under still other federal programs, eligible applicants and beneficiaries are the same. Examples include certain veterans, small business, and student programs.

The distinction between programs offering assistance specifically to eligible applicants, eligible beneficiaries, and eligible applicants/beneficiaries is clear in the program entries presented in PART II.

The point to be understood is that the distinction between eligible applicants and eligible beneficiaries is very important to those seeking assistance. Many deserving persons have not obtained assistance to which they were entitled because this distinction was not understood. Being ineligible to *apply* to a federal agency for assistance under certain programs does not necessarily mean that one cannot *benefit* from those programs. The following actual example illustrates the point.

"The Case of the Muffin Machine"

Several years ago, a baker in a small city used his savings to establish a franchised doughnut business. The city was economically depressed; it managed to obtain relatively large sums of federal money for economic development from several federal agencies.

In a relatively short time after starting, the business did well enough for the owner to meet expenses while employing eleven persons, mostly waiters and waitresses for its 24-hour operation.

The owner was notified by the franchise company of a new product, muffins, that was boosting other franchise owners' sales and profits substantially in market test areas. The franchise company offered an $11,000 package that would include the necessary equipment to begin making and selling muffins. The owner's assets were tied up in the business and in keeping it solvent. So, he applied to a bank for an $11,000 loan to finance purchase of the package. The bank told the owner that it would lend him only $5,500 toward the purchase. The owner did not have the $5,500 balance that he needed, nor would any other bank lend him more because his assets were heavily mortgaged.

Meanwhile, the city's success in obtaining federal funds to help in the creation of new jobs was publicized in the local media. The owner phoned the Department of Housing and Urban Development's nearest office for information about obtaining the funds, because he had heard that HUD was the source of much of the money received by the city. Unfortunately, whoever answered the phone at HUD told the owner that only the city could receive that type of funds from HUD.

Several weeks passed before the owner "badmouthed" the HUD program to the right customer. The customer happened to be another small business owner who had obtained some of the HUD funds to finance the expansion of his business. The customer told the owner whom to contact *locally* to apply for funds. Following a short meeting with an official in the city's economic development organization, the baker-owner had an entirely different attitude toward the program he had been complaining about.

Three weeks later, financing had been arranged to purchase the "muffin machine." The bank loaned the small businessman $5,500 at its commercial interest rate. From the city's funds received from HUD, he obtained $4,400 at 5 percent interest. And, he scraped up the remaining $1,100, or 10 percent of the total investment, on his own. One full-time job and two part-time jobs resulted from this loan.

In this particular program (**14.228**) only small cities may *apply* for the available project grants, which may be used for quite a broad range of activities, including revolving loan funds with interest rates established locally. However, as an *eligible beneficiary* of the program the small business owner was able to obtain the assistance; the city accomplished its objectives of creating jobs and "leveraging" private funds through its economic development efforts; and, most important perhaps, three persons received jobs generated by the program.

The importance of this example to persons seeking federal assistance is the distinction between eligible *applicants* and eligible *beneficiaries*.

If only certain types of applicants may apply for a program and you are not eligible, but you are eligible to *benefit*—say, under a training program—find out who has obtained funds and apply there for the training. If it cannot be established who has received funds by contacting organizations at the community level, contact the appropriate federal field office listed in PART IV of this book; if there is no field office, contact the program headquarters listed in PART II.

Organization of the Federal Programs in This Book

PART II of *GOVERNMENT ASSISTANCE ALMANAC* uses the same numerical system of listing federal programs followed in the CFDA. The system is not totally logical, in that the programs are not listed alphabetically, functionally, or by type of assistance. They are organized according to their administering department or agency; this makes this book's MASTER INDEX especially useful in identifying available assistance.

Each program is identified by a five-digit number. The first two digits identify the administrative entity responsible for the program. The last three digits identify the administrative sub-unit, if any, and the program. Using as examples the programs described in PART II, beginning on page 109, illustrate the numerical system:

DEPARTMENT OF COMMERCE

This administrative entity has responsibility for all programs that begin with the digits "11."

BUREAU OF THE CENSUS

This administrative sub-unit of the Department of Commerce has management responsibility for the programs outlined. **11.001** through **11.006** are the numbers identifying programs managed by the Bureau of the Census.

All programs with "**12**" as their first two digits, beginning on page 143, are administered by the Department of Defense. The system continues throughout PART II and PART III, as well as PART IV which provides field contact information.

PART III. Program Funding Levels—Summary Tables lists the departments, agencies, commissions, and other governmental entities in the order in which they are presented in PART II.

Note, however, that PARTS II and III provide headings for administrative sub-units only when the sub-unit's program series is uninterrupted in the CFDA. The *ALMANAC*'s AGENCY INDEX lists all administrative units and sub-units alphabetically, and it includes the program numbers within their respective purviews.

(The numerical system originated in the 1960s when the first edition of the *Catalog of Federal Domestic Assistance* was published. It was organized alphabetically by the name of the administering agency. Many numbers were not used, to allow for inclusion of new programs. Through the years, new agencies and programs were established and existing ones were terminated. The new agencies were added to the end of the list, to avoid changing the numerical sequence within the numbering system. Program numbers for terminated agencies or programs were removed altogether, and reserved in case they are reinstated eventually.)

Red Tape—Should You Hire a Consultant?

Federal laws, regulations, statutory provisions, policies, forms, criteria, procedures, processes, standards, deadlines, audits, certifications, documentation, appeals, authorizations, records, credentials, formulas, obligations, guidelines—these terms and many others signify the "red tape" of federal programs.

The terms form an important part of the language used in administering federal programs. Expect to encounter the language in seeking federal assistance. Depending on the program pursued, none, some, or all of the terms may be encountered.

The following general principles concerning "red tape" are understood by persons experienced in applying for federal assistance.

1. *Programs involving financial benefits in any form involve more red tape than other types of assistance.*

2. *The more persons served by a given program, the less red tape to the beneficiaries.* For example, applicants for basic Social Security benefits must produce certain information to enable federal officials to verify their eligibility and to calculate their benefits. Because millions of persons participate in the Social Security program, red tape has been minimized and usually is simple enough to overcome.

3. *Programs providing for one-on-one contacts between federal officials and applicants usually involve less red tape.* Examples: persons applying for some types of farming assistance or fellowships, training, veterans benefits, and similar assistance. In such cases, the applicant/ beneficiary usually can easily arrange to provide the required information.

4. *Programs with relatively few participants nationwide and with large benefit amounts involve extensive lengths of red tape.* Examples: programs addressing the problem of toxic waste; multi-year intensive research projects; financial assistance programs based on the recipient's promise to perform certain tasks, such as construction projects involving federal mortgage insurance.

5. *Programs with several parties to an application for assistance involve increased red tape.* For example, a housing developer applying for a mortgage guaranty on apartments to receive rental subsidies will be required to produce documents from a lender, attorneys, architects, housing management experts, local housing officials, and others—with each party needing to satisfy various requirements. Such applications must be "packaged" into a single application. Moreover, the approval process requires "sign-off" (i.e., approval) by several officials both outside and within the administering federal agency.

6. *Programs that provide federal assistance to beneficiaries through nonfederal offices may or may not have added red tape.* The five preceding principles apply. Examples: information about drug abuse might be obtained easily through a federally-funded state agency, but obtaining federal funds through the same state agency to establish a local drug abuse program could be more difficult than dealing with a federal office because of complex state requirements *in addition to* federal requirements; a student applying to a college financial aid office for federal educational assistance could have to meet federal, state, *and* the institution's requirements.

For most programs, paid consultants are not needed to apply for federal assistance. Generally, the official receiving the application will guide applicants in meeting requirements. Many programs require that applications be submitted through public administering agencies, private organizations, banks, or similar entities. Personnel in these organizations might well be considered the "consultant" or advocate for the application.

Programs involving complicated applications may require expert assistance to assure favorable action by the funding agency. Applicants without the time or patience to learn about and fulfill all requirements may find it advantageous to hire an experienced consultant.

In selecting a consultant, verify his or her credentials, experience, and record in obtaining federal assistance *of the type to be sought*. Check with the consultant's other clients and with federal offices to confirm that the qualifications are pertinent to the specific program. A consultant's impressive background in one field or with one federal agency is not necessarily a recommendation in another field or with a different federal agency. Most federal offices will provide advice about the need for a consultant's help in applying for given programs.

Keep the red tape in perspective. Try to understand its necessity. Federal requirements are intended to assure the proper use of federal funds. Virtually everyone agrees that many federal programs involve excessive red tape. Separate complaints and constructive recommendations about program requirements from the application process.

Obtaining Federal Assistance: How to Use PART II

Identifying and obtaining federal assistance is a reasonably straightforward process when one proceeds carefully and resourcefully. The previous section commented generally on the most complicated part of the process: the requirements that must be met to obtain assistance from the federal government. Complications can be minimal if a few basic steps are followed.

STEP ONE: USE THE MASTER INDEX

Thumb through the MASTER INDEX at the end of this book. Each program appears in the index an average of ten times. Together with the cross-references, the index assures that users will be able to identify *all* available assistance programs. Become familiar with the types of headings, sub-headings, and cross references. The index presents:

- subjects (shown in bold face);
- official program titles (in capital letters); bracketed agency identifiers are added to program titles to clarify the federal agency involved in cases where the program title alone is indistinct;

- popular titles of programs;
- miscellaneous (abbreviations, agency names, names of Acts, etc.);

The numbers following the headings refer to the program numbers in PART II where they appear in the left column. *Indexed programs that offer financial assistance are italicized, distinguishing them from programs that do not,* to further assist users in quickly identifying programs most pertinent to their needs.

Finding programs by title, popular name, abbreviation, or administrative entity is a simple procedure of looking in the index alphabetically, and then turning to PART II where the program descriptions are presented in numerical order. The introductory notes preceding the MASTER INDEX may prove useful.

Finding programs by subject involves looking for a main term and then scanning the indented entries under it. Generally, programs *intended* for the benefit of certain groups of people, such as women, youth, Indians, the disadvantaged, the disabled or handicapped, etc., are indexed directly under the common name of the group. Many programs are available to group members even though not targeted primarily for them. For example, programs relating to housing for Indians will be found under "Indian housing;" however, programs listed under the more general headings beginning with "Housing"—such as "Housing, rental" or "Housing, construction"—may also be applicable. To ascertain that every possible available program has been identified, both approaches should be followed.

The MASTER INDEX also includes section and title numbers of certain Acts, as well as the names of the Acts themselves. So if an *ALMANAC* user is interested in "section 109," for example, but does not know or cannot remember the exact name of the Act, in looking under "Section" numerous section numbers will be found with their corresponding program numbers.

Finding programs by administrative entity, such as "Department of Labor," can be done through the MASTER INDEX for all agencies. Or, the AGENCY INDEX might be consulted instead. The AGENCY INDEX also shows programs administered by sub-units. "PART III. Program Funding Levels—Summary Tables" gives the names of all the agencies, arranged by government department, in the order in which the programs are presented in PARTS II and IV.

For other programs, the recommended procedure is to check first under the specific term, and then under more general terms. "*See*" and "*see also*" references have been used liberally to direct searches. For example, under "Aquaculture" a "*see also*" reference suggests looking under such other headings as "Farm, nonfarm enterprises," "Fish," and "Fisheries industry" for more entries of possible interest.

Or, if a scholarship to attend podiatry school is sought, users should look first under "Podiatry" where one or more programs will be found; but the *see also* reference directs users to "Health professions" where more general programs will be found that may be of interest; users also will be referred to "Fellowships, scholarships, traineeships" for still other related programs.

The index includes some terms indicating permitted uses of programs, which may not be mentioned in the program entry. These terms are included in the index for programs where it is known that program funds possibly may be used for activities embodied in the indexed term. "Block grant" programs frequently are indexed in this manner.

Often, more than one program will be found providing assistance under a given heading. Read all program entries in PART II carefully, and pursue the most pertinent.

After perusing the index, if no reference is found to a program providing assistance for a specific purpose, it is almost certain that such federal assistance is unavailable. There is one more step that might be taken: contact the federal office most apt to know about assistance available for specific purposes. Many programs can be "stretched" to cover activities that are not found in the program entry or in the index.

STEP TWO: "READ" A FEDERAL PROGRAM

PART II provides outlines of all available domestic programs. Properly "reading" the information on a given program—that is, understanding the program entry—will facilitate decisions on whether to pursue the available assistance. The following explanation of the program entries explains how to "read" the entries to greatest advantage. Program **14.239** on page 179 serves as the example.

① **COMMUNITY PLANNING AND DEVELOPMENT**

② **14.239 HOME INVESTMENT PARTNERSHIPS PROGRAM**
③ **("HOME Program")**
④ **Assistance:** formula grants (67-75 percent/2-5 years).
⑤ **Purposes:** pursuant to the National Affordable Housing Act as amended, to support partnerships among all levels of government and the private sector, including profit and nonprofit organizations, in the production and operation of affordable housing, particularly rental housing for low- and very-low-income families. Funds may be used for: planning; development of model projects; technical assistance; housing rehabilitation; tenant-based rental assistance; assistance to homebuyers; new construction of housing; site acquisition and improvements including improved energy efficiency, demolition, relocation. As of FY 03, the American Dream Downpayment Initiative (ADDI) may provide funds for low-income families to make down payments on suitable housing. Ineligible funds uses include: public housing modernization; matching funds for other federal programs; rental housing operating subsidies; activities under the Low Income Housing Preservation Act, except for priority purchasers.

⑥ **Eligible applicants:** formula allocations—states, cities, urban counties, or consortia of general local government units; Insular Areas. Technical Assistance—nonprofit and profit firms; public purpose organizations; nonprofit national and regional HOME organizations; community housing development organizations (CHDOs).

⑦ **Eligible beneficiaries:** rental housing—90 percent of funds for families with incomes at 60 percent of area median, and the remainder for families below 80 percent. Homeownership assistance—families with incomes below 80 percent of the area median.

⑧ **Range:** $287,000 to $137,354,000; ADDI, $13,000 to $2,699,000. **Average:** $1,170,000.

⑨ **Activity:** cumulatively through FY 04, 552,000 units completed; 111,000 tenants received rental assistance.

⑩ **HQ:** Director, Office of Affordable Housing Programs, CPD-HUD, 451 Seventh St. SW - Rm.7164, Washington, DC 20410. Phone: (202)708-2470. **Internet:** "www.hud.gov/offices/cpd/affordablehousing/index.cfm".

---

① *Administrative sub-unit* with management responsibility for all programs under the heading.

② *Program number,* and *official program title.*

③ *popular title.*

Many program titles in PART II are followed by one or more *popular titles*, shown within parentheses and quotation marks as in this illustration. Field office officials and others may refer to programs only by their popular titles.

④ *Classification of assistance* available through the program. (The fifteen "Types of Federal Assistance Available" are defined beginning on page 4.)

Many programs provide more than one type of assistance. When financial assistance is provided this line indicates the percentage of assistance provided by the federal agency, as well as the usual project term *when the term is other than for one year*. For some programs, the percentage and project term are clarified under "⑤ **Purposes**."

Project grants usually are awarded either through competitions or solicitations of proposals by the sponsoring federal agency; however, authorizing statutes for some programs allocate funds on the basis of a formula, as in the "HOME Program," in which case the federal administrative agency notifies eligible applicants of the availability of funds. It is necessary for prospective applicants for competitive, solicited, or unsolicited proposals to remain aware of available programs.

Although the percentage of federal assistance may say "100 percent," most programs have maintenance of effort ("MOE") or "non-supplementation" requirements—meaning that federal funds may not supplant existing nonfederal funding allocated to the effort for which federal funds are sought. Also, some level of cost sharing by the applicant almost always is required, if only through the provision of administrative space and services supporting project activities; such contributions by applicants are known as "in-kind" contributions. *Frequently, the level of "MOE" or of cost sharing by applicants will influence the approval of applications.*

⑤ Description of the *basic objectives* and *permitted uses* of the program, as well as *restrictions* on the use of funds. Examples of funded projects also are included when they help to explain the types of activities that are eligible.

The information on the purposes of program **14.239** should be sufficient to permit a decision on whether to pursue it. Note that many programs include more than a single program purpose. Other program features also are included in program descriptions.

⑥ *Who may apply* for the available assistance.

⑦ *Who may benefit* from the program.

Thus, the headings setting forth the eligibility for program **14.239** indicate that only states, cities, urban counties, or consortia or general local government units, and Insular Areas may apply directly for available formula grants; however, other types of applicants are eligible to apply for technical assistance funding. And, when program assistance is sought for rental housing, 90 percent of approved funds must benefit families with incomes at 60 percent of area median, and the remainder for families below 80 percent; when assistance is approved for homeownership projects, families with incomes below 80 percent of the area median may benefit.

It follows that someone interested in participating in this program, if not an eligible applicant, should contact appropriate state or local officials to learn more about it. Contact the state or city public information office to find out whom to contact for details; if that fails, contact the nearest HUD Community Planning and Development field office listed in PART IV.

Frequently, there is no distinction between eligible applicants and eligible beneficiaries, because they are one and the same. Many program descriptions name the intended beneficiaries; those beneficiaries need not apply because services will (or should) be provided to them by the applicants—for instance, programs intended to benefit elderly persons, children and youth, substance abusers, and other general categories of beneficiaries. Such programs have the following eligibility heading:

Eligible applicants/beneficiaries:

Review the section beginning on page 10 entitled "Who May Obtain Federal Assistance?" for a discussion and example of the significance of eligible applicants vs. eligible beneficiaries.

Occasionally a notation in this heading will indicate "same as for" another program. In "reading" program entries, take such a notation to

OBTAINING FEDERAL ASSISTANCE   21

mean that the two programs probably have related purposes—suggesting that, if the one being considered does not meet certain needs, perhaps the other will.

⑧ Indicates the *range and average amounts* provided to applicants or, sometimes, to beneficiaries for programs that provide financial assistance. Numbers over 10,000 under this heading are rounded to the nearest 1,000.

Knowing range and average amounts helps in assessing the chances of obtaining a certain sum. Often, applying for a sum that is outside the range shown is pointless, whether the sum sought is below or above the range.

Complementing the "Range" heading are the tables in PART III. *Used together*, the amounts provide a perspective of the funding available nationally for a given activity, and how much an applicant or a beneficiary might expect to obtain through that program.

In "reading" the tables, remember that the U.S. government's fiscal year begins on October 1 and ends on September 30. Fiscal years are expressed in the ending date; thus, FY 06 ends September 30, 2006. Table 1 shows the following funding available for program **14.239**:

(FY 03) $1,753,940,000;   (FY 04) $2,005,597,000;   (FY 05) $1,899,680,000 e;   (FY 06) $1,941,000,000 e

Note that amounts are rounded to the nearest $1,000 in Tables 1, 2, and 3 (but not in the line above).

The information on funding for the four years: (1) indicates the amount available nationally; (2) shows whether, from year to year, a program's funding level remains relatively consistent or if it is increasing or decreasing.

"·" following an amount indicates that the amount is a "credit" rather than an actual outlay of funds. For purposes of the tables, amounts loaned or insured by the government were classified as credits. Program **14.239** provides formula grants and, therefore, is classified as an outlay.

"e" next to an amount indicates that it is *estimated*. In the example, the amounts shown are actual for FY 03 and FY 04; the FY 05 and FY 06 amounts are estimated.

Estimated amounts could mean that Congress had not approved a specific amount when the information was compiled, or that the amount obligated for a program fluctuates depending on demands for the funds.

Estimates of "$0" also may indicate that the program has been proposed for termination.

Amounts shown in the tables must meet demands nationwide. The total often is allocated geographically by government agencies to regions, states, districts, or areas, according to legislative or administrative policy. Therefore, it could be useful to learn the amount available in a given geographical area, from the officials contacted concerning a specific program—for an indication of the extent of competition to be expected.

The tables offer a perspective of government support for agencies and programs, in relation to one another and to other federal domestic activities. The introduction to the tables further discusses their usefulness in "reading" federal programs.

⑨ *Activity within the program* in the most recent period reported by the administering entity, including such information as the number of assistance awards or of persons benefiting. Numbers over 10,000 under this heading are rounded to the nearest 1,000. It is also noted when the program is new, with or without reported activity.

In combination with the information provided under *Range/Average* and in the Tables, "reading" the level of activity provides an indication of the participation nationally in given programs.

⑩ *Program headquarters address, phone number, and web sites* of the administering agency. FAX numbers and generic e-mail addresses are included when provided in the source material.

Occasionally, a notation in this heading will indicate "same address/phone as" another program (e.g., in program **10.069**). In "reading" program entries, such a notation probably indicates that the two programs have closely related purposes—suggesting that, if the one being considered does not meet certain needs, perhaps the other will.

THE FIRST CONTACT WITH A FEDERAL AGENCY ABOUT A PROGRAM SHOULD ALWAYS BE WITH THE FIELD OFFICE IF

ONE EXISTS. The "HQ" entry always indicates when there are no field offices for a given program with "(Note: no field offices for this program.)" following the HQ address. If the notation does not appear, field office contact information is provided in PART IV.

Contacting field offices has advantages for both applicants and federal officials: the nearer a federal office is to applicants, the more probable it is that the officials will be able to provide pertinent information; field office personnel usually are more aware of needs in the area they serve; contacts with them add to this awareness.

Also, they are more apt to know who else in a given area has similar interests; they could provide leads to others experienced with the program. It is important for the field offices to know the extent of interest in the programs that they manage. Generally, headquarters personnel are more involved with "big picture" matters than with handling individual contacts from throughout the country.

PART IV provides contact information for regional, state, and area or district offices. The hierarchy should be followed upwards when deciding which office to contact—that is, if there is a district, branch, or area office, it should be contacted before state or regional offices; state offices should be contacted before regional offices.

When contacting a field office, address the "Director" unless the entry in PART IV suggests otherwise. Include the full name of the agency. For example, correspondence with HUD's Chicago state office, concerning program **14.239**, should be addressed as follows:

> Director, State Office
> Community Planning and Development
> Department of Housing and Urban Development
> Metcalfe Federal Bldg.
> 77 W. Jackson Blvd.
> Chicago, IL 60604-3507

PART IV also provides contact information for specialized field service offices such as research centers, laboratories, and testing stations.

STEP THREE: ASK THE RIGHT QUESTIONS

"STEP ONE" and "STEP TWO" involve the selection of programs to pursue. The process of obtaining federal assistance begins when those steps are completed. Hundreds of programs involve very little red tape. They require little or no additional "homework", especially those involving nonfinancial assistance. For nonfinancial programs, one or two contacts with the right federal official usually will bring the desired assistance.

This "step" is meant for newcomers to federal programs, deciding to pursue the more complicated programs involving awards of funds. All the points discussed will not be pertinent to all the programs, obviously.

Before formally applying for financial assistance under all but the least complicated programs, a preliminary contact with the responsible federal office is always advisable; indeed, some programs *require* a preapplication conference. An appointment with the responsible official should be requested; when making this request, the eligibility criteria for the program being pursued should be discussed generally. At this first meeting at least the following should be accomplished:

1. *Verify the eligibility of the applicant*—whether as an individual or as an organization. This should have been done verbally when the appointment was made. If the official mentioned credentials required to document eligibility, these should be shown at the meeting. The required credentials could include documents such as a birth certificate, academic certificates, a financial statement, endorsements, a copy of the organization's charter or license, etc. If the required credentials are not ready, evidence that they be can produced should be shown—e.g., publications, sample products, leaflets describing the organization, a good resume.

2. *Explain the applicant's specific need for the assistance in very basic terms*. Prior to the meeting an outline for using the assistance should be prepared, and it should be shown to the official. This will open a discussion of the program, its objectives, the permitted uses of funds, program restrictions, etc. All possible questions about the program should be posed, including the availability of funding. The official should be allowed to do most of the talking—the purpose of the meeting is for the applicant to obtain information, not give it. On the

other hand, prospective applicants should answer all questions honestly to reveal potential problems early in the process; if problems do surface, the official's advice should be sought on how to resolve them. *Written* notes should be made, both during and immediately after the meeting.

3. *Obtain all available written information pertaining to the program.* The following could be useful in preparing a thorough application:

- a copy of the law establishing the program;
- policy statements;
- procedural guidelines and instructions to applicants;
- regulations governing the program, including those published in the *Federal Register* and those pertaining mainly to the processing requirements that federal agencies themselves must fulfill—the latter often provide instructions for "scoring" the merits of applications, giving insights into what those reviewing an application will look for;
- statements of application deadlines, if any;
- general literature describing the program and the experiences of others that have obtained funds under the same or similar programs;
- a copy of a sample successful application;
- most important, copies of any pertinent circulars governing the program issued by the Office of Management and Budget, as well as Executive Orders or other regulations issued by federal or state agencies that will coordinate or review applications—e.g., the Environmental Protection Agency;
- lists of requirements for records to be kept and reports to be filed if the application is approved—including copies of pertinent accounting procedures;
- a description of the "appeal process," in case the application is not approved and the decision is appealed.

4. *If the program requires cost sharing or a matching contribution* by the applicant, it should be determined whether any portion of this sum can be provided through "in-kind" services, use of facilities or equipment, or other noncash contributions. Review the explanation of the program description entry heading "Assistance" on page 19 for insights on cost sharing.

5. *Ask to be placed on the office's mailing list* to receive announcements, news releases, notifications of invitations to apply or of awards, changes in regulations or deadlines, and the like.

6. Keep the meeting as brief as possible.

STEP FOUR: COMPLETE YOUR HOMEWORK

Examine carefully all the material obtained in "STEP THREE." Make a list of the most important points. Note especially items that are not readily understood, and follow through on each of them. Follow all instructions carefully. In your application, projecting an ability to adhere carefully and fully to instructions and regulations is all-important. "Dot every i, cross every t."

At this point, the "grantsmanship" process begins. Grantsmanship is a term often used inaccurately to describe *obtaining* federal assistance. Successful grantsmanship necessitates thorough familiarity with program and project planning, development, and operations. A good application will reflect complete understanding of program purposes and requirements, *as well as sound project management capability*. The grantsmanship process is both an art and a science; its productive outcome requires extensive research, discipline, precise work, sound psychology, effective presentation, a good sense of business, and persistence.

The *ALMANAC*'s author/editor and publisher wish users success in their quest, trusting that this book points them in the right direction.

Finding More Information

Several sources might be checked for more information on obtaining federal assistance.

1. The principal source providing additional details about the programs outlined in the *ALMANAC* is the *Catalog of Federal Domestic Assistance* ("CFDA"), subscriptions to which may be ordered from:

   Superintendent of Documents
   U.S. Government Printing Office
   Washington, DC 20402

CFDA-2005 is the main source of the information in this edition of the *ALMANAC*. The "Catalog" is published every year, pursuant to federal statute; it contains some 2,500 pages and is mailed unbound for filing in a loose-leaf binder. Subscriptions no longer include the "Update to the Catalog of Federal Domestic Assistance," formerly published in December and numbering several hundred additional pages; the General Services Administration, which maintains the data base for the CFDA, discontinued preparation of a printed version of the Update in 2001. GSA also no longer offers the CFDA on CD-ROM.

GSA recommends now that interested parties use its "on-line version" of the CFDA to obtain updated information, which may be accessed through the following web site: "http://www.cfda.gov". The edition of the *ALMANAC* at-hand reflects all added and deleted programs according to the CFDA web site through January 2006.

It should be noted that the CFDA web site provides most of the information presented in the ALMANAC only in printer definition file ("PDF") format, including the CFDA's several indexes; the CFDA on-line version provides ongoing updates only for individual programs—i.e., the version in PDF format has been updated only annually in recent years.

The catalog contains a brief section with "Suggestions for Proposal Writing and Following Grant Application Procedures," which could be helpful to newcomers to federal programs.

Until 2003 GSA distributed free copies of the CFDA to the entities listed below; however, this policy was changed, requiring the recipients to purchase subscriptions; presumably, many of them did so and would have copies available for examination:

> Members of Congress
> Congressional staff
> All federal Depository Libraries (see program **40.002**)
> Federal offices
> Governors
> State coordinators of federal-state relations
> Directors of state departments of administration
> Directors of state agricultural extension services
> Directors of state departments of community affairs

Directors of state planning agencies
State budget offices
State municipal leagues
State associations of counties
Chief state school officers
State employment security agencies
Mayors
County chairmen
Chairmen of boards of commissioners
City planners
Some other state and local government agencies and officials

Federal Information Centers and *Federal Regional Councils* also may have copies available for examination.

2. *The United States Government Manual* is a useful reference source for persons wanting to better understand the federal government. The manual describes the basic functions and operations of all government agencies, including the judicial, legislative, and executive branches. Most libraries have copies available for reference. The current manual may be purchased from the Government Printing Office.

3. *The Federal Register,* published daily, provides the public with federal agency regulations and other legal documents covering government activities, including *proposed* changes in regulations. Newly authorized programs and the availability of funding also are announced in *The Federal Register.*

The Federal Register Index, published monthly, consolidates entries appearing in the basic publication, with broad references to the contents.

Additional *Federal Register* resources include "Weekly Compilation of Presidential Documents" and "The Federal Register: What It Is and How to Use It."

The *Code of Federal Regulations* ("CFR") codifies the general and permanent rules published in the *The Federal Register* by federal executive departments and agencies. The CFR includes all statutory regulations; it is updated by *The Federal Register.*

The foregoing publications are available for examination in federal depository libraries and major libraries, or for purchase from the Government Printing Office.

4. *Libraries* are obvious places to look for additional information about government programs, "grantsmanship," proposal writing, and similar topics. Larger or more specialized libraries also will have available directories of trade or professional associations and of commercial publishers specializing in information on various government activities, which might provide assistance or guidance concerning certain federal assistance programs. Directories of consultants and consulting organizations also are available.

5. *Government Phone Book USA—A Comprehensive Guide to Federal, State, County, and Local Government Offices in the United States*, provides standard and e-mail addresses, as well as web sites, and phone and FAX numbers, totaling some 164,000 listings. Published annually by Omnigraphics, Inc., this comprehensive reference should be available at libraries.

6. *Congressional offices* may or may not be able to provide help in obtaining additional information or actual assistance. Some senators and representatives are more anxious to do so than others, depending on the capacity, interest, and capabilities of their staffs.

Many elected officials respond more quickly to requests for assistance from other elected officials, or from campaign supporters. Keep this in mind when deciding to seek a congressman's intercession. The first contact should be with district or state offices. The Washington addresses for offices of Members of Congress are:

        United States Senate   House of Representatives
        Washington, DC 20510   Washington, DC 20515

The best source of more information about given programs and obtaining the assistance they provide usually is someone experienced in those programs or similar ones.

PART II

Program Information

DEPARTMENT OF AGRICULTURE

10.001 AGRICULTURAL RESEARCH—BASIC AND APPLIED RESEARCH ("Extramural Research")

Assistance: project grants (100 percent).

Purposes: for agricultural discovery research; to provide scientific technical information. Most projects are conducted with in-house staff; limited discretionary research funds are available.

Eligible applicants/beneficiaries: nonprofit IHEs and other research organizations.

Range: $1,000 to $25,000. **Average:** $3,000.

Activity: N.A.

HQ: Administrator, Agriculture Research Service (ARS)-USDA, Washington, DC 20250. Phone: (202)720-3656; Extramural Agreements Division, (301) 504-1147. **Internet:** "www.ars.usda.gov".

10.025 PLANT AND ANIMAL DISEASE, PEST CONTROL, AND ANIMAL CARE

Assistance: project grants (cost sharing/1 year).

Purposes: pursuant to the Plant Protection Act, Farm Security and Rural Investment Act of 2002 (FSRIA), and Animal Welfare Act as amended, for surveys, demonstration projects, and inspections to detect, appraise, eradicate, and control plant and animal diseases and pests injurious to agriculture, including brucellosis and tuberculosis; to ensure the safety and potency of veterinary biologics. Emphasis is on prevention of interstate spread of infestations and diseases.

Eligible applicants/beneficiaries: foreign, state, local, and territorial government agencies; nonprofit IHEs and other organizations.

Range/Average: N.A.

Activity: FY 06 estimate, 52 states brucellosis-free, 47 tuberculosis-free.

HQ: Agreement Services Center, Marketing and Regulatory Programs, Animal and Plant Health Inspection Service-USDA, USDA Center, 4700 River Rd. - Unit 55-Station 4B80, Riverdale, MD 20737. Phone: (301)734-8792. **Internet:** "www.aphis.usda.gov".

10.028 WILDLIFE SERVICES

Assistance: project grants (cost sharing/1 year).

Purposes: pursuant to the Animal Damage Control Act of 1931 as amended, to reduce damage caused by nuisance mammals and birds, including those carrying zoonotic diseases. Project examples: predator control programs in the western states, including coyote, mountain lion, and bear; aerial blackbird hazing program protecting the sunflower crop; control of beaver, deer, and cormorants against damage to aquaculture in the eastern and southern states. Most direct technical assistance is provided through state fish and game, agriculture, and health departments.

Eligible applicants/beneficiaries: state, local, territorial, and tribal governments; public or private nonprofit organizations; nonprofit IHEs; individuals.

Range/Average: N.A.

Activity: FY 03 estimate, 88,000 projects.

HQ: same as **10.025**.

10.029 AVIAN INFLUENZA INDEMNITY PROGRAM ("AII")

Assistance: direct payments/unrestricted use.

Purposes: to provide indemnity payments to owners of animals required to be destroyed because of foot-and-mouth disease, pleuropneumonia, rinderpest, exotic Newcastle disease, highly pathogenic avian influenza, infectious salmon anemia, or any other communicable disease of livestock or poultry that constitutes an emergency and threatens the U.S. livestock or poultry population. Payment for animals destroyed is based on fair market value.

Eligible applicants/beneficiaries: poultry owners and contract growers.

Range/Average: 100 percent of eligible losses, up to the eligible amount before grower compensation is deducted.

Activity: N.A.

HQ: Animal and Plant Health Inspection Service-USDA, 1400 Independence Ave. SW, Washington, DC 20250. Phone: (no number provided). **Internet:** "www.fsa.usda.gov".

10.051 COMMODITY LOANS AND LOAN DEFICIENCY PAYMENTS ("Price Supports")

Assistance: direct payments/unrestricted use; direct loans/to 9 months.

Purposes: pursuant to the Agricultural Adjustment Act of 1938, Commodity Credit Corporation Charter Act, Food, Agriculture, Conservation, and Trade Act of 1990 (FACTA), Federal Agriculture Improvement and Reform Act of 1996 (FAIRA), Agricultural Risk Protection Act of 2000, amendments, and other acts, to help growers stabilize their income from commodities through a system of price supports involving loans and purchases by the CCC. Producers may receive nonrecourse loans against the support price established for crops serving as loan collateral; if market prices exceed the support price, farmers may market the commodity and repay the loan principal plus interest; if market prices are low, the loan is repaid through forfeiture of the collateral to the CCC in return for a loan deficiency payment (LDP) for the difference between the support and the market prices. Commodities eligible for loans include feed grains, wheat, rice, peanuts, tobacco, upland cotton, extra-long staple cotton, sugar, soybeans, canola, flaxseed, mustard seed, rapeseed, safflower, and sunflower seed. LDPs are offered for feed grains, wheat, upland cotton, rice, soybeans, canola, flaxseed, mustard seed, rapeseed, safflower, and sunflower seed. If the loan repayment rates are less than the established loan levels, producers may forego the loan and elect to receive LDPs which are equal to the amount by which the loan rate exceeds the loan repayment rate in effect on the delivery date. Recourse loans may be made for low quality grain or unginned seed cotton; such loans require repayment at maturity.

Eligible applicants/beneficiaries: owners, landlords, tenants, or sharecroppers on farms producing eligible commodities; for sugar, processors or refiners meeting USDA program requirements.

Range: loans, $162 to $1,006,000; purchases, N.A. **Average:** $23,000. Note: maximum total LDP and any gain from repaying a loan at a level lower than the original loan per "person", $75,000 ($150,000 in for 1999 crops).

Activity: FY 01, 178,000 new loans, 2,855,000 LDPs.

HQ: Price Support Division, FSA-USDA, 1400 Independence Ave. SW, Washington, DC 20250-0512. Phone: (202)720-7901. **Internet:** same as **10.029**.

10.053 DAIRY INDEMNITY PROGRAM

Assistance: direct payments/unrestricted use (100 percent).

Purposes: pursuant to the Agricultural Act of 1970, Agriculture and Consumer Protection Act of 1973, FACTA, amendments, and other acts, to indemnify dairy farmers and dairy product manufacturers against losses when their milk or dairy products are contaminated by pesticides, chemicals, toxic substances, or nuclear radiation or fallout, if the cause was outside their control; in such cases CCC pays the fair market value of the product.

Eligible applicants/beneficiaries: dairy farmers and manufacturers with products removed from the market by a public agency. Available also in PR.

Range: $88 to $95,000. **Average:** $40,000.

Activity: FY 01, payments to 7 dairy farmers in 4 states.

HQ: FSA-USDA, 1400 Independence Ave. SW, Washington, DC 20250-0512. Phone: (202)720-7641. **Internet:** same as **10.029**.

10.054 EMERGENCY CONSERVATION PROGRAM ("ECP")

Assistance: direct payments/specified use.

Purposes: pursuant to the Agricultural Credit Act of 1978 as amended, for emergency conservation measures to control wind erosion; to rehabilitate farmlands damaged by wind, floods, or other natural disasters; to take water enhancing or conservation measures during drought. Assistance is limited basically to new conservation problems created by natural disasters. Cost-sharing payment rates vary.

Eligible applicants/beneficiaries: owners, landlords, tenants, or sharecroppers on farms or ranches, including associated groups. Available also in Guam, Northern Marianas, PR, and VI.

Range: $50 to $64,000. **Average:** $2,681.

Activity: FY 01, payments made in 44 states, PR, and VI.

HQ: FSA-USDA (CEPD), 1400 Independence Ave. SW, Washington, DC 20250-0513. Phone: (202)720-6221. **Internet:** same as **10.029**.

10.055 DIRECT AND COUNTER-CYCLICAL PAYMENTS PROGRAM ("DCP")

Assistance: direct payments/specified use.

Purposes: pursuant to the FSRIA, to provide CCC income support to producers of covered commodities. Contract payments equal the contract payment rate, times 85 percent of the contract acreage, times the farm program payment yield. Participants must: share the risk of producing a crop on base acres and be entitled to share in the crop available for marketing from the base acres; comply with conservation, wetland, and similar requirements; comply with planting flexibility requirements; use the base acres for agricultural or related activities.

Eligible applicants/beneficiaries: owners, operators, landlords, tenants, or sharecroppers on producing farms—enrolled in DCP for the 2002-2007 crop years. FSA offices should be consulted for specifics.

Range: N.A.

Activity: N.A.

HQ: Compliance Branch, Production Emergencies and Compliance Division, FSA-USDA, 1400 Independence Ave. SW, Washington, DC 20250-0514. Phone: (202)720-9882. **Internet:** same as **10.029**.

10.056 FARM STORAGE FACILITY LOANS

Types: direct loans (85 percent/7 years).

Purposes: for new, remodeled, or refinanced farm grain storage structures and drying equipment; to meet handling requirements for genetically enhanced production.

Eligible applicants/beneficiaries: owner, landlord, tenant, or sharecropper producing one or more of the CCC-approved commodities, participating in the Federal Crop Insurance program, and producing proof of flood insurance.

Range: $1,000 to $100,000.

Activity: FY 01, 1,500 loans obligated (program deleted from CFDA in 1989, reinstated in 2001).

HQ: same address as **10.051**. Phone: (202)720-7935. **Internet:** "www.fsa.usda.gov/dafp/psd/FSFL.html".

10.062 WATER BANK PROGRAM

Assistance: direct payments/specified use (to 20 years).

Purposes: pursuant to the Water Bank Act, to conserve surface waters; to preserve and improve wetlands; to improve nesting, breeding, and feeding areas of migratory waterfowl—in accordance with approved conservation plans. Participants must agree not to use designated areas for agricultural purposes, nor to drain, burn, fill, or otherwise destroy their wetlands character for a ten-year period. This program is coordinated with DOI's wetlands programs.

Eligible applicants/beneficiaries: landowners and operators of specified types of wetlands in designated areas.

Range: $7 to $75 per acre. **Average:** $13 per acre.

Activity: cumulatively since 1985, 4,953 agreements covering 615,000 acres.

HQ: Natural Resources Conservation Service (NRCS)-USDA, P.O. Box 2890, Washington, DC 20013. Phone: (202)720-7157. **Internet:** "www.nrcs.usda.gov".

10.064 FORESTRY INCENTIVES PROGRAM ("FIP")

Assistance: direct payments/specified use (to 65 percent).

Purposes: pursuant to the Cooperative Forestry Assistance Act of 1978, for tree planting, timber stand improvement, and site preparation for natural regeneration on private nonindustrial forest land. Program is limited to eligible land ownerships of not more than 1,000 acres capable of producing at least 50 cubic feet of wood per acre per year, except by special approval.

Eligible applicants/beneficiaries: individuals, groups, associations, tribes or other native groups, corporations whose stocks are not publicly traded, and other legal entities. Available also in PR.

Range: $50 to $10,000 per year. **Average:** $1,781.

Activity: FY 01, funds awarded to owners of 151,000 acres.

HQ: same address/web site as **10.062**. Phone: (202)720-1845.

10.066 LIVESTOCK ASSISTANCE PROGRAM ("LAP")

Assistance: direct payments/unrestricted use.

Purposes: for cash payments to livestock producers that suffered grazing losses of at least 40 percent during calendar year 2000 because of disease, insect infestation, natural disasters, droughts, or other emergencies.

Eligible applicants/beneficiaries: in counties with a declared severe natural disaster—U.S. citizens or legal resident aliens, farm cooperatives, private domestic corporations or partnerships or joint operations, or Indian tribes or tribal organizations, that: are actively engaged in farming; do not have gross annual income exceeding $2,500,000; receive at least 10 percent of their total gross income from livestock production.

Range: $10 to $40,000. **Average:** $875.

Activity: not quantified specifically.

HQ: Emergency Preparedness and Program Branch, Production Emergencies and Compliance Division, FSA-USDA, 1400 Independence Ave. SW, Washington, DC 20250-0517. Phone: (202)720-7641. **Internet:** same as **10.029**.

10.069 CONSERVATION RESERVE PROGRAM ("CRP")

Assistance: direct payments/specified use (10-15 years).

Purposes: pursuant to the Food Security Act of 1985 as amended, FACTA, and FAIRA, to convert highly erodible or environmentally sensitive cropland to less intensive uses such as grasses, legumes, shrubs, trees. Basic program objectives include reducing soil erosion or sedimentation, and improving water quality and wildlife habitat. Participants must institute approved conservation plans and reduce the aggregate total of acreage bases, allotments, and quotas for the contract period.

Eligible applicants/beneficiaries: individuals, partnerships, associations, tribal ventures corporations, estates, trusts, other businesses and legal entities; states and their political subdivisions.

Range: $50 to $50,000. **Average:** $4,000; contracts, rental rate, $45.95/acre.

Activity: 33,500,000 acres under active contracts; average of 74 acres/contract.

HQ: same as **10.054**.

10.070 COLORADO RIVER BASIN SALINITY CONTROL PROGRAM ("CRBSCP")

Assistance: direct payments/specified use (to 70 percent/3-10 years).

Purposes: pursuant to the Colorado River Basin Salinity Control Act of 1974 as amended, for salinity control activities in the Colorado River basin, toward the improvement of water quality in the U.S. and Mexico. Assistance may be financial or technical, to: identify salt source areas; employ conservation practices to reduce salt loads; conduct research, education, and demonstration projects.

Eligible applicants/beneficiaries: owners, landlords, operators, or tenants of eligible lands; individuals, tribes, partnerships, firms, associations, corporations, joint stock companies, conservation or irrigation districts, estates, trusts, states, local public or nonpublic entities.

Range/Average: $20,000.

Activity: FY 01, 118 active contracts covering 6,370 acres in Colorado, Utah, and Wyoming.

HQ: same address/web site as **10.062**. Phone: (202)720-1873.

10.072 WETLANDS RESERVE PROGRAM ("WRP")

Assistance: direct payments/specified use (to 100 percent/5-30 years).

Purposes: pursuant to the Food Security Act of 1985 as amended, FACTA, FAIRA, and other acts, to install restoration practices needed to protect farmed or converted wetlands, certain riparian areas, and buffer areas. Landowners must: place the wetlands under permanent or long-term easement with USDA; provide an access road to the land to enable easement management and monitoring. Landowners receive payments based on the fair agricultural market value of the land or 75 percent of such value.

Permitted land uses after installing restoration or protective practices include haying, grazing, and buffer areas.

Eligible applicants/beneficiaries: individual landowners, partnerships, associations, corporations, estates, trusts; other businesses or legal entities; states and their political subdivisions.

Range/Average: N.A.

Activity: FY 01 estimate, 140,000 acres enrolled.

HQ: Watersheds and Wetlands Division, NRCS-USDA, P.O. Box 2890, Washington, DC 20013. Phone: (202)690-0848. **Internet:** same as **10.062**.

10.073 CROP DISASTER PROGRAM ("CDP")

Assistance: direct payments/unrestricted use.

Purposes: for producers that suffered crop losses greater than 35 percent during the 2000 crop year, because of adverse weather, disaster conditions, drought, insect infestation, or similar causes—preventing planting, or reducing production, or resulting in value loss crops, including in nursery and aquaculture. Crops eligible for federal crop insurance are covered regardless of whether insurance was purchased.

Eligible applicants/beneficiaries: producers meeting FSA requirements. "Persons" with gross annual revenues exceeding $2,500,000 for the 2000 tax year are ineligible for 2000 CDP benefits.

Range: to $80,000 per "person."

Activity: N.A.

HQ: same as **10.055**.

10.075 SPECIAL APPLE PROGRAM

Assistance: direct loans (to 3 years).

Purposes: pursuant to the Agricultural Risk Protection Act, for apple producers suffering from low prices for apples. Loan funds may be used for purposes related to the production or marketing of apples including: farm reorganization; payment of operating expenses or loan closing costs; purchases of equipment or fixtures, real estate, related cooperative stock; capital improvements.

Eligible applicants/beneficiaries: U.S. citizens or legal permanent residents that: are not delinquent on any federal debt; have not caused a loss to FSA by receiving debt forgiveness; have no outstanding indebtedness to the U.S.

Range: to $300 per acre; maximum per applicant, $500,000.

Activity: 2,000 to 4,000 loans anticipated.

HQ: Director, Loan Making Division, FSA-USDA, Washington, DC 20250-0522. Phone: (202)720-1632. **Internet:** same as **10.029**.

10.076 EMERGENCY LOAN FOR SEED PRODUCERS

Assistance: direct loans (to 18 months).

Purposes: pursuant to the Agricultural Risk Protection Act of 2000, to assist seed producers adversely impacted by the bankruptcy filing of AgriBioTech. Loans may be obtained to cover up to 65 percent of the amount of an applicant's valid claim in bankruptcy court, based on seed produced under contract to AgriBioTech in 1999, and may be used for any purpose except those specifically prohibited as contributing to the conversion of wetlands, excessive erosion of highly erodible lands, or for lobbying.

Eligible applicants/beneficiaries: U.S. citizens or legal permanent residents not delinquent on any federal debt and with no outstanding indebtedness to the U.S.

Range/Average: N.A.

Activity: N.A.

HQ: same as **10.075**.

10.077 LIVESTOCK COMPENSATION PROGRAM ("LCP")

Assistance: direct payments/unrestricted use.

Purposes: pursuant to the Act of August 24, 1935 as amended by the Agricultural Assistance Act of 2003, to provide immediate assistance to livestock producers in counties that have received primary disaster designation due to drought in 2001 and 2002.

Eligible applicants/beneficiaries: producers of cattle, sheep, goats, buffalo, and catfish in designated counties—subject to a gross revenue limitation of $2,500,000 during the preceding tax year, with payments limited to $40,000 "per person."

Range/Average: payments vary according to the type of livestock or feed lost—ranging from $4.50 per head for sheep and goats born prior to 1 June 2002 to $31.50 per head for adult dairy cattle, and $34.00 per ton for catfish feed.

Activity: new program listing in 2003.

HQ: Production Emergencies and Compliance Division, FSA-USDA, Washington, DC 20250. Phone: (no number provided). **Internet:** same as **10.029**.

10.078 BIOENERGY PROGRAM ("BIO")

Assistance: direct payments/specified use.

Purposes: pursuant to FSRIA, to encourage increased purchases of eligible commodities toward expansion of bioenergy (fuel grade ethanol and biodiesel) through conversion of crops grown in the U.S. and its territories. Eligible commodities include barley, corn, grain sorghum, oats, rice, wheat, soybeans, sunflower seed, canola, crambe, rapeseed, safflower, sesame seed, flaxseed, mustard seed, and cellulosic crops such as switchgrass and short rotation trees grown on farms for the purpose of producing ethanol and/or biodiesel or any other commodity or commodity by-product approved by the CCC.

Eligible applicants/beneficiaries: all bioenergy producers that can provide evidence of increased production, purchase, and utilization to meet program purposes. Producers with less than 65,000,000 gallons annual production capacity are favored.

Range/Average: based on rate of increased production, reimbursements at 50 percent of the rate.

Activity: N.A.

HQ: Kansas City Commodity Office, FSA-USDA, Kansas City, MO 64141-6205. Phone: (816)926-6525. **Internet:** "www.fsa.usda.gov/daco/bio_daco.htm". (Note: the field office serves as headquarters.)

10.079 BILL EMERSON HUMANITARIAN TRUST ("EHT")

Assistance: direct payments/unrestricted use.

Purposes: pursuant to the Agricultural Act of 1980 as amended, to provide a trust solely to meet emergency humanitarian food needs in developing countries—consisting of a trust stock of wheat, rice, corn, or sorghum, or any combination, and totaling not more than 4,000,000 metric tons. Commodities may be released when domestic supplies are insufficient to meet availability criteria or in instances when unanticipated needs cannot be met in a timely manner under normal means.

Eligible applicants/beneficiaries: developing countries that suffer from natural disasters, prolonged war or diseases, and/or acute hunger.

Range/Average: N.A.

Activity: new program listing in 2003. (Note: program was originally authorized as the Food Security Wheat Reserve, and was renamed in 1998.)

HQ: Kansas City Commodity Office, FSA-USDA, 6501 Beacon Dr., Kansas City, MO 64131-4676. Phone: (816)926-6715. **Internet:** "www.fsa.usda.gov/daco/default.htm". (Note: the field office serves as headquarters.)

10.080 MILK INCOME LOSS CONTRACT PROGRAM ("MIL")

Assistance: direct payments/unrestricted use.

Purposes: pursuant to FSRIA, to provide payments to milk producers for milk produced and marketed between 1 December 2001 and 30 September 2005—when the prices under milk marketing orders fall below $16.94 per cwt.

Eligible applicants/beneficiaries: U.S. dairy producers with MIL contracts; foreign producers with a working U.S. visa or other valid taxpayer identification number.

Range/Average: N.A.

Activity: new program listing in 2004.

HQ: Price Support Division, FSA-USDA, 1400 Independence Ave. SW, Washington, DC 20250-0517. Phone: (202)720-1919. **Internet:** "www.fsa.usda.gov/dafp/psd/MILC.htm".

10.081 LAMB MEAT ADJUSTMENT ASSISTANCE PROGRAM ("LMA")

Assistance: direct payments/unrestricted use.

Purposes: pursuant to the Act of August 24, 1935 as amended, for sheep and lamb producers to: in Year 1 of the program, purchase eligible rams for breeding and enroll herds in a sheep improvement program; improve production facilities; in Years 2-4, market eligible slaughtered lambs, feeder lambs or ewe lambs.

Eligible applicants/beneficiaries: producers of eligible sheep and lambs, with 1999 gross annual revenue of $2,500,000 or less, and that marketed their products between 1 August 2001 and 31 July 2003.

Range/Average: varies (consult FSA for details).

Activity: new program listing in 2004.

HQ: same address/phone as **10.080**. **Internet:** "www.fsa.usda.gov/dafp/psd/lamb.htm".

10.082 TREE ASSISTANCE PROGRAM ("TAP")

Assistance: direct payments/unrestricted use.

Purposes: pursuant to FSRIA, for payments to tree, bush, and vine owners that lost crops due to natural disasters. Payments are restricted to owners that produce annual crops from trees for commercial purposes and that actually replant or rehabilitate eligible crops within 12 months of application approval. Payments may not exceed 75 percent of eligible costs—i.e., that loss over and above the calculated 15 percent mortality.

Eligible applicants/beneficiaries: private stand owners with gross annual revenue not exceeding $2,500,000 for the previous tax year.

Range: to $75,000 per program year for planting up to 500 acres.

Activity: new program in FY 04.

HQ: Production, Emergencies, and Compliance Division, FSA-USDA, Washington, DC 20250-0517. Phone: (202)720-7641. **Internet:** same as **10.029**.

10.083 TOBACCO LOSS ASSISTANCE PROGRAM ("TLAP")

Assistance: direct payments/unrestricted use.

Purposes: to defray tobacco production costs and enhance solvency of producers and quota-holders.

Eligible applicants/beneficiaries: "persons" owning, controlling, or growing eligible tobacco on farms with an established marketing quota or allotment for the 2001 crop year.

Range: formula based.

Activity: new program listing in 2004.

HQ: Tobacco Branch, FSA-USDA, 1400 Independence Ave. SW, Washington, DC 20250-0540. Phone: (202)720-2715. **Internet:** same as **10.029**.

10.084 DAIRY MARKET LOSS ASSISTANCE PROGRAM ("DMLA III")

Assistance: direct payments/unrestricted use.

Purposes: pursuant to the Military Construction Appropriations and Emergency Hurricane Supplemental Appropriations Act of 2005, to provide financial assistance to dairy operations affected by a declared hurricane disaster in 2004, in connection with normal milk production sold on the commercial market.

Eligible applicants/beneficiaries: dairy producers that were paid under DMLA II and new producers that began production in calendar 2000.

Range: to $25,225. **Average:** $8,300.

Activity: new program in FY 05.

HQ: same address/phone as **10.080**. **Internet:** "www.fsa.usda.gov/dafp/psd/dairy.htm".

10.085 TOBACCO TRANSITION PAYMENT PROGRAM ("TTPP")

Assistance: direct payments/unrestricted use.

Purposes: pursuant to the Fair and Equitable Tobacco Reform Act of 2004 (FETRA) which repeals the federal tobacco price support control program, to compensate tobacco quota owners for the elimination of their government-created asset—i.e., quota—through a system of transition payments by the CCC.

Eligible applicants/beneficiaries: tobacco producers owning, controlling, or growing eligible tobacco on farms with an established marketing quota or allotment for the 2004 marketing year, or their assignees.

Range/Average: according to formula based on the FSA-established basic quota.

Activity: new program in FY 05.

HQ: same address/phone as **10.083**. **Internet:** "www.fsa.usda.gov/tobacco"; "www.fsa.usda.gov/pas/publications/facts/html/ttpp05.htm".

10.153 MARKET NEWS

Assistance: technical information.

Purposes: pursuant to the Agricultural Marketing Act of 1946, Food Security Act of 1985, amendments, and other acts, to provide reports on prices, demand, movement, volume, and quality of all major U.S. agricultural commodities. Information is disseminated through news media and through printed reports, bulletin boards, phone, facsimile machines, data networks, and telegraph.

Eligible applicants/beneficiaries: anyone may subscribe.

Activity: FY 03 estimate, 1,213 markets covered.

HQ: Associate Administrator, AMS-USDA, Washington, DC 20250. Phone: (202)720-4276. **Internet:** "www.ams.usda.gov".

10.155 MARKETING AGREEMENTS AND ORDERS

Assistance: specialized services; advisory services/counseling.

Purposes: pursuant to the Agricultural Marketing Agreement Act of 1937 as amended, Agriculture and Food Act of 1981, and other acts, to help maintain adequate prices to producers of agricultural products by issuing federal marketing orders or agreements relating to marketing and economic problems of the commodity or area covered by the federal actions. Marketing orders are issued by USDA only after a public hearing where milk, fruit, and vegetable producers, marketers, and consumers testify, and after farmers vote approval through a referendum.

Eligible applicants/beneficiaries: generally, growers of certain fruits, vegetables, and specialty crops (e.g., nuts, raisins, olives, hops); dairy farmers.

Activity: FY 04, $23.7 billion in marketings.

HQ: same as **10.153**. (Note: no field offices for this program.)

10.156 FEDERAL-STATE MARKETING IMPROVEMENT PROGRAM

Assistance: project grants (50 percent).

Purposes: pursuant to the Agricultural Marketing Act of 1946, for state pilot marketing service projects to improve the marketability of agricultural products, expand export markets, and improve economic and physical marketing efficiency and competitive trading.

Eligible applicants/beneficiaries: state agencies.

Range: $12,000 to $74,000. **Average:** $50,000.

Activity: FY 05 estimate, 28 projects funded.

HQ: Staff Officer, Federal-State Marketing Improvement Program, AMS-USDA, Washington, DC 20250. Phone: (202)720-2704. **Internet:** "www.ams.usda.gov/tmd/fsmip.htm". (Note: no field offices for this program.)

10.162 INSPECTION GRADING AND STANDARDIZATION ("Agricultural Fair Practices Act")

Assistance: specialized services.

Purposes: pursuant to the Agricultural Marketing Act of 1946, Food Security Act of 1985, amendments, and other acts, to develop and apply standards of quality and condition for agricultural commodities, for use used by owners and dealers; to help develop international standards; to conduct quarterly inspections of egg handlers and hatcheries.

Eligible applicants/beneficiaries: agricultural commodity owners or dealers with a financial interest in the commodity to be graded; egg hatcheries and shell egg handlers with an annual production from 3,000 or more hens, packing for the retail consumer—located within the U.S. or its territories.

Activity: FY 04, 18,306,000 bales of cotton classed; 100 tobacco auctions and 1,246,000,000 pounds of imported and domestic tobacco inspected; 12,623 million pounds of poultry products graded; 39,745 million pounds of meat graded; 2,620 billion dozens of shell eggs graded; 20,131 million pounds of processed fruit and vegetables graded; 76 billion pounds of fresh fruit and vegetables graded; 40,000,000 pounds of livestock graded; 1.6 billion pounds of dairy products graded.

HQ: same as **10.153**.

10.163 MARKET PROTECTION AND PROMOTION

Assistance: specialized services; advisory services/counseling; training.

Purposes: pursuant to the Agricultural Marketing Act of 1946, Agricultural Fair Practices Act, amendments, and other acts, to assure a fair and open marketing distribution system for agricultural products, through the prevention and elimination of deceptive, unfair, or fraudulent trade practices. Various activities fall under the national dairy promotion research and nutrition education program, the Federal Seed Program, the Plant Variety Protection Program, the Research and Promotion Program, and the Pesticide Data Program.

Eligible applicants/beneficiaries: any state government, public or private organization, business, or individual.

Activity: FY 06 estimates, 2,600 seed samples tested, 325 plant variety certificates of protection issued, 11,000 pesticide data samples collected.

HQ: same as **10.153**.

10.164 WHOLESALE FARMERS AND ALTERNATIVE MARKET DEVELOPMENT

Assistance: advisory services/counseling; training.

Purposes: pursuant to the Agricultural Marketing Act of 1946, to provide marketing assistance to food producers through studies on wholesaling, conducted in cooperation with other government agencies and private industry. Project examples: central refrigeration systems in modern food centers; wholesale and farmers markets for distributing produce.

Eligible applicants: government agencies and private industry. Cooperative agreements—states, trade associations, universities, and other nonprofit organizations.

Eligible beneficiaries: producers, processors, marketing agencies, and consumers.

Activity: FY 05 estimate, 12 projects and studies.

HQ: Deputy Administrator, Transportation and Marketing Programs, AMS-USDA, Washington, DC 20250. Phone: (202)690-1305. **Internet:** same as **10.153**. (Note: no field offices for this program.)

10.165 PERISHABLE AGRICULTURAL COMMODITIES ACT ("PACA")

Assistance: investigation of complaints.

Purposes: pursuant to the Act of 1930 as amended and Produce Agency Act, to suppress unfair and fraudulent practices in the marketing of perishable agricultural commodities in interstate and foreign commerce, such as dumping or destruction of farm produce.

Eligible applicants/beneficiaries: businesses or individuals may apply for a PACA license.

Activity: FY 03 estimate, 58,000 license actions completed.

HQ: same as **10.153**.

10.167 TRANSPORTATION SERVICES

Assistance: advisory services/counseling; training.

Purposes: pursuant to the Agricultural Adjustment Act of 1938, Agricultural Marketing Act of 1946, Rural Development Act of 1972, and other acts, for the development and promotion of efficient agricultural transportation policies and systems, toward improved farm income and expanded exports. Assistance is provided in cases of significant regional impact or with broad policy implications.

Eligible applicants/beneficiaries: any state government, public or private organization, business or industry, individual.

Activity: FY 06 estimate, 12 research projects, 12 publications, 25 workshops to be completed.

HQ: same as **10.164**. (Note: no field offices for this program.)

10.200 GRANTS FOR AGRICULTURAL RESEARCH, SPECIAL RESEARCH GRANTS
("Special Research Grants")

Assistance: project grants (1-3 years).

Purposes: for applied research, extension, and education projects toward breakthroughs in the food and agricultural sciences, and for ongoing state-federal programs. Current priority areas include integrated pest management and pest management alternatives. Project examples: small fruit crops research; arid rangelands.

Eligible applicants/beneficiaries: state agricultural experiment stations; U.S. IHEs, federal agencies, private organizations and corporations, individuals.

Range: $57,000 to $9,549,000. **Average:** $46,000.

Activity: not quantified specifically.

HQ: Proposal Services Unit, Competitive Programs, CSREES-USDA, 1400 Independence Ave. SW, Washington, DC 20250-2245. Phone: (202)401-5048. **Internet:** "www.reusda.gov". (Note: no field offices for this program.)

10.202 COOPERATIVE FORESTRY RESEARCH
("McIntire-Stennis Act")

Assistance: formula grants (50 percent).

Purposes: pursuant to the Cooperative Forestry Research Act of 1962 and other acts, for forestry research and research training at state forestry schools, in such categories as reforestation, forest and watershed management, rangeland management, production of wildlife and domestic livestock forage, forest pest control, outdoor recreation, wood products development, and protection against fire, insects, and diseases.

Eligible applicants/beneficiaries: governor-designated state institutions; territories and possessions.

Range: $30,000 to $694,000. **Average:** $323,000.

Activity: not quantified specifically.

HQ: Deputy Administrator/Natural Resources and Environment, CSREES-USDA, Washington, DC. 20250. Phone: (202)720-4318. **Internet:** same as **10.200**. (Note: no field offices for this program.)

10.203 PAYMENTS TO AGRICULTURAL EXPERIMENT STATIONS UNDER THE HATCH ACT
("Hatch Act")

Assistance: formula grants (50 percent).

Purposes: pursuant to the Hatch Act of 1887 as amended and other acts, for basic and applied research in broad subject areas at state agricultural experiment stations—to promote efficient production, marketing, distribution, and use of farm products. Funds also may be used to pay for administrative planning and direction, and for such purposes as purchasing or renting land and acquiring or constructing or repairing buildings used for research. The stations may contract with agencies and individuals for research projects.

Eligible applicants/beneficiaries: state agricultural experiment stations; territories and possessions.

Range: $612,000 to $5,832,000. **Average:** $2,796,000.

Activity: not quantified specifically.

HQ: Deputy Administrator/Partnerships, CSREES-USDA, Washington, DC 20250-2201. Phone: (202)720-5623. **Internet:** same as **10.200**. (Note: no field offices for this program.)

10.205 PAYMENTS TO 1890 LAND-GRANT COLLEGES AND TUSKEGEE UNIVERSITY

Assistance: formula grants (50 percent).

Purposes: pursuant to the National Agricultural Research, Extension, and Teaching Policy Act of 1977 as amended (NARETPA) and other acts, for continuing agricultural research and research training, toward the promotion of efficient production, marketing, distribution, and utilization of farm products, and toward sound agriculture and rural life. Funds may be used to pay for developmental costs, retirement programs, administrative planning and direction, and for such purposes as purchasing or renting land and acquiring or constructing or repairing buildings used for research. Recipients may contract with agencies and individuals.

Eligible applicants/beneficiaries: Tuskegee University and the "1890" land grant colleges in Alabama, Arkansas, Delaware, Florida, Georgia, Kentucky, Louisiana, Maryland, Mississippi, Missouri, North Carolina, Oklahoma, South Carolina, Tennessee, Texas, Virginia, and West Virginia.

Range: $518,000 to $1,540,000. **Average:** $1,571,000.

Activity: not quantified specifically.

HQ: National Program Leader, MultiCultural Alliances, CSREES-USDA,

1400 Independence Ave. SW, Washington, DC 20250-2251. Phone: (202) 720-3511. **Internet:** same as **10.200**. (Note: no field offices for this program.)

10.206 GRANTS FOR AGRICULTURAL RESEARCH—COMPETITIVE RESEARCH GRANTS
("National Research Initiative Competitive Grants Program")

Assistance: project grants (100 percent/to 4 years).

Purposes: for research, education and extension grants in food, agriculture, and related areas. Priority areas for funding include agricultural security, plant science and plant pathology, animal science, entomology and nematology, nanotoechnology, obesity, natural resources and environment, nutrition, rural development, and new products and processes.

Eligible applicants/beneficiaries: same as for **10.200**.

Range: $4,000 to $5,000,000. **Average:** $184,000.

Activity: not quantified specifically.

HQ: Chief Scientist, National Research Initiative Competitive Grants Program, CSREES-USDA, 14th & Independence Ave. SW, Washington, DC 20250-2241. Phone: (202)401-5022. **Internet:** same as **10.200**. (Note: no field offices for this program.)

10.207 ANIMAL HEALTH AND DISEASE RESEARCH

Assistance: formula grants (50 percent matching above base amount).

Purposes: pursuant to NARETPA, amendments, and other acts, for research on health and disease of food animals and horses. Focus is on: infectious diseases; internal and external parasites; noninfectious diseases, toxins, poisons, transportation losses, predators, and other hazards; diseases and parasites of wildlife and other animals transmissible to food animals, horses, or humans.

Eligible applicants/beneficiaries: public nonprofit schools and colleges of veterinary medicine; state agricultural experiment stations.

Range: $1,586 to $409,000. **Average:** $66,000.

Activity: not quantified specifically.

HQ: Deputy Administrator/Plant and Animal Science, CSREES-USDA, Washington, DC. 20250. Phone: (202)401-4329. **Internet:** same as **10.200**. (Note: no field offices for this program.)

10.210 FOOD AND AGRICULTURAL SCIENCES NATIONAL NEEDS GRADUATE FELLOWSHIP GRANTS

Assistance: project grants (100 percent/to five years).

Purposes: pursuant to NARETPA as amended, to support graduate degree candidates and professionals in the food and agricultural sciences. Fellowships are awarded to outstanding students pursuing graduate degrees in fields for which there is a national need for the development of scientific expertise. Doctoral and masters fellows may receive three and two years of support, respectively. The targeted national need areas include: animal, plant biotechnology; food science; human nutrition; food, forest product, or agricultural engineering; water science; agribusiness marketing or management.

Eligible applicants: U.S. public and private nonprofit IHEs.

Eligible beneficiaries: graduate students.

Range: N.A.

Activity: not quantified specifically.

HQ: National Program Leader, Higher Education Programs, CSREES-USDA, 1400 Independence Ave. SW, Washington, DC 20250-2251. Phone: (202) 720-7854. **Internet:** same as **10.200**. (Note: no field offices for the program.)

10.212 SMALL BUSINESS INNOVATION RESEARCH ("SBIR Program")

Assistance: project grants (100 percent).

Purposes: pursuant to the Small Business Innovation Development Act of 1982 as amended, for research by small businesses to stimulate technological innovation, mainly in the areas of: forests and related resources; plant, animal production and protection; air, water, and soils; food science and nutrition; rural and community development; industrial applications; aquaculture; industrial applications; marketing and trade. Previous phase I grants have ranged up to $65,000 for six months of activity; phase II, to $300,000 for up to two years; phase III covers pursuit of commercialization of research products, and receives no federal funding. An objective of SBIR programs is to foster and encourage participation by women-owned and socially disadvantaged firms.

Eligible applicants/beneficiaries: small, U.S. for-profit businesses.

Range: $46,000 to $300,000. **Average:** $95,000.

Activity: not quantified specifically.

HQ: SBIR Director, CSREES-USDA, 14th & Independence Ave. SW, Washington, DC 20250-2243. Phone: (202)401-4002. **Internet:** same as **10.200**. (Note: no field offices for this program.)

10.215 SUSTAINABLE AGRICULTURE RESEARCH AND EDUCATION

Assistance: project grants (100 percent/1-5 years).

Purposes: pursuant to NARETPA and FACTA, for scientific investigations and education to: reduce the use of chemical pesticides, fertilizers, and toxic materials; improve management of farm resources to enhance productivity and competitiveness; promote crop, livestock, and enterprise diversification; facilitate research projects designed to study agricultural production systems located in areas with various soil, climatic, and physical characteristics; study farms that are managed using production practices optimizing on-farm resources and conservation practices. Funds may not be used to pay indirect costs or tuition.

Eligible applicants/beneficiaries: land grant colleges or universities, other universities, state agricultural experiment and cooperative extension stations, nonprofit organizations, individuals, federal or state government entities.

Range: $8,000 to $1,752,000. **Average:** $856,000.

Activity: not quantified specifically.

HQ: Deputy Administrator/Economic and Community Systems, CSREES-USDA, Washington, DC. 20250. Phone: (202)720-7948. **Internet:** same as **10.200**. (Note: no field offices for this program.)

10.216 1890 INSTITUTION CAPACITY BUILDING GRANTS

Assistance: project grants (100 percent/1-5 years).

Purposes: pursuant to NARETPA as amended, to build research and teaching capacities at "1890" land grants institutions and Tuskegee University. Teaching grants may support: curricula design and materials development; faculty development; instruction delivery systems; scientific instrumentation; student recruitment and retention; student experiential learning. Research grants may support studies and experimentation in food and agricultural sciences, centralized research support systems, and technology delivery systems. CSREES encourages cost-sharing by grant recipients.

Eligible applicants/beneficiaries: "1890" land grant institutions, Tuskegee University.

Range: teaching grants, $88,000 to $225,000; research, $108,000 to $350,000. **Average:** teaching, $171,000; research, $243,000.

Activity: not quantified specifically.

HQ: same address, web site as **10.210**. Phone: (202)720-2186. (Note: no field offices for this program.)

10.217 HIGHER EDUCATION CHALLENGE GRANTS

Assistance: project grants (50 percent/1-5 years).

Purposes: pursuant to NARETPA as amended, to increase institutional capacity to respond to state, regional, national, or international educational needs in food and agricultural sciences. Funds may be used for curriculum design and materials development, faculty development, instruction delivery systems, scientific instrumentation, student recruitment and retention.

Eligible applicants/beneficiaries: U.S. colleges and universities.

Range: $48,000 to $152,000. **Average:** $89,000.

Activity: not quantified specifically.

HQ: National Program Leader/Higher Education Challenge Grants, Higher Education Programs, CSREES-USDA, 1400 Independence Ave. SW, Washington, DC 20250-2251. Phone: (202)720-1973, FAX (202)720-2030. **Internet:** "www.reusda.gov/1700/funding/ourfund.htm". (Note: no field offices for this program.)

10.219 BIOTECHNOLOGY RISK ASSESSMENT RESEARCH

Assistance: project grants (100 percent/1-5 years).

Purposes: for research focusing on environmental effects of agricultural biotechnology. Project examples: gene crop flow and introgression into natural populations; hazard of pest evolution.

Eligible applicants/beneficiaries: any public or private research or educational institution or organization.

Range: $50,000 to $223,000. **Average:** $148,000.

Activity: not quantified specifically.

HQ: Deputy Administrator, Competitive Programs, CSREES-USDA, Washington, DC 20250. Phone: (202)401-1761. **Internet:** same as **10.210**. (Note: no field offices for this program.)

10.220 HIGHER EDUCATION MULTICULTURAL SCHOLARS PROGRAM ("Minority Scholars Program")

Assistance: project grants (75 percent/5 years).

Purposes: pursuant to NARETPA as amended and the Food and Agriculture Act of 1977, for four-year undergraduate scholarships supporting minority students pursuing baccalaureate degrees in the food and agricultural sciences, including natural resources, forestry, veterinary medicine, home economics, and closely allied disciplines.

Eligible applicants: all U.S. colleges and universities with appropriate baccalaureate or higher degree programs and with significant minority enrollments.

Eligible beneficiaries: full-time students from groups traditionally underrepresented in the fields of study in which funds are awarded.

Range: $20,000 to $80,000. **Average:** $52,000.

Activity: not quantified specifically.

HQ: same address, web site as **10.210**. Phone:(202)720-1973. (Note: no field offices for this program.)

10.221 TRIBAL COLLEGES EDUCATION EQUITY GRANTS

Assistance: formula grants (1-2 years).

Purposes: pursuant to the Equity in Educational Land-Grant Status Act of 1994 as amended, to enhance educational opportunities at the 30 tribal colleges designated as the "1994 Land-Grant Institutions" by strengthening their teaching programs in the food and agricultural sciences in targeted need areas. Funds may support: curricula design and instructional materials development; faculty development; instruction delivery systems; scientific instrumentation; student experiential learning; student recruitment and retention.

Eligible applicants/beneficiaries: the 30 designated tribal colleges.

Range/Average: $50,000 to each institution.

Activity: N.A.

HQ: Science and Education Resources Development, Higher Education Programs, CSREES-USDA, 800 Ninth St.SW - Rm.3901, Washington, DC 20250-2251. Phone: (202)720-1973. **Internet:** same as **10.200**. (Note: no field offices for this program.)

10.222 TRIBAL COLLEGES ENDOWMENT PROGRAM

Assistance: formula grants (100 percent).

Purposes: pursuant to the Equity in Educational Land-Grant Status Act of 1994, to enhance educational opportunities at the 30 tribal colleges designated as the "1994 Land-Grant Institutions" by strengthening their teaching programs in the food and agricultural sciences in targeted need areas. Funds may be used to establish an endowment supporting activities described in **10.221**.

Eligible applicants/beneficiaries: same as for **10.221**.

Range: $7,932 to $40,000. **Average:** $15,000.

Activity: N.A.

HQ: same as **10.221**. (Note: no field offices for this program.)

10.223 HISPANIC SERVING INSTITUTIONS EDUCATION GRANTS

Assistance: project grants (some matching/1-3 years).

Purposes: pursuant to NARETPA as amended, to support activities by a consortium of Hispanic serving institutions to enhance educational equity for under-represented students, by strengthening their capacities to respond to identified state, regional, national, or international needs in the food and agricultural sciences. Funds may support cooperative initiatives between two or more institutions and units of state government or the private sector, for activities such as: student mentoring beginning at the high school level and continuing with the provision of financial support for students through graduate training; library resources; curricula design and materials development; faculty development; instruction delivery systems; scientific instrumentation; student experiential learning; student recruitment and retention.

Eligible applicants/beneficiaries: Hispanic-serving IHEs with an enrollment of at least 25 percent Hispanic students, and providing postsecondary programs for which a two-year associate, baccalaureate, or higher degree is awarded.

Range: $25,000 to $75,000.

Activity: N.A.

HQ: Multicultural Alliances, Science and Education Resources Development, Higher Education Programs, CSREES-USDA, Waterfront Center - Rm. 3240, Washington, DC 20250-2251. Phone: (202)720-1254. **Internet:** same as **10.200**. (Note: no field offices for this program.)

10.224 FUND FOR RURAL AMERICA—RESEARCH, EDUCATION, AND EXTENSION ACTIVITIES

Assistance: project grants (50 percent/6 months-4 years).

Purposes: pursuant to FAIRA, for research, education, and extension projects to aid farmers, ranchers, and rural communities in addressing changes resulting from fundamental reforms to federal farm programs. Funded projects are expected to: increase international competitiveness, efficiency, and farm profitability; reduce economic and health risk; conserve and enhance natural resources; develop new crops, crop uses, and agricultural applications of biotechnology; enhance animal agricultural resources; preserve plant and animal germplasm; increase economic opportunities in farming and rural communities; and, expand locally-owned, value-added processing. Funds may support: applied, developmental, and adaptive research; technology transfer; extension and related activities; and, education—with emphasis on biological, physical, and social sciences to address systems-based problems; planning costs toward development of Fund for Rural America (FRA) Centers.

Eligible applicants: federal research agencies; national laboratories; IHEs and their research foundations; private research organizations.

Eligible beneficiaries: producers, commodity groups, environmental interests, rural communities, others.

Range: $25,000 to $600,000. **Average:** standard grants, $271,000; center planning grants, $25,000.

Activity: N.A.

HQ: same as **10.219**. (Note: no field offices for this program.)

10.225 COMMUNITY FOOD PROJECTS

Assistance: project grants (50 percent/1-3 years).

Purposes: pursuant to the Food Stamp Act of 1977 as amended and FAIRA, for community food projects designed to provide food to low-income persons; to increase self-reliance in communities; to promote comprehensive responses to local food, farm, and nutrition issues. Funds may support: improving access to affordable food by low-income households; local food systems such as urban gardening and obtaining food from local farms; expanding economic opportunities for community residents through local businesses or other economic development, job training, youth apprenticeships, school-to-work transitions. Projects should link the food sector to community development, economic opportunity, and environmental enhancement.

Eligible applicants/beneficiaries: experienced private nonprofit entities and partnerships thereof.

Range: $10,000 to $250,000.

Activity: 2001, 16 grants.

HQ: same as **10.219**. (Note: no field offices for this program.)

10.226 SECONDARY AND TWO-YEAR POSTSECONDARY AGRICULTURE EDUCATION CHALLENGE GRANTS

Assistance: project grants (50 percent/1-5 years).

Purposes: pursuant to FAIRA as amended, to promote excellence in agriscience and agribusiness education, and to encourage increased pursuit of undergraduate and higher degrees in the food and agricultural sciences. Funds may be used for such targeted areas as curricula design and materials development, promotion of teaching competency, student experiential learning, increasing the diversity of students enrolling.

Eligible applicants/beneficiaries: public secondary schools; public, private nonprofit junior and community colleges.

Range: $15,000 to $40,000. **Average:** $21,000.

Activity: not quantified specifically.

HQ: National Program Leader/Secondary and Two-Year Postsecondary Agriculture Education Challenge Grants, Higher Education Programs, same address/phones, web site as **10.217**. (Note: no field offices for this program.)

10.227 1994 INSTITUTIONS RESEARCH PROGRAM

Assistance: project grants (100 percent/to 3 years).

Purposes: pursuant to the Equity in Educational Land-Grant Status Act of 1994 as amended, for competitive research grants to the 30 institutions designated as "1994 Institutions," to conduct agricultural research addressing high priority concerns of tribal, national, or multi-state significance.

Eligible applicants/beneficiaries: the 30 institutions designated as "1994 Institutions" (i.e., specified Indian colleges and institutions).

Range: $41,000 to $150,000. **Average:** $66,000.

Activity: not quantified specifically.

HQ: Administrator, CSREES-USDA, 14th & Independence Ave. SW, Washington, DC. 20250-2201. Phone: (202)720-4423. **Internet:** same as **10.200**. (Note: no field offices for this program.)

10.228 ALASKA NATIVE SERVING AND NATIVE HAWAIIAN SERVING INSTITUTIONS EDUCATION GRANTS

Assistance: project grants (100 percent/1-3 years).

Purposes: to recruit, support, and educate under-represented scientists and professionals, and to advance the educational capacity of Alaska native- and Hawaii native-serving institutions in the food, agricultural, and natural resource systems and careers. Funds may support: curriculum, faculty and library development; scientific instrumentation; instruction delivery systems; student recruitment and retention; and, cooperative initiatives between institutions, state governments, the private sector.

Eligible applicants/beneficiaries: Alaska native- and Hawaii native-serving IHEs.

Range: $100,000 to $150,000.

Activity: N.A.

HQ: Multicultural Alliances, Science and Education Resources Development, CSREES-USDA, Waterfront Center - Rm.3901, 1400 Independence Ave. SW, Washington, DC 20250-2251. Phone: (202)720-1973. **Internet:** same as **10.200**. (Note: no field offices for this program.)

10.250 AGRICULTURAL AND RURAL ECONOMIC RESEARCH

Assistance: technical information.

Purposes: to provide economic and other social science information and analysis related to U.S. and world agriculture, food, natural resources, and rural America. Reports are prepared by USDA staff, and are available in printed or electronic form. Fees may be charged.

Eligible applicants/beneficiaries: anyone in the U.S. and territories.

Activity: FY 03, 244 active projects; responses to 50,000 requests for information; 200 reports published.

HQ: Director, Extramural Agreement Division, Economic Research Service-

USDA, Sunnyside Ave. - ARS Rm.5601, Beltsville, MD 20705-5110. Phone: (301)504-1147; *sales through NTIS,* (800)999-6779. **Internet:** "www.ers.usda.gov". (Note: no field offices for this program.)

10.303 INTEGRATED PROGRAMS

Assistance: project grants (100 percent/to 3 years).

Purposes: pursuant to the Food Stamp Act of 1977, for competitive integrated and multi-functional research, education, and extension projects addressing priorities in U.S. agriculture.

Eligible applicants/beneficiaries: same as for **10.200**.

Range: $20,000 to $2,080,000. **Average:** $499,000.

Activity: not quantified specifically.

HQ: same as **10.227**. (Note: no field offices for this program.)

10.304 HOMELAND SECURITY—AGRICULTURAL

Assistance: project grants (100 percent/1-3 years).

Purposes: pursuant to NARETPA as amended, to protect the food supply and agricultural production; to protect USDA facilities and other agricultural infrastructure; and to protect USDA staff and manage emergency preparedness. Project examples: establishment of two diagnostic networks—one each for plant and animal diseases and pests. Research projects may not be funded.

Eligible applicants/beneficiaries: recipients eligible under Section 1472(c) of NARETPA.

Range: $250,000 to $2,000,000.

Activity: new program listing in 2003.

HQ: Office of the Administrator, CSREES-USDA, 14th & Independence Ave. SW - Rm.305-A, Washington, DC. 20250-2201. Phone: (no number provided). **Internet:** same as **10.200**. (Note: no field offices for this program.)

10.305 INTERNATIONAL SCIENCE AND EDUCATION GRANT PROGRAM

Assistance: project grants (1-4 years).

Purposes: pursuant to NARETPA as amended, to strengthen the global competence of students, faculty, and staff in agriculture and related areas, and to enhance business performance in international agriculture and related sectors—through extension, research, and teaching programs. Projects should be designed to: enhance the international content of curricula; enable U.S. faculty to work beyond the U.S. and bring back lessons learned; promote international partnerships; enhance the use of foreign technologies in the U.S.; strengthen the role of IHEs in maintaining U.S. competitiveness.

Eligible applicants/beneficiaries: accredited public or other nonprofit U.S. IHEs that award bachelor's or higher degrees

Range/Average: N.A.

Activity: new program listing in 2005 (CFDA on-line version).

HQ: International Programs, CSREES-USDA, 14th & Independence Ave. SW, Washington, DC. 20250-2203. Phone: (202)720-3801. **Internet:** "www.csrees.usda.gov". (Note: no field offices for this program.)

10.306 BIODIESEL

Assistance: project grants (100 percent/5 years).

Purposes: to educate governmental and private entities that operate vehicle fleets, as well as the general public, about the benefits of biodiesel fuel use—through education and outreach activities.

Eligible applicants/beneficiaries: nonprofit organizations or IHEs.

Range: $190,000 to $770,000.

Activity: new program listing in 2005 (CFDA on-line version).

HQ: Plant and Animal Systems, CSREES-USDA, 14th & Independence Ave. SW, Washington, DC. 20250-2220. Phone: (202)401-5877. **Internet:** same as **10.305**. (Note: no field offices for this program.)

10.307 ORGANIC AGRICULTURE RESEARCH AND EXTENSION INITIATIVE

Assistance: project grants (50-100 percent).

Purposes: pursuant to FSRIA as amended and FACTA, for projects emphasizing research and outreach activities that assist farmers and ranchers with whole farm planning and ecosystem integration. Field work for both program areas must be done on certified organic land or land in transition to certification. Projects should: facilitate the development of organic agriculture production, breeding, and processing methods; explore both barriers to and opportunities for marketing, both domestically and abroad; be designed to study and apply most related aspects of organic agriculture.

Eligible applicants/beneficiaries: state agricultural experiment stations, IHEs, other research institutions and organizations, federal agencies, national laboratories, private organizations and corporations, individuals.

Range/Average: N.A.

Activity: new program listing in 2005 (CFDA on-line version).

HQ: same address, web site as **10.306**. Phone: (202)401-3356. (Note: no field offices for this program.)

10.308 RESIDENT INSTRUCTION GRANTS FOR INSULAR AREA ACTIVITIES

Assistance: project grants (100 percent).

Purposes: pursuant to FSRIA, to enhance teaching programs in extension programs in U.S. insular areas, including PR, VI, Guam, Samoa, Northern Marianas, Micronesia, Marshall Islands, and Palau. Funded activities should be similar to those funded under **10.228**, and they facilitate cooperative initiatives between two or more insular area institutions and organizations.

Eligible applicants/beneficiaries: institutions with demonstrated commitment to higher education in the food and agricultural sciences.

Range/Average: N.A.

Activity: new program in FY 05.

HQ: Science and Education Resources Development, CSREES-USDA, 1400 Independence Ave. SW, Washington, DC 20250-2250. Phone: (no number provided). **Internet:** same as **10.305**. (Note: no field offices for this program.)

10.350 TECHNICAL ASSISTANCE TO COOPERATIVES

Assistance: specialized services; advisory services/counseling; training; technical information.

Purposes: pursuant to the Cooperative Marketing Act of 1926 and Agricultural Marketing Act of 1946, to provide research, technical assistance, and educational programs on the financial, organization, management, legal, social, and economic aspects of rural cooperatives. Assistance may include publications, workshops, audiovisual materials, computer systems.

Eligible applicants/beneficiaries: farmer cooperatives and groups of rural residents, including in the territories.

Activity: not quantified.

HQ: Deputy Administrator/Cooperative Services, RBCS-USDA, Washington, DC 20250-3250. Phone: (202)720-7558, FAX (202)720-4641. **Internet:** "www.rurdev.usda.gov/rbs/coops/esdir.htm".

10.352 VALUE-ADDED PRODUCER GRANTS ("VAPG")

Assistance: project grants (50 percent).

Purposes: pursuant to Agricultural Risk Protection Act of 2000 as amended and FSRIA, to refine agricultural commodity product values and enhance returns to producers. Grants may cover either: planning activities to prepare feasibility studies, marketing strategies, business plans, and legal evaluations; or, working capital for operating expenses of ventures.

Eligible applicants/beneficiaries: agricultural commodity producers and producer groups, farmer and rancher cooperatives, and majority-controlled, producer-based business ventures—including producer steering committees, producer-owned corporations and associations with an ownership interest in the product subject to the value-added activity.

Range: planning, to $100,000; working capital, to $150,000. **Average:** $125,000.

Activity: new program listing in 2005. FY 04, 97 awards.

HQ: same address/phone as **10.350**. **Internet:** "www.rurdev.usda.gov/rbs/".

10.404 EMERGENCY LOANS

Assistance: direct loans (80-100 percent/15-40 years).

Purposes: pursuant to the Consolidated Farm and Rural Development Act of 1987 (CFRDA) and other acts, to repair, restore, or replace damaged or destroyed farm property, required as a result of declared natural disasters; for farm operating expenses and other costs necessary to return disaster victims' farming operations to financially sound condition, including debt refinancing. Loans at 3.75 percent interest may cover: 100 percent of the cost of physical loss for up to 40 years; 80 percent of actual production loss for up to 15 years.

Eligible applicants/beneficiaries: established family farmers, ranchers, or aquaculture operators (tenant- or owner-operator) conducting a farming operation at the time of the disaster, as proprietors, partnerships, cooperatives, corporations, or joint operations—and that: are U.S. citizens or legal resident aliens, or entities operated by citizens owning over a 50 percent interest; are unable to obtain necessary credit from other sources to qualify for subsidized loss loans; are capable of managing the operation; have county committee eligibility certification; provide suitable collateral to secure the loan; have crop insurance if available for affected crops; have not caused a loss to FSA, nor received FSA debt forgiveness on more than one occasion, after 4 April 1996. Available also in most territories when those areas are designated. Prospective applicants should contact FSA county offices immediately after sustaining the loss.

Range: $500 to $500,000. **Average:** $58,000.

Activity: FY 01, 2,451 loans obligated.

HQ: same as **10.075**.

10.405 FARM LABOR HOUSING LOANS AND GRANTS
("Labor Housing" - "Sections 514 and 516")

Assistance: project grants (to 90 percent); guaranteed/insured loans (1 percent/to 33 years).

Purposes: pursuant to the Housing Act of 1949 as amended, to construct, repair, or purchase basic year-round or seasonal housing and related support facilities for domestic farm laborers. Funds may be used for land acquisition, recreation areas, central cooking and dining facilities, small infirmaries, laundry facilities, day care centers. Grants are available only when there is a pressing need and when facilities could not be developed otherwise.

Eligible applicants: loans—farmers, family farm partnerships or corporations, associations of farmers. Loans and grants—states and their political subdivisions, PR, VI, broad-based public or private nonprofit organizations, tribes, and nonprofit corporations of farm workers.

Eligible beneficiaries: domestic farm laborers that are U.S. citizens or legal permanent residents.

Range: initial grants, $43,000 to $12,270,000; initial loans, individuals, $58,000 to $300,000; initial loans/organizations, $58,000 to $3,000,000; **Average:** grants, $882,000; loans/individuals, $35,000; loans/organizations, $925,000.

Activity: FY 04, 818 new, 579 new, 2,063 rehabilitated units provided.

HQ: Multifamily Housing Processing Division, RHS-USDA, Washington, DC 20250. Phone: (202)720-1604. **Internet:** "www.rurdev.usda.gov".

10.406 FARM OPERATING LOANS

Assistance: direct loans; guaranteed/insured loans (7-22 years).

Purposes: pursuant to CFRDA and other acts, to enable family farm operators to: purchase livestock, poultry, fur-bearing and other farm animals, fish, and bees; purchase farm, forestry, recreation, or nonfarm enterprise equipment and provide operating funds for such enterprises; meet family subsistence needs; purchase essential home equipment; refinance certain secured and unsecured debts; pay property taxes and property insurance premiums;

finance youth projects. The interest rate on guaranteed loans may be subsidized at 4 percent; direct loans are awarded at one percent interest above the federal borrowing rate.

Eligible applicants/beneficiaries: U.S. citizens or permanent residents with: experience or training to operate a farm; an acceptable credit history; legal capacity to incur a loan obligation; inability to obtain a reasonable loan elsewhere; and, that will become owners or tenants operating family farms through the program; except for youth projects, no history of causing a loss to FSA, nor of receiving FSA debt forgiveness more than three times after 4 April 1996. Certain corporations, cooperatives, partnerships, and joint operations conducting family farms. Available also in most territories.

Range: direct loans, to $200,000; guaranteed, to $731,000. **Average:** direct, $47,000; guaranteed, $157,000.

Activity: FY 01, 14,000 direct, 11,000 guaranteed loans.

HQ: same as **10.075**.

10.407 FARM OWNERSHIP LOANS

Assistance: direct loans; guaranteed/insured loans (to 40 years).

Purposes: pursuant to CFRDA and other acts, to: purchase, enlarge, and improve family farms; provide necessary water and water facilities; take necessary basic soil treatment and land conservation measures; construct, repair, or improve buildings needed in farm operations; provide facilities to produce fish under controlled conditions.

Eligible applicants/beneficiaries: applicants must meet the criteria for **10.406** and: if an individual, not have a combined farm ownership loan, soil and water loan, and recreation loan indebtedness to FSA of more than $200,000 for direct loans, and $717,000 for guaranteed loans, or a total indebtedness against the property securing the loan of more than the market value of the security, whichever is the lesser amount.

Range: direct, to $200,000; guaranteed, to $731,000. **Average:** direct, $112,000; guaranteed, $250,000.

Activity: FY 01, 2,085 direct, 3,488 guaranteed loans.

HQ: same as **10.075**.

10.410 VERY LOW TO MODERATE INCOME HOUSING LOANS ("Section 502 Rural Housing Loans")

Assistance: guaranteed loans (to 30 years); direct loans (to 38 years).

Purposes: pursuant to the Housing Act of 1949 and CFRDA as amended and other acts, for below-market-rate loan financing to lower-income rural families to: purchase, construct, improve, or repair housing to be used as a permanent residence; to finance the cost of sewage disposal, water supply facilities, weatherization, and essential household equipment; and, under certain conditions, to refinance housing debts, finance the purchase of manufactured homes and sites for their location. Loans can be subsidized through interest credits to as low as an effective rate of one percent, depending on the loan amount and applicant income and family size; interest subsidies are subject to recapture if property is liquidated.

Eligible applicants/beneficiaries: applicants determined to be very low income (below 50 percent of area median), low income (between 50 and 80 percent or area median), or moderate income (below 115 percent of area median)—with adequate and dependable available income to meet operating and family living expenses, including taxes, insurance, maintenance, and repayments on debts including the proposed loan, and without sufficient resources to obtain the necessary housing or related facilities. For direct loans, applicants must be eligible for interest credit, with income not above established limits. Available in territories and possessions.

Range: $1,000 to $105,000. **Average:** direct loans, $73,000; guaranteed, $93,000—more in high-cost areas.

Activity: FY 04, 15,000 direct, 31,000 guaranteed loans.

HQ: Director, Single Family Housing Direct Loan Division *or* Director, Single Family Housing Guaranteed Loan Division, RHS-USDA, Washington, DC 20250. Phone: *direct loans,* (202)720-1474; *guaranteed loans,* (202)720-1452. **Internet:** same as **10.405**.

10.411 RURAL HOUSING SITE LOANS AND SELF-HELP HOUSING LAND DEVELOPMENT LOANS
("Section 523 and 524 Site Loans")

Assistance: direct loans (2 years).

Purposes: pursuant to the Housing Act of 1949 as amended, to buy land for housing sites and to install improvements thereon—to be sold to low- or very-low-income households. Loans also may cover the costs of water and sewer facilities, walks, driveways, parking areas, landscaping, engineering and legal fees, and closing costs.

Eligible applicants: private or public nonprofit organizations that will provide the developed sites to qualified borrowers without profit, in open country or towns of 10,000 population or less, or in places up to 25,000 population under certain conditions. Available also in PR, VI, Guam, and the Northern Marianas.

Eligible beneficiaries: Section 524—low- and very-low-income families, nonprofit organizations, public agencies, cooperatives. Sites developed under Section 523 must be used for housing built under the self-help method.

Range: to $200,000 (unless with RHS approval). **Average:** Section 523, $9,380; Section 524, $12,000.

Activity: FY 04, 3 Section 523, 1 Section 524 loans.

HQ: Director, Single-Family Housing Processing Division, RHS-USDA, Washington, DC 20250. Phone (202)720-1474. **Internet:** same as **10.405**.

10.415 RURAL RENTAL HOUSING LOANS
("Sections 515 and 521")

Assistance: direct loans (30 years).

Purposes: pursuant to the Housing Act of 1949 as amended, for the purchase, construction, or substantial rehabilitation of rural rental or cooperative housing with two or more family units, including manufactured housing, and certain related uses including recreational and service facilities. Loans may be made in communities with up to 10,000 population, and up to 20,000 under certain conditions. Tenants pay basic rent or 30 percent of adjusted income, whichever is greater; RHS rental assistance subsidies can be used to limit rental payments to 30 percent of income (see **10.427**). Loans may not cover nursing, special care, or institutional homes.

Eligible applicants: individuals, cooperatives, nonprofit organizations, state or local public agencies, profit corporations, trusts, partnerships, limited partnerships and, except for state or local public agencies, unable to finance the housing either with their own resources or with credit obtained from private sources. Available also in territories.

Eligible beneficiaries: very-low-, low-, and moderate-income households, elderly, and handicapped or disabled persons.

Range: to $1,000,000 per application; to $2,500,000 per state.

Activity: FY 04, 902 new, 6,737 rehabilitated units provided.

HQ: same as **10.405**.

10.417 VERY LOW-INCOME HOUSING REPAIR LOANS AND GRANTS ("Section 504 Rural Housing Loans and Grants")

Assistance: direct loans (1 percent interest/to 20 years); project grants (formula based).

Purposes: pursuant to the Housing Act of 1949 as amended, to provide loans of up to $20,000 to very low-income rural owner-occupants and/or grants of up to $7,500 to eligible elderly persons—to repair or modernize their existing homes, including weatherization, and to upgrade water and waste disposal systems.

Eligible applicants/beneficiaries: owner-occupants of rural homes, with sufficient income to repay loans, and that are U.S. citizens or legal residents or on indefinite parole. Applicant's income may not exceed very-low-income limits set forth in USDA instructions. Grant recipients must be at least age 62 and unable to repay the part of the assistance received as a grant. Available also in territories.

Range/Average: loans, $5,894; grants, $5,128.

Activity: FY 04, 5,594 loans, 5,988 grants.

HQ: same as **10.411**.

10.420 RURAL SELF-HELP HOUSING TECHNICAL ASSISTANCE ("Section 523 Technical Assistance")

Assistance: project grants (100 percent/2 years).

Purposes: pursuant to the Housing Act of 1949 as amended, for the organizational, administrative, and basic costs of carrying out mutual self-help housing programs in rural areas. Grant funds may be used to pay the costs of training self-help group members and of purchasing tools and equipment—but not to hire construction personnel, nor to buy real estate or building materials.

Eligible applicants: states or political subdivisions, public or private nonprofit corporations. Available also in PR, VI, Guam, Northern Marianas.

Eligible beneficiaries: very-low- and low-income rural families, usually in groups of 6 to 10 families.

Range/Average: $34,000.

Activity: FY 04, 104 grants.

HQ: same as **10.411**.

10.421 INDIAN TRIBES AND TRIBAL CORPORATION LOANS

Assistance: direct loans (100 percent/to 40 years).

Purposes: pursuant to the Loans to Indian Tribes and Tribal Corporations Act, to buy land within tribal reservations and Alaskan communities. Loan funds may be used to acquire land and for related costs, for such purposes as rounding out farming or ranching units or to eliminate fractional heirships. Loan funds may not be used for development, improvements, or operating costs.

Eligible applicants/beneficiaries: recognized tribes and tribal corporations or Alaska communities.

Range: $450,000 to $2,000,000. **Average:** $224,000.

Activity: FY 02 estimate, 1 loan.

HQ: Director, Loan Servicing and Property Management Division, FSA-USDA, Ag Box 0523, Washington, DC 20250. Phone: (202)720-4572. **Internet:** same as **10.029**.

10.427 RURAL RENTAL ASSISTANCE PAYMENTS
("Rental Assistance" - "Section 521")

Assistance: direct payments/specified use (5 years).

Purposes: pursuant to the Housing Act of 1949 as amended, to subsidize rents paid by low-income senior citizens, families, and domestic farm laborers occupying eligible RHS-assisted units, and whose rents exceed 30 percent of an adjusted annual income figure established for each state.

Eligible applicants: basically, state and local agencies and nonprofit or limited-profit sponsors of certain rural rental housing projects financed by RHS. (New construction and rehabilitation projects receiving Section 8 assistance from HUD are ineligible.)

Eligible beneficiaries: low- or very-low-income families and handicapped or senior citizens occupying eligible rural rental, cooperative, or farm labor housing.

Range: N.A.

Activity: FY 05 estimate, 42,000 households to be assisted.

HQ: Director, Multifamily Housing Portfolio Management Division, RHS-USDA, Washington, DC 20250. Phone: (202)720-1615. **Internet:** same as **10.405**.

10.433 RURAL HOUSING PRESERVATION GRANTS
("HPG" - "Section 533")

Assistance: project grants (formula based).

Purposes: pursuant to the Housing Act of 1949 as amended, to assist low- and very-low-income rural homeowners, rental property owners, and cooperatives to repair or rehabilitate their housing. Generally, assistance is used in conjunction with other federal funding, such as HUD's CDBG or HHS's weatherization programs, or with programs sponsored by states. Revolving loan funds may be established. Applicants may use up 20 percent of funds for project operating costs, including training of project personnel; the remaining 80 percent must be used as loans or grants for housing improvements.

Eligible applicants/beneficiaries: authorized public or private nonprofit organizations; city and county agencies, state governments; tribes; consortia of eligible entities—in communities with up to 10,000 population, or up to 20,000 under certain conditions. Available also in territories and possessions.

Range/Average: N.A.

Activity: FY 04, 151 grants obligated to provide assistance for 2,105 units.

HQ: same as **10.405**.

10.435 STATE MEDIATION GRANTS

Assistance: project grants (70 percent).

Purposes: pursuant to the Agricultural Credit Act of 1987, FACTA, Agricultural Credit Improvement Act of 1992, Federal Crop Insurance Reform and Department of Agriculture Reorganization Act of 1994, and United States Grain Standards Act of 2000, to cover state operating and administrative costs in connection with certified agricultural loan mediation programs for producers, creditors, and others affected by USDA actions.

Eligible applicants: state governments.

Eligible beneficiaries: agricultural producers and their creditors; others directly affected by USDA actions.

Range: $5,000 to $392,000.

Activity: FY 02 estimate, 26 states certified.

HQ: FSA-USDA (Stop 0539), Washington, DC 20250. Phone: (202)720-1471, FAX (202)690-0644. **Internet:** same as **10.029**. (Note: no field offices for this program.)

10.437 INTEREST ASSISTANCE PROGRAM

Assistance: guaranteed/insured loans (to 90 percent/to 10 years).

Purposes: pursuant to CFRDA as amended, for interest rate buy-downs on behalf of family farms indebted to conventional lenders. Essentially, FSA pays up to four percent of a farm-borrower's interest costs on loans taken for operations including livestock, farm and home equipment, family living expenses, water system development, and similar costs.

Eligible applicants/beneficiaries: individuals, partnerships, joint operations, legal resident aliens, corporations, and cooperatives. Loans may be obtained through lender.

Range: to $731,000. **Average:** $158,000.

Activity: FY 01, 4,646 farmers assisted.

HQ: same as **10.075**.

10.438 SECTION 538 RURAL RENTAL HOUSING GUARANTEED LOANS

Assistance: guaranteed/insured loans.

Purposes: pursuant to the Housing Act of 1949 as amended, for partnerships between RHS and major lenders including state and local housing finance agencies and bond insurers, resulting in an increased supply of new, affordable, multifamily, rural housing consisting of two or more family units. Projects must provide new forms of credit enhancements for housing development. Nursing, special care, and industrial type housing are ineligible.

Eligible applicants: lenders approved by the Federal National Mortgage Association, Federal Home Loan Mortgage Corporation, HUD, or state housing finance agencies.

Eligible beneficiaries: rural households with income not exceeding 115 percent of the median.

Range/Average: N.A.

Activity: FY 04, 150 awards to provide 2,600 units.

HQ: same as **10.405**.

10.441 TECHNICAL AND SUPERVISORY ASSISTANCE GRANTS ("Section 525(a)")

Assistance: project grants (100 percent/1-2 years).

Purposes: pursuant to the Housing Act of 1949 as amended, for housing delivery and counseling projects to assist low-income rural persons obtain adequate rental housing, homeownership, or continued occupancy in existing housing—through technical and supervisory assistance provided by grantees. Project funds may cover such costs as staff salaries, travel, administrative and office expenses, training. Grant funds may not be used for real estate acquisition or improvement, vehicles, equipment, or for financial assistance to families participating in the projects.

Eligible applicants/beneficiaries: public or private nonprofit corporations, organizations, agencies, institutions, tribal governments, and other associations; sponsored organizations including community development, model cities, and community action agencies; IHEs, hospitals.

Range/Average: N.A.

Activity: N.A.

HQ: RHS-USDA, 14th & Independence Ave. SW, Washington, DC 20250. Phone: (202)720-1474. **Internet:** same as **10.405**.

10.442 HOUSING APPLICATION PACKAGING GRANTS ("Section 509 Grants")

Assistance: project grants.

Purposes: pursuant to the Housing Act of 1949 as amended, to package applications for single-family housing for very-low- and low-income rural residents wishing to buy, build, or repair houses for their own use—in colonias and designated counties; to package applications for organizations developing rental units for lower-income families. Funds may cover operating, administrative, and coordinating costs.

Eligible applicants/beneficiaries: states, state and local agencies, local government units, private nonprofit housing organizations.

Range/Average: N.A.

Activity: N.A.

HQ: same as **10.411**.

10.443 OUTREACH AND ASSISTANCE FOR SOCIALLY DISADVANTAGED FARMERS AND RANCHERS

Assistance: project grants (100 percent/1-5 years).

Purposes: pursuant to FACTA, to provide outreach, training, and technical assistance socially disadvantaged farmers and ranchers—toward their ownership and operation of farms and their participation in farm programs.

Eligible applicants: experienced "1890" land-grant colleges and Tuskegee University; tribal community colleges and Alaska native cooperative colleges, Hispanic-serving and other postsecondary educational institutions, and community-based organizations.

Eligible beneficiaries: socially disadvantaged farmers or ranchers including Blacks, women, American Indians, Alaska natives, Hispanics, Asians, and Pacific Islanders.

Range: $66,000 to $277,000. **Average:** $200,000.

Activity: cumulatively, 27 awards assisting 8,686 farmers, outreach to 108,000 constituents.

HQ: Office of Outreach (1710), USDA, 1400 Independence Ave. SW, Washington, DC 20250. Phone: (202)720-6350, FAX (202)720-7489. **Internet:** "www.usda.gov/agency/outreach".

10.444 DIRECT HOUSING—NATURAL DISASTER LOANS AND GRANTS ("Section 504 Rural Housing Loans and Grants")

Assistance: direct loans; project grants (100 percent).

Purposes: pursuant to the Housing Act of 1949 as amended, to meet emergency housing assistance needs of very-low-income owner-occupants, resulting from natural disasters. Funds may be used to repair or replace damaged property, only to the extent that funds are not provided by FEMA.

Eligible applicants/beneficiaries: loans—very-low income owner-occupants with sufficient income to repay the loans. Grants—owner-occupants at least age 62 and unable to repay loans.

Range/Average: loans, $4,860,000; grants, $5,093,000.

Activity: FY 04, 990 houses improved.

HQ: same as **10.411**.

10.445 DIRECT HOUSING—NATURAL DISASTER ("Section 502 Very Low and Low Income Loans")

Assistance: direct loans.

Purposes: pursuant to the Housing Act of 1949 and CFRDA as amended and other acts, to meet emergency housing assistance needs of lower-income families, resulting from natural disasters. Funds may be used to buy, build, rehabilitate, or improve dwellings in rural areas. Subsidies may be available to eligible low- and very-low-income applicants, in the form of payment assistance or interest credits, to effectively reduce interest payments to as low as one percent—and are subject to recapture if the borrower transfers title or ceases to occupy the property. Funds are available only to the extent that funds are not provided by FEMA.

Eligible applicants/beneficiaries: households without adequate resources to obtain housing or related facilities, and unable to secure credit from other sources.

Range/Average: loans, $54,000.

Activity: FY 04, 519 loans.

HQ: same as **10.411**.

10.446 RURAL COMMUNITY DEVELOPMENT INITIATIVE

Assistance: project grants (50 percent/3 years).

Purposes: for capacity building toward the improvement of rural housing, community facilities, and community and economic development projects. Grant funds may be used to train and provide technical assistance to subgrantees in such areas as: conducting homeownership education and minority entrepreneurial programs, and developing child care facilities; strategic planning, obtaining alternative funding, fund raising, board training. Funds may also be used to develop training tools including videos, workbooks, and reference guides.

Eligible applicants/beneficiaries: private, public, or tribal organizations with three years of pertinent rural experience, including in territories and possessions.

Range: $50,000 to $1,000,000. **Average:** $300,000.

Activity: FY 04, 26 awards.

HQ: Deputy Administrator/Community Programs, RHS-USDA, Washington, DC 20250-3222. Phone: (202)720-1490. **Internet:** "www.rurdev.usda.gov/rhs/rcdi/index.htm".

10.449 BOLL WEEVIL ERADICATION LOAN PROGRAM

Assistance: direct loans (1-7 years).

Purposes: to eradicate boll weevils from the U.S. Loan funds may be used to: purchase or lease supplies and equipment; pay operating expenses, salaries, and benefits—but not for lobbying, public relations, or similar activities.

Eligible applicants/beneficiaries: nonprofit entities authorized under appropriate state law.

Range: $1,000,000 to $46,000,000. **Average:** $7,000,000.

Activity: FY 02, 13 loans.

HQ: same as **10.075**. (Note: no field offices for this program.)

10.450 CROP INSURANCE

Assistance: insurance.

Purposes: pursuant to the Federal Crop Insurance Act, Agricultural Adjustment

Act of 1938, Federal Crop Insurance Reform Act of 1994, FAIRA, AREERA, Agriculture Risk Protection Act of 2000, amendments, and other acts, to insure farmers against losses resulting from unavoidable causes and uncontrollable events. Producers must obtain at least the catastrophic level of coverage to be eligible under the price support or production adjustment programs, the Conservation Reserve Program, or farm credit programs. The premium is fully subsidized on catastrophic crop insurance, except for a processing fee. Coverage compensates producers for yield losses exceeding 50 percent, at a price equal to 55 percent of maximum price. Additional protection at higher levels of coverage is also offered. The program provides for ongoing research to devise and establish crop insurance protection programs, as well as risk management education for producers including futures and options trading. Pilot insurance programs currently are being tested for various crops. Various insurance programs in certain areas cover specific crops; regulations concerning crops and insurance coverage may be obtained from USDA regional offices or private industry crop insurance agents.

Eligible applicants/beneficiaries: owners or operators of farmland, with an insurable interest in a crop in a county where insurance is offered on that crop. The Noninsured Assistance Program is available in other areas (see **10.451**). Note: applications are to be submitted to companies reinsured by FCIC.

Range/Average: N.A.

Activity: crop year 2003 estimate, 207,900,000 acres covered, with protection of $34.3 billion.

HQ: Administrator, RMA-USDA, Ag Box 0801, Washington, DC 20250. Phone: (202)690-2803. **Internet:** "www.rma.usda.gov".

10.451 NONINSURED ASSISTANCE ("NAP")

Assistance: direct payments/unrestricted use.

Purposes: pursuant to FAIRA as amended, to provide producers with protection comparable to the catastrophic risk protection plan of crop insurance (see **10.450**) and to help reduce production risks faced by crop producers for which federal insurance is not available under the Federal Crop Insurance Act; to reduce financial losses that occur when natural disasters cause catastrophic loss of production or prevent planting of an eligible crop. Payment eligibility is based on an expected yield for the area and the producer's approved yield based on actual production history, or a transitional yield if sufficient records are unavailable. Yields must fall below specified percentages to be eligible for payment. Eligible areas may be located within or outside the continental U.S., as determined by USDA; generally, areas within the continental U.S. are eligible if they have suffered a greater than 35 percent loss of eligible production because of damaging weather or of an adverse natural occurrence. Eligible crops include any commercial agricultural crop (excluding livestock and their by-products, tobacco, and trees grown for wood, paper, or pulp), commodity, or acreage of a commodity grown for food or fiber for which catastrophic coverage is unavailable; included also are floriculture, ornamental nursery, Christmas tree crops, turfgrass sod, seed crops, aquaculture including ornamental fish, and industrial crops.

Eligible applicants/beneficiaries: producers including owners, landlords, tenants, or sharecroppers with total annual gross revenue less than $2,000,000 for the preceding tax year.

Range/Average: N.A.

Activity: not quantified specifically.

HQ: Noninsured Assistance Program Branch (0517), Production, Emergency, and Compliance Division, FSA-USDA, 1400 Independence Ave. SW, Washington, DC 20250-0526. Phone: (202)720-5172. **Internet:** same as **10.029.**

10.452 DISASTER RESERVE ASSISTANCE ("DRAP")

Assistance: direct payments/specified use.

Purposes: pursuant to the Agricultural Act of 1970 as amended, to provide emergency assistance to livestock owners in USDA-approved areas where livestock emergencies exist because of disease, insect infestation, flood, drought, fire, hurricane, earthquake, hail storm, hot or cold weather, freeze, snow, ice, winterkill, or other natural disaster. Assistance may be provided for losses of feed grain crops, forage, and grazing. Direct payments are for unrestricted use; feed obtained must be fed to the producer's livestock, may not be resold, and must be used during the established feeding period.

Eligible applicants/beneficiaries: U.S. citizens or legal resident aliens, cooperatives, private domestic corporations, partnerships, or joint operations, tribal organizations that: (1) do not have total annual gross revenue in excess of $2,500,000; (2) are actively engaged in farming with at least 10 percent of gross revenue derived from producing grain or livestock; (3) have suffered a 40 percent or greater loss of normal feed production; (4) have insufficient feed for eligible livestock for the duration of the emergency. Applicants must choose whether to receive disaster assistance program benefits or benefits under another USDA program for the same crop loss (applicants are not eligible for both).

Range/Average: N.A.

Activity: not quantified specifically.

HQ: Emergency and Noninsured Assistance Program Division, FSA-USDA, 1400 Independence Ave. SW, Washington, DC 20250-0526. Phone: (202) 720-3168. **Internet:** same as **10.029.**

10.454 DAIRY OPTIONS PILOT PROGRAM ("DOPP")

Assistance: direct payments/specified use (80 percent).

Purposes: pursuant to FAIRA, Agricultural Market Transition Act, and Agricultural Risk Protection Act of 2000, to educate and assist dairy producers in certain regions in managing their price risk by purchasing options on milk futures. Payments, including some fee costs, are made to commodities brokers for options contracts purchased by participants.

Eligible applicants/beneficiaries: dairy farmers producing at least 100,000 pounds of milk during the consecutive six-month period preceding application—including individuals, entities, or joint operations, owners, operators, landlords, tenants, or sharecroppers.

Range: the farmer pays 20 percent of the premium and broker fees exceeding $30 per contract.

Activity: Round III, 790 producers bought 2,816 milk put options.

HQ: RMA-USDA, 1400 Independence Ave. SW, Washington, DC 20250-0808. Phone: (202)690-0520, FAX (202)690-3605. **Internet:** "www.rma.usda.gov"; e-mail, "rma.options@wdc.usda.gov". (Note: no field offices for this program.)

10.455 RMA COMMUNITY OUTREACH AND ASSISTANCE PARTNERSHIP PROGRAM

Assistance: project grants (90 percent).

Purposes: pursuant to the Federal Crop Insurance Act as amended, for partnerships to develop and implement community outreach programs for women, limited-resource, socially disadvantaged, and other traditionally underserved producers of priority commodities—providing them with information and training necessary to use financial management, crop insurance, marketing contracts and other existing and emerging risk management tools to mitigate risks associated with farming.

Eligible applicants/beneficiaries: educational institutions, community-based organizations, and associations of farmers, ranchers, and other nonprofit organizations.

Range: $5,000 to $300,000. **Average:** $75,000.

Activity: new program listing in 2004. FY 04 estimate, 30,000 producers assisted.

HQ: Commodity Outreach and Assistance Partnership Program, RMA-USDA (Stop 0805), 1400 Independence Ave. SW, Washington, DC 20250. Phone: (202)690-2686. **Internet:** same web site as **10.454**.

10.456 PARTNERSHIP AGREEMENTS TO DEVELOP NON-INSURANCE RISK MANAGEMENT TOOLS FOR PRODUCERS (FARMERS)

Assistance: project grants (100 percent/to 3 years).

Purposes: pursuant to the Federal Crop Insurance Act and Agricultural Market Transition Act, for research partnerships to develop noninsurance risk management tools for agricultural producers, emphasizing producers of specialty crops, livestock, rangeland, and underserved commodities.

Eligible applicants/beneficiaries: public and private entities including: IHEs; federal, state, and local government agencies; tribal organizations; nonprofit and profit organizations or corporations; other qualified entities.

Range: $143,000 to $2,329,000. **Average:** $585,000.

Activity: new program listing in 2004. FY 03, 18 partnerships funded.

HQ: Research and Evaluation Division (0813), RMA-USDA, 6501 Beacon Dr., Kansas City, MO 64133-4676. Phone: (816)926-6343, FAX, 926-7343. **Internet:** same web site as **10.454**; e-mail, "applications@rma.usda.gov". (Note: the field office serves as headquarters.)

10.457 COMMODITY PARTNERSHIPS FOR RISK MANAGEMENT EDUCATION

Assistance: project grants (100 percent).

Purposes: pursuant to the Federal Crop Insurance Act as amended, for programs delivering training and information in the management of production, marketing, and financial risk to agricultural producers and agribusiness professionals—with priority for producers of crops not insurable by RMA, specialty crops, and underserved commodities. Funds may be used for planning, instructional materials development, outreach, and educational activities.

Eligible applicants/beneficiaries: state departments of agriculture, universities, nonprofit agricultural organizations, other public and private organizations.

Range: $50,000 to $500,000.

Activity: new program listing in 2004. FY 04, 30,000 producers assisted.

HQ: Risk Management Education Division, same address/web site as **10.454**. Phone: (202)720-6356. **Internet:** e-mail, "rma.risk-ed@usda.gov".

10.458 CROP INSURANCE IN TARGETED STATES
("Targeted States")

Assistance: project grants.

Purposes: pursuant to the Federal Crop Insurance Act as amended, to deliver crop insurance education and information to agricultural producers in designated states historically underserved by crop insurance—including specifically Connecticut, Delaware, Maine, Maryland, Massachusetts, Nevada, New Hampshire, New Jersey, New York, Pennsylvania, Rhode Island, Utah, Vermont, West Virginia, and Wyoming.

Eligible applicants/beneficiaries: same as **10.457**.

Range: $150,000 to $750,000. **Average:** $300,000.

Activity: new program listing in 2004. FY 04 estimate, training provided to 60,000 producers.

HQ: same as **10.457**.

10.459 COMMODITY PARTNERSHIPS FOR SMALL AGRICULTURAL RISK MANAGEMENT EDUCATION SESSIONS
("Commodity Partnerships Small Sessions Program")

Assistance: project grants (100 percent/to 1 year).

Purposes: pursuant to the Federal Crop Insurance Act as amended, to deliver training and information during small sessions in the management, production, marketing, and financial risk to U.S. agricultural producers, with priority to producers of crops not insurable with federal crop insurance, specialty crops, and underserved commodities. Funding is through cooperative agreements, covering such costs as program planning, development of instructional materials, awareness promotion, educational activities, and project documentation.

Eligible applicants/beneficiaries: same as **10.457**.

Range: $1,000 to $10,000.

Activity: new program in FY 05. Some 3,000 producers estimated to be trained in FY 05.

HQ: same as **10.457**.

10.475 COOPERATIVE AGREEMENTS WITH STATES FOR INTRASTATE MEAT AND POULTRY INSPECTION
("Meat and Poultry Inspection State Programs")

Assistance: project grants (to 50 percent).

Purposes: pursuant to the Federal Meat Inspection Act, Federal-State Cooperative Act ("Talmadge-Aiken"), and Poultry Products Inspection Act, to cover cooperating states' costs of meat and poultry inspection programs.

Eligible applicants/beneficiaries: state or territorial agencies administering meat or poultry inspection programs under applicable laws equivalent to federal acts.

Range: $204,000 to $5,356,000. **Average:** $1,622,000.

Activity: FY 05 estimate, 28 states participating under the Federal Meat Inspection Act, 25 under the Poultry Products Inspection Act; 500,000,000 pounds of products inspected.

HQ: Director, Federal-State Relations Staff, Field Operations, Food Safety and Inspection Service-USDA, Congressional Quarterly Bldg. - Rm.329, Washington, DC 20250-3700. Phone: (202)418-8897. **Internet:** "www.fsis.usda.gov".

10.477 MEAT, POULTRY, AND EGG PRODUCTS INSPECTION

Assistance: specialized services.

Purposes: pursuant to the Federal Meat Inspection Act, Poultry Products Inspection Act, and other acts, to provide inspection by USDA personnel of the slaughtering, processing, and labeling of meat, poultry, and egg products shipped in commerce. All U.S. plants are required to be under continuous USDA inspection, including in the territories.

Eligible applicants/beneficiaries: any meat or poultry plant engaging in slaughtering or processing meat, poultry, and all egg products processing—for shipment in commerce.

Activity: FY 04, some 100.4 billion pounds of products inspected at some 6,300 establishments.

HQ: Assistant Administrator/Field Operations, Food Safety and Inspection Service-USDA, Washington, DC 20250. Phone: (202)720-8803. **Internet:** same as **10.475**.

10.500 COOPERATIVE EXTENSION SERVICE

Assistance: formula grants; project grants (matching).

Purposes: pursuant to the Smith-Lever Act, Food and Agriculture Act of 1977, FACTA, FAIRA, AREERA, FSRIA, amendments, and other acts, for land grant institutions to operate state and county agricultural extension service programs providing educational and technical assistance to: farmers, producers, and marketing firms in applying technical developments ensuing from research; community organizations to develop natural, economic, and human resources; homemakers and youth regarding food and nutrition, home economics, child development, and parent education; 4-H youth programs. "1890" institutions may receive funds to construct, renovate, plan, and develop new facilities and to purchase equipment.

Eligible applicants/beneficiaries: designated state land grant institutions including in the territories; "1890" and "1994" institutions, and Tuskegee extension programs.

Range: $890,000 to $19,962,000. **Average:** $7,210,000.

Activity: not quantified specifically.

HQ: Deputy Administrator/Planning and Accountability, same address/phone, web site as **10.203**. (Note: no field offices for this program.)

10.550 FOOD DONATION

Assistance: sale, exchange, or donation of property and goods.

Purposes: pursuant to the National School Lunch Act, Food and Agriculture Act of 1965, Child Nutrition Act of 1966, Older Americans Act of 1965, amendments, and other legislation, to provide food without charge for distribution to qualifying outlets, such as emergency feeding organizations, soup kitchens, food banks, child feeding programs, schools, child and adult day care, charitable institutions, nutrition programs for the elderly, nonprofit summer camps and food services for children. Food distributed under the program may be acquired under USDA surplus removal or price support operations.

Eligible applicants/beneficiaries: state, territorial, and federal agencies designated as distributing agencies by the governor, legislature, or other authority. Qualifying entities apply to state agencies.

Activity: not quantified specifically.

HQ: Director, Food Distribution Division, FNS-USDA, Alexandria, VA 22302. Phone: (703)305-2680. **Internet:** "www.fns.usda.gov/fdd".

10.551 FOOD STAMPS

Assistance: direct payments/specified use (100 percent).

Purposes: pursuant to the Food Stamp Act of 1977 as amended, to enable low-income households to purchase food. Eligible recipients receive a coupon allotment, varying according to household size and income, to be used to buy food or seeds and plants to produce food for their personal consumption. Coupons may also be used to purchase meals by special categories of recipients, including the elderly, handicapped, homeless, alcoholics and drug addicts participating in rehabilitation programs, disabled or blind, specific categories of noncitizens, and residents of shelters for battered women and children.

Eligible applicants: state or territorial agencies.

Eligible beneficiaries: households receiving welfare assistance in some form, or unemployed, part-time employed, working for low wages, receiving limited pensions. Able-bodied adults must meet a work requirement. At their option, states may pay the cost of providing food stamps to noncitizens that are made ineligible by welfare reform and to individuals disqualified by the new work requirement.

Range/Average: FY 04, $86.02 per person per month.

Activity: FY 04 monthly participation average, 23,860,000 persons.

HQ: Deputy Administrator/Food Stamp Program, FNS-USDA, Alexandria, VA 22302. Phone: (703)305-2026. **Internet:** "www.fns.usda.gov".

10.553 SCHOOL BREAKFAST PROGRAM

Assistance: formula grants.

Purposes: pursuant to the Child Nutrition Act of 1966 as amended, to reimburse participating entities for the cost of providing breakfasts to eligible public and private nonprofit school children through the high school grades, through cash grants and food donations. Breakfasts are served free or at a reduced price to children determined by local school authorities to be unable to pay the full price, based on income eligibility guidelines. Reimbursements rates are based on the "Food Away From Home" series of the Consumer Price Index. The maximum reduced price charged for breakfast is 30 cents.

Eligible applicants/beneficiaries: state and territorial agencies; public and nonprofit private schools and residential child care institutions except Job Corps Centers; residential summer camps that participate in the Summer Food Service Program; private foster homes.

Range: FY 01, per meal reimbursement of 21 cents to 147 cents. **Average:** 110.5 cents per meal.

Activity: FY 04, 1.523 billion breakfasts served.

HQ: Director, Child Nutrition Division, FNS-USDA, Alexandria, VA 22302. Phone: (703)305-2590. **Internet:** "www.fns.usda.gov/cnd".

10.555 NATIONAL SCHOOL LUNCH PROGRAM ("School Lunch Program")

Assistance: formula grants (70 percent).

Purposes: pursuant to the National School Lunch Act as amended, to reimburse participating entities for the cost of providing school lunches to public and private nonprofit school children through the high school grades, through cash grants and food donations. Eligible schools also may be reimbursed for snacks served to children in after-school-hour care programs. Meals are served free or at a reduced price to children determined by local school authorities to be unable to pay the full price, based on income eligibility guidelines. Reimbursement rates are based on the "Food Away from Home" series of the Consumer Price Index. The maximum reduced price charge for lunch is 40 cents.

Eligible applicants/beneficiaries: same as for **10.553**.

Range:: FY 04, 5 cents for snacks to 226 cents per meal.

Activity: FY 01 estimate, 4.543 billion lunches served.

HQ: same address/phone as **10.553**. **Internet:** "www.fns.usda.gov".

10.556 SPECIAL MILK PROGRAM FOR CHILDREN

Assistance: formula grants.

Purposes: pursuant to the Child Nutrition Act of 1966 as amended, to reimburse the cost of milk served to primary and secondary pupils in public and private nonprofit schools and institutions. A portion of the cost of the milk is subsidized for non-needy children; milk is free to students meeting certain income guidelines. Nonprofit schools with split-session kindergartens and pre-kindergartens that do not have access to the meal service program operating in the school may receive milk subsidies. States bear the costs in excess of the federal reimbursement.

Eligible applicants/beneficiaries: state or territorial agencies; public or private nonprofit schools or child care institutions of high school grade or under, including nursery schools, child-care centers, settlement houses, summer camps, and similar institutions devoted to the care and training of children, except Job Corps Centers—provided they do not participate in a meal service program authorized under the National School Lunch Act or the Child Nutrition Act of 1966.

Range/Average: FY 01 reimbursements, 13.4 cents per subsidized half-pint, 17 cents for half-pints served free.

Activity: FY 04, 103.4 million half-pints served.

HQ: same as **10.553**.

10.557 SPECIAL SUPPLEMENTAL NUTRITION PROGRAM FOR WOMEN, INFANTS, AND CHILDREN
("WIC Program")

Assistance: formula grants (100 percent).

Purposes: pursuant to the Child Nutrition Act of 1966 as amended, to supply supplemental foods, nutrition education, and health care referrals at no cost to low-income pregnant, postpartum, and breast-feeding women, infants, and children under age five, identified as at nutritional risk. Grants are awarded to state health or comparable agencies and certain tribes or Indian groups; in turn, funds and food are distributed through local public or nonprofit agencies.

Eligible applicants: local public or private nonprofit health or human service agencies. Applications must be submitted to the responsible state or territorial agency.

Eligible beneficiaries: pregnant, postpartum, or breast-feeding women, infants and children to age five—determined to be in need of supplemental foods, meeting an income standard or receiving benefits under the Food Stamp,

Medicaid, or Temporary Assistance to Needy Families Program, and residents of the state in which they receive benefits.

Range: $56,000 to $718,922,000. **Average:** $46,854,000; cost, $32.94 per person per month.

Activity: participation by 88 state, territorial, and Indian agencies. FY 01 monthly average, 7,197,000 participants.

HQ: Director, Supplemental Food Programs Division, FNS-USDA, Alexandria, VA 22302. Phone: (703)305-2746. **Internet:** same as **10.551**.

10.558 CHILD AND ADULT CARE FOOD PROGRAM

Assistance: formula grants.

Purposes: pursuant to the National School Lunch Act as amended, to provide funding and commodity foods to institutional food service programs that serve meals to eligible children, including in emergency shelters, or to elderly or impaired adults receiving care in nonresidential day care facilities.

Eligible applicants: state and territorial agencies. In Virginia where the state does not administer the program, institutions may receive funds directly from USDA.

Eligible beneficiaries: public and private nonprofit organizations, including day care centers, outside-school-hour centers, settlement houses, recreation centers, family and group day care home programs, Head Start programs, institutions providing day care services for mentally or physically handicapped children; certain licensed private for-profit centers that receive compensation under Title XX for at least 25 percent of the children, or under Title XIX or XX for at least 25 percent of the adults, enrolled in nonresidential day care services.

Range: state grants, $92,000 to $203,695,000.

Activity: FY 04, over 1 billion meals served.

HQ: same as **10.553**.

10.559 SUMMER FOOD SERVICE PROGRAM FOR CHILDREN

Assistance: formula grants.

Purposes: pursuant to the National School Lunch Act as amended, to provide funding and other donations to nonprofit food service programs for needy children age 18 and under and for disabled persons, when schools are closed for summer vacation or for periods of 15 days or more during the regular school year. Funds are available to institutions conducting regularly scheduled programs for children in areas where at least 50 percent of the children meet the family income eligibility criteria for free and reduced-price lunches. Disbursements equal the full cost of food service operations, but cannot exceed per meal rates.

Eligible applicants: state and territorial agencies. Where states do not administer the program, beneficiary agencies may apply directly.

Eligible beneficiaries: public and private nonprofit school food authorities, residential summer camps serving eligible children, and IHEs operating the National Youth Sports Program; units of local, municipal, county, or state government; shelters for homeless children and families; homeless feeding sites regardless of location. Other organizations may participate under certain conditions.

Range/Average: state grants, $71,000 to $42,469,000.

Activity: FY 04, 130,600,000 meals served.

HQ: same as **10.553**.

10.560 STATE ADMINISTRATIVE EXPENSES FOR CHILD NUTRITION

Assistance: formula grants.

Purposes: pursuant to the Child Nutrition Act of 1966 as amended, for the costs of administering various child nutrition programs, including technical assistance to operating agencies. Program funds may be used to purchase supplies, equipment, and services.

Eligible applicants/beneficiaries: state and territorial agencies administering child nutrition programs, and agencies distributing USDA donated commodities to schools.

Range: $307,000 to $17,864,000. **Average:** $2,715,000.

Activity: not quantified specifically.

HQ: same as **10.553**.

10.561 STATE ADMINISTRATIVE MATCHING GRANTS FOR FOOD STAMP PROGRAM

Assistance: formula grants (from 50-60 percent).

Purposes: pursuant to the Food Stamp Act of 1977 as amended, for the administrative costs of operating the food stamp program, including for fraud investigations and for developing computer systems. States also conduct an employment and training program requiring no state matching funds. Reimbursements are made to participants for up to 50 percent their dependent care costs, not exceeding $25 monthly per participant; states also receive 50 percent of case management costs.

Eligible applicants/beneficiaries: state and territorial cooperators.

Range: $3,600,000 to $426,200,000. **Average:** $46,500,000.

Activity: not quantified specifically.

HQ: same as **10.551**.

10.565 COMMODITY SUPPLEMENTAL FOOD PROGRAM

Assistance: sale, exchange, or donation of property and goods; formula grants.

Purposes: pursuant to the Agriculture and Consumer Protection Act of 1973 and Food and Agriculture Act of 1977 as amended, for the donation of supplemental foods to low-income persons. Grant funds may be used only for administrative costs incurred in making the donated goods and nutrition education services available to beneficiaries.

Eligible applicants: state agencies; recognized tribes, bands, or groups—which distribute funds to local public or nonprofit agencies.

Eligible beneficiaries: infants or children to age 6; pregnant, postpartum, or breast-feeding women; or, elderly persons age 60 or older—certified as income-eligible for benefits under existing federal, state, or local food, health, or welfare programs for low-income persons, and at nutritional risk.

Range: $5,937 to $4,672,000 per state.

Activity: FY 04, 63,000 women, infants, and children and 459,000 elderly persons participated monthly.

HQ: same address/phone as for **10.550**. **Internet:** "www.fns.usda.gov/fdd/programs/csfp".

10.566 NUTRITION ASSISTANCE FOR PUERTO RICO ("NAP")

Assistance: direct payments/specified use.

Purposes: for low-income Puerto Ricans to purchase food—as an alternative to Food Stamps.

Eligible applicants: only the Commonwealth of PR.

Eligible beneficiaries: low-income Puerto Rican individuals and families.

Range/Average: $104.00/person/month.

Activity: FY 04, 1,010,000 persons assisted monthly.

HQ: same as **10.551**.

10.567 FOOD DISTRIBUTION PROGRAM ON INDIAN RESERVATIONS

Assistance: project grants (75 percent); sale, exchange, or donation of property and goods.

Purposes: pursuant to the Agricultural Act of 1949, Food and Agriculture Act of 1963, Food Stamp Act of 1977, amendments, and other legislation, to provide food to needy persons living on or near Indian reservations, and funds for the administrative costs incurred by organizations operating the program. Donated foods may be acquired under USDA's surplus removal or price support operations.

Eligible applicants: state agencies; tribal organizations.

Eligible beneficiaries: households living on Indian reservations; Indian households living near an Indian reservation (or, for Oklahoma, living in Indian country)—certified by local authorities as having inadequate income and resources. Upper limits of allowable income and resources vary with family size.

Range: $79,000 to $4,938,000.

Activity: FY 04, 107,000 persons participating monthly; 97 tribal organizations and 5 states administering the program for 246 participating tribes.

HQ: same as for **10.550**.

10.568 EMERGENCY FOOD ASSISTANCE PROGRAM (ADMINISTRATIVE COSTS)

Assistance: formula grants.

Purposes: pursuant to the Emergency Food Assistance Act of 1983 as amended and other acts, to cover state and local costs of processing, storage, and distribution of food used to feed needy persons.

Eligible applicants: state agencies.

Eligible beneficiaries: public or private organizations that operate USDA food programs.

Range: $9,202 to $5,717,000. **Average:** $822,000.

Activity: not quantified specifically.

HQ: same address/phone as **10.550**. **Internet:** "www.fns.usda.gov/fdd/programs/tefap".

10.569 EMERGENCY FOOD ASSISTANCE PROGRAM (FOOD COMMODITIES)

Assistance: formula grants (100 percent).

Purposes: pursuant to the Emergency Food Assistance Act of 1983 and Hunger Prevention Act of 1988, to make food commodities available to needy persons, including for meals served at congregate meal sites.

Eligible applicants: designated state food commodity distributing agencies.

Eligible beneficiaries: needy persons including the unemployed, welfare recipients, and the low-income.

Range: $20,000 to $12,437,000. **Average:** $1,818,000.

Activity: not quantified specifically.

HQ: same address/phone as **10.568**. **Internet**"www.fns.usda.gov/fncs/".

10.572 WIC FARMERS' MARKET NUTRITION PROGRAM ("FMNP")

Assistance: formula grants (70 percent; tribal organizations, 70-90 percent).

Purposes: pursuant to the WIC Farmers' Market Nutrition Act of 1992 and Child Nutrition Act of 1966 as amended, to provide fresh and nutritious unprepared foods (such as fruits and vegetables) from farmers' markets to low-income women, infants, and children at nutritional risk—through the use of FMNP coupons; to expand awareness and use of farmers' markets. States may meet matching fund requirements through state contributions to similar programs.

Eligible applicants: state health, agriculture, and other agencies; recognized Indian organizations.

Eligible beneficiaries: WIC program participants (i.e., pregnant, postpartum, or breast-feeding women, infants over age 4 months, children to age 5). At the discretion of the states, WIC program applicants may also participate.

Range: $6,337 to $4,452,000. **Average:** $621,000.

Activity: FY 05, 46 programs approved.

HQ: Branch Chief, Supplemental Food Programs Division, FCS-USDA, 3101 Park Center Dr. - Rm. 540, Alexandria, VA 22302. Phone: (703)305-2746. **Internet:** "www.fns.usda.gov/wic/".

10.574 TEAM NUTRITION GRANTS ("TN Training Grants")

Assistance: project grants (100 percent/2 years).

Purposes: pursuant to the National School Lunch Act and amendments, to establish and enhance nutrition training and technical assistance programs to school food service professionals, as well as to children and parents. The program provides start-up money for projects, and may include a cafeteria-classroom link to support nutrition education and healthy food choices. States may use funds to provide comprehensive, action-oriented delivery of training programs for schools.

Eligible applicants/beneficiaries: state agencies—applying individually or as coalitions.

Range: $50,000 to $200,000. **Average:** $188,000.

Activity: FY 04, 21 grants.

HQ: Grants Management Division, FNS-USDA, Alexandria, VA 22302. Phone: (703)305-2867. **Internet:** same as **10.553**.

10.576 SENIOR FARMERS MARKET NUTRITION PROGRAM ("SFMNP")

Assistance: project grants.

Purposes: pursuant to FSRIA, to expand, develop, or aid domestic farmers markets, roadside stands, and community-supported agriculture programs serving low-income seniors. Grants are competitive, and may support costs of food only.

Eligible applicants: states, territories, and tribal governments, which may make subgrants to local governments and nonprofit organizations.

Eligible beneficiaries: low-income seniors, generally defined as individuals at least age 60 with household income not exceeding 185 percent of federal poverty guidelines.

Range: $6,440 to $1,500,000. **Average:** $421,000.

Activity: new program listing in 2004. FY 05, 47 state agencies and tribal governments operated programs.

HQ: Grant Officer, Grants Management Division, FNS-USDA, Alexandria, VA 22302. Phone: (703)305-2760. **Internet:** "www.fns.usda.gov/fns".

10.578 WIC GRANTS TO STATES ("WGS")

Assistance: project grants (100 percent/1-3 years).

Purposes: pursuant to the Child Nutrition Act of 1966 as amended, to provide funding to WIC state agencies for Electronic Benefit Transfer Projects (EBT) and pilots exploring the technical and financial feasibility of providing WIC benefits electronically; for WIC state agencies and tribal governments to fund, implement, and evaluate innovative projects that improve WIC services provisions and impact the nutrition and health of WIC participants. Grants are competitive. Special projects examples: motivational interviewing in nutrition education; increasing breastfeeding among Indians.

Eligible applicants/beneficiaries: state WIC program agencies; state coalitions.

Range: EBT, $262,000 to $2,300,000; discretionary grants, $20,000 to $1,076,000. **Average:** EBT, $907,000; discretionary, $475,000.

Activity: new program listing in 2004.

HQ: same address as **10.576**. Phone: (no number provided). **Internet:** "www.fns.usda.gov".

10.579 CHILD NUTRITION DISCRETIONARY GRANTS LIMITED AVAILABILITY

Assistance: project grants (100 percent).

Purposes: pursuant to National School Lunch Act, Child Nutrition Act of 1966 and amendments, to assist states through cash and food donations in making food and milk service programs available, by providing school breakfasts and lunches—and through nutrition programs for children, the elderly, and impaired adults in nonresidential day care facilities and child emergency shelters. Program emphasis is on the school breakfast program.

Eligible applicants/beneficiaries: determined legislatively.

Range/Average: determined legislatively.

Activity: new program listing in 2004.

HQ: same address, web site as **10.574**. Phone: (703)305-2867.

10.580 FOOD STAMP PROGRAM OUTREACH GRANTS

Assistance: project grants (100 percent).

Purposes: pursuant to the Food Stamp Act of 1977, for research into food stamp outreach activities, methods, or technologies, directed to targeted groups that are eligible but that traditionally under-use food stamp benefits—involving new technology and partnerships to educate eligible beneficiaries about the nutrition benefits of the program and about how to apply.

Eligible applicants/beneficiaries: non-food stamp governmental authorities, nonprofit organizations.

Range/Average: N.A.

Activity: new program listing in 2004.

HQ: same address/phone as **10.574**. **Internet:** same as **10.552**.

10.582 FRESH FRUIT AND VEGETABLE PROGRAM ("FFVP")

Assistance: project grants (100 percent).

Purposes: pursuant to the National School Lunch Act as amended, to reimburse states providing free fresh fruits and vegetables to school children of high school grade and under in designated public and private schools.

Eligible applicants/beneficiaries: state agencies specified in Section 18(g) of the National School Lunch Act or selected by USDA, including Indian tribal organizations and public and private schools participating in the National School Lunch Program or School Breakfast Program. States must ensure that the majority of schools have 50 percent or more students eligible for free or reduced price meals, with priority to schools with partnerships with nonfederal resources, except for schools previously participating in the Fresh Fruit and Vegetable Pilot Program prior to 1 May 2004.

Range/Average: N.A.

Activity: new program in FY 05.

HQ: same as **10.553**.*And:* Director, Grants Management Division, Special Nutrition Programs, FNS-USDA, Alexandria, VA 22302. Phone: (703)305-2161. (Note: no field offices for this program.)

10.600 FOREIGN MARKET DEVELOPMENT COOPERATOR PROGRAM

Assistance: direct payments/specified use (50 percent/1-3 years).

Purposes: pursuant to the Agricultural Trade Act of 1978, for CCC projects abroad to develop, expand, and maintain long-term export markets for U.S. agricultural products, usually conducted by U.S. nonprofit trade associations ("Cooperators"). Funded activities may include trade servicing, market research, and technical assistance to actual or potential foreign purchasers. (FAS administers the program for the CCC.)

Eligible applicants/beneficiaries: U.S. nonprofit nationwide or industry-wide agricultural trade groups.

Range: $11,000 to $7,000,000. **Average:** $1,243,000.

Activity: FY 04, 23 cooperator programs in 100 foreign countries.

HQ: Deputy Administrator, Commodity and Marketing Programs, FAS-USDA, Washington, DC 20250. Phone: (202)720-4761. **Internet:** "www.fas.usda.gov/mos/programs/fmd.html". (Note: no field offices for this program.)

10.601 MARKET ACCESS PROGRAM ("MAP")

Assistance: direct payments/specified use (50-90 percent/1-3 years).

Purposes: pursuant to the Agricultural Trade Act of 1978 as amended, to develop, expand, and maintain export markets for U.S. agricultural commodities. Projects may involve generic (90 percent funding) or brand-specific (50 percent) promotions. Activities may include consumer advertising, point-of-sale demonstrations, public relations, trade fairs, exhibits, market research, or technical assistance. Funding is through CCC reimbursements for authorized activities.

Eligible applicants/beneficiaries: U.S. nonprofit agricultural trade organizations, state regional trade groups, agricultural cooperatives, state agencies, small private entities.

Range: $22,000 to $9,611,000. **Average:** $1,375,000.

Activity: 2004, allocations to 66 groups.

HQ: same address/phone as **10.600**. **Internet:** "www.fas.usda.gov/mos/programs/mapprog.html". (Note: no field offices for this program.)

10.603 EMERGING MARKETS PROGRAM ("EMP")

Assistance: direct payments/specified use.

Purposes: pursuant to FACTA as amended and FAIRA, to promote, enhance, or expand U.S. agricultural commodity exports to emerging markets abroad. Project funds may finance feasibility studies, market research, sector assessments, orientation visits, specialized training, business workshops, and similar activities. Funding is provided through the Commodity Credit Corporation. Implementors contribute a share of project costs.

Eligible applicants/beneficiaries: U.S. agricultural or agribusiness organizations, nonprofit trade associations, universities, state departments of agriculture, certain consultant groups.

Range: $5,000 to $500,000.

Activity: FY 03, 62 projects funded.

HQ: Director, Marketing Operations Staff, FSA-USDA, Washington, DC 20250. Phone: (202)720-4327. **Internet:** "www.fas.usda.gov/mos/em-markets/em-markets.html". (Note: no field offices for this program.)

10.604 TECHNICAL ASSISTANCE FOR SPECIALTY CROPS PROGRAM ("TASC")

Assistance: direct payments/specified use.

Purposes: pursuant to FSRIA, for projects addressing sanitary, phytosanitary, and technical barriers that prohibit or threaten the export of U.S. specialty crops. Activities eligible for funding include initial preclearance programs, export protocol and work plan support, seminars and workshops, study tours, field surveys, pest lists development, pest and disease research, data base development, logistical and administrative support, and travel costs. Costs are reimbursed by CCC.

Eligible applicants/beneficiaries: federal and state government agencies; U.S. nonprofit trade associations, universities, agricultural cooperatives, private companies, and other organizations.

Range: to $250,000 per year for projects.

Activity: new program listing in 2004; 21 organizations funded in 2004.

HQ: same address/phone as **10.603**. **Internet:** no web site. (Note: no field offices for this program.)

10.605 QUALITY SAMPLES PROGRAM ("QSP")

Assistance: direct payments/specified use.

Purposes: pursuant to the CCC Charter Act, to develop and expand export markets for U.S. agricultural commodities by assisting U.S. entities in providing commodity samples to potential foreign importers. Costs of purchasing and transporting the samples may be reimbursed by the CCC; technical assistance costs may not.

Eligible applicants/beneficiaries: U.S. entities.

Range: to $75,000 for projects.

Activity: new program listing in 2004. 20 organizations assisted in 2004.

HQ: same address/phone as **10.603**. **Internet:** "www.fas.usda.gov/mos/programs/qspfact.html". (Note: no field offices for this program.)

10.606 FOOD FOR PROGRESS

Assistance: project grants (100 percent/1-3 years).

Purposes: pursuant to the Food for Progress Act of 1985, to provide agricultural commodities to developing countries and emerging democracies committed to introducing and expanding free enterprise in the agricultural sector.

Eligible applicants/beneficiaries: "Cooperating Sponsors" including: foreign governments; entities registered with USAID; entities demonstrating satisfactory experience and other qualifications to the CCC.

Range/Average: N.A.

Activity: new program listing in 2003.

HQ: Director, Programming Division, FAS-USDA, 1400 Independence Ave. SW, Washington, DC 20250-1034. Phone: (202)720-4221. **Internet:** "www.fas.usda.gov/". (Note: no field offices for this program.)

10.607 SECTION 416(B)

Assistance: project grants (100 percent/1-3 years).

Purposes: pursuant to the Agricultural Act of 1949, essentially same as **10.606**.

Eligible applicants/beneficiaries: same as **10.606**.

Range/Average: N.A.

Activity: new program listing in 2003.

HQ: same as **10.606**. (Note: no field offices for this program.)

10.608 FOOD FOR EDUCATION ("FFE")

Assistance: project grants (100 percent/1-3 years).

Purposes: pursuant to the FSRIA, to reduce hunger and improve literacy and primary education, especially for girls, with a focus on developing countries. Projects may provide for such activities as school meals, teacher training, and related support including nutrition programs for pregnant women, nursing mothers, and pre-school youngsters.

Eligible applicants/beneficiaries: same as **10.606**.

Range/Average: N.A.

Activity: N.A.

HQ: same as **10.606**. (Note: no field offices for this program.)

10.609 TRADE ADJUSTMENT ASSISTANCE ("TAA")

Assistance: direct payments/unrestricted use.

Purposes: pursuant to the Trade Act of 1974 as amended by the Trade Act of 2002, to provide technical assistance and cash benefits to farmers, ranchers, fish farmers, and fishermen competing with imported aquaculture products, if increased imports have contributed to a price decline of at least 20 percent. Technical assistance may be provided by CSREES in cooperation with county Extension Services, in helping producers respond proactively to import competition through training, cash benefits, and employment services.

Eligible applicants/beneficiaries: producers of raw commodities that: are owners, operators, landlords, tenants, or sharecroppers—sharing in production risk and entitled to share in the crop availability; have been adversely affected by import competition; are covered by a certification of eligibility; have average adjusted annual gross income below $2,500,000; have received free technical assistance from the Extension Service.

Range: to $10,000 per year.

Activity: new program listing in 2004.

HQ: Trade Adjustment Assistance, FAS-USDA, 1400 Independence Ave. SW, Washington, DC 20250-1021. Phone: (202)720-2916. **Internet:** "www.fas.usda.gov/itp/taa/taaindex.htm".

10.652 FORESTRY RESEARCH
("Research Grants & Agreements")

Assistance: project grants (1-5 years).

Purposes: pursuant to the Forest and Rangeland Renewable Resources Research Act of 1978, for fundamental research in: management of forests, watersheds, forest ranges, wildlife habitat; recreation; fire protection; insect and disease protection and control; forest products utilization; forest engineering; forest production economics and marketing; forest surveying; urban forestry; and social/cultural influences.

Eligible applicants, beneficiaries: state agricultural experiment stations, IHEs, state and local governments, territories; profit, nonprofit, and international organizations; individuals.

Range: $2,000 to $300,000. **Average:** $35,000.

Activity: FY 01, 425 grants awarded.

HQ: Deputy Chief/Research and Development, Forest Service-USDA, Washington, DC 20090-6090. Phone: (202)205-1075. **Internet:** "www.fs.fed.us/links/research.html".

10.664 COOPERATIVE FORESTRY ASSISTANCE

Assistance: formula grants; project grants (50-80 percent).

Purposes: pursuant to the Cooperative Forestry Assistance Act of 1978 and FACTA as amended, for state forest stewardship programs on private, local, state, and other nonfederal forest and rural lands. Programs may include: timber production: insect and disease control; processing of wood products; producing and distributing tree seeds and seedlings, urban forestry; conversion of wood to energy; improvement and maintenance of fish and wildlife habitat; financial and technical assistance for rural firefighting; organizational improvement; technology transfer; acquisition and loan of federal surplus property.

Eligible applicants: states, tribes, municipalities, territories and possessions, nonprofit organizations.

Eligible beneficiaries: owners of nonfederal lands; rural community firefighting forces; urban and municipal governmental and other state, local, and private agencies acting through state foresters or equivalent state officials.

Range: $25,000 to $6,000,000. **Average:** $1,000,000.

Activity: estimated 2003 activities (representative): 37,000 landowners enrolled, covering 3,914,000 acres.

HQ: Deputy Chief, State and Private Forestry, Forest Service-USDA, Washington, DC 20090-6090. Phone: (202)205-1657. **Internet:** "www.fs.fed.us/spf/coop".

10.665 SCHOOLS AND ROADS—GRANTS TO STATES ("25 Percent Payments to States")

Assistance: formula grants.

Purposes: to return 25 percent of revenues from the national forests to states and U.S. territories, for the benefit of public schools and public roads of the counties in which the forests are located.

Eligible applicants/beneficiaries: states or territories with national forest land.

Range: $35 to $161,889,000.

Activity: N.A.

HQ: Acquisitions Management, Grants and Agreements, Forest Service-USDA, RPE - Rm.706, Washington, DC 20090-6090. Phone: (703)605-4776. **Internet:** "www.fs.fed.us".

10.666 SCHOOLS AND ROADS—GRANTS TO COUNTIES ("Payments to Counties")

Assistance: formula grants.

Purposes: to return 25 percent of revenues from national grasslands and land utilization projects, for the benefit of public schools and roads of the counties in which they are located.

Eligible applicants/beneficiaries: U.S. counties with national grasslands or land utilization projects.

Range: $5 to $1,707,000. **Average:** $69,000.

Activity: N.A.

HQ: Director/Procurement and Property, same address/web site as **10.665**. Phone: (202)605-4662.

10.670 NATIONAL FOREST-DEPENDENT RURAL COMMUNITIES ("Economic Recovery")

Assistance: project grants (80 percent); use of property, facilities, and equipment; training.

Purposes: pursuant to the National Forest Dependent Rural Communities Economic Diversification Act of 1990 as amended, to provide accelerated assistance to rural communities with acute economic problems associated with federal, state, or private sector forest management policies. Assistance is coordinated with other USDA agencies and may be provided through a community action team to identify and develop opportunities to promote economic improvement, diversification, and revitalization. Funds may support costs of technical assistance, planning, and community training related to the upgrading of existing industries, and development of new economic activities in industries unrelated to the forests.

Eligible applicants/beneficiaries: general purpose local governments or tribes represented by state-authorized nonprofit corporations, with not more than

10,000 population; counties not within metropolitan statistical areas—located inside or within 100 miles of a national forest, and whose economies are strongly related to activities in the forest.

Range: $1,000 to $30,000.

Activity: FY 01, 800 communities receiving assistance.

HQ: same address/phone as **10.664**. **Internet:** "www.fs.fed.us/spf".

10.671 SOUTHEAST ALASKA ECONOMIC DISASTER FUND

Assistance: direct payments/specified use (formula based).

Purposes: to counter the effects of the declining timber program of the Tongass National Forest. Funds may be used to employ former timber workers and for related community development projects. Note: this program is scheduled to end with the expenditure of FY 03 payments.

Eligible applicants/beneficiaries: local communities/boroughs named in PL 104-134.

Range: $500,000 to $4,000,000.

Activity: N.A.

HQ: Forest Service-USDA, 3301 C St. - Ste.522, Anchorage, AK 99503-3956. Phone: (907)271-2519. **Internet:** same as **10.665**. (Note: the field office serves as headquarters.)

10.672 RURAL DEVELOPMENT, FORESTRY, AND COMMUNITIES ("Rural Development Through Forestry")

Assistance: project grants (to 5 years).

Purposes: for projects to analyze and assess forest resource opportunities, maximize local economic potential through market development and expansion, and diversify the community economic base. Funds may support costs such as for technical assistance, training and education, equipment, marketing, and related expenses.

Eligible applicants/beneficiaries: state foresters; tribal, state, and federal agencies; local governments, nonprofit organizations; others.

Range: $1,000 to $50,000.

Activity: FY 99, 2,200 communities, 1,000 organizations assisted (latest data reported).

HQ: Forest Service-USDA, Washington, DC 20090. Phone: same as **10.664**. **Internet:** "www.fs.fed.us/spf/coop/programs/eap.shtml".

10.673 WOOD IN TRANSPORTATION PROGRAM ("WIT")

Assistance: project grants (50 percent).

Purposes: pursuant to FACTA, to construct demonstration modern timber bridges and related technology transfer projects for structures to be built on public lands—toward the development and commercialization of new technologies that incorporate under-utilized timber and related resources.

Eligible applicants/beneficiaries: nonfederal agencies, state and local governments, nonprofit organizations, tribal nations.

Range: commercialization projects, to $150,000; single vehicle bridges, to 50,000; pedestrian bridges, to $20,000; special projects, $30,000.

Activity: new program listing in 2003. FY 02, 42 projects.

HQ: Forest Service-USDA, 180 Canfield St., Morgantown, WV 26505. Phone: (304)285-1591, FAX (304)285-1587. **Internet:** "www.fs.fed.us/na/wit"; e-mail, "na-wit@fs.us". (Note: the field office serves as headquarters.)

10.674 FOREST PRODUCTS LAB: TECHNOLOGY MARKETING UNIT (TMU) ("TMU Biomass Grant/Assistance Program")

Assistance: project grants (80 percent/to 3 years).

Purposes: to turn small diameter and under-utilized wood species into marketable forest products, including biomass energy. Programs may include: technical assistance for processing and manufacturing; prototype development of potential new products; demonstration projects showcasing innovative uses; economic feasibility and market assessments. Land treatment must be adjacent to national forest system lands, and may include other lands as part of treatment activities.

Eligible applicants/beneficiaries: nonprofit organizations; local, state, and tribal, governments; special purpose districts; profit businesses.

Range: $50,000 to $250,000.

Activity: new program listing in 2003.

HQ: Technology Marketing Unit, State and Private Forestry, Forest Service-USDA, 1 Gifford Pinchot Dr., Madison, WI 53276-2398. Phone: (608)231-9200. **Internet:** "www.fpl.fs.fed.us/tmu". (Note: the field office serves as headquarters.)

10.675 URBAN COMMUNITY FORESTRY PROGRAM ("UCF")

Assistance: project grants (50 percent).

Purposes: pursuant to the Cooperative Forestry Assistance Act of 1978 as amended, to improve urban livability through projects to: plan, establish, and protect trees, forests, green spaces, and related resources in and adjacent to cities and towns; link governmental, private, and grass-roots organizations and resources to address environmental issues at the local, regional, and national levels; engage people in citizen-based, grass-roots volunteer efforts to assist in retaining and protecting their natural environment to provide a balance between quality of life and land consumption associated with urban sprawl; improve the ecological function and social and economic stability of cities and communities.

Eligible applicants/beneficiaries: state forestry or equivalent state agencies; interested members of the public; private nonprofit organizations. Available also in territories and possessions.

Range/Average: N.A.

Activity: new program listing in 2003. FY 04 estimate, 10,500 communities assisted.

HQ: Deputy Chief, State and Private Forestry, Forest Service-USDA, 1400

Independence Ave. SW, Washington, DC 20090-1123. Phone: same as **10.664**. **Internet:** "www.fs.fed.us/ucf/".

10.676 FOREST LEGACY PROGRAM ("FLP")

Assistance: project grants (75 percent/2 years).

Purposes: pursuant to Cooperative Forestry Assistance Act of 1978 FACTA, FAIRA, and amendments, to protect and conserve environmentally important forest areas threatened by conversion to nonforest uses, through conservation easements and other mechanisms. Projects must be conducted on a strictly voluntary basis—i.e., without eminent domain or other legal compulsions.

Eligible applicants: state lead agencies in consultation with state forest stewardship coordinating committees, including in territories and possessions.

Eligible beneficiaries: private forest landowners and land trust organizations.

Range/Average: N.A.

Activity: new program listing in 2003. As of April 2005, more than 1,000,000 acres protected.

HQ: Cooperative Forestry (1123), State and Private Forestry, Forest Service-USDA, 1400 Independence Ave. SW Washington, DC 20250. Phone: (202) 605-1469. **Internet:** "www.fs.fed.us/spf/coop/programs/loa/flp.shtml".

10.677 FOREST LAND ENHANCEMENT PROGRAM ("FLEP")

Assistance: project grants (100 percent).

Purposes: pursuant to FSRIA, for sustainable forest management of nonindustrial private forest and other suitable rural lands. Funds may be used for: technical and educational assistance; practices such as management plan development, tree planting, forest stand improvement, agro-forestry implementation, water quality improvement and watershed protection, fish and wildlife habitat improvement, forest health protection, invasive species control, wildfire and catastrophic protection, and approved special practices. Landowners and managers may not receive grants exceeding 75 percent of project costs.

Eligible applicants: state forestry or equivalent agencies in the states, territories, and possessions; municipalities; nonprofits.

Eligible beneficiaries: owners of nonfederal lands, nonprofit organizations, other state and local private organizations and agencies acting through states.

Range: $1,100 to $832,000.

Activity: 7,800 owners of 610,000 acres to benefit.

HQ: none. **Internet:** "www.fs.fed.us/contactus/regions.shtml". (Note: all contacts are with field offices.)

10.678 FOREST STEWARDSHIP PROGRAM ("FSP")

Assistance: project grants (12-18 months).

Purposes: pursuant to the Cooperative Forestry Assistance Act of 1978 and FACTA as amended, to provide financial, technical, educational, and related assistance to promote and enable the long-term active management of nonindustrial private and other nonfederal forest land.

Eligible applicants/beneficiaries: same as **10.677**.

Range: $25,000 to $2,000,000. **Average:** $450,000.

Activity: new program listing in 2003. FY 02, 186,000 landowners assisted, 18,000 plans completed, 1,640,000 acres encompassed.

HQ: Forest Stewardship Program Manager, State & Private/Cooperative Forestry, Forest Service-USDA, Washington, DC 20090-6090. Phone: (202) 205-6206. **Internet:** "www.na.fs.fed.us/spfo/stewardship/index.htm".

10.679 COLLABORATIVE FOREST RESTORATION

Assistance: project grants (80 percent/to 4 years).

Purposes: pursuant to Secure Rural Schools and Community Self-Determination Act of 2000, to promote healthy watersheds and to reduce high intensity wildfires, insect infestation, and diseases in federal, tribal, state, county, and municipal forest lands in New Mexico; to improve the forests' ecosystems functioning and enhance plant and wildlife biodiversity by reducing the high number and density of small diameter trees; to improve communication and joint problem-solving among interested groups. Funds may support costs of technical assistance, training and education, equipment, marketing, and related services.

Eligible applicants/beneficiaries: local and tribal governments, educational institutions, landowners, conservation associations, and other public and private entities that include a diverse and balanced group of stakeholders, including public officials.

Range: $66,000 to $360,000.

Activity: new program listing in 2005. 2001-04, 62 proposals recommended for funding.

HQ: Cooperative and International Forestry Staff, Southwestern Region, Forest Service-USDA, 333 Broadway SE, Albuquerque, NM 87122. Phone: (505) 842-3289. **Internet:** "www.fs.fed.us/r3/spf/cfrp". (Note: the field office serves as headquarters.)

10.680 FOREST HEALTH PROTECTION ("FHP")

Assistance: formula grants; project grants (50-100 percent).

Purposes: pursuant to the Cooperative Forestry Assistance Act of 1978 and FACTA as amended, to protect nonfederal forest and tree resources from damaging insects, disease-causing agents, and invasive plants; to develop or improve forest health protection technologies. Project funds may be used for project planning, surveys, assessments, monitoring, technical assistance, technology and applied methods development.

Eligible applicants/beneficiaries: state forestry, agriculture, and equivalent agencies, including in territories; municipalities; profit and nonprofit organizations; Alaska native corporations, tribal governments.

Range: $25,000 to $6,000,000. **Average:** $1,000,000.

Activity: new program listing in 2005. 2001-03, all applications for base funding approved.

HQ: same as **10.664**.

10.700 NATIONAL AGRICULTURAL LIBRARY

Assistance: technical information.

Purposes: to provide agricultural information products and services through traditional library functions and through electronic distribution. Publications are available through interlibrary loan or photo-reproduction.

Eligible applicants/beneficiaries: general public.

Activity: 3,300,000 items available.

HQ: Office of the Director, National Agricultural Library, ARS-USDA, Beltsville, MD 20705-2351. Phone: (301)504-6780. **Internet:** "www.nal.usda.gov". (Note: no field offices for this program.)

10.760 WATER AND WASTE DISPOSAL SYSTEMS FOR RURAL COMMUNITIES

Assistance: project grants (45-75 percent); direct loans, guaranteed/insured loans (40 years).

Purposes: pursuant to CFRDA as amended, to install, repair, improve, or expand rural water facilities and waste disposal systems including the collection and treatment of sanitary, storm, and solid wastes. Funds may be used to pay for distribution lines, well-pumping facilities, and their related costs. Loans have varying interest rates beginning as low as 4.5 percent, depending on area median income. Grants are made only when necessary to reduce the average annual benefited user charges to a reasonable level, with the matching percentage based on the applicant area's median income. Grant funds may not be used to pay loan interest, operation and maintenance costs, nor to acquire or refinance existing systems. Grants funding for this program includes **10.761** and **10.770**.

Eligible applicants/beneficiaries: municipalities, counties, state political subdivisions such as districts and authorities; associations, cooperatives, and nonprofit corporations; tribes on federal and state reservations and other federally recognized tribes. Authorized also in territories.

Range: direct loans, $500 to $9,509,000; grants, $3,423 to $9,900,000. **Average:** loans, $1,090,000; grants, $457,000.

Activity: FY 05 estimate, 900 direct, 2 guaranteed loans; 800 grants.

HQ: Assistant Administrator, Water and Environmental Programs, RUS-USDA, Washington, DC 20250. Phone: (202)690-2670. **Internet:** "www.rurdev.usda.gov".

10.761 TECHNICAL ASSISTANCE AND TRAINING GRANTS

Assistance: project grants (100 percent).

Purposes: pursuant to CFRDA as amended, to identify and evaluate solutions to rural water problems relating to source, storage, treatment, and waste disposal; to provide training to improve the management, operation, and maintenance of water and waste disposal facilities. Funding for this program is included in **10.760**.

Eligible applicants: tax-exempt nonprofit organizations.

Eligible beneficiaries: state political subdivisions such as counties, municipalities, districts, and authorities; tribes; cooperatives; nonprofit corporations.

Range: $40,000 to $7,903,000. **Average:** $1,105,000.

Activity: FY 04, 16 grants.

HQ: same as **10.760**.

10.762 SOLID WASTE MANAGEMENT GRANTS

Assistance: project grants (100 percent).

Purposes: pursuant to CFRDA as amended, to evaluate landfill conditions to determine threats to water resources in rural areas; to provide technical assistance and training in the operation of landfills, and to reduce the solid waste stream; to provide planning assistance for closing landfill sites and for future uses of such sites. Funds may not be used to pay for capital assets.

Eligible applicants/beneficiaries: tax-exempt nonprofit organizations; public bodies including local government-based multijurisdictional organizations.

Range: $5,000 to $720,000. **Average:** $75,000.

Activity: FY 04, 46 grants awarded.

HQ: same as **10.760**.

10.763 EMERGENCY COMMUNITY WATER ASSISTANCE GRANTS

Assistance: project grants (100 percent).

Purposes: pursuant to CFRDA and FACTA, to assist rural areas experiencing a significant decline in quality or quantity of water, in complying with the Safe Drinking Water Act. Funds may be used to: extend or repair water lines on existing systems; construct new lines, new wells, reservoirs, transmission lines, treatment plants, storage tanks; and, for similar projects and related activities and costs.

Eligible applicants/beneficiaries: public bodies, private nonprofit corporations, state political subdivisions, tribes—in communities with populations not above 10,000, with household income below the statewide nonmetropolitan median.

Range: $9,000 to $500,000. **Average:** $238,000.

Activity: FY 04, 64 grants.

HQ: same as **10.760**.

10.766 COMMUNITY FACILITIES LOANS AND GRANTS

Assistance: direct loans; guaranteed loans; project grants.

Purposes: pursuant to CFRDA as amended, to construct, enlarge, extend, or improve public facilities serving rural residents, including child care, food recovery and distribution, assisted living, group homes, mental health clinics, shelters, fire and rescue services, industrial park sites, transportation, access ways, utility extensions, educational facilities.

Eligible applicants/beneficiaries: state agencies, counties, cities, state political and quasi-political subdivisions, tribes, associations including nonprofit corporations—in communities with populations under 20,000. Available also in territories.

Range: direct loans, $50,000 to $4,500,000; guaranteed, $50,000 to $12,000,000; grants, $100 to $100,000. **Average:** direct, $442,000; guaranteed, $859,000; grants $32,000.

Activity: FY 04, 551 direct, 103 guaranteed loans; 596 grants.

HQ: same address/phone as **10.446**. **Internet:** same as **10.760**.

10.767 INTERMEDIARY RELENDING PROGRAM

Assistance: direct loans (75 percent at 1 percent interest/to 30 years).

Purposes: pursuant to the Health and Human Services Act of 1986, Food Security Act of 1985, and Community Economic Development Act of 1981, and amendments, for business facilities and community development in rural areas with under 25,000 population. Successful applicants become intermediary lenders that may make loans to ultimate recipients to finance up to 75 percent of project costs, but not more than $150,000 to any one recipient.

Eligible applicants: private nonprofit organizations, state or local governments, recognized tribes, cooperatives.

Eligible beneficiaries: individuals, public and private profit or nonprofit organizations.

Range: $3,000 to $615,000. **Average:** $20,000.

Activity: FY 05 estimate, 73 loan approvals.

HQ: RBCS-USDA, South Agriculture Bldg. - Rm.6867, Washington, DC 20250-3225. Phone: (202)690-4100. **Internet:** same as **10.760**.

10.768 BUSINESS AND INDUSTRY LOANS

Assistance: direct loans (75-80 percent); guaranteed/insured loans (to 80-90 percent).

Purposes: pursuant to CFRDA as amended, for the development or improvement of rural businesses, industry, and employment. Loan funds may cover such costs as business and industrial acquisition, construction, conversion, enlargement, repair, modernization, equipment, machinery, supplies, pollution control and abatement—for 30 years for real estate, up to 15 years for machinery and equipment, and 7 years for working capital. Assistance is unavailable for community antenna TV services or facilities, charitable and educational institutions, hotels and tourist facilities, large businesses, or uses other than those that will protect or create jobs, improve existing business and industry, and provide economic stability to rural areas. Project examples: agri-business expansion; radio station start-up; catfish farm operating loan; printing company expansion.

Eligible applicants/beneficiaries: cooperatives, corporations, partnerships, trusts, or other for-profit enterprises; certain nonprofit entities; tribes, municipalities, counties, or other state political subdivisions; individuals. Applicants must be U.S. citizens or legal permanent residents; if corporations,

51 percent ownership must be held by U.S. citizens. Available also in some territories. Projects must be in rural jurisdictions under 50,000 population, with preference to those under 25,000.

Range: direct loans, $35,000 to $10,000,000; guaranteed loans, $35,000 to $25,000,000. **Average:** direct, $559,000; guaranteed, $2,100,000.

Activity: FY 05 estimate, 286 guaranteed loans. (Note: no funds have been available for direct loans since FY 01.)

HQ: Administrator, RBCS-USDA, Washington, DC 20250-3201. Phone: (202) 690-4730, FAX (202)690-4737. **Internet:** same as **10.760**.

10.769 RURAL BUSINESS ENTERPRISE GRANTS ("RBEG")

Assistance: project grants (formula based).

Purposes: pursuant to CFRDA as amended, to facilitate the development of small and emerging private business, industry, and related employment—toward economic improvement of rural areas. Grants may be used to: create, expand, or operate distance learning networks or programs providing educational or job training instruction; to establish revolving loan funds, provide operating capital, and finance industrial sites—including land acquisition; construction, conversion, enlargement, repair, or modernization of buildings, plants, machinery, equipment; access streets and roads, parking areas, transportation serving the site; utility extensions; water supply and waste disposal facilities, pollution control and abatement; technical assistance, fees, and refinancing. Television demonstration grants (TDG) may be used for programming demonstrating the effectiveness of providing information on agriculture and other issues of importance to farmers and other rural residents.

Eligible applicants: RBEG—public bodies and nonprofit corporations serving rural areas, such as states, counties, cities, townships, and incorporated towns and villages, boroughs, authorities, districts, and tribes on federal and state reservations serving rural areas. TDG—statewide nonprofit public television systems whose coverage is predominantly rural. For this program, "rural area" is defined as all territory of a state not within the outer boundary of any city with a population over 50,000. Priority is accorded to projects: in areas of under 25,000 population with a large number of low-income persons; designed to save existing or to create new jobs; in areas with high unemployment.

Eligible beneficiaries: private businesses that will employ 50 or fewer new employees, and with under $1,000,000 in projected revenue.

Range: $2,000 to $500,000. **Average:** $83,000.

Activity: FY 05 estimate, 455 grants.

HQ: Director, Specialty Lenders Division, RBCS-USDA, Washington, DC 20250-3222. Phone: (202)720-1400. **Internet:** same as **10.760**.

10.770 WATER AND WASTE DISPOSAL LOANS AND GRANTS ("Section 306C")

Assistance: project grants; direct loans (100 percent).

Purposes: pursuant to CFRDA as amended and FACTA, to develop water and waste disposal facilities and services for rural low-income communities facing significant health risks. Funds may be used to: construct, enlarge, extend, or improve community water or sewer systems; connect residences to community systems; enable individuals to install plumbing and related fixtures and to construct bathrooms within their dwellings. Funded projects must primarily serve residents of counties with per capita incomes not more than 70 percent of the national average, and with unemployment not less than 125 percent of the national average rate. Grant funds for this program are included in **10.760**, and may be used only in colonias.

Eligible applicants/beneficiaries: local governments, tribes, nonprofit associations, cooperatives—including territories and possessions.

Range/Average: $702,000.

Activity: FY 04, 34 infrastructure projects, 247 individual connections funded.

HQ: same as **10.760**.

10.771 RURAL COOPERATIVE DEVELOPMENT GRANTS ("RCDG")

Assistance: project grants (75 percent).

Purposes: pursuant to the FACTA, CFRDA, and FAIRA, to establish and operate centers for rural cooperative development to improve economic conditions by promoting development of new cooperatives, or to improve existing cooperatives. Funds may be used for basic feasibility studies, technical assistance, advisory services, and research or technical support for individuals, small businesses, cooperatives, or rural industries

Eligible applicants/beneficiaries: nonprofit corporations and IHEs serving rural areas beyond the outer boundary of any city with population 50,000 or more.

Range: $85,000 to $300,000. **Average:** $264,000.

Activity: FY 04, 24 grants.

HQ: Assistant Deputy Administrator/Cooperative Services, RBCS-USDA, Washington, DC 20250. Phone: (202)720-8460. **Internet:** same as **10.760**.

10.772 EMPOWERMENT ZONES PROGRAM ("Empowerment Zones and Enterprise Communities")

Assistance: project grants (100 percent/to 10 years).

Purposes: pursuant to the Taxpayer Relief Acts of 1997 and 2000 and other acts, to establish job creation zones in rural areas toward the revitalization of economically distressed areas for the benefit of the disadvantaged and long-term unemployed. Through national competitions among applicants demonstrating a certain level of distress, designated rural Empowerment Zones and Enterprise Communities became eligible for private activity tax exempt bonding authority to finance qualifying enterprises and facilities. Some Round I Empowerment Zones designated in 1994 are eligible for: employer wage credits; accelerated IRS Section 179 expensing for eligible property; priority funding or special consideration under other federal programs; empowerment zone/enterprise community social service block grants

(EZ/EC-SSBG) from HHS, based on activities identified in strategic plans. Round II designations were made in late 1998; provisions changed slightly. (Urban area programs are described under **14.244**.)

Eligible applicants/beneficiaries: generally, rural areas with pervasive poverty, unemployment, general distress, and with a maximum population of 30,000, no larger than 1,000 square miles, located entirely within no more than three contiguous states, and not including any portion of an Indian reservation. No new designations are authorized currently; additional details should be obtained from RDA state offices.

Range: $500,000 to $40,000,000. **Average:** $6,300,000.

Activity: cumulatively, 57 rural areas designated as EZs and ECs.

HQ: Deputy Administrator, Office of Community Development-USDA, Reporters Bldg. - Rm.266, 300 Seventh St. SW, Washington, DC 20024. Phone: (202)619-7980; **Internet:** "www.ezec.gov", *and* same as **10.760**.

10.773 RURAL BUSINESS OPPORTUNITY GRANTS ("RBOG")

Assistance: project grants (2 years).

Purposes: pursuant to FAIRA, to promote sustainable economic development in rural communities with exceptional needs. Grants may support technical assistance, training, and planning costs.

Eligible applicants/beneficiaries: public bodies, nonprofit corporations, tribes, cooperatives.

Range: $3,000 to $615,000. **Average:** $99,000.

Activity: FY 04, 55 grants.

HQ: Specialty Lenders Division, RBCS-USDA, 1400 Independence Ave. SW - Rm.6767, Washington, DC 20250-1521. Phone: (202)720-1400. **Internet:** same as **10.760**.

10.774 NATIONAL SHEEP INDUSTRY IMPROVEMENT CENTER ("NSIIC")

Assistance: direct loans, guaranteed/insured loans (80 percent/to 40 years); direct payments/specified use (50 percent); project grants.

Purposes: pursuant to FAIRA, for the sheep and goat industries to strengthen and enhance production and marketing. Funds may support such activities as making capital available to increase production or improve efficiency, coordination of marketing systems, and public communication programs. An appropriated revolving fund supports this program.

Eligible applicants/beneficiaries: public, private, cooperative, and nonprofit organizations; tribes; public and quasi-public agencies.

Range: loans, to $1,000,000.

Activity: not quantified specifically.

HQ: NSIIC-USDA, 1400 Independence Ave. SW - Rm.2117, Washington, DC 20250. Phone: (202)690-0632, FAX (207)236-6576. **Internet:** "www.rurdev.usda.gov/rbs/coops/cssheep.htm". (Note: no field offices for this program.)

10.775 RENEWABLE ENERGY SYSTEMS AND ENERGY EFFICIENCY IMPROVEMENTS PROGRAM ("RES and EEI")

Assistance: project grants (25 percent); guaranteed loans and direct loans (50 percent).

Purposes: pursuant to the FSRIA, for farmers, ranchers, and small rural businesses to purchase renewable energy systems or energy efficiency improvements. Projects combining grant and loan funds may not receive more than 50 percent federal funding.

Eligible applicants/beneficiaries: agricultural producers and small rural businesses that are U.S. citizens or legally admitted permanent residents.

Range: $2,500 to $500,000. **Average:** $125,000.

Activity: 280 projects to date.

HQ: RBCS-USDA, 1400 Independence Ave. SW, Washington, DC 20013. Phone: (202)720-1400. **Internet:** "www.rurdev.usda.gov/rbs".

10.850 RURAL ELECTRIFICATION LOANS AND LOAN GUARANTEES

Assistance: direct loans (70-90 percent/to 35 years).

Purposes: pursuant to the Rural Electrification Act of 1936 (REA) as amended, to supply or improve central station electric services in rural areas—i.e., any farm or nonfarm area not within the boundaries of an urban area. RUS also guarantees loans used primarily for generation and transmission projects.

Eligible applicants/beneficiaries: rural electric cooperatives, public utility districts, power companies, municipalities, and other qualified power suppliers, including in territories.

Range: direct loans, $676,000 to $104,324,000; FFB guarantees, $860,000 to $320,921,000. **Average:** direct, $22,149,000; FFB, $36,771,000.

Activity: FY 04, 173 direct, 48 guaranteed loans.

HQ: Administrator, RUS-USDA, Washington, DC 20250-1500. Phone: (202) 720-9540. **Internet:** same as **10.760**. (Note: no field offices for this program.)

10.851 RURAL TELEPHONE LOANS AND LOAN GUARANTEES

Assistance: direct loans; guaranteed/insured loans.

Purposes: pursuant to REA as amended, to improve, expand, construct, acquire, and operate telecommunications systems in rural areas—i.e., any area of the U.S. not within the boundaries of a city, village, or borough with over 5,000 population. Average loan term, 18 years.

Eligible applicants/beneficiaries: telephone companies or cooperatives; nonprofit, limited dividend, or mutual associations; public bodies—including in territories.

Range: direct loans, $48,000 to $44,537,000; guaranteed, $60,000 to $45,100,000. **Average:** direct, $4,719,000; guaranteed, $11,429,000.

Activity: FY 04, 65 loans.

HQ: Assistant Administrator, same address/web site as **10.850**. Phone: (202)720-9554, FAX (202)720-0810. (Note: no field offices for this program.)

10.852 RURAL TELEPHONE BANK LOANS ("RTB Loans")

Assistance: direct loans (to 35 years).

Purposes: pursuant to REA as amended, to provide supplemental financing to supply or improve telecommunications services in rural areas—i.e., any area of the U.S. not within the boundaries of a city, village, or borough with over 5,000 population.

Eligible applicants/beneficiaries: borrowers with a current RUS loan or loan commitment, including in territories and possessions.

Range: $34,000 to $73,399,000. **Average:** $5,861,000.

Activity: FY 04, 29 loans.

HQ: same as **10.851**. (Note: no field offices for this program.)

10.853 LOCAL TELEVISION LOAN GUARANTEE PROGRAM ("Local TV Program")

Assistance: guaranteed/insured loans (80 percent/to 25 years).

Purposes: pursuant to the Local Television Act of 2000 as amended, to facilitate access to signals of local television stations for households located in nonserved and underserved areas. Loans may finance the acquisition, improvement, enhancement, construction, deployment, launch, or rehabilitation of the means by which local television stations will be delivered. Loan funds may not be used for operating, advertising, or promotion expenses—nor for the acquisition of licenses.

Eligible applicants/beneficiaries: corporations, partnerships, joint venture trustees; government entities, agencies, or instrumentalities.

Range/Average: N.A.

Activity: new program in FY 04.

HQ: Secretary, Local Television Loan Guarantee Board, RUS-USDA, 1400 Independence Ave. SW - Rm. 2919-S, Washington, DC 20250-1575. Phone: (202)720-0530, FAX (202)720-3724. **Internet:** "www.usda.gov/rus/localtvboard/"; e-mail, "localtv@usda.gov". (Note: no field offices for this program.)

10.854 RURAL ECONOMIC DEVELOPMENT LOANS AND GRANTS

Assistance: direct loans (80 percent, no interest/10 years); project grants (80 percent).

Purposes: pursuant to REA as amended, for rural economic and job development projects, including the costs of feasibility studies, project start-up, and other reasonable expenses. Project examples: business incubators; establishment or expansion of factories or businesses; revolving loan funds.

Eligible applicants/beneficiaries: electric and telephone utilities with current RUS loans.

Range: loans, $200,000 to $450,000; grants, $10,000 to $300,000. **Average:** loans, $375,000; grants, $260,000.

Activity: cumulatively 1989-FY 04, 638 loans, 282 grants approved.

HQ: same as **10.769**.

10.855 DISTANCE LEARNING AND TELEMEDICINE LOANS AND GRANTS

Assistance: project grants (85 percent/3 years); direct loans (100 percent/3 years).

Purposes: pursuant to FAIRA, for telecommunications, computer networks, and related technologies in rural areas, providing educational and/or medical benefits to students, teachers, medical professionals, and rural residents—through distance learning and telemedicine projects.

Eligible applicants/beneficiaries: legally organized corporations, partnerships; tribes and tribal organizations; state and local governments; schools, libraries, hospitals, medical centers, and similar organizations.

Range: from $50,000.

Activity: FY 01, 89 projects funded (latest data reported in CFDA).

HQ: Assistant Administrator/Telecommunications Program, same address/phone as **10.851**. **Internet:** "www.usda.gov/rus/telecom/dit/dlt.htm". (Note: no field offices for this program.)

10.856 1890 LAND GRANT INSTITUTIONS RURAL ENTREPRENEURIAL OUTREACH PROGRAM
("1890 Outreach")

Assistance: direct payments/specified use (75 percent).

Purposes: pursuant to the Rural Development Act of 1972 as amended by FAIRA, to promote rural development programs; to provide outreach and technical assistance, advisory services, training, counseling, and disseminate technical information; to develop programs to develop future entrepreneurs and businesses in rural America—in communities with the greatest economic need. Project activities may include assistance in: business start-up; best practices in community economic development; computer technology outreach and network systems.

Eligible applicants: 1890 land grant institutions, Tuskegee University.

Eligible beneficiaries: rural residents in areas with economic need and in Empowerment Zones, Enterprise Communities, Champion Communities; tribal groups.

Range: $75,000 to $150,000. **Average:** $136,000.

Activity: new program listing in 2004. FY 03, 15 cooperative agreements awarded.

HQ: RBS Land Grant Outreach Manager, Cooperative Services, RBCS-USDA, 1400 Independence Ave. SW, Washington, DC 20250-3252. Phone: (202)690-3407. **Internet:** same as **10.775**.

10.857 STATE BULK FUEL REVOLVING FUND

Assistance: project grants (100 percent/3 years).

Purposes: pursuant to REA as amended, for states to establish revolving funds to enable cost-effective fuel purchases for communities where fuel cannot be shipped by surface transportation.

Eligible applicants/beneficiaries: state entities in existence as of 9 November 2000, including in territories and possessions.

Range/Average: FY 01, $5,000,000 (single competitive grant).
Activity: 1 grant.
HQ: Assistant Administrator, same address/phone as **10.850**. **Internet:** "www.usda.gov/rus/electric/hecgp/index.htm". (Note: no field offices for this program.)

10.858 RUS DENALI COMMISSION GRANTS AND LOANS
Assistance: project grants (from 3 years); direct loans.
Purposes: pursuant to REA as amended, for the Denali Commission to finance facilities serving several rural communities in Alaska where average residential energy expenditures are at least 275 percent of the national average—in coordination with state rural development initiatives. Project examples: improvements in bulk fuel storage and handling facilities; electric distribution system improvements.
Eligible applicants: Denali Commission only.
Eligible beneficiaries: Alaska rural residents.
Range/Average: $10,000,000 to $18,500,000 (single grant).
Activity: 1 grant.
HQ: same as **10.850**. (Note: no field offices for this program.)

10.859 ASSISTANCE TO HIGH ENERGY COST—RURAL COMMUNITIES ("RUS High Energy Cost Grant")
Assistance: project grants; direct loans.
Purposes: pursuant to REA as amended, for projects in rural communities with high energy costs to acquire, construct, extend, upgrade, and improve energy generation, transmission, or distribution facilities—where the average residential home energy expenditure is at least 275 percent of the national average.
Eligible applicants/beneficiaries: states, state political subdivisions, and state entities including profit and nonprofit businesses, partnerships, associations, cooperatives, public bodies, tribal entities, and individuals—including in territories and possessions.
Range: $75,000 to $5,000,000. **Average:** N.A.
Activity: FY 04, 6 projects funded.
HQ: Assistant Administrator, Electric Program, RUS-USDA, Washington, DC 20250-1500. Phone: (202)720-9545. **Internet:** same as **10.857**. (Note: no field offices for this program.)

10.860 RURAL BUSINESS INVESTMENT PROGRAM ("RBIP")
Assistance: guaranteed/insured loans (to 10 years); project grants (5 years).
Purposes: pursuant to CFRDA as amended, to promote economic development and create wealth and job opportunities in rural areas. USDA licenses newly formed Rural Business Investment Companies (RBICs), and guarantees their debentures to fund their investments in rural areas; in turn, RBICs use the proceeds to make equity capital investments in mostly smaller enterprises.

The program also provides operational assistance grants to RBICs, enabling them to provide operational and technical assistance to the enterprises in which they invest.

Eligible applicants: RBICs—newly formed, for-profit entities or their subsidiaries with appropriate community development or venture capital financing expertise, and with at least $10,000,000 in private equity capital.

Eligible beneficiaries: rural individual businesses, enterprises, or tribal groups that are public, private, or cooperative profit or nonprofit organizations; other persons or entities.

Range/Average: debentures, $20,000,000; grants, $1,000,000.

Activity: new program listing in 2005 (CFDA on-line version).

HQ: same address/phone as **10.768**. **Internet:** "www.sba.gov/INV/RBIP".

10.861 PUBLIC TELEVISION STATION DIGITAL TRANSITION GRANT PROGRAM

Assistance: project grants (100 percent/3-4 years).

Purposes: to convert rural analog public television broadcasting to digital signals, pursuant to FCC regulations. Project funds may be used to cover such costs as digital transmitters and translators, transmitting antennas, towers and tower improvement, and some production and management equipment.

Eligible applicants/beneficiaries: public television stations serving rural areas, or consortia, eligible to be licensed as noncommercial educational broadcast stations owned and operated by public agencies or nonprofit private foundations, corporations, or associations, or municipalities.

Range: individual stations, to $2,000,000; consortia, to $2,000,000 for the first station and $1,000,000 for each additional station to a maximum of $5,000,000;. **Average:** $851,000.

Activity: new program listing in 2005. FY 04, 34 grants awarded.

HQ: Assistant Administrator, Telecommunications Program, RUS-USDA, 1400 Independence Ave. SW, Washington, DC 20250-1590. Phone: (202) 720-9554, FAX (202)720-0810. **Internet:** "www.usda.gov/rus/telecom/index.htm". (Note: no field offices for this program.)

10.862 HOUSEHOLD WATER WELL SYSTEM GRANT PROGRAM ("HWWS Program")

Assistance: project grants.

Purposes: pursuant to CFRDA as amended, to establish and maintain revolving loan funds to make loans, in turn, to eligible rural homeowners to construct, refurbish, and service individually owned household water well systems

Eligible applicants: experienced private nonprofit corporations.

Eligible beneficiaries: households with a combined income not exceeding 100 percent of the nonmetropolitan median for the area.

Range/Average: $500,000.

Activity: new program listing in 2005 (CFDA on-line version); FY 04 estimate, 2 grants.

HQ: same as **10.760**.

10.863 COMMUNITY CONNECT GRANT PROGRAM

Assistance: project grants (to 85 percent/3 years).

Purposes: to deploy broadband transmission services to critical rural community facilities such as schools, education centers, libraries, hospitals, health care providers, law enforcement agencies, public safety organizations, fire and rescue services, and residents and businesses that will operate a community center providing free and open access to area residents. Funds may cover costs of construction, acquisition, expansion, and operation of centers for at least 2 years.

Eligible applicants/beneficiaries: incorporated profit or nonprofit organizations; tribes and tribal organizations, state or local governments.

Range: from $50,000.

Activity: new program listing in 2004. FY 05, 16 grants approved.

HQ: Assistant Administrator/Telecommunications, same address/phone **10.851**. **Internet:** "www.usda.gov/rus/telecom/commconnect.htm". (Note: no field offices for this program.)

10.864 GRANT PROGRAM TO ESTABLISH A FUND FOR FINANCING WATER AND WASTEWATER PROJECTS

Assistance: project grants (80 percent).

Purposes: pursuant to CFRDA as amended, to establish and maintain a revolving loan fund to finance small and short-term predevelopment costs of proposed or existing water and wastewater projects or systems, including costs of replacement equipment and small-scale extension of services—in rural communities with populations not higher 10,000.

Eligible applicants: private nonprofit organization.

Eligible beneficiaries: municipalities, counties, other state political subdivisions including districts and authorities; associations, cooperatives, nonprofit corporations; tribes.

Range/Average: $497,000 (single grant).

Activity: new program listing in 2005. Single grant.

HQ: same as **10.760**.

10.886 RURAL BROADBAND ACCESS LOANS AND LOAN GUARANTEES

Assistance: direct loans (4 percent); guaranteed/insured loans (5 years).

Purposes: pursuant to REA as amended, for rural communities to finance the construction, improvement, and acquisition of telecommunications facilities and equipment to provide broadband service comparable in reliability and quality to the rest of the nation.

Eligible applicants/beneficiaries: cooperative, nonprofit, limited dividend, or mutual associations; limited liability companies; commercial organizations; tribes and tribal organizations; state and local governments; territories and possessions—serving communities with population not exceeding 20,000 population.

Range: $100,000 to $168,406,000. **Average:** $18,271,000.

Activity: new program listing in 2005. FY 04, 34 loans approved.

HQ: same address/phone as **10.861**. **Internet:** "www.usda.gov/rus/telecom/broadband.htm ". (Note: no field offices for this program.)

10.900 GREAT PLAINS CONSERVATION

Assistance: direct payments/specified use (50-80 percent/3-10 years); advisory services/counseling.

Purposes: pursuant to the Soil Conservation and Domestic Allotment Act of 1936 as amended and the Great Plains Act of 1956, for technical and financial assistance in the conservation and development of soil and water resources on the Great Plains, including: agriculture-related pollution abatement; enhancement of fish, wildlife, recreational resources; promotion of economic land use.

Eligible applicants/beneficiaries: farmers, ranchers, and others in the 556 designated counties of the ten states in the Great Plains area.

Range: to $35,000 per farm operating unit.

Activity: as of FY 04, 930 active contracts covering 3,906,000 acres.

HQ: Deputy Chief/Natural Resources Conservation Programs, NRCS-USDA, same address, web site as **10.062**. Phone: (202)720-1873.

10.901 RESOURCE CONSERVATION AND DEVELOPMENT ("RC&D")

Assistance: advisory services/counseling.

Purposes: to encourage and improve capabilities to plan, develop, and execute programs for resource conservation and development, in approved RC&D areas. Assistance is available for approved measures for land conservation, water management, community development, and environmental enhancement. Project examples include: promotion of economic development, cluster zoning, land conservation easements, historic preservation; formation of water quality associations; use of low-grade timber for housing development; fertilizer development from composting.

Eligible applicants/beneficiaries: state and local governments and nonprofit organizations in multi-jurisdictional areas. Available also in PR, VI, Guam, Northern Marianas.

Activity: 52,000 completed projects as of FY 02.

HQ: Deputy Chief/Programs, Resource Conservation and Community Development Division, same address/web site as **10.062**. Phone: (202)720-2847.

10.902 SOIL AND WATER CONSERVATION

Assistance: advisory services/counseling.

Purposes: pursuant to the Soil Conservation and Domestic Allotment Act of 1936 as amended, to assist in planning and applying soil and water conservation practices, systems, and treatment; to provide technical natural resource conservation information.

Eligible applicants/beneficiaries: land users and owners, community organizations, state and local governments. Available also in PR, VI, and Western Pacific Trust Territories.

Activity: FY 00, 34,000,000 acres covered by NRCS services to landowners and users (latest data reported).

HQ: same address/web site as **10.900**. Phone: (202)720-4527.

10.903 SOIL SURVEY

Assistance: technical information.

Purposes: to produce and maintain current published soil surveys and related data bases of counties and areas of comparable size for use by environmentalists, engineers, planners, zoning and tax commissions, homeowners, farmers, ranchers, land developers, and others—in selecting and implementing appropriate use and treatment of the soils surveyed.

Eligible applicants/beneficiaries: anyone needing soil surveys.

Activity: FY 03-04 estimate, 22,000,000 acres surveyed.

HQ: Deputy Chief/Soil Survey and Resource Assessment, same address, web site as **10.062**. Phone: (202)690-4616.

10.904 WATERSHED PROTECTION AND FLOOD PREVENTION ("Small Watershed Program" - "PL-566 Operations Phase")

Assistance: project grants (50-100 percent); advisory services/counseling.

Purposes: pursuant to the Watershed Protection and Flood Prevention Act as amended and other acts, to plan and execute projects to protect, develop, and utilize land and water resources in small watersheds (250,000 acres or less). Funds may support watershed protection measures, flood prevention, irrigation, drainage, agricultural water management, sedimentation control, and public water-based fish, wildlife, and recreation resources; also, to extend long-term credit to help local interests with their share of costs. Single structure capacity is limited to 25,000 acre-feet of total capacity and 12,500 acre-feet of flood-water detention capacity.

Eligible applicants/beneficiaries: any authorized state agency, county or groups of counties, municipality, town or township, soil and water conservation district, flood prevention or flood control district, tribe or tribal organization, or nonprofit agency. Available also in territories.

Range: to $2,164,000. **Average:** $650,000.

Activity: FY 02 estimate, 8 projects approved for operations; 512 projects under construction; 931 projects completed.

HQ: Watersheds and Wetlands Division, NRCS-USDA, same address, web site as **10.062**. Phone: (202)720-3534.

10.905 PLANT MATERIALS FOR CONSERVATION

Assistance: specialized services.

Purposes: pursuant to the Soil Conservation and Domestic Allotment Act of 1936 as amended, to assemble, evaluate, select, release, and introduce into commerce the use of new and improved plant materials such as grasses, legumes, forbs, shrubs, and trees for soil, water, and related resource conservation and environmental improvement programs—including erosion control, roadside and stream bank protection, surface-mined land reclamation, and wildlife food and cover. Plant materials are produced only for field testing and to provide commercial producers with breeder and foundation quality seed or propagules. Free plants or seed are not provided to the general public under this program.

Eligible applicants/beneficiaries: cooperating state and federal agencies and cooperators of conservation districts; commercial seed growers and nurseries interested in the production of selected plant materials, including in PR and VI.

Activity: to date, over 450 releases for commercial increase.

HQ: Deputy Chief/Science and Technology, same address, web site as **10.062**. Phone: (202)720-4630.

10.906 WATERSHED SURVEYS AND PLANNING ("Small Watershed Program" - "PL-566")

Assistance: specialized services; advisory services/counseling.

Purposes: pursuant to the Watershed Protection and Flood Prevention Act as amended and other acts, to assist in the planning and development of coordinated water and related land resource programs in watersheds and river basins to help solve such problems as those involving upstream rural community flooding, agricultural nonpoint source pollution, wetlands preservation, and drought management—through such disciplines as engineering, economics, social sciences, landscape architecture, agronomy, range management, forestry, biology, waste management, hydrology, archaeology. The program emphasizes assisting communities wishing to adopt floodplain management regulations meeting National Flood Insurance Program requirements, and to assist states in developing a strategic water resource plan.

Eligible applicants/beneficiaries: any local or state water resource agency or federal agency concerned with water and related land resource development. Available also in territories.

Activity: since 1954 program inception, 1,660 watershed plans, 550 flood insurance studies, 602 flood plain management studies, 461 river basin studies, 171 resource plans completed.

HQ: same as **10.904**.

10.907 SNOW SURVEY AND WATER SUPPLY FORECASTING

Assistance: technical information.

Purposes: pursuant to the Soil Conservation and Domestic Allotment Act of 1936 as amended, to provide information on forthcoming seasonal water supplies from streams that derive most of their runoff from snowmelt in the mountain states and the far west—assisting farm operators, rural communities, municipalities, and others in planning for and managing water resources. Data are used in the regulation of small and large reservoirs for irrigation, flood control, power generation, recreation, industry, and municipal supplies.

Eligible applicants/beneficiaries: general public, including in the territories.

Activity: daily snow and precipitation data gathered from 670 automated snow telemetry sites and 1,100 manual snow courses in the U.S. and Alaska; 11,000 forecasts of seasonal volume streamflows at 575 streamgaging points provided to water users.

HQ: same as **10.905**.

10.910 RURAL ABANDONED MINE PROGRAM ("RAMP")

Assistance: direct payments/specified use (25-100 percent/5-10 years).

Purposes: pursuant to the Surface Mining Control and Reclamation Act of 1977, Abandoned Mine Reclamation Act of 1990, and Energy Policy Act of 1992, for conservation practices needed for the reclamation, conservation, and development of abandoned rural coal mine land or lands and waters affected by coal mining activities. Up to 320 acres per owner may be assisted.

Eligible applicants/beneficiaries: individuals, groups, or units of government that own or control the surface or water rights of abandoned coal land or lands and water affected by coal mining practices before August 3, 1977. (These areas are ineligible if: (1) reclamation responsibility on the part of the mine operator or the state is continuing; (2) the lands are in federal ownership; and (3) surface rights are under easement or lease to be remined.)

Range/Average: N.A.

Activity: as of FY 01, 20 active projects.

HQ: same as **10.900**.

10.912 ENVIRONMENTAL QUALITY INCENTIVES PROGRAM ("EQIP")

Assistance: direct payments/specified use (to 75 percent/5-10 years).

Purposes: pursuant to FSRIA, FAIRA, and Food Security Act of 1985, to assist farmers and ranchers in complying with environmental laws and to encourage environmental enhancement by providing technical, educational, and financial assistance to implement structural, vegetative, and land management practices that address soil, water, and related natural resource concerns. Program is funded through the CCC. Fifty percent of available funding must be targeted at practices relating to livestock production.

Eligible applicants/beneficiaries: agricultural producers including owners, landlords, operators, or tenants of eligible lands—with special encouragement to apply to limited resource producers, small-scale producers, and minority groups, tribal governments, Alaska natives, and Pacific Islanders.

Range: to $10,000 per person per year; to $50,000 for life of contract. **Average:** $15,000.

Activity: since FY 98 program inception, 655 priority areas approved, 20,000 long-term contracts.

HQ: same address, web site as **10.900**. Phone: (202)720-1845, FAX (202)720-4265.

10.913 FARM AND RANCH LANDS PROTECTION PROGRAM

Assistance: direct payments/specified use (50 percent).

Purposes: pursuant to Food Security Act of 1985, to purchase conservation easements or other interests in lands to limit nonagricultural uses of farm land with prime, unique, or other productive soils—with a minimum 30-year duration.

Eligible applicants/beneficiaries: local or state agencies, counties, municipalities, towns, local government units, tribes, soil and water conservation districts—with a farmland protection program. Available also in territories.

Range: $2,700 to $1,000,000. **Average:** $97,000.

Activity: FY 02, 89 cooperative agreements to protect over 71,000 acres.

HQ: Farmland Protection and Community Planning Staff, NRCS-USDA, P.O. Box 2890, Washington, DC 20013. Phone: (202)720-9476, FAX (202)720-0745. **Internet:** same as **10.062**.

10.914 WILDLIFE HABITAT INCENTIVE PROGRAM ("WHIP")

Assistance: direct payments/specified use (to 75 percent/5-10 years minimum).

Purposes: pursuant to FAIRA, to develop habitats for upland and wetland wildlife, threatened and endangered species, and fish. Technical assistance is provided to prepare a Wildlife Habitat Development Plan.

Eligible applicants/beneficiaries: owners, landlords, operators, tenants of eligible lands. Limited resource producers, small-scale producers, and minority groups, tribal governments, Alaska natives, and Pacific Islanders are encouraged to apply.

Range/Average: $4,500.

Activity: since FY 98, 1,400,000 acres enrolled, with average agreement covering 165 acres.

HQ: Director, Watersheds and Wetlands Division, NRCS-USDA, P.O. Box 2890, Washington, DC 20013. Phone: (202)720-3534, (202)720-7157, FAX (202)720-2143. **Internet:** same as **10.062**.

10.916 WATERSHED REHABILITATION PROGRAM ("PL-566 Watershed Program")

Assistance: project grants (65-100 percent); advisory services/counseling.

Purposes: pursuant to the Watershed Protection and Flood Prevention Act and other acts, to plan, design, and implement watershed rehabilitation and improvement projects involving dams originally constructed with USDA assistance. Projects may include reconstruction or decommissioning of dams and relocation or flood proofing or downstream property.

Eligible applicants/beneficiaries: state agencies, counties or groups of counties, towns or townships, soil and water conservation districts, flood prevention or flood control districts, tribes or tribal organizations, other state-authorized nonprofit organizations.

Range: to $6,451,000 per state. **Average:** $770,000.

Activity: new program listing in 2003; FY 03, 3 projects completed, 6 under construction, 14 in design.

HQ: same as **10.904**.

10.917 AGRICULTURAL MANAGEMENT ASSISTANCE

Assistance: direct payments/specified use (75 percent/3-10 years).

Purposes: pursuant to the Agricultural Risk Protection Act of 2000, for producers on private lands to: construct or improve water management or irrigation structures; plant trees for windbreaks or to improve water quality; mitigate financial risk through production or marketing diversification or resource conservation practices including soil erosion control, integrated pest management, or transition to organic farming.

Eligible applicants/beneficiaries: applicants with control of the land during the contract period—i.e., 3-10 years—only in Connecticut, Delaware, Maine, Maryland, Massachusetts, Nevada, New Hampshire, New Jersey, New York, Pennsylvania, Rhode Island, Utah, Vermont, West Virginia, and Wyoming.

Range: to $50,000 per year; to $150,000 per contract period.

Activity: new program listing in 2004. As of FY 03, 1,176 active contracts covering 287,000 acres in all 15 states.

HQ: Conservation Operations Division, NRCS-USDA, P.O. Box 2890, Washington, DC 20013. Phone: (202)720-1873, FAX (202)720-4265. **Internet:** same as **10.062**.

10.918 GROUND AND SURFACE WATER CONSERVATION—ENVIRONMENTAL QUALITY INCENTIVES PROGRAM ("EQIP-G&SW")

Assistance: direct payments/specified use (75-90 percent/to 10 years).

Purposes: pursuant to the Food Security Act of 1985, FAIRA, and FSRIA, to help farmers and ranchers achieve net savings of water usage on their agricultural lands in an environmentally beneficial and cost-effective manner, through: technical assistance in conservation planning; incentive payments to install structural and land management practices that comply with federal, state, and tribal environmental laws. Limited-resource producers and beginning farmers may receive up to 90 percent of project costs. Funding is through the CCC.

Eligible applicants/beneficiaries: same as for **10.914**. (Program may not be available in all states.)

Range: to $450,000 per entity for 10-year contract period.

Activity: new program listing in 2004. FY 02, 20,000 applications funded.

HQ: same as **10.912**.

10.919 KLAMATH BASIN—ENVIRONMENTAL QUALITY INCENTIVES PROGRAM ("EQIP-KB")

Assistance: direct payments/specified use (75-90 percent/to 10 years).

Purposes: same as for **10.918**.

Eligible applicants/beneficiaries: same as for **10.914** only in the Klamath Basin area of California and Oregon.

Range: same as for **10.918**.

Activity: new program listing in 2004. Activity included in report for **10.918**.

HQ: same as **10.912**.

10.920 GRASSLAND RESERVE PROGRAM ("GRP")

Assistance: project grants.

Purposes: to restore and protect eligible grasslands and certain other lands through rental agreements and easements that: permit controlled grazing; permit controlled haying, mowing, or harvesting for seed production; allow for fire rehabilitation and construction of firebreaks, fencing, water facilities; prohibit production of row crops, fruit trees, vineyards, and the like.

Eligible applicants/beneficiaries: easements—owners of eligible lands; rental agreements—entities with sufficient control of land.

Range/Average: easements, $382 per acre; rental agreements, $134 per acre.

Activity: new program listing in 2004. FY 03, 240,000 acres enrolled.

HQ: same address, web site as **10.900**. Phone: (202)720-4527; NRCS program manager, (202)720-0242; FSA program manager, (202)720-9652.

10.921 CONSERVATION SECURITY PROGRAM ("CSP")

Assistance: direct payments/specified use (5-10 years).

Purposes: pursuant to the Food Security Act of 1985 and FSRIA, for the conservation and improvement through approved appropriate stewardship of soil, water, air, energy, and plant and animal life on tribal and working lands—including cropland, grassland, prairie land, improved pasture, and rangeland, as well as forested land incidental to an agricultural operation. Funding is provided through the CCC.

Eligible applicants/beneficiaries: individual producers, partnerships, associations, corporations, estates, trusts, and other business entities enrolling eligible lands.

Range/Average: N.A.

Activity: new program listing in 2004. FY 04 estimate, 3,000 to 5,000 contracts.

HQ: Financial Assistance Programs Division, same address, web site as **10.062**. Phone: (202)690-0848.

10.950 AGRICULTURAL STATISTICS REPORTS ("Agricultural Estimates")

Assistance: technical information.

Purposes: to collect and publish statistics related to agriculture, resources, and rural communities. Reports cover crops, agricultural chemical usage, livestock and poultry estimates, prices received by farmers, prices for commodities and services, data on farm employment and wage rates.

Eligible applicants/beneficiaries: farmers and agricultural producers, marketing and processing groups, transportation and handler groups, consumers, state governments, educational institutions, and the general public, including in the territories.

Activity: annually, estimates on some 120 crops and 45 livestock items, published in 400 reports.

HQ: Administrator, National Agricultural Statistics Service-USDA, Washington, DC 20250. Phone: (202)720-2707. **Internet:** "www.usda.gov/nass". (Note: no field offices for this program.)

10.960 TECHNICAL AGRICULTURAL ASSISTANCE

Assistance: project grants (100 percent/1-2 years).

Purposes: pursuant to NARETPA and Food Security Act of 1985 as amended, for technical research and assistance projects dealing with international agricultural problems in developing countries. Program is conducted in cooperation with the State Department's Agency for International Development.

Eligible applicants/beneficiaries: U.S. IHEs, public and private nonprofit scientific research organizations—including in territories.

Range: $30,000 to $600,000. **Average:** $160,000.

Activity: not quantified specifically.

HQ: Development Resources Division, Office of International Cooperation and Development, FAS-USDA, Washington, DC 20250-1089. Phone: (202) 690-1924. **Internet:** same as **10.606**. (Note: no field offices for this program.)

10.961 SCIENTIFIC COOPERATION AND RESEARCH
("International Collaborative Research and Scientific Exchanges" - "Scientific Cooperation Program")

Assistance: project grants (cost sharing); direct payments/specified use.

Purposes: pursuant to NARETPA and Food Security Act of 1985 as amended, for research on international agriculture and the environment in collaboration with foreign scientists—through short- (2-4 weeks) and long-term (1-3 years) exchanges.

Eligible applicants/beneficiaries: same as for **10.960**—and federal or state agencies; designated international agricultural research centers.

Range: long-term, to $45,000.

Activity: projects ongoing in 53 countries.

HQ: Director, Research and Scientific Exchanges Division, Office of International Cooperation and Development, FAS-USDA, Washington, DC 20250-1084. Phone: (202)690-4872. **Internet:** "www.fas.usda.gov/icd/grants/scrp.htm". (Note: no field offices for this program.)

10.962 INTERNATIONAL TRAINING—FOREIGN PARTICIPANT

Assistance: project grants (100 percent).

Purposes: pursuant to NARETPA and Food Security Act of 1985 as amended, for international research training and extension in food, agricultural, and related subjects, including in the areas of course development and evaluation. Funding currently supports projects involving short-term agricultural and trade-related training and orientation for senior and mid-level officials, including marketing and production of forestry and wood products, soybean utilization, rice processing, food safety, and dairy production and livestock management.

Eligible applicants/beneficiaries: U.S. IHEs or nonprofit organizations.

Range: $10,000 to $40,000. **Average:** $19,000.

Activity: not quantified specifically.

HQ: Food Industries Division, Office of International Cooperation and Development, FAS-USDA, Washington, DC 20250-1086. Phone: (202)690-1339. **Internet:** same as **10.606**. (Note: no field offices for this program.)

10.994 PEANUT QUOTA BUYOUT PROGRAM ("PQB")

Assistance: direct payment/unrestricted use (5 years).

Purposes: pursuant to FSRIA, to terminate the marketing quota program for peanuts and offer compensation to peanut quota holders for losses in quota asset value.

Eligible applicants/beneficiaries: peanut producers that owned a farm and were eligible for a permanent peanut quota for the 2002-2006 crop years.

Range/Average: $0.11 per pound or $220 per ton, based on producer's eligible quota.

Activity: new program listing in 2005.

HQ: Production Emergency and Compliance Division, FSA-USDA, 1400 Independence Ave. SW. Washington, DC 202500512. Phone: (no number provided). **Internet:** "www.fsa.usda.gov".

10.995 HARD WHITE WHEAT INCENTIVE PROGRAM ("HWW")

Assistance: direct payment/unrestricted use.

Purposes: pursuant to the Agricultural Assistance Act of 2002, to increase the production of both spring and winter varieties of hard white wheat during the 2003 through 2005 crop years.

Eligible applicants/beneficiaries: hard white wheat producers with an interested buyer that will use the wheat for all purposes except for feed.

Range/Average: $0.20 per bushel; planting incentive, $2.00 per acre—within stipulated program maximum.

Activity: new program listing in 2005.

HQ: same address, web site as **10.994**. Phone: (202)720-7641.

DEPARTMENT OF COMMERCE

BUREAU OF THE CENSUS

11.001 CENSUS BUREAU DATA PRODUCTS

Assistance: technical information.

Purposes: pursuant to the Act of August 31, 1954, to provide statistical results of censuses, surveys, and other programs. Data cover population, housing, American Community Survey, retail and wholesale trade, service and construction industries, transportation, communications, utilities, manufacturing, mineral industries, governments, foreign trade statistics, and financial, insurance, real estate industries. Certain estimates, projections, and boundary and code maps covering various types of geographic areas also are available. Reports include statistical compendia, directories, indexes, catalogues, and guides—distributed both in print form and on computer disks and tapes, CD-ROMs, DVDs, online, and other media.

Eligible applicants/beneficiaries: anyone may purchase Census products.

Activity: publications.

HQ: Customer Services Center, Marketing Services Office, Bureau of the Census-USDC, Washington, DC 20233. Phone: (301)763-4636. **Internet:** "www.census.gov".

11.002 CENSUS CUSTOMER SERVICES

Assistance: advisory services/counseling; technical information; training.

Purposes: pursuant to the Act of August 31, 1954, to assist census data users in the access to and use of census data—through newsletters, on-line catalogues, conferences, training courses, and related activities including development of informational and data products to meet specific user needs. Staff are available to participate in conferences and workshops on the censuses and other Census Bureau programs.

Eligible applicants/beneficiaries: materials and consultation at the Census Bureau—anyone. User training—officials of federal, state, and local governments, universities, community organizations, the private sector; nominal fees may be charged.

Activity: not quantified specifically.

HQ: same as **11.001**. *Training opportunities,* phone: (301)457-4081.

11.003 CENSUS GEOGRAPHY
("Census Mapping and Statistical Areas")

Assistance: specialized services; technical information.

Purposes: pursuant to the Act of August 31, 1954, to prepare computer-generated maps for use in conducting censuses and surveys, and to show their results geographically; to determine names and current boundaries of selected statistical areas; to develop geographic code systems; to provide maps and area reports for states and local areas throughout the U.S. including territories and possessions; to develop computer files of area measurements, geographic boundaries, and map features with address ranges. The "TIGER" (Topologically Integrated Geographic Encoding and Referencing) system, an automated cartographic data base developed in cooperation with the U.S. Geological Survey, covers the entire U.S. and its possessions; the system generates maps and other geographic products; geographic base files, called TIGER/Line files, are available on computer tape, CD-ROM, and online. Published maps are sold by GPO; unpublished maps are sold directly by the Census Bureau.

Eligible applicants/beneficiaries: anyone.

Activity: publications.

HQ: Geography Division, Bureau of the Census-USDC, Washington, DC 20233-7400. Phone: (301)457-1128. Customer Services, same as **11.001**. **Internet:** same as **11.001**; *and,* e-mail, "geography@geo.census.gov".

11.004 CENSUS INTERGOVERNMENTAL SERVICES ("Intergovernmental Services Program")

Assistance: advisory services/counseling; technical information; training.

Purposes: pursuant to the Act of August 31, 1954, to provide technical assistance and information on methods of making population estimates and projections. Consultation services are available to local officials to plan and conduct special surveys. Special surveys are taken on a cost reimbursement basis. Assistance is provided to states in establishing and operating State Data Centers and Business and Industry Data Centers (BIDC).

Eligible applicants/beneficiaries: federal, state, local government officials; community organizations.

Activity: currently, all states, DC, and PR participating in Federal-State Cooperative Program for the preparation of county population estimates; all states participating in the State Data Center Program, along with DC, Guam, Northern Marianas, PR, and VI; 1,800 state and local governmental agencies, universities, and other organizations participating in the BIDC Program.

HQ: Bureau of the Census-USDC, Washington, DC 20233. Phone: *special censuses,* Office of Special Censuses, (301)457-1429; *population estimates and projections,* Population Division, (301)457-2422; *State Data Center and BIDC Programs,* Customer Liaison Office Staff, (301)457-1305. **Internet:** same as **11.001**.

11.005 CENSUS SPECIAL TABULATIONS AND SERVICES

Assistance: technical information; specialized services.

Purposes: pursuant to the Act of August 31, 1954, to provide customized census tabulations in a variety of output forms to meet user needs and to conduct statistical surveys, on a reimbursable basis.

Eligible applicants/beneficiaries: federal, state, local government officials; community and private organizations; individuals.

Activity: not quantified specifically.

HQ: Director, Bureau of the Census-USDC, Washington, DC 20233. Phone: *demographic and household special surveys*, Chief, Demographic Surveys Division, (301)763-3773; Office of Special Censuses, (301)763-1429; *special economic surveys*, Chief, Economic Planning and Coordination Division, (301)763-2558; *special tabulations (demographic)*, Population Division, (301)457-2447; *special tabulations (housing)*, Housing and Household Economic Statistics Division, (301)763-3204. **Internet:** same as **11.001**.

11.006 PERSONAL CENSUS SEARCH ("Age Search")

Assistance: specialized services.

Purposes: pursuant to the Act of August 31, 1954, to provide data for proof of age, family relationship, or citizenship, for such purposes as qualifying for: government program benefits (e.g., Medicare, Social Security, pensions); certain types of employment; inheritances, annuities, and other rights or benefits. A $40 fee is charged for searches.

Eligible applicants/beneficiaries: personal information from census records is confidential and may be furnished only upon written request by the person to whom it relates, or, for a proper purpose, to a legal representative of an estate. Information regarding a child not of legal age may be obtained upon written request by either parent. For records of a deceased person, application must be signed by either: (1) a blood relative in the immediate family; (2) the surviving spouse; (3) a beneficiary; or, (4) the administrator or executor of the estate. Appropriate certifications are required.

Activity: FY 02, 5,000 requests processed.

HQ: Technical Services Supervisor, Personal Census Search Unit, Bureau of the Census-USDC, P.O. Box 1545, Jeffersonville, IN 47131. Phone (812) 218-3046. **Internet:** "www.census.gov/genealogy". (Note: the field office serves as headquarters.)

ECONOMICS AND STATISTICS ADMINISTRATION

11.025 MEASURES AND ANALYSES OF THE U.S. ECONOMY

Assistance: technical information.

Purposes: to produce measures and analyses of national economic accounts statistics, as well as a series of related economic data analyses, used to formulate and execute fiscal, financial, international, and other policies. The principal analyses include: gross domestic product; corporate profits; personal income by state and region; U.S. balance of payments; international trade; gross domestic product by industry. Regular and special reports are produced, including the monthly "Survey of Current Business," available by subscription through GPO. On-line services and CD-ROMs are available.

Eligible applicants/beneficiaries: general public.

Activity: publications.

HQ: Public Information Office, Bureau of Economic Analysis (BE-53), Economics and Statistics Administration-USDC, 1441 L St. NW, Washington, DC 20230. Phone: (202)606-9900; TDD (202)606-5335; *Order Desk,* (800) 704-0415, (202)606-9666. **Internet:** "www.bea.doc.gov"; e-mail, "webmaster@bea.gov". (Note: no field offices for this program.)

11.026 NATIONAL TRADE DATA BANK ("NTDB")

Assistance: technical information.

Purposes: pursuant to the Omnibus Trade and Competitiveness Act of 1988, to provide a comprehensive source of international trade and export data through the "GLOBUS" (Global Business Opportunities) program, offering daily trade leads from the "TOPS" (Trade Opportunities Program) program, as well as USDA, the Defense Logistics Agency, United Nations, and Commerce Business Daily leads. Access also is provided to Country Commercial Guides, Market Research reports, Best Market reports, and other programs. The NTDB contains over 100,000 documents as part of STAT-USA/Internet that are updated daily and available on-line by subscription, and at federal depository libraries (see **40.001**). Funding for this program is derived from revolving fund proceeds from product sales.

Eligible applicants/beneficiaries: subscriptions available to the general public.

Activity: currently, over 120 program titles including market research, country profiles, export and import statistics, and export "how-to" guides.

HQ: Director, STAT-USA, ESA-USDC, HCHB - Rm.4885, Washington, DC 20230. Phone: (202)482-3429; *subscriptions,* 202)482-1986, FAX (202) 482-2164. **Internet:** "www.stat-usa.gov/ntdb"; e-mail (*subscriptions,*) "statmail@esa.doc.gov". (Note: no field offices for this program.)

11.027 STATE OF THE NATION ("SOTN")

Assistance: technical information.

Purposes: pursuant to the Omnibus Trade and Competitiveness Act of 1988, to maintain an on-line computer service providing access to over 8,000 files containing trade leads, official economic and financial press releases, and statistical data prepared by numerous federal agencies. Files are continually updated. Annual subscriptions are available from ESA. Funding for this program is derived from revolving fund proceeds from product sales. (NOTE: as of the 2002 CFDA, this program replaces the former Economic Bulletin Board ["EBB"].)

Eligible applicants/beneficiaries: general public.

Activity: not quantified specifically.

HQ: same address/phones/e-mail as **11.026**. **Internet:** "www.stat-usa.gov/sotn". (Note: no field offices for this program.)

… PROGRAM INFORMATION   113

INTERNATIONAL TRADE ADMINISTRATION

11.106 REMEDIES FOR UNFAIR FOREIGN TRADE PRACTICES—ANTIDUMPING AND COUNTERVAILING DUTY INVESTIGATIONS

Assistance: specialized services; investigation of complaints.

Purposes: pursuant to the Tariff Act of 1930 as amended, Trade Agreements Act of 1979, Trade and Tariff Act of 1984, and Uruguay Round Agreements Act, to protect U.S. industries against economic injury from the sale of foreign merchandise at less than fair value and by unfair subsidies provided by foreign governments. Import duties are assessed against such merchandise if "dumping" or countervailing subsidies are found to occur, which may be revoked five years after violations of the act have ceased.

Eligible applicants/beneficiaries: any interested party may file a complaint on behalf of an affected U.S. industry.

Activity: not quantified specifically.

HQ: Office of Policy, Import Administration, ITA-USDC, 14th & Constitution Ave. NW, Washington, DC 20230. Phone: (202)482-4412. **Internet:** "www.ita.doc.gov". (Note: no field offices for this program.)

11.108 COMMERCIAL SERVICE

Assistance: advisory services/counseling.

Purposes: pursuant to the Omnibus Trade and Competitiveness Act of 1988, to expand export markets by providing information and guidance on overseas trade markets and opportunities to U.S. firms, through: nonfinancial assistance in export promotion with displays, trade and industrial exhibits, trade missions, catalog shows, and foreign buyer shows; information on trade statistics, foreign tariffs, customs regulations and procedures; overseas government-to-government advocacy and representation; assistance on sources of export finance available from the U.S. Export-Import Bank, SBA, and USAID—in U.S. Export Assistance Centers.

Eligible applicants/beneficiaries: any U.S. citizen, firm, organization or branch of government.

Activity: not quantified specifically.

HQ: none; all contacts are with USDC Export Assistance Centers listed in Part IV. **Internet:** same as **11.106**.

11.110 MANUFACTURING AND SERVICES

Assistance: advisory services/counseling.

Purposes: to provide a central federal source of industry-specific expertise, negotiation and enforcement of bilateral and multilateral trade agreements, and industry and trade competitiveness analysis. Principal services include regular statistical reports, forecasts of industry/sector outputs and cost trends, information on technological developments, and other foreign market information.

Eligible applicants/beneficiaries: anyone.

Activity: not quantified specifically.

HQ: ITA-USDC, 14th & Constitution Ave. NW, Washington, DC 20230. Phone: *manufacturing,* (202)482-1872; *aerospace, automotive affairs,* (202)482-0554; *energy, environment, materials,* (202)482-5225; *health, consumer goods,* (202)482-1176; *materials, machinery,* (202)482-0575; *technology, electronic commerce,* (202)482-0216; *service industries,* (202)482-3375; *travel, tourism industries,*, (202)482-0140; *finance,* (202)482-3277; *export trading company affairs,* (202)482-5131; *industry and advisory analysis,* (202)482-5145; *advisory committees,* (202)482-2474; *planning, coordination, management,* (202) 482-4921. **Internet:** "www.export.gov".

11.111 FOREIGN-TRADE ZONES IN THE UNITED STATES

Assistance: specialized services.

Purposes: pursuant to the Foreign Trade Zones Act of 1934 as amended, to stimulate domestic production of export goods by encouraging domestic warehousing, manufacturing, and processing activity in foreign trade zones (FTZs). States and local communities establish FTZs that are operated by local public or quasi-public corporations. The FTZs function like public utilities, subject to U.S. Customs and other requirements, providing access to businesses and manufacturers.

Eligible applicants/beneficiaries: public and private corporations in states with enabling legislation.

Activity: annually, 60-80 FTZ orders issued, covering zones, sub-zones, and expansions.

HQ: Executive Secretary, Foreign-Trade Zones Board, ITA-USDC, 1401 Constitution Ave. NW - Rm.FCB-4100W, Washington, DC 20230. Phone: (202)482-2862. **Internet:** "www.ia.ita.doc.gov/ftzpage".

11.112 EXPORT PROMOTION MARKET DEVELOPMENT COOPERATION ("MDCP")

Assistance: project grants (33 percent/to 3 years).

Purposes: pursuant to the Omnibus Trade and Competitiveness Act of 1988, to develop, maintain, and expand foreign markets for nonagricultural goods and services produced in the U.S. "Cooperators" conduct activities abroad to promote certain industries, including outreach campaigns, conferences, consultative services, exhibitions, training, market research. Project funds support direct costs only.

Eligible applicants/beneficiaries: nonprofit industry organizations, trade associations, state departments of trade and their regional associations, and, if approved, private industry firms or groups of firms.

Range: $10,000 to $400,000. **Average:** $298,000.

Activity: not quantified specifically.

HQ: MDCP Manager, Trade Development, Management and Planning Division, Office of Planning, Coordination and Management, ITA-USDC, HCHB - Rm.3215, Washington, DC 20230. Phone: (202)482-2969, FAX (202)482-5828. **Internet:** "www.ita.doc/gov/mdcp". (Note: no field offices for this program.)

11.113 ITA SPECIAL PROJECTS

Assistance: project grants (100 percent).

Purposes: to assist organizations identified by Congress to provide information and conduct research and development activities assisting small- and medium-sized businesses in expanding exports.

Eligible applicants/beneficiaries: organizations or individuals specifically identified by Congress.

Range: $500,000 to $10,000,000.

Activity: not quantified specifically.

HQ: Trade Development, Management and Planning Division, same address as **11.112**. Phone: (202)482-3197, FAX (202)482-4462. **Internet:** (none). (Note: no field offices for this program.)

11.114 SPECIAL AMERICAN BUSINESS INTERNSHIP TRAINING PROGRAM ("SABIT")

Assistance: project grants (100 percent).

Purposes: pursuant to the Foreign Assistance Act of 1961, to train Eurasian business executives and scientists. Mid- to senior-level interns participate in 3- to 6-month internships with public and private sector companies in various fields including agribusiness, defense conversion, environmental technology, financial services, telecommunications, energy.

Eligible applicants/beneficiaries: profit or nonprofit U.S. corporations, associations, organizations, or other public or private entities.

Range: $8,400 to $40,000 per project. **Average:** $18,000.

Activity: since 1997 program inception, 3,500 interns trained in 2,500 host companies.

HQ: SABIT Program, ITA-USDC, 1401 Constitution Ave. NW - Rm.4100W, Washington, DC 20230. Phone: (202)482-0073, FAX (202)482-2443. **Internet:** "www.mac.doc.gov/sabit". (Note: no field offices for this program.)

BUREAU OF INDUSTRY AND SECURITY

11.150 EXPORT LICENSING SERVICE AND INFORMATION ("Export Control" - "Exporter Assistance Program")

Assistance: advisory services/counseling.

Purposes: pursuant to the Export Administration Act of 1979 as amended and extended under the International Emergency Economic Powers Act, to provide information, training, seminars, and other assistance on export licensing requirements, regulations, and policies; to expedite export applications when priority action is warranted.

Eligible applicants/beneficiaries: anyone.

Activity: FY 05 estimate, 3,200 exporters counseled; 42 export licensing seminars.

HQ: Outreach and Educational Services Division, Office of Exporter Services,

Bureau of Industry and Security-USDC, Rm.1099, P.O. Box 273, Washington, DC 20044. Phone: (202)482-4811. **Internet:** "www.bis.doc.gov".

ECONOMIC DEVELOPMENT ADMINISTRATION

11.300 GRANTS FOR PUBLIC WORKS AND ECONOMIC DEVELOPMENT FACILITIES

Assistance: project grants (50-100 percent).

Purposes: pursuant to the Public Works and Economic Development Act of 1965 (PWEDA) as amended, to construct or improve public works and economic development facilities to create or retain permanent jobs in the private sector in areas experiencing substantial economic distress. Projects may involve water and sewer systems, railroad spurs, industrial parks, access roads, other business infrastructure, port facilities, tourism facilities, vocational schools, renovation and recycling of old industrial buildings, business incubator facilities, technology infrastructure, projects enabling telecommunications, redevelopment of brownfields. Projects must be consistent with approved Comprehensive Economic Development Strategies. Grants cover 50 percent of costs; severely depressed areas may receive 80 percent; designated tribes receive 100 percent; projects in redevelopment areas supporting Economic Development Districts may receive 80 percent and a 10 percent bonus for public works projects.

Eligible applicants/beneficiaries: states, cities, counties, other political subdivisions; IHEs; consortia; tribes; private or public nonprofit organizations or associations; territories and possessions.

Range/Average: $1,313,000.

Activity: FY 03, 159 projects approved.

HQ: no address/phone provided; contact regional offices listed in Part IV. **Internet:** "www.commerce.gov/eda/".

11.302 ECONOMIC DEVELOPMENT—SUPPORT FOR PLANNING ORGANIZATIONS

("Section 203 Grants for Planning and Administrative Expenses")

Assistance: project grants (from 50 percent; tribes, to 100 percent).

Purposes: pursuant to PWEDA as amended, for economic development planning and to formulate and establish comprehensive economic development, process, and strategies to reduce unemployment and increase incomes. Funds may be used to pay administrative expenses.

Eligible applicants/beneficiaries: economic development districts, tribes, states, cities, IHEs, public or private nonprofit organizations.

Range: $500 to $175,000. **Average:** $59,000.

Activity: FY 04, 395 grantees funded.

HQ: same as **11.300**. **Internet:** "www.eda.gov".

11.303 ECONOMIC DEVELOPMENT—TECHNICAL ASSISTANCE ("National, University Center and Local Technical Assistance")

Assistance: project grants (from 50 percent).

Purposes: pursuant to PWEDA as amended, to provide technical assistance in developing data and expertise in evaluating and planning specific economic development projects and programs in depressed areas. Technical assistance is provided through: university economic development centers; innovative projects; information dissemination and studies of issues of national significance; feasibility studies and other projects leading to local economic development.

Eligible applicants/beneficiaries: public or private nonprofit organizations, educational institutions; tribal, state, municipal, county, and territorial governments.

Range: $10,000 to $220,000. **Average:** university programs, $96,000; national technical assistance projects, $247,000; local projects, $47,000.

Activity: FY 04, 98 projects funded.

HQ: *university and local projects,* no address/phone provided; contact regional offices listed in Part IV. *National grants,* Office of External Affairs and Communication, EDA-USDC, HCHB - Rm.7822, Washington, DC 20230. Phone: (202)482-5631. **Internet:** same as **11.302**.

11.307 ECONOMIC ADJUSTMENT ASSISTANCE

Assistance: project grants (from 50 percent).

Purposes: pursuant to PWEDA as amended, to design and implement strategies to address problems stemming from serious structural deterioration of local economies, such as result from corporate or industrial restructuring, new requirements in federal laws, reduction in defense expenditures, natural disasters, or depletion of natural resources. Strategy Investments may be used for plan development resulting in a Comprehensive Economic Development Strategy. Implementation Investments may be used for development of organizational capacity, business development and financing including through the capitalization of revolving loan funds, infrastructure improvement, and market or industry research and analysis.

Eligible applicants/beneficiaries: same as for **11.302**.

Range: no specific minimum or maximum.

Activity: FY 04, 128 projects funded.

HQ: same as **11.302**.

11.312 RESEARCH AND EVALUATION PROGRAM

Assistance: project grants (100 percent).

Purposes: pursuant to PWEDA as amended, for studies, training, research, and program evaluations to determine the causes of unemployment and underemployment in various regional areas; to develop related national, state, and local programs.

Eligible applicants/beneficiaries: IHEs, other research institutions.

Range: $12,000 to $209,000. **Average:** $114,000.

Activity: FY 04, 4 projects funded.

HQ: Office of External Affairs and Communication, EDA-USDC, HCHB. - Rm.7822, Washington, DC 20230. Phone: (202)482-3566. **Internet:** same as **11.302**. (Note: no field offices for this program.)

11.313 TRADE ADJUSTMENT ASSISTANCE ("TAA")

Assistance: project grants (50-100 percent).

Purposes: pursuant to the Trade Act of 1974 as amended, for trade adjustment assistance to firms and industries adversely affected by increased imports, in the form of technical assistance for which participants must share the expense. Assistance may consist of such detailed aid as industrial engineering, marketing studies, product diversification, and the like. To receive Trade Act certification, firms must demonstrate that increased imports of articles like or directly competitive with those that they produce contribute significantly to declines in sales or production, and to separation or threat of separation of their workers. Firms must submit an acceptable adjustment proposal to be eligible to apply. Industry associations or other organizations must submit evidence demonstrating import competition, and that the industry includes a substantial number of Trade Act-certified firms or workers.

Eligible applicants: intermediary organizations including Trade Adjustment Assistance Centers or industry groups that can demonstrate injury from imports.

Eligible beneficiaries: private firms with Trade Act certification.

Range: $888,000 to $1,827,000.

Activity: FY 04, 162 firms certified; 177 adjustment proposals accepted.

HQ: Office of Strategic Initiatives, EDA-USDC, HCHB Rm.7812, 14th & Constitution Ave. NW, Washington, DC 20230. Phone: (202)482-2127. **Internet:** same as **11.302**; *and* "www.taacenters.org".

NATIONAL OCEANIC AND ATMOSPHERIC ADMINISTRATION

11.400 GEODETIC SURVEYS AND SERVICES
("Geodesy and Applications of the National Geodetic Reference System")

Assistance: project grants (cost sharing/1-5 years).

Purposes pursuant to the Coast and Geodetic Survey Act, to assist in the development and implementation of Multipurpose Land Information Systems/Geographic Information Systems (MPLIS/GIS) into areas inadequately covered by the national networks. The networks consist of horizontal and vertical geodetic reference monuments at various specified intervals, providing scale, orientation, coordinated positions, and elevations of specific points—for use in surveying, boundary delineation and demarcation, mapping, planning, and development. The system provides the standards of reference which provide the basis for state plane coordinate systems, land and public utility records, and boundary delineations—and from which restricted coastal and other boundaries are marked. This program also provides funding to the University of New Hampshire for research and other programs at the Joint Hydrographic Center (JHC).

Eligible applicants/beneficiaries: state, local, municipal, or regional agencies and universities. JHC funding, University of New Hampshire only.

Range/Average: N.A.

Activity: FY 05, 8 continuation, 2 new projects.

HQ: Grant Program Office, Geodetic Service Division, National Ocean Service, NOAA-USDC, Silver Spring, MD 20910. Phone: (301)713-3228. **Internet:** "www.ngs.noaa.gov/"; JHC, "http://chartmaker.ncd.noaa.gov/". (Note: no field offices for this program.)

11.405 ANADROMOUS FISH CONSERVATION ACT PROGRAM

Assistance: project grants (50-90 percent).

Purposes: pursuant to the 1965 act as amended, for the conservation, development, and enhancement of anadromous fish stocks and fish in the Great Lakes and Lake Champlain that ascend streams to spawn; to control sea lamprey. Permissible uses of funds include: spawning area improvement; fishways installation; construction of fish protection devices and hatcheries; research to improve anadromous fish resources.

Eligible applicants/beneficiaries: interested persons or organizations, in coordination with state fishery agencies.

Range: $2,000 to $400,000. **Average:** $40,000.

Activity: not quantified specifically.

HQ: Director, Office of Sustainable Fisheries, NMFS-NOAA-USDC, 1315 East-West Hwy., Silver Spring, MD 20910. Phone: (301)713-2334, FAX (301)713-0596. **Internet:** "www.nmfs.noaa.gov/sfa/state_federal/state_federal.htm".

11.407 INTERJURISDICTIONAL FISHERIES ACT OF 1986

Assistance: formula grants (75-90 percent).

Purposes: pursuant to the act of 1986 as amended, to manage interjurisdictional fisheries resources. Permissible uses of funds include research, management planning, enforcement, restoration of resources damaged by natural disasters.

Eligible applicants/beneficiaries: state agencies; the Pacific, Atlantic, and Gulf Interstate Marine Fisheries Commissions.

Range: $12,000 to $250,000. **Average:** $63,000.

Activity: FY 03 estimate, 40 projects.

HQ: same as **11.405**.

11.408 FISHERMEN'S CONTINGENCY FUND
("Title IV")

Assistance: direct payments/unrestricted use.

Purposes: pursuant to the Outer Continental Shelf Lands Act Amendments of 1978, to compensate U.S. commercial fishermen for damage to or loss of fishing gear, and 50 percent of resulting financial loss caused by oil- and gas-related activities in Outer Continental Shelf areas.

Eligible applicants/beneficiaries: U.S. commercial fishermen.

Range: $500 to $54,000. **Average:** $6,000.

Activity: FY 05 estimate, 28 claims paid.

HQ: Chief, Financial Services Division, NMFS-NOAA-USDC, 1315 East-West Hwy., Silver Spring, MD 20910. Phone: (301)713-2396, FAX (301) 713-1306. **Internet:** "www.noaa.gov".

11.413 FISHERY PRODUCTS INSPECTION AND CERTIFICATION
("Inspection and Grading of Fishery Products")

Assistance: specialized services.

Purposes: pursuant to the Agricultural Marketing Act of 1946 and Fish and Wildlife Act of 1956 as amended, to provide voluntary inspection, grading, and certification of seafood harvesting and processing operations to ensure adherence to minimum public health requirements, as well as product identity, condition, quality, and quantity. Fees are charged for the service, in support of program costs.

Eligible applicants/beneficiaries: individuals; federal, state, county, or municipal agencies; carriers with a financial interest in the commodity.

Activity: 2004, contract inspections at 325 plants, 175 establishments participating voluntarily.

HQ: Inspection Services Division, NMFS-NOAA-USDC, 1315 East-West Hwy., Silver Spring, MD 20910. Phone: (301)713-2355, (800)422-2750. **Internet:** "www.seafood.nmfs.noaa.gov". (Note: no field offices for this program.)

11.415 FISHERIES FINANCE PROGRAM

Assistance: direct loans (to 80 percent/to 25 years).

Purposes: for certain fisheries costs including: purchase or reconstruction of used vessels; refinancing of existing debt; financing or refinancing of shoreside fishery and aquaculture facilities; financing of Individual Fishing Quota (IFQ) for first-time purchasers and small vessel operators in the Halibut Sablefish industries and to Community Development Quota (CDQ) groups fisheries investments in the Bering Sea Aleutian Islands Pollock fishery; long-term fishery buyback financing to retire fishing permits or fishing vessels in overcapitalized fisheries. Funds may not be used for loans that add to fishing capacity or that over-capitalize the industry.

Eligible applicants/beneficiaries: commercial fishermen, fishery products processors or distributors.

Range: $10,000 to $100,000,000. **Average:** $1,000,000.

Activity: 25 direct, 47 quota share, 1 buyback loans.

HQ: same address/web site as **11.408**. Phone: (301)713-2390, FAX (301)713-1306.

11.417 SEA GRANT SUPPORT

Assistance: project grants (67-100 percent).

Purposes: pursuant to the Sea Grant College Program Improvement Act of 1976 as amended, for marine resources research, education, training, and advisory services. Some institutions may obtain coherent area, institutional, or Sea Grant College support. Project examples: cardiovascular, anti-cancer, and central nervous system drugs from marine organisms; marine fouling and corrosion in seawater; marine finfish and shellfish aquaculture; seafood quality and safety; coastal erosion. Funds may not be used to purchase or construct ships or facilities.

Eligible applicants/beneficiaries: IHEs, junior colleges, technical schools, institutes, laboratories; public or private corporations, partnerships, or other associations or entities; states or political subdivisions or agencies; individuals.

Range: $5,000 to $3,900,000.

Activity: FY 04, 800 projects funded.

HQ: Director, National Sea Grant College Program, NOAA-USDC, 1315 East-West Hwy., Silver Spring, MD 20910. Phone: (301)713-2448. **Internet:** same as **11.408**. (Note: no field offices for this program.)

11.419 COASTAL ZONE MANAGEMENT ADMINISTRATION AWARDS

Assistance: formula grants (cost sharing/18 months).

Purposes: pursuant to the Coastal Zone Management Act of 1972 and amendments, to administer various elements of approved Coastal Zone Management programs, including such activities as management and protection of coastal wetlands, natural hazards management, public access improvements, reduction of marine debris, ocean resource planning, siting of coastal energy facilities.

Eligible applicants/beneficiaries: coastal states including those bordering the Great Lakes; territories and possessions.

Range: $300,000 to $2,000,000. **Average:** $1,300,000.

Activity: 34 coastal states and U.S. island territories participating.

HQ: Chief, Coastal Programs Division, Office of Ocean and Coastal Resource Management, NOS-NOAA-USDC, 1305 East-West Hwy.- 11th floor, Silver Spring, MD 20910. Phone: (301)713-3155. **Internet:** "www.coastalmanagement.nos.noaa.gov/czm/". (Note: no field offices for this program.)

11.420 COASTAL ZONE MANAGEMENT ESTUARINE RESEARCH RESERVES

Assistance: project grants (to 50 percent/from 18 months).

Purposes: pursuant to the Coastal Zone Management Act of 1972 and amendments, to acquire, monitor, develop, and operate national estuarine research reserves; for data gathering, research, and educational purposes.

Eligible applicants/beneficiaries: acquisition, development, construction operating grants—coastal states including those bordering the Great Lakes; territories. Research or monitoring grants—qualified scientists, educators, students, and entities.

Range: $20,000 to $6,000,000. **Average:** $300,000.

Activity: FY 03, 26 designated reserves.

HQ: Chief, Estuarine Reserves Division, Office of Ocean and Coastal Resource Management, same address/phone as **11.419**. **Internet:** "www.nerrs.nos.noaa.gov/". (Note: no field offices for this program.)

11.426 FINANCIAL ASSISTANCE FOR NATIONAL CENTERS FOR COASTAL OCEAN SCIENCE

Assistance: project grants (100 percent/to 5 years).

Purposes: pursuant to the Marine Protection, Research, and Sanctuaries Act of 1972 and National Ocean Pollution Planning Act of 1978, for research to determine the long-term consequences of human activities affecting the coastal and marine environment; to assess the ecological, economic, and social impacts of these activities upon human, physical, and biotic environments; to define and evaluate management alternatives that minimize adverse consequences of human use of marine environments and resources. Project examples: analyses of estuarine and marine contaminants, habitats, and natural resources; data set of characteristics of coasts and oceans including erosion rates, coastal vulnerability indices, and coastal hazards for incorporation into a geographic information system.

Eligible applicants/beneficiaries: IHEs, junior colleges, technical schools, institutes, laboratories, public or private profit or nonprofit entities, state and local government agencies, individuals.

Range: $20,000 to $550,000. **Average:** $250,000.

Activity: not quantified specifically.

HQ: National Centers for Coastal Ocean Science (N/SCI), NOS-NOAA-USDC, 1305 East-West Hwy., Rockville, MD 20910. Phone: (no number provided). **Internet:** "www.nccos.noaa.gov". (Note: no field offices for this program.)

11.427 FISHERIES DEVELOPMENT AND UTILIZATION RESEARCH AND DEVELOPMENT GRANTS AND COOPERATIVE AGREEMENTS PROGRAM

Assistance: project grants (50-90 percent/2 years).

Purposes: pursuant to the Saltonstall-Kennedy Act as amended, for research to develop and strengthen the U.S. fishing industry. Project examples: risk management of a new oyster disease threat; engineering design and analysis for more secure salmon net pen systems.

Eligible applicants/beneficiaries: U.S. citizens or nationals including in the territories and possessions; state and local governments. Federal and Regional Fishery Management Council employees are ineligible.

Range: $3,400 to $180,000. **Average:** $84,000.

Activity: N.A.

HQ: Federal Program Officer, State/Federal Liaison Branch, NMFS-NOAA-USDC, 263 13th Ave. South, St. Petersburg, FL 33701. Phone: (727)824-5324, FAX (727)824-5364. **Internet:** "www.nmfs.noaa.gov/sfweb/skhome.html".

11.428 INTERGOVERNMENTAL CLIMATE—PROGRAM (NESDIS) ("National Environmental Satellite, Data, and Information Service" - "Regional Climate Centers")

Assistance: project grants (100 percent).

Purposes: pursuant to the National Climate Program Act as amended, to establish regional climate centers to supply guidance and data to users in the private and public sectors, and to perform research on regional climate problems.

Eligible applicants/beneficiaries: states or groups of states, public or private educational institutions, state agencies, and other persons or institutions.

Range: $148,000 for each of 6 centers.

Activity: 6 continuation grants awarded.

HQ: Regional and State Climate Program Manager, National Climate Data Center, NOAA-USDC, 151 Patton Ave., Asheville, NC 28801-5001. Phone: (828)271-4358. **Internet:** "www.rdc.noaa.gov"; *regional centers,* "www.ncdc.noaa.gov/regionalclimatecenters.html"; *agency,* "www.ncdc.noaa.gov". (Note: the field office serves as headquarters.)

11.429 MARINE SANCTUARY PROGRAM

Assistance: project grants (100 percent).

Purposes: pursuant to the Marine Protection, Research, and Sanctuaries Act of 1972 and amendments, for research and educational programs in the marine sanctuary system; for enforcement activities at sanctuary sites; for projects enhancing public awareness, appreciation, and wise use of the marine environment. Scholarships are available for masters and doctorate level studies, particularly by women and minorities pursuing degrees in marine biology, maritime archaeology, and oceanography.

Eligible applicants/beneficiaries: project grants—states, local, and tribal governments; regional and interstate agencies, K-12 public and independent schools and school systems; IHEs; commercial and nonprofit organizations; other persons. Agreements to solicit private donation—nonprofit organizations. Scholarships—U.S. citizens, particularly women and minorities with financial needs.

Range: cooperative agreements, $200,000 to $3,940,000; competitive awards, $10,000 to $50,000. **Average:** agreements, $1,695,000; scholarships, $32,000.

Activity: currently, 13 designated sanctuaries, management plan reviews under way at 7 sites.

HQ: Director, National Marine Sanctuary Program, NOS-NOAA-USDC, 1305 East-West Hwy., Silver Spring, MD 20910. Phone: (301)713-3125, ext.

2731; scholarships, (301)713-4204; Monterey Bay program, (831647-4204). **Internet:** "www.sanctuaries.nos.noaa.gov/"; *scholarships,* "www.fosterscholars.noaa.gov".

11.430 UNDERSEA RESEARCH

Assistance: project grants (100 percent).

Purposes: pursuant to the Coast and Geodetic Act, for undersea research and development projects. Funds may be used to acquire necessary technology. Examples: Nutrient Cycling and Primary Productivity of Marine Ecosystems; diving safety and physiology research; submarine venting of liquids and gases.

Eligible applicants/beneficiaries: IHEs, junior colleges, technical schools, institutes, laboratories; states, political subdivisions, agencies; individuals.

Range: $15,000 to $2,225,000.

Activity: FY 03, 13 grants awarded.

HQ: Director, Office of Undersea Research, NOAA-USDC, 1315 East-West Hwy., Silver Spring, MD 20910. Phone: (301)713-2427. **Internet:** same as **11.408**. (Note: no field offices for this program.)

11.431 CLIMATE AND ATMOSPHERIC RESEARCH

Assistance: project grants (95-100 percent/1-5 years).

Purposes: pursuant to the Federal Aviation Act and National Climate Program Act as amended, and Weather Service Organic Act, for research and development, advisory services, and operational systems designed to establish a predictive capability for short- and long-term climate fluctuations and trends. Projects funded to date have ranged from some with a global scope to specific activities in the Indian Ocean and the S.W. Tropical Pacific Ocean.

Eligible applicants/beneficiaries: IHEs and other nonprofits, commercial and international organizations; state, local, tribal governments.

Range: $50,000 to $200,000. **Average:** $85,000.

Activity: FY 04, 62 new grants awarded.

HQ: Director, Office of Global Programs, NOAA-USDC, 1100 Wayne Ave., Silver Spring, MD 20910. Phone: (301)427-2089. **Internet:** "www.ogp.noaa.gov". (Note: no field offices for this program.)

11.432 OFFICE OF OCEANIC AND ATMOSPHERIC RESEARCH (OAR) JOINT AND COOPERATIVE INSTITUTES
("OAR Cooperative Institutes")

Assistance: project grants (cost sharing/5 years).

Purposes: for research and development, education, training, advisory services, and operational systems as they relate to specific programs in the environmental sciences. Projects involve research in oceanography, atmospherics, limnology, and the solar, Arctic, near-space environments.

Eligible applicants/beneficiaries: universities or nonprofit research institutions, usually located near NOAA environmental research laboratories or facilities.

Range: individual proposals, $3,000 to $60,000; group proposals, $60,000 to $150,000. **Average:** individual, $25,000; group, $80,000.

Activity: FY 05 estimate, 13 cooperative agreements.

HQ: Program Manager, OAR (R/OSSX5), NOAA-USDC, 1315 East-West Hwy., Silver Spring, MD 20910. Phone: (301)713-2465, ext. 206. **Internet:** "www.oarhq.noaa.gov/OSS_Jl.html". (Note: no field offices for this program.)

11.433 MARINE FISHERIES INITIATIVE ("MARFIN")

Assistance: project grants (100 percent/to 3 years).

Purposes: pursuant to the Fish and Wildlife Act of 1956, Magnuson Fishery Conservation and Management Act, and Saltonstall-Kennedy Act, for fisheries research and development projects involving harvest methods, economic analyses, processing methods, and fish stock assessment and enhancement in the Gulf of Mexico, South Atlantic, and New England fisheries.

Eligible applicants/beneficiaries: state or local governments, IHEs, profit and nonprofit entities, U.S. citizens.

Range: $21,000 to $374,000. **Average:** $64,000.

Activity: not quantified specifically.

HQ: State/Federal Liaison Office, NMFS-NOAA-USDC, 263 13th Ave. South, St. Petersburg, FL 33701. Phone: (727)824-5324. *Or:* Northeast Regional Office, NMFS-NOAA-USDC, One Blackburn Drive, Gloucester, MA 01930. Phone: (978)281-9267. **Internet:** e-mail, "grants.information@noaa.gov". (Note: the field offices serve as headquarters.)

11.434 COOPERATIVE FISHERY STATISTICS

Assistance: project grants (100 percent/to 5 years).

Purposes: pursuant to the Fish and Wildlife Act of 1956, for cooperative state-federal programs to collect, analyze, and distribute statistics on commercial and recreational fishing in the States' Territorial Sea and the U.S. Exclusive Economic Zone—supporting the Magnuson-Stevens Fishery Conservation and Management Act.

Eligible applicants/beneficiaries: fisheries conservation agencies in the southeast and Gulf states, and PR and VI; Gulf States Marine Fisheries Commission.

Range: $59,000 to $124,000—not including award of $3,305,000 to Gulf States Marine Fisheries Commission. **Average:** $80,000.

Activity: not quantified specifically.

HQ: Fisheries Statistics and Economics Division, Office of Science and Technology (SSMC3), NMFS-NOAA-USDC, 1315 East-West one: (301)713-2328; (301)713-4137. Hwy. - Rm.12441, Silver Spring, MD 20910. Ph **Internet:** "www.st.nmfs.gov/st1/"; "http://caldera.sero.nmfs.gov/grants/programs/csp.htm".

11.435 SOUTHEAST AREA MONITORING AND ASSESSMENT PROGRAM ("SEAMAP")

Assistance: project grants (100 percent/to 5 years).

Purposes: pursuant to the Fish and Wildlife Act of 1956, to collect, manage, and disseminate independent information on marine fisheries, and to participate in inter-jurisdictional fisheries management programs, exclusively in the Gulf of Mexico, South Atlantic, and U.S. Caribbean—supporting the Magnuson-Stevens Fishery Conservation and Management Act.

Eligible applicants/beneficiaries: same as for **11.434**.

Range: $25,000 to $299,000. **Average:** $111,000.

Activity: not quantified specifically.

HQ: State/Federal Liaison Office, NMFS-NOAA/USDC, 263 13th Ave. South, St. Petersburg, FL 33701. Phone: (727)824-5324. **Internet:** "http://caldera.sero.nmfs.gov/grants/programs/seamap.htm". (Note: the field office serves as headquarters.)

11.436 COLUMBIA RIVER FISHERIES DEVELOPMENT PROGRAM

Assistance: project grants (100 percent).

Purposes: pursuant to the Mitchell Act, to develop measures to protect and enhance salmon and steelhead resources in the Columbia River Basin, using the facilities and personnel of state fisheries agencies.

Eligible applicants/beneficiaries: state governments, quasi-public nonprofit organizations.

Range: $57,000 to $4,912,000. **Average:** $1,991,000.

Activity: not quantified specifically.

HQ: Director, Columbia River Fisheries Development Program, Hatcheries and Inland Fisheries Branch, Salmon Recovery Division, NMFS-NOAA-USDC, 1201 NE Lloyd Blvd., Portland, OR 97232-1274. Phone: (503)231-2009, FAX (503)872-2737. *And* Program Manager, Northwest Fisheries Science Center, NMFS-NOAA-USDC, 2725 Montlake Blvd. E, Seattle, WA 98112-2097. Phone: (206)860-3234, FAX (206)860-3467. **Internet:** same as **11.408**. (Note: the field offices serve as headquarters.)

11.437 PACIFIC FISHERIES DATA PROGRAM

Assistance: project grants (100 percent).

Purposes: pursuant to the Magnuson-Stevens Fishery Conservation and Management Act as amended, to enhance state fishery data collection and analysis systems to respond to Pacific coastwide and insular fisheries management needs, including projects providing catch, effort, and economic and biological data on federally managed species.

Eligible applicants/beneficiaries: same as for **11.436**, and Guam, Samoa, and Northern Marianas.

Range: $36,000 to $7,694,000. **Average:** $3,775,000.

Activity: not quantified specifically.

HQ: same address/phone as **11.434**. **Internet:** "www.st.nmfs.gov/st1/".

PROGRAM INFORMATION   127

11.438 PACIFIC COAST SALMON RECOVERY—PACIFIC SALMON TREATY PROGRAM

Assistance: project grants (75-100 percent).

Purposes: pursuant to the Pacific Coast Salmon Treaty Act, to fund state fishery agencies assisting the U.S. in fulfilling its administrative and management responsibilities for salmon recovery.

Eligible applicants/beneficiaries: state governments, treaty tribes.

Range: $58,000 to $17,850,000. **Average:** $8,954,000.

Activity: not quantified specifically.

HQ: program administered by field offices; see Part IV. **Internet:** Alaska office, "www.fakr.noaa.gov".

11.439 MARINE MAMMAL DATA PROGRAM

Assistance: project grants (75-100 percent/to 3 years).

Purposes: pursuant to the Marine Mammal Act of 1972 and Marine Mammal Rescue Assistance Act of 2000, to collect and analyze information on the abundance and distribution of marine mammals and their interactions with fisheries and other marine resources, toward the conservation of such mammals. Funds may be available for related research projects.

Eligible applicants/beneficiaries: state governments, quasi-public nonprofit organizations; U.S. Marine Mammal Stranding Network participants including state and local governments, academia, aquaria, nonprofits, individuals, and organizations.

Range: $50,000 to $2,807,000. **Average:** $531,000.

Activity: FY 05 estimate, 41 awards.

HQ: Office of Protected Resources, NMFS-NOAA-USDC, 1315 East-West Hwy., Silver Spring, MD 20910. Phone: (301)713-2322, ext. 178. **Internet:** "www.nmfs.noaa.gov/prot_res/PR2/".

11.440 ENVIRONMENTAL SCIENCES, APPLICATIONS, DATA, AND EDUCATION

Assistance: project grants (100 percent/1-5 years).

Purposes: for applied research, data assimilation and management, technology development, and education in environmental science. Funds also may support advisory services and long-term partnerships between the federal government and research institutions and IHEs for cooperative science and education.

Eligible applicants/beneficiaries: any state IHE, institute, laboratory; any public or private nonprofit institution or consortium.

Range: projects, to $200,000; cooperative agreements, $250,000 to $5,000,000.

Activity: FY 05 estimate, 15 continuation grants, some additional awards.

HQ: Office of Research and Applications, NESDIS-NOAA-USDC, 5200 Auth Rd. - Rm.701, Camp Springs, MD 20746-4304. Phone: (301)763-8127, FAX (301)763-8108. **Internet:** same as **11.408**; *and,* ORA, "http://orbit-net.

nesdis.noaa.gov/ora/"; grant applications, "www.ofa.noaa.gov/%eago/index. html". (Note: no field offices for this program.)

11.441 REGIONAL FISHERY MANAGEMENT COUNCILS

Assistance: project grants (100 percent/to 5 years).

Purposes: pursuant to the Magnuson-Stevens Fishery Conservation and Management Act as amended, for the eight regional fishery management councils to prepare, monitor, and revise fishery management plans and data collection programs for domestic and foreign fishing within the 200-mile U.S. Exclusive Economic Zone.

Eligible applicants/beneficiaries: Regional Fishery Management Councils (New England, Mid-Atlantic, South Atlantic, Gulf of Mexico, Caribbean, Pacific, North Pacific, and Western Pacific).

Range: $891,000 to $2,035,000. **Average:** $1,638,000.

Activity: 2002, 1 new fishery management plan, 8 amendments.

HQ: same address/phone as **11.427**. **Internet:** "www.nmfs.noaa.gov/sfa/domes_fish/index/index.htm".

11.443 SHORT TERM CLIMATE FLUCTUATIONS

Assistance: project grants (95 percent).

Purposes: for studies relevant to the diagnosis and prediction of short-term climate fluctuations.

Eligible applicants/beneficiaries: public and private educational institutions; qualified institutional personnel.

Range/Average: N.A.

Activity: FY 01, 1 renewal grant.

HQ: Climate Prediction Center, National Centers for Environmental Prediction, National Weather Service, NOAA-USDC, World Weather Bldg., 5200 Auth Rd., Camp Springs, MD 20746. Phone: (301)763-8000, ext. 7512. **Internet:** same as **11.408**. (Note: no field offices for this program.)

11.444 HAWAII SUSTAINABLE FISHERIES DEVELOPMENT (AQUACULTURE PROGRAM)

Assistance: project grants (100 percent).

Purposes: to develop commercially feasible technology for high-value marine finfish in the U.S., to increase availability for aquaculture and stock enhancement in the U.S.—through the Hawaiian Fisheries Development Project.

Eligible applicants/beneficiaries: Oceanic Institute.

Range: $440,000 to $869,000. **Average:** $654,000.

Activity: funding restricted to one applicant.

HQ: Pacific Islands Fisheries Science Center, NMFS-NOAA-USDC, 2570 Dole St., Honolulu, HI 96822. Phone: (808)983-5374, FAX (808)983-2902. **Internet:** "www.pifsc.noaa.gov". (Note: the field office serves as headquarters.)

11.445 HAWAII STOCK MANAGEMENT PROGRAM ("SEMFISH")

Assistance: project grants (100 percent).

Purposes: pursuant to the Magnuson Fishery Conservation and Management Act, to develop and test the technology of a marine stock enhancement program in Hawaii, as a management option to protect and enhance depleted near-shore fishery resources.

Eligible applicants/beneficiaries: private nonprofit institutions.

Range: $439,000 to $475,000. **Average:** $457,000.

Activity: funding to date restricted to one applicant.

HQ: same as **11.444**. (Note: the field office serves as headquarters.)

11.449 INDEPENDENT EDUCATION AND SCIENCE PROJECTS AND PROGRAMS

Assistance: project grants (100 percent).

Purposes: to increase minority high school student enrollment in college and majoring in math, science, and engineering, and to recruit scientists and engineers to serve as volunteer tutors primarily for high school girls and minority students. Funds are used for: student stipends, tutoring, and field trips to government facilities; advisors training.

Eligible applicants/beneficiaries: Colorado Minority Engineering Achievement Association/Mathematics, Engineering, Science Achievement (CMEA/MESA).

Range: grants, $5,000 to $10,000; cooperative agreements, $45,000 to $172,000.

Activity: funding suspended in FY 04 for two years.

HQ: Program Officer, Office of Atmospheric Research, NOAA-USDC, Bldg. 22, 325 Broadway, Boulder, CO 80303. Phone: (303)497-6731. **Internet:** same as **11.408**. (Note: the field office serves as headquarters.)

11.450 AUTOMATED FLOOD WARNING SYSTEMS ("AFWS")

Assistance: project grants (to 100 percent).

Purposes: to improve flood warning capabilities. Program funds are used for initial costs of acquiring equipment, software development, personnel training, developing technical procedures, and implementation personnel.

Eligible applicants/beneficiaries: states, counties, municipalities, educational institutions, nonprofit organizations.

Range: $25,000 to $97,000. **Average:** $73,000.

Activity: not quantified specifically.

HQ: AFWS Program Office, Hydrologic Services Division, National Weather Service (W/OS3), NOAA-USDC, 1325 East-West Hwy., Silver Spring, MD 20910. Phone: (301)713-0006, ext. 154. **Internet:** "http://ofa.noaa.gov/grants/index.html".

11.452 UNALLIED INDUSTRY PROJECTS

Assistance: project grants (to 100 percent).

Purposes: pursuant to the Fish and Wildlife Coordination Act of 1956 and the Saltonstall-Kennedy Act, for biological, economic, sociological, public policy, and other research and administration projects benefiting the U.S. fisheries; to develop innovative approaches and methods to ensure the safety, quality, and integrity of fishery products; to develop, test, and apply new technology in molecular biology for use in the management of commercial and recreational marine fisheries, emphasizing the development of molecular genetics techniques. Project funds may support research and management activities for high-priority marine and estuarine resources, especially for species and habitats currently under or proposed for federal or interjurisdictional management.

Eligible applicants/beneficiaries: state and local governments, IHEs, territorial agencies, tribal governments, private profit and nonprofit research and conservation organizations, individuals.

Range: $50,000 to $150,000. **Average:** $100,000.

Activity: not quantified specifically.

HQ: Management and Administration Division, NMFS-NOAA-USDC, 1315 East-West Hwy., Silver Spring, MD 20910. Phone: (301)713-1364, FAX (301)713-2258. **Internet:** same as **11.408**.

11.454 UNALLIED MANAGEMENT PROJECTS

Assistance: project grants (to 100 percent).

Purposes: pursuant to the Fish and Wildlife Coordination Act of 1956 and the Magnuson Fishery Conservation and Management Act, for fisheries management and conservation activities by providing economic, sociological, public policy, and other information relating to fishery resources and protected species and their environments—in federal, state, and territorial waters. Activities are intended to benefit high-priority marine and estuarine resources, especially for species and habitats currently under or proposed for federal or interjurisdictional management.

Eligible applicants/beneficiaries: same as for **11.452**.

Range: $147,000 to $1,225,000. **Average:** $539,000.

Activity: not quantified specifically.

HQ: same as **11.452**.

11.455 COOPERATIVE SCIENCE AND EDUCATION PROGRAMS

Assistance: project grants (to 100 percent).

Purposes: pursuant to the Fish and Wildlife Coordination Act of 1956 and Fish and Wildlife Act, to support partnerships with NMFS for cooperative science and education on marine issues, especially living marine resources and their habitat, confronting local, regional, and national resources managers; to develop innovative approaches and methods for marine and estuarine science and education—through programs including: Cooperative Marine Education and Research Programs (CMER); Joint Institute for Marine Observation

(JIMO); Cooperative Unit of Fisheries Education and Research (CUFER); Cooperative Institute of Fishery Oceanography (CIFO); Cooperative Education and Research Program (CERP); Cooperative Institute Agreement (CIA); Cooperative Institute for Marine Resources Studies (CIMRS); Cooperative Institute for Marine and Atmospheric Studies (CIMAS); Cooperative Institute for Arctic Research (CIFAR); Joint Institute for the Study of the Atmosphere and Oceans (JISAO).

Eligible applicants/beneficiaries: state, territorial, and private IHEs; private and public research organizations affiliated with IHEs; national and international organizations.

Range: $33,000 to $1,777,000. **Average:** $136,000.

Activity: not quantified specifically.

HQ: contact regional NMFS science and research directors (addresses in Part IV).

11.457 CHESAPEAKE BAY STUDIES

Assistance: project grants (to 100 percent/to 3 years).

Purposes: pursuant to the Fish and Wildlife Act of 1956 and NOAA Authorization Act of 1992, for research and development projects providing information for the living marine resources of Chesapeake Bay; for the Chesapeake Bay Watershed Education and Training Initiative, providing environment-based education to students, teachers, and communities.

Eligible applicants/beneficiaries: IHEs, hospitals, other nonprofits, commercial organizations; state, local, and tribal governments; international organizations; foreign governments and their jurisdictional entities.

Range: $8,000 to $350,000. **Average:** $85,000.

Activity: not quantified specifically.

HQ: Chesapeake Bay Office, NOAA-USDC, 410 Severn Ave. Ste.107A, Annapolis, MD 21403. Phone: (410)267-5660, FAX (410)267-5666. **Internet:** "www.noaa.chesapeakebay.net/". (Note: the field office serves as headquarters.)

11.459 WEATHER AND AIR QUALITY RESEARCH

Assistance: project grants (100 percent).

Purposes: pursuant to the Federal Aviation Act, Weather Service Organic Act, and National Climate Program Act as amended, and Clean Air Act Amendments of 1990, for research and development, science assessments, advisory services, and operational systems to establish a predictive capability for short- and long-term climate and air quality fluctuations and trends.

Eligible applicants/beneficiaries: IHEs, technical schools, institutions, laboratories; states, political subdivisions, agencies; individuals.

Range: (no funding available in recent years).

Activity: 1-3 contracts per year.

HQ: Director, Office of Weather and Air Quality, Office of Oceanic and Atmospheric Research, NOAA-USDC, 1315 East-West Hwy., Silver

Spring, MD 20910. Phone: (301)713-9397, -9121. **Internet:** same as **11.408**. (Note: no field offices for this program.)

11.460 SPECIAL OCEANIC AND ATMOSPHERIC PROJECTS

Assistance: project grants (100 percent).

Purposes: pursuant to the National Weather Service and Related Agencies Authorization Act of 1999 as amended, for research and development, education and training, advisory services, and operational systems relating to oceanic and atmospheric resources.

Eligible applicants/beneficiaries: organizations and individuals specified in NOAA special announcements.

Range/Average: N.A.

Activity: not quantified specifically.

HQ: Director, Planning and Evaluation, OAR-NOAA-USDC, 1315 East-West Hwy., Silver Spring, MD 20910. Phone: (301)713-2465, ext. 119. **Internet:** same as **11.408**.

11.462 HYDROLOGIC RESEARCH

Assistance: project grants (to 100 percent).

Purposes: pursuant to the Weather Service Organic Act, for research and development on issues relating to the forecasting of surface hydrologic conditions. Project examples: automated calibration of hydrologic models; flash flood guidance procedures and models.

Eligible applicants/beneficiaries: IHEs, state and local government agencies, quasi-public institutions such as water supply or power companies, and hydrologic consultants and companies.

Range: $5,000 to $100,000. **Average:** $25,000.

Activity: not quantified specifically.

HQ: Chief, Hydrology Laboratory, National Weather Service (W/OHD-1), NOAA-USDC, 1325 East-West Hwy., Silver Spring, MD 20910. Phone: (301)713-0640. **Internet:** same as **11.408**. (Note: no field offices for this program.)

11.463 HABITAT CONSERVATION

Assistance: project grants (50-100 percent).

Purposes: pursuant to the Fish and Wildlife Coordination Act of 1956 and Coral Reef Conservation Act, for biological, economic, sociological, public policy, and other research, and for administration, public education, and construction activities relating to marine and estuarine habitats, especially for species currently under or proposed for federal or interjurisdictional management.

Eligible applicants/beneficiaries: same as for **11.452**.

Range: $14,000 to $8,057,000. **Average:** $764,000.

Activity: not quantified specifically.

HQ: Office of Habitat Conservation, NMFS-NOAA-USDC, 1315 East-West Hwy., Silver Spring, MD 20910. Phone: Community-based Restoration Program, (301)713-0174, FAX (301)713-0184; General Coral Reef Conservation Grant Program, (301)713-3159, FAX (301)713-1594; International Coral Reef Conservation Grant Program, (301)713-3078. **Internet:** "www. nmfs.noaa.gov/habitat/ecosystem/index.htm".

11.467 METEOROLOGIC AND HYDROLOGIC MODERNIZATION DEVELOPMENT
("Hydrometeorological Development")

Assistance: project grants (to 100 percent); direct payments/specified use; direct payments/unrestricted use; technical information; training.

Purposes: pursuant to the Weather Service Organic Act, to maintain a cooperative university-federal partnership to conduct meteorological training, education, professional development, and research and development on hydrometeorological issues. Funding supports the Cooperative Program for Operational Meteorology, Education and Training (COMET) and outreach.

Eligible applicants/beneficiaries: IHEs and consortia; state or local government agencies including school systems, quasi-public institutions; consultants, companies.

Range: $15,000 to $4,000,000. **Average:** small projects, $8,500; collaborative projects, $35,000.

Activity: FY 02, 37 projects funded.

HQ: Chief, Training Division, National Weather Service (OS6), NOAA-USDC, 1325 East-West Hwy., Silver Spring, MD 20910. Phone: (301)713-0280, FAX (301)713-1598. **Internet:** same as **11.408**. (Note: no field offices for this program.)

11.468 APPLIED METEOROLOGICAL RESEARCH

Assistance: project grants (to 100 percent/1-3 years).

Purposes: for the Collaborative Science, Technology, and Applied Research (CSTAR) program, designed to create a cost-effective transition from basic and applied research to operations and services. Project examples include: operational system for probalistic quantitative precipitation forecasts to improve prediction of warm- and cold-season heavy precipitation events; forecasts of topographically-forced weather systems; improving operational radar algorithms.

Eligible applicants/beneficiaries: U.S. IHEs.

Range: $100,000 to $3,700,000. **Average:** $460,000.

Activity: not quantified specifically.

HQ: CSTAR Program Manager (SSMC2 - W/OST12), National Weather Service, NOAA-USDC, 1325 East-West Hwy. - Rm.15326, Silver Spring, MD 20910. Phone: (301)713-5570, ext. 150. **Internet:** "www.noaa.nws.gov". (Note: no field offices for this program.)

11.469 CONGRESSIONALLY IDENTIFIED AWARDS AND PROJECTS

Assistance: project grants (to 100 percent).

Purposes: to facilitate education, research, and development in the atmospheric and marine sciences; for related construction of facilities.

Eligible applicants/beneficiaries: same as for **11.452** (except territorial agencies).

Range: $140,000 to $28,500,000.

Activity: no future competitive funding identified.

HQ: Chief, Grants Management Division, (OFA62 - SSMC2), NOAA-USDC, 1325 East-West Hwy., Silver Spring, MD 20910. Phone: (301)713-0926. **Internet:** same as **11.408**. (Note: no field offices for this program.)

11.472 UNALLIED SCIENCE PROGRAM

Assistance: project grants (to 100 percent).

Purposes: pursuant to the Fish and Wildlife Coordination Act of 1956 and Fish and Wildlife Act, for biological, socio-economic, and physical science research on the stocks of U.S. fishery and protected resources and their environment, contributing to their optimal management; to develop innovative approaches and methods for marine and estuarine science.

Eligible applicants/beneficiaries: same as for **11.452**.

Range: $25,000 to $2,455,000. **Average:** $546,000.

Activity: not quantified specifically.

HQ: same as **11.452**.

11.473 COASTAL SERVICES CENTER ("CSC")

Assistance: project grants (100 percent/1-3 years).

Purposes: to develop a science-based, multi-dimensional approach allowing for the maintenance or improvement of environmental quality while allowing for economic growth. Funds may be used for such activities as: outreach; coastal fellowships and apprenticeships; training materials development and information dissemination; development of geographic information system and tabular and spatial data bases; to generate, archive, interpret, and validate aircraft, satellite, and other remotely sensed data and derived products; related purposes.

Eligible applicants/beneficiaries: same as **11.457**.

Range: $10,000 to $300,000.

Activity: not quantified specifically.

HQ: Assistant Administrator, Coastal Services Center, NOS-NOAA-USDC, 1305 East-West Hwy., Silver Spring, MD 20910. Phone: (301)713-3074. **Internet:** "www.csc.noaa.gov".

11.474 ATLANTIC COAST FISHERIES COOPERATIVE MANAGEMENT ACT

Assistance: project grants (to 100 percent).

Purposes: pursuant to the act, to develop, implement, and enforce interstate conservation and management plans pertaining to Atlantic Coastal fishery resources, and for activities required by such plans including: collection, management, and analysis of fishery data; law enforcement; habitat conservation; fishery research and management planning.

Eligible applicants/beneficiaries: Atlantic States Marine Fisheries Commission; Atlantic Coast state governments; Potomac River Fisheries Commission; DC.

Range: $14,000 to $1,926,000. **Average:** $150,000.

Activity: not quantified specifically.

HQ: same as **11.405**.

11.477 FISHERIES DISASTER RELIEF

Assistance: project grants (75 percent).

Purposes: pursuant to the Magnuson-Stevens Fishery Conservation and Management Act of 1966, to assess the effects of commercial fishery failures caused by natural or man-made disasters; to restore fisheries or prevent future failures; to assist communities affected by the failures. Funded activities may not expand assisted commercial fishery failures.

Eligible applicants/beneficiaries: state agencies; fishing communities including vessel owners, operators, crew; U.S. fish processors.

Range: $344,000 to $7,000,000. **Average:** $2,781,000.

Activity: not quantified specifically/

HQ: same address/phone as **11.427**. **Internet:** same as **11.408**.

11.478 CENTER FOR SPONSORED COASTAL OCEAN RESEARCH—COASTAL OCEAN PROGRAM ("CSCOR/COP")

Assistance: project grants (100 percent/1-5 years).

Purposes: to provide a predictive capability for managing coastal ecosystems, including in Great Lakes areas. Funds support research and inter-agency initiatives in coastal ecosystem oceanography, cumulative coastal impacts, and forecasting coastal and natural hazards

Eligible applicants/beneficiaries: IHEs; nonprofit institutions; state, local, and tribal governments; federal agencies.

Range: $25,000 to $1,000,000.

Activity: currently, 68 projects funded.

HQ: Financial Services Division (F/CS2), NMFS-NOAA-USDC, 1315 East-West Hwy., Silver Spring, MD 20910. Phone: (301)713-2358, FAX (301) 713-1939. **Internet:** same as **11.408**. (Note: no field offices for this program.)

11.480 NATIONAL OCEAN SERVICE INTERN PROGRAM ("NOS Program")

Assistance: project grants (100 percent/5 years).

Purposes: to establish internship programs providing opportunities for cooperative study, research and development—to increase the number and diversity of skilled engineers, scientists, and managers in the environmental arena, in the techniques and technologies used by the National Ocean Service. Funds may support: recruitment and evaluation of candidates; stipends for a maximum of two years.

Eligible applicants: nonprofit organizations.

Eligible beneficiaries: recent college graduates.

Range: $40,000 to $1,800,000/year to support 1-50 interns.

Activity: FY 03, 12 new internships, 13 extensions supported.

HQ: Office of Coast Survey, National Ocean Service, NOAA-USDC, 1305 East-West Hwy. - 6th floor, Silver Spring, MD 20910. Phone: (301)713-2780, ext. 137. **Internet:** (none). (Note: no field offices for this program.)

11.481 EDUCATIONAL PARTNERSHIP PROGRAM

Assistance: project grants (100 percent/1-5 years).

Purposes: to develop programs to increase research and educational partnerships between NOAA and minority-serving institutions, by establishing: new cooperative science centers in atmospheric, oceanic, environmental sciences, and remote sensing (AOES); an environmental entrepreneurship program supporting restoration projects in environmentally depleted zones and program development in AOES. Funds may support a distinguished professor, research and development programs, and students undertaking NOAA-related sciences course work and/or research.

Eligible applicants/beneficiaries: DOED-approved minority serving institutions with AOES graduate programs; non-minority institutions in partnerships with minority-serving institutions.

Range: $20,000 to $2,500,000 per year.

Activity: 4 centers funded.

HQ: Education Partnership Program (SSMC 3), Office of Oceanic and Atmospheric Research, NOAA-USDC, 1315 East-West Hwy. - Rm.10600, Silver Spring, MD 20910. Phone: (301)713-9437. **Internet:** same as **11.408**. (Note: no field offices for this program.)

NATIONAL TELECOMMUNICATIONS AND INFORMATION ADMINISTRATION

11.550 PUBLIC TELECOMMUNICATIONS FACILITIES PLANNING AND CONSTRUCTION ("PTFP")

Assistance: project grants (75-100 percent/to 2 years).

Purposes: pursuant to the Communications Act of 1934 as amended, to plan, acquire, install, or modernize public telecommunications facilities including conversion to digital broadcasting. Planning grants may cover 100 percent of costs. Construction grant funds, requiring a 25 percent match, may be applied against costs of apparatus needed for production, dissemination, interconnection, and reception of noncommercial educational and cultural radio and television programs. Real estate, operating, or indirect expenses are ineligible.

Eligible applicants/beneficiaries: public or noncommercial educational broadcast stations, entities, or systems; nonprofit foundations, corporations, institutions, or associations organized primarily for educational or cultural purposes; state, local, tribal governmental agencies. Applications for facilities involving ownership, operation, and participation by minorities and women receive special consideration.

Range: $4,900 to $1,854,000. **Average:** $145,000.

Activity: FY 04, 143 grants awarded.

HQ: Director, Public Telecommunications Facilities Program, Office of Telecommunications and Information Applications, NTIA-USDC, 1401 Constitution Ave. NW - Rm.4625, Washington, DC 20230. Phone: (202)482-5802. **Internet:** "http://www.ntia.doc.gov/ptfp". (Note: no field offices for this program.)

11.552 TECHNOLOGY OPPORTUNITIES PROGRAM ("TOP")

Assistance: project grants (50-75 percent/1-3 years).

Purposes: for innovative applications of telecommunications and information technology in the public and nonprofit sectors, fostering improved communication, resource sharing, and economic development. Awards are highly competitive. Project examples: wireless lending initiative benefiting minority entrepreneurs; videoconferencing network providing supportive services to frail elderly residing independently at home.

Eligible applicants/beneficiaries: state, local, and tribal governments; IHEs; nonprofit entities including national and community-based organizations, health care providers, schools, libraries, museums, public safety providers.

Range: $266,000 to $700,000. **Average:** $543,000.

Activity: FY 04, 27 grants awarded.

HQ: Director, Technology Opportunities Program, Office of Telecommunications and Information Applications, NTIA-USDC, 1401 Constitution Ave. NW - Rm.4096, Washington, DC 20230. Phone: (202)482-2048. **Internet:** "www.ntia.doc.gov/top/". (Note: no field offices for this program.)

NATIONAL INSTITUTE OF STANDARDS AND TECHNOLOGY

11.601 CALIBRATION PROGRAM

Assistance: specialized services.

Purposes: pursuant to the National Bureau of Standards Organic Act (NBSOA) as amended, to provide a national consistent system of physical measurements used for assurance of interchangeability and uniformity of manufactured items, for process control, for informational and scientific purposes, and for fairness and objectivity in commerce and regulation. Fees are charged for tests and calibrations.

Eligible applicants/beneficiaries: state and local governments, academic institutions, laboratories, industrial firms, corporations, individuals.

Activity: FY 05 estimate, 12,000 tests conducted.

HQ: Calibration Program, NIST-USDC, 100 Bureau Drive, Gaithersburg, MD 20899-2330. Phone: (301)975-2002, FAX (301)869-3548. **Internet:** "http://ts.nist.gov/ts/htdocs/230/233/calibration"; e-mail, "calibrations@nist.gov". (Note: no field offices for this program.)

11.603 NATIONAL STANDARD REFERENCE DATA SYSTEM ("NSRDS")

Assistance: sale, exchange, or donation of property and goods.

Purposes: pursuant to the Standard Reference Data Act and NBSOA as amended, to provide evaluated scientific and technical data on the chemical, physical, and other properties of substances and systems. Publications, data bases, and online services may be purchased, subject to copyright restrictions.

Eligible applicants/beneficiaries: federal agencies, firms, corporations, universities, industrial laboratories, research establishments, general public.

Activity: annually, some 10 publications and computerized data bases issued.

HQ: Standard Reference Data Group, NIST-USDC, 100 Bureau Drive, Gaithersburg, MD 20899-2320. Phone: (301)975-2208, FAX (301)926-0416. **Internet:** "www.nist.gov/srd".

11.604 STANDARD REFERENCE MATERIALS ("SRM")

Assistance: sale, exchange, or donation of property and goods.

Purposes: pursuant to NBSOA as amended, to develop accurate methods of analysis and to calibrate measurement systems, through the certification and dissemination of reference materials used to: facilitate the exchange of goods; institute quality control; determine material performance characteristics; measure materials at state-of-the-art limits; assure the long-term adequacy and integrity of measurement quality assurance programs. SRMs are used as primary reference measurement standards for such purposes as: clinical laboratories testing; monitoring of air, water, and low-level radioactive pollution; quality control in the production of basic materials such as steel, rubber, cement, and plastics. Materials may be purchased from NIST.

Eligible applicants/beneficiaries: federal agencies, state and local governments, societies, institutions, firms, corporations, individuals.

Activity: FY 05 estimate, sales of 31,000 units.

HQ: SRM Program, NIST-USDC, Bldg. 820 - Rm.113, 100 Bureau Dr., Gaithersburg, MD 20899-2322. Phone: (301)975-6776, FAX (301)948-3730. **Internet:** "www.nist.gov/srm"; e-mail, "srminfo@nist.gov".

11.606 WEIGHTS AND MEASURES SERVICE

Assistance: advisory services/counseling; specialized services; technical information; training.

Purposes: pursuant to NBSOA as amended, to provide education, technical and other assistance, and training to states, users and manufacturers of weights and measures devices, and other devices users—concerning: weights and measures operations development of model laws and regulations; upgrading of state laboratories; administration of device evaluation; promotion of a uniform national weights and measures system; harmonization of national and international legal metrology standards; transition to the metric system.

Eligible applicants/beneficiaries: states, political subdivisions, private industry, general public.

Activity: not quantified specifically.

HQ: Chief, Weights and Measures Division, NIST-USDC, 100 Bureau Drive, Gaithersburg, MD 20899-2600. Phone: (301)975-4004. **Internet:** "http://ts.nist.gov/ts/htdocs/230/235/ownhome.htm". (Note: no field offices for this program.)

11.609 MEASUREMENT AND ENGINEERING RESEARCH AND STANDARDS

Assistance: project grants (100 percent/1-3 years).

Purposes: pursuant to NBSOA as amended, for scientific research and technology transfer for measurement and engineering research and standards, in such areas as fire prevention, building construction, precision measurement, automation manufacturing, materials science, chemistry, physics, biotechnology, electronics, optical technologies, mathematics, communications and information.

Eligible applicants/beneficiaries: IHEs, professional institutes and associations, nonprofit and commercial organizations, state and local governments.

Range: N.A.

Activity: FY 05-06 estimate, 220 grant, cooperative agreement, and amendment awards.

HQ: NIST-USDC, Bldg. 411 - Rm.A120, 100 Bureau Drive, Gaithersburg, MD 20899-3580. Phone: (301)975-6328. **Internet:** "www.nist.gov". (Note: no field offices for this program.)

11.610 NATIONAL CENTER FOR STANDARDS AND CERTIFICATION INFORMATION ("NCSCI")

Assistance: technical information.

Purposes: pursuant to NBSOA as amended and the Trade Agreements Act of 1979, to serve as an information center and referral service—maintaining a reference collection of standards and specifications, regulations, certification rules, directories, reference books, special publications, copyrights, lending restrictions, and similar data; information relating to foreign trade. NCSCI does not analyze, evaluate, translate, or interpret standards. Published directories, indexes, and bibliographies are available from GPO, NTIS, and NCSCI.

Eligible applicants/beneficiaries: state and local governments; private, public, profit and nonprofit organizations; individuals.

Activity: not quantified specifically.

HQ: Global Standards and Information Group, NIST-USDC, 100 Bureau Dr., Gaithersburg, MD 20899-2100. Phone: (301)975-4040, FAX (301)926-

1559; Standards Information Program, (301)975-2573. **Internet:** "http://ts.nist.gov/ncsci"; e-mail, "ncsci@nist.gov". (Note: no field offices for this program.)

11.611 MANUFACTURING EXTENSION PARTNERSHIP

Assistance: project grants (50 percent/to 2 years); technical information.

Purposes: pursuant to the Omnibus Trade and Competitiveness Act of 1988, American Technology Preeminence Act of 1991, and Technology Administration Act of 1998, to establish and maintain extension centers and services for the transfer of appropriate manufacturing technology to smaller U.S. manufacturing firms. Funding may support: demonstrations and technology deployment especially to firms with fewer than 500 employees; statewide planning and pilot testing projects.

Eligible applicants/beneficiaries: extension services—U.S. nonprofit organizations. Planning and pilot services grants—state and local governments, state-affiliated nonprofit organizations, consortia.

Range: extension planning, testing, $25,000 to $100,000; extension centers, $200,000 to $6,500,000.

Activity: not quantified specifically.

HQ: Director, Manufacturing Extension Partnership, NIST-USDC, 100 Bureau Drive, Gaithersburg, MD 20899-4800. Phone: (301)975-5020. **Internet:** "www.mep.nist.gov". (Note: no field offices for this program.)

11.612 ADVANCED TECHNOLOGY PROGRAM ("ATP")

Assistance: project grants (from 40 percent/3-5 years).

Purposes: pursuant to the Omnibus Trade and Competitiveness Act of 1988 and American Technology Preeminence Act of 1991, to foster development and broad dissemination of high-risk technologies offering potential for significant, broad-based, national economic benefits. Project examples: printed wiring board; flat panel display manufacturing; magneto-resistive random access memories; deep ultraviolet lasers; high temperature superconducting material processes.

Eligible applicants/beneficiaries: U.S. businesses, joint research and development ventures, certain foreign-owned businesses. IHEs, governmental entities, and nonprofit independent research organizations may participate in joint ventures that include at least two profit companies.

Range: $434,000 to $31,000,000. **Average:** $2,900,000.

Activity: since 1990 program inception, 768 awards.

HQ: ATP, NIST-USDC, 100 Bureau Drive, Gaithersburg, MD 20899-4701. Phone: (301)975-4447, FAX (301)869-1150; *application kit*, (800)ATP-FUND. **Internet:** "www.atp.nist.gov"; *application kit*, e-mail, "atp@nist.gov". (Note: no field offices for this program.)

11.617 CONGRESSIONALLY-IDENTIFIED PROJECTS

Assistance: project grants.

Purposes: to assist organizations identified by Congress to achieve objectives specified by Congress. Project examples: windstorm mitigation initiative; biocommodity engineering initiative.

Eligible applicants/beneficiaries: organizations specifically identified by Congress.

Range: $500,000 to $20,000,000.

Activity: new program listing in 2003.

HQ: Office of the Director (MS 1001), NIST-USDC, Bldg. 101 - Rm.A1126, 100 Bureau Drive, Gaithersburg, MD 20899. Phone: (301)975-2397, FAX (301)869-8972. **Internet:** "http://www.nist.gov". (Note: no field offices for this program.)

NATIONAL TECHNICAL INFORMATION SERVICE

11.650 NATIONAL TECHNICAL INFORMATION SERVICE ("NTIS")

Assistance: technical information.

Purposes: pursuant to the Research and Technical Services Act, Omnibus Trade and Competitiveness Act of 1988, National Institute of Standards and Technology Authorization Act, National Technical Information Act of 1988, and American Technology Preeminence Act of 1991, to serve as the principal source for the sale of federally-sponsored technical information products, related business information, register of research in progress, machine-processed data files, and computer software. NTIS operates the National Audiovisual Center which distributes videotapes, slide sets, and multimedia kits—covering subjects ranging from foreign languages and history to law enforcement and natural resources. NTIS recently established the Homeland Security Information Center, directing users to information products on homeland security. Fees are charged, supporting a revolving fund.

Eligible applicants/beneficiaries: any U.S. and most foreign organizations; individuals.

Activity: not quantified specifically.

HQ: Director, NTIS-USDC, Sills - Rm.1014, 5285 Port Royal Rd., Springfield, VA 22161. Phone: (703)605-6400; Sales Division, (800)553-6847. **Internet:** "http://www.ntis.gov"; Homeland Security Information Center, "http://www.ntis.gov/hs"; Sales Division, e-mail, "info@ntis.gov". (Note: no field offices for this program.)

OFFICE OF THE SECRETARY

11.702 INTERNSHIP PROGRAM FOR POSTSECONDARY STUDENTS ("Postsecondary Internship Program")

Assistance: project grants (100 percent/3 years).

Purposes: to aid and promote experiential training activities through internships fostering future employment at USDC or the federal government in general—primarily in the Washington, DC area.

Eligible applicants: 2- and 4-year IHEs including graduate and law schools, nonprofit organizations.

Eligible beneficiaries: postsecondary students.

Range: $196,000 to $514,000. **Average:** $289,000.

Activity: FY 04, 78 internships.

HQ: Office of Human Resources Management, OS-USDC, Washington, DC 20230. Phone: (202)482-1445. **Internet:** "www.ohrm.doc.gov/intern-website/htm". (Note: no field offices for this program.)

MINORITY BUSINESS DEVELOPMENT AGENCY

11.800 MINORITY BUSINESS DEVELOPMENT CENTERS ("MBDC")

Assistance: project grants (85 percent/1-3 years).

Purposes: for the operation of electronic MBDCs—i.e., organizations offering electronic and one-on-one business development services and technical assistance in all phases of business development and management by existing or proposed minority firms. No loans are offered to businesses. Client service fees may be charged.

Eligible applicants/beneficiaries: state and local governments, tribes, educational institutions, nonprofit and profit organizations, individuals.

Range: $155,000 to $400,000.

Activity: FY 05 estimate, 26 MBDCs funded.

HQ: Office of Business Development, MBDA-USDC, 14th & Constitution Ave. NW, Washington, DC 20230. Phone: (202)482-1940. **Internet:** "http://www.mbda.gov".

11.801 NATIVE AMERICAN BUSINESS DEVELOPMENT CENTERS ("NABDC")

Assistance: project grants (100 percent/1-3 years).

Purposes: for eight designated Native American Business Development Centers (NABDCs) to provide electronic and one-on-one business development and technical assistance of all types to new or existing American Indian businesses. No loans or grants are awarded to individual businesses under this program; however, businesses may be helped in obtaining financial assistance for their operations.

Eligible applicants/beneficiaries: same as for **11.800**.

Range: $155,000 to $288,000.

Activity: 2004, 687 clients obtained $199,394,000 in financings and contracts.

HQ: same as **11.800**.

11.803 MINORITY BUSINESS OPPORTUNITY COMMITTEE ("MBOC")

Assistance: project grants (from 50 percent/1-3 years).

Purposes: for MBOCs to provide minority businesses and individuals with enhanced access to markets by identifying and facilitating procurement and contract awards, marketing and sales opportunities, financing resources, potential joint venture partners, timely market leads, and other business information.

Eligible applicants/beneficiaries: federal, state, local government or quasi-governmental entities; tribes, IHEs, and nonprofit and profit organizations.

Range: $150,000 to $300,000.

Activity: FY 06 estimate, $600,000,000 in financial transactions generated.

HQ: same as **11.800**.

U.S. PATENT AND TRADEMARK OFFICE

11.900 PATENT AND TRADEMARK TECHNICAL INFORMATION DISSEMINATION

Assistance: technical information.

Purposes: to support the growth of American commerce and technology through the utilization and dissemination of technical information available through patents and trademarks, and for the maintenance of public search centers. The office examines patent and trademark applications, and grants patents and approves trademarks when legal requirements are met. Fees are charged for services.

Eligible applicants/beneficiaries: general public.

Activity: annually (representative), processing of more than 839,000 customer requests for general patent and trademark information.

HQ: General Information Services, U.S. Patent and Trademark Office-USDC, Alexandria, VA 20313-1450. Phone: General Information Services, (703) 308-4357, (800)786-9199. **Internet:** "http://www.uspto.gov".

DEPARTMENT OF DEFENSE

DEFENSE LOGISTICS AGENCY

12.002 PROCUREMENT TECHNICAL ASSISTANCE FOR BUSINESS FIRMS ("PTA Cooperative Agreement Program")

Assistance: project grants (50-75 percent).

Purposes: to establish and operate new or existing procurement technical assistance programs to assist business firms in selling their goods and services to DOD, other federal agencies, and state and local governments.

Eligible applicants/beneficiaries: state and local governments, private nonprofit organizations, tribal organizations, profit or nonprofit Indian economic enterprises.

Range: $30,000 to $300,000. **Average:** $160,000.

Activity: FY 02 estimate, 66 cooperative agreements.

HQ: Office of Small and Disadvantaged Business Utilization (DDAS), Defense Logistics Agency-DOD, 8725 John J. Kingman Rd. - Ste.2533, Ft. Belvoir, VA 22060-6221. Phone: (703)767-1650. **Internet:** "www.d/a.mil/ddas". (Note: no field offices for this program.)

DEPARTMENT OF THE ARMY
OFFICE OF THE CHIEF OF ENGINEERS

12.100 AQUATIC PLANT CONTROL

Assistance: specialized services; technical information.

Purposes: pursuant to the River and Harbor Act of 1958 as amended, to assist in controlling and eradicating obnoxious aquatic plants in rivers, harbors, and allied waters. Localities must provide 50 percent matching funds.

Eligible applicants/beneficiaries: states, political subdivisions, instrumentalities.

Activity: no funding during the last several years.

HQ: Commander, U.S. Army Corps of Engineers - Attn: CECW-ON, DOD, Washington, DC 20314-1000. Phone: (202)272-0247. **Internet:** "http://www.usace.army.mil/business.html".

12.101 BEACH EROSION CONTROL PROJECTS
("Small Beach Erosion Control Projects")

Assistance: specialized services; technical information.

Purposes: pursuant to the River and Harbor Act of 1962 as amended, to design and construct beach and shore erosion control projects not specifically authorized by Congress. The Corps funds the first $100,000 in planning costs, and 50 percent of additional study costs; localities must provide the balance. Cost-sharing is required for construction, with a $2,000,000 maximum federal share.

Eligible applicants/beneficiaries: states, political subdivisions, other authorized local agencies.

Activity: N.A.

HQ: U.S. Army Corps of Engineers - Attn: CECW-PM, DOD, Washington, DC 20314-1000. Phone: (202)761-1975. **Internet:** same as **12.100**.

12.102 EMERGENCY REHABILITATION OF FLOOD CONTROL WORKS OR FEDERALLY AUTHORIZED COASTAL PROTECTION WORKS
("Public Law 84-99, Code 300 Program")

Assistance: specialized services.

Purposes: pursuant to the Flood Control Act of 1941 as amended, to assist in the emergency repair or rehabilitation of flood control works damaged by flood, or federally authorized hurricane flood and shore protection works damaged by extraordinary wind, wave, or water action. Nonfederal sources must provide 20 percent of project costs.

Eligible applicants/beneficiaries: owners of damaged flood protective works, or state and local public entities responsible for their maintenance, repair, and operation.

Activity: 200 individual projects since 1993 Midwest flood.

HQ: Commander, U.S. Army Corps of Engineers - Attn: CECW-OE, DOD, Washington, DC 20314-1000. Phone: (202)272-0251. **Internet:** same as **12.100**.

12.103 EMERGENCY OPERATIONS FLOOD RESPONSE AND POST FLOOD RESPONSE
("Public Law 84-99, Code 200 Program")

Assistance: specialized services.

Purposes: pursuant to the Flood Control Act of 1941 as amended, to provide emergency assistance in all phases of flood fighting, and post-flood response and rescue operations in times of flood or coastal storm.

Eligible applicants/beneficiaries: state or local public agencies.

Activity: annually, 50 to 250 operations.

HQ: same as **12.102**.

12.104 FLOOD PLAIN MANAGEMENT SERVICES
("FPMS")

Assistance: advisory services/counseling; technical information.

Purposes: pursuant to the Flood Control Act of 1960 as amended, to promote recognition of flood hazards in land and water use planning and development, by providing and interpreting historical data maintained by the Corps on floods and flood plains areas subject to flooding and flood losses from streams, lakes, and oceans. Services are available to states and local governments on a reimbursable basis; fees are charged to private parties.

Eligible applicants/beneficiaries: states, political subdivisions, general public.

Activity: N.A.

HQ: U.S. Army Corps of Engineers - Attn: CECW-PF, DOD, Washington, DC 20314-1000. Phone: (202)761-0169. **Internet:** same as **12.100**.

12.105 PROTECTION OF ESSENTIAL HIGHWAYS, HIGHWAY BRIDGE APPROACHES, AND PUBLIC WORKS
("Emergency Bank Protection")

Assistance: specialized services.

Purposes: pursuant to the Flood Control Act of 1946 as amended, to design and construct projects protecting highways, highway bridges, essential public works, churches, hospitals, schools, and other nonprofit public services endangered by flood-caused erosion. Federal costs are limited to $1,000,000 per project; localities are responsible for costs in excess.

Eligible applicants/beneficiaries: same as for **12.101**.

Activity: N.A.

HQ: same as **12.101**.

12.106 FLOOD CONTROL PROJECTS
("Small Flood Control Projects")

Assistance: specialized services.

Purposes: pursuant to the Flood Control Act of 1948 as amended, to design and construct flood control projects not specifically authorized by Congress. The Corps funds the first $100,000 in planning costs, and 50 percent of additional study costs; localities must provide the balance. Cost-sharing is required for construction, with a $7,000,000 maximum federal share.

Eligible applicants/beneficiaries: same as for **12.101**.

Activity: N.A.

HQ: same as **12.101**.

12.107 NAVIGATION PROJECTS
("Small Navigation Projects")

Assistance: specialized services.

Purposes: pursuant to the River and Harbor Act of 1960 as amended, to design and construct small general navigation projects not specifically authorized by Congress. The federal cost limit is $4,000,000 per project; localities must provide a share of study costs, and pay construction costs exceeding the federal maximum.

Eligible applicants/beneficiaries: same as for **12.101**.

Activity: N.A.

HQ: same as **12.101**.

12.108 SNAGGING AND CLEARING FOR FLOOD CONTROL
("Section 208")

Assistance: specialized services.

Purposes: pursuant to the Flood Control Act of 1937 as amended, to design and construct snagging and clearing projects for flood control. The federal cost limit is $500,000 per project; localities must share in construction costs.

Eligible applicants/beneficiaries: same as for **12.101**.

Activity: N.A.

HQ: same as **12.101**.

12.109 PROTECTION, CLEARING AND STRAIGHTENING CHANNELS
("Section 3 Emergency Dredging Projects")

Assistance: specialized services.

Purposes: pursuant to the River and Harbor Act of 1945 as amended, for the emergency protection, clearing, and straightening of navigation channels in rivers, harbors, and other waterways, including for flood control purposes. Localities must provide maintenance.

Eligible applicants/beneficiaries: same as for **12.101**.

Activity: no current projects.

HQ: Commander, U.S. Army Corps of Engineers - Attn: CECW-OD, DOD, Washington, DC 20314-1000. Phone: (202)272-8835. **Internet:** same as **12.100**.

12.110 PLANNING ASSISTANCE TO STATES ("Section 22")

Assistance: specialized services.

Purposes: pursuant to the Water Resources Development Act of 1974 as amended, to assist states in preparing comprehensive plans for the development, utilization, or conservation of water and related land resources of drainage basins. No state may receive more than $500,000 in assistance in any one year; 50 percent cost sharing is required.

Eligible applicants/beneficiaries: states, tribes, territories.

Activity: N.A.

HQ: same as **12.104**.

12.111 EMERGENCY ADVANCE MEASURES FOR FLOOD PREVENTION ("Public Law 84-99, Code 500 Program")

Assistance: specialized services.

Purposes: pursuant to the Flood Control Act of 1941 as amended, to provide assistance when there is an immediate threat of unusual flooding, including such work as removal of waterway obstructions, dam failure prevention, and work necessary to prepare for abnormal snowmelt.

Eligible applicants/beneficiaries: state governors.

Activity: N.A.

HQ: same as **12.102**.

12.112 PAYMENTS TO STATES IN LIEU OF REAL ESTATE TAXES

Assistance: formula grants (100 percent).

Purposes: pursuant to the Flood Control Acts of 1941, 1946, and 1954 as amended, to compensate local taxing units for loss of real estate taxes lost as the result of federal acquisition of land for flood control, navigation, hydroelectric power projects, and allied purposes. Funds are derived from federal receipts from leases covering such lands, 75 percent of which are distributed through this program.

Eligible applicants: state governments.

Eligible beneficiaries: state, county governments.

Range/Average: N.A.

Activity: N.A.

HQ: Headquarters - Attn: CERM-FC, U.S. Army Corps of Engineers, DOD, 20 Massachusetts Ave. NW, Washington, DC 20314-1000. Phone: (202)

272-1931. **Internet:** same as **12.100**. (Note: no field offices for this program.)

12.113 STATE MEMORANDUM OF AGREEMENT PROGRAM FOR THE REIMBURSEMENT OF TECHNICAL SERVICES ("DSMOA")

Assistance: project grants (100 percent/2 years).

Purposes: pursuant to CERCLA as amended and Superfund amendments, to reimburse states for costs incurred to provide technical services in support of the DOD Environmental Restoration Program, in cleaning up DOD hazardous wastes sites.

Eligible applicants: state, territorial governments.

Eligible beneficiaries: state, local, territorial governments; public, private, nonprofit and profit organizations.

Range: $104,000 to $11,400,000.

Activity: FY 02, 4 states and territories entered program; 44 states participating to date.

HQ: Corps of Engineers, CEMP-RI, DOD, 20 Massachusetts Ave. NW, Washington, DC 20314. Phone: (202)504-4950. **Internet:** same as **12.100**. (Note: no field offices for this program.)

12.114 COLLABORATIVE RESEARCH AND DEVELOPMENT ("Construction Productivity Advanced Research Program" - "CPAR")

Assistance: project grants (50 percent).

Purposes: pursuant to the Water Resources Development Act of 1988, to improve construction productivity through research and development and application of advanced technologies involving collaborative projects, field demonstrations, licensing agreements, and other means of commercialization and technology transfer. Corps laboratories must perform a significant portion of projects.

Eligible applicants/beneficiaries: U.S. private firms including corporations, partnerships, and industrial development organizations; public and private foundations; nonprofit organizations; units of state or local government; academic institutions; others.

Range: $200,000 to $900,000. **Average:** $400,000.

Activity: 76 projects to date.

HQ: Headquarters - Attn: CERD-C, U.S. Army Corps of Engineers, DOD, 20 Massachusetts Ave. NW, Washington, DC 20314-1000. Phone: (202)272-1846. **Internet:** same as **12.100**.

12.116 DEPARTMENT OF DEFENSE APPROPRIATION ACT 2003 ("Section 8044")

Assistance: specialized services.

Purposes: pursuant to the Act, to develop a system for prioritization of environmental impacts mitigation and costs to complete estimates for mitigation on Indian lands resulting from DOD activities, including: training and technical assistance to tribes; related administrative support; information gathering; documenting environmental damage.

Eligible applicants/beneficiaries: states, tribes, territories and possessions.

Range: N.A.

Activity: new program listing in FY 03.

HQ: U.S. Army Corps of Engineers - Attn: CEMP-RF, DOD, Washington, DC 20314-1000. Phone: (202)761-5145. **Internet:** none.

DEPARTMENT OF THE NAVY
OFFICE OF NAVAL RESEARCH

12.300 BASIC AND APPLIED SCIENTIFIC RESEARCH

Assistance: project grants (100 percent).

Purposes: for basic and applied research and training in the physical, mathematical, environmental, engineering, and life sciences, leading to the improvement of naval operations; for programs encouraging careers in those disciplines by supporting outstanding graduate, undergraduate, and high school students; to increase the number of graduates from under-represented minority groups; to assist universities in buying major high-cost research equipment; for symposia.

Eligible applicants/beneficiaries: nonprofit private and public IHEs and other research organizations.

Range: $1,000 to $15,000,000. **Average:** $111,000.

Activity: FY 02 estimate, 1,200 new grants.

HQ: Office of Naval Research (ONR 22), Department of the Navy-DOD, 800 N. Quincy St., Arlington, VA 22217-5000. Phone: (703)696-2570. **Internet:** "http://www.onr.navy.mil". (Note: no field offices for this program.)

NATIONAL GUARD BUREAU

12.400 MILITARY CONSTRUCTION, NATIONAL GUARD

Assistance: project grants (75-100 percent).

Purposes: to provide facilities for training and administering Army and Air Force National Guard units. Funds may be used for armories or to provide offices, storage, assembly areas, rifle ranges, and classrooms. For non-armories, funds may provide for maintenance, supply, training, and other logistical and administrative expenses.

Eligible applicants/beneficiaries: states, DC, territories and possessions.

Range: from $300,000.

Activity: FY 02 estimate, 5 armory, 23 non-armory projects.

HQ: Chief of Installations (NGB-ARI), National Guard Bureau, Department of the Army-DOD, ARNG Readiness Center, DOD, 111 S. George Mason

Drive, Arlington, VA 22204-1382. Phone: (703)607-7900. **Internet:** "http://www.ngb.dtic.mil/indexshtm/". (Note: no field offices for this program.)

12.401 NATIONAL GUARD MILITARY OPERATIONS AND MAINTENANCE (O&M) PROJECTS

Assistance: project grants (75-100 percent).

Purposes: for services provided by states for such National Guard activities as real property maintenance and repair, environmental resources management and services, security guard services, electronic security systems, telecommunications services, air traffic control, automated target systems, recruitment, fire protection, and related activities.

Eligible applicants/beneficiaries: states, DC, PR, VI, Guam.

Range: from $100,000.

Activity: not quantified specifically.

HQ: *National Guard Bureaus*—Army National Guard Bureau, Department of the Army-DOD, ARNG Readiness Center, 111 S. George Mason Drive, Arlington, VA 22204-1382. Phone: Real Property O&M Projects, (703)607-7922; Environmental Resources Management, (703)607-7977; Security Guard Activities, (703)607-7158; Electronic Security System, (703)607-7449; Telecommunications, (703)607-7672; Aviation Operations, (703)607-7752; Automated Target Systems, (703)607-7346; Full Time Dining Facility Operations, (703)607-7408; Store Front Recruiting Office Lease, (703)607-7199; Printing and Duplication, (703)681-3758. *And,* Air National Guard Bureau, Department of the Air Force-DOD, 3500 Fletcher Ave., Andrews Air Force Base, MD 20331-5157. Phone: Facilities O&M, (301)836-8723; Environmental, (301)836-8146; Security Guard, (301)836-8542; Fire Protection, (301)836-8170. **Internet:** same as **12.400**. (Note: no field offices for this program.)

12.404 NATIONAL GUARD CIVILIAN YOUTH OPPORTUNITIES ("National Guard ChalleNGe Program")

Assistance: formula grants (60 percent).

Purposes: to use the National Guard to provide military-based training to civilian youth that have graduated from secondary school, including supervised work experience in community service and conservation projects—to improve their life skills and employment potential. Funds may support civilian personnel hired to conduct the program.

Eligible applicants/beneficiaries: states and territories.

Range/Average: N.A.

Activity: 25 states participating; 22,000 graduates to date.

HQ: Youth Programs Division (NGB/NGB-YP), National Guard Bureau, Department of the Army-DOD, 1411 Jefferson Davis Hwy (JP1), Arlington, VA 22202-3221. Phone: (703)607-5975. **Internet:** same as **12.400**. (Note: no field offices for this program.)

DEPARTMENT OF THE ARMY
ARMY RESEARCH AND MATERIAL COMMAND

12.420 MILITARY MEDICAL RESEARCH AND DEVELOPMENT

Assistance: project grants (100 percent/to 5 years).

Purposes: for fundamental basic and applied medical research projects that expand the technology base or understanding of biological-medical processes. Project examples: analysis of investigational drugs in biological fluids; altered response to infection induced by severe injury; conferences and symposia.

Eligible applicants/beneficiaries: public, quasi-public, or private nonprofit institutions and organizations; specialized groups.

Range: $100,000 to $5,000,000. **Average:** $650,000.

Activity: not quantified specifically.

HQ: U.S. Army Medical Research and Material Command-DOD (ATTN: MCMR-ACQ-BA), Fort Detrick, Frederick, MD 21702-5012. Phone: (301) 619-7216; Army Medical Research Acquisition Activity (ATTN: SGRD-RMA-RC), (301)619-2036. **Internet:** "http://mrmc-www.army.mil"; "http://cdmrp.army.mil". (Note: the field office serves as headquarters for this program.)

ARMY RESEARCH OFFICE

12.431 BASIC SCIENTIFIC RESEARCH

Assistance: project grants (100 percent/3-5 years).

Purposes: for basic research in the mathematical, physical, engineering, biological, and geosciences related to the improvement of Army programs or operations. Funds may support: programs encouraging careers for outstanding graduate, undergraduate, and high school students; increases in the number of graduates from under-represented minority groups; symposia; purchases of major high-cost research equipment.

Eligible applicants/beneficiaries: educational institutions, nonprofit scientific research organizations.

Range: $25,000 to $1,000,000.

Activity: FY 02 estimate, 500 awards.

HQ: U.S. Army Research Office-DOD (ATTN: AMXRO-RT), Research Triangle Park, NC 27709-2211. Phone: (919)549-4204. **Internet:** "http://www.amc.army.mil". (Note: no field offices for this program.)

OFFICE OF ASSISTANT SECRETARY/ STRATEGY AND REQUIREMENTS

12.550 INTERNATIONAL EDUCATION—U.S. COLLEGES AND UNIVERSITIES ("National Security Education Program" - "NSEP")

Assistance: project grants (100 percent/1-2 years).

Purposes: to develop and strengthen IHE capabilities in critical language education, area studies, and international fields. International exchanges are ineligible for funding. The National Security Education Trust Fund supports this program.

Eligible applicants/beneficiaries: U.S. IHEs. Others may be included in proposals, but may not receive direct grants.

Range/Average: to $200,000 per year for two years.

Activity: N.A.

HQ: NSEP, Under Secretary of Defense/Policy, Assistant Secretary/Strategy and Requirements, DOD, 1101 Wilson Blvd. - Ste.1210, Arlington, VA 22209-2248. Phone: (703)696-1991. **Internet:** "www.ndu.edu/nsep". (Note: no field offices for this program.)

12.551 NATIONAL SECURITY EDUCATION—SCHOLARSHIPS

Assistance: project grants (100 percent/2 academic terms per year).

Purposes: for undergraduate scholarships in critical languages and world area studies. Recipients must agree to work in a federal organization or in higher education for a time equal to the award period. Studies may be conducted abroad. International exchanges are ineligible for funding. The National Security Education Trust Fund supports this program.

Eligible applicants/beneficiaries: U.S. citizens enrolled in public or private two- or four-year IHEs. Students in federal government schools are ineligible.

Range: to $8,000/academic term.

Activity: since 1993 program inception, 800 awards.

HQ: same as **12.550**. (Note: no field offices for this program.)

OFFICE OF ECONOMIC ADJUSTMENT

12.600 COMMUNITY ECONOMIC ADJUSTMENT

Assistance: specialized services; advisory services/counseling.

Purposes: for communities, regions, and states to alleviate serious economic impacts resulting from DOD program changes—e.g., base openings, expansions, or closings, contract changes, personnel increases or reductions. Typically, assistance consists of assessing the impact and formulating strategies to relieve problems, including involving other federal departments, identifying alternative resources and solutions, and developing an action plan.

Eligible applicants/beneficiaries: local governments or states on their behalf, regional organizations.

Activity: not quantified specifically.

HQ: Director, Office of Economic Adjustment, DOD, 400 Army-Navy Dr. - Ste.200, Arlington, VA 22202-4704. Phone: (703)604-6020. **Internet:** "www.oea.gov"; e-mail, "oeafeedback@osd.gov".

12.607 COMMUNITY ECONOMIC ADJUSTMENT PLANNING ASSISTANCE ("Community Planning Assistance")

Assistance: project grants (75 percent).

Purposes: for community economic adjustment planning activities in coordination with communities, concerning military installation closures or realignment. Funds may be used for staffing, operating and administrative costs, studies.

Eligible applicants/beneficiaries: in DOD-approved areas—local governments or states on their behalf; regional organizations; tribes, DC, PR, Guam.

Range: $36,000 to $226,000. **Average:** $100,000.

Activity: 1990-2002, 73 communities reporting creation of 87,000 new jobs replacing 130,000 lost jobs.

HQ: same as **12.600**.

12.610 COMMUNITY ECONOMIC ADJUSTMENT PLANNING ASSISTANCE FOR JOINT LAND USE STUDIES

Assistance: project grants (75 percent).

Purposes: pursuant to the Defense Authorization Act, to prepare joint military/community comprehensive land use plans concerning public or private land development around military installation, to assure that land uses are compatible with both military operations and plans of nonmilitary jurisdictions; in certain cases, to carry out the recommendations of such a study.

Eligible applicants/beneficiaries: same as for **12.607**.

Range: $45,000 to $90,000. **Average:** $70,000.

Activity: not quantified specifically

HQ: same as **12.600**.

12.611 COMMUNITY ECONOMIC ADJUSTMENT PLANNING ASSISTANCE FOR REDUCTIONS IN DEFENSE INDUSTRY EMPLOYMENT

Assistance: project grants (75 percent).

Purposes: for communities to undertake economic adjustment planning activities to respond to major reductions in defense industry employment resulting from the cancellation, termination, or failure to proceed with DOD spending under a previously approved program. Funds may be used for planning expenses including staffing, operating and administrative costs, studies.

Eligible applicants/beneficiaries: states on behalf of local governments, local governments, tribes, DC, PR, Guam—if the spending reduction involves the loss of at least: 2,500 full-time contractor employee jobs in a metropolitan statistical area; or 1,000 jobs outside a metropolitan statistical area; or one percent of the total number of jobs in that area.

Range: $100,000 to $200,000. **Average:** $150,000.

Activity: no funding in recent years.

HQ: same as **12.600**.

12.612 COMMUNITY BASE REUSE PLANS ("Community Planning Assistance")

Assistance: project grants (75 percent).

Purposes: pursuant to the Defense Base Closure and Realignment Act of 1990, to prepare community base reuse plans at closing or realigning military installations—required as part of the Environmental Impact Statement for disposal and reuse of such installations.

Eligible applicants/beneficiaries: same as for **12.607**.

Range: $25,000 to $400,000. **Average:** $150,000.

Activity: not quantified specifically.

HQ: same as **12.600**.

12.613 GROWTH MANAGEMENT PLANNING ASSISTANCE ("Community Planning Assistance")

Assistance: project grants (90 percent).

Purposes: for growth management planning activities to respond to military base opening or expansion resulting in large-scale military-related population growth requiring additional public facilities and services off-base. Funds may support staffing, operating and administrative costs, studies—if expansions involve assignment of more than 2,000 personnel, or if they equal 10 percent or more of existing employment within 15 miles of the installation.

Eligible applicants/beneficiaries: same as for **12.607**.

Range: $100,000 to $300,000. **Average:** $150,000.

Activity: no funding FY 94-06.

HQ: same as **12.610**.

12.614 COMMUNITY ECONOMIC ADJUSTMENT ASSISTANCE FOR ADVANCE PLANNING

Assistance: project grants (90 percent).

Purposes: for community economic adjustment planning activities to lessen dependence on military base-related defense spending; to prepare strategies and schematic plans for the potential reuse of redevelopment of active bases.

Eligible applicants/beneficiaries: states; local governments or states on their behalf; regional governmental organizations.

Range: to $175,000.

Activity: new program listing in 2005. Not quantified specifically.

HQ: Deputy Director, same address, web site as **12.600**. Phone: (703)604-4828.

OFFICE OF THE SECRETARY

12.630 BASIC, APPLIED, AND ADVANCED RESEARCH IN SCIENCE AND ENGINEERING

Assistance: project grants.

Purposes: for research in areas that cut across traditional academic disciplines, in mathematical, physical, engineering, environmental, life sciences, and other fields—with long-term potential for contributing to technology for DOD missions; for fellowships and research traineeships for graduate education.

Eligible applicants: private and public educational institutions.

Eligible beneficiaries: graduate and undergraduate students in science and engineering disciplines important to DOD.

Range: $1,000 to $3,000,000. **Average:** $120,000.

Activity: not quantified specifically.

HQ: contact the executive agents listed under "HQ" for programs **12.300**, **12.431**, **12.800**, or **12.910**. **Internet:** "http://www.usace.army.mil/business.html". (Note: no field offices for this program.)

SECRETARIES OF MILITARY DEPARTMENTS

12.700 DONATIONS/LOANS OF OBSOLETE DOD PROPERTY

Assistance: use of property, facilities, and equipment.

Purposes: to donate or lend obsolete combat materiel and other specified items for historical, ceremonial, or display purposes—including books, manuscripts, models, vessels. Recipients must pay packing and handling costs.

Eligible applicants/beneficiaries: veterans' organizations recognized by the Office of the Deputy Under Secretary of Defense (LIMDM); libraries, historical societies, educational institutions, and tax-exempt museums operated and maintained only for education purposes; municipalities; states, territories, and possessions.

Activity: none.

HQ: appropriate military department, DOD, Pentagon, Washington, DC 20301. **Internet:** "http://www.usace.army.mil/business.html".

DEPARTMENT OF THE AIR FORCE MATERIEL COMMAND

12.800 AIR FORCE DEFENSE RESEARCH SCIENCES PROGRAM

Assistance: project grants (1-3 years).

Purposes: for research to maintain technological superiority in scientific areas relevant to Air Force needs; to prevent technology surprise to the nation and to create it for adversaries; to maintain a strong research infrastructure composed of Air Force laboratories, industry, and universities; to complement the national research effort. Projects may be in such areas as the aerospace, engineering, chemistry and materials, and life, environmental, mathematical, and computer sciences.

Eligible applicants/beneficiaries: private and public educational institutions; private and public nonprofit organizations; commercial concerns.

Range: $50,000 to $5,000,000. **Average:** $500,000.

Activity: FY 02 estimate, 600 new grants.

HQ: HQ-Air Force Materiel Command/PKT, DOD, 4375 Childlaw Rd. - Ste.6, Wright-Patterson AFB, OH 45433-5006. Phone: (513)257-8934. **Internet:** "http://www.usace.army.mil/business.html".

NATIONAL SECURITY AGENCY

12.900 LANGUAGE GRANT PROGRAM

Assistance: project grants (100 percent).

Purposes: to foster foreign language training of Americans. Funded projects have included documentation of low density languages, foreign language reference works, and research in training methods and computer-assisted instruction technologies.

Eligible applicants/beneficiaries: employees of U.S. private or public IHEs and nonprofit organizations operated primarily for language training.

Range: $5,000 to $500,000.

Activity: not quantified specifically.

HQ: Chief, Language Training, National Security Agency (ATTN: E41), DOD, Fort George Meade, MD 20755-6000. Phone: (410)859-6087. **Internet:** "http://www.darpa.mil/cmo". (Note: no field offices for this program.)

12.901 MATHEMATICAL SCIENCES GRANTS PROGRAM

Assistance: project grants (100 percent/to 2 years).

Purposes: pursuant to the National Security Act of 1959, to stimulate developments and promote careers in areas of mathematics identified with cryptography, including number theory, discrete mathematics, statistics, probability. Funds may support summer salary (one month maximum), professional travel, publishing costs, graduate or postgraduate student support, conferences.

Eligible applicants/beneficiaries: employees and graduate students at U.S. IHEs, that are U.S. citizens, permanent residents, or intending to apply for citizenship.

Range: $5,000 to $60,000. **Average:** $15,000.

Activity: none.

HQ: National Security Agency (ATTN: R51A), DOD, Fort George Meade, MD

20755-6000. Phone: (301)688-0400. **Internet:** same as **12.900**. (Note: no field offices for this program.)

12.902 INFORMATION SECURITY GRANT PROGRAM
("Information Security University Research Program" - "URP")

Assistance: project grants (100 percent/1-2 years).

Purposes: for research to design, build, and maintain secure computing systems involving unclassified information; to develop and train computer science graduates to be recruited by NSA. Project examples: "Multilevel Secure Distributed Systems Security;" "Computer Misuse and Anomaly Detection." Funds may support summer salary (two months maximum), professional travel, publishing costs, graduate and postdoctoral student support, conferences.

Eligible applicants/beneficiaries: same as **12.901**.

Range: $50,000 to $100,000. **Average:** $80,000.

Activity: 2002, 45 proposals received.

HQ: Program Director, INFOSEC University Research Program, National Security Agency (ATTN: R23), DOD, 9840 O'Brien Rd., Fort George Meade, MD 20755-6000. Phone: (301)688-0847, FAX (301)688-0255. **Internet:** "http://www.darpa.mil/cmo"; e-mail, "urp@tycho.ncsc.mil". (Note: no field offices for this program.)

DEFENSE ADVANCED RESEARCH PROJECTS AGENCY

12.910 RESEARCH AND TECHNOLOGY DEVELOPMENT

Assistance: project grants (50 percent/3-5 years).

Purposes: for basic and applied research and development in science and technology; for projects advancing the state of the art or resulting in fundamental changes in technology—in areas that may have military or dual-use applications. Funds may also support: symposia and conferences; programs encouraging careers in science, technology, and engineering, and an increase in the number of graduates from under-represented minority groups; university research instrumentation.

Eligible applicants/beneficiaries: grants—public and private educational institutions and nonprofit organizations. Cooperative agreements—educational institutions, nonprofit organizations, commercial firms.

Range: $100,000 to $100,000,000. **Average:** $1,150,000.

Activity: FY 02 estimate, 30 grant awards and 20 "other transactions."

HQ: Director, Contract Management Office (CMO), Defense Advanced Research Projects Agency, DOD, 3701 N. Fairfax Drive, Arlington, VA 22203. Phone: (703)696-2399. **Internet:** "http://www.darpa.mil/cmo". (Note: no field offices for this program.)

DEPARTMENT OF HOUSING AND URBAN DEVELOPMENT

> **NOTE**: *For most HUD mortgage insurance programs, applications should be submitted to HUD-approved lenders authorized to act on mortgages covering single-family housing. Multifamily project proposals generally require HUD approval of prospective sponsors; pre-application conferences are held with HUD field offices to determine project feasibility, particularly if housing subsidies are sought.*

14.103 INTEREST REDUCTION PAYMENTS—RENTAL AND COOPERATIVE HOUSING FOR LOWER INCOME FAMILIES
("Section 236")

Assistance: direct payments/specified use; guaranteed/insured loans (40 years).

Purposes: pursuant to the National Housing Act (NHA) as amended, to subsidize interest costs for mortgages on rental or cooperative housing developed for the low- and moderate-income. Subsidies are paid directly to lenders during the term of the mortgage; payments are adjusted to equal the difference between market rate interest costs and as low as one percent, depending on the incomes of tenants who must pay at least 30 percent of their adjusted gross incomes toward rent. The program now is inactive except for commitments to existing projects; no new projects have been insured since 1992.

Eligible applicants: nonprofit, cooperative, builder-seller, investor-sponsor, and limited-distribution sponsors. Public bodies were ineligible.

Eligible beneficiaries: within certain locally determined income limits, families and individuals including the elderly or handicapped or those displaced by government action or natural disaster. Families with incomes exceeding eligibility for subsidies may occupy apartments, but with no benefit from subsidy payments.

Range: N.A.

Activity: FY 92 status, 378,000 rental units insured, valued at $6.5 billion.

HQ: Director, Office of Multifamily Housing Management, Housing- HUD, Washington, DC 20410. Phone: (202)708-3730. **Internet:** "www.hud.gov/offices/hsg//mfh/progdesc.cfm".

14.108 REHABILITATION MORTGAGE INSURANCE
("Section 203(k)")

Assistance: guaranteed/insured loans (30 years).

Purposes: pursuant to NHA as amended, to insure loans for rehabilitation, acquisition and rehabilitation, acquisition and relocation from another site and rehabilitation, or rehabilitation and debt refinancing—for existing oneto four-unit residential buildings. Rehabilitation cost must be at least $5,000. Certain application fees must be paid by purchasers.

Eligible applicants/beneficiaries: individual purchasers (*see NOTE preceding* **14.103**).

Range: same as for **14.117**.

Activity: FY 05 estimate, 4,000 loans insured.

HQ: (no address provided). Phone: (202)708-2121. **Internet:** "www.hud.gov/offices/hsg/sfh/ins/singlefamily.cfm".

14.110 MANUFACTURED HOME LOAN INSURANCE—FINANCING PURCHASE OF MANUFACTURED HOMES AS PRINCIPAL RESIDENCES OF BORROWERS ("Title I")

Assistance: guaranteed/insured loans (to 90 percent/15-25 years).

Purposes: pursuant to NHA as amended, to insure loans to manufactured home purchasers when the unit will be used as the principal residence. 5 percent down payments and fees must be provided by purchasers. Funding for this program includes **14.162**.

Eligible applicants/beneficiaries: anyone (*see NOTE preceding* **14.103**).

Range: to $48,600 (whether single or multiple modules).

Activity: FY 05 estimate, 1,980 loans.

HQ: Chief, Home Mortgage Insurance Division, Housing-HUD, 451 7th St. SW - Rm. 9272, Washington, DC 20410. Phone: same as **14.108**. **Internet:** "www.hud.gov/progdesc/manuf14.cfm".

14.112 MORTGAGE INSURANCE FOR CONSTRUCTION OR SUBSTANTIAL REHABILITATION OF CONDOMINIUM PROJECTS ("Section 234(d) Condominiums")

Assistance: guaranteed/insured loans (to 90 percent/to 40 years).

Purposes: pursuant to NHA and Housing Act of 1964 as amended, to insure for the construction or substantial rehabilitation of multifamily housing structures by sponsors intending to sell individual units as condominiums; in turn, purchasers may obtain mortgage insurance through **14.133**. Funding for this program is included in **14.135**.

Eligible applicants/beneficiaries: private profit-motivated developers, public bodies, certain other sponsors (*see NOTE preceding* **14.103**).

Range/Average: to 90 percent of replacement cost within statutory limits.

Activity: no loans insured in recent years.

HQ: Office of Multifamily Development, Housing-HUD, 451 Seventh St. SW, Washington, DC 20410. Phone: (202)708-1142. **Internet:** "www.hud.gov/offices/hsg/hsgmulti.cfm".

14.117 MORTGAGE INSURANCE—HOMES ("Section 203(b)")

Assistance: guaranteed/insured loans (to 30 years).

Purposes: pursuant to NHA as amended, to insure loans to purchasers acquiring existing or newly constructed one- to four-unit housing. Mortgage indebtedness on existing housing owned by applicants may also be refinanced. Small down payments, certain closing costs, and other expenses must be covered by purchasers. Funding for this program includes **14.119, 14.126, 14.159, 14.163, 14.172,** and **14.175.**

Eligible applicants/beneficiaries: purchasers that will occupy insured units (*see NOTE preceding* **14.103**).

Range: $172,632 maximum insurable loans for single-family units, $220,992 for two-family housing, $267,120 for three-family, $312,895 for four-family—which may be increased in high-cost areas (details available from HUD area offices).

Activity: FY 04, 894,000 loans insured.

HQ: none; all contacts are with Homeownership Centers at field offices listed in Part IV. **Internet:** "www.hud.gov/offices/hsg/sfh/ins/sfh203b.cfm".

14.119 MORTGAGE INSURANCE—HOMES FOR DISASTER VICTIMS ("Section 203(h)")

Assistance: guaranteed/insured loans (100 percent/to 30-35 years).

Purposes: pursuant to NHA as amended, to insure loans to enable disaster victims to acquire new or reconstructed existing single-family housing. Certain fees must be paid by purchasers. Funding for this program is included in **14.117.**

Eligible applicants/beneficiaries: victims of major disasters that will occupy acquired housing as their principal residence (*see NOTE preceding* **14.103**).

Range: to 100 per cent of the maximum limits for **14.117.**

Activity: FY 04, 51 loans insured.

HQ: none; all contacts are with Homeownership Centers at field offices listed in Part IV. **Internet:** "www.hud.gov80/progdesc/203h-dft.cfm".

14.122 MORTGAGE INSURANCE—HOMES IN URBAN RENEWAL AREAS ("Section 220 Homes")

Assistance: guaranteed/insured loans (to 30-35 years).

Purposes: pursuant to the Housing Act of 1954, to insure loans for new, existing, or rehabilitated, owner-occupied one- to 11-unit housing acquired or rehabilitated in approved urban renewal or code enforcement areas. Small down payments and fees must be paid by purchasers. Funding for this program is included in **14.133.**

Eligible applicants/beneficiaries: all families (*see NOTE preceding* **14.103**).

Range: same as for **14.117**, plus $9,165 for each unit over four.

Activity: FY 04, one mortgage endorsement.

HQ: none; all contacts are with Homeownership Centers at field offices listed in Part IV. **Internet:** "www.hud.gov/fha/sfh/sf_home.html".

14.123 MORTGAGE INSURANCE—HOUSING IN OLDER, DECLINING AREAS ("Section 223(e)")

Assistance: guaranteed/insured loans.

Purposes: pursuant to NHA as amended, for purchasers of existing, new, or rehabilitated single-family or multifamily housing in older declining areas where conditions are such that certain normal eligibility requirements for mortgage insurance cannot be met. HUD insures loans made under other programs (e.g., **14.135**); claims are paid from the Special Risk Insurance Fund. Small down payments and insurance fees may be required of beneficiaries. Funding for this program is included in **14.133**.

Eligible applicants: HUD-approved mortgagees.

Eligible beneficiaries: single-family houses—individuals or families. Multifamily sponsorship eligibility is determined by applicable program requirements.

Range: varies according to program under which mortgage is insured.

Activity: FY 00-05, no loans insured.

HQ: none; all contacts are with field offices listed in Part IV. **Internet:** same as **14.122**.

14.126 MORTGAGE INSURANCE—COOPERATIVE PROJECTS ("Section 213 Cooperatives")

Assistance: guaranteed/insured loans (90-98 percent).

Purposes: pursuant to NHA as amended, Housing Acts of 1950 and 1956, and other acts, to insure loans for existing, new, or rehabilitated cooperative housing consisting of detached, semi-detached, row, walk-up, or elevator structures, with five units minimum. Certain fees must be paid by purchasers. Maximum mortgage term: "management-type" projects, 40 years; "sales-type," 35 years. Funding for this program is included in **14.117**.

Eligible applicants: nonprofit cooperatives, ownership housing corporations, or trusts that may sponsor projects directly, sell individual units to cooperative members, or purchase projects from investor-sponsors (*see NOTE preceding* **14.103**).

Eligible beneficiaries: members of cooperatives.

Range: $1,321,000 to $11,039,000; maximum mortgage to investor-sponsor, 90 percent of replacement cost; cooperative member, 98 percent—within statutory maximums for individual units under program **14.117**. **Average:** $6,300,000.

Activity: FY 04, 4 projects with 167 total units.

HQ: same as **14.112**.

14.127 MORTGAGE INSURANCE—MANUFACTURED HOME PARKS ("Section 207 Manufactured Home Parks")

Assistance: guaranteed/insured loans (90 percent/to 40 years).

Purposes: pursuant to NHA as amended, to insure loans for manufactured home park development, new or rehabilitated, with five or more spaces. Funding for this program is included in **14.135**.

Eligible applicants: investors, builders, developers, others (*see NOTE preceding* **14.103**).

Eligible beneficiaries: families or individuals owning manufactured houses and leasing spaces.

Range: to $11,250 per space (higher in high-cost areas); loans, $1,890,000 to $7,830,000. **Average:** $4,500,000.

Activity: FY 05, no activity.

HQ: same as **14.112**.

14.128 MORTGAGE INSURANCE—HOSPITALS
(Section 242 Hospitals")

Assistance: guaranteed/insured loans (to 90 percent/to 25 years).

Purposes: pursuant to NHA as amended, to insure loans for acute care hospital construction, rehabilitation, or refinancing, including the costs of major movable equipment—including facilities designated as "Critical Access Hospitals."

Eligible applicants/beneficiaries: profit or nonprofit hospitals licensed or regulated by the state, municipality, or other political subdivision.

Range: $10,000,000 to $94,020,000. **Average:** $40,698,000.

Activity: FY 04, 12 mortgages.

HQ: Office of Insured Health Care Facilities, Housing-HUD, 451 Seventh St. SW - Rm.9224, Washington, DC 20410. Phone: (202)708-0599. *Or*: Division of Facilities Loans, HHS, Bethesda, MD 20814. Phone: (301)443-5317. **Internet:** "www.hud.gov/groups/healthcare.cfm". (Note: no field offices for this program.)

14.129 MORTGAGE INSURANCE—NURSING HOMES, INTERMEDIATE CARE FACILITIES, BOARD AND CARE HOMES AND ASSISTED LIVING FACILITIES
("Section 232 Nursing Homes")

Assistance: guaranteed/insured loans.

Purposes: pursuant to NHA and Housing Act of 1959 as amended, and Housing and Urban Development Act of 1969, to insure loans for the purchase, construction, rehabilitation, or refinancing of nursing homes providing skilled nursing care or intermediate care facilities accommodating 20 or more patients, or board and care homes and assisted living facilities with five or more accommodations or units, or a combination of the foregoing types of facilities. Loans also may cover the cost of fire safety equipment and major equipment.

Eligible applicants/beneficiaries: investors, builders, developers, public entities, nursing homes, and private nonprofit corporations or associations (*see NOTE preceding* **14.103**).

Range: 40-year mortgage insurance on 90 percent loans for new or substantially rehabilitated facilities (95 percent for nonprofit sponsors); 35 years on 85 percent loans for refinanced existing HUD-insured facilities not requiring substantial rehabilitation (to 90 percent for nonprofit sponsors).

Activity: FY 04, 279 loans insured, with 34,000 beds total.

HQ: same as **14.112**.

14.132 MORTGAGE INSURANCE—PURCHASE OF SALES-TYPE COOPERATIVE HOUSING UNITS ("Section 213 Sales")

Assistance: guaranteed/insured loans (30-35 years).

Purposes: pursuant to NHA as amended and Housing Act of 1950, to insure loans for purchases of new dwelling units by members of cooperatives in projects with at least five units. Small down payments are required. Funding for this program is included in **14.135**.

Eligible applicants/beneficiaries: members of nonprofit cooperative ownership housing corporations or trusts (*see NOTE preceding* **14.103**).

Range: same as for **14.117**.

Activity: included in report for **14.117**.

HQ: none; all contacts are with Homeownership Centers at field offices listed in Part IV. **Internet:** "www.hud.gov/progdesc/coops213.cfm".

14.133 MORTGAGE INSURANCE—PURCHASE OF UNITS IN CONDOMINIUMS ("Section 234(c)")

Assistance: guaranteed/insured loans (to 30-35 years).

Purposes: pursuant to NHA as amended, to insure loans to purchase new or existing individual units in condominium projects containing four or more dwellings. Units converted from rental to condominiums are insurable, provided: the conversion occurred more than one year prior to the application for insurance; mortgagor occupied the rental housing; conversion was sponsored by an approved tenants organization. Small down payments and fees must be paid by purchasers. Funding for this program includes **14.122**, **14.123**, **14.165**, **14.183**, and **14.184**.

Eligible applicants/beneficiaries: condominium purchasers (*see NOTE preceding* **14.103**).

Range: same as for **14.117**.

Activity: FY 04, 62,000 units insured.

HQ: none; all contacts are with Homeownership Centers at field offices listed in Part IV. **Internet:** "www.hud.gov/progdesc/234c-df.cfm".

14.134 MORTGAGE INSURANCE—RENTAL HOUSING ("Section 207")

Assistance: guaranteed/insured loans (90 percent/to 40 years).

Purposes: pursuant to NHA as amended, to insure loans for the construction or rehabilitation of middle-income rental housing in detached, semi-detached, row, walk-up, or elevator structures, with five units minimum. Funding for this program is included in **14.135**.

Eligible applicants/beneficiaries: investors, builders, developers, others (*see NOTE preceding* **14.103**).

Range: to 90 percent of value.

Activity: no projects insured in several years; Sections 221(d)(3) and 221(d)(4) (**14.135**) are used instead.

HQ: same as **14.112**.

14.135 MORTGAGE INSURANCE—RENTAL AND COOPERATIVE HOUSING FOR MODERATE INCOME FAMILIES AND ELDERLY, MARKET INTEREST RATE
("Section 221(d)(3) and (4) Multifamily - Market Rate Housing")

Assistance: guaranteed/insured loans (90-100 percent/to 40 years).

Purposes: pursuant to NHA as amended, to insure loans to sponsors of new or rehabilitated market-rate rental or cooperative housing developed for moderate-income families, the elderly, and the handicapped, including for "single-room occupancy" (**14.184**). Units may be in detached, semi-detached, row, walk-up, or elevator structures containing five units minimum. Funding for this program includes **14.112, 14.127, 14.132, 14.134, 14.138,** and **14.139**.

Eligible applicants: public, profit-motivated, limited-distribution, nonprofit, cooperative, builder-seller, investor, and general sponsors (*see NOTE preceding* **14.103**).

Eligible beneficiaries: all households regardless of income.

Range: Section 221(d)(3), to 90 percent of replacement cost for profit-motivated or limited-distribution sponsors; to 100 percent for public, cooperative, or nonprofit sponsors. Section 221(d)(4), to 90 percent of replacement cost—within statutory maximums; loans, $675,000 to $45,000,000. **Average:** $12,100,000.

Activity: FY 04, 221 projects with 38,000 units insured.

HQ: same as **14.112**.

14.138 MORTGAGE INSURANCE—RENTAL HOUSING FOR THE ELDERLY
("Section 231")

Assistance: guaranteed/insured loans (90-100 percent/to 40 years).

Purposes: pursuant to NHA as amended, to insure loans for rental housing for elderly or handicapped persons—in new or rehabilitated detached, semi-detached, walk-up, or elevator structures with a minimum of five units. Funding for this program is included in **14.135**.

Eligible applicants/beneficiaries: private profit-motivated investors, non-profit sponsors (*see NOTE preceding* **14.103**).

Range: within statutory maximum per unit costs—nonprofit and public sponsors, 100 percent of replacement cost; other sponsors, 90 percent.

Activity: FY 01-05, no loans insured. (NOTE: in recent years, program **14.135** has been used instead of this program.)

HQ: same as **14.112**.

14.139 MORTGAGE INSURANCE—RENTAL HOUSING IN URBAN RENEWAL AREAS
("Section 220 Multifamily")

Assistance: guaranteed/insured loans (90 percent/40 years).

Purposes: pursuant to NHA as amended, to insure loans for new or rehabilitated rental housing located in urban renewal, code enforcement, or other approved public program areas including disaster areas; loans may also cover existing properties rehabilitated by a local public agency. Projects must include a minimum of two units, and may involve detached, semi-detached, walk-up, or elevator structures. Funding for this program is included in **14.135**.

Eligible applicants: private profit entities, public bodies, others (*see NOTE preceding* **14.103**).

Eligible beneficiaries: all families.

Range: to 90 percent of replacement cost; loans, $1,366,000 to $45,495,000. **Average:** $17,900,000.

Activity: FY 04, 9 projects insured with 1,583 total units.

HQ: same as **14.112**.

14.142 PROPERTY IMPROVEMENT LOAN INSURANCE FOR IMPROVING ALL EXISTING STRUCTURES AND BUILDING OF NEW NONRESIDENTIAL STRUCTURES
("Title I")

Assistance: guaranteed/insured loans (90 percent/20-30 years).

Purposes: pursuant to NHA as amended, to insure loans for property improvement for existing housing, including the cost of erecting new nonresidential structures that substantially protect or improve the livability or utility of the properties.

Eligible applicants/beneficiaries: owners of properties to be improved; lessees with a lease extending at least six months beyond loan maturity; purchasers under a land installment contract (*see NOTE preceding* **14.103**).

Range: $25,000 maximum for one-family dwelling or nonresidential structure; $12,000 maximum per unit for multifamily structures, not to exceed $60,000.

Activity: FY 04, 4,847 loans insured.

HQ: none; all contacts are with Homeownership Centers at field offices listed in Part IV. **Internet:** "www.hud.gov/offices/hsg/sfh/titlei_home.cfm".

14.149 RENT SUPPLEMENTS—RENTAL HOUSING FOR LOWER INCOME FAMILIES

Assistance: direct payments/specified use (to 40 years).

Purposes: pursuant to the Housing and Urban Development Act of 1965, to subsidize rents paid by lower-income tenants of certain HUD-insured and other housing. Assistance covers the difference between the rent paid by the tenant and up to 70 percent of the market rent, with the tenant paying between 25 and 30 percent of monthly adjusted income. This program is inactive except for commitments to existing projects.

Eligible applicants: eligible sponsors included nonprofit, cooperative, builder-seller, investor-sponsor, and limited-distribution mortgagors.

Eligible beneficiaries: families with income within the limits for admission to Section 8 housing (see **14.856**). Families may continue in occupancy if 30 percent of adjusted monthly income exceeds market rents, but subsidy may be adjusted downward or eliminated.

Range: N.A.
Activity: FY 92 cumulative commitments, 19,270 units.
HQ: same as **14.103**.

14.151 SUPPLEMENTAL LOAN INSURANCE—MULTIFAMILY RENTAL HOUSING
("Section 241(a)")

Assistance: guaranteed/insured loans (90 percent/varying term).

Purposes: pursuant to NHA as amended, to insure loans for expansion or improvement of existing multifamily housing and health care facilities, including hospitals, group practice facilities, or nursing homes, already covered by HUD mortgage insurance—including energy conservation and purchase of major movable equipment for health facilities.

Eligible applicants/beneficiaries: owners of multifamily projects or facilities subject to a HUD-insured mortgage (*see NOTE preceding* **14.103**).

Range: to 90 percent of the value of the improvements; loans, $755,000 to $1,153,000. **Average:** $954,000.

Activity: FY 04, 1 loan insured, with 180 units/beds total.

HQ: same address, web site as **14.112**. Phone: (202)708-2556.

14.155 MORTGAGE INSURANCE FOR THE PURCHASE OR REFINANCING OF EXISTING MULTIFAMILY HOUSING PROJECTS
("Sections 223(f) and 207")

Assistance: guaranteed/insured loans (85 percent/10-35 years).

Purposes: pursuant to NHA and Housing and Community Development Act of 1974 as amended, to insure loans for the purchase or refinancing existing rental multifamily housing not requiring substantial rehabilitation. The property must have five or more living units; three years must have elapsed from the later of completion of project construction or substantial rehabilitation, or beginning of occupancy to date of application for mortgage insurance; the remaining economic life must be long enough to permit at least a ten-year mortgage term.

Eligible applicants/beneficiaries: private or public mortgagors (*see NOTE preceding* **14.103**).

Range: repairs, maximum of 15 percent of estimated value after repairs or $6,500 per unit—more in high-cost areas; loans, $425,000 to $31,750,000. **Average:** $5,500,000.

Activity: FY 04, 189 projects with 23,000 total units insured.

HQ: same as **14.112**.

14.157 SUPPORTIVE HOUSING FOR THE ELDERLY
("Section 202")

Assistance: direct payments/specified use.

Purposes: pursuant to the Housing Act of 1959 as amended, Housing and Community Development Act of 1992, and American Homeownership and Economic Opportunity Act of 2000, for the acquisition, construction, or substantial rehabilitation of rental or cooperative housing with supportive services and related facilities (e.g., central dining) for the very low-income elderly. Capital advances are provided by HUD to meet development costs; these advances need not be repaid, provided the project is available to the very-low-income elderly for 40 years. HUD project rental assistance payments may cover the difference between per-unit operating cost and the rent amount paid by tenants, under five-year contracts with project sponsors. Funding for this program includes **14.191** and **14.314**.

Eligible applicants/beneficiaries: private nonprofit organizations and consumer cooperatives. Also, profit-motivated limited partnerships may participate in projects with mixed financing.

Range: $424,000 to $13,830,000. **Average:** $4,349,000.

Activity: FY 04, 5,852 units assisted.

HQ: Office of Housing Assistance and Grants Administration, Housing-HUD, Washington, DC 20410. Phone: (202)708-3000. **Internet:** "www.hud.gov/offices/hsg/mfh/progrdesc/eld202.cfm".

14.159 SECTION 245 GRADUATED PAYMENT MORTGAGE PROGRAM

Assistance: guaranteed/insured loans (30 years).

Purposes: pursuant to NHA, Housing and Community Development Acts of 1974 and 1979, and amendments, to insure loans for existing or new single-family housing, and condominiums financed with graduated payment mortgages—allowing smaller monthly payments initially, and with increased amounts over time as the borrower's income increases. Small down payments are required, and mortgagors must pay certain closing costs. Funding for this program is included in **14.117**.

Eligible applicants/beneficiaries: prospective owner-occupants (*see NOTE preceding* **14.103**).

Range: basically, 97 percent of appraised value and closing costs minus deferred interest during graduated term.

Activity: FY 03-05 estimate, no loans insured.

HQ: none; all contacts are with Homeownership Centers at field offices listed in Part IV. **Internet:** "www.hud.gov/progdesc/245-dft.cfm".

14.162 MORTGAGE INSURANCE—COMBINATION AND MANUFACTURED HOME LOT LOANS
("Title I")

Assistance: guaranteed/insured loans (90 percent).

Purposes: pursuant to NHA as amended, to insure loans to purchase manufactured homes and lots. The maximum term is 20 years for a single module and lot, 25 years for a double module, and 15 years for a lot only. Funding for this program is included in **14.110**.

Eligible applicants/beneficiaries: purchasers intending to use property as their principal place of residence (*see NOTE preceding* **14.103**).

Range: to $64,800 for a manufactured home and lot; to $16,200 for a developed lot only—more in high-cost areas.

Activity: FY 04, 1,980 loans insured.

HQ: same address/phone, web site as **14.110**; *and,* general information, phone: (800)767-7468. (Note: no field offices for this program.)

14.163 MORTGAGE INSURANCE—SINGLE FAMILY COOPERATIVE HOUSING ("Section 203(n)")

Assistance: guaranteed/insured loans (to 30 years).

Purposes: pursuant to NHA as amended and the Emergency Home Purchase Assistance Act of 1974, to insure loans to purchase the Corporate Certificate and Occupancy Certificate for a unit in a HUD-insured cooperative housing project covered by a blanket mortgage, giving purchasers the right to occupy the unit. Funding for this program is included in **14.117**.

Eligible applicants/beneficiaries: potential owner-occupant mortgagors (*see NOTE preceding* **14.103**).

Range: to maximums stipulated for **14.117**.

Activity: included in report for **14.117**.

HQ: none; all contacts are with Homeownership Centers at field offices listed in Part IV. **Internet:** "www.hud.gov80/progdesc/203n-df.cfm".

14.164 OPERATING ASSISTANCE FOR TROUBLED MULTIFAMILY HOUSING PROJECTS
("Flexible Subsidy Fund" - "Troubled Projects")

Assistance: direct payments/specified use (75-100 percent/1 year).

Purposes: pursuant to the Housing and Community Development Amendments of 1978 as amended, to restore or maintain the physical and financial soundness of HUD-assisted (i.e., subsidized) low- and moderate-income multifamily rental projects—through repairs, augmentation of replacement reserves, or funding of operating deficits. Owners, except nonprofits, must contribute at least 25 percent of the total needed.

Eligible applicants/beneficiaries: nonprofit owners with existing assisted housing program loans. Public bodies are ineligible. Field offices recommend projects to be assisted.

Range/Average: N.A.

Activity: FY 04, no activity anticipated.

HQ: same address as **14.157**. Phone: (202)708-2866. **Internet:** "www.hud.gov/offices//hsg/mfh/progdesc/progdesc.cfm".

14.165 MORTGAGE INSURANCE—HOMES—MILITARY IMPACTED AREAS ("Section 238(c)")

Assistance: guaranteed/insured loans (30-35 years).

Purposes: pursuant to NHA as amended, to insure loans for the purchase of existing, new, or to refinance one- to four-unit structures in areas impacted by military facilities. Small down payments are required, and mortgagors must pay certain closing costs. Funding for this program is included in **14.133**.

Eligible applicants/beneficiaries: purchasers in approved areas, intending to occupy the housing (*see NOTE preceding* **14.103**).

Range: same as for **14.117**.

Activity: FY 04, 607 loans insured.

HQ: none; all contacts are with Homeownership Centers at field offices listed in Part IV. **Internet:** "www.hud.gov80/progdesc/snglindx.cfm".

14.167 MORTGAGE INSURANCE—TWO YEAR OPERATING LOSS LOANS, SECTION 223(D)
("Two Year Operating Loss Loans")

Assistance: guaranteed/insured loans.

Purposes: pursuant to NHA as amended, to insure loans covering operating losses incurred during the first two years of occupancy of HUD-insured multifamily projects, and/or for any other two-year period within 10 years of project completion. Such loans may extend for the unexpired term of the original mortgage.

Eligible applicants/beneficiaries: owners of multifamily projects or facilities subject to a HUD-insured mortgage (*see NOTE preceding* **14.103**).

Range: 2-year loans, essentially to the maximum loss amount supported by debt service limitations; 10-year loans, 80 percent of unreimbursed funds invested; loans, $721,000 to $3,099,000. **Average:** loans, $1,900,000.

Activity: FY 04, 2 loans insured.

HQ: same as **14.112**.

14.168 LAND SALES—CERTAIN SUBDIVIDED LAND
("Interstate Land Sales Registration Program")

Assistance: technical information; investigation of complaints.

Purposes: pursuant to the Interstate Land Sales Full Disclosure Act as amended, to provide consumer protection in subdivision lot sales through enforcement of fraud prohibitions and full disclosure requirements. The law requires developers that engage in interstate land sales consisting of 100 or more nonexempt lots to register with HUD; prospective purchasers must be given a property report with pertinent facts about the development and the developer. Anti-fraud provisions of the act apply to subdivisions of 25 lots or more. Affected land developers are required to submit a filing in compliance with registration requirements. Lot purchasers are entitled to certain rights and remedies.

Eligible applicants/beneficiaries: lot purchasers.

Activity: FY 04 (representative), 531 filings processed, 436 annual reports, 46 exemption requests.

HQ: Office of RESPA and Interstate Land Sales, Housing-HUD, 451 Seventh St. SW - Rm.9154, Washington, DC 20410. Phone: (202)708-0502. **Internet:** "www.hud.gov/offices/hsg/sfh/ils/ilshome.cfm". (Note: no field offices for this program.)

14.169 HOUSING COUNSELING ASSISTANCE PROGRAM

Assistance: project grants.

Purposes: pursuant to the Housing and Urban Development Act of 1968 as amended, to provide counseling services to homeowners, homebuyers, and prospective tenants in HUD-assisted or -insured housing and other housing—toward the prevention and reduction of mortgage or rental delinquencies, defaults, and foreclosures.

Eligible applicants/beneficiaries: HUD-approved national, regional, multistate, or state agencies.

Range: $15,000 to local agencies to $3,400,000 to intermediaries. **Average:** $40,000 to local agencies, $1,100,000 to intermediaries.

Activity: grant activity not quantified specifically.

HQ: Program Support Division, Office of Insured Single Family Housing, Housing-HUD, 451 Seventh St. SW, Washington, DC 20410. Phone: (202) 708-0317. **Internet:** "www.hud.gov/offices/hsg/sfh/hcc/ hcc_home cfm".

14.171 MANUFACTURED HOME CONSTRUCTION AND SAFETY STANDARDS

Assistance: technical information; investigation of complaints.

Purposes: pursuant to the National Manufactured Housing Construction and Safety Standards Act as amended, to provide consumer protection for manufactured homes purchasers and residents, by enforcing standards covering safety, quality, durability, and installation—through certifications, testing, in-plant inspections, design review, and investigations of complaints against manufacturers or dealers. Siting and other local activity are considered to be under state or local jurisdiction, and are not covered by the program; however, model siting standards are under development; in the interim such work must meet at least minimum standards established by HUD.

Eligible applicants/beneficiaries: purchasers of manufactured homes built since June 15, 1976.

Activity: annually, 200,000 homes produced.

HQ: Office Manufactured Housing Programs, Office of Regulatory Affairs and Manufactured Housing, Housing-HUD - Rm.9164, Washington, DC 20410-8000. Phone: (202)708-6409, consumer hotline, (800)927-2891 (messages only), FAX (202)708-4213. **Internet:** "www.hud.gov/offices/hsg/sfh/mhs/mhshome.cfm"; e-mail, "mhs@hud.gov". (Note: no field offices for this program.)

14.172 MORTGAGE INSURANCE—GROWING EQUITY MORTGAGES ("GEMs" - "Section 245(a)")

Assistance: guaranteed/insured loans (varying term).

Purposes: pursuant to NHA as amended, to insure loans to purchase existing, new, or refinanced single-family housing including condominiums, with growing equity mortgages providing for a rapid principal reduction and shorter mortgage terms, by gradually increasing monthly payments over a 10-year period. Small down payments are required, and mortgagors must pay certain closing costs. Funding for this program is included in **14.117**.

Eligible applicants/beneficiaries: prospective purchasers (*see NOTE preceding* **14.103**).

Range: same as for **14.117**.

Activity: FY 02-05 estimate, no loans insured.

HQ: none; all contacts are with Homeownership Centers at field offices listed in Part IV. **Internet:** "www.hud.gov/progdesc/245a-df.cfm".

14.175 ADJUSTABLE RATE MORTGAGES ("ARMs" - "Section 251")

Assistance: guaranteed/insured loans (30 years).

Purposes: pursuant to NHA as amended and Housing and Urban-Rural Recovery Act of 1983, to insure loans with adjustable rate mortgages financing the purchase of new, existing, or refinanced one- to four-family housing including condominiums—offering lenders more assurance of long-term profitability than fixed rate mortgages. Interest rates may not increase more than one percent per year or five percent over the mortgage term. Small down payments are required, and mortgagors must pay certain closing costs. Funding for this program is included in **14.117**.

Eligible applicants/beneficiaries: prospective owner-occupants (*see NOTE preceding* **14.103**).

Range: same as for **14.117**.

Activity: FY 05 estimate, 140,000 loans insured.

HQ: none; all contacts are with Homeownership Centers at field offices listed in Part IV. **Internet:** "www.hud.gov/progdesc/251-df.cfm".

14.181 SUPPORTIVE HOUSING FOR PERSONS WITH DISABILITIES ("Section 811")

Assistance: direct payments/specified use (100 percent).

Purposes: pursuant to the National Affordable Housing Act and American Homeownership and Economic Opportunity Act of 2000, to provide capital advances to construct, acquire, or rehabilitate supportive housing for persons with disabilities, including group homes, for 40-year projects. Project Rental Assistance Contract payments may be obtained for 5-year periods (renewable), and may cover operating costs not met from project income; payments cover the difference between approved operating costs and tenant rental contributions of 30 percent of adjusted income.

Eligible applicants: "501(c)(3)" nonprofit corporations. Also, profit-motivated limited dividend organizations may participate in projects with mixed financing.

Eligible beneficiaries: very-low-income physically or developmentally disabled or chronically mentally ill persons, age 18 or older.

Range: $288,000 to $3,221,000. **Average:** $990,000.

Activity: FY 04, 1,379 units receiving rental assistance.

HQ: same address/phone as **14.157**. **Internet:** "www.hud.gov/progdesc/811main.cfm".

14.183 HOME EQUITY CONVERSION MORTGAGES ("Section 255")

Assistance: guaranteed/insured loans.

Purposes: pursuant to NHA as amended and Housing and Community Development Act of 1987, to insure "reverse mortgage" loans obtained by elderly homeowners to convert equity in their homes to monthly streams of income or (except in Texas) lines of credit. Eligible properties are one- to four-unit dwellings including condominiums and manufactured homes. Borrowers must pay loan origination charges and other fees. Funding for this program is included in **14.133**.

Eligible applicants/beneficiaries: homeowners at least age 62 (*see NOTE preceding* **14.103**).

Range: determined by calculating the limit of the principal, established by using a factor corresponding to the age of the borrower, the interest rate, and the value of the property.

Activity: FY 04, 38,000 units insured.

HQ: Director, Insured Family Development Division, Office of Single Family Housing, Housing-HUD, Washington, DC 20410. Phone: (202)708-2121. **Internet:** "www.hud.gov/progdesc/hecm-df.cfm".

14.184 MORTGAGE INSURANCE FOR SINGLE ROOM OCCUPANCY (SRO) PROJECTS
("Section 221(d) Single Room Occupancy")

Assistance: guaranteed/insured loans (90-100 percent/to 40 years).

Purposes: pursuant to NHA as amended, to insure loans for the construction or substantial rehabilitation of multifamily properties with at least five single-room occupancy residential units—intended to provide housing for tenants with income insufficient to enable them to rent a standard apartment. Projects may have no more than 10 percent of total gross floor space dedicated to commercial use (20 percent for substantial rehabilitation). Funding for this program is included in **14.133**.

Eligible applicants: nonprofit entities; builder-sellers with a nonprofit purchaser; limited-distribution, private profit, or public sponsors (*see NOTE preceding* **14.103**).

Eligible beneficiaries: anyone, subject to normal tenant selection procedures.

Range: 100 percent of replacement cost financing for nonprofits, 90 percent for others.

Activity: FY 03-04, no loans insured.

HQ: same as **14.112**.

14.188 HOUSING FINANCE AGENCIES (HFA) RISK SHARING
("Section 542(c) Risk Sharing Program")

Assistance: guaranteed/insured loans.

Purposes: pursuant to the Housing and Community Development Act of 1992 as amended, to provide HUD mortgage insurance to state and local housing finance agencies on affordable multifamily projects for which they share in the insurance risk. The program provides for HUD and HFAs to share between 10 and 90 percent of the financial risk.

Eligible applicants: state and local housing finance agencies.

Eligible beneficiaries: investors, builders, developers, public entities, private nonprofit corporations or associations. Applications are submitted to qualified housing finance agencies.

Range: $465,000 to $24,052,000 (for projects with 33 to 745 units). **Average:** 136 units.

Activity: FY 03, 71 projects with 9,649 total units insured.

HQ: same as **14.112**.

14.189 QUALIFIED PARTICIPATING ENTITIES (QPE) RISK SHARING ("Section 542(b) Risk Sharing Program")

Assistance: guaranteed/insured loans (50 percent).

Purposes: pursuant to the Housing and Community Development Act of 1992 as amended, for projects in which HUD provides reinsurance on multifamily housing projects whose loans covering affordable housing are originated, underwritten, serviced, and disposed of by QPEs or approved lenders. In the event of default, the QPE will pay all costs associated with loan disposition, 50 percent of which may be reimbursed by HUD.

Eligible applicants/beneficiaries: HUD-approved lenders and QPEs. Investors, builders, developers, public entities, private nonprofit corporations or associations submit applications to the lender.

Range: $1,800,000 to $6,600,000 (for projects with 64-133 units). **Average:** $3,500,000 (98 units).

Activity: FY 04, 41 loans insured with 5,526 total units.

HQ: same as **14.112**.

14.191 MULTIFAMILY HOUSING SERVICE COORDINATORS

Assistance: project grants (100 percent).

Purposes: pursuant to the National Affordable Housing Act and Housing and Community Development Act of 1992 as amended and American Homeownership and Economic Opportunity Act of 2000, to hire multifamily housing service coordinators—to link elderly, especially the frail and disabled, or disabled non-elderly, assisted-housing residents to community supportive or medical services; to prevent premature and unnecessary institutionalization; and, to assess individual service needs, determine eligibility for public services, and make resource allocation decisions enabling residents to remain in the community longer. Coordinators are social service staff persons providing such services as: formal case management; resident and management education; monitoring of services; and, resident advocacy. Project funds may not be used to pay coordinators to serve as recreational or activities director, nor to provide supportive services directly or perform administrative duties. Funding for this program is included in **14.157**.

Eligible applicants: owners of HUD-assisted housing projects, including in rural areas, that are under management and current in mortgage payments. Congregate Housing Service Programs, Section 202 Capital Advance, or Section 811 projects are ineligible.

Eligible beneficiaries: residents of approved projects, at least age 62 and frail (unable to perform at least three activities of daily living), disabled, or *at risk* (i.e., deficient in one or two activities of daily living).

Range: $27,000 to $381,000. **Average:** $155,000.

Activity: FY 04, 123 grants awarded to serve 14,000 units.

HQ: same address as **14.157**. Phone: (202)708-2866. **Internet:** "www.hud.gov/offices/hsg/mfh/scp/schome.cfm"; e-mail, "sercoor@hud.com".

14.195 SECTION 8 HOUSING ASSISTANCE PAYMENTS PROGRAM—SPECIAL ALLOCATIONS
("Project-based Section 8")

Assistance: direct payments/specified use (to 20 years).

Purposes: pursuant to the U.S. Housing Act of 1937, to reduce claims on HUD's insurance fund by aiding insured or Secretary-held projects mortgages with immediate or potentially serious financial difficulties. HUD makes payments to owners of assisted housing on behalf of tenants, representing the difference between the contract and tenant rent. Assistance is available only on a renewable basis; current projects receive a one-year renewal upon expiration of a Section 8 contract.

Eligible applicants/beneficiaries: only Section 8 project owners of record, with an expiring Section 8 contract. No funding is available to new applicants.

Range/Average: tenants pay no more than 30 percent or their adjusted monthly income for rent.

Activity: FY 04, 1,500,000 units assisted.

HQ: same address/phone as **14.157**. **Internet:** "www.hud.gov/fha/mfh/mfhsec8.html".

14.197 MULTIFAMILY ASSISTED HOUSING REFORM AND AFFORDABILITY ACT
("Market-to-Market")

Assistance: direct payments/specified use.

Purposes: pursuant to the Multifamily Assisted Housing and Affordability Act of 1997 as amended and Market-to-Market Extension Act of 2001, to retain affordable housing resources represented by existing FHA-insured Section 8 assisted housing, maintain such housing in good physical and financial condition, and reduce ongoing federal subsidies. HUD assists participating owners in restructuring their mortgages, and works with willing owners and lenders to reduce the Section 8 rents and operating expenses to true market levels, while providing for the project's capital improvement needs. Participating owners must commit to maintaining project affordability for 30 years.

Eligible applicants/beneficiaries: owners of FHA-insured project mortgages supported by Section 8 contracts, with rent levels exceeding comparable market rents.

Range: to the amount of the unpaid principal mortgage balance.

Activity: FY 04, assistance to 483 projects with 35,000 total units.

HQ: Director, Office of Multifamily Housing Assistance Restructuring, HUD,

1280 Maryland Ave. SW - Ste.4000, Washington, DC 20024. Phone: (202) 708-0001. **Internet:** "www.hud.gov/offices/omhar"; e-mail, "m2minfo@hud.gov".

14.198 OFFICER NEXT DOOR SALES PROGRAM

Assistance: sale, exchange, donation of property and goods.

Purposes: to improve security in HUD-designated revitalization areas, by providing 50 percent discounts to law enforcement officers purchasing homes in those neighborhoods. Officers must agree to occupy the homes as their sole residence for at least 3 years; if they do not, a proportion of the discount must be returned to HUD. Available homes are listed on the Internet; purchasers are selected by lottery when more than one officer indicates an interest in a property.

Eligible applicants/beneficiaries: federal, state, county, municipal, and academic institution law enforcement officers possessing general arrest powers. NOTE: CFDA August 2005 states (within program description for **14.310**) that Housing Notice 99-30 authorizing this program has expired; check with HUD about current program status.

Range: to 50 percent discount off list price.

Activity: FY 04, 569 properties sold.

HQ: Asset Management and Disposition Division, Housing-HUD, 451 Seventh St. SW, Washington, DC 20410. Phone: (202)708-1672. **Internet:** "www.hud.gov/offices/hsg/sfh/reo/ond.ond.cfm".

14.199 MULTIFAMILY PROPERTY DISPOSITION

Assistance: sale, exchange, donation of property and goods.

Purposes: pursuant to the National Housing Act and subsequent legislation, to provide for the sales of multifamily properties owned or held by HUD to new owners, with Section 8 contracts remaining in place. Properties may be: purchased by governmental entities or nonprofits without competition, or sold to others through bidding procedures; sold with tenant-based Section 8 vouchers (**14.871**) allowing tenants to remain on-site or to relocate; sold with up-front rehabilitation grants of the lesser of 50 percent of development costs or $40,000 per unit, provided the housing remains affordable for at least 20 years.

Eligible applicants/beneficiaries: governmental entities, private individuals, corporations, nonprofit organizations.

Range/Average: N.A.

Activity: annually, 50-125 HUD-owned projects sold.

HQ: Multifamily Housing Programs, Office of Asset Management, Housing-HUD, 451 Seventh St. SW - Rm. 6160, Washington, DC 20410. Phone: (202)708-0614, ext.2680. **Internet:** same as **14.103**.

14.218 COMMUNITY DEVELOPMENT BLOCK GRANTS/ENTITLEMENT GRANTS ("CDBG")

Assistance: formula grants (100 percent).

Purposes: pursuant to the Housing and Community Development Act of 1974 as amended, for a broad range of activities designed to result in decent housing and suitable living environments, neighborhood revitalization, economic development, and improved community facilities and services. Program policy requires that the "principal benefit" of projects be to low- and moderate-income persons—i.e., at least 70 percent of the grant allocation. Projects may be operated by the locality or through subgrantees, including public or nonprofit agencies, neighborhood-based organizations, local development corporations, small business investment companies, and other groups. Permitted uses of funds include: virtually any aspect of residential or nonresidential rehabilitation, including historic preservation and energy conservation; energy development; grants or loans to businesses; revolving loan funds for rehabilitation or for economic development purposes; real property acquisition; relocation of households or businesses; demolition; redevelopment site clearance and preparation for re-use; improvement or installation of public works; certain public service programs; housing code enforcement; meeting urgent community needs that present an immediate threat to health or welfare; city planning and related studies. Ineligible uses include: facilities for the general conduct of government; community-wide facilities; new housing construction; housing subsidies paid directly to occupants; income maintenance payments. Cities must: include citizen participation in program planning; have an approved comprehensive housing assistance plan. For "entitlement" communities CDBG grant amounts are based on a statutory formula.

Eligible applicants: cities in metropolitan areas with populations over 50,000; qualified urban counties of at least 200,000 (excluding the population in entitlement cities); and cities with populations under 50,000 that are central cities in Metropolitan Statistical Areas. NOTE: small cities obtain CDBG funds under **14.219** or **14.228**.

Eligible beneficiaries: low- and moderate-income residents, including those benefiting from projects sponsored by CDBG subgrantees or others awarded CDBG funds.

Range: N.A.

Activity: FY 05, 1,100 eligible local government units. *NOTE: CFDA 2005 states that the President's FY 06 budget requests no funding for this program in FY 06.*

HQ: Entitlement Communities Division, Office of Block Grant Assistance, CPD-HUD, 451 Seventh St. SW, Washington, DC 20410. Phone: (202)708-1577. **Internet:** "www.hud.gov/offices/cpd/indx.cfm".

14.219 COMMUNITY DEVELOPMENT BLOCK GRANTS/SMALL CITIES PROGRAM
("Small Cities")

Assistance: formula grants (100 percent).

Purposes: pursuant to the Housing and Community Development Act of 1974 as amended, to provide funding to small cities for the same purposes and eligible uses as for program **14.218**.

Eligible applicants: small cities only in the state of Hawaii; other small cities may obtain funding under **14.228**. ("Small cities" are defined as local government units including counties with populations under 50,000 and that are not central cities within metropolitan areas; there is no minimum population.)

Eligible beneficiaries: same as for **14.218**.

Range: $892,000 (Kauai County) to $2,672,000 (Hawaii County).

Activity: N.A. *NOTE: CFDA 2005 states that the President's FY 06 budget requests no funding for this program in FY 06.*

HQ: State and Small Cities Division, same address as **14.218**. Phone: (202) 708-1322. **Internet:** "www.hud.gov/offices/cpd/communitydevelopment/programs/smallcities/index.cfm".

14.225 COMMUNITY DEVELOPMENT BLOCK GRANTS/SPECIAL PURPOSE GRANTS/INSULAR AREAS

Assistance: project grants (formula based, 100 percent).

Purposes: pursuant to the Housing and Community Development Act of 1974 as amended, basically, the same as for program **14.218**.

Eligible applicants/beneficiaries: Samoa, Guam, Northern Marianas, VI.

Range: $1,022,000 (Samoa) to $2,764,000 (Guam).

Activity: N.A. NOTE: CFDA 2005 states that the President's FY 06 budget requests no funding for this program in FY 06.

HQ: Office of Block Grant Assistance, same address/phone as **14.219**. **Internet:** "www.hud.gov/offices/cpd/aboutcpd_programs.cfm/".

14.227 COMMUNITY DEVELOPMENT BLOCK GRANTS/TECHNICAL ASSISTANCE PROGRAM

Assistance: project grants (100 percent/1-3 years).

Purposes: pursuant to the Housing and Community Development Act of 1974 as amended, for technical assistance and training in planning and administering CDBG programs—through publications, training sessions, and consultations.

Eligible applicants/beneficiaries: states, general local government units, areawide planning organizations, educational institutions; certain national or regional nonprofit organizations; profit and nonprofit professional and technical services companies or firms.

Range: $10,000 to $369,000. **Average:** $60,000.

Activity: no funding FY 99-03; FY 04, assistance to 50 states and 986 CDBG entitlement communities.

HQ: Technical Assistance Division, CPD-HUD, 451 Seventh St. SW, Washington, DC 20410. Phone: (202)708-3176.

Internet: "www.hud.gov/offices/cpd/communitydevelopment/programs/index.cfm".

14.228 COMMUNITY DEVELOPMENT BLOCK GRANTS/STATE'S PROGRAM

Assistance: formula grants (100 percent).

Purposes: pursuant to the Housing and Community Development Act of 1974 as amended, to provide funding to states—to be granted, in turn, to small cities for uses permitted in program **14.218**.

Eligible applicants/beneficiaries: state governments electing to administer program **14.219**, or to leave program administration to HUD; all states except Hawaii have so elected. Funds must be distributed to units of general local government in non-entitlement areas, including counties, with populations under 50,000 and that are not central cities within metropolitan areas; there is no minimum population.

Range: $2,296,000 to $83,737,000. **Average:** $24,542,000.

Activity: FY 04, 17,000 total housing benefits and 36,000 jobs created. *NOTE: CFDA 2005 states that the President's FY 06 budget requests no funding for this program in FY 06.*

HQ: same address/phone as **14.219**. **Internet:** same as **14.225**.

14.231 EMERGENCY SHELTER GRANTS PROGRAM ("ESG")

Assistance: formula grants (50 percent/to 2 years).

Purposes: pursuant to the McKinney-Vento Homeless Assistance Act of 1987 (MVHAA) as amended, to improve existing or to develop additional emergency shelters, transitional housing, and homeless assistance programs. Funds may be used for: renovation, major rehabilitation, or conversion of existing buildings; essential social services; certain maintenance and operating costs; activities to prevent homelessness.

Eligible applicants/beneficiaries: states, metropolitan cities, urban counties, territories. Other local government units and nonprofit organizations apply to states for funds rather than to HUD. Grantees may, in turn, subcontract with nonprofit entities to conduct program activities.

Range: $80,000 to $8,144,000. **Average:** $431,000.

Activity: FY 05 estimate, 364 grants.

HQ: Deputy Director, Office of Special Needs Assistance Programs, CPD-HUD, 451 Seventh St. SW - Rm.7262, Washington, DC 20410. Phone: (202)708-4300. **Internet:** "www.hud.gov/offices/cpd/homeless/programs/esg/index.cfm".

14.235 SUPPORTIVE HOUSING PROGRAM

Assistance: project grants (from 50 percent/to 3 years).

Purposes: pursuant to MVHAA as amended, to develop transitional housing and supportive services to assist homeless persons in the transition from homelessness and to enable them to live as independently as possible. Funds support the following categories of projects: Transitional Housing, for a 24-month period and up to six months of follow-up services; Permanent Housing for Homeless Persons with Disabilities, to maximize participants' ability to live as independently as possible; Innovative Supportive Housing, to develop alternative methods of meeting the immediate and long-term needs of homeless individuals and families; Supportive Services for Homeless Persons Not in Conjunction with Supportive Housing; and, Safe Havens, for homeless persons with serious mental illness. Projects may include facilities acquisition and rehabilitation, limited new construction, operating costs and supportive services.

Eligible applicants/beneficiaries: state, local, and other governmental entities; private nonprofit organizations; public community mental health associations.

Range: acquisition/rehabilitation, to $200,000 ($400,000 in high-cost areas); new construction, to $400,000; to 75 percent of operating costs; leasing costs, to three years.

Activity: FY 04, 3,600 applications received.

HQ: same address/phone as **14.231**. **Internet:** "www.hud.gov/offices/cpd/homeless/programs/shp/index.cfm".

14.238 SHELTER PLUS CARE

Assistance: project grants (50 percent/5-10 years).

Purposes: pursuant to MVHAA as amended, to provide rental assistance in connection with supportive services available through other programs, to homeless persons with disabilities and their families—primarily those with serious mental illness, with substance addictions, or AIDS and related diseases. Four program components include: Tenant-based Rental Assistance (TRA); Sponsor-based Rental Assistance (SRA); Project-based Rental Assistance (PRA); Single Room Occupancy for Homeless Individuals (SRO). Grant funds must be matched by supportive services equal in value to the grant amount.

Eligible applicants/beneficiaries: states, local government units, public housing agencies.

Range: $14,000 to $3,900,000. **Average:** $405,000.

Activity: FY 04, 184 new, 610 renewal grants awarded.

HQ: same address/phone as **14.231**. **Internet:** "www.hud.gov/offices/cpd/homeless/index.cfm".

14.239 HOME INVESTMENT PARTNERSHIPS PROGRAM ("HOME Program")

Assistance: formula grants (67-75 percent/2-5 years).

Purposes: pursuant to the National Affordable Housing Act as amended, to support partnerships among all levels of government and the private sector, including profit and nonprofit organizations, in the production and operation of affordable housing, particularly rental housing for low- and very-low-income families. Funds may be used for: planning; development of model projects; technical assistance; housing rehabilitation; tenant-based rental assistance; assistance to homebuyers; new construction of housing; site acquisition and improvements including improved energy efficiency, demolition, relocation. As of FY 03, the American Dream Downpayment Initiative (ADDI) may provide funds for low-income families to make down payments on or to rehabilitate suitable housing. Ineligible funds uses include: public housing modernization; matching funds for other federal programs; rental housing operating subsidies; activities under the Low Income Housing Preservation Act, except for priority purchasers.

Eligible applicants: formula allocations—states, cities, urban counties, or consortia of general local government units; Insular Areas. Technical Assistance—nonprofit and profit firms; public purpose organizations; nonprofit national and regional HOME organizations; community housing development organizations (CHDOs).

Eligible beneficiaries: rental housing—90 percent of funds for families with incomes at 60 percent of area median, and the remainder for families below 80 percent. Homeownership assistance—families with incomes below 80 percent of the area median.

Range: $287,000 to $137,354,000; ADDI, $13,000 to $2,699,000. **Average:** $1,170,000.

Activity: cumulatively through FY 04, 552,000 units completed; 111,000 tenants received rental assistance.

HQ: Director, Office of Affordable Housing Programs, CPD-HUD, 451 Seventh St. SW - Rm.7164, Washington, DC 20410. Phone: (202)708-2470. **Internet:** "www.hud.gov/offices/cpd/affordablehousing/index.cfm".

14.241 HOUSING OPPORTUNITIES FOR PERSONS WITH AIDS ("HOPWA")

Assistance: formula grants; project grants (to 3 years).

Purposes: pursuant to the AIDS Housing Opportunity Act, to develop long-term comprehensive strategies to meet the housing needs of low-income persons with AIDS or related diseases, and their families. Eligible funds uses include: resource identification to establish, coordinate, and develop housing assistance; information services including counseling and referral; acquisition, rehabilitation, conversion, lease, and repair of facilities to provide housing and services; new construction of single-room occupancy and community residences; project- or tenant-based rental assistance including for shared housing arrangements; short-term rent, mortgage, and utility payments to prevent the homelessness of a tenant or mortgagor; supportive services including health, mental health, assessment, permanent housing placement, alcohol and drug abuse treatment and counseling, nutritional services, day care, intensive care; housing operating costs; training; technical assistance. Resident rent payments are required.

Eligible applicants/beneficiaries: entitlement (formula) grants—states and eligible metropolitan areas with the largest number of AIDS cases; communities in metropolitan areas must designate one unit of local government to serve as the applicant/grantee for the area. Competitive project grants—states, local governments, and nonprofit organizations for projects of national significance; states and localities not qualifying for formula grants.

Range: formula grants, $105,000 to $47,056,000; competitive, $299,000 to $1,370,000. **Average:** formula, $2,336,000; competitive, $916,000.

Activity: FY 05 estimate, housing assistance to 74,000 households.

HQ: Director, Office of HIV/AIDS Housing, CPD-HUD, 451 Seventh St. SW - Rm.7212, Washington, D.C. 20410. Phone: (202)708-1934, TTY (800) 877-8339. *Technical assistance,* AIDS Housing of Washington, 2014 E. Madison. - Ste.200, Seattle, WA 98122. Phone: (206)322-9444. **Internet:** "www.hud.gov/offices/cpd/aidshousing".

14.243 OPPORTUNITIES FOR YOUTH—YOUTHBUILD PROGRAM ("Youthbuild Program")

Assistance: project grants (100 percent/2.5 years).

Purposes: pursuant to the National Affordable Housing Act as amended and Housing and Community Development Act of 1992, to help economically disadvantaged high school dropouts obtain the education and employment skills necessary to achieve economic self-sufficiency, and to develop leadership skills and a commitment to community involvement in low-income communities; to provide on-site training in constructing or rehabilitating housing as a community service; to expand the supply of permanent affordable housing for homeless persons and for low- and very-low-income families. Project funds are intended to support: educational and supportive services including basic skills development, counseling, referral, and support services. Although the following are discouraged, funds may also be used for: architectural and engineering fees; housing acquisition, construction, rehabilitation; operating expenses, replacement reserves, and related costs.

Eligible applicants: public or private nonprofit agencies including community-based organizations, Job Training and Partnership Act agencies, community action agencies, state or local housing authorities, community development corporations, and other entities including states, local government units.

Eligible beneficiaries: very-low-income young adults age 16-24 that have dropped out of high school, with special emphasis on eligible young women. Up to 25 percent of project participants not meeting the foregoing criteria but requiring educational services may be allowed.

Range: $400,000 to $700,000. **Average:** $550,000.

Activity: FY 04, 3,896 youth participants, 373 new housing units constructed, 1,069 housing units rehabilitated.

HQ: Director, Grants Management Division, CPD-HUD, 451 Seventh St. SW - Rm.7149, Washington, D.C. 20410. Phone: (202)708-2035. **Internet:** "www.hud.gov/progdesc/cpdindx.cfm". (Note: no field offices for this program.)

14.244 EMPOWERMENT ZONES PROGRAM ("Empowerment Zones and Enterprise Communities")

Assistance: project grants (100 percent).

Purposes: pursuant to the Community Renewal Tax Relief Act of 2000, Taxpayer Relief Act of 1997, and other acts, to establish Empowerment Zones, Enterprise Communities, and Renewal Communities in urban and rural areas—to stimulate the creation of new jobs particularly for the disadvantaged and long-term unemployed and to promote revitalization of distressed areas. Areas designated in Round I receive Social Services Block Grant funds from HHS, special tax benefits to employers, and special consideration in obtaining funds under other federal programs; Round III communities and Renewal Communities receive tax incentives only.

Eligible applicants/beneficiaries: urban zones—basically, areas, including noncontiguous parcels meeting certain criteria, with 200,000 maximum population or the greater of 50,000 or 10 percent of the population of the most populous city, with pervasive poverty, unemployment, and general distress. Renewal Community criteria may differ slightly. Rural zones are defined by USDA (see **10.772**).

Range: FY 05 Round II Empowerment Zones, $661,000 each.

Activity: FY 02, 8 new urban Round III Empowerment Zones, 40 Renewal Communities designated.

HQ: RC/EZ/EC Office, CPD-HUD, Washington, DC 20410. Phone: (202)708-6339; *general information*, (800)998-9999. **Internet:** "www.hud.gov/cr".

14.246 COMMUNITY DEVELOPMENT BLOCK GRANTS/BROWNFIELDS ECONOMIC DEVELOPMENT INITIATIVE ("Section 108" - "BEDI")

Assistance: project grants (3-5 years).

Purposes: pursuant to the Housing and Community Development Act of 1974 as amended, to enhance the security of loans or improve the viability of projects financed under the Section 108 loan guarantee program (**14.248**)—including: commercial, industrial, and economic development revolving loan funds; qualified "brownfields" projects. Activities must be consistent with local CDBG plans and meet citizen participation requirements.

Eligible applicants/beneficiaries: local government units eligible under the Section 108 loan guarantee program.

Range: $290,000 to $2,000,000.

Activity: FY 04, 17 brownfields grants.

HQ: Economic Development Specialist, Office of Economic Development, CPD-HUD, 451 Seventh St. SW, Washington, DC 20410. Phone: (202)708-3484, ext.4445. **Internet:** "www.hud.gov/offices/cpd/economicdevelopment/programs/".

14.247 SELF-HELP HOMEOWNERSHIP OPPORTUNITY PROGRAM ("SHOP")

Assistance: project grants (2-3 years).

Purposes: pursuant to the Housing Opportunity Extension Act of 1996 as amended, for innovative projects enabling low-income families to become homeowners under the self-help concept, by contributing "sweat equity" toward the construction of dwellings. Program funds may be used for land acquisition and infrastructure improvements, with a maximum of 20 percent of grants for administrative costs.

Eligible applicants/beneficiaries: nonprofit national or regional organizations or consortia.

Range: $2,841,000 to $14,000,000; to $15,000 maximum per dwelling on average. **Average:** $8,947,000.

Activity: FY 04, 1,778 units completed, 3,200 under development.

HQ: same address as **14.239**. Phone: (202)708-2684. **Internet:** "www.hud.gov/progdesc/cpdindx.html". (Note: no field offices for this program.)

14.248 COMMUNITY DEVELOPMENT BLOCK GRANTS—SECTION 108 LOAN GUARANTEES ("Section 108")

Assistance: guaranteed/insured loans (to 20 years).

Purposes: pursuant to the Housing and Community Development Act of 1974 as amended, to provide communities with a source of financing for economic development, housing rehabilitation, public facilities, and large-scale physical development projects—provided the "principal benefit" of such projects: is to low- or moderate-income persons; aids in the elimination or prevention of slums and blight; or, meets urgent community needs. Maximum approvable loan amounts generally are five times the latest CDBG amount received by the public entity, minus any outstanding Section 108 commitment or principal balances.

Eligible applicants/beneficiaries: CDBG recipients. The public entity may be the borrower, or it may designate a public agency.

Range: $280,000 to $24,250,000. **Average:** $4,380,000.

Activity: FY 04 estimate, 74 loan commitments, generating some 13,000 jobs.

HQ: Financial Management Division, CPD-HUD, 451 Seventh St. SW - Rm.7180, Washington, DC 20410. Phone: (no number provided). **Internet:** "www.hud.gov/offices/cpd/communitydevelopment/programs/".

14.249 SECTION 8 MODERATE REHABILITATION SINGLE ROOM OCCUPANCY

Assistance: project grants (100 percent/11-year contracts).

Purposes: pursuant to MVHAA as amended, to provide rental assistance for homeless individuals to occupy single-room dwelling units rehabilitated under this program.

Eligible applicants/beneficiaries: local public housing agencies; private nonprofit organizations under contract with PHAs.

Range: $250,000 to $2,228,000. **Average:** $1,151,000.

Activity: cumulatively FY 98-04, 442 grants.

HQ: same address/phone as **14.231**. **Internet:** "www.hud.gov/offices/cpd/homeless/programs/sro/index.cfm".

14.250 RURAL HOUSING AND ECONOMIC DEVELOPMENT

Assistance: project grants (100 percent/3 years).

Purposes: to build capacity to expand the supply of affordable housing and access to economic opportunities in rural areas. Funds may support capacity building and innovative housing and economic development activities.

Eligible applicants/beneficiaries: local rural nonprofit organizations; community development corporations; tribes; state housing finance, community, and economic development agencies.

Range: $150,000 to $400,000. **Average:** $250,000.

Activity: FY 03, 1,475 jobs created, 6,980 persons trained, 275 new businesses assisted, 897 existing businesses assisted, 3,070 new housing units constructed, 2,995 existing housing units rehabilitated.

HQ: Office of Rural Housing and Economic Development, CPD-HUD, 451 Seventh St. SW - Rm.7137, Washington, D.C. 20410. Phone: (202)708-2290. **Internet:** same as **14.246**.

14.310 TEACHER NEXT DOOR INITIATIVE

Assistance: sale, exchange, donation of property and goods.

Purposes: to encourage and enable teachers to live in HUD-designated revitalization areas within the school districts in which they teach, by providing 50 percent discounts to teachers purchasing HUD-owned homes in those neighborhoods. Teachers must contract to occupy the homes as their sole residence for at least 36 months; if they do not, a proportion of the discount must be repaid to HUD. Available homes are listed on the Internet; purchasers are selected randomly.

Eligible applicants/beneficiaries: full-time public and private school grades K-12 teachers.

Range: to 50 percent discount off list price.

Activity: FY 04, 557 units sold.

HQ: same address/phone as **14.198**. **Internet:** "www.hud.gov/offices/hsg/sfh/reo/tnd.ond.cfm"; e-mail, "teacher_next_door@hud.gov".

14.311 SINGLE FAMILY PROPERTY DISPOSITION ("Good Neighbor Initiative")

Assistance: sale, exchange, donation of property and goods.

Purposes: pursuant to NHA as amended, to reduce the inventory of HUD-acquired properties, expand homeownership opportunities, and strengthen neighborhoods and communities, especially in revitalization areas established in consultation with local governments and nonprofit organizations, in urban or rural areas. Discounts of 30 percent off the list price are granted to sponsors in designated areas—and ten percent outside such areas. Ultimate eligible purchasers acquire and occupy one- to four-unit properties with low down payments, under the FHA Section 203(b) or 203(k) programs, and agree to rehabilitate the properties according to specified standards with funds included in the mortgage amount; generally, such loans include up to $5,000 placed in escrow, to improve the property to minimum standards. In addition, FHA may sell such homes to HUD contractors that, in turn, offer them to the general public. The collective "Good Neighbor Initiative" includes **14.198**, **14.310**, and the "Discount Sales to Nonprofits and Local Governments" and "$ HOME to Local Governments Sales" (**14.313**) programs. Funding for this program includes **14.313**.

Eligible applicants: local governments and nonprofit organizations; others on a competitive basis.

Eligible beneficiaries: purchasers meeting FHA requirements.

Range: local governments and nonprofit organizations, 10 to 30 percent discounts off list price.

Activity: FY 02, 60,000 homes sold.

HQ: same address/phone as **14.198**. **Internet:** "www.hud.gov/offices/hsg/sfh/reo/reo_home.cfm".

14.313 DOLLAR HOME SALES

Assistance: sale, exchange, or donation of property and goods.

Purposes: to expand HUD's partnership with local governments to foster housing opportunities for low- to moderate-income families. Under the program, FHA-foreclosed single-family homes, remaining unsold for at least six months, may be sold to local governments for $1.00 plus closing costs—and then sold or rented to low- to moderate-income families, first-time homebuyers, or groups that will use the homes to provide such services as child care, shelters, or job training centers. Funding for this program is included in **14.311**.

Eligible applicants/beneficiaries: local governments.

Range/Average: $50,000 in market value per home.

Activity: FY 04, 1,800 home sales.

HQ: same address/phone as **14.198**. **Internet:** "www.hud.gov/offices/hsg/sfh/reo/goodn/dhmaabout.cfm".

14.314 ASSISTED LIVING CONVERSION FOR ELIGIBLE MULTIFAMILY HOUSING PROJECTS ("ALCP")

Assistance: project grants.

Purposes: pursuant to the HUD Reform Act of 1989 and Housing Act of 1959 as amended, to enable owners of eligible elderly housing developments to convert some or all units in such facilities into Assisted Living Facilities (ALFs) serving frail elderly and disabled persons, designed to accommodate persons able to live independently but needing assistance with activities of daily living. ALFs must provide support services such as personal care, transportation, meals, housekeeping, and laundry. Funds may be used: for physical reconfiguration of individual units; to develop common, services, and administrative spaces, including central kitchens and dining areas, lounges, and recreation spaces; for necessary remodeling. Funding for the supportive services must be provided by the owners or borrowers, either directly or through a third party. Funding for this program is included in **14.157**.

Eligible applicants/beneficiaries: qualified private nonprofit owners of Section 202, 202/8, and 202 Project Rental Assistance Contracts, Section 515/8 projects; Section 236 projects, Section 221(d)(3) that have been in occupancy for at least 5 years; private nonprofit owners of certain unused or under-utilized commercial structures.

Range: $521,000 to $2,859,00. **Average:** $338,000.

Activity: FY 04, 232 units funded

HQ: Office of Grant Policy and Management, Housing-HUD, 451 Seventh St. SW - Rm.6138, Washington, DC 20410. Phone: (202)708-3000. **Internet:** "www.hud.gov/offices/hsg/mfh/progdesc/alcp.html".

14.400 EQUAL OPPORTUNITY IN HOUSING ("Fair Housing")

Assistance: investigation of complaints.

Purposes: pursuant to the Fair Housing Act, to enforce the protection of the right to choose housing suited to one's needs and financial ability, in areas where one chooses to live, without discrimination because of race, color, religion, sex, family status, handicap, or national origin, in the sale, lease, advertising, financing, or appraisal—including multifamily housing occupied after 13 March 1991, which must comply with accessibility guidelines. Complaints are investigated and conciliated; if discrimination is established and conciliation is unsuccessful, complainants receive legal representation in taking further legal action. Suits may be filed in a federal court, seeking injunctive relief and actual or punitive damages together with court costs and reasonable attorney fees. Litigation may be initiated by the individual, by HUD on behalf of the individual, or, under certain conditions, by the Attorney General. Technical assistance is available to attorneys, developers, real estate brokers, and the general public.

Eligible applicants/beneficiaries: aggrieved persons may file a complaint with HUD or with a HUD-approved state or local fair housing agency.

Activity: FY 04, 2,817 cases filed by HUD, 6,370 by state and local agencies; $11,955,000 in monetary relief obtained.

HQ: OFHEO-HUD, 451 Seventh St. SW - Rm.5226, Washington, DC 20410. Phone: (202)708-0836; *complaint lines*, (800)669-9777, TTY (800)927-9275. **Internet:** "www.hud.gov/complaints/housediscrm.cfm".

14.401 FAIR HOUSING ASSISTANCE PROGRAM—STATE AND LOCAL ("FHAP")

Assistance: project grants (100 percent).

Purposes: pursuant to the Fair Housing Act, for state and local complaint processing, technical assistance, training, education, outreach, data and information systems, special enforcement efforts, and for the National Fair Housing Training Academy—to handle complaints regarding violations of fair housing laws.

Eligible applicants/beneficiaries: state and local enforcement agencies administering state and local fair housing laws and ordinances certified by HUD as providing substantially equivalent rights and remedies as those provided by the Fair Housing Act.

Range/Average: capacity building, $120,000.

Activity: 103 jurisdictions funded.

HQ: Director, FHAP Support Division, OFHEO-HUD, 451 Seventh Street SW - Rm.5221, Washington, DC 20410. Phone: (202)708-2288, ext.7044. **Internet:** "www.hud.gov/offices/fheo/partners/FHAP/index.cfm".

14.402 NON-DISCRIMINATION IN FEDERALLY-ASSISTED PROGRAMS (ON THE BASIS OF AGE)

Assistance: investigation of complaints.

Purposes: pursuant to the Age Discrimination Act of 1975 as amended, to enforce the act prohibiting discrimination on the basis of age, in programs or activities receiving HUD financial assistance. Complaints are referred to FMCS; investigations are conducted by HUD if complaints cannot be mediated successfully.

Eligible applicants/beneficiaries: aggrieved persons may file a complaint with HUD. Complainants may file civil actions following exhaustion of administrative remedies.

Activity: FY 04, 6 complaints received.

HQ: OFHEO-HUD, 451 Seventh St. SW - Rm.5240, Washington, DC 20410. Phone: (202)708-2333, ext.7057. **Internet:** "www.hud.gov/prodesc/fheoindx.html".

14.404 NON-DISCRIMINATION IN FEDERALLY ASSISTED AND CONDUCTED PROGRAMS (ON THE BASIS OF DISABILITY) ("Section 504")

Assistance: investigation of complaints.

Purposes: pursuant Section 504 of the Rehabilitation Act of 1973 as amended, to enforce provisions of the act as it pertains to discrimination against persons with disabilities, in HUD programs except contracts of insurance and guaranty.

Eligible applicants/beneficiaries: aggrieved persons.

Activity: FY 04, 836 Section 504 complaints received, 504 compliance reviews initiated.

HQ: same as **14.402**.

14.405 NON-DISCRIMINATION IN FEDERALLY ASSISTED PROGRAMS (ON THE BASIS OF RACE, COLOR, OR NATIONAL ORIGIN) ("Title VI")

Assistance: investigation of complaints.

Purposes: pursuant to Title VI of CRA as amended, to enforce provisions prohibiting discrimination on the basis race, color, or national origin, as it pertains to HUD assistance programs except contracts of insurance and guaranty.

Eligible applicants/beneficiaries: aggrieved persons.

Activity: FY 04, 535 complaints received, 76 compliance reviews initiated.

HQ: OFHEO-HUD, 451 Seventh St. SW - Rm.5214, Washington, DC 20410. Phone: (202)619-8041, ext.6995. **Internet:** same as **14.402**.

14.406 NON-DISCRIMINATION IN THE COMMUNITY DEVELOPMENT BLOCK GRANT PROGRAM (ON THE BASIS OF RACE, COLOR, NATIONAL ORIGIN, RELIGION, OR SEX) ("Section 109")

Assistance: investigation of complaints.

Purposes: pursuant to Title I of the Housing and Community Development Act of 1974 as amended, to enforce all nondiscrimination provisions of the CDBG program, including employment, on the basis of race, color, national origin, religion, or sex.

Eligible applicants/beneficiaries: aggrieved persons.

Activity: FY 04, 70 complaints received, 109 compliance reviews initiated.

HQ: same as **14.405**.

14.407 ARCHITECTURAL BARRIERS ACT ENFORCEMENT
("Section 502 Architectural Barriers Act")

Assistance: investigation of complaints.

Purposes: pursuant to the Architectural Barriers Act of 1968 as amended, to assure that facilities assisted by the federal government are accessible to physically disabled persons, in programs involving HUD including its leased or owned facilities such as public housing.

Eligible applicants/beneficiaries: aggrieved persons. Complaints may be sent to HUD or to the Architectural and Transportation Barriers Compliance Board.

Activity: FY 04, 1 complaint received.

HQ: same address/phone as **14.402**. **Internet:** "www.hud.gov/sec8.html". (Note: no field offices for this program.)

14.408 FAIR HOUSING INITIATIVES PROGRAM
("FHIP")

Assistance: project grants (100 percent/to 5 years).

Purposes: pursuant to the Housing and Community Development Acts of 1987 and 1992 as amended, to develop, execute, or coordinate specialized programs or activities designed to obtain enforcement of the Fair Housing Act or state or local laws certified by HUD as providing substantially equivalent rights and remedies for discriminatory housing practices.

Eligible applicants/beneficiaries: experienced state and local fair housing agencies.

Range/Average: N.A.

Activity: FY 04, 106 grants to 42 states, DC, PR, and 93 cities.

HQ: Director, FIP/FHAP Support Division, OFHEO-HUD, 451 Seventh Street SW - Rm.5224, Washington, DC 20410. Phone: (202)708-2288, ext.7095. **Internet:** "www.hud.gov/offices/fheo/partners/FHIP/fhip.cfm".

14.412 EMPLOYMENT OPPORTUNITIES FOR LOWER INCOME PERSONS AND BUSINESSES
("Section 3")

Assistance: investigation of complaints.

Purposes: pursuant to the Housing and Urban Development Act of 1968, to enforce provisions requiring development of opportunities for job training and employment to lower-income residents in connection with HUD-funded projects in their neighborhoods—as well as for contract opportunities to local businesses. Section 3 also applies to financial assistance in the form of insurance or guaranty, or assistance to tenant-based organizations.

Eligible applicants/beneficiaries: aggrieved lower-income persons residing, or businesses located, in or substantially owned by persons residing in Section 3 areas.

Activity: FY 04, 34 complaints closed.

HQ: OFHEO-HUD, 451 Seventh Street SW - Rm.5222, Washington, DC 20410. Phone: (202)708-3633, ext.6949. **Internet:** "www.hud.gov/offices/fheo/section3/section3.cfm".

14.414 NON-DISCRIMINATION ON THE BASIS OF DISABILITY BY PUBLIC ENTITIES
("Title II of the ADA")

Assistance: investigation of complaints.

Purposes: to enforce the provisions of Title II of the Americans with Disabilities Act of 1990, prohibiting discrimination against persons with disabilities, in all programs, services, and regulatory activities relating to state and local government, public housing, and housing assistance and referral.

Eligible applicants/beneficiaries: aggrieved persons.

Activity: FY 04, 160 complaints received, 11 compliance reviews conducted.

HQ: same address/phone as **14.402**. **Internet:** "www.hud.gov/sec8.html".

14.415 NON-DISCRIMINATION ON THE BASIS OF SEX IN EDUCATION PROGRAMS AND ACTIVITIES RECEIVING FEDERAL FINANCIAL ASSISTANCE

Assistance: investigation of complaints.

Purposes: pursuant to Title IX of the Education Amendments Act of 1972 as amended, to investigate discrimination complaints on the basis of sex in HUD's education programs, including academic, research, training, employment, and related activities.

Eligible applicants/beneficiaries: aggrieved persons. Complaints may be filed on behalf of specific groups or individuals.

Activity: FY 00-04, no complaints received.

HQ: same address/phone as **14.405**. **Internet:** same as **14.402**.

14.506 GENERAL RESEARCH AND TECHNOLOGY ACTIVITY

Assistance: project grants.

Purposes: pursuant to the Housing Act of 1970 as amended, for research, demonstration, and program evaluation and monitoring, in such HUD program-related areas as national housing needs, advancing technology, government-sponsored enterprises, international activities, and urban economic development.

Eligible applicants/beneficiaries: researchers, research organizations, state and local governments, academic institutions, public and private profit and nonprofit organizations.

Range: $13,000 to $1,400,000.

Activity: not quantified specifically.

HQ: Budget, Contracts, and Program Control Division, OPDR-HUD, 451 Seventh St. SW, Washington, DC 20410. Phone: (202)708-1796. **Internet:** "www.huduser.org". (Note: no field offices for this program.)

14.511 COMMUNITY OUTREACH PARTNERSHIP CENTER PROGRAM

Assistance: project grants (outreach, 75 percent; research, 50 percent/3-5 years).

Purposes: pursuant to the Community Outreach Partnership Act of 1992 and Housing and Community Development Act of 1992, for partnerships among IHEs and communities to address urban problems through research, outreach, and exchange of information. Projects must focus on housing, economic development, neighborhood revitalization, infrastructure, health care, job training, education, crime prevention, planning, community organizing, and similar areas.

Eligible applicants/beneficiaries: IHEs.

Range: $200,000 to $400,000.

Activity: FY 04, 14 new grants, 7 renewals.

HQ: Office of University Partnerships, OPDR-HUD, 451 Seventh St. SW, Washington, DC 20410. Phone: (202)708-3061, ext.7495. **Internet:** "www.hud.gov"; "www.oup.org". (Note: no field offices for this program.)

14.512 COMMUNITY DEVELOPMENT WORK-STUDY PROGRAM

Assistance: project grants (100 percent/2 years).

Purposes: pursuant to the Housing and Community Development Acts of 1987 and 1974 as amended, for community development work-study programs for minority and economically disadvantaged college students. Students must be enrolled full-time in graduate programs in community and economic development, community or urban planning or management, public administration, urban economics, or related fields. Such fields as law, economics, psychology, education, or history are excluded.

Eligible applicants/beneficiaries: IHEs; states and areawide planning organizations for programs conducted by two or more IHEs.

Range/Average: to $150,000 for 5 students for two years.

Activity: annually, 120 students assisted.

HQ: same address, web site as **14.511**. Phone: (202)708-3061, ext.5969. (Note: no field offices for this program.)

14.514 HISPANIC-SERVING INSTITUTIONS ASSISTING COMMUNITIES

Assistance: project grants (100 percent/to 3 years).

Purposes: for Hispanic-serving IHEs to expand their activities in addressing community development needs in their localities, including neighborhood revitalization, housing, and economic development consistent with the purposes Title I of the Housing and Community Development Act of 1974.

Eligible applicants/beneficiaries: nonprofit IHEs meeting statutory requirements.

Range/Average: $600,000 per grantee.

Activity: FY 05 estimate, 12 grants.

HQ: same address, web site as **14.512**. Phone: (202)708-3061, ext.5939. **Internet:** "www.hud.gov/grants". (Note: no field offices for this program.)

14.515 ALASKA NATIVE/NATIVE HAWAIIAN INSTITUTIONS ASSISTING COMMUNITIES

Assistance: project grants (100 percent/to 3 years).

Purposes: for Alaska and Hawaii native IHEs to enhance their ability to address community development needs including neighborhood revitalization, housing, and economic development, consistent with Housing and Community Development Act of 1974 purposes.

Eligible applicants/beneficiaries: nonprofit Alaska and Hawaii native IHEs meeting statutory requirements.

Range/Average: $800,000 per grantee.

Activity: FY 05 estimate, 5 organizations to be funded.

HQ: same address, web site as **14.511**. Phone: (202)708-3061, ext.4200. (Note: no field offices for this program.)

14.516 DOCTORAL DISSERTATION RESEARCH GRANTS

Assistance: project grants (2 years).

Purposes: pursuant to the Housing and Community Development Act of 1970, to assist Ph.D. candidates in completing their research and dissertations on housing and urban development issues. Funds may be used for stipends, software, data purchases, travel, compensation for interviews—but not for tuition, computer hardware, or meals.

Eligible applicants/beneficiaries: graduate students with approved dissertation proposals, whose institutions provide support.

Range: to $25,000.

Activity: annually, 16 candidates assisted.

HQ: same address, web site as **14.511**. Phone: (202)708-3061, ext.3852. (Note: no field offices for this program.)

14.517 EARLY DOCTORAL STUDENT RESEARCH GRANTS

Assistance: project grants (100 percent/1 year).

Purposes: pursuant to the Housing and Community Development Act of 1970, to assist doctoral students in completing their research manuscripts on housing and urban development issues. Funds may be used for stipends, software, data purchases, travel, compensation for interviews—but not for tuition, computer hardware, or meals.

Eligible applicants/beneficiaries: doctoral candidates with: at least two completed graduate semesters or three terms; approved dissertation proposals; and, whose institutions provide support.

Range: to $15,000.

Activity: annually, 10 students assisted.

HQ: same as **14.516**. (Note: no field offices for this program.)

14.519 TRIBAL COLLEGES AND UNIVERSITIES PROGRAM

Assistance: project grants (100 percent/3 years).

Purposes: for tribal colleges and universities to build, expand, renovate, and equip their facilities.

Eligible applicants/beneficiaries: tribal IHEs.

Range/Average: $600,000.

Activity: not quantified specifically.

HQ: same as **14.514**. (Note: no field offices for this program.)

14.520 HISTORICALLY BLACK COLLEGES AND UNIVERSITIES PROGRAM

Assistance: project grants (100 percent/to 3 years).

Purposes: pursuant to the Housing and Community Development Act of 1974 as amended, to assist HBCUs in addressing community needs, including neighborhood revitalization, housing, and economic development.

Eligible applicants/beneficiaries: HBCUs.

Range: to $400,000 (new applicants); to $600,000 (previously funded applicants).

Activity: FY 04, 13 HBCUs received grants.

HQ: same address, web site as **14.511**. Phone: (202)708-3061, ext.4390, FAX (202)708-0309.

14.521 UNIVERSITIES REBUILDING AMERICA PROGRAM—COMMUNITY DESIGN

Assistance: project grants (100 percent/to 2 years).

Purposes: pursuant to the Housing and Community Development Act of 1974, for schools of architecture, urban planning and design, or construction to establish and operate partnerships with and for communities affected by Hurricanes Katrina or Rita or both, to: develop long-range neighborhood designs and plans addressing both reconstruction and future growth needs within a municipality or established neighborhoods; develop architectural design assessment and rehabilitation or reconstruction planning for housing and community amenities damaged or elimnated by the hurricanes to address resettlement needs. Activities must primarily benefit low- and moderate-income families.

Eligible applicants/beneficiaries: accredited IHEs granting two- or four-year degrees in architecture, urban planning and design, or construction.

Range: $100,000 to $300,000 for two years.

Activity: new program in FY 06.

HQ: same address, web sites as **14.511**. Phone: (202)708-3061, FAX (202)708-0309. (Note: no field offices for this program.)

14.850 PUBLIC AND INDIAN HOUSING

Assistance: direct payments/specified use.

Purposes: pursuant to the Housing Act of 1937 as amended, to support lower-income housing projects operated by local public housing agencies. For projects approved prior to 1 October 1986, HUD may award payments for up to 30 years (to 20 years for modernization) to meet debt service requirements that cannot be paid with rental revenue; for contracts executed after 1 October 1986, for up to 40 years. Operating subsidies may be used to achieve and maintain adequate operating and maintenance services and reserves. Localities make contributions through forgiveness of property taxes or payments in lieu of taxes (PILOTs). Note: development and reconstruction projects now are financed through **14.866**.

Eligible applicants: public housing agencies. (Note: per the Native American Housing Assistance and Self-Determination Act of 1996 (NAHASDA), Indian housing authorities now are ineligible.)

Eligible beneficiaries: lower-income families including families with or without children, the elderly and near-elderly, remaining members of a tenant family, certain single persons, the handicapped, and the displaced.

Range/Average: N.A.

Activity: FY 04, subsidies provided for 1,188,000 existing public housing units.

HQ: Assistant Secretary/Public and Indian Housing-HUD, Washington, DC 20410. Phone: (202)708-0950. **Internet:**
"www.hud.gov/progdesc/pihindx.html".

14.856 LOWER INCOME HOUSING ASSISTANCE PROGRAM—SECTION 8 MODERATE REHABILITATION
("Section 8 Housing Assistance Payments Program for Very Low Income Families - Moderate Rehabilitation")

Assistance: direct payments/specified use.

Purposes: pursuant to the Housing Act of 1937, Housing and Urban-Rural Recovery Act of 1983, Department of Housing and Urban Development Reform Act of 1989, Housing Opportunity Program Extension Act of 1996, Multifamily Assisted Housing Reform and Affordability Act of 1997, and other housing acts and amendments, to pay rent subsidies to property owners, covering the difference between very-low-income renters' adjusted family income and the market rent for moderately rehabilitated housing. Payments to owners may be made for up to 180 days, and extended for 12 months at a time. Families must pay toward the rent the highest of: 30 percent of their adjusted monthly family income; ten percent of gross monthly family income; or, the portion of welfare assistance designated for their monthly housing cost. The program is inactive; no new projects are being approved.

Eligible applicants/beneficiaries: state, county, municipal, or other authorized public housing agencies. Housing owners coordinate with HUD and/or local agencies to obtain the subsidies for their tenants.

Range/Average: N.A.

Activity: currently, 40,000 units available for occupancy or receiving subsidies, per CFDA August 2005.

HQ: Housing Voucher Management and Operations Division, Deputy Assistant Secretary/Housing and Voucher Programs, Public and Indian Housing-HUD, Washington, DC 20410. Phone: (202)708-0477. **Internet:** same as **14.850**.

14.862 INDIAN COMMUNITY DEVELOPMENT BLOCK GRANT PROGRAM

Assistance: project grants (100 percent/to 2 years).

Purposes: pursuant to the Housing and Community Development Act of 1974 as amended, basically, the same as for program **14.218**.

Eligible applicants/beneficiaries: any tribe, band, group, or nation, including Alaska Indians, Aleuts, and Eskimos, and any Alaskan native village eligible for assistance under the Indian Self-Determination and Education Assistance Act or, previously, under the Local Fiscal Assistance Act of 1972.

Range: $177,000 to $4,951,000. **Average:** $600,000.

Activity: FY 03, 124 awards.

HQ: Office of Native American Programs, Public and Indian Housing-HUD, Public and Indian Housing-HUD, 451 Seventh St. SW - Rm.4126, Washington, DC 20410. Phone: (202)401-7914. **Internet:** "www.hud.gov/offices/pih/ih/grants/icbdg.cfm".

14.865 PUBLIC AND INDIAN HOUSING—INDIAN LOAN GUARANTEE PROGRAM
("Loan Guarantees for Indian Housing")

Assistance: guaranteed/insured loans (to 30 years).

Purposes: pursuant to the Housing and Community Development Act of 1992 as amended, for native Americans and tribal organizations to acquire new, existing, or rehabilitated homes in Indian areas—using guaranteed mortgage loans available through private financial institutions. Such homes may be sold or rented to families. Individual applicant's total debts should not exceed 41 percent of income, including amount of loan.

Eligible applicants/beneficiaries: native Americans including Alaska natives, or tribes, TDHEs, and Indian housing authorities (*see NOTE preceding* **14.103**).

Range: to 97.75 percent of appraised value if over $50,000; to 98.75 percent if under $50,000. **Average:** $101,000.

Activity: cumulatively 1995-March 2005, 2,207 loans guaranteed.

HQ: Director, Office of Loan Guaranty, same address/phone (ext.4978) as **14.862**. **Internet:** "www.codetalk.fed.us/loan184.html". (Note: no field offices for this program.)

14.866 DEMOLITION AND REVITALIZATION OF SEVERELY DISTRESSED PUBLIC HOUSING
("HOPE VI")

Assistance: project grants (95 percent).

Purposes: pursuant to the U.S. Housing Act of 1937 as amended by the HOPE VI Program Reauthorization and Small Community Mainstreet Revitalization Housing Act of 2003, to revitalize severely distressed public housing through: demolition of obsolete projects or portions thereof; where appropriate, revitalization of demolition sites by reducing concentrations of very-low-income families. Grant funds may be used for community and supportive services programs, including: relocation of affected residents; disposition activities; rehabilitation of existing public housing units and community facilities. HOPE VI "Mainstreet" funds may be used to develop affordable housing in so-designated rejuvenation areas.

Eligible applicants/beneficiaries: public housing agencies that operate housing projects, not including agencies that administer only Section 8 programs.

Range: revitalization, $1,800,000 to $20,000,000; demolition-only, $60,000 to $4,800,000 ($6,000 per unit maximum). **Average:** revitalization, $17,700,000; demolition, $1,030,000.

Activity: FY 03 (cumulative totals), 35 planning, 193 revitalization, 218 demolition-only grants.

HQ: Office of Urban Revitalization, Deputy Assistant Secretary/Public Housing Investments, Public and Indian Housing- HUD, Washington, DC 20410. Phone: (202)401-8812. **Internet:** "www.hud.gov/offices/pih/programs/ph/hope6/".

14.867 INDIAN HOUSING BLOCK GRANTS

Assistance: formula grants (100 percent/2 years).

Purposes: pursuant to NAHASDA as amended, for affordable housing activities such as: Indian housing assistance; development; housing management services; crime prevention and safety; model activities.

Eligible applicants/beneficiaries: tribes or TDHEs.

Range: $25,000 to $88,388,000. **Average:** $1,663,000.

Activity: N.A.

HQ: same as **14.862**. **Internet:** "www.hud.gov/progdesc/ihbg1208.cfm".

14.869 TITLE VI FEDERAL GUARANTEES FOR FINANCING TRIBAL HOUSING ACTIVITIES

Assistance: guaranteed/insured loans (from 20 years).

Purposes: pursuant to NAHASDA, to assist tribes or TDHEs to obtain financing for affordable housing where an obligation cannot be completed without such guaranty. Assistance is limited to eligible affordable housing activities listed in Section 202 of the Act, including housing assistance, development, services, crime prevention and safety activities, model activities.

Eligible applicants/beneficiaries: approved recipients of program **14.867** funds.

Range: to five times the amount of program **14.867** funds received.

Activity: N.A.

HQ: Director, Economic Development Access Center, Office of Native American Programs, Public and Indian Housing-HUD, 451 Seventh St. SW - Rm.4126, Washington, DC 20410. Phone: (202)708-0614. **Internet:** "www.hud.gov/codetalk". (Note: no field offices for this program.)

14.870 RESIDENT OPPORTUNITY AND SUPPORTIVE SERVICES ("ROSS")

Assistance: project grants (some matching/3 years).

Purposes: pursuant to the U.S. Housing Act of 1937, to assist public housing residents through employment development and supportive services activities, including the employment of service coordinators or case managers. The primary focus is on "welfare to work," and on independent living for the elderly and disabled.

Eligible applicants/beneficiaries: public and Indian housing agencies, TDHEs, resident management corporations; resident councils or organizations in partnerships to leverage resources.

Range: $125,000 to $1,000,000.

Activity: annually, 323 grants.

HQ: Office of Public and Voucher Programs, Public and Indian Housing-HUD, 451 Seventh St. SW - Rm.4204, Washington, DC 20410. Phone: (202)708-1380; TDD (202)708-0850. **Internet:** same as **14.850**.

14.871 SECTION 8 HOUSING CHOICE VOUCHERS

Assistance: direct payments/specified use.

Purposes: pursuant to the Housing Act of 1937 as amended, Quality Housing and Work Responsibility Act of 1998, and other acts, to consolidate previous Section 8 rental assistance programs into a market-driven program, making tenant-based rental assistance available to low-income families and increasing their housing choices. Payments are made to participating owners, representing the difference between the local standard rent and 30 percent of the family's adjusted income.

Eligible applicants: entities qualifying as public housing agencies including certain public and nonprofit entities that administer Section 8 voucher programs.

Eligible beneficiaries: very low income families—i.e., with income not exceeding 50 percent of the area median); lower income families—i.e., with income not exceeding 80 percent of the area median. Criteria are adjusted for smaller or larger families. For Welfare-to-Work vouchers, families must also meet special Welfare-to-Work criteria.

Range: amount necessary to make housing assistance payments and cover related administrative expenses.

Activity: current estimate in CFDA August 2005, 2,000,000 vouchers in effect.

HQ: same address/phone as **14.856**. **Internet:** "www.hud.gov/offices/pih/programs/hcv/index.html".

14.872 PUBLIC HOUSING CAPITAL FUND ("CFP")

Assistance: formula grants (100 percent/to 4 years).

Purposes: pursuant to the U.S. Housing Act of 1937 as amended and Quality Housing and Work Responsibility Act of 1998, for public housing agencies to pay for their capital and management activities including public housing modernization and development.

Eligible applicants/beneficiaries: public housing agencies.

Range: $8,500 to $366,600,000. **Average:** $725,000.

Activity: not quantified.

HQ: same address/phone as **14.850**. **Internet:** "www.hud.gov/offices/pih/programs/ph/capfund/index.cfm".

14.873 NATIVE HAWAIIAN HOUSING BLOCK GRANTS

Assistance: project grants.

Purposes: pursuant to the Hawaiian Homelands Homeownership Act of 2000, to provide housing assistance to native Hawaiian families. Grants may support development, housing services, crime prevention and safety activities, and model activities

Eligible applicants: Hawaii Department of Native Hawaiian Home Lands.

Eligible beneficiaries: native Hawaiian families eligible to reside on the Hawaiian Home Lands.

Range/Average: N.A.

Activity: new program listing in 2003; FY 04, 1 grant awarded.

HQ: Office of Native American Programs, Public and Indian Housing-HUD, 500 Ala Moana Blvd. - Ste. 3A, Honolulu, HI 96813. Phone: (808)522-8175, ext.223. **Internet:** "www.hud.gov/codetalk". (Note: no other field offices for this program.)

14.874 LOAN GUARANTEES FOR NATIVE HAWAIIAN HOUSING ("Section 184A")

Assistance: guaranteed/insured loans (to 30 years).

Purposes: pursuant to the Hawaiian Homelands Homeownership Act of 2000 and Housing and Community Act of 1992, for Hawaii natives to construct, purchase, or rehabilitate one- to four-family housing located on Hawaiian Home Lands. Small down payments are required.

Eligible applicants/beneficiaries: native Hawaiian families; Department of Hawaiian Homes Lands; Office of Hawaiian Affairs; experienced private nonprofit organizations (*see NOTE preceding* **14.103**).

Range: N.A.

Activity: new program in 2004.

HQ: same as **14.873**. (Note: no other field offices for this program.)

14.875 PUBLIC HOUSING NEIGHBORHOOD NETWORK GRANTS

Assistance: project grants (75 percent/3 years).

Purposes: pursuant U.S. Housing Act of 1937, Section 9(d)(1)(E), for public housing authorities to establish community technology centers to provide internet access, job training, and other supportive services to public housing residents.

Eligible applicants/beneficiaries: public housing authorities.

Range: $150,000 to $600,000.

Activity: new program listing in 2005. FY 05 estimate, 70 awards.

HQ: Director, HOPE VI Community and Supportive Services, Public and Indian Housing-HUD, Washington, DC 20410. Phone: (202)401-8812, ext. 4258. **Internet:** "www.hud.gov/pih/programs/ph/ross/aboutnn.cfm". (Note: no field offices for this program.)

14.900 LEAD-BASED PAINT HAZARD CONTROL IN PRIVATELY-OWNED HOUSING

Assistance: project grants (90 percent/3 years).

Purposes: pursuant to the Housing and Community Development Act of 1992, for programs to identify and control lead-based paint hazards in housing owned by or rented to by low- or very-low-income families, and to prevent childhood lead poisoning caused by lead-based paint. Program objectives include: capacity building; integrating comprehensive community approaches; establishing public registries of lead-safe housing; promoting related job training and employment for low-income area residents. Projects must be conducted by certified contractors and inspectors.

Eligible applicants/beneficiaries: local general government units and tribes with a current, approved "Consolidated Plan."

Range: $1,000,000 to $3,000,000.

Activity: FY 04 estimate, 32-40 grants.

HQ: Director, Program Management and Assistance Division, Office of Lead Hazard Control-HUD, 451 Seventh St. SW - Rm.P-3206, Washington, DC 20410. Phone: *control grants,* (202)755-1785, ext.126; TTY (800)-877-8339. **Internet:** "www.hud.gov/offices/lead/". (Note: no field offices for this program.)

14.901 HEALTHY HOMES DEMONSTRATION GRANTS

Assistance: project grants (100 percent/to 3 years).

Purposes: pursuant to the Housing and Urban Development Act of 1970, to develop, demonstrate, and promote cost-effective preventive measures to correct multiple safety and health hazards particularly in low-income home environments, with special focus on children, through: (1) demonstration projects implementing housing assessment, maintenance, renovation, and construction techniques to identify and correct housing-related illness and injury risk factors; (2) outreach and education activities.

Eligible applicants/beneficiaries: nonprofit institutions, profit firms (operating without profit), state and local governments, tribes.

Range: $250,000 to $1,000,000. **Average:** $959,000.

Activity: FY 05 estimate, 4 to 6 grants.

HQ: same address, web site as **14.900**. Phone: (336)547-4002, ext.2067; TTY, (800)877-8339. (Note: no field offices for this program.)

14.902 LEAD TECHNICAL STUDIES GRANTS

Assistance: project grants (100 percent/3-4 years).

Purposes: pursuant to the Housing and Community Development Act of 1992, to improve methods for detecting and controlling lead-based paint and other residential health and safety hazards. Project examples: measuring lead in soil using portable X-ray fluorescence analyzers.

Eligible applicants/beneficiaries: same as for **14.901**; and, HBCUs for set-aside funds.

Range: $200,000 to $750,000.

Activity: new program listing in 2003. FY 04 estimate, 6-10 awards.

HQ: Office of Healthy Homes and Lead Hazard Control-HUD, 451 Seventh St. SW - Rm.P-3206, Washington, DC 20410. Phone: (202)755-1785, ext. 115; TTY (800)-877-8339. **Internet:** "www.hud.gov/offices/lead/techstudies/index.cfm". (Note: no field offices for this program.)

14.903 OPERATION LEAD ELIMINATION ACTION PROGRAM ("LEAP")

Assistance: project grants (100 percent/3 years).

Purposes: pursuant to the Housing and Community Development Act of 1992, to provide seed money to leverage private sector resources to eliminate lead poisoning as a major public health threat to young children, on both a preventive and remedial basis. Funds have been awarded to such organizations as the National Safety Council, Neighborhood Improvement Development Corporation, and Energy Program Consortium.

Eligible applicants/beneficiaries: tax exempt ("501(c)(3)"), other nonprofit or profit entities or firms, including IHEs. State and local governments are ineligible.

Range: to $2,000,000.

Activity: new program listing in 2003. 7 grants awarded to date per CFDA August 2005.

HQ: same as **14.900**. (Note: no field offices for this program.)

14.904 LEAD OUTREACH GRANTS

Assistance: project grants (100 percent/1-2 years).

Purposes: pursuant to the Housing and Community Development Act of 1992, to increase enrollment of low-income housing units for treatment via the HUD lead hazard control grant program or another lead treatment program; to develop and distribute outreach and educational materials to raise public awareness of childhood lead poisoning, its prevention and proper lead hazard identification and control methods among at-risk communities and populations of children and workers in the housing maintenance or rehabilitation fields; and, to encourage occupants to identify potential lead-based paint hazards and report them to property managers, and public health and/or housing officials, as appropriate.

Eligible applicants/beneficiaries: community-based organizations; states, tribes, and local government units. Partnerships are encouraged, including with educational institutions.

Range: $200,000 to $500,000.

Activity: 4-10 grants anticipated.

HQ: same as **14.900**. (Note: no field offices for this program.)

14.905 LEAD HAZARD REDUCTION DEMONSTRATION GRANT PROGRAM

Assistance: project grants (75 percent/3-4 years).

Purposes: pursuant to the Housing and Community Development Act of 1992, for areas with the highest lead paint abatement needs to undertake programs for abatement, inspections, risk assessments, temporary relocations, and interim control of lead-based hazards in eligible private-owned units and multifamily buildings that are occupied by low-income families. Projects must be conducted using certified contractors and inspectors, as well as workers trained through EPA authorized programs.

Eligible applicants/beneficiaries: states, local government units, tribes with approved Consolidated Plan; consortia.

Range: $2,000,000 to $4,000,000.

Activity: FY 04, 13 to 25 grants anticipated.

HQ: same as **14.901**. (Note: no field offices for this program.)

14.906 HEALTHY HOMES TECHNICAL STUDIES GRANTS

Assistance: project grants (100 percent/3-4 years).

Purposes: pursuant to the Housing and Urban Development Act of 1970, for technical studies to improve methods for detecting and controlling housing-related health and safety hazards.

Eligible applicants/beneficiaries: U.S. academic, nonprofit and profit (operating without profit) institutions; state, local governments; tribes.

Range: $250,000 to $1,000,000.

Activity: new program listing in 2004. FY 04 estimate, 2-8 awards.

HQ: same as **14.902**. (Note: no field offices for this program.)

DEPARTMENT OF THE INTERIOR

BUREAU OF INDIAN AFFAIRS

15.020 AID TO TRIBAL GOVERNMENTS

Assistance: direct payments/specified use.

Purposes: pursuant to the Indian Self-Determination and Education Assistance Act (ISDEAA) as amended, for general tribal government operations, to maintain up-to-date tribal enrollment records, to conduct tribal elections, and to develop tribal policies, legislation, and regulations.

Eligible applicants/beneficiaries: recognized tribal governments.

Range: $10,000 to $700,000. **Average:** $80,000.

Activity: not quantified specifically.

HQ: Deputy Director, Office of Tribal Services (MS-320 SIB), BIA-DOI, 1849 C St. NW, Washington, DC 20240. Phone: (202)513-7640. **Internet:** "www.

doi.gov/bia/tribegovserv/tribegov.htm"; "www.doi.gov/bureau-indian-affairs.html".

15.021 CONSOLIDATED TRIBAL GOVERNMENT PROGRAM

Assistance: direct payments/specified use.

Purposes: pursuant to ISDEAA as amended, to combine funding for certain ongoing programs into a single agreement, thus allowing greater flexibility in planning programs and lowering costs of administration—such as scholarships, adult education, job placement, and training.

Eligible applicants/beneficiaries: recognized tribal governments.

Range: $1,300 to $2,400,000. **Average:** $500,000.

Activity: not quantified specifically.

HQ: same as **15.020**.

15.022 TRIBAL SELF-GOVERNANCE

Assistance: direct payments/specified use.

Purposes: pursuant to ISDEAA as amended, for tribal law enforcement, social services, scholarships, welfare payments, housing improvement, road maintenance, and other programs previously administered by DOI—but not for the operation of educational institutions.

Eligible applicants/beneficiaries: recognized tribal governments and consortia.

Range: $330,000 to $9,000,000. **Average:** $6,000,000.

Activity: FY 05, 88 agreements covering 232 tribes.

HQ: Office of Self-Governance (MS-4618 MIB), BIA-OS-DOI, 1849 C St. NW, Washington, DC 20240. Phone: (202)219-0244. **Internet:** "www.doi.gov/bureau-indian-affairs.html".

15.024 INDIAN SELF-DETERMINATION CONTRACT SUPPORT ("Contract Support")

Assistance: direct payments/specified use.

Purposes: pursuant to ISDEAA as amended, to cover indirect costs incurred in administering federal programs.

Eligible applicants/beneficiaries: recognized tribal governments and authorized organizations.

Range: $10,000 to $8,000,000. **Average:** $190,000.

Activity: annually, 500 tribal governments and organizations funded.

HQ: same address/phone as **15.020**. **Internet:** "www.doi.gov/bia/self-determ/idc.htm".

15.025 SERVICES TO INDIAN CHILDREN, ELDERLY AND FAMILIES ("Social Services")

Assistance: direct payments/specified use.

Purposes: pursuant to the Snyder Act of 1921 and ISDEAA as amended, to administer welfare assistance programs for adults and children including foster care placement; to reduce substance abuse. Funds may support caseworkers and counselors, staffing and operation of emergency shelters, and similar costs.

Eligible applicants/beneficiaries: recognized tribal governments.

Range: $10,000 to $4,800,000. **Average:** $100,000.

Activity: not quantified specifically.

HQ: Chief, Division of Social Services (MS-320 SIB), BIA-DOI, 1849 C St. NW, Washington, DC 20240. Phone: (202)513-7642. **Internet:** "www.doi.gov/bia/childw-2.htm".

15.026 INDIAN ADULT EDUCATION

Assistance: direct payments/specified use.

Purposes: pursuant to the Snyder Act of 1921 and ISDEAA as amended, to provide Indian adult education courses, programs, and related activities promoting opportunities for productive employment.

Eligible applicants/beneficiaries: recognized tribal governments.

Range: $100 to $629,000. **Average:** $25,000.

Activity: annually, 140 tribes funded.

HQ: Office of Indian Education Programs (MS-3609 MIB), BIA-DOI, 1849 C St. NW, Washington, DC 20240. Phone: (202)208-3478. **Internet:** "www.oeip.bia.edu/contact.htm".

15.027 ASSISTANCE TO TRIBALLY CONTROLLED COMMUNITY COLLEGES AND UNIVERSITIES

Assistance: project grants (100 percent).

Purposes: pursuant to the Tribally Controlled Community College Assistance Act, to operate and improve tribally controlled community colleges, including expansion of their physical resources.

Eligible applicants/beneficiaries: nonprofit, nonsectarian colleges sponsored by recognized tribal governments and organizations, offering certificates or associate, baccalaureate, or graduate degrees.

Range: $213,000 to $11,118,000 (based on enrollment). **Average:** $2,080,000.

Activity: annually, 20,000 Indian students enrolled; 1,000 graduates.

HQ: same address/phone as **15.026**. **Internet:** "www.oeip.bia.edu".

15.028 TRIBALLY CONTROLLED COMMUNITY COLLEGE ENDOWMENTS

Assistance: project grants (50 percent).

Purposes: pursuant to the Tribally Controlled College Assistance Act, to establish endowments for tribally controlled community colleges. Interest earned may be used to defray college operating costs, but not to benefit private persons.

Eligible applicants/beneficiaries: colleges chartered by recognized tribes, offering certificates or associate, baccalaureate, or graduate degrees.

Range: $10,000 to $64,000. **Average:** $47,000.

Activity: annually, 25 colleges receive grants

HQ: same as **15.027**.

15.029 TRIBAL COURTS

Assistance: direct payments/specified use.

Purposes: pursuant to ISDEAA as amended, to operate judicial systems. Funds may support salaries and related expenses of judges, prosecutors, defenders, clerks, probation and juvenile officers, and other court personnel.

Eligible applicants/beneficiaries: recognized tribal governments.

Range: $15,000 to $800,000. **Average:** $50,000.

Activity: annually, 250 tribal systems and Courts of Indian Offenses funded, serving 40 tribes.

HQ: same address/phone as **15.020**. **Internet:** "www.doi.gov/bia/ots/otshome.htm".

15.030 INDIAN LAW ENFORCEMENT

Assistance: direct payments/specified use.

Purposes: pursuant to ISDEAA as amended and Indian Law Enforcement Reform Act, to operate tribal police departments and detention facilities. Funds may be used for salaries and related expenses of criminal investigators, uniformed officers, detention personnel, radio dispatchers, administrative costs.

Eligible applicants/beneficiaries: recognized tribal governments.

Range: $20,000 to $20,000,000. **Average:** $200,000.

Activity: annually, 200 tribes funded; 58 detention facilities operated.

HQ: Deputy Director, Law Enforcement Services, (MS-2429 MIB), BIA-DOI, 1849 C St. NW, Washington, DC 20240. Phone: (202)208-5787. **Internet:** "www.bialaw.fedworld.gov/".

15.031 INDIAN COMMUNITY FIRE PROTECTION

Assistance: direct payments/specified use.

Purposes: pursuant to ISDEAA as amended, for fire protection services when tribal governments do not receive support for such services from state or local governments. Funds may cover costs of staff, volunteer firefighters training, equipment purchases and repairs, and to purchase smoke detectors, fire extinguishers, fire escapes, and emergency lighting for public buildings.

Eligible applicants/beneficiaries: recognized tribal governments.

Range: $200 to $138,000. **Average:** $10,000.

Activity: annually, 40 tribal fire protection programs on reservations.

HQ: same address/phone as **15.020**. **Internet:** same as **15.029**.

15.032 INDIAN ECONOMIC DEVELOPMENT

Assistance: direct payments/specified use.

Purposes: pursuant to the Snyder Act of 1921, ISDEAA as amended, and other acts, to administer revolving loan and loan guaranty programs, including assistance to Indian-owned businesses in obtaining private financing—toward improvement of tribal economies. Administered programs may include BIA's Loan Guaranty and Insurance Fund, Indian Business Development Program, and Community and Economic Development Program.

Eligible applicants/beneficiaries: recognized tribal governments.

Range: $5,000 to $300,000. **Average:** $215,000.

Activity: not quantified specifically.

HQ: Deputy Assistant Secretary/Policy and Economic Development (MS-4071 MIB), BIA-DOI, 1849 C St. NW, Washington, DC 20240. Phone: (202)219-0005. **Internet:** "www.doi.gov/bia/ecodev/index.htm".

15.033 ROAD MAINTENANCE—INDIAN ROADS

Assistance: direct payments/specified use.

Purposes: pursuant to the Federal Highway Act of 1921 and ISDEAA as amended, for limited routine maintenance of roads, bridges, and airstrips serving Indian reservations, emphasizing school bus routes and arterial highways.

Eligible applicants/beneficiaries: recognized tribal governments and authorized organizations.

Range: $300 to $500,000. **Average:** $100,000.

Activity: annually, maintenance of 50,000 miles of roads, 745 bridges, and numerous airstrips, and operation of a ferry.

HQ: Division of Transportation, Office of Trust Responsibilities (MS-4058 MIB), BIA-DOI, 1849 C St. NW, Washington, DC 20240. Phone: (202)208-4359. **Internet:** "www.doi.gov/bia/otrhome.htm".

15.034 AGRICULTURE ON INDIAN LANDS

Assistance: direct payments/specified use; advisory services/counseling; specialized services.

Purposes: pursuant to ISDEAA as amended and American Indian Agriculture Resource Management Act, to protect and restore agronomic and rangeland resources on trust lands; to facilitate the development of renewable agricultural resources. Noxious weed eradication requires 50 percent local matching funds.

Eligible applicants/beneficiaries: recognized tribal governments and authorized organizations.

Range: $200 to $575,000; noxious weed eradication, $500 to $300,000. **Average:** $50,000; weed eradication, $20,000.

Activity: annually, 30,000 farmers, ranchers, and landowners assisted; 50 noxious weed eradication awards, treating 80,000 acres.

HQ: Branch of Agriculture and Range, Division of Water and Land Resources, Office of Trust Responsibilities (MS-4513 MIB), BIA-DOI, 1849 C St. NW, Washington, DC 20240. Phone: (202)208-3598. **Internet:** same as **15.033**.

15.035 FORESTRY ON INDIAN LANDS

Assistance: direct payments/specified use; advisory services/counseling; specialized services.

Purposes: pursuant to the Snyder Act of 1921, ISDEAA as amended, and other acts, to maintain, protect, enhance, and develop Indian forest resources.

Funds may be used for reforestation, commercial stand improvement, timber sales management, forest planning, and protection activities.

Eligible applicants/beneficiaries: recognized tribal governments and authorized organizations.

Range: $10,000 to $1,000,000. **Average:** $100,000.

Activity: to date, 122 management plans developed.

HQ: Division of Forestry, Office of Trust Responsibilities (MS-4513 MIB), BIA-DOI, 1849 C St. NW, Washington, DC 20240. Phone: (202)208-4837. **Internet:** "www.doi.gov/bia/otrhome.htm#Forests".

15.036 INDIAN RIGHTS PROTECTION

Assistance: direct payments/specified use.

Purposes: pursuant to ISDEAA as amended and other acts, to protect Indian rights guaranteed through treaty or statute, by obtaining the services or information needed by the federal government to litigate challenges to these rights. Project examples include research and data collection concerning water and land title disputes, hunting and fishing rights, environmental problems.

Eligible applicants/beneficiaries: recognized tribal governments and authorized organizations.

Range: $1,000 to $100,000. **Average:** $25,000.

Activity: not quantified specifically.

HQ: Office of Trust Responsibilities (MS-4510 MIB), BIA-DOI, 1849 C St. NW, Washington, DC 20240. Phone: (202)208-7737. **Internet:** "www.doi.gov/bia/Rightsprot.htm".

15.037 WATER RESOURCES ON INDIAN LANDS

Assistance: direct payments/specified use; advisory services/counseling; specialized services.

Purposes: pursuant to the Snyder Act of 1921 and ISDEAA as amended, to assist tribes in the management, planning, and development of their water and related land resources. Water Management, Planning, and Development funds are awarded competitively. Project examples: geographic, hydrologic quantitative and qualitative analysis of water, ground, surface water monitoring; aquifer classification and stream gauging.

Eligible applicants/beneficiaries: recognized tribal governments and authorized organizations.

Range: $50,000 to $1,000,000. **Average:** $50,000.

Activity: annually, 70 litigation and negotiation activities.

HQ: Division of Water and Land Resources, Office of Trust Responsibilities (MS-4513 MIB), BIA-DOI, 1849 C St. NW, Washington, DC 20240. Phone: (202)208-6042. **Internet:** same as **15.034**.

15.038 MINERALS AND MINING ON INDIAN LANDS

Assistance: direct payments/specified use; specialized services; technical information.

Purposes: pursuant to the Snyder Act of 1921, ISDEAA as amended, and other acts, to assist and support the inventory and development of energy and minerals on Indian lands. Funds may be used to inventory, develop, and produce nonrenewable resources. Mineral Assessment funds, awarded competitively, may be used for inventory programs and to develop baseline data. Project examples: feasibility studies; lease compliance; environmental reviews; training; seismic explorations; mapping systems.

Eligible applicants/beneficiaries: recognized tribal governments and authorized organizations.

Range: assessments, $25,000 to $150,000. **Average:** $75,000.

Activity: annually, 10-15 assessment projects funded.

HQ: Division of Energy and Minerals, Office of Trust Responsibilities, BIA-DOI, 12136 W. Bayaud Ave. - Ste.300, Lakewood, CO 80228. Phone: (303) 969-5270, ext.222. **Internet:** "www.doi.gov/bia/otrhome.htm#Energy". (Note: this field office serves as headquarters for this program.)

15.039 FISH, WILDLIFE, AND PARKS PROGRAMS ON INDIAN LANDS ("Wildlife and Parks")

Assistance: direct payments/specified use.

Purposes: pursuant to the Snyder Act of 1921 and ISDEAA as amended, to promote the conservation, development, and utilization of fish, wildlife, and recreational resources for sustenance, cultural enrichment, economic support, and maximum benefit of Indians. Tribes participate in resource planning and management with their state and federal counterparts. The program supports continuing activities; generally, no new projects are funded.

Eligible applicants/beneficiaries: recognized tribal governments and authorized organizations.

Range: $5,000 to $800,000; fish hatchery maintenance, $1,500 to $22,000. **Average:** hatcheries, $12,000.

Activity: annually, awards to 8 intertribal fish and wildlife commissions and authorities, 11 fish-producing tribes, 100 tribal fish hatcheries, 32 individual fish and wildlife resource tribes, 6 tribal fish and wildlife organizations.

HQ: Branch of Fish, Wildlife, and Recreation, Division of Water and Land Resources, Office of Trust Responsibilities (MS-3061 MIB), BIA-DOI, 1849 C St. NW, Washington, DC 20240. Phone: (202)208-4088. **Internet:** "www.doi.gov/bia/otrhome.htm#Fish".

15.040 REAL ESTATE PROGRAMS—INDIAN LANDS

Assistance: direct payments/specified use.

Purposes: pursuant to ISDEAA as amended, Indian Land Consolidation Act, and other acts, to provide real property management, counseling, and land use planning services to individual Indian allottees and tribal and Alaska native entities owning an interest in the almost 56,000,000 acres of trust land; to provide appraisal services required in processing land transactions; to protect and enhance the Indian leasehold estate by providing individual landowners and tribes with lease compliance activities.

Eligible applicants/beneficiaries: recognized tribal governments and authorized organizations; individual American Indians.

Range: services, $1,000 to $500,000; appraisals, $500 to $2,500; lease compliance, $250 to $30,000. **Average:** lease compliance, to $5,000.

Activity: cumulatively, 12,000 surface leases approved; 7,800 acquisitions, 4,000 land sales processed; 20,000 appraisals; 25,000 inspections completed on 100,000 leases.

HQ: Division of Real Estate Services, same address/phone as **15.036**. **Internet:** "www.doi.gov/bia/otrhome.htm#Land".

15.041 ENVIRONMENTAL MANAGEMENT—INDIAN PROGRAMS

Assistance: direct payments/specified use.

Purposes: pursuant to ISDEAA as amended, CERCLA, SWDA, RCRA, and other acts, to determine environmental impacts of federal projects on Indian lands and to identify hazardous waste sites—to determine compliance with the National Environmental Policy Act; to prepare Environmental Assessments; to obtain information for compliance with the National Historic Preservation Act and the Archeological Resources Protection Act.

Eligible applicants/beneficiaries: recognized tribal governments and authorized organizations.

Range: $5,000 to $250,000. **Average:** $25,000.

Activity: annually, 3,000 compliance issues addressed, 50 emergency responses.

HQ: Division of Environmental and Cultural Resources Management, Office of Trust Responsibilities (MS-4513 MIB), BIA-DOI, 1849 C St. NW, Washington, DC 20240. Phone: (202)208-5696. **Internet:** same as **15.022**.

15.042 INDIAN SCHOOL EQUALIZATION PROGRAM ("ISEP")

Assistance: direct payments/specified use.

Purposes: pursuant to ISDEAA as amended, Indian Education Amendments of 1978, and Tribally Controlled Schools Act, for primary and secondary education including residential programs for Indian students not served by public or sectarian schools.

Eligible applicants/beneficiaries: recognized tribes or tribal organizations currently served by a BIA-funded school.

Range: $120,000 to $7,091,000. **Average:** $1,700,000 per school.

Activity: annually, 30,000 students served by 122 tribally operated schools.

HQ: same address as **15.026**. Phone: (202)208-7658. **Internet:** same as **15.027**

15.043 INDIAN CHILD AND FAMILY EDUCATION ("Family and Child Education" - "FACE")

Assistance: project grants (100 percent); training.

Purposes: pursuant to the Indian Education Amendments of 1978, to conduct early childhood education, adult education, and parenting skills programs. Funds may not be used for administration costs.

Eligible applicants/beneficiaries: same as for **15.042**.

Range/Average: $250,000 per site.

Activity: annually, 1,800 children, 1,800 adults, and 1,700 families receive services.

HQ: Center for School Improvement, Office of Indian Education Programs, BIA-DOI, 500 Gold Ave. SW - 7th floor, Albuquerque, NM 87102. Phone: (505)248-7552. **Internet:** "www.oeip.bia.edu/sirc.htm". (Note: this field office serves as headquarters for this program.)

15.044 INDIAN SCHOOLS—STUDENT TRANSPORTATION

Assistance: direct payments/specified use.

Purposes: pursuant to ISDEAA as amended, Indian Education Amendments of 1978, and Tribally Controlled Schools Act, to provide round-trip transportation of students between home and schools.

Eligible applicants: same as for **15.042**.

Eligible beneficiaries: Indian children age 5 to 21, enrolled in schools eligible for assistance under **15.042**.

Range: $2,000 to $1,133,000. **Average:** $204,000.

Activity: annually, 20,000 students served.

HQ: same as **15.042**.

15.045 ASSISTANCE FOR INDIAN CHILDREN WITH SEVERE DISABILITIES ("Institutionalized Handicapped")

Assistance: direct payments/specified use.

Purposes: pursuant to ISDEAA as amended, Indian Education Amendments of 1978, and IDEA, for special education and related services to Indian children with severe disabilities, including: physical, occupational, and speech therapy; counseling; direct academic services; administration and staff development.

Eligible applicants/beneficiaries: members or direct descendants of members of recognized tribes, age 5 to 21, enrolled in BIA-funded schools, and determined to need specialized services available only in residential settings.

Range: $140 to $300 per day.

Activity: annually, institutional services to 170 students requiring 24-hours/day attention.

HQ: same address as **15.043**. Phone: (505)248-6942. **Internet:** "www.oeip.bia.edu/sped.htm".

15.046 ADMINISTRATIVE COST GRANTS FOR INDIAN SCHOOLS

Assistance: project grants (100 percent).

Purposes: pursuant to ISDEAA as amended, Indian Education Amendments of 1978, and Tribally Controlled Schools Act, to pay school operating costs including administration, property and procurement management, insurance, safety, and related expenses.

Eligible applicants/beneficiaries: recognized tribes or tribal organizations operating BIA-funded schools.

Range: $49,000 to $1,785,000. **Average:** $363,000.

Activity: annually, funding for 122 tribally operated schools.

HQ: same address/phone as **15.042**. **Internet:** "www.oeip.bia.edu/administration.htm".

15.047 INDIAN EDUCATION FACILITIES, OPERATIONS, AND MAINTENANCE

Assistance: direct payments/specified use.

Purposes: pursuant to ISDEAA as amended, Indian Education Amendments of 1978, and Tribally Controlled Schools Act, to pay facilities operations and maintenance costs including personnel, utilities, minor repairs, equipment, and similar costs.

Eligible applicants/beneficiaries: recognized tribal governments or organizations currently served by BIA-funded elementary or secondary schools or peripheral dormitories.

Range: $9,600 to $1,326,000. **Average:** $360,000.

Activity: annually, 100 schools funded.

HQ: same address as **15.043**. Phone: (505)346-6954. **Internet:** same as **15.027**.

15.048 BUREAU OF INDIAN AFFAIRS FACILITIES—OPERATIONS AND MAINTENANCE

Assistance: direct payments/specified use.

Purposes: pursuant to ISDEAA as amended, for basic operating and maintenance services provided to BIA-owned or -operated noneducation facilities, including expenses incurred for personnel, supplies, planning, utility costs, telecommunications equipment, and similar costs.

Eligible applicants/beneficiaries: recognized tribal governments with BIA-owned or -operated facilities on their reservations.

Range/Average: N.A.

Activity: annually, funding for 1,263 buildings, excluding quarters.

HQ: Director, Office of Facilities Management and Construction, BIA-DOI, 201 Third St. NW - Ste.500, P.O. Box 1248, Albuquerque, NM 87103. Phone: (505)346-6522. **Internet:** "www.doi.gov/bia/ofmc/om/htm".

15.049 IRRIGATION OPERATIONS AND MAINTENANCE ON INDIAN LANDS

Assistance: direct payments/specified use; specialized services; use of property, facilities, and equipment.

Purposes: pursuant to ISDEAA as amended, American Indian Agriculture Resource Management Act, Indian Dams Safety Act of 1994, and other acts, and other acts, to operate and maintain existing Indian irrigation projects and the Indian Dams Safety Maintenance Program.

Eligible applicants/beneficiaries: recognized tribal governments and authorized organizations.

Range: $8,000 to $3,000,000.

Activity: not quantified specifically.

HQ: Branch of Irrigation, Power, and Safety of Dams, Division of Water and Land Resources, Office of Trust Responsibilities (MS-4513 MIB), BIA-

DOI, 1849 C St. NW, Washington, DC 20240. Phone: (202)208-5480. **Internet:** same as **15.022**.

15.050 UNRESOLVED INDIAN HUNTING AND FISHING RIGHTS

Assistance: direct payments/specified use.

Purposes: pursuant to the Snyder Act of 1921 and ISDEAA as amended, to assist tribes in negotiations with other fish and wildlife resource management authorities in clarifying and defining their off-reservation hunting, fishing, and gathering rights.

Eligible applicants/beneficiaries: recognized tribal governments and authorized organizations.

Range: $50,000 to $320,000.

Activity: generally, only 1 competitive award annually, supporting 20 tribes.

HQ: same address/phone as **15.039**. **Internet:** same as **15.022**.

15.051 ENDANGERED SPECIES ON INDIAN LANDS

Assistance: direct payments/specified use; technical information; advisory services/counseling.

Purposes: pursuant to the Snyder Act of 1921, ISDEAA as amended, and the Endangered Species Act, to enable compliance with the Endangered Species Act, the Northern Spotted Owl Recovery Plan, and to implement the Cheyenne River Prairie Management Plan on Indian lands. Project examples: water impoundments, cross fencing and vegetative management; owl and habitat surveys.

Eligible applicants/beneficiaries: recognized tribal governments and authorized organizations whose reservations are inhabited by specific endangered species.

Range: $20,000 to $1,000,000. **Average:** $500,000.

Activity: annually, 12 tribes funded.

HQ: Branch of Environmental and Cultural Resources Management, same address/web site as **15.034**. Phone: (202)208-5037.

15.052 LITIGATION SUPPORT FOR INDIAN RIGHTS

Assistance: direct payments/specified use.

Purposes: pursuant to ISDEAA as amended, Indian Claims Limitation Act of 1982, and other acts, to establish or defend Indian property or treaty rights through judicial, administrative, or settlement actions. Funds may be used to pay for expert witnesses, research, data collection, technical support, and other evidence-gathering activities required to defend such rights issues as: hunting, fishing, and gathering; trespass; titles; allotment claims; mineral entry; Equal Access to Justice Act settlements.

Eligible applicants/beneficiaries: recognized tribal governments and authorized organizations.

Range: $2,000 to $220,000. **Average:** $76,000.

Activity: annually, 20-25 requests funded.

HQ: same address as **15.036**. Phone: (202)208-5831. **Internet:** same as **15.033**.

15.053 ATTORNEY FEES—INDIAN RIGHTS

Assistance: direct payments/specified use.

Purposes: pursuant to the Indian Claims Limitation Act of 1982 and other acts, to support tribes in protecting their treaty rights and other rights established through executive order or court action, by providing assistance in obtaining legal representation. Project examples: environmental damage claims; water rights negotiation or litigation; boundary disputes.

Eligible applicants/beneficiaries: recognized tribal governments.

Range: $20,000 to $237,000. **Average:** $60,000.

Activity: N.A.

HQ: same as **15.052**.

15.055 ALASKAN INDIAN ALLOTMENTS AND SUBSISTENCE PREFERENCE—ALASKA NATIONAL INTEREST LANDS CONSERVATION ACT ("ANILCA")

Assistance: direct payments/specified use.

Purposes: pursuant to the Indian Claims Limitation Act of 1982, Alaska National Interest Lands Conservation Act of 1980, ISDEAA as amended, and other acts, to assist Alaska natives in acquiring title to lands they occupy; to study past subsistence uses and conduct population studies on subsistence resources.

Eligible applicants/beneficiaries: recognized tribal governments in Alaska and authorized organizations; individual Alaska natives.

Range: allotments, $12,000 to $221,000; subsistence preferences, $15,000 to $40,000.

Activity: cumulatively, 9,000 parcels finalized, 2,800 parcels awaiting final action.

HQ: same address/phone as **15.052**. **Internet:** same as **15.022**.

15.057 NAVAJO-HOPI INDIAN SETTLEMENT PROGRAM

Assistance: direct payments/specified use.

Purposes: pursuant to the Navajo-Hopi Settlement Act and ISDEAA as amended, to restore the grazing potential of rangeland within the former Navajo/Hopi Joint Use Area, including: livestock monitoring; issuance of grazing permits; implementation of range management plans and grazing control methods; establishment of range units and grazing capacity; removal of trespass livestock on the Hopi Partitioned Lands; initiation of grazing control on the Navajo Partitioned Lands; natural resources restoration.

Eligible applicants/beneficiaries: recognized tribal governments of the Navajo and Hopi tribes and organizations authorized by either tribe.

Range: $5,000 to $150,000. **Average:** $75,000.

Activity: activities are ongoing.

HQ: Office of Trust Responsibilities (MS-3061 MIB), BIA-DOI, 1849 C St. NW, Washington, DC 20240. Phone: (202)208-6464. **Internet:** same as **15.022**.

15.058 INDIAN POST SECONDARY SCHOOLS ("Haskell Indian Nations University and Southwestern Indian Polytechnic Institute - "SIPI")

Assistance: training.

Purposes: pursuant to the Snyder Act of 1921, to enable American Indian students to attend either of the BIA-operated postsecondary schools with minimal charge for tuition or room and board: Haskell Indian Nations University and Southwestern Indian Polytechnic Institute (SIPI).

Eligible applicants/beneficiaries: members of recognized tribes.

Activity: annually, 900 students enrolled at Haskell, 174 graduates; 600 students enrolled at SIPI, 100 graduates.

HQ: Haskell Indian Nations University, 155 Indian Ave., Lawrence, KS 66046. Phone: (913)749-8454. *Or,* SIPI, 9169 Coors Rd. NW, Albuquerque, NM 81774. Phone: (505)346-2348. **Internet:** same as **15.027**; *and,* "www.Haskell.edu".

15.059 INDIAN GRADUATE STUDENT SCHOLARSHIPS ("Special Higher Education Scholarships")

Assistance: project grants.

Purposes: pursuant to the Snyder Act of 1921, to provide financial aid to Indian students, enabling them to obtain advanced degrees.

Eligible applicants/beneficiaries: Indian students that are members of recognized tribal governments, admitted to a graduate program.

Range: $250 to $4,000 annually. **Average:** $3,200.

Activity: annually, 325 students assisted.

HQ: American Indian Graduate Center, BIA-DOI, 4520 Montgomery Blvd. - Ste.1-B, Albuquerque, NM 87109. Phone: (505)881-4584. **Internet:** same as **15.026**. (Note: no other field offices for this program.)

15.060 INDIAN VOCATIONAL TRAINING—UNITED TRIBES TECHNICAL COLLEGE

Assistance: training; direct payments/unrestricted use.

Purposes: pursuant to the Snyder Act of 1921, ISDEAA as amended, and Indian Adult Vocational Training Act of 1956, to provide vocational training to American Indians through the United Tribes Technical College in Bismarck, North Dakota.

Eligible applicants: the United Tribes Technical College.

Eligible beneficiaries: members of recognized tribes, residing on or near reservations under BIA jurisdiction and needing financial assistance.

Range: $500 to $3,000. **Average:** $2,500.

Activity: annually, 160 students admitted.

HQ: Division of Job Placement and Training, Office of Self-Governance and Self-Determination (MS-2542 MIB), BIA-DOI, 1849 C St. NW, Washington, DC 20240. Phone: (202)219-5270. **Internet:** "www.united-tribes.tec.nd.us/".

15.061 INDIAN JOB PLACEMENT—UNITED SIOUX TRIBES DEVELOPMENT CORPORATION
("United Sioux Tribes")

Assistance: direct payments/specified use; advisory services/counseling.

Purposes: pursuant to the Snyder Act of 1921, ISDEAA as amended, and Indian Adult Vocational Training Act of 1956, to assist Indians in finding permanent employment through job development programs, counseling, and referrals to job training programs—through the United Sioux Tribes Development Corporation in Pierre, South Dakota. Participants receive stipends.

Eligible applicants: United Sioux Tribes Development Corporation.

Eligible beneficiaries: members of federally recognized tribes, residing on or near reservations under BIA jurisdiction.

Range: $500 to $1,200. **Average:** $1,000.

Activity: not quantified specifically.

HQ: Division of Job Placement and Training, Office of Economic Development (MS-2412 MIB), BIA-DOI, 1849 C St. NW, Washington, DC 20240. Phone: same as **15.060**. **Internet:** "www.doi.gov".

15.062 REPLACEMENT AND REPAIR OF INDIAN SCHOOLS

Assistance: direct payments/specified use.

Purposes: pursuant to ISDEAA and Tribally Controlled Schools Act of 1988 as amended, and Tribal Self-Governance Act of 1994, for advanced planning, design, and construction of major expansion or replacement projects or improvement and repair projects—involving BIA-owned or -funded education facilities for the direct support of primary and secondary schools and dormitories.

Eligible applicants/beneficiaries: recognized tribal governments and organizations, including school boards.

Range: expansion/replacement, $6,000,000 to $25,000,000; improvement/repair, to $7,000,000.

Activity: not quantified specifically.

HQ: same as **15.048**.

15.063 IMPROVEMENT AND REPAIR OF INDIAN DETENTION FACILITIES

Assistance: direct payments/specified use.

Purposes: pursuant to ISDEAA as amended and Tribal Self-Governance Act of 1994, for advanced planning, design, and construction, and improvements, repair, additions to, BIA adult or juvenile detention facilities.

Eligible applicants/beneficiaries: recognized tribal governments.

Range: to $1,000,000.

Activity: not quantified specifically.

HQ: Director, Office of Law Enforcement Services, P.O. Box 66, Albuquerque,

NM 87103. Phone: (505)248-7937. *Or* **15.048**. **Internet:** "www.doi.gov/bia/ofmc/cm/htm#3".

15.064 STRUCTURAL FIRE PROTECTION—BUREAU OF INDIAN AFFAIRS FACILITIES
("Fire Protection")

Assistance: direct payments/specified use.

Purposes: pursuant to ISDEAA and Tribally Controlled Schools Act of 1988 as amended, and the Tribal Self-Governance Act of 1994, to install fire protection and varied prevention equipment in schools, dormitories, detention centers, and other BIA facilities. Funds also may be used for personnel training, to conduct inventories, and to retrofit equipment.

Eligible applicants/beneficiaries: same as **15.062**.

Range: $5,000 to $250,000. **Average:** $120,000.

Activity: not quantified specifically.

HQ: Structural Fire Protection Program Manager, same address/phone as **15.048**. **Internet:** "www.doi.gov/bia/ofmc/sp/htm".

15.065 SAFETY OF DAMS ON INDIAN LANDS

Assistance: direct payments/specified use (100 percent/1-5 years).

Purposes: pursuant to the Snyder Act of 1921, ISDEAA as amended, and Indian Dams Safety Act of 1994, to improve the structural integrity of the 116 dams on Indian lands, for which BIA has responsibility, including inspection, hazard classification, and modification construction.

Eligible applicants/beneficiaries: recognized tribal governments and authorized organizations.

Range: design, $100,000 to $300,000; construction, $1,000,000 to $17,000,000.

Activity: FY 03, 4 final design completions.

HQ: same address/phone as **15.049**. **Internet:** same as **15.033**.

15.108 INDIAN EMPLOYMENT ASSISTANCE

Assistance: direct payments/specified use.

Purposes: pursuant to the Snyder Act of 1921, ISDEAA, Indian Adult Vocational Training Act, amendments, and other acts, for American Indians to obtain vocational training and employment opportunities. Funds may be used for subsistence, tuition, and related training costs. Payments may extend for up to two years—three years for registered nurses training.

Eligible applicants: federally recognized tribal governments and authorized organizations.

Eligible beneficiaries: unemployed or under-employed members of recognized tribes, residing on or near an Indian reservation under BIA jurisdiction.

Range: tribal awards, $7,000 to $350,000; individuals, $200 to $10,000 per year. **Average:** tribal, $46,000; individuals, $5,100.

Activity: annually, 175 tribal awards assisting 1,500 persons.

HQ: same address/phone as **15.061**. **Internet:** same as **15.032**.

15.113 INDIAN SOCIAL SERVICES—WELFARE ASSISTANCE

Assistance: direct payments/specified use.

Purposes: pursuant to the Snyder Act of 1921, for cash payments to needy Indians to pay for: food, clothing, shelter, etc.; adult nonmedical institutional or custodial care; foster home care; burial expenses; emergency assistance—when such assistance is unavailable from state or local public agencies. Extra benefits are provided when recipients are receiving general assistance and work under the Tribal Work Experience Program.

Eligible applicants/beneficiaries: needy members of recognized tribes, living on or near reservations.

Range: to several hundred dollars monthly.

Activity: monthly average of 41,000 persons receiving general assistance payments, 3,000 children receiving Indian Child Welfare Assistance, 1,100 disabled adults receiving nonmedical institutional or custodial care.

HQ: Deputy Director, Office of Tribal Services (MS-520 MIB), same address/phone, web site as **15.025**.

15.114 INDIAN EDUCATION—HIGHER EDUCATION GRANT PROGRAM

Assistance: project grants (100 percent/to 5 years).

Purposes: pursuant to the Snyder Act of 1921, to provide financial assistance to Indian undergraduate college students, supplementing aid packages awarded by colleges.

Eligible applicants/beneficiaries: recognized tribal governments and authorized organizations; members of tribes in financial need, enrolled in or accepted by an accredited college.

Range: $300 to $5,000. **Average:** $3,000.

Activity: annually, 9,800 students assisted.

HQ: same address/phone as **15.026**. **Internet:** "www.oeip.bia.edu/scholarships.htm".

15.124 INDIAN LOANS—ECONOMIC DEVELOPMENT ("Loan Guaranty Program")

Assistance: guaranteed/insured loans (to 90 percent/to 30 years).

Purposes: pursuant to the Snyder Act of 1921, ISDEAA as amended, and other acts, for economic development on or near federal Indian reservations, through projects on or near reservations, involving business, industry, or agriculture. Borrowers must have 20 percent equity in businesses being financed.

Eligible applicants/beneficiaries: recognized tribal governments and authorized organizations; individual American Indians.

Range: individuals and tribal enterprises, $2,500 to $500,000; tribes, $10,000 to $12,000,000. **Average:** individuals and tribal enterprises, $125,000; tribes, $1,500,000.

Activity: cumulatively, $385,000,000 in guaranteed loans awarded.

HQ: Office of Tribal Services (MS-320 SIB), BIA-DOI, 1849 C St. NW,

Washington, DC 20240. Phone: (202)513-7681. **Internet:** "www.doi.gov/bia/ecodev/loanpgm.html".

15.130 INDIAN EDUCATION—ASSISTANCE TO SCHOOLS ("Johnson-O'Malley")

Assistance: direct payments/specified use.

Purposes: pursuant to the Johnson-O'Malley Act of 1934 as amended and ISDEAA, for supplemental education programs for Indians in public schools. Project examples: home-school coordinators; remedial tutoring; educational field trips; cultural programs.

Eligible applicants: tribal organizations, Indian corporations, school districts, or states with eligible Indian Education Committees.

Eligible beneficiaries: children age 3 through grade 12, of one-fourth or more degree of Indian blood and descendants of members of recognized tribes—with priority to those residing on or near reservations.

Range: $700 to $4,359,000. **Average:** $72,000.

Activity: annually, 272,000 students in 33 states served.

HQ: same address/phone as **15.026**. **Internet:** "www.oeip.bia/edu/jom.htm".

15.141 INDIAN HOUSING ASSISTANCE

Assistance: project grants (100 percent); technical information.

Purposes: pursuant to ISDEAA as amended, for home improvements, for housing construction in certain situations, and for technical assistance in establishing housing plans. The HHS Indian Health Service may supplement this program by funding water and sanitary systems. Program is restricted to use within reservations and approved tribal service areas.

Eligible applicants/beneficiaries: recognized tribal governments and organizations; Indians needing Housing Improvement Program assistance.

Range: repairs/renovations, to $35,000; interim improvements, $2,500. **Average:** repairs, $18,000; new housing, $55,000.

Activity: annually, 500 families receive assistance.

HQ: same address/phone as **15.021**. **Internet:** "www.doi.gov/bia/tservices/hip/housing.htm".

15.144 INDIAN CHILD WELFARE ACT—TITLE II GRANTS

Assistance: project grants (100 percent).

Purposes: pursuant to the Indian Child Welfare Act, for the operation and maintenance of counseling programs and facilities related to child and family services, including: family assistance; protective day and after-school care; recreational activities; respite care; foster care subsidies; preparation and administration of child welfare codes, including legal representation; education and training; related services and programs.

Eligible applicants/beneficiaries: recognized tribal governments.

Range: $26,000 to $750,000. **Average:** $60,000.

Activity: annually, 27,000 referrals to 500 child abuse and neglect investigation programs.

HQ: same address/phone as **15.113**. **Internet:** same as **15.029**.

15.146 IRONWORKER TRAINING PROGRAM

Assistance: project grants (100 percent/to 12 weeks).

Purposes: pursuant to the Snyder Act of 1921 and the Indian Adult Vocational Training Act of 1956 as amended, to pay stipends to native Americans to permit them to obtain vocational training and apprenticeships as ironworkers at the National Ironworker Training Program in Broadview, Illinois, and to provide job placement assistance.

Eligible applicants/beneficiaries: American Indian members of recognized tribes, at least age 20, with a high school diploma or equivalent certificate, residing on or near an Indian reservation under BIA jurisdiction, and in good physical health.

Range/Average: $185/week.

Activity: cumulatively, 120 participants.

HQ: same address/phone as **15.061**. **Internet:** same as **15.032**.

15.147 TRIBAL COURTS—TRUST REFORM INITIATIVE

Assistance: project grants (formula-based).

Purposes: pursuant to ISDEAA as amended and the American Indian Trust Fund Management Reform Act of 1994, to supplement funds available to tribal governments assuming specific increased responsibilities such as: appointing guardians; determining competency; awarding child support from Indian Individual Money (IIM) accounts; determining paternity; sanctioning adoptions, marriages, and divorces; making presumptions of death; adjudicating claims involving trust assets. Funds may not be used for general operating costs.

Eligible applicants/beneficiaries: federally-recognized tribal governments.

Range: $3,000 to $216,000. **Average:** $50,000.

Activity: new program listing in 2003.

HQ: Office of Tribal Government Services (MS-320 SIB), BIA-DOI, 1849 C St. NW, Washington, DC 20240. same address as **15.124**. Phone: (202)513-7641. **Internet:** same as **15.029**.

BUREAU OF LAND MANAGEMENT

15.214 NON-SALE DISPOSALS OF MINERAL MATERIAL ("Free Use of Mineral Material")

Assistance: sale, exchange, or donation of property and goods.

Purposes: pursuant to the Materials Act of 1947 as amended, to grant free use permits to extract mineral material from BLM lands for use in public projects. Such material may not be bartered or sold.

Eligible applicants/beneficiaries: federal or state agencies, municipalities; nonprofit entities.

Activity: N.A.

HQ: Team Leader, Use Authorization Team, BLM-DOI, Washington, DC 20240. Phone: (202)452-0350. **Internet:** "www.blm.gov/nhp/index.htm".

15.222 COOPERATIVE INSPECTION AGREEMENTS WITH STATES AND TRIBES
("Section 202 Agreements")

Assistance: project grants (to 100 percent).

Purposes: pursuant to the Federal Oil and Gas Royalty Act of 1982, for inspections of oil and gas leases on Indian lands, by tribal inspectors.

Eligible applicants/beneficiaries: tribes with producing oil and gas leases on Indian lands for which the federal government has trust responsibility; states with tribal permission.

Range: $664 to $260,000. **Average:** $68,000.

Activity: to date, 4 inspection agreements; 655 inspections, 394 violations detected.

HQ: Assistant Director, Resource Use and Protection (300), BLM-DOI, Washington, DC 20240. Phone: (202)208-4201. **Internet:** same as **15.222**.

15.224 CULTURAL RESOURCE MANAGEMENT

Assistance: project grants (to 100 percent); sale, exchange, donation, of property or goods; use of property, facilities, and equipment; specialized services; advisory services/counseling; technical information; training; investigation of complaints.

Purposes: pursuant to the Federal Land Policy and Management Act, Archaeological Resources Protection Act, and National Historic Preservation Act of 1966 as amended, to manage and protect cultural resources on BLM lands, and to increase public awareness of the resources, mainly in western states and Alaska. Project example: universities conducting management-focused archaeological field schools and scholarly research.

Eligible applicants/beneficiaries: anyone.

Range: to $75,000. **Average:** $10,000.

Activity: 20 field schools participating; 7,000 new cultural properties identified; interpretive signing for 300 properties.

HQ: Group Administrator, Cultural and Recreation Group (WO 340), BLM-DOI, 1849 C St. NW, Washington, DC 20240. Phone: (202)452-0330. **Internet:** "www.blm.gov".

15.225 RECREATION RESOURCE MANAGEMENT

Assistance: project grants (cost sharing); use of property, facilities, and equipment; specialized services; advisory services/counseling; technical information; training.

Purposes: pursuant to the Federal Land Policy and Management Act, to manage and upgrade recreational resources and related facilities on BLM lands, mainly in western states and Alaska; for related public education. Project examples: promotion of effective cave management; Back Country Byways program; "watchable" wildlife and recreational fishing programs.

Eligible applicants/beneficiaries: anyone.

Range: $500 to $250,000. **Average:** $10,000.

Activity: not quantified specifically.

HQ: Manager, Recreation Group (WO 250), BLM-DOI, 1849 C St. NW - 204LS, Washington, DC 20240-9998. Phone: (202)452-5041. **Internet:** same as **15.214**.

15.226 PAYMENTS IN LIEU OF TAXES ("PILT")

Assistance: direct payments/unrestricted use; direct payments/restricted use.

Purposes: to compensate local governmental taxing units for the loss of taxes from federal lands. Funds may be used for any governmental purpose.

Eligible applicants/beneficiaries: local government units with eligible lands.

Range/Average: N.A.

Activity: N.A.

HQ: PILT Specialist, Office of Budget, BLM-DOI, 1849 C St. NW - Rm.4012, Washington, DC 20240. Phone: (202)208-3157. **Internet:** "www.blm.gov/budget/pilt". (Note: no field offices for this program.)

15.227 DISTRIBUTION OF RECEIPTS TO STATE AND LOCAL GOVERNMENTS ("Revenue Sharing, Public Lands and Resources")

Assistance: direct payments/specified use; direct payments/unrestricted use.

Purposes: pursuant to the Mineral Lands Leasing Act, Outer Continental Shelf Lands Act, Federal Land Policy and Management Act of 1976, Mineral Revenue Payments Clarification Act of 2000, amendments, and other acts, to share federal revenues from fees charged for sale or use of public lands, minerals, and vegetation. Payments are formula-based.

Eligible applicants/beneficiaries: same as for **15.226**.

Range/Average: N.A.

Activity: N.A.

HQ: Distribution of Receipts Specialist (BC-621), BLM-DOI, Bldg. 50, Denver Federal Center, Denver, CO 80225. Phone: (303)236-7135. **Internet:** same as **15.224**. (Note: no other field offices for this program.)

15.228 NATIONAL FIRE PLAN—WILDLAND URBAN INTERFACE COMMUNITY FIRE ASSISTANCE

Assistance: project grants (matching); use of property, facilities, and equipment; specialized services; advisory services/counseling; technical information; training.

Purposes: to implement the National Fire Plan and assist communities at risk from catastrophic wildland fires affecting BLM-managed lands, through community capability building including: assessment, planning, and mitigation activities; community and homeowner education and action; planning and implementation of hazardous fuels reduction including training, monitoring or maintenance; increasing the effectiveness of rural fire district protection; purchase of protective clothing and equipment.

Eligible applicants/beneficiaries: state and local governments, tribes, public and private education institutions, nonprofit organizations, rural fire departments serving communities under 10,000 population in the wildland/urban interface.

Range: $1,000 to $50,000.

Activity: not quantified specifically.

HQ: Chief, Community Protection and Assistance, Planning-Resources Group, National Interagency Fire Center (FA-130), BLM-DOI, 3833 S. Development Ave., Boise, ID 83705. Phone: (208)387-5150. **Internet:** "www.blm.gov/nhp/index.htm"; "www.nifc.gov". (Note: the field office serves as headquarters.)

15.229 WILD HORSE AND BURRO RESOURCE MANAGEMENT

Assistance: project grants (to 100 percent); use of property facilities, and equipment; advisory services/counseling; technical information; training.

Purposes: pursuant to Wild Free-Roaming Horse and Burros Act of 1971 and Federal Land Policy and Management Act, to manage and protect wild free-roaming horses and burros, toward achievement and maintenance of natural ecological balance on public lands. Funds may be used in research activities for improved census techniques and fertility control methods, and for adopting excess animals removed from the range. Project example: development of the National Wild Horse and Burro Foundation and its pertinent activities.

Eligible applicants/beneficiaries: anyone.

Range: partnership projects, $10,000 to $400,000. **Average:** $60,000.

Activity: new program listing in 2005 (CFDA on-line version).

HQ: Group Manager, Wild Horses and Burros Group (WO260), BLM, 1848 C St. NW - 402 LS, Washington, DC 20240-9998. Phone: (202)452-5073. **Internet:** "www.wildhorseandborro.blm.gov".

15.231 FISH, WILDLIFE AND PLANT CONSERVATION RESOURCE MANAGEMENT

Assistance: project grants (to 100 percent); use of property facilities, and equipment; advisory services/counseling; technical information; training.

Purposes: Federal Land Policy and Management Act of 1976, Endangered Species Act of 1973, Sikes Act, Fish and Wildlife Conservation and Water Resources Development Coordination Act, Oceans Act of 1992, Wyden Amendment, and other amendments, to manage fish, wildlife, and plant conservation resources on the public lands administered by BLM, and on certain other public or private lands. Funds may be used for activities involving protection, restoration, enhancement, and conservation, and to provide related public contact and education opportunities. Most projects are conducted by BLM staff; however, management partnerships are supported through challenge grants. No regular discretionary funding is available.

Eligible applicants/beneficiaries: anyone.

Range: $1,000 to $100,000. **Average:** $10,000.

Activity: new program listing in 2005 (CFDA on-line version).

HQ: Manager, Fish, Wildlife and Botany Group, (WO230), BLM, 1848 C St. NW - LSB 204, Washington, DC 20240-9998. Phone: (202)452-5133. **Internet:** "www.blm.gov/nhp/index.htm".

15.242 NATIONAL FIRE PLAN—RURAL FIRE ASSISTANCE

Assistance: project grants (matching); use of property, facilities, and equipment; specialized services; advisory services/counseling; technical information; training.

Purposes: to implement the National Fire Plan by increasing firefighter safety and enhancing the knowledge and fire protection capability of rural fire departments near BLM-managed lands, through: education and training, protective clothing and equipment purchases, public education.

Eligible applicants/beneficiaries: same as for **15.228**.

Range: $1,000 to $20,000. **Average:** $6,000.

Activity: new program listing in 2005. Annually, 1,200 rural fire departments assisted.

HQ: same address as **15.228**. Phone: National Interagency Fire Center, (208) 387-5169; Assistant Director, BIA Fire Operations, (208)387-5372; Fire Management Specialist, Fish and Wildlife Service, (208)387-5976; National Fire Operations Program Leader, National Park Service, (208)387-5226. **Internet:** "www.nifc.gov/rfa/index.html".

OFFICE OF SURFACE MINING RECLAMATION AND ENFORCEMENT

15.250 REGULATION OF SURFACE COAL MINING AND SURFACE EFFECTS OF UNDERGROUND COAL MINING

Assistance: project grants (50-100 percent/to 3 years); direct payments/specified use.

Purposes: pursuant to the Surface Mining Control and Reclamation Act of 1977, for regulatory activities to control surface impacts of coal mining. Grants may be used to develop state legislation, programs, and regulations, as well as for enforcement activities; also, to provide hydrologic and geologic data for small coal operators.

Eligible applicants/beneficiaries: state governors. Small coal mine operators (annual production under 300,000 tons) may apply for assistance in meeting technical permit application requirements.

Range: $104,000 to $12,578,000. **Average:** $2,384,000.

Activity: currently, 24 states receive grants.

HQ: Chief, Division of Regulatory Support, Office of Surface Mining Reclamation and Enforcement, DOI, 1951 Constitution Ave. NW, Washington, DC 20240. Phone: (202)208-2788. **Internet:** "www.osmre.gov/".

15.252 ABANDONED MINE LAND RECLAMATION (AMLR) PROGRAM

Assistance: formula grants; project grants (100 percent/to 3 years).

Purposes: pursuant to the Surface Mining Control and Reclamation Act of 1977, for reclamation projects to correct environmental damage caused or affected by coal and other mining and related processes on eligible lands and waters—occurring prior to 3 August 1977, and certain post-1977 lands and waters beginning 1 October 1991. Subsidence insurance grants, limited to $3,000,000, are also available to states to insure private property against damages caused by underground coal mining.

Eligible applicants/beneficiaries: states and tribes with eligible lands and coal mining operations, and paying reclamation fees.

Range: $101,000 to $30,321,000. **Average:** $5,874,000.

Activity: 23 states, 3 tribes with approved programs.

HQ: Chief, Division of Reclamation Support, same address/phone, web site as **15.250**.

15.253 NOT-FOR-PROFIT AMD RECLAMATION ("Acid Mining Drainage" - "AMD")

Assistance: project grants (100 percent/2 years).

Purposes: pursuant to the Surface Mining Control and Reclamation Act of 1977, for local acid mine drainage reclamation projects, especially in watershed areas, where lands and water were impacted by coal mining activities. Eligibility is limited to areas where mining and related damage occurred prior to 3 August 1977, and where there is no continuing state or federal legal responsibility.

Eligible applicants/beneficiaries: existing nonprofit organizations.

Range: $8,000 to $160,000.

Activity: not quantified specifically.

HQ: same as **15.252**.

15.254 SUMMER WATERSHED INTERN

Assistance: direct payments/specified use (12-24 weeks).

Purposes: pursuant to the Surface Mining Control and Reclamation Act of 1977, to hire summer interns to work on specified watershed projects toward the remediation of acid mine drainage. Funds may cover stipends and project expenses.

Eligible applicants: private and public nonprofit organizations and established watershed organizations in Alabama, Illinois, Indiana, Iowa, Kentucky, Maryland, Missouri, Ohio, Oklahoma, Pennsylvania, Tennessee, Virginia, West Virginia.

Eligible beneficiaries: undergraduate and graduate students.

Range/Average: $2,000 stipend per 12-week full-time internship, plus $500 for related expenses (part-time hires may extend award to 24 weeks).

Activity: FY 05, 22 interns placed.

HQ: same address/phone as **15.252**. **Internet:** "www.osmre.gov.acsi/intern-index.htm".

BUREAU OF RECLAMATION

15.504 WATER RECLAMATION AND REUSE PROGRAM

Assistance: formula grants (25 to 50 percent).

Purposes: pursuant to the Reclamation Wastewater and Groundwater Study and Facilities Act as amended other acts, for appraisals and feasibility studies (50 percent federal funding) on water reclamation and re-use projects, mainly in the western states; for research and demonstration programs and for construction of re-use projects (25 percent federal funding).

Eligible applicants/beneficiaries: projects—legally organized nonfederal entities such as irrigation districts, municipalities. Research—IHEs; architectural and engineering firms.

Range: to $20,000,000.

Activity: not quantified specifically.

HQ: Office of the Commissioner (D-5000), Bureau of Reclamation-DOI, Denver Federal Center, P.O. Box 25007, Denver, CO 80225. Phone: (303) 445-3710. **Internet:** "www.usbr.gov/pmts/writing/guidelines/". (Note: the field office serves as headquarters.)

15.506 WATER DESALINATION RESEARCH AND DEVELOPMENT PROGRAM ("Desal R& D Program")

Assistance: project grants (to 50 percent).

Purposes: pursuant to the Water Desalination Act of 1966, for water desalination studies, research, demonstrations, development projects, and related activities—to develop more cost-effective, technologically efficient, and implementable methods of producing usable water from saline or otherwise contaminated water.

Eligible applicants/beneficiaries: individuals, academic institutions, commercial and industrial organizations; other profit, nonprofit and public entities including state, local, and tribal governments.

Range: $20,000 to $150,000. **Average:** $85,000.

Activity: FY 02, 6 awards.

HQ: Water Treatment Engineering and Research Group, Bureau of Reclamation-DOI, Federal Center (D-8230), P.O. Box 25007, Denver, CO 80225. Phone: *technical information (MC D-8230),* (303)445-2260, FAX (303)445-6329; *solicitation documents,* Acquisitions Operations Group (MC D-7810), (303)445-2432, FAX (303)445-6345. **Internet:** "www.usbr.gov/water/desal.html". (Note: no other field offices for this program.)

15.507 WATER 2025 ("Water 2025 Challenge Grant Program")

Assistance: project grants (50-100 percent/from 2 years).

Purposes: to prevent crisis and conflict over water in western United States through projects (50 percent funding) that will conserve water, increase water use efficiency, or enhance water management—using advanced technology, improvements to existing facilities, and water banks and markets. Up to 100 percent funding may be available for water use efficiency research.

Eligible applicants/beneficiaries: projects—irrigation or water districts in the western U.S. Research grants—IHEs and nonprofit institutions.

Range: challenge grants, $19,000 to $300,000. **Average:** $140,000; research, $1,000,000.

Activity: new program listing in 2005 (CFDA on-line version). FY 04, 19 awards.

HQ: Office of Program & Policy Services (D-5500), Bureau of Reclamation-DOI, Federal Center, P.O. Box 25007, Denver, CO 80225. Phone: (303)445-2906, FAX (303)445-6683. **Internet:** "www.doi.gov/water2025/". (Note: no other field offices for this program.)

15.508 PROVIDING WATER TO AT-RISK NATURAL DESERT TERMINAL LAKES ("Desert Terminal Lakes")

Assistance: project grants.

Purposes: pursuant to FSRIA and appropriations acts, for activities to provide water only to Walker Lake, Pyramid Lake, and Summit Lake in Nevada.

Eligible applicants/beneficiaries: state and local public agencies, tribes, nonprofit organizations, individuals.

Range/Average: N.A.

Activity: new program listing in 2005 (CFDA on-line version). FY 04, 6 awards.

HQ: *technical program information,* Lahontan Basin Area Office, Bureau of Reclamation-DOI, 705 N. Plaza St. - Rm.320, Carson City, NV 89701-4015. Phone: (775)882-3436. *Acquisition services,* Mid-Pacific Regional Office, Bureau of Reclamation-DOI, 2800 Cottage Way - Rm.E-1815, Sacramento, CA 95825-1898. Phone: (916)978-5130, FAX (916)978-5175, -5182. **Internet:** "www.usbr.gov". (Note: the field offices serve as headquarters.)

U.S. FISH AND WILDLIFE SERVICE

15.602 CONSERVATION LAW ENFORCEMENT TRAINING ASSISTANCE

Assistance: training.

Purposes: pursuant to the Fish and Wildlife Coordination Act of 1958 and Fish and Wildlife Improvement Act of 1978, for state conservation officer training in criminal law and in principles, techniques, and procedures of wildlife law enforcement.

Eligible applicants/beneficiaries: state agencies.

Activity: not quantified specifically.

HQ: Assistant Director, Office of Law Enforcement, FWS-DOI, 4401 N.

Fairfax Dr. - Rm.520, Arlington, VA 22203. Phone: (703)358-1949. **Internet:** "www.le.fws.gov".

15.605 SPORT FISH RESTORATION
("Dingell-Johnson Program" - "D-J Program")

Assistance: formula grants (to 75 percent/2 years).

Purposes: pursuant to the Federal Aid in Sport Fish Restoration Act of 1950 as amended, to restore, conserve, manage, or enhance sport fish populations for the preservation and improvement of sport fishing and related uses of fisheries resources. Funds may be used for acquisition of boating access to public waters, fresh water fish habitat improvement, lake and stream rehabilitation, research, operations and maintenance, similar uses.

Eligible applicants/beneficiaries: fish and wildlife agencies in states with laws prohibiting diversion of revenues from fishing licenses to uses other than administration of the agency; territories.

Range: $900,000 to $13,600,000. **Average:** $4,800,000.

Activity: not quantified specifically.

HQ: Sport Fish Restoration Program Coordinator, Division of Federal Aid (MS MBSP-4020), FWS-DOI, 4401 N. Fairfax Dr., Arlington, VA 22203. Phone: (703)358-2156, FAX (703)358-1837. **Internet:** "www.fa.r9.fws.gov".

15.608 FISH AND WILDLIFE MANAGEMENT ASSISTANCE

Assistance: specialized services.

Purposes: pursuant to the Fish and Wildlife Act of 1956 and Sikes Act of 1974 as amended, Fish and Wildlife Coordination Act of 1958, and other acts, for: conservation and management of fish and wildlife resources, based on biological, chemical, and physical examinations of land and waters; stocking of fishes from national fish hatcheries; co-management by Alaska natives of marine mammals for subsistence use. Services are provided on a cost recoverable basis.

Eligible applicants/beneficiaries: state agencies, local governments, native American organizations, public nonprofit and other organizations, federal agencies.

Activity: assistance to 100 native American tribes, 254 national wildlife refuges, 150 DOD installations.

HQ: Chief, Division of Fish and Wildlife Management and Habitat Restoration, FWS-DOI, ARLSQ - Rm.840, Washington, DC 20240. Phone: (703)358-1718. **Internet:** "www.fisheries.fws.gov".

15.611 WILDLIFE RESTORATION
("Pittman-Robertson Program" - "P-R Program")

Assistance: formula grants (to 75 percent/2 years).

Purposes: pursuant to the Federal Aid in Wildlife Restoration Act of 1937 as amended, to restore or manage wildlife populations and to provide facilities and services for hunter safety programs. Funds may be used for land acquisition, development, research, and coordination.

Eligible applicants/beneficiaries: fish and wildlife agencies in states with laws prohibiting diversion of hunting license revenues to uses other than administration of the agency; territories.

Range: $268,000 to $7,187,000. **Average:** $2,750,000.

Activity: not quantified specifically.

HQ: Chief, Division of Federal Aid, FWS-DOI, 1849 C St. NW, Washington, DC 20240. Same phone, web site as **15.605**.

15.614 COASTAL WETLANDS PLANNING, PROTECTION AND RESTORATION ACT
("National Coastal Wetlands Conservation Grants")

Assistance: project grants (50-75 percent).

Purposes: pursuant to the act, for coastal wetlands conservation projects. Funds may be used to acquire interests in lands or waters, and for restoration, enhancement, or management of coastal wetlands ecosystems, including conservation of fish and wildlife.

Eligible applicants/beneficiaries: states bordering the Atlantic, Pacific, Great Lakes, or Gulf coasts (except Louisiana); territories and possessions.

Range: $75,000 to $1,000,000. **Average:** $753,000.

Activity: FY 04 estimate, 18,000 acres acquired or restored.

HQ: Program Coordinator, same address/phone as **15.605** or **15.608**. **Internet:** "www.r9.fws.gov"; "www.fws.gov/cep/cwgcover.html".

15.615 COOPERATIVE ENDANGERED SPECIES CONSERVATION FUND

Assistance: project grants (75-90 percent).

Purposes: pursuant to the Endangered Species Act of 1973 as amended, for programs for the conservation of endangered and threatened species of animals and plants. Funds may cover the costs of habitat surveys, research, planning, monitoring, management, land acquisition, habitat protection, and public education.

Eligible applicants/beneficiaries: states and territories with cooperative agreements with DOI.

Range: $1,000 to $14,363,000.

Activity: FY 03, 72 projects funded.

HQ: Chief, Endangered Species, Division of Consultation, Habitat Conservation, Planning, and Recovery (MS-420 ARLSQ), FWS-DOI, 1849 C St. NW, Washington, DC 20240. Phone: (703)358-2171, FAX (703)358-1735. **Internet:** "www.endangered.fws.gov/grants/section6/index.html".

15.616 CLEAN VESSEL ACT
("Clean Vessel Act Pumpout Grant Program")

Assistance: project grants (75 percent).

Purposes: pursuant to the 1992 act, for surveys and plans for installing pumpout/dump stations to protect sensitive areas in the coastal zone from recreational boat sewage; for station construction; for related public education programs.

Eligible applicants/beneficiaries: states bordering the Atlantic, Pacific, or Gulf coasts, or the Great Lakes; territories and possessions.

Range: $1,000 to $900,000. **Average:** $171,000.

Activity: FY 93-03, 3,000 pumpout and 1,900 dump stations constructed in 49 states.

HQ: Chief, Division of Federal Aid, FWS-DOI, Washington, DC 20240. Same phone, web site as **15.605**.

15.619 RHINOCEROS AND TIGER CONSERVATION FUND

Assistance: project grants (some matching).

Purposes: pursuant to the Rhinoceros and Tiger Conservation Act of 1994 as amended by the Rhino and Tiger Product Labeling Act of 1998, for rhinoceros and tiger conservation projects including: surveys and monitoring; conservation training and education; wildlife inspection, law enforcement, and forensic skills; research; protected area management; sustainable development in buffer zones surrounding rhinoceros and tiger habitat; management of human behavior and livestock to decrease conflicts; use of substitutes for tiger and rhinoceros products in oriental medicine.

Eligible applicants/beneficiaries: appropriate government agencies; experienced organizations and individuals.

Range/Average: generally, to $50,000.

Activity: FY 04, 40 grants in 15 countries.

HQ: Chief, Division of International Conservation, FWS-DOI, ARLSQ 730, 4401 N. Fairfax Dr., Arlington, VA 22203. Phone: (703)358-1754, FAX (703)358-2849. **Internet:** "www.fws.gov/international/grants/grants.html". (Note: no field offices for this program.)

15.620 AFRICAN ELEPHANT CONSERVATION FUND

Assistance: project grants (some matching).

Purposes: pursuant to the African Elephant Conservation Act, for African elephant conservation projects including research, management, and protection activities. Project examples: meritorious service awards program for game wardens in Africa; training in elephant biology and ecology; providing anti-poaching equipment.

Eligible applicants/beneficiaries: African government agencies; experienced organizations and individuals.

Range: generally, to $50,000.

Activity: FY 04, 26 grants in 12 countries.

HQ: same as **15.619**. (Note: no field offices for this program.)

15.621 ASIAN ELEPHANT CONSERVATION FUND

Assistance: project grants (some matching).

Purposes: pursuant to the Asian African Elephant Conservation Act, for Asian elephant conservation projects including research, management, and protection activities.

Eligible applicants/beneficiaries: Asian government agencies; experienced organizations and individuals.

Range: generally, to $50,000.

Activity: FY 04, 33 grants awarded in 10 countries.

HQ: same as **15.619**. (Note: no field offices for this program.)

15.622 SPORTFISHING AND BOATING SAFETY ACT ("Boating Infrastructure Grant Program")

Assistance: project grants (75 percent).

Purposes: pursuant to the act, to construct, renovate, or maintain tie-up facilities for transient, nontrailerable recreational vessels.

Eligible applicants/beneficiaries: states, possessions and territories.

Range: $10,000 to $1,500,000. **Average:** $300,000.

Activity: not quantified specifically.

HQ: Boating Infrastructure Grant Program Coordinator, same address/phone, web site as **15.605**.

15.623 NORTH AMERICAN WETLANDS CONSERVATION FUND ("NAWCF")

Assistance: project grants (50 percent/2 years).

Purposes: pursuant to the North American Wetlands Conservation Act, for wetlands conservation projects in the U.S., Canada, and Mexico, including: acquisition of interests in lands or waters for fish and wildlife protection; restoration, management, or enhancement of wetland ecosystems and habitats—only in coastal wetlands ecosystems in coastal states.

Eligible applicants/beneficiaries: entities and individuals recommended by the North American Wetlands Conservation Council and approved by the Migratory Bird Conservation Commission.

Range: small grants, to $50,000; standard grants, $50,000 to $1,000,000. **Average:** small grants, $42,000; standard, $710,000.

Activity: FY 04, 125 new projects.

HQ: Chief, Division of Bird Habitat Conservation (MBSP 4075), FWS-DOI, 4401 N. Fairfax Dr., Arlington, VA 22203. Phone: (703)358-1784, FAX (703)358-2282. **Internet:** "www.birdhabitat.fws.gov/NAWCA/grants.htm".

15.626 HUNTER EDUCATION AND SAFETY PROGRAM

Assistance: formula grants (75 percent).

Purposes: pursuant to the Federal Aid in Wildlife Restoration Act of 1937 as amended, to enhance hunter, bow, and archery education programs, and to construct firearm shooting and archery ranges.

Eligible applicants/beneficiaries: same as for **15.611**.

Range: $12,500 to $225,000.

Activity: not quantified specifically.

HQ: same address/phone as **15.616**. **Internet:** "www.grants.fws.gov".

15.628 MULTI-STATE CONSERVATION GRANTS

Assistance: project grants (100 percent/to 3 years).

Purposes: pursuant to the Wildlife and Sport Fish Restoration Act of 2000 as amended and other acts, for sport fish and wildlife restoration projects identified by the International Association of Fish and Wildlife Agencies. Funds may be used for research, boating access development, hunter safety, aquatic education, habitat improvements, and similar purposes.

Eligible applicants/beneficiaries: states or groups of states; nongovernmental organizations.

Range: $25,000 to $500,000. **Average:** $140,000.

Activity: annually, 10-20 grants.

HQ: Multistate Conservation Grant Program Coordinator, Division of Federal Assistance, FWS-DOI, 4401 N. Fairfax Dr.-Rm.4020, Arlington, VA 22203. Phone: (703)358-2156. **Internet:** same as **15.626**.

15.629 GREAT APES CONSERVATION FUND

Assistance: project grants (matching).

Purposes: pursuant to the Great Ape Conservation Act of 2000, for great apes research, conservation, management, and protection programs and projects in countries within their range.

Eligible applicants/beneficiaries: same as for **15.619**.

Range: generally, to $50,000.

Activity: FY 04, 35 grants in 15 countries.

HQ: same as **15.619**. (Note: no field offices for this program.)

15.630 COASTAL PROGRAM

Assistance: project grants.

Purposes: pursuant to the Fish and Wildlife Act of 1956 and Fish and Wildlife Coordination Act of 1958, to provide financial and technical assistance via partnerships to identify, protect, and restore habitats in priority coastal areas. Funds may be used for assessments and acquisition of private or public lands.

Eligible applicants/beneficiaries: federal, state, interstate, and intrastate agencies; local and tribal governments; sponsored organizations; public nonprofit institutes and organizations such as watershed councils, land trusts, schools and IHEs; territories and possessions; individuals, families, minority groups, businesses.

Range: $5,000 to $50,000.

Activity: FY 94-03, restoration of 94,000 acres of coastal wetlands, 25,000 acres of coastal uplands, and 961 miles of coastal riparian habitat.

HQ: Chief, Branch of Habitat Restoration, FWS-DOI, 4401 N. Fairfax Dr. - Rm.400, Arlington, VA 22203. Phone: (703)358-2201, FAX (703)358-2232. **Internet:** "www.fws.gov/cep/coastweb.html".

15.631 PARTNERS FOR FISH AND WILDLIFE

Assistance: direct payments/specified use (50 percent).

Purposes: pursuant to the Fish and Wildlife Act of 1956 as amended and Fish and Wildlife Coordination Act of 1958, to provide financial and technical assistance to private landowners and tribes to voluntarily restore or improve native fish and wildlife habitats. Landowners must enter into 10-year cooperative agreements.

Eligible applicants/beneficiaries: private landowners, local governments, tribal organizations, educational institutions.

Range: $200 to $25,000. **Average:** $5,400.

Activity: FY 93, 4,000 landowner agreements completed.

HQ: same address/phones as **15.630**. **Internet:** "www.partners.fws.gov".

15.632 CONSERVATION GRANTS PRIVATE STEWARDSHIP FOR IMPERILED SPECIES
("Private Stewardship Grants Program" - "PSGP")

Assistance: project grants (90 percent).

Purposes: pursuant to the Endangered Species Act of 1973 as amended, for the voluntary restoration, management, or enhancement of habitat on private lands—for endangered, threatened, proposed, or other at-risk species.

Eligible applicants/beneficiaries: sponsored organizations, individuals, families, specialized groups, public or private nonprofit organizations, small businesses.

Range: $4,000 to $300,000. **Average:** $70,000.

Activity: FY 03, 113 awards in 43 states.

HQ: same address/phone as **15.615**. **Internet:** "www.endangered.fws.gov".

15.633 LANDOWNER INCENTIVE

Assistance: project grants (75 percent).

Purposes: pursuant to the Land and Water Conservation Fund Act of 1965, to establish new or supplement existing landowner incentive programs providing technical or financial assistance for habitat protection, restoration, and management—to benefit federally listed, proposed, or at-risk species on private lands; to encourage states to enhance private landowner conservation efforts.

Eligible applicants/beneficiaries: fish and wildlife agencies of the states, tribes, territories, and possessions.

Range: "Tier 2" grants, $165,000 to $1,750,000. **Average:** "Tier 2," $1,170,000; "Tier 1" grants, $1,170,000.

Activity: not quantified specifically.

HQ: Land Owner Incentive Program Coordinator, Division of Federal Aid, FWS-DOI, same address/phone as **15.605**. **Internet:** "www.international.fws.gov".

15.634 STATE WILDLIFE GRANTS
("SWG")

Assistance: formula grants (planning, 75 percent; implementation, 50 percent/2 years).

Purposes: to develop and implement programs for the benefit of wildlife and their habitat, including species that are not hunted or fished.

Eligible applicants/beneficiaries: same as **15.633**.

Range/Average: N.A.

Activity: FY 04, 56 grants anticipated.

HQ: State Wildlife Program Coordinator, Division of Federal Aid, same address/phone as **15.605**. **Internet:** same as **15.633**.

15.635 NEOTROPICAL MIGRATORY BIRD CONSERVATION

Assistance: project grants (25 percent/to 2 years).

Purposes: pursuant to the Neotropical Migratory Bird Conservation Act of 2000, for projects that: enhance the conservation of neotropical bird species in the U.S., Latin America, or the Caribbean; ensure adequate local public participation in project development and implementation; are conducted in consultation with relevant wildlife management authorities and other appropriate government officials; are sensitive to local historic and cultural resources and comply with applicable laws; and, promote sustainable effective, long-term programs. 75 percent of available funds must be expended outside the U.S.

Eligible applicants/beneficiaries: individuals, corporations, partnerships, trusts, or other private entities; officers, employees, agents, departments, or instrumentalities of any state, municipality, or political subdivision of state, or of any foreign government; entities subject to the jurisdiction of the U.S. or any foreign government; international organizations with an interest in neotropical migratory bird conservation.

Range: $2,000 to $250,000. **Average:** $88,000.

Activity: new program listing in 2003. FY 02-04, 109 awards to entities in 34 countries.

HQ: same address/phone as **15.623**. **Internet:** "www.birdhabitat.fws.gov/". (Note: no field offices for this program.)

15.636 ALASKA SUBSISTENCE MANAGEMENT

Assistance: project grants (100 percent).

Purposes: pursuant to the Alaska National Interest Lands Conservation Act of 1980, for approved fish and wildlife subsistence management, fisheries monitoring, and traditional ecological knowledge projects—involving partnerships within the ranges of designated fish and wildlife species. Project examples include tagging, studies, harvest surveys.

Eligible applicants/beneficiaries: individuals, families, profit and nonprofit organizations, federal and Alaska state employees and agents or instrumentalities, tribal governments.

Range: $3,000 to $513,000.

Activity: new program listing in 2004.

HQ: Administrative Specialist, Office of Subsistence Management, Fisheries Information Service Division, FWS-DOI, 3501 C St. - Ste.1030, Anchorage,

AK 99503. Phone: (907)786-3387. **Internet:** "www.alaska.fws.gov/asm/home.html". (Note: the field office serves as headquarters.)

15.637 MIGRATORY BIRD JOINT VENTURES

Assistance: direct payments/specified use; project grants (100 percent/1-5 years).

Purposes: pursuant to the Fish and Wildlife Act of 1956, Fish and Wildlife Coordination Act of 1958, Fish and Wildlife Conservation Act, Migratory Bird Treaty Act, and amendments, to protect, restore, and enhance wetland and upland ecosystems for the conservation of migratory birds. Project funds must be matched by joint ventures and may be used for costs of administration, coordination, bird habitat landscape planning, monitoring, evaluation, applied research, training, communications and outreach, and project implementation.

Eligible applicants/beneficiaries: federal, state, local, and tribal governments; public, private, profit, and nonprofit organizations; inter- and intrastate entities; individuals or families owning lands.

Range: $250 to $900,000. **Average:** $12,000.

Activity: new program listing in 2004. As of 2003, 17 joint ventures focusing on regions with critical habitats, 3 focused on individual species—in the U.S., Canada, and Mexico.

HQ: Joint Venture Liaison Officer, Division of Bird Habitat Conservation (MS 4075), FWS-DOI, 4401 N. Fairfax Dr., Arlington, VA 22203. Phone: (703) 358-1784, FAX (703)358-2282. **Internet:** "www.birdhabitat.fws.gov/NAWMP/jv.htm".

15.638 TRIBAL LANDOWNER INCENTIVE PROGRAM ("TLIP")

Assistance: project grants (75 percent).

Purposes: pursuant to the Land and Water Conservation Fund Act of 1965, to establish new or supplement existing programs providing technical or financial assistance to tribal governments for habitat protection and management, to benefit federally listed, proposed, or candidate species or other at-risk species—whether on tribal trust or private lands.

Eligible applicants/beneficiaries: tribal governments.

Range: to $150,000.

Activity: new program in FY 04. FY 04 estimate, 23 proposals selected for funding.

HQ: Native American Liaison, Division of External Affairs (MS-3251), FWS-DOI, 1849 C St. NW, Washington, DC 20240. Phone: (202)208-4133, FAX (202)501-3524. **Internet:** "http://grants.fws.gov/tribal.html".

15.639 TRIBAL WILDLIFE GRANTS PROGRAM ("TWG")

Assistance: project grants (to 100 percent).

Purposes: pursuant to the Land and Water Conservation Fund Act of 1965, to develop and implement programs for the benefit of wildlife and their habitat, including species that are not hunted or fished—whether on tribal trust or private lands.

Eligible applicants/beneficiaries: tribal governments.

Range: to $250,000.

Activity: new program listing in 2004. FY 04 estimate, 24 proposals selected for funding.

HQ: same as **15.638**.

15.640 WILDLIFE WITHOUT BORDERS—LATIN AMERICA AND THE CARIBBEAN

Assistance: project grants (cost sharing).

Purposes: pursuant to the Endangered Species Act of 1973 as amended, for the management of fish, plant, and wildlife resources in the Western Hemisphere. Priority is accorded to projects to strengthen capacity to conserve and use sustainable biological resources, and result in specific measurable on-the-ground management actions in agreement with the Convention on Nature Protection and Wildlife Preservation in the Western Hemisphere ("Western Hemisphere Convention, 1940"). Activities should be conducted on-site, and may include work such as: academic and technical training; applied research; community-level education; technology transfer and information exchange; promotion of networks, partnerships, and coalitions.

Eligible applicants/beneficiaries: federal, state, and local governments; nonprofit, nongovernmental organizations; public and private IHEs.

Range/Average: preference to projects requesting less than $50,000.

Activity: new program listing in 2004. FY 04, 34 awards for projects in 18 countries.

HQ: same as **15.619**. (Note: no field offices for this program.)

15.641 WILDLIFE WITHOUT BORDERS—MEXICO

Assistance: project grants (cost sharing).

Purposes: pursuant to the Endangered Species Act of 1973 as amended, for the conservation and sustainable use of Mexico's wildlife and plant resources through projects that strengthen Mexico's capacity. Activities should be conducted in Mexico, and may include work such as: academic and technical training; applied research; community-level education; technology transfer and information exchange; promotion of networks, partnerships, and coalitions.

Eligible applicants/beneficiaries: same as for **15.640**.

Range/Average: same as for **15.640**.

Activity: new program listing in 2004. FY 04, 14 awards.

HQ: same as **15.619**. (Note: no field offices for this program.)

15.642 CHALLENGE COST SHARE ("CCS")

Assistance: project grants (50 percent).

Purposes: to encourage partnerships to support the mission of the U.S. Fish and Wildlife Service through projects involving conservation, protection, and enhancement of fish, wildlife, and plants, including recreational and educational activities—whether on or off FWS lands.

Eligible applicants/beneficiaries: individuals, families, and virtually any organization, whether public or private, profit or nonprofit—including territories and possessions.

Range: $300 to $25,000. **Average:** $7,800.

Activity: new program listing in 2004. FY 03, 1,400 approved partners provided $10,500,000 in matching funds.

HQ: Assistant Director, National Wildlife Refuge System, FWS-DOI, 4401 N. Fairfax Dr. - Ste.670, Arlington, VA 22203. Phone: (703)358-1744, FAX (703)358-2248. **Internet:** "www.fws.gov".

15.643 ALASKA MIGRATORY BIRD CO-MANAGEMENT COUNCIL ("AMBCC")

Assistance: project grants (100 percent).

Purposes: pursuant to the Fish and Wildlife Coordination Act of 1958 and Migratory Bird Treaty Act, to facilitate and administer programs to involve subsistence hunters of migratory birds in the management and regulation of migratory birds.

Eligible applicants/beneficiaries: native American and public nonprofit organizations, other public institutions, tribal and local governments.

Range: $14,000 to $33,000.

Activity: new program listing in 2005 (CFDA on-line version); 11 regional management bodies established.

HQ: Office of the Alaska Migratory Bird Co-Management Council (201), FWS-DOI, 1011 E. Tudor Rd., Anchorage, AK 99503. Phone: (907)786-3499, FAX (907)786-3641. **Internet:** "http://Alaska.fws/ambcc/index.htm".

15.644 FEDERAL JUNIOR DUCK STAMP CONSERVATION AND DESIGN ("Junior Duck Stamp Contest")

Assistance: direct payments/specified use; sale, exchange, or donation of property and goods.

Purposes: pursuant to the reauthorized Junior Duck Stamp Conservation and Design Program Act of 1994, for a nationwide design contest to teach K-12 students environmental science, wildlife management, wetlands ecology, and the importance of habitat conservation. Assistance may be used to: provide awards and scholarships to student-winners in state-territory contest rounds; provide awards to schools and other participants; pay costs of outreach and marketing. Cash awards are provided for scholarships to national round winners.

Eligible applicants/beneficiaries: U.S. and territorial K-12 students attending public, private, or home schools.

Range: state-territorial level, to $2,350; national level, $200 to $5,000.

Activity: new program listing in 2005 (CFDA on-line version). Program in existence since 1994. Annually, 26,500 participants from all states, DC, Samoa, and VI.

HQ: National Program Coordinator, Federal Duck Stamp Office (MBSP-4070), FWS-DOI, 4401 N. Fairfax Dr., Arlington, VA 22203. Phone: (703) 358-2000, FAX (703)358-2009. **Internet:** "http://duckstamps.fws.gov"; e-mail, "duckstamps@fws.gov".

15.645 MARINE TURTLE CONSERVATION FUND

Assistance: project grants (to 100 percent).

Purposes: pursuant to the Marine Turtle Conservation Act of 2004, for foreign countries to conduct projects to conserve marine turtles and their nesting habitats; to address other threats to marine turtle survival. Applied research projects should address specific management needs and activities.

Eligible applicants/beneficiaries: appropriate responsible government agencies; other qualified organizations and individuals.

Range: preference to projects requesting less than $25,000.

Activity: new program in FY 05.

HQ: same as **15.619**.

15.647 MIGRATORY BIRD CONSERVATION

Assistance: project grants (1-5 years); direct payments/specified use.

Purposes: pursuant to the Fish and Wildlife Act of 1956, Fish and Wildlife Coordination Act of 1958, Fish and Wildlife Conservation Act, Migratory Bird Treaty Act, and amendments, to maintain and enhance populations and habitats of migratory bird species found in the Upper Midwest, including Illinois, Indiana, Iowa, Michigan, Minnesota, Missouri, Ohio, and Wisconsin. Funds may be used for population surveys and monitoring, applied research, compilation of technical information.

Eligible applicants/beneficiaries: federal, state, local, and tribal governments; public, private, profit, and nonprofit organizations

Range: $1,000 to $50,000. **Average:** $7,000.

Activity: new program listing in 2005. FY 05 estimate, 16 proposals funded.

HQ: Division of Migratory Birds, FWS-DOI, 1 Federal Drive, Fort Snelling, MN 55111-4056. Phone: (612)713-5473, -5470, FAX (612)713-5393. **Internet:** "http://midwest.fws.gov.MidwestBird". (Note: no other field offices for this program.)

U.S. GEOLOGICAL SURVEY

15.805 ASSISTANCE TO STATE WATER RESOURCES RESEARCH INSTITUTES ("Water Research Institute Program")

Assistance: formula grants (33 percent); project grants (50 percent).

Purposes: pursuant to the Water Resources Research Act of 1984 as amended, for basic or applied research, conferences, studies, student training, and related activities concerning regional, state, or local water problems. Project funds may not support formal instructional activities, general education, or costs of permanent buildings.

Eligible applicants/beneficiaries: university water research institutes in states and territories. Other IHEs may participate in cooperation with the designated state institute.

Range: $92,000 to $449,000.

Activity: FY 05, 54 formula grants, 8 competitive awards.

HQ: Chief, Office of External Research, USGS-DOI, 424 National Center, Reston, VA 20192. Phone: (703)648-6800, FAX (703)648-5070. **Internet:** "www.water/usgs.gov/wrri". (Note: no field offices for this program.)

15.807 EARTHQUAKE HAZARDS REDUCTION PROGRAM

Assistance: project grants (cost sharing/to 2 years).

Purposes: for mitigation of earthquake losses. Projects may include providing earth science data and assessments, land use planning, engineering design, emergency preparedness systems.

Eligible applicants/beneficiaries: IHEs, profit and nonprofit organizations, state and local governments.

Range: $5,887 to $1,100,000. **Average:** $76,000.

Activity: N.A.

HQ: External Research Program Manager, Earthquakes Hazards Program Office, Geologic Division, USGS-DOI, 905A National Center, Reston, VA 20192. Phone: (703)648-6696, FAX (703)648-6642. **Internet:** "http://erp-web.er.usgs.gov/"; e-mail, "gd-erp-coordinator@usgs.gov". (Note: no field offices for this program.)

15.808 U.S. GEOLOGICAL SURVEY—RESEARCH AND DATA ACQUISITION

Assistance: project grants (from 50 percent).

Purposes: pursuant to the Organic Act of 1879, for scientific research complementing USGS programs in classification of the public lands and examination of the geological structure, water, mineral, and biological resources and products of the national domain. Most funded research involves enhancing existing, long-term collaborative projects, including coastal and marine geology studies, volcano monitoring, and earth science research facilities.

Eligible applicants/beneficiaries: profit and nonprofit organizations; state and local governments. Note: funding for external projects is limited; applicants are urged to consult USGS prior to submitting proposals.

Range: $1,000 to $582,000. **Average:** $50,000.

Activity: FY 05 estimate, 288 grants and cooperative agreements.

HQ: none; all contacts are with field offices listed in Part IV. **Internet:** "www.usgs.gov/contracts".

15.809 NATIONAL SPATIAL DATA INFRASTRUCTURE COOPERATIVE AGREEMENTS PROGRAM

Assistance: project grants (from 50 percent).

Purposes: pursuant to the Organic Act of 1879, for collaborative projects to

PROGRAM INFORMATION 237

improve the discovery, access, transfer, and use of geospatial data, through the National Geospatial Data Clearinghouse to further development and implementation of the National Spatial Data Infrastructure (NSDI). Project funds may be used: to develop and promulgate the use of standards in data collection, documentation, transfer, and search and query; for educational outreach programs.

Eligible applicants/beneficiaries: collaborations of federal, state, and local government agencies; educational institutions; private firms and foundations; nonprofit organizations; recognized tribes or native American groups.

Range: $20,000 to $75,000. **Average:** $29,000.

Activity: FY 06 estimate, 50 awards.

HQ: Federal Geographic Data Committee Secretariat (MS 590), USGS-DOI, 12201 Sunrise Valley Dr., Reston, VA 20192. Phone: (703)648-5514, FAX (703)648-5755. **Internet:** "www.fgdc.gov/funding/cap2002.html"; e-mail, "gdc@usgs.gov". (Note: no field offices for this program.)

15.810 NATIONAL COOPERATIVE GEOLOGIC MAPPING PROGRAM ("STATEMAP" - "EDMAP")

Assistance: project grants (50 percent/1-2 years).

Purposes: pursuant to the National Geologic Mapping Reauthorization Act of 1997, to produce geologic maps of areas important to the economic, social, or scientific welfare of individual states. "STATEMAP" supports projects: (1) producing new geologic maps with attendant explanatory information; (2) compiling existing geologic data in a digital form at a scale of 1 to 100,000 for inclusion in the National Digital Geologic Map Database. "EDMAP") provides funding: (1) for graduate students in academic research programs involving geologic mapping and scientific data analysis as major components; (2) to expand research and educational capacity of graduate programs; (3) for publication and distribution of geologic maps generated in field-based graduate academic research programs.

Eligible applicants/beneficiaries: state geological surveys. State IHEs may apply on behalf of the state survey.

Range: STATEMAP, $15,000 to $356,000; EDMAP, $3,676 to $15,000 per graduate student and $2,500 to $15,000 per student. **Average:** STATEMAP, $134,000.

Activity: FY 04, 46 STATEMAP awards, 62 EDMAP students funded at 39 institutions.

HQ: Coordinator, National Cooperative Geologic Mapping Program, USGS-DOI, 908 National Center, 12201 Sunrise Valley Dr., Reston, VA 20192. Phone: (no number provided). **Internet:** "www.ncgmp.usgs.gov". (Note: no field offices for this program.)

15.811 GAP ANALYSIS PROGRAM ("GAP")

Assistance: project grants.

Purposes: pursuant to the Endangered Species Act of 1973, Fish and Wildlife

Act of 1956, and Fish and Wildlife Conservation Act, for studies where native animal species and natural plant communities occur—to identify gaps in their representation in support of the conservation of biodiversity. Studies are used by federal, state, and other governmental organizations to develop land use or acquisition plans that incorporate information about the presence and distribution of biodiversity.

Eligible applicants/beneficiaries: profit organizations, public and private nonprofit organizations, state and local governments.

Range: $40,000 to $380,000. **Average:** $192,000.

Activity: new program listing in 2003. FY 04, 9 cooperative agreements.

HQ: Coordinator, National GAP Program, USGS-DOI, 530 S. Asbury - Ste.1, Moscow, ID 83843. Phone: (no number provided). **Internet:** "www.gap.uidaho.edu". (Note: no other field offices.)

15.812 COOPERATIVE RESEARCH UNITS PROGRAM ("CRUP")

Assistance: project grants (to 5 years).

Purposes: pursuant to the Cooperative Research Units Act as amended by the Fish and Wildlife Improvement Act of 1978, for research, technical assistance, and education projects addressing the information needs of local, state, and federal fish, wildlife, and natural resource agencies. Project examples: gopher tortoise relocation; Caspian terns in San Francisco Bay; black bear genetics; fish community response to pump-storage; Great Lakes colonial waterbirds.

Eligible applicants/beneficiaries: universities hosting CRUPs.

Range: $5,000 to $700,000. **Average:** $47,000.

Activity: new program listing in 2003. FY 05 estimate, 530 research work orders.

HQ: Cooperative Research Units, USGS-DOI, Sunrise Valley Dr., Reston, VA 20192. Phone: (703)648-4261, -4262, FAX (703)648-4269. **Internet:** "www.coopunits.org". (Note: no field offices for this program.)

INDIAN ARTS AND CRAFTS BOARD

15.850 INDIAN ARTS AND CRAFTS DEVELOPMENT

Assistance: use of property, facilities, and equipment; advisory services/counseling; investigation of complaints.

Purposes: pursuant to the Act to Promote the Development of Indian Arts and Crafts as amended, Indian Arts and Crafts Act of 1990, and Indian Arts and Crafts Enforcement Act of 2000, to provide program planning assistance in promoting the development of American Indian and native Alaskan arts and crafts. Assistance is nonfinancial including: development of innovative educational, promotional, production, and economic concepts related to native culture; investigations of misrepresentation of handicrafts. No financial assistance is provided through this program.

Eligible applicants/beneficiaries: American Indian and Alaska native individuals and organizations; recognized tribal governments; state and local governments; nonprofit organizations.

Activity: annually, 6,500 native artists and craftsmen served. Also, operation of the Sioux Indian Museum in Rapid City, South Dakota, the Museum of the Plains Indian in Browning, Montana, and the Southern Plains Indian Museum in Anadarko, Oklahoma.

HQ: Director, Indian Arts and Crafts Board, DOI, Main Interior Bldg. - Rm.4004, Washington, DC 20240. Phone: (202)208-3773. **Internet:** "www.iacb.doi.gov". (Note: no field offices for this program.)

OFFICE OF INSULAR AFFAIRS

15.875 ECONOMIC, SOCIAL, AND POLITICAL DEVELOPMENT OF THE TERRITORIES

Assistance: project grants (100 percent).

Purposes: pursuant to the Act of February 20, 1929 and other acts, to promote the economic, social, and political development of the U.S. territories and freely associated states, toward their self-government and self-sufficiency. Operational costs and capital improvements may be funded, such as the construction of water systems, roads, schools, hospitals, and power and sewer facilities. A small percentage of funding may be available for discretionary grants.

Eligible applicants/beneficiaries: Guam, VI, American Samoa, Northern Mariana Islands.

Range: N.A.

Activity: not quantified specifically.

HQ: Director, Financial Management Division, Office of Insular Affairs-DOI, Washington, DC 20240. Phone: (202)208-6971, FAX (202)208-7585. **Internet:** "www.doi.gov/oia". (Note: no field offices for this program.)

NATIONAL PARK SERVICE

15.904 HISTORIC PRESERVATION FUND GRANTS-IN-AID

Assistance: formula grants; project grants (60 percent/to 2 years; territories, 100 percent).

Purposes: pursuant to the National Historic Preservation Act of 1966 as amended, to provide matching grants for the identification, evaluation, and protection of historic properties listed or eligible for listing in the National Register of Historic Places (see **15.914**). Historic properties may include districts, sites, buildings, structures, and objects significant in American history, architecture, archaeology, engineering, and culture at national, state, and local levels. Grants may finance studies and reports, preservation plans, state staff salaries, equipment, materials, necessary travel, acquisition, or repair. Development projects must involve preservation, restoration, rehabilitation, or nonmajor reconstruction. Certain tax incentives are available to owners of listed properties.

Eligible applicants/beneficiaries: states and territories operating programs administered by a state historic preservation officer, which may subgrant to public and private parties including local governments, profit and nonprofit organizations, or individuals to accomplish program objectives. Tribal Grant Program—tribal governments, Alaska or Hawaii native corporations.

Range: $197,000 to $1,194,000. **Average:** $661,000.

Activity: FY 03, 59 state grants and, in turn, 850 subgrants; 3,400 tax credit applications reviewed.

HQ: Associate Director, Cultural Resource Stewardship and Partnerships, NPS-DOI, Washington, DC 20240. Phone: (202)354-2054. **Internet:** "www.family.info.gov.cfda.index.htm"; *State Historic Preservation Offices,* "www.2cr.nps.gov".

15.910 NATIONAL NATURAL LANDMARKS PROGRAM

Assistance: specialized services; technical information.

Purposes: pursuant to the Historic Sites Act of 1935, General Authorities Act of 1970, and Mining in National Parks Act of 1976, to identify and recognize nationally significant natural areas and to encourage their preservation. Designation of natural landmarks renders them eligible for registration on the National Registry of Natural Landmarks. Technical assistance is available to landmark owners and administrators. No financial assistance is provided.

Eligible applicants/beneficiaries: anyone may suggest an area for inclusion.

Activity: cumulatively as of 2004, 587 natural landmarks designated.

HQ: Natural Landmarks Program, Natural Systems Management Office (2320), NPS-DOI, Washington, DC 20240. Phone: (202)513-7166. **Internet:** "www.family.info.gov\cfda\index.htm".

15.912 NATIONAL HISTORIC LANDMARK

Assistance: advisory services/counseling.

Purposes: pursuant to the Historic Sites Act of 1935, National Historic Preservation Act of 1966, and amendments, to study, identify, and encourage preservation of nationally-significant historic properties. Designation of historic landmarks and registration on the National Register of Historic Places (see **15.914**) renders them eligible for federal protection, some grants-in-aid programs, and certain tax benefits. Properties of only state or local significance do not qualify.

Eligible applicants/beneficiaries: anyone may suggest properties for inclusion. Property owners may be individuals, governments, or corporate bodies.

Activity: cumulatively as of April 2004, 2,365 National Historic Landmarks designated.

HQ: National Historic Landmarks Survey (MS 2280), NRHE-NPS-DOI, 1849

C St. NW, Washington, DC 20240. Phone: (202)354-2210. **Internet:** "www.cr.nps.gov/nhl".

15.914 NATIONAL REGISTER OF HISTORIC PLACES ("National Register")

Assistance: advisory services/counseling.

Purposes: pursuant to the Historic Preservation Act of 1966 and Amendments of 1980 and 1992, Economic Recovery Tax Act of 1981, Tax Reform Act of 1986, and other acts, to expand and maintain the National Register of Historic Places which serves as a planning tool and source of information on sites, buildings, districts, structures, and objects of historical, architectural, engineering, archaeological, and/or cultural significance. Designation of historic landmarks and registration on the National Register renders them eligible for federal protection, some grants-in-aid and loan programs, and certain tax benefits. Federal agencies are required to consider and nominate historic properties within their jurisdiction.

Eligible applicants/beneficiaries: states and territories operating programs administered by state historic preservation officers; tribal preservation officers; federal agencies. Applicants eligible for federal tax benefits include owners of individually listed properties and properties certified by NPS as historic and in a district certified as historic.

Activity: cumulatively as of FY 04, 77,000 properties listed in the National Register, with some 125 entries added monthly; 31,000 projects representing $31 billion in rehabilitation work had received Tax Reform Act certifications.

HQ: Keeper of the National Register of Historic Places, same address as **15.912**. Phone: (202)345-2213. **Internet:** "www.cr.nps.gov/nr".

15.915 TECHNICAL PRESERVATION SERVICES

Assistance: advisory services/counseling; specialized services; technical information.

Purposes: pursuant to the Federal Property and Administrative Services Act of 1949 and National Historic Preservation Act of 1966, amendments, Mining in National Parks Act of 1976, Tax Reform Act of 1986, and other acts, to offer technical information pertaining to the treatment and maintenance of historic properties. The program provides for the development of policies and standards and for distribution of publications on the technical and design aspects of preservation and rehabilitation, as well as for monitoring acquisition and development grant awards under **15.904**; the service also includes general technical assistance concerning preservation efforts, including certification for eligibility for tax credits.

Eligible applicants/beneficiaries: federal agencies, state and local governments, and individual owners.

Activity: not quantified specifically.

HQ: Chief, Heritage Preservation Services Program (ORG 2255), NPS-DOI, 1849 C St. NW, Washington, DC 20240. Phone: (202)513-7270. **Internet:** "www.cr.nps.gov".

15.916 OUTDOOR RECREATION—ACQUISITION, DEVELOPMENT AND PLANNING
("Land and Water Conservation Fund Grants")

Assistance: project grants (50 percent/to 3 years).

Purposes: pursuant to the Land and Water Conservation Fund Act of 1965 as amended and other acts, to plan, acquire, and develop public outdoor recreation areas and facilities, including picnic areas, inner city parks, campgrounds, tennis courts, boat launching ramps, bike trails, outdoor swimming pools, roads, water supply, etc.; for studies, surveys, and data collection and analysis related to refinement and improvement of Statewide Comprehensive Outdoor Recreation Plans (SCORPs). Grant funds are not available to cover operating and maintenance costs.

Eligible applicants/beneficiaries: planning grants—only state agencies and territories. Acquisition and development grants—state agencies may apply for direct assistance, or on behalf of other state agencies or political subdivisions, such as cities, counties, and park districts; tribes functioning as general purpose units of government.

Range: $150 to $5,450,000. **Average:** $68,000.

Activity: not quantified specifically.

HQ: Chief, Recreation Programs (2225), NPS-DOI, 1849 C St. NW, Washington, DC 20240. Phone: (202)354-6900, FAX (202)371-5179. **Internet:** "www.ncrc.nps.gov/lwcf".

15.918 DISPOSAL OF FEDERAL SURPLUS REAL PROPERTY FOR PARKS, RECREATION, AND HISTORIC MONUMENTS
("Surplus Property Program" - "Federal Land-to-Parks Program" - "Historic Surplus Property Program")

Assistance: use of property, facilities, and equipment.

Purposes: pursuant to the Federal Property and Administrative Services Act of 1949 as amended and Federal Lands for Parks and Recreation Act, to transfer surplus federal real property for public park and recreation use, or for use as historic real property. Recipients must agree to manage the property in the public interest and for public use. Only properties listed on the National Register or so eligible may be transferred through the Historic Surplus Property Program. Examples of new uses include nature study areas, wildlife conservation areas, youth and senior citizen areas; arts and crafts centers.

Eligible applicants/beneficiaries: only states or local government units.

Activity: since 1949, 1,400 properties transferred for park and recreation uses, comprising over 156,000 acres; 130 properties for historic purposes. FY 04, 25 properties transferred.

HQ: Historic Surplus Property Program, Heritage Preservation Services (ORG 2255), NPS-DOI, 1849 C St. NW, Washington, DC. Phone: (202)354-2044. Federal Land-to-Parks Program, Recreation Programs Division, NPS-DOI, same address. Phone: (202)354-6915. **Internet:** Historic Surplus Property Program, "www.cr.nps.gov/tps/hspp_p.htm"; Federal Land-to-Parks Program, "www.cr.nps.gov/flp".

15.921 RIVERS, TRAILS AND CONSERVATION ASSISTANCE ("RTCA")

Assistance: advisory services/counseling.

Purposes: pursuant to the Wild and Scenic Rivers Act of 1968 and National Trails System Act as amended, Outdoor Recreation Act of 1963, and the Federal Power Act, to support activities between government and citizens to conserve rivers, preserve open space, and develop trails and greenways.

Eligible applicants/beneficiaries: private nonprofit organizations; federal, state, and local government agencies.

Activity: not quantified specifically.

HQ: Chief, Rivers, Trails and Conservation Assistance (ORG 2235), NPS-DOI, 1849 C St. NW, Washington, DC 20240. Phone: (202)354-6900. **Internet:** "www.nps.gov/rtca".

15.922 NATIVE AMERICAN GRAVES PROTECTION AND REPATRIATION ACT ("NAGPRA")

Assistance: project grants (100 percent/to 18 months).

Purposes: pursuant to the act of 1990, for the documentation, inventory, and repatriation of native American human remains and cultural items including sacred objects, objects of cultural patrimony, funerary objects. Funds may be used: to involve specialists including lineal descendants, traditional religious leaders, and other officials; for staff training; for travel costs; to construct appropriate containers to transport finds. Ineligible uses of funds include documentation or repatriation of items from the Smithsonian Institution, care and curation of repatriated items, facilities construction or renovation, or real estate purchases.

Eligible applicants/beneficiaries: museum documentation—any institution or state or local government agency including IHEs with possession of, or control over, native American human remains or cultural items. Tribal documentation and repatriation—recognized tribes, Alaska native villages or corporations, native Hawaiian organizations.

Range: documentation, $5,000 to $75,000; repatriation, $5,000 to $15,000.
Average: documentation, $60,000; repatriation, $8,635.

Activity: not quantified specifically.

HQ: National Center for Cultural Resources, NPS-DOI, 1849 C St. NW - Rm.NC-340, Washington, DC 20240. Phone: (202)343-8161, FAX (202) 343-5260. **Internet:** "www.cr.nps.gov/nagpra/grants"; e-mail, "NAGPRA.grants@nps.gov". (Note: no field offices for this program.)

15.923 NATIONAL CENTER FOR PRESERVATION TECHNOLOGY AND TRAINING

Assistance: project grants (100 percent).

Purposes: pursuant to the National Historic Preservation Act Amendments of 1992, to develop and distribute preservation and conservation skills and technologies for the identification, evaluation, conservation, and interpretation of prehistoric and historic resources; to develop and facilitate training of federal, state, and local professional, managerial, maintenance, and other personnel; and for international cooperation efforts. Funds may support projects involving: information management; training and education in such disciplines as archeology, historic architecture, historic landscapes, object and materials conservation and interpretation; applied and fundamental research; pollutant research and treatment; analytical facilities; conferences; publications. Ineligible projects include: those focused on specific sites, structures, objects, or collections; internships and fellowships when integrated into funded projects; current projects.

Eligible applicants/beneficiaries: IHEs; nonprofit and quasi-public organizations; federal, state, local, and tribal preservation offices; profit organizations.

Range: $7,856 to $50,000. **Average:** $36,000.

Activity: FY 04, 9 awards.

HQ: Grants Administrator, Heritage Preservation Services Program, National Center for Cultural Resource Stewardship and Partnership (MS 2255), NPS-DOI, 1849 C St. NW, Washington, DC 20240. Phone: (202)354-2088. **Internet:** same as **15.910**.

15.925 NATIONAL MARITIME HERITAGE GRANTS

Assistance: project grants (50 percent/to 2 years).

Purposes: pursuant to the National Maritime Heritage Act of 1994, to preserve historic maritime resources and increase public awareness and appreciation for the maritime heritage of the U.S. Eligible preservation activities include: acquisition; planning; documentation; protection and stabilization; preservation, restoration, or rehabilitation; maintenance of properties; reporting and publicity projects. Eligible education activities include: enhancement of public access, use, and appreciation for maritime heritage collections; activities focusing on heritage trails and corridors; field programs; preservation of traditional maritime skills; minor construction projects to improve access, use, and appreciation of educational and exhibit spaces; reconstruction or reproduction of well-documented properties. Generally, costs of staff training or professional development are ineligible.

Eligible applicants/beneficiaries: state and local governments, private nonprofit organizations.

Range: $2,500 to $50,000.

Activity: not quantified specifically.

HQ: National Maritime Initiative, NPS-DOI, Washington, DC 20240. Phone: (no number provided). **Internet:** "www.cr.nps.gov/maritime/grants.htm". (Note: no field offices for this program.)

15.926 AMERICAN BATTLEFIELD PROTECTION

Assistance: project grants (100 percent).

Purposes: pursuant to the Omnibus Parks and Public Lands Management Act of 1996 and American Battlefield Protection Act of 1996, for the protection and preservation of battlefield lands on American soil by supporting nonacquisition preservation methods such as planning, education, and survey and inventory. Project examples: preparation of Vision and Protection Plan; preparation of National Register nomination; archeological survey. Funds may not be used for such activities as battlefield reenactments, any construction, permanent staff positions, curation, or other ongoing activities.

Eligible applicants/beneficiaries: federal, intrastate, interstate, state, and local agencies; public and private nonprofit organizations; recognized tribal governments and organizations; territories and possessions; public and private IHEs. Multi-organizational applications are encouraged.

Range: $1,000 to $75,000. **Average:** $25,000.

Activity: FY 92-01 (latest data reported), 260 projects funded.

HQ: American Battlefield Protection Program (MS 2255), NPS-DOI, 1849 C St. NW, Washington, DC 20240. Phone: (202)354-2037, -2023, FAX (202) 371-1616. **Internet:** "www.zcr.nps.gov/abpp/"; "www.cr.nps.gov/abpp". (Note: no field offices for this program.)

15.927 HYDROPOWER RECREATION ASSISTANCE ("Rivers and Trails, Hydropower Licensing")

Assistance: advisory services/counseling.

Purposes: pursuant to the Federal Power Act, Wild and Scenic Rivers Act of 1968 as amended, and Outdoor Recreation Act of 1963, to serve as a national technical resource to support government, industry, and nonprofit partnerships, concerning applications for hydropower licensing; to meet present and future outdoor recreation needs; to maintain and enhance a project's riparian areas.

Eligible applicants/beneficiaries: private nonprofit organizations; federal, state, and local government agencies; hydropower licensing applicants.

Activity: not quantified specifically.

HQ: Rivers and Hydro Leader, Rivers, Trails, and Conservation Assistance (2220), NPS-DOI, 1849 C St. NW, Washington, DC 20240. Phone: (202) 354-6900. **Internet:** "www.nps.gov/hydro".

15.928 CIVIL WAR BATTLEFIELD LAND ACQUISITION GRANTS

Assistance: project grants (50 percent).

Purposes: pursuant to the American Battlefield Protection Act of 1996, to help states and communities acquire and preserve threatened Civil War battlefields. Grants may cover costs of fee simple acquisition of land and protective interests in land at Civil War Battlefields listed in the Civil War Sites Advisory Commission's 1993 report on the Nation's Civil War Battlefields. Administrative costs are ineligible.

Eligible applicants/beneficiaries: state and local governments, which may subgrant funds to private nonprofit organizations that convey perpetual protective easements to the state historic preservation officer or other agency acceptable to NPS.

Range: $47,000 to $540,000. **Average:** $287,000.

Activity: new program listing in 2003. FY 02, funds obligated to protect 590 acres at 5 battlefields.

HQ: American Battlefield Protection Program (2255), NPS-DOI, 1849 C St. NW, Washington, DC 20240-0001. Phone: (202)354-2023, FAX (202)371-1794. **Internet:** "www2.cr.nps.gov/abpp/"; *interim guidelines,* "www2.cr.nps.gov/abpp/lwcf2002.htm". (Note: no field offices for this program.)

15.929 SAVE AMERICA'S TREASURES

Assistance: project grants (50 percent/2 years).

Purposes: pursuant to the Omnibus Parks and Lands Management Act of 1996 and National Historic Preservation Act of 1966 as amended, for preservation and conservation work on nationally significant intellectual and cultural artifacts, as well as historic structures and sites listed on the National Register. Funds may not be used for costs of acquisition or rent.

Eligible applicants/beneficiaries: federal, intrastate, interstate, state, and local agencies; public or private nonprofit organizations and IHEs; tribes.

Range: $50,000 to $500,000. **Average:** $200,000.

Activity: new program listing in 2004. FY 03, 60 projects funded.

HQ: Save America's Treasures Program, NPS-DOI, 1849 C St. NW, Washington, DC 20240. Phone: (202)513-7270, ext,6, FAX (202)371-1794. **Internet:** "www2.cr.nps.gov/treasures". (Note: no field offices for this program.)

15.978 UPPER MISSISSIPPI RIVER SYSTEM LONG TERM RESOURCE MONITORING PROGRAM ("LTRMP")

Assistance: project grants (100 percent).

Purposes: pursuant to the Upper Mississippi River Management Act of 1986, to maintain the Upper Mississippi River System as a sustainable large river ecosystem—through monitoring of trends and effects related to resources, and through research as specified in the LTRMP Operations Plan.

Eligible applicants/beneficiaries: states, local governments, intra- and interstate agencies, sponsored organizations, private nonprofit organizations.

Range: $218,000 to $609,000. **Average:** $392,000.

Activity: FY 04, 6 awards.

HQ: Upper Midwest Environmental Sciences Technical Center, USGS-DOI, 2630 Fanta Reed Rd. LaCrosse, WI 54603. Phone: Center Director, (608)781-6221; Management Analyst, (608)781-6229, FAX (608)783-6066. **Internet:** "www.umesc.usgs.gov"; "www.usgs.gov/ltrmp.html". (Note: no other field offices for this program.)

DEPARTMENT OF JUSTICE

16.001 LAW ENFORCEMENT ASSISTANCE—NARCOTICS AND DANGEROUS DRUGS—LABORATORY ANALYSIS

Assistance: specialized services; advisory services/counseling; technical information.

Purposes: pursuant to the Comprehensive Drug Abuse Prevention and Control Act of 1970 (CDAPCA), to provide drug evidence analysis, expert court testimony, and technical assistance to law enforcement agencies concerning narcotics and other abused drugs.

Eligible applicants/beneficiaries: state and local governments, law enforcement officials, forensic laboratories.

Activity: FY 04, 5,889 drug samples analyzed.

HQ: Deputy Assistant Administrator, Office of Forensic Sciences, DEA-DOJ, Washington, DC 20537. Phone: (202)307-8866. **Internet:** "www.usdoj.gov".

16.003 LAW ENFORCEMENT ASSISTANCE—NARCOTICS AND DANGEROUS DRUGS TECHNICAL LABORATORY PUBLICATIONS ("Microgram")

Assistance: technical information.

Purposes: pursuant to CDAPCA, to disseminate scientific information on the detection and analysis of narcotics and dangerous drugs, published monthly in "Microgram."

Eligible applicants/beneficiaries: forensic laboratories; scientists working for law enforcement agencies.

Activity: mail-subscription services; distribution via the internet.

HQ: same as **16.001**. *And,* **Internet:** "www.usdoj.gov/dea/program/forensicsci/microgram/index.html". (Note: no field offices for this program.)

16.004 LAW ENFORCEMENT ASSISTANCE—NARCOTICS AND DANGEROUS DRUGS TRAINING

Assistance: training.

Purposes: pursuant to CDAPCA, for DEA training of accredited professional and enforcement personnel in: drug investigations techniques; physical security aspects of legitimate drug distribution; evidence analysis; pharmacology, socio-psychology of drug abuse, and drug education; management and supervisory training of drug unit commanders.

Eligible applicants/beneficiaries: state, local, military, and other federal law enforcement and regulatory officials; crime laboratory technicians and forensic chemists.

Activity: FY 05 estimate, 37,000 participants.

HQ: Office of Training, DEA-DOJ, Quantico, VA 22134-1475. Phone: (703) 632-5141. **Internet:** same as **16.001**.

16.005 PUBLIC EDUCATION ON DRUG ABUSE—INFORMATION

Assistance: specialized services; training; technical information.

Purposes: pursuant to CDAPCA, to coordinate and facilitate the involvement of law enforcement and communities in drug abuse prevention and public education, through DEA field offices. No financial assistance is provided.

Eligible applicants/beneficiaries: anyone. Law enforcement agencies and community anti-drug coalitions receive priority.

Activity: annually, 50 states and several foreign countries assisted.

HQ: Demand Reduction Section, Congressional and Public Affairs Staff, DEA-DOJ, Washington, DC 20537. Phone: (202)307-7936, FAX (202)307-4559. **Internet:** "www.dea.gov".

16.012 ALCOHOL, TOBACCO, AND FIREARMS—TRAINING ASSISTANCE

Assistance: training.

Purposes: pursuant to OCCSSA as amended, Gun Control Act of 1968, and Organized Crime Control Act of 1970, to provide training in the enforcement of laws relating to alcohol, tobacco, firearms, arson, explosives, and organized crime. Programs include identification of firearms problems, laboratory capability, undercover, interviewing, investigation techniques, case management.

Eligible applicants/beneficiaries: state, county, and local law enforcement agencies. Participation is limited to nonuniformed police personnel.

Activity: annually, 600 officers participate.

HQ: Chief, Local and International Training Division, Bureau of Alcohol, Tobacco and Firearms-DOJ, 800 Seventh St. NW - Rm.600, Washington, DC 20226. Phone: (202)927-3160. **Internet:** "www.atf.gov". (Note: no field offices for this program.)

16.100 DESEGREGATION OF PUBLIC EDUCATION

Assistance: specialized services.

Purposes: pursuant to Title IV of the Civil Rights Act of 1964 (CRA), Equal Educational Opportunities Act of 1974, and amendments, to secure equal educational opportunities in public schools and colleges, for all persons regardless of their race, color, religion, sex, or national origin. DOJ may: seek court orders to desegregate pubic schools or colleges; intervene in cases in which plaintiffs allege discriminatory practices; litigate referrals from DOED involving such discrimination, as well as on the basis of disability pursuant to the Rehabilitation Act of 1973; seek court orders to ensure that local school districts take steps to overcome language barriers in their instructional programs.

Eligible applicants/beneficiaries: public school parents or groups of parents; public college students or their parents.

Activity: annually (sampling), compliance monitoring of school districts covered by desegregation orders; responses to routine citizen inquiries, Congressional referrals.

HQ: Educational Opportunities Litigation Section, Civil Rights Division-DOJ, Washington, DC 20530. Phone: (202)514-4092; Office of Public Affairs, (202)514-2007, TDD (202)514-1888. **Internet:** "www.usdoj.gov/crt/edo/index.html". (Note: no field offices for this program.)

16.101 EQUAL EMPLOYMENT OPPORTUNITY

Assistance: specialized services.

Purposes: pursuant to Title VII of CRA as amended, to initiate legal processes enforcing the Act's provisions and regulations concerning equal employment opportunities, including authorized affirmative action programs—for all persons, regardless of their race, religion, national origin, or sex. Discrimination is forbidden by employers, labor organizations, employment agencies, state and local governments, public agencies, and government contractors and subcontractors.

Eligible applicants/beneficiaries: all persons.

Activity: FY 04, 11 complaints filed, 5 court cases settled.

HQ: Employment Litigation Section, Civil Rights Division-DOJ, Washington, DC 20530. Phone: (202)514-3831, TDD (800)578-5404; Office of Public Affairs, (202)514-2007, TDD (202)514-1888. **Internet:** "www.usdoj.gov/crt/emp/index.html". (Note: no field offices for this program.)

16.103 FAIR HOUSING AND EQUAL CREDIT OPPORTUNITY

Assistance: specialized services.

Purposes: pursuant to the Acts cited below, to initiate legal processes assuring enforcement of the provisions of: Title VIII of the Civil Rights Act of 1968 as amended by the Fair Housing Amendments Act of 1988—assuring equal housing opportunities for all in the sale, rental, financing, and related housing activities—regardless of race, color, religion, sex, national origin, family status, or handicap (HUD investigates and attempts conciliation of fair housing cases; if unsuccessful, HUD may file administrative charges; DOJ brings suit in federal court); the Equal Credit Opportunity Act (ECOA) which prohibits discrimination in credit transactions on the basis of race, color, religion, sex, national origin, marital status, or age—because any part of the applicant's income is derived from public assistance, or because the applicant has in good faith exercised a right under the Consumer Credit Protection Act; Title II of CRA, prohibiting discrimination in places of public accommodation including hotels, motels, restaurants, gas stations, and places of entertainment; and, Section 2 of the Religious Land Use and Institutionalized Persons Act of 2000 prohibiting local governments from significantly burdening the exercise of religion or discriminating against religious institutions in their land use and zoning decisions.

Eligible applicants/beneficiaries: all persons.

Activity: FY 04 (sampling), 22 pattern or practice cases filed and 22 cases resolved; enforcement of "New Freedom Initiative."

HQ: Housing and Civil Enforcement Section, Civil Rights Division-DOJ,

Washington, DC 20530. Phone: (202)514-4713; Office of Public Affairs, (202)514-2007, TDD (202)514-1888. **Internet:** "www.usdoj.gov/crt/housing/hcehome.html". (Note: no field offices for this program.)

16.104 PROTECTION OF VOTING RIGHTS

Assistance: specialized services.

Purposes: pursuant to the Voting Rights Act of 1965, amendments, and related laws, to enforce the provisions of the Act regarding voter registration and voting in local, state, and federal elections. The laws protect the rights of all persons to register and vote, without discrimination based on race, color, membership in a language minority group, age, handicap, literacy, or residence overseas.

Eligible applicants/beneficiaries: all U.S. citizens of voting age.

Activity: (sampling) participation in redistricting challenges, changes in voting practices and procedures, polling place monitoring.

HQ: Voting Section, Civil Rights Division-DOJ, Washington, DC 20530. Phone: (202)307-3143, (800)253-3931; Office of Public Affairs, (202)514-2007, TDD (202)514-1888. **Internet:** "www.usdoj.gov/crt/voting/index.htm". (Note: no field offices for this program.)

16.105 CIVIL RIGHTS OF INSTITUTIONALIZED PERSONS
("Equal Enjoyment of Rights in Public Facilities" - "Protection of Rights to Reproductive Health Services")

Assistance: specialized services.

Purposes: pursuant to the Civil Rights of Institutionalized Persons Act (CRIPA), RLUIPA, Freedom of Access to Clinic Entrances Act (FACE), VCCLEA, OCCSSA, and related laws, to enforce the provisions of the Acts. CRIPA assures the right of equal utilization of any public facility owned or operated by any state or subdivision thereof, without regard to race, religion, or national origin—including facilities for the mentally ill or for the retarded or chronically ill, prisons, jails, pretrial detention facilities, juvenile facilities, and homes for the elderly. FACE authorizes the Attorney General to investigate and, where appropriate, to initiate actions for relief from certain violent, threatening, obstructive, and destructive actions intended to injure, intimidate, or interfere with persons seeking reproductive health services, or deny religious freedom or destruction of property at places of religious worship. RLUIPA prohibits government entities from imposing a substantial burden on the religious exercise of a person residing in or confined to a publicly operated institution.

Eligible applicants/beneficiaries: anyone.

Activity: (sampling), CRIPA compliance monitoring; police misconduct investigations initiated.

HQ: Special Litigation Section, Civil Rights Division-DOJ, Washington, DC 20530. Phone: (202)514-6255; Office of Public Affairs, (202)514-2007, TDD (202)514-1888. **Internet:** "www.usdoj.gov/crt/split/index.html". (Note: no field offices for this program.)

16.108 AMERICANS WITH DISABILITIES ACT TECHNICAL ASSISTANCE PROGRAM ("ADA")

Assistance: project grants (100 percent); technical information; training; investigation of complaints.

Purposes: pursuant to the Americans with Disabilities Act (ADA), to ensure that public accommodations and commercial facilities and state and local governments learn and understand the requirements of the ADA. Publications, conferences, seminars, training, and other educational services and materials are developed and disseminated through technical assistance grants and contracts.

Eligible applicants/beneficiaries: nonprofit organizations including trade and professional associations; state and local government agencies; national and state organizations representing the disabled; individuals.

Range/Average: N.A.

Activity: (sampling), services through the ADA telephone information line; publications distribution through libraries; maintenance of ADA web site.

HQ: Disability Rights Section, Civil Rights Division-DOJ, Washington, DC 20530. Phone: (800)514-0301, TDD (800)514-0383; Office of Public Affairs, (202)514-2007, TDD (202)514-1888. **Internet:** "www.ada.gov". (Note: no field offices for this program.)

16.109 CIVIL RIGHTS PROSECUTION ("Criminal Section")

Assistance: investigation of complaints.

Purposes: to prosecute cases of national significance involving the deprivation of personal liberties that cannot be or are not sufficiently addressed by state or local authorities. The Criminal Section's jurisdiction includes: acts of racial violence; misconduct by local, state, or federal law enforcement officers; violations of the peonage and involuntary servitude statutes protecting migrant workers and others held in bondage; violations of the FACE Act.

Eligible applicants/beneficiaries: all persons.

Activity: FY 04, 96 cases filed charging 156 defendants; 111 defendants successfully prosecuted.

HQ: Criminal Section, Civil Rights Division-DOJ, Washington, DC 20530. Phone: (202)514-3204; Office of Public Affairs, (202)514-2007, TDD (202) 514-1888; **Internet:** "www.usdoj.gov/crt/crim/index.html".

16.110 EDUCATION AND ENFORCEMENT OF THE ANTIDISCRIMINATION PROVISION OF THE IMMIGRATION AND NATIONALITY ACT

Assistance: project grants (100 percent); specialized services; investigation of complaints.

Purposes: pursuant to the Immigration and Nationality Act, to educate employers and workers about their rights and responsibilities under the Act, to prevent employment discrimination based on citizenship status or national origin, and unfair documentary practices with respect to verification or employment eligibility. Eligible funded project activities include outreach and education to workers and employers, and to immigrant service providers. For charges relating to national origin, the Office of the Special Counsel has jurisdiction only over employers with four to fourteen employees—with respect to the hiring, firing, recruiting, or referral for a fee of protected individuals and aliens authorized to work in the U.S.; employers with 15 or more employees are under the jurisdiction of the Equal Employment Opportunity Commission.

Eligible applicants/beneficiaries: local, regional, or national ethnic and immigrants' rights advocacy organizations; labor organizations; trade associations; industry groups; professional organizations; state and local government agencies; employer organizations; others including profit entities—providing information services to employers or potential victims of discrimination.

Range: FY 05, $35,000 to $100,000. **Average:** FY 03, $61,000.

Activity: FY 04 (sampling), staff participation in 807 outreach presentations, 15,000 calls handled.

HQ: Office of Special Counsel/Immigration-Related Unfair Employment Practices, Civil Rights Division-DOJ, Washington, DC 20530. Phone: (202)616-5594, (800)225-7688; TDD (202)616-5525, (800)237-2515. **Internet:** "www.usdoj.gov/crt/osc/index.html". (Note: no field offices for this program.)

16.200 COMMUNITY RELATIONS SERVICE ("CRS")

Assistance: specialized services.

Purposes: pursuant to CRA as amended, Title X, to provide conciliation, mediation, training, and technical services to communities in resolving community tensions, conflicts, and civil disorders perceived to be based on race, ethnicity, or national origin. Technical assistance, resource materials, and publications are available. No funds are provided.

Eligible applicants/beneficiaries: representatives of groups, communities; federal, state, or local governmental units.

Activity: annually, 1,200 cases.

HQ: Community Relations Service-DOJ, 600 E St. NW - Ste.6000, Washington, DC 20530. Phone: (202)305-2935. **Internet:** "www.usdoj.gov/crs".

16.202 OFFENDER REENTRY PROGRAM

Assistance: project grants (100 percent/2 years).

Purposes: to assist jurisdictions in facing challenges presented by the return of offenders from prison to the community, through enhanced surveillance and monitoring, strengthened individual and community support systems, and repairing harm to victims. Program is a combined effort of DOJ, HHS, and DOL.

Eligible applicants/beneficiaries: partnerships that include state and local corrections or juvenile justice and mental health and substance abuse agencies, and Workforce Investment Boards. Private, community, and religious organizations may be included. Recognized tribes may also apply with similar partnerships.

Range/Average: $3,100,000.

Activity: 25 grants.

HQ: Associate Deputy Director, Corrections Program Office, BJA-OJP-DOJ, 810 Seventh St. NW, Washington, DC 20531. Phone: (202)616-6500. **Internet:** "www.ojp.usdoj.gov/bja". (Note: no field offices for this program.)

16.203 SEX OFFENDER MANAGEMENT DISCRETIONARY GRANT ("SOM")

Assistance: project grants (75 percent/to 2 years).

Purposes: pursuant VCCLEA, to implement comprehensive approaches to the effective management of juvenile and adult sex offenders, or to enhance existing programs. Projects must focus on the continuum of activities and services targeted to community reintegration and management of offenders released from incarceration, rather than on institutional services.

Eligible applicants/beneficiaries: state, local, or tribal units of government, including possessions and territories.

Range: $40,000 to $250,000.

Activity: N.A

HQ: same as **16.202**. (Note: no field offices for this program.)

16.300 LAW ENFORCEMENT ASSISTANCE—FBI ADVANCED POLICE TRAINING ("FBI Academy, Advanced Specialized Courses")

Assistance: training (1-11 weeks).

Purposes: pursuant to the OCCSSA as amended, Crime Control Act of 1973, Comprehensive Crime Control Act of 1984, and VCCLEA, to provide advanced training at the FBI Academy in such topics as criminal law and investigations, behavioral science, forensic science, education, management, and fitness and health—emphasizing development of managers and administrators. Specialized advanced courses and seminars include firearms administration, white-collar and computer related crimes, latent fingerprint examination, police legal issues, hostage negotiations, executive development, technology, laboratory matters, budgeting, scientific technical analysis, death investigations, bombing and arson investigations, violent crimes against the elderly, sexual exploitation of children. Participants may be reimbursed for round-trip travel costs to Washington, DC; housing, food, laundry and dry cleaning are furnished to students at FBI Academy, Quantico, VA.

Eligible applicants/beneficiaries: regular full-time personnel of municipal, county, or state criminal justice agencies; qualified representatives of federal agencies—meeting age, experience, education, physical, and character requirements.

Activity: FY 05, -06 estimates, 1,675 participants.

HQ: Director, FBI-DOJ, Washington, DC 20535. Phone: (202)324-3000. **Internet:** "www.fbi.gov".

16.301 LAW ENFORCEMENT ASSISTANCE—FBI CRIME LABORATORY SUPPORT ("FBI Laboratory")

Assistance: specialized services; training.

Purposes: pursuant to OCCSSA as amended, to provide FBI Laboratory facilities and forensic assistance in examining evidence in criminal matters, technology transfer and access to information and forensic data bases, surveillance capabilities, related expert testimony, and specialized training in forensic disciplines.

Eligible applicants/beneficiaries: state and local law enforcement agencies in the U.S. or possessions.

Activity: FY 04, 47,000 nonfederal scientific examinations.

HQ: same as **16.300**.

16.302 LAW ENFORCEMENT ASSISTANCE—FBI FIELD POLICE TRAINING ("FBI Field Police Training")

Assistance: training.

Purposes: pursuant to the OCCSSA as amended, Crime Control Act of 1973, Comprehensive Crime Control Act of 1984, and VCCLEA, to provide training courses by FBI instructors for criminal justice personnel, covering such areas as fingerprinting, legal topics, police-community relations, hostage negotiation, white collar crime, organized crime, computer fraud, management techniques, investigative support.

Eligible applicants/beneficiaries: municipal, county, local, and state criminal justice personnel.

Activity: FY 04, 88,000 personnel attending.

HQ: same as **16.300**.

16.303 LAW ENFORCEMENT ASSISTANCE—FBI FINGERPRINT IDENTIFICATION ("FBI Criminal Justice Information Services Division")

Assistance: specialized services.

Purposes: to provide FBI fingerprint and arrest-record services. Besides criminal identification, services include locating missing persons and identifying unknown living or deceased persons and victims of major disasters.

Eligible applicants/beneficiaries: criminal justice agencies, federal government, and other authorized governmental and nongovernmental entities.

Activity: FY 04, 18,624,000 fingerprint cards processed.

HQ: Assistant Director, Criminal Justice Information Services Division, FBI-DOJ, 1000 Custer Hollow Rd., Clarksburg, WV 26306. Phone: (304)625-2222. **Internet:** same as **16.300**.

16.304 LAW ENFORCEMENT ASSISTANCE—NATIONAL CRIME INFORMATION CENTER ("NCIC")

Assistance: specialized services.

Purposes: to operate the FBI NCIC, complementing the development of similar metropolitan and statewide criminal justice information systems. Located in Washington, D.C., NCIC is a computerized index of crimes and criminals of nationwide interest, serving as a nucleus of a high-speed communications network that includes criminal justice agencies throughout the U.S., Canada, and some territories and possessions. The service can also be used to locate wanted or missing persons and stolen property. Technical assistance, consultant services, and training are provided to state agencies.

Eligible applicants/beneficiaries: local, state, and federal criminal justice agencies may participate through their individual control terminal agency.

Activity: FY 04, 1.515 billion transactions.

HQ: same as **16.300**. (Note: no field offices for this program.)

16.305 LAW ENFORCEMENT ASSISTANCE—UNIFORM CRIME REPORTS

Assistance: technical information.

Purposes: to collect, analyze, and publish nationwide crime statistics providing such information as crime trends, offenses known to police, demographic characteristics of arrested persons, police disposition of juveniles arrested, police employee information.

Eligible applicants/beneficiaries: all participating law enforcement agencies including state and local governments receive the annual publication and semiannual releases. Limited copies of semiannual releases are available to any interested individual; the annual publication may be purchased from GPO.

Activity: annually, 25,000 copies of "Crime in the United States" distributed, plus 2,500 CD-ROM copies.

HQ: same address/web site as **16.303**. Phone: (304)625-2000. (Note: no field offices for this program.)

16.307 COMBINED DNA INDEX SYSTEM ("CODIS")

Assistance: project grants.

Purposes: pursuant to the DNA Identification Act of 1994, to develop and maintain a national data base containing DNA records from convicted offenders, unsolved crime scenes, and missing persons. CODIS software allows storage and matching of DNA records; installation, training, and user support are provided. The FBI administers the Forensic Laboratory Improvement grant program jointly with the DOJ National Institute of Justice, providing funds for required equipment, supplies, and contractual services.

Eligible applicants/beneficiaries: software and technical assistance—publicly funded state or local forensic science laboratories performing DNA analysis, or private laboratories under contract. DNA grants—publicly funded state or local forensic laboratories.

Range/Average: N.A.

Activity: as of March 2005, 17 state and local laboratories; CODIS installed in 50 states, PR, and U.S. Army Crime Laboratory.

HQ: *FBI CODIS Program,* Director, FBI-DOJ, Washington, DC 20535. Phone: (no number provided). *DNA grants program,* Director, Forensic Science Systems Unit, Laboratory Division, National Institute of Justice-DOJ, Washington, DC 20531. Phone: (202)324-9440. **Internet:** same as **16.300**. (Note: no field offices for this program.)

16.308 INDIAN COUNTRY INVESTIGATIONS

Assistance: training.

Purposes: pursuant to VCCLEA, to train BIA and tribal law enforcement officers in conducting investigations in Indian country, in coordination with the Federal Law Enforcement Training Center (FLETC) and the BIA—including in death investigations, child sexual/physical abuse, gaming, evidence recovery, supervision and management, street officer safety.

Eligible applicants/beneficiaries: BIA investigators, tribal and other law enforcement officers.

Activity: FY 05, 5500 students trained.

HQ: FBI-DOJ, 935 Pennsylvania Ave. NW, Washington, DC 20535. Phone: (202)324-3802. **Internet:** same as **16.300**. (Note: no field offices for this program.)

16.309 LAW ENFORCEMENT ASSISTANCE—NATIONAL INSTANT CRIMINAL BACKGROUND CHECK SYSTEM ("NICS")

Assistance: specialized services.

Purposes: pursuant to the Gun Control Act and National Firearms Act, to provide a system through which federal firearm licensees may obtain information on whether prospective buyers would violate federal or state laws, by telephone or other electronic means. Background checks are conducted by the NICS Operations Center; also provided are technical and operational support to users and State Points of Contacts.

Eligible applicants/beneficiaries: firearms licensees and purchasers.

Activity: FY 04, 34,077,000 inquiries; 268,000 prohibited purchasers identified.

HQ: same as **16.303**. (Note: no other field offices for this program.)

16.320 SERVICES FOR TRAFFICKING VICTIMS

Assistance: project grants (75 percent/1-3 years); direct payments/specified use.

Purposes: pursuant to the Victims of Trafficking and Violence Prevention Act of 2000 (VTVPA), to provide assistance to victims of severe forms of trafficking, primarily to meet victims' pre-certifications needs as victims, through: comprehensive services awards to support the creation or enhancement of collaborative networks within given regions or communities, providing or coordinating services including shelter and sustenance, general health and mental health care, legal assistance, job skills training, cultural support, and educational services; and, supplemental and specialized services awards to support discrete, rapid response whenever and wherever trafficking victims are identified. Limited funding also is available for training, technical assistance, and research and evaluation projects.

Eligible applicants: state and local governments; tribes; nonprofit, nongovernmental victims services organizations.

Eligible beneficiaries: victims of severe forms of trafficking without regard to the victim's immigration status. ("Trafficking" is defined by DOJ as: sex trafficking in which a commercial sex act is induced by force, fraud, or coercion, or in which the person induced to perform such act is under age 18; or, the recruitment, harboring, transportation, provision, or obtaining of a person for labor or services through the use of force, fraud, or coercion for the purpose of subjection to involuntary servitude, peonage, debt bondage, or slavery.)

Range: services, $200,000 to $500,000.

Activity: as of 1 January 2005, 18 comprehensive services, 3 supplemental, 1 technical assistance grants awarded; 557 victims pre-certified assisted; 25,000 personnel trained.

HQ: Office for Victims of Crime, OJP-DOJ, 810 Seventh St. NW, Washington, DC 20531. Phone: (202)307-5983; Program Development and Dissemination Division, (202)305-1715. **Internet:** "www.ovc.gov". (Note: no field offices for this program.)

16.321 ANTITERRORISM EMERGENCY RESERVE

Assistance: project grants (to 100 percent/to 3 years); direct payments/specified use.

Purposes: pursuant to VOCA, ATEDPA, VTVPA, and USA Patriot Act of 2001, to provide assistance for victims of mass violence and terrorism occurring within and outside the United States, and a compensation program for victims of international terrorism—through: (1) Antiterrorism and Emergency Assistance Program (AEAP), providing assistance and compensation benefits for victims of domestic and international terrorism, mass violence, including emergency relief, crisis response efforts, training and technical assistance; (2) International Terrorism Victim Expense Reimbursement Program (ITVERP), to compensate victims for expenses associated with acts occurring outside the U.S. Victims all may receive appropriate support services and compensation specifically for medical, mental health, funeral and burial, lost wages, and loss of support.

Eligible applicants: AEAP—victim services organizations; federal, state, and local governments; nongovernmental organizations and similar organizations.

Eligible beneficiaries: ITVERP—generally, victims, family members, and dependents that are U.S. nationals or U.S. government officers or employees as of the date on which the international terrorism act occurred—on or after 21 December 1988, with respect to which an investigation or prosecution was ongoing after 24 April 1996. (Final regulations are still being developed.)

Range/Average: N.A.

Activity: assistance provided to victims such as of the Oklahoma City bombing, "9/11," U.S. Embassy bombings, and other terrorism incidents.

HQ: same as **16.320**. (Note: no field offices for this program.)

16.523 JUVENILE ACCOUNTABILITY INCENTIVE BLOCK GRANTS ("JABG")

Assistance: formula grants (90 percent/3 years); project grants (100 percent/1-3 years).

Purposes: to develop programs promoting greater accountability in the juvenile justice system. Formula grant funds may be used for such purposes as: building, expanding, renovating, or operating temporary or permanent juvenile correction or detention facilities, including personnel training; to develop and administer accountability-based sanctions for juvenile offenders; to hire additional judges, probation officers, court-appointed defenders, and prosecutors; to enable prosecutors to address drug, gang, and youth violence problems more effectively; to acquire related technology, equipment, and training; to establish juvenile "gun courts" and "drug courts;" to establish and maintain interagency information-sharing programs involving the juvenile and criminal justice systems, schools, and social services agencies; for programs to protect students and school personnel from drug, gang, and youth violence; to implement a policy of controlled substance testing for appropriate categories of juveniles. Discretionary project grants may be awarded for pertinent research, demonstrations, evaluations, and training and technical assistance.

Eligible applicants/beneficiaries: formula grants—states, territories and possessions (except Palau), and local government units. Discretionary grants—public or private agencies, organizations, individuals.

Range/Average: N.A.

Activity: FY 02, 15 training and technical assistance awards (most recent quantified data reported).

HQ: OJJDP, OJP-DOJ, 810 Seventh St. NW, Washington, DC 20531. Phone: State Relations and Assistance Division, (202)307-5924, (202)514-9292; Demonstration Programs Division, (202)616-3646. **Internet:** "www.usdoj.gov". (Note: no field offices for this program.)

16.524 LEGAL ASSISTANCE FOR VICTIMS

Assistance: project grants (100 percent/to 2 years).

Purposes: pursuant to the Violence Against Women Act of 2000 (VAWA), to increase direct legal services available to victims of domestic violence, sexual assault, and stalking—through innovative collaborative programs and services within the civil legal system, promoting victim safety and increased victim economic autonomy, including representation in such matters as protection orders, family law, or housing matters. Funded activities also may include training, technical assistance, and data collection.

Eligible applicants/beneficiaries: private nonprofit entities, tribal governments, publicly funded organizations not acting in their governmental capacity.

Range: N.A.

Activity: not quantified specifically.

HQ: Office on Violence Against Women, OJP-DOJ, 800 K St. NW, Washington, DC 20530. Phone: (202)307-6026. **Internet:** "www.ojp.usdoj.gov/vawo". (Note: no field offices for this program.)

16.525 GRANTS TO REDUCE VIOLENT CRIMES AGAINST WOMEN ON CAMPUS

Assistance: project grants (100 percent/to 2 years).

Purposes: pursuant to Higher Education Amendments of 1998, Title VIII, as amended and VAWA, to develop and strengthen security and investigation strategies to combat violent crimes against women on campuses, including domestic and dating violence, sexual assault, and stalking; for victim services programs. Funds may support such costs as: apprehension, investigation, and adjudication; personnel training; public education for prevention; lighting and communications systems; coordination with local law enforcement. Grant recipients must meet strict crime reporting requirements.

Eligible applicants/beneficiaries: IHEs or IHE consortia.

Range; $143,000 to $550,000. **Average:** $360,000.

Activity: not quantified specifically.

HQ: same as **16.524**. (Note: no field offices for this program.)

16.526 TECHNICAL ASSISTANCE AND TRAINING INITIATIVE

Assistance: project grants (100 percent/to 2 years).

Purposes: pursuant to VAWA, to provide expertise and support to communities in: responding to violent crimes against women, including domestic violence, sexual assault, or stalking; increasing victim safety; and, bolstering offender accountability. Grantees participate in educational initiatives, conferences, peer-to-peer consultations, and targeted assistance from experts. Program aim also is to build the capacity of national criminal justice and victim advocacy organizations.

Eligible applicants/beneficiaries: public or private nonprofit victim advocacy and national criminal justice constituency organizations, judicial organizations and related agencies.

Range/Average: N.A.

Activity: 56 cooperative agreements in effect.

HQ: same as **16.524**. (Note: no field offices for this program.)

16.527 SUPERVISED VISITATION, SAFE HAVENS FOR CHILDREN

Assistance: project grants (100 percent/to 2 years).

Purposes: pursuant to VTVPA, for projects enabling supervised visitation and safe exchange of children by and between parents, in situations involving domestic violence, child abuse, sexual assault, or stalking. Projects should involve collaborative relationships among courts, local victim coalitions and shelters, and related entities.

Eligible applicants/beneficiaries: states, tribal governments, local government units.

Range/Average: N.A.
Activity: N.A.
HQ: same as **16.524**. (Note: no field offices for this program.)

16.528 TRAINING GRANTS TO STOP ABUSE AND SEXUAL ASSAULT OF OLDER INDIVIDUALS OR INDIVIDUALS WITH DISABILITIES
("Elder Abuse, Neglect, and Exploitation")

Assistance: project grants (100 percent/to 2 years).

Purposes: pursuant to VTVPA, to train law enforcement officers, prosecutors, and court personnel to recognize, address, investigate, and prosecute cases of elder abuse, neglect, financial exploitation, and violence against individuals with disabilities—including domestic violence and sexual assault. Projects must include coordination among appropriate services agencies and organizations.

Eligible applicants/beneficiaries: states, tribes, local government units; state or local government agencies; private nonprofit victim advocacy organizations; public or private nonprofit service organizations for older persons or the disabled; national criminal justice constituency or judicial organizations.

Range/Average: to $300,000.
Activity: N.A.
HQ: same as **16.524**. (Note: no field offices for this program.)

16.529 EDUCATION AND TRAINING TO END VIOLENCE AGAINST AND ABUSE OF WOMEN WITH DISABILITIES
("Women with Disabilities")

Assistance: project grants (100 percent/to 2 years).

Purposes: pursuant to VTVPA, to provide education, training, consultation, and information to organizations and programs that provide services to individuals with disabilities that are victims of domestic violence, stalking, or sexual assault—including independent living centers and disability-related service organizations. Funds may support outreach activities and cost-effective ways that shelters and victim services may accommodate the needs of the disabled. Projects must include coordination among appropriate services agencies and organizations.

Eligible applicants/beneficiaries: states, local government units, tribal governments, private nongovernmental entities.

Range/Average: N.A.
Activity: N.A.
HQ: same as **16.524**. (Note: no field offices for this program.)

16.540 JUVENILE JUSTICE AND DELINQUENCY PREVENTION—ALLOCATION TO STATES
("State Formula Grants")

Assistance: formula grants, project grants (50-100 percent/to 3 years).

Purposes: pursuant to JJDPA as amended, for state and local programs to prevent juvenile delinquency and improve the juvenile justice system, including: deinstitutionalization of status offenders; separation of adults and juveniles in secure custody; removal of juveniles from adult jails and lockups; community-based services such as group homes and halfway houses; personnel education and training; monitoring and evaluation; elimination of disproportionate contact of minority juveniles. Applicants must have three-year comprehensive plans for meeting program purposes. States must distribute two-thirds of formula funds to local governments, private nonprofit agencies, and tribes performing law enforcement functions.

Eligible applicants/beneficiaries: formula grants—designated state and territorial agencies. Technical assistance contracts—experienced organizations, agencies, and individuals.

Range: formula minimum—territories, $100,000; states, $600,000.

Activity: FY 01, 54 formula grant awards (latest data reported).

HQ: OJJDP-DOJ, Washington, DC 20531. Phone: (202)307-5924. **Internet:** same as **16.523**. (Note: no field offices for this program.)

16.541 DEVELOPING, TESTING AND DEMONSTRATING PROMISING NEW PROGRAMS

Assistance: project grants (100 percent/to 18 months); specialized services.

Purposes: pursuant to JJDPA as amended, for programs to design, test, and demonstrate approaches, techniques, and methods of preventing and controlling juvenile delinquency, such as: community-based alternatives to institutional confinement; diverting juveniles from the traditional justice and correctional system; advocacy activities; programs to strengthen the family unit; prevention and treatment programs for juveniles that commit serious crimes; hate crimes, gun and gang violence prevention programs; after-care and reintegration programs.

Eligible applicants/beneficiaries: public and private nonprofit agencies and organizations; individuals; state, local, and tribal government units or combinations thereof.

Range: N.A.

Activity: not quantified specifically.

HQ: same address, web site as **16.523**. Phone: (202)307-5914. (Note: no field offices for this program.)

16.542 PART D—RESEARCH, EVALUATION, TECHNICAL ASSISTANCE AND TRAINING

Assistance: project grants (100 percent/1-3 years).

Purposes: pursuant to JJDPA as amended, to: coordinate and conduct research and evaluation of justice and delinquency prevention activities; serve as a clearinghouse and information center for collecting and distributing information; conduct national training programs and provide technical assistance to federal, state, and local governments, judges and other court personnel, law enforcement executives, correctional administrators, probation officers, and volunteers. Projects may involve such activities as: developing programs addressing high-risk youth and missing and exploited children; prevention and treatment of drug and alcohol abuse by juveniles; effective parenting strategies for families of high-risk youth; reduction of drugs and crime in schools; longitudinal research on the causes and correlates of delinquency and juvenile court statistics.

Eligible applicants/beneficiaries: public or private agencies, organizations, or individuals.

Range: N.A.

Activity: FY 04 (sampling), 50 publications produced, training sessions, technical assistance.

HQ: Demonstration Programs Division, OJJDP-DOJ, Washington, DC 20531. Phone: (202)307-5940. **Internet:** same as **16.523**. (Note: no field offices for this program.)

16.543 MISSING CHILDREN'S ASSISTANCE

Assistance: project grants (100 percent/1-3 years).

Purposes: pursuant to JJDPA as amended, to coordinate federal programs related to missing and exploited children and to establish and operate a national resource center and clearinghouse to: provide technical assistance and training in locating and recovering missing children; provide a toll-free hotline; disseminate information about innovative and model programs, services, and legislation; conduct national incidence studies. Research, demonstration, or service program contracts may be awarded for public education programs, services to missing children and their families, location and return of adults with Alzheimer's or related diseases, statewide clearinghouses, and related purposes.

Eligible applicants/beneficiaries: state and local governments, public and private nonprofit organizations; individuals.

Range: N.A.

Activity: FY 04 (sampling), 10 new awards to state and local agencies; support for the National Center for Missing and Exploited Children and the Cyber Tipline; 150,000 calls received on the toll-free hotline; 500 law enforcement and prosecutors trained.

HQ: same address, web site as **16.540**. Phone: (202)307-5911. (Note: no field offices for this program.)

16.544 GANG-FREE SCHOOLS AND COMMUNITIES—COMMUNITY-BASED GANG INTERVENTION

Assistance: project grants (100 percent/to 18 months).

Purposes: pursuant to JJDPA as amended, to establish and operate programs and activities involving families and community agencies, designed to: reduce the participation of juveniles in gang-related crimes; improve adjudicatory, correctional, and treatment systems addressing the problems of juveniles convicted of serious drug and gang-related offenses; provide individual, peer, family, and group counseling, including provision of life skills training and preparation for living independently, and cooperation with social services, educational, welfare, and health care agencies; reduce juvenile participation in gangs, particularly those involving drug distribution; provide education and training to program personnel; accomplish similar program objectives.

Eligible applicants/beneficiaries: same as **16.542**.

Range/Average: N.A.

Activity: FY 01 (sampling), support for the National Youth Gang Center, Rural Gang Initiative, Boys and Girls Clubs of America programs (latest data reported).

HQ: same address/web site as **16.540**. Phone: (no number provided). (Note: no field offices for this program.)

16.547 VICTIMS OF CHILD ABUSE
("Judicial Child Abuse Training - Investigation and Prosecution of Child Abuse Through the Criminal Justice System - Court Appointed Special Advocates ("CASA") - Children's Advocacy Centers ("CACs")")

Assistance: project grants (100 percent/1-3 years).

Purposes: pursuant to the Victims of Child Abuse Act of 1990, to develop model technical assistance and training programs to improve court handling of child abuse and neglect cases; to facilitate the adoption of laws to protect child abuse victims against the potential "second assault" of courtroom proceedings; to address situations in which states have laws and procedures that outpace federal law, leaving children entering the federal system inadequately protected; to address inconsistencies and disparities among pertinent state laws; to train criminal justice system personnel on the latest investigative and prosecuting techniques; to promote a multi-disciplinary approach to coordinating the investigation and prosecution of cases, by limiting the number of pre-trial interviews of child victims and better assuring interview accuracy; to provide technical assistance, information, and support to local CASA programs, and to assist communities in developing new programs; and, for similar projects and programs.

Eligible applicants/beneficiaries: per congressional designations—National Court Appointed Special Advocates (100 W. Harrison St. - Ste.500, Seattle, WA 98119-4123); National Children's Alliance (1612 K St. NW - Ste.500, Washington, DC 20006). Local nonprofit agencies, organizations, and children's advocacy centers may apply to the national organizations.

Range: N.A.

Activity: FY 04 (sampling), technical assistance to 910 local CASA and all state organizations; 81 training events.

HQ: Director, Child Protection Division, OJJDP-DOJ, Washington, DC 20531. Phone: (202)616-3637. **Internet:** same as **16.523**. (Note: no field offices for this program.)

16.548 TITLE V—DELINQUENCY PREVENTION PROGRAM

Assistance: formula grants (50 percent/3 years).

Purposes: pursuant to Incentive Grants for Local Delinquency Prevention Program Act of 2002, to increase the capacity of state and local governments to support more effective programs in the prevention of juvenile delinquency through risk and protective factor programming approaches—including such activities as mentoring, tutoring, after-school programs, gang prevention outreach, community team training.

Eligible applicants/beneficiaries: designated state and territorial agencies—for transmittal to local government units.

Range/Average: N.A.

Activity: FY 02, 55 states and territories participated. FY 03 (sampling), 63 communities received team orientation training, 54 received data collection and analysis training, 40 received program and plan development training.

HQ: same address/phone as **16.540**. **Internet:** "www.ojjdp.ncjrs.org/titleV". (Note: no field offices for this program.)

16.549 PART E—STATE CHALLENGE ACTIVITIES ("Challenge Grants")

Assistance: formula grants (100 percent/3 years).

Purposes: pursuant to JJDPA as amended, to provide incentives to states to develop, adopt, and approve policies and programs in one or more specified challenge activities. Examples include: developing curricula on gender-specific issues for female offenders, juvenile justice personnel, and service providers; drafting program regulations and policies for the needs of runaways; developing mental health referral checklists, risk assessments, screening instruments for placements; developing case review systems and ombudsman programs.

Eligible applicants/beneficiaries: state and territorial agencies participating in the OJJDP Formula Grants Program (**16.548**).

Range: to 10 percent of formula grant allocation for each challenge activity, not exceeding total amount of state Part E allocation.

Activity: FY 01, 54 states and territories participated (latest data reported).

HQ: same as **16.540**. (Note: no field offices for this program.)

16.550 STATE JUSTICE STATISTICS PROGRAM FOR STATISTICAL ANALYSIS CENTERS ("SACs")

Assistance: project grants (100 percent).

Purposes: pursuant to OCCSSA as amended, to establish and operate Statistical Analysis Centers for the collection, analysis, and dissemination of statistics pertaining to crime and criminal justice.

Eligible applicants/beneficiaries: state agencies.

Range/Average: $50,000.

Activity: FY 04, 34 cooperative agreement awards.

HQ: Bureau of Justice Statistics (BJA), DOJ, Washington, DC 20531. Phone: (202)514-9012. **Internet:** "www.ojp.usdoj.gov/bjs". (Note: no field offices for this program.)

16.554 NATIONAL CRIMINAL HISTORY IMPROVEMENT PROGRAM ("NCHIP")

Assistance: project grants (80 percent).

Purposes: pursuant to OCCSSA, for states to: establish or improve computerized criminal history record systems; to collect data on stalking and domestic violence; to improve data accessibility and transmission to the National Instant Criminal Background Check System (NICS). Projects are to permit immediate identification of persons prohibited from purchasing firearms, or subject to domestic violence protective orders, or ineligible to hold positions of responsibility involving children, the elderly, or the disabled. Funds may support participation in the Interstate Automated Identification System and the FBI's Sex Offender Registry.

Eligible applicants/beneficiaries: designated state agencies, which may allocate funds to other state or local agencies or courts. Private organizations may receive contracts.

Range/Average: N.A.

Activity: N.A.

HQ: Administrative Officer, Bureau of Justice Statistics-DOJ, Washington, DC 20531. Phone: (202)616-3632. **Internet:** "www.ojp.usdoj.gov". (Note: no field offices for this program.)

16.560 NATIONAL INSTITUTE OF JUSTICE RESEARCH, EVALUATION, AND DEVELOPMENT PROJECT GRANTS

Assistance: project grants (100 percent/to 2 years); technical information.

Purposes: pursuant to OCCSSA as amended and Anti-Drug Abuse Act of 1988 (ADAA), for research, development, and evaluation projects relating to the causes and correlates of crime and violence and the improvement of the criminal justice system. Priorities include violent crime, alcohol- and drug-related crime, community crime prevention, criminal justice system improvement, forensic science research, and technology development.

Eligible applicants/beneficiaries: state, local, and tribal governments; profit and nonprofit organizations; IHEs; qualified individuals—including in the territories.

Range: N.A.

Activity: FY 06 estimate, 80 awards.

HQ: National Institute of Justice, OJP-DOJ, 810 Seventh St. NW, Washington, DC 20531. Phone: (202)307-2942, FAX (202)307-6394. **Internet:** "www.usdoj.gov/nij". (Note: no field offices for this program.)

16.561 NATIONAL INSTITUTE OF JUSTICE VISITING FELLOWSHIPS

Assistance: project grants (100 percent/6-18 months).

Purposes: pursuant to OCCSSA as amended and ADAA, to award fellowships to conduct research at the National Institute of Justice, on crime and the criminal justice system including juvenile delinquency, crime causation, crime measurements, law enforcement, criminal justice administration, and other topics.

Eligible applicants/beneficiaries: experienced practitioners and researchers or their parent agencies or organizations including criminal justice agencies, universities, or colleges. Recipients must have at least a bachelor's degree.

Range: N.A.

Activity: FY 03, 2 awards.

HQ: same as **16.560**. (Note: no field offices for this program.)

16.562 CRIMINAL JUSTICE RESEARCH AND DEVELOPMENT—GRADUATE RESEARCH FELLOWSHIPS

Assistance: project grants (100 percent/6-18 months).

Purposes: pursuant to the OCCSSA as amended and ADAA, for fellowships to doctoral candidates to conduct research related to law enforcement, crime, or criminal justice—covering stipends, project costs, and certain university fees.

Eligible applicants/beneficiaries: IHEs.

Range: to $15,000.

Activity: FY 03, 5 awards.

HQ: same as **16.560**. (Note: no field offices for this program.)

16.563 CORRECTIONS AND LAW ENFORCEMENT FAMILY SUPPORT

Assistance: project grants (50 percent/12-18 months).

Purposes: pursuant to VCCLEA, to research the effects of stress on corrections and law enforcement personnel and their families; to identify and evaluate model programs providing support services; for demonstration and training projects to develop stress reduction and family support programs; for dissemination of information and research findings.

Eligible applicants/beneficiaries: state and local agencies; organizations representing law enforcement or correctional personnel in employment matters, including national, state, or local labor unions or associations. IHEs, independent research enterprises, professional associations, health care providers, and others may obtain subcontracts to provide consulting or technical assistance.

Range: agencies, to $100,000; organizations, to $250,000.

Activity: FY 01, 2 awards (latest data reported).

HQ: same address, web site as **16.560**. Phone: DOJ Response Center, (202)307-1480, (800)421-6770, FAX (202)616-9249. (Note: no field offices for this program.)

16.564 CRIME LABORATORY IMPROVEMENT—COMBINED OFFENDER DNA INDEX SYSTEM BACKLOG REDUCTION

Assistance: project grants (to 75 percent).

Purposes: pursuant to OCCSSA as amended, ADAA, and DNA Identification Act of 1994, to increase state and local forensic laboratory capacity to conduct DNA testing. Funds may be used for: laboratory equipment, supplies, and necessary space modifications; outside training including approved graduate courses; contracted DNA testing services; CODIS equipment. Personnel, new construction, and indirect costs are ineligible.

Eligible applicants/beneficiaries: state or local governments, local or state crime laboratories, consortia.

Range/Average: N.A.

Activity: not quantified specifically.

HQ: same as **16.560**. (Note: no field offices for this program.)

16.565 NATIONAL INSTITUTE OF JUSTICE DOMESTIC ANTI-TERRORISM TECHNOLOGY DEVELOPMENT PROGRAM (COUNTERTERRORISM RESEARCH AND DEVELOPMENT)

Assistance: project grants (100 percent/6-18 months).

Purposes: pursuant to OCCSSA as amended, ADAA, and Anti-Terrorism and Effective Death Penalty Act of 1996 (ATEDPA), to develop counter-terrorism technologies for state and local law enforcement. Project examples: interactive computer-based training tools for bomb technicians; flying plate disrupter technology to disrupt capability of large explosive devices; electro-magnetic portal for detection of concealed weapons.

Eligible applicants/beneficiaries: same as for **16.560**.

Range/Average: N.A.

Activity: not quantified specifically.

HQ: same as **16.560**. *And,* **Internet:** NIJ Technology Information Network ("JUSTNET"), "www.nletc.org". (Note: no field offices for this program.)

16.566 NATIONAL INSTITUTE OF JUSTICE W.E.B. DUBOIS FELLOWSHIP PROGRAM

Assistance: project grants (100 percent/6-12 months).

Purposes: pursuant to OCCSSA as amended and ADAA, for research fellowships concerning justice system administration, delinquency prevention, violence reduction, and related topics. Studies are conducted at the National Institute of Justice.

Eligible applicants/beneficiaries: individuals or their parent agencies or organizations on their behalf. Candidates must have a doctoral-level or legal degree of J.D. or higher.

Range/Average: N.A.

Activity: N.A.

HQ: same as **16.560**. (Note: no field offices for this program.)

16.571 PUBLIC SAFETY OFFICERS' BENEFITS PROGRAM

Assistance: direct payments/unrestricted use.

Purposes: pursuant to OCCSSA as amended, to pay disability benefits to officers disabled in the line of duty, or death benefits to survivors of federal, state, or local public safety officers whose death results from a personal injury sustained in the line of duty.

Eligible applicants/beneficiaries: totally and permanently disabled officers or their surviving spouses and children (or their parents if there is no spouse or children). Public safety officers, including law enforcement officers, firefighters and public rescue squad or ambulance crew members, both paid and volunteer; law enforcement officers, including police, corrections, probation, parole, and judicial officers; FEMA personnel; state, local, and tribal emergency management and civil defense personnel. Available also in territories and possessions. (Note: eligibility by category of recipient varies by date of incident; a proportional distribution formula applies in instances of multiple beneficiaries. Details are available from the program headquarters.)

Range: FY 05, $275,658 death or disability benefit.

Activity: not quantified specifically.

HQ: Benefits Office, Public Safety Officers' Benefits Program, BJA-OJP-DOJ, Washington, DC 20531. Phone: (202)616-6500; (888)744-6513. **Internet:** "www.usdoj.gov/bja/psob". (Note: no field offices for this program.)

16.575 CRIME VICTIM ASSISTANCE

Assistance: formula grants (to 4 years).

Purposes: pursuant to VOCA and Children's Justice and Assistance Act of 1986 (CJAA) as amended, VCCLEA, ADAA, ATEDPA, VTVPA, USA Patriot Act of 2001 (USAPA), and other acts, for crime victim assistance programs. Primary program purposes include: to stimulate state participation and support for victim direct services programs; to promote victim cooperation with law enforcement; to provide direct compensation and services to victims of violent crimes, sexual assault, spousal abuse, or child abuse, or other crimes. Project examples: domestic violence shelter services; rape crisis programs; support groups for survivors of homicide victims and DUI/DWI crash victims.

Eligible applicants: states, all territories and possessions. Funds are subgranted to public agencies and nonprofit organizations.

Eligible beneficiaries: crime victims or their survivors.

Range: base amounts—states, $500,000 minimum; territories, possessions, $200,000 minimum. Additional amounts are based on population.

Activity: not quantified specifically.

HQ: Director, State Compensation and Assistance Division, Office for Victims of Crime, OJP-DOJ, 810 Seventh St. NW, Washington, DC 20531. Phone: (202)616-3579. **Internet:** "www.usdoj.gov/ovc". (Note: no field offices for this program.)

16.576 CRIME VICTIM COMPENSATION

Assistance: formula grants (to 4 years).

Purposes: pursuant to VOCA and CJAA as amended, VCCLEA, ADAA, ATEDPA, VTVPA, USAPA, and other acts, for awards by states to crime victims (other than for property damage excluding damage to prosthetic devices, eyeglasses or corrective lenses, or dental devices); to support victim compensation programs, including for survivors of terrorism, drunk driving, and domestic violence. Compensation may be made for such expenses as medical costs including mental health counseling and care, loss of wages, funeral expenses, costs incurred by nonresidents of the jurisdictions with operating programs.

Eligible applicants: states, territories, and possessions with established crime victim compensation programs.

Eligible beneficiaries: victims of crime resulting in death or physical or personal injury.

Range: states receive 60 percent of their prior year payout from state funds.

Activity: not quantified specifically.

HQ: same address/phone as **16.575**. **Internet:** "www.usdoj.gov". (Note: no field offices for this program.)

16.577 EMERGENCY FEDERAL LAW ENFORCEMENT ASSISTANCE

Assistance: project grants (100 percent).

Purposes: pursuant to the Justice Assistance Act of 1984, for assistance to state and local governments that experience law enforcement emergencies threatening to become of serious or epidemic proportions, enabling more adequate response through federal law enforcement activities.

Eligible applicants/beneficiaries: states, territories, and possessions.

Range: N.A.

Activity: no activity since 1997 due to lack of funding.

HQ: BJA-OJP-DOJ, 810 Seventh St. NW - 4th floor, Washington, DC 20531. Phone: (202)616-6500. **Internet:** same as **16.576**.

16.578 FEDERAL SURPLUS PROPERTY TRANSFER PROGRAM

Assistance: sale, exchange, or donation of property and goods.

Purposes: pursuant to the Comprehensive Crime Control Act of 1984, Surplus Federal Property Amendments of 1984, and other acts, to transfer or convey surplus federal real or other property for use in correctional or law enforcement programs and projects involving the care or rehabilitation of criminal offenders.

Eligible applicants/beneficiaries: state, local, and territorial governments; political subdivisions.

Activity: 27 properties conveyed to date.

HQ: BJA-OJP-DOJ, 810 Seventh St. NW - 4th floor, Washington, DC 20531. Phone: (202)616-6500. **Internet:** same as **16.576**. (Note: no field offices for this program.)

16.579 BYRNE FORMULA GRANT PROGRAM

Assistance: formula grants (base amount plus 75 percent of project costs/3 years; tribes, 100 percent).

Purposes: pursuant to OCCSSA as amended, to reduce and prevent illegal drug activity, crime, and violence, and to improve the functioning of the criminal justice system. Funds may support costs of: additional personnel; equipment;

facilities including upgraded and additional corrections and law enforcement crime laboratories; personnel training—to increase the apprehension, prosecution, and adjudication of persons that violate state and local laws relating to the production, possession, and transfer of controlled substances.

Eligible applicants/beneficiaries: states, territories, possessions.

Range: $500,000 to $52,000,000.

Activity: not quantified specifically.

HQ: same address/phone as **16.578**. **Internet:** "www.usdoj.gov/bja". (Note: no field offices for this program.)

16.580 EDWARD BYRNE MEMORIAL STATE AND LOCAL LAW ENFORCEMENT ASSISTANCE DISCRETIONARY GRANTS PROGRAM ("Discretionary Drug and Criminal Justice Assistance Program")

Assistance: project grants (to 100 percent/12-18 months).

Purposes: pursuant to OCCSSA as amended and Crime Control Act of 1990, to control the use and availability of illegal drugs and to improve the functioning of the criminal justice system, emphasizing violent crime and serious offenders. Funds may be used for: replicable demonstration programs that develop new concepts or strategies, national or multi-jurisdictional in scope; personnel education and training.

Eligible applicants/beneficiaries: state and local government agencies, public and private nonprofit organizations, tribal governments.

Range: $25,000 to $16,000,000.

Activity: annually, 200 awards.

HQ: Associate Director, same address/phone, web site as **16.579**. (Note: no field offices for this program.)

16.582 CRIME VICTIM ASSISTANCE/DISCRETIONARY GRANTS

Assistance: project grants (75-90 percent/6 months to 2 years); direct payments/specified use.

Purposes: pursuant to VOCA and CJAA as amended, VCCLEA, ADAA, ATEDPA, VTVPA, USAPA, and other acts, for programs to improve the overall quality of services delivered to crime victims including victims of terrorism domestically and abroad, through: demonstration projects and technical assistance to and training of services providers; support of victims services programs including direct compensation benefits. Project focus examples: religious organizations' response to crime victims; victims of crimes in urban and rural areas and in Indian country (requiring 10 percent local matching share); working with grass roots organizations to identify and replicate promising practices; practitioners training; special populations programs.

Eligible applicants/beneficiaries: states, U.S. Attorneys offices, university sites and colleges, victim service agencies, private nonprofit agencies; tribes and tribal organizations.

Range: Federal Crime Victims Division, $40,000 to $275,000; Program Development and Dissemination Division (PDDD), $25,000, $1,000,000. **Average:** PDDD, $100,000.

Activity: not quantified specifically.

HQ: same as **16.320**. (Note: no field offices for this program.)

16.583 CHILDREN'S JUSTICE ACT PARTNERSHIPS FOR INDIAN COMMUNITIES

Assistance: project grants (90 percent/1-3 years); direct payments/specified use.

Purposes: pursuant to VOCA and CJAA as amended, VCCLEA, ADAA, ATEDPA, VTVPA, and other acts, for Indian tribes to develop, establish, and operate programs to improve the handling of child abuse cases, particularly cases of sexual abuse, and to improve the investigation and prosecution of such cases.

Eligible applicants/beneficiaries: tribal governments, nonprofit Indian organizations.

Range/Average: N.A.

Activity: 75 programs funded.

HQ: Director, Federal Assistance Division, Office for Victims of Crime, OJP-DOJ, 810 Seventh St. NW, Washington, DC 20531. Phone: (202)616-3578; Program Manager, (202)616-3218. **Internet:** same as **16.523**. (Note: no field offices for this program.)

16.585 DRUG COURT DISCRETIONARY GRANT PROGRAM

Assistance: project grants (75 percent/2-3 years).

Purposes: pursuant to OCCSSA, to establish and develop drug courts to handle cases involving nonviolent adult and juvenile offenders. Program funds may support projects providing early and continuous judicial supervision and integrated administration of sanctions and services, including: mandatory periodic testing for controlled or addictive substance use during any period of supervised release or probation; treatment; diversion, probation, or other supervised release; offender management and after-care services.

Eligible applicants/beneficiaries: states, local government units, state and local courts, tribal governments; joint applicants.

Range: implementation, to $500,000 for 3 years; enhancements, to $300,000.

Activity: cumulatively, 75 planning, 52 implementation, 21 enhancement, 12 continuation, 3 mini-grants.

HQ: Associate Deputy Director, BJA-OJP-DOJ, Washington, DC 20531. Phone: (202)616-6500. **Internet:** same as **16.202**. (Note: no field offices for this program.)

16.586 VIOLENT OFFENDER INCARCERATION AND TRUTH IN SENTENCING INCENTIVE GRANTS
("Prison Grants")

Assistance: formula grants (90 percent/to 5 years).

Purposes: pursuant to VCCLEA as amended, to build, renovate, or expand:

adult or juvenile correctional facilities for violent offenders; temporary or permanent correctional facilities, including on military bases, prison barges, and "boot camps," for confinement of nonviolent offenders; jails. As of FY 99, ten percent of funds may be used for approved drug testing programs.

Eligible applicants/beneficiaries: states; multi-state compacts; territories and possessions. Subgrants may be awarded to local government units.

Range: states, from $1,533,000; VI, Guam, Samoa, Northern Marianas, $102,000 each.

Activity: N.A.

HQ: same as **16.202**. (Note: no field offices for this program.)

16.587 VIOLENCE AGAINST WOMEN DISCRETIONARY GRANTS FOR INDIAN TRIBAL GOVERNMENTS

Assistance: project grants (75 percent).

Purposes: pursuant to VCCLEA and OCCSSA as amended and VAWA, to develop and strengthen law enforcement and prosecution strategies to combat violent crimes against women, and to augment victim services. Funding may be used to pay costs of personnel, training, technical assistance, data collection, equipment, and victim services.

Eligible applicants/beneficiaries: tribal governments.

Range: $50,000 to $150,000.

Activity: 10 new and 35 continuation awards.

HQ: Office on Violence Against Women, OJP-DOJ, 810 Seventh St. NW, Washington, DC 20531. Same phone, web site as **16.524**. (Note: no field offices for this program.)

16.588 VIOLENCE AGAINST WOMEN FORMULA GRANTS

Assistance: formula grants (75 percent).

Purposes: pursuant to VCCLEA and OCCSSA as amended and VAWA, to develop and strengthen law enforcement and prosecution strategies to combat violent crimes against women, and to augment victim services. Grants may support costs of personnel, training, technical assistance, data collection and other equipment for apprehension, prosecution, and adjudication, and victim services.

Eligible applicants/beneficiaries: states, territories, and possessions. Subgrants will be awarded to local government units, nonprofit nongovernmental victim services programs, and tribal governments.

Range: base grant, $600,000 per recipient plus an amount based on population.

Activity: not quantified specifically.

HQ: same as **16.524**. (Note: no field offices for this program.)

16.589 RURAL DOMESTIC VIOLENCE AND CHILD VICTIMIZATION ENFORCEMENT GRANT PROGRAM

Assistance: project grants (100 percent/to 2 years).

Purposes: pursuant to VCCLEA as amended and VAWA, for rural states to implement, expand, and establish cooperative efforts and projects among law enforcement officers, prosecutors, victim advocacy groups, and others—to: investigate and prosecute incidents of domestic violence, dating violence, and child victimization, including in immigration matters; provide treatment and counseling to victims; develop community education and prevention strategies.

Eligible applicants/beneficiaries: state agencies; local governments, tribal governments, and public and private entities in rural states—i.e., those with a population density of 52 or fewer persons per square mile, or in which the largest county's population is less than 150,000, including Alaska, Arkansas, Arizona, Colorado, Idaho, Iowa, Kansas, Maine, Montana, Nebraska, Nevada, New Mexico, North Dakota, Oklahoma, Oregon, South Dakota, Utah, Vermont, and Wyoming.

Range: local, tribal projects, $50,000 to $500,000; statewide, multijurisdictional, tribal consortium projects, $50,000 to $900,000.

Activity: FY 01, 78 grants (latest data reported).

HQ: same as **16.524**. (Note: no field offices for this program.)

16.590 GRANTS TO ENCOURAGE ARREST POLICIES AND ENFORCEMENT OF PROTECTION ORDERS

Assistance: project grants (100 percent/to 2 years).

Purposes: pursuant to VCCLEA as amended and VAWA, to implement mandatory arrest or pro-arrest programs and policies in police departments in cases of domestic violence including for protection order violations, dating violence, and assaults against older persons and the disabled; to develop related educational and training programs; to improve tracking of cases; to centralize and coordinate police enforcement in groups or units of police, probation, and parole officers, prosecutors, or judges; to coordinate computer tracking systems; to strengthen legal advocacy service programs for victims; to improve judicial handling or such cases.

Eligible applicants/beneficiaries: states, local government units, state or local courts, and tribal governments.

Range: $80,000 to $1,600,000.

Activity: FY 01, 90 awards (latest data reported).

HQ: same as **16.524**. (Note: no field offices for this program.)

16.592 LOCAL LAW ENFORCEMENT BLOCK GRANTS PROGRAM

Assistance: formula grants (90 percent/2 years).

Purposes: pursuant to the Local Law Enforcement Block Grants Act of 1996 and subsequent appropriations acts, to enable local governments to: (1) hire and train new, additional permanent law enforcement officers and necessary support personnel, pay overtime to presently employed officers and personnel, and acquire equipment, technology, and other material directly related to basic law enforcement; (2) enhance security measures in and around schools and other high-risk locations; (3) establish and support drug courts; (4) enhance the adjudication of cases involving violent offenders including juveniles; (5) establish multijurisdictional law enforcement task forces to prevent and control crime, particularly in rural areas; (6) establish crime prevention programs involving cooperation among community residents and law enforcement personnel; (7) defray costs of indemnification insurance of law enforcement officers.

Eligible applicants/beneficiaries: local government units including in PR; recognized tribes, Alaska native villages.

Range: $10,000 to $25,000,000.

Activity: FY 01, 3,300 jurisdictions awarded funds (latest data reported).

HQ: same address/phone as **16.585**. **Internet:** same as **16.579**. (Note: no field offices for this program.)

16.593 RESIDENTIAL SUBSTANCE ABUSE TREATMENT FOR STATE PRISONERS ("RSAT")

Assistance: formula grants (75 percent/to 3 years).

Purposes: pursuant to OCCSSA as amended, to develop and implement residential substance abuse treatment programs within state and local correctional facilities, including individual and group programs to develop cognitive, behavioral, social, vocational, and other skills—and lasting six to twelve months.

Eligible applicants/beneficiaries: states, possessions, territories. Subgrants may be awarded to state and local government units.

Range: $259,000 (Northern Marianas) to $6,802,000 (California).

Activity: N.A.

HQ: same as **16.202**. (Note: no field offices for this program.)

16.595 COMMUNITY CAPACITY DEVELOPMENT OFFICE

Assistance: project grants (100 percent); specialized services.

Purposes: in cooperation with several other federal departments and agencies, to implement "Operation Weed and Seed"—a comprehensive, multidisciplinary approach to combat violent crime, drug use, and gang activity in high-crime neighborhoods. The goal is to identify drug activity and then to "seed" the sites with an array of crime and drug prevention programs, along with human service resources to prevent crime from reoccurring. The strategy is to bring together federal, state, and local government, the community, and the private sector in a partnership.

Eligible applicants/beneficiaries: coalitions of community residents and local, county, state, and federal agencies, and the private sector.

Range: initial award, $175,000; continuation awards, $225,000.

Activity: cumulatively, 300 sites involved with DOJ funding, plus others without.

HQ: Community Capacity Development Office, OJP-DOJ, 810 Seventh St. NW, Washington, DC 20531. Phone: (202)616-1152, FAX (202)616-1159. **Internet:** "www.usdoj.gov/ccdo". (Note: no field offices for this program.)

16.596 CORRECTIONAL GRANT PROGRAM FOR INDIAN TRIBES

Assistance: project grants (90 percent/2 years).

Purposes: pursuant to VCCLEA as amended, to construct or expand jails on tribal lands for the incarceration of adult or juvenile offenders subject to tribal jurisdiction.

Eligible applicants/beneficiaries: tribes—defined as any Indian or Alaska native tribe, band, nation, pueblo, village, or community recognized by DOI.

Range/Average: N.A.

Activity: N.A.

HQ: Senior Policy Advisor, same as **16.202**. (Note: no field offices for this program.)

16.597 MOTOR VEHICLE THEFT PROTECTION ACT PROGRAM ("Watch Your Car")

Assistance: project grants (100 percent/to 24 months).

Purposes: pursuant to VCCLEA and Motor Vehicle Theft Protection Act of 1994, to develop a national voluntary motor vehicle theft prevention program as a cooperative initiative among states, local governments, and DOJ. The Watch Your Car program allows owners to voluntarily display decals or devices alerting police that the vehicle normally is not driven between 1:00 a.m. and 5:00 a.m., nor across or in proximity of international borders or ports. Grant funds may be used: to print, purchase, and distribute decals and registration and consent forms; for public information campaigns; for law enforcement personnel training and overtime costs; for computer database upgrading; related costs.

Eligible applicants/beneficiaries: states; local government units (when states do not apply).

Range/Average: N.A.

Activity: 16 states with active programs.

HQ: Deputy Director, same address/phone as **16.585**. **Internet:** same as **16.579**. (Note: no field offices for this program.)

16.601 CORRECTIONS—TRAINING AND STAFF DEVELOPMENT

Assistance: project grants (100 percent); specialized services; technical information; training.

Purposes: pursuant to JJDPA as amended, to upgrade operation of state and local correctional programs through training seminars, workshops, or other programs for law enforcement officers, judges and judicial personnel, probation and parole personnel, corrections personnel, welfare workers, lay ex-offenders, and paraprofessionals—involved in the treatment and rehabilitation of criminal and juvenile offenders; to develop technical training teams.

Eligible applicants/beneficiaries: states, local government units, public and private agencies, educational institutions, organizations, and individuals.

Range: $1,500 to $300,000. **Average:** $100,000.

Activity: FY 04, 69,000 participants, including through video conference and "E-Learning".

HQ: National Institute of Corrections-DOJ, 320 First St. NW - Rm.5007,

Washington, DC 20534. Phone: (202)307-3106, (800)995-6423, FAX (202) 307-3361; TDD (202)307-3156. **Internet:** "www.usdoj.gov".

16.602 CORRECTIONS—RESEARCH AND EVALUATION AND POLICY FORMULATION

Assistance: project grants (100 percent); specialized services; technical information.

Purposes: pursuant to JJDPA as amended, for research and evaluation projects on the corrections system, including the causes, prevention, diagnosis, and treatment of criminal offenders. Project examples: classification systems and methods; community corrections options; communications audits.

Eligible applicants/beneficiaries: same as for **16.601**.

Range: $1,500 to $200,000. **Average:** $75,000.

Activity: not quantified specifically.

HQ: same as **16.601**.

16.603 CORRECTIONS—TECHNICAL ASSISTANCE/CLEARINGHOUSE

Assistance: project grants (100 percent); specialized services; technical information.

Purposes: pursuant to JJDPA as amended, to upgrade the operation of state and local correctional facilities, programs, and services for criminal and juvenile offenders; to provide consultation to federal, state, and local courts, departments, and agencies. Examples of funded projects: improved programs for female offenders; evaluation of offender classification systems; development of community sanctions.

Eligible applicants/beneficiaries: same as for **16.601**.

Range: $1,500 to $50,000. **Average:** $7,500.

Activity: FY 04, technical assistance responding to 359 requests.

HQ: Technical Assistance Coordinator/Prisons-Community Corrections, same address/phones/web site as **16.601**.

16.606 STATE CRIMINAL ALIEN ASSISTANCE PROGRAM ("SCAAP")

Assistance: direct payments/unrestricted use (100 percent).

Purposes: pursuant to the Immigration and Nationality Act as amended and VCCLEA, to reimburse states and localities for costs incurred to imprison undocumented aliens convicted of felonies or of two or more misdemeanors; to expedite the transfer of illegal aliens to federal custody for deportation.

Eligible applicants/beneficiaries: states, DC, PR, Guam, VI; authorized localities and local jurisdictions.

Range/Average: N.A.

Activity: cumulative 9-year reimbursement of $4-billion to 660 jurisdictions.

HQ: SCAAP, BJA-OJP-DOJ, 810 Seventh St. NW, Washington, DC 20531. Phone: (202)616-6500. **Internet:** same as **16.579**. (Note: no field offices for this program.)

PROGRAM INFORMATION   277

16.607 BULLETPROOF VEST PARTNERSHIP PROGRAM

Assistance: direct payments/specified use (50 percent/to 4 years).

Purposes: pursuant to the Bulletproof Vest Partnership Grant Act of 1998 and Bulletproof Vest Program Act of 2000, to purchase armored vests for law enforcement officers, including costs of vest carriers, attachments, inserts, essential covers, and fitting, shipping, handling, and tax charges.

Eligible applicants/beneficiaries: chief executives of states, local governments units, recognized tribes, territories, possessions.

Range/Average: N.A.

Activity: 4-year cumulative estimate, 5,129 applications approved covering the purchase of 190,000 vests.

HQ: BJA-OJP-DOJ, 810 Seventh St. NW - 4th floor, Washington, DC 20531. Phone: (202)616-6500, FAX (202)616-0314; Justice Response Center, (800)421-6770; Vest Technical Support Help Desk, (877)758-3787. **Internet:** same as **16.579** *and* "http://vests.ojp.gov"; e-mail, "askbja@ojp.usdoj.gov/bja". (Note: no field offices for this program.)

16.608 TRIBAL COURT ASSISTANCE PROGRAM

Assistance: project grants (100 percent/to 18 months).

Purposes: to develop, enhance, and operate tribal courts, including inter-tribal systems.

Eligible applicants/beneficiaries: tribal governments.

Range/Average: N.A.

Activity: not quantified specifically.

HQ: same as **16.596**. (Note: no field offices for this program.)

16.609 COMMUNITY PROSECUTION AND PROJECT SAFE NEIGHBORHOODS ("Community Prosecution Program")

Assistance: project grants (100 percent/to 18 months).

Purposes: pursuant to OCCSSA as amended and the Crime Control Act of 1990, to enable community leaders and residents to work with prosecutors and other justice officials in the identification of local priorities, problem solving, and strategic planning for public safety—through "Community Gun Violence Prosecution" projects. "Project Safe Neighborhoods" is designed to remove gun-wielding criminals from local neighborhoods. Funds may be used: to hire additional prosecutors to work on cases of firearm-related violent crime; for investigations; for training; for outreach efforts.

Eligible applicants/beneficiaries: state, county, city, and tribal public prosecutor offices.

Range: $50,000 to $480,000, depending on population.

Activity: as of FY 01, 34 awards (latest reported data).

HQ: Associate Deputy Director, same address/phone/web site as **16.580**. (Note: no field offices for this program.)

16.610 REGIONAL INFORMATION SHARING SYSTEMS ("RISS")

Assistance: project grants (100 percent).

Purposes: pursuant to OCCSSA, to enhance the ability of state and local criminal justice agencies to identify, target, and remove criminal conspiracies and activities that span interjurisdictional boundaries—by exchanging and sharing information among federal, state, and local law enforcement agencies, pertaining to known or suspected criminals or criminal activity; to provide technical resources, specialized equipment, and training.

Eligible applicants/beneficiaries: Middle Atlantic-Great Lakes Organized Crime Law Enforcement Center, Mid-States Organized Crime Information Center, New England State Police Information Network, Regional Organized Crime Information Center, Rocky Mountain Information Network, and Western States Information Network.

Range/Average: N.A.

Activity: FY 01 (sampling), 3,000 arrests, $100,000,000 in illegal controlled substances, property, and currency seized or recovered, 125,000 match hits (latest data reported).

HQ: same address/phone as **16.609**. (Note: no field offices for this program.)

16.611 CLOSED-CIRCUIT TELEVISING OF CHILD VICTIMS OF ABUSE ("CCTV")

Assistance: project grants (75 percent).

Purposes: pursuant to the Victims of Child Abuse Act as amended, to purchase equipment and provide personnel training for the closed-circuit televising and videotaping of the testimony of children in criminal proceedings for the violation of laws relating to the abuse of children.

Eligible applicants/beneficiaries: state or local units of government with enabling laws in effect.

Range: $50,000 to $100,000.

Activity: not quantified specifically.

HQ: same as **16.579**. (Note: no field offices for this program.)

16.612 NATIONAL WHITE COLLAR CRIME CENTER ("NWCCC")

Assistance: project grants.

Purposes: pursuant to OCCSSA as amended, to support the NWCCC, a nationwide support system for the prevention, investigation, and prosecution of economic crime—through research, training, and investigative support services including the Internet Fraud Complaint Center (IFCC).

Eligible applicants/beneficiaries: state and local law enforcement authorities.

Range: $7,000,000 to $10,000,000.

Activity: 1,300 personnel trained.

HQ: Program Development Division, same address/phone/web site as **16.607**. (Note: no field offices for this program.)

16.613 SCAMS TARGETING THE ELDERLY

Assistance: project grants (100 percent/12-18 months).

Purposes: pursuant to VCCLEA, to assist law enforcement in preventing and stopping marketing scams against senior citizens, through: training and technical assistance including a telemarketing fraud task force; state and local demonstration programs; public awareness initiatives and assistance through the National Fraud Information Center.

Eligible applicants/beneficiaries: public and private nonprofit organizations operating programs that are national in scope.

Range: $70,000 to $1,000,000.

Activity: not quantified specifically.

HQ: Associate Deputy Director, same address/phone/web site as **16.579**. (Note: no field offices for this program.)

16.614 STATE AND LOCAL ANTI-TERRORISM TRAINING ("SLATT")

Assistance: training; technical information; advisory services/counseling.

Purposes: pursuant to ATEDPA, to provide specialized multi-agency anti-terrorism preparedness training, covering both domestic and international threats and incidents. Training focus includes crisis and consequence management, anti-terrorist research, operational issues development, and technical assistance and support.

Eligible applicants/beneficiaries: state and local law enforcement and prosecution authorities.

Activity: 50 workshop and training sessions with 7,600 line officers and 586 law enforcement officers participating.

HQ: Senior Policy Advisor, same address/phone/web site as **16.579**. (Note: no field offices for this program.)

16.615 PUBLIC SAFETY OFFICERS' EDUCATIONAL ASSISTANCE ("PSOEA")

Assistance: direct payments/unrestricted use (100 percent/45 months).

Purposes: to provide financial assistance for higher education to dependents of public safety officers killed or totally disabled in the line of duty.

Eligible applicants/beneficiaries: spouses and surviving children under age 27—of federal, state, or local public safety officers including those who served public agencies with or without compensation in law enforcement, firefighting, or as members of public rescue squads or ambulance crews; effective November 1, 2000, FEMA personnel and state, local, and tribal emergency management and civil defense employees also became eligible. Categorical eligibility dates vary with service of victim; contact BJA for details.

Range/Average: $140 monthly for less than half-time students to $600 monthly for full-time.

Activity: FY 02, 233 dependents received assistance (latest data reported).

HQ: same address/phone as **16.571**. **Internet:** "www.ojp.usdoj.gov/bja/topics/psobprogram.html". (Note: no field offices for this program.)

16.616 INDIAN COUNTRY ALCOHOL DRUG PREVENTION

Assistance: project grants (100 percent/18 months).

Purposes: to assist tribal governments in the development and implementation of programs to reduce alcohol abuse and crime.

Eligible applicants/beneficiaries: tribal governments.

Range/Average: N.A.

Activity: N.A.

HQ: Senior Policy Advisor, same address/phone as **16.578**. **Internet:** "www.ojp.gov/bja". (Note: no field offices for this program.)

16.710 PUBLIC SAFETY PARTNERSHIP AND COMMUNITY POLICING GRANTS ("'COPS' Grants")

Assistance: project grants (75 percent/3 years).

Purposes: pursuant to OCCSSA as amended and VCCLEA, to increase police presence in communities, to expand and improve cooperation between law enforcement agencies and communities in addressing problems of crime and disorder, and to enhance public safety. Funds may be used to hire or rehire career law enforcement officers and to procure equipment, technology, or support systems. Grants may also cover costs of programs or projects to: increase the number of officers interacting with community members on proactive crime control and prevention; train officers to increase their skills in conflict resolution, mediation, problem solving; increase participation in multidisciplinary early intervention teams; develop new technologies; support similar activities including innovative approaches to fulfilling the duties of police officers.

Eligible applicants/beneficiaries: states, local government units, tribal governments, other public and private entities, multijurisdictional or regional consortia. Available also in territories and possessions.

Range: $2,000 to $6,250,000. **Average:** $354,000.

Activity: FY 04, 1,167 awards.

HQ: Office of Community Oriented Policing Services, DOJ, 1100 Vermont Ave. NW, Washington, DC 20530. Phone: (202)307-1480; DOJ Response Center, (800)421-6770. **Internet:** "www.usdoj.gov/cops". (Note: no field offices for this program.)

16.712 POLICE CORPS

Assistance: project grants (100 percent).

Purposes: pursuant to VCCLEA, for scholarships and reimbursement of expenses for advanced education and training on community patrol—of police personnel or of students pursuing careers in law enforcement, or dependents of officers killed in the line of duty. Individual participants may receive assistance for baccalaureate or graduate study (but not both) in preparation for police service. Undergraduate participants must first attend college and earn a baccalaureate degree. All recipients must complete 16-24 weeks of Police Corps training program and serve for four years as a state or local police officer. Graduate participants must complete their service and training obligations in advance. Dependents of officers killed in the line of duty need not fulfill the service obligation.

Eligible applicants/beneficiaries: states; state and local police forces; U.S. citizens or lawful permanent residents pursuing undergraduate or graduate study; dependents of officers killed in the line of duty. (NOTE: applications should be directed to the state lead agencies in participating states.)

Range: to $30,000 per participant. **Average:** state training costs, $25,000.

Activity: cumulatively as of 1 January 2004, 24 states participating; 1,522 participants receiving educational assistance, 60 scholarships to dependents.

HQ: Office of the Police Corps and Law Enforcement Education, OJP-DOJ, 810 Seventh St. NW, Washington, DC 20531. Phone: (202)353-8953; (888) 94CORPS; DOJ Response Center, (800)421-6770. **Internet:** "www.usdoj.gov/opclee/". (Note: no field offices for this program.)

16.726 JUVENILE MENTORING PROGRAM ("JUMP")

Assistance: project grants (100 percent/3 years).

Purposes: pursuant to JJDPA as amended, to develop, implement, and pilot-test mentoring strategies and programs for youth in the juvenile justice system, re-entry youth, and those in foster care.

Eligible applicants/beneficiaries: states, territories, and possessions in partnership with mentoring and other public or private nonprofit organizations.

Range: $650,000 for 5 project sites, and $350,000 for training and technical assistance supporting the sites; evaluation, $400,000.

Activity: not quantified specifically.

HQ: same as **16.541**. (Note: no field offices for this program.)

16.727 ENFORCING UNDERAGE DRINKING LAWS PROGRAM

Assistance: project grants (1-3 years).

Purposes: to enforce state laws prohibiting alcohol purchase, possession, and use by minors—through projects conducted by partnerships among state and local governments, organizations, and agencies, including for training and technical assistance.

Eligible applicants/beneficiaries: states, DC.

Range: from $360,000.

Activity: all states and DC funded.

HQ: same address/phone as **16.540**. **Internet:** "www.ojjdp.ncjrs.org". (Note: no field offices for this program.)

16.728 DRUG PREVENTION PROGRAM

Assistance: project grants (100 percent/12-18 months).

Purposes: to reduce drug use through projects: promoting multiple approaches to educating and motivating young adolescents to pursue healthy lifestyles; fostering interpersonal and decision making skills to help them choose alternatives to high-risk behaviors; providing the motivation and tools to build constructive lives.

Eligible applicants/beneficiaries: public and private agencies and organizations; states and territories; local governments units.

Range/Average: N.A.

Activity: 105 sites selected for training and technical assistance, involving 430 schools.

HQ: OJJDP-DOJ, Washington, DC 20531. Phone: (202)307-5911. **Internet:** same as **16.727**. (Note: no field offices for this program.)

16.730 REDUCTION AND PREVENTION OF CHILDREN'S EXPOSURE TO VIOLENCE
("Safe Start")

Assistance: project grants (100 percent/1-5 years).

Purposes: for a demonstration initiative to prevent and reduce the impact of family and community violence on young children, primarily from birth to age 6, by expanding existing community partnerships between service providers such as law enforcement, mental health, early childhood education agencies and others. Funds may be used to: establish or enhance a broad range of local intervention and treatment services; develop multi-agency protocols; develop community-wide systems.

Eligible applicants/beneficiaries: public agencies applying on behalf of collaboratives including private agencies and organizations.

Range/Average: N.A.

Activity: FY 05 estimate, 14 sites to be awarded funds.

HQ: Child Protection Division, OJJDP, Office of Justice Programs-DOJ, 810 Seventh St. NW, Washington, DC 20531. Phone: (202)616-7323. **Internet:** same as **16.523**. (Note: no field offices for this program.)

16.731 TRIBAL YOUTH PROGRAM
("TYP")

Assistance: project grants (100 percent/3 years).

Purposes: to reduce, control, and prevent crime by or against native American youth; to provide interventions for court-involved tribal youth; to improve tribal juvenile justice systems; to provide prevention programs focusing on alcohol and drugs.

Eligible applicants/beneficiaries: tribes and Alaska native villages, including partnerships.

Range: $300,000 to $500,000.

Activity: FY 04, 3,929 tribal communities funded.

HQ: Program Manager, State and Tribal Assistance Division, same address/phone/web site as **16.523**. (Note: no field offices for this program.)

16.732 NATIONAL EVALUATION OF THE SAFE SCHOOLS-HEALTHY STUDENTS INITIATIVE
("SS/HS National Evaluation")

Assistance: project grants (100 percent/5 years).

Purposes: to evaluate the Safe Schools/Healthy Students Initiative.

Eligible applicants/beneficiaries: public or private agencies, organizations, and individuals. For-profit organizations may apply, but must waive profits or fees.

Range/Average: N.A.

Activity: to date, 1 award for five-year project.

HQ: OJJDP, OJP-DOJ, Washington, DC 20531. Phone: (202)307-5929. **Internet:** same as **16.523**. (Note: no field offices for this program.)

16.734 SPECIAL DATA COLLECTIONS AND STATISTICAL STUDIES

Assistance: project grants.

Purposes: pursuant to OCCSSA, to produce official national statistics on crime and the administration of justice to guide federal, state, and local policymaking; to improve the quality of and access to the information. Projects may involve: data collection and processing activities; statistical and methodological research; technical assistance to state, local, and tribal governments; dissemination and clearinghouse services.

Eligible applicants/beneficiaries: state, local, and tribal governments; private and public nonprofit and profit organizations, IHEs, and qualified individuals—including in territories.

Range: $50,000 to $600,000.

Activity: new program listing in 2003.

HQ: same address as **16.550**. Phone: (202)616-3561. **Internet:** same as **16.554**. (Note: no field offices for this program.)

16.735 PROTECTING INMATES AND SAFEGUARDING COMMUNITIES DISCRETIONARY GRANT PROGRAM
("Prison Rape Elimination")

Assistance: project grants (100 percent/2 years).

Purposes: pursuant to the Prison Rape Elimination Act of 2003, to protect male and female inmates in adult and juvenile facilities from prison rape; to safeguard communities to which inmates return. Funds may be used for such costs as: under the Protecting Inmates component—personnel, training, technical assistance, data collection, victim service and treatment, and equipment necessary for the proper prevention, investigation, and prosecution; Safeguarding Communities component—training and technical assistance to states on moderating the growth of prison populations, education of state and local governments on the risks of inmate reentry, developing state and local government collaborative efforts, programs reducing rates of parole and probation revocation.

Eligible applicants/beneficiaries: states—in coordination with stakeholders.

Range: to $1,000,000.

Activity: new program in FY 04.

HQ: same address/phone as **16.585**. **Internet:** "www.ojp.usdoj.gov". (Note: no field offices for this program.)

16.736 TRANSITIONAL HOUSING ASSISTANCE FOR VICTIMS OF DOMESTIC VIOLENCE, STALKING, OR SEXUAL ASSAULT ("Transitional Housing")

Assistance: project grants (100 percent/to 2 years).

Purposes: pursuant to the Prosecutorial Remedies and Other Tools to End the Exploitation of Children Today Act of 2003 (PROTECT Act), for transitional housing assistance and related support services to minors, adults, and the dependents that are homeless or in need of such assistance as a result of fleeing from domestic violence, or for whom emergency shelter or other crisis intervention services are unavailable or insufficient. Funds may be used to pay for short-term rental or utilities and related expenses, and for transportation, counseling, child care, case management, employment counseling, and other assistance.

Eligible applicants/beneficiaries: states, local and tribal governments, other organizations.

Range/Average: N.A.

Activity: new program in FY 04.

HQ: same as **16.524**. (Note: no field offices for this program.)

16.737 GANG RESISTANCE EDUCATION AND TRAINING ("GREAT")

Assistance: project grants (100 percent/to 18 months).

Purposes: to help prevent youth crime, violence, and gang association, while developing positive relationships among law enforcement, families, and young persons. Funds may support personnel training and purchase of program materials and supplies.

Eligible applicants/beneficiaries: state, county, tribal, and municipal law enforcement agencies—including in territories; other special purpose law enforcement agencies (i.e., independent school districts).

Range: $3,500 to $500,000.

Activity: as of mid-2004 (sampling), 7,027 officers from 5,485 agencies funded; 3,900,000 youth trained.

HQ: Policy Office, same address/phone as **16.577**. **Internet:** "www.ojp.usdoj.gov/bja/great.html".

16.738 EDWARD BYRNE MEMORIAL JUSTICE ASSISTANCE GRANT PROGRAM

Assistance: formula grants; project grants (4 years).

Purposes: to acquire additional personnel, equipment, supplies, contractual support, training, technical assistance, and information systems—related to programs of law enforcement, prosecution and courts, prevention and education, corrections, drug treatment, planning, evaluation.

Eligible applicants/beneficiaries: state, territorial, and local government units.

Range: $10,000 to $37,000,000.

Activity: new program in FY 05.

HQ: Programs Office, BJA-OJP-DOJ, 810 Seventh St. NW - 4th floor, Washington, DC 20531. Phone: (202)616-6500. **Internet:** same as **16.579**. (Note: no field offices for this program.)

16.739 NATIONAL PRISON RAPE STATISTICS PROGRAM

Assistance: project grants (100 percent/12-18 months).

Purposes: pursuant to OCCSA as amended and Prison Rape Elimination Act, to collect and analyze data on the incidence of sexual assault among individuals held in federal and state prisons, local jails, and juvenile facilities, as well as on former inmates.

Eligible applicants/beneficiaries: state and local governments, private and public nonprofit and profit organizations, IHEs, individuals.

Range: $1,000,000 to $3,500,000.

Activity: new program listing in 2005.

HQ: same address as **16.550**. Phone: (202)616-3561. **Internet:** same as **16.554**. (Note: no field offices for this program.)

16.740 STATEWIDE AUTOMATED VICTIM INFORMATION NOTIFICATION (SAVIN) PROGRAM ("SAVIN")

Assistance: project grants (50 percent/2 years); technical information.

Purposes: for states to build, implement, or improve their statewide automated victim notification systems, enabling them to provide critical information to victims in near-real time and to build a nationwide information sharing capability. Funding may support program staffing, facilities, communication infrastructure, and equipment.

Eligible applicants/beneficiaries: designated state agencies, including tribal governments and territories.

Range/Average: N.A.

Activity: new program in FY 05.

HQ: Senior Policy Advisor, BJA-OJP-DOJ, 810 Seventh St. NW- 4th floor, Washington, DC 20531. Phone: (202)616-7829. **Internet:** "www.ojp.usdoj.gov/BJA". (Note: no field offices for this program.)

16.741 FORENSIC DNA CAPACITY ENHANCEMENT PROGRAM

Assistance: formula grants (75 percent/12-18 months).

Purposes: to improve the infrastructure and analysis capacity of existing crime laboratories. Eligible project costs include: upgrading, replacing, and purchasing equipment, instrumentation, and computer hardware and software; supplies such as offender-related evidence collection kits; certain contracted services; facilities renovation; accreditation; personnel training and continuing education.

Eligible applicants/beneficiaries: state and local government units with existing crime labs complying with DOJ requirements.

Range/Average: N.A.

Activity: new program in FY 05 (CFDA on-line version).

HQ: same as **16.560**. (Note: no field offices for this program.)

16.742 PAUL COVERDELL FORENSIC SCIENCES IMPROVEMENT GRANT PROGRAM

Assistance: formula grants.

Purposes: pursuant to the Paul Coverdell National Forensic Sciences Improvement Act of 2000, to improve the capacity of state and local forensic science and medical examiner services, including elimination of analysis backlogs by training and employing additional personnel. Funds may be used for personnel, computerization, laboratory equipment, supplies, accreditation, education, training, and certification.

Eligible applicants/beneficiaries: state administering agencies and local government units with approved plans.

Range/Average: N.A.

Activity: new program listing in 2005 (CFDA on-line version).

HQ: same as **16.560**. (Note: no field offices for this program.)

16.743 FORENSIC CASEWORK DNA BACKLOG REDUCTION PROGRAM

Assistance: formula grants (75-100 percent).

Purposes: to provide funds to state and local units of government with existing crime laboratories to identify and test backlogged forensic DNA casework samples and for post-conviction testing. Funds may be used to hire new directly associated project personnel, as well as certain directly related project costs including overtime pay to current laboratory and law enforcement staff.

Eligible applicants/beneficiaries: state and local government units with existing crime labs that conduct DNA analysis whether in accredited government-owned labs or through accredited fee-for-service vendors.

Range/Average: N.A.

Activity: new program listing 2005 in (CFDA on-line version).

HQ: same as **16.560**. (Note: no field offices for this program.)

DEPARTMENT OF LABOR

BUREAU OF LABOR STATISTICS

17.002 LABOR FORCE STATISTICS

Assistance: project grants (100 percent); technical information.

Purposes: to provide statistical data on and analyses of labor force activities— e.g., employment and unemployment, wages, occupations, layoffs, plant closings. Quarterly and monthly reports are produced, providing national, state, and local analyses. The data and analyses appear in BLS publications such as "Monthly Labor Review," "Unemployment in States and Local Areas," and "Handbook of Labor Statistics" published by BLS.

Eligible applicants/beneficiaries: cooperative agreement grants—State Workforce Agencies (SWAs) or alternate agencies. Information—anyone (from SWAs and BLS).

Range: $41,000 (Guam) to $8,223,000 (California). **Average:** $1,612,000.

Activity: monthly (sampling), labor force survey of 60,000; 400,000 establishments reporting on employment, hours, and earnings; 7,000 labor areas covered by reports on state and local employment statistics.

HQ: Office of Employment and Unemployment Statistics, BLS-DOL, Washington, DC 20212. Phone: (202)691-6400. **Internet:** "www.bls.gov".

17.003 PRICES AND COST OF LIVING DATA

Assistance: technical information.

Purposes: to provide statistical data for use in evaluating consumer, producer, export, and import prices and price changes, and consumer expenditures. Data are published periodically in the "Consumer Price Index," "Producer Price Index," international price indexes, and "Consumer Expenditure Surveys," as well as in other research and study reports.

Eligible applicants/beneficiaries: general public.

Activity: BLS indexes and analyses refined continuously.

HQ: Office of Prices and Living Conditions, BLS-DOL, Washington, DC 20212. Phone: (202)606-6960. **Internet:** same as **17.002**.

17.004 PRODUCTIVITY AND TECHNOLOGY DATA

Assistance: technical information.

Purposes: to provide and analyze data and trends on productivity and technology in major sectors of the U.S. economy and specific industries, and in selected countries. Pertinent reports are published, found in "Major Programs-Bureau of Labor Statistics." Also produced periodically are: consumer price indexes in foreign countries; international comparisons of productivity, labor costs, and the labor force and unemployment.

Eligible applicants/beneficiaries: general public.

Activity: FY 05 estimate, 29 reports, studies, and articles completed, 2,993 individual statistical series updated.

HQ: Office of Productivity and Technology, BLS-DOL, 2 Massachusetts Ave. NE, Washington, DC 20212. Phone: (202)691-5600. **Internet:** same as **17.002**.

17.005 COMPENSATION AND WORKING CONDITIONS

Assistance: project grants (50 percent); technical information.

Purposes: to develop and publish data on levels and trends in wages, employee benefits, compensation, occupational safety and health, and work stoppages.

Eligible applicants/beneficiaries: cooperative agreements—state and local governments to operate statistical programs concerning occupational health and safety. Technical information—general public.

Range: $4,100 (Idaho) to $658,000 (California). **Average:** $113,000.

Activity: annually, 110 bulletins, reports, studies, and research articles.

HQ: none; all contacts are with field offices listed in Part IV. **Internet:** same as **17.002**.

EMPLOYEE BENEFITS SECURITY ADMINISTRATION

17.150 EMPLOYEE BENEFITS SECURITY ADMINISTRATION "(EBSA)"

Assistance: technical information.

Purposes: pursuant to the Employee Retirement Income Security Act of 1974 as amended (ERISA), to protect the pension, health care, and other employee benefit plans of workers and their families, by: requiring reporting and disclosure of plan and financial information; developing and enforcing fiduciary standards; providing technical assistance, advisory and informational services, workshops and conferences; deterring and correcting violations of statutes through education, voluntary compliance, and civil and criminal enforcement actions. More than $4.8 trillion in assets are under control of ERISA, covering some 6,700,000 benefit plans with 150,000,000 participants.

Eligible applicants/beneficiaries: plan administrators, trustees, participants, beneficiaries.

Activity: annually, 150,000 participants, employers, and plan administrators assisted. FY 02, $832,000,000 in monetary recoveries.

HQ: EBSA-DOL, 200 Constitution Ave. NW - Rm.N5656, Washington, DC 20210. Phone: (202)693-8666; *publications hotline,* (866)444-3272. **Internet:** "www.dol.gov/dol/ebsa".

EMPLOYMENT AND TRAINING ADMINISTRATION

17.201 REGISTERED APPRENTICESHIP AND OTHER TRAINING

Assistance: advisory services/counseling.

Purposes: pursuant to the National Apprenticeship Act of 1937 as amended, to assist industry in developing, expanding, and improving apprenticeship and other training programs; to register apprentices and programs; to provide technical assistance to state apprenticeship councils; to ensure equal employment opportunities in registered apprenticeship and other training programs. (Apprentice wage rates are exempt from prevailing wages requirements of the Davis-Bacon Act and the Service Contract Act when federal and state programs are registered.)

Eligible applicants: employers, groups or associations of employers, and individual employers—with or without union participation.

Eligible beneficiaries: individuals at least age 16 with sufficient ability, aptitude, and education to master the rudiments of the trade or occupation and to satisfactorily complete required theoretical instruction.

Activity: FY 04, 405,000 apprentices (including in the military) trained in 28,000 registered programs; 139,000 new apprentices registered.

HQ: Administrator, Office of Apprenticeship Training, Employer and Labor Services (OATELS), ETA-DOL, 200 Constitution Ave. NW - Rm.N-4671, Washington, DC 20210. Phone: (202)693-2796; FAX (202)693-2808. **Internet:** "www.doleta.gov/atels_bat".

17.202 CERTIFICATION OF FOREIGN WORKERS FOR TEMPORARY AGRICULTURAL EMPLOYMENT

Assistance: specialized services.

Purposes: pursuant to the Immigration and Nationality Act of 1952 as amended and Immigration Reform and Control Act of 1986, to certify and assist agricultural and other employers in obtaining temporary alien workers for specific seasonal jobs when domestic workers are unavailable. Funding for this program includes **17.203** and **17.252**.

Eligible applicants/beneficiaries: organizations and individual employers.

Activity: FY 03, 45,000 foreign workers certified.

HQ: Director, Office of National Programs, U.S. Employment Service, ETA-DOL, 200 Constitution Ave. NW - Rm.C-4312, Washington, DC 20210. Phone: (202)693-3010. **Internet:** "www.dol.gov".

17.203 LABOR CERTIFICATION FOR ALIEN WORKERS

Assistance: specialized services.

Purposes: pursuant to the Immigration and Nationality Act of 1952 as amended, to certify aliens seeking nonagricultural employment, provided U.S workers similarly employed will not be adversely affected. ETA coordinates certification applications with the Department of State and DHS. Funding for this program is included in **17.202**.

Eligible applicants/beneficiaries: employers unable to find qualified domestic workers to meet their needs; aliens whose category of employment is included in the DOL "Schedule A" list of precertified occupations.

Activity: FY 04, 89,000 new permanent, 11,000 temporary applications received.

HQ: Director, same address, web site as **17.202**. Phone: (202)693-3502.

17.207 EMPLOYMENT SERVICE

Assistance: formula grants (100 percent); specialized services; advisory services/counseling.

Purposes: pursuant to the Wagner-Peyser Act of 1933 as amended and Workforce Investment Act of 1998 (WIA), for states to provide "One-Stop" job finding, counseling, recruitment, referral, re-employment, and placement services, including a computerized interstate listing of hard-to-fill openings, and testing services for job seekers and employers seeking qualified workers—in cooperation with the DOL's U.S. Employment Service nationwide network of public employment offices. Specialized services may be provided for groups such as veterans, migrant and seasonal farm workers, ex-offenders, and the disabled, disadvantaged, youth, minorities, and older workers.

Eligible applicants: states, DC, VI, PR, Guam.

Eligible beneficiaries: employers seeking workers; persons seeking employment; associated groups. Veterans receive priority, with handicapped veterans receiving preferential treatment.

Range: N.A.

Activity: formula based on average state civilian labor force and unemployment.

HQ: Administrator, Office of Workforce Security, U.S. Employment Service, ETA-DOL, Washington, DC 20210. Phone: (202)693-3046. **Internet:** "www.doleta.gov".

17.225 UNEMPLOYMENT INSURANCE

Assistance: formula grants; direct payments/unrestricted use.

Purposes: pursuant to SSA, Trade Act of 1974, Federal Unemployment Tax Act, Federal Employees and Ex-Service Members Act, Robert T. Stafford Disaster Relief and Emergency Assistance Act, and amendments, to administer state programs providing unemployment compensation, trade adjustment and disaster unemployment assistance, and unemployment compensation for eligible workers, federal employees, and ex-service members. State unemployment insurance tax collections fund benefit payments; federal unemployment insurance tax collections fund state administrative costs, and reimburse states for one-half the costs of extended benefits paid under SSA and the Federal Unemployment Tax Act; benefits to former federal civilian employees and ex-service members are paid out of the Federal Employees Compensation Account in the Unemployment Trust Fund, and reimbursed by the former employing agency; Trade Adjustment Assistance payments and training costs are paid out of the Federal Unemployment Benefits and Allowance Appropriation account in the Unemployment Trust Fund; Disaster Unemployment Assistance is paid by FEMA.

Eligible applicants: state workforce agencies, including in DC, PR, and VI.

Eligible beneficiaries: workers with wages subject to state unemployment laws, federal civilian employees, ex-servicemembers, workers whose unemployment resulted from trade imports, workers whose unemployment resulted from a Presidentially declared disaster—all are eligible if they are involuntarily unemployed, able to and available for work, and meet state eligibility and qualifying requirements. Individual state eligibility requirements are available from local "One-Stop" employment centers.

Range: $2,000,000 to $355,000,000. **Average:** $42,500,000.

Activity: not quantified specifically.

HQ: Administrator, Office of Workforce Security, ETA-DOL, 200 Constitution Ave. NW, Washington, DC 20210. Phone: (202)693-3029. **Internet:** "www.workforcesecurity.doleta.gov/".

17.235 SENIOR COMMUNITY SERVICE EMPLOYMENT PROGRAM ("SCSEP" - "Older Worker Program")

Assistance: formula grants; project grants (90 percent).

Purposes: pursuant to the Older Americans Act of 1965 as amended, to provide, foster, and promote useful part-time (usually 20 hours weekly) training and work opportunities for unemployed persons age 55 or over—in community service activities such as schools, hospitals, day care centers, park systems, public housing projects, weatherization and nutrition programs, libraries, etc. Training, counseling, and other supportive services may be provided. The program also assists and promotes the transition of enrollees into unsubsidized employment.

Eligible applicants: states; national public and private nonprofit agencies and organizations other than political parties; tribal organizations.

Eligible beneficiaries: adults age 55 or older, with family income at or below 125 percent of the HHS poverty level.

Range: $330,000 to $86,000,000.

Activity: 2004 estimate, 103,000 part-time positions supported; 69 grant awards annually.

HQ: Division of Older Worker Programs, Office of National Programs, ETA-DOL, 200 Constitution Ave. NW - Rm.S4209, Washington, DC 20210. Phone: (202)693-3842; FAX (202)693-3817. **Internet:** "http://doleta.gov/seniors/". (Note: no field offices for this program.)

17.245 TRADE ADJUSTMENT ASSISTANCE—WORKERS

Assistance: direct payments/unrestricted use (to 78 weeks); specialized services.

Purposes: pursuant to the Trade Act of 1974 as amended, Omnibus Trade and Competitiveness Act of 1988, North American Free Trade Agreement Implementation Act, and other acts, to provide "adjustment assistance" payments to and assistance for workers adversely affected by increased imports—including relocation allowances, job testing, counseling, training, and placement services. Payments may be made only after state unemployment compensation benefits have been exhausted. The maximum number of weeks of state unemployment compensation, extended benefits, and trade readjustment allowances may not exceed 52—except that benefits may be paid for an additional 26 weeks to workers participating in approved training.

Eligible applicants: groups of three of more workers, or their union or authorized representative, working with designated state agencies.

Eligible beneficiaries: unemployed workers certified by DOL as eligible to apply for adjustment assistance, and meeting specific other requirements.

Range: same as weekly amount of state unemployment benefits.

Activity: cumulatively 1975-2004, 31,000 certifications covering 4,003,000 workers.

HQ: Director, Division of Trade Adjustment Assistance, ETA-DOL, 200 Constitution Ave. NW - Rm.C-5311, Washington, DC 20210. Phone: (202)693-3560. **Internet:** same as **17.207**.

17.252 ATTESTATIONS BY EMPLOYERS USING NON-IMMIGRANT ALIENS IN SPECIALTY OCCUPATIONS

Assistance: specialized services.

Purposes: pursuant to the Immigration and Nationality Acts of 1952 and 1990 as amended, to process attestations by employers of the working conditions and wages of aliens to be employed in specialty occupations. Documentation must be available for public inspection at the employer's principal place of business, as well as at the ETA. Funding for this program is included in **17.202**.

Eligible applicants/beneficiaries: employers; aliens to be employed in specialty occupations or as fashion models.

Activity: FY 04, 340,000 attestations received and processed.

HQ: same as **17.202**.

17.258 WIA ADULT PROGRAM

Assistance: formula grants (100 percent/to 3 years).

Purposes: pursuant to WIA, for workforce investment activities that increase the unsubsidized employment, retention and earnings, and occupational skill attainment of participants, through One Stop Career Centers providing three levels of services: (1) "core," including outreach, job search and placement assistance, and labor market information; (2) "intensive," with comprehensive assessments, individual employment plans, counseling, and career planning; (3) "training," including occupation and basic skills, linked to job opportunities. Such supportive services as transportation and child care may also be provided.

Eligible applicants: states, DC, PR, and outlying areas, which allocate funds to Workforce Investment Boards.

Eligible beneficiaries: adults age 18 or older, with priority to public assistance recipients and other low-income individuals.

Range/Average: N.A.

Activity: 2004 estimate, 460,000 participants.

HQ: Director, Division of Adult and Dislocated Workers, ETA-DOL, 200 Constitution Ave. NW - Rm.C4318, Washington, DC 20210. Phone: (202) 693-3375. **Internet:** same as **17.207**.

17.259 WIA YOUTH ACTIVITIES
("WIA Formula Youth")

Assistance: formula grants.

Purposes: pursuant to WIA, to help low-income youth acquire the educational and occupational skills, training, and support needed to achieve academic and employment success and make the transition to successful careers and productive adulthood. Funds may be used by local workforce investment boards for: employment and training activities; mentoring; supportive services; and, to develop opportunities for leadership development, citizenship, and community service.

Eligible applicants: state governors.

Eligible beneficiaries: individuals age 14-21 whose total family income does not exceed the higher of the poverty line or 70 percent of the lower living standard income, and are deficient in basic literacy skills, or school dropouts, homeless, runaways, foster children, pregnant or parents, offenders, or require additional assistance to complete their education or secure and hold employment.

Range/Average: N.A.

Activity: 2003, 370,000 youth enrolled.

HQ: Chief, Division of Program Planning and Operations, ETA-DOL, 200 Constitution Ave. NW, Washington, DC 20210. Phone: (202)693-3608; FAX (202)693-3532. **Internet:** "www.doleta.gov/youth_services/formulagrants.cfm".

17.260 WIA DISLOCATED WORKERS

Assistance: formula grants (100 percent/3 years); project grants (100 percent).

Purposes: pursuant to WIA, to assist dislocated workers in obtaining essentially the services available under **17.258**. National Emergency Grant funds also are available under this program (see eligibility factors below).

Eligible applicants: states, DC, PR, and outlying areas, including for National Emergency Grant funds.

Eligible beneficiaries: workers that have lost their jobs, including those dislocated because of plant closings or mass layoffs, and unlikely to return to their previous industry or occupations; formerly self-employed individuals; displaced, dependent homemakers no longer supported by the other's income. National Emergency Grant funds—same eligibility; also includes certain military defense employees and individuals affected by mass layoffs, natural disasters, federal government actions, and other specified circumstances.

Range/Average: N.A.

Activity: 2003, 365,000 participants.

HQ: same as **17.258**.

17.261 EMPLOYMENT AND TRAINING ADMINISTRATION PILOTS, DEMONSTRATIONS, AND RESEARCH PROJECTS

Assistance: project grants (to 100 percent/1-2 years).

Purposes: pursuant to WIA, for pilot and demonstration projects with interstate validity, addressing national employment and training problems. Projects must include direct services to individuals to enhance employment opportunities, and an evaluation component. Eligible activities include: establishing advanced manufacturing technology skill centers involving local partnerships; training to upgrade the skills of employed workers or to increase employment of out-of-school youth residing in enterprise communities or empowerment zones; joint programs with DOD to develop training programs using innovative learning technology; distance learning projects; partnerships with national organizations experienced in employment and training programs; assistance to public housing authorities providing resident job training; local project evaluation.

Eligible applicants/beneficiaries: state and local governments, federal agencies, private nonprofit and profit organizations including religious and community-based, and educational institutions.

Range: $100,000 to $1,750,000.

Activity: FY 05 estimate, 50 new projects approved.

HQ: Division of Pilots, Demonstrations and Research, Office of Policy and Research, ETA-DOL, 200 Constitution Ave. NW - Rm.N-4470, Washington, DC 20210. Phone: (202)693-3676. **Internet:** same as **17.207**.

17.262 EMPLOYMENT AND TRAINING ADMINISTRATION EVALUATIONS

Assistance: project grants (100 percent/1-6 years).

Purposes: pursuant to WIA, for continuing evaluations of WIA programs and activities to improve program management and effectiveness.

Eligible applicants/beneficiaries: qualified applicants.

Range: $80,000 to $20,000,000. **Average:** $1,000,000.

Activity: FY 04, 15 ongoing, 5 new evaluations.

HQ: Office of Performance and Technology, ETA-DOL, 200 Constitution Ave. NW - Rm.S-5206, Washington, DC 20210. Phone: (202)693-3912. **Internet:** same as **17.207**.

17.263 YOUTH OPPORTUNITY GRANTS ("YOG")

Assistance: project grants (100 percent/to 5 years).

Purposes: pursuant to WIA, for projects with purposes and activities similar to those described in **17.259**, targeted to youth living in empowerment zones, enterprise communities, and areas of high poverty. Funds may also be used for intensive placement services and for follow-up services for not less than two years after completion of participation.

Eligible applicants: local workforce investment boards or entities: serving empowerment zones or enterprise communities; or, that are states with a zone but designated a high poverty area by the governor; or, that consist of one or two poverty areas designated by the governor that may apply; or, that are located on an Indian reservation or serves Oklahoma Indians or Alaska native villages or native groups.

Eligible beneficiaries: youth age 14-21 residing in target areas, that are legal U.S. residents, regardless of family income. Males age 18 and above must meet Selective Service Act requirements.

Range: to $11,000,000.

Activity: 80,000 youth served.

HQ: Office of Youth Opportunities, ETA-DOL, 200 Constitution Ave. NW - Rm.N-4459, Washington, DC 20210. Phone: (202)693-3604. **Internet:**

"www.doleta.gov/youth_services/opportunities.asp". (Note: no field offices for this program.)

17.264 MIGRANT AND SEASONAL FARMWORKERS ("National Farmworker Jobs Program")

Assistance: formula grants; project grants (100 percent/1-4 years).

Purposes: pursuant to WIA, for individual employability development assistance and related services to migrant and seasonal farm workers and their dependents suffering chronic unemployment and under-employment. Services may include initial assessment, "One-Stop" Center services, job placement, eligibility determination, intensive case management, basic education, drop-out prevention assistance, allowance payments, training including classroom and on-the-job, and emergency and other supportive services.

Eligible applicants: public agencies and state and local government units; private nonprofit organizations.

Eligible beneficiaries: individuals who, during any consecutive 12 months in the prior 24-month period, were seasonal or migrant farm workers, and are legally available for work in compliance with Selective Service Act requirements.

Range: $100,000 to $7,000,000.

Activity: 2003, 53 grants awarded.

HQ: Division of Seasonal Farmworker Programs, Office of National Programs, ETA-DOL, 200 Constitution Ave. NW - Rm.S-4206, Washington, DC 20210. Phone: (202)693-3843; FAX (202)693-3945. **Internet:** "http://wdsc.doleta.gov/msfw/". (Note: no field offices for this program.)

17.265 NATIVE AMERICAN EMPLOYMENT AND TRAINING ("Section 166 Program" - "Indian Program")

Assistance: formula grants (100 percent/1-3 years).

Purposes: pursuant to WIA, for employment and training activities for native Americans, including classroom and on-the-job training, work experience, youth employment programs. Grant funds may be used to pay for such services as day care, health care, job search, relocation and transportation allowances.

Eligible applicants/beneficiaries: tribes, bands, or groups; Alaska native villages or groups; Hawaiian native communities; consortia of the foregoing groups.

Range: $12,000 to $6,489,000. **Average:** $292,000.

Activity: 2003, 18,000 participants.

HQ: Division of Indian and Native American Programs, Office of National Programs, same address as **17.264**. Phone: (202)693-3737; FAX (202)693-3818. **Internet:** "http://wdsc.doleta.gov/dinap". (Note: no field offices for this program.)

17.266 WORK INCENTIVES GRANT

Assistance: project grants (100 percent/2 years).

Purposes: pursuant to WIA and the Wagner-Peyser Act, to develop a "One-Stop" system infrastructure toward the achievement of model seamless and comprehensive services for the disabled, increasing their employability, job retention, earning capacity, and occupational skill attainment. Funds support expanding the capacity within the One-Stop system through "Disability Program Navigator" (DPN) positions to better coordinate employment services available to the handicapped; DOL program activities are coordinated with SSA.

Eligible applicants/beneficiaries: states and tribal entities capable of launching DPN initiatives; consortia.

Range: $400,000 to $2,000,000.

Activity: 2004, 227 DPN positions funded in 17 participating states.

HQ: Division of Disability and Workforce Programs, ETA-DOL, 200 Constitution Ave. NW, Washington, DC 20210. Phone: (202)693-3844; FAX (202)693-3818; TTY (202)693-2871. **Internet:** "www.doleta.gov/disability".

17.267 WIA INCENTIVE GRANTS—SECTION 503 GRANTS TO STATES

Assistance: project grants (100 percent/to 3 years).

Purposes: pursuant to WIA and the Carl D. Perkins Vocational and Applied Technology Education Amendments of 1998, for innovative programs furthering the purposes of the authorizing acts—including services and activities beyond those provided with regular WIA funding. Applicants should plan activities promoting cooperation and collaboration among administering agencies.

Eligible applicants/beneficiaries: states, DC, VI, PR, Guam—provided their performance under WIA exceeds expected outcome levels.

Range: $750,000 to $3,000,000.

Activity: new program listing in 2003.

HQ: Chief, Division of System Accomplishments and Accountability, Office of Performance and Technology, ETA-DOL, 200 Constitution Ave. NW - Rm.S5206, Washington, DC 20210. Phone: (202)693-3031. **Internet:** same as **17.207**. (Note: no field offices for this program.)

EMPLOYMENT STANDARDS ADMINISTRATION

17.301 NON-DISCRIMINATION AND AFFIRMATIVE ACTION BY FEDERAL CONTRACTORS AND FEDERALLY ASSISTED CONSTRUCTION CONTRACTORS
("Office of Federal Contract Compliance Programs" - "OFCCP")

Assistance: investigation of complaints.

Purposes: pursuant to the Rehabilitation Act of 1973, Vietnam Era Readjustment Assistance Act of 1974, Veterans Codification Act of 1991, ADA, Immigration Reform and Control Act of 1986, and amendments, to enforce nondiscrimination and affirmative action regulations covering employment by federal contractors including subcontractors and those involved in federally-assisted construction. Complaints alleging employment discrimination on the basis of race, sex, religion, color, national origin, disability, or covered veteran status may be filed with OFCCP. Technical advice and assistance are available to employers.

Eligible applicants/beneficiaries: employment applicants, employees, and former employees of federal contractors or federally involved contractors performing work in the U.S., Panama Canal Zone, and possessions and territories—including those recruited in the U.S. to perform work abroad.

Activity: FY 04, $34,400,000 in financial remedies to minority, female, and handicapped workers.

HQ: Deputy Assistant Secretary, OFCCP, Employment Standards Administration-DOL, Washington, DC 20210. Phone: (202)693-0101. **Internet:** "www.dol.gov".

17.302 LONGSHORE AND HARBOR WORKERS' COMPENSATION

Assistance: direct payments/unrestricted use.

Purposes: pursuant to the Longshore and Harbor Workers Compensation Act as extended, to replace and supplement income to compensate for permanent disability or death resulting from injury, including occupational disease; to provide benefits for certain medical expenses including hospital care, and funeral expenses up to $3,000. Benefits are paid by private insurers or self-insured employers; federal funds are available in certain cases of permanent total disability and death.

Eligible applicants/beneficiaries: longshore and harbor workers; certain maritime employees working on U.S. navigable waters and in pier and dock areas; employees working on the Outer Continental Shelf, of nonappropriated fund instrumentalities, of private employers working in DC within specified periods or abroad under U.S. government contracts; survivors. PR is not covered.

Range: disability—two-thirds of average weekly wage; death benefits—50 percent of average wages of deceased, to widow or widower, plus 16.7 percent for each surviving child with a 66.7 percent limit. Benefits are limited to 200 percent of national average weekly wage. Payments are made for the period of total or partial disability, with no monetary limit; death benefits are paid to the spouse until death or remarriage, and to children until age 18—or 23 if qualified as a student.

Activity: annually, 20,000 new lost-time injury claims.

HQ: Division of Longshore and Harbor Workers' Compensation, Office of Workers' Compensation Programs, Employment Standards Administration-DOL, Washington, DC 20210. Phone: (202)693-0038. **Internet:** same as **17.301**.

17.303 WAGE AND HOUR STANDARDS
("Federal Wage-Hour Laws")

Assistance: advisory services/counseling; investigation of complaints.

Purposes: pursuant to the Fair Labor Standards Act, Walsh-Healy Public Contracts Act, Davis-Bacon Act, Immigration and Nationality Acts, Family and Medical Leave Act of 1993, amendments, and other acts, to provide and enforce standards protecting wages and working conditions of working persons with respect to minimum rate of pay, overtime pay, prevailing hourly wage rates, fringe benefits, child labor, and family and medical leave including for adoptive parents; to enforce wage payment standards for professional performers and related professional employees, as well as for students, nonimmigrant agricultural and certain nonagricultural workers and employees, seasonal workers, handicapped workers, apprentices, and other employment categories; to curtail employer use of lie detector tests. Generally, federal wage and hour standards apply to employees engaged in interstate or foreign commerce, or in the production of goods for such commerce, and to government employees at all levels. Funding for this program includes **17.306** and **17.308**.

Eligible applicants/beneficiaries: any covered employee in the U.S., territories, possessions, and Outer Continental Shelf lands. Family and medical leave provisions apply to all public employers and private employers with 50 or more employees within 75-mile radius of worksite.

Activity: FY 04, $196,000,000 in back wages recovered.

HQ: Administrator, Wage and Hour Division, Employment Standards Administration-DOL, Washington, DC 20210. Phone: (202)693-0051. **Internet:** same as **17.301**.

17.306 CONSUMER CREDIT PROTECTION
("Federal Wage Garnishment Law")

Assistance: advisory services/counseling; investigation of complaints.

Purposes: pursuant to the Consumer Credit Protection Act as amended, to enforce federal restrictions on the amount of a person's earnings that may be garnished, and prohibiting employers from discharging employees by reason of garnishment for any one indebtedness. Earnings are defined as compensation paid or payable for personal services, whether as wages, salary, commission, bonuses, including periodic payments under a pension or retirement program. Funding for this program is included in **17.303**.

Eligible applicants/beneficiaries: persons with earnings subjected to garnishment—in the U.S., territories, and possessions.

Activity: not quantified specifically.

HQ: same as **17.303**.

17.307 COAL MINE WORKERS' COMPENSATION
("Black Lung")

Assistance: direct payments/unrestricted use.

Purposes: pursuant to the Federal Mine Safety and Health Amendments Act of 1977 as amended, to pay monthly cash benefits to coal miners totally disabled with black lung disease, and to their surviving dependents.

Eligible applicants/beneficiaries: disabled coal miners; widows, and other surviving dependents. Included are some workers involved in coal transportation in and around mines, and in coal mine construction. Beneficiaries must have become "totally disabled" from coal workers' pneumoconiosis, as defined in the Act. Applicants may work in areas other than coal mines and remain eligible for benefits. Benefits may be reduced in cases of excess earnings.

Range: effective January 2005, $562 monthly for claimant only, to $1,125 for three or more dependents (not including medical services). **Average:** $574.30 monthly.

Activity: 2004, 102,000 beneficiaries, 18,000 dependents received benefits.

HQ: Director, Division of Coal Mine Workers' Compensation, Office of Workers' Compensation Programs, Employment Standards Administration-DOL, Washington, DC 20210. Phone: (202)693-0046. **Internet:** same as **17.301**.

17.308 FARM LABOR CONTRACTOR REGISTRATION ("Crew Leader")

Assistance: advisory services/counseling; investigation of complaints.

Purposes: pursuant to the Migrant and Seasonal Agricultural Worker Protection Act as amended, to enforce regulations covering farm labor contractors, agricultural employers, and agricultural associations regarding such factors as wages, records, transportation, health, safety, liability insurance, and housing provided for migrant and seasonal agricultural workers. Funding for this program is included in **17.303**.

Eligible applicants/beneficiaries: contractors and their full-time or regular employees that recruit, solicit, hire, furnish, or transport migrant or seasonal agricultural workers for employment for a fee in any form must register with DOL.

Activity: FY 04, $1,194,000 in back pay collected for 3,700 agricultural workers.

HQ: same as **17.303**.

17.309 LABOR ORGANIZATION REPORTS ("Landrum-Griffin Act")

Assistance: advisory services/counseling; technical information; investigation of complaints.

Purposes: pursuant to the Labor-Management Reporting and Disclosure Act of 1959 as amended, to provide for reporting and disclosure of financial transactions and administrative practices of labor organizations, employers, labor consultants, and others required to report under the Landrum-Griffin Act; to provide standards for the election of union officers, administration of trusteeships, fiduciary responsibilities of union officers, and rights of union members; for court enforcement of safeguards pertaining to union organizations.

Eligible applicants/beneficiaries: union officers, members, organizations. All required reports are available for disclosure to the general public.

Activity: FY 04, 36,000 reports received and processed; 3,100 investigations; 785 compliance audits; 46 elections supervised.

HQ: Office of Labor-Management Standards-DOL, 200 Constitution Ave. NW, Washington, DC 20210. Phone: (202)693-0123; *Public Disclosure Room (N-5608)*, (202)693-0125. **Internet:** same as **17.301**.

OCCUPATIONAL SAFETY AND HEALTH ADMINISTRATION

17.502 OCCUPATIONAL SAFETY AND HEALTH—SUSAN HARWOOD TRAINING GRANTS

Assistance: project grants.

Purposes: pursuant to the Occupational Safety and Health Act, to provide occupational safety and health training and education to employees and employers, particularly in the recognition, avoidance, and abatement of workplace hazards.

Eligible applicants/beneficiaries: nonprofit organizations.

Range: $33,000 to $545,000.

Activity: FY 05 estimate, 67 grants.

HQ: Assistant Secretary, OSHA-DOL, Washington, DC 20210. Phone: (202) 693-2000; (847)297-4810. **Internet:** "www.osha.gov".

17.503 OCCUPATIONAL SAFETY AND HEALTH—STATE PROGRAM

Assistance: project grants (50 percent).

Purposes: pursuant to the Occupational Safety and Health Act, for state administration and enforcement of approved occupational safety and health programs.

Eligible applicants/beneficiaries: designated state agencies.

Range: $203,000 to $23,135,000.

Activity: FY 06 estimate, 58,000 state enforcement inspections.

HQ: same address, web site as **17.502**. Phone: (202)693-1919.

17.504 CONSULTATION AGREEMENTS

Assistance: project grants (90 percent).

Purposes: pursuant to the Occupational Safety and Health Act, for consultative workplace safety and health services by states to smaller employers, primarily those with hazardous operations.

Eligible applicants: designated state agencies.

Eligible beneficiaries: any private employer.

Range: $199,000 to $5,089,000.

Activity: FY 06 estimate, 32,000 consultation visits.

HQ: same as **17.503**.

17.505 OSHA DATA INITIATIVE

Assistance: project grants.

Purposes: pursuant to the Occupational Safety and Health Act, for cooperative agreements for the collection of injury and illness data from employers in specified industries—for OSHA use in targeting interventions.

Eligible applicants/beneficiaries: designated state agencies.

Range: $5,750 to $186,000. **Average:** $51,000.

Activity: new program listing in 2004. FY 06 estimate, 80,000 employer samples collected.

HQ: same as **17.503**.

MINE SAFETY AND HEALTH ADMINISTRATION

17.600 MINE HEALTH AND SAFETY GRANTS

Assistance: project grants (80 percent).

Purposes: pursuant to the Federal Mine Safety and Health Amendments Act of 1977 as amended, to develop and enforce state laws and regulations related to the health and safety of miners; to improve workmen's compensation and occupational disease laws and programs; for miner training.

Eligible applicants/beneficiaries: any mining state.

Range: $3,700 to $603,000. **Average:** $162,000.

Activity: not quantified specifically.

HQ: Assistant Secretary/Mine Safety and Health, Mine Safety and Health Administration-DOL, 1100 Wilson Blvd., Arlington, VA 22209. Phone: (202)693-9572, -9580. **Internet:** "www.msha.gov". (Note: no field offices for this program.)

17.601 MINE HEALTH AND SAFETY COUNSELING AND TECHNICAL ASSISTANCE

Assistance: advisory services/counseling; technical information.

Purposes: pursuant to the Federal Mine Safety and Health Amendments Act of 1977 as amended, to establish or improve health and safety conditions in and around coal, metal, and nonmetallic mines and mineral facilities—through special studies, technical assistance, investigations, equipment testing.

Eligible applicants/beneficiaries: states, organizations, or individuals.

Activity: not quantified specifically.

HQ: same address, web site as **17.600**. Phone: (202)693-9472, -9478.

17.602 MINE HEALTH AND SAFETY EDUCATION AND TRAINING

Assistance: training.

Purposes: pursuant to the Federal Mine Safety and Health Amendments Act of 1977 as amended, to provide initial and advanced technical mine safety and health training of federal mine inspectors, miners, and others. Curriculum materials and audiovisual programs are available.

Eligible applicants/beneficiaries: mine operators, miners, or their agents.

Activity: 1,495 course days of federal employee training; mining industry, 244 days.

HQ: Director, Educational Policy and Development, same address, web site as **17.600**. Phone: (202)693-9572, (304)256-3201.

WOMEN'S BUREAU, OFFICE OF THE SECRETARY

17.700 WOMEN'S BUREAU

Assistance: advisory services/counseling.

Purposes: to develop training and employment policies and programs affecting the employment of women and their retirement security; to expand employment opportunities for women and promote their entry into better paying jobs, especially in new technology and nontraditional occupations. Project examples: online newsletter; apprenticeship programs; Work and Family projects; planning for employer-sponsored child care; Girls 'E-Mentoring in Science, Engineering & Technology, and in nursing.

Eligible applicants/beneficiaries: any individual or group, including in territories.

Activity: not quantified specifically.

HQ: Director, Women's Bureau, OS-DOL, Washington, DC 20210. Phone: (202)693-6710; Office of Information and Support Services (Rm.S3305), (202)693-6727. **Internet:** "www.dol.gov".

OFFICE OF DISABILITY EMPLOYMENT POLICY

17.720 DISABILITY EMPLOYMENT POLICY DEVELOPMENT

Assistance: project grants.

Purposes: to promote employment opportunities for persons with disabilities by providing disability employment policy leadership to DOL and other federal agencies, through: research and dissemination activities; outreach initiatives; coordination with such other initiatives as Workforce Investment Act projects and programs; technical information about the provisions of the ADA to business leaders, organized labor, and others; and, a range of related activities.

Eligible applicants/beneficiaries: varies according to grant.

Range: $15,000 to $1,500,000.

Activity: new program listing in 2002 (replacing former program 53.001, operated by the President's Committee on Employment of People with Disabilities).

HQ: Office of Disability Employment Policy, DOL, 200 Constitution Ave. NW - Rm.S1303, Washington, DC 20210. Phone: (202)693-7880; TTY

(202)693-7881; FAX (202)693-7888. **Internet:** "www.dol.gov/odep"; e-mail, "infoodep@dol.gov". (Note: no field offices for this program.)

OFFICE OF ASSISTANT SECRETARY/VETERANS' EMPLOYMENT AND TRAINING

17.801 DISABLED VETERANS' OUTREACH PROGRAM ("DVOP")

Assistance: formula grants (100 percent).

Purposes: pursuant to the Veterans' Rehabilitation and Education Amendments of 1980, to pay the salaries and expenses of DVOP specialists assigned to meet the employment needs of eligible veterans, with emphasis on those that are economically or educationally disadvantaged including the homeless and those with barriers to employment.

Eligible applicants/beneficiaries: state employment security agencies.

Range: $106,000 to $11,900,000. **Average:** $1,543,000.

Activity: FY 04, 282,000 veterans and other eligibles entered employment, including 33,000 disabled veterans.

HQ: Assistant Secretary/Veterans' Employment and Training-DOL, 200 Constitution Ave. NW - Rm.S-1312, Washington, DC 20210. Phone: (202)693-4708. **Internet:** "www.dol.gov/dol/vets".

17.802 VETERANS' EMPLOYMENT PROGRAM ("Veterans' Workforce Investment Program" - "VWIP")

Assistance: project grants (to 100 percent).

Purposes: pursuant to WIA, to enhance services to veterans in employment and training programs and related services; to provide innovative employment and training services and projects; for outreach and public information programs.

Eligible applicants: governors, public agencies, private nonprofit and community-based organizations. Discretionary funds—all applicants.

Eligible beneficiaries: service-connected disabled veterans, veterans with significant employment barriers, and those recently separated from military service.

Range: $200,000 to $850,000. **Average:** $487,000.

Activity: 2004, 2,561 veterans of 3,728 enrolled entered employment.

HQ: same as **17.801**.

17.803 UNIFORMED SERVICES EMPLOYMENT AND REEMPLOYMENT RIGHTS

Assistance: advisory services/counseling; technical information; investigation of complaints.

Purposes: to assist in the employment and reemployment of non-career veterans or candidates for the uniformed services. (Discrimination in employment and acts of reprisal by employers are prohibited—against persons because of their obligation in the uniformed services, filing a claim, seeking assistance concerning an alleged violation, testifying in a proceeding, or otherwise participating in an investigation.) Unresolved complaints are referred to DOJ or to the DOL Office of Special Counsel for representation in federal district courts.

Eligible applicants/beneficiaries: persons that have served voluntarily or involuntarily on active duty, active duty for training, or training duty with the uniformed services, including reservists and National Guard members. Entitlement ceases upon termination of service with a bad conduct or dishonorable discharge, or upon separation under other than honorable conditions.

Activity: FY 04, 895 new complaint cases processed, 1,440 cases closed; responses to 187,000 public inquiries.

HQ: same address, web site as **17.801**. Phone: (202)693-4701.

17.804 LOCAL VETERANS' EMPLOYMENT REPRESENTATIVE PROGRAM ("LVER Program")

Assistance: formula grants (100 percent).

Purposes: pursuant to the Servicemen's Readjustment Act of 1944, to fund salaries and expenses of Local Veterans' Employment Representatives assigned to conduct outreach to employers concerning employment, training, and job placement services and opportunities for veterans.

Eligible applicants/beneficiaries: state employment agencies.

Range: $57,000 to $7,147,000. **Average:** $1,476,000.

Activity FY 04, 287,000 entered employment through the LVER program, including 29,000 disabled veterans.

HQ: same as **17.801**.

17.805 HOMELESS VETERANS REINTEGRATION PROJECT

Assistance: project grants (100 percent).

Purposes: pursuant to the SBMHAA as amended, for projects to reintegrate homeless veterans into the labor force—through activities including employment and training services, support services, linkages with other service providers, and outreach performed by formerly homeless veterans.

Eligible applicants/beneficiaries: state and local Workforce Investment Boards and public agencies, private nonprofit and profit organizations and entities.

Range/Average: $100,000 to $300,000.

Activity: FY 03, 8,191 homeless veterans of 13,000 enrolled entered employment.

HQ: same as **17.801**.

17.806 VETERAN'S PREFERENCE IN FEDERAL EMPLOYMENT

Assistance: federal employment.

Purposes: pursuant to the Veterans Preference Act of 1944, to assist persons who perform services in the uniformed services to secure federal employment and to ensure a higher retention standing in the event of reduction-in-force; to assist veterans, employers, labor organizations, and others concerned with such preference; to investigate related complaints. A point system accords levels of preference to eligible veterans, based on such factors as when they served, receipt of the Purple Heart medal, disability if any, conditions of discharge. Details are available from federal agencies.

Eligible applicants/beneficiaries: veterans and certain of their dependents and survivors. Applicants should indicate their level of preference on job application forms.

Activity: FY 04, 351 veterans preference cases processed.

HQ: same address as **17.801**. Phone: (202)693-4700. **Internet:** "www.dol.gov/dol/vets/public/programs/programs/preference/main.htm".

17.807 TRANSITION ASSISTANCE PROGRAM ("TAP")

Assistance: project grants.

Purposes: pursuant to the Defense Reauthorization Act of 1991, to provide employment instruction, information, and assistance to separating military personnel ad their spouses by offering job search and related services such as resume preparation and service benefits—through TAP workshops at military installations worldwide. Funding is not appropriated separately, and is derived from other funded accounts.

Eligible applicants: state employment agencies; contractors.

Eligible beneficiaries: service members within two years of retirement or one year of separation.

Range/Average: N.A. (Project funds are used to purchase training manuals.)

Activity: new program listing in 2005. FY 03, 110,000 individuals participated.

HQ: same as **17.801**.

DEPARTMENT OF STATE

BUREAU OF OCEANS AND INTERNATIONAL ENVIRONMENTAL AND SCIENTIFIC AFFAIRS

19.204 FISHERMEN'S GUARANTY FUND ("Section 7")

Assistance: insurance.

Purposes: pursuant to the Fishermen's Protective Act of 1967 as amended and other acts, to reimburse U.S. commercial fishing vessel owners for losses resulting from the seizure of the vessel by a foreign country on the basis of rights or claims in territorial waters or on the high seas, not recognized by the U.S. (Effective 28 November 1990, the U.S. acknowledges the authority of coastal states to manage highly migratory species, reducing the basis for claims.)

Eligible applicants/beneficiaries: U.S. citizen-owners or -charterers of a documented or certified fishing vessel. Claimants must have paid a premium for the year in which the seizure occurs, if required.

Range: limited to the market value of fish caught before seizure, to the market value of the confiscated vessel or gear, and up to 50 percent of gross income lost as a result of seizure.

Activity: FY 05, no agreements. FY 06 estimate, 10 guaranty agreements.

HQ: Office of Marine Conservation, Bureau of Oceans and International Environmental and Scientific Affairs, Department of State, Rm.5806, Washington, DC 20520-7818. Phone: (202)647-3941; FAX (202)736-7350. **Internet:** "www.state.gov". (Note: no field offices for this program.)

BUREAU OF INTELLIGENCE AND RESEARCH

19.300 PROGRAM FOR STUDY OF EASTERN EUROPE AND THE INDEPENDENT STATES OF THE FORMER SOVIET UNION ("Title VIII")

Assistance: project grants (100 percent/to 3 years).

Purposes: pursuant to the Research and Training for Eastern Europe and the Independent States of the Former Soviet Union Act of 1983 as amended, for advanced research, graduate training, language training, and related activities—toward the development of American expertise on the countries of the former Soviet Union and Southeast Europe. Funds may support short-term research projects, fellowships, conferences, travel, and publication costs.

Eligible applicants: nonprofit organizations, IHEs.

Eligible beneficiaries: graduate students, scholars.

Range: $129,000 to $1,210,000. **Average:** $300,000.

Activity: not quantified specifically.

HQ: Executive Director *or* Program Officer, Program for Study of Eastern Europe and the Independent States of the Former Soviet Union (INR/RES), Department of State, 2201 C St. - Rm.2251, Washington, DC 20520-6510. Phone: (202)736-4572; FAX (202)736-4851. **Internet:** "www.state.gov". (Note: no field offices for this program.)

BUREAU OF EDUCATIONAL AND CULTURAL AFFAIRS

19.400 EDUCATIONAL EXCHANGE—GRADUATE STUDENTS ("Fulbright Program")

Assistance: project grants (100 percent/from 1 year).

Purposes: pursuant to the Mutual Educational and Cultural Exchange Act of 1961 (MECEA) as amended, for one-year scholarships to graduate students for one year of academic studies abroad, in the humanities and social sciences—covering costs of tuition, maintenance, transportation, books, insurance. Travel grants may supplement awards obtained from others.

Eligible applicants/beneficiaries: U.S. citizens with: B.A. degree or equivalent, with certain exceptions; no doctoral degree; the majority of their high school and undergraduate college education received at U.S. institutions; language proficiency; good health.

Range: $1,200 to $35,000. **Average:** $20,000.

Activity: FY 04, 1,100 grants.

HQ: Institute of International Education, 809 United Nations Plaza, New York, NY 10017. Phone: (no number provided). **Internet:** "http://exchanges.state.gov".

19.401 EDUCATIONAL EXCHANGE—UNIVERSITY LECTURERS (PROFESSORS) AND RESEARCH SCHOLARS ("Fulbright-Hays Program")

Assistance: project grants (100 percent/3 months to 1 year).

Purposes: pursuant to MECEA as amended, for lectureships for university lecturers to serve as visiting professors abroad, and for research grants for scholars for postdoctoral work abroad—covering costs of travel for the grantee (and, in some cases, dependents), maintenance, books, and services.

Eligible applicants/beneficiaries: U.S. citizens with foreign language proficiency and, for lecturing, college or university teaching experience. Research grants—doctoral degree or, in some fields, recognized professional standing as demonstrated by faculty rank, publications, compositions, exhibition record, concerts, etc. Doctoral and other predoctoral candidates should contact the Institute of International Education (see **19.400**).

Range: $3,500 to $80,000. **Average:** $28,000.

Activity: FY 04, 875 full-, 450 short-term grants.

HQ: Council for International Exchange of Scholars, 3007 Tilden St. NW - Ste.5M, Washington, DC 20008. Phone: (202)686-4000. **Internet:** same as **19.400**. (Note: no field offices for this program.)

19.402 INTERNATIONAL VISITORS PROGRAM ("Fulbright-Hays Program")

Assistance: project grants (cost sharing).

Purposes: pursuant to MECEA as amended, to plan and conduct programs of travel, observation, consultation, study, and practical experience for foreign visitors selected and assigned by the Department of State upon recommendations from U.S. embassies—to bring visitors into contact with influential Americans and representative organizations and institutions, and increase communication and mutual understanding between the foreign and domestic parties.

Eligible applicants/beneficiaries: incorporated U.S. nonprofit organizations with at least four years experience.

Range: $137,000 to $4,497,000. **Average:** $137,000.

Activity: N.A.

HQ: Community Relations Branch, Office of International Visitors, BECA-Department of State, 301 Fourth St. SW - Rm.255, Washington, DC 20547. Phone: (202)619-5220. **Internet:** "www.exchanges.state.gov.education". (Note: no field offices for this program.)

19.403 AMERICAN COUNCIL OF YOUNG POLITICAL LEADERS ("ACYPL")

Assistance: project grants (50 percent).

Purposes: pursuant to MECEA as amended, to enable two-way exchanges with emerging U.S. and foreign political leaders, enabling them to experience firsthand the cultural and political dynamics of the countries visited, usually for two-week programs. Grants cover costs of travel, insurance, program activities, and orientation.

Eligible applicants: ACYPL (1612 K St. NW - Ste.300, Washington, DC 20006. Phone: (202)857-0999).

Eligible beneficiaries: generally, state and local elected officials, staff and party activists—to age 41, and selected by a Delegate Selection Committee with Democratic and Republican co-chairs.

Range/Average: N.A.

Activity: FY 04, 30 countries involved, with 270 participants.

HQ: Youth Programs Division (ECA/PE/C/PY), Office of Citizen Exchanges, BECA-Department of State, 301 Fourth St. SW, Washington, DC 20547. Phone: (202)203-7507; FAX (202)203-7529. **Internet:** same as **19.400**. (Note: no field offices for this program.)

19.408 EDUCATIONAL EXCHANGE—TEACHERS FROM SECONDARY AND POSTSECONDARY LEVELS AND SCHOOL ADMINISTRATORS ("Fulbright Program Teacher and Administrator Program")

Assistance: project grants (100 percent).

Purposes: pursuant to MECEA as amended, to enable U.S. and foreign educators to live and teach in a foreign country. Participants from primary, secondary, or junior/community colleges exchange classroom assignments for six weeks, one semester, or one academic year. Generally, participants receive leave with pay and benefits from their respective employers; grants support transportation, maintenance, accident and health insurance.

Eligible applicants/beneficiaries: teachers and administrators with at least a B.A., 3 years full-time experience, English and foreign language proficiency, and U.S. citizenship (for U.S. participants).

Range: $2,000 to $27,000.

Activity: FY 05-06 estimate, 566 individual, 8 institutional grants.

HQ: Fulbright Teacher and Administrator Exchange Branch (ECA/A/S/X), BECA (SA-44), Department of State, 301 Fourth St. SW, Washington, DC 20547. Phone: (202)619-4556; FAX (202)401-1433. *Application booklet,* Fulbright Teacher Exchange Program, USDA Graduate School, 600 Maryland Ave. SW, Washington, DC 20024. Phone: (202)314-3520; FAX (202)

479-6806. **Internet:** "www.fulbrightexchanges.org"; e-mail, "fulbright@grad.usda.gov". (Note: no field offices for this program.)

19.409 ARTS EXCHANGES ON INTERNATIONAL ISSUES

Assistance: project grants (70 percent/1-3 years).

Purposes: pursuant to MECEA as amended, for cooperative international group projects that introduce American and foreign participants to each other's cultural and artistic life and traditions—including composers, choreographers, playwrights, theater designers, writers, poets, filmmakers, visual artists, and arts administrators. Ineligible projects include those focussed on youth, speaking tours, research, amateurs or semi-professionals, community-level presentations, or vocational and technical long-term academic study.

Eligible applicants: public or private "501(c)(3)" nonprofit organizations with four years experience.

Eligible beneficiaries: professional artists and arts administrators over age 25.

Range: $60,000 to $300,000.

Activity: FY 05 estimate, 8 grants.

HQ: Creative Arts Exchanges Program, Office of Citizen Exchanges, BECA-Department of State, 301 Fourth St. SW, Washington, DC 20547. Phone: (202)203-7500. **Internet:** same as **19.400**. (Note: no field offices for this program.)

19.410 EDUCATIONAL EXCHANGE—CONGRESS-BUNDESTAG YOUTH EXCHANGE ("CBYX")

Assistance: projects grants (to 100 percent/18 months).

Purposes: pursuant to MECEA as amended, to foster interaction between young people from the U.S. and Germany to promote mutual understanding through reciprocal exchanges of groups of high school students and practical trainees. Grants support costs of travel, insurance, orientation, selection, and administration. (The German government conducts a reciprocal counterpart program.)

Eligible applicants: nonprofit organizations with at least four years experience and with a German partner.

Eligible beneficiaries: generally, high school students and young professionals demonstrating language ability, social skills, academic achievement.

Range/Average: N.A.

Activity: 2004-05, 380 U.S. and 400 German participants

HQ: same address as **19.403**. Phone: (202)619-6299; FAX (202)619-5311. **Internet:** "http://usagermanyscholarships.org". (Note: no field offices for this program.)

19.413 CULTURAL EXCHANGE (PERFORMING ARTS) ("Fund for U.S. Artists at International Festivals and Exhibitions - Performing Arts")

Assistance: project grants.

Purposes: pursuant to MECEA as amended, for the creative and professional development of U.S. performing artists and organizations, including support for the presentation of their work at significant international festivals outside the U.S. (Funding is augmented by the federal NEA, and privately by the Rockefeller Foundation, Doris Duke Charitable Foundation, and the Pew Charitable Trust.)

Eligible applicants/beneficiaries: U.S. citizens or permanent residents that are creative, interpretive, or traditional performing artists working at a professional level.

Range: organizations, $2,000 to $25,000.

Activity: FY 04 estimate, 110 grants.

HQ: Arts International for the Fund for U.S. Artists at International Festivals and Exhibitions, 251 Park Ave. South - 5th floor, New York, NY 10010. Phone: (212)674-9744; FAX (212)674-9092. **Internet:** same as **19.400**; *and, for guidelines, applications,* "www.artsinternational.org". (Note: no field offices for this program.)

19.415 PROFESSIONAL EXCHANGES—ANNUAL OPEN GRANT
("Office of Citizen Exchanges")

Assistance: project grants (cost sharing).

Purposes: pursuant to MECEA as amended, to foster, improve, and strengthen U.S. international relations by promoting mutual understanding among the peoples of the world through educational and professional exchanges. Grant funds should support: development of lasting institutional links; establishment of consortia, associations, and information networks; information transfer; development of internships.

Eligible applicants: public and private nonprofit organizations meeting the provisions of IRS regulation 26CFR1.501(c).

Eligible beneficiaries: U.S. citizens and foreign nationals.

Range: to $150,000; developing organizations, to $60,000.

Activity: FY 06 estimate, 20 grants.

HQ: Office of Citizen Exchanges, BECA-Department of State, 301 Fourth St. SW - Rm.220, Washington, DC 20547. Phone: (202)453-8181; FAX (202) 453-8168. **Internet:** "http://exchanges.state.gov/education/citizens/". (Note: no field offices for this program.)

19.418 EDUCATIONAL EXCHANGE—FULBRIGHT AMERICAN STUDIES INSTITUTES
("Study of the U.S. Program - Office of Academic Exchange Programs")

Assistance: project grants (to 100 percent/6-8 months).

Purposes: pursuant to MECEA as amended, to provide foreign educators with a deeper understanding of American society, culture, and institutions to improve courses and teaching about the U.S. abroad. Participants attend an integrated series of lectures, readings, interactive discussions, research and independent study, faculty mentoring, and site visits. Grant recipients are responsible for institute design and implementation, as well as all logistical program aspects.

Eligible applicants: IHEs or consortia, other nonprofit academic organizations—with four years of pertinent experience.

Eligible beneficiaries: foreign university faculty nominated by a U.S. embassy, consulate, or Fulbright Commission.

Range: $182,000 to $255,000. **Average:** $182,000.

Activity: FY 02, 10 institutional cooperative agreements, hosting 200 foreign participants (latest data reported).

HQ: Study of the U.S. Branch (ECA/A/E/USS), BECA-Department of State, Rm.252 State Annex 44, 301 Fourth St. SW, Washington, DC 20547. Phone: (202)619-4562; FAX (202)619-6790. **Internet:** "http://exchanges.state.gov/education/amstudy". (Note: no field offices for this program.)

19.421 EXCHANGE—ENGLISH LANGUAGE FELLOW PROGRAM ("English Language Programs")

Assistance: project grants (100 percent/to 1 year).

Purposes: pursuant to MECEA as amended, to provide highly qualified ESL/EFL teachers abroad to offer professional expertise in current English language methods and theory to host institutions; to provide specially designed courses for targeted high level groups, such as members and staffs of parliaments, and judicial, finance, and business officials; to develop communication skills among teachers and students that they need to participate in the global economy, to improve their access to diverse perspectives on a broad variety of issues, and to better understand America and its values and institutions. Grants support costs of participant travel, medical insurance, related living and project expenses, and a basic stipend.

Eligible applicants/beneficiaries: U.S. citizens with an M.A. or Ph.D. in TESL/TEFL, applied linguistics, or closely related field, and with specific teacher training experience.

Range: $45,000 to $65,000.

Activity: FY 05 estimate, 100 grants.

HQ: World Learning, Inc., School for International Training, Kipling Rd., Brattleboro, VT 05302-0676. Phone: (802)258-3311. **Internet:** "http://exchanges.state.gov/education/engteaching/fellows.htm". (Note: no field offices for this program.)

19.423 EXCHANGE—ENGLISH LANGUAGE SPECIALIST/SPEAKER PROGRAM

Assistance: project grants (100 percent/2-6 weeks).

Purposes: pursuant to MECEA as amended, for short-term projects to improve the teaching and learning of English abroad, through curriculum development, teacher training seminars, textbook development, program evaluation, and "English for Specific Purposes" programs. Grants cover travel, living, materials, and related costs, and a $200/day honorarium.

Eligible applicants/beneficiaries: same as for **19.421**.

Range: $1,500 to $9,000. **Average:** $5,500.

Activity: FY 04, 100 specialists assigned to 20 countries.

HQ: Programs Officer, Office of English Language Programs, BECA-Department of State, 301 Fourth St. SW, Washington, DC 20547. Phone: (202)205-3636; FAX (202)401-1250. **Internet:** "http://exchanges.state.gov/education/engteaching/specialists.htm". (Note: no field offices for this program.)

19.425 BENJAMIN GILMAN INTERNATIONAL SCHOLARSHIP

Assistance: project grants (100 percent).

Purposes: pursuant to MECEA as amended, for scholarships to financially needy U.S. undergraduates to pursue study abroad for one semester or one academic year.

Eligible applicants/beneficiaries: U.S. citizens enrolled as undergraduates and receiving federal financial aid for schooling.

Range/Average: $4,000.

Activity: FY 03, 351 scholarships awarded to recipients from 48 states, studying in 50 foreign countries.

HQ: Educational Information and Resources (ECA/A/S/A), BECA-Department of State, 301 Fourth St. SW (SA-44), Washington, DC 20547. Phone: (202)619-5434; FAX (202)401-1433. **Internet:** same as **19.400**.

19.430 INTERNATIONAL EDUCATION TRAINING AND RESEARCH

Assistance: project grants.

Purposes: pursuant to MECEA as amended, for training of international education professionals on U.S. campuses; for research on specified international exchange programs.

Eligible applicants/beneficiaries: experienced incorporated U.S. nonprofit organizations.

Range/Average: research, $190,000; training. $535,000.

Activity: new program listing in 2005. FY 05 estimate, 60 new trainees

HQ: same as **19.425**.

19.431 EDUCATIONAL EXCHANGE—SCHOLAR-IN-RESIDENCE (U.S. INSTITUTIONS OF HIGHER EDUCATION HOST LECTURING FACULTY FROM ABROAD)

Assistance: project grants (cost sharing/to 10 months).

Purposes: pursuant to MECEA as amended, for U.S. IHEs to host scholars-in-residence to teach on global issues at the undergraduate level, as well as to participate in other internal institutional and community outreach activities. Project funds are paid to the scholar, not to the host institution.

Eligible applicants/beneficiaries: U.S. IHEs—with preference to those traditionally less involved in international exchange programs, and with priority to HBCUs, Hispanic-serving institutions, tribal IHEs, small liberal arts colleges, and community colleges; consortia.

Range: $16,000 to $40,000. **Average:** $27,000.

Activity: new program listing in 2005. FY 05 estimate, 36 grants.

HQ: same address/phone as **19.401**. **Internet:** "www.cies.org/sir/sir.htm". (Note: no field offices for this program.)

19.432 OVERSEAS EDUCATIONAL ADVISING

Assistance: project grants.

Purposes: pursuant to MECEA as amended, to establish an overseas network of "Education USA" educational advising and information centers, to ensure that prospective students in specific locations abroad receive unbiased, ethical, and current information on U.S. higher education. Project funds support program implementation including adviser orientation and training.

Eligible applicants/beneficiaries: experienced incorporated U.S. nonprofit organizations.

Range: $60,000 to $450,000. **Average:** $200,000.

Activity: new program listing in 2005. 2004, field offices established in 10 countries.

HQ: same address/phone as **19.425**. **Internet:** "www.educationusa.state.gov". (Note: no field offices for this program.)

BUREAU OF NEAR EASTERN AFFAIRS

19.500 MIDDLE EAST PARTNERSHIP INITIATIVE ("MEPI")

Assistance: project grants.

Purposes: pursuant to the Foreign Assistance Act of 1961 as amended, to support economic, political, and educational reform efforts in the Middle East and North Africa, promoting opportunity especially for women and youth. Projects usually involve partnerships to provide training programs and projects involving local nongovernmental organizations (NGOs) and government officials. Some cost sharing is expected.

Eligible applicants: experienced nonprofit and profit organizations, state and local governments.

Eligible beneficiaries: Morocco, Algeria, Tunisia, Egypt, West Bank/Gaza, Jordan, Lebanon, Kuwait, Iraq, Saudi Arabia, Qatar, Bahrain, UAE, Oman, and Yemen.

Range: N.A.

Activity: new program listing in 2004. 100 programs funded.

HQ: Office of MEPI, Bureau of Near Eastern Affairs, Department of State, 2201 C St. NW - Rm.5253A, Washington, DC 20520. Phone: (no number provide). **Internet:** "www.mepi.state.gov". (Note: no field offices for this program.)

BUREAU OF POPULATION, REFUGEES, AND MIGRATION

19.510 U.S. REFUGEE ADMISSIONS PROGRAM

Assistance: project grants.

Purposes: pursuant to the Immigration and Nationality Act and Migration and Refugee Assistance Act of 1962 as amended (MRA), to provide initial reception and placement services for refugees approved for admission in the U.S., including: resettlement activities; providing basic necessities and core services for a 90-day period; employment services coordinated with publicly sponsored assistance programs. The program provides a fixed $800 reimbursement per resettled refugee; sponsors are expected to contribute private funds toward actual costs.

Eligible applicants/beneficiaries: state governments, private nonprofit organizations.

Range: $20,000 to $2,873,000. **Average:** $1,021,000.

Activity: new program listing in 2004. FY 03, 28,000 refugees resettled through 9 private organizations, 1 state government.

HQ: Office of Refugee Admissions, Bureau of Population, Refugees, and Migration, Department of State, SA-1 - Ste.L505, Washington, DC 20522-0105. Phone: (202)663-1056; Comptroller, (202)663-1022. **Internet:** "www.state.gov/g/prm". (Note: no field offices for this program.)

19.511 OVERSEAS REFUGEE ASSISTANCE PROGRAMS FOR EAST ASIA

Assistance: project grants.

Purposes: pursuant to MRA, for humanitarian activities and services for refugees in East Asia—particularly in Thailand along the Burmese border. Projects must be complementary to and coordinated with United Nations programs, as well as other organizations.

Eligible applicants/beneficiaries: United Nations; international and nongovernmental organizations.

Range: NGOs, $1,150,000 to $3,410,000; international organizations, $850,000 to $7,500,000.

Activity: new program listing in 2005.

HQ: same address as **19.510**. Phone: Director, (202)663-1063; Deputy Director, (202)663-1065; Southeast Asia, (202)663-1012; Northeast Asia, (202)663-1950; Comptroller, (202)663-1022. **Internet:** (none provided). (Note: no field offices for this program.)

19.517 OVERSEAS REFUGEE ASSISTANCE PROGRAMS FOR AFRICA

Assistance: project grants.

Purposes: pursuant to MRA, for humanitarian activities and services for refugees across the African continent. Project must be complementary to and coordinated with United Nations programs.

Eligible applicants/beneficiaries: same as for **19.511**.

Range: NGOs, $105,000 to $2,300,000. **Average:** NGOs, $740,000.

Activity: new program listing in 2005.

HQ: same address as **19.511**. Phone: Director, (202)663-1027; Deputy Director/Sahel, North Africa, Southern Africa, Horn of Africa,(202)663-1014; Coastal West Africa, (202)663-1031; Great Lakes-Central Africa, (202)663-1476; Chad (Sudanese Refugees), (202)663-3344; Comptroller, (202)663-1022. **Internet:** (none provided). (Note: no field offices for this program.)

19.518 OVERSEAS REFUGEE ASSISTANCE PROGRAMS FOR WESTERN HEMISPHERE

Assistance: project grants.

Purposes: pursuant to MRA, for humanitarian activities and services for refugees in the Western Hemisphere—particularly in Columbia. Projects must be complementary to and coordinated with United Nations programs, as well as other organizations.

Eligible applicants/beneficiaries: same as for **19.511**.

Range: overall, $37,000 to $6,000,000; NGOs, $7,000 to $3,200,000. **Average:** overall, $1,400,000; NGOs, $451,000.

Activity: new program listing in 2005.

HQ: same address as **19.510**. Phone: Director, (202)663-1062; FAX (202)663-1530. Phone: Comptroller, (202)663-1022. **Internet:** same web site as **19.510**; e-mail, "prm-eca@state.gov". (Note: no field offices for this program.)

19.519 OVERSEAS REFUGEE ASSISTANCE PROGRAMS FOR NEAR EAST AND SOUTH ASIA

Assistance: project grants.

Purposes: pursuant to MRA, for humanitarian activities and services for refugees in the Near East and South Asia—including those in and from Afghanistan, India, Iran, Iraq, Palestine, and Tibet. Projects must be complementary to and coordinated with United Nations programs.

Eligible applicants/beneficiaries: same as for **19.511**.

Range: overall, $100,000 to $52,000,000; NGOs, $80,000 to $2,000,000. **Average:** overall, $5,300,000. NGOs, $734,000.

Activity: new program listing in 2005.

HQ: same address as **19.511**. Phone: Director, (202)663-1063; Deputy Director/Iraq Team, (202)663-1065; Afghan Team, (202)663-3717, -3442; South/Northeast Asia, Pacific, (202)663-1950; Near East/UNRWA, (202)663-1531; Iraq Team, (202)663-3442; Comptroller, (202)663-1022. **Internet:** (none provided). (Note: no field offices for this program.)

19.520 OVERSEAS REFUGEE ASSISTANCE PROGRAMS FOR EUROPE

Assistance: project grants.

Purposes: pursuant to MRA, for humanitarian activities and services for refugees in Europe and Central Asia, including Armenia, Azerbaijan, the Balkans, the North and South Caucasus, Chechnya, Georgia, Kosovo, Macedonia, Serbia-Montenegro. Projects must be complementary to and coordinated with United Nations programs, as well as other organizations.

Eligible applicants/beneficiaries: same as for **19.511**.

Range: overall, $24,000 to $12,600,000; NGOs, $24,000 to $2,700,000. **Average:** overall, $1,800,000; NGOs, $702,000.

Activity: new program listing in 2005.

HQ: same as **19.518**. (Note: no field offices for this program.)

19.522 OVERSEAS REFUGEE ASSISTANCE PROGRAMS FOR STRATEGIC GLOBAL PRIORITIES

Assistance: project grants.

Purposes: pursuant to MRA, for humanitarian activities and services promoting PRM's initiatives in areas that are cross-cutting, core priorities—including refugee women and children, prevention and response to gender-based violence, enhancing refugee protection and health including HIV/AIDS protection. Projects must be complementary to and coordinated with United Nations programs, as well as other organizations. (Most funding under this program is allocated to the United Nations High Commissioner for Refugees and the International Committee of the Red Cross.)

Eligible applicants/beneficiaries: same as for **19.511**.

Range: overall, $54,000 to $11,700,000; NGOs, $56,000 to $296,000. **Average:** overall, $2,500,000; NGOs, $221,000.

Activity: new program listing in 2005.

HQ: same address as **19.511**. Phone: Director, (202)663-1075; Refugee Children, (202)663-1713; Refugee Women, GBV/NGO Liaison, (202)663-1481; Office Director, (202)663-3954; Policy Office, (202)663-3881, -3104; Comptroller, (202)663-1022. **Internet:** (none provided). (Note: no field offices for this program.)

DEPARTMENT OF TRANSPORTATION

FEDERAL AVIATION ADMINISTRATION

20.100 AVIATION EDUCATION

Assistance: advisory services/counseling.

Purposes: pursuant to the Airport and Airway Development Act of 1970 as amended, for a broad range of public civil aviation education, career awareness, and related programs, from the elementary through college levels in all regions of the country. Also for: clearinghouse, data gathering and dissemination, communications, teacher training activities; conferences; and, publications on aviation including aviation mathematics, science, technology, computer literacy; Internet services.

Eligible applicants/beneficiaries: aviation and education administrators, IHE officials, officers of civil organizations, domestic and international governments, aviation industry, education organizations.

Activity: not quantified specifically.

HQ: Assistant Administrator/Region and Center Operations, FAA-DOT, 800 Independence Ave. SW, Washington, DC 20590. Phone: (no number provided). *National HQ office for program implementation,* Regional Administrator, FAA-DOT, 12 New England Executive Park, Burlington, MA 01893. Phone: (no number provided). **Internet:** "www.faa.dot.gov/education".

20.106 AIRPORT IMPROVEMENT PROGRAM ("AIP")

Assistance: project grants (75-90 percent); advisory services/counseling.

Purposes: for planning, construction, or rehabilitation of public-use airports and related facilities and equipment, including for commercial passenger and cargo service, heliports, and seaplane landing bases. Eligible expenditures include airport master planning, land acquisition, site preparation, runway and related construction and improvement, noise reduction programs, weather reporting equipment, security and snow-removal equipment, firefighting and rescue equipment, lighting, and projects to comply with the ADA, Clean Air Act, and Federal Water Pollution Control. Ineligible uses of funds include hangar and most automobile parking facilities, buildings unrelated to safety, landscaping or artwork, routine maintenance and repair.

Eligible applicants/beneficiaries: development grants for airports listed in the National Plan of Integrated Airport Systems (NPIAS)—states, counties, municipalities, territories and possessions, and other public agencies including tribes or pueblos; private owners of public-use reliever airports or airports enplaning over 2,500 passengers annually.. Noise compatibility grants—certain local government units.

Range: $6,785 to $31,673,000. **Average:** $570,000.

Activity: FY 03, 2,234 grant agreements.

HQ: Financial Assistance Division (APP-500), Office of Airport Planning and Programming, FAA-DOT, 800 Independence Ave. SW, Washington, DC 20591. Phone: (202)267-3831. **Internet:** "www.faa.gov".

20.108 AVIATION RESEARCH GRANTS

Assistance: project grants (to 100 percent/1 year minimum); use of property, facilities, and equipment.

Purposes: pursuant to the Federal Aviation Administration Research, Engineering and Development Authorization and the Aviation Security Improvement Act of 1990, for advanced applied research and development projects in: Capacity and Air Traffic Management Technology; Communications, Navigation, and Surveillance; Aviation Weather; Airport Technology; Aircraft Safety Technology; System Security Technology; Human Factors and Aviation Medicine; Environment and Energy; Systems Science and Operations Research; Commercial Space Transportation.

Eligible applicants/beneficiaries: IHEs, nonprofit institutions. Profit organizations may apply in the area of Aviation Security.

Range: $25,000 to $5,000,000 (multi-year). **Average:** $50,000 to $150,000.

Activity: not quantified specifically.

HQ: Aviation Research Grants Program (ACT-50), FAA-DOT, Hughes Technical Center, Atlantic City International Airport, NJ 08405. Phone: (609)485-4424, FAX (609)485-6509. **Internet:** "www.its.tc.faa.gov/logistics/grants". (Note: no other field offices for this program.)

20.109 AIR TRANSPORTATION CENTERS OF EXCELLENCE
("FAA Centers of Excellence")

Assistance: project grants (50 percent/to 10 years); use of property, facilities, and equipment; specialized services.

Purposes: pursuant to the Federal Aviation Administration Research, Engineering and Development Authorization Act of 1990, for centers conducting long-term continuing research in such areas as catastrophic failure of aircraft, airspace and airport planning and design, airport capacity enhancement techniques, human performance, aviation safety and security, air transportation personnel training.

Eligible applicants/beneficiaries: IHEs, which may partner with industry affiliates and other government laboratories.

Range/Average: from $500,000 per year per center.

Activity: not quantified specifically.

HQ: Director, Centers of Excellence Program (AAR-400), Office of Aviation Research, Technical Center, Atlantic City International Airport, NJ 08405. Phone: (609)485-5043, FAX (609)485-9430. **Internet:** same as **20.106**. (Note: no other field offices for this program.)

FEDERAL HIGHWAY ADMINISTRATION

20.205 HIGHWAY PLANNING AND CONSTRUCTION
("Federal-Aid Highway Program")

Assistance: formula grants; project grants (80-100 percent/to 4 years).

Purposes: for highway and related projects in the interstate and national highway systems, and for bridge and safety improvements on nonfederal-aid roads and within federal lands. Eligible fund uses include costs of planning, design, right-of-way acquisition, relocation assistance, construction, reconstruction, repair (but not maintenance), improvement of interstate and primary and secondary highways, bridge repairs, roads, and streets in urban systems, congestion mitigation and air quality improvement, and research. Related projects may involve railroad grade crossings, roadside beautification, bridges, bicycle paths, pedestrian walkways, carpool projects, fringe and corridor parking, wetland mitigation, forest highways, rest areas, scenic and historic highway improvements. In some cases, funds may be used for public mass transit improvements. Funding is derived from the Highway Trust Fund. Funding for this program includes **20.215** and **20.219**.

Eligible applicants/beneficiaries: state transportation agencies; territories, possessions. Projects related to Indian reservations, parkways and park roads, and public lands highways, certain projects in urban areas or off the state highway systems—tribal governments, counties, other political subdivisions or agencies and federal agencies applying through state agencies.

Range: $115,343,000 to $1,246,084,000. **Average:** $601,708,000.

Activity: FY 04 (sampling), emergency assistance to 17 disaster areas in 31 states and territories.

HQ: Director, Office of Program Administration, FHWA-DOT, 400 Seventh St. SW, Washington, DC 20590-0001. Phone: (202)366-4853; *forest highways, Indian reservation roads, park roads and parkways,* Federal Lands Highways, (202)366-9494. **Internet:** "www.fhwa.dot.gov".

20.215 HIGHWAY TRAINING AND EDUCATION

Assistance: project grants (80-100 percent/3 months to 5 years); training.

Purposes: pursuant to the Transportation Equity Act for the 21st Century, to develop and administer training, educational, and technical assistance programs related to federal-aid highway work. Faculty, graduate, research, and minority fellowships may be awarded under the Dwight David Eisenhower Transportation Fellowship Program. Courses and study programs may be obtained from IHEs, government agencies, private entities, or the National Highway Institute. Funding for this program is included in **20.205**.

Eligible applicants/beneficiaries: training—state and local transportation agency employees. Fellowships—persons matriculating at U.S. IHEs in transportation-related disciplines.

Range/Average: N.A.

Activity: 1992-2004, 2,000 fellowships awarded.

HQ: Director, National Highway Institute, FHWA-DOT, 4600 N. Fairfax Dr. - Ste.800, Arlington, VA 22203-1553. Phone: (703)235-0500. **Internet:** "www.nhi.fhwa.dot.gov".

20.217 MOTOR CARRIER SAFETY

Assistance: investigation of complaints; training.

Purposes: pursuant to the Transportation Act, Department of Transportation Act of 1966, Hazardous Materials Transportation Act, Motor Carrier Act of 1991, amendments, and other acts, for enforcement of and training in commercial motor carrier safety regulations, including those applying to the transport of hazardous materials and incident response.

Eligible applicants/beneficiaries: anyone may file a complaint. Safety and hazardous materials training—state and local police, rescue, and firefighting units.

Activity: FY 02, 11,000 federal and state personnel participated in training; 6,654 federal, 2,524 state compliance reviews (latest data reported).

HQ: Federal Motor Carrier Safety Administration-DOT, 400 Seventh St. SW, Washington, DC 20590. Phone: (202)366-2519. **Internet:** "www.dot.gov".

20.218 NATIONAL MOTOR CARRIER SAFETY ("MCSAP")

Assistance: formula grants (to 80-100 percent).

Purposes: pursuant to the Surface Transportation Assistance Act of 1982, Motor Carrier Safety Act of 1991, and Transportation Equity Act for the 21st Century, for programs involving the development and enforcement of uniform rules, regulations, and standards concerning inter- and intrastate commercial motor vehicle safety, and of state hazardous materials regulations compatible with federal standards.

Eligible applicants/beneficiaries: states; territories and possessions (100 percent funding).

Range: N.A.

Activity: FY 04, 9,200 state personnel supported.

HQ: State Programs (MC-ESS), Federal Motor Carrier Safety Administration-DOT, 400 Seventh St. SW, Washington, DC 20590. Phone: (202)366-9579. **Internet:** "www.fmcsa.dot.gov".

20.219 RECREATIONAL TRAILS PROGRAM

Assistance: formula grants; project grants (80-95 percent/to 4 years).

Purposes: to provide new and maintain existing recreational trails and related facilities for motorized and nonmotorized uses. Project funds may be used to: maintain and restore existing trails; construct new trails; develop trail-side and trail-head facilities and trail linkages; acquire easements identified in state trail plans; acquire fee simple title from willing sellers; pay limited administrative and public education costs. Funds may not be used for property condemnation, nor to provide access by motorized users to trails used mainly by nonmotorized users. Funding for this program is included in **20.205**.

Eligible applicants/beneficiaries: state agencies, which may accept applications from private organizations, or city, county, or other governmental organizations including federal agencies. States must have an advisory committee representing both motorized and nonmotorized users.

Range: $400,000 to $2,751,000. **Average:** $767,000.

Activity: not quantified specifically.

HQ: Office of Planning and Environment (HEPN-50), FHWA-DOT, 400 Seventh St. SW - Rm.3240, Washington, DC 20590. Phone: (202)366-5013, FAX (202)366-3409. **Internet:** "www.fhwa.dot.gov/environment/rectrails.html".

20.230 CRASH DATA IMPROVEMENT PROGRAM

Assistance: project grants (100 percent/to 2 years).

Purposes: pursuant to the Motor Carrier Improvement Act of 1999, to implement programs providing data on truck and bus crashes for analysis.

Eligible applicants/beneficiaries: states.

Range/Average: N.A.

Activity: new program listing in 2005. Since 2002, grants awarded to 27 states.

HQ: same address as **20.217**. Phone: (202)366-5387. **Internet:** same as **20.218**. (Note: no field offices for this program.)

20.232 COMMERCIAL DRIVER LICENSE STATE PROGRAMS

Assistance: project grants (100 percent).

Purposes: to prevent truck and bus accidents, fatalities, and injuries through programs requiring drivers to have a single commercial motor vehicle license, and by disqualifying drivers that operate commercial motor vehicles in an unsafe manner. Project examples: Social Security online verification; covert operations for third-party tester.

Eligible applicants/beneficiaries: states.

Range/Average: N.A.

Activity: new program listing in 2005. FY 03, 6 states funded.

HQ: same as **20.218**.

20.233 BORDER ENFORCEMENT GRANTS

Assistance: project grants (100 percent/2 years).

Purposes: pursuant to the Safe, Accessible, Feasible, and Efficient Equity Act, to ensure that commercial motor carriers entering the U.S. from foreign country comply with U.S. commercial vehicle safety and financial standards, regulations, and requirements, and that their drivers are qualified and properly licensed; for enforcement activities and projects.

Eligible applicants/beneficiaries: entities and states sharing a land border with a foreign country.

Range/Average: N.A.

Activity: new program in FY 06.

HQ: Borders Division, (MC-ESB), Federal Motor Carrier Safety Administration-DOT, 400 Seventh St. SW, Washington, DC 20590. Phone: (202)366-4049. **Internet:** same as **20.218**.

FEDERAL RAILROAD ADMINISTRATION

20.303 GRANTS-IN-AID FOR RAILROAD SAFETY—STATE PARTICIPATION ("State Participation in Railroad Safety")

Assistance: project grants (50 percent).

Purposes: pursuant to the Federal Railroad Safety Act of 1970 as amended and Hazardous Materials Transportation Uniform Safety Act of 1990, to subsidize costs of personnel, equipment, and activities related to enforcement of railroad safety standards, including the inspection of equipment, operating practices, signal and train control, and hazardous materials transport. Classroom training costs for state inspectors are reimbursed at 100 percent.

Eligible applicants/beneficiaries: states.

Range: $2,000 to $16,000 per inspector in FY 88 (no funds available since). **Average:** $9,000.

Activity: FY 04, 30 states participating with 153 inspectors.

HQ: Associate Administrator/Safety (MS 25), Federal Railroad Administration-DOT, 1120 Vermont Ave. NW, Washington, DC 20590. Phone: (202) 493-6300. **Internet:** "www.fra.dot.gov".

20.312 HIGH SPEED GROUND TRANSPORTATION—NEXT GENERATION HIGH SPEED RAIL PROGRAM ("HSGT")

Assistance: project grants.

Purposes: pursuant to the Transportation Equity Act for the 21st Century, to implement high speed passenger rail systems. Projects must benefit research, development, design, or operation of incremental high speed passenger rail systems. Project examples: high speed, high acceleration fossil-fueled locomotives; highway-rail grade crossing sensor and warning systems.

Eligible applicants/beneficiaries: any U.S. private business, educational institution, state or local government or public authority, or federal agency.

Range: $100,000 to $7,000,000. **Average:** $250,000.

Activity: not quantified specifically.

HQ: Office of Railroad Development (RDV-13), Federal Railroad Administration-DOT, 1120 Vermont Ave. NW, Washington, DC 20590. Phone: (no number provided). **Internet:** same as **20.303**. (Note: no field offices for this program.)

20.313 RAILROAD RESEARCH AND DEVELOPMENT

Assistance: project grants.

Purposes: for research advancing rail safety, by university organizations.

Eligible applicants/beneficiaries: academic research institutions with at least five years relevant experience.

Range: $50,000 to $250,000. **Average:** $100,000.

Activity: N.A.

HQ: Office of Research and Development (RDV-31), Federal Railroad Administration-DOT, 1120 Vermont Ave. NW, Washington, DC 20590. Phone: (no number provided). **Internet:** "www.fra.dot.gov/o/hsgt/index.htm". (Note: no field offices for this program.)

FEDERAL TRANSIT ADMINISTRATION

20.500 FEDERAL TRANSIT—CAPITAL INVESTMENT GRANTS

Assistance: formula grants; project grants (80-90 percent).

Purposes: for public transportation project costs in the following categories: fixed guideway modernization formula grants; bus and bus facilities discretionary grants and "New Starts" discretionary grants covering new systems and extensions, if specifically designated by Congress. Eligible costs include: acquisition, construction, reconstruction, and improvement of facilities and equipment; purchases of land, buses or other rolling stock; planning and engineering; new technological methods and techniques; park-and-ride lots; projects to meet the needs of the elderly and the disabled; certain projects enhancing urban economic development.

Eligible applicants/beneficiaries: public agencies including states, municipalities, and other state subdivisions; public agencies and instrumentalities of one or more states; public corporations, boards, and commissions established under state law. Private transportation companies may participate through contracts.

Range/Average: N.A.

Activity: not quantified specifically.

HQ: Office of Program Management, FTA-DOT, 400 Seventh St. SW, Washington, DC 20590. Phone: (202)366-2053. **Internet:** "www.fta.dot.gov/htl/grants.htm".

20.505 FEDERAL TRANSIT—METROPOLITAN PLANNING GRANTS ("Metropolitan Planning")

Assistance: formula grants (80 percent/3 years).

Purposes: to develop transportation improvement projects, long-range transportation plans, and other technical studies related to management systems, capital requirements, and economic feasibility.

Eligible applicants/beneficiaries: states (for distribution to metropolitan planning organizations).

Range: $20,000 to $5,000,000.

Activity: not quantified specifically.

HQ: Office of Planning and Environment (TPE-11), FTA-DOT, 400 Seventh St. SW, Washington, DC 20590. Phone: (202)366-1648. **Internet:** "www.fta.dot.gov".

20.507 FEDERAL TRANSIT—FORMULA GRANTS ("Urbanized Area Formula Program")

Assistance: formula grants (50-90 percent/3 years).

Purposes: to plan, acquire, construct or reconstruct, improve, and maintain transit facilities and equipment. Transit projects may involve bringing equipment into compliance with the ADA and the Clean Air Act; also, they may involve bicycles (90 percent funding). Grants subsidizing operating costs may not exceed 50 percent.

Eligible applicants/beneficiaries: urbanized areas of 200,000 or more population—public entities jointly designated by the governor, responsible local officials, and publicly-owned operators of mass transportation services. Urbanized areas of 50,000 to 200,000 population—governors or their designees.

Range: N.A.

Activity: not quantified specifically.

HQ: Director, Office of Resource Management and State Programs, Office of Program Management, FTA-DOT, 400 Seventh St. SW, Washington, DC 20590. Phone: (202)366-1659. **Internet:** same as **20.505**.

20.509 FORMULA GRANTS FOR OTHER THAN URBANIZED AREAS ("Nonurbanized Area Formula Program")

Assistance: formula grants (50-90 percent/2 years).

Purposes: for public transportation systems in nonurbanized areas—i.e., rural and small areas under 50,000 population, for uses similar to **20.507**.

Eligible applicants/beneficiaries: designated state agencies. Sub-grants may be awarded to state agencies, local public bodies and agencies, nonprofit organizations, tribes, and operators of public transportation services, including intercity bus service—in rural and small urban areas. Private operators may receive subcontracts.

Range: N.A.

Activity: not quantified specifically.

HQ: Office of Capital and Formula Assistance, Office of Program Management, FTA-DOT, 400 Seventh St. SW, Washington, DC 20590. Phone: (202)366-0893. **Internet:** same as **20.505**.

20.513 CAPITAL ASSISTANCE PROGRAM FOR ELDERLY PERSONS AND PERSONS WITH DISABILITIES

Assistance: formula grants (80-90 percent).

Purposes: to cover capital costs of providing specialized transportation services for elderly and handicapped persons. Specially designed vehicles may be purchased with grant funds. Awards favor projects involving private profit operators.

Eligible applicants/beneficiaries: designated states. Subgrants may be awarded to private nonprofit organizations or public bodies.

Range: $300,000 to $10,000,000.

Activity: cumulatively since 1975 program inception, funds to 1,000 organizations to purchase vehicles, involving some 4,000 subrecipients.

HQ: Program Coordinator, Office of Resource Management and State Programs, Office of Program Management, FTA-DOT, 400 Seventh St. SW, Washington, DC 20590. Phone: (202)366-1630. **Internet:** same as **20.505**.

20.514 TRANSIT PLANNING AND RESEARCH ("National Planning and Research Programs")

Assistance: project grants (to 100 percent); technical information; training.

Purposes: for research on mobility management, transit operational efficiency, safety and emergency preparedness, transit capacity building, energy independence and environmental protection, infrastructure and equipment protection and innovation, and strategic program planning. Projects may involve research, development, demonstrations, training, planning studies, and human resource programs.

Eligible applicants/beneficiaries: public bodies, state and local agencies, nonprofit institutions, universities, profit organizations, and operators of public transportation services.

Range: N.A.

Activity: not quantified specifically.

HQ: Associate Administrator/Research, Demonstration and Innovation (TRI-1), FTA-DOT, 400 Seventh St. SW - Rm.9401, Washington, DC 20590. Phone: (202)366-4052, -4209. **Internet:** "www.fta.dot.gov/research". (Note: no field offices for this program.)

20.515 STATE PLANNING AND RESEARCH

Assistance: formula grants (80 percent).

Purposes: to develop cost-effective multimodal transportation improvement programs, including the planning, engineering, and design of federal transit projects and other technical studies and training, within a unified or officially coordinated state-wide transportation system. States may authorize use of funds to supplement metropolitan planning funds. This program operates as a block grant program, for projects identified by states to accomplish planning and research objectives.

Eligible applicants/beneficiaries: states.

Range: $45,000 to $1,000,000 (plus per-state formula allocations).

Activity: not quantified specifically.

HQ: same as **20.505**.

20.516 JOB ACCESS—REVERSE COMMUTE

Assistance: project grants (50-80 percent).

Purposes: pursuant to the Transportation Equity Act for the 21st Century, to develop transportation services to connect welfare recipients and low-income persons to employment and support services. Funds may be used: for capital projects; to finance equipment, facilities, and associated support costs related to providing access to jobs—associated with adding reverse commute bus, train, carpool or service from urban areas, urbanized areas, and other areas to suburban work places.

Eligible applicants/beneficiaries: state and local government agencies, nonprofit agencies, transit providers.

Range: $24,000 to $1,500,000. **Average:** $356,000.

Activity: cumulatively, 300 grants.

HQ: Office of Program Management, FTA-DOT, 400 Seventh St. SW - Rm. 9315, Washington, DC 20590. Phone: (202)366-2053, -1622; Office of Research and Innovation (Rm.9407), (202)366-1666. **Internet:** same as **20.505**.

20.518 CAPITAL AND TRAINING ASSISTANCE PROGRAM FOR OVER-THE-ROAD BUS ACCESSIBILITY

Assistance: project grants (to 90 percent/3 years).

Purposes: pursuant to the Transportation Equity Act for the 21st Century, for private operators of over-the-road buses to finance the incremental capital and training costs of complying with DOT's "Transportation for Individuals with Disabilities" rule. Project costs may cover: adding wheelchair lifts and other accessibility components to new vehicle purchases; retrofitting existing vehicles; training in equipment operation and maintenance, boarding assistance, handling, and storage.

Eligible applicants/beneficiaries: certain private operators of over-the-road buses.

Range: $10,000 to $50,000. **Average:** $20,000.

Activity: cumulatively, 74 companies funded involving 129 vehicles.

HQ: Program Manager, same address, web site as **20.507**. Phone: (202)366-4345.

NATIONAL HIGHWAY TRAFFIC SAFETY ADMINISTRATION

20.600 STATE AND COMMUNITY HIGHWAY SAFETY

Assistance: formula grants (80 percent).

Purposes: pursuant to the Highway Safety Act of 1966 as amended, for highway traffic safety enforcement program costs, such as police equipment purchases, training, and overtime pay; emergency medical services training and equipment purchases; public education projects. Program priority areas include alcohol and other drug countermeasures, police traffic services, occupant protection, traffic records, emergency medical services, motorcycle safety, pedestrian/bicycle safety, speed control, roadway safety, pupil transportation safety.

Eligible applicants/beneficiaries: states, tribes, territories, possessions.

Range: $340,000 to $13,000,000. **Average:** $2,200,000.

Activity: not quantified specifically.

HQ: Associate Administrator/Injury Control Operations and Resources, National Highway Traffic Safety Administration-DOT, Washington, DC 20590. Phone: (202)366-2121. *Or:* Transportation Specialist, Safety Technology Division, Office of Highway Safety, FHWA-DOT, Washington, DC 20590. Phone: (202)366-2161. **Internet:** "www.nhtsa.whatsup.fedassist/index.html".

20.601 ALCOHOL TRAFFIC SAFETY AND DRUNK DRIVING PREVENTION INCENTIVE GRANTS

Assistance: project grants (25-75 percent/six years).

Purposes: pursuant to the Highway Safety Act of 1998 as amended, for state programs to reduce crashes resulting from persons driving under the influence of alcohol and other controlled substances. Grant amounts are based on apportionments by states. Funds may be used: to purchase breath testing devices; to train law enforcement personnel; for public education; to pay for overtime by police personnel.

Eligible applicants/beneficiaries: states, DC.

Range/Average: $262,000 to $4,500,000.

Activity: N.A.

HQ: same as **20.600** (for NHTSA).

20.602 OCCUPANT PROTECTION

Assistance: project grants (25-75 percent/to 5 years).

Purposes: pursuant to the Highway Safety Act of 1998 as amended, for states to implement and enforce automobile occupant protection programs.

Eligible applicants/beneficiaries: states, DC, PR, VI, Samoa, Northern Marianas, Guam, BIA.

Range: $100,000 to $300,000. **Average:** $200,000.

Activity: N.A.

HQ: same as **20.601**.

20.603 FEDERAL HIGHWAY SAFETY DATA IMPROVEMENTS INCENTIVE GRANTS

Assistance: project grants (25-75 percent/to 5 years).

Purposes: pursuant to the Highway Safety Act of 1998 as amended, to improve the timeliness, accuracy, completeness, and accessibility of state data.

Eligible applicants/beneficiaries: same as for **20.602**.

Range: $25,000 to $250,000. **Average:** $50,000.

Activity: N.A.

HQ: same as **20.601**.

20.604 SAFETY INCENTIVE GRANTS FOR USE OF SEATBELTS

Assistance: project grants (formula based/to 7 years).

Purposes: pursuant to the Highway Safety Act of 1998 as amended, for states to implement and enforce automobile occupant seat belt programs.

Eligible applicants/beneficiaries: same as for **20.602**.

Range: $100,000 to $1,200,000. **Average:** $350,000.

Activity: N.A.

HQ: same as **20.601**.

20.605 SAFETY INCENTIVES TO PREVENT OPERATION OF MOTOR VEHICLES BY INTOXICATED PERSONS

Assistance: project grants (100 percent/to 7 years).

Purposes: pursuant to the Highway Safety Act of 1998 as amended, for states to implement programs establishing a 0.08 percent blood alcohol concentration as the legal limit for drunk driving. Funds may be used to cover law enforcement personnel training and overtime pay, equipment purchases, and public education.

Eligible applicants/beneficiaries: same as for **20.602**.

Range: $1,000,000 to $4,000,000. **Average:** $1,850,000.
Activity: N.A.
HQ: same as **20.601**.

20.607 ALCOHOL OPEN CONTAINER REQUIREMENTS

Assistance: project grants (to 6 years).

Purposes: pursuant to the Highway Safety Act of 1998 as amended, to encourage states to enact and enforce alcohol open container laws. Funding is based on the calculated annual savings in medical costs to the federal government, including in the Medicare and Medicaid programs.

Eligible applicants/beneficiaries: states, DC, and PR—provided they have Repeat Intoxicated Driver Laws in effect.

Range: $2,500,000 to $13,700,000. **Average:** $5,500,000.

Activity: new program listing in 2004.

HQ: same as **20.601**.

20.608 MINIMUM PENALTIES FOR REPEAT OFFENDERS FOR DRIVING WHILE INTOXICATED

Assistance: project grants (to 6 years).

Purposes: pursuant to the Highway Safety Act of 1998 as amended, to encourage states to enact Repeat Intoxicated Driver Laws. Program funding is based on the calculated annual savings in medical costs to the federal government, including in the Medicare and Medicaid programs.

Eligible applicants/beneficiaries: same as for **20.607**.

Range: $2,400,000 to $47,500,000. **Average:** $7,000,000.

Activity: new program listing in 2004.

HQ: same as **20.601**.

PIPELINES AND HAZARDOUS MATERIALS SAFETY ADMINISTRATION

20.700 PIPELINE SAFETY

Assistance: formula grants (to 50 percent).

Purposes: pursuant to the Natural Gas Pipeline Safety Act of 1968 as amended and related acts, to pay personnel, inspection, equipment, training, and research costs related to natural gas, liquefied natural gas, and hazardous liquids pipeline safety programs.

Eligible applicants/beneficiaries: state agencies.

Range: $4,522 to $1,123,000.

Activity: FY 01, 49 grants (latest data reported).

HQ: Pipelines and Hazardous Materials Safety Administration-DOT, 400 Seventh St. SW, Washington, DC 20590. Phone: (202)366-4595. **Internet:** "www.phmsa.dot.gov/".

20.703 INTERAGENCY HAZARDOUS MATERIALS PUBLIC SECTOR TRAINING AND PLANNING GRANTS
("Hazardous Materials Emergency Preparedness Training and Planning Grants" - "HMEP")

Assistance: project grants (80 percent/to 6 years).

Purposes: pursuant to the Federal Hazardous Materials Transportation Act, for the development, improvement, and implementation of emergency response plans to handle hazardous materials accidents and incidents; to enhance implementation of the Emergency Planning and Community Right-to-Know Act of 1986 (EPCRA); for related training of public sector employees.

Eligible applicants/beneficiaries: states, tribes, territories.

Range: $4,000 to $968,000. **Average:** $180,000.

Activity: all states, territories, and 41 tribes funded since program inception.

HQ: HMEP Grants Manager (PHM-64), Research and Special Programs Administration-DOT, 400 Seventh St. SW, Washington, DC 20590. Phone: (202)366-0001. **Internet:** same as **20.700**. (Note: no field offices for this program.)

MARITIME ADMINISTRATION

20.801 DEVELOPMENT AND PROMOTION OF PORTS AND INTERMODAL TRANSPORTATION
("Ports and Domestic Shipping and Intermodal Development")

Assistance: advisory services/counseling; technical information.

Purposes: pursuant to Merchant Marine Acts, Defense Production Act of 1950, and amendments, to make federal personnel available to help promote and plan for the development and utilization of domestic waterways, ports, port facilities, and intermodal transportation systems by conducting studies in cooperation with port authorities and others—toward the enhancement of related economic development, as well as national security under national mobilization conditions. No grants are awarded under this program.

Eligible applicants/beneficiaries: state and local government agencies, metropolitan planning organizations, public port and intermodal authorities, trade associations, private terminal and intermodal operators.

Activity: not quantified specifically.

HQ: Director, Office of Ports and Domestic Shipping, Maritime Administration-DOT, Washington, DC 20590. Phone: (202)366-4357, FAX (202)366-6988; Director, Office of Intermodal Development, (202)366-8888, FAX (202)366-6988. **Internet:** "www.marad.dot.gov".

20.802 FEDERAL SHIP FINANCING GUARANTEES
("Title XI")

Assistance: guaranteed/insured loans (87.5 percent/to 25 years).

Purposes: pursuant to the Merchant Marine Act of 1936 as amended, to finance or refinance: construction, reconstruction, reconditioning, or refinancing of ships built in U.S. shipyards, used in foreign or domestic commerce, in research, or as ocean thermal energy conversion facilities—in coast-wide or intercoastal trade, on the Great Lakes or on bays, sounds, rivers, harbors, inland lakes, or as floating dry-docks; for advanced shipbuilding technology of general shipyard facilities. Vessels must be larger than five net tons—other than towboats, barges, scows, lighters, car floats, canal boats, or tank vessels of less than 25 gross tons.

Eligible applicants/beneficiaries: qualified individuals, U.S. shipyards, U.S. and foreign ship owners.

Range: from less than $1,000,000 to several hundred million.

Activity: FY 05, 1 approval, 10 applications pending.

HQ: Associate Administrator/Shipbuilding, Office of Ship Financing, Maritime Administration-DOT, Washington, DC 20590. Phone: (202)366-5744. **Internet:** same as **20.801**.

20.803 MARITIME WAR RISK INSURANCE ("Title XII, MMA, 1936")

Assistance: insurance.

Purposes: pursuant to the Merchant Marine Act of 1936 as amended, to provide war risk insurance binders or policies on vessels in operation or under construction. Insurance is available at nominal cost in peacetime.

Eligible applicants/beneficiaries: owners of U.S. flag vessels and certain foreign flag vessels.

Range: N.A.

Activity: as of FY 04, 350 vessels covered.

HQ: Director, Office of Insurance and Shipping Analysis, Maritime Administration-DOT, 400 Seventh St. SW, Washington, DC 20590. Phone: (202) 366-2400. **Internet:** same as **20.801**.

20.806 STATE MARINE SCHOOLS

Assistance: direct payments/specified use (50 percent); use of property, facilities, and equipment.

Purposes: for the operation and maintenance of state marine schools; for loans to the schools of training vessels by the federal government, as well as their maintenance and repair; for incentive payments to selected cadets. States must admit out-of-state students.

Eligible applicants/beneficiaries: states (limited to one academy per state).

Range: states, $200,000 annually; student stipends, $4,000 per academic year for up to four years.

Activity: FY 04, 406 officers graduated; incentive payments to 45 graduates.

HQ: Director, Office of Policy and Plans, Maritime Administration-DOT, Washington, DC 20590. Phone: (202)366-5755. **Internet:** same as **20.801**.

20.807 U.S. MERCHANT MARINE ACADEMY
("Kings Point")

Assistance: training.

Purposes: for the operation and maintenance of the federal maritime academy, including subsistence payments to students training to become merchant marine officers—as well as their quarters, medical care, program travel, and other expenses.

Eligible applicants/beneficiaries: U.S. citizens that are high school graduates; eligible international students.

Range: allowance prescribed for all personnel for uniforms and textbooks. (During the sea year a midshipman will earn $700 monthly from his/her steamship company employer.)

Activity: 2003, 200 graduates.

HQ: same address, web site as **20.806**. Phone: (202)366-5484.

20.808 CAPITAL CONSTRUCTION FUND
("CCF")

Assistance: direct payments/specified use.

Purposes: pursuant to the Merchant Marine Act of 1936 as amended, to provide tax deferment incentives to shipbuilders to acquire, construct, or reconstruct vessels built in the U.S. for use in the U.S. foreign, Great Lakes, or noncontiguous domestic trades.

Eligible applicants/beneficiaries: U.S. citizens that own or lease one or more eligible vessels, with appropriate plans and financial capabilities.

Range: N.A.

Activity: as of March 2005, 132 active agreements; cumulatively since program inception, over $2.7 billion in tax deferments. FY 04, 2 applications approved.

HQ: same as **20.802**.

20.810 SUPPLEMENTARY TRAINING

Assistance: training.

Purposes: pursuant to the Merchant Marine Act of 1936 as amended, to train seafarers in shipboard firefighting, intermodal freight transportation, maritime defense, and safety-related subjects. Training is provided on a fee-paid basis.

Eligible applicants/beneficiaries: qualified U.S. merchant seafarers; operators of inland waterway, offshore drilling, and mining vessels; maritime academy students; NOAA, USCG, U.S. Army Corps of Engineers, and Naval Reserve personnel; qualified representatives of marine industry; state and local governments.

Activity: FY 04, 469 firefighting training, 24 intermodal freight transportation, 35 national sealift training participants.

HQ: Associate Administrator/Policy and International Trade, Maritime Administration-DOT, Washington, DC 20590. Phone: (202)366-5755. **Internet:** same as **20.801**.

20.812 CONSTRUCTION RESERVE FUND ("CRF")

Assistance: direct payments/specified use.

Purposes: pursuant to the Merchant Marine Act of 1936 as amended, to provide tax deferment incentives to shipbuilders to construct, reconstruct, recondition, or acquire vessels necessary for national defense or U.S. commerce.

Eligible applicants/beneficiaries: U.S. citizens that own in whole or in part one or more vessels operating in the foreign or domestic commerce of the U.S. or in the fisheries; citizens operating such vessel or vessels owned by another individual.

Range: N.A.

Activity: as of March 2004, 24 active contracts with deposits totaling $85,300,000.

HQ: same as **20.802**.

20.813 MARITIME SECURITY FLEET PROGRAM

Assistance: direct payments/specified use.

Purposes: pursuant to the Merchant Marine Act of 1936 as amended and Maritime Security Act of 2003, to maintain a U.S. flag merchant fleet crewed by U.S. citizens to serve both commercial and national security needs, including container ships, lighter-aboard ships, and roll-on/roll-off vessels.

Eligible applicants/beneficiaries: U.S. citizens and certain specified foreign corporations.

Range/Average: FY 06-08, $2,600,000 per vessel per year.

Activity: as of 12 January 2005, 60 vessels enrolled.

HQ: Director, Office of Sealift Support, Maritime Administration-DOT, 400 Seventh St. SW, Washington, DC 20590. Phone: (202)366-2323, FAX (202)366-3128. **Internet:** same as **20.801**. (Note: no field offices for this program.)

OFFICE OF THE SECRETARY

20.900 TRANSPORTATION—CONSUMER AFFAIRS

Assistance: investigation of complaints.

Purposes: pursuant to the Federal Aviation Act of 1958 as amended, to provide assistance and information to consumers with complaints of all types against domestic and foreign air carriers, travel agents, and tour operators; to investigate alleged violations of airline passengers' civil rights.

Eligible applicants/beneficiaries: all users of air transportation.

Activity: 2004, 10,217 complaints and information requests received.

HQ: Aviation Consumer Protection Division (C-75), DOT, 400 Seventh St. SW

- Rm.4107, Washington, DC 20590. Phone: (202)366-5957. **Internet:** "http://airconsumer.ost.dot.gov".

20.901 PAYMENTS FOR ESSENTIAL AIR SERVICES

Assistance: direct payments/specified use.

Purposes: to subsidize air carriers providing commuter services to unserved communities, covering operating losses and a profit element.

Eligible applicants/beneficiaries: carriers selected by DOT.

Range: for continental U.S., $291,000 to $1,872,000. **Average:** $840,000 annually per point.

Activity: currently, some 145 affected communities receiving subsidies.

HQ: Director, Office of Aviation Analysis (X-50), DOT, 400 Seventh St. SW, Washington, DC 20590. Phone: (202)366-1030. **Internet:** "www.ost.dot.gov". (Note: no field offices for this program.)

20.903 SUPPORT MECHANISMS FOR DISADVANTAGED BUSINESSES ("Minority Resource Center")

Assistance: project grants.

Purposes: for outreach, technical assistance, and referral services supporting participation by small disadvantaged business enterprises in transportation-related contract opportunities. Short-term lending and bonding assistance also may be provided to minority-, disadvantaged-, and women-owned businesses.

Eligible applicants/beneficiaries: tax-exempt chambers of commerce, trade associations, business organizations, profit entities.

Range/Average: $134,000.

Activity: FY 04, 9 new cooperative agreements.

HQ: Office of Small and Disadvantaged Business Utilization (S-40), Office of the Secretary-DOT, 400 Seventh St. SW, Washington, DC 20590. Phone: (202)366-1930, (800)532-1169. **Internet:** "www.osdbuweb.dot.gov". (Note: no field offices for this program.)

20.905 DISADVANTAGED BUSINESS ENTERPRISES—SHORT TERM LENDING PROGRAM

Assistance: direct loans (1 year).

Purposes: to provide lines of credit to disadvantaged business enterprises to obtain accounts receivable financing for the performance of transportation-related contracts from DOT, its grantees, and recipients, and their contractors and subcontractors—including for maintenance, rehabilitation, restructuring, improvement, or revitalization of any mode of transportation with any public or commercial provider of transportation or any federal, state, or local transportation agency.

Eligible applicants/beneficiaries: certified disadvantaged business enterprises, minority- and women-owned enterprises; all SBA "Section 8(a)" firms; HUBZONE Empowerment-eligible and disabled veterans.

Range: to $750,000.

Activity: FY 03, 23 approvals.

HQ: same address, web site as **20.903**. Phone: (202)366-2852, (800)532-1169. (Note: no field offices for this program.)

20.907 MINORITY INSTITUTIONS ("Entrepreneurial Training and Technical Assistance Program" - "ETTAP")

Assistance: project grants (100 percent).

Purposes: for minority institutions to develop educational, training and technical assistance programs to encourage, promote, and assist minority and disadvantaged entrepreneurs and businesses, including women-owned businesses, in obtaining transportation-related contracts, subcontracts, and projects. Funds may also support student internships and mentorships.

Eligible applicants/beneficiaries: accredited minority institutions, defined as IHEs with over 50 percent minority enrollment.

Range: $80,000 to $94,000.

Activity: 2003, 4 awards.

HQ: Program Coordinator, same address (Rm.9414), web site as **20.904**. Phone: (202)366-2852, (800)532-1169. (Note: no field offices for this program.)

OFFICE OF AVIATION ANALYSIS

20.930 PAYMENTS FOR SMALL COMMUNITY AIR SERVICE DEVELOPMENT

Assistance: project grants (to 100 percent/to 3 years).

Purposes: pursuant to the Wendell H. Ford Aviation Investment and Reform Act for the 21st Century and Vision 100-Century in Aviation Reauthorization Act, for smaller communities to enhance their air service and increase access to the national transportation system—through such activities as: marketing, advertising, and promotion; air service deficiency studies, measuring traffic loss or diversion to other communities; providing financial incentives including subsidies or revenue guarantees to cover air carrier's prospective operating losses or to ground service access providers.

Eligible applicants/beneficiaries: communities or consortia with airports not larger than a small hub airport, including in territories and possessions.

Range: $20,000 to $1,500,000. **Average:** $497,000.

Activity: new program in 2004. 12 communities participating

HQ: Associate Director/Small Community Air Service Development Program, Office of Aviation Analysis (X-50), OS-DOT, 400 Seventh St. SW, Washington, DC 20590. Phone: (202)366-1032, FAX (202)366-7638. **Internet:** "http://ostpxweb.dot.aviation/index.html". (Note: no field offices for this program.)

DEPARTMENT OF THE TREASURY

INTERNAL REVENUE SERVICE

21.003 TAXPAYER SERVICE

Assistance: advisory services/counseling.

Purposes: to provide information and guidance on income tax matters, including taxpayer obligations and rights. Besides toll-free phone and Internet services and information offices, IRS sponsors volunteer programs, and offers films, seminars, and other services. Special educational programs are available to assist small businesses, secondary school teachers, adult education classes, colleges, and the elderly. Special procedures become effective for victims of natural disasters.

Eligible applicants/beneficiaries: individuals, groups.

Activity: annually, 30,000,000 additional taxpayer contacts through partnership programs.

HQ: Commissioner, IRS, 1111 Constitution Ave. NW - Rm.3000IR, Washington, DC 20224. Phone: *general inquiries,* (800)829-1040; National Taxpayer Advocate's Help Line, (877)777-4778; TDD (800)829-4059. **Internet:** "www.irs.gov".

21.004 EXCHANGE OF FEDERAL TAX INFORMATION WITH STATE TAX AGENCIES
("Agreement on Coordination of Tax Administration")

Assistance: specialized services.

Purposes: to increase taxpayer compliance and to reduce duplication of resources—through the confidential exchange of tax data, models, and extracts with states and municipalities for tax administration purposes.

Eligible applicants/beneficiaries: states, territories, and municipalities with over 250,000 population that impose taxes on income or wages.

Activity: 50 state and several municipal and territorial agencies participating.

HQ: Director, Governmental Liaison and Disclosure, IRS, 1111 Constitution Ave. NW - Rm.1603, Washington, DC 20224. Phone: (202)622-6200. **Internet:** "www.irs.gov/foia".

21.006 TAX COUNSELING FOR THE ELDERLY

Assistance: project grants.

Purposes: pursuant to the Revenue Act of 1978, to reimburse volunteers for their out-of-pocket expenses in receiving training and in providing tax counseling to elderly taxpayers.

Eligible applicants/beneficiaries: experienced private or public nonprofit organizations. Governmental agencies are ineligible.

Range: N.A.

Activity: annually, 60 sponsors funded; 1,800,000 taxpayers assisted.

HQ: Program Analyst, Tax Counseling for the Elderly, IRS, 5000 Ellin Rd., Lanham, MD 20706. Phone: (202)283-0189. **Internet:** same as **21.003**. (Note: no field offices for this program.)

21.008 LOW-INCOME TAXPAYER CLINICS

Assistance: project grants (50 percent/to 3 years).

Purposes: to enable organizations to represent low-income taxpayers in controversies with the IRS, or to inform individuals with limited English language abilities of their tax rights and responsibilities.

Eligible applicants/beneficiaries: private nonprofit organizations; educational institutions with accredited law, business, or accounting schools.

Range/Average: N.A.

Activity: FY 05, 153 organizations funded.

HQ: Program Manager, Low-Income Taxpayer Clinics (MS 211D), IRS, 401 W. Peachtree St. NW, Atlanta, GA 30308. Phone: (404)338-7900. **Internet:** "www.irs.gov/advocate"; e-mail, "LITCProgramOffice@irs.gov". (Note: the field office serves as headquarters.)

UNDER SECRETARY/DOMESTIC FINANCE

21.020 COMMUNITY DEVELOPMENT FINANCIAL INSTITUTIONS PROGRAM ("CDFI")

Assistance: project grants (50 percent/to 3 years).

Purposes: to provide financial and technical assistance through CDFIs, promoting economic revitalization and community development, including for: CDFI staff training; acquiring products and services including technology; consulting services.

Eligible applicants/beneficiaries: private nonprofit institutions and organizations, and profit organizations that are or seek to become CDFIs. Governmental entities are ineligible.

Range: $50,000 to $3,000,000. **Average:** $800,000.

Activity: not quantified specifically

HQ: Program Manager, CDFI Fund, Department of the Treasury, 601 13th St. NW - Ste.200-S, Washington, DC 20005. Phone: (202)622-6355, FAX (202)622-7754. **Internet:** "www.cdfifund.gov". (Note: no field offices for this program.)

21.021 BANK ENTERPRISE AWARD PROGRAM ("BEA")

Assistance: project grants (100 percent).

Purposes: to encourage insured depository institutions to increase their level of community development activities in the form of loans, investments, services, and technical assistance within distressed communities; to provide assistance to community development financial institutions through grants, stock purchases, loans, deposits, and other forms of financial and technical assistance. Award amounts are based on a percentage of increases by the institutions in qualifying activities. Project example: multifamily housing financing.

Eligible applicants/beneficiaries: Federal Deposit Insurance Corporation-insured depository institutions.

Range: $1,100 to $1,500,000. **Average:** $73,000.

Activity: FY 04, 49 awards.

HQ: same address, web site as **20.020**. Phone: (202)622-6355, FAX (202)622-7754. (Note: no field offices for this program.)

APPALACHIAN REGIONAL COMMISSION

23.001 APPALACHIAN REGIONAL DEVELOPMENT (SEE INDIVIDUAL APPALACHIAN PROGRAMS)
("Appalachian Program")

Assistance: project grants.

Purposes: pursuant to the Appalachian Regional Development Act of 1965 (ARDA) and amendments, for programs and projects to stimulate public investments in public services, facilities, and institutions in the Appalachian region, through federal-state-local efforts. Priorities are established by the Appalachian Regional Commission, comprising the 13 state governors within the region or their alternates. All proposed projects must meet the requirements of the state Appalachian plan and the annual state investment program, both of which must be approved annually by the commission. (See individual Appalachian program descriptions). Funding is through the commission's various programs (**23.002 - 23.011**).

Eligible applicants/beneficiaries: only in the Appalachian region—states and, through the states, public bodies and private nonprofit organizations.

Range/Average: see individual programs.

Activity: see individual programs.

HQ: Executive Director, Appalachian Regional Commission, 1666 Connecticut Ave. NW, Washington, DC 20009 Phone: (202)884-7700. **Internet:** "www.arc.gov".

23.002 APPALACHIAN AREA DEVELOPMENT
("Supplemental and Direct Grants")

Assistance: project grants (10-80 percent).

Purposes: pursuant to ARDA and amendments, to supplement other federal project funding supporting self-sustaining development in the region's most distressed counties. Projects must hold high priority in the state's Appalachian development plan. Examples include water and sewer systems, industrial parks, entrepreneurship, export promotion, training, vocational education, health care, child development, revolving loan funds, and business incubator projects—in conjunction with private sector commitments.

Eligible applicants/beneficiaries: (Appalachia only) states, state subdivisions and instrumentalities, private nonprofit agencies.

Range: $55,000 to $1,500,000. **Average:** $161,000

Activity: FY 04, 471 projects funded.

HQ: same as **23.001**.

23.003 APPALACHIAN DEVELOPMENT HIGHWAY SYSTEM ("Appalachian Corridors")

Assistance: project grants (80 percent).

Purposes: pursuant to ARDA as amended, to develop a highway system within the Appalachian region where commerce and communication have been inhibited by inadequate access. Grants may cover preliminary engineering, right-of-way acquisition, and construction costs. Additional funding for this program may be provided from the DOT Highway Trust Fund.

Eligible applicants/beneficiaries: (Appalachia only) state governments.

Range: N.A.

Activity: cumulatively through FY 04, 2,627 miles completed or under construction.

HQ: same as **23.001**.

23.009 APPALACHIAN LOCAL DEVELOPMENT DISTRICT ASSISTANCE ("LDD")

Assistance: project grants (50-75 percent).

Purposes: pursuant to ARDA and amendments, for development planning and activities relating to local economic development. Funds may be used for: administrative expenses including technical services of local development districts; with ARC approval, real estate and vehicle purchases, construction and space improvement.

Eligible applicants/beneficiaries: (Appalachia only) multicounty organizations.

Range: $12,000 to $304,000. **Average:** $84,000.

Activity: FY 04, 72 planning districts assisted.

HQ: same as **23.001**.

23.011 APPALACHIAN RESEARCH, TECHNICAL ASSISTANCE, AND DEMONSTRATION PROJECTS ("State Research")

Assistance: project grants.

Purposes: pursuant to ARDA and amendments, for research, planning, demonstration, and technical assistance projects relating to concerted economic and community development. Priority is on technical assistance projects leading to job creation.

Eligible applicants/beneficiaries: Appalachian states, state consortia; local public bodies; state instrumentalities.

Range: $1,758 to $359,000. **Average:** $56,000.

Activity: not quantified specifically.

HQ: same as **23.001**.

OFFICE OF PERSONNEL MANAGEMENT

27.001 FEDERAL CIVIL SERVICE EMPLOYMENT

Assistance: federal employment.

Purposes: pursuant to the Civil Service Reform Act of 1978, to fill federal job vacancies, usually through competitive exams and without discrimination on any nonmerit basis. Veterans receive preference. Special programs help place the physically handicapped, the mentally retarded or mentally restored, and the disadvantaged.

Eligible applicants/beneficiaries: U.S. citizens age 18 or older (age 16 in certain cases).

Activity: FY 01, 10,212,000 inquiries answered (latest data reported).

HQ: Office of Personnel Management (no address provided). Phone: (202)606-2700; *nation-wide,* (912)757-3000, TTD (912)744-2299; Federal Job Opportunities Bulletin Board (FJOB), (912)757-3100. **Internet:** USA JOBS site, "www.usajobs.opm.gov"; OPM, "www.opm.gov".

27.002 FEDERAL EMPLOYMENT ASSISTANCE FOR VETERANS

Assistance: federal employment.

Purposes: pursuant to the Veterans Preference Act of 1944, to assist veterans in obtaining federal employment, with preferences according to their discharge status.

Eligible applicants/beneficiaries: nondisabled and disabled veterans, and certain spouses, widows, widowers, and mothers of veterans.

Activity: as of FY 02, 480,000 veterans assisted, constituting 26.9 percent of non-postal federal workers (latest data available).

HQ: *Disabled Veterans Affirmative Action Programs,* Office of Diversity, Employment Service, OPM, 1900 E St. NW - Rm.2445, Washington, DC 20415. Phone: (202)606-1059; *veterans preference and special hiring programs,* Office of Staffing Reinvention, (same address - Rm.6500), (202)606-0830. **Internet:** "www.opm.gov". (Note: no field offices for this program.)

27.003 FEDERAL STUDENT TEMPORARY EMPLOYMENT PROGRAM

Assistance: federal employment (to 1 year).

Purposes: to provide temporary federal employment for youth during school terms (full-time during extended vacation periods). OPM coordinates this program, but it is carried out by other participating federal agencies.

Eligible applicants/beneficiaries: students accepted for or enrolled at least half-time in a secondary, vocational, or technical school or IHE through the graduate level.

Activity: FY 01, 32,000 participants (latest data reported).

HQ: *information available from personnel offices of the agencies of interest. For inquiries on policy issues,* Staffing Reinvention Office, Employment Service, OPM, 1900 E St. NW, Washington, DC 20415. Phone: (202)606-0830. **Internet:** same as **27.002**. (Note: no field offices for this program.)

27.005 FEDERAL EMPLOYMENT FOR INDIVIDUALS WITH DISABILITIES ("Selective Placement Program")

Assistance: federal employment.

Purposes: pursuant to the Rehabilitation Act of 1973 as amended, to provide special OPM assistance to federal agencies to assist persons with disabilities, including veterans, in obtaining or retaining federal employment. Federal agencies have coordinators responsible for expanding employment opportunities under this program, to work with state vocational rehabilitation agencies, DVA facilities, and other public and private agencies. Funding is by the accounts of individual agencies.

Eligible applicants/beneficiaries: persons with physical, cognitive, or mental disabilities.

Activity: as of FY 02, 127,000 federal employees with targeted and nontargeted disabilities; 12,000 full-time position hires (latest data reported).

HQ: *information available from personnel offices of the agencies of interest. For inquiries on policy issues,* same as **27.002**. (Note: no field offices for this program.)

27.006 FEDERAL SUMMER EMPLOYMENT ("Summer Jobs in Federal Agencies")

Assistance: federal employment.

Purposes: pursuant to the Civil Service Reform Act of 1978, to provide summer employment primarily for college and high school students, in clerical, craft or trade, administrative, and subprofessional jobs. Summer jobs are filled through agency staffing plans, with funding by the participating agencies.

Eligible applicants/beneficiaries: any U.S. citizen at least age 16 at time of appointment.

Activity: N.A.

HQ: same as **27.001**.

27.011 INTERGOVERNMENTAL PERSONNEL ACT (IPA) MOBILITY PROGRAM

Assistance: specialized services; advisory services/counseling.

Purposes: pursuant to the Act of 1970 as amended and ISDEAA, to enable temporary assignments of professional, administrative, or technical personnel back and forth between federal, state, local, and tribal governments, IHEs, and other organizations. Assignments may be for up to two years, with one two-year extension. Upon completion of assignments, assigned federal employees must serve in the Civil Service for a period equal to that of the assignment. Cost sharing is negotiable.

Eligible applicants/beneficiaries: federal agencies; state, local, and tribal governments; IHEs. Other organizations include: national, regional, statewide, areawide, or metropolitan organizations of state or local governments; associations of state or local public officials; nonprofit organizations offering professional advisory, research, educational, or development services, or related services to governments or universities concerned with public management.

Activity: annually, 1,400 mobility assignments with participation by all states, PR, VI, Samoa, Guam, Northern Marianas, DC, 519 local governments, 512 universities, 106 tribal governments, and 161 other organizations.

HQ: Office of Merit Systems Oversight and Effectiveness, OPM, 1900 E St. NW - Rm.7463, Washington, DC 20415-0001. Phone: (202)606-1181. **Internet:** same as **27.002**.

27.013 PRESIDENTIAL MANAGEMENT INTERN PROGRAM

Assistance: federal employment; training; specialized services.

Purposes: to attract graduate students of exceptional potential to the federal service. Two-year internships may be awarded for work in federal agencies (exceptionally, for three years). Awardees may be assigned to work temporarily for state or local governments. Nominations for awards are submitted by deans of graduate level programs. Participating entities reimburse OPM for certain program costs through a revolving loan fund.

Eligible applicants/beneficiaries: state and local governments and organizations eligible for **27.011**.

Activity: FY 01, 350 interns hired (latest data reported).

HQ: Presidential Management Intern Program, Philadelphia Service Center, OPM, 600 Arch St., Philadelphia, PA 19106. Phone: (215)597-7136, (215) 597-1920. **Internet:** same as **27.002**.

COMMISSION ON CIVIL RIGHTS

29.001 CLEARINGHOUSE SERVICES, CIVIL RIGHTS DISCRIMINATION COMPLAINTS

Assistance: technical information.

Purposes: pursuant to the Civil Rights Commission Reauthorization Act of 1991, to serve as a national clearinghouse concerning the civil rights of individuals, entitling them to equal protection of the laws regardless of their race, color, religion, sex, age, handicap, or national origin; to provide related research, liaison, publications, and public information services to private and public groups and the media; and to process complaints for referral to appropriate federal agencies.

Eligible applicants/beneficiaries: anyone may seek information.

Activity: FY 02-03 estimate (both years), 10,000 complaints processed, 12 publications completed.

HQ: Commission on Civil Rights, 624 Ninth St. NW, Washington, DC 20425. Phone: (202)376-8177, TDD (202)376-8116; *complaints,* (202)376-8582, (800)552-6843. **Internet:** "www.opm.gov".

EQUAL EMPLOYMENT OPPORTUNITY COMMISSION

30.001 EMPLOYMENT DISCRIMINATION—TITLE VII OF THE CIVIL RIGHTS ACT OF 1964

Assistance: advisory services/counseling; investigation of complaints.

Purposes: pursuant to the Acts of 1964 and 1991 and amendments, to for provide education, technical assistance, and enforcement of federal prohibitions against employment discrimination in the public and private sectors, based on race, sex, color national origin, or religion. Complaints are investigated and, if reasonable cause is found, mediation is offered; if mediation is not used or successful, charges are conciliated; if unsuccessful, civil action may be brought against named respondents. If conciliation fails on a charge against a state or local government, EEOC may refer the case to DOJ for further action. Funding for this program includes **30.008, 30.010,** and **30.011**.

Eligible applicants/beneficiaries: any individual or any labor union, association, legal representative, or organization filing on behalf of an individual with reason to believe that an unlawful employment practice has been committed by an employer with more than 15 employees, an employment agency, a labor organization, or a joint labor-management committee controlling apprenticeship or other training activities.

Activity: FY 04 (including **30.008, 30.010,** and **30.011** for litigation and systemic data), 48,000 charges received to process, 51,000 cases resolved with $128,597,000 in benefits to 7,796 persons; 379 suits filed, 347 resolved; 45 appellate briefs filed.

HQ: Communications Staff, Office of Communications and Legislative Affairs, EEOC, 1801 L St. NW, Washington, DC 20507. Phone: (202)663-4900, TTY (202)663-4494. **Internet:** "www.eeoc.gov".

30.002 EMPLOYMENT DISCRIMINATION—STATE AND LOCAL FAIR EMPLOYMENT PRACTICES AGENCY CONTRACTS

Assistance: direct payments/specified use (100 percent/1-3 years).

Purposes: pursuant to the Civil Rights Acts of 1964 and 1991, Age Discrimination in Employment Act of 1967, amendments, and ADA, for state and local fair employment practices agencies to assist in the enforcement and resolution of charges of violation of civil rights laws prohibiting discrimination in employment, based on race, color, national origin, sex, religion, disability, or age. Funding for this program includes **30.009**.

Eligible applicants: state and local government agencies designated as fair employment practices agencies.

Eligible beneficiaries: covered applicants, employees, and former employees.

Range: $10,000 to $2,775,000.

Activity: FY 04, 92 agencies funded to resolve 58,000 charges.

HQ: Director, State and Local Programs, Office of Field Programs, EEOC, 1801 L St. NW - Rm.8030, Washington, DC 20507. Phone: (202)663-4944. **Internet:** same as **30.001**.

30.005 EMPLOYMENT DISCRIMINATION—PRIVATE BAR PROGRAM

Assistance: specialized services.

Purposes: pursuant to the Civil Rights Acts of 1964 and 1991 and amendments, to assist aggrieved individuals in locating lawyers to represent them in suits involving employment discrimination under provisions of Title VII of the Civil Rights Act of 1964, the Equal Pay Act, the Age Discrimination in Employment Act, or the ADA; to provide technical assistance to aggrieved parties and their attorneys.

Eligible applicants/beneficiaries: individuals filing charges.

Activity: N.A.

HQ: Office of General Counsel, EEOC, 1801 L St. NW, Washington, DC 20507. Phone: (202)663-4702. **Internet:** same as **30.001**.

30.008 EMPLOYMENT DISCRIMINATION—AGE DISCRIMINATION IN EMPLOYMENT

Assistance: advisory services/counseling; investigation of complaints.

Purposes: pursuant to the Age Discrimination in Employment Act of 1967, amendments, and Civil Rights Act of 1991, to enforce regulations concerning arbitrary employment discrimination on the basis of age; to promote the employment of older workers. Individuals age 40 or older are protected from discrimination by: private commercial employers with 20 or more employees; federal, state, local governments; employment agencies; labor organizations. Funding for this program is included in **30.001**.

Eligible applicants/beneficiaries: persons age 40 or over.

Activity: FY 04, 15,000 charges received; 16,000 charges resolved with $68,993,000 in benefits to 2,272 persons. (Information on systemic charges and suits filed is included under **30.001**.)

HQ: same as **30.001**.

30.009 EMPLOYMENT DISCRIMINATION PROJECT CONTRACTS—INDIAN TRIBES

Assistance: direct payments/specified use.

Purposes: pursuant to the Civil Rights Acts of 1964 and 1991 and amendments, for Tribal Employment Rights Offices (TEROs) to protect the employment rights of Indians working or seeking work on or near reservations. Funding for this program is included in **30.002**.

Eligible applicants/beneficiaries: land-based tribes with approved TEROs.

Range/Average: $25,000 to each tribe.

Activity: FY 04-05 estimate, 64 offices funded.

HQ: same as **30.002**.

30.010 EMPLOYMENT DISCRIMINATION EQUAL PAY ACT

Assistance: advisory services/counseling; investigation of complaints.

Purposes: pursuant to the Equal Pay Act of 1963 as amended and Fair Labor Standards Act Amendment of 1974, to enforce laws prohibiting discrimination on the basis of sex in the payment of wages to men and women performing equal work in the same establishment, which is illegal for: employers engaged in commerce or in the production of goods; federal, state, and local governments. Also, labor organizations are prohibited from causing or attempting to cause employers to violate the law. Exceptions are permitted only where payments are based on systems recognizing seniority, merit, quantity or quality of production, or differentials based on factors other than sex. Funding for this program is included in **30.001**.

Eligible applicants/beneficiaries: employees believing that they or others have been or are being paid in violation of the Act, in any state, territory, or possession.

Activity: FY 04, 821 complaints received, 996 complaints resolved with $6,421,000 in benefits to 192 persons. (Information on systemic charges and suits filed is included under **30.001**.)

HQ: same as **30.001**.

30.011 EMPLOYMENT DISCRIMINATION—TITLE I OF THE AMERICANS WITH DISABILITIES ACT

Assistance: advisory services/counseling; investigation of complaints.

Purposes: to enforce the ADA as amended, prohibiting employment discrimination by private employers and state and local governments against qualified individuals with disabilities. The commission investigates complaints and, if reasonable cause is found, mediation is offered; if mediation is not used or successful, charges are conciliated; if unsuccessful, legal action may be taken by DOJ against private respondents. If conciliation fails on a charge against a state or local government, EEOC refers the case to DOJ for further action. Funding for this program is included in **30.001**.

Eligible applicants/beneficiaries: same as for **30.001**.

Activity: FY 04, 15,000 charges received, 17,000 charges resolved with

$47,698,000 in benefits to 2,419 persons. (Information on systemic charges and suits filed is included under **30.001**.)

HQ: same as **30.001**.

FEDERAL COMMUNICATIONS COMMISSION

32.001 COMMUNICATIONS INFORMATION AND ASSISTANCE AND INVESTIGATION OF COMPLAINTS

Assistance: technical information; investigation of complaints.

Purposes: pursuant to the Communications Act of 1934 as amended, for public information, education, and investigation of complaints concerning public communications systems. FCC services relate to rates, broadcast signal interference, equal time for political candidates, and the presentation of issues.

Eligible applicants/beneficiaries: anyone.

Activity: FY 01, received 23,000 broadcast and cable, 32,000 common carrier, and 30,000 interference complaints; 3,098 comments and information requests received (latest data reported).

HQ: Public Service Division, Federal Communications Commission, 1919 M St. NW - Rm.244, Washington, DC 20554. Phone: *Fees,* (202)418-0220; *Cable,* (202)418-0190. **Internet:** "www.fcc.gov".

FEDERAL MARITIME COMMISSION

33.001 SHIPPING—INVESTIGATION OF COMPLAINTS

Assistance: investigation of complaints.

Purposes: pursuant to the Shipping Act of 1984 as amended, to provide a forum for settling disputes between carriers, shippers concerning maritime shipping and ocean transportation, including: cruise passengers seeking reimbursement of deposits when a cruise is canceled; complaints about unlawful rates or practices. Reparations may be awarded for violations.

Eligible applicants/beneficiaries: anyone.

Activity: FY 03, responses to 2,389 informal inquiries and complaints.

HQ: Director, Office of Consumer Complaints, Federal Maritime Commission, 800 N. Capitol St. NW, Washington, DC 20573. Phone: (202)523-5807, FAX (202)523-0059; Dispute Resolution Specialist, (202)523-5787, FAX (202)523-5830. **Internet:** no web site. E-mail, Office of Consumer Complaints, "COMPLAINTS@fmc.gov"; Dispute Resolution Specialist, "ADR@fmc.gov".

FEDERAL MEDIATION AND CONCILIATION SERVICE

34.001 LABOR MEDIATION AND CONCILIATION
Assistance: specialized services; advisory services/counseling.

Purposes: pursuant to the Labor-Management Relations Act of 1947 as amended and other acts, to prevent or minimize work stoppages caused by disputes between labor and management in industries affecting commerce, including federal labor disputes—through mediation of collective bargaining disputes, arbitration assistance, public education, conciliation.

Eligible applicants/beneficiaries: employers involved in interstate commerce, related labor organizations, federal agencies.

Activity: FY 04 estimate, 18,000 arbitration panels handled.

HQ: FMCS, 2100 K St. NW, Washington, DC 20427. Phone: (202)606-8100; Public Affairs Specialist, (202)606-8091. **Internet:** "www.fmcs.gov".

34.002 LABOR-MANAGEMENT COOPERATION
Assistance: project grants (12-18 months).

Purposes: pursuant to the Labor-Management Cooperation Act of 1978, to establish, expand, and operate joint labor-management committees in the public or private sectors at the work-site, area, and industry-wide levels—to improve labor-management relations and productivity.

Eligible applicants/beneficiaries: private nonprofit labor-management committees; labor organizations and private companies or public agencies applying jointly; private nonprofit entities.

Range: work-site, $10,000 to $65,000; others, $10,000 to $125,000. **Average:** work-site, $50,000; others, $100,000.

Activity: annually, approximately 17 grants.

HQ: Grants Program Office, Labor Management Cooperation Program, FMCS, 2100 K St. NW, Washington, DC 20427. Phone: (202)606-8181. **Internet:** same as **34.001**. (Note: no field offices for this program.)

FEDERAL TRADE COMMISSION

36.001 FAIR COMPETITION COUNSELING AND INVESTIGATION OF COMPLAINTS
Assistance: advisory services/counseling; investigation of complaints.

Purposes: pursuant to the Federal Trade Commission Act of 1914, amendments, and related acts, to prevent and eliminate anticompetitive, deceptive, and other practices adversely affecting consumers. The FTC's concerns include price-fixing, boycotts, price discrimination, illegal mergers and acquisitions, false and misleading advertising, consumer credit transactions and reporting, debt collection practices, food and drug advertising, and other practices affecting the consuming public.

Eligible applicants/beneficiaries: anyone.

Activity: FY 06 estimate, 500 formal investigations initiated, 609 closed; 21 orders to cease and desist issued; 7 trade regulations promulgated or amended.

HQ: Federal Trade Commission, 600 Pennsylvania Ave. NW, Washington, DC 20580. Phone: Director, Bureau of Consumer Protection, (202)326-3430; Director, Bureau of Competition, (202)326-3175. **Internet:** "www.ftc.gov/".

GENERAL SERVICES ADMINISTRATION

39.002 DISPOSAL OF FEDERAL SURPLUS REAL PROPERTY

Assistance: sale, exchange, or donation of property and goods.

Purposes: pursuant to the Federal Property and Administrative Services Act of 1949, Surplus Property Act of 1944, SBMHAA, and amendments, to dispose of surplus federal real and related personal property for public purposes, at discounts of up to 100 percent, through leases, permits, sale, exchange, or donation. Applicants for property coordinate with appropriate other federal agencies. Surplus property not deeded to public bodies is generally offered for sale to the public on a competitive bid basis.

Eligible applicants/beneficiaries: surplus real property for park, recreation, correctional facility, historic monument, public airport uses, for health, educational, or homeless programs, and for replacement housing and general public purposes—state and local government agencies. Property for wildlife conservation use—states. Property for health, educational, and homeless program uses—tax-supported and nonprofit medical and educational institutions exempt from taxation under IRS Section 501(c)(3).

Activity: FY 04, value of $1.4 billion for 376 property disposals.

HQ: Assistant Commissioner, Office of Property Disposal, Public Building Service, GSA, Washington, DC 20405. Phone: (202)501-0084. **Internet:** "www.propertydisposal.gsa.gov/property".

39.003 DONATION OF FEDERAL SURPLUS PERSONAL PROPERTY

Assistance: sale, exchange, or donation of property and goods.

Purposes: pursuant to the Federal Property and Administrative Services Act of 1949, Surplus Property Act of 1944, Older Americans Act of 1965, and amendments, to donate surplus federal personal property to state and local public agencies for public purposes, to qualifying nonprofit entities for tax-exempt activities, or for educational and research activities. Examples of surplus property include office machines and supplies, furniture, hardware, textiles, special purpose motor vehicles, boats, airplanes, construction equipment. Participation requires prior GSA approval of state plans for distribution to eligible recipients. Items not donated are made available for sale to the general public (see **39.007**).

Eligible applicants/beneficiaries: state and local agencies, departments, instrumentalities, economic development districts, instrumentalities; multi-jurisdictional substate districts; tribes, bands, groups, pueblos; nonprofit, tax-exempt organizations such as schools, colleges, universities, public libraries, schools for the handicapped, educational radio or TV stations, child care centers, museums, hospitals, health centers, clinics, programs for the elderly or homeless; public airports; private service and educational organizations.

Activity: FY 06 estimate, $320,000,000 in original acquisition cost of property donated.

HQ: Director, Property Management Division, Office of Transportation and Property Management, Federal Supply Service, GSA, Washington, DC 20406. Phone: (703)605-5610. *Service educational activities information,* Deputy Under Secretary of Defense/Production and Logistics (L/MDM), The Pentagon, Washington, DC 20301.) **Internet:** "www.gsa.gov/property".

39.007 SALE OF FEDERAL SURPLUS PERSONAL PROPERTY

Assistance: sale, exchange, or donation of property and goods.

Purposes: pursuant to the Federal Property and Administrative Services Act of 1949 as amended, to sell surplus federal personal property on behalf of most federal civil agencies—including vehicles, aircraft, hardware, electronic and electrical equipment, office supplies and equipment, scrap goods. Disposal is by competitive bid.

Eligible applicants/beneficiaries: general public.

Activity: FY 06 estimate, $51,000,000 in proceeds from sales.

HQ: same address/phone as **39.003**. **Internet:** "www.gsa.gov"; *GSA auctions,* "www.gsaauctions.gov".

39.009 FEDERAL CITIZEN INFORMATION CENTER

Assistance: technical information.

Purposes: to assist federal agencies in releasing information of interest to consumers through: toll-free phone services, publications including a quarterly catalog of consumer-oriented publications, and several web sites including those cited under "HQ," below. Fees are charged for some products. A revolving fund partially supports the program.

Eligible applicants/beneficiaries: general public.

Activity: FY 04, 242,000,000 public contacts.

HQ: Director, Federal Citizen Information Center, GSA, Washington, DC 20405. Phone: (202)501-1794; Federal Citizen Information Center, (800) 333-4636. **Internet:** "www.FirstGov.gov"; *www.pueblo.gsa.gov*; *www.consumeraction.gov*; "www.kids.gov"; *www.espanol.gov*. (Note: no field offices for this program.)

GOVERNMENT PRINTING OFFICE

40.001 DEPOSITORY LIBRARIES FOR GOVERNMENT PUBLICATIONS

Assistance: technical information.

Purposes: to provide government publications and other information products, including electronic products, for public reference in 1,270 depository libraries in the U.S. and its possessions.

Eligible applicants: libraries designated by members of Congress (two Representative designations in each congressional district, four Senatorial designations in each state). By law, all state, highest state appellate court, land-grant college, and law school libraries are eligible for designation.

Eligible beneficiaries: general public.

Activity: FY 05, 11,000 titles distributed in paper, microfiche, and CD-ROM; 285,000 on-line searches on GPO servers.

HQ: Information Dissemination Department, Superintendent of Documents, GPO, 732 N. Capitol St., Washington, DC 20402. Phone: (202)512-1114. **Internet:** "www.access.gpo.gov/su_docs/fdlp/librpro.html".

40.002 GOVERNMENT PUBLICATIONS SALES AND DISTRIBUTION ("The Government Bookstore")

Assistance: sale, exchange, or donation of property and goods; technical information.

Purposes: to make available government publications, including 233 subscription services, for sale to the general public. Discounts are available to dealers and other purchasers of large quantities. A revolving fund supports this program.

Eligible applicants/beneficiaries: general public.

Activity: FY 04, 228,000 mail orders processed.

HQ: Superintendent of Documents, GPO, 732 N. Capitol St., Washington, DC 20402. Phone: Order Desk, (202)512-1800, FAX (202)512-2250; *toll-free*, (866)512-1800. **Internet:** "www.bookstore.gpo.gov"; e-mail, "orders@gpo.gov" *or* "gpo@cuthelp.com".

LIBRARY OF CONGRESS

42.001 BOOKS FOR THE BLIND AND PHYSICALLY HANDICAPPED
Assistance: use of property, facilities, and equipment.
Purposes: to provide library services to blind and physically handicapped persons—consisting of books on cassette, music scores, discs, and instructional materials in braille, large type, and on recorded formats, in 57 regional and 77 subregional libraries.
Eligible applicants/beneficiaries: U.S. residents and citizens living abroad, providing a certificate of inability to read or manipulate conventional printed material, from a competent authority.
Activity: FY 03, 766,000 blind and physically handicapped readers served, from a collection of 402,000 titles.
HQ: Director, National Library Service for the Blind and Physically Handicapped, LC, 1291 Taylor St. NW, Washington, DC 20542. Phone: (202)707-5100. **Internet:** "www.loc.gov/nls"; e-mail, "nls@loc.gov".

42.002 COPYRIGHT SERVICE
Assistance: technical information.
Purposes: to administer the U.S. Copyright Law, including: processing of applications, renewals, transfers, searches, and distribution of regulations; processing of compulsory licenses for satellite carriers and cable systems, and digital audio recording products, and collection and distribution of royalties; to administer the Copyright Arbitration Royalty Panels. Fees are charged for certain services. Funding for this program also supports **42.008**.
Eligible applicants/beneficiaries: anyone. Registration may be made by authors, their assignees, or their exclusive licensees, and others designated by law, or by their agents.
Activity: FY 06 estimate (sampling), 580,000 registrations.
HQ: Register of Copyrights, Copyright Office, LC, 101 Independence Ave. SE, Washington, DC 20559-6000. Phone: (202)707-3000. **Internet:** "www.gov/copyright". (Note: no field offices for this program.)

42.008 SEMICONDUCTOR CHIP PROTECTION SERVICE
Assistance: technical information.
Purposes: to administer the provisions of the Semiconductor Chip Protection Act of 1984. The Copyright Office staff: examines and decides on the acceptability of applications and identifying materials for registration of claims of protection; records and publishes legal facts or data pertaining to registered works; furnishes pertinent information to the public; and, records transfer documents. Fees are charged for some services. Program operating costs are absorbed in the budget of the Copyright Office; fees collected are returned to the U.S. Treasury to offset program costs.
Eligible applicants: general public.

Eligible beneficiaries: owners of qualified mask works.

Activity: FY 06 estimate, 350 mask work registrations.

HQ: same address, web site as **42.002**. Phone: (202)707-1497. (Note: no field offices for this program.)

42.009 VESSEL HULL DESIGN PROTECTION SERVICE

Assistance: technical information.

Purposes: to administer the Vessel Hull Design Protection Act of 1998. The LC Copyright Office: examines and decides the acceptability of applications and identifying material for registration of claims; records and publishes legal facts or data pertaining to registered works. Fees are charged for services. Program operating costs are absorbed in the budget of the Copyright Office; fees collected are returned to the U.S. Treasury to offset program costs.

Eligible applicants/beneficiaries: registration may be made by owners of qualified vessel hull designs, or their agents. Information is available to anyone.

Activity: new program listing in 2004. FY 05 estimate, 45 registrations.

HQ: same as **42.008**. (Note: no field offices for this program.)

NATIONAL AERONAUTICS AND SPACE ADMINISTRATION

43.001 AEROSPACE EDUCATION SERVICES PROGRAM ("Spacemobile")

Assistance: technical information.

Purposes: pursuant to the National Aeronautics and Space Act of 1958 as amended, to support instruction and to initiate systemic change in mathematics, science, and technology education, using NASA specialists to provide inservice and preservice workshops for K-12 teachers, lectures, classroom demonstrations, and media broadcasts.

Eligible applicants/beneficiaries: schools, teacher training institutions, IHEs, civic groups, museums, planetaria.

Activity: FY 04 (sampling), presentations in 1,786 schools, 3,298,000 programming recipients.

HQ: Office of Education, NASA, Washington, DC 20546. Phone: (202)358-1110. **Internet:** "www.nasa.gov".

43.002 TECHNOLOGY TRANSFER

Assistance: technical information.

Purposes: pursuant to the National Aeronautics and Space Act of 1958 as amended, to disseminate information about government-sponsored civilian aerospace research and development, including inventions, discoveries, innovations, and other improvements—through: NASA's "TechTracs" data system, via the Internet; publications including "Tech Briefs;" Regional Technology Transfer Centers; commercial technology field center offices.

Eligible applicants/beneficiaries: Tech Briefs subscriptions (no charge)—engineers, domestic enterprise managers, professionals, and others involved in technology transfer. Technical information search and retrieval services and computer programs/documentation—domestic organizations (fees charged for services beyond those available on the Internet); Technology Transfer Projects—those demonstrating a national public need.

Activity: annually, information to 200,000 persons and firms.

HQ: Innovative Partnerships Program, Office of Exploration Systems, NASA, Washington, DC 20546-0001. Phone: (202)358-2560. **Internet:** "www.nctn.hq.nasa.gov".

NATIONAL CREDIT UNION ADMINISTRATION

44.001 CREDIT UNION CHARTER, EXAMINATION, SUPERVISION, AND INSURANCE

Assistance: insurance; specialized services; advisory services/counseling.

Purposes: pursuant to the Federal Credit Union Act as amended, to assist in establishing and operating chartered federal credit unions; to provide $100,000 deposit insurance on individual accounts. Approval of applications is based on a combination of interests by group, economic feasibility, and other factors. Fees and insurance premiums support this program.

Eligible applicants/beneficiaries: generally, associations, employee groups, and communities with 500 or more potential members. State-chartered credit unions may apply for depositor insurance.

Activity: 2004, 2 new charters granted. As of 2005, 5,572 federal credit unions operating, 3,442 state credit unions insured.

HQ: Board Chairman, NCUA, 1775 Duke St., Alexandria, VA 22314-3428. Phone: (703)518-6300. **Internet:** "www.ncua.gov".

44.002 COMMUNITY DEVELOPMENT REVOLVING LOAN FUND PROGRAM FOR CREDIT UNIONS ("CDCU")

Assistance: direct loans (50-67 percent/1 to 3 percent interest/to 5 years).

Purposes: to stimulate economic development activities by: increasing income, business ownership, and employment opportunities among the low-income; providing basic financial and related services to community residents, such as financial counseling, membership and participation drives. Loans can also involve housing, including cooperatives and self-help. Funding is derived from a revolving loan fund.

Eligible applicants/beneficiaries: established state- and federally-chartered credit unions serving low-income communities. Available also in territories and possessions.

Range: $25,000 to $300,000.

Activity: FY 02, $2,000,000 in new loans (latest data reported).

HQ: Community Development Revolving Loan Program for Credit Unions, NCUA, 1775 Duke St., Alexandria, VA 22314-3428. Phone: (703)518-6610. **Internet:** same as **44.001**. (Note: no field offices for this program.)

NATIONAL FOUNDATION ON THE ARTS AND THE HUMANITIES

NATIONAL ENDOWMENT FOR THE ARTS

45.024 PROMOTION OF THE ARTS—GRANTS TO ORGANIZATIONS AND INDIVIDUALS

Assistance: project grants (organizations, to 50 percent/to 2-3 years; individuals, 100 percent/to 2 years).

Purposes: pursuant to the National Foundation on the Arts and the Humanities Act of 1965 (NFAHA) as amended, to foster and preserve excellence in the arts, provide public access to the arts, and advance arts education for children and youth. Funds support national, regional, and field-wide organizations in the visual, literary, media, design, and performing arts—in projects involving one of more aspects of: creativity; organizational capacity including technology; heritage and preservation; access; arts learning; international exchanges; and, for national arts programs for television or radio. Also, to support published writers through fellowships for creative writing (fiction and nonfiction), poetry, and literary translations.

Eligible applicants/beneficiaries: organizations—nonprofit tax-exempt entities such as arts institutions and arts service organizations, local arts agencies, state and local governments, tribal organizations; consortia. Individuals—U.S. citizens or permanent residents with exceptional talent; currently, however, only published creative writers are eligible.

Range: organizations, $5,000 to $500,000. **Average:** $25,000.

Activity: FY 05 estimate, 2,200 grants.

HQ: NEA, 1100 Pennsylvania Ave. NW, Washington, DC 20056-0001. Phone: (202)682-5400, TTY (202)682-5496; *audio recordings of guidelines*, (202) 682-5532. **Internet:** "www.arts.gov". (Note: no field offices for this program.)

45.025 PROMOTION OF THE ARTS—PARTNERSHIP AGREEMENTS

Assistance: formula grants, project grants (50 percent); advisory services/counseling.

Purposes: pursuant to NFAHA as amended, for development of basic state arts plans; for elements of state plans addressing arts learning and fostering arts in underserved areas; to provide basic support through Partnership Agreements for regional arts planning and for presenting and touring. Limited partnership funds are available for national services provided by membership organizations of state and regional arts organizations.

Eligible applicants/beneficiaries: state arts agencies in the states and in six special U.S. jurisdictions; regional and national arts organizations.

Range: states, $238,000 to $953,000; regions, $861,000 to $1,300,000. **Average:** states, $589,000; regions, $1,301,000.

Activity: FY 05, 63 partnership awards, supporting 28,000 projects in 5,500 communities.

HQ: State and Regional Director, NEA, 1100 Pennsylvania Ave. NW, Washington, DC 20056-0001. Phone: (202)692-5429; voice/TT (202)682-5496; *audio recordings of guidelines*, (202)682-5532. **Internet:** same as **45.024**. (Note: no field offices for this program.)

NATIONAL ENDOWMENT FOR THE HUMANITIES

45.129 PROMOTION OF THE HUMANITIES—FEDERAL/STATE PARTNERSHIP

Assistance: project grants (formula based, 50 percent/3 years).

Purposes: pursuant to NFAHA as amended, for humanities councils for regranting to local groups and individuals to conduct local, statewide, and regional projects. Project examples: youth partnership programs with Boy and Girl Scouts of America, Boys and Girls Clubs, YMCA-YWCA; traveling exhibits; scholar-led seminars; elder reading initiative.

Eligible applicants: state and territorial nonprofit citizen councils. If the state matches a certain percentage of the federal grant, the governor may designate the existing council as a state agency.

Eligible beneficiaries: state and local governments, sponsored organizations, public and private nonprofit organizations, tribal governments, native American organizations, territories, minority organizations and other specialized groups, quasi-public nonprofit institutions.

Range: $230,000 to $1,528,000. **Average:** $653,000.

Activity: annually, grants to 56 nonprofit organizations.

HQ: Federal/State Partnership, NEH (Rm.603), Washington, DC 20506. Phone: (202)606-8254, FAX (202)606-8365. **Internet:** "www.neh.gov"; e-mail, "fedstate@neh.gov". (Note: no field offices for this program.)

45.130 PROMOTION OF THE HUMANITIES—CHALLENGE GRANTS

Assistance: project grants (20-25 percent/1-4 years).

Purposes: pursuant to NFAHA as amended, for educational and cultural institutions and organizations to increase their financial stability and to sustain or improve humanities programs, services, or resources. Principally, project funds are used to establish endowments; also, for library acquisitions, technological enhancement, construction and renovation, or debt retirement. Grants may not fund general operating costs, projects eligible for other NEH support, or undergraduate scholarships or prizes.

Eligible applicants/beneficiaries: public or private nonprofit organizations including: two- and four-year IHEs; museums; historical or professional societies; research or public libraries; advanced study centers; university presses; media organizations; other similar and related organizations. States, local governments, and territories may apply on their own behalf or on behalf of organizations within their jurisdictions. Individuals and public and private elementary and secondary schools are ineligible.

Range: $40,000 to $1,000,000. **Average:** $400,000.

Activity: FY 03, 30 grants.

HQ: Office of Challenge Grants, NEH (Rm.420), Washington, DC 20506. Phone: (202)606-8309. **Internet:** same as **45.129**. (Note: no field offices for this program.)

45.149 PROMOTION OF THE HUMANITIES—DIVISION OF PRESERVATION AND ACCESS

Assistance: project grants (50-80 percent/to 5 years).

Purposes: pursuant to NFAHA as amended, for the preservation of and activities to provide intellectual access to library, museum, archival, and other humanities collections, including still and moving images and recorded sound collections; for preservation practices and activities including microfilming, archival surveys, cataloguing; for a national program to catalog and preserve U.S. newspapers; for training; for research; for related uses.

Eligible applicants/beneficiaries: state and local governments, sponsored organizations, public and private nonprofit organizations, tribal governments, native American organizations, territories, minority organizations and other specialized groups, quasi-public nonprofit institutions.

Range: $5,000 to $700,000. **Average:** $84,000.

Activity: FY 06 estimate, 213 awards.

HQ: Division of Preservation and Access, NEH (Rm.411), Washington, DC 20506. Phone: (202)606-8570, FAX (202)606-8639. **Internet:** same as **45.129**; e-mail, "PRESERVATION@NEH.GOV". (Note: no field offices for this program.)

45.160 PROMOTION OF THE HUMANITIES—FELLOWSHIPS AND STIPENDS

Assistance: project grants.

Purposes: pursuant to NFAHA as amended, for six- to twelve-month fellowships and two-month summer stipends to scholars to undertake full-time independent research and writing in the humanities. Two-year faculty research awards are available to historically black, Hispanic-serving, and tribal IHEs.

Eligible applicants/beneficiaries: college, university, and other institutional faculty and staff, and independent scholars and writers that have completed their professional training. Degree candidates are ineligible. All applicants must be U.S. citizens or nationals, or foreign nationals with at least three years of U.S. legal residence.

Range: fellowships, research, to $40,000 for 9-12 months, $24,000 for 6-8 months; summer stipends, $5,000; faculty research, to $40,000.

Activity: FY 06 estimate, 325 awards.

HQ: Division of Research Programs, NEH (Rm.318), Washington, DC 20506. Phone: (202)606-8200. **Internet:** same as **45.129**. (Note: no field offices for this program.)

45.161 PROMOTION OF THE HUMANITIES—RESEARCH

Assistance: project grants (cost sharing/to 3 years).

Purposes: pursuant to NFAHA as amended, to support collaboration by scholars, and postdoctoral fellowship programs at independent humanities research centers. Grants may cover the costs of salaries, travel, supplies, and appropriate research assistance and consultation.

Eligible applicants: collaborative research, scholarly editions—U.S. IHEs, nonprofit professional associations, scholarly societies, other nonprofit organizations. Fellowships—U.S. independent research centers, scholarly societies, and international research organizations with existing fellowships programs.

Eligible beneficiaries: U.S. citizens and residents, state and local governments, sponsored organizations, public and private nonprofit organizations, tribal governments, native American organizations, territories, minority organizations and other specialized groups, quasi-public nonprofit institutions.

Range: $18,000 to $280,000. **Average:** $112,000.

Activity: FY 06 estimate, 55 awards.

HQ: Division of Research and Education, NEH (Rm.318), Washington, DC 20506. Phone, web site: same as **45.160**. (Note: no field offices for this program.)

45.162 PROMOTION OF THE HUMANITIES—TEACHING AND LEARNING RESOURCES AND CURRICULUM DEVELOPMENT

Assistance: project grants (to 3 years).

Purposes: pursuant to NFAHA as amended, to fund curriculum and materials development projects to create durable tools for teachers at all educational levels, to engage their students in substantive study in the humanities. Institutional grants are available to historically black, Hispanic-serving, and tribal IHEs, for faculty study programs, institutional planning, construction, acquisition of library and advanced technology resources.

Eligible applicants/beneficiaries: state and local governments, sponsored organizations, public and private nonprofit organizations, tribal governments, native American organizations, territories, minority organizations and other specialized groups, quasi-public nonprofit institutions. Institutional grants—historically black, Hispanic-serving, and tribal IHEs designated by the White House.

Range: curriculum and materials development, to $200,000; institutional grants, to $25,000.

Activity: FY 05 estimate, 45 awards.

HQ: Teaching and Learning Resources and Curriculum Development Program, NEH (Rm.302), Washington, DC 20506. Phone: (202)606-8380; *institutional grants* (202)606-8463. **Internet:** same as **45.129**. (Note: no field offices for this program.)

45.163 PROMOTION OF THE HUMANITIES—PROFESSIONAL DEVELOPMENT

Assistance: project grants (to 18 months).

Purposes: pursuant to NFAHA as amended, to promote better teaching and research in the humanities through summer seminars and national institutes, as well Landmarks of American History workshops. Grants may support salaries, participant stipends, travel, and related direct costs. Projects dealing with pedagogical theory or intended to improve writing and speaking normally are not supported.

Eligible applicants: distinguished humanities scholars and teachers applying through sponsoring institutions to direct a program for teachers. Landmarks of American History and Faculty Humanities workshops—state and local governments, sponsored organizations, public and private nonprofit organizations, tribal governments, native American organizations, territories, minority organizations and other specialized groups, quasi-public nonprofit institutions.

Eligible beneficiaries: teachers in grades K-12 or colleges.

Range: seminars, $60,000 to $120,000; institutes, $100,000 to $180,000; Landmarks of American History (two one-week sessions minimum), $150,000 to $300,000; Faculty Humanities workshops, $30,000 to $75,000.

Activity: FY 05 estimate, 110 grants.

HQ: Professional Development, Division of Education Programs, NEH, Washington, DC 20506. Phone: (202)606-8463; Faculty Humanities Workshops, (202)606-8380. **Internet:** same as **45.129**. (Note: no field offices for this program.)

45.164 PROMOTION OF THE HUMANITIES—PUBLIC PROGRAMS

Assistance: project grants (6-24 months).

Purposes: pursuant to NFAHA as amended, for planning and implementation costs of humanities programs in museums, historical organizations, libraries, community centers, as well as on public television and radio.

Eligible applicants/beneficiaries: same as for **45.149**.

Range: $1,000 to $800,000. **Average:** $60,000.

Activity: FY 05 estimate, 191 grants.

HQ: Division of Public Programs, NEH (Rm.426), Washington, DC 20506. Phone: (202)606-8267. **Internet:** same as **45.129**. (Note: no field offices for this program.)

45.168 PROMOTION OF THE HUMANITIES—WE THE PEOPLE

Assistance: project grants; direct payments/unrestricted use.

Purposes: pursuant to NFAHA as amended, for scholarly, educational, preservation, and public projects that explore events and themes in U.S. history and culture and that advance principles defining America. Eligible activities include: Idea of America Essay Contest for U.S. high school juniors; We the People Bookshelf for community programs by libraries, conducted in collaboration with the American Library Association; Landmarks of American History projects; school teacher workshops; challenge grants.

Eligible applicants/beneficiaries: public libraries; K-12 school libraries including public, private, parochial, and charter schools—including in the territories.

Range: essay, $5,000 grand prize, $1,000 to finalist.

Activity: new program listing in 2004. FY 06 estimate, 6 awards.

HQ: Office of Public Information, NEH (Rm.402), Washington, DC 20506. Phone: (202)606-8400; *challenge grants,* (202)606-8309; *education programs,* (202)606-8463; *"Bookshelf,"* (202)606-8589, American Library Association, (800)545-2433, ext.5045; TDD (866)372-2930. **Internet:** web site, same as **45.129**; e-mail, info@neh.gov. (Note: no field offices for this program.)

FEDERAL COUNCIL ON THE ARTS AND THE HUMANITIES

45.201 ARTS AND ARTIFACTS INDEMNITY

Assistance: insurance.

Purposes: pursuant to NFAHA as amended, to provide indemnification against loss or damage to eligible art works, artifacts, and objects exhibited abroad or borrowed from abroad for display in the U.S. Deductibles and maximum amounts apply.

Eligible applicants/beneficiaries: federal, state, and local government entities; nonprofit agencies, institutions; individuals.

Range: $1,000,000 to $8,000,000,000.

Activity: FY 06 estimate, 43 indemnity certificates issued.

HQ: Indemnity Administrator, Museum Program, NEA, Washington, DC 20506-0001. Phone: (202)682-5574. **Internet:** "www.arts.gov". (Note: no field offices for this program.)

… PROGRAM INFORMATION 359

INSTITUTE OF MUSEUM AND LIBRARY SERVICES

45.301 MUSEUM FOR AMERICA GRANTS

Assistance: project grants (50 percent/to 3 years); direct payments/unrestricted use.

Purposes: pursuant to the Museum and Library Services Act of 1996 (MSLA), for museums to conserve the nation's historic, scientific, and cultural heritage; to maintain and expand the educational roles of museums and libraries in their educational role. Funds may be used for projects to: sustain cultural heritage; support lifelong learning; or serve as centers of community.

Eligible applicants/beneficiaries: generally, museums in the states, territories, and possessions that have provided museum services for at least two years. Public or private nonprofit agencies, such as a municipality, college, or university responsible for operating a museum, may apply on behalf of museums. Under the IMS definition, a museum is a public or private nonprofit institution organized on a permanent basis for educational or aesthetic purposes, and which: owns or uses and cares for tangible objects, whether animate or inanimate; exhibits them to the general public on a regular basis. "Museums" includes aquariums and zoological parks, botanical gardens and arboreta, and nature centers; art, history (including historic buildings and sites), natural history, children's, general, and specialized museums; science and technology centers; and planetariums. Federal museums are ineligible.

Range/Average: $5,000 to $150,000.

Activity: FY 04 estimate, 190 grants.

HQ: IMLS, 1800 M St. NW - 9th fl., Washington, DC 20036-5802. Phone: (202)653-4674, -4689, -4702; Public Affairs, (202)653-4757; *general library programs information,* (202)653-4700; *museum programs,* (202)653-4789; TDD, (202)653-4699. **Internet:** "www.imls.gov"; e-mail, "imlsinfo@imls.gov". (Note: no field offices for this program.)

45.302 MUSEUM ASSESSMENT PROGRAM ("MAP")

Assistance: project grants; direct payments/specified use.

Purposes: pursuant to MSLA, for assessments of various aspects of museum collections and operations, including institutional, public dimensions, and governance.

Eligible applicants/beneficiaries: same as for **45.301**. (NOTE: applicants must complete a self-study questionnaire provided by the American Association of Museums, 1575 Eye St. NW - Ste.400, Washington, DC 20005. Phone: 202-289-9118.)

Range/Average: $2,325 to $3,820.

Activity: FY 04, 144 awards.

HQ: IMLS, 1100 Pennsylvania Ave, NW, Washington, DC 20506. Phone: (202)606-8548, -0515; Public Affairs, (202)606-8339; *library programs,* (202)606-5226; *museum programs,* (202)606-8539, TTY (202)606-8636. **Internet:** same web site as **45.301** (Note: no field offices for this program.)

45.303 CONSERVATION PROJECT SUPPORT ("CPS")

Assistance: project grants (50 percent/to 3 years).

Purposes: pursuant to MSLA, for projects involving the safekeeping of living and nonliving museum and library collections, including: surveys of collections and environmental conditions; collections treatment; research; staff training.

Eligible applicants/beneficiaries: same as for **45.301**.

Range/Average: $57,000.

Activity: FY 05, 49 awards.

HQ: same address/web site/e-mail as **45.301**. Phone: (202)653-4641; Public Affairs, (202)653-4757; *library programs,* (202)653-4700; museum programs, (202)653-4789; TDD (202)653-4699. (Note: no field offices for this program.)

45.304 CONSERVATION ASSESSMENT PROGRAM ("CAP")

Assistance: direct payments/specified use (cost sharing).

Purposes: pursuant to MSLA, for overall assessments of the conditions of museum environments and collections to identify their conservation needs and priorities.

Eligible applicants/beneficiaries: same as for **45.301**.

Range/Average: $6,000.

Activity: FY 04, 119 awards.

HQ: same as **45.303**. (Note: no field offices for this program.)

45.307 21ST CENTURY MUSEUM PROFESSIONALS

Assistance: project grants (50 percent/to 3 years).

Purposes: for professional training projects in all areas of museum operations and in personnel and leadership development; for related assessment and information collection and dissemination, including through workshops, seminars, and courses or indirect communication through publications and web sites. Projects should reflect community needs and address issues facing museums of similar size and type.

Eligible applicants/beneficiaries: same generally as for **45.301**.

Range: $87,000 to $441,000. **Average:** $249,000.

Activity: new program listing in 2005 (CFDA on-line version). FY 05, 4 projects funded.

HQ: same address, web site as **45.301**. Phone: (202)653-4634; *library programs,* (202)653-4700; museum programs, (202)653-4789; TDD (202)653-4699. (Note: no field offices for this program.)

45.308 NATIVE AMERICAN/NATIVE HAWAIIAN MUSEUM SERVICES PROGRAM

Assistance: project grants (to 2 years).

Purposes: pursuant to MSLA as amended, for strengthening of museum programming, professional development, and museum services provided to native Americans and Hawaii natives.

Eligible applicants/beneficiaries: Indian tribes, bands, nations. or other organized groups or communities including Alaska native villages, regional corporations, or village corporations—eligible for BIA programs; nonprofit organizations serving and representing Hawaii natives. Museums, libraries, schools, and IHEs are ineligible; however, they may participate in project partnerships.

Range: $6,700 to $20,000. **Average:** $18,000.

Activity: new program listing in 2005 (CFDA on-line version). FY 05, 45 grants awarded.

HQ: same as **45.307**. (Note: no field offices for this program.)

45.310 STATE LIBRARY PROGRAM

Assistance: formula grants (66 percent).

Purposes: pursuant to MSLA, to support a broad range of library and information services, either directly or through subgrants, including: establishing or enhancing electronic linkages among or between libraries and with educational, school, or information services; promoting targeted services to diverse geographic, cultural, and socio-economic audiences in urban and rural communities; acquiring or sharing computer systems and telecommunications technologies. Recipients must have an approved five-year state plan.

Eligible applicants/beneficiaries: state library administrative agencies, including in territories and possessions.

Range: formula based on population. No range reported.

Activity: FY 04, 59 awards.

HQ: Office of Library Services, same address, web site as **45.301**. Phone: (202)653-4602. (Note: no field offices for this program.)

45.311 NATIVE AMERICAN AND NATIVE HAWAIIAN LIBRARY SERVICES

Assistance: project grants (100 percent/to 2 years).

Purposes: pursuant to the Museum and Library Services Act of 2003, to provide library services to native Americans, including: support of core library operations; technical assistance projects for training tribal library staff; establishing or enhancing electronic linkages among libraries and with educational, school, or information services; acquiring or sharing computer systems and telecommunications technologies; targeted services to those having difficulty using a library and to under-served communities.

Eligible applicants/beneficiaries: recognized tribes, Alaska native villages, organizations primarily serving Hawaii natives.

Range/Average: N.A.

Activity: FY 04, 222 grants.

HQ: same address/web site as **45.310**. Phone: (202)653-4665. (Note: no field offices for this program.)

45.312 NATIONAL LEADERSHIP GRANTS

Assistance: project grants (67 percent; above $250,000, 50 percent/to 3 years).

Purposes: pursuant to MSLA, to enhance the quality of library and museum services nationwide and to provide coordination between libraries and museums. Funded activities may include: research and demonstration projects; preservation or digitization of library materials and resources; model cooperative library-museum programs; Building Digital Resources projects.

Eligible applicants/beneficiaries: libraries including those that are nonfederal, public, school, academic, archives, and private nonprofit; also, special libraries, research libraries, library agencies; consortia, and IHEs—applying individually or in partnerships, including with other public, nonprofit organizations; museums as defined in **45.301**.

Range: libraries, $50,000 to $1,000,000; museums, $25,000 to $1,000,000.

Activity: FY 04, 18 library, 8 museum, 19 museum/library project grants.

HQ: same address, web site as **45.301**. Phone: Library Building Digital Resources, Research, Demonstration, (202)653-4667; Advanced Learning Communities, (202)653-4768; Museums, (202)653-4644. (Note: no field offices for this program.)

45.313 LIBRARIANS FOR THE 21ST CENTURY

Assistance: project grants (to 3 years).

Purposes: pursuant to Museum and Library Services Act of 2003, to recruit and educate new librarians and faculty prepared to teach masters of library science students; to support pertinent research. Current priorities include master's level programs, doctoral programs, preprofessional programs, research, building institutional capacity, continuing education. Grants require a 50 percent match, minus funds for student support; the matching requirement is waived for projects involving research only.

Eligible applicants/beneficiaries: same as for **45.312**.

Range: $50,000 to $1,000,000.

Activity: new program in FY 03. FY 05, 37 projects funded.

HQ: same address, web site as **45.301**. Phone: Doctoral, Research, Capacity Building Programs, (202)653-4662; Master's, Preprofessional, Continuing Education Programs, (202)653-4663. (Note: no field offices for this program.)

NATIONAL LABOR RELATIONS BOARD

46.001 LABOR-MANAGEMENT RELATIONS ("NLRB")

Assistance: specialized services; investigation of complaints.

Purposes: pursuant to the Labor-Management Relations Act of 1947 as amended, to avoid or minimize industrial strife affecting interstate commerce, by providing orderly procedures to protect the rights of employers, employees, labor organizations, and the general public; to prevent unlawful interference with those rights. Services are provided to employee organizations voting on whether to be represented by a labor organization, and to employers or unions regarding unfair labor practices—only after charges or petitions are filed.

Eligible applicants/beneficiaries: any covered employer, employee, labor organization, or person believing that a violation has occurred, or wishing to vote on whether to be represented by a labor organization. "Employees" exclude: agricultural laborers and domestic workers; persons employed by spouse or parent; independent contractors; employees subject to the Railway Labor Act; certain others not covered by the Act. Federal, state, and local governments and most government corporations, except the U.S. Postal Service, are ineligible employers.

Activity: FY 04, intake 32,000 cases.

HQ: Division of Information, National Labor Relations Board, 1099 14th St. NW, Washington, DC 20570. Phone: (202)273-1991. **Internet:** "www.nlrb.gov".

NATIONAL SCIENCE FOUNDATION

47.041 ENGINEERING GRANTS ("ENG")

Assistance: project grants (67-100 percent/6 months-3 years).

Purposes: pursuant to the National Science Foundation Act of 1950 (NSFA) as amended, for engineering research and education programs in virtually all phases of engineering science and technological innovation and practice. Funding may support such activities as: research in emerging areas; industry-university cooperative research centers; biomedical engineering research; research equipment and instrumentation grants; undergraduate student research; graduate fellowships; faculty enhancement; inter-disciplinary studies; small business innovation research; small business technology transfer programs. Cost sharing is required except for solicited proposals, conferences, publications, travel, and logistical support. Funds may not support inventions, product development, marketing, or research requiring security classifications.

Eligible applicants/beneficiaries: public and private IHEs; nonprofit institutions; profit organizations including small businesses; state, and local government agencies; unaffiliated individuals.

Range: $5,000 to $4,000,000. **Average:** $120,000.

Activity: FY 06 estimate, 3,675 grants.

HQ: Program Director, Grant Opportunities for Academic Liaison with Industry, Directorate for Engineering-NSF, 4201 Wilson Blvd., Arlington, VA 22230. Phone: (703)292-7082. **Internet:** "www.eng.nsf.gov/"; e-mail, *general inquiries,* "enginfo@nsf.gov". (Note: no field offices for this program.)

47.049 MATHEMATICAL AND PHYSICAL SCIENCES ("MPS")

Assistance: project grants (to 100 percent/3-5 years).

Purposes: pursuant to NSFA as amended, for mostly basic research in physics, chemistry, astronomical and mathematical sciences, and materials, including multidisciplinary research. Grants may support: start-of-the-art user facilities; science and technology centers; institutes; undergraduate student research; developing research opportunities for women, minority, and disabled scientists and engineers; instrumentation; laboratory improvement; research workshops, symposia, and conferences; faculty enhancement; curriculum development. Cost sharing is required, except for symposia, conferences, publications, travel, education, training, or facilities.

Eligible applicants/beneficiaries: public and private IHEs; nonprofit, nonacademic research institutions; private profit organizations; foreign institutions; state and local governments; other federal agencies; certain unaffiliated scientists.

Range: $10,000 to $45,000,000. **Average:** $130,000.

Activity: FY 06 estimate, 2,110 grants.

HQ: Assistant Director, MPS-NSF, same address as **47.041**. Phone: (703)292-8801. **Internet:** "www.mps.nsf.gov/". (Note: no field offices for this program.)

47.050 GEOSCIENCES ("GEO")

Assistance: project grants (to 100 percent/1-5 years).

Purposes: pursuant to NSFA as amended, for basic research and studies in the atmospheric (e.g., meteorology, climate, paleoclimate), earth, and ocean sciences and in related biological, chemical, and physical disciplines. Grants may support science and technology centers, undergraduate student research, facility enhancement, instrumentation, laboratory equipment, and research opportunities for women, minority, and disabled scientists and engineers. Cost sharing is required, except for symposia, conferences, publications, travel, education, training, facilities, ship operations, or equipment.

Eligible applicants/beneficiaries: public and private IHEs, nonprofit nonacademic research institutions, private profit organizations, certain unaffiliated scientists.

Range: $1,000 to $60,000,000. **Average:** $149,000.

Activity: FY 06 estimate, 1,400 awards.

HQ: NSF, same address as **47.041**. Phone: *atmospheric sciences,* (703)292-8520, FAX (703)292-9022; *earth sciences,* (703)292-8550, FAX (703)292-9025; *ocean sciences,* (703)292-8580, FAX (703)292-9085. **Internet:** URL,

NSF, "www.nsf.gov/"; *geosciences,* "www.geo.nsf.gov/". (Note: no field offices for this program.)

47.070 COMPUTER AND INFORMATION SCIENCE AND ENGINEERING ("CISE")

Assistance: project grants (cost sharing/6 months-3 years).

Purposes: pursuant to NSFA as amended, for research improving the fundamental understanding of computer and information science and engineering; to enhance the training and education of scientists and engineers; and, to provide access to very advanced computing and networking capabilities. Ineligible uses of funds include fellowships, scholarships, product development and marketing.

Eligible applicants/beneficiaries: public and private IHEs; nonprofit and profit organizations; small businesses; state and local government agencies.

Range: $1,000 to $20,000,000. **Average:** $165,000.

Activity: FY 06 estimate, 1,050 awards.

HQ: Assistant Director, CISE-NSF, same address as **47.041**. Phone: (703)292-8900. **Internet:** "www.cise.nsf.gov/". (Note: no field offices for this program.)

47.074 BIOLOGICAL SCIENCES ("BIO")

Assistance: project grants (to 100 percent/to 5 years).

Purposes: pursuant to NSFA as amended, for mostly basic research in the biological sciences, including cellular and molecular biosciences, integrative organismal biology, environmental biology, biological infrastructure, and plant genomes. Grants may be used to purchase multi-user scientific equipment and for instrument development; research workshops, symposia, and conferences; doctoral, postdoctoral fellowships including for minority scientists. Cost sharing is required, except for symposia, conferences, publications, travel, education, or training.

Eligible applicants/beneficiaries: same as for **47.050**.

Range: $2,000 to $11,890,000. **Average:** $140,000.

Activity: FY 06 estimate, 1,419 grants.

HQ: Assistant Director, BIO-NSF, same address as **47.041**. Phone: (703)292-8400. **Internet:** "www.nsf.gov/bio/". (Note: no field offices for this program.)

47.075 SOCIAL, BEHAVIORAL, AND ECONOMIC SCIENCES ("SBE")

Assistance: project grants (to 100 percent/to 5 years).

Purposes: pursuant to NSFA as amended, for basic research in the social, behavioral and economic sciences in such disciplines as: anthropological and geographic sciences; cognitive, psychological, and language science; economic, decision, and management sciences; social and political science; infrastructure, methods, and science studies; educational attainment in science, mathematics, and engineering. Grants may support: science and technology centers, including climate change; science of learning centers, workshops, symposia, and conferences; doctoral and postdoctoral fellowships; junior faculty research; graduate traineeships; mid-career development; undergraduate student research; research opportunities for women, minorities, and disabled scientists and engineers.

Eligible applicants/beneficiaries: same as for **47.050**.

Range: $1,100 to $4,980,000. **Average:** $85,000.

Activity: FY 06 estimate, 1,013 grants.

HQ: Directorate for Social, Behavioral and Economic Sciences-NSF, same address as **47.041**. Phone: (703)292-8700; Division of Science Resources Statistics, (703)292-8780; Division of Social and Economic Sciences, (703)292-8760; Division of Behavioral and Cognitive Sciences, (703)292-8740. **Internet:** "www.nsf.gov"; *science resources,* "www.nsf.gov/sbe/srs"; *social, economic sciences,* "www.nsf.gov/sbe/ses"; *behavioral, cognitive sciences,* "www.nsf.gov/sbe/bcs". (Note: no field offices for this program.)

47.076 EDUCATION AND HUMAN RESOURCES ("EHR")

Assistance: project grants (50-100 percent/to 5 years).

Purposes: pursuant to NSFA as amended, for programs improving the effectiveness of science, mathematics, engineering, and technology education—through programs that support research and the development of models and strategies, including in: elementary, secondary, informal science education, and lifelong learning; undergraduate, graduate, and postdoctoral education; human resource development; research, evaluation, and dissemination; experimental programs. Grants may support fellowships for up to three years, scholarships, equipment purchases, salaries, and other expenses.

Eligible applicants: public and private two- and four-year IHEs; SEAs and LEAs; tribal entities; nonprofit and private organizations; professional societies; science academies and centers; science museums and zoological parks; research laboratories; other informal science education institutions.

Eligible beneficiaries: pre-school, elementary, secondary, and undergraduate science, mathematics, and engineering teachers and faculty; secondary, undergraduate, and graduate students.

Range: $3,000 to $15,000,000. **Average:** $262,000.

Activity: FY 06 estimate, 800 awards; FY 04, 115 H1-B Nonimmigrant Petitioner institutional awards for 9,600 scholarships.

HQ: Assistant Director, EHR-NSF, same address (Rm.805) as **47.041**. Phone: (703)292-8600. **Internet:** "www.ehr.nsf.gov/dir/index.jsp?org=EHR". (Note: no field offices for this program.)

47.078 POLAR PROGRAMS ("OPP")

Assistance: project grants (to 100 percent/1-3 years).

Purposes: pursuant to NSFA as amended, for basic research in the arctic and antarctic regions, focused on the solid earth, glacial and sea ice, terrestrial ecosystems, the oceans, the atmosphere and beyond. Support is available for science and technology centers, undergraduate student research, postdoctoral fellowships, facility enhancement, instrumentation, laboratory equipment, and research opportunities for women, minority, and handicapped scientists and engineers. Cost sharing is required, except for symposia, conferences, publications, travel, education, training, facilities, ship operations, or equipment.

Eligible applicants/beneficiaries: same as for **47.050**.

Range: $1,000 to $5,000,000. **Average:** $198,000.

Activity: FY 06 estimate, 200-300 awards.

HQ: National Science Foundation, same address as **47.041**. Phone: Arctic Sciences, (703)292-8029, FAX (703)292-9082; Antarctic Sciences, (703) 292-8033, FAX (703)292-9079; Polar Research, (703)292-8032, FAX (703) 292-9080. **Internet:** "www.nsf.gov/od/opp/". (Note: no field offices for this program.)

47.079 INTERNATIONAL SCIENCE AND ENGINEERING (OISE)

Assistance: project grants (to 100 percent/to 3 years).

Purposes: pursuant to NSFA as amended, for international partnerships fostering scientific basic research collaborations, discovery, and education abroad for U.S. students and junior faculty. Activities eligible for funding include graduate traineeships, postdoctoral fellowships, undergraduate research experiences, workshops, planning visits, and research opportunities for women, minorities, and scientists and engineers with disabilities—in all disciplinary fields supported by NSF.

Eligible applicants/beneficiaries: public and private IHEs, nonprofit nonacademic research institutions, profit organizations, certain unaffiliated scientists, multilateral science and technology organizations.

Range: $500 to $2,000,000. **Average:** $40,000.

Activity: new program listing in 2005. FY 06 estimate, 270 awards.

HQ: Office of International Science and Engineering-NSF, same address (Rm.935) as **47.078**. Phone: (703)292-8710. **Internet:** 169www.nsf.gov/div/index.jsp?org=OISE". (Note: no field offices for this program.)

RAILROAD RETIREMENT BOARD

57.001 SOCIAL INSURANCE FOR RAILROAD WORKERS

Assistance: direct payments/unrestricted use.

Purposes: pursuant to the Social Security Act, Railroad Unemployment Insurance Act, Railroad Retirement Act of 1974, and amendments, to pay benefits to railroad workers and their beneficiaries, including retirement, death, disability, unemployment, or sickness insurance.

Eligible applicants/beneficiaries: Railroad Retirement Act benefits—for employee, spouse, and survivor benefits, the employee must have had 10 or more years of railroad service. Annuities—beginning January 2002 or later, 5 years of railroad service rendered after 1995. For survivors, the employee must have been insured at death. Railroad Unemployment Insurance Act—employees with certain minimum earnings in railroad wages; new employees must have worked for a railroad at least five months in a calendar (base) year.

Range/Average: age annuities, monthly maximum $3,379, average $1,619; disability, monthly maximum $3,341, average $1,751; employee supplemental annuities, monthly maximum $70, average $42; spouse benefits, monthly maximum $1,612, average $626; widows/widowers, monthly maximum $3,399, average $1,020; widowed mothers/fathers, monthly maximum $2,398, average $1,337; children, monthly maximum $1,927, average $766; unemployment and sickness, weekly maximum $280, average $280.

Activity: FY 04, 677,000 total beneficiaries; 36,000 retirement awards; 32,000 unemployment insurance beneficiaries.

HQ: Public Affairs, Railroad Retirement Board, 844 N. Rush St., Chicago, IL 60611-2092. Phone: (312)751-4737. **Internet:** "www.rrb.gov".

SECURITIES AND EXCHANGE COMMISSION

58.001 SECURITIES—INVESTIGATION OF COMPLAINTS AND SEC INFORMATION
("Complaints and Inquiries")

Assistance: technical information; investigation of complaints.

Purposes: pursuant to the Securities Act of 1933, Securities and Exchange Act of 1934, Securities Investor Protection Act of 1970, amendments, and related acts, to provide assistance to or on behalf of securities investors, including educational materials and public educational activities; to represent individual investors in SEC rule-making proceedings. SEC's public files contain financial and other information about companies, broker-dealers, investment companies, investment advisers, transfer agents, and banks, which may be examined at SEC offices; or, copies may be obtained from SEC's Public Reference Branch. Investors believing they have been defrauded, or that another party has violated the federal securities laws, may present their complaint and/or information to the SEC. A public action taken by SEC does not necessarily result in monetary benefits to investors; however, aggrieved investors may find the information disclosed by the commission in its actions helpful in any private action brought to recover losses.

Eligible applicants/beneficiaries: anyone may seek information or file a complaint.

Activity: FY 04, 73,000 complaints, inquiries, and other investor contacts.

HQ: Office of Investor Education and Assistance, SEC, 100 F St. NE, Washington, DC 20549-0213. Phone: (202)551-6551, FAX (202)772-9295; Public Reference Branch (MS 1-2), (202)551-8090, FAX (202)777-1027. **Internet:** "www.sec.gov"; *questions, complaints,* "www.sec.gov/complaint.shtml"; e-mail, "help@sec.gov"; e-mail, Public Reference Branch, "publicinfo@sec.gov".

SMALL BUSINESS ADMINISTRATION

NOTE: *In the following SBA program descriptions, "small business" means a business independently owned and operated, not dominant in its field, and meeting certain size standards in terms of numbers of employees and annual revenues. Unless otherwise indicated, SBA excludes from its financial assistance programs: nonprofit enterprises (except for disaster loans and sheltered workshops); lending or investment enterprises; gambling enterprises; and, real estate speculators.*

59.002 ECONOMIC INJURY DISASTER LOANS ("EIDL")

Assistance: direct loans (4 percent/to 30 years).

Purposes: pursuant to Small Business Act of 1953 as amended and Disaster Relief Act of 1970, to help small businesses recover from federally declared disasters. Funds may be used for debt payments and working capital, but not realty, equipment acquisition or repair, or debt refinancing. Loans may not be provided to cover merely lost income or profits.

Eligible applicants/beneficiaries: small business, small agricultural cooperative, or nursery victims in declared disaster areas, unable to obtain credit elsewhere, with evidence of the cause and extent of economic injury.

Range: to $1,500,000. **Average:** $78,000.

Activity: FY 04, 29,000 loans approved.

HQ: Office of Disaster Assistance, SBA, 409 Third St. SW, Washington, DC 20416. Phone: (202)205-6734. **Internet:** "www.sba.gov/DISASTER"; e-mail, "disaster.assistance@sba.gov".

59.005 INTERNET-BASED TECHNICAL ASSISTANCE

Assistance: technical information.

Purposes: pursuant to the Small Business Act of 1953 as amended, to provide advice on management and operation of small businesses, through on-line training and counseling, educational materials, and referrals to SBDCs, Service Corps of Retired Executives (SCORE), women's business centers, and other programs and services.

Eligible applicants/beneficiaries: anyone.

Activity: FY 05 estimate, 285,000 small businesses counseled on-line.

HQ: Director, e-Small Business, Office of Entrepreneurial Development, SBA, 409 Third St. SW, Washington, DC 20416. Phone: (202)205-6706. **Internet:** "www.sba.gov"; "www.business.gov".

59.006 8(A) BUSINESS DEVELOPMENT ("Section 8(a) Program")

Assistance: specialized services.

Purposes: pursuant to the Small Business Act of 1953 as amended, for SBA to enter into procurement contracts with other federal agencies and for subcontracts, in turn, with socially and economically disadvantaged businesses. The program incorporates contract, technical, and managerial assistance to participants, and access to financial resources.

Eligible applicants/beneficiaries: small businesses at least 51 percent owned, controlled, and managed by U.S. citizens, determined by SBA to be socially and economically disadvantaged; disadvantaged tribes, Alaska native corporations, or native Hawaiian organizations.

Activity: FY 01, 32,000 contract actions valued at $6.59 billion (latest data reported).

HQ: Associate Administrator/8(a) Business Development, SBA, 409 Third St. SW, Washington, DC 20416. Phone: (no number provided). **Internet:** "www.sba.gov".

59.007 7(I) TECHNICAL ASSISTANCE ("Section 7(j) Program")

Assistance: project grants (100 percent).

Purposes: pursuant to the Small Business Act of 1953 as amended, for projects conducted by qualified entities to provide business management, technical assistance, and services in obtaining financing—to businesses that are socially and economically disadvantaged, located in areas of high unemployment or low income, or participants in program **59.006**. Funds also may be used to establish and strengthen business service agencies including trade associations and cooperatives.

Eligible applicants/beneficiaries: state and local governments; educational institutions; public or private organizations and businesses; lending and financial institutions and sureties; tribes; qualified individuals.

Range/Average: N.A.

Activity: FY 01, 14 cooperative agreement, 3 contract awards (latest data reported).

HQ: Associate Administrator/Management and Technical Assistance, Office of Business Development, SBA, 409 Third St. SW, Washington, DC 20416. Phone: (202)205-7343. **Internet:** same as **59.006**.

59.008 PHYSICAL DISASTER LOANS ("DL" - "Section 7(b) Loans")

Assistance: direct loans (to 4-8 percent/3-30 years).

Purposes: pursuant to the Small Business Act of 1953 as amended and the Disaster Relief Act of 1970, for victims of declared physical disasters to restore or replace uninsured damaged or destroyed real or personal property. Loan terms depend on the applicant's access to credit. Provisions of the Flood Disaster Protection Act of 1973 and National Flood Insurance Reform Act of 1994 apply. Collateral is required on loans of more than $10,000.

Eligible applicants/beneficiaries: homeowners, renters, businesses, and charitable and nonprofit organizations. Agricultural enterprises are ineligible.

Range: homes, to $240,000, plus $200,000 in special cases to refinance existing liens, and $48,000 additional for protective measures; businesses, to $1,500,000 with higher amounts available for major source of employment. **Average:** homes, $25,000; businesses, $75,000.

Activity: FY 04, 25,000 loans.

HQ: same as **59.002**.

59.009 PROCUREMENT ASSISTANCE TO SMALL BUSINESSES

Assistance: specialized services.

Purposes: pursuant to the Small Business Act of 1953 as amended and the Economic Opportunity Act of 1964, to assist small businesses in all phases of obtaining government procurement contracts and subcontracts, as well as of federal property sold. SBA: advocates small business participation in federal contracts and subcontracts, including application of small business "set-asides;" consults with other federal procuring agencies to optimize small business participation; manages the Central Contractor Registration's Dynamic Small Business Search, a nationwide Internet information database on small businesses interested in obtaining federal contracts or subcontracts.

Eligible applicants/beneficiaries: existing and potential small businesses.

Activity: FY 04, $11.2 billion in set-asides.

HQ: Associate Administrator/Government Contracting, SBA, 409 Third St. SW, Washington, DC 20416. Phone: (202)205-6460. **Internet:** same as **59.006**.

59.011 SMALL BUSINESS INVESTMENT COMPANIES ("SBIC - SSBIC")

Assistance: direct loans, guaranteed/insured loans (to 10-15 years); advisory services/counseling.

Purposes: pursuant to the Small Business Investment Act of 1958 as amended, for privately owned and managed SBA-licensed small business investment companies, including specialized SBICs (SSBICs) assisting socially or economically disadvantaged enterprises, to provide equity capital, in turn, to small businesses—through long-term loans or equity purchases. SBA guarantees debentures issued by the investment companies to maximize leveraging of private funds, by up to 300 percent within maximums established by SBA and for terms of 10 years; participating securities may be guaranteed for up to 15 years. The investment companies provide continuing management and other assistance to firms that obtain the loans.

Eligible applicants: chartered SBICs with private capital of at least $3,000,000 for those not receiving SBA leveraging, or $5,000,000 if receiving SBA leveraging.

Eligible beneficiaries: small businesses (single proprietorship, partnership, or corporation); SSBIC beneficiaries must also be socially or economically disadvantaged enterprises.

Range: $50,000 to $119,000,000. **Average:** $18,200,000.

Activity: as of FY 05, participation by 448 SBICs with capital resources of $25.7 billion.

HQ: Associate Administrator/Investment, Investment Division, SBA, 409 Third St. SW, Washington, DC 20416. Phone: (202)205-6510. **Internet:** same as **59.006**. (Note: no field offices for this program.)

59.012 SMALL BUSINESS LOANS
("Regular Business Loans" - "Section 7(a) Loans")

Assistance: guaranteed/insured loans.

Purposes: pursuant to the Small Business Act of 1953 as amended, for small businesses to construct, expand, or convert business facilities; to purchase equipment or materials; for working capital. Eligible loan uses also include design, manufacture, marketing, installation, or servicing of specific energy measures. Program components include SBA's: Low Documentation Loan Program (Low Doc); Cap Line Program; SBAExpress Program; International Trade.

Eligible applicants/beneficiaries: small businesses.

Range: to $2,000,000. **Average:** $150,000.

Activity: FY 04, 81,000 loans guaranteed.

HQ: Director, Loan Programs Division, SBA, 409 Third St. SW, Washington, DC 20416. Phone: (202)205-6570. **Internet:** "www.sba.gov/financing".

59.016 BOND GUARANTEES FOR SURETY COMPANIES
("Surety Bond Guarantee")

Assistance: insurance (70-90 percent).

Purposes: pursuant to the Small Business Act of 1953 as amended and the Inspector General Act of 1978, to guarantee bonds issued by commercial surety companies for bid, payment, and performance or other bonds provided to small businesses on contracts up to $2,000,000.

Eligible applicants: surety companies holding certificates of authority from the Secretary of the Treasury.

Eligible beneficiaries: small contractors with gross annual receipts of no more than $6,000,000 as averaged for the last three fiscal years; certain manufacturers. (Applications are submitted directly to insurance agents or brokers.)

Range: $475 to $2,000,000. **Average:** contract, $268,000; guarantee, $213,000.

Activity: FY 04, 5,573 bid bonds approved, 2,230 final bond guarantees issued.

HQ: Associate Administrator, Office of Surety Guarantees, SBA, 409 Third St. SW, Washington, DC 20416. Phone: (202)205-6540. **Internet:** same as **59.006**.

59.026 SERVICE CORPS OF RETIRED EXECUTIVES ("SCORE")

Assistance: advisory services/counseling; training.

Purposes: pursuant to the Small Business Act of 1953 as amended, to operate the SCORE program through which retired or active business executives volunteer their services to counsel and train new and existing small business persons. Out-of-pocket expenses of volunteers may be reimbursed.

Eligible applicants/beneficiaries: existing and potential small businesses.

Activity: 11,500 volunteers serve in the 50 states and in possessions.

HQ: Office of Business and Community Initiatives, SBA, 409 Third St. SW, Washington, DC 20024. Phone: (202)205-6665, (800)634-0245; National SCORE Office, (same address), (202)205-6762; (800)634-0245. **Internet:** same as **59.006**; SCORE, "www.score.org".

59.037 SMALL BUSINESS DEVELOPMENT CENTER ("SBDC")

Assistance: project grants (formula based, 50 percent); specialized services; advisory services/counseling; technical information.

Purposes: pursuant to the Small Business Act of 1953 as amended, for SBDCs to provide management counseling, training, and technical assistance to existing or potential small businesses.

Eligible applicants/beneficiaries: public or private IHEs including land grant, community, or junior colleges; certain existing SBDCs.

Range: $500,000 to $5,927,000. **Average:** $1,298,000.

Activity: FY 04, 280,000 individuals counseled, 27,000 training sessions.

HQ: SBDC Office, SBA, 409 Third St. SW - 6th floor, Washington, DC 20416. Phone: (202)205-6766, FAX (202)205-7727. **Internet:** "www.sba.gov/sbdc".

59.041 CERTIFIED DEVELOPMENT COMPANY LOANS (504 LOANS) ("Section 504 Loans")

Assistance: guaranteed/insured loans (10-20 years).

Purposes: pursuant to the Small Business Investment Act of 1958 as amended, to assist small businesses in acquiring fixed assets, through the sale of debentures to private investors. Loans may cover acquisition of land, buildings, equipment, construction, expansion, renovation, or modernization. Ten percent of project costs must be provided by the small business concern, and 50 percent by a private lender.

Eligible applicants/beneficiaries: nonprofit certified development companies.

Range: to $1,000,000. **Average:** $480,000.

Activity: FY 04, 8,168 loans approved.

HQ: Office of Financial Assistance, SBA, 409 Third St. SW, Washington, DC 20416. Phone: (202)205-6490. **Internet:** same as **59.006**.

59.043 WOMEN'S BUSINESS OWNERSHIP ASSISTANCE

Assistance: project grants (50-67 percent/to 5 years).

Purposes: pursuant to the Small Business Act of 1953 as amended, Women's Business Ownership Act of 1988, and Women's Business Center Sustainability Act of 1999, to establish women's business centers to assist new or existing small businesses owned and controlled by women, through financial, management, procurement, marketing, training, and counseling services. Services are also provided through the Online Women's Business Center.

Eligible applicants/beneficiaries: experienced private nonprofit organizations.

Range: $75,000 to $150,000.

Activity: FY 04, 123,000 clients trained and counseled at 104 funded centers.

HQ: Office of Women's Business Ownership, SBA, 409 Third St. SW, Washington, DC 20416. Phone: (202)205-6673. **Internet:** "www.sba.gov/womeninbusiness"; "www.onlinewbc.gov".

59.044 VETERANS ENTREPRENEURIAL TRAINING AND COUNSELING ("Veterans Business Outreach Program" - "VBOP")

Assistance: project grants (matching/1-5 years).

Purposes: pursuant to the Small Business Act of 1953 as amended, to establish and operate Veterans Business Outreach Centers to provide long-term training, counseling, and mentoring to veterans starting or operating small businesses.

Eligible applicants/beneficiaries: educational institutions; private businesses; veterans nonprofit community-based organizations; federal, state, and local entities.

Range: $75 to $1,500 per client.

Activity: N.A.

HQ: Associate Administrator, Office of Veterans Business Development, SBA, 409 Third St. SW - 5th Floor, Washington, DC 20416. Phone: (202)205-6773. **Internet:** same as **59.006**.

59.046 MICROLOAN PROGRAM

Assistance: formula grants; direct loans (to 10 years).

Purposes: to provide loan funds or loan guaranties to eligible intermediary lenders that, in turn, will make short-term, fixed-rate loans to newly established or growing small businesses for working capital or for the acquisition of supplies or equipment; to make grants to intermediaries to provide intensive marketing, management, and technical assistance to borrowers; to make grants to nonprofit entities to assist low-income individuals in obtaining private sector financing for their businesses.

Eligible applicants: intermediary lenders meeting SBA requirements.

Eligible beneficiaries: small businesses, minority entrepreneurs, nonprofit entities, women, low-income and other persons.

Range: to $35,000. **Average:** $12,000.

Activity: not quantified specifically.

HQ: Microenterprise Development Branch (MC 7881), Office of Financial Assistance, SBA, 409 Third St. SW - 8th Floor, Washington, DC 20416. Phone: (202)205-6490. **Internet:** same as **59.006**.

59.049 OFFICE OF SMALL DISADVANTAGED BUSINESS CERTIFICATION AND ELIGIBILITY ("OSBDC&E")

Assistance: direct loans (from 3 years).

Purposes: pursuant to the Small Business Act of 1953 as amended, to ensure compliance with "Adarand vs. Pena," relative to federal action programs that use racial or ethnic criteria as a basis for decision-making. The program assists the government in finding firms capable of providing services under procurement contracts.

Eligible applicants/beneficiaries: certified socially and economically disadvantaged small business concerns.

Range/Average: N.A.

Activity: FY 04, 1,000 new certifications issued.

HQ: OSBDC&E, SBA, 409 Third St. SW, Washington, DC 20416. Phone: (no number provided). **Internet:** "www.sba.gov/sdb". (Note: no field offices for this program.)

59.050 MICROENTERPRISE DEVELOPMENT GRANTS ("PRIME")

Assistance: project grants (50 percent/1-5 years).

Purposes: pursuant to the Riegle Community Development and Regulatory Improvement Act of 1994 as amended and Gramm-Leach-Bliley Act, to increase the number of microenterprises and enhance their management capabilities, by: providing training and technical assistance in starting or expanding their businesses; providing training and capacity building services to enhance existing or new microenterprise development organizations (MDOs) that provide training programs and services; conducting research and development of "best practices" in the field.

Eligible applicants: established nonprofit MDOs or programs, including collaboratives, that are accountable to local communities and working in conjunction with a state or local government or tribe; certain tribes acting on their own.

Eligible beneficiaries: disadvantaged entrepreneurs and microenterprises.

Range/Average: N.A.

Activity: N.A.

HQ: same address as **59.041**. Phone: (202)205-6491. **Internet:** "www.sba.gov/inv"; "www.sba.gov/financing/sbaloan/microloans.html". (Note: no field offices for this program.)

59.051 NEW MARKETS VENTURE CAPITAL PROGRAM, OPERATIONAL ASSISTANCE (OA) GRANTS

Assistance: project grants (50 percent/to 10 years); guaranteed/insured loans (to 10 years).

Purposes: pursuant to the Small Business Investment Act of 1958 as amended, to promote economic development and the creation of wealth and job opportunities in low-income areas—through development venture capital investments in smaller enterprises located in such areas. Program loan recipients must match 30 percent of capital funds obtained from SBA (derived from SBA-guaranteed debentures); they may make equity capital investments in the enterprises at 1 percent interest above the cost of federal borrowing, requiring no repayment in years 1 to 5, interest-only payments in years 6 to 10, and a balloon payment at maturity, and with no prepayment penalty after year 1. Grant recipients provide related management and technical assistance to the enterprises.

Eligible applicants/beneficiaries: new for-profit companies; existing specialized small business investment companies (SSBICs).

Range: from $1,500,000.

Activity: N.A.

HQ: New Markets Venture Capital Program, Investment Division, SBA, 409 Third St. SW - Ste.6300, Washington, DC 20416. Phone: (202)205-6510. **Internet:** "www.sba.gov/INV/NMVC". (Note: no field offices for this program.)

59.052 NATIVE AMERICAN ECONOMIC DEVELOPMENT ASSISTANCE

Assistance: project grants.

Purposes: pursuant to the Small Business Act as amended, for entrepreneurial development programs and services provided to American Indians and Alaska and Hawaii natives, located in disadvantaged and under-served reservations and tribal areas, and seeking to establish, develop, and expand small businesses. Projects must include a strong outreach component stressing participation in under-served areas. Project examples: small business incubator activities; training; marketing outreach.

Eligible applicants/beneficiaries: organizations with experience in training, counseling, developing, and measuring small business development in Indian country.

Range/Average: N.A.

Activity: new program listing in 2005.

HQ: Office of Native American Affairs, SBA, 409 Third St. SW, Washington,

DC 20416. Phone: (no number provided). **Internet:** "www.sba.gov/naa/". (Note: no field offices for this program.)

59.053 SMALL BUSINESS AND AGRICULTURE REGULATORY ENFORCEMENT OMBUDSMAN AND SMALL BUSINESS REGULATORY FAIRNESS BOARDS

Assistance: project grants.

Purposes: pursuant to the Small Business Regulatory Fairness Act of 1996, to serve the small business community by receiving comments regarding unfair or excessive actions by federal agencies or agency employees conducting compliance or enforcement activities. Comments may be confidential or not, and be discussed with appropriate federal agency personnel to seek a timely response to an excessive or unfair federal regulatory issue. Hearings may be held throughout the country to receive testimony and commentary. Comments also may be submitted online, by FAX, mail, or personal delivery.

Eligible applicants/beneficiaries: small businesses, nonprofit organizations, or small government entities (representing fewer than 50,000 persons).

Range/Average: N.A.

Activity: new program listing in 2005.

HQ: Office of the National Ombudsman, SBA, 409 Third St. SW, Washington, DC 20416. Phone: (no number provided). **Internet:** "www.sba.gov/ombudsman". (Note: no field offices for this program.)

59.054 7(A) LOANS (EXPORT LOANS)
("Export Loans")

Assistance: guaranteed/insured loans.

Purposes: pursuant to the Small Business Act of 1953 as amended, for small businesses to increase their ability to compete in international markets by enhancing their ability to export, through: the Export Working Capital Program, providing 90 percent loan guarantees; the Export Express Loan Program, with 85 percent loan guarantees; the International Trade Loan Program, with 75 percent loan guarantees. Loans may be used: to construct, expand, or convert facilities; to purchase building equipment or materials; for export working capital.

Eligible applicants/beneficiaries: small businesses meeting SBA size standards, that are independently owned and operated, and not dominant in their field.

Range/Average: N.A.

Activity: new program listing in 2005. FY 04, 2,316 loans to exporters.

HQ: Associate Administrator, Office of International Trade, SBA, 409 Third St. SW, Washington, DC 20416. Phone: (202)205-6720. **Internet:** same as **59.006.**

DEPARTMENT OF VETERANS AFFAIRS

> **NOTE:** *In DVA programs providing benefits directly to veterans, eligibility factors may include all or some of the following: discharge under other than dishonorable conditions; former prisoners of war; Medal of Honor award in peacetime and unable to pay the cost of necessary care; wartime service resulting in need of treatment for a full or partial service-connected or nonservice-connected disability, or for a disease; receiving a DVA pension or age 65 or older and with wartime or peacetime active service; discharged for a disability, or receiving compensation for and suffering from a permanent disability, with no adequate means of support; degree of disability; receiving compensation or allowances based on need of regular aid and attendance or housebound; income within certain limits, although eligibility based on financial income may be established by making a copayment for some services. For some programs, time and duration of service may affect eligibility.*
>
> *Details may be obtained from DVA medical centers or outpatient clinics, from DVA Veterans Benefits Administration field offices (see **64.115** or other centers listed in Part IV).*

VETERANS HEALTH ADMINISTRATION

64.005 GRANTS TO STATES FOR CONSTRUCTION OF STATE HOME FACILITIES
("State Home Construction")

Assistance: project grants (to 65 percent/to 5 years).

Purposes: to acquire or construct state domiciliary or nursing home facilities for veterans; to expand, remodel, alter, or equip existing buildings to provide domiciliary, nursing home, or hospital care to veterans in state homes.

Eligible applicants/beneficiaries: states.

Range: $23,000 to $14,312,000. **Average:** $2,532,000.

Activity: FY 03 estimate, 42 grant approvals.

HQ: Chief Consultant, Geriatrics and Extended Care Strategic Healthcare Group (114), DVA, Washington, DC 20420. Phone: (202)273-8356. **Internet:** "www.va.gov". (Note: no field offices for this program.)

64.007 BLIND REHABILITATION CENTERS

Assistance: specialized services.

Purposes: to provide personal and social adjustment programs and medical or health-related services to blind veterans at DVA medical centers with blind rehabilitation centers.

Eligible applicants/beneficiaries: blind veterans meeting certain general requirements (*see NOTE preceding* **64.005**). Active duty armed forces personnel may be transferred to a center.

Activity: FY 02, 2,119 veterans benefited at the 10 centers (latest data reported).

HQ: Blind Rehabilitation Service (117B), Patient Care Services, DVA, Washington, DC 20420. Phone: (202)273-8482, -8483. **Internet:** "www.va.gov/blindrehab".

64.008 VETERANS DOMICILIARY CARE

Assistance: specialized services.

Purposes: to provide inpatient medical care and physical, social, and psychological support services to ambulatory veterans disabled by age or illness, and not requiring acute care or skilled nursing services; for rehabilitation services preparing veterans for independent community living, or assisting them in reaching their optimal level of functioning in a protective environment.

Eligible applicants/beneficiaries: veterans meeting specific criteria (*see NOTE preceding* **64.005**).

Activity: FY 06 estimate, 29,000 veterans served; average daily census, 11,000.

HQ: Domiciliary Care Program Chief, Geriatrics and Extended Care Strategic Healthcare Group (114A), DVA, Washington, DC 20420. Phone: (202)273-8543, -8545. **Internet:** same as **64.005**.

64.009 VETERANS MEDICAL CARE BENEFITS ("Hospitalization and Medical Services")

Assistance: specialized services.

Purposes: to provide hospital outpatient medical, dental, medicine, medical supplies, home health, podiatric, optometric, surgical, and mental health services to enrolled veterans and their dependents, including reimbursement for some travel costs. Services are provided at DVA facilities or under fee-basis hometown care programs when properly authorized.

Eligible applicants/beneficiaries: veterans meeting specific criteria (*see NOTE preceding* **64.005**); veterans dependents and survivors that are ineligible for Medicare, CHAMPUS (Civilian Health and Medical Program of the Uniformed Service), or CHAMPVA (Civilian Health and Medical Program, Veterans Affairs).

Activity: FY 06 estimate, 772,000 inpatients served in VA, state, and contract facilities; 61,555,000 total outpatient visits.

HQ: Director, Health Administration Services (10C3), DVA, Washington, DC 20420. Phone: (202)273-8302, -8303. **Internet:** same as **64.005**.

64.010 VETERANS NURSING HOME CARE

Assistance: specialized services.

Purposes: to provide skilled nursing home care to veterans in DVA, state, or contracts facilities. Also provided are related medical services, supportive personal care, and individual adjustment services.

Eligible applicants/beneficiaries: veterans requiring skilled nursing care and related medical services, and meeting specific criteria (*see NOTE preceding* **64.005**).

Activity: FY 06 estimate, 61,000 patients treated; average daily census, 21,000.

HQ: Nursing Home Care Program Chief, Geriatrics and Extended Strategic Health Group (114), DVA, Washington, DC 20420. Phone: (202)273-8544. **Internet:** same as **64.005**.

64.011 VETERANS DENTAL CARE

Assistance: specialized services.

Purposes: to provide dental services for veterans.

Eligible applicants/beneficiaries: veterans meeting specific criteria (*see NOTE preceding* **64.005**).

Activity: FY 06 estimate, 570,000 staff examinations, and 172,000 staff treatments by DVA staff, 36,000 fee cases.

HQ: same as **64.009**.

64.012 VETERANS PRESCRIPTION SERVICE
("Medicine For Veterans")

Assistance: sale, exchange, or donation of property and goods.

Purposes: to provide prescription drugs and expendable medical supplies from DVA pharmacies to veterans and certain dependents and survivors. Small co-payments may be required.

Eligible applicants/beneficiaries: veterans meeting specific criteria (*see NOTE preceding* **64.005**); wives and dependent children under CHAMPVA (Civilian Health and Medical Program, Veterans Affairs)

Activity: N.A.

HQ: Chief Consultant, Pharmacy Benefits Management, DVA, Washington, DC 20420. Phone: (202)273-8429. **Internet:** same as **64.005**.

64.013 VETERANS PROSTHETIC APPLIANCES
("Prosthetics Services")

Assistance: sale, exchange, or donation of property and goods.

Purposes: to provide prosthetic and related appliances, equipment, and services to disabled veterans, including artificial limbs, artificial eyes, wheelchairs, aids for the blind, hearing aids, braces, orthopedic shoes, eyeglasses, crutches and canes, automobile adaptive equipment, and medical equipment, implants, and supplies—as well as training in the use of the foregoing.

Eligible applicants/beneficiaries: disabled veterans meeting specific criteria (*see NOTE preceding* **64.005**).

Range: $10 to $25,000. **Average:** $118.

Activity: FY 01, 2,800,000 prosthetic items and services provided (latest data reported).

HQ: Chief Consultant, Prosthetic and Sensory Aids Strategic Health Care Group (113), DVA, Washington, DC 20420. Phone: (202)273-8515, FAX (202)273-9110. **Internet:** same as **64.005**.

64.014 VETERANS STATE DOMICILIARY CARE

Assistance: formula grants (to 50 percent).

Purposes: pursuant to the Act of August 27, 1888 as amended, to provide domiciliary care services in state homes to veterans disabled by age or illness—to assist them in attaining physical, mental, and social well-being through rehabilitative programs.

Eligible applicants: states.

Eligible beneficiaries: veterans meeting specific criteria (*see NOTE preceding* **64.005**) including state admission requirements.

Range: $5,000 to $3,600,000. **Average:** $427,000.

Activity: FY 06 estimate, 5,300 patients treated; average daily census, 6,000.

HQ: Chief, State Home Per Diem Program, Assistant Chief Medical Director/Geriatrics and Extended Care (114B), DVA, Washington, DC 20420. Phone: (202)273-8538. **Internet:** same as **64.005**.

64.015 VETERANS STATE NURSING HOME CARE

Assistance: formula grants (to 50 percent).

Purposes: to provide skilled nursing home care and related medical services to veterans in state veterans homes.

Eligible applicants: states.

Eligible beneficiaries: veterans eligible for care in a DVA facility, needing nursing home care, and meeting other specific criteria (*see NOTE preceding* **64.005**), including state admission requirements.

Range: $416,000 to $7,879,000. **Average:** $2,410,000.

Activity: FY 05 estimate, 26,000 patients treated; average daily census, 19,000.

HQ: same as **64.014**.

64.016 VETERANS STATE HOSPITAL CARE

Assistance: formula grants (to 50 percent).

Purposes: to provide inpatient hospital care to veterans in state veterans homes.

Eligible applicants: states.

Eligible beneficiaries: veterans meeting specific criteria (*see NOTE preceding* **64.005**), including state requirements.

Range: $42,000 to $2,900,000. **Average:** $790,000.

Activity: FY 06 estimate, 942 patients treated; average daily census, 187.

HQ: same as **64.014**.

64.018 SHARING SPECIALIZED MEDICAL RESOURCES

Assistance: specialized services.

Purposes: for exchanges between DVA and communities, or mutual use of, advanced medical techniques and specialized resources which otherwise might not be available to DVA or to the communities.

Eligible applicants/beneficiaries: medical schools; federal, state, local, public or private hospitals; clinics; research centers; blood and organ banks.

Activity: FY 04, 2,818 contracts.

HQ: Director, Sharing and Purchasing Office (175), Veterans Health Administration, DVA, 810 Vermont Ave. NW, Washington, DC 20420. Phone: (202)273-8406. **Internet:** same as **64.005.**

64.019 VETERANS REHABILITATION—ALCOHOL AND DRUG DEPENDENCE ("Substance Abuse Treatment Program, Mental Health and Behavioral Sciences Service")

Assistance: specialized services.

Purposes: to provide medical, social, vocational, and rehabilitation therapies to alcohol- and drug-dependent veterans, in DVA medical centers and clinics. Services include detoxification, substance abuse rehabilitation, individual and group and family therapy, psychotropic medications, psychiatric counseling, social services, vocational rehabilitation.

Eligible applicants/beneficiaries: veterans meeting specific criteria (*see NOTE preceding* **64.005**).

Activity: FY 03, 100,000 veterans served (latest data reported).

HQ: Director, Mental Health and Behavioral Sciences Services (11C), DVA, Washington, DC 20420. Phone: (202)273-8437. **Internet:** same as **64.005.**

64.022 VETERANS HOME BASED PRIMARY CARE

Assistance: specialized services.

Purposes: to provide primary health care services through DVA interdisciplinary teams to homebound veterans whose caregivers are capable and willing to assist in their care.

Eligible applicants/beneficiaries: veterans requiring intermittent skilled nursing care and related medical services, and meeting specific criteria (*see NOTE preceding* **64.005**).

Activity: FY 04, 9,825 veterans received home care on the average day.

HQ: Home Based Primary Care Program Coordinator, Geriatrics and Extended Care Strategic Healthcare Group (114), DVA, Washington, DC 20420. Phone: (202)273-6488, -8540. **Internet:** same as **64.005**. (Note: no field offices for this program.)

64.024 VA HOMELESS PROVIDERS GRANT AND PER DIEM PROGRAM

Assistance: project grants (to 65 percent).

Purposes: pursuant to the Homeless Veterans Comprehensive Service Programs Act of 1992, to establish new programs and service centers to provide supportive housing and services for homeless veterans. Funds may be used to: acquire, renovate, or alter facilities; provide outreach and transportation services; pay operating costs. Per diem payments may be provided on behalf of VA-referred or -authorized veterans. Operating costs may be partially supported with grant funds.

Eligible applicants/beneficiaries: project grants—public or private nonprofit entities. For per diem payments, programs must have been established after 10 November 1992.

Range: $13,000 to $541,000.

Activity: cumulative estimate since program inception, 14 services centers, 2,500 new community-based beds, 20 vans purchased.

HQ: Program Manager, Homeless Providers Grant and Per Diem Program, Mental Health Strategic Healthcare Group (116E), DVA, 810 Vermont Ave. NW, Washington, DC 20420. Phone: (202)273-8966, -8443; *toll-free*, (877) 322-0334. **Internet:** same as **64.005**. (Note: no field offices for this program.)

64.026 VETERANS STATE ADULT DAY HEALTH CARE

Assistance: project grants (50 percent).

Purposes: for community-based, nonresidential programs providing skilled nursing and rehabilitative therapy services to veterans with medical or disabling conditions, including at least physical or occupational therapy, or speech-language pathology or audiology, and personal and psychological or counseling services as appropriate.

Eligible applicants/beneficiaries: veterans meeting state as well as DVA requirements (*see NOTE preceding* **64.005**).

Range: $35.17 per diem per veteran; state grants, $113,000 to $124,000. **Average:** $119,000.

Activity: new program listing in 2005 (CFDA on-line). FY 06 estimate, 96 participant slots at 2 recognized program locations.

HQ: same as **64.024**.

VETERANS BENEFITS ADMINISTRATION

64.100 AUTOMOBILES AND ADAPTIVE EQUIPMENT FOR CERTAIN DISABLED VETERANS AND MEMBERS OF THE ARMED FORCES

Assistance: direct payments/specified use.

Purposes: for disabled veterans and service-persons to purchase automobiles or other conveyances with adaptive equipment. Funds also may be used for repairs, replacements, or reinstallation. Adaptive equipment may be provided for no more than two conveyances during any four-year period, unless one of the vehicles becomes unavailable to the veteran.

Eligible applicants/beneficiaries: active duty personnel and veterans with honorable service and service-persons with a service-connected disability caused by loss of use or permanent loss of one or both feet, one or both hands, or a permanent impairment of vision of both eyes to a prescribed degree. Adaptive equipment—service-connected ankylosis of one or both knees or hips.

Range: no maximum for adaptive equipment; 11,000 maximum for automobile or other conveyance.

Activity: FY 06 estimate, 1,585 vehicles purchased.

HQ: DVA, Washington, DC 20420. Phone: (202)273-7210. **Internet:** same as **64.005**.

64.101 BURIAL EXPENSES ALLOWANCE FOR VETERANS

Assistance: direct payments/specified use.

Purposes: for the plot or internment expenses of certain veterans not buried in a national cemetery; for funeral and burial expenses of veterans whose death results from a service-connected disability; for transportation of the remains of service-connected, disabled veterans to a national cemetery. Headstones or markers and an American flag to drape the casket may also be provided.

Eligible applicants/beneficiaries: burial and plot allowances—the person bearing the veteran's burial expense or the funeral director, if unpaid, on behalf of veterans: discharged under other than dishonorable conditions; discharged or released from active duty for a disability incurred or aggravated in line of duty; or, at time of death, entitled to compensation or pension or indigent or properly hospitalized at VA expense. Flags—next of kin, friend, or associate.

Range: to $300 for plot or interment expenses; to $300 for burial allowance if death is not service-connected; to $2,000 if death is service-connected.

Activity: FY 06 estimate, 96,000 burial allowances; 542,000 flags.

HQ: same as **64.100**.

64.102 COMPENSATION FOR SERVICE-CONNECTED DEATHS FOR VETERANS' DEPENDENTS
("Death Compensation")

Assistance: direct payments/unrestricted use.

Purposes: for dependents or survivors of veterans whose death resulted from a service-connected disability.

Eligible applicants/beneficiaries: unmarried surviving spouses, unmarried children, and dependent parent(s) of veterans deceased before January 1, 1957. Compensation for later deaths is payable under Dependency and Indemnity Compensation (DIC) (see **64.110**).

Range: monthly, $87 for surviving spouses to $121 for widows or widowers with one child, plus $29 for each additional child; dependent parent(s), $75 for one alone, $80 for two, with additional $79 if aid and attendance is required.

Activity: FY 06 estimate, benefits to 12 spouses and 452 parents.

HQ: same as **64.100**.

64.103 LIFE INSURANCE FOR VETERANS
("GI Insurance")

Assistance: direct loans; insurance.

Purposes: pursuant to the War Risk Insurance Act, World War Veterans Act, National Service Life Insurance Act, and Servicemen's Indemnity and Insurance Act, and amendments, to provide: life insurance protection for veterans of WW-I and -II, the Korean, Vietnam, and Gulf era conflicts, and for those with service-connected disabilities, separated from active duty on April 25, 1951 or later, and current members of the uniformed services and their spouses; mortgage protection life insurance for veterans receiving specially adapted housing; policy loans at varying interest rates. The programs are closed for new issues except Service-Disabled Veterans Insurance, Mortgage Protection Life Insurance, Service Members' Group Life Insurance, and Veterans Group Life Insurance.

Eligible applicants/beneficiaries: veterans meeting specific criteria (*see NOTE preceding* **64.005**). If the eligible applicant is mentally incompetent, a fiduciary recognized by DVA may apply of the veteran for Service-Disabled Veterans Insurance—benefits of which may also be granted under certain conditions for mentally incompetent veterans who were otherwise eligible for such insurance but, due to their incompetence, died without filing an application. Souses and dependent children are automatically covered unless the member declines or reduces the coverage.

Range: N.A.

Activity: as of FY 05, 1,800,000 policies in force.

HQ: Regional Office and Insurance Center, DVA, P.O. Box 42954, Philadelphia, PA 19101. Phone: (800)669-8477. **Internet:** "www.insurance.va.gov". (Note: no other field offices for this program.)

64.104 PENSION FOR NON-SERVICE-CONNECTED DISABILITY FOR VETERANS

Assistance: direct payments/unrestricted use.

Purposes: for wartime veterans with total and permanent nonservice-connected disabilities. Income and asset restrictions are prescribed.

Eligible applicants/beneficiaries: veterans with 90 days or more of honorable active wartime service in the Armed Forces or, if less than 90 days, released or discharged from service because of a service-connected disability, or permanently and totally disabled for reasons not due to service. Pension is not payable to those whose estates are so large that it is reasonable they use the estate for maintenance.

Range: $10,162 annually, reduced by countable income for veteran without dependents ($16,955 if in need of aid and attendance, and $12,419 if housebound); $13,309 for a veteran with one dependent ($20,099 if in need of aid and attendance, and $15,566 if housebound) plus $1,734 for each additional dependent. Also, an additional $2,305 if a veteran of WW-I or Mexican Border Period.

Activity: FY 06 estimate, pensions to 336,000 veterans.

HQ: same as **64.100**.

64.105 PENSION TO VETERANS SURVIVING SPOUSES, AND CHILDREN ("Death Pension")

Assistance: direct payments/unrestricted use.

Purposes: for needy dependents of deceased wartime veterans whose deaths were not due to service.

Eligible applicants/beneficiaries: unmarried surviving spouses and children of deceased veterans with at least 90 days of honorable active wartime service or, if less than 90 days, discharged for a service-connected disability.

A child must be unmarried and under age 18, between age 18 and 23 if in school, or disabled before age 18 and continuously incapable of self-support. Pensions are not payable to those whose estates are so large that it is reasonable they use the estate for maintenance.

Range: $6,814 annually, reduced by countable income for a spouse without children ($10,893 if in need of aid and attendance, and $8,328 if housebound), $8,928 for spouse with one child ($12,966 if in need of aid and attendance, and $10,432 if housebound), plus $1,734 for each additional child.

Activity: FY 06 estimate, 203,000 cases.

HQ: same as **64.100**.

64.106 SPECIALLY ADAPTED HOUSING FOR DISABLED VETERANS ("SAH" - "Paraplegic Housing")

Assistance: direct payments/specified use.

Purposes: to provide suitable adapted housing with special fixtures and facilities to severely disabled veterans, including construction, remodeling, or mortgage reduction payments.

Eligible applicants/beneficiaries: veterans with permanent, total, and compensable disabilities.

Range: 50 percent of cost to purchase, construct, or remodel a suitable housing unit, with $50,000 maximum; to $10,000 for special residential adaptations.

Activity: FY 05 estimate, 600 grants.

HQ: DVA, Washington, DC 20420. Phone: (202)273-7355. **Internet:** same as **64.005**.

64.109 VETERANS COMPENSATION FOR SERVICE-CONNECTED DISABILITY ("Compensation")

Assistance: direct payments/unrestricted use.

Purposes: for disabled veterans, in amounts reflecting the average impairment in the earning capacity the disability would cause in civilian occupations.

Eligible applicants/beneficiaries: persons suffering disabilities during service in the Armed Forces, incurred in or aggravated by service in the line of duty. Separation from service must have been under other than dishonorable conditions.

Range: monthly, from $108 for a 10 percent degree of disability, to $6,514 for very severe disabilities.

Activity: FY 04, 2,519,000 cases.

HQ: same as **64.100**.

64.110 VETERANS DEPENDENCY AND INDEMNITY COMPENSATION FOR SERVICE-CONNECTED DEATH ("DIC")

Assistance: direct payments/unrestricted use.

Purposes: for survivors of deceased veterans whose death resulted from a service-connected disability or while on active duty.

Eligible applicants/beneficiaries: surviving spouses, children, and parent(s) of deceased veterans.

Range: monthly, from $421 for one child when no spouse is entitled; $993 to $2,272 for a surviving spouse, with $247 additional if in need of aid and attendance, or $118 if housebound; surviving spouse is entitled to an additional $247 for each child under age 18; parents, $5 to $487 depending on income and whether single or married, with $263 additional if in need aid and attendance. NOTE: effective January 2005, surviving spouses that receive DIC and have one of more children under age 18 receive an additional $250 monthly—for months occurring during the two-year period beginning on the date of their DIC entitlement, and ceasing at the expiration of the two-year period when the dependent child reaches age 18 or becomes no longer entitled to the award.

Activity: FY 06 estimate, 335,000 cases.

HQ: DVA, Washington, DC 20420. Phone: (202)273-7203. **Internet:** same as **64.005**.

64.114 VETERANS HOUSING—GUARANTEED AND INSURED LOANS ("VA Home Loans")

Assistance: guaranteed/insured loans.

Purposes: for housing for veterans, certain service personnel, or their surviving unremarried spouses—covering home construction or purchases, repairs, improvements, or refinancing. Eligible loans include those covering standard single-family units, condominiums, or manufactured homes and lots—for their own use; also, for solar heating or cooling or other energy conservation improvements. Applicants must have sufficient present and prospective income to meet loan repayment terms, and a satisfactory credit record.

Eligible applicants/beneficiaries: veterans meeting specific criteria (*see NOTE preceding* **64.005**). Also, unremarried surviving spouses of eligible veterans deceased in service or as a result of service-connected disabilities.

Range/Average: to 50 percent for loans of $45,000 or less; $22,500 for loans between $45,000 and $56,250; $36,000 or 40 percent, whichever is less, for loans between $56,250 to $144,000; for loans greater than $144,000 or for VA loan refinancing, basically 25 percent of established loan limits.

Activity: FY 05 estimate, 150,000 insured loans.

HQ: DVA, Washington, DC 20420. Phone: (202)273-7390. **Internet:** same as **64.005**.

64.115 VETERANS INFORMATION AND ASSISTANCE ("Veterans Services")

Assistance: advisory services/counseling.

Purposes: to provide information and assistance to all veterans—including of the PHS, NOAA, and certain WW-II Merchant Marines—relating to the full range of benefits to which they are entitled.

Eligible applicants/beneficiaries: generally, veterans, their dependents or beneficiaries, their representatives or other interested parties.

Activity: annually, 10,000,000 contacts.
HQ: same as **64.100**.

64.116 VOCATIONAL REHABILITATION FOR DISABLED VETERANS

Assistance: direct payments/unrestricted use; direct payments/specified use; direct loans; advisory services/counseling.

Purposes: pursuant to the Veterans' Rehabilitation and Education Amendments of 1980, to provide counseling, no-interest loans, and payments for tuition, fees, related costs, and subsistence for up to four years to disabled veterans and hospitalized service-members pending discharge—to obtain vocational training and suitable employment and to achieve maximum independence in daily living.

Eligible applicants/beneficiaries: veterans of WW-II and later service, with a compensable service-connected disability; certain hospitalized service-members pending discharge or release from service, in need of vocational rehabilitation because of an employment handicap.

Range: full cost of tuition, books, fees, supplies, and services; monthly full-time allowances range from $474.27 for a single veteran to $695.23 for a veteran with two dependents, plus $50.54 for each additional dependent; no-interest loans of up to $948.54 and a work-study allowance not higher than 25 times the minimum hourly wage times the number of weeks of the veteran's period of enrollment.

Activity: FY 06 estimate, 99,000 participants, 4,634 loans.

HQ: Vocational Rehabilitation and Employment Service (28), Veterans Benefits Administration, DVA, Washington, DC 20420. Phone: (202)273-7419.
Internet: same as **64.005**.

64.117 SURVIVORS AND DEPENDENTS EDUCATIONAL ASSISTANCE

Assistance: direct payments/specified use (to 45 months).

Purposes: to provide educational opportunities for dependents of certain deceased or disabled veterans—covering pursuit of associate, bachelor, or graduate degree, licensing and certification tests, diplomas, apprenticeships and on-the-job training, preparatory courses, restorative or vocational training. Education must be completed within ten years of the date that the disability was incurred, or from the date of death of the veteran.

Eligible applicants/beneficiaries: spouses, surviving spouses, and children between age 18 and 26—of veterans deceased because of service-connected disabilities; of living veterans with service-connected disabilities considered permanently and totally disabling; of those deceased because of any cause while such disabilities were in existence; of service-members listed for more than 90 days as missing in action; or, of prisoners of war.

Range: monthly, institutional training—full time, $803; three-quarters time, $603; half-time, $401. Tutorial assistance, to $1,200. Work-study allowances also may be paid.

Activity: FY 06 estimate, 80,000 participants.

HQ: DVA, Washington, DC 20420. Phone: (202)273-7132. **Internet:** "www.gibill.va.gov".

64.118 VETERANS HOUSING—DIRECT LOANS FOR CERTAIN DISABLED VETERANS

Assistance: direct loans (below-market interest).

Purposes: for disabled veterans to purchase, construct, or improve homes, including farm residences, with specially adapted features and facilities. Loans are coordinated with grants obtained under **64.106**.

Eligible applicants/beneficiaries: disabled veterans serving on active duty on or after September 16, 1940, and eligible under **64.106**.

Range: to $33,000.

Activity: FY 06 estimate, 1 loan.

HQ: same as **64.114**.

64.119 VETERANS HOUSING—MANUFACTURED HOME LOANS

Assistance: guaranteed/insured loans (to 95 percent/15-25 years).

Purposes: for manufactured homes (new or used), or homes and lots, or lots only—purchased or refinanced for their own use by veterans, service-members, and certain unremarried surviving spouses of veterans.

Eligible applicants/beneficiaries: same as for **64.114**.

Range: maximum guaranteed amount, $20,000 or 40 percent of the loan, whichever is less. **Average:** loan amount, $30,000.

Activity: FY 05-06, no loans.

HQ: same as **64.114**.

64.120 POST-VIETNAM ERA VETERANS' EDUCATIONAL ASSISTANCE ("Voluntary-Contributory Matching Program")

Assistance: direct payments/specified use.

Purposes: for educational, vocational, or professional training to persons entering the Armed Services after 31 December 1976 and before 1 July 1985, as well as those who served during certain other periods. Payments are provided on the basis of a $2 to $1 match of federal to participant contribution. Enrollments in avocational or recreational courses may not be covered. Participants must have satisfactorily contributed to the program, consisting of a monthly deduction of $25 to $100 from military pay, up to a maximum of $2,700, for deposit in a special training fund. Participants may make lump-sum contributions. Applicants must complete their education within ten years after release from service, with certain exceptions.

Eligible applicants/beneficiaries: basically, veterans serving honorably on active duty for more than 180 days beginning on or after 1 January 1977, or discharged after such date because of a service-connected disability; veterans serving for more than 180 days and continuing on active duty and completing their first period of obligated service (or six years of active duty, whichever comes first). No persons on active duty may initiate contributions to this program after March 31, 1987. Certain more recent veterans may elect

Montgomery GI Bill benefits (see **64.124**), provided their basic pay was reduced by $1,200, based on dates of duty periods.

Range: $8,100 maximum; $1,200 maximum tutorial assistance. Work study allowances also may be provided.

Activity: FY 06 estimate, 650 participants.

HQ: same as **64.117**.

64.124 ALL-VOLUNTEER FORCE EDUCATIONAL ASSISTANCE ("Montgomery GI Bill Active Duty" - "MGIB" - "Chapter 30")

Assistance: direct payments/specified use.

Purposes: for the educational expenses of veterans enrolling in approved educational, professional, or vocational programs, including flight training if already licensed. Participants must have agreed to reductions in their military pay while in service, as nonrefundable contributions toward their participation. $100 monthly is deducted from the basic pay for the first twelve months, unless the veteran specifically elects not to participate in the program; such deductions are nonrefundable except in the case of the death of the veteran within a certain time frame. DOD may provide supplementary contributions to participants' funds as inducements to reenlist, paid while they are enrolled in educational programs. Applicants must complete their education within ten years after release from service, with certain exceptions.

Eligible applicants/beneficiaries: basically, veterans with an honorable discharge and military personnel on active duty on or after 1 July 1985, and with a minimum of two years service. Participants without the required obligated service must have been discharged for a service-connected disability, for hardship, for a pre-existing medical or physical or mental condition, or for involuntary separation due to reduction in force. Certain others may also meet eligibility requirements as described in **64.120**; full criteria may be obtained from DVA.

Range: monthly, $816 to $1,900 for 36 months full-time; work-study allowances based on minimum wage rates; tutorial assistance, to $1,200.

Activity: FY 06 estimate, 346,000 trainees.

HQ: same as **64.117**.

64.125 VOCATIONAL AND EDUCATIONAL COUNSELING FOR SERVICEMEMBERS AND VETERANS ("Chapter 36 Counseling")

Assistance: advisory services/counseling.

Purposes: pursuant to Veterans Education and Employment Programs Amendments, to provide vocational and educational counseling to service-members or veterans, in the identification of personal objectives including the development of employment plans.

Eligible applicants/beneficiaries: service-members applying within 180 days of projected discharge or release from active duty; veterans within one year of discharge or release.

Activity: FY 04, 8,903 participants.

HQ: same as **64.116**.

64.126 NATIVE AMERICAN VETERAN DIRECT LOAN PROGRAM ("VA Native American Veterans Housing Loan Program")

Assistance: direct loans.

Purposes: for certain native American veterans to purchase, construct, improve, or refinance homes that they will occupy, including manufactured homes, located on trust lands.

Eligible applicants/beneficiaries: qualifying native American veterans certified by a recognized tribal government, and their surviving unremarried native American spouses.

Range/Average: to $80,000 (more in high-cost areas).

Activity: FY 06 estimate, 30 loans.

HQ: DVA, Washington, DC 20420. Phone: (202)273-7377. **Internet:** same as **64.005**.

64.127 MONTHLY ALLOWANCE FOR CHILDREN OF VIETNAM VETERANS BORN WITH SPINA BIFIDA

Assistance: direct payments/unrestricted use.

Purposes: to provide financial assistance to children of Vietnam veterans, born with spina bifida.

Eligible applicants/beneficiaries: natural children of Vietnam veterans, born with spina bifida, except spina bifida occulta, regardless of age or marital status, conceived after the date on which the veteran first served in Vietnam (between 9 January 1962 and 2 May 1975).

Range: $244 to $1,440 monthly, based on the degree of disability.

Activity: FY 06 estimate, 1,175 children assisted.

HQ: same as **64.100**.

64.128 VOCATIONAL TRAINING AND REHABILITATION FOR VIETNAM VETERANS' CHILDREN WITH SPINA BIFIDA AND OTHER COVERED BIRTH DEFECTS

Assistance: direct payments/specified use.

Purposes: to provide vocational training and rehabilitation to certain children of Vietnam and Korea veterans, born with spina bifida or other covered birth defects.

Eligible applicants/beneficiaries: same as for **64.127** (and some Korea veterans). DVA must determine that it is feasible for the child to achieve a vocational goal within 2 to 4 years.

Range/Average: N.A.

Activity: FY 04 estimate, 49 cases.

HQ: same as **64.116**.

NATIONAL CEMETERY ADMINISTRATION

64.201 NATIONAL CEMETERIES

Assistance: specialized services.

Purposes: pursuant to the National Cemeteries Act of 1973, to provide burial space, headstones and markers, and perpetual care for deceased veterans, members of the Armed Forces, Reservists, and National Guard members whose service was terminated other than dishonorably, and certain dependents—in national cemeteries.

Eligible applicants/beneficiaries: next of kin or, if there is no living kin, a friend of the decedent or public assistance officer on their behalf, of deceased: veterans, members of the Armed Forces (Army, Navy, Air Force, Marine Corps, Coast Guard) dying while on active duty; members of the Reserve or Army or Air National Guard dying while on active duty for training; 20-year reservists and National Guard and certain of their dependents; enlisted personnel entering military duty after September 7, 1980, and/or becoming commissioned officers after October 16, 1981, and serving for a minimum of two years; spouses of eligible veterans or members of the Armed Forces lost or buried at sea or determined to be permanently missing or missing in action; minor children and certain unmarried adult children of eligible veterans; U.S. citizens serving in the Armed Forces of any government allied with the U.S. during any war, and holding U.S. citizenship at time of death; certain commissioned officers of the PHS, NOAA, and others.

Activity: FY 04, 93,000 interments in the 120 national cemeteries under DVA jurisdiction.

HQ: Director, Memorial Programs Service (41A), National Cemetery Administration-DVA, 810 Vermont Ave. NW, Washington, DC 20420. Phone: (202)273-5226. **Internet:** same as **64.005**.

64.202 PROCUREMENT OF HEADSTONES AND MARKERS AND/OR PRESIDENTIAL MEMORIAL CERTIFICATES

Assistance: direct payments/specified use; specialized services.

Purposes: pursuant to the National Cemeteries Act of 1973 and Veterans' Disability Compensation and Survivors' Benefits Act of 1978, for headstones and markers for the graves or memorial plots in national, post, and state veterans cemeteries, or for the unmarked graves or memorial plots in private cemeteries—of deceased eligible veterans; also, costs of transportation and installation and maintenance, replacement of illegible markers. Presidential Memorial Certificates may also be provided.

Eligible applicants: private cemetery burials—next of kin or nonmembers of the deceased's family, after ascertaining that the grave is unmarked and that a government monument is preferred over a privately purchased one. Monuments must be of a type permitted on the grave of the deceased. If burial or memorial plot is in a national cemetery or state veterans cemetery, the director of the cemetery orders the headstone or marker, after completion of the interment in the cemetery, or upon need for replacement.

Eligible beneficiaries: deceased veterans of wartime or peacetime service, discharged under conditions other than dishonorable; members of the Reserve and the Army and Air National Guard dying while performing or as a result of performing active duty for training; commissioned officers of the PHS and the NOAA, Merchant Marine Seamen, and certain others participating in wartime activities. Spouses and certain dependents also may be eligible.

Activity: FY 04, 351,000 applications; 349,000 markers or headstones, and 436,000 Certificates.

HQ: Director, Memorial Programs Service (41A1), National Cemetery Administration-DVA, 5109 Russell Rd., Quantico, VA 22134-3903. Phone: (202)501-3100; *issues relating to headstone and marker,* (202)501-3027; *application assistance, tracer information, problems with shipments arriving C.O.D., eligibility matters, inscription matters,* (800)697-6947; *Presidential Certificates,* (202)565-4259. **Internet:** same as **64.005**.

64.203 STATE CEMETERY GRANTS

Assistance: project grants (to 100 percent/to 3 years).

Purposes: pursuant to the Veterans Housing Benefits Act of 1978, to establish, expand, or improve state-owned veterans cemeteries for the interment of eligible veterans and their dependents.

Eligible applicants/beneficiaries: states.

Range: $4,305 to $10,966,000. **Average:** $1,534,000.

Activity: FY 05-06 estimate, 5 to 10 applications.

HQ: Director, State Cemetery Grants Service (41E), National Cemetery Administration-DVA, 810 Vermont Ave. NW, Washington, DC 20420. Phone: (202)565-6152, -6801, FAX (202)565-6141. **Internet:** same as **64.005**. (Note: no field offices for this program.)

ENVIRONMENTAL PROTECTION AGENCY

66.001 AIR POLLUTION CONTROL PROGRAM SUPPORT

Assistance: formula grants (60 percent; tribes, 90-95 percent).

Purposes: pursuant to the Clean Air Act of 1990 (CAA) as amended, to plan, establish, improve, and maintain air pollution prevention and control programs. Funding priorities: attain and maintain national ambient standards for criteria pollutants (ozone, particulate matter, visibility, carbon monoxide, lead, sulfur dioxide, and nitrogen dioxide) that endanger human health and the environment; eliminate unacceptable risks of cancer and other health problems from air toxics emissions; reduce the destructive effects of acid rain deposition on land and water systems. Projects involve such strategies as: regulation of stationary sources, mobile source emissions testing and trip reduction measures, participation in interstate emissions trading program, and other innovative early reduction and voluntary measures taken locally. Funding supports cost of monitoring, personnel, training, and operations; construction costs are ineligible.

Eligible applicants/beneficiaries: municipal, intermunicipal, state, tribal, interstate, and intertribal agencies, including possessions and territories.

Range: $7,500 to $7,000,000. **Average:** $900,000.

Activity: FY 04, 110 agencies funded.

HQ: National Air Grant Coordinator (MC 6102A), OAR-EPA, Washington, DC 20460. Phone: *state/local,* (202)564-1349, FAX (202)564-1327; *tribal,* (202)564-7416, FAX (202)501-1153. **Internet:** "www.epa.gov".

66.032 STATE INDOOR RADON GRANTS ("SIRG")

Assistance: project grants (to 50 percent/to 5 years; tribes, 100 percent).

Purposes: pursuant to the Indoor Radon Abatement Act and Toxic Substances Control Act (TSCA), to develop and implement programs and projects to reduce radon risks in homes, schools, and other buildings. Eligible activities include radon surveys, public information and educational materials, radon control programs, purchase and maintenance of analytic equipment, training, administrative costs, data storage and management, mitigation demonstrations, toll-free hotlines, and promotion of environmental justice through outreach to low-income and culturally-diverse populations. Financial assistance may be provided to individuals only if such costs relate to demonstration projects or to the purchase and analysis of radon measurement devices.

Eligible applicants: states, territories and possessions, tribes.

Eligible beneficiaries: local, municipal, district, or areawide organizations; IHEs; nonprofit organizations; low-income persons, homeowners.

Range: $10,000 to $500,000. **Average:** states, $150,000; tribes, $10,000.

Activity: currently, 49 states, DC, Guam, and 35 tribal nations with radon programs.

HQ: Office of Radiation and Indoor Air (6604J), OAR-EPA, 1310 L St. NW, Washington, DC 20005. Phone: (202)343-9117, FAX (202)343-2394. **Internet:** "www.epa.gov/iaq".

66.033 OZONE TRANSPORT

Assistance: project grants (60-100 percent/to 5 years).

Purposes: pursuant to Section 106 (interstate pollution) and Section 111 (interstate ozone pollution) of CAA of 1990 as amended, to develop or recommend regional air quality control implementation plans for reducing ozone pollution. Funds may be used to support interstate pollution projects, including public education and outreach.

Eligible applicants/beneficiaries: state agencies or commissions designated by the governors of the New England and Mid-Atlantic states, and DC, representing affected states and political subdivisions.

Range/Average: $635,000 (single grant).

Activity: single grant.

HQ: OAR-EPA (6102A), 1200 Pennsylvania Ave. NW, Washington, DC 20460. Phone: (202)564-1082, FAX (202)564-1352. **Internet:** "www.epa.gov/air/".

66.034 SURVEYS, STUDIES, INVESTIGATIONS, DEMONSTRATIONS AND SPECIAL PURPOSE ACTIVITIES RELATING TO THE CLEAN AIR ACT

Assistance: project grants (100 percent/to 5 years).

Purposes: pursuant to CAA of 1963 as amended, for surveys, studies, investigations, demonstrations, and special purpose assistance relating to the causes, effects (including upon health and welfare), extent, prevention, and control of air pollution—including air quality, acid deposition, climate change, global programs, indoor environments, mobile source technology, and community-driven approaches to transportation. Funding priorities include: indoor environments, especially those affecting children; air toxics, including the National Air Toxics Assessment program, National Toxics Inventory, and Air Toxics Monitoring Network; mobile source technologies; truck engine idle reduction technologies; National Clean Diesel Campaign; climate protections, including outreach and public education efforts; other issues.

Eligible applicants/beneficiaries: states, territories and possessions, tribes; international organizations; IHEs; other public and private nonprofit institutions.

Range: $5,000 to $750,000. **Average:** $150,000.

Activity: not quantified specifically.

HQ: *Program information,* same address as **66.033**. Phone: (202)564-1514, FAX (202)564-1352. *Grants management information*: Grants Administration Division (3903R), EPA, 1200 Pennsylvania Ave. NW, Washington, DC 20460. Phone: (no number provided). **Internet:** same as **66.001**.

66.035 COMMUNITY ACTION FOR A RENEWED ENVIRONMENT (CARE) PROGRAM ("CARE")

Assistance: project grants (cost sharing/to 5 years).

Purposes: pursuant to CAA, Clean Water Act (CWA), Solid Waste Disposal Act (SWDA), TSCA, Federal Insecticide Fungicide, and Rodenticide Act (FIFRA), Safe Drinking Water Act (SDWA), Marine Protection, Research, and Sanctuaries Act (MPRSA), and amendments, for analyses, studies, evaluations, surveys, investigations, conferences, demonstrations, and special projects that empower communities to reduce risks from exposure to toxic pollutants in the air, water, and land—through collaborative local action. "Level I" agreements support problem assessments and identification of potential solutions; "Level II" agreements support risk reduction projects.

Eligible applicants/beneficiaries: local public, private, and quasi-public nonprofit institutions and organizations; tribal governments and native American organizations; interstate and intrastate organizations.

Range: to $450,000. **Average:** "Level I," $75,000; "Level II," $300,000.

Activity: new program in FY 05.

HQ: *Grants management information*: same address as **66.034**. Phone: (202) 564-9226, FAX (202)564-7739. **Internet:** "http://cfpub.epa.gov/care/".

66.036 CLEAN SCHOOL BUS USA ("CSBUSA")

Assistance: project grants (95 percent/2 years).

Purposes: to minimize children's exposure to diesel exhaust through necessary upgrades to diesel school bus fleets, through partnerships with educators, industry, transportation experts, public health officials, and community leaders. Projects involve: reducing school bus idling; retrofit of 1991-2004 model year buses with devices that reduce pollution; replacement of pre-1990 buses with new, clean-technology buses.

Eligible applicants/beneficiaries: local and tribal governments.

Range: to $750,000. **Average:** $200,000 to $300,000.

Activity: new program in FY 05.

HQ: OAR-EPA, 1200 Pennsylvania Ave. NW, Washington, DC 20460. Phone: (202)343-9541, FAX (202)343-2804. **Internet:** "www.epa.gov/cleanschoolbus".

66.110 HEALTHY COMMUNITIES GRANT PROGRAM

Assistance: project grants (95 percent/1-2 years).

Purposes: pursuant to CAA, CWA, Resource Conservation and Recovery Act (RCRA), TSCA, SDWA, FIFRA, National Environmental Education Act, Pollution Prevention Act (PPA), MPRSA, CERCLA, Indian Environmental General Assistance Program Act, and amendments, for projects only in the New England states that: are located in and directly benefit one or more EPA-designated "Target Investment Areas," "Environmental Justice Areas of Potential Concern," "Places with High Risks from Toxic Air Pollution," "Sensitive Populations," or "Urban Areas;" and, that will achieve measurable environmental and public health results as defined by EPA. Current program priorities include projects involving asthma, capacity building, healthy indoor/outdoor environments, healthy schools, preserving and restoring urban natural resources and open/green space, smart growth, and water quality monitoring or analyses. Projects may provide or support educational opportunities for students, interns, or citizens to learn more about science, biology, and water quality monitoring.

Eligible applicants/beneficiaries: for activities only within the New England states—local public, private, and quasi-public nonprofit institutions and organizations; tribal governments; K-12 schools or school districts; grass-roots and community-based organizations; IHEs with substantial community involvement.

Range/Average: N.A.

Activity: new program in 2005.

HQ: Region 1-EPA, 1 Congress St. - Ste.1100, Boston, MA 02114. **Phone:** (617)918-1797. **Internet:** "www.epa.gov/ne/eco/uep/grants.html". (Note: the field office serves as headquarters.)

66.111 REGIONAL ENVIRONMENTAL PRIORITY PROJECTS

Assistance: project grants (to 5 years).

Purposes: pursuant to CWA, FIFRA, CAA, SWDA, SDWA, and TSCA, for investigations, experiments, training, demonstrations, surveys, studies, and special purpose assistance to protect public health and prevent, reduce, and eliminate pollution—only in Iowa, Kansas, Missouri, and Nebraska. Projects may be single or multi-media, addressing places, sectors, or innovations, and focused on critical ecosystems, sensitive populations, or agriculture.

Eligible applicants/beneficiaries: for activities only within EPA Region 7—states, territories, possessions, tribes; IHEs, hospitals, laboratories; other public or private nonprofit organizations; profit groups; individuals.

Range/Average: N.A.

Activity: new program listing in 2005 (CFDA on-line version).

HQ: Region 7-EPA, 901 N, Fifth St., Kansas City, Kansas 66101. **Phone:** (913)551-7782, -7193; **FAX** (913)551-9782, -9183. **Internet:** "www.epa.gov/region07/economics/index.htm". (Note: the field office serves as headquarters.)

66.305 COMPLIANCE ASSISTANCE SUPPORT FOR SERVICES TO THE REGULATED COMMUNITY AND OTHER ASSISTANCE PROVIDERS ("Compliance Assistance Centers")

Assistance: project grants (to 100 percent/to 5 years).

Purposes: pursuant to SWDA as amended and RCRA, to develop projects to improve environmental compliance within identified commercial or industrial sectors. Funds may be used to create compliance assistance tools utilizing industry and commercial communication channels to deliver the assistance tools, including internet communications, toll-free telephone assistance lines, satellite training, other interactive technologies.

Eligible applicants/beneficiaries: nonprofit organizations, IHEs, and state, local, and tribal governments.

Range: $65,000 to $150,000 per year. **Average:** $90,000.

Activity: FY 05, 14 centers supported through 7 cooperative agreements.

HQ: OECA-EPA, 1200 Pennsylvania Ave. NW, Washington, DC 20460. **Phone:** Compliance Centers Team, Platform Development, U.S.-Mexico Border Environmental Issues Leads, (202)564-7076, FAX (202)564-0037; Industry Leads, (202)564-1459, FAX (202)564-0009; Chemical Manufacturing Center Lead, (202)564-7071, FAX (202)564-0037; Local Government Center Lead, (202)564-7049, FAX (202)564-0037; **Internet:** "www.epa.gov/compliance/assistance/centers/index.html"; "www.assistancecenters.net". (Note: no field offices for this program.)

66.306 ENVIRONMENTAL JUSTICE COLLABORATIVE PROBLEM-SOLVING COOPERATIVE AGREEMENT PROGRAM ("EJCPS")

Assistance: project grants (100 percent/3 years).

Purposes: pursuant to the CWA, SDWA, SWDA, CAA, TSCA, FIFRA, and MPRSA, for projects by affected groups demonstrating the utility of the Federal Interagency Working Group Model on Collaborative Problem-Solving, toward the solution of community environmental and public health issues. Funds may support such activities as: capacity-building; partnerships and collaborative involvement with industry and federal, state, and local governments, academia, and environmental organizations; establishing health clinics or medical screening programs or replacing diesel buses with buses using clean fuels; outreach and community education.

Eligible applicants/beneficiaries: incorporated community-based, grassroots, nonprofit organizations.

Range/Average: $100,000 for 3 years.

Activity: new program listing in 2004; 30 projects approved.

HQ: Director, Office of Environmental Justice (2201A), EPA, 1200 Pennsylvania Ave. NW, Washington, DC 20460. Phone: (202)564-2515; Environmental Justice Hotline (800)962-6215. **Internet:** "www.epa.gov/compliance/environmentaljustice/".

66.307 ENVIRONMENTAL JUSTICE TRAINING AND FELLOWSHIP ASSISTANCE ("EJTF")

Assistance: project grants (100 percent).

Purposes: pursuant to CWA, SDWA, SWDA, CAA, FIFRA, CERCLA, and amendments, for training and fellowship programs for occupational and professional development relating to environmental and public health issues, emphasizing environmental justice.

Eligible applicants/beneficiaries: states, territories, possessions, and public and private IHEs, hospitals, libraries, and other institutions.

Range/Average: N.A.

Activity: new program in FY 06 (CFDA on-line version); 10 awards anticipated.

HQ: *program information,* same address, web site as **66.306**. Phone: (202)564-2602, FAX (202)501-1162. *Grants management information:* same as in **66.034**. (Note: no field offices for this program.)

66.308 ENVIRONMENTAL JUSTICE RESEARCH ASSISTANCE ("EJRA")

Assistance: project grants (100 percent/1-5 years).

Purposes: pursuant to the CWA, SDWA, SWDA, CAA, TSCA, FIFRA, MPRSA, and CERCLA, for research projects addressing broad environmental and public health issues, emphasizing environmental justice—with "environment justice" defined as the fair treatment and meaningful involvement of all people regardless of race, color, national origin, or income, with respect to the development, implementation, and enforcement of environmental laws, regulations, and policies. Multi-media awards (citing two or more environmental statutes) are permitted.

Eligible applicants/beneficiaries: same as for **66.307**.

Range/Average: N.A.

Activity: new program in FY 06 (CFDA on-line version); 10 awards anticipated.

HQ: *program information,* same as **66.307**. (Note: no field offices for this program.)

66.309 SURVEYS, STUDIES, INVESTIGATIONS AND SPECIAL PURPOSE ACTIVITIES RELATING TO ENVIRONMENTAL JUSTICE ("EJSS")

Assistance: project grants (100 percent/1-5 years).

Purposes: pursuant to the CWA, SDWA, SWDA, CAA, TSCA, FIFRA, MPRSA, and CERCLA, for surveys, studies, investigations, and special activities addressing broad environmental and public health issues, emphasizing environmental justice—along lines similar to **66.308**.

Eligible applicants/beneficiaries: same as for **66.308**.

Range/Average: N.A.

Activity: new program in FY 06 (CFDA on-line version); 10 awards anticipated.

HQ: same as **66.308**. (Note: no field offices for this program.)

66.310 CAPACITY BUILDING GRANTS AND COOPERATIVE AGREEMENTS FOR COMPLIANCE ASSURANCE ACTIVITIES IN INDIAN COUNTRY AND OTHER TRIBAL AREAS
("Office of Enforcement and Compliance Assurance Tribal Resources")

Assistance: project grants (100 percent/multi-year).

Purposes: pursuant to CWA, FIFRA, CAA, SWDA, SDWA, TSCA, MPRSA, National Environmental Policy Act, and Indian Environmental General Assistance Program Act, to build and improve the capacity to foster environmental enforcement and compliance assurance activities in Indian country and other tribal areas including in Alaska. Eligible project activities include: inspections; assessment; surveys; performance measurement; data quality improvement; enforcement; training including through fellowships, scholarships, traineeships, conferences, and technical assistance; experiments and demonstrations; construction; dissemination and information exchange. Funds should support activities directly related to the National Tribal Compliance Assurance Priority and other specified priorities in Indian country.

Eligible applicants/beneficiaries: responsible tribal, federal, and state organizations; consortia.

Range: $5,000 to $100,000 per year.

Activity: new program listing in 2005 (CFDA on-line version). Not quantified specifically.

HQ: Office of Compliance, OECA-EPA, 1200 Pennsylvania Ave. NW, Washington, DC 20460. Phone: (202)564-2516, FAX (202)564-7083. **Internet:** "www.epa.gov/compliance/state/grants/index.html".

66.418 CONSTRUCTION GRANTS FOR WASTEWATER TREATMENT WORKS

Assistance: project grants (55-85 percent; insular areas, 100 percent).

Purposes: pursuant to CWA as amended, for construction of municipal wastewater treatment works, including privately owned individual systems, required to meet state or federal water quality standards. Projects may include industrial wastes, provided pretreatment or entry prevention into funded projects is included. Users must be charged.

Eligible applicants/beneficiaries: any municipal, intermunicipal, state, or interstate agency; Indian tribal governments. Also available to each U.S. territory and possession. (Currently, only DC, VI, and Outer Pacific Islands being newly funded; others apply to state revolving funds—see **66.458**.)

Range: $100,000 to $15,000,000 per fiscal year. **Average:** $7,550,000.

Activity: FY 05 estimate, 2 grants.

HQ: Municipal Assistance Branch (4204M), Municipal Support Division, Office of Wastewater Management, OW-EPA, 1200 Pennsylvania Ave. NW, Washington, DC 20460. Phone: (202)564-0648, FAX (202)501-2396. **Internet:** "www.epa.gov/owm.cwfinance/index.htm".

66.419 WATER POLLUTION CONTROL STATE AND INTERSTATE PROGRAM SUPPORT
("Section 106 Grants")

Assistance: formula grants (matching).

Purposes: pursuant to CWA as amended, for activities to prevent and abate surface- and groundwater pollution from point and nonpoint sources, including: planning, monitoring, assessments, permitting, studies, surveillance and enforcement, training, technical assistance, and public information; restoration of impaired watersheds. Funds may not be used for waste treatment plant construction, operation, or maintenance.

Eligible applicants/beneficiaries: state, interstate, tribal, and territorial agencies.

Range: $60,000 to $10,200,000 per fiscal year. **Average:** $5,630,000.

Activity: not quantified specifically.

HQ: State, Interstate and Tribal Coordinator, Office of Wastewater Management (4201), OW-EPA, 1200 Pennsylvania Ave. NW, Washington, DC 20460. Phone: (202)564-8831, FAX (202)501-2399. **Internet:** "www.epa.gov/owm".

66.424 SURVEYS, STUDIES, DEMONSTRATIONS AND SPECIAL PURPOSE GRANTS—SECTION 1442 OF THE SAFE DRINKING WATER ACT

Assistance: project grants.

Purposes: pursuant to SDWA Section 1442 as amended, to support research, studies, and demonstrations associated with source water and drinking water;

to develop and expand capabilities of pertinent programs. Priorities include: contaminants in drinking water; source water protection and treatment methods; measures to protect water quality in the distribution system and at the tap; tribal source water program support; tribal operator certification program; tribal capacity development; tribal administration of the Drinking Water Infrastructure Grants to identify health effects associated with drinking water contaminants.

Eligible applicants/beneficiaries: states, territories and possessions, tribes, IHEs, hospitals, laboratories, other public and private nonprofit institutions, and individuals.

Range: $10,000 to $1,800,000 per fiscal year. **Average:** $905,000.

Activity: FY 04, 4 grants.

HQ: *Program information,* Office of Groundwater and Drinking Water, OW-EPA (no address provided). Phone: (202)564-3817, FAX (202)564-3754; Immediate Office, (202)564-4633, FAX (202)564-0348. *Grants management information*: same as in **66.034**. **Internet:** "www.epa.gov/safewater".

66.432 STATE PUBLIC WATER SYSTEM SUPERVISION

Assistance: formula grants (75 percent).

Purposes: pursuant to the Public Health Service Act (PHSA), SDWA, and amendments, to develop and implement programs implementing public water system supervision adequate to enforce SDWA provisions, including program plan development, adoption of applicable regulations, data management, system inventories, public participation, technical assistance, laboratory certification, and enforcement.

Eligible applicants/beneficiaries: state agencies, territories and possessions, tribes treated as states.

Range: $124,000 to $6,198,000. **Average:** $1,724,000.

Activity: FY 04, 55 grants.

HQ: Office of Ground Water and Drinking Water (4604M), OW-EPA, Washington, DC 20460. Phone: (202)564-3829, FAX (202)564-3755. **Internet:** "www.epa.gov/safewater/pws/pwsgrant.html".

66.433 STATE UNDERGROUND WATER SOURCE PROTECTION

Assistance: formula grants (75 percent; tribes, 90 percent).

Purposes: pursuant to SDWA and amendments, to develop and implement underground injection control programs. Funds may be used for such purposes as state regulation review, plan development, data management, inventory of injection facilities, identification of aquifers, technical assistance, public participation, enforcement activities.

Eligible applicants/beneficiaries: states, tribes.

Range: $33,000 to $951,000. **Average:** $174,000.

Activity: FY 04, funding to 43 states and tribes with primary responsibility for 36 full and 7 partial programs.

HQ: Prevention Branch, Drinking Water Protection Division (4606M), Office of Ground Water and Drinking Water, OW-EPA, 1200 Pennsylvania Ave.

NW, Washington, DC 20460. Phone: (202)564-3868, FAX (202)564-3756. **Internet:** "www.epa.gov/OGWDW/Safewater/UIC.html".

66.436 SURVEYS, STUDIES, INVESTIGATIONS, DEMONSTRATIONS, AND TRAINING GRANTS AND COOPERATIVE AGREEMENTS—SECTION 104(B)(3) OF THE CLEAN WATER ACT

Assistance: project grants.

Purposes: pursuant to CWA Section 104(b)(3) as amended, for coordination and acceleration of research, investigations, experiments, training, demonstrations, surveys, and studies relating to the causes, effects including health and welfare effects, extent, prevention, reduction, and elimination of water pollution. Priorities include: water quality improvement, watersheds management, aquatic ecosystem restoration, pollutant trading, fish contamination and consumption, nonpoint source management, wetlands protection, coastal and estuarine management, treatment technologies, and environmental management systems. Project examples: watershed education program for broadcast meteorologists; atmospheric mercury deposition study; watershed protection and restoration guides.

Eligible applicants/beneficiaries: same as for **66.424**.

Range: $15,000 to $4,970,000 per fiscal year. **Average:** $2,493,000.

Activity: not quantified specifically.

HQ: same as **66.424** *and* phone: Office of Wetlands, Oceans and Watersheds, (202)566-1254; Office of Wastewater Management, (202)564-0672; Office of Science and Technology, (202)566-1453; Immediate Office, (202)566-4633. **Internet:** same as **66.419**.

66.437 LONG ISLAND SOUND PROGRAM ("Long Island Sound Study" - "LISS")

Assistance: project grants (50-95 percent).

Purposes: pursuant to CWA as amended by the Long Island Sound Restoration Act of 2000, to implement elements of the Long Island Sound Study (LISS) Comprehensive Conservation and Management Plan (CCMP), with special emphasis on implementation projects, research and planning, enforcement, and citizen involvement and education projects.

Eligible applicants/beneficiaries: state, interstate, and regional water control agencies and organizations.

Range: $20,000 to $600,000. **Average:** $310,000.

Activity: new program listing in 2004. FY 05 estimate, 5 awards.

HQ: Ocean and Coastal Protection Division, Office of Wetlands, Oceans and Watersheds, OW-EPA, 1301 Pennsylvania Ave. NW, Washington, DC 20004. Phone: (202)566-1256, FAX (202)566-1334. **Internet:** "www.longislandsoundstudy.net".

66.439 TARGETED WATERSHED GRANTS

Assistance: project grants (75 percent; tribes, to 100 percent).

Purposes: pursuant to CWA as amended, for watershed partnerships to develop innovative, community-based approaches aimed at preventing, reducing, or eliminating water pollution—involving local, state, tribal, and interstate agencies and other public or nonprofit organizations. Funds may be used for research, investigations, experiments, training, demonstrations, surveys, and studies.

Eligible applicants/beneficiaries: state, local, interstate, public agencies; private nonprofit institutions and organizations; tribal governments; territories, possessions; IHEs, individuals

Range: $300,000 to $1,300,000. **Average:** $800,000.

Activity: FY 05, 10-15 awards.

HQ: Office of Wetlands, Oceans, and Watersheds, OW-EPA, 1200 Pennsylvania Ave. NW - Rm.7136E, Washington, DC 20460. Phone: (202)566-1304, FAX (202)566-1326. **Internet:** "www.epa.gov/owow/watershed/initiative/".

66.454 WATER QUALITY MANAGEMENT PLANNING ("Section 205(j)(2)")

Assistance: formula grants (100 percent).

Purposes: pursuant to CWA as amended and Water Quality Act of 1987, for water quality management planning, with priority encouraged for watershed restoration. States must allocate 40 percent of funds to regional and interstate agencies. Program examples: performing waste load allocations; point and nonpoint source planning.

Eligible applicants/beneficiaries: state and territorial agencies.

Range: $100,000 to $1,500,000. **Average:** $800,000.

Activity: FY 04, 57 state and territorial grants awarded.

HQ: Assessment and Watershed Protection Division (4503T), OW-EPA, 1200 Pennsylvania Ave. NW, Washington, DC 20004. Phone: (301)694-7329. **Internet:** "www.epa.gov/ow/owow.htm".

66.456 NATIONAL ESTUARY PROGRAM ("NEP")

Assistance: project grants (50-75 percent/to 3 years).

Purposes: pursuant to CWA as amended, to develop and implement comprehensive conservation and management plans to protect and restore the coastal resources of 28 estuaries holding priority for funding. Funds must be used to develop master environmental plans based on relationships between pollutant loading and ecological impacts.

Eligible applicants/beneficiaries: within the priority geographic areas—regional, interstate, state water pollution control agencies; state coastal zone management agencies; public or private nonprofit organizations; individuals.

Range/Average: base grant of $512,000 for each NEP.

Activity: not quantified specifically.

HQ: Chief, Coastal Management Branch, Oceans and Coastal Protection Division, Office of Wetlands, Oceans, and Watersheds (4504T), OW-EPA, Washington, DC 20460. Phone: (202)566-1240, FAX (202)566-1366. **Internet:** "www.epa.gov/owow/estuaries/".

66.458 CAPITALIZATION GRANTS FOR CLEAN WATER STATE REVOLVING FUNDS
("CW State Revolving Fund")

Assistance: formula grants (80 percent).

Purposes: pursuant to CWA as amended and Water Quality Act of 1987, to establish state revolving loan funds to finance wastewater treatment facilities and other water quality management activities. Capitalization grants deposited in the revolving funds may be used to provide loans to finance construction of publicly owned wastewater treatment works, to execute a nonpoint source management program, and to develop and execute estuary conservation and management plans.

Eligible applicants: states, PR. (DC and territorial agencies use **66.418**.)

Eligible beneficiaries: loans from revolving funds—community, intermunicipal, interstate, and tribal agencies.

Range: $6,500,000 to $147,000,000. **Average:** $26,000,000.

Activity: annually, 51 grants.

HQ: State Revolving Fund Branch, Municipal Support Division (4204M), Office of Wastewater Management, OW-EPA, Washington, DC 20460. Phone: (202)564-0686, FAX (202)501-2403. **Internet:** same as **66.419**.

66.460 NONPOINT SOURCE IMPLEMENTATION GRANTS
("Section 319 Program")

Types: formula grants (60 percent; tribes, to 90 percent).

Purposes: pursuant to CWA, to implement EPA-approved nonpoint source management programs, with priority to watershed-based plans. Project examples: "best management practices" (BMP) installation for animal wastes and sediment, pesticide, and fertilizer control; design and implementation of BMP systems for stream, lake, and estuary watersheds; basin-wide landowner and homeowner education programs.

Eligible applicants: states, territories and possessions, tribes.

Eligible beneficiaries: state and local governments; interstate and intrastate agencies; public and private nonprofit organizations.

Range: states, territories, $541,000 to $10,701,000; tribes, $30,000 to $50,000; competitive grants, to $150,000. **Average:** states, territories, $3,577,000.

Activity: grants to all states and selected tribes.

HQ: Nonpoint Source Control Branch, Assessment and Watershed Protection Division, Office of Wetlands, Oceans and Watersheds (4503-T), OW-EPA, 1200 Pennsylvania Ave. NW, Washington, DC 20460. Phone: (202)566-1203, FAX (202)566-1545. **Internet:** "www.epa.gov/owow/nps".

66.461 REGIONAL WETLAND PROGRAM DEVELOPMENT GRANTS

Assistance: project grants (75 percent).

Purposes: pursuant to CWA as amended, to develop new or enhance existing regional wetlands protection management and restoration programs, with priority to: strengthening comprehensiveness of programs; monitoring and assessment; compensatory mitigation; protection of vulnerable wetlands and aquatic resources. Funds may support research, investigations, experiments, training, demonstrations, surveys, and studies—relating to the causes, effects, extent, prevention, reduction and elimination of water pollution.

Eligible applicants/beneficiaries: appropriate state, interstate, and local agencies—including those involved with wetlands or water quality regulation, planning offices, wild and scenic rivers, fish and wildlife, agriculture and transportation departments, coastal zone management, similar functions; inter-tribal consortia.

Range: $11,000 to $496,000. **Average:** $254,000.

Activity: not quantified specifically.

HQ: Wetlands Division, Office of Wetlands, Oceans and Watersheds (4502T), OW-EPA, 1200 Pennsylvania Ave. NW, Washington, DC 20460. Phone: (202)566-1378, FAX (202)566-1375. **Internet:** "www.epa.gov/owow/wetlands/initiative/#financial/".

66.462 NATIONAL WETLAND PROGRAM DEVELOPMENT GRANTS

Assistance: project grants (75 percent).

Purposes: pursuant to CWA as amended, for comprehensive national wetlands program development by promoting the coordination and acceleration of research, investigations, experiments, training, and studies—relating to the causes, effects, extent, prevention, reduction and elimination of water pollution. Projects also may involve such activities as training and information dissemination.

Eligible applicants/beneficiaries: nonprofit, nongovernmental capable of advancing programs on a national basis; interstate and intertribal agencies.

Range: $10,000 to $140,000. **Average:** $75,000.

Activity: new program in FY 05.

HQ: same address, web site as **66.461**. Phone: (202)566-1383, FAX (202)566-1375.

66.463 WATER QUALITY COOPERATIVE AGREEMENTS

Assistance: project grants.

Purposes: pursuant to CWA as amended, to develop, implement, and demonstrate innovative approaches relating to the causes, effects, extent, prevention, reduction, and elimination of water pollution, including watershed approaches for combined sewer overflow, sanitary sewer overflows, and storm water discharge problems, pretreatment and sludge program activities, alternative ways to measure the effectiveness of point source programs, trading, water efficiency, asset management, and sustainable infrastructure. Projects should promote the coordination and acceleration of research, investigations, experiments, training, and studies—relating to the causes, effects, extent, prevention, reduction and elimination of water pollution. In most EPA regions, funds also may be used for internships to high school students working at wastewater treatment plants, under the Youth and the Environment Program.

Eligible applicants/beneficiaries: state, interstate agencies; tribes; IHEs; individuals; other public or nonprofit organizations.

Range $10,000 to $300,000. **Average:** EPA HQ awards, $100,000; regional awards, $120,000.

Activity: not quantified specifically.

HQ: Office of Wastewater Management (4204M), OW-EPA, 1200 Pennsylvania Ave NW - Rm.7324J, Washington, DC 20460. Phone: (202)564-0672, FAX (202)501-2397. **Internet:** same as **66.419**.

66.466 CHESAPEAKE BAY PROGRAM

Assistance: project grants (50-95 percent).

Purposes: pursuant to CWA, for research, experiments, investigations, training, demonstrations, surveys, or studies related to reducing pollution and improving the quality of living resources in the Chesapeake Bay; for the implementation of Chesapeake Bay interstate management programs; for small watershed grants to local organizations to build citizen-based stewardship. Project examples: nonpoint source implementation programs; biological nutrient removal; living resources restoration studies and surveys; mainstem monitoring.

Eligible applicants/beneficiaries: within the Chesapeake Bay basin—state and local governments, interstate agencies, IHEs, other nonprofit organizations, individuals.

Range: $8,200 to $2,800,000. **Average:** $1,404,000.

Activity: FY 05 awards, 13 grants.

HQ: Office of Water (4101M), EPA, 1200 Pennsylvania Ave. NW, Washington, DC 20460. Phone: (202)546-4633. **Internet:** "www.epa.gov/region03-chesapeake".

66.467 WASTEWATER OPERATOR TRAINING GRANT PROGRAM (TECHNICAL ASSISTANCE)

Assistance: project grants (75 percent/to 3 years).

Purposes: pursuant to the Federal Water Pollution Control Act as amended, to provide on-site technical assistance to operations and maintenance (O&M) personnel at publicly owned wastewater treatment works, as well as classroom training.

Eligible applicants/beneficiaries: state agencies; possessions, territories, and tribes; state-designated nonprofit agencies.

Range: $14,000 to $71,000. **Average:** $30,000.

Activity: FY 04, 700 small facilities assisted.

HQ: same address/phone as **66.418**. **Internet:** "www.epa.gov/owm/mab/smcomm/104g/index.htm".

66.468 CAPITALIZATION GRANTS FOR DRINKING WATER STATE REVOLVING FUND
("Drinking Water State Revolving Fund" - "DWSRF")

Assistance: formula grants (80 percent).

Purposes: pursuant to SDWA Amendments of 1966, to capitalize DWSRFs to finance infrastructure needed to achieve and maintain compliance with SDWA requirements, through loans or other assistance; to establish new programs to prevent contamination through source water protection and enhanced water systems management.

Eligible applicants: capitalization grants—states, PR. Direct grants—DC, territories, tribes.

Eligible beneficiaries: loans—public, private, or nonprofit community drinking water systems.

Range: $14,000 (for tribes) to $84,848,000 (for states). **Average:** states, $46,567,000; tribes, $330,000; territories, $685,000.

Activity: DWSRFs established in all states and PR. FY 04, states made 633 loans; 4 awards to territories, 38 awards to tribes.

HQ: Infrastructure Branch (4606M), Drinking Water Protection Division, Office of Groundwater and Drinking Water, OW-EPA, 1200 Pennsylvania Ave. NW, Washington, DC 20460. Phone: (202)564-3848, FAX (202)564-1836. **Internet:** "www.epa.gov/safewater/dwsrf.html".

66.469 GREAT LAKES PROGRAM

Assistance: project grants (65-100 percent/1-2 years); use of property, facilities, and equipment; technical information.

Purposes: pursuant to CWA, to restore and maintain the chemical, physical, and biological integrity of the Great Lakes Basin Ecosystem. Funds may be used for such activities as surveys, research, experiments, training, studies, and demonstrations relating to: contaminated sediment remediation; pollution prevention, reduction, or elimination; habitat protection and restoration; invasive aquatic and terrestrial species, emphasizing prevention; and, similar efforts. Great Lakes Legacy Act projects, requiring a 35 percent match, entail cooperative agreements for contaminant remediation.

Eligible applicants/beneficiaries: state water pollution control agencies; interstate and other public and private nonprofit agencies; institutions; organizations; individuals.

Range: $4,000 to $700,000. **Average:** $352,000.

Activity: FY 05 estimate, 75 awards.

HQ: Great Lakes National Program Office (G-17J), OW-EPA, 77 W. Jackson Blvd., Chicago, IL 60604-3590. Phone: (312)886-4013. **Internet:** "www.epa.gov/glnpo/fund". (Note: no other field offices for this program.)

66.471 STATE GRANTS TO REIMBURSE OPERATORS OF SMALL WATER SYSTEMS FOR TRAINING AND CERTIFICATION GRANTS ("Operator Certification Expense Reimbursement Grants")

Assistance: formula grants (80-100 percent/2 years).

Purposes: pursuant to SDWA Amendments, to reimburse operators of community and nontransient noncommunity water systems serving 3,300 or fewer persons—for costs of training and certification needed to meet EPA guidelines.

Eligible applicants: states, PR, and territories.

Eligible beneficiaries: small systems operators, tribes, Alaska native villages.

Range: $14,000 to $9,643,000. **Average:** $4,829,000.

Activity: to date, all states, PR, Northern Marianas, Guam funded.

HQ: Protection Branch, same address as **66.433**. Phone: (202)564-3836, FAX (202)564-3755. **Internet:** "www.epa.gov/safewater/opcert/opcert.htm".

66.472 BEACH MONITORING AND NOTIFICATION PROGRAM IMPLEMENTATION GRANTS

Assistance: project grants.

Purposes: pursuant to CWA as amended and Beaches Environmental Assessment and Coastal Health Act of 2000, to develop and implement water quality monitoring and public notification programs for coastal recreation waters adjacent to beaches or similar points of public access—including developing protocols, public outreach and education to users.

Eligible applicants/beneficiaries: coastal and Great Lakes states, territories, tribes. Local governments may receive grants after the first year of program operation.

Range: $150,000 to $530,000. **Average:** $340,000.

Activity: not quantified specifically.

HQ: OW-EPA (4305T), 1200 Pennsylvania Ave. NW, Washington, DC 20460. Phone: (202)566-0399, FAX (202)566-0409. **Internet:** "www.epa.gov/waterscience/beaches".

66.473 DIRECT IMPLEMENTATION TRIBAL COOPERATIVE AGREEMENTS ("DITCA")

Assistance: project grants (100 percent/1-3 years).

Purposes: to build tribal capacity to carry out EPA-approved environmental programs for tribes, including such activities as developing protocols for interfacing inspections, permit and enforcement actions, training tribal employees to receive federal credentials.

Eligible applicants/beneficiaries: tribes and inter-tribal consortia.

Range: $10,000 to $100,000. **Average:** $55,000.

Activity: FY 05 estimate, 6 awards.

HQ: *program information:* American Indian Environmental Office (4104M), OW-EPA, 1200 Pennsylvania Ave. NW, Washington, DC 20460. Phone: (202)564-0289, FAX (202)564-0298. *Grants management information,* same as in **66.034**. Phone: (202)564-5084, FAX (202)565-2467. **Internet:** "www.epa.gov/indian/index.htm". (Note: no field offices for this program.)

66.474 WATER PROTECTION GRANTS TO THE STATES

Assistance: formula grants (from 1 year).

Purposes: pursuant to SDWA and Department of Defense and Emergency Supplemental Appropriations for Recovery from and Response to Terrorist Acts on the Unites States Act of 2002, for coordination of protection activities pertaining to critical water infrastructure, including work with water utilities and local, state, and federal agencies. Funded activities may include vulnerability assessments and related security enhancements, communications improvement, duty officer programs, toll-free numbers, emergency response and recovery planning, technical assistance, training, and education.

Eligible applicants/beneficiaries: states, tribes, territories, possessions.

Range: $17,000 to $272,000. **Average:** $144,000.

Activity: not quantified specifically.

HQ: Water Security Division (4601M), OW-EPA, 1200 Pennsylvania Ave. NW, Washington, DC 20460. Phone: (202)564-3824, FAX (202)564-3755. **Internet:** "http://cfpub.epa.gov/safewater/watersecurity/financeassist.cfm".

66.475 GULF OF MEXICO PROGRAM

Assistance: project grants.

Purposes: pursuant to CWA, to expand and strengthen cooperative efforts to restore and protect the health and productivity of the Gulf of Mexico and its region—including activities in the Mississippi River Basin designed to reduce Gulf hypoxia. Funded activities may include surveys, studies, investigations, research, and demonstrations that are approved by the Gulf of Mexico Program Office. Project examples include: implementation of restoration actions for impaired coastal segments; shellfish habitat restoration; water quality monitoring; characterization of mercury data.

Eligible applicants/beneficiaries: state and local governments, interstate agencies, tribes, IHEs, individuals, and other public or nonprofit organizations.

Range: $5,000 to $225,000. **Average:** $115,000.

Activity: FY 04, 25 agreements funded.

HQ: same address/phone as **66.466**. **Internet:** "www.epa.gov/gmpo/".

66.478 WATER SECURITY TRAINING AND TECHNICAL ASSISTANCE

Assistance: project grants.

Purposes: pursuant to SDWA as amended, Public Health Security and Bioterrorism Preparedness and Response Act of 2002, and Department of Defense and Emergency Supplemental Appropriations for Recovery from and Response to Terrorist Attacks on the United States Act of 2002, to improve drinking water system security through training and technical assistance for water utilities, provided by eligible nonprofit organizations. Program focus is helping states, tribes, and local authorities in completing vulnerability assessments, emergency response plans, security enhancements.

Eligible applicants/beneficiaries: capable public and private nonprofit organizations.

Range: $20,000 to $850,000. **Average:** $435,000.

Activity: FY 03, 5 grants for systems serving populations under 50,000; 2 grants estimated for systems serving populations between 50,000 and 100,000. FY 04, continuation grants issued.

HQ: same as **66.474**.

66.479 WETLAND PROGRAM GRANTS—STATE/TRIBAL ENVIRONMENTAL OUTCOME WETLAND DEMONSTRATION PROGRAM

Assistance: project grants (75 percent).

Purposes: pursuant to CWA as amended, for projects proposing to demonstrate the extent to which the implementation of both regulatory and nonregulatory wetland programs result in positive environmental outcomes—in particular, no net loss, net gain, and protection of vulnerable wetlands. Projects may involve the coordination and acceleration of research, investigations, experiments, training, surveys, and studies relating to the causes, effects, extent, prevention, reduction, and elimination of water pollution.

Eligible applicants/beneficiaries: state and tribal wetland agencies.

Range: $200,000 to $300,000. **Average:** $250,000.

Activity: new program in FY 05.

HQ: same address/phone as **66.462**. **Internet:** "www.epa.gov/owow/wetlands/grantpilot/".

66.480 ASSESSMENT AND WATERSHED PROTECTION PROGRAM GRANTS

Assistance: project grants (to 5 years).

Purposes: pursuant to CWA, to coordinate and accelerate watershed research, investigations, experiments, training, demonstrations surveys, and studies relating to the causes, effects, extent, prevention, reduction, and elimination of water pollution. Current program priorities include: Total Maximum Daily Load (TMDL) technical conference; advancing the TMDL program nationally; TMDL technical support.

Eligible applicants/beneficiaries: state, local governments; tribes; territories and possessions; interstate or intertribal consortia; public or private nonprofit, nongovernmental organizations; individuals.

Range: $1,000 to $500,000. **Average:** $251,000.

Activity: new program listing in 2005. FY 04, 22 pre-proposals funded, involving watershed planning tools and training.

HQ: *program information,* OWOW-EPA, (no address provided). Phone: (202) 566-1254; Assessment and Watershed Protection Division, (202)566-1206. *Grants management information:* same as in **66.424**. **Internet:** "www.epa.gov/owow/funding.html".

66.481 LAKE CHAMPLAIN BASIN PROGRAM

Assistance: project grants (75 percent).

Purposes: pursuant to CWA as amended, to assist the states of New York and Vermont in protecting and preserving the Lake Champlain ecosystem, through implementation of elements of the "Lake Champlain Basin Management Plan, Opportunities for Action." Funds may be used to assist research, surveys, studies, modeling, technical, field, restoration, and other supporting work.

Eligible applicants/beneficiaries: state, interstate, and regional water pollution control agencies; public or nonprofit agencies and organizations.

(Awards are made in consultation with the Lake Champlain Program Steering Committee.)

Range: $75,000 to $1,199,000. **Average:** $637,000.

Activity: new program listing in 2005. (Program began in 1991; awards are not quantified specifically.)

HQ: New England Regional Office, EPA, 1 Congress St. - Ste.1100-CWN, Boston, MA 02114-2023. Phone: (617)918-1606. *Or,* Region 2 Office, EPA, 290 Broadway - 24th floor, New York, NY 10007-1866. Phone: (212)637-3779, FAX (212)637-3889. **Internet:** "www.epa.gov/NE/eco/lakechamplain/index.html". (Note: the field offices serve as headquarters for this program.)

66.508 SENIOR ENVIRONMENTAL EMPLOYMENT PROGRAM ("SEE")

Assistance: project grants (100 percent/1-3 years).

Purposes: pursuant to the Environmental Programs Assistance Act of 1984, to employ older Americans in temporary full- or part-time jobs to provide technical assistance in pollution prevention, abatement, and control projects. Funded project examples: nonagricultural pesticide surveys; monitoring asbestos compliance in schools; research, general administrative, and clerical tasks; review and monitoring of the import car program.

Eligible applicants: nonprofit organizations designated by DOL under the Older Americans Act of 1965.

Eligible beneficiaries: individuals age 55 or older.

Range: $2,900 to $2,291,000. **Average:** $185,000.

Activity: FY 05 estimate, 350 cooperative agreements.

HQ: Director, Customer Services Support Center (3661A), Office of Administration and Resources Management, EPA, 1200 Pennsylvania Ave. NW, Washington, DC 20460. Phone: (202)564-3182, FAX (202)564-0356; Director, SEE Program, (202)564-0410, (202)564-0735. **Internet:** "www.epa.gov/epahrist/see/brochure". (Note: no field offices for this program.)

66.509 SCIENCE TO ACHIEVE RESULTS (STAR) RESEARCH PROGRAM ("STAR Program")

Assistance: project grants (2-5 years).

Purposes: pursuant to CAA, CWA, SWDA, SDWA, FIFRA, and TSCA, for research: to determine the environmental and human health effects of air and water quality, hazardous waste, toxic substances, and pesticides; to identify, develop, and demonstrate effective pollution control techniques; to explore and develop strategies and mechanisms for use by those in economic, social, governmental, and environmental systems in decision-making. Support may be provided for environmental research centers. Awards are made only in response to requests for competitive proposals; unsolicited proposals are not accepted.

Eligible applicants/beneficiaries: U.S. IHEs and nonprofit organizations; state, local, tribal governments.

Range: new grants, $150,000 to $950,000; centers, to $1,500,000. **Average:** new grants, $400,000.

Activity: FY 04, 82 grants.

HQ: Office of Research and Development-EPA (no additional address provided). *Grants management information*: Grants Administration Division (3903R), EPA, 1200 Pennsylvania Ave. NW, Washington, DC 20460. Phone: *eligibility questions,* (202)343-9862, FAX (202)233-0680. **Internet:** "www.epa.gov.ncer".

66.510 SURVEYS, STUDIES, INVESTIGATIONS AND SPECIAL PURPOSE GRANTS WITHIN THE OFFICE OF RESEARCH AND DEVELOPMENT

Assistance: project grants (100 percent/to 5 years).

Purposes: pursuant to CAA, CWA, SWDA, RCRA, SDWA, FIFRA, TSCA, amendments, and MPRSA, to determine the environmental effects of air quality, drinking water, water quality, hazardous waste, toxic substances, and pesticides; to identify, develop, and demonstrate effective pollution control techniques. Generally, awards are made only in response to requests for competitive proposals, and unsolicited proposals are not funded.

Eligible applicants/beneficiaries: state, local, tribal governments and agencies; territories, possessions; IHEs, hospitals, laboratories, nonprofit organizations; individuals.

Range: $5,000 to $500,000. **Average:** $100,000.

Activity: annually, 50 awards.

HQ: Office of Research and Development-EPA, 1200 Pennsylvania Ave. NW, Washington, DC 20460. Phone: *applications, procedures information,* (202) 564-4763, FAX (202)565-2903. **Internet:** "www.epa.gov/ord/htm/grantopportunity.htm".

66.511 OFFICE OF RESEARCH AND DEVELOPMENT CONSOLIDATED RESEARCH/TRAINING

Assistance: project grants (100 percent/to 5 years).

Purposes: pursuant to CAA, CWA, SWDA, RCRA, SDWA, FIFRA, TSCA, CERCLA, amendments, and MPRSA, for research and engineering to determine the environmental effects of air quality, drinking water, water quality, hazardous waste, toxic substances, and pesticides; to identify, develop, and demonstrate effective pollution control techniques; to perform risk assessments to characterize the potential adverse health effects of human exposures to environmental hazards—in broad areas such as environmental chemistry and physics, environmental engineering, health and ecological effects of pollution, environmental economics and decision sciences. Generally, unsolicited proposals are not funded.

Eligible applicants/beneficiaries: same as for **66.509**.

Range: $75,000 to $950,000. **Average:** $250,000.

Activity: annually, 125 awards.

HQ: same as **66.510**.

66.512 REGIONAL ENVIRONMENTAL MONITORING AND ASSESSMENT PROGRAM (REMAP) RESEARCH PROJECTS ("REMAP Research Projects")

Assistance: project grants (to five years).

Purposes: pursuant to the Clean Water Act, Section 104, as amended, for statistical monitoring of the conditions of national ecological resources, toward the testing of the applicability of EMAP's probalistic approach to answer questions about ecological conditions at regional and local levels—resulting in improved monitoring tools and probability-based data for resolving issues.

Eligible applicants/beneficiaries: states, territories, possessions, local and tribal governments; IHEs, hospitals, other nonprofit organizations; consortia.

Range: $10,000 to $278,000 annually, per region.

Activity: new program listing in 2005. Not quantified specifically.

HQ: Mid-Continent Ecology Division, Office of Research and Development-EPA, 6201 Congdon Blvd., Duluth, MN 55804. Phone: *applications, procedures information,* (218)529-5198; *administrative questions,* (218)529-5016. **Internet:** "www.epa.gov/emap/remap/".

66.513 GREATER RESEARCH OPPORTUNITIES FELLOWSHIP PROGRAM

Assistance: project grants (100 percent).

Purposes: pursuant to CAA, CWA, SWDA, SDWA, TSCA, and FIFRA, to provide graduate and undergraduate fellowships in fields of study related to the environment, including environmental engineering, atmospheric sciences, geology, economics, geography, urban/regional planning, biochemistry, biological sciences, genetics, public health, ecological sciences, and related fields—to strengthen the research capacity especially of IHEs that receive limited funding in the field, including particularly institutions with substantial minority enrollment. Two years of study in specific disciplines may be supported for undergraduates and master's students; doctoral candidates, for three years. Awards are competitive.

Eligible applicants/beneficiaries: U.S. citizens and lawfully admitted permanent residents demonstrating high scientific ability.

Range: undergraduates, $12,000 to $17,000 annually; graduates, $26,000 to $37,000. **Average:** undergraduates, $15,000; graduates, $30,000.

Activity: new program listing in 2004. Annually, 35 new fellowships awards.

HQ: *Grants management information:* same address, web site as **66.509**. Phone: *graduate fellowships information,* (202)343-9737, FAX (202)343-0680; *undergraduate fellowships information,* (202)343-9741, FAX (202) 343-0680. (Note: no field offices for this program.)

66.514 SCIENCE TO ACHIEVE RESULTS (STAR) FELLOWSHIP PROGRAM ("STAR Program")

Assistance: project grants (100 percent).

Purposes: pursuant to CAA, CWA, SWDA, SDWA, TSCA, and FIFRA, to provide graduate fellowships in the fields of study cited under **66.514**. Two years of study may be supported for master's students; doctoral candidates, for three years. Awards are competitive.

Eligible applicants/beneficiaries: same as for **66.513**.

Range: $26,000 to $37,000 annually. **Average:** $30,000.

Activity: new program listing in 2004. FY 04, 124 awards.

HQ: same as **66.513**. (Note: no field offices for this program.)

66.515 GREATER OPPORTUNITIES RESEARCH PROGRAM

Assistance: project grants (2-5 years).

Purposes: pursuant to CAA, CWA, SWDA, RCRA, SDWA, TSCA, and FIFRA, to stimulate and nurture environmental and educational opportunities at IHEs that receive limited funding in environmental fields, particularly institutions with substantial minority enrollment. Projects are invited for research concerning the applications of nanotechnology in environmentally benign manufacturing and processing, monitoring devices and sensors, and treatment and remediation technology. Generally, awards are made only in response to requests for competitive proposals; unsolicited proposals are not funded.

Eligible beneficiaries/beneficiaries: four-year IHEs as described under "Purposes".

Range: $300,000 to $450,000. **Average:** $325,000.

Activity: new program listing in 2004. FY 04, 6 awards.

HQ: same address, web site as **66.509**. Phone: (202)343-9858, FAX (202)233-0680.

66.516 P3 AWARD: NATIONAL STUDENT DESIGN COMPETITION FOR SUSTAINABILITY

Assistance: project grants.

Purposes: pursuant to CAA, CWA, SWDA, SDWA, TSCA, and FIFRA, for design projects in wide-ranging categories, conducted by interdisciplinary student teams to: define a technical challenge to environmental sustainability; discuss the relationship of the challenge to people, prosperity, and the planet; and, develop a design approach to address the challenge. Categories may include such topics as water quality and quantity, protection of ecosystem health, green chemistry and engineering, biotechnology, energy production and distribution, conservation of materials and energy, product design, mobility, information technology, and delivery of resources.

Eligible applicants/beneficiaries: teams of graduate and undergraduate students attending U.S. IHEs. (*For additional details, see request for applications at web site*: "http://es.epa.gov.ncer/rfa/".)

Range: $7,000 to $10,000. **Average:** $10,000.

Activity: new program in FY 04. FY 04, 65 competitive grants.

HQ: same address, web site as **66.509**. Phone: (202)343-9689, FAX (202)233-0680.

66.518 STATE SENIOR ENVIRONMENTAL EMPLOYMENT PROGRAM ("SSEE")

Assistance: project grants (100 percent/1-3 years).

Purposes: pursuant to the Environmental Programs Assistance Act of 1984, for states to employ Americans, age 55 or older, in temporary full- or part-time positions to provide technical assistance to federal, state, and local environmental agencies for projects involving pollution prevention, abatement, and control—ranging from inspections of large capacity cesspools to clerical work for environmental staff offices.

Eligible applicants: private, nonprofit organizations designated by the DOL secretary under OAA.

Eligible beneficiaries: state environmental agencies; individuals age 55 or older.

Range/Average: $50,000.

Activity: new program listing in 2005. FY 04, 1 cooperative agreement (with the state of Hawaii).

HQ: same as **66.508**. (Note: no field offices for this program.)

66.600 ENVIRONMENTAL PROTECTION CONSOLIDATED GRANTS—PROGRAM SUPPORT

Assistance: project grants.

Purposes: pursuant to CAA, CWA, SWDA, RCRA, SDWA, FIFRA, SWDA, MPRSA, CERCLA, amendments, and other acts, to provide an alternative funding mechanism to territories and possessions within the purview of EPA Regions 2 and 9 to develop an integrated approach to pollution control programs, by consolidating activities funded under such programs as **66.001, 66.418, 66.419, 66.432, 66.433, 66.454, 66.468, 66.473, 66.700, 66.801**. Applicants eligible for two or more of the programs may consolidate applications into one, and receive a single total award. Funding for this program is the aggregate total of the programs that may be consolidated; it is not appropriated separately.

Eligible applicants/beneficiaries: agencies in territories and possessions within the purview of EPA Regions 2 and 9.

Range/Average: N.A.

Activity: FY 05, consolidated awards to 3 Samoa, Northern Marianas, and Guam.

HQ: *for information on programs of interest, contact appropriate HQ or field offices for individual programs.* **Internet:** Region 2, "www.epa.gov.region2/"; Region 9, "www.epa.gov/region9/".

66.604 ENVIRONMENTAL JUSTICE SMALL GRANT PROGRAM ("EJCGP")

Assistance: project grants (100 percent/1 year).

Purposes: pursuant to pursuant to CWA, SDWA, SWDA, CAA, TSCA, FIFRA, MPRSA, AND CERCLA, to design, demonstrate, or disseminate practices, methods, or techniques related to environmental justice, including multi-media projects. Funding is available for activities that examine issues related to a community's exposure to multiple environmental harms and risks, extending to socio-economic, institutional, and public policy issues and the natural sciences. Research training may be supported. Ineligible uses of funds include: research related only to contamination from petroleum products unless other issues also are involved; organizational support; capacity building; program development; any construction activities; lobbying; underwriting legal actions.

Eligible applicants/beneficiaries: only affected nonprofit, incorporated community-based organizations unaffiliated with larger national, state, or regional organizations.

Range/Average: $25,000.

Activity: FY 05, 30 awards.

HQ: Office of Environmental Justice (2201A), EPA, 1200 Pennsylvania Ave. NW, Washington, DC 20460. Phone: (202)564-2515; Environmental Justice Hotline, (800)962-6215. **Internet:** "www.epa.gov/compliance/environmentaljustice/grants".

66.605 PERFORMANCE PARTNERSHIP GRANTS ("PPGs")

Assistance: project grants.

Purposes: to provide an alternative assistance delivery mechanism giving grant recipients greater flexibility in addressing environmental priorities; to improve environmental performance; to achieve savings in administrative costs; and, to strengthen partnerships between EPA and grant recipients. For application and administrative purposes, recipients may combine two or more grant programs specifically identified by EPA. Funding for this program is included in the grant programs that may be involved; it is not appropriated separately.

Eligible applicants/beneficiaries: states, interstate agencies; territories; tribes—eligible to combine two or more of 20 specific EPA categorical grant programs.

Range/Average: N.A.

Activity: FY 04, 125 new and continuation grants, including 38 to state environmental agencies, 28 to state agricultural agencies, and 58 to tribal agencies.

HQ: Office of Congressional and Intergovernmental Relations (1306A), Office of the Administrator-EPA, 1200 Pennsylvania Ave. NW, Washington DC 20460. Phone: Program Manager, (202)564-3792, FAX (202)501-1545; *tribes,* Office of Water, American Indian Environmental Office, (202)564-0303, FAX (202)564-0298.

Internet: "www.epa.gov/ocir".

66.606 SURVEYS, STUDIES, INVESTIGATIONS AND SPECIAL PURPOSE GRANTS

Assistance: project grants (to 5 years).

Purposes: pursuant to CAA, CWA, SWDA, SDWA, TSCA, FSRIA, MPRSA, CERCLA, National Environmental Policy Act, and Indian Environmental General Assistance Program Act, for Congressionally earmarked surveys, studies, investigations, training, demonstrations, technical assistance, and special purpose assistance associated with air quality, acid deposition, drinking water quality, water quality, hazardous waste, toxic substances, and pesticides, including multimedia projects; to develop and demonstrate pollution control techniques; to evaluate the economic and social consequences of alternative mechanisms.

Eligible applicants/beneficiaries: states, tribes, territories, possessions; IHEs, hospitals, laboratories, other public or private nonprofit institutions; individuals.

Range/Average: N.A.

Activity: N.A.

HQ: *grants management information*: same as in **66.034**. Phone: *program information,* Office of Water, (202)564-4633; Office of Environmental Information, (202)564-1024. **Internet:** same as **66.001**.

66.608 ENVIRONMENTAL INFORMATION EXCHANGE NETWORK GRANT PROGRAM

Assistance: project grants (100 percent/2-3 years).

Purposes: to develop a nationwide Environmental Information Exchange Network, an internet- and standards-based information network—facilitating electronic reporting, exchange, and integration of environmental data from many sources, concerning the natural environment and related human health issues. Funds support development of: related information technology infrastructure and management capabilities; exchanging data with EPA and other users, through the development of data standards and formats; collaborative innovative projects address the business needs of government agencies at all levels.

Eligible applicants/beneficiaries: states, territories and possessions, tribes and tribal consortia; authorized regional air pollution control agencies

Range: $75,000 to $500,000 for two years. **Average:** $300,000.

Activity: currently, 9 operational state nodes, 26 nodes under development; all states and 30 tribes engaged at some level.

HQ: Program Manager, Office of Information Collection, Office of Environmental Information (2823T), EPA, 1200 Pennsylvania Ave. NW, Washington, DC 20460. Phone: (202)566-1679, -0196, FAX (202)566-1684, -1624. **Internet:** "www.epa.gov/oei". (Note: no field offices for this program.)

66.609 PROTECTION OF CHILDREN AND OLDER ADULTS (ELDERLY) FROM ENVIRONMENTAL HEALTH RISKS

Assistance: project grants (cost sharing/to 5 years).

Purposes: pursuant to CAA, CWA, SDWA, TSCA, SWDA, FIFRA, MPRSA, CERCLA, and National Environmental Policy Act, to reduce environmental health threats to children or the elderly, through such activities as: supporting efforts to create health school environments; building capacity to address childhood asthma and other children's environmental health issues, as well as to reduce environmental health hazards affecting older persons; implementing a National Agenda for the Environment and the Aging to help protect the health of older persons; civic engagement in pertinent activities and projects; related international efforts; public outreach and communications.

Eligible applicants/beneficiaries: states and state agencies, territories and possessions, tribes, IHEs, hospitals, laboratories, public and private non-profit organizations.

Range: $5,000 to $150,000. **Average:** aging initiatives, $23,000; children, $145,000.

Activity: FY 05, 19 awards to aging initiatives, 7 awards for child-related projects.

HQ: Office of Children's Health Protection (1107A), Office of the Administrator-EPA, 1200 1200 Pennsylvania Ave. NW, Washington, DC 20460. Phone: FAX (202)564-2763; Children's Health, (202)564-2192; Aging Initiative, (202)564-3651. **Internet:** "www.epa.gov/children". (Note: no field offices for this program.)

66.610 SURVEYS, STUDIES, INVESTIGATIONS AND SPECIAL PURPOSE GRANTS WITHIN THE OFFICE OF THE ADMINISTRATOR

Assistance: project grants (cost sharing/to 5 years).

Purposes: pursuant to CAA, CWA, SDWA, TSCA, SWDA, FIFRA, MPRSA, CERCLA, and National Environmental Policy Act, for surveys, studies, investigations, and special purpose assistance associated with air quality, acid deposition, drinking water quality, hazardous waste, toxic substances, and pesticides; to identify, develop and demonstrate necessary pollution control techniques; to evaluate the economic and social consequences of alternative strategies and mechanisms. Current funding priorities include: providing environmental health information and analysis to state legislatures; building state capacity to reduce environmental hazards affecting health and the environment; supporting environmental education training.

Eligible applicants/beneficiaries: same as for **66.609**.

Range: $500 to $500,000. **Average:** $150,000.

Activity: not quantified specifically.

HQ: *grants management information*: same as in **66.034**. *Program information*, Office of the Administrator-EPA. Phone: (202)564-1347, FAX (202)564-2733. **Internet:** "www.epa.gov/adminweb". (Note: no field offices for this program.)

66.611 ENVIRONMENTAL POLICY AND INNOVATION GRANTS

Assistance: project grants (cost sharing/to 5 years).

Purposes: pursuant to CAA, CWA, SDWA, TSCA, SWDA, FIFRA, and CERCLA, for analyses, studies, evaluations, and conferences leading to reduced pollutants generated and to conservation of natural resources; to improve economic information and analytic methods to support studies, surveys, analyses, evaluations, conferences, workshops, and demonstration projects relating to the benefits, costs, and impacts of environmental programs, as well as of incentive-based and voluntary environmental management strategies and mechanisms. Current funding priorities include innovative projects relating to smart growth, performance result demonstrations, economic analysis, economic analytical and statistical methods development.

Eligible applicants/beneficiaries: same as for **66.606**.

Range: $15,000 to $200,000. **Average:** $45,000.

Activity: not quantified specifically.

HQ: *grants information,* same as in **66.034**. *Program information,* Office of Policy, Economics and Innovation, Office of the Administrator-EPA, (202) 566-0949, FAX (202)566-3001. **Internet:** "www.epa.gov/opei".

66.700 CONSOLIDATED PESTICIDE ENFORCEMENT COOPERATIVE AGREEMENTS

Assistance: project grants (100 percent).

Purposes: pursuant to FIFRA as amended, to develop and maintain comprehensive pesticide programs addressing all aspects of enforcement, and special initiatives; to sponsor cooperative surveillance, monitoring, and analytical procedures; to encourage state regulatory activities. Funding priorities include: worker protection; pesticides used to protect public health; inspection of production facilities, retailing, and application practices; civil and criminal prosecution of violations. Grant funds may be used to pay for inspection and laboratory equipment and supplies, personnel salaries, other administrative costs.

Eligible applicants/beneficiaries: state agencies, territories and possessions, tribes.

Range: $32,000 to $747,000. **Average:** $250,000.

Activity: annually, 85 awards.

HQ: same address (MC 2225A) as **66.310**. Phone: (202)564-5033, FAX (202)564-0085. **Internet:** "www.epa.gov/compliance/state/grants/fifra.html".

66.701 TOXIC SUBSTANCES COMPLIANCE MONITORING COOPERATIVE AGREEMENTS

Assistance: project grants (75-100 percent).

Purposes: pursuant to TSCA as amended, to: establish and operate

compliance toxic substance monitoring and enforcement programs, including PCBs, asbestos in schools, lead-based paint, and sector-based activities; encourage state regulatory activities; establish worker training and accreditation standards. Grant funds may cover costs of inspection supplies and equipment, personnel, and administration.

Eligible applicants/beneficiaries: same as for **66.700**.

Range: $17,000 to $273,000. **Average:** $145,000.

Activity: annually, 72 awards.

HQ: OECA-EPA, 1200 Pennsylvania Ave. NW, Washington, DC 20460. **Phone:** *PCB, asbestos programs,* Chief, National Compliance Monitoring Policy Branch (2223A), Compliance Assessment and Media Programs Division, (202)564-4131, FAX (202)564-0050; *lead-based paint,* Sector Analysis and Implementation Branch (2224A), Compliance Assistance and Sector Programs Division, (202)564-7037, FAX (202)564-0009. **Internet:** "www.epa.gov/compliance/state/grants/tsca.html".

66.707 TSCA TITLE IV STATE LEAD GRANTS CERTIFICATION OF LEAD-BASED PAINT PROFESSIONALS ("State Lead Certification Grants")

Assistance: project grants.

Purposes: pursuant to TSCA as amended, to develop and conduct accredited training and certification programs for persons and contractors engaged in lead-based paint activities, and accredit training programs; for pre-renovation education programs, requiring distribution of lead-hazard information prior to building renovations.

Eligible applicants/beneficiaries: same as for **66.700**.

Range: $16,000 to $350,000. **Average:** $200,000.

Activity: as of FY 04, 39 states and territories, 3 tribes with approved training and certification programs, 2 states with pre-renovation education programs.

HQ: Director, National Program Chemicals Division (7404T), Office of Pollution Prevention and Toxics, OPPTS-EPA, 1200 Pennsylvania Ave. NW, Washington, DC 20460. Phone: (202)566-0500. **Internet:** "www.epa.gov/leadoffl.htm".

66.708 POLLUTION PREVENTION GRANTS PROGRAM ("P2 Grant Program")

Assistance: project grants (50 percent/to 3 years).

Purposes: pursuant to the Pollution Prevention Act of 1990, to support two programs. Pollution Prevention Grants ("P2") cover innovative activities promoting preventative approaches to environmental performance and addressing various sectors of concern, including industrial toxics, agriculture, energy, transportation; projects focus on institutionalizing multimedia pollution prevention, establishing prevention goals, providing direct technical assistance and outreach to businesses, and collecting and analyzing data. Pollution Prevention Information Network ("PPIN") Grants seek to coordinate work among technical assistance providers, to minimize duplication of effort in information collection, synthesis, dissemination, and training.

Eligible applicants/beneficiaries: same as for **66.700**. Participation is encouraged through partnerships with business and other environmental assistance providers.

Range: $20,000 to $200,000. **Average:** $80,000.

Activity: annually, 70 P2, 10 PPIN grants awarded.

HQ: Pollution Prevention Division, Office of Pollution Prevention, Pesticides and Toxics (7409-M), OPPTS-EPA, 1200 Pennsylvania Ave. NW, Washington, DC 20460. Phone: (202)564-8857, FAX (202)564-8899. **Internet:** P2 Grants, "www.epa.gov/p2/grants/ppis/ppis.htm"; PPIN Grants, "www.epa.gov//p2/grants/ppin/ppin.htm".

66.709 MULTI-MEDIA CAPACITY BUILDING GRANTS FOR STATES AND TRIBES

Assistance: project grants (100 percent/2-3 years).

Purposes: pursuant to CWA, FIFRA, CAA, SWDA, SDWA, TSCA, MPRSA, National Environmental Policy Act, and Indian Environmental General Assistance Program Act, to build and improve capacity to foster environmental enforcement and compliance assurance activities—including through economic, social science, statistical research, development, studies, demonstrations, investigations, public education, training, and fellowships. Program emphasis: inspector training, program planning and performance measurement, outcome measurement, public access to information, data management, permit compliance system modernization.

Eligible applicants/beneficiaries: state agencies, territories, multijurisdictional state organizations, tribes.

Range: $35,000 to $250,000. **Average:** $130,000.

Activity: FY 04, 12 projects funded.

HQ: Office of Compliance, OECA-EPA, 1200 Pennsylvania Ave. NW, Washington, DC 20460. Phone: (202)564-8318, FAX (202)564-0034. **Internet:** "www.epa.gov/compliance/state/grants/stag/index.html".

66.714 PESTICIDE ENVIRONMENTAL STEWARDSHIP REGIONAL GRANTS ("PESP Regional Grants")

Assistance: project grants (100 percent/to 2 years).

Purposes: pursuant to FIFRA as amended, to reduce risk from the use of pesticides in agricultural and nonagricultural settings, through research, monitoring, demonstration, and related activities.

Eligible applicants/beneficiaries: states, state universities, territories, possessions, tribes.

Range: $20,000 to $47,000. **Average:** $47,000.

Activity: FY 04, 13 grants.

HQ: Pesticide Environmental Stewardship Program, Biopesticides and Pollution Prevention Division (7511-C), OPPTS-EPA, 1200 Pennsylvania Ave. NW, Washington, DC 20460. Phone: (703)308-8107, (800)972-7717, FAX (703)308-7026. **Internet:** "www.epa.gov/oppbppd1/PESP/regional_grants.html".

66.715 CHILDHOOD BLOOD-LEAD SCREENING AND LEAD AWARENESS (EDUCATIONAL) OUTREACH FOR INDIAN TRIBES ("Tribal Lead Grants")

Assistance: project grants (100 percent/2 years).

Purposes: pursuant to TSCA as amended, for activities relating to blood-lead screening of tribal children; for outreach to educate Indian families about lead-based paint hazards.

Eligible applicants/beneficiaries: tribes, tribal consortia.

Range: assessment projects, to $75,000; outreach/education, to $50,000; combined, to $125,000.

Activity: FY 04 estimate, 15-30 grants estimated.

HQ: same address as **66.707**. Phone: (202)566-0516, FAX (202)566-0469. **Internet:** "www.epa.gov/lead/".

66.716 SURVEYS, STUDIES, INVESTIGATIONS, TRAINING DEMONSTRATIONS AND EDUCATIONAL OUTREACH

Assistance: project grants.

Purposes: pursuant to FIFRA and TSCA, to protect the public health, the environment, ecosystems, and most threatened species from potential risk from future toxic chemicals; to explore such emerging issues as risks to the environment and ecosystems from biotechnology, endocrine disrupters, and lead poisoning.

Eligible applicants/beneficiaries: states, territories, possessions, tribal governments, native American organizations; public and private IHEs, hospitals, laboratories, and other nonprofit institutions; individuals.

Range: $1,000 to $500,000. **Average:** $250,000.

Activity: FY 05 estimate, 10 awards.

HQ: *grants management information*: same as in **66.034**. Phone: *Program information,* Immediate Office, OPPTS, (202)564-0547, FAX (202)564-0550; Office of Pollution Prevention and Toxics, (202)564-0911, FAX (202)564-8251; Office of Pesticide Programs, (703)305-7711, FAX (703) 305-5060; Office of Science Coordination Policy, (202)564-8430, FAX (202)564-8452. **Internet:** "www.epa.gov/oppts.html".

66.717 SOURCE REDUCTION ASSISTANCE

Assistance: project grants (95 percent/to 2 years).

Purposes: pursuant to CAA, CWA, FIFRA, SDWA, SWDA, TSCA, amendments, and Executive Orders, for source reduction, pollution prevention, and resource conservation activities that: promote integration of pollution prevention into environmental media regulatory programs; disseminate pollution prevention news, innovative technologies, and technical assistance; encourage and promote activities to assist in the purchasing of environmentally preferable products and services; support the pollution prevention information network through work in measurement of "P2" information activities and services (re **66.708**).

Eligible applicants/beneficiaries: state, local, tribal, and special districts governments, territories and possessions, independent school districts, state IHEs, nonprofits including community-based grassroots organizations.

Range: $5,000 to $50,000. **Average:** $40,000.

Activity: FY 05 estimate, 55 awards.

HQ: same address as **66.708**. Phone: (202)564-8857. **Internet:** "www.epa.gov/p2/grants".

66.801 HAZARDOUS WASTE MANAGEMENT STATE PROGRAM SUPPORT

Assistance: formula grants (75 percent).

Purposes: pursuant to SWDA and RCRA as amended, to develop and implement authorized hazardous waste management programs to control the generation, transportation, treatment, storage, and disposal of hazardous wastes, including: permitting; oversight of corrective actions; facilities inspection; inspection of wastes generators; waste minimization.

Eligible applicants/beneficiaries: state agencies, territories, possessions.

Range: $200,000 to $8,400,000. **Average:** $2,085,000.

Activity: not quantified specifically.

HQ: Office of Solid Waste (5303W), OSWER-EPA, Washington, DC 20460. Phone: (703)308-8630. *Grants management information*: same as in **66.034**. **Internet:** "www.epa.gov/epaoswer/osw".

66.802 SUPERFUND STATE, POLITICAL SUBDIVISION, AND INDIAN TRIBE SITE-SPECIFIC COOPERATIVE AGREEMENTS ("Superfund")

Assistance: project grants (50-100 percent; tribes, 100 percent).

Purposes: pursuant to CERCLA as amended, to conduct site characterization activities at potential or confirmed hazardous waste sites; to undertake remedial planning and implementation at sites on the National Priorities List (NPL) of the National Oil and Hazardous Substances Contingency Plan. Project funds may be used to: conduct nontime-critical removal actions; inspect, assess, investigate, study, and prepare remedial designs; conduct remedial actions at uncontrolled sites listed on the NPL; identify responsible parties, conduct settlement negotiations, and take enforcement actions. Matching fund requirements: none if site was privately owned and operated at time of waste disposal prior to development of the NPL, and 10 percent for subsequent activities; 50 percent for sites state or locally operated; 10 percent for infrastructure development.

Eligible applicants/beneficiaries: states, political subdivisions, tribal governments, territories and possessions.

Range: $30,000 to $1,000,000. **Average:** $500,000.

Activity: not quantified specifically.

HQ: State, Tribe and Site Identification Branch, Assessment and Remediation Division, Office of Superfund Remediation and Technology Innovation (5204G), OSWER-EPA, Washington, DC 20460. Phone: (703)299-3438. **Internet:** "www.epa.gov/superfund".

66.804 STATE AND TRIBAL UNDERGROUND STORAGE TANKS PROGRAM ("UST Program")

Assistance: project grants (75 percent; tribes, 100 percent).

Purposes: pursuant to SWDA, RCRA, Demonstration Cities and Metropolitan

Development Act, and amendments, to develop and implement underground hazardous substances storage tank programs to operate in lieu of the federal program. Funds may be used to: promote effective compliance; ensure routine and correct monitoring by owners and operators; establish state statutory and regulatory authority.

Eligible applicants/beneficiaries: state and territorial agencies, tribes, intertribal consortia.

Range: $80,000 to $187,000. **Average:** states, $187,000; territories, $80,000.

Activity: annually, 66 awards.

HQ: Immediate Office, Office of Underground Storage Tanks (5401G), OSWER-EPA, 1200 Pennsylvania Ave. NW, Washington, DC 20460. Phone: (703)603-7148, FAX (703)603-0175. **Internet:** "www.epa.gov/oust/".

66.805 LEAKING UNDERGROUND STORAGE TANK TRUST FUND PROGRAM ("LUST")

Assistance: project grants (90 percent; tribes, 100 percent).

Purposes: pursuant to SWDA, RCRA, Demonstration Cities and Metropolitan Development Act, and amendments, to correct releases of petroleum from underground storage tanks; to conduct related enforcement and cost recovery activities; to oversee clean-ups by responsible parties. Trust funds may be used for responses where tank owners and operators are unknown, unwilling, or unable to undertake corrective actions; owners and operators are liable to states for costs incurred when the trust fund is used, and are subject to cost recovery actions.

Eligible applicants/beneficiaries: same as for **66.804**.

Range: $43,000 to $3,400,000. **Average:** states, $910,000; territories, $45,000.

Activity: FY 04, 50 states, 6 territories, 10 tribes funded; 14,000 clean-ups completed.

HQ: same as **66.804**.

66.806 SUPERFUND TECHNICAL ASSISTANCE GRANTS FOR CITIZEN GROUPS AT NATIONAL PRIORITY LIST (NPL) SITES ("Superfund TAG Grants")

Assistance: project grants (from 80 percent/3 years).

Purposes: pursuant to CERCLA and SARA as amended, for community groups to hire technical advisors to assist in: interpreting technical information concerning the assessment of potential hazards at waste sites; selecting and designing appropriate remedies at sites eligible for clean-up under the Superfund program; providing community information. Grant funds may not pay the costs of developing new information, underwriting legal actions or political activity, or travel by recipients.

Eligible applicants/beneficiaries: qualified, incorporated groups affected by an actual or threatened release at any Superfund facility.

Range/Average: initial award, $50,000.

Activity: cumulatively since 1988 program inception, 282 awards. FY 04, 7 new, 12 continuation awards.

HQ: Community Involvement and Outreach Center, Office of Superfund Remediation and Technology Innovation (5204G), OSWER-EPA, 1200 Pennsylvania Ave. NW, Washington, DC 20460. Phone: (703)603-8889, FAX (703)603-9102. **Internet:** "www.epa.gov/superfund/action/community/index.htm"; "www.epa.gov/superfund/tools/tag/index.htm".

66.808 SOLID WASTE MANAGEMENT ASSISTANCE GRANTS

Purposes: project grants (95-100 percent/3 years).

Assistance: pursuant to SWDA and RCRA as amended, to promote use of integrated solid waste management systems to solve municipal generation and management problems at the local, regional, and national levels. Funds may be used for training, surveys, public education materials and programs, studies, and demonstrations. Funding priorities include developing partnerships and education and outreach activities.

Eligible applicants/beneficiaries: federal, state, interstate, intrastate, and local public authorities; private nonprofit organizations and agencies, institutions, individuals; tribes.

Range: $5,000 to $1,367,000. **Average:** $100,000.

Activity: FY 05 estimate, 75 project awards.

HQ: *grants management information*, Grants Administration Division (3903F), EPA, Washington, DC 20460. Phone: (202)260-9266. *Program information*, OSWER-EPA (5305W), Washington, DC 20460. Phone: (703)308-8460. **Internet:** same as **66.801**.

66.809 SUPERFUND STATE AND INDIAN TRIBE CORE PROGRAM COOPERATIVE AGREEMENTS

Assistance: project grants (90 percent).

Purposes: pursuant to CERCLA as amended, for CERCLA response actions that are not site-specific. Funding supports personnel hiring and training, emergency response procedural planning, enforcement, legislative development.

Eligible applicants/beneficiaries: states, territories and possessions, tribal governments, tribal consortia.

Range: $50,000 to $500,000. **Average:** $200,000.

Activity: not quantified specifically.

HQ: same as **66.802**.

66.810 CHEMICAL EMERGENCY PREPAREDNESS AND PREVENTION (CEPP) TECHNICAL ASSISTANCE GRANTS PROGRAM
("CAA Section 112 and SARA Title III State Grants Program")

Assistance: project grants (75 percent/1-2 years).

Purposes: pursuant to CAA and TSCA, for chemical accident emergency preparedness and prevention planning (CEPP) activities relating to the Risk Management Program under CAA; for community right-to-know programs established to prevent or eliminate unreasonable risk to community health and environment. Funding priorities are: capacity building to implement and enforce CAA chemical accident prevention provisions, and to integrate chemical accident prevention activities, planning efforts, and community right-to-know programs; community issues; and, partnerships among states and tribes and local emergency planning committees, industry, emergency responders, and the general public. Project funds may be used to develop technical assistance and materials to be used directly or by others. Project examples: educational videos; Hazardous Vulnerability Analysis Plans.

Eligible applicants: states, local agencies, tribes, DC, PR, VI, Northern Marianas.

Eligible beneficiaries: local emergency planning committees, local emergency responders.

Range: $14,000 to $44,000 for 2 years. **Average:** $12,000 per year.

Activity: FY 04, 4 awards.

HQ: Grant Program Manager, Office of Emergency Management (5104A), OSWER-EPA, 1200 Pennsylvania Ave. NW, Washington, DC 20460. Phone: (202)564-6174, FAX (202)564-8211. **Internet:** "www.epa.gov/emergencies".

66.812 HAZARDOUS WASTE MANAGEMENT GRANT PROGRAM FOR TRIBES

Assistance: project grants (100 percent).

Purposes: to develop and implement hazardous waste management programs, including: building capacity to improve and maintain regulatory compliance; developing solutions to address waste mismanagement affecting tribal lands.

Eligible applicants/beneficiaries: tribal governments, including those involving Alaska natives; consortia.

Range: $18,000 to $100,000. **Average:** $56,000.

Activity: FY 05, 8 awards.

HQ: same address as **66.801**. Phone: (703)308-8458, FAX (703)308-8638. **Internet:** "www.epa.gov/tribalmsw"; *grants information,* "www.epa.gov/ogd".

66.813 ALTERNATIVE OR INNOVATIVE TREATMENT TECHNOLOGY RESEARCH, DEMONSTRATION, TRAINING, AND HAZARDOUS SUBSTANCE RESEARCH GRANTS

Assistance: project grants (cost sharing/to 5 years).

Purposes: pursuant to CERCLA as amended, for programs involving: research, evaluation, testing, development, and demonstration of alternative or innovative treatment technologies that may be used in response actions to achieve more permanent protection of human health and welfare and the environment; technology transfer including the development, collection, evaluation, coordination, and dissemination of information for response action; training and evaluation of training needs in handling and removal of hazardous substances; research on the detection, assessment, and evaluation of human health and environmental risks of hazardous substances.

Eligible applicants/beneficiaries: states, territories, possessions, tribes; public and private IHEs, hospitals, laboratories, and other nonprofits; individuals; certain projects by profit organizations.

Range: $30,000 to $500,000. **Average:** $40,000.

Activity: FY 04, 3 grants.

HQ: *grants information,* same as in **66.034**. *Program information,* Contracts Management Branch, Resources Management Division (5202G), same address as **66.807**. Phone: (703)603-8861, FAX (703)603-9133. **Internet:** "www.epa.gov/superfund/index.htm".

66.814 BROWNFIELDS TRAINING, RESEARCH, AND TECHNICAL ASSISTANCE GRANTS AND COOPERATIVE AGREEMENTS

Assistance: project grants (to 100 percent/1-5 years).

Purposes: pursuant to CERCLA as amended, for training, research, and technical assistance to individuals and organizations to facilitate the inventory of brownfield properties, assessments, clean-up, community involvement, or site preparation. Grant matching requirements have not been established.

Eligible applicants/beneficiaries: general purpose local government units; land clearance authorities or other quasi-governmental entities operating under the supervision of, or as agent of a local government; regional councils or groups of local governments; redevelopment agencies established by state legislatures; tribes, Alaska native corporations, and the Metlakatla Indian Community; nonprofit organizations including IHEs.

Range: to $750,000. **Average:** $200,000.

Activity: FY 03, 19 awards.

HQ: Office of Brownfields Cleanup and Redevelopment, OSWER-EPA, Washington, DC 20460. Phone: (202)566-2777, FAX (202)566-2757. **Internet:** "www.epa.gov/brownfields".

66.815 BROWNFIELD JOB TRAINING COOPERATIVE AGREEMENTS

Assistance: project grants (to 100 percent/2 years).

Purposes: pursuant to CERCLA as amended, for training, research, and technical assistance to individuals and organizations to facilitate the inventory of brownfield properties, assessments, clean-up, community involvement, or site preparation. Proposed projects showing evidence of leveraged funding receive priority consideration for approval.

Eligible applicants/beneficiaries: same as for **66.814**.

Range: to $200,000.

Activity: FY 04, 16 grants.

HQ: same as **66.814**.

66.816 HEADQUARTERS AND REGIONAL UNDERGROUND STORAGE TANKS PROGRAM

Assistance: project grants (100 percent/to 5 years).

Purposes: pursuant to SWDA, Hazardous and Solid Waste Amendments of 1984, SARA, RCRA, Demonstration Cities and Metropolitan Development Act, and amendments, for activities promoting the prevention, identification, corrective action, enforcement, and management of releases from underground storage tank systems, including: training on a regional and national scale; an "electronic newsletter" to provide technical information to state and tribal regulators, the general public, and the regulated community; state-federal partnerships providing technical assistance and forums for information exchange.

Eligible applicants/beneficiaries: public authorities including state, inter- and intrastate, tribal, intertribal, and local consortia; public and private nonprofit agencies and institutions.

Range: $50,000 to $500,000. **Average:** $275,000.

Activity: FY 04, 2 awards.

HQ: same as **66.804**.

66.817 STATE AND TRIBAL RESPONSE PROGRAM GRANTS

Assistance: project grants (80-100 percent).

Purposes: pursuant to CERCLA as amended and Small Business Liability Relief and Brownfields Revitalization Act, to establish or enhance state and tribal capacity for brownfields response programs; to capitalize revolving loan funds for clean-up activities; and, to support insurance mechanisms. Programs must ensure maintenance of a public record of completed projects and of planned sites. Applicants must provide a 20 percent share of the cost projects that capitalize a revolving loan fund; otherwise, the federal share is 100 percent.

Eligible applicants/beneficiaries: states and tribes.

Range: $50,000 to $1,500,000. **Average:** $500,000.

Activity: FY 05 estimate, 100 grants.

HQ: same as **66.814**.

66.818 BROWNFIELDS ASSESSMENT AND CLEANUP COOPERATIVE AGREEMENTS

Assistance: project grants (80-100 percent/2-5 years).

Purposes: pursuant to CERCLA as amended by the Small Business Liability Relief and Brownfields Revitalization Act, to conduct inventories, characterizations, assessments, planning, and community involvement activities related to brownfield sites; to capitalize revolving loan funds and provide subgrants (maximum, 40 percent of grants funds) for clean-up activities; to carry out clean-up activities at brownfield sites owned by the grant recipient. Assessment grants do not require matching funds; grants to establish revolving loan funds or provide subgrants require a 20 percent match, which may be waived by EPA in cases of financial hardship.

Eligible applicants/beneficiaries: same as for **66.814**.

Range: assessment grants, to $200,000 per site for sites contaminated by hazardous substances or pollutants; to $350,000 for sites contaminated by petroleum; revolving loan funds, to $1,000,000. **Average:** assessments, clean-ups, $200,000; revolving funds, $1,000,000.

Activity: FY 05, 302 grants awarded.

HQ: same as **66.814** Additional phone: (202)566-2744; Superfund Call Center, (800)553-7672.

66.926 INDIAN ENVIRONMENTAL GENERAL ASSISTANCE PROGRAM (GAP) ("GAP for Tribes")

Assistance: project grants (100 percent/to 4 years).

Purposes: pursuant to the Indian Environmental General Assistance Program Act of 1992 as amended, to administer environmental regulatory programs on Indian lands; to provide EPA technical assistance in the development of multimedia programs to address environmental issues. Funds may be used: to plan, develop, and establish capability to implement environmental protection programs including development and implementation of solid and hazardous waste programs; to conduct assessments and monitoring; to foster compliance with federal environmental statutes. Project examples: water quality assessment program; environmental assessment inventory; establishment of environmental codes; radon and underground storage tank projects.

Eligible applicants/beneficiaries: tribal governments, including those involving Alaska natives; consortia.

Range: $75,000 to $400,000. **Average:** $110,000.

Activity: FY 04, 490 tribes benefited.

HQ: American Indian Environmental Office (4104M), EPA, 1200 Pennsylvania Ave. NW, Washington, DC 20460. Phone: (202)564-0303, FAX (202) 564-0298. **Internet:** "www.epa.gov/indian/grant.htm".

66.931 INTERNATIONAL FINANCIAL ASSISTANCE PROJECTS SPONSORED BY THE OFFICE OF INTERNATIONAL AFFAIRS

Assistance: project grants (to 100 percent/to 5 years).

Purposes: pursuant to CWA, SWDA, RCRA, CAA, TSCA, FIFRA, SDWA, amendments, National Environmental Policy Act, and MPRSA, for multilateral international efforts to reduce significant risks to human health and ecosystems, caused by pollution that crosses national boundaries—including: issues concerning air quality, water, and toxins relating to the borders between the U.S. and Mexico, Canada (particularly the Great Lakes region), and the Arctic region; reviews and analytical studies of environmental aspects of international trade issues; and, providing technical assistance, capacity building, and on-the-ground projects in priority countries—including those conducted in cooperation with such organizations as the World Health Organization and the United Nations Environment Program, concerning such issues as global climate and clean fuels,.

Eligible applicants/beneficiaries: states, territories, possessions, tribes; public and private IHEs, hospitals, laboratories, and other nonprofit organizations.

Range: $15,000 to $325,000. **Average:** $90,000.

Activity: not quantified specifically.

HQ: *grants information,* same as in **66.034**. *Program information,* Office of International Affairs-EPA, 1200 Pennsylvania Ave. NW, Washington, DC. Phone: (no phone number provided). **Internet:** "www.oia.epa.gov". (Note: no field offices for this program.)

66.940 ENVIRONMENTAL POLICY AND STATE INNOVATION GRANTS

Assistance: project grants (100 percent/to 3 years).

Purposes: pursuant to CAA, CWA, SWDA, SDWA, TSCA, FIFRA, CERCLA, and amendments, for projects involving: analyses, studies, evaluations, and conferences leading to reduced generation of pollutants and conservation of natural resources; promotion of comprehensive cross-media approaches; encouragement and promotion of stewardship programs reflecting "beyond compliance" performance and offering incentives for superior environmental performance; systems-oriented change enabling better results from programs, processes, or sector-wide innovation; building in measurement and evaluation essential to transferability of the innovation.

Eligible applicants/beneficiaries: state environmental regulatory agencies including in territories and possessions. (EPA may make a separate competition available to federally certified Tribes.)

Range: $50,000 to $250,000. **Average:** $150,000.

Activity: new program in FY 05.

HQ: same address/phone as **66.611**. **Internet:** "www.epa.gov/innovation/stategrants".

66.950 ENVIRONMENTAL EDUCATION AND TRAINING PROGRAM ("EETP")

Assistance: project grants (75 percent/5 years).

Purposes: pursuant to the National Environmental Education Act, to train professionals in the development and delivery of environmental education programs. Funds may be used to develop programs involving such activities as: classroom training; demonstration projects; program and curriculum development; international exchanges involving the U.S., Mexico, and Canada; library acquisitions; conferences; networking.

Eligible applicants/beneficiaries: states, territories, public and private IHEs, hospitals, laboratories, and other nonprofit institutions; consortia.

Range/Average: single grant awarded.

Activity: 1 grant only, to the University of Wisconsin/Stevens Point (funded through 30 September 2005).

HQ: Environmental Education Specialist, Office of Environmental Education (1704A), EPA, 1200 Pennsylvania Ave. NW, Washington, DC 20460. Phone: (202)564-0454, FAX (202)564-2754. **Internet:** "www.epa.gov/enviroed".

66.951 ENVIRONMENTAL EDUCATION GRANTS ("EEG")

Assistance: project grants (75 percent/1-2 years).

Purposes: pursuant to the National Environmental Education Act, to design, demonstrate, or disseminate practices, methods, or techniques related to environmental education and training, including: development of curricula and educational tools and materials; teacher and faculty training programs; international exchanges involving the U.S., Mexico, and Canada; projects to understand and assess specific environmental and ecological issues or problems. Funding priorities include: capacity building across a state or multiple states; education reform; community issues focus; health and threats to health from environmental pollution, especially as children are affected; teaching skills; career development; environmental justice.

Eligible applicants/beneficiaries: same as for **66.950**.

Range: $2,000 to $150,000. **Average:** $85,000.

Activity: FY 04, 12 grants from HQ, 145 from regional offices.

HQ: Environmental Education Grant Program (1704A), Office of Environmental Education, EPA, 1200 Pennsylvania Ave. NW, Washington, DC 20460. Phone: (202)564-0451, FAX (202)564-2754. **Internet:** same as **66.950**.

66.952 NATIONAL NETWORK FOR ENVIRONMENTAL MANAGEMENT STUDIES FELLOWSHIP PROGRAM ("NEMS Fellowship Program")

Assistance: project grants (100 percent/to 3 years).

Purposes: pursuant to CAA, CWA, SDWA, SWDA, FIFRA, CERCLA, and amendments, to enable students to participate in research projects directly related to their fields of study. Current priorities include: environmental policy, regulation, and law; environmental management and administration; environmental science; public relations and communications; computer programming and development. Stipends are awarded for three months full-time to three years part-time, throughout the fellowship period—for work performed at EPA headquarters, regional offices, or laboratories.

Eligible applicants/beneficiaries: U.S. citizens and permanent residents enrolled at accredited IHEs as graduate or undergraduate students, with satisfactory educational performance and appropriate related course completion.

Range: 3-months/full-time, $7,100 to $11,300. **Average:** $10,000.

Activity: new program listing in 2005 (CFDA on-line version). Annually, 35 NEMS research projects eligible for participation by fellowship awardees. Since 1986, 1,370 fellowships awarded. FY 06 estimate, 30 awards.

HQ: same address, web site as **66.950**. Phone: (202)564-0452, FAX (202)564-2754. *Or,* NNEMS Fellowship Program, Tetra Tech EM, Inc., 1881 Campus Commons Dr. - Ste.200, Reston, VA 20191. Phone: (800)358-8769. (Note: no field offices for this program.)

NATIONAL GALLERY OF ART

68.001 NATIONAL GALLERY OF ART EXTENSION SERVICE

Assistance: use of property, facilities, and equipment.

Purposes: to provide educational materials from the National Gallery of Art for use in art and humanities programs. Available audiovisual materials relate to collections of paintings, sculptures, and special exhibitions in the gallery; included are video cassettes, CD-ROMS, DVDs, slide programs, teaching packets. The service is free of charge, except for return mailing costs.

Eligible applicants/beneficiaries: schools, colleges, libraries, museums, clubs, community organizations, noncommercial educational television stations, and individuals.

Activity: FY 03-04 estimate, 134,000 showings with a total audience of some 13,440,000 persons.

HQ: Department of Education Resources, National Gallery of Art, Washington, DC 20565. Phone: (202)842-6273, (202)737-4215. **Internet:** "www.nga.gov/resources"; e-mail, "ExtProg@nga.gov". (Note: no field offices for this program.)

OVERSEAS PRIVATE INVESTMENT CORPORATION

70.002 FOREIGN INVESTMENT FINANCING

Assistance: guaranteed/insured loans (5-15 years).

Purposes: pursuant to the Foreign Assistance Act of 1969, to finance investments in developing countries and emerging economies. Projects must contribute to the economic and social development of host countries and have a positive impact on the U.S. economy. Borrowers must provide a significant equity investment. Direct loans may be approved only for private sector projects with significant involvement by U.S. small businesses. Examples of funded projects include power generation, cellular telephone networks, retail petroleum.

Eligible applicants/beneficiaries: U.S. citizens, corporations, partnerships, other associations beneficially owning more than 50 percent of the entity, or foreign corporations at least 95 percent owned be such entity, or any other 100 percent U.S.-owned foreign entity.

Range: $10,000,000 to $400,000,000; small businesses, $100,000 to

$29,500,000; non-small businesses, $$40,950,000 to $190,000,000. **Average:** small businesses, $6,300,000; non-small businesses, $9,000,000.

Activity: since 1971, $164 billion in investments supported in more than 150 countries.

HQ: Information Officer, OPIC, 1100 New York Ave. NW, Washington, DC 20527. Phone: (202)336-8799. **Internet:** "www.opic.gov"; e-mail, "info@opic.gov". (Note: no field offices for this program.)

70.003 FOREIGN INVESTMENT INSURANCE ("Political Risk Insurance")

Assistance: insurance (90 percent/to 20 years).

Purposes: pursuant to the Foreign Assistance Act of 1969, to insure U.S. investments in developing countries and emerging markets against the political risks of inconvertibility, expropriation, and political violence. The investments must contribute to the economic and social development of host countries, and not adversely affect U.S. employment or the economy. Special programs insure: contractors and exporters against arbitrary drawings of letters of credit posted as bid, performance, or advance payment guarantees; petroleum exploration, development, and production; leasing operations; debt financing including securities.

Eligible applicants/beneficiaries: same as for **70.002**.

Range: to $250,000,000.

Activity: included in **70.002**.

HQ: same as **70.002**. (Note: no field offices for this program.)

COMMODITY FUTURES TRADING COMMISSION

78.004 COMMODITY FUTURES REPARATIONS CLAIMS

Assistance: investigation of complaints.

Purposes: pursuant to the Commodity Exchange Act as amended, Futures Trading Acts, Commodity Futures Modernization Act of 2000, related acts, and amendments, to respond to customer complaints and inquiries concerning commodity futures trading; to conduct hearings and rulings on reparations complaints regarding monetary damages resulting from violations of the acts or regulations, by persons or firms registered under the Act.

Eligible applicants/beneficiaries: market users and the general public.

Activity: FY 04 estimate, 100 reparations complaints accepted.

HQ: Office of the Executive Director, Office of Proceedings, Commodity Futures Trading Commission, 1155 21st St. NW, Washington, DC 20581. Phone: (202)418-5250. **Internet:** "www.cftc.gov".

DEPARTMENT OF ENERGY

81.003 GRANTING OF PATENT LICENSES
("DOE Patents Available for Licensing")

Assistance: technical information.

Purposes: pursuant to the Atomic Energy Act of 1954 and Department of Energy Organization Act of 1977 (DOEOA) as amended, to license some 1,200 DOE-owned U.S. and 200 foreign patents, encouraging widespread use of the licensed inventions. Licenses usually are nonexclusive and revocable, but may be exclusive or partially so under some circumstances such as for commercialization. Copies of patents may be obtained for a modest fee from the U.S. Patent and Trademark Office (see **11.900**).

Eligible applicants/beneficiaries: individuals, firms, or corporations with satisfactory commercialization plans.

Activity: FY 06 estimate, 6 licenses to be granted.

HQ: Office of Assistant General Counsel/Technology Transfer and Intellectual Property, DOE, Washington, DC 20585. Phone: (202)586-2802. **Internet:** "www.doe.gov". (Note: no field offices for this program.)

81.022 USED ENERGY-RELATED LABORATORY EQUIPMENT GRANTS

Assistance: sale, exchange, or donation of property and goods.

Purposes: pursuant to the Atomic Energy Act of 1954, DOEOA, and Energy Reorganization Act of 1974 as amended, to grant used energy-related laboratory equipment for use in energy-oriented research or instructional programs in the life, physical, and environmental sciences and engineering.

Eligible applicants/beneficiaries: U.S. nonprofit IHEs, hospitals, technical institutes, museums.

Activity: not quantified specifically.

HQ: Office of Science, DOE, 1000 Independence Ave. SW, Washington, DC 20585. Phone: (202)586-7231. **Internet:** "www.erle.osti.gov/erle".

81.036 INVENTIONS AND INNOVATIONS
("I&I")

Assistance: project grants (to 100 percent/1-2 years); technical information; advisory services/counseling.

Purposes: pursuant to the Federal Nonnuclear Energy Research and Development Act of 1974 and DOEOA as amended, to support development and commercialization of energy-saving inventions, by providing limited financial assistance and technical assistance in evaluating and launching promising concepts. Funding may not include equity capital.

Eligible applicants/beneficiaries: U.S. citizens and small businesses.

Range/Average: $83,000.

Activity: since 1977 program inception, 500 inventions supported.

HQ: Weatherization and Intergovernmental Program (EE-2K), OEERE-DOE, 1000 Independence Ave. SW, Washington, DC 20585. Phone: (202)586-2212. **Internet:** "www.eere.energy/gov/inventions/".

81.039 NATIONAL ENERGY INFORMATION CENTER ("NEIC")

Assistance: technical information.

Purposes: pursuant to the Federal Energy Administration Act of 1974 and DOEOA as amended, to operate the NEIC as a comprehensive source and referral service for statistical and analytical energy data, computer models, publications, on-line services, and information. Clearinghouse services are provided for registration of information products.

Eligible applicants/beneficiaries: federal, state, and local governments; academic and other nonprofit institutions; industrial and commercial organizations; general public.

Activity: annually, 33,000 inquiries.

HQ: Energy Information Administration-DOE (no additional contact info provided). **Internet:** "www.eia.doe.gov" (Note: no field offices for this program.)

81.041 STATE ENERGY PROGRAM

Assistance: formula grants (100 percent).

Purposes: pursuant to the Energy Policy and Conservation Act, DOEOA as amended, and related acts, to develop, implement, or modify state energy conservation plans. Funds may cover costs of plan development or modification, but not research, demonstrations, subsidies, or tax credits.

Eligible applicants/beneficiaries: states, territories, possessions.

Range: $200,000 to $2,000,000.

Activity: 56 states and territories participate.

HQ: same address as **81.036**. Phone: (no number provided). **Internet:** "www.eree.energy.doe.gov/state_energy_program/".

81.042 WEATHERIZATION ASSISTANCE FOR LOW-INCOME PERSONS

Assistance: formula grants (100 percent).

Purposes: pursuant to the Energy Conservation and Production Act, DOEOA, Energy Security Act of 1980, State Energy Efficiency Programs Improvement Act of 1990, amendments, and other acts, for weatherization measures in the homes of low-income households, especially the elderly and the handicapped. Funds may cover such costs as attic insulation, storm windows, furnace and cooling system modifications, replacement furnaces and boilers.

Eligible applicants/beneficiaries: states and certain tribal organizations. If a state does not apply, general purpose local government units, community action agencies, or other nonprofit agencies may apply.

Range: to $2,500 per dwelling unit. **Average:** states, $4,400,000.

Activity: to date, 5,000,000 homes weatherized.

HQ: same address as **81.022.** Phone: (202)586-4074. **Internet:** "www.eree. doe.gov/weatherization/".

81.049 OFFICE OF SCIENCE FINANCIAL ASSISTANCE PROGRAM

Assistance: project grants (to 100 percent/to 5 years).

Purposes: pursuant to the Atomic Energy Act of 1954, Federal Nonnuclear Energy Research and Development Act of 1974, DOEOA, Energy Reorganization Act of 1974, and amendments, for fundamental energy research, training, and related activities in the basic sciences and in advanced technology concepts and assessments in related fields. Funds may be obtained for work in such fields as basic energy sciences, high energy and nuclear physics, fusion energy, biological and environmental research, advanced scientific computing. Graduate student support may be provided.

Eligible applicants/beneficiaries: IHEs, profit and nonprofit organizations, state and local governments, unaffiliated individuals.

Range: $10,000 to $2,000,000. **Average:** $200,000.

Activity: not quantified specifically.

HQ: Grants and Contracts Division (SC-64), Office of Science-DOE, 19901 Germantown Rd., Germantown, MD 20874-1290. Phone: (301)903-5212. **Internet:** "www.science.doe.gov/production/grants/grants.html".

81.057 UNIVERSITY COAL RESEARCH

Assistance: project grants (75-100 percent/to 3 years).

Purposes: pursuant to the Atomic Energy Act of 1954 as amended, Federal Nonnuclear Energy Research and Development Act of 1974, DOEOA, and Energy Reorganization Act of 1974, for research on the physics and chemistry involved in the conversion and utilization of coal. Projects must involve teaching faculty and funded student participation.

Eligible applicants/beneficiaries: U.S. IHEs.

Range: $50,000 to $400,000. **Average:** $154,000.

Activity: FY 04, 22 grants.

HQ: Office of Advanced Research, Assistant Secretary/Fossil Energy-DOE, Washington, DC 20585. Phone: (301)903-2786. **Internet:** "www.netl.doe. gov/coal/Advanced%20Research/".

81.064 OFFICE OF SCIENTIFIC AND TECHNICAL INFORMATION ("OSTI")

Assistance: technical information.

Purposes: for OSTI to conduct its centralized technical information management program for the collection, organization, preservation, and distribution of domestic and international nuclear and other energy research findings in electronic and printed form; to provide pertinent technical services and information to DOE and its contractors.

Eligible applicants/beneficiaries: state and local governments, universities that are DOE contractors, and other organizations. Public access is available through NTIS and GPO.

Activity: FY 04, 18,600,000 user transactions for OSTI web products.

HQ: Office of Program Integration, OSTI-DOE, 1 Science.gov Way, Oak Ridge, TN 37831. Phone: Program Integration, (865)576-1194. **Internet:** "www.osti.gov". (Note: the field office serves as headquarters for this program.)

81.065 NUCLEAR WASTE DISPOSAL SITING

Assistance: direct payments/specified use; project grants (to 100 percent).

Purposes: pursuant to the Nuclear Waste Policy Act and amendments, to develop repositories for the disposal of high-level radioactive waste and spent nuclear fuel; for related research, development, and demonstration projects. Funds may be used to: review potential economic, social, health and safety, and environmental impacts; develop requests for impact and mitigation assistance; monitor, test, or evaluate activities; provide public information.

Eligible applicants/beneficiaries: Nevada and affected local governments and tribes where DOE is considering nuclear waste disposal activities.

Range: $40,000 to $5,000,000.

Activity: approximately 10 grants.

HQ: Office of Repository Development, Office of Civilian Radioactive Waste Management-DOE, Las Vegas, NV. Phone: (702)794-1368. **Internet:** "www.ocrwn.doe.gov". (Note: the field office serves as headquarters for this program.)

81.079 REGIONAL BIOMASS ENERGY PROGRAMS

Assistance: project grants (to 100 percent/2 months-1 year).

Purposes: pursuant to DOEOA as amended, to develop and transfer biomass energy technologies to the scientific and industrial communities; for outreach, public education, and behavior modification activities. Regional programs are tailored to specific regions—for feedstock production, conversion technologies, and feasibility studies.

Eligible applicants/beneficiaries: profit and nonprofit organizations; intrastate, interstate, state, local government agencies; universities.

Range: N.A.

Activity: not quantified specifically.

HQ: Office of Biomass Program, OEERE-DOE, Washington, DC 20585. Phone: (no number provided). **Internet:** "www.eere.energy.gov".

81.086 CONSERVATION RESEARCH AND DEVELOPMENT

Assistance: project grants (to 100 percent/2 months to 2 years).

Purposes: pursuant to DOEOA as amended and Federal Nonnuclear Energy Research and Development Act of 1974, for long-term research in energy conservation technology in buildings, industry, "FreedomCar" and vehicle technologies and hydrogen, fuel cells, and infrastructure. Project examples include research on high-performance heat pumps, thermally efficient commercial buildings, vehicle engines, high temperature materials, industrial separation processes.

Eligible applicants/beneficiaries: profit and nonprofit organizations, state and local governments.

Range: $50,000 to $500,000.

Activity: not quantified specifically.

HQ: OEERE-DOE (no additional contact info provided). **Internet:** "www.eere.doe.gov" (Note: no field offices for this program.)

81.087 RENEWABLE ENERGY RESEARCH AND DEVELOPMENT

Assistance: project grants (to 100 percent/2 months-1 year).

Purposes: pursuant to DOEOA, for research and development projects in energy technologies, including solar, distributed energy and electric reliability, biomass, wind and hydropower, hydrogen, and geothermal.

Eligible applicants/beneficiaries: profit and nonprofit organizations; intrastate, interstate, and local agencies; universities.

Range: $50,000 to $1,000,000.

Activity: not quantified specifically.

HQ: same as **81.086**. (Note: no field offices for this program.)

81.089 FOSSIL ENERGY RESEARCH AND DEVELOPMENT

Assistance: project grants.

Purposes: pursuant to the Federal Nonnuclear Energy Research and Development Act of 1974, Energy Policy and Conservation Act, DOEOA, and other acts, for fundamental research and technology development to promote the use of environmentally and economically superior technologies for supply, conversion, delivery, and utilization of fossil fuels.

Eligible applicants/beneficiaries: states, local governments, universities, governmental entities, consortia, nonprofit institutions, commercial corporations, joint federal-industry corporations, territories, individuals.

Range: $10,000 to $25,000,000.

Activity: FY 02, 87 awards (latest data reported).

HQ: Fossil Energy Program (FE-3), DOE, 19901 Germantown Rd., Germantown, MD 20874. Phone: (301)903-3514. **Internet:** "www.fe.doe.gov".

81.104 OFFICE OF ENVIRONMENTAL CLEANUP AND ACCELERATION

Assistance: project grants (to 100 percent/to 5 years).

Purposes: pursuant to the Atomic Energy Act, DOEOA, Hazardous Materials Transportation Uniform Safety Act of 1990, amendments, and other acts, to develop new or improved technology systems to: eliminate or reduce known or recognized potential risks to the public and to the environment; reduce overall clean-up costs; develop new clean-up methods. Major remediation and waste management areas include: transuranic waste; high-level waste; groundwater and soils; deactivation and decommissioning; nuclear materials.

Eligible applicants/beneficiaries: public and quasi-public agencies, private industry, individuals, groups, educational institutions, nonprofit organizations, state and local governments, tribal governments, territories and possessions.

Range: $200,000 to $7,000,000.

Activity: not quantified specifically.

HQ: Office of Environmental Cleanup and Acceleration, Office of Environmental Management, DOE, Washington, DC 20585. Phone: (no number provided). **Internet:** "www.em.doe.gov". (Note: no field offices for this program.)

81.105 NATIONAL INDUSTRIAL COMPETITIVENESS THROUGH ENERGY, ENVIRONMENT, AND ECONOMICS ("NICE3")

Assistance: project grants (50 percent/to 3 years).

Purposes: pursuant to DOEOA and Energy Policy Act of 1992 as amended, to develop new processes and/or equipment to reduce the generation of high-volume wastes and greenhouse gases in industry, including agriculture and mining, and to conserve energy and energy-intensive feed stocks. Emphasis is on states with industries with the highest energy consumption and the greatest levels of generation of pollutants. State funding must include industrial partner monies.

Eligible applicants/beneficiaries: commercial firms with proposals endorsed by state agencies; state agencies, territories, possessions, tribes.

Range: $455,000 to $525,000. **Average:** $475,000.

Activity: not quantified specifically.

HQ: same address/phone as **81.036**. **Internet:** "www.eere.energy.gov/wip/program/nice3.html".

81.106 TRANSPORT OF TRANSURANIC WASTE TO THE WASTE ISOLATION PLANT: STATES AND TRIBAL CONCERNS, PROPOSED SOLUTIONS ("WIPP")

Assistance: project grants (100 percent).

Purposes: pursuant to the National Security and Military Application of Nuclear Energy Authorization Act and Waste Isolation Pilot Land Withdrawal Act as amended, to support cooperative efforts among the tribes, states, and DOE on the Waste Isolation Pilot Plant shipping corridors—in developing plans and procedures for the safe transportation of transuranic waste from temporary storage facilities to the plant. Project elements include accident prevention, emergency preparedness training, and public information activities.

Eligible applicants/beneficiaries: Western Governors' Association, Southern Governors' Association, State of New Mexico, and affected tribal governments.

Range: $50,000 to $2,150,000.

Activity: not quantified specifically.

HQ: Federal Disposition Options, Office of Environmental Management-

DOE, Washington, DC 20585. Phone: (301)903-7416. **Internet:** same as **81.104**.

81.108 EPIDEMIOLOGY AND OTHER HEALTH STUDIES FINANCIAL ASSISTANCE PROGRAM

Assistance: project grants (100 percent).

Purposes: pursuant to the Atomic Energy Act of 1954, Federal Nonnuclear Energy Research and Development Act of 1977, Energy Reorganization Act of 1974, and amendments, for research, education, conferences, communication, and other activities relating to the health of DOE workers and others potentially exposed to health hazards associated with energy production, transmission, and use. Grant funds may support costs relating to project administration, training, publications, and epidemiological studies and research.

Eligible applicants/beneficiaries: IHEs, businesses, nonprofit institutions.

Range: $50,000 to $7,000,000. **Average:** $1,000,000.

Activity: not quantified specifically.

HQ: Office of Health Programs (EH-6/270CC), Office of Environment, Safety and Health-DOE, Germantown, MD 20874-1290. Phone: (301)903-1244. **Internet:** "http://tis.eh.doe.gov/health". (Note: no field offices for this program.)

81.112 STEWARDSHIP SCIENCE GRANT PROGRAM ("Defense Science")

Assistance: project grants (100 percent).

Purposes: pursuant to the Atomic Energy Act of 1954, Federal Nonnuclear Energy Research and Development Act of 1974, DOEOA, amendments, and other laws, for basic and applied research in science and technology relevant to stockpile stewardship; to promote inter-action among researchers and scientists at DOE laboratories; to train scientists in specific areas related to long-term research; to complement the DOE Advanced Simulation and Computing Academic Strategic Alliances Program by emphasizing primarily experimental research in forefront areas.

Eligible applicants/beneficiaries: U.S. public and private IHEs.

Range: $100,000 to $2,000,000. **Average:** $380,000.

Activity: not quantified specifically.

HQ: Office of Defense Science (NA-113/Forrestal), National Nuclear Security Administration-DOE, 1000 Independence Ave, Washington, DC 20585. Phone: (202)586-5782, FAX (202)586-8005. **Internet:** "www.nnsa.doe.gov/ssaa".

81.113 DEFENSE NUCLEAR NONPROLIFERATION RESEARCH

Assistance: project grants (100 percent/to 3 years).

Purposes: pursuant to the Atomic Energy Act of 1954, Federal Nonnuclear Energy Research and Development Act of 1974, DOEOA, National Defense Authorization Act of 2000, amendments, and other acts, for basic and applied research and development on verification technologies that enhance U.S. national security and reduce global danger from the proliferation of special nuclear materials and weapons of mass destruction.

Eligible applicants/beneficiaries: public and private nonprofit IHEs and non-governmental organizations; federal agencies.

Range: $100,000 to $250,000/year.

Activity: 20 grants expected per year.

HQ: Office of Nonproliferation Research and Engineering (NA-22), Office of Defense Nuclear Nonproliferation, National Nuclear Security Administration-DOE, Washington, DC 20585. Phone: (202)586-5751. **Internet:** "www.nnsa.doe.gov/na-20". (Note: no field offices for this program.)

81.114 UNIVERSITY REACTOR INFRASTRUCTURE AND EDUCATION SUPPORT

Assistance: project grants (to 100 percent).

Purposes: pursuant to the Atomic Energy Act of 1954, DOEOA, amendments, and Energy Reorganization Act of 1974, for research design, equipment upgrades, graduate and undergraduate student support, analysis, and assessments in science and technology in fields related to nuclear energy.

Eligible applicants/beneficiaries: individuals, partnerships, corporations, associations, joint ventures, IHEs, nonprofit organizations.

Range: $50,000 to $300,000.

Activity: not quantified specifically.

HQ: Office of Nuclear Energy, Science and Technology (NE-30), DOE, 19901 Germantown Rd., Germantown, MD 20874. Phone: (301)903-1536. **Internet:** "http://ne.doe.gov/university1.html".

81.117 ENERGY EFFICIENCY AND RENEWABLE ENERGY INFORMATION DISSEMINATION, OUTREACH, TRAINING AND TECHNICAL ANALYSIS/ASSISTANCE

Assistance: project grants (to 100 percent/6 months-5 years).

Purposes: pursuant to DOEOA, Energy Policy Act of 1992, Energy Reorganization Act of 1974, and amendments, to stimulate increased energy efficiency and use of renewable and alternative energy in transportation, buildings, industry, and the federal sector—through information dissemination, outreach, training, and related technical assistance.

Eligible applicants/beneficiaries: public and private profit and nonprofit organizations, state and local governments, tribal organizations, Alaska native American organizations, universities.

Range: N.A.

Activity: FY 02, 34 awards (most recent data reported).

HQ: Program Execution Support, Office of Business Administration (EE-3A), OEERE-DOE, 1000 Independence Ave, SW, Washington, DC 20585. Phone: (no number provided). **Internet:** same as **81.086**. (Note: no field offices for this program.)

81.119 STATE ENERGY PROGRAM SPECIAL PROJECTS

Assistance: project grants (to 100 percent).

Purposes: pursuant to DOEOA and National Energy Conservation Policy Act of 1978, amendments, and other acts, to assist states in implementing specific DOE deployment activities and initiatives in such programmatic areas as building codes and standards, alternative fuels, industrial efficiency, and solar and renewable energy technologies.

Eligible applicants/beneficiaries: states, territories, and possessions.

Range: $20,000 to $1,000,000. **Average:** $100,000.

Activity: not quantified specifically.

HQ: same as **81.041**.

81.121 NUCLEAR ENERGY RESEARCH, DEVELOPMENT AND DEMONSTRATION ("NE RD&R")

Assistance: project grants (to 100 percent).

Purposes: pursuant to the Atomic Energy Act of 1954, DOEOA, amendments, and Energy Reorganization Act of 1974, for research, development, demonstrations, and deployment in science and technology fields related to nuclear energy to address key issues affecting the future world-wide use of nuclear energy—including such areas as advanced reactors, proliferation-resistant fuel and reactor concepts, modeling and analysis, reactor physics. Projects may include development, demonstrations, studies, economic analyses, new regulatory or licensing requirements, and similar activities.

Eligible applicants/beneficiaries: federal, state, and local governments; public or private nonprofit or profit organizations, IHEs; consortia; individuals.

Range: $100,000 to $500,000. **Average:** $350,000.

Activity: not quantified specifically.

HQ: Office of Nuclear Energy, Science and Technology, 1000 Independence Ave. SW, Washington, DC 20585-1290. Phone: (301)903-3097. **Internet:** "www.nuclear.gov".

81.122 ELECTRICITY DELIVERY AND ENERGY RELIABILITY, RESEARCH, DEVELOPMENT AND ANALYSIS

Assistance: project grants (100 percent/to 3 years).

Purposes: pursuant to DOEOA as amended, Energy Tax Act of 1978, Energy Security Act of 1980, Superconductivity and Competitiveness Act of 1988, and Energy Policy Act of 1992, for research, development, demonstration, technology transfer, and education and outreach activities intended to: modernize and expand the national electricity delivery system; assure the security of the energy infrastructure and reduce its vulnerability; develop an effective emergency response system to protect and restore its capabilities in case of disruption or attack.

Eligible applicants/beneficiaries: private profit and nonprofit organizations, state and local governments.

Range: $2,000,000 to $3,000,000 over 3 years. **Average:** $2,500,000.

Activity: new program in FY 05.

HQ: Office of Electricity Delivery and Energy Reliability, DOE, Washington, DC. Phone: (202)586-1411. **Internet:** "www.electricity.doe.gov". (Note: no field offices for this program.)

81.123 NATIONAL NUCLEAR SECURITY ADMINISTRATION (NNSA) HISTORICALLY BLACK COLLEGES AND UNIVERSITIES (HBCU) PROGRAM ("NNSA HBCU")

Assistance: project grants (100 percent/to 3 years).

Purposes: pursuant to the Atomic Energy Act of 1954, DOEOA, Energy Reorganization Act of 1974, National Nuclear Security Administration Act, and amendments, to establish a research partnership with HBCUs to increase their participation in national security-related research, and to train HBCU graduates for NNSA employment.

Eligible applicants/beneficiaries: HBCUs.

Range: $210,000 to $2,000,000 for 1-3 years. **Average:** $1,000,000.

Activity: new program listing in 2005 (CFDA on-line version). FY 05, 24 awards.

HQ: Office of Diversity and Outreach, NNSA-DOE, 1000 Independence Ave. SW, Washington, DC 20585. Phone: (202)586-8023. FAX (202)586-2531. **Internet:** "www.nnsa.doe.gov/"; e-mail, "diversity.outreach@nnsa,doe.gov". (Note: no field offices for this program.)

DEPARTMENT OF EDUCATION

84.002 ADULT EDUCATION—STATE GRANT PROGRAM

Assistance: formula grants (75 percent/to 27 months; territories, 88 percent).

Purposes: pursuant to the Adult Education and Family Literacy Act, Chapter 2, and WIA, for education and workplace, family, and English literacy services, and civics education programs—for adults and out-of-school youth at least age 16 lacking mastery of basic educational skills or without a high school diploma or English language proficiency. Portions of grant amounts may be spent for: state leadership activities; professional development; teacher training; correctional education and services to other institutionalized individuals.

Eligible applicants/beneficiaries: SEAs including in certain territories and possessions. LEAs and other public or private nonprofit organizations may receive subgrants, including libraries, public housing authorities, IHEs, literacy organizations.

Range: $843,000 to $63,213,000.

Activity: FY 03, 2,800,000 participants.

HQ: Division of Adult Education and Literacy, OVAE-DOED, 400 Maryland Ave. SW, Washington, DC 20202-7100. Phone: (202)205-5698. **Internet:** "www.ed.gov/fund/grant//find//AdultEd/f-ogrant.html". (Note: no field offices for this program.)

84.004 CIVIL RIGHTS TRAINING AND ADVISORY SERVICES

Assistance: project grants (100 percent/3 years).

Purposes: pursuant to the Civil Rights Act of 1964 as amended, Title IV, for educational equity assistance centers to provide technical assistance and training services to school districts, relating to compliance with civil rights laws pertaining to race, gender, and national origin. Project funds may be used for information dissemination, staff and community training, and developing curriculum materials specifically for the instruction of students with limited English proficiency relevant to program purposes.

Eligible applicants/beneficiaries: private nonprofit organizations, public agencies.

Range/Average: $724,000.

Activity: FY 04, 10 centers grants awarded.

HQ: School Support and Technology Programs, OESE-DOED, 400 Maryland Ave. SW, Washington, DC 20202. Phone: (202)260-2638. **Internet:** "www.ed.gov/programs/equitycenters/index.html"; "www.ed.gov/about/contacts/gen/othersites/equity.html". (Note: no field offices for this program.)

84.007 FEDERAL SUPPLEMENTAL EDUCATIONAL OPPORTUNITY GRANTS ("FSEOG" - "SEOG")

Assistance: direct payments/specified use (75 percent).

Purposes: pursuant to the Higher Education Act of 1965 (HEA) as amended, Title IV, for undergraduate postsecondary study by students in financial need. Institutions may receive an administrative cost allowance.

Eligible applicants: public, private nonprofit, postsecondary vocational, and proprietary IHEs.

Eligible beneficiaries: needy undergraduate students meeting citizenship or residency requirements, enrolled or enrolling as regular students, maintaining satisfactory academic progress, in compliance with Selective Service requirements, and neither owing a refund nor in default on a Title IV grant or loan.

Range: $100 to $4,000/year, plus up to $400 additional. **Average:** $763.

Activity: FY 04, 1,278,000 student awards.

HQ: FSA-DOED, 400 Maryland Ave. SW, Washington, DC 20202-5446. Phone: Student Financial Aid Information Center, (800)443-3243. **Internet:** "http://ifap.ed.gov".

84.010 TITLE 1 GRANTS TO LOCAL EDUCATIONAL AGENCIES ("Title 1 Basic, Concentration, and Targeted Education Finance Incentive Grants")

Assistance: formula grants (100 percent).

Purposes: pursuant to the Elementary and Secondary Education Act of 1965 (ESEA), Title I, Part A, to supplement state and local funding for extra instructional activities for children failing to meet academic standards or at-risk. Programs in schools with at least a 40 percent poverty rate may be operated on a schoolwide basis; other schools must operate targeted assistance programs for children failing or at-risk of failing to meet challenging state academic standards.

Eligible applicants/beneficiaries: SEAs including in outlying areas; BIA. LEAs and tribal schools are subgrantees.

Range: $27,919,000 to $1,765,538,000.

Activity: 15,800,000 public and nonpublic (1.3 percent) school children in 51,000 schools served.

HQ: OESE-DOED, 400 Maryland Ave. SW, Washington, DC 20202-6132. Phone: (202)260-0826. **Internet:** "www.ed.gov/programs/titleiparta/index.html". (Note: no field offices for this program.)

84.011 MIGRANT EDUCATION—STATE GRANT PROGRAM

Assistance: formula grants (100 percent).

Purposes: pursuant to ESEA as amended, Title I, Part C, for comprehensive educational programs for migratory children, including: academic, remedial, bilingual, compensatory, multicultural, and vocational instruction; preschool services; health services; career education services.

Eligible applicants: SEAs; consortia.

Eligible beneficiaries: children age 0-21, of migratory agricultural workers or fishers that have moved across school districts during the last 36 months.

Range: $70,000 to $127,573,000. **Average:** $7,376,000.

Activity: 2004 school year, 738,000 students served.

HQ: Office of Migrant Education, OESE-DOED, 400 Maryland Ave. SW, Washington, DC 20202-6135. Phone: (202)260-1334. **Internet:** "www.ed.gov/programs/mep/index.html". (Note: no field offices for this program.)

84.013 TITLE I PROGRAM FOR NEGLECTED AND DELINQUENT CHILDREN

Assistance: formula grants (100 percent).

Purposes: pursuant to ESEA as amended, Title I, Part D, for education programs and related services for institutionalized neglected or delinquent children, including children under age 21 in state institutions, adult correctional institutions, or state-operated community day schools. Funds may cover supplemental instruction in core academic subjects, tutoring, counseling, services facilitating transition to schools. Juvenile institutions must provide at least 20 hours of instruction per week; adult institutions, at least 15 hours—from nonfederal funds.

Eligible applicants/beneficiaries: SEAs. Related state agencies may receive subgrants.

Range: $64,000 to $3,240,000.

Activity: FY 04, 171,000 children served in 400 institutions.

HQ: Student Achievement and School Accountability Programs, OESE-DOED, FOB-6 - Rm.3W214, 400 Maryland Ave. SW, Washington, DC 20202-6132. Phone: (202)260-4412. **Internet:** "www.ed.gov/programs/titleipartd/index.html". (Note: no field offices for this program.)

84.015 NATIONAL RESOURCE CENTERS AND FELLOWSHIPS PROGRAM FOR LANGUAGE AND AREA OR LANGUAGE AND INTERNATIONAL STUDIES

Assistance: project grants (100 percent/to 3 years).

Purposes: pursuant to HEA as amended, Title VI, for instruction in modern foreign languages and in area and international studies. Center grants may be awarded for undergraduate training only, or they may be comprehensive involving undergraduate, graduate, and professional training—supporting costs of instruction programs, administration, library resources and staff, lectures and conferences. Fellowships may be awarded for graduate language study combined with area studies and world affairs, covering tuition, fees, and basic subsistence.

Eligible applicants: U.S. IHEs.

Eligible beneficiaries graduate students that are U.S. citizens, nationals, or permanent residents; training must be undertaken at a school with an allocation of Foreign Language and Area Studies Fellowships (FLAS).

Range/Average: centers, $239,000; fellowship awards, $217,000.

Activity: FY 04, 120 centers funded; 124 fellowships grants.

HQ: OPE-DOED, 400 Maryland Ave. SW, Washington, DC 20202-5331. Phone: (202)502-7630. **Internet:** "www.ed.gov/programs/iegpsnrc/"; "www.ed.gov/programs/iegpsflasf". (Note: no field offices for this program.)

84.016 UNDERGRADUATE INTERNATIONAL STUDIES AND FOREIGN LANGUAGE PROGRAMS

Assistance: project grants (50 percent/1-3 years).

Purposes: pursuant to HEA as amended, Title VI, for undergraduate international studies and foreign language program strengthening and improvement. Funds may cover costs of administration, curriculum and faculty development, lectures and conferences, library enhancement, travel.

Eligible applicants/beneficiaries: accredited IHEs, public and private nonprofit agencies and organizations.

Range/Average: new awards $75,000; continuations, $77,000.

Activity: FY 04, 59 grants.

HQ: International Studies Branch, International Education and Graduate Programs Service, Office of International Education and Foreign Language Studies, OPE-DOED, 400 Maryland Ave. SW, Washington, DC 20202-5332. Phone: (202)502-7629. **Internet:** "www.ed.gov/programs/iegpsugisf". (Note: no field offices for this program.)

84.017 INTERNATIONAL RESEARCH AND STUDIES

Assistance: project grants (100 percent/1-3 years).

Purposes: pursuant to HEA as amended, Title VI, to improve education and training in modern foreign languages, area, and other international studies—through studies, surveys, research, experimentation, and development of specialized instructional materials and publications. Funds may not support student or teacher training.

Eligible applicants/beneficiaries: public and private agencies, organizations, institutions; individuals.

Range/Average: new awards, $135,000; continuations, $130,000.

Activity: FY 04, 43 grants; 1 SBIR project.

HQ: International Education and Graduate Programs Service, same address as **84.015**. Phone: (202)502-7636. **Internet:** "www.ed.gov/programs/iegpsirs/". (Note: no field offices for this program.)

84.018 OVERSEAS PROGRAMS—SPECIAL BILATERAL PROJECTS

Assistance: project grants (100 percent/4-6 weeks).

Purposes: pursuant to MECEA as amended, to pay the travel and tuition costs of educators participating in short-term training seminars abroad, on topics in the social sciences and humanities.

Eligible applicants/beneficiaries: U.S. citizens or permanent residents with appropriate language proficiency and a bachelor's degree, that are: undergraduate faculty members or full-time elementary or junior high school teachers, administrators, or supervisors with at least three years of professional experience in U.S. school systems. (DOED recommends applicants to the Fulbright scholarship board for approval.)

Range/Average: $217,000.

Activity: FY 04, 158 participants in 10 projects.

HQ: same address as **84.016**. Phone: (202)502-7691. **Internet:** "www.ed.gov/programs/iegpssap/". (Note: no field offices for this program.)

84.019 OVERSEAS—FACULTY RESEARCH ABROAD

Assistance: project grants (100 percent/3-12 months).

Purposes: pursuant to MECEA as amended, for fellowships for research abroad by college faculty members, relevant to foreign languages and cultures. Generally, grants are unavailable for projects focusing primarily on Western Europe, nor in countries where the U.S. has no formal diplomatic relations. Awards provide stipends in lieu of salary and cover travel costs, fees to foreign institutions, expenses for expendable materials and supplies, services.

Eligible applicants: IHEs.

Eligible beneficiaries: U.S. citizens, nationals, or permanent residents that: are IHE employees; have been engaged in teaching relevant to the foreign language or area specialization for the previous two years; are not engaged in dissertation research for a Ph.D.; have appropriate language skills. (DOED recommends applicants to the Fulbright scholarship board for approval.)

Range/Average: $60,000.

Activity: FY 04, 26 fellowships.

HQ: Advanced Training and Research Team, same address as **84.017**. Phone: (202)502-7633. **Internet:** "www.ed.gov/programs/iegpsfra/". (Note: no field offices for this program.)

84.021 OVERSEAS—GROUP PROJECTS ABROAD

Assistance: project grants (100 percent/5 weeks to 36 months).

Purposes: pursuant to MECEA, for groups of teachers, faculty, and graduate or upper-classmen to conduct studies abroad in modern foreign languages and area studies. Funds may cover costs incurred abroad including round-trip travel, rent for instructional facilities, maintenance stipends, books, teaching materials, clerical, and related costs.

Eligible applicants: IHEs; state departments of education; private nonprofit educational organizations; consortia.

Eligible beneficiaries: U.S. citizens, nationals, or permanent residents that are faculty members or teachers at all levels, or graduate students or upper-classmen planning teaching careers in foreign language or area studies. (DOED recommends applicants to the Fulbright scholarship board for approval.)

Range/Average: new awards, $65,000; continuations, $96,000.

Activity: FY 04, 59 projects with 986 participants.

HQ: International Studies Team, International Education and Grants Programs Service, OPE-DOED, 400 Maryland Ave. SW, Washington, DC 20202-5332. Phone: (202)502-7624. **Internet:** "www.ed.gov/programs/iegpsgpa/". (Note: no field offices for this program.)

84.022 OVERSEAS—DOCTORAL DISSERTATION

Assistance: project grants (100 percent/6-12 months).

Purposes: pursuant to MECEA as amended, for fellowships to graduate students to complete dissertation research abroad in modern foreign languages and area studies—to develop research knowledge and capability in areas not widely included in American curricula. Generally, no grants are available for projects focusing primarily on Western Europe, nor in countries where the U.S. has no formal diplomatic relations. Grants may cover stipends, travel costs, tuition to host institutions, dependents allowances, insurance, project expenses.

Eligible applicants: IHEs.

Eligible beneficiaries: U.S. citizens, nationals, or permanent residents that are graduate students already admitted to a doctoral degree candidacy program, plan teaching careers in the U.S. upon graduation, and have appropriate language skills. (DOED recommends applicants to the Fulbright scholarship board for approval.)

Range/Average: $30,000.

Activity: FY 04, 150 fellowships.

HQ: International Education Programs Service, same address as **84.015**. Phone: (202)502-7632. **Internet:** "www.ed.gov/programs/iegsddrap/". (Note: no field offices for this program.)

84.027 SPECIAL EDUCATION—GRANTS TO STATES

Assistance: formula grants (100 percent).

Purposes: pursuant to the Individuals with Disabilities Act (IDEA) as amended, to provide special education and related services to children and youth, age 3-21, with disabilities, including those in private schools.

Eligible applicants/beneficiaries: SEAs; territories and possessions; BIA. LEAs apply to SEAs for funds.

Range: $14,038,000 to $1,072,637,000.

Activity: FY 04, 6,700,000 children served.

HQ: Division of Monitoring and State Improvement Planning, OSERS-DOED, 400 Maryland Ave. SW, Washington, DC 20202. Phone: (202)245-7629. **Internet:** "www.ed.gov/about/offices/list/osers/osep/index.html".

84.031 HIGHER EDUCATION—INSTITUTIONAL AID

Assistance: project grants (50-100 percent/to 5 years).

Purposes: pursuant to HEA as amended, Title III, to help colleges and universities address their fiscal and management problems. The Strengthening Institutions Program includes tribally controlled and Alaska native- and Hawaii native-serving institutions; funds may be used to plan, develop, and implement programs for faculty development, and for administrative expenses, improvement of academic programs, library and equipment purchases, and student services. The Historically Black Colleges and Universities (HBCU) Program provides funds for undergraduate and graduate programs, which may be used: to acquire scientific equipment; to construct, maintain, and improve classroom, library, and other instructional facilities; for faculty exchanges and fellowships; to purchase library materials; to provide tutoring, counseling, and other student services; for administrative management and equipment. Graduate HBCU program funds may be used to establish or maintain endowments. HBCU projects over $1,000,000 require a 50 percent match.

Eligible applicants/beneficiaries: IHEs with a low average educational and general expenditure, substantial percentage of students receiving Pell Grants or other federal need-based financial aid; HBCUs established prior to 1964.

Range: HBCU, from $500,000.

Activity: FY 04, 500 grants.

HQ: Office of Higher Education Programs, OPE-DOED, 1990 K St. NW, Washington, DC 20006-8500. Phone: (202)502-7777. **Internet:** "www.ed.gov/programs/iduestitle3a/". (Note: no field offices for this program.)

84.032 FEDERAL FAMILY EDUCATION LOANS ("FFELP")

Assistance: guaranteed/insured loans (100 percent/ 5-30 years).

Purposes: pursuant to HEA as amended, Title IV, to provide federal reinsurance on loans insured by state or private nonprofit guaranty agencies—for vocational, graduate, or undergraduate student educational expenses. Loans are obtained from banks, credit unions, savings and loan associations, pension funds, insurance companies, and schools. Repayment of Stafford loans begins six months after termination of at least half-time enrollment; for PLUS loans, repayment begins 60 days after disbursement of the last installment, and generally extends five to ten years, except that Consolidation Loans may extend up to 30 years. Deferments and forbearance of payment may be granted for certain periods.

Eligible applicants/beneficiaries: Stafford loans—generally, any U.S. citizen, national, or permanent resident enrolled or accepted for enrollment for at least half-time as an undergraduate, graduate, professional, or vocational student at a participating postsecondary school. Federal PLUS program—parents on behalf of dependent students. Federal Unsubsidized Stafford program—graduate, professional, and independent undergraduate students, including half-time students seeking elementary or secondary teacher certification; exceptionally, dependent undergraduate students. Consolidation loans—graduates including married couples; school enrollment is not required. U.S. citizens or nationals may obtain loans to attend eligible foreign postsecondary schools. Applicants for subsidized loans must meet needs criteria. Applicants must maintain satisfactory academic performance, and may neither owe a refund nor be in default on a Title IV grant or loan.

Range: varies according to type of loan.

Activity: FY 04, 10,800,000 loans.

HQ: same as **84.007**.

84.033 FEDERAL WORK-STUDY PROGRAM ("FWS")

Assistance: direct payments/specified use (50-75 percent).

Purposes: pursuant to HEA as amended, Title IV, to provide part-time employment to postsecondary students. The program contributes up to 75 percent of student earnings in jobs in public or nonprofit organizations, or 50 percent when a profit organization hires the student—plus administrative cost allowances to the educational institution. At least 5 percent of allocated funds must support students employed in community service.

Eligible applicants: public, private nonprofit, postsecondary vocational, and proprietary IHEs.

Eligible beneficiaries: undergraduate, graduate, or professional students meeting citizenship and residency requirements, demonstrating financial need, maintaining satisfactory academic progress, in compliance with Selective Service requirements, and neither owing a refund nor in default on a Title IV grant or loan.

Range/Average: students, $1,446 per award.
Activity: FY 04, 826,000 student jobs supported.
HQ: same as **84.007**.

84.037 PERKINS LOAN CANCELLATIONS

Assistance: direct payments/specified use; direct payments/unrestricted use.

Purposes: pursuant to HEA as amended, Title IV, to reimburse institutions for their share of loans canceled for Perkins loan recipients that: become teachers; perform full-time active military service; and, certain other recipients.

Eligible applicants: same as for **84.033**.

Eligible beneficiaries: Federal Perkins and National Direct and Defense Loan borrowers for loans made 23 July 1992 or after, with an outstanding balance as of 7 October 1998—loan cancellation is available for full-time service as: teachers in designated elementary or secondary schools with a high enrollment of children from low-income families; Head Start Programs staff; members of the Armed Forces in areas of hostilities; volunteers in the Peace Corps or in ACTION programs; law enforcement or corrections officers serving state, local, or federal agencies; special education teachers of children with disabilities or professional providers of early intervention services; teachers of mathematics, science, foreign languages, bilingual education, or certain other fields; nurses or medical technicians; or, employees of public or private child or family service agencies providing services to high-risk children from low-income communities and their families.

Range/Average: N.A.
Activity: N.A.
HQ: same as **84.007** (use zip code 20202-5347).

84.038 FEDERAL PERKINS LOAN PROGRAM—FEDERAL CAPITAL CONTRIBUTIONS

Assistance: direct payments/specified use (75 percent).

Purposes: pursuant to HEA as amended, Title IV, for educational institutions to make low-interest loans to needy undergraduate, graduate, and professional students for their educational expenses. The institutions receive an administrative cost allowance.

Eligible applicants/beneficiaries: same as for **84.033**.

Range: graduate, professional students, to $6,000 annually and $40,000 cumulative maximum including undergraduate loans; undergraduates, to $4,000 annually and $20,000 cumulative maximum. (Maximums may be 20 percent more for study abroad.) **Average**: $2,003 annually.

Activity: FY 04, 630,000 student awards.
HQ: same as **84.007**.

84.040 IMPACT AID—FACILITIES MAINTENANCE

Assistance: project grants (100 percent).
Purposes: pursuant to ESEA as amended, Title VIII, to construct, enlarge,

maintain, restore, or improve school facilities owned by DOED and operated by LEAs, and to transfer such facilities to LEAs.

Eligible applicants/beneficiaries: LEAs.

Range/Average: N.A.

Activity: not quantified specifically.

HQ: Impact Aid Programs, OESE-DOED, 400 Maryland Ave. SW - Rm.3E105, Washington, DC 20202-6244. Phone: (202)260-3858. **Internet:** "www.ed.gov/about/offices/list/oese/impactaid/index.html"; e-mail, "impact.aid@ed.gov". (Note: no field offices for this program.)

84.041 IMPACT AID

Assistance: formula grants (100 percent).

Purposes: pursuant to ESEA as amended, Title VIII, for operating costs of LEAs where enrollments or the tax base are adversely affected by federal activities including: federal acquisition of real property; employment of parents on federal property or in the uniformed services; significant numbers of children residing on federal land including Indian lands; sudden increases in school enrollment. Special additional funds are provided based on related enrollments of handicapped children, which must be used for special programs. Payments for construction may be used for construction and renovation, debt service, or other capital fund activities.

Eligible applicants/beneficiaries: LEAs.

Range: N.A.

Activity: FY 04, 1,250 grants serving 1,038,000 children.

HQ: same as **84.040**. (Note: no field offices for this program.)

84.042 TRIO—STUDENT SUPPORT SERVICES

Assistance: project grants (100 percent/4-5 years).

Purposes: pursuant to HEA as amended, Title IV, to provide supportive services to disadvantaged college students to enhance their potential to complete their programs, to facilitate their transition from two-year to four-year programs of study, or to graduate or professional programs. Projects may include personal and academic counseling, career guidance, instruction, mentoring, tutoring, and special services to students with limited language proficiency. Grants may be awarded to students under certain conditions. At least two-thirds of project participants must be physically handicapped or low-income, first-generation college students.

Eligible applicants/beneficiaries: IHEs and consortia.

Range/Average: $281,000.

Activity: FY 04, 935 awards, 196,000 students served.

HQ: Federal TRIO Programs, OPE-DOED, 400 Maryland Ave. SW, Washington, DC 20202-5249. Phone: (202)502-7694, -7097. **Internet:** "www.ed.gov/programs/triostusupp/"; e-mail, "trio@ed.gov".

84.044 TRIO—TALENT SEARCH

Assistance: project grants (100 percent/to 5 years).

Purposes: pursuant to HEA as amended, Title IV, to identify disadvantaged youth with potential for postsecondary education; to encourage them to return to or continue in and graduate from secondary schools and enroll in postsecondary education; to publicize the availability of financial aid; to provide special tutoring. Two-thirds of project participants must be low-income, potential first-generation college students.

Eligible applicants: IHEs; public and private agencies and organizations; combinations of IHEs and others; some secondary schools.

Eligible beneficiaries: individuals residing in target areas or attending a target school. Participants must be age 11-27 (exceptions allowed).

Range/Average: new awards, $372,000; continuations, $307,000.

Activity: FY 04, 469 grants; 383,000 individuals served.

HQ: same address as **84.042**. Phone: (202)502-7539. **Internet:** "www.ed.gov/programs/triotalent/"; e-mail, "trio@ed.gov". (Note: no field offices for this program.)

84.047 TRIO—UPWARD BOUND

Assistance: project grants (100 percent/to 5 years).

Purposes: pursuant to HEA as amended, Title IV, for programs providing academic instruction, personal and academic counseling, tutoring, career guidance, and special instruction—to prepare participants for postsecondary education and for careers in which persons from disadvantaged backgrounds are under-represented. Stipends may be paid to students ($40 monthly during the academic year, $60 monthly during special summer residential programs). Two-thirds of the participants must be low-income, potential first-generation college students.

Eligible applicants: same as for **84.044**.

Eligible beneficiaries: low-income individuals and potential first-generation college students. Except for veterans, eligible regardless of age, participants must be age 13-19 and have completed the eighth grade but not have entered the twelfth grade (exceptions allowed).

Range/Average: new awards, $346,000; new math/science, $269,000.

Activity: FY 04, 805 awards; 62,000 students served; 127 awards for math/science centers projects.

HQ: same address as **84.042**. Phone: (202)502-7545. **Internet:** "www.ed.gov/programs/trioupbound/"; e-mail, "trio@ed.gov".

84.048 VOCATIONAL EDUCATION—BASIC GRANTS TO STATES

Assistance: formula grants (states, 50 percent/27 months; outlying areas, 100 percent).

Purposes: pursuant to the Carl D. Perkins Vocational and Technical Education Act of 1998 (CDPVTEA), Title I, to expand and improve vocational education programs, including special programs for single parents, single pregnant women, displaced homemakers, criminal offenders in correctional institutions, and for individuals participating in programs to eliminate sex bias and stereotyping.

Eligible applicants/beneficiaries: states, outlying areas. Subgrants may be awarded to LEAs and postsecondary institutions.

Range: $4,215,000 to $127,705,000.

Activity: not quantified specifically.

HQ: Division of High School, Postsecondary and Career Education, OVAE-DOED, 400 Maryland Ave. SW, Washington, DC 20202-7241. Phone: (202)245-7781. **Internet:** "www.ed.gov/students/prep/job/cte/index.html". (Note: no field offices for this program.)

84.051 VOCATIONAL EDUCATION—NATIONAL PROGRAMS

Assistance: project grants (100 percent/to 5 years).

Purposes: pursuant to CDPVTEA as amended, for research, development, demonstration, dissemination, evaluation, and assessment activities to improve vocational and technical education.

Eligible applicants/beneficiaries: universities; university consortia and a public or private nonprofit organization.

Range/Average: N.A.

Activity: support for the National Center for Research and related activities.

HQ: Policy, Research and Evaluation Staff, OVAE-DOED, 400 Maryland Ave. SW, Washington, DC 20202-7242. Phone: (202)245-7818. **Internet:** "www.ed.gov/about/offices/list/ovae/index.html". (Note: no field offices for this program.)

84.060 INDIAN EDUCATION—GRANTS TO LOCAL EDUCATIONAL AGENCIES

Assistance: formula grants; project grants (100 percent/to 5 years).

Purposes: pursuant to ESEA as amended, Title VII, for education programs serving Indian students to assure that they are based on state content and student performance standards. Among the types of activities that may be funded are culturally related programs including native languages, early childhood and family programs emphasizing school readiness, enrichment programs, school-to-work transition, drop-out prevention.

Eligible applicants/beneficiaries: LEAs that enroll at least 10 Indian children or in which Indians constitute at least 25 percent of the total enrollment—except those serving Indian children in Alaska, California, and Oklahoma or located on or near an Indian reservation; BIA-funded schools.

Range: $4,000 to $2,180,000. **Average:** $209 per student.

Activity: FY 04, awards to 1,072 LEAs, 46 BIA grant/contract, 46 BIA-operated schools—serving 458,000 Indian students.

HQ: Office of Indian Education, OESE-DOED, 400 Maryland Ave. SW, Washington, DC 20202. Phone: (202)260-1683. **Internet:** "www.ed.gov/about/offices/list/ous/oie/programs.html#fgrants". (Note: no field offices for this program.)

84.063 FEDERAL PELL GRANT PROGRAM
("Pell Grants")

Assistance: direct payments/specified use.

Purposes: pursuant to HEA as amended, Title IV, for grants to undergraduate postsecondary students demonstrating financial need—to attend public or private nonprofit colleges, vocational-technical schools, universities, hospital schools of nursing, or for-profit proprietary institutions. Award amount reflects family income and assets.

Eligible applicants/beneficiaries: U.S. citizens or eligible noncitizens with a high school diploma, enrolled as undergraduate students and making satisfactory academic progress. Eligible males, age 18 or over and born after December 31, 1959, must have registered with the Selective Service. Students may not owe a refund nor be in default on a Title IV grant or loan.

Range: $400 to $4,050 annually. **Average:** $2,469.

Activity: FY 04, 5,302,000 grants awarded.

HQ: same as **84.007**.

84.066 TRIO—EDUCATIONAL OPPORTUNITY CENTERS

Assistance: project grants (100 percent/to 5 years).

Purposes: pursuant to HEA as amended, Title IV, to establish and operate educational opportunity centers to provide academic and financial information to qualified adults interested in pursuing postsecondary education, and to assist them in applying for admission. Tutoring and counseling may be provided for participants not enrolled in an Upward Bound or a Student Support Services project. Two-thirds of the participants must be low-income potential first-generation college students.

Eligible applicants: same as for **84.044**.

Eligible beneficiaries: residents of target areas, at least age 19 (exceptions allowed).

Range/Average: new awards, $495,000; continuations, $345,000.

Activity: FY 04, 139 awards assisting 217,000 participants.

HQ: same address as **84.042**. Phone: (202)502-7547. **Internet:** "www.ed.gov/programs/trioeoc/"; e-mail, "ope.trio@ed.gov". (Note: no field offices for this program.)

84.069 LEVERAGING EDUCATIONAL ASSISTANCE PARTNERSHIP ("LEAP")

Assistance: formula grants (50 percent).

Purposes: pursuant to HEA as amended, Title IV, to provide scholarships of up to $5,000 to postsecondary students with substantial financial need, enrolled at postsecondary institutions. Grant amounts are reduced for students enrolled less than full time.

Eligible applicants/beneficiaries: state and territorial agencies.

Range: student awards, to $5,000. **Average:** $1,000.

Activity: FY 04, awards to 169,000 students.

HQ: same as **84.007** (use zip code 20202-5447).

84.083 WOMEN'S EDUCATIONAL EQUITY ACT PROGRAM

Assistance: project grants (100 percent/to 4 years).

Purposes: pursuant to ESEA as amended, Title V, to promote gender equity for women and girls at all levels of education, including their increased participation in such areas as math, science, and computer science courses. Grants may be awarded for implementation projects or for research to develop model programs.

Eligible applicants/beneficiaries: public and private nonprofit agencies, institutions, and organizations; student and community groups; individuals.

Range/Average: implementation, $270,000.

Activity: FY 04, 9 implementation awards.

HQ: Office of Innovation and Improvement, OESE-DOED, 400 Maryland Ave. SW, Washington, DC 20202. Phone: (202)260-0964. **Internet:** "www.ed.gov/programs/equity/index.html". (Note: no field offices for this program.)

84.101 VOCATIONAL EDUCATION—INDIANS SET-ASIDE

Assistance: project grants (100 percent/to 2 years).

Purposes: pursuant to CDPVTEA, Title I, to plan, conduct, and administer Indian vocational and technical education programs or portions of programs.

Eligible applicants/beneficiaries: tribes, tribal organizations, Alaska native entities.

Range/Average: N.A.

Activity: 35 projects funded.

HQ: Division of High School, Postsecondary and Career Education, OVAE-DOED, 400 Maryland Ave. SW, Washington, DC 20202-7242. Phone: (202)205-9353. **Internet:** "www.ed.gov/programs/cteivep/index.html". (Note: no field offices for this program.)

84.103 TRIO STAFF TRAINING PROGRAM")

Assistance: project grants (100 percent/1-2 years).

Purposes: pursuant to HEA as amended, Title IV, to train present or new staff and leadership personnel for federal TRIO programs (special programs for students from disadvantaged backgrounds—**84.042, 84.044, 84.047, 84.066, 84.217**). Grants support seminars, workshops, internships, and publications.

Eligible applicants/beneficiaries: IHEs, public and nonprofit private agencies and organizations.

Range/Average: $408,000.

Activity: FY 04, 13 grants involving 3,688 TRIO projects staff.

HQ: same address as **84.042**. Phone: (202)502-7733, -7735. **Internet:** "www.ed.gov/programs/triotrain/"; e-mail, "trio@ed.gov". (Note: no field offices for this program.)

84.116 FUND FOR THE IMPROVEMENT OF POSTSECONDARY EDUCATION ("FIPSE")

Assistance: project grants (to 100 percent/1-3 years).

Purposes: pursuant to HEA as amended, Title VII, to develop innovative programs to improve access to and quality of postsecondary education.

Examples of funded projects include cooperation between colleges and business, uses of technology, improved access for Blacks, Hispanics, and other minorities.

Eligible applicants/beneficiaries: two- and four-year IHEs, community organizations, libraries, museums, consortia, student groups, local government agencies.

Range/Average: new grants, $194,000; continuations, $147,000.

Activity: FY 04, 150 grants.

HQ: FIPSE, OPE-DOED, Washington, DC 20202-5175. Phone: (202)502-7506. **Internet:** "www.ed.gov/programs/fipsecomp/". (Note: no field offices for this program.)

84.120 MINORITY SCIENCE AND ENGINEERING IMPROVEMENT ("MSEIP")

Assistance: project grants (to 100 percent/1-3 years).

Purposes: pursuant to HEA as amended, Title III, to improve undergraduate science and engineering education programs at predominantly minority institutions to better prepare their students, particularly women, for graduate work or careers in which they are under-represented. Eligible uses of funds include salaries, purchase of equipment and instructional materials, faculty development, and inservice training.

Eligible applicants/beneficiaries: private and public nonprofit two- and four-year IHEs whose enrollments are predominantly American Indian, Alaska native, Black, Hispanic, Pacific Islander, or any combination of these or other under-represented disadvantaged ethnic minorities. Also, nonprofit science-oriented organizations, professional scientific societies, and other accredited IHEs that provide needed services to eligible applicants.

Range/Average: new awards, $122,000; continuations, $73,000.

Activity: FY 04, 96 awards.

HQ: Institutional Development and Undergraduate Education Service, OPE-DOED, Washington, DC 20202. Phone: (202)502-7598. **Internet:** "www.ed.gov/programs/iduesmsi/". (Note: no field offices for this program.)

84.126 REHABILITATION SERVICES—VOCATIONAL REHABILITATION GRANTS TO STATES

Assistance: formula grants (79 percent).

Purposes: pursuant to the Rehabilitation Act of 1973 as amended, for vocational rehabilitation services to persons with mental and/or physical disabilities resulting in employment handicaps that may reasonably be expected to increase their employability. Services include: assessment; counseling; vocational and other training; reader services for the blind, interpreter services for the deaf; job placement; medical and related services, prosthetic and orthotic devices; rehabilitation technology; transportation to obtain services; construction and establishment of community rehabilitation facilities; services to families of handicapped persons.

Eligible applicants/beneficiaries: state agencies, territories, possessions.

Range: $7,399,000 to $247,893,000.

Activity: FY 04, 1,037,000 persons served.

HQ: Rehabilitation Services Administration, OSERS-DOED, 400 Maryland Ave. SW, Washington, DC 20202-2500. Phone: (202)245-7533. **Internet:** "www.ed.gov/programs/rsabvrs.html".

84.128 REHABILITATION SERVICES—SERVICE PROJECTS

Assistance: project grants (50-100 percent/3-5 years).

Purposes: pursuant to the Rehabilitation Act of 1973 as amended, for vocational rehabilitation demonstrations and special projects for disabled persons, holding promise of expanding and otherwise improving services over and above those provided by **84.126**. Special programs include recreation projects, migrant and seasonal worker projects.

Eligible applicants/beneficiaries: recreational projects—states, public agencies, nonprofit organizations. Migrant and seasonal farm worker projects—designated state agencies including territories and possessions; nonprofit and local agencies in collaboration with state agencies.

Range/Average: N.A.

Activity: FY 04, 26 recreational, 13 migrant and seasonal farm worker projects.

HQ: Rehabilitation Services Administration, OSERS-DOED, 400 Maryland Ave. SW, Washington, DC 20202-2647. Phone: *migrant, seasonal workers,* (202)245-7421; (202)245-7320. **Internet:** "www.ed.gov/programs/rsamigrant/index.html"; "www.ed.gov/programs/rsarecreation/index.html".

84.129 REHABILITATION LONG-TERM TRAINING

Assistance: project grants (90 percent/to 5 years).

Purposes: pursuant to the Rehabilitation Act of 1973 as amended, for academic training programs for personnel involved in vocational rehabilitation for the disabled. Training grants cover such specialties as rehabilitation counseling, independent living, rehabilitation medicine, physical and occupational therapy, prosthetics-orthotics, speech-language, pathology and audiology, rehabilitation of the deaf and the blind, rehabilitation technology. At least 75 percent of grant funds must be used for scholarships.

Eligible applicants/beneficiaries: IHEs, state vocational rehabilitation agencies including territories and possessions; other public or nonprofit agencies and organizations.

Range: $70,000 to $100,000. **Average:** $100,000.

Activity: annually, 1,500 students supported.

HQ: Rehabilitation Services Administration, OSERS-DOED, 400 Maryland Ave. SW, Washington, DC 20202-2649. Phone: (202)245-7458. **Internet:** "www.ed.gov/offices/OSERS/RSA".

84.132 CENTERS FOR INDEPENDENT LIVING

Assistance: project grants (to 100 percent/to 5 years).

Purposes: pursuant to the Rehabilitation Act of 1973 as amended, to establish and operate centers for independent living for significantly disabled persons—providing a broad range of services to residents such as information and referrals, training in independent living skills, peer counseling, and individual and systems advocacy. Individuals with disabilities must be employed by and substantially involved in policy direction and management of the centers. Personnel training may be provided with grants funds.

Eligible applicants: principally, previously funded private nonprofit agencies. If funds are available, other centers for independent living and state agencies, including territories and possessions, become eligible.

Eligible beneficiaries: persons with such significant physical, mental cognitive, or sensor impairments that independent living services are needed to attain independence in the home or community.

Range: $775,000 to $7,233,000. **Average:** $1,360,000.

Activity: 320 centers supported.

HQ: Rehabilitation Services Administration, OSERS-DOED, 400 Maryland Ave. SW, Washington, DC 20202. Phone: (202)245-7585. **Internet:** "www.ed.gov/programs/cil/index.html".

84.133 NATIONAL INSTITUTE ON DISABILITY AND REHABILITATION RESEARCH

Assistance: project grants (cost sharing/to 5 years).

Purposes: pursuant to the Rehabilitation Act of 1973 as amended, for research, demonstrations, dissemination and utilization projects, rehabilitation personnel career training, and research fellowships—involving broad ranges of programs and services for persons of all ages with physical and mental disabilities, especially the severely disabled.

Eligible applicants/beneficiaries: states; public, private, or nonprofit agencies and organizations; IHEs; tribes and tribal organizations. Individuals may obtain fellowships.

Range/Average: N.A.

Activity: FY 04, 245 projects funded.

HQ: National Institute on Disability and Rehabilitation Research, OSERS-DOED, 400 Maryland Ave. SW, Washington, DC 20202-2500. Phone: (202)245-7462. **Internet:** "www.ed.gov/about/offices/list/nidrr/index.html". (Note: no field offices for this program.)

84.141 MIGRANT EDUCATION—HIGH SCHOOL EQUIVALENCY PROGRAM ("HEP")

Assistance: project grants (100 percent/to 5 years).

Purposes: pursuant to HEA, Title IV, to assist migrant students obtain the equivalent of a secondary school diploma and subsequently to gain employment or to attend college or obtain other postsecondary education or training. Program funds may be used to recruit students and to provide academic and support services and stipends.

Eligible applicants: IHEs or private nonprofit agencies in cooperation with IHEs.

Eligible beneficiaries: students age 16 or older, lacking a high school diploma, in migrant or seasonally employed families, or that participated or were eligible to participate in the Title I Migrant Education Program or JTPA 402.

Range/Average: $2,642 per student.

Activity: 2004, 7,150 students served in 54 projects.

HQ: Office of Migrant Education, OESE-DOED, 400 Maryland Ave. SW - Rm.3E227, Washington, DC 20202. Phone: (202)260-1396. **Internet:** "www.ed.gov/programs/hep/index.html". (Note: no field offices for this program.)

84.144 MIGRANT EDUCATION—COORDINATION PROGRAM

Assistance: project grants (100 percent/to 5 years).

Purposes: pursuant to ESEA, Title I, to improve interstate and intrastate coordination of migrant education among SEAs and LEAs. Incentive grants may be provided to SEAs that participate in an approved consortium.

Eligible applicants/beneficiaries: SEAs, LEAs, IHEs, other public or non-profit private entities.

Range/Average: N.A.

Activity: FY 03, 35 consortium incentive grants.

HQ: same address (Rm.3E331) as **84.011**. Phone: (202)260-1391. **Internet:** "www.ed.gov/about/offices/oese/ome/index.html". (Note: no field offices for this program.)

84.145 FEDERAL REAL PROPERTY ASSISTANCE PROGRAM

Assistance: sale, exchange, or donation of property and goods.

Purposes: pursuant to the Federal Property and Administrative Services Act of 1949 as amended and Department of Education Organization Act of 1979, to convey surplus federal real property for educational purposes, including all educational levels, vocational education or rehabilitation, libraries, central administration facilities, educational radio and television, rehabilitation and training, research, correctional education centers. Examples include: improved or unimproved land; former Nike sites; total military bases.

Eligible applicants/beneficiaries: states and their political subdivisions and instrumentalities; tax-supported or tax-exempt organizations or private non-profit institutions.

Activity: annually, 10 transfers.

HQ: Federal Real Property Assistance Program, Office of the Administrator/Management Services, DOED, 400 Maryland Ave. SW, Washington, DC 20202. Phone: (202)401-0500. **Internet:** "www.ed.gov".

84.149 MIGRANT EDUCATION—COLLEGE ASSISTANCE MIGRANT PROGRAM ("CAMP")

Assistance: project grants (100 percent/to 5 years).

Purposes: pursuant to HEA, Title IV, to provide supportive and instructional services and other assistance to migrants enrolling full-time in college for the first academic year. Funds may be used to provide tutoring, counseling, assistance in obtaining financial aid, follow-up services, and inservice training for project staff.

Eligible applicants: same as for **84.141**.

Eligible beneficiaries: first-year college students engaged, or whose families are engaged, in migrant or other seasonal farm work, or that participated or were eligible to participate in the Title I Migrant Education Program or JTPA 402.

Range/Average: $6,500 per student.

Activity: 2,400 students currently being served at 45 institutions.

HQ: same address/phone as **84.141**. **Internet:** "www.ed.gov/programs/ camp/index.html". (Note: no field offices for this program.)

84.153 BUSINESS AND INTERNATIONAL EDUCATION PROJECTS

Assistance: project grants (50 percent/1-2 years).

Purposes: pursuant to HEA as amended, Title VI, for innovations and improvements in international business education curricula. Participating institutions must enter into agreements with businesses, trade organizations, or associations engaged in international economic activity.

Eligible applicants/beneficiaries: IHEs.

Range/Average: continuations, $82,000; new awards, $73,000.

Activity: FY 04, 58 awards.

HQ: International Education and Graduate Programs Service, OPE-DOED, 400 Maryland Ave. SW, Washington, DC 20202-5332. Phone: (202)502-7626. **Internet:** "www.ed.gov/programs/iegpsbie/". (Note: no field offices for this program.)

84.160 TRAINING INTERPRETERS FOR INDIVIDUALS WHO ARE DEAF AND INDIVIDUALS WHO ARE DEAF-BLIND

Assistance: project grants (cost sharing/to 5 years).

Purposes: pursuant to the Rehabilitation Act of 1973 as amended, to train prospective or improve the skills of present manual, oral, and cued speech interpreters providing services to deaf or deaf-blind persons—through classroom instruction, workshops, seminars, and field placement. Curriculum may include such specialty areas as interpreting in medical, legal, or rehabilitation settings.

Eligible applicants/beneficiaries: public or private nonprofit agencies and organizations; IHEs.

Range: $120,000 to $160,000.

Activity: N.A.

HQ: Rehabilitation Services Administration, OSERS-DOED, 400 Maryland Ave. SW, Washington, DC 20202-2736. Phone: (202)245-7489. **Internet:** "www.ed.gov/students/college/aid/rehab/catinter.html". (Note: no field offices for this program.)

84.161 REHABILITATION SERVICES—CLIENT ASSISTANCE PROGRAM ("CAP")

Assistance: formula grants (100 percent).

Purposes: pursuant to the Rehabilitation Act of 1973 as amended, to help persons with disabilities obtain information about and benefits of Rehabilitation Act and ADA projects, programs, facilities, and services, whether as clients or applicants for services—and to help them overcome problems with service delivery systems including assistance and advocacy in pursuing legal, administrative, and other appropriate remedies. Grants may not support class action suits.

Eligible applicants/beneficiaries: states and territories, through public or private agencies designated by the governor.

Range: $122,000 to $1,232,000.

Activity: FY 04, 54,000 clients served.

HQ: same address as **84.126**. Phone: (202)245-7258. **Internet:** "www.ed.gov/programs/rsacap/index.html".

84.165 MAGNET SCHOOLS ASSISTANCE

Assistance: project grants (100 percent/to 3 years).

Purposes: pursuant to ESEA as amended, Title V, for magnet school projects that are part of approved desegregation plans designed to bring together students from different social, economic, racial, and ethnic backgrounds. Funds may be used for planning and promotional activities to develop, expand, continue, or enhance academic instruction; to pay or subsidize teacher and staff salaries; to purchase books, materials, equipment. Funds may not be used for transportation or activities that do not augment academic improvement. Project examples: science and math magnet projects; performing arts magnet programs; Montessori programs.

Eligible applicants/beneficiaries: LEAs.

Range: $357,000 to $3,385,000.

Activity: FY 04, 52 awards.

HQ: Magnet Schools Assistance Program, School Improvement Programs, Office of Innovation and Improvement, OESE-DOED, 400 Maryland Ave. SW, Washington, DC 20202-6140. Phone: (202)260-2476. **Internet:** "www.ed.gov/programs/magnet/index.html". (Note: no field offices for this program.)

84.169 INDEPENDENT LIVING—STATE GRANTS

Assistance: formula grants (50 percent).

Purposes: pursuant to the Rehabilitation Act of 1973 as amended, for states to maximize the leadership, empowerment, independence, and productivity of individuals with disabilities and their integration into the mainstream American society—through independent living services. Funds may be used to: support statewide independent living councils; support center operations; demonstrate ways to expand and improve services; increase the capacities of public or nonprofit organizations and agencies to develop comprehensive approaches and systems; conduct studies and analyses; train the disabled and service personnel; provide outreach to unserved or underserved populations.

Eligible applicants/beneficiaries: designated state agencies, territories, possessions.

Range/Average: $417,000.

Activity: 78 state units funded.

HQ: same address as **84.132**. Phone: (202)245-7404. **Internet:** "www.ed.gov/programs/rsailstate/index.html".

84.170 JAVITS FELLOWSHIPS

Assistance: project grants (100 percent/to 4 years).

Purposes: pursuant to HEA as amended, Title VII, for fellowships to graduate degree candidates demonstrating exceptional promise, financial need, and intending to pursue doctoral degrees in the arts, humanities, or social sciences—or terminal master's degrees.

Eligible applicants/beneficiaries: U.S. citizens, nationals, or permanent residents.

Range/Average: $30,000; institutional allowance, $12,000.

Activity: FY 04, 234 awards.

HQ: International Education and Graduate Programs, OPE-DOED, Washington, DC 20202. Phone: (202)502-7767. **Internet:** "www.ed.gov/programs/iegpsjavits/"; e-mail, "ope-javits-programs@ed.gov". (Note: no field offices for this program.)

84.173 SPECIAL EDUCATION—PRESCHOOL GRANTS

Assistance: formula grants (100 percent).

Purposes: pursuant to IDEA as amended, for free appropriate public educational programs for preschool children with disabilities, requiring special education and related services. States may also use funds to develop and implement elements of comprehensive statewide service delivery systems.

Eligible applicants: SEAs, DC, PR.

Eligible beneficiaries: children age 3-5 (optionally, age 2 and to reach age 3 during the school year), determined to be mentally retarded, hearing impaired, speech or language impaired, visually handicapped, seriously emotionally disturbed, autistic, orthopedically impaired, or other health-impaired.

Range: $255,000 to $39,551,000.

Activity: all eligible agencies funded; 680,000 children served.

HQ: Office of Special Education Programs, OSERS-DOED, 400 Maryland Ave. SW, Washington, DC 20202. Phone: (202)245-7553. **Internet:** "www.ed.gov/about/offices/list/osers/osep/programs.html".

84.177 REHABILITATION SERVICES—INDEPENDENT LIVING SERVICES FOR OLDER INDIVIDUALS WHO ARE BLIND

Assistance: project grants (90 percent/to 5 years).

Purposes: pursuant to the Rehabilitation Act of 1973 as amended, to provide independent living services for blind persons age 55 or older, whose vision impairments make competitive employment extremely difficult, but for whom independent living in their own homes or communities is feasible. Program funds may be used to pay such costs as: vision correction or modification; eyeglasses or other visual aids; services and equipment to enhance mobility and self-care; training in braille; teaching services in household management; public education activities.

Eligible applicants/beneficiaries: state agencies, territories, possessions.

Range/Average: $603,000.

Activity: 56 projects funded.

HQ: same address (Rm.5057 PCP) as **84.132**. Phone: (202)245-7454. **Internet:** "www.ed.gov/programs/rsailob/index.html".

84.181 SPECIAL EDUCATION—GRANTS FOR INFANTS AND FAMILIES WITH DISABILITIES

Assistance: formula grants (100 percent).

Purposes: pursuant to IDEA as amended, to develop and implement statewide, comprehensive, coordinated, multidisciplinary, inter-agency systems to provide early intervention services for handicapped infants and toddlers and their families. Grants may support expanded or improved services.

Eligible applicants/beneficiaries: states, territories, possessions.

Range: $2,194,000 to $54,397,000. **Average:** $8,388,000.

Activity: FY 04, 272,000 participants served.

HQ: Office of Special Education Programs, same address/phone, web site as **84.027**. (Note: no field offices for this program.)

84.184 SAFE AND DRUG-FREE SCHOOLS AND COMMUNITIES—NATIONAL PROGRAMS

Assistance: project grants (to 100 percent/1-4 years).

Purposes: pursuant to ESEA as amended, Title IV, for prevention and education activities concerning the illegal use of drugs and violence at all educational levels.

Eligible applicants/beneficiaries: public and private and nonprofit organizations, individuals.

Range: N.A.

Activity: FY 04, 93 safe schools/healthy students initiative, 19 coordinator initiative, 208 mentoring awards; 150 other grants.

HQ: Office of Safe and Drug-Free Schools, DOED, 400 Maryland Ave. SW, Washington, DC 20202-6123. Phone: (202)260-3954. **Internet:** "www.ed.gov/about/offices/list/osdfs/programs.html#state". (Note: no field offices for this program.)

84.185 BYRD HONORS SCHOLARSHIPS

Assistance: formula grants (100 percent/to 4 years).

Purposes: pursuant to HEA as amended, Title IV, for $1,500 annual merit scholarships to recognize and promote student excellence and achievement.

Each participating state is allotted at least 10 scholarships, based on population.

Eligible applicants: SEAs including territories and possessions.

Eligible beneficiaries: U.S. citizens or residents that are public or private high school graduates, accepted for enrollment at IHEs, demonstrating promise of continued outstanding academic achievement.

Range/Average: scholarships, $1,500.

Activity: FY 04, 27,000 scholarships.

HQ: Higher Education Programs, OPE-DOED, 400 Maryland Ave. SW, Washington, DC 20024-5251. Phone: (202)502-7583. **Internet:** "www.ed.gov/programs/iduesbyrd/". (Note: no field offices for this program.)

84.186 SAFE AND DRUG-FREE SCHOOLS AND COMMUNITIES—STATE GRANTS

Assistance: formula grants (100 percent).

Purposes: pursuant to ESEA as amended, Title IV, to establish alcohol, drug, tobacco, and violence prevention and education programs in local school systems, coordinated with related federal, state, and community efforts and resources including parent involvement. At least 20 percent of awarded funds must be distributed to community-based organizations.

Eligible applicants: state departments of education, governors, insular areas, native Hawaiian organizations.

Eligible beneficiaries: SEAs, LEAs, tribal governments, public and private nonprofit organizations including community action agencies, parent groups, and other community-based organizations.

Range: $2,153,000 to $53,257,000. **Average:** $8,279,000.

Activity: awards to all states, insular areas, and BIA.

HQ: same address, web site as **84.184**. Phone: (202)205-8134. (Note: no field offices for this program.)

84.187 SUPPORTED EMPLOYMENT SERVICES FOR INDIVIDUALS WITH SEVERE DISABILITIES

Assistance: formula grants (100 percent).

Purposes: pursuant to the Rehabilitation Act of 1973 as amended, for time-limited services leading to supported employment for severely handicapped persons whose potential to engage in a training program has been properly evaluated. Funds may be used for most program operating costs including systematic client training, skilled job trainers to accompany workers for intensive on-the-job training, job development, follow-up services.

Eligible applicants/beneficiaries: state vocational rehabilitation agencies, territories and possessions.

Range: states, $300,000 to $4,124,000.

Activity: 37,000 individuals served.

HQ: same address/phone as **84.126**. **Internet:** "www.ed.gov/programs/rsasupemp/index.html".

84.191 ADULT EDUCATION—NATIONAL LEADERSHIP ACTIVITIES

Assistance: project grants (100 percent/12-18 months).

Purposes: pursuant to the Adult Education and Family Literacy Act as amended, for the improvement and expansion nationally of adult basic education through applied research, development, demonstration, dissemination, evaluation, and related activities. Project examples: evaluations of "what works" for adult basic education and ESL, the funding set-aside for corrections education, and distance learning initiative.

Eligible applicants/beneficiaries: public or private agencies, institutions, organizations; business concerns; individuals.

Range/Average: N.A.

Activity: not quantified specifically.

HQ: Division of Adult Education and Literacy, OVAE-DOED, 400 Maryland Ave. SW, Washington, DC 20202-7240. Phone: (202)245-7758. **Internet:** "www.ed.gov/about/offices/list/ovae/pi/AdultEd/index.html". (Note: no field offices for this program.)

84.196 EDUCATION FOR HOMELESS CHILDREN AND YOUTH

Assistance: formula grants (100 percent).

Purposes: pursuant to MVHAA, to develop and implement plans to coordinate and improve education programs for homeless children and youth; to identify homeless children and ensure that they enroll in, attend, and achieve success in school. States may provide subgrants to LEAs for direct services to homeless children and youth including tutoring, summer enrichment programs, purchases of supplies, school personnel training.

Eligible applicants/beneficiaries: state departments of education and outlying areas; schools funded by DOI, serving Indian students.

Range/Average: states, $1,125,000.

Activity: awards to 50 states, DC, PR, VI, Guam, Samoa, Palau, Northern Marianas, and BIA.

HQ: OESE-DOED, 400 Maryland Ave. SW, Washington, DC 20202-6132. Phone: (202)260-4412. **Internet:** "www.ed.gov/programs/homeless/index.html". (Note: no field offices for this program.)

84.200 GRADUATE ASSISTANCE IN AREAS OF NATIONAL NEED ("GAANN")

Assistance: project grants (75 percent/3 years).

Purposes: pursuant to HEA as amended, Title VII, for graduate fellowships for up to five years that will help sustain and enhance the capacity for teaching and research in academic areas of national need, designated by the Secretary of Education.

Eligible applicants: IHEs.

Eligible beneficiaries: needy graduate students with excellent academic records and planning teaching or research careers. They must be U.S. citizens, nationals, permanent residents, or permanent residents of the Trust Territory of the Pacific Islands or citizens of the Freely Associated States.

Range/Average: new institutional grants, $189,000; fellowships, $42,000.

Activity: FY 04, 145 grants awarded providing 736 fellowships.

HQ: International Education and Graduate Programs Service, OPE-DOED, 400 Maryland Ave. SW, Washington, DC 20202-5247. Phone: (202)502-7638. **Internet:** "www.ed.gov/programs/iegpsgaann/"; e-mail, "ope.gaann.program@ed.gov". (Note: no field offices for this program.)

84.203 STAR SCHOOLS

Assistance: project grants (50-75 percent/to 5 years).

Purposes: pursuant to ESEA as amended, Title V, for telecommunications partnerships to encourage improved instruction in mathematics, science, foreign languages, vocational education, literacy skills, and other subjects. Funds may be used: to develop telecommunications facilities and to acquire equipment, instructional programming; for technical assistance; for teacher training. Priority is given to projects that will meet the needs of traditionally underserved populations.

Eligible applicants/beneficiaries: partnerships organized on a statewide or multistate basis (1) by public agencies or corporations or, (2) that include at least one SEA or LEA, and three or more of the following: LEAs with a significant number of schools eligible for Title I funds (or operated by DOI for Indian children); SEAs; adult and family education programs; IHEs or state higher education agencies; teacher training centers; public or private agencies with relevant experience, or public broadcasting entities; or a public or private elementary or secondary school.

Range: N.A.

Activity: FY 04, 13 grants.

HQ: OII-DOED, 555 New Jersey Ave. NW, Washington, DC 20208-5645. Phone: (202)205-5633. **Internet:** "www.ed.gov/programs/starschools/index.html". (Note: no field offices for this program.)

84.206 JAVITS GIFTED AND TALENTED STUDENTS EDUCATION GRANT PROGRAM

Assistance: project grants (100 percent/to 3 years).

Purposes: pursuant to ESEA as amended, Title V, for programs designed to meet the special educational needs of gifted and talented elementary and secondary students, including: personnel professional development; exemplary programs; innovative learning strategies; SEA leadership and assistance to local entities in planning, operating, and improving programs; research, technical assistance, and information dissemination.

Eligible applicants/beneficiaries: SEAs, LEAs, IHEs, public and private agencies and organizations, including tribes and Hawaii native organizations.

Range: N.A.

Activity: FY 04, 15 awards; National Center for Research and Development in the Education of Gifted and Talented Children and Youth also funded.

HQ: Jacob J. Javits Gifted and Talented Students Education, OESE-DOED, 400 Maryland Ave. SW, Washington, DC 20202. Phone: (202)260-1541.

Internet: "www.ed.gov/programs/javits/index.htm/". (Note: no field offices for this program.)

84.213 EVEN START—STATE EDUCATIONAL AGENCIES

Assistance: formula grants; project grants (subgrants, 50-90 percent/to 4 years).

Purposes: pursuant to ESEA as amended, Title I, for education projects involving low-income parents in the early education of their children, and to provide literacy training and adult and parenting education. Subgrants may support participant recruitment and screening, program design and coordination, instruction of children and parents, staff training.

Eligible applicants/beneficiaries: SEAs. Subgrants—partnerships of LEAs and community-based organizations, public agencies, IHEs, or other nonprofit organizations, with priority to projects in Empowerment Zones or Enterprise Communities.

Range: $1,113,000 to $31,451,000. **Average:** $4,282,000.

Activity: 1,000 projects funded in all states.

HQ: same address as **84.013**. Phone: (202)260-2533. **Internet:** "www.ed.gov/programs/evenstartformula/index.html". (Note: no field offices for this program.)

84.214 EVEN START—MIGRANT EDUCATION

Assistance: project grants (60-90 percent/to 4 years).

Purposes: pursuant to ESEA as amended, Title I, for education projects involving parents of migratory children in the early education of their children from birth-age 7, including adult literacy and adult basic and parenting education. Funds may support participant recruitment and screening, program design and coordination, instruction of children and parents, staff training.

Eligible applicants/beneficiaries: SEAs, LEAs, other entities including nonprofit community-based organizations.

Range/Average: N.A.

Activity: 28 projects operating.

HQ: Office of Migrant Education, OESE-DOED, FOB 6 - Rm.3E313, 400 Maryland Ave. SW, Washington, DC 20202-6134. Phone: (202)260-9533. **Internet:** same as **84.011**. (Note: no field offices for this program.)

84.215 FUND FOR THE IMPROVEMENT OF EDUCATION ("FIE")

Assistance: project grants (100 percent).

Purposes: pursuant to ESEA as amended, Title V, for projects of national significance to improve the quality of education, to assist all students to meet challenging state content standards, and contribute to the achievement of elementary and secondary students. Projects may support a wide range of activities.

Eligible applicants/beneficiaries: SEAs, LEAs, IHEs, public and private organizations.

Range: N.A.

Activity: N.A.

HQ: OERI-DOED, 555 New Jersey Ave. NW, Washington, DC 20208-5645. Phone: (202)205-4746. **Internet:** "www.ed.gov/offices/OERI". (Note: no field offices for this program.)

84.217 TRIO—MCNAIR POST-BACCALAUREATE ACHIEVEMENT

Assistance: project grants (100 percent/4-5 years).

Purposes: pursuant to HEA as amended, Title IV, to prepare low-income, first-generation college students and students from under-represented groups for graduate study. Services may include: opportunities for research and other scholarly activities; summer internships; seminars; tutoring; academic counseling; securing graduate admission and financial assistance; mentoring; exposure to cultural events.

Eligible applicants/beneficiaries: IHEs or combinations of IHEs.

Range/Average: new awards, $248,000; continuations, $233,000.

Activity: FY 04, 179 grants, serving 4,133 students.

HQ: same address as **84.042**. Phone: (202)502-7730, -7694. **Internet:** "www.ed.gov/programs/triomcnair/"; e-mail, "trio@ed.gov". (Note: no field offices for this program.)

84.220 CENTERS FOR INTERNATIONAL BUSINESS EDUCATION

Assistance: project grants (50-90 percent/3 years).

Purposes: pursuant to HEA as amended, Title VI, for inter-disciplinary faculty research to promote international competitiveness of U.S. business. Activities must include: center advisory councils to plan and design activities and programs; collaboration in the center's establishment and operation among the business, management, foreign language, international studies, and other professional schools or departments; assurance that the center's programs are open to students concentrating in these areas.

Eligible applicants/beneficiaries: public and nonprofit private IHEs, or combinations thereof.

Range/Average: $357,000.

Activity: FY 04, 30 grants.

HQ: International Studies Branch, Center for International Education, same address as **84.016**. Phone: (202)502-7700. **Internet:** "www.ed.gov/programs/iegpscibe/". (Note: no field offices for this program.)

84.224 ASSISTIVE TECHNOLOGY

Assistance: project grants; technical information.

Purposes: pursuant to the Assistive Technology Act of 1998, to develop and implement comprehensive consumer-responsive statewide programs of technology-related assistance and services for persons of all ages with disabilities, and to their family members, guardians, advocates, and authorized representatives. States may provide assistance directly to individuals or to statewide community-based organizations.

Eligible applicants/beneficiaries: states, DC, PR, outlying areas.

Range/Average: N.A.

Activity: awards to all states.

HQ: same address, web site as **84.133**. Phone: (202)245-7319. (Note: no field offices for this program.)

84.229 LANGUAGE RESOURCE CENTERS

Assistance: project grants (100 percent/to 3 years).

Purposes: pursuant to HEA as amended, Title VI, to establish, strengthen, and operate foreign language resource centers to improve teaching and learning at IHEs, through: research on the use of advanced educational technology; development of new teaching materials based on the research; development and application of performance testing; teacher training; publication of instructional materials in the less commonly taught languages; dissemination of project results.

Eligible applicants/beneficiaries: IHEs or combinations of IHEs.

Range/Average: $346,000.

Activity: FY 04, 14 awards.

HQ: International Education and Graduate Programs Service, same address as **84.015**. Phone: (202)502-7636. **Internet:** "www.ed.gov/programs/iegpslrc/". (Note: no field offices for this program.)

84.234 PROJECTS WITH INDUSTRY ("PWI")

Assistance: project grants (80 percent/to 5 years).

Purposes: pursuant to the Rehabilitation Act of 1973 as amended, for programs preparing persons with disabilities for employment in the competitive labor market, by partnering with private industry to provide job training, placement, and career advancement services.

Eligible applicants/beneficiaries: employers, profit and nonprofit organizations, labor unions, state vocational rehabilitation agencies. New awards are available only in unserved or under-served areas.

Range/Average: $235,000.

Activity: FY 04, 86 awards.

HQ: OSERS-DOED, 400 Maryland Ave. SW, Washington, DC 20202-2740. Phone: (202)245-7281. **Internet:** "www.ed.gov/programs/rsapwi/index.html".

84.235 REHABILITATION SERVICES DEMONSTRATION AND TRAINING PROGRAMS

Assistance: project grants (100 percent/to 5 years).

Purposes: pursuant to the Rehabilitation Act of 1973 as amended, to expand and improve vocational rehabilitation and related services for the disabled and severely disabled. Projects may include demonstrations involving such activities as: increasing client choice; service delivery; technical assistance; systems change; special studies and evaluations; transition services; supportive employment; services to unserved, underserved, or populations, and to low-incidence disabilities; transportation; parent information and training; Braille training.

Eligible applicants/beneficiaries: states, public or nonprofit organizations.

Range/Average: N.A.

Activity: FY 04, 80 projects funded.

HQ: same address as **84.126**. Phone: (202)245-7485. **Internet:** "www.ed.gov/offices/OSERS/RSA/Programs/Discretionary/demotrain.html".

84.240 PROGRAM OF PROTECTION AND ADVOCACY OF INDIVIDUAL RIGHTS ("PAIR")

Assistance: project grants (100 percent).

Purposes: pursuant to the Rehabilitation Act of 1973 as amended, for systems for protection and advocacy of the rights of persons with disabilities—including services upholding their individual legal and human rights beyond the scope of the Client Assistance Program, and for persons ineligible for programs under the Developmental Disabilities Assistance (DDA) and Bill of Rights Act and the Protection and Advocacy for Individuals with Mental Illness Act (PAIMI).

Eligible applicants/beneficiaries: state-designated protection and advocacy agencies, including territories.

Range: $168,000 to $1,692,000.

Activity: FY 04, 89,000 persons served.

HQ: same address/phone as **84.161**. **Internet:** "www.ed.gov/programs/rsapair/index.html".

84.243 TECH-PREP EDUCATION

Assistance: formula grants, project grants (100 percent/27 months).

Purposes: pursuant to CDPVTEA, for planning and demonstrations by educational consortia to develop and operate four-year programs to provide "tech-prep" education programs leading to two-year associate degrees or certificates, establishing proficiency in mathematics, science, communications, and technologies. The four years must include the two years preceding and following graduation from secondary school, including apprenticeships. Funds may support curriculum development, inservice teacher and counselor training.

Eligible applicants/beneficiaries: state vocational education boards. Subgrants—consortia of LEAs, intermediate education agencies or area vocational education schools serving secondary students, BIA-funded secondary schools, nonprofit and proprietary IHEs offering two-year associate degrees, and two-year apprenticeship programs that follow secondary instruction.

Range: $60,000 to $11,563,000.

Activity: Tech-Prep consortia in 50 states, DC, PR, and VI.

HQ: same address as **84.048**. Phone: (202)205-9441. **Internet:** "www.ed.gov/about/offices/ovae/pi/cte/tphome.html". (Note: no field offices for this program.)

84.245 TRIBALLY CONTROLLED POSTSECONDARY VOCATIONAL AND TECHNICAL INSTITUTIONS

Assistance: project grants (100 percent/to 5 years).

Purposes: pursuant to CDPVTEA, for the maintenance and operation of tribally controlled postsecondary vocational and technical institutions.

Eligible applicants/beneficiaries: chartered and accredited tribally controlled postsecondary vocational institutions that: have operated for at least three years; enroll at least 100 full-time students (a majority of which are Indians); and, meet other requirements.

Range: $3,000,000 to $4,200,000.

Activity: FY 04, 2 awards.

HQ: same address as **84.101**. Phone: (202)205-9962. **Internet:** "www.ed.gov/programs/tcpvi/index.html". (Note: no field offices for this program.)

84.246 REHABILITATION SHORT-TERM TRAINING

Assistance: project grants (cost sharing/1-3 years).

Purposes: pursuant to the Rehabilitation Act of 1973 as amended, for special training seminars, institutes, workshops, and other short-term courses in technical matters relating to the delivery of vocational, medical, social, and psychological services—in fields directly related to the vocational and independent living rehabilitation of persons with disabilities.

Eligible applicants/beneficiaries: same as for **84.129**.

Range: $100,000 to $250,000.

Activity: not quantified specifically.

HQ: same as **84.129**.

84.250 REHABILITATION SERVICES—AMERICAN INDIANS WITH DISABILITIES

Assistance: project grants (90 percent/to 5 years).

Purposes: pursuant to the Rehabilitation Act of 1973 as amended, to establish and operate tribal vocational rehabilitation service projects serving American Indians with disabilities, residing on reservations.

Eligible applicants/beneficiaries: tribal governments or consortia on federal or state reservations.

Range: $250,000 to $400,000.

Activity: FY 04, 70 projects funded.

HQ: same address/phone as **84.235**. **Internet:** same as **84.027**.

84.255 LITERACY PROGRAMS FOR PRISONERS

Assistance: project grants (100 percent/to 3 years).

Purposes: pursuant to the National Literacy Act of 1991, to establish and operate programs to assist persons incarcerated in prisons, jails, or detention centers to achieve functional literacy; to reduce prisoner recidivism through the development and improvement of their life skills necessary for reintegration into society.

Eligible applicants/beneficiaries: state or local correctional agencies or state correctional educational agencies.

Range/Average: $400,000.

Activity: FY 04, 12 awards.

HQ: Office of Safe and Drug-Free Schools, DOED, 400 Maryland Ave. SW, Washington, DC 20202-7242. Phone: (202)219-1806. **Internet:** "www.ed.gov/programs/lifeskills/index.html". (Note: no field offices for this program.)

84.256 FREELY ASSOCIATED STATES—EDUCATION GRANT PROGRAM

Assistance: project grants (100 percent/3 years).

Purposes: pursuant to ESEA as amended, Title I, for educational activities including teacher training, curriculum development, instructional materials, general school improvement, and schoolwide reform.

Eligible applicants/beneficiaries: LEAs in Micronesia, Marshall Islands, Palau.

Range/Average: $250,000 to $500,000.

Activity: annually, 7-10 awards.

HQ: School Support and Technology Programs, OESE-DOED, FOB 6 - Rm.3E245, 400 Maryland Ave. SW, Washington, DC 20202-6140. Phone: (202)260-2543. **Internet:** "www.ed.gov/programs/tfasegp/index.html".

84.257 NATIONAL INSTITUTE FOR LITERACY ("NIL")

Assistance: project grants (100 percent).

Purposes: pursuant to the Adult Education and Family Literacy Act, to coordinate literacy services and services; to serve as a national resource for adult education and literacy programs through dissemination. Program is governed by an interagency group made up of DOED, DOL, and HHS. Project examples: inter-agency systems; internet-based literacy information system.

Eligible applicants/beneficiaries: public and private nonprofit institutions.

Range/Average: N.A.

Activity: not quantified specifically.

HQ: National Institute for Literacy, DOED, 1775 I St. NW, Washington, DC 20006. Phone: (202)233-2025. **Internet:** "www.nifl.gov". (Note: no field offices for this program.)

84.258 EVEN START—INDIAN TRIBES AND TRIBAL ORGANIZATIONS

Assistance: project grants (50-90 percent/to 4 years).

Purposes: pursuant to ESEA as amended, Title I, to operate family-centered education projects involving low-income parents in the early education of their children from birth-age 7, and to provide literacy training, and adult and parenting education. Funds may support participant recruitment and screening, program design and coordination, instruction of children and parents, staff training.

Eligible applicants/beneficiaries: tribes and tribal organizations.

Range: $100,000 to $200,000.

Activity: FY 05 estimate, 21 grants.

HQ: same address as **84.010**. Phone: (202)260-0999. **Internet:** "www.ed.gov/programs/evenstartindian/index.html". (Note: no field offices for this program.)

84.259 NATIVE HAWAIIAN VOCATIONAL EDUCATION

Assistance: project grants (100 percent/to 5 years).

Purposes: pursuant to CDPVTEA, for vocational education projects conducted by organizations primarily serving and representing Hawaii natives.

Eligible applicants/beneficiaries: organizations recognized by the governor, primarily serving and representing Hawaii natives.

Range: N.A.

Activity: not quantified specifically.

HQ: same address as **84.101**. Phone: (202)245-7768. **Internet:** "www.ed.gov/programs/ctenhvep/index.html". (Note: no field offices for this program.)

84.263 REHABILITATION TRAINING—EXPERIMENTAL AND INNOVATIVE TRAINING

Assistance: project grants (cost sharing/to 5 years).

Purposes: pursuant to the Rehabilitation Act of 1973 as amended, to develop new and improved methods of training rehabilitation personnel, relating to vocational and independent living services provided to persons with disabilities.

Eligible applicants/beneficiaries: same as for **84.129**.

Range: N.A.

Activity: not quantified specifically.

HQ: same as **84.129**.

84.264 REHABILITATION TRAINING—CONTINUING EDUCATION

Assistance: project grants (cost sharing/to 5 years).

Purposes: pursuant to the Rehabilitation Act of 1973 as amended, for regional or area training centers providing continuing education for rehabilitation counselors, administrators, independent living specialists, audiologists, rehabilitation teachers for the blind, and rehabilitation technology specialists—providing vocational, independent living, and client assistance services to the disabled.

Eligible applicants/beneficiaries: same as for **84.129**.

Range/Average: N.A.

Activity: not quantified specifically.

HQ: same as **84.129**.

84.265 REHABILITATION TRAINING—STATE VOCATIONAL REHABILITATION UNIT IN-SERVICE TRAINING

Assistance: project grants (90 percent/to 3 years).

Purposes: pursuant to the Rehabilitation Act of 1973 as amended, for special projects to train state vocational rehabilitation unit personnel. Projects must address: recruitment and retention of professionals; planning needs; issues of leadership development and capacity building; training on provisions of the Act and amendments.

Eligible applicants/beneficiaries: state vocational rehabilitation agencies including territories and possessions.

Range: $7,400 to $240,000. **Average:** $70,000.

Activity: 13,000 rehabilitation personnel participating.

HQ: same as **84.129**.

84.268 FEDERAL DIRECT STUDENT LOANS

Assistance: direct loans (10-30 years).

Purposes: pursuant to HEA as amended, Title IV, to provide education loans for any school year to vocational, undergraduate, professional, and graduate postsecondary students and their parents—directly from DOED rather than through private lenders. Subsidized loans are based on financial need; unsubsidized loans are not. Standard, extended, consolidated, and graduated repayment plans are available. Generally, repayment begins six months after termination of at least half-time enrollment.

Eligible applicants/beneficiaries: U.S. citizens, nationals, or permanent residents enrolled or accepted for at least half-time enrollment at a participating postsecondary school. Parents may borrow for dependent students under the Direct PLUS program. School enrollment is not required for Direct Consolidation Loans which are available to students, married couples, or parents if they are unable to obtain consolidated loans under **84.032**. Students must maintain satisfactory academic progress, be in compliance with Selective Service requirements, and neither owe a refund nor be in default on a Title IV grant or loan.

Range/Average: $6,190.

Activity: FY 03, 3,200,000 loans.

HQ: Federal Direct Loans, OFSA-DOED, Washington, DC 20202. Same phone, web site as **84.007**.

84.269 INSTITUTE FOR INTERNATIONAL PUBLIC POLICY

Assistance: project grants (50 percent/to 5 years).

Purposes: pursuant to HEA as amended, Title VI, to establish an institute of international public policy to conduct a program to increase the numbers of African-Americans and other under-represented minorities in the international service, including with private international voluntary organizations and the U.S. Foreign Service. Funds may support a junior year abroad, graduate fellowships, internships, intensive academic programs such as summer institutes, or intensive language training.

Eligible applicants/beneficiaries: a consortium of institutions eligible for assistance under HEA Title III, Part B, and an IHE serving substantial numbers of African-Americans or other under-represented minority students.

Range/Average: one award only.

Activity: FY 04, 1 award.

HQ: same address/phone as **84.153**. **Internet:** "www.ed.gov/programs/iegpsiipp/". (Note: no field offices for this program.)

84.274 AMERICAN OVERSEAS RESEARCH CENTERS

Assistance: project grants (100 percent/3 years).

Purposes: pursuant to HEA as amended, Title VI, to establish or operate overseas research centers that are consortia of IHEs to promote postgraduate research, exchanges, and area studies. Funds may cover the costs of: faculty and staff stipends, salaries, travel, and research; student travel; maintenance and operations; teaching and research materials; conferences; publications.

Eligible applicants/beneficiaries: tax-exempt permanent overseas centers receiving over 50 percent of their funding from public or private U.S. sources.

Range/Average: $83,000.

Activity: FY 04, 12 awards.

HQ: International Education and Graduate Programs Service, same address as **84.015**. Phone: (202)502-7634. **Internet:** "www.ed.gov/programs/iegpsaorc/". (Note: no field offices for this program.)

84.275 REHABILITATION TRAINING—GENERAL TRAINING

Assistance: project grants (100 percent/1-5 years).

Purposes: pursuant to the Rehabilitation Act of 1973 as amended, for education programs for rehabilitation personnel providing services to persons with disabilities through such programs as: vocational, medical, social, and psychological rehabilitation; supported employment; independent living client assistance. Specialties include rehabilitation counselors, administrators, audiologists, teachers of the blind, rehabilitation teachers, and rehabilitation technology specialists.

Eligible applicants/beneficiaries: same as for **84.129**.

Range/Average: N.A.

Activity: clearinghouse for rehabilitation training materials.

HQ: same as **84.129**.

84.282 CHARTER SCHOOLS

Assistance: project grants (100 percent/to 3 years).

Purposes: pursuant to ESEA as amended, Title V, for the planning, development, and initial implementation of charter schools—which provide enhanced parental choice while exempt from many statutory and regulatory requirements, in return for which the schools establish plans to improve student academic achievement and stimulate the creativity and commitment of teachers, parents, and the public.

Eligible applicants/beneficiaries: SEAs. If SEAs do not participate, authorized public chartering agencies or other public entities may apply.

Range/Average: SEAs, $3,000,000.

Activity: FY 1,200 schools supported.

HQ: Parental Options and Information, OII-DOED, 400 Maryland Ave. SW, Washington, DC 20202. Phone: (202)260-1882. **Internet:** "www.ed.gov/programs/charter/index.html". (Note: no field offices for this program.)

84.283 COMPREHENSIVE CENTERS

Assistance: project grants (100 percent/to 5 years); technical information.

Purposes: pursuant to the Education Sciences Reform Act of 2002, to support not less than 20 comprehensive centers provide training, technical assistance, and professional development in reading, mathematics, and technology—particularly to school districts and schools that fail to meet their state's definition of adequate yearly progress. Sixteen centers focus on such areas as: implementation and administration of programs authorized under ESEA; using scientifically valid teaching methods and assessment tools in mathematics, science, reading and language arts, English language acquisition, education technology; facilitating communication between education experts, school officials, teachers, parents, and librarians; related information dissemination. Five content centers focus on accountability, instruction, teacher quality, innovation and improvement, and high schools.

Eligible applicants/beneficiaries: public or private nonprofit entities or consortia.

Range/Average: $1,854,000.

Activity: FY 03, 15 center awards.

HQ: School Support and Technology Programs, OESE-DOED, 400 Maryland Ave. SW, Washington, DC 20202-6140. Phone: (202)205-9198. **Internet:** "www.ed.gov/about/contacts/gen/othersites/compcenters.html"; "www.ed.gov/pubs/ExcellAcctTeach/Part-5.html". (Note: no field offices for this program.)

84.286 READY TO TEACH

Assistance: project grants (50 percent/to 3 years).

Purposes: pursuant to ESEA as amended, Title V, for a national telecommunications-based program to improve teaching in core curriculum areas. Projects must: use the public broadcasting infrastructure, the internet, and school digital networks to deliver video and data in an integrated service to train teachers in the use of materials and learning technologies; be conducted in cooperation with appropriate SEAs, LEAs, state, and local profit public telecommunications entities; ensure that a significant portion of project benefits will be available to schools with a high percentage of children counted for the purpose of ESEA Title I, Part A. The program also provides digital educational programming grants, enabling development, production, and distribution of innovative educational video programming.

Eligible applicants/beneficiaries: public telecommunications entities or partnership of such entities.

Range/Average: N.A.

Activity: FY 04, 2 national, 3 digital programming awards.

HQ: Technology in Education Programs, OII-DOED, 400 Maryland Ave. SW,

Washington, DC 20202. Phone: (202)205-5880. **Internet:** "www.ed.gov/programs/readyteach/index.html". (Note: no field offices for this program.)

84.287 TWENTY-FIRST CENTURY COMMUNITY LEARNING CENTERS

Assistance: formula grants (100 percent).

Purposes: pursuant to ESEA as amended, Title IV, for community learning centers to provide academic enrichment opportunities in core subjects for children and literacy programs for families, in rural and inner-city areas.

Eligible applicants/beneficiaries: state departments of education.

Range: $4,895,000 to $136,981,000.

Activity: FY 04, 1,320,000 students served.

HQ: 21st Century Community Learning Centers, OESE-DOED, 400 Maryland Ave. SW, Washington, DC 20202-6100. Phone: (202)260-0982. **Internet:** "www.ed.gov/programs/21stcclc/index.html". (Note: no field offices for this program.)

84.293 FOREIGN LANGUAGE ASSISTANCE

Assistance: project grants (50 percent/3 years).

Purposes: pursuant to ESEA as amended, Title V, for innovative model programs of foreign language study in public elementary and secondary schools.

Eligible applicants/beneficiaries: SEAs, LEAs.

Range/Average: $140,000.

Activity: FY 04, 117 awards.

HQ: Office of English Language Acquisition, OESE-DOED, 400 Maryland Ave. SW, Washington, DC 20202. Phone: (202)245-7153. **Internet:** "www.ed.gov/programs/flap/index.html". (Note: no field offices for this program.)

84.295 READY-TO-LEARN TELEVISION

Assistance: project grants (100 percent/to 5 years).

Purposes: pursuant to ESEA as amended, Title II, to develop: educational programming for preschool and early elementary school children and their families; educational television, programming, and ancillary materials to increase school readiness for young children with limited English proficiency; family literacy programs; support materials and services promoting effective use of educational programming.

Eligible applicants/beneficiaries: qualified public telecommunications entities.

Range/Average: single grant to the Corporation for Public Broadcasting.

Activity: 1 five-year award in 2000.

HQ: Technology in Education Programs, OII-DOED, 500 Maryland Ave. SW, Washington, DC 20202. Phone: (202)205-5449. **Internet:** "www.ed.gov/programs/rtltv/index.html". (Note: no field offices for this program.)

84.298 STATE GRANTS FOR INNOVATIVE PROGRAMS

Assistance: formula grants (100 percent).

Purposes: pursuant to ESEA as amended, Title V, for reforms in elementary and secondary education by LEAs and SEAs. Funds may be used for such related purposes as: implementing programs that rely on scientifically-based research; providing library services and instructional and media materials; improving services to disadvantaged students; class-size reduction programs.

Eligible applicants/beneficiaries: states, DC, PR, and insular areas.

Range: $1,472,000 to $36,430,000. **Average:** $5,663,000.

Activity: not quantified specifically.

HQ: same address as **84.256**. Phone: (202)260-2551. **Internet:** "www.ed.gov/programs/innovative/index.html"; "www.ed.gov/policy/elsec/leg/esea02/pg57.html". (Note: no field offices for this program.)

84.304 CIVIC EDUCATION—COOPERATIVE EDUCATION EXCHANGE PROGRAM

Assistance: project grants (100 percent).

Purposes: pursuant to ESEA as amended, Title II, for international K-12 education exchange activities between the U.S. and eligible countries, in civics, government, and economics education—in Eastern and Central European countries, Lithuania, Latvia, Estonia, the independent states of the former Soviet Union, Republic of Ireland, Northern Ireland, and approved developing countries.

Eligible applicants/beneficiaries: Center for Civic Education and the National Council Economic Education (each receiving 37.5 of available funds); independent nonprofit education organizations experienced in program areas.

Range: N.A.

Activity: FY 04, 4 awards.

HQ: Office of Safe and Drug-Free Schools, DOED, 400 Maryland Ave. SW, Washington, DC 20202. Phone: (202)205-8061. **Internet:** "www.ed.gov/programs/coopedexchange/index.html". (Note: no field offices for this program.)

84.305 EDUCATION RESEARCH, DEVELOPMENT AND DISSEMINATION

Assistance: project grants (100 percent/1-5 years).

Purposes: pursuant to the Education Sciences Reform Act of 2002, to develop and distribute research-based information supporting learning and improved academic achievement. Grants may fund basic and applied research, development, dissemination, evaluations, and demonstrations.

Eligible applicants/beneficiaries: SEAs, LEAs, IHEs, public and private agencies and organizations, institutions, individuals, or consortia.

Range/Average: N.A.

Activity: not quantified specifically.

HQ: Institute of Education Sciences, DOED, 555 New Jersey Ave. NW, Washington, DC 20202. Phone: (202)219-2079. **Internet:** "www.ed.gov/about/offices/list/ies/index.html"(Note: no field offices for this program.)

84.310 PARENTAL ASSISTANCE CENTERS

Assistance: project grants (first year, 100 percent/1-4 years).

Purposes: pursuant to ESEA as amended, Title V, to establish parental information and resource centers to: (1) assist parents in helping their children to meet state and local standards; (2) obtain information about the range of programs, services, and resources available nationally and locally to parents and school personnel; (3) help parents use the technology applied in their children's education; (4) plan, implement, and fund activities for parents that coordinate child education with other appropriate programs; (5) coordinate and integrate early childhood and school-age education programs. At least 50 percent of grant funds must be used to serve areas with high concentrations of low-income families, to serve parents that are severely educationally or economically disadvantaged. After the first year of grant-funded activities, cost sharing is required.

Eligible applicants/beneficiaries: nonprofit organizations; nonprofit organizations in consortia with LEAs.

Range/Average: $501,000.

Activity: FY 04, 82 awards.

HQ: Parental Options and Information, OII-DOED, FOB 6 - Rm.3E209, 400 Maryland Ave. SW, Washington, DC 20202. Phone: (202)260-2476. **Internet:** "www.ed.gov/programs/pirc/index.html". (Note: no field offices for this program.)

84.315 CAPACITY BUILDING FOR TRADITIONALLY UNDERSERVED POPULATIONS

Assistance: project grants (100 percent/1-5 years).

Purposes: pursuant to the Rehabilitation Act of 1973 as amended, to enhance the capacity and increase the participation of HBCUs, Hispanic serving IHEs, other IHEs where minority enrollment is at least 50 percent, and tribes in competitions for Rehabilitation Act funds. Projects should focus on recruiting minorities into vocational rehabilitation and related service careers.

Eligible applicants/beneficiaries: states; public and nonprofit agencies; profit organizations.

Range: $200,000 to $300,000.

Activity: not quantified specifically.

HQ: same address as **84.129**. Phone: (202)245-7300. **Internet:** "www.ed.gov/about/offices/list/osers/rsa/index.html".

84.318 EDUCATION TECHNOLOGY STATE GRANTS ("Enhancing Education through Technology Program")

Assistance: formula grants.

Purposes: pursuant to ESEA as amended, Title II, to improve student academic achievement through the use of technology in schools; to assist students to become technologically literate by the end of the eighth grade; to integrate technology with teacher training and curriculum development to establish successful research-based instructional methods. At least 95 percent of grant funds to SEAs must be subgranted to LEAs.

Eligible applicants/beneficiaries: states, territories and possessions, BIA.

Range: $3,215,000 to $89,960,000.

Activity: not quantified specifically.

HQ: same address (Rm.3E241) as **84.256**. Phone: (202)401-0039. **Internet:** "www.ed.gov/programs/edtech/index.html". (Note: no field offices for this program.)

84.319 EISENHOWER REGIONAL MATH AND SCIENCE CONSORTIA

Assistance: project grants (80 percent/to 5 years).

Purposes: pursuant to the Educational Technical Assistance Act of 2002, to establish and operate regional mathematics and science education consortia, to: disseminate exemplary curriculum materials; provide technical assistance to implement teaching methods and assessment tools for K-12 students, teachers, and administrators.

Eligible applicants/beneficiaries: SEAs, LEAs, elementary or secondary schools, IHEs, nonprofit organizations, regional education laboratories, or combinations of such entities.

Range/Average: $1,490,000.

Activity: FY 03, 10 grants.

HQ: School Support and Technology Programs, OESE-DOED, 400 Maryland Ave. SW, Washington, DC 20208-5645. Phone: (202)260-7405. **Internet:** "www.ed.gov/programs/enconsortia/index.htm". (Note: no field offices for this program.)

84.323 SPECIAL EDUCATION—STATE PERSONNEL DEVELOPMENT

Assistance: project grants (100 percent/1-5 years).

Purposes: pursuant to IDEA as amended, to reform and improve systems for providing educational, early intervention, and transitional services to infants, toddlers, and children with disabilities and their families—including professional development, technical assistance, and information dissemination about best practices.

Eligible applicants/beneficiaries: SEAs.

Range/Average: N.A.

Activity: FY 03, 50 grants.

HQ: Office of Special Education Programs, OSERS-DOED, 400 Maryland Ave. SW, Washington, DC 20202-2500. Phone: (202)205-5390. **Internet:** same as **84.027**. (Note: no field offices for this program.)

84.324 RESEARCH IN SPECIAL EDUCATION

Assistance: project grants (to 100 percent/1-5 years).

Purposes: pursuant to the Education Sciences Reform Act of 2002, for applied research to improve services provided and results achieved under IDEA, for infants, toddlers, and children with disabilities—including educational and early intervention services and professional practices.

Eligible applicants/beneficiaries: SEAs, LEAs, IHEs, public agencies, private nonprofit organizations, tribes and tribal organizations, profit organizations, outlying areas.

Range: $150,000 to $1,000,000 per year.

Activity: annually, 75-100 awards.

HQ: same address, web site as **84.323**. Phone: (202)205-7329. (Note: no field offices for this program.)

84.325 SPECIAL EDUCATION—PERSONNEL PREPARATION TO IMPROVE SERVICES AND RESULTS FOR CHILDREN WITH DISABILITIES

Assistance: project grants (to 100 percent/1-5 years).

Purposes: pursuant to IDEA as amended, to prepare personnel to serve infants, toddlers, and children with disabilities—in special and regular education, related services, and early intervention. Projects must emphasize use of skills and knowledge derived from research and experience.

Eligible applicants/beneficiaries: same as for **84.324** (excluding Marshall Islands, Micronesia, and Palau after FY 01).

Range: $200,000 to $250,000 per year.

Activity: estimate, 65 awards.

HQ: same address, web site as **84.323**. Phone: (202)401-7659. (Note: no field offices for this program.)

84.326 SPECIAL EDUCATION—TECHNICAL ASSISTANCE AND DISSEMINATION TO IMPROVE SERVICES AND RESULTS FOR CHILDREN WITH DISABILITIES

Assistance: project grants (to 100 percent/1-5 years).

Purposes: pursuant to IDEA as amended, to provide technical assistance and disseminate information to improve early intervention, education, and transitional services and results for children with disabilities and their families—through institutes, regional resource centers, clearinghouses, and similar methods.

Eligible applicants/beneficiaries: same as for **84.325**.

Range: N.A.

Activity: FY 04 estimate, 75 awards.

HQ: same address, web site as **84.323**. Phone: (202)245-7291. (Note: no field offices for this program.)

84.327 SPECIAL EDUCATION—TECHNOLOGY AND MEDIA SERVICES FOR INDIVIDUALS WITH DISABILITIES

Assistance: project grants (to 100 percent/1-5 years).

Purposes: pursuant to IDEA as amended, for the development, demonstration, and utilization of technology; for educational media activities designed to be of educational value; and, for captioning, video description, and cultural activities—for children with disabilities and their families.

Eligible applicants/beneficiaries: same as for **84.325**.

Range: $150,000 to $1,000,000 per year.

Activity: N.A.

HQ: same address, web site as **84.323**. Phone: (202)245-7473. (Note: no field offices for this program.)

84.328 SPECIAL EDUCATION—PARENT INFORMATION CENTERS

Assistance: project grants (to 100 percent/1-5 years).

Purposes: pursuant to IDEA as amended, to ensure that children with disabilities and their parents: receive training and information on their rights under the Act; can participate effectively in planning and decision-making related to early intervention, special education, and transitional services, including the development of Individual Education Programs (IEPs).

Eligible applicants/beneficiaries: parent organizations as defined in IDEA.

Range/Average: N.A.

Activity: FY 04, 100 awards.

HQ: same as **84.324**. (Note: no field offices for this program.)

84.329 SPECIAL EDUCATION—STUDIES AND EVALUATIONS

Assistance: project grants (to 100 percent/1-5 years).

Purposes: pursuant to IDEA as amended, to evaluate progress in implementing IDEA. Projects cover state and local efforts to provide a free appropriate public education to children with disabilities and early intervention services to infants and toddlers that would be at risk of having substantial development delays without such services.

Eligible applicants/beneficiaries: same as for **84.325**.

Range/Average: N.A.

Activity: N.A.

HQ: same as **84.327**. (Note: no field offices for this program.)

84.330 ADVANCED PLACEMENT PROGRAM

Assistance: project grants.

Purposes: pursuant to ESEA as amended, Title I, to cover part or all of the cost of Advanced Placement Test Fees for low-income persons enrolled in an advanced placement class and planning to take a test.

Eligible applicants/beneficiaries: SEAs, LEAs, nonprofit organizations.

Range/Average: N.A.

Activity: FY 04, 41 incentive grants with 34 states participating.

HQ: Improvement Programs, OII-DOED, 400 Maryland Ave. SW, Washington, DC 20202-6140. Phone: (202)260-2502. **Internet:** "www.ed.gov/programs/apfee/index.html". (Note: no field offices for this program.)

84.331 GRANTS TO STATES FOR INCARCERATED YOUTH OFFENDERS

Assistance: formula grants (100 percent/2 years).

Purposes: pursuant to HEA as amended, Title VIII, to assist and encourage incarcerated youth offenders to acquire postsecondary education and vocational training, and to provide them with employment counseling and related services during their incarceration and pre-release periods, and subsequently.

Eligible applicants: designated state correctional education agencies, territories and possessions.

Eligible beneficiaries: persons age 25 or younger, incarcerated in state prisons including pre-release facilities or alternative programs such as boot camps, eligible for release or parole within five years, and possessing a secondary school diploma or equivalent.

Range: $36,000 to $2,179,000.

Activity: FY 04, 48 grants.

HQ: same address as **84.255**. Phone: (202)219-1743. **Internet:** "www.ed.gov/programs/transitiontraining/index.html". (Note: no field offices for this program.)

84.332 COMPREHENSIVE SCHOOL REFORM DEMONSTRATION ("CSRD")

Assistance: formula grants (100 percent; subgrants, to 3 years).

Purposes: pursuant to ESEA as amended, Title I, to substantially improve student achievement, particularly in Title I schools, through implementation of comprehensive school reform programs that are based on reliable research and effective practices and that emphasize basic academics and parental involvement. Funded projects must also include: comprehensive schools designs with aligned components; professional development; measurable goals and benchmarks; support within the school; parental and community involvement; external technical support and assistance; evaluation strategies; coordination of resources.

Eligible applicants/beneficiaries: SEAs. Subgrants—LEAs applying as collaboratives.

Range/Average: $4,267,000.

Activity: N.A.

HQ: CSRD, OESE-DOED, 400 Maryland Ave. SW, Washington, DC 20202. Phone: (202)260-1335. **Internet:** "www.ed.gov/programs/compreform/index.html". (Note: no field offices for this program.)

84.333 DEMONSTRATION PROJECTS TO ENSURE STUDENTS WITH DISABILITIES RECEIVE A HIGHER EDUCATION

Assistance: project grants (to 100 percent/3 years).

Purposes: pursuant to HEA as amended, Title VII, for model demonstration projects providing technical assistance or professional development for higher education faculty, to provide students with disabilities a quality postsecondary education.

Eligible applicants/beneficiaries: IHEs of which at least two provide professional development for students with learning disabilities.

Range/Average: $256,000.

Activity: 27 grants awarded.

HQ: OPE-DOED, 400 Maryland Ave. SW, Washington, DC 20202-5131. Phone: (202)502-7808. **Internet:** "www.ed.gov/programs/disabilities/". (Note: no field offices for this program.)

84.334 GAINING EARLY AWARENESS AND READINESS FOR UNDERGRADUATE PROGRAMS ("GEAR-UP")

Assistance: project grants (50 percent/to 5 years).

Purposes: pursuant to HEA, Title IV, to assist low-income students with a secondary diploma, or equivalent, in obtaining the financial assistance necessary to attend an IHE; to provide supportive services to elementary, middle, and secondary students at risk of becoming school drop-outs, including counseling, mentoring, academic support; to provide outreach and relevant information to students and their parents. Services are provided under the Early Intervention Component. Federal grants may be provided under the Scholarship Component, to students participating in the Early Intervention component or in a TRIO program.

Eligible applicants/beneficiaries: states; partnerships of LEAs, IHEs, and at least two community organizations including businesses, professional associations, philanthropic organizations, state agencies, parent groups.

Range/Average: continuations—state grants, $2,573,000; partnerships, $746,000.

Activity: FY 04, 36 state, 274 partnership grants.

HQ: GEAR-UP, same address as **84.333**. Phone: (202)502-7676. **Internet:** "www.ed.gov/programs/gearup/"; e-mail, "gearup@ed.gov". (Note: no field offices for this program.)

84.335 CHILD CARE ACCESS MEANS PARENTS IN SCHOOL

Assistance: project grants (4 years).

Purposes: pursuant to HEA as amended, Title IV, to support participation of low-income parents in postsecondary education by providing campus-based child care services. Grants may be used to support or establish child care programs, including before or after-school services—but not for construction other than minor renovations. Grant amounts may not exceed one percent of the total amount of Pell grants awarded by the IHE for the preceding year.

Eligible applicants/beneficiaries: IHEs that awarded $350,000 or more in Pell grants for the preceding year.

Range/Average: continuations, $47,000.

Activity: FY 04, 341 awards.

HQ: Higher Education Programs, same address as **84.333**. Phone: (202)502-7634. **Internet:** "www.ed.gov/programs/campisp/". (Note: no field offices for this program.)

84.336 TEACHER QUALITY ENHANCEMENT GRANTS

Assistance: project grants (50-75 percent/3-5 years).

Purposes: pursuant to HEA, Title II, for projects to reform teacher preparation programs and certification and licensure requirements, providing alternatives to traditional preparation for teaching, and to develop and implement effective mechanisms for teacher recruitment, pay, removal, and social promotion.

Eligible applicants/beneficiaries: states and partnerships with LEAs with high percentages of households below the poverty line and of secondary teachers not teaching within their specialty, and high rate of teacher turn-over. IHEs must demonstrate specific teacher training performance standards.

Range/Average: continuations—states, $2,105,000; partnerships, $1,059,000; teacher recruitment, $462,000.

Activity: FY 04, 19 state, 38 partnership, 19 teacher recruitment grants.

HQ: Teacher Quality Programs, OPE-DOED, 400 Maryland Ave. SW, Washington, DC 20202. Phone: (202)502-7719. **Internet:** "www.ed.gov/programs/heatqp/"; e-mail, "teacherquality@ed.gov". (Note: no field offices for this program.)

84.337 INTERNATIONAL EDUCATION—TECHNOLOGICAL INNOVATION AND COOPERATION FOR FOREIGN INFORMATION ACCESS

Assistance: project grants (67 percent).

Purposes: pursuant to HEA as amended, Title VI, to develop innovative techniques or programs using new electronic technologies to collect, organize, preserve, and disseminate information on world regions and countries other than the U.S.—addressing U.S. teaching and research needs in international education and foreign languages.

Eligible applicants/beneficiaries: IHEs, public or nonprofit private libraries, or consortia.

Range/Average: $170,000.

Activity: 10 awards.

HQ: same address as **84.153**. Phone: (202)502-7628. **Internet:** "www.ed.gov/programs/iegpsticfia/". (Note: no field offices for this program.)

84.341 COMMUNITY TECHNOLOGY CENTERS

Assistance: project grants (100 percent/to 3 years).

Purposes: pursuant to ESEA as amended, Title V, to develop or expand community technology centers to provide access and training in their use in distressed rural and urban areas.

Eligible applicants/beneficiaries: SEAs, LEAs, IHEs, other public and private nonprofit and profit agencies and organizations, or groups of same.

Range: $195,000 to $500,000.

Activity: FY 04, 25 awards.

HQ: OVAE-DOED, 400 Maryland Ave. SW, Washington, DC 20202-7240. Phone: (202)245-7708. **Internet:** "www.ed.gov/fund/grant/apply/AdultEd/CTC/index.html". (Note: no field offices for this program.)

84.343 ASSISTIVE TECHNOLOGY—STATE GRANTS FOR PROTECTION AND ADVOCACY

Assistance: project grants (100 percent/to 6 years).

Purposes: pursuant to the Assistive Technology Act of 1998, for protection and advocacy services related to acquiring, using, or maintaining assistive technology services and devices for persons with disabilities, as provided in the Developmental Disabilities Assistance and Bill of Rights Act.

Eligible applicants/beneficiaries: designated protection and advocacy agencies in states and outlying areas.

Range: $50,000 to $436,000.

Activity: annually, 56 grants.

HQ: same address as **84.133**. Phone: (202)245-7258. **Internet:** same as **84.240**. (Note: no field offices for this program.)

84.344 TRIO—DISSEMINATION PARTNERSHIP GRANTS

Assistance: project grants (100 percent/3 years).

Purposes: pursuant to HEA as amended, Title IV, to establish partnerships between TRIO projects and institutions and community-based organizations serving low-income and first-generation college students without TRIO grants—toward replication or adaptation of successful TRIO program components and practices, including the use of educational technology, business and community partnerships and K-12 collaborations, program evaluation and student outcome assessments.

Eligible applicants/beneficiaries: IHEs and other public and private nonprofit organizations with TRIO projects.

Range/Average: $191,000.

Activity: FY 04, 23 awards.

HQ: same address/web site as **84.042**. Phone: (202)502-7730, -7735. **Internet:** "www.ed.gov/programs/triodissem/index.html". (Note: no field offices for this program.)

84.345 UNDERGROUND RAILROAD EDUCATIONAL AND CULTURAL PROGRAM

Assistance: project grants (20 percent).

Purposes: pursuant to HEA as amended, Title VIII, to support research, display, interpretation, and collection of artifacts relating to the history of the underground railroad.

Eligible applicants/beneficiaries: nonprofit educational organizations meeting program purposes.

Range/Average: $555,000.

Activity: FY 04, 4 awards.

HQ: OPE-DOED, 400 Maryland Ave. SW, Washington, DC 20202. Phone: (202)502-7507. **Internet:** "www.ed.gov/programs/ugroundrr/index.html". (Note: no field offices for this program.)

84.346 VOCATIONAL EDUCATION—OCCUPATIONAL AND EMPLOYMENT INFORMATION STATE GRANTS

Assistance: project grants (100 percent/to 4 years).

Purposes: pursuant to CDPVTEA, to promote improved career and education decision making by individuals. Funds must be used for such activities as: supporting career guidance and academic counseling programs; pertinent personnel professional development; improving coordination and communication among administrators; parent and student involvement.

Eligible applicants/beneficiaries: designated state and outlying area agencies.

Range: $70,000 to $336,000.

Activity: annually, 59 awards.

HQ: Division of High School, Postsecondary and Career Education, OVAE-DOED, 400 Maryland Ave. SW, Washington, DC 20202-7100. Phone: (202)401-6225. **Internet:** "www.ed.gov/about/offices/list/ovae/pi/cte/acrn.html". (Note: no field offices for this program.)

84.349 EARLY CHILDHOOD EDUCATOR PROFESSIONAL DEVELOPMENT

Assistance: project grants (100 percent/to 4 years).

Purposes: pursuant to ESEA as amended, Title II, for professional development of early childhood educators working in urban or rural high-poverty communities and serving primarily low-income families. Training must be research-based and designed to improve pedagogy that will improve children's language ability and literacy skills.

Eligible applicants/beneficiaries: IHEs, state higher education agencies, LEAs, SEAs; other public and private agencies and organizations including child care consortia and Head Start programs.

Range/Average: $1,815,000.

Activity: FY 04, 8 awards.

HQ: Early Childhood Educator Professional Development, OESE-DOED, 400 Maryland Ave. SW, Washington, DC 20202-6132. Phone: (202)260-0792. **Internet:** "www.ed.gov/programs/eceducator/index.html"; "e-mail, eceprofdev@ed.gov". (Note: no field offices for this program.)

84.350 TRANSITION TO TEACHING

Assistance: project grants (100 percent/3 years).

Purposes: pursuant to ESEA, Title II, to recruit, train, and place talented individuals from other fields, as well as recent college graduates, into licensed teaching positions in K-12 classrooms in high-need areas, and to support them during their first years in the classroom.

Eligible applicants/beneficiaries: LEA, SEAs, educational service centers, nonprofit agencies and other organizations; partnerships of the foregoing.

Range/Average: $363,000.

Activity: FY 04, 92 continuation, 32 new awards.

HQ: Teacher Quality Programs, OII-DOED, 400 Maryland Ave. SW, Washington, DC 20202-6100. Phone: (202)260-0223. **Internet:** "www.ed.gov/

programs/transitionteach/index.html". (Note: no field offices for this program.)

84.351 ARTS IN EDUCATION

Assistance: project grants (100 percent/3-5 years).

Purposes: pursuant to ESEA as amended, Title V, to improve systemic education reform by strengthening arts education as an integral part of elementary and secondary school curricula; to assist students in learning to challenge state content standards in the arts; to enable students to demonstrate competence in the arts in accordance with the National Education Goals; to improve the educational performance and future potential of at-risk students; to provide comprehensive and coordinated educational and cultural services. Project selection is coordinated with NEA, NEH, and other arts organizations.

Eligible applicants/beneficiaries: SEAs, LEAs, IHEs; museums and other cultural institutions; other public and private agencies; private profit organizations for certain activities.

Range: N.A.

Activity: FY 04, 85 awards.

HQ: OESE-DOED, 400 Maryland Ave. SW, Washington, DC 20202. Phone: (202)260-2487. **Internet:** "www.ed.gov/programs/artsed/index.html". (Note: no field offices for this program.)

84.353 TECH-PREP DEMONSTRATION GRANTS

Assistance: project grants (100 percent/3 years).

Purposes: pursuant to CDPVTEA, for consortia to conduct tech-prep demonstration programs at secondary schools located on the sites of community colleges, involving a business as a consortium member and with the voluntary participation of secondary students. Summer business internships may be provided for students or teachers.

Eligible applicants/beneficiaries: consortia of an LEA, an intermediate educational agency or area vocational and technical education school serving secondary students, or a BIA-funded secondary school, and a nonprofit IHE offering a two-year associate degree program, or a two-year certificate program.

Range/Average: N.A.

Activity: FY 04 estimate, 6-7 awards.

HQ: same address as **84.346**. Phone: (202)245-7840. **Internet:** "www.ed.gov/programs/techprepdemo/index.html". (Note: no field offices for this program.)

84.354 CREDIT ENHANCEMENT FOR CHARTER SCHOOL FACILITIES

Assistance: project grants (100 percent/to 5 years).

Purposes: pursuant to ESEA as amended, Title V, for charter schools to leverage funds to finance the cost of acquiring, constructing, and renovating facilities. Grant funds must be deposited in approved reserve accounts, to be used to access private sector capital through bond or other financing instruments.

Eligible applicants/beneficiaries: public governmental or private nonprofit entities, or consortia.

Range: $5,000,000 to $8,000,000.

Activity: FY 04, 10 awards.

HQ: same address (Rm.3C140) as **84.282**. Phone: (202)401-0307. **Internet:** "www.ed.gov/programs/charterfacilities/index.html". (Note: no field offices for this program.)

84.356 ALASKA NATIVE EDUCATIONAL PROGRAM

Assistance: project grants (100 percent).

Purposes: pursuant to ESEA as amended, Title VII, for projects that recognize and address the unique education needs of Alaska native students, parents, and teachers. Activities eligible for funding include: curriculum and education development programs; student enrichment programs in science and mathematics; professional development; Even Start and Headstart activities; family literacy services; dropout prevention programs.

Eligible applicants/beneficiaries: Alaska native educational organizations or entities with experience in developing programs, or partnerships including Alaska native organizations.

Range: N.A.

Activity: FY 04, 46 awards.

HQ: School Improvement Programs, OESE-DOED, 400 Maryland Ave. SW, Washington, DC 20202-6140. Phone: (202)260-1541. **Internet:** "www.ed.gov/programs/alaskanative/index.html". (Note: no field offices for this program.)

84.357 READING FIRST STATE GRANTS

Assistance: project grants (100 percent/to 6 years).

Purposes: pursuant to ESEA as amended, Title I, to ensure that every student can read at grade level or above by the end of the third grade, by establishing reading programs for students in kindergarten through third grade that are based on scientific reading research. Projects also focus on teacher development, including special education teachers, preparing them to identify specific reading barriers facing their students.

Eligible applicants/beneficiaries: SEAs, BIA, territories, and possessions.

Range: $2,452,000 to $146,146,000. **Average:** $18,858,000.

Activity: all eligible agencies funded.

HQ: Reading First Program, OESE-DOED, FOB 6 - Rm.3W311, 400 Maryland Ave. SW, Washington, DC 20202-6100. Phone: (202)401-4877. **Internet:** "www.ed.gov/programs/readingfirst/index.html". (Note: no field offices for this program.)

84.358 RURAL EDUCATION ("REAP")

Assistance: formula grants.

Purposes: pursuant to ESEA as amended, Title VI, to help improve the quality of teaching and learning in rural school districts. Components include: "Small, Rural School Achievement Program," for activities including Improving Teacher Quality, Educational Technology, Language Instruction for Limited English Proficient and Immigrant Students, Safe and Drug-Free Schools and Communities, 21st Century Community Learning Centers, and Innovative Programs; "Rural and Low-Income School Program," for teacher recruitment and retention, professional development, educational technology, and parental involvement.

Eligible applicants/beneficiaries: Small, Rural Achievement—essentially, LEAs where average daily attendance at all schools is less than 600, or in counties with population density less than 10 persons per square mile. Rural and Low-Income Schools—SEAs, for redistribution to LEAs ineligible for Small, Rural Achievement funds and meeting other criteria. If an SEA does not apply, funds may be awarded to eligible LEAs.

Range/Average: Small, Rural Achievement, $21,000; Rural and Low-Income Schools, $64,000.

Activity: FY 04, 3,948 Small, Rural achievement grants; Rural, Low-Income, 1,308 grants.

HQ: same address as **84.283**. Phone: (202)401-3778. **Internet:** "www.ed. gov/nclb/freedom/local/reap.html"; e-mail, "reap@ed.gov". (Note: no field offices for this program.)

84.359 EARLY READING FIRST

Assistance: project grants (100 percent/to 6 years).

Purposes: pursuant to ESEA as amended, Title I, to enhance the early language, literacy, and prereading development of preschool age children, particularly those from low-income families, through instructional strategies and professional development based on scientific reading research—with monitoring and assessment components. Funds must be used in existing public or private preschool programs serving low-income families.

Eligible applicants/beneficiaries: LEAs eligible for a subgrant under **84.357**; public or private organizations of agencies serving Head Start, child care, Even Start Family Literacy, school labs, or similar agencies; collaboratives.

Range/Average: $2,829,000.

Activity: FY 04, 6,700 children, 790 teachers served.

HQ: Early Reading First Program, OESE-DOED, 400 Maryland Ave. SW, Washington, DC 20202. Phone: (202)260-4555. **Internet:** "www.ed.gov/programs/earlyreading/index.html". (Note: no field offices for this program.)

84.360 DROPOUT PREVENTION PROGRAMS

Assistance: project grants (100 percent/to 3 years).

Purposes: pursuant to ESEA as amended, Title I, to help schools implement effective dropout prevention and re-entry programs, including: identifying at-risk students including in middle schools; providing special services to at-risk students; identifying drop-outs and encouraging them to re-enter school; implementing other comprehensive approaches such as breaking large schools into smaller learning communities. Authorized activities include: professional development; reduction in pupil-teacher ratios; counseling and mentoring for at-risk students; implementing comprehensive school reform models.

Eligible applicants/beneficiaries: SEAs and LEAs serving communities with dropout rates above the state average.

Range/Average: $197,000.

Activity: FY 04, 23 grants.

HQ: OVAE-DOED, 400 Maryland Ave. SW, Washington, DC 20202-6100. Phone: (202)205-9477. **Internet:** "www.ed.gov/about/offices/list/ovae/pi/hs/dropout.html". (Note: no field offices for this program.)

84.361 VOLUNTARY PUBLIC SCHOOL CHOICE

Assistance: project grants (100 percent/to 5 years).

Purposes: pursuant to ESEA as amended, Title V, to establish or expand programs of public school choice, with funding for: planning or designing programs; making tuition transfer payments to public elementary or secondary schools to which students transfer; capacity-enhancing activities that enable high-demand public elementary or secondary schools to accommodate transfers; public education campaigns to inform students and parents about the program; similar costs.

Eligible applicants/beneficiaries: SEAs; LEAs; partnerships of SEAs, LEAs, or other public, nonprofit, or profit entities.

Range: N.A.

Activity: FY 04, 13 awards.

HQ: same address as **84.282**. Phone: (202)260-1999. **Internet:** "www.ed.gov/programs/choice/index.html". (Note: no field offices for this program.)

84.362 NATIVE HAWAIIAN EDUCATION

Assistance: project grants (100 percent/to 5 years).

Purposes: pursuant to ESEA as amended, Title VII, to develop innovative educational programs to assist native Hawaiians and to supplement and expand education programs and authorities. Funds may support: early education and care programs; operation of family-based education centers; beginning reading and literacy activities; programs addressing the needs of gifted and talented students; professional development; assistance enabling students to enter and complete postsecondary education.

Eligible applicants/beneficiaries: native Hawaiian educational organizations or community-based organizations; experienced public and private nonprofit organizations, agencies, and institutions; consortia.

Range: N.A.

Activity: FY 04, 40 awards.

HQ: Academic Improvement and Teacher Quality Programs, same address as **84.356**. Phone: (202)260-1091. **Internet:** "www.ed.gov/programs/native-hawaiian/index.html". (Note: no field offices for this program.)

84.363 SCHOOL LEADERSHIP

Assistance: project grants.

Purposes: pursuant to ESEA as amended, Title II, to develop innovative programs that recruit, train, and mentor principals and assistant principals. Funds may be used for: financial incentives to aspiring new principals; stipends to principals to mentor new principals; professional development programs in instructional leadership and management; incentives for teachers or individuals from other fields wanting to become principals and that are effective in training new principals.

Eligible applicants/beneficiaries: high-need LEAs applying singly or in consortia or partnerships that include nonprofit organizations and IHEs.

Range/Average: $512,000.

Activity: FY 04, 24 awards.

HQ: Teacher Quality Programs, OII-DOED, 400 Maryland Ave. SW, Washington, DC 20202-6140. Phone: (202)260-2614. **Internet:** "www.ed.gov/programs/leadership/index.html". (Note: no field offices for this program.)

84.364 LITERACY THROUGH SCHOOL LIBRARIES

Assistance: project grants.

Purposes: pursuant to ESEA as amended, Title I, to improve student literacy skills and achievement by increasing access to up-to-date school library materials, technologically advanced school library media centers, and well-trained professionally certified school library media specialists. Funds may be used for pertinent library acquisitions, internet links and other resource-sharing networks, professional development and collaborative activities, and student library access during non-school hours.

Eligible applicants/beneficiaries: LEAs with a child poverty rate of at least 20 percent.

Range/Average: N.A.

Activity: FY 04, 92 awards for 600 schools.

HQ: Academic Improvement and Teacher Quality Programs, OESE-DOED, 400 Maryland Ave. SW, Washington, DC 20202-6100. Phone: (202)401-3751. **Internet:** "www.ed.gov/program/lsl/index.html". (Note: no field offices for this program.)

84.365 ENGLISH LANGUAGE ACQUISITION GRANTS

Assistance: formula grants; project grants.

Purposes: pursuant to ESEA as amended, Title III, to ensure that limited English proficient (LEP) children and youth, including immigrants, attain proficiency and meet the same state academic content and achievement standards as all children. Outlying areas and native American applicants may use project funds for appropriate special activities for up to five years, including: hiring tutors and for special professional development and training; developing students' native language skills. Training must be based upon scientifically based research and improve teacher instruction and enhance their ability to understand and use curricula, assessment measures, and instruction strategies for LEP students.

Eligible applicants/beneficiaries: formula funds (95 percent of which must be allocated as subgrants to SEAs)—states and outlying areas with approved state plans. Project grants—tribal educational authorities, BIA-operated or -funded elementary or secondary schools, nonprofit native Hawaiian or native American Pacific Islander language organizations.

Range: formula grants, $500,000 to $161,549,00.

Activity: new program in FY 03. All SEAs funded annually. FY 04, 148 project grants.

HQ: Office of English Language Acquisition, OESE-DOED, 400 Maryland Ave. SW, Washington, DC 20202-6150. Phone: (202)245-7149. **Internet:** "www.ed.gov/programs/sfgp/nrgcomp.html". (Note: no field offices for this program.)

84.366 MATHEMATICS AND SCIENCE PARTNERSHIPS

Assistance: project grants (100 percent/to 3 years).

Purposes: pursuant to ESEA as amended, Title II, to improve student academic achievement in mathematics and science through projects supporting partnerships of organizations representing preschool through higher education. Funds may be used for such activities as: developing more rigorous curricula aligned with state and local content standards; distance learning projects for teachers; teacher recruitment among mathematics, science, and engineering majors through the use of signing and performance incentives, stipends, and scholarships.

Eligible applicants/beneficiaries: partnerships of SEAs with IHE mathematics, science, or engineering departments, and a high-need LEA. Other organizations may participate.

Range: $742,000 to $20,617,000. **Average:** $2,853,000.

Activity: new program in FY 03. FY 04, all states supported.

HQ: Academic Improvement and Teacher Quality Programs, OESE-DOED, 400 Maryland Ave. SW, Washington, DC 20202-6254. Phone: (202)260-3710. **Internet:** "www.ed.gov/programs/mathsci/index.html". (Note: no field offices for this program.)

84.367 IMPROVING TEACHER QUALITY STATE GRANTS

Assistance: formula grants (to 2 years).

Purposes: pursuant to ESEA as amended, Title II, to increase student achievement by improving teacher and principal quality and increasing their numbers, through such efforts as: recruiting and retaining highly qualified teachers, principals, and assistant principals; professional development addressing subject matter knowledge and related activities.

Eligible applicants/beneficiaries: states with approved consolidated state plans.

Range/Average: $55,506,000.

Activity: new program listing in 2003. All SEAs funded.

PROGRAM INFORMATION 495

HQ: OESE-DOED, 400 Maryland Ave. SW, Washington, DC 20202. Phone: (202)260-9737. **Internet:** "www.ed.gov/programs/teacherqual/index.html". (Note: no field offices for this program.)

84.369 GRANTS FOR STATE ASSESSMENTS AND RELATED ACTIVITIES

Assistance: formula grants (to 27 months).

Purposes: pursuant to ESEA as amended, Title VI, for the development of the additional state assessments and standards required currently by ESEA—or, if a state has developed those assessments, to support their administration or to carry out other activities related to ensuring that the state's schools and LEAs are held accountable for results.

Eligible applicants/beneficiaries: states.

Range: $249,000 to $32,268,000. **Average:** $7,425,000.

Activity: new program in FY 03.

HQ: Compensatory Education Programs, OESE-DOED, 400 Maryland Ave. SW, Washington, DC 20202-6132. Phone: (202)260-1824. **Internet:** (none provided). (Note: no field offices for this program.)

84.370 DC SCHOOL CHOICE INCENTIVE PROGRAM

Assistance: project grants (100 percent/to 5 years).

Purposes: pursuant to the DC School Choice Incentive Act of 2003, to establish scholarship programs to provide students with expanded elementary and secondary school choice options. Scholarship funds may be used to pay tuition and fees and transportation expenses to participating DC nonpublic schools of their choice.

Eligible applicants: an educational entity of the District of Columbia government; a nonprofit organizations or a consortium of same.

Eligible beneficiaries: elementary and secondary students residing in DC, from households with income not exceeding 185 percent of the poverty line.

Range/Average: $6,252,000.

Activity: new program listing in 2005.

HQ: same address/phone as **84.361**. **Internet:** "www.ed.gov/about/offices/list/oese/programs.html". (Note: no field offices for this program.)

SCHOLARSHIP AND FELLOWSHIP FOUNDATIONS

HARRY S TRUMAN SCHOLARSHIP FOUNDATION

85.001 HARRY S TRUMAN SCHOLARSHIP PROGRAM

Assistance: direct payments/specified use.

Purposes: pursuant to the Harry S Truman Memorial Scholarship Act, for scholarships for full-time students pursuing careers in public service, financed by a permanent trust fund endowment.

Eligible applicants/beneficiaries: U.S. citizens or nationals in their college junior year, nominated by their IHEs. Applicants must rank in the upper quarter of their class, and their studies should permit admission to a graduate or professional program leading to a public service career.

Range: $2,000 to $15,000/year. **Average:** $12,000/year.

Activity: since 1977 program inception, 2,405 scholarships.

HQ: Executive Secretary, Harry S Truman Scholarship Foundation, 712 Jackson Pl. NW, Washington, DC 20006. Phone: (202)395-4831. **Internet:** "www.truman.gov". (Note: no field offices for this program.)

CHRISTOPHER COLUMBUS FELLOWSHIP FOUNDATION

85.100 CHRISTOPHER COLUMBUS FELLOWSHIP PROGRAM

Assistance: project grants; specialized services.

Purposes: pursuant to the Christopher Columbus Quincentenary Coins and Fellowship Foundation Act, for research, study, and labor designed to produce new discoveries in all fields, for the benefit of mankind.

Eligible applicants/beneficiaries: U.S. citizens.

Range: $10,000 to $50,000.

Activity: awards honor and sponsor individual inventors, as well as group efforts.

HQ: Executive Director, Christopher Columbus Scholarship Foundation, 110 Genesee St. - Ste.390, Auburn, NY 13021. Phone: (315)258-0090, FAX (315)258-0093. **Internet:** "www.columbusfdn.org". (Note: no field offices for this program.)

BARRY M. GOLDWATER SCHOLARSHIP AND EXCELLENCE IN EDUCATION FOUNDATION

85.200 BARRY M. GOLDWATER SCHOLARSHIP PROGRAM

Assistance: direct payments/specified use.

Purposes: for scholarships to outstanding students to pursue careers in mathematics, the natural sciences, and engineering—financed by a permanent trust fund endowment.

Eligible applicants/beneficiaries: U.S. citizens, nationals, or lawful resident aliens that are full-time college sophomores and juniors at two- and four-year IHEs, ranking in the upper fourth of their class.

Range: to $7,500/year. **Average:** $6,650.

Activity: since 1988 program inception, 3,962 scholars selected.

HQ: President, Barry M. Goldwater Scholarship Foundation, 6225 Brandon Ave. - Ste.315, Springfield, VA 22150-2519. Phone: (703)756-6012, FAX (703)756-6015. **Internet:** "www.act.org/goldwater"; e-mail, "goldh2o@erols.com". (Note: no field offices for this program.)

WOODROW WILSON INTERNATIONAL CENTER FOR SCHOLARS

85.300 WOODROW WILSON CENTER FELLOWSHIPS IN THE HUMANITIES AND SOCIAL SCIENCES

Assistance: project grants (4-9 months).

Purposes: pursuant to the Woodrow Wilson Memorial Act of 1968, to foster scholarship and promote exchange of views between scholars and decision makers. The Center sponsors research, meetings, and publications in such areas as history, economics, politics, international relations, the environment, the humanities, and other areas. Fellows are in residence at the Center's main offices in Washington, D.C., where they receive office space, use of special libraries and personal computers, part-time research assistance, and publications services.

Eligible applicants/beneficiaries: citizens of any country, with backgrounds in government, business, the professions, or academia—with English language proficiency. For academic participants, eligibility is limited to the postdoctoral level. Degree candidates are ineligible.

Range: $7,000 to $85,000 including travel, support for dependents, health insurance.

Activity: 2004-2005, 23 fellows supported.

HQ: Woodrow Wilson International Center for Scholars, 1300 Pennsylvania Ave. NW, Washington, DC 20004. Phone: (202)691-4000. **Internet:** "www.wilsoncenter.org"; e-mail, "fellowships@wwics.si.edu". (Note: no field offices for this program.)

MORRIS K. UDALL SCHOLARSHIP AND EXCELLENCE IN NATIONAL ENVIRONMENTAL POLICY FOUNDATION

85.400 MORRIS K. UDALL SCHOLARSHIP PROGRAM

Assistance: direct payments/specified use.

Purposes: pursuant to the Morris K. Udall Scholarship and Excellence in National Environmental and Native American Public Policy Act of 1992, for internships, scholarships, and fellowships to develop increased opportunities for young Americans to prepare for careers related to the environment; for native Americans and Alaska natives intending to pursue careers in health care and tribal public policy. The program is financed by a permanent trust fund endowment.

Eligible applicants/beneficiaries: U.S. citizens, nationals, or permanent resident aliens that are college sophomores or juniors, nominated by accredited IHEs.

Range/Average: to $5,000/year.

Activity: as of FY 05, 756 scholarships awarded.

HQ: Executive Director, Morris K. Udall Foundation, 130 S. Scott Ave., Tucson, AZ 85701. Phone: (520)670-5529, -5542, FAX (520)670-5530. **Internet:** "www.udall.gov". (Note: no field offices for this program.)

85.401 MORRIS K. UDALL FELLOWSHIP PROGRAM

Assistance: direct payments/specified use.

Purposes: same generally as for **85.400**.

Eligible applicants/beneficiaries: U.S. citizens and permanent residents that are full-time doctoral degree candidates in their final year of writing their dissertation in environmental public policy and conflict resolution.

Range/Average: $24,000/year.

Activity: as of FY 05, 20 fellowships.

HQ: same address, web site as **85.400**. Phone: (520)670-5529, -5609, FAX (520)670-5530. (Note: no field offices for this program.)

85.402 MORRIS K. UDALL NATIVE AMERICAN CONGRESSIONAL INTERNSHIP PROGRAM

Assistance: direct payments/specified use.

Purposes: same generally as for **85.400**. Interns receive round-trip air fare to Washington, D.C., lodging, a per diem for meals and incidentals, and a $1,200 stipend at the conclusion of the internship.

Eligible applicants/beneficiaries: members of recognized tribes or Alaska natives that are matriculated college seniors or graduate or law students with a minimum 3.2 GPA, and interested in tribal government and policy.

Range/Average: $3,160 to $3,685 per intern per 10-week program.

Activity: as of FY 05, 112 internships in various Congressional offices and the White House.

HQ: same as **85.400**. (Note: no field offices for this program.)

JAMES MADISON MEMORIAL FELLOWSHIP FOUNDATION

85.500 JAMES MADISON MEMORIAL FELLOWSHIP PROGRAM

Assistance: direct payments/specified use.

Purposes: pursuant to the James Madison Memorial Fellowship Act, for fellowships to future and current secondary school (grades 7-12) American history, government, or social studies teachers—toward a deeper understanding of American government, as well the spirit of civic participation that inspired the nation's founders. Recipients are obligated to perform one year of teaching for each year of study supported by a fellowship. Payments cover actual costs of tuition, room and board, fees, and books.

Eligible applicants/beneficiaries: Junior Fellows (2-year maximum)—college seniors or college graduates. Senior Fellows (5-year maximum)—experienced, full-time teachers of grades 7-12, pursuing a Master's level degree. All candidates must be U.S. citizens or nationals.

Range: to $12,000 for one year; $24,000 maximum total award.

Activity: since 1992 program inception, 800 fellowship awards. Currently, 83 active junior, 268 active senior fellowships.

HQ: Director of Administration and Finance, James Madison Memorial Fellowship Foundation, 2000 K St. NW - Ste.303, Washington, DC 20006. Phone: (202)653-8700, FAX (202)653-6045. **Internet:** "www.jamesmadison.com". (Note: no field offices for this program.)

SMITHSONIAN INSTITUTION

NOTE: inclusion of this program in the CFDA as of August 2005 marks the resumption of Smithsonian Institution program listings, which had been included [series 60.000] until CFDA 1987 when several Smithsonian Institution programs were deleted.

85.601 SMITHSONIAN INSTITUTION FELLOWSHIP PROGRAM

Assistance: project grants (10 weeks to 1 year).

Purposes: for graduate and predoctoral students and postdoctoral and senior investigators to conduct research in association with Smithsonian professional staff. Fellowships and internships presently cover: animal behavior; ecology; environmental science emphasizing the tropics; anthropology and archaeology; astrophysics and astronomy; earth sciences and paleobiology; evolutionary and systemic biology; history of science and technology, history of art, especially American, contemporary African, and Asian art, American crafts, decorative arts; social and cultural history of the U.S.; folklife.

Eligible applicants/beneficiaries: postdoctoral fellowships—scholars holding the degree or equivalent for less than 7 years. Senior fellowships—scholars holding the degree or equivalent for 7 years of more. Predoctoral fellowships—candidates with completed course worse and examinations. Graduate fellowships—students enrolled in graduate programs, with one completed semester of work. There are no citizenship requirements.

Range: $4,500 to $40,000.

Activity: new program in FY 05.

HQ: Office of Fellowships, Smithsonian Institution, Victor Bldg. - Ste.9300, Washington, DC 20013-7012. Phone: (202)275-0655. **Internet:** "www.si.edu/research+study". (Note: no field offices for this program.)

PENSION BENEFIT GUARANTY CORPORATION

86.001 PENSION PLAN TERMINATION INSURANCE ("ERISA")

Assistance: insurance.

Purposes: pursuant to the Employee Retirement Income Security Act of 1974 as amended (ERISA), Pension Protection Act of 1987, Retirement Protection Act of 1994, Job Creation and Worker Assistance Act of 2002, Pension Funding Act Equity Act of 2004, and other acts, to insure voluntary private pension plans; to provide for uninterrupted payment of pension benefits to participants and beneficiaries in PBGC-covered plans; to maintain premiums charged by PBGC at the lowest level consistent with fulfilling its obligations. Insurance coverage is mandatory for any pension plan established or maintained by an employer or an employee organization engaged in or affecting commerce, except such plans as those covering: individual accounts; federal, state, local employees; church employees; nonresident aliens; select groups of management or highly compensated employees; professional service employers with fewer than 25 participants; other specific groups. Single-employer plans may terminate in a standard termination only if sufficient assets exist to provide all benefits—and in a voluntary distress termination only if the sponsoring employer can satisfy specified distress criteria. Benefits are paid within limits limits specified by law.

Eligible applicants/beneficiaries: private businesses and organizations that maintain defined benefit plans; participants in such plans.

Range: $10 to $3,801 in monthly benefits per retiree. **Average:** $483.68 monthly.

Activity: 31,000 plans insured with 44,400,000 participants; FY 04, 518,000 participants received benefits.

HQ: Pension Benefit Guaranty Corporation, 1200 K St. NW, Washington, DC 20005-4026. Phone: (202)326-4000. **Internet:** "www.pbgc.gov".

ARCHITECTURAL AND TRANSPORTATION BARRIERS COMPLIANCE BOARD

88.001 ARCHITECTURAL AND TRANSPORTATION BARRIERS COMPLIANCE BOARD ("ATBCB"- "Access Board")

Assistance: technical information.

Purposes: pursuant to the ADA, Rehabilitation Act of 1973, and Architectural Barriers Act of 1968 as amended, and other laws, to enforce federal laws requiring accessibility for physically handicapped persons in federally funded buildings and facilities; to establish related guidelines and requirements; to provide technical assistance and training on design guidelines and standards; to conduct pertinent research.

Eligible applicants/beneficiaries: general public; federal, state, and local agencies.

Activity: not quantified specifically.

HQ: Director, Office of Technical and Information Services, ATBCB, 1331 F St. NW - Ste.1000, Washington, DC 20004-1111. Phone: (202)272-0080, TTY (202)272-0082, FAX (202)272-0081; *technical assistance,* (800)872-2253, TTY (800)993-2822. **Internet:** "www.access-board.gov"; e-mail, "info@access-board.gov". (Note: no field offices for this program.)

NATIONAL ARCHIVES AND RECORDS ADMINISTRATION

89.001 NATIONAL ARCHIVES REFERENCE SERVICES—HISTORICAL RESEARCH

Assistance: use of property, facilities, and equipment; advisory services/counseling; technical information.

Purposes: pursuant to the National Archives and Records Administration Act of 1984 and other acts, to provide reference services to the public and researchers in obtaining access to records and historical materials of the federal government in the National Archives, Presidential Libraries, and Regional Records Services. Conferences, workshops, and other outreach activities may be conducted. Restrictions apply to records subject to the Freedom of Information Act, such as national security.

Eligible applicants/beneficiaries: general public.

Activity: FY 04 (aggregate of all sources), 13,232,000 reference services.

HQ: Office of Records Services, National Archives and Records Administration, College Park, MD 20740-6001. Phone: (301)837-3110; Office of Regional Records Services, (301)837-1982; Office of Presidential Libraries, (301)837-3250. **Internet:** "www.archives.gov".

89.003 NATIONAL HISTORICAL PUBLICATIONS AND RECORDS GRANTS

Assistance: project grants.

Purposes: pursuant to the National Archives and Records Administration Act of 1984 and other acts, for preservation, publication, and use of documentary sources relating to U.S. history. Projects may involve: collaborative efforts with the states, including training; publication in book, microform, or electronic editions of papers and documents of national historical significance.

Eligible applicants/beneficiaries: state and local governments, territorial agencies, tribes; educational and other nonprofit institutions including IHEs, libraries, historical societies, museums, university presses, archives; individuals.

Range: $5,000 to $750,000. **Average:** $85,000.

Activity: FY 06 estimate, no grants.

HQ: National Historical Publications and Records Commission, National Archives and Records Administration, National Archives Bldg., Washington, DC 20408. Phone: (202)501-5610, FAX (202)501-5601. **Internet:** "www.archives.gov/grants"; e-mail, "nhprc@nara.gov". (Note: no field offices for this program.)

INDEPENDENT BOARDS AND COMMISSIONS

DENALI COMMISSION

90.100 DENALI COMMISSION PROGRAM

Assistance: project grants.

Purposes: pursuant to the Denali Commission Act of 1998, to support the Denali Commission as a federal-state partnership to provide critical utilities and infrastructure throughout Alaska, particularly in distressed communities. Project examples: bulk fuel tank storage at isolated site; remote hydroelectric generation; health care infrastructure planning and construction.

Eligible applicants/beneficiaries: Alaska state and local government agencies, public and private profit and nonprofit organizations, individuals.

Range: $200,000 to $10,000,000. **Average:** $5,000,000.

Activity: not quantified specifically.

HQ: Denali Commission, 510 L St. - Ste.410, Anchorage, AK 99501. Phone: (907)271-1414. **Internet:** "www.denali.gov". (Note: no field offices for this program.)

DELTA REGIONAL AUTHORITY

90.200 DELTA REGIONAL DEVELOPMENT ("Delta Program")

Assistance: project grants.

Purposes: pursuant to FSRIA, for 240 specific counties in the eight states in the Delta Region (Mississippi River), in partnership with the federal government, to remedy severe and chronic economic distress by stimulating economic development in distressed communities—by leveraging other federal and state programs focused on: basic infrastructure development transportation improvements; business development; and job training services. States each prepare annual development plans related to a strategic program for which funding is requested in that year; the plans are submitted for approval to the Delta Regional Authority (DRA) which is led by a federal co-chairman and the eight state governors; once approved, individual projects are administered by the federal agency involved, a local development district, or the DRA. Funding is reflected in programs **90.201** and **90.202**.

Eligible applicants/beneficiaries: eight states, public and nonprofit entities in the Delta region. Inquiries and proposals should be submitted to appropriate Local Development Districts (listed on the DRA web site, below).

Range/Average: N.A.

Activity: new program listing in 2005 (CFDA on-line).

HQ: Executive Director, Delta Regional Authority, 236 Sharkey Ave. - Ste.400, Clarksdale, MS 38614. Phone: (662)624-8600. **Internet:** "www.dra.gov". (Note: no field offices for this program.)

90.201 DELTA AREA ECONOMIC DEVELOPMENT

Assistance: project grants (50-90 percent/to 18 months).

Purposes: pursuant to FSRIA, to provide supplemental funds under federal grant-in-aid programs for high-priority projects in state development plans as described in **90.200**. Projects must involve: basic public infrastructure in distressed counties and isolated areas of distress; transportation infrastructure to facilitate economic development; business development emphasizing entrepreneurship; job training or employment-related education, using existing public educational institutions in the region. Recent project examples: water and sewer systems for industrial parks, with tenants committed; IHE workforce training with committed company participation; business incubators.

Eligible applicants/beneficiaries: same as for **90.200**.

Range: $25,000 to $200,000.

Activity: new program listing in 2005 (CFDA on-line). FY 04, 69 projects approved.

HQ: same as **90.200**. (Note: no field offices for this program.)

90.202 DELTA LOCAL DEVELOPMENT DISTRICT ASSISTANCE ("LDD")

Assistance: project grants (50 percent/1 year).

Purposes: pursuant to FSRIA, for the administrative and technical services costs of certified development districts in multicounty districts, including pertinent professional and technical development—in furtherance of projects and programs outlined in **90.200**.

Eligible applicants/beneficiaries: certified multicounty organizations in the Delta Region

Range: $5,100 to $20,000. **Average:** $9,209.

Activity: new program listing in 2005 (CFDA on-line). FY 04, 43 planning districts aided.

HQ: same as **90.200**. (Note: no field offices for this program.)

JAPAN-U.S. FRIENDSHIP COMMISSION

90.300 JAPAN-U.S. FRIENDSHIP COMMISSION GRANTS

Assistance: project grants (cost sharing/6-18 months).

Purposes: to promote educational, artistic, and cultural exchange and research between Japan and the U.S.

Eligible applicants/beneficiaries: public, state, and private IHEs; "501(c)(3)" organizations other than IHEs.

Range/Average: N.A.

Activity: new program listing in 2004.

HQ: Japan-U.S. Friendship Commission, 1201 15th St. NW - Ste.330, Washington, DC 20005. Phone: (no number provided). **Internet:** "www.jusfc.gov". (Note: no field offices for this program.)

ELECTIONS ASSISTANCE COMMISSION

90.400 HELP AMERICAN VOTE COLLEGE POLLWORKER PROGRAM

Assistance: project grants.

Purposes: pursuant to the Help America Vote Act of 2002, to recruit and train college students to assist state and local governments in the administration of elections by serving as nonpartisan poll workers or assistants.

Eligible applicants/beneficiaries: state and private IHEs; "501(c)(3)" organizations other than IHEs; other nonprofit organizations.

Range: to $150,000.

Activity: new program in FY 04.

HQ: Director, Help America Vote College Program, U.S. Elections Assistance Commission, 1225 New York Ave. NW - Ste.1100, Washington, DC 20005. Phone: (202)566-3100. **Internet:** "www.eac.gov ". (Note: no field offices for this program.)

90.401 HELP AMERICA VOTE ACT REQUIREMENT PAYMENTS

Assistance: direct payments/specified use (95 percent).

Purposes: pursuant to the Help America Vote Act of 2002, to reimburse states for costs incurred in obtaining voting equipment and in meeting standards required by the Act.

Eligible applicants/beneficiaries: states, DC, and outlying areas.

Range/Average: N.A.

Activity: new program listing in 2005 (CFDA on-line).

HQ: same as **90.400**. (Note: no field offices for this program.)

UNITED STATES INSTITUTE OF PEACE

91.001 UNSOLICITED GRANT PROGRAM

Assistance: project grants.

Purposes: pursuant to the United States Institute of Peace Act and the Department of Defense Authorization Act of 1985, for education, training, research, and public information projects in international peace and conflict resolution. Unsolicited grant awards may support: research by scholars; curricula and materials development for secondary through postgraduate programs; media programming, including materials for television and radio; development of data bases, bibliographies, collections.

Eligible applicants/beneficiaries: domestic or foreign nonprofit organizations; official public institutions; individuals including U.S. citizens and foreign nationals.

Range/Average: $38,000.

Activity: since FY 89, 1,150 awards.

HQ: Unsolicited Grant Program, U.S. Institute of Peace, 1200 17th St. NW - Ste.200, Washington, DC 20036-3006. Phone: (202)429-3842. **Internet:** "www.usip.org"; e-mail, "grants@usip.org". (Note: no field offices for this program.)

91.002 SOLICITED GRANT PROGRAM

Assistance: project grants (100 percent).

Purposes: pursuant to the United States Institute of Peace Act and the Department of Defense Authorization Act of 1985, for competitive grants to support research, education, library and information technology—on international peace and conflict resolution and on themes and topics identified by the Institute.

Eligible applicants/beneficiaries: same as for **91.001**.

Range/Average: $45,000.

Activity: since 1989, 450 awards.

HQ: Solicited Grant Program, same address/phone, web site as **91.001**. (Note: no field offices for this program.)

DEPARTMENT OF HEALTH AND HUMAN SERVICES

NOTES

In HHS programs:

"NRSA" *refers to National Research Service Awards available to institutions, individuals, or both. Only domestic nonprofit organizations may apply for institutional awards. Individual applicants must: be U.S. citizens, noncitizen nationals, or lawful permanent residents; have a professional or scientific degree (M.D., Ph.D., D.D.S., D.V.M., Sc.D., D.Eng., or equivalent domestic or foreign degree); arrange sponsorship by a public or private nonprofit institution with appropriate staff and facilities; comply with applicable service or payback requirements. Predoctoral awards may be available to recipients with a baccalaureate degree and some work completed toward a graduate degree.*

"SBIR" *refers to the Small Business Innovation Research program. SBIR grants fund the development of technological innovations that may lead to commercialization of products and processes. Phase I contracts, usually up to $100,000 covering six months of research activity, are to establish technical merit and feasibility. Phase II funding, ranging to $750,000 for up to two years, is for continuation of Phase I activities. Primary employment of the principal investigator named in the firm's proposal must be with the small business.*

"STTR" *refers to the Small Business Technology Transfer program. STTR Phase I grants, up to $100,000 for one year of activity, fund cooperative research and development by small businesses and research institutions to determine scientific, technical, and commercial merit and feasibility. Phase II funding, up to $500,000 for two years, reflects results of Phase I research. At least 40 percent of project activities must be performed by the small business concern, and at least 30 percent by the research institution.*

SBIR *and* **STTR** *program contracts must involve domestic small businesses—i.e., for-profit, independently owned, not dominant in the field, and with no more than 500 employees—conducting research in the U.S. or its possessions. Participation by minority, women-owned, and socially and economically disadvantaged businesses is fostered and encouraged.*

Internet: *NIH SBIR and STTR program basic grant solicitation and contract information: e-mail, "ASKNIH@odrockml.od.nih.gov".*

93.001 CIVIL RIGHTS AND PRIVACY RULE COMPLIANCE ACTIVITIES

Assistance: investigation of complaints.

Purposes: pursuant to the Civil Rights Act, Age Discrimination Act of 1975, ADA, Small Business Job Protection Act of 1996 (SBJPA), Health Insurance Portability and Accountability Act of 1996 (HIPAA), related acts, and amendments, to ensure equal opportunities for, and nondiscrimination on any basis against, applicants for or beneficiaries of HHS assistance through any HHS-assisted program or facility—and that the privacy of their health information will be protected under the HIPAA Privacy Rule; to encourage compliance with nondiscrimination regulations by providing technical assistance to recipients of HHS assistance, through workshops, designing model compliance plans, and training responsible state and local officials. Under SBJPA, the Office of Civil Rights investigates complaints and takes steps to assure that individuals are not discriminated against in adoption or foster care placement decisions.

Eligible applicants/beneficiaries: anyone believing that they have been discriminated against in any HHS program, or wanting information or technical assistance to assure compliance with applicable laws.

Activity: FY 04 (sampling), 9,189 discrimination complaints filed, 7,046 complaint actions completed; 2,407 grant compliance reviews.

HQ: Deputy Director, Management Operations Division, Office for Civil Rights, OS-HHS, HHH Bldg. - Rm.509-F6, 200 Independence Ave. SW, Washington, DC 20201. Phone: (202)619-1333; Director, Office for Civil Rights, (same address), (202)619-0403; *Hotlines,* (800)368-1019, TDD (800)537-7697, HIPAA (866)627-7728. **Internet:** "www.hhs.gov/ocr".

93.003 PUBLIC HEALTH AND SOCIAL SERVICES EMERGENCY FUND

Assistance: project grants (100 percent).

Purposes: pursuant to the Public Health Service Act (PHSA), to provide supplemental funding for public health and social service emergencies resulting from disasters. Funds are allocated to HHS agencies for award. (Note: see planned additional uses under "Activity," below.)

Eligible applicants/beneficiaries: federal agencies, state and local governments, service providers in disaster areas.

Range/Average: N.A.

Activity: FY 05-06, funds to be used to prepare the public health system and hospitals for future emergencies, for a reserve of medical supplies for use in possible mass casualty events, for research into new treatments and diagnostic tools to cope with possible bioterrorism incidents.

HQ: Director, Division of Financial Management, SAMHSA-HHS, Parklawn Bldg., 1 Choke Cherry Rd., Rockville, MD 20857. Phone: (240)276-1660. Deputy Director, Financial Management Office, CDCP-HHS, 1600 Clifton Rd., Atlanta, GA 30333. Phone: (404)639-7400. Director, Office of Financial Management, ACF-HHS, Aerospace Bldg. - 6th floor, 370 L'Enfant Promenade SW, Washington, DC 20447. Phone:(202)401-9238. Director, Office of Emergency, 12300 Twinbrook Pkwy. - Ste.360, Rockville, MD 20875. Phone: (301)443-1167. **Internet:** "www.hhs.gov". (Note: no field offices for this program.)

93.004 COOPERATIVE AGREEMENTS TO IMPROVE THE HEALTH STATUS OF MINORITY POPULATIONS

Assistance: project grants (100 percent/to 5 years).

Purposes: pursuant to PHSA as amended, for activities to improve the health status and quality of life of racial and ethnic minorities, consistent with the mission of the HHS Office of Minority Health. Funds may not be used to provide health care, for construction, or to supplant ongoing project activities. Project example: provider education and sensitivity training on cultural practices and their influence on patient compliance with medication and therapeutic treatment interventions.

Eligible applicants/beneficiaries: public and private nonprofit entities.

Range: $25,000 to $614,000. **Average:** $186,000.

Activity: FY 06 estimate, 7 continuation awards.

HQ: Director, Division of Program Operations, Office of Minority Health, Office of Public Health and Science, OS-HHS, 1101 Wooten Pkwy. - Ste.700, Rockville, MD 20852. Phone: (301)594-0769. *Grants management information*: Grants Management Officer, Office of Public Health and Science-HHS, 1101 Wooten Pkwy. - Ste.550, Rockville, MD 20852. Phone: (301)594-0758. **Internet:** "www.omhrc.gov". (Note: no field offices for this program.)

93.006 STATE AND TERRITORIAL AND TECHNICAL ASSISTANCE CAPACITY DEVELOPMENT MINORITY HIV/AIDS DEMONSTRATION PROGRAM

Assistance: project grants (100 percent/to 3 years).

Purposes: pursuant to PHSA as amended, for demonstrations involving state offices of minority health and community-based organizations in HIV/AIDS health education and prevention strategies—to coordinate statewide responses to the crisis in minority communities; to increase access to services and treatment for minorities; to provide technical assistance and capacity development to minority community-based organizations. Funds may not be used to provide health care, for construction, or to supplant ongoing project activities.

Eligible applicants/beneficiaries: state and territorial offices of minority health, or agencies functioning in that capacity; minority-serving community-based organizations.

Range: $144,000 to $1,200,000. **Average:** $431,000.

Activity: FY 06 estimate, 7 continuation awards.

HQ: same as **93.004**. (Note: no field offices for this program.)

93.007 PUBLIC AWARENESS CAMPAIGNS ON EMBRYO ADOPTION

Assistance: project grants (100 percent/to 1 year).

Purposes: for public awareness campaigns on embryo adoption.

Eligible applicants/beneficiaries: "particular" experienced public agencies, nonprofit, and profit organizations; collaboratives. Subgrants may be awarded.

Range: $200,000 to $250,000.

Activity: FY 05, 3-4 new, 4 continuation awards.

HQ: Office of Population Affairs, Office of Public Health and Science, OS-HHS, 1101 Wooten Pkwy. - Ste.700, Rockville, MD 20852. Phone: (301) 594-4001. *Grants management information*: same address/phone as **93.004**. **Internet:** "www.osophs.dhhs.gov/ophs". (Note: no field offices for this program.)

93.008 MEDICAL RESERVE CORPS SMALL GRANT PROGRAM

Assistance: project grants (100 percent/to 3 years).

Purposes: pursuant to PHSA as amended, for development of community Medical Reserve Corps (MRCs) units to increase capacity at the community level to respond to emergencies that have medical consequences, and to improve public health through volunteerism on an ongoing basis. Funds may be used: to establish community-based, citizen-volunteer MRCs; for organizing, volunteer recruitment, assessment of risks and vulnerability, strategy development, planning, training, drills and practices, supplies, and equipment.

Eligible applicants/beneficiaries: local government entities; local nonprofit, nongovernmental community-based organizations, including nonprofit Citizen Corps Councils of the USA Freedom Corps.

Range: $10,000 to $50,000. **Average:** $50,000.

Activity: new program listing in FY 03. FY 06 estimate, 40-75 new awards.

HQ: Office of the Surgeon General, USPHS, OS-HHS, 5600 Fishers Lane - Rm.18-66, Rockville, MD 20817. Phone: (301)443-2910. *Grants management information*: same as **93.004**. **Internet:** "www.medicalreservecorps.gov". (Note: no field offices for this program.)

93.009 COMPASSION CAPITAL FUND
("CCF")

Assistance: project grants (80-100 percent/to 3 years).

Purposes: pursuant to SSA as amended, for charitable organizations to emulate model social service programs; for research on the "best practices" of social service organizations. Funds are provided to intermediary organizations, experienced in capacity building, to provide long-term technical assistance to smaller so-called faith-based and community organizations in such areas as strategic planning, financial management, board development, fund development, and outcome measurement. The intermediary organizations provide one-time $50,000 (unmatched) sub-awards to the smaller organizations, with priority to those that: have not received federal funds; will serve the homeless, elders in need, families in transition from welfare to work, at-risk youth, those in need of intensive rehabilitation such as addicts or prisoners, provide marriage education and preparation services. The sub-awards may not fund direct services; rather, they must improve efficiency and capacity.

Eligible applicants/beneficiaries: intermediaries—county, municipal, special district, and tribal governments; IHEs; profit and nonprofit "501(c)(3)" organizations; faith-based organizations. Sub-awards—nonprofit organizations with and without "501(c)(3)" status, other than IHEs; tribal governments; faith-based organizations

Range: from $50,000 to $100,000.

Activity: new program listing in 2004 (CFDA on-line). FY 04, 14 intermediary grants, 102 sub-awards.

HQ: Program Manager, Office of Community Services, ACF-HHS, 370 L'Enfant Promenade - 5th floor west, Washington, DC 20447. Phone: (202)260-2583, FAX (202)401-4839. **Internet:** "www.acf.dhhs.gov". (Note: no field offices for this program.)

93.010 COMMUNITY-BASED ABSTINENCE EDUCATION ("CBAE")

Assistance: project grants (100 percent/to 3 years).

Purposes: pursuant to SSA, Section 510(a-h), for community-based abstinence education projects to reduce out-of-wedlock childbearing and sexually-transmitted disease among adolescents age 9-18. (Note: program provisions approximate **93.235**.)

Eligible applicants/beneficiaries: public and private nonprofit organizations, state and local government agencies, tribal or ethnic and faith-based organizations, hospitals, clinics, school districts.

Range: $200,000 to $800,000. **Average:** $459,000.

Activity: new program listing in 2005. FY 06 estimate, 233 grants.

HQ: Family and Youth Services Bureau, ACF-HHS, 370 L'Enfant Promenade SW, Washington, DC 20447. Phone: (no number provided). *Grants management information:* Office of Grants Management, Division of Discretionary Grants, same address. Phone: (no number provided) **Internet:** "www.acf.hhs.gov/programs/fysb". (Note: no field offices for this program.)

93.012 IMPROVING, ENHANCING, AND EVALUATING OUTCOMES OF COMPREHENSIVE HEART HEALTH CARE PROGRAMS FOR HIGH-RISK WOMEN

Assistance: project grants.

Purposes: pursuant to PHSA, to improve and enhance existing heart health care programs and to enable tracking and evaluation of outcome data through demonstration projects. Projects must provide a continuum of services through the integration of five inter-related components: Education and Awareness; Screening and Risk Assessment; Diagnostic Testing and Treatment; Lifestyle Modification and Rehabilitation; Tracking and Evaluation. Grantees must target high-risk women in at least of the following groups: age 60 or older; racial and ethnic minorities; women living in rural communities. Funds may cover such costs as personnel and consultants; supplies and software; domestic travel; educational, promotional, and evaluation materials. Funds may not support direct health care services or equipment for patients nor building costs.

Eligible applicants/beneficiaries: existing public or private hospitals, clinics, or health centers; academic health centers and state, county, and local health departments—providing heart health care services to women and with three of the five components previously mentioned in place. Special encouragement to apply is given to enterprise communities and empowerment zones, tribal organizations, religious organizations and those serving rural or frontier communities.

Range: $50,000 to $150,000.

Activity: new program in FY 05; 5 awards anticipated.

HQ: Senior Science Advisor, Office on Women's Health, Office of Public Health and Science, OS-HHS, 200 Independence Ave. SW - Rm.719E, Washington, DC 20201. Phone: (no number provided). *Grants management information*: same address/phone as **93.004**. **Internet:** "www.4woman.gov/owh". (Note: no field offices for this program.)

93.041 SPECIAL PROGRAMS FOR THE AGING—TITLE VII, CHAPTER 3—PROGRAMS FOR PREVENTION OF ELDER ABUSE, NEGLECT, AND EXPLOITATION
("Elder Abuse Prevention")

Assistance: formula grants (100 percent/1-4 years).

Purposes: pursuant to the Older Americans Act of 1965 (OAA) as amended, to develop, strengthen, and carry out comprehensive and coordinated programs for the prevention and treatment of abuse, neglect, and exploitation of older persons. Eligible project activities include public education and outreach, counseling, development and analysis of information and data systems, technical assistance and training for professionals and paraprofessionals. States must submit plans covering 2-4 years.

Eligible applicants/beneficiaries: states and territories with state agencies on aging, designated by the governors.

Range: $3,197 to $512,000. **Average:** $92,000.

Activity: annually, 56 grants.

HQ: Director, Office of Deputy Assistant Secretary/Policy and Programs, AOA-HHS, Washington, DC 20001. Phone: (202)401-4634. **Internet:** "www.aoa.gov".

93.042 SPECIAL PROGRAMS FOR THE AGING—TITLE VII, CHAPTER 2—LONG-TERM CARE OMBUDSMAN SERVICES FOR OLDER INDIVIDUALS
("State Grants for Long-Term Care Ombudsman Services")

Assistance: formula grants.

Purposes: pursuant to OAA as amended, to develop or strengthen ombudsman services programs for older persons living or seeking to live in nursing homes or long-term care facilities, to: provide for the investigation and resolution of complaints by or on behalf of residents; promote policies and practices to improve the quality of life and care; consumer and provider education activities. States must submit plans covering 2-4 years.

Eligible applicants/beneficiaries: same as for **93.041**.

Range: $8,833 to $1,415,000. **Average:** $255,000.

Activity: annually, 55 grants.

HQ: same as **93.041**.

93.043 SPECIAL PROGRAMS FOR THE AGING—TITLE III, PART D—DISEASE PREVENTION AND HEALTH PROMOTION SERVICES

Assistance: formula grants (85 percent/1-4 years).

Purposes: pursuant to OAA as amended, to develop or strengthen programs for preventive health services ineligible for reimbursement under Medicare and for health promotion, at senior centers or alternative sites. Eligible project activities include health risk assessments, routine health and nutrition screening, home injury control and safety screening, physical fitness programs, coordination of community mental health services, gerontological counseling, referrals and follow-ups. States must submit plans covering 2-4 years.

Eligible applicants/beneficiaries: same as for **93.041**.

Range: $14,000 to $2,172,000. **Average:** $389,000.

Activity: annually, 56 grants.

HQ: Office for Community-Based Services, AOA-HHS, Washington, DC 20001. Phone: (202)357-3546. **Internet:** same as **93.041**.

93.044 SPECIAL PROGRAMS FOR THE AGING—TITLE III, PART B—GRANTS FOR SUPPORTIVE SERVICES AND SENIOR CENTERS

Assistance: formula grants (85 percent/1-4 years).

Purposes: pursuant to OAA as amended, to provide comprehensive and coordinated supportive services and to operate multipurpose facilities for older persons, including senior centers, developed according to approved 2-4 year state plans; to maximize support provided to older Americans to enable them to remain in their homes and communities. In addition to supportive nutrition services, funds may cover transportation service, in-home services, and caregiver support, as well as acquisition, construction, or renovation costs.

Eligible applicants/beneficiaries: same as for **93.041**.

Range: $220,000 to $34,820,000. **Average:** $6,319,000.

Activity: annually, 56 grants.

HQ: same as **93.043**.

93.045 SPECIAL PROGRAMS FOR THE AGING—TITLE III, PART C—NUTRITION SERVICES

Assistance: formula grants (85 percent/1-4 years).

Purposes: pursuant to OAA as amended, to provide meals, nutrition education, and related services for the elderly—including at least one hot or other appropriate meal per day, five or more days per week (except in rural areas). Meals may be served in a congregate setting or delivered to the home.

Eligible applicants/beneficiaries: same as for **93.041**.

Eligible beneficiaries: persons age 60 and over and their spouses; certain disabled or handicapped persons under age 60.

Range: congregate services, $240,000 to $34,937,000; home services, $112,000 to $17,931,000. **Average:** congregate, $6,899,000; home, $3,213,000.

Activity: annually, 56 grants.

HQ: same as **93.043**.

93.047 SPECIAL PROGRAMS FOR THE AGING—TITLE VI, PART A, GRANTS TO INDIAN TRIBES—PART B, GRANTS TO NATIVE HAWAIIANS

Assistance: project grants (formula-based - 100 percent).

Purposes: pursuant to OAA as amended, for supportive services to older Indians and Alaska and Hawaii natives, including nutrition services, multipurpose center improvements and staffing, transportation, information and referral assistance, and multifaceted caregiver services.

Eligible applicants: tribal organizations and public or private nonprofit organizations that serve native Hawaiian elders, serving at least 50 clients.

Eligible beneficiaries: Indians age 60 or older and, for nutrition services, their spouses; certain others under age 60.

Range: tribes, $74,000 to $180,000; Hawaii natives, $95,000 to $1,718,000; caregiver grants, $14,000 to $57,000. **Average:** tribes, $102,000; Hawaii, $906,000; caregivers, $36,000.

Activity: FY 03-04 estimate, 2 native Hawaii, 241 tribal organizations funded.

HQ: Director, Office of American Indian, Alaskan Native, and Native Hawaiian Programs, AOA-HHS, Washington, DC 20201. Phone: (202)357-3500. **Internet:** same as **93.041**.

93.048 SPECIAL PROGRAMS FOR THE AGING—TITLE IV— AND TITLE II— DISCRETIONARY PROJECTS

Assistance: project grants (75 percent/1-3 years).

Purposes: pursuant to OAA as amended, for development and testing of innovative programs in the field of aging—to develop knowledge of the problems and needs of the elderly. Funds may be used to: demonstrate new methods and practices; evaluate existing programs and services; conduct applied research and analysis; train professionals.

Eligible applicants/beneficiaries: public or private nonprofit agencies, organizations, and institutions.

Range: $9,694 to $2,943,000. **Average:** $250,000.

Activity: FY 05 estimate, 400 awards.

HQ: Public Inquiries Unit, Center for Communications and Consumer Services, AOA-HHS, Washington, DC 20201. Phone: (202)619-0724. **Internet:** same as **93.041**.

93.051 ALZHEIMER'S DISEASE DEMONSTRATION GRANTS TO STATES

Assistance: project grants (55-75 percent/3 years).

Purposes: pursuant to PHSA as amended, Home Health Care and Alzheimer's Disease Amendments Act of 1990, and HPEPA, to plan, establish, and operate model programs for persons with Alzheimer's disease and related disorders, their families, and care-givers, including home health and personal care, companion services, short-term care in health facilities, other respite care services.

Eligible applicants/beneficiaries: state agencies.

Range: $250,000 to $325,000. **Average:** $288,000.

Activity: FY 03, 7 new grants. Cumulatively, first 10 years of program, 15,000 client families served.

HQ: Center for Wellness and Community-Based Services, AOA-HHS, Washington, DC 20201. Phone: (202)357-3452. **Internet:** "www.aoa.gov/alz".

93.052 NATIONAL FAMILY CAREGIVER SUPPORT

Assistance: formula grants (75 percent/1-4 years); project grants (100 percent).

Purposes: pursuant to OAA as amended, to provide multi-faceted systems of support services for family caregivers and grandparents or older individuals who are relative-caregivers, including: information about, and assistance in gaining access to, available services; individual counseling, organizational support groups, caregiver training in making decisions and solving problems relating to their roles; temporary respite care relief for the caregivers; supplemental complementary services.

Eligible applicants/beneficiaries: formula grants—state and territorial governments, with subgrants to area agencies on aging. Project grants—tribal organizations, native Hawaiian organizations.

Range: $95,000 to $15,153,000. **Average:** $2,840,000.

Activity: annually, 56 awards.

HQ: *formula grants,* Center for Wellness of Community-Based Services, AOA-HHS, Washington, DC 20201. Phone: (202)357-3586. *Project grants,* same as **93.047**. Phone: (202)357-3501. **Internet:** same as **93.041**.

93.053 NUTRITION SERVICES INCENTIVE PROGRAM ("NSIP")

Assistance: formula grants.

Purposes: pursuant to OAA as amended, to reward effective performance by states and tribes in the efficient delivery or meals to older adults, through the use of cash or USDA commodities in congregate or home-delivered meals. The funding incentives are based on the number of meals served in the prior fiscal year in proportion to all other states and tribes.

Eligible applicants/beneficiaries: state agencies and tribal organizations receiving funds through OAA Titles III and VI.

Range: $68,000 to $14,042,000. **Average:** $2,646,000.

Activity: new program listing in 2003. FY 03, 248,000,000 meals served. (Note: USDA administered this program during FY 02-03.)

HQ: same as **93.043**.

93.061 INNOVATIONS IN APPLIED HEALTH RESEARCH

Assistance: project grants (100 percent/to 3 years).

Purposes: pursuant to PHSA as amended, for applied public health research to translate biomedical science results into effective programs that directly affect the quality and length of life. Preference in project selection is given to proposals with participatory research involving affected communities.

Eligible applicants/beneficiaries: public and private profit and nonprofit organizations; governments and their agencies including territories and possessions; IHEs, hospitals, community-based organizations, women- and minority-owned businesses, tribes and tribal organizations.

Range/Average: N.A.

Activity: new program in FY 04.

HQ: Office of Public Health Research (D-72), CDCP-HHS, 1600 Clinton Rd., Atlanta, GA 30333. Phone: (404)371-5480. *Grants management information*: Grants Management Specialist, Procurement and Grants Office, CDCP-HHS, 2920 Brandywine Rd., Atlanta, GA 30341. Phone: (770)488-2696. **Internet**: "www.cdc.gov". (Note: no field offices for this program.)

93.063 CENTERS FOR GENOMICS AND PUBLIC HEALTH

Assistance: project grants (100 percent/1-4 years).

Purposes: pursuant to PHSA as amended, to provide information, technical assistance, and training to community, state, and regional organizations in genomics and population health for the health workforce. Funds may not support direct patient care, capital outlays, or research involving human subjects.

Eligible applicants/beneficiaries: IHEs, research institutions.

Range: $400,000 to $600,000.

Activity: new program in FY 04; 3 public health schools funded.

HQ: Office of Genomics and Disease Prevention (E-82), CDCP-HHS, 1600 Clifton Rd. N.E., Atlanta, GA 30333. Phone: (no number provided). Grants management contact address, web site: same as **93.061**. Phone: (770)488-2722. (Note: no field offices for this program.)

93.064 LABORATORY TRAINING, EVALUATION, AND QUALITY ASSURANCE PROGRAMS
("Quality Assurance in Pathology and Laboratory Medicine")

Assistance: project grants (100 percent/to 3 years).

Purposes: pursuant to PHSA as amended, to improve laboratory genetic testing practices relevant to clinical and public health settings; to determine standardized approaches to quality assurance in pathology and laboratory medicine, applicable in diverse settings including community hospitals, academic medical centers, and independent laboratories.

Eligible applicants/beneficiaries: public and private nonprofit organizations, IHEs, research institutions, hospitals, community organizations; state and local governments and their agents, including in territories and possessions.

Range: $100,000 to $225,000.

Activity: new program in FY 04.

HQ: PHPPO-DLS, CDCP-HHS, 4770 Buford Hwy, Atlanta, GA 30333. Phone: (770)488-8070, FAX (770)488-8278. *Grants management information*:

same address as **93.061**. Phone: (770)488-2748. **Internet:** "www.cdc.gov"; e-mail, "sqr2@cdc.gov".

93.065 LABORATORY LEADERSHIP, WORKFORCE TRAINING AND MANAGEMENT DEVELOPMENT, IMPROVING PUBLIC HEALTH LABORATORY INFRASTRUCTURE

Assistance: project grants (100 percent/to 5 years).

Purposes: pursuant to PHSA as amended, to improve public health laboratory infrastructure; for state-of-the-art training to prepare laboratorians to deal with public health threats with emerging infectious diseases or other biologic and chemical threats; to improve laboratory leadership capabilities; to enhance inter-laboratory communications.

Eligible applicants/beneficiaries: state governments, specifically state public health laboratories; organizations representing state public health laboratories with an established training network.

Range: $4,200,000 to $4,800,000. **Average:** $4,700,000.

Activity: new program listing in 2005.

HQ: Project Officer, CDCP-HHS, Atlanta, GA. Phone: (770)488-8098. *Grants management information*: same as **93.064**. **Internet:** "www.cdc.gov"; "www.phppo.cdc.gov/dls". (Note: no field offices for this program.)

93.066 VITAL STATISTICS RE-ENGINEERING PROGRAM

Assistance: project grants (100 percent/1-3 years).

Purposes: pursuant to PHSA as amended, to assist states in improving the timeliness, quality, and sustainability of the decentralized vital statistics system by adopting national consensus standards and guidelines, in all 57 registration areas. These will be systems that can: provide quality and timely data for public health surveillance and medical research; meet citizen needs for legal copies of their birth and death records, as well as meet federal needs for related record verification and authentication; produce comparable vital registration and statistics systems in each state; use national standards and guidelines, including certificates of birth, death, and fetal death; support national security and privacy requirements; integrate with other public health systems; use internet technology.

Eligible applicants/beneficiaries: appropriate public and private nonprofit organizations.

Range/Average: $172,000.

Activity: new program listing in 2004.

HQ: Project Officer, Division of Vital Statistics, National Center for Health Statistics, CDCP-HHS, 3311 Toledo Rd. - Rm.7311, Hyattsville, MD 20782. Phone: (301)458-4468. *Grants management information*: Grants Management Specialist, Acquisition and Assistance Field Branch, Procurement and Grants Office, CDCP-HHS, Cochran Mill Rd., P.O. Box 18070, Pittsburgh, PA 15236. Phone: (412)386-6826. **Internet:** ""www.cdc.gov"". (Note: no field offices for this program.)

93.067 GLOBAL AIDS

Assistance: project grants (100 percent/1-5 years).

Purposes: pursuant to PHSA as amended, for activities conducted with other countries, international organizations, U.S. Department of State, USAID, and other partners to achieve the United Nations General Assembly Special Session on HIV/AIDS goal of reducing prevalence among persons age 15-24. Research may not be funded under this program.

Eligible applicants/beneficiaries: limited competition, or single eligibility by authorizing legislation.

Range: $75,000 to $775,000.

Activity: new program in FY 05.

HQ: Lead Contract Specialist, International Branch, CDCP-HHS, 2920 Brandywine Rd., Atlanta, GA 30341. Phone: (770)488-2632. **Internet:** "www.cdc.gov". (Note: no field offices for this program.)

93.068 CHRONIC DISEASES: RESEARCH, CONTROL AND PREVENTION

Assistance: project grants (to 100 percent; 1-5 years).

Purposes: pursuant to PHSA as amended, to prevent and control chronic diseases and disorders through research, development, capacity building, and intervention; to use research data to improve detection, diagnosis, treatment, and care of chronic diseases and their complications; to develop new related knowledge that will improve health and quality of life and eliminate health disparities among segments of the population. CDCP will have substantial involvement in project activities.

Eligible applicants/beneficiaries: state and local governments or their bona fide agents, including in territories and possessions; public, private, profit, and nonprofit organizations including small, minority and women-owned businesses, IHEs, research institutions, hospitals, community-based organizations, tribal governments, tribes, tribal organizations. Foregoing applicants may not be eligible for all programs.

Range: $100,000 to $1,500,000. **Average:** $500,000.

Activity: new program listing in 2005 (CFDA on-line).

HQ: Office of Extramural Research (K-92), National Center for Chronic Disease Prevention and Health Promotion, CDCP-HHS, 4770 Buford Hwy. NE, Atlanta, GA. Phone: (770)488-8390. *Grants management information*: Grants Management Specialist, same address/phone as **93.063**. **Internet:** "www.cdc.gov". (Note: no field offices for this program.)

93.100 HEALTH DISPARITIES IN MINORITY HEALTH

Assistance: project grants (100 percent/to 2 years).

Purposes: pursuant to PHSA as amended and Disadvantaged Minority Health Improvement Act of 1990, to support elimination of health disparities among racial and ethnic populations through small-scaled projects addressing a demonstrated health problem or issue. Funds may not support health care, construction, or ongoing project costs.

Eligible applicants: private nonprofit community-based minority organizations.

Eligible beneficiaries: Pacific islanders, Blacks, African-Americans, Hispanics, Latinos, native Americans, Alaska natives, native Hawaiians, or their subgroups.

Range: $30,000 to $50,000. **Average:** $49,000.

Activity: FY 05 (final program year), noncompeting applications only.

HQ: same as **93.004**. (Note: no field offices for this program.)

93.103 FOOD AND DRUG ADMINISTRATION—RESEARCH

Assistance: project grants (100 percent/1-5 years).

Purposes: pursuant to PHSA and Small Business Innovation Research Program Reauthorization Act of 1992 (SBIRPRA) as amended and Radiation Control for Health Safety Act of 1968, for research, demonstration, education, and dissemination activities in a broad range of areas, AIDS, biologics, blood and blood products, therapeutics, vaccine and allergenic projects, drug hazards, human and veterinary drugs, medical devices and diagnostics products, orphan product development, and radiation-emitting devices and materials, food safety and additives. SBIR awards are made (*see Notes preceding 93.001*).

Eligible applicants/beneficiaries: public or private nonprofit IHEs, institutions, state and local governments, hospitals, laboratories, commercial and nonprofit organizations.

Range: $889 to $3,000,000. **Average**: $226,000.

Activity: FY 06 estimate, 23 new, 65 continuation grants; SBIR, 3 Phase I, 1 Phase II awards.

HQ: Chief Grants Management Officer, Division of Contracts and Procurement Management, Office of Acquisition and Grant Services, FDA-HHS (HFA-500), 5600 Fishers Lane - Rm.2107, Rockville, MD 20857. Phone: (301)827-7182; *SBIR information,* (301)827-7179, FAX (301)827-7101. **Internet:** "www.fda.gov". (Note: no field offices for administration of this program; however, district offices are listed in Part IV for information purposes.)

93.104 COMPREHENSIVE COMMUNITY MENTAL HEALTH SERVICES FOR CHILDREN WITH SERIOUS EMOTIONAL DISTURBANCES (SED) ("CMHS Child Mental Health Service Initiative")

Assistance: project grants (33-75 percent/to 6 years).

Purposes: pursuant to PHSA as amended, for community-based care systems for children and adolescents with serious emotional disturbances, and their families—ensuring that: services are provided collaboratively across child-serving systems; each child or adolescent served receives an individualized service plan developed with the participation of the family and, where appropriate, of the child; each plan designates a case manager; funding is provided for the required mental health services. Project funds may be used to pay: administrative costs including staff salaries, travel, supplies, communications, and space and equipment rental; for pertinent training including in providing therapeutic foster or group home care, intensive home-based or intensive day treatment services. Ineligible expenses include real estate-related costs, residential care or services in centers serving more than 10 children, unrelated training, non-mental health services including medical and educational services, and protection and advocacy.

Eligible applicants: states and their political subdivisions, tribal governments.

Eligible beneficiaries: children under age 22 with diagnosed SED or serious behavioral or mental disorders.

Range: to $4,383,000. **Average:** $3,700,000.

Activity: FY 06 estimate, 44 continuation awards.

HQ: Chief, Child Adolescent and Family Branch, Division of Knowledge Development and Systems Change, CMHS-SAMHSA-HHS, 1 Choke Cherry Rd., Rockville, MD 20857. Phone: (no number provided). *Grants management information*: Grants Management Officer, SAMHSA-HHS, same address. Phone: (240)276-1421. **Internet:** "www.hhs.gov". (Note: no field offices for this program.)

93.105 BILINGUAL/BICULTURAL SERVICE DEMONSTRATION GRANTS

Assistance: project grants (100 percent/3 years).

Purposes: pursuant to PHSA as amended, to improve and expand the capacity for bilingual/bicultural competence of health care professionals in providing services to minority communities with limited English proficiency (LEP), including professional and paraprofessional staff training and providing interpreters and translators—but not providing health care services or augmentation of ongoing project activities.

Eligible applicants/beneficiaries: public or private nonprofit minority community-based organizations or health care facilities serving targeted LEP communities.

Range: $80,000 to $150,000. **Average:** $142,000.

Activity: FY 05 estimate, 20 new awards; FY 06-07, continuation awards only.

HQ: same as **93.004**. (Note: no field offices for this program.)

93.107 MODEL STATE-SUPPORTED AREA HEALTH EDUCATION CENTERS ("Model AHEC")

Assistance: formula grants (50 percent/to 3 years).

Purposes: pursuant to PHSA as amended and HPEPA, to encourage regionalization of health professions schools by establishing model Area Health Education Centers (see **93.824**), involving collaborative partnerships of university health centers with local planning, educational, and clinical resources; for health careers programs for students in grades 9-12. Emphasis is on recruitment and community-based training of primary care students, residents, and providers.

Eligible applicants/beneficiaries: schools of allopathic medicine or osteopathy and consortia operating AHECs and no longer receiving assistance under **93.824**.

Range: $173,000 to $865,000. **Average:** $380,000.

Activity: FY 04, 36 grants.

HQ: Chief, AHEC Branch, Division of State, Community and Public Health, Bureau of Health Professions, HRSA-HHS, Parklawn Bldg. - Rm.9-05, 5600 Fishers Lane, Rockville, MD 20857. Phone: (301)443-6950. *Grants management information*: Director, Division of Grants Management Operations, HRSA-HHS, 5600 Fishers Lane - Rm.11A-16, Rockville, MD 20857. Phone: Health Services Branch, (301)443-2385; Research and Training Branch, (301)443-3099; Government and Special Focus Branch, (301)443-3288. **Internet:** "www.hrsa.gov". (Note: no field offices for this program.)

93.110 MATERNAL AND CHILD HEALTH FEDERAL CONSOLIDATED PROGRAMS
("Special Projects of Regional and National Significance" - "SPRANS")

Assistance: project grants.

Purposes: pursuant to the Social Security Act of 1935 (SSA) as amended, for special projects of regional or national significance involving training, services, research, and demonstrations in maternal and child health services, including: genetic disease testing, counseling, and information dissemination; operation of comprehensive hemophilia diagnosis and treatment centers. A portion of grant funds, if appropriated, may be used to provide other services including home visitations, increased participation of obstetricians and pediatricians, maternal and child health centers for women and infants, rural health services, community-based services for children with special health care needs.

Eligible applicants/beneficiaries: training grants—public or private nonprofit IHEs. Research grants—public or private nonprofit IHEs, agencies, and organizations. Hemophilia and genetics grants and other special project grants—any public or private entity.

Range: $14,000 to $1,500,000. **Average:** $179,000.

Activity: FY 06 estimate, 500-600 projects.

HQ: Associate Administrator, Maternal and Child Health Bureau, HRSA-HHS, 5600 Fishers Lane - Rm.18-05, Rockville, MD 20857. Phone: (301)443-2170. *Grants management information*: same as **93.107**. **Internet:** "www.hrsa.gov".

93.111 ADOLESCENT FAMILY LIFE RESEARCH GRANTS

Assistance: project grants (100 percent/to 3 years).

Purposes: pursuant to PHSA as amended, for research and information dissemination activities concerning societal causes and consequences of adolescent sexual activity, contraceptive use, pregnancy and child rearing.

Eligible applicants/beneficiaries: state and local government agencies; private nonprofit and profit organizations; IHEs.

Range: $108,000 to $151,000. **Average:** $145,000

Activity: FY 06 estimate, 5 continuation, 3 new project awards.

HQ: Office of Adolescent Pregnancy Programs, Office of Population Affairs, OS-HHS, 1101 Wootton Pkwy. - Ste.700, Rockville, MD 20852. Phone:

(301)594-4008. *Grants management information*: same as **93.004**. **Internet:** "www.opa.osophs.dhhs.gov". (Note: no field offices for this program.)

93.113 BIOLOGICAL RESPONSE TO ENVIRONMENTAL HEALTH HAZARDS

Assistance: project grants (100 percent/to 5 years).

Purposes: pursuant to PHSA as amended and Small Business Research and Development Enhancement Act of 1992 (SBRDEA), for research and research training on the chemical and physical causes of pathological changes in molecules, cells, tissues, and organs, toward the prevention of neurological, behavioral, and developmental abnormalities, and respiratory diseases, cancer, and other disorders. Grants also support studies of toxicity in metals, natural and synthetic chemicals, pesticides, asbestos and silica, and natural toxins—and their effects on human organ systems, metabolism, endocrine and immune systems, and other biological functions. The Environmental Health Sciences Education Program may fund projects to improve student understanding of environmental health issues and to expand career awareness in health sciences research and services occupations, by developing educational materials for grades K-12. Independent Scientist Awards, Mentored Research Scientist Development Awards, Mentored Clinical Scientist Development Awards, Academic Career Awards, and other programs may also be funded including centers on children's health and disease. SBIR and STTR awards are made (*see Notes preceding* **93.001**).

Eligible applicants/beneficiaries: research grants and cooperative agreements, science education grants, independent scientist awards, mentored clinical and research scientist awards, academic career awards—IHEs, hospitals, state or local governments, nonprofit research institutions, or profit organizations for research by a named principal investigator. Candidates for academic career development awards must have a clinical or research doctorate and peer-reviewed independent research support, and they must devote at least 75 percent effort. Candidates for mentored clinical scientist awards must have clinical training; those holding a Ph.D. degree are ineligible, as are researchers that have served as principal investigators on PHS-supported research projects.

Range: research grants, $39,000 to $2,033,000. **Average:** projects, $350,000.

Activity: FY 06 estimate, 523 awards.

HQ: Division of Extramural Research and Training, NIEHS, NIH-HHS, P.O. Box 12233, Research Triangle Park, NC 27709. Phone: Director, Center for Risk & Integrated Sciences, (919)541-0797; Chief, Cellular, Organ and Systems Pathobiology Branch, (919)541-3289; *environmental justice, science education grants,* Chief, Susceptibility and Population Health, (919) 541-4980; *individual awards,* Program Administrator, Cellular, Organ and Systems Pathobiology Branch, (919)541-1445; *AREA, SBIR, STTR awards,* Program Administrator, Cellular, Organ and Systems Pathobiology Branch, (919)541-0781. *Grants management information*: Grants Management Branch, Division of Extramural Research and Training, same address. Phone: (919)541-2749. **Internet:** "www.niehs.nih.gov". (Note: no field offices for this program.)

93.114 APPLIED TOXICOLOGICAL RESEARCH AND TESTING ("Bioassay of Chemicals and Test Development")

Assistance: project grants (100 percent/to 5 years).

Purposes: pursuant to PHSA as amended and SBRDEA, to develop scientific information about potentially toxic and hazardous chemicals, through research, testing and test development, and validation efforts. Program goals include the development and validation of existing and emerging methodologies that can be employed successfully to predict human response to toxic agents. SBIR and STTR awards are made (*see Notes preceding* **93.001**). Awards for individuals generally are in the categories and amounts outlined in **93.113**.

Eligible applicants/beneficiaries: same as for **93.113**.

Range: projects, $142,000 to $1,602,000. **Average:** $333,000.

Activity: FY 05 estimate, 82 awards.

HQ: same as **93.113**. (Note: no field offices for this program.)

93.115 BIOMETRY AND RISK ESTIMATION—HEALTH RISKS FROM ENVIRONMENTAL EXPOSURES

Assistance: project grants (100 percent/to 5 years).

Purposes: pursuant to PHSA as amended and SBRDEA, for research and research training in statistics, biomathematics, epidemiology, and risk estimation, toward the estimation of probable health risks of cancer, reproductive and neurological effects, and other adverse effects—from various environmental hazards including air and water pollution and lead poisoning. Major emphasis is on refining methods for estimating human risk from data derived from studying laboratory animals, and on examining the quantitative issues involved in designing short-term tests and interpreting the data from the tests. The Environmental Health Sciences Education Program funds one- to three-year projects to improve student understanding of environmental health issues and to expand career awareness in health sciences research and services occupations, by developing educational materials for grades K-12. SBIR and STTR awards are made (*see Notes preceding* **93.001**). Awards for individuals generally are in the categories and amounts outlined in **93.113**.

Eligible applicants/beneficiaries: same as for **93.113**.

Range: projects, $68,000 to $3,661,000. **Average:** $479,000.

Activity: FY 06 estimate, 92 awards.

HQ: same as **93.113**. (Note: no field offices for this program.)

93.116 PROJECT GRANTS AND COOPERATIVE AGREEMENTS FOR TUBERCULOSIS CONTROL PROGRAMS

Assistance: projects grants (to 100 percent/to 5 years).

Purposes: pursuant to PHSA as amended, TB Prevention Amendments Act of 1990 as amended, and other acts, for tuberculosis control and prevention activities. Funds may cover such costs as patient outreach, directly observed therapy to assure its completion, morbidity surveillance, personnel, equipment, supplies, program assessment, and services. Costs of construction and inpatient care are ineligible uses.

Eligible applicants/beneficiaries: official public health agencies of state and local governments, territories and possessions.

Range: $61,000 to $17,421,000. **Average:** $1,509,000.

Activity: annually, 68 continuation awards.

HQ: National Center for HIV, STD, and TB Prevention, CDCP-HHS, 1600 Clifton Rd. NE, Atlanta, GA 30333. Phone: (404)639-5336. Grants management contact address, web site: same as **93.061**. Phone: (770)498-1912. (Note: no field offices for this program.)

93.117 GRANTS FOR PREVENTIVE MEDICINE ("Preventive Medicine")

Assistance: project grants (100 percent/3 years).

Purposes: pursuant to PHSA as amended and HPEPA, to plan, develop, maintain, or improve postgraduate training programs in preventive medicine. Financial assistance may be provided to residency trainees. Grants may not used for construction or direct patient services.

Eligible applicants: public or private schools of medicine, osteopathy, or public health.

Eligible beneficiaries: U.S. citizens, nationals, and lawful permanent residents.

Range: $102,000 to $430,000. **Average:** $207,000.

Activity: FY 04 estimate, 7 new and continuation awards.

HQ: Division of State, Community, and Public Health, Center for Public Health, Bureau of Health Professions, HRSA-HHS, Parklawn Bldg. - Rm. 8A-19, 5600 Fishers Lane, Rockville, MD 20857. Phone: (301)443-0157. Grants management information, web site, same as **93.107**. (Note: no field offices for this program.)

93.118 ACQUIRED IMMUNODEFICIENCY SYNDROME (AIDS) ACTIVITY

Assistance: project grants (100 percent/to 5 years).

Purposes: pursuant to PHSA as amended, to develop and implement HIV prevention programs of public education and information.

Eligible applicants/beneficiaries: public and private nonprofit and profit organizations including IHEs and research institutions; state and local governments, territories and possessions; small and minority- and women-owned businesses.

Range: $45,000 to $2,000,000. **Average:** $390,000.

Activity: FY 03, 28 awards for epidemiological research studies, national partnerships, and evaluation.

HQ: Division of HIV/AIDS Prevention (A43), CDCP-HHS, 1600 Clifton Rd., Atlanta, GA 30333. Phone: (404)639-0900. Grants management contact address, web site: same as **93.061**. Phone: (770)488-1911. (Note: no field offices for this program.)

93.121 ORAL DISEASES AND DISORDERS RESEARCH

Assistance: project grants (100 percent/to 5 years).

Purposes: pursuant to PHSA as amended and SBRDEA, for research and research training in the oral health sciences, in such areas as craniofacial, oral, and dental health promotion and disease prevention, diagnostics, and therapeutics. Grant programs support basic, clinical, and transitional research, from molecular biology to patient-oriented and community-based clinical investigations—including etiology, pathogenesis, epidemiology, prevention, diagnosis, and treatment—within overlapping programs: Inherited Diseases and Disorders (e.g., cleft lip and palate, other craniofacial birth defects, developmentally related disorders), as well as occlusion defects acquired through trauma; Infectious Diseases such as dental caries, periodontitis, oral manifestations of HIV/AIDS, herpes, hepatitis, and other diseases; Neoplastic Diseases; Chronic Disabling Diseases; Biomaterials, Biomimetics and Tissue Engineering; Behavior, Health Promotion and Environment. Also supported are: Comprehensive Oral Research Centers of Discovery; Research Training and Careers; Diversity in Research; Clinical Trials and Clinical Core Centers; and Technology Transfer. NRSA, SBIR, and STTR awards are available (*see Notes preceding* **93.001**).

Eligible applicants/beneficiaries: research grants—scientists at universities, medical and dental schools, hospitals, laboratories, other public, private, nonprofit, or profit institutions. Career development award candidates must comply with requirements similar to those applying to the NRSA program.

Range: projects, $1,000 to $5,613,000; NRSA, $8,000 to $677,000. **Average:** projects, $318,000; NRSA, $154,000.

Activity: FY 03 estimate, 453 noncompeting, 177 competing research grants; 13 research centers; 107 career development, 303 NRSA positions; 15 other research grants; 57 SBIR/STTR awards.

HQ: Division of Extramural Research, National Institute of Dental and Craniofacial Research, NIH-HHS, Bethesda, MD 20892. Phone: Division of Basic and Translational Sciences, (301)594-2419; Division of Extramural Activities, (301)594-2904; Division of Population and Health Promotion Sciences, (301)496-9469; Division of Intramural Research, (301)496-2687. **Internet:** "www.hhs.gov". (Note: no field offices for this program.)

93.123 HEALTH PROFESSIONS PREGRADUATE SCHOLARSHIP PROGRAM FOR INDIANS

Assistance: project grants (100 percent).

Purposes: pursuant to the Indian Health Care Improvement Act as amended, for four-year scholarships for American Indians and Alaska natives to complete pregraduate education leading to a baccalaureate degree in pre-medicine or pre-dentistry. Part-time attendance may be supported for a maximum of eight years.

Eligible applicants/beneficiaries: American Indians or Alaska natives accepted or enrolled in a pregraduate program.

Range: $19,000 to $27,000. **Average:** $20,000.

Activity: FY 05-06 estimate, 31 awards.

HQ: IHS Scholarship Program, IHS-HHS, 801 Thompson Ave. - Ste.120, Rockville, MD 20852. Phone: (301)443-6197. *Grants management information*: Grants Management Officer, Division of Acquisition and Grants Operations, IHS-HHS, same address. Phone: (301)443-0243. **Internet:** "www.ihs.gov". (Note: no field offices for this program.)

93.124 NURSE ANESTHETIST TRAINEESHIPS

Assistance: project grants (100 percent/1 year).

Purposes: pursuant to PHSA as amended and HPEPA, for nurse anesthetist traineeships for up to 18 months of full-time study by registered nurses in nurse anesthetist master's education programs.

Eligible applicants: accredited schools of nursing, academic health centers, and other public and private nonprofit institutions.

Eligible beneficiaries: U.S. citizens, noncitizen nationals, or permanent residents with 12 months of completed nurse anesthetist master's training.

Range: $1,800 to $29,000. **Average:** $15,000.

Activity: FY 04 estimate, 73 awards.

HQ: Division of Nursing, Bureau of Health Professions, HRSA-HHS, Parklawn Bldg. - Rm.9-36, 5600 Fishers Lane, Rockville, MD 20857. Phone: (301)443-5787. Grants management information, web site: same as **93.107**. (Note: no field offices for this program.)

93.127 EMERGENCY MEDICAL SERVICES FOR CHILDREN ("EMS for Children")

Assistance: project grants (100 percent/to 3 years).

Purposes: pursuant to PHSA as amended, for demonstration projects to expand and improve emergency medical services for children needing critical care or treatment for trauma.

Eligible applicants/beneficiaries: states, schools of medicine.

Range: $96,000 to $1,100,000. **Average:** $178,000.

Activity: FY 05 estimate, 83 projects funded. FY 06 estimate, no funding available.

HQ: EMSC Program Director, Maternal and Child Health Bureau, HRSA-HHS, 5600 Fishers Lane - Rm.18A-38, Rockville, MD 20857. Phone: (no number provided). Grants management information, web site: same as **93.107**. (Note: no field offices for this program.)

93.129 TECHNICAL AND NON-FINANCIAL ASSISTANCE TO HEALTH CENTERS ("State and Regional Primary Care Associations")

Assistance: project grants (100 percent/to 5 years).

Purposes: pursuant to PHSA as amended, to provide technical and nonfinancial assistance to health centers and NHSC delivery sites, relative to: collaborative activities on state or market area levels; involvement of state agencies in providing primary care to medically underserved populations; developing shared services and joint purchasing arrangements; providing training, assessment of community health needs, expertise in dealing with the homeless, public housing residents, farm workers, and rural and other special populations, as well as in managing and maximizing nonfederal resources; expanding the health center network.

Eligible applicants/beneficiaries: state primary care associations currently working with BHPC-supported providers; other community-based providers.

Range: $175,000 to $800,000.

Activity: FY 05 estimate, 50 associations funded.

HQ: Director, Division of State and Community Assistance, Bureau of Primary Health Care, HRSA-HHS, 5600 Fishers Lane - Rm.15C-26, Rockville, MD 20857. Phone: (301)594-4488. Grants management information, web site: same as **93.107**. (Note: no field offices for this program.)

93.130 PRIMARY CARE SERVICES RESOURCE COORDINATION AND DEVELOPMENT
("State Primary Care Offices")

Assistance: project grants.

Purposes: pursuant to PHSA, to coordinate local, state, and federal resources contributing to primary care service delivery and workforce issues to meet the needs of medically under-served populations, through health centers and other community-based providers. Emphasis is on: coordination of Medicaid, Children's Health Insurance program, state offices of rural health, and other health care financing services, maternal and child health; health systems development; National Health Service Corps monitoring; and recruitment and retention of primary care practitioners.

Eligible applicants/beneficiaries: states, state agencies, statewide public or nonprofit entities operating in one state only.

Range/Average: $192,000.

Activity: annually, 53 awards.

HQ: Shortage Designation Branch, Office of Workforce, Evaluation and Quality Assurance, Bureau of Health Professions, HRSA-HHS, 5600 Fishers Lane - Rm.8C-26, Rockville, MD 20857. Phone: (301)594-0816. Grants management information, web site: same as **93.107**. (Note: no field offices for this program.)

93.134 GRANTS TO INCREASE ORGAN DONATIONS

Assistance: project grants (100 percent/3 years).

Purposes: pursuant to PHSA as amended, for activities to increase the number of organ donors. Funds may not be used for activities reimbursable under Medicare.

Eligible applicants/beneficiaries: public and private nonprofit organ procurement, donation, and transplantation organizations.

Range: clinical interventions, $185,000 to $638,000; social, behavioral interventions, $165,000 to $510,000. **Average:** clinical, $371,000; social, behavioral, $377,000.

Activity: FY 05 estimate, 11 noncompeting clinical intervention awards; 19 noncompeting, 4-5 competing social, behavioral intervention awards.

HQ: Division of Transplantation, Healthcare Systems Bureau, HRSA-HHS, 5600 Fishers Lane - Rm.12C-06, Rockville, MD 20857. Phone: *clinical interventions,* (301)443-3124; *social, behavioral interventions* (301)443-3622. Grants management information, web site: same as **93.107**. (Note: no field offices for this program.)

93.135 CENTERS FOR RESEARCH AND DEMONSTRATION FOR HEALTH PROMOTION AND DISEASE PREVENTION ("Prevention Research Centers")

Assistance: project grants (100 percent/1-5 years).

Purposes: pursuant to PHSA as amended, to establish, maintain, and operate academic-based centers for research and demonstration programs in health promotion and disease prevention; to establish linkages between ongoing related basic and applied research; for field testing and evaluation of new methods and strategies; to streamline the development and delivery of new techniques; to involve communities in prevention research.

Eligible applicants/beneficiaries: schools of medicine, osteopathy, and public health.

Range: $740,000 to $770,000. **Average:** $755,000.

Activity: FY 05 estimate, 28 continuation, 5 new grants.

HQ: Director, Prevention Research Center Program, Division of Adult and Community Health (K-45), National Center for Chronic Disease Prevention and Health Promotion, CDCP-HHS, 4770 Buford Hwy. NE, Atlanta, GA 30341-3724. Phone: (770)488-5919. *Grants management information:* Grants Management/Contracting Officer, Procurement and Grants Office (E-18), CDCP-HHS, 2920 Brandywine Rd., Atlanta, GA 30341. Phone: (770)488-2754. **Internet:** "www.cdc.gov/prs". (Note: no field offices for this program.)

93.136 INJURY PREVENTION AND CONTROL RESEARCH AND STATE AND COMMUNITY BASED PROGRAMS

Assistance: project grants (100 percent/1-5 years).

Purposes: pursuant to PHSA as amended and other acts, for injury prevention and control research and demonstrations; to integrate aspects of engineering, public health, behavioral sciences, medicine, and other disciplines; to apply and evaluate current and new interventions, methods, and strategies; for injury control research centers in academic institutions to develop improved approaches to research and training; for public health programs for injury control; to develop and evaluate existing and new methods and techniques of injury surveillance, and to develop, expand, or improve injury control programs to reduce morbidity, mortality, severity, disability, and cost from injuries.

Eligible applicants/beneficiaries: research and centers grants—nonprofit and profit organizations. State and community program grants—official state public health agencies; territories and possessions; jurisdictions of more than

1,000,000 population. Community-based programs—public and private nonprofit and profit organizations.

Range: research projects, $200,000 to $300,000; injury control, $200,000 to $300,000; state, community-based projects, $40,000 to $300,000; state/community-based control programs, $40,000 to $300,000; youth violence prevention programs, $150,000 to $425,000; violence against women prevention, $85,000 to $800,000; traumatic brain injury research, $100,000 to $150,000; surveillance and brain injury follow-up registry, $16,000 to $500,000; other unintentional injuries, $50,000 to $1,050,000. **Average:** centers, $905,000; injury control, $250,000; projects, $250,000; state, community-based, $170,000; youth violence prevention, $275,000; violence against women, $600,000; traumatic brain injury research, $125,000; surveillance/brain injury, $258,000; other, $550,000.

Activity: FY 04-05 estimate (sampling), 11 centers, 38 individual grants; most existing grants continued.

HQ: National Center for Injury Prevention and Control, CDCP-HHS, 4770 Buford Hwy. NE, Atlanta, GA 30341-3724. Phone: *individual research grants,* (770)488-1508, FAX (770)488-1670; *research centers,* (770)488-4823, FAX (770)488-1670; *state/community-based,* (770)488-4037, FAX (770)488-1662; Grants management address, web site: same as **93.061**. Phone: (770)488-2645. (Note: no field offices for this program.)

93.137 COMMUNITY PROGRAMS TO IMPROVE MINORITY HEALTH GRANT PROGRAM

Assistance: project grants (100 percent/3 years).

Purposes: pursuant to PHSA as amended, for demonstration projects conducted by minority community health coalitions to modify behavioral or environmental conditions implicated in the health problems of minority groups—including HIV/AIDS, cancer, cardiovascular disease and stroke, chemical dependency, diabetes, homicide, suicide, unintentional injuries, infant mortality. Projects involve: coordination of integrated community-based screening and outreach services to minority groups and low-income communities; linkages for access and treatment to those at high risk; overcoming sociocultural and linguistic barriers; working with nontraditional partners in projects to increase educational understanding of health issues. No health care services are provided under this program.

Eligible applicants/beneficiaries: private nonprofit community-based organizations serving Asians, Pacific islanders, African Americans, Latinos, Hispanics, native Americans, Alaska natives, native Hawaiians, or subgroups.

Range: $132,000 to $150,000. **Average:** $149,000.

Activity: FY 06 estimate, 40-45 continuation awards.

HQ: same as **93.004**. (Note: no field offices for this program.)

93.138 PROTECTION AND ADVOCACY FOR INDIVIDUALS WITH MENTAL ILLNESS ("PAIMI")

Assistance: formula grants (100 percent/2 years).

Purposes: pursuant to PHSA, Protection and Advocacy for Individuals with Mental Illness Act of 1986, and Developmental Disabilities Assistance and Bill of Rights Act, as amended, to plan, develop, administer, and expand programs to protect and advocate the rights of the mentally ill, and to investigate incidents of their abuse and neglect including in public and private care and treatment facilities and nonmedical community-based facilities for children and youth. Limited funds may be used for training and technical assistance provided to staff.

Eligible applicants: state and local government agencies, public or private organizations designated by governors; territories, possessions.

Eligible beneficiaries: mentally ill persons with severe emotional impairments while inpatients or residents in care or treatment facilities, in their own homes, or living in the community; persons in process of being admitted or transported to such facilities, or involuntarily confined in detention facilities, jails, or prisons.

Range: $190,000 to $2,658,000. **Average:** $384,000.

Activity: annually, 57 grants (to all states and territories).

HQ: Program Officer, Protection and Advocacy Program, Division of State and Community Systems Development, CMHS-SAMHSA-HHS, 1 Choke Cherry Rd., Rockville, MD 20857. Phone: (240)276-1741. *Grants management information*: Division of Grants Management, SAMHSA-HHS, same address (Rm.7-1091). Phone: (240)276-1404. **Internet:** "www.samhsa.gov". (Note: no field offices for this program.)

93.140 INTRAMURAL RESEARCH TRAINING AWARD ("IRTA")

Assistance: project grants.

Purposes: pursuant to HPEPA, to provide developmental training and practical research experience at the NIH for pre- or post-doctoral participants, in disciplines related to biomedical research, medical library research, and related fields. IRTA components include: postdoctoral (1-5 years), for physicians and other doctoral researchers; predoctoral (1 month-3 years), for students enrolled in doctoral degree programs in biomedical sciences, or accepted into graduate, doctoral, or medical degree programs; postbaccalaureate (1-2 years), for recent college graduates, particularly minorities, women, and persons with disabilities; technical (2-3 years), for training of professionals; student (1 month-1 year), for promising high school, undergraduate, and graduate students.

Eligible applicants/beneficiaries: postdoctoral awards—candidates with a Ph.D., M.D., D.D.S., D.M.D., D.V.M., or equivalent degree and not more than five years of postdoctoral research experience; predoctoral awards—students applying for, enrolled in, or accepted into graduate, doctoral, or medical degree programs; postbaccalaureate—candidates that graduated no more than one year prior to activation of the traineeship and intending to apply to graduate or medical school in biomedical research within one year; technical—candidates that graduated from a U.S. college or university with a bachelor's or master's degree in any discipline; student—candidates at least age 16 and enrolled at least half-time in high school, or accepted for or enrolled in an accredited U.S. college or university. Recipients must be U.S. citizens or permanent resident aliens.

Range: postdoctoral stipends, $34,000 to $67,000; predoctoral, $23,000 to $30,000; postbaccalaureate, $20,000-$25,000; technical, $22,000 to $31,000; student, $1,200 to $2,900.

Activity: FY 06 estimate, 4,048 awards.

HQ: Executive Director/Intramural Research, NIH-HHS, Shannon Bldg. - Rm. 140, Bethesda, MD 20892. Phone: (301)496-4920. **Internet:** "www.nih.gov". (Note: no field offices for this program.)

93.142 NIEHS HAZARDOUS WASTE WORKER HEALTH AND SAFETY TRAINING
("Superfund Worker Training Program")

Assistance: project grants (100 percent/to 5 years).

Purposes: pursuant to PHSA and SARA as amended, to develop and administer model education and training programs in worker health and safety practices for persons involved in hazardous waste generation, treatment, storage, removal, disposal, containment, transportation, or emergency response. Direct costs of classroom and practical training may be supported. Some SBIR and STTR awards may be made (*see Notes preceding* **93.001**).

Eligible applicants/beneficiaries: public or private nonprofit entities. Small business may apply for SBIR and STTR awards.

Range: $528,000 to $5,328,000. **Average:** $1,158,000.

Activity: FY 05 estimate, 18 noncompeting renewal grants.

HQ: Program Director, Worker Training and Education Program, NIEHS, NIH-HHS, P.O. Box 12233, Research Triangle Park, NC 27709. Phone: (919)541-0217. *Grants management information*: same address as **93.113**. Phone: (919)541-1373. **Internet:** "www.niehs.nih.gov/wetp/home.htm". (Note: no field offices for this program.)

93.143 NIEHS SUPERFUND HAZARDOUS SUBSTANCES—BASIC RESEARCH AND EDUCATION
("NIEHS Superfund Research Program")

Assistance: project grants (100 percent/to 5 years).

Purposes: pursuant to PHSA, CERCLA, and SARA, as amended, to establish linkages between biomedical research and related engineering, geoscience, and ecological research. Funds may support basic research and advanced or graduate training activities on an inter-disciplinary, multi-project basis, covering: methods and technologies to detect hazardous substances in the environment; advanced techniques for the detection, assessment, and evaluation of the effects of hazardous substances on humans; environmental and occupational health and safety and the engineering aspects of hazardous waste control; related graduate training in the geosciences. SBIR awards are available (*see Notes preceding* **93.001**).

Eligible applicants/beneficiaries: IHEs. Subcontracts are permitted with state and local governments, public or private organizations, or persons or organizations involved with the generation, assessment, treatment of hazardous substances, or operation or ownership of facilities containing hazardous substances.

Range: $156,000 to $3,419,000. **Average:** $1,315,000.

Activity: FY 04, 26 noncompeting grants.

HQ: Director, Superfund Hazardous Substance Basic Research and Training Program, Division of Extramural Research and Training, NIEHS-NIH-HHS, P.O. Box 12233, Research Triangle Park, NC 27709. Phone: (919)541-0797. Grants management information, web site: same as **93.113**. (Note: no field offices for this program.)

93.145 AIDS EDUCATION AND TRAINING CENTERS

Assistance: project grants (100 percent/3-5 years).

Purposes: pursuant to PHSA as amended and Ryan White CARE Act Amendments of 2000, for the education and training of primary care providers and others, on the diagnosis, treatment and prevention of HIV disease; for faculty training in related disciplines; to develop and disseminate pertinent curricula and resource materials; to develop protocols for the medical care of women with HIV disease, including prenatal and other gynocological care.

Eligible applicants/beneficiaries: public and private nonprofit entities, schools, academic health science centers.

Range: $450,000 to $5,120,000. **Average:** $2,237,000.

Activity: FY 05 estimate, 15 noncompetitive awards; some 155,000 personnel participating in training.

HQ: Division of Training and Technical Assistance/AIDS ETCs, HIV/AIDS Bureau, HRSA-HHS, 5600 Fishers Lane - Rm.7-46, Rockville, MD 20857. Phone: (301)443-6364, FAX (301)443-9887. Grants management information, web site: same as **93.107**. (Note: no field offices for this program.)

93.150 PROJECTS FOR ASSISTANCE IN TRANSITION FROM HOMELESSNESS ("PATH")

Assistance: formula grants (75 percent; territories, 100 percent).

Purposes: pursuant to PHSA as amended and SBMHAA, to support services for homeless persons with serious mental illness, with serious mental illness and substance abuse, or at imminent risk of so becoming. Funds may support such services as: outreach; community mental health; screening and diagnosis; habilitation and rehabilitation; substance abuse treatment services; referrals to housing, primary health, job training; staff training; case management; supportive and supervisory services in residential settings. Funds may not be used for emergency shelters or construction, inpatient psychiatric of substance abuse treatment, cash payments to recipients of mental health or substance abuse services.

Eligible applicants/beneficiaries: states, territories, possessions. Subgrants must be provided to political subdivisions and private nonprofit entities including veterans and other community-based organizations.

Range: $50,000 to $1,680,000. **Average:** $347,000.

Activity: annually, 56 grants.

HQ: PATH Program, Homeless Programs Branch, Division of Knowledge Development and Systems Change, CMHS-SAMHSA-HHS, 1 Choke Cherry Rd., Rockville, MD 20857. Phone: (240)276-1894. Grants management information, web site: same as **93.138**. (Note: no field offices for this program.)

93.153 COORDINATED SERVICES AND ACCESS TO RESEARCH FOR WOMEN, INFANTS, CHILDREN, AND YOUTH ("Ryan White CARE Act Title IV Program")

Assistance: project grants (100 percent/to 5 years).

Purposes: pursuant to PHSA as amended and Ryan White CARE Amendments Act of 2000, to improve access to primary medical care, research, and support services within for women, infants, children, and youth with HIV/ AIDS or at risk, and to provide support services for their families; to link care systems with proven clinical research; to provide related client education.

Eligible applicants/beneficiaries: public and private nonprofit entities providing primary care.

Range: $230,000 to $2,569,000. **Average:** $766,000.

Activity: FY 05 estimate, 88 projects.

HQ: Division of Community Based Programs, HIV-AIDS Bureau, HRSA-HHS, 5600 Fishers Lane - Rm.7A-30, Rockville, MD 20857. Phone: (301) 443-9051. Grants management information, web site: same as **93.107**. (Note: no field offices for this program.)

93.155 RURAL HEALTH RESEARCH CENTERS

Assistance: project grants (100 percent/to 4 years).

Purposes: to operate rural health research centers and to provide one-year research grants to new investigators to establish an information base and policy analysis capability on the full range of rural health issues, including financing, recruitment and retention of health professionals, access to care, and rural delivery systems.

Eligible applicants/beneficiaries: public and private nonprofit and profit entities including IHEs, research organizations, foundations, and community entities.

Range: centers, $400,000 to $600,000; research grants, $100,000 to $200,000. **Average:** centers, $500,000; research, $150,000.

Activity: FY 06 estimate, 8 center, 6 research awards.

HQ: Director, Rural Research Centers, Office of Rural Health Policy, HRSA-HHS, Parklawn Bldg. - Rm.9A-55, 5600 Fishers Lane, Rockville, MD 20857. Phone: (301)443-0835. Grants management information, web site: same as 93.107. (Note: no field offices for this program.)

93.156 GERIATRIC TRAINING FOR PHYSICIANS, DENTISTS AND BEHAVIORAL/MENTAL HEALTH PROFESSIONALS ("Geriatric Fellowships")

Assistance: project grants (100 percent/5 years).

Purposes: pursuant to PHSA as amended and HPEPA, for training programs for current and future faculty in geriatric medicine, dentistry, and behavioral and mental health professionals. Funds may support: one-year retraining programs for physician faculty members in departments of internal or family medicine, gynecology, geriatrics, behavioral or mental health, and dentist faculty members at schools of dentistry or hospital departments of dentistry; two-year fellowships for physicians and dentists with relevant advanced training or experience in medical or dental education.

Eligible applicants/beneficiaries: public or private nonprofit schools of medicine or osteopathy, teaching hospitals, graduate medical education programs.

Range: $178,000 to $633,000. **Average:** $375,000

Activity: FY 04, 1 new, 12 continuation awards.

HQ: Division of State, Community, and Public Health, Bureau of Health Professions, HRSA-HHS, Parklawn Bldg. - Rm.8A-09, 5600 Fishers Lane, Rockville, MD 20857. Phone: (301)443-8681. Grants management information, web site: same as **93.107**. (Note: no field offices for this program.)

93.157 CENTERS OF EXCELLENCE ("COEs")

Assistance: project grants (100 percent/3 years).

Purposes: pursuant to PHSA as amended and HPEPA, to establish, strengthen, or expand programs to enhance the academic performance of under-represented minority students in the health professions, though linkages with IHEs, local school districts, and other community-based entities. Funds may be used for such costs as: faculty recruitment, training, and retention, including through the payment of stipends and fellowships; library resource development and enhancement; student recruitment and academic performance enhancement programs; curriculum development; facilitating faculty and student research on issues particularly affecting minority groups; student stipends.

Eligible applicants/beneficiaries: schools of medicine, osteopathy, dentistry, pharmacy; private nonprofit schools with graduate training programs in behavioral and mental health; certain HBCUs.

Range: $280,000 to $5,280,000. **Average:** $733,000.

Activity: FY 05, 16 continuation, 22 competitive grants.

HQ: Chief, Diversity Branch, Division of Health Careers Diversity and Development, Bureau of Health Professions, HRSA-HHS, Parklawn Bldg. - Rm.8-55, 5600 Fishers Lane, Rockville, MD 20857. Phone: (301)443-2100. Grants management information, web site: same as **93.107**. (Note: no field offices for this program.)

93.161 HEALTH PROGRAM FOR TOXIC SUBSTANCES AND DISEASE REGISTRY

Assistance: project grants (100 percent/1-5 years).

Purposes: pursuant to CERCLA and RCRA as amended, to reduce or eliminate illness, disability, and death resulting from public or worker exposure to toxic substances at spill and waste disposal sites. Services may include: health assessments; health effects studies; exposure and disease registries; technical assistance; consultation; information dissemination; specialized services and assistance including responses to public health emergencies; training; research of chemical toxicity.

Eligible applicants/beneficiaries: states and their political subdivisions, territories, possessions, IHEs, tribal governments.

Range: $130,000 to $300,000. **Average:** $200,000.

Activity: FY 05 estimate, 14 continuation grants.

HQ: Office of Financial and Administrative Services, Agency for Toxic Substances and Disease (E-28), CDCP-HHS, 1600 Clifton Rd. NE, Atlanta, GA 30333. Phone: (404)498-0270, FAX (404)498-0059. *Grants management information:* same address as **93.061**. Phone: (770)488-2745, FAX (770) 488-2777. **Internet:** "www.atsdr.cdc.gov". (Note: no field offices for this program.)

93.162 NATIONAL HEALTH SERVICE CORPS LOAN REPAYMENT PROGRAM ("NHSC Loan Repayment Program")

Assistance: project grants.

Purposes: pursuant to PHSA as amended and National Health Service Corps Amendments Act of 1987, for the repayment of NHSC participants' qualifying government and commercial health professions undergraduate and graduate education loans. Up to $25,000 per year may be awarded during the first two years of practice at selected NHSC service sites, and up to $35,000 in the third and subsequent years—plus a 39 percent tax assistance payment. Priority currently is given to primary care physicians, dentists, certified nurse-midwives and nurse practitioners, physician assistants, clinical psychologists, clinical social workers, psychiatric nurse specialists, marriage and family therapists, licensed professional counselors, dental hygienists.

Eligible applicants/beneficiaries: U.S. citizens with a degree in health professions or in professional practice, licensed in a state, and eligible for appointment in the federal civil service or holding a commission in the PHS. Applicants may not: be in default on any federal debt; have a court judgment against them; have an existing service obligation.

Range: $9,163 to $75,000; new awards, $3,671 to $52,000; amended contracts, $27,000 to $65,000. **Average:** $66,000; new, $44,000; amendments, $38,000.

Activity: FY 06 estimate, 1,520 awards.

HQ: Chief, Applications and Award Branch, NHSC Division, Bureau of Health Professions, HRSA-HHS, 5600 Fishers Lane - Rm.8A-55, Rockville, MD 20857. Phone: (301)594-4400; *public information,* (800)221-9393. Grants management information, web site: same as **93.107**. (Note: no field offices for this program.)

93.164 INDIAN HEALTH SERVICE EDUCATIONAL LOAN REPAYMENT ("IHS Loan Repayment Program")

Assistance: project grants (100 percent).

Purposes: pursuant to the Indian Health Care Amendments of 1988, for payments of up to $20,000 annually toward participants' health professions education loans during each year of service at IHS priority sites or certain other sites—plus 20 percent for tax liability on the grant award. A minimum of two years of service is required.

Eligible applicants/beneficiaries: students enrolled in their final year in a program leading to a degree, or graduate students enrolled in approved programs; or, degreed and licensed professionals, eligible for or holding a PHS or civil service appointment in the IHS; or employees of an Indian health program.

Range: $3,000 to $48,000 for a two-year service obligation. **Average:** $43,000.

Activity: FY 06 estimate, 230 new, 220 continuation awards.

HQ: Chief, Loan Repayment Program, IHS-HHS, same address, web site as **93.123**. Phone: (301)443-3396.

93.165 GRANTS TO STATES FOR LOAN REPAYMENT PROGRAM ("State Loan Repayment Program")

Assistance: project grants (50 percent/to 5 years).

Purposes: pursuant to PHSA, for state educational loan repayment programs for health professionals agreeing to serve full-time for a minimum of two years in a health manpower shortage area. State programs must be similar to **93.162**.

Eligible applicants/beneficiaries: states.

Range: $50,000 to $1,000,000. **Average:** $250,000.

Activity: FY 06 estimate, 40 awards.

HQ: Division of State, Community and Public Health, Bureau of Health Professions, HRSA-HHS, Parklawn Bldg. - Rm.9-05, 5600 Fishers Lane, Rockville, MD 20857. Phone: (301)443-1648. Grants management information, web site: same as **93.107**. (Note: no field offices for this program.)

93.172 HUMAN GENOME RESEARCH

Assistance: project grants (100 percent/1-5 years).

Purposes: pursuant to PHSA as amended and SBRDEA, to obtain genetic and physical maps and to determine the deoxyribonucleic acid (DNA) sequences of the genomes of humans and model organisms to be used as resources in biomedical research, medicine, and biotechnology—including consideration of the ethical, legal, and social implications. NRSA, SBIR, and STTR awards are available (*see Notes preceding* **93.001**).

Eligible applicants/beneficiaries: public or private, profit or nonprofit IHEs, hospitals, laboratories, other institutions; state and local governments; small businesses.

Range: $7,148 to $9,587,000. **Average:** $610,000.

Activity: FY 05 estimate, 76 competing research project grants; 31 research center, 28 research career, 18 other research-related, and 157 full-time research trainee position awards.

HQ: National Human Genome Research Institute, NIH-HHS, Bethesda, MD 20892. Phone: *program, research centers, SBIR*, (301)496-7531; *ethical, legal, and social implications*, 402-4997. *Grants management information*: Grants Management Officer, same address. Phone: (301)402-0733. **Internet:** "www.nih.gov". (Note: no field offices for this program.)

93.173 RESEARCH RELATED TO DEAFNESS AND COMMUNICATION DISORDERS

Assistance: project grants (100 percent/to 5 years).

Purposes: pursuant to PHSA as amended and SBRDEA, to investigate solutions to problems of patients with deafness or disorders of human communication such as hearing, balance, voice, speech, language, and the senses of taste, touch, and smell. Focus may be on etiology, pathology, detection, treatment, and prevention of all forms of hearing disorders and other communication processes, primarily through basic and applied research in anatomy, audiology, biochemistry, bioengineering, epidemiology, genetics, immunology, microbiology, molecular biology, the neurosciences, otolaryngology, psychology, pharmacology, physiology, speech and language pathology, and other scientific disciplines. Funds may support research centers, as well as mentored and unmentored career awards. NRSA, SBIR, and STTR awards are available (*see Notes preceding* **93.001**).

Eligible applicants/beneficiaries: public, private, nonprofit, or profit institutions; SBIR firms; individuals.

Range: $23,000 to $1,632,000. **Average:** $296,000.

Activity: FY 06 estimate, 1,179 grants.

HQ: National Institute on Deafness and Other Communication Disorders, NIH-HHS, Executive Plaza South - Rm.400-C, Bethesda, MD 20892-7180. Phone: (301)496-5061. *Grants management information*: same address (Rm. 400-B). Phone: (301)402-0909. **Internet:** "www.nidcd.nih.gov". (Note: no field offices for this program.)

93.178 NURSING WORKFORCE DIVERSITY

Assistance: project grants (100 percent/3 years).

Purposes: pursuant to PHSA as amended and HPEPA, to increase nursing education opportunities for individuals from disadvantaged backgrounds, by providing student $250 monthly stipends, with a $7,000 annual maximum scholarship, and pre-entry preparation and retention activities. Funds also may be used for project personnel salaries, consultant fees, supplies and equipment, travel, and related costs.

Eligible applicants/beneficiaries: schools of nursing, nursing centers, academic health centers, state and local governments, and other public and nonprofit private entities—with above average rates of admission, retention, and graduation of individuals from disadvantaged backgrounds and ethnic and racial minorities, or with plans for improving such rates.

Range: $59,000 to $519,000. **Average:** $255,000.

Activity: FY 05 estimate, 33 new, 46 continuation grants.

HQ: same address as **93.124**. Phone: (301)443-6193. Grants management information, web site: same as **93.107**. (Note: no field offices for this program.)

93.181 PODIATRIC RESIDENCY TRAINING IN PRIMARY CARE

Assistance: project grants (100 percent/to 3 years).

Purposes: pursuant to PHSA as amended and HPEPA, for preventive and primary care residency training programs for podiatrists, including financial assistance to residents.

Eligible applicants/beneficiaries: collaboratives of health professions schools, academic health centers, state or local governments, public and private nonprofit entities, community-based organizations.

Range $205,000 to $286,000. **Average:** $246,000.

Activity: FY 05, 2 continuation awards.

HQ: Dentistry, Psychology and Special Projects Branch, Division of Medicine and Dentistry, Bureau of Health Professions, HRSA-HHS, 5600 Fishers Lane - Rm.9A-27, Rockville, MD 20857. Phone: (301)443-1568. Grants management information, web site: same as **93.107**. (Note: no field offices for this program.)

93.184 DISABILITIES PREVENTION
("Disability and Health")

Assistance: project grants (to 100 percent/3-5 years).

Purposes: pursuant to PHSA as amended, to provide a national focus for the prevention of secondary conditions in persons with selected disability domains, including mobility, personal care, communication, and learning—through cooperative agreements and research projects designed to: build state capacity to coordinate prevention and education activities and to conduct surveillance; provide related technical assistance to communities; employ epidemiological methods to set priorities and target interventions; conduct research on the disabled and their physical, medical, cognitive, emotional, or psychosocial conditions; support a national limb loss information center to serve as an information clearinghouse and to conduct peer education and training sessions with hospitals and limb loss support groups; support the National Center on Physical Activity and Disability to provide information and promote physical activity for the disabled; conduct related activities.

Eligible applicants/beneficiaries: cooperative agreements—state health departments or other state agencies, including in territories or possessions with existing agreements. Research grants—public and private nonprofit entities, universities, nonprofit medical centers, rehabilitation hospitals, disability service organizations, tribal governments.

Range: state capacity projects, $130,000 to $460,000. **Average:** $310,000.

Activity: FY 02 (latest data reported), 16 state capacity continuation, 12 continuation research grants.

HQ: Project Officer, Division of Human Development and Disability, National Center on Birth Defects and Developmental Disabilities (E88), CDCP-HHS, 1600 Clifton Rd. NE., Atlanta, GA 30333. Phone: (404)498-3957. Grants management information, web site: same address as **93.061**. Phone: (770) 488-2728. (Note: no field offices for this program.)

93.185 IMMUNIZATION RESEARCH, DEMONSTRATION, PUBLIC INFORMATION AND EDUCATION—TRAINING AND CLINICAL SKILLS IMPROVEMENT PROJECTS

Assistance: project grants (100 percent/1-5 years).

Purposes: pursuant to PHSA as amended, for research, demonstration, and information dissemination projects on vaccine-preventable diseases and conditions. Funds may be used to conduct project activities including, in certain circumstances, purchasing vaccine.

Eligible applicants/beneficiaries: states and their political subdivisions, other public and private nonprofit entities.

Range: $5,000 to $500,000. **Average:** $185,000.

Activity: not quantified specifically.

HQ: Associate Director/Management and Operations, National Immunization Program (E-05), CDCP-HHS, 1600 Clifton Rd. NE, Atlanta, GA 30333. Phone: (404)639-8900, FAX (404)639-8626. Grants management address (Rm.3623), web site: same as **93.061**. Phone: (770)488-2716. (Note: no field offices for this program.)

93.186 NATIONAL RESEARCH SERVICE AWARD IN PRIMARY CARE MEDICINE

Assistance: project grants (100 percent/3-5 years).

Purposes: pursuant to PHSA as amended and the National Institutes of Health Revitalization Act of 1993, for postdoctoral research training programs in primary medical care. Individuals receiving awards incur one month of service obligation for each of the first 12 months of the NRSA support, after which no further service obligation is incurred; the continued training serves to discharge the payback obligation (*see Notes preceding* **93.001**).

Eligible applicants/beneficiaries: domestic public or private nonprofit organizations; state or local governments and territories. Individuals must be U.S. citizens, noncitizen nationals, or lawful permanent residents.

Range: $258,000 to $538,000. **Average:** $390,000.

Activity: FY 05 estimate, 19 continuation awards.

HQ: same address as **93.181**. Phone: (202)443-6785. Grants management information, web site: same as **92.107**. (Note: no field offices for this program.)

93.187 UNDERGRADUATE SCHOLARSHIP PROGRAM FOR INDIVIDUALS FROM DISADVANTAGED BACKGROUNDS ("NIH Undergraduate Scholarship Program" - "UGSP")

Assistance: project grants (100 percent/to 4 years).

Purposes: pursuant to PHSA as amended, for scholarships to persons from disadvantaged backgrounds, pursuing undergraduate education preparing them for professions in the biomedical or bio-behavioral sciences at NIH. Recipients must agree: to serve full-time for at least ten consecutive weeks as an NIH employee during each year of the scholarship period; within 60 days of obtaining a degree, to serve one year as a full-time NIH employee for each year of scholarship assistance received, unless deferred.

Eligible applicants/beneficiaries: U.S. citizens, nationals, or permanent residents from disadvantaged backgrounds, enrolled or accepted at IHEs for full-time study, and maintaining good academic standing.

Range: $1,714 to $20,000 per academic year. **Average:** $12,000 per scholar.

Activity: FY 06 estimate, 20 awards.

HQ: Office of Loan Repayment and Scholarship, NIH-HHS, 2 Center Dr. - Rm.2E24, Bethesda, MD 20892-0230. Phone: (800)528-7689, FAX (301) 480-3123. **Internet:** "http://ugsp.info.nih.gov"; e-mail, "ugsp@nih.gov". (Note: no field offices for this program.)

93.189 HEALTH EDUCATION AND TRAINING CENTERS ("HETC")

Assistance: project grants (100 percent/to 3 years).

Purposes: pursuant to PHSA as amended and HPEPA, establish, maintain, and operate multi-disciplinary HETCs to improve the supply, distribution, quality, and efficiency of personnel providing health services—in rural and inner-city communities, in Florida, and in U.S.-Mexico border areas. Funds must be expended mainly in the service area of the recipient's program.

Eligible applicants/beneficiaries: schools of allopathic or osteopathic medicine or nursing; consortia.

Range: border-HETC, $92,000 to $525,000; non-border, $152,000 to $241,000. **Average:** border, $376,000; non-border, $215,000.

Activity: FY 04, 13 continuation awards.

HQ: same as **93.107**. (Note: no field offices for this program.)

93.191 ALLIED HEALTH SPECIAL PROJECTS

Assistance: project grants (100 percent/3 years).

Purposes: pursuant to PHSA as amended and HPEPA, to establish and expand training programs in the allied health professions that will: expand enrollments in disciplines in short supply or most needed by the elderly; provide rapid transition training programs for participants with baccalaureate degrees in health-related sciences; provide career advancement training for practicing allied health professionals; establish or expand clinical training sites in medically underserved or rural communities; develop curriculum in prevention and health promotion, geriatrics, long-term care, home health and hospice care, and ethics; expand or establish interdisciplinary and training programs; link academic centers to clinical centers; support graduate programs in behavioral and mental health practice. Funds may be used for the costs of personnel, equipment, consultants, guest lecturers, space rental, or renovation—but not for construction, land acquisition, financial support to students.

Eligible applicants/beneficiaries: health professions schools, academic health centers, state or local governments, public or private nonprofit entities.

Range: $54,000 to $190,000. **Average:** $130,000.

Activity: FY 04, 14 new, 20 continuation awards.

HQ: Division of State, Community and Public Health, Bureau of Health Professions, HRSA-HHS, Parklawn Bldg. - Rm.8C-09, 5600 Fishers Lane, Rockville, MD 20857. Phone: (301)443-3353, -0062. Grants management information, web site: same as **93.107**. (Note: no field offices for this program.)

93.192 QUENTIN N. BURDICK PROGRAM FOR RURAL INTERDISCIPLINARY TRAINING
("Interdisciplinary Training for Health Care for Rural Areas")

Assistance: project grants (100 percent/to 3 years).

Purposes: pursuant to PHSA as amended and HPEPA, for interdisciplinary training projects for health care professionals in rural areas, in delivering health services; for relevant demonstration and research projects; to recruit and retain health care practitioners. Grants may be used for student stipends, postdoctoral fellowships, faculty training, and purchase or rental of transportation and telecommunications equipment.

Eligible applicants/beneficiaries: health professions schools; academic health centers; state or local governments; public and private nonprofit entities. Applications must be submitted jointly by at least two eligible applicants, designating rural health care agencies for clinical treatment or training hospitals, community or migrant health centers, long-term care facilities, or facilities operated by the IHS, tribal, or native Hawaiian health care providers.

Range: $134,000 to $344,000. **Average:** $250,000.

Activity: FY 04, 5 new, 18 continuation awards.

HQ: same address as **93.156**. Phone: (301)443-6867. Grants management information, web site: same as **93.107**. (Note: no field offices for this program.)

93.193 URBAN INDIAN HEALTH SERVICES

Assistance: project grants (100 percent/to 5 years).

Purposes: pursuant to the Indian Health Care Improvement Act as amended, for health-related services to Indians residing in urban areas, including: alcohol and substance abuse prevention, treatment, rehabilitation, and education; mental health needs assessment and services; health promotion and disease prevention; immunization.

Eligible applicants/beneficiaries: urban Indian organizations.

Range: $115,000 to $573,000. **Average:** $210,000.

Activity: FY 06 estimate, 34 continuation grants.

HQ: Urban Programs, IHS-HHS, 801 Thompson Ave. - Ste.200, Rockville, MD 20852. Phone: (301)443-4680. Grants management information, web site: same as **93.123**. Phone: (301)443-5204. (Note: no field offices for this program.)

93.197 CHILDHOOD LEAD POISONING PREVENTION PROJECTS—STATE AND LOCAL CHILDHOOD LEAD POISONING PREVENTION AND SURVEILLANCE OF BLOOD LEVELS IN CHILDREN ("CLPPP")

Assistance: project grants (100 percent/to 3 years).

Purposes: pursuant to PHSA as amended, Preventive Health Amendments of 1992, and Children's Health Act of 2000, for childhood lead poisoning prevention projects in communities with demonstrated high-risk populations. Funds are to be used: for screening and testing; to identify sources of lead exposure; to monitor medical and environmental management of cases, including follow-up; for public and technical education activities, including staff training; to enhance primary prevention activities in collaboration with other government and community-based organizations; to establish state-based surveillance systems. Ineligible uses of funds include medical care or treatment, remediation of lead sources; however, an acceptable plan must be submitted with assurances that such activities will be carried out.

Eligible applicants/beneficiaries: state health or other departments or agencies; territories and possessions; tribal governments; consortia of the foregoing; five specified local governments.

Range: $75,000 to $1,700,000.

Activity: annually, 61 state, local grants.

HQ: Program Services Team Leader, Lead Poisoning Prevention Branch, National Center for Environmental Health, CDCP-HHS (F-30), 4770 Buford Hwy., Atlanta, GA 30341. Phone: (770)488-7493, FAX (770)498-3635. *Grants management information*: same as **93.161**. **Internet:** "www.cdc.gov". (Note: no field offices for this program.)

93.202 CAPACITY BUILDING AMONG AMERICAN INDIAN TRIBES

Assistance: project grants (100 percent/1-5 years).

Purposes: pursuant to CERCLA as amended, to enhance tribal ability to collaborate with the Agency for Toxic Substances and Disease Registry in conducting public health activities related to potential human exposures from the Hanford Nuclear Reservation, including outreach materials to community members.

Eligible applicants/beneficiaries: affected tribal governments.

Range: $40,000 to $60,000. **Average:** $50,000.

Activity: FY 03 estimate, 9 continuation awards. No new awards anticipated.

HQ: Division of Health Assessment and Consultation, Agency for Toxic

Substances and Disease (E-32), CDCP-HHS, 1600 Clifton Rd. NE, Atlanta, GA 30333. Phone: (404)498-0457. Grants management information address, web site: same as **93.161**. Phone: (770)488-2743, FAX (770)488-2777. (Note: no field offices for this program.)

93.204 SURVEILLANCE OF HAZARDOUS SUBSTANCE EMERGENCY EVENTS

Assistance: project grants (100 percent/1-5 years).

Purposes: pursuant to CERCLA as amended and SARA, to develop state-based surveillance systems for monitoring hazardous substance emergency events, to enable states to: assess the burden of adverse health effects created by unexpected, sudden releases; describe the situations and persons most likely impacted; define the risk factors; and, work with appropriate agencies to implement prevention activities. Funds may cover the costs of personnel, travel, supplies, and services.

Eligible applicants/beneficiaries: state public health departments, tribal governments, possessions and territories.

Range: $60,000 to $80,000. **Average:** $79,000.

Activity: FY 03 estimate, 16 continuation awards.

HQ: Division of Health Studies, Agency for Toxic Substances and Disease Registry, CDCP-HHS (E-31), 1600 Clifton Rd. NE, Atlanta, GA 30333. Phone: (404)498-0268, FAX (404)498-0058. Grants management information, web site: same as **93.161**. (Note: no field offices for this program.)

93.206 HUMAN HEALTH STUDIES—APPLIED RESEARCH AND DEVELOPMENT

Assistance: project grants (100 percent/1-5 years).

Purposes: pursuant to CERCLA as amended and SARA, for studies on human health effects of hazardous substances identified at hazardous waste sites, as identified by the Agency for Toxic Substances and Disease Registry, including: birth defects and reproductive disorders; cancers; immune function disorders; kidney and liver dysfunction; lung and respiratory diseases; neurotoxin disorders.

Eligible applicants/beneficiaries: same as for **93.204**, and state research institutions and IHEs.

Range: $50,000 to $500,000. **Average:** $100,000.

Activity: FY 05, 20 continuation awards.

HQ: *program information,* same as **93.161**. *Program technical assistance*: Director, Division of Health Studies, same address as **93.204**. Phone: (404) 498-0105, FAX (770)498-0077. Grants management information, web site: same as **93.161**. (Note: no field offices for this program.)

93.208 GREAT LAKES HUMAN HEALTH EFFECTS RESEARCH

Assistance: project grants (100 percent/1-3 years).

Purposes: pursuant to CERCLA as amended, SARA, and Great Lakes Critical Programs Act of 1990, for research on the impact on human health of fish consumption in the Great Lakes basin, focusing on populations identified as having a higher risk of long-term adverse health effects from exposure to contaminants—especially native Americans and other minority groups, sport anglers, the urban poor, the elderly. The research is intended to study the effects of contaminants on human reproductive and developmental, behavioral, immunologic, neurologic, and endocrinologic health. Findings are coordinated with other Public Health Service research programs and activities, to ameliorate adverse impacts of persistent toxic substances.

Eligible applicants/beneficiaries: in the Great Lakes states—state and local health agencies, state IHEs and research institutions, and tribal governments.

Range: $72,000 to $175,000. **Average:** $119,000.

Activity: annually, 10 continuation grants.

HQ: Division of Toxicology, Agency for Toxic Substances and Disease Registry, HHS (E-29), 1600 Clifton Rd. NE, Atlanta, GA 30333. Phone: (404) 498-0717, FAX (404)498-0094. Grants management information, web site: same as **93.161**. (Note: no field offices for this program.)

93.209 CONTRACEPTION AND INFERTILITY RESEARCH LOAN REPAYMENT PROGRAM ("CIR-LRP")

Assistance: direct payments/specified use.

Purposes: pursuant to PHSA as amended, to provide incentives to health professionals to work in reproductive research related to contraceptive development or infertility diagnosis and treatment, by providing assistance in repaying their education loans. The program pays up to $35,000 of loan principal and interest for each year of service commitment, not to exceed one-half of remaining loan balance—plus up to 39 percent to offset tax liability. Participants must agree to commit to a period of obligated service of at least two years.

Eligible applicants/beneficiaries: U.S. citizens, nationals, or permanent residents that are health and allied health professionals, including physicians, Ph.D.-level scientists, nurses, physician assistants, or graduate students and postgraduate research fellows.

Range: $4,179 to $70,000. **Average:** $61,000.

Activity: FY 06 estimate, 17 contracts.

HQ: Director, Office of Extramural Research, National Institute of Child Health and Human Development, NIH-HHS, Bldg.61E - Rm.2C01, Bethesda, MD 20892-7510. Phone: (301)435-6856. **Internet:** "www.nichd.nih.gov/". (Note: no field offices for this program.)

93.210 TRIBAL SELF-GOVERNANCE PROGRAM: PLANNING AND NEGOTIATION COOPERATIVE AGREEMENTS AND IHS COMPACTS/FUNDING AGREEMENTS

Assistance: project grants.

Purposes: pursuant to ISDEAA as amended, to establish and operate programs to provide planning and negotiation resources to tribes interested in participating in the Tribal Self-Governance Program—enabling them to enter into compacts to assume programs, services, and functions of the IHS and HHS that are otherwise available to Indians or tribes.

Eligible applicants/beneficiaries: recognized tribes.

Range: N.A.

Activity: FY 04, 62 compact, 82 funding agreements awards covering 11 hospitals, 64 health centers, 1 school health center, 189 health stations.

HQ: Director, Office of Tribal Self-Governance, IHS-HHS, 801 Thompson Ave. - Ste.240, Rockville, MD 20852. Phone: (301)443-7821. Grants management information address, web site: same as **93.123**. Phone: (301)443-5204. (Note: no field offices for this program.)

93.211 TELEHEALTH NETWORK GRANTS

Assistance: project grants (100 percent/to 3 years).

Purposes: pursuant to PHSA as amended by the Health Care Safety Net Amendments of 2002, to demonstrate the use of telehealth technologies to support and promote long-distance clinical health care, patient and professional health-related education; to collect information for a systematic evaluation of such projects. Projects are meant for rural areas, frontier communities, and medically-underserved populations. Up to 40 percent of grant funds may be used for equipment (non-transmission).

Eligible applicants/beneficiaries public nonprofit health care providers or consortia, that are members of an existing or proposed telemedicine network including for-profit entities.

Range: to $250,000. **Average:** $250,000.

Activity: FY 03, 15 three-year grants.

HQ: Office for the Advancement of Telehealth, HRSA-HHS, 5600 Fishers Lane - Rm.7C-22, Rockville, MD 20857. Phone: (301)443-1730. Grants management information, web site: same as **93.107**. (Note: no field offices for this program.)

93.212 CHIROPRACTIC DEMONSTRATION PROJECT GRANTS

Assistance: project grants (100 percent/3 years).

Purposes: pursuant to PHSA as amended and HPEPA, for demonstration projects in which chiropractors and medical doctors collaborate to identify and treat spinal and lower-back conditions. Project funds may be used for related research activities, personnel, equipment, supplies, domestic travel, consultants and guest lecturers, rent, renovations, and other direct project costs—but not for land acquisition, facilities construction, foreign travel, or student support.

Eligible applicants/beneficiaries: health professions schools, academic health centers, state or local governments, public or private nonprofit entities, and nonprofit colleges and schools of chiropractic.

Range: $381,000 to $389,000. **Average:** $386,000.

Activity: FY 05 estimate, 3 continuation awards, no new awards.

HQ: same address as **93.156**. Phone: (301)443-0908. Grants management information, web site: same as **93.107**. (Note: no field offices for this program.)

93.213 RESEARCH AND TRAINING IN COMPLEMENTARY AND ALTERNATIVE MEDICINE
("National Center for Complementary and Alternative Medicine")

Assistance: project grants (100 percent/to 5 years).

Purposes: pursuant to PHSA as amended, to foster collaboration between biomedical researchers and practitioners of alternative, complementary, or unconventional medical treatments, by: supporting and coordinating evaluations of alternative medical practices; identifying areas of clinical and preclinical research needing further development; developing clinical databases in conjunction with the National Library of Medicine; developing further international contacts; establishing an intra- and extramural clinical research fellowship program in alternative medicine. Grants may support costs of personnel, consultants, equipment, supplies, patient costs, animals, travel, and related items.

Eligible applicants/beneficiaries: IHEs, hospitals, public agencies, nonprofit research institutions, profit organizations, individuals.

Range: training, $22,000 to $412,000; projects, $125,000 to $3,000,000. **Average:** projects, $317,000.

Activity: FY 06 estimate, 291 grants.

HQ: Division of Extramural Research, National Center for Complementary and Alternative Medicine, NIH-HHS, 6707 Democracy Blvd. - Ste.401, Bethesda, MD 20892-5475. Phone: (301)496-4792, FAX (301)402-4741. **Internet:** "http://nccam.nih.gov". (Note: no field offices for this program.)

93.217 FAMILY PLANNING—SERVICES

Assistance: project grants (from 90 percent/3-5 years).

Purposes: pursuant to PHSA as amended and Family Planning Services and Population Research Acts, for educational, counseling, and comprehensive medical and social services involving family planning, with priority to the low-income. Grants may be used for contraceptive, infertility, and special services to adolescents. Funds may not be used in programs where abortion is a method of family planning, nor for personnel salaries paid from other federal funds, nor for building construction.

Eligible applicants/beneficiaries: city, county, local, regional, or state governmental or private nonprofit entities in states, territories, and possessions; "faith-based" organizations.

Range: $48,000 to $16,962,000. **Average:** $2,520,000.

Activity: annually, 91 grantees funded.

HQ: Director, Office of Family Planning, Office of Population Affairs, same address/phone, web site as **93.111**. *Grants management information:* same as **93.004**.

93.219 MATCHING GRANTS FOR HEALTH PROFESSIONS SCHOLARSHIPS TO INDIAN TRIBES
("Health Professions Scholarships")

Assistance: project grants (80 percent).

Purposes: pursuant to the Indian Health Care Improvement Act as amended, to establish and operate programs providing for undergraduate or graduate scholarships to Indians to serve as health professionals in Indian communities. Scholarship recipients must: maintain satisfactory academic standing; meet service requirements equal to the number of years covered by the scholarships, but not less than two years.

Eligible applicants/beneficiaries: tribes or tribal organizations.

Range: $57,000 to $75,000. **Average:** $66,000.

Activity: FY 06, 5 continuation awards.

HQ: same addresses/phone, web site as **93.123**. *Grants management information*: same address. Phone: (301)443-5204. (Note: no field offices for this program.)

93.220 CLINICAL RESEARCH LOAN REPAYMENT PROGRAM FOR INDIVIDUALS FROM DISADVANTAGED BACKGROUNDS ("NIH Clinical Research Loan Repayment Program" - "CR-LRP")

Assistance: project grants (100 percent/2 years minimum).

Purposes: pursuant to PHSA as amended, for repayment of extant educational loans incurred by persons from disadvantaged backgrounds, engaged in clinical research as employees of the NIH. Payments may be made up to $35,000 per year, plus $13,650 annually for tax reimbursements.

Eligible applicants/beneficiaries: U.S. citizens, nationals, or permanent residents from disadvantaged backgrounds, with: an M.D., Ph.D., D.O., D.D.S., D.M.D., D.P.M., B.S.N., A.D.N., or equivalent degree; qualified undergraduate or graduate educational loan debt exceeding 20 percent of their NIH salary; a contract commitment of at least two years of service to NIH; no existing service obligation to federal, state, or other entities.

Range: $4,000 to $70,000; tax reimbursements, $1,977 to $35,000. **Average:** $68,000.

Activity: FY 06 estimate, 19 awards.

HQ: Office of Loan Repayment and Scholarship, NIH-HHS, 6011 Executive Blvd. - Rm.206, Bethesda, MD 20892-7650. Phone: *helpline,* (866)849-4047, FAX (866)849-4046. **Internet:** "www.lrp.nih.gov"; e-mail, "lrp@nih.gov". (Note: no field offices for this program.)

93.223 DEVELOPMENT AND COORDINATION OF RURAL HEALTH SERVICES

Assistance: project grants (100 percent/3 years).

Purposes: pursuant to PHSA, to develop and disseminate information to assist rural communities and rural health care organizations in developing and coordinating rural health care services—including information from federal and state agencies, workshops, conferences, research reports, recruitment efforts, and reports from national health care associations.

Eligible applicants/beneficiaries: nonprofit private organizations representing national, state, and local rural health constituencies.

Range/Average: one award only.

Activity: FY 06, 1 continuation award.

HQ: Director, Office of Rural Health Policy, same addresses/phones, web site as **93.155**. (Note: no field offices for this program.)

93.224 CONSOLIDATED HEALTH CENTERS
("Community Health Centers" - "Migrant Health Centers" - "Health Care for the Homeless" - "Public Housing Primary Care" - "School-Based Health Centers")

Assistance: project grants (to 5 years).

Purposes: pursuant to PHSA and Health Centers Consolidation Act of 1996, to increase access to comprehensive primary and preventive health care and improve the health status of underserved and vulnerable populations, including at centers providing care through or to community, migrant, homeless, public housing, and school-based populations. Projects should improve the availability, accessibility, and organization of health care. Project funds may not be used for inpatient services or to make cash payments to service recipients.

Eligible applicants/beneficiaries: public or private nonprofit entities.

Range: $100,000 to $8,000,000.

Activity: FY 04, 13,200,000 patients served.

HQ: Director, Division of Health Center Management, Bureau of Primary Health Care, HRSA-HHS, 5600 Fishers Lane - Rm.16C-26, Rockville, MD 20857. Phone: (301)594-4420. Grants management information, web site: same as **93.007**. (Note: no field offices for this program.)

93.225 NATIONAL RESEARCH SERVICE AWARDS—HEALTH SERVICES RESEARCH TRAINING

Assistance: project grants (100 percent/3-5 years).

Purposes: pursuant to PHSA, for fellowships for full-time postdoctoral training in health services research for up to three years, and to predoctoral candidates from under-represented minority groups for up to five years—with grants to institutions providing the training (*see Notes preceding* **93.001**). Training is in health services research and research methods, epidemiology, biostatistics, geriatrics, health administration and public health, medical information sciences, health policy and management, organizational behavior, clinical outcomes and effectiveness, primary care, health care quality, health economics and financing, child health, and vulnerable populations. Postdoctoral fellowship recipients must meet service payback requirements.

Eligible applicants/beneficiaries: domestic public or private nonprofit organizations including state and local governments and territories—with existing training programs. Fellowship recipients must be U.S. citizens, noncitizen nationals, or lawful permanent residents.

Range: individuals, $35,000 to $75,000; institutions, $120,000 to $500,000.
Average: individuals, $50,000; institutions, $250,000.

Activity: FY 06 estimate, 10 fellowships, 27 institutional grants.

HQ: Division of Research Education, Agency for Healthcare Research and Quality, HHS, 540 Gaither Rd., Rockville, MD 20850. Phone: (301)427-

1527, -1528; Grants Management Specialist, (301)427-1454, -1704. **Internet:** "www.ahrq.gov". (Note: no field offices for this program.)

93.226 RESEARCH ON HEALTHCARE COSTS, QUALITY AND OUTCOMES

Assistance: project grants (100 percent/to 5 years).

Purposes: pursuant to PHSA as amended, for research and evaluations, demonstration projects, research networks, multidisciplinary centers, and information dissemination on health care and systems for delivery of care. Major issue categories include: quality measurement and improvement; outcomes and cost-effectiveness; clinical practice including primary and practice-oriented research; health care technologies, facilities, and equipment; costs, productivity, organization, and market forces; health promotion and disease prevention, including clinical preventive services; health statistics, surveys, data base development, epidemiology; medical liability.

Eligible applicants/beneficiaries: federal, state, local government agencies; tribal governments; territories and possessions; sponsored organizations; public or private nonprofit organizations; minority and specialized groups; IHEs; individuals; and, profit organizations for cooperative agreements.

Range: $5,000 to $2,800,000. **Average:** $310,000.

Activity: FY 06 estimate, 306 grants.

HQ: same address, web site as **93.225**. Phone: Center for Outcomes and Evidence, (301)427-1600; Center for Quality Improvement and Patient Safety, (301)427-1349; Center for Primary Care, Prevention and Partnerships, (301)427-1500; Center for Financing, Access, and Cost Trends, (301)427-1406; Center for Organization, Delivery, and Markets, (301)427-1410; Grants Management Officer, (301)427-1447. (Note: no field offices for this program.)

93.228 INDIAN HEALTH SERVICE—HEALTH MANAGEMENT DEVELOPMENT PROGRAM

Assistance: project grants.

Purposes: pursuant to ISDEAA, to increase the capability of American Indians and Alaska natives to operate existing IHS health care programs involving curative, preventive, and rehabilitative health services. Funds may be used for feasibility studies, planning, tribal health management structure development, evaluation.

Eligible applicants/beneficiaries: tribes and tribal organizations.

Range: management, $50,000 to $100,000; services projects, $85,000 to $185,000. **Average:** management, $80,000; services, $182,000.

Activity: FY 06, estimate, 23 new, 7 continuing tribal management project awards; 20 continuing health services awards.

HQ: *management programs,* Program Analyst, Office of Tribal Programs, IHS-HHS, same address as **93.123**. Phone: (301)443-1104. *Health services projects, grants management information:* same address as **93.123**. Phone: (301)443-5204. **Internet:** "www.ihs.gov/nonmedicalprograms/tmg/index.asp".

93.229 DEMONSTRATION COOPERATIVE AGREEMENTS FOR DEVELOPMENT AND IMPLEMENTATION OF CRIMINAL JUSTICE TREATMENT NETWORKS

Assistance: project grants (100 percent/to 5 years).

Purposes: pursuant to PHSA as amended, for integrated criminal justice treatment networks of a consortium of criminal justice, substance abuse treatment, primary health and mental health care, and allied social services and job placement agencies involved with adult male or female offenders and juvenile justice populations. Each network must develop strategies to link existing partnerships into a comprehensive continuum of services in metropolitan areas with populations of 200,000 to 1,000,000, with the pivotal points of referral and supervision either in the courts or community probations and parole agencies.

Eligible applicants/beneficiaries: state alcohol and drug abuse agencies applying on behalf of consortia state and local officials and public and nonprofit private entities. If the state does not apply, consortia may submit applications through nonprofit entities, in coordination with state agencies.

Range/Average: one award only.

Activity: FY 03, 1 award.

HQ: Division of Practice and Systems Development, CSAT-SAMHSA-HHS, 1 Choke Cherry Rd., Rockville, MD 20857. Phone: (240)276-1576. *Grants management information*: Grants Management Officer, Office of Program Support, SAMHSA-HHS, 1 Choke Cherry Rd., Rockville, MD 20857. Phone: (240)276-1421. **Internet:** "www.samhsa.gov". (Note: no field offices for this program.)

93.230 CONSOLIDATED KNOWLEDGE DEVELOPMENT AND APPLICATION (KD&A) PROGRAM ("KD&A")

Assistance: project grants (100 percent/3 years).

Purposes: pursuant to PHSA as amended, to provide immediately usable, practical knowledge to services providers on the efficacy of substance abuse and mental health services in crucial selected areas—based on questions arising from consumers and their families, providers, and public and private agencies and organizations including at state and federal policymaking and legislative levels. Activities are undertaken in service settings. Dissemination occurs through multiple channels including technology. Specific study topics are announced annually.

Eligible applicants/beneficiaries: state and local governments; private nonprofit and profit entities such as community-based organizations, IHEs, and hospitals.

Range: $163,000 to $1,200,000. **Average:** $352,000.

Activity: FY 01, 303 CMHS, 318 CSAP, 318 CSAT awards. FY 02-03 estimate, no awards.

HQ: *general address,* SAMHSA-HHS, 1 Choke Cherry Rd., Rockville, MD 20857. Phone: CSAP, (240)276-2018; CSAT, (240)276-1421. Grants management information, web site: same as **93.229**. (Note: no field offices for this program.)

93.231 EPIDEMIOLOGY COOPERATIVE AGREEMENTS

Assistance: project grants (100 percent/to 3 years).

Purposes: pursuant to the Indian Health Care Improvement Act as amended, to develop tribal epidemiology centers and public health infrastructure to coordinate and participate in disease surveillance and prevention projects, as well as investigations and studies of national scope. Project activities include convening of meetings, technical assistance and consultation, training, site visits, coordination on a national basis.

Eligible applicants/beneficiaries: tribes; tribal, urban tribal organizations; consortia.

Range: $400,000 to $540,000. **Average:** $470,000.

Activity: FY 06 estimate, 11 continuation projects.

HQ: Division of Epidemiology, IHS Headquarters West, HHS, 5300 Homestead Rd. NE, Albuquerque, NM 87110. Phone: (505)248-4132. Grants management information, web site: same as **93.123**. Phone: (301)443-5204. (Note: no other field offices for this program.)

93.232 LOAN REPAYMENT PROGRAM FOR GENERAL RESEARCH ("NIH General Loan Repayment Program" - "GR-LRP")

Assistance: project grants (100 percent/3 years).

Purposes: pursuant to PHSA as amended, for repayment of extant educational loans incurred by scientific professionals engaged in laboratory or clinical research as employees of the NIH for a minimum of three years.

Eligible applicants/beneficiaries: same as for **93.220**.

Range: $6,000 to $105,000 per year, plus $2,966 to $52,000 for tax reimbursements. **Average:** $85,000 including tax reimbursement.

Activity: FY 06 estimate, 89 awards.

HQ: same as **93.220**. (Note: no field offices for this program.)

93.233 NATIONAL CENTER ON SLEEP DISORDERS RESEARCH

Assistance: project grants (100 percent/1-5 years).

Purposes: pursuant to PHSA, for research, training, information dissemination, and other activities relating to sleep and sleep disorders, including biological and circadian rhythm research, basic understanding of sleep, chronobiological and other sleep related research; to coordinate center activities with other federal agencies and with public and nonprofit organizations. NRSA, SBIR, and STIR funding is available (*see Notes preceding* **93.001**).

Eligible applicants/beneficiaries: nonprofit and profit organizations; individuals.

Range: $86,000 to $964,000. **Average:** $350,000.

Activity: FY 06 estimate, 173 research grants, 10 NRSAs.

HQ: Director, National Center on Sleep Disorders Research, National Heart, Lung, and Blood Institute, NIH-HHS, Bethesda, MD 20892. Phone: (301)

435-0199; Administrative Office, (301)435-6373; *SBIR,* Deputy Director, Division of Extramural Affairs, (301)435-0266. *Grants management information*: Grants Management Officer, Grants Operations Branch, Office of Program Policy and Procedures, National Heart, Lung, and Blood Institute, NIH-HHS, Bethesda, MD 20892. Phone: (301)435-0144. **Internet:** "www.nih.gov/sleep". (Note: no field offices for this program.)

93.234 TRAUMATIC BRAIN INJURY STATE DEMONSTRATION GRANT PROGRAM ("TBI")

Assistance: project grants (67 percent/1-3 years).

Purposes: pursuant to PHSA as amended, to improve access to health and other TBI-related service for persons of all ages and their families. Planning grants support development of four state-level core capacity components to provide TBI services. Implementation grants are for states with the four core capacity components in place. Post-demonstration grants fund activities begun during the state implementation phase.

Eligible applicants/beneficiaries: state governments.

Range: $73,000 to $200,000. **Average:** $136,000.

Activity: FY 05 estimate, 13 projects supported; FY 06, no projects.

HQ: Division of Services for Children with Special Health Care Needs, Maternal and Child Health Bureau, same address as **93.127**. Phone: (301) 443-2370. Grants management information, web site: same as **93.107**. (Note: no field offices for this program.)

93.235 ABSTINENCE EDUCATION PROGRAM

Assistance: formula grants (57 percent).

Purposes: pursuant to SSA, Section 510, to provide abstinence education and, at state option, mentoring, counseling, and adult supervision to promote abstinence from sexual activity outside of marriage—focussing on groups most likely to bear children out of wedlock. (Note: program provisions approximate **93.010**.)

Eligible applicants/beneficiaries: governor-designated agencies.

Range: $14,000 to $7,055,000. **Average:** $847,000.

Activity: FY 06, 59 grants.

HQ: same as **93.010**. (Note: no field offices for this program.)

93.236 GRANTS FOR DENTAL PUBLIC HEALTH RESIDENCY TRAINING ("Dental Residency Training Grants")

Assistance: project grants (100 percent/3 years).

Purposes: pursuant to PHSA and HPEPA, to plan and develop new or to maintain and improve existing dental public health residency training programs; to provide financial assistance to trainees. Grants may not be used for construction or for direct patient services.

Eligible applicants/beneficiaries: public or private schools of public health or dentistry; experienced, qualified nonprofit and community-based organizations.

Range: $47,000 to $153,000. **Average:** $74,000.

Activity: FY 05 estimate, 7 continuation awards.

HQ: Division of Medicine and Dentistry, Bureau of Health Professions, HRSA-HHS, Parklawn Bldg. - Rm.9A-27, 5600 Fishers Lane, Rockville, MD 20857. Phone: (301)443-1707. Grants management information, web site: same as **93.107**. (Note: no field offices for this program.)

93.237 SPECIAL DIABETES PROGRAM FOR INDIANS—DIABETES PREVENTION AND TREATMENT PROJECTS

Assistance: project grants (100 percent/to 5 years).

Purposes: for primary, secondary, and tertiary diabetes prevention and treatment services and related data collection among American Indians and Alaskan natives.

Eligible applicants/beneficiaries: tribes, tribal and urban Indian organizations operating IHS health programs.

Range: $46,000 to $5,000,000. **Average:** $350,000.

Activity: FY 06 estimate, 286 grants.

HQ: Director, Diabetes Program, IHS-HHS, 5300 Homestead Rd. NE, Albuquerque, NM 87110. Phone: (505)248-4182, FAX (505)248-4188. Grants management contact address, web site: same as **93.123**. Phone: (301)443-5204, FAX (301)443-9602. (Note: no other field offices for this program.)

93.238 COOPERATIVE AGREEMENTS FOR STATE TREATMENT OUTCOMES AND PERFORMANCE PILOT STUDIES ENHANCEMENT

Assistance: project grants (100 percent/3 years).

Purposes: pursuant to PHSA as amended, to collect information on treatment services funded with Substance Abuse Pilot Treatment Block Grant; to monitor common substance abuse treatment effectiveness data across various state management information systems; for evaluation programs to design or enhance state management information systems or outcome management systems that examine treatment effectiveness and costs through standardized performance and outcome measures while incorporating common data measures on an interstate basis.

Eligible applicants/beneficiaries: projects—single state authorities. Technical assistance centers—domestic nonprofit and profit entities including community-based organizations, IHEs, and hospitals.

Range: $300,000 to $500,000. **Average:** $460,000.

Activity: FY 04 estimate, 6 awards.

HQ: Division for State and Community Assistance, CSAT-SAMHSA-HHS, 1 Choke Cherry Rd., Rockville, MD 20857. Phone: (240)276-2406. Grants management information, web site: same as **93.229**. (Note: no field offices for this program.)

93.239 POLICY RESEARCH AND EVALUATION GRANTS

Assistance: project grants (to 100 percent).

Purposes: pursuant to the Social Security Act, for research relevant to policy development and evaluation of current and proposed programs, covering: issues of long-term care, disability, and personal assistance services including informal care giving; health care delivery issues including financing; welfare reform outcomes and policies affecting children and youth; community development; science policy development; reduction of poverty.

Eligible applicants/beneficiaries: nonprofit organizations, state and local government agencies, IHEs, individuals, some profit organizations.

Range: $300,000 to $1,200,000. **Average:** $575,000.

Activity: FY 04 estimate, 7 awards.

HQ: Grants Officer, Assistant Secretary/Planning and Evaluation, OS-HHS, HHH Bldg. - Rm.405F, 200 Independence Ave. SW, Washington, DC 20201. Phone: (202)690-8794. **Internet:** "www.aspe.hhs.gov". (Note: no field offices for this program.)

93.240 STATE CAPACITY BUILDING
("Site Specific Activities Cooperative Agreement Program")

Assistance: project grants (100 percent/3-5 years).

Purposes: pursuant to CERCLA, SARA, and RCRA as amended, for public health agency capacity building in coordination with the Agency for Toxic Substances and Disease Registry, to conduct: health consultations; public health assessments; exposure investigations; community involvement; health education; public health studies.

Eligible applicants/beneficiaries: state public health agencies including possessions and territories, tribal governments.

Range: $151,000 to $700,000. **Average:** $350,000.

Activity: FY 05 estimate, 33 continuation awards.

HQ: Funding Resource Specialist, Office of Financial and Administrative Services, Agency for Toxic Substances and Disease Registry, same address as **93.161**. Phone: (404)498-0624, FAX (404)498-0059. Grants management information, web site: same as **93.161**. (Note: no field offices for this program.)

93.241 STATE RURAL HOSPITAL FLEXIBILITY PROGRAM

Assistance: project grants.

Purposes: for states to work with rural communities and hospitals to develop and implement rural health plans and integrated care networks, to improve emergency medical services, and to designate critical access hospitals.

Eligible applicants/beneficiaries: states with rural health plans already submitted to the Centers for Medicare and Medicaid Services (CMS). Other states submit applications to CMS regional offices.

Range: $200,000 to $700,000. **Average:** $485,000.

Activity: annually, 45 continuation awards.

HQ: Health Systems Advisor, Office of Rural Health Policy, same address/phone as **93.155**. Grants management information, web site: same as **93.107**. (Note: no field offices for this program.)

93.242 MENTAL HEALTH RESEARCH GRANTS

Assistance: project grants (100 percent/to 5 years).

Purposes: pursuant to PHSA as amended and SBRDEA, for research on basic brain and behavioral processes underlying mental and behavioral disorders and mental health—employing theoretical, laboratory, clinical, methodological, and field studies involving clinical, subclinical, and normal subjects and populations of all age ranges, as well as animal, computational, and mathematical models. Areas eligible for support include HIV/AIDS behavior, neurosciences including molecular genetics, behavioral sciences, epidemiology, clinical assessment, etiology, treatment, prevention, and services. Grants support clearly defined projects or small groups of related research activities, and research conferences. Program Project and Center grants support large-scale, broad-based interdisciplinary research programs. Small grants (to $50,000 for two years) support small-scale exploratory and pilot studies or exploration of an unusual research opportunity. SBIR and STTR awards are made (*see Notes preceding* **93.001**).

Eligible applicants/beneficiaries: public, private, profit, or nonprofit agencies including state and local governments, federal agencies, IHEs, hospitals, academic or research institutions.

Range: $29,000 to $6,331,000. **Average:** $336,000.

Activity: FY 06 estimate, 2,533 grants.

HQ: NIMH, NIH-HHS, 6001 Executive Blvd., Bethesda, MD 20892. Phone: (301)443-9700; *Grants management information*: Grants Management Officer, NIMH, NIH-HHS, 6001 Executive Blvd. - Rm.6115, Bethesda, MD 20892-9605. Phone: (301)443-2811. **Internet:** "www.nih.gov". (Note: no field offices for this program.)

93.243 SUBSTANCE ABUSE AND MENTAL HEALTH SERVICES—PROJECTS OF REGIONAL AND NATIONAL SIGNIFICANCE ("PRNS")

Assistance: project grants (100 percent/1-5 years).

Purposes: pursuant to PHSA as amended and Children's Health Act of 2000, to address priority substance abuse treatment, prevention, and mental health needs of regional and national significance, through grants and cooperative agreements for: knowledge, development, and application projects for treatment and rehabilitation, and their evaluation; training and technical assistance; targeted capacity response programs; systems change, including projects involving statewide family networks and client-oriented and consumer-run self-help activities; programs to foster child health and development.

Eligible applicants/beneficiaries: same as for **93.230**.

Range/Average: $1,083,000.

Activity: FY 04-05 estimate, 600 grants.

HQ: same as **93.230**. (Note: no field offices for this program.)

93.244 MENTAL HEALTH CLINICAL AND AIDS SERVICE-RELATED TRAINING GRANTS

Assistance: project grants (100 percent/to 5 years).

Purposes: pursuant to PHSA as amended, for training programs in the mental health professions, including administrative costs, trainee stipends, and other allowances to trainees—with payback agreements required in some instances. Specific program objectives are to increase the number of qualified minority personnel in the field, and the number of mental health personnel trained to deal with the special problems of children, adolescents, the elderly, the seriously mentally ill, and rural populations. Eligible disciplines include: psychiatry, psychology, social work, psychiatric nursing, and marriage and family therapy. Awards may be made to faculty scholars and for state human resource development.

Eligible applicants: public or private nonprofit institutions and organizations, state and local government agencies.

Eligible beneficiaries: U.S. citizens, nationals, lawful permanent residents.

Range: institutional, $225,000 to $300,000; predoctoral trainees, $10,000; postdoctoral, $19,600 to $32,300; faculty scholars, salary support, $25,000 in educational expenses. **Average:** institutional, $250,000.

Activity: FY 03 estimate, 4 awards.

HQ: Human Resource Planning and Development Branch, CMHS-SAMHSA-HHS, 1 Choke Cherry Rd., Rockville, MD 20857. Phone: *clinical*, (240)276-1387; HIV/AIDS Program, (240)276-1962. Grants management information, web site: same as **93.229**. (Note: no field offices for this program.)

93.247 ADVANCED EDUCATION NURSING GRANT PROGRAM

Assistance: project grants (100 percent/3 years).

Purposes: pursuant to PHSA as amended and HPEPA, to enhance advanced nursing education and practice including: master's and doctoral programs; combined RN and master's degree programs; post-nursing master's certificate programs; or, for nurse midwives, in certificate programs existing on 12 November 1998, to serve as nurse practitioners, clinical nurse specialist, nurse midwives, nurse administrators, public health nurses, or other specialties.

Eligible applicants/beneficiaries: schools of nursing, academic health centers; other public or private nonprofit or profit entities including community-based organizations.

Range: $90,000 to $451,000. **Average:** $250,000.

Activity: FY 04, 82 new, 75 continuation awards.

HQ: Division of Nursing, Bureau of Health Professions, HRSA-HHS, Parklawn Bldg. - Rm.9-36, 5600 Fishers Lane, Rockville, MD 20857. Phone: (301)443-6333. Grants management information, web site: same as **93.107**. (Note: no field offices for this program.)

93.249 PUBLIC HEALTH TRAINING CENTERS GRANT PROGRAM

Assistance: project grants (100 percent/5 years).

Purposes: pursuant to PHSA as amended and HPEPA, for graduate-level and specialized public health educational programs to strengthen the technical, scientific, managerial, and leadership competencies of the current and future public health work force—particularly with respect to providing health care services to medically underserved populations including such groups as the elderly, immigrants, refugees, and the disadvantaged. Centers must: designate specific geographic service areas in a location removed from the main teaching facilities; assess personnel needs of such areas and design programs to meet those needs; establish or strengthen field placements for students; involve faculty members and students in collaborative projects to enhance services. Project funds may not be used for student stipends, construction, or patient services.

Eligible applicants/beneficiaries: accredited schools of public health and other public or private nonprofit institutions.

Range: $250,000 to $500,000. **Average:** $350,000.

Activity: FY 04 estimate, 14 continuation awards.

HQ: Public Health Advisor, Division of Community, State and Public Health, same address (Rm.8A-17) as **93.156**. Phone: (301)443-6864. Grants management information, web site: same as **93.107**. (Note: no field offices for this program.)

93.250 GERIATRIC ACADEMIC CAREER AWARDS

Assistance: direct payments/specified use (100 percent/5 years).

Purposes: pursuant to PHSA as amended and HPEPA, to provide financial incentives for junior faculty at schools of allopathic and osteopathic medicine to pursue academic careers in geriatrics.

Eligible applicants/beneficiaries: junior faculty members of accredited schools of allopathic and osteopathic medicine who: are board-certified or -eligible in internal medicine, family practice, or psychiatry; have completed geriatrics fellowship programs; are U.S. citizens, nationals, or lawful permanent residents.

Range/Average: $58,000.

Activity: FY 04, 1 new, 12 continuation awards.

HQ: same as **93.156**. (Note: no field offices for this program.)

93.251 UNIVERSAL NEWBORN HEARING SCREENING

Assistance: project grants (100 percent/3-5 years).

Purposes: pursuant to PHSA, to implement universal newborn child hearing screening prior to hospital discharge with linkage to a medical home, and diagnostic evaluation and enrollment in a program of early intervention.

Eligible applicants/beneficiaries: states; one technical assistance organization.

Range: $44,000 to $515,000. **Average:** $161,000.

Activity: FY 05 estimate, 1 new, 53 continuation state projects; 1 continuation technical assistance grant.

HQ: Integrated Services Branch, Division of Services for Children with Special Needs, Maternal and Child Health Bureau, HRSA-HHS, 5600 Fishers Lane - Rm.18A-18, Rockville, MD 20857. Phone: (301)443-2370. Grants management information, web site: same as **93.107**. (Note: no field offices for this program.)

93.252 HEALTHY COMMUNITIES ACCESS PROGRAM

Assistance: project grants (100 percent/to 3 years).

Purposes: pursuant to PHSA, for communities and consortia of health care providers to develop or strengthen integrated health care systems that coordinate health services for the uninsured or under-insured, including those with chronic conditions. Grants may support activities directly providing or ensuring the provision of primary, secondary, and tertiary services, as well as substance abuse treatment and mental health services. A maximum of 15 percent of granted funds may be used to provide direct patient care and services, including reimbursable services, supplies, capital equipment. Grants funds may not be used for construction or reserve requirements for state licensure.

Eligible applicants/beneficiaries: consortia or networks of community-wide health care providers, including local and tribal governments, hospitals, medical and dental societies, foundations, and community-based nonprofit organizations.

Range: $355,000 to $1,200,000.

Activity: FY 05 estimate, 35 new. Since program inception, 228 grantees funded in 45 states, DC, VI.

HQ: Health Center Infrastructure Branch, Division of Health Center Development, Bureau of Primary Health Care, HRSA-HHS, 5600 Fishers Lane, Rockville, MD 20857. Phone: (301)594-4300. Grants management information, web site: same as **93.107**. (Note: no field offices for this program.)

93.253 POISON CONTROL STABILIZATION AND ENHANCEMENT GRANTS ("Poison Control Centers" - "PCC")

Assistance: project grants.

Purposes: pursuant to the Poison Control Center Enhancement and Awareness Act, Amendments of 2003, to strengthen poisoning prevention and treatment programs and services; to enable non-certified or new centers to obtain certification; to create collaborative approaches among PCCs and with other health entities; to expand access to services. Previous projects also have established a toll-free phone number and nationwide media campaign, developed uniform patient management guidelines.

Eligible applicants/beneficiaries: state-designated poison control centers.

Range: $30,000 to $2,100,000. **Average:** $300,000.

Activity: FY 05-06 estimate, 69 grants.

HQ: Poison Control Program, Healthcare Systems Bureau, HRSA-HHS, 5600

Fishers Lane - Rm.13-103, Rockville MD 20857. Phone: (301)443-6192. (Note: no field offices for this program.)

93.254 INFANT ADOPTION AWARENESS TRAINING ("IAATP")

Assistance: project grants (100 percent/1-3 years).

Purposes: pursuant to PHSA and Children's Health Act of 2000, to develop and implement programs to train designated health center staff in providing adoption information and referrals to pregnant women on an equal basis, with all other courses of action included in nondirective counseling.

Eligible applicants/beneficiaries: private nonprofit national, regional, or local organizations whose primary purposes are adoption.

Range: $400,000 to $6,000,000. **Average:** $600,000.

Activity: FY 04, 6 awards; to date.

HQ: Children's Bureau, Administration for Children, Youth, and Families, HRSA-HHS, 330 C St. SW - Rm.2428, Washington, DC 20447. Phone: (202)205-8060, FAX (202)401-5917. **Internet:** "www.acf.hhs.gov/programs/cb". (Note: no field offices for this program.)

93.255 CHILDREN'S HOSPITALS GRADUATE MEDICAL EDUCATION PAYMENT ("CHGME Payment Program")

Assistance: direct payments/specified use.

Purposes: pursuant to SSA, PHSA as amended, Children's Health Act of 2000, and Healthcare Research and Quality Act of 1999, to operate graduate medical residency programs in pediatrics and other specialties at children's teaching hospitals—to help offset the disparity in funding levels versus other types of federally supported teaching hospitals.

Eligible applicants/beneficiaries: public or private nonprofit and profit children's teaching hospitals with accredited residency training programs, with a Medicare provider agreement in effect and excluded from the Medicare Inpatient Prospective Payment system.

Range: $6,687 to $22,674,000. **Average:** $4,755,000.

Activity: FY 05 estimate, 60 hospitals funded.

HQ: Chief, Graduate Medical Education Branch, Division of Medicine and Dentistry, Bureau of Health Professions, HRSA-HHS, 5600 Fishers Lane - Rm.9A-05, Rockville, MD 20857. Phone: (301)443-1058. Grants management information, web site: same as **93.107**. (Note: no field offices for this program.)

93.256 STATE PLANNING GRANTS HEALTH CARE ACCESS FOR THE UNINSURED

Assistance: project grants.

Purposes: for states to develop plans to provide access to health insurance coverage for all citizens. Plans must set forth proposed programs that are similar in scope to the Federal Employees Health Benefit Plan, Medicaid, state employee plans, or similar plans.

Eligible applicants/beneficiaries: governor-designated agencies or individuals, including in territories, that have not previously a state planning grant.

Range: $175,000 to $800,000.

Activity: FY 05 estimate, 2 new grants. FY 06 estimate, no funding.

HQ: Director, State Planning Grants Program, Healthcare Systems Bureau, HRSA-HHS, 5600 Fishers Lane - Rm.11C-26, Rockville, MD 20857. Phone: (301)443-0938, FAX (301)443-8196. Grants management information, web site: same as **93.107**. (Note: no field offices for this program.)

93.257 GRANTS FOR EDUCATION, PREVENTION, AND EARLY DETECTION OF RADIOGENIC CANCERS AND DISEASES
("Radiation Exposure Screening and Education Program")

Assistance: project grants.

Purposes: pursuant to PHSA, for new or expanded programs to: screen individuals, as described in the Radiation Exposure Compensation Act, for cancer as a preventative health measure; provide referrals for medical treatment and provide follow-up services; develop and disseminate public information and education for the detection, prevention, and treatment of radiogenic cancers and diseases; facilitate putative applicants in the documentation of claims under the Radiation Exposure Compensation Act. Project funds may not support inpatient services or cash payments to patients.

Eligible applicants/beneficiaries: within states with uranium mines or mills or involved in uranium transport (Arizona, Colorado, Idaho, New Mexico, North Dakota, Oregon, South Dakota, Texas, Utah, Washington, and Wyoming)—cancer centers designated by the National Cancer Institute, DVA health facilities, federally qualified health centers, state or local agencies currently providing health care services, IHS health care facilities, nonprofit organizations.

Range/Average: $300,000.

Activity: FY 05 estimate, 6-8 grants.

HQ: same as **93.224**. (Note: no field offices for this program.)

93.259 RURAL ACCESS TO EMERGENCY DEVICES GRANT
("AEDs")

Assistance: project grants.

Purposes: pursuant to the Cardiac Arrest Survival Act of 2000, for state community partnerships to purchase Access to Emergency Devices (AEDs) and to obtain training on their use. Funds may also support: medical dispatcher training addressing the use of AEDs for the lay person until arrival of EMS personnel; maintenance costs; data reporting costs.

Eligible applicants/beneficiaries: rural community partnerships including first response entities (e.g., fire, EMS, police), profit and nonprofit entities, statewide or regional offices.

Range: $50,000 to $300,000.

Activity: FY 06 estimate, 49 continuation awards.

HQ: Office of Rural Health Policy, same address/phone, web site as **93.155**. (Note: no field offices for this program.)

93.260 FAMILY PLANNING—PERSONNEL TRAINING

Assistance: project grants (100 percent/to 3-5 years).

Purposes: pursuant to PHSA and the Family Planning Services and Population Research Act of 1970 as amended, to train paramedical and paraprofessional personnel in family planning services, particularly in rural areas. Programs where abortion as a method of family planning are ineligible for assistance.

Eligible applicants/beneficiaries: city, county, local, regional, or state governments and private nonprofit entities in states, territories, and possessions.

Range: $238,000 to $472,000. **Average:** $355,000.

Activity: FY 04-05 estimate, 11 grants.

HQ: Director, Office of Family Planning, Office of Population Affairs, same as **93.111**.

93.262 OCCUPATIONAL SAFETY AND HEALTH PROGRAM

Assistance: project grants (100 percent/1-5 years).

Purposes: pursuant to PHSA as amended and Occupational Safety and Health Act of 1970, for research in occupational disease and injury prevention, including projects involving new or improved procedures, methods, techniques, or systems; to train specialized professional and paraprofessional personnel in occupational medicine, nursing, safety, and in industrial hygiene and occupational safety. Grants may be used for: educational resource centers to provide primarily graduate multidisciplinary training; long-term training programs for undergraduate, graduate, technical, or professional trainees. SBIR awards are made (*see Notes preceding* **93.001**).

Eligible applicants/beneficiaries: domestic and foreign public or private profit and nonprofit organizations; federal, state, local, tribal governments agencies; IHEs; research institutions; hospitals; individuals, with special encouragement to apply to women, minorities, and persons with disabilities.

Range: research, $50,000 to $5,000,000; training, $28,000 to $1,500,000.

Activity: FY 05 estimate, 275 grants.

HQ: Office of Extramural Programs, NIOSH (E74), CDCP-HHS, 1600 Clifton Rd. NE, Atlanta, GA 30333. Phone: (404)498-2530. Grants management information, web site: same as **93.066**. (Note: no field offices for this program.)

93.264 NURSE FACULTY LOAN PROGRAM ("NFLP")

Assistance: direct loans (90 percent/1 year).

Purposes: pursuant to PHSA as amended and Nurse Reinvestment Act of 2002, for schools of nursing to capitalize student loan funds to increase the number of nursing faculty. The program provides up to 90 percent funding for such funds; in turn, schools may award loans of to $30,000 per academic year to students, or the amount of the student's financial need. Loan cancellation ensues for students completing a four-year employment service requirement as nursing faculty, up to 85 percent of the total principal and interest.

Eligible applicants: public and private nonprofit and profit schools of nursing offering full-time advanced degree programs.

Eligible beneficiaries: full-time, graduate nursing students that are U.S. citizens, nationals, or lawful permanent residents.

Range: $21,000 to $194,000. **Average:** $51,000.

Activity: new program in FY 03. FY 04, 61 agreements.

HQ: same address, grants management contact, web site as **93.247**. Phone: (301)443-1399, FAX (301)443-0791. (Note: no field offices for this program.)

93.265 COMPREHENSIVE GERIATRIC EDUCATION PROGRAM ("CGEP")

Assistance: project grants (100 percent/3 years).

Purposes: pursuant to PHSA as amended and Nurse Reinvestment Act of 2002, for programs to train and educate nursing personnel in providing geriatric care. Funds may support student and faculty training programs, curriculum development, continuing education, salaries, travel costs, supplies, and equipment.

Eligible applicants/beneficiaries: schools of nursing, academic health centers, health care facilities, programs leading to certified nurse assistant, partnerships, and other public or private nonprofit and profit entities.

Range: $58,000 to $216,000. **Average:** $157,000.

Activity: new program in FY 03. FY 04, 17 continuation awards.

HQ: same as **93.247**. (Note: no field offices for this program.)

93.266 RAPID EXPANSION OF ANTIRETROVIRAL THERAPY PROGRAMS FOR HIV-INFECTED PERSONS IN SELECTED COUNTRIES OF AFRICA AND THE CARIBBEAN UNDER THE PRESIDENT'S EMERGENCY PLAN FOR AIDS RELIEF ("Global AIDS" - "PEDFAR")

Assistance: project grants (100 percent/1-5 years).

Purposes: pursuant to PHSA as amended and United States Leadership Against HIV/AIDS, Tuberculosis and Malaria Act of 2003, to rapidly expand antiretroviral therapy ("ART") to low-income HIV-infected persons in the 15 countries targeted under the President's Emergency Plan for AIDS Relief (PEDFAR); to develop sustainable indigenous capacity to continue such programs after projects end.

Eligible applicants/beneficiaries: organizations with three years experience in providing ART in three or more of the targeted countries.

Range: $25,000,000 to $50,000,000. **Average:** $25,000,000.

Activity: new program in FY 04; 2 awards.

HQ: Global Program, HIV/AIDS Bureau, HRSA-HHS, 5600 Fishers Lane - Ste. 7-05, Rockville, MD 20857. Phone: (301)443-1993. Grants management information, web site: same as **93.107**. (Note: no field offices for this program.)

93.267 STATE GRANTS FOR PROTECTION AND ADVOCACY SERVICES

Assistance: formula grants (100 percent/2 years).

Purposes: pursuant to PHSA as amended, for state protection and advocacy systems to provide outreach and services to individuals with traumatic brain injury, including: information, referrals, and advice; individual and family advocacy; legal representation; specific assistance in self-advocacy.

Eligible applicants/beneficiaries: state protection and advocacy systems including in territories.

Range: $20,000 to $124,000. **Average:** $53,000.

Activity: new program listing in 2004. Annually beginning in FY 03, 57 awards.

HQ: Program Officer, Protection and Advocacy for Traumatic Brain Injury Program, Division of Services for Children with Special Healthcare Needs, same address/phone, grants management contact, web site as **93.251**. (Note: no field offices for this program.)

93.268 IMMUNIZATION GRANTS
("Section 301 and 317, Public Health Service Act" - "Section 1928 - Social Security Act" - "Vaccines for Children Program" - "VCF")

Assistance: project grants (to 100 percent).

Purposes: pursuant to PHSA as amended, Health Services and Centers Amendments of 1978, Preventive Health Amendments of 1984, and SSA, to plan, organize, and conduct immunization programs for the control of vaccine-preventable diseases; to purchase, store, supply, and deliver vaccine; for assessment, surveillance, outbreak control, information and education, and volunteer activities; compliance with compulsory school immunization laws. Vaccine purchased with grant funds may be given to private practitioners but may not be sold to patients.

Eligible applicants/beneficiaries: states and, in consultation with state health authorities, political subdivisions and other public entities.

Range: Section 317 grants, $167,000 to $41,919,000; VCF, $248,000 to $153,808,000. **Average:** "317," $6,362,000; VCF, $16,300,000.

Activity: annually, 64 "317," 61 VCF grants.

HQ: Director, Immunization Services Division, CDCP-HHS, 1600 Clifton Rd. NE, Atlanta, GA 30333. Phone: (404)639-8208, FAX (404)639-8627. Grants management contact address, web site, same as **93.061**. Phone: (770)488-2738. (Note: no field offices for this program.)

93.271 ALCOHOL RESEARCH CAREER DEVELOPMENT AWARDS FOR SCIENTISTS AND CLINICIANS
("Research Career Awards" - "'K' Awards")

Assistance: project grants (100 percent/5 years).

Purposes: pursuant to PHSA as amended, for research training related to alcohol abuse and alcoholism prevention, treatment, and rehabilitation.

Funds may support five-year fellowships and some research costs, including work by senior investigators. Programs include Mentored Research Scientist Development, Mentored Clinical Scientist Development, Independent Scientist, Mentored Patient-Oriented Career Development, Mid-career Investigator in Patient Oriented Research, Mentored Quantitative Research Career Development, Senior Scientist, and Academic Career Awards.

Eligible applicants/beneficiaries: research centers, medical schools, departments of psychiatry, nonmedical academic departments, psychiatric hospitals or hospitals with psychiatric services, community mental health centers, biomedical research institutes, and departments of behavioral science. Researchers must have scholastic degree and previous training, and they must be U.S. citizens, nationals, or lawful permanent residents.

Range: $89,000 to $196,000. **Average:** $122,000.

Activity: FY 06 estimate, 94 awards.

HQ: same as NIAAA, NIH-HHS, 5635 Fishers Lane, Bethesda, MD 20892-9304. Phone: Division of Metabolism and Health Effects, (301)443-0799; Division of Treatment and Recovery, (301)443-1208; Division of Epidemiology and Prevention Research, (301)443-1274; Division of Neuroscience and Behavior, (301)443-7722. *Grants management information*: Grants Management Officer, NIAAA, NIH-HHS, same address. Phone: (301)443-4704. **Internet:** "www.nih.gov". (Note: no field offices for this program.)

93.272 ALCOHOL NATIONAL RESEARCH SERVICE AWARDS FOR RESEARCH TRAINING

Assistance: project grants (100 percent/to 6 years).

Purposes: pursuant to PHSA as amended, for NRSA programs providing training in clinical research, treatment assessment research, problems of health promotion and alcoholism prevention, and basic biological and behavioral processes (*see Notes preceding* **93.001**). Individual grants may cover up to five years for predoctoral or up to three years of postdoctoral full-time research training; M.D. and Ph.D. fellowships are for up to 6 years; senior fellowships are for up to two years. Special predoctoral fellowships are available for students with disabilities and for minority students. Postdoctoral recipients must meet payback requirements through a period of research and/or teaching after training is completed.

Eligible applicants/beneficiaries: domestic public or private nonprofit organizations. Predoctoral applicants must be enrolled in a doctoral degree program. Postdoctoral applicants must have a doctoral degree. Awardees must be U.S. citizens, nationals, or lawful permanent residents.

Range: $16,000 to $462,000. **Average:** institutional, $134,000.

Activity: FY 06 estimate, 55 fellowship, 30 institutional grants.

HQ: same as **93.271**, *except,* Division of Treatment and Recovery Research— Phone: (301)402-4344. (Note: no field offices for this program.)

93.273 ALCOHOL RESEARCH PROGRAMS

Assistance: project grants (100 percent/to 5 years).

Purposes: pursuant to PHSA as amended and SBRDEA, for research on alcoholism and alcohol-related problems in such disciplines and subject areas as biomedical and genetic factors, psychological and environmental factors, medical disorders, health services, and prevention and treatment. Research Project Grants support clearly defined projects or small groups of related research activities, and research conferences. Program Project grants support large-scale, broad-based interdisciplinary research programs. Small Grants, limited to $50,000 for up to two years, are for small-scale exploratory and pilot studies or exploration of an unusual research opportunity. Exploratory/Developmental Grants are for a maximum of $275,000 total for up to two years. SBIR and STTR awards are available (*see Notes preceding* **93.001**).

Eligible applicants/beneficiaries: public, private profit and nonprofit agencies including state, local, or regional government agencies, IHEs, hospitals, academic or research institutions.

Range: $74,000 to $2,014,000. **Average:** $328,000.

Activity: FY 06 estimate, 801 grants.

HQ: same as **93.271**. (Note: no field offices for this program.)

93.275 SUBSTANCE ABUSE AND MENTAL HEALTH SERVICES—ACCESS TO RECOVERY ("ATR")

Assistance: project grants (100 percent/1-3 years).

Purposes: pursuant to PHSA as amended, to implement voucher programs for substance abuse clinical treatment and recovery support services, enabling clients to obtain free services from providers of their choice.

Eligible applicants/beneficiaries: chief executives of states, territories, and tribal organizations.

Range: to $15,000,000.

Activity: new program listing in FY 04. FY 06 estimate, 15 grants.

HQ: CSAT-SAMHSA-HHS, 1 Choke Cherry Rd., Rockville, MD 20857. Phone: (240)276-1575. Grants management contact address, web site: same as **93.229**. Phone: (240)276-1407, FAX (240)276-1430. (Note: no field offices for this program.)

93.276 DRUG-FREE COMMUNITIES SUPPORT PROGRAM GRANTS ("Drug-Free Community Grants")

Assistance: project grants (to 50 percent/1 year).

Purposes: pursuant to the Drug-Free Communities Act of 1997, to increase the capacity of community coalitions to reduce substance abuse among adults through collaborative activities; to disseminate state-of-the-art information on practices and initiatives proven to be effective in reducing substance abuse among youth.

Eligible applicants/beneficiaries: nonprofit, charitable, educational community coalitions collaborating with community entities, including government agencies, in a substantial voluntary effort—established for at least six months and with a five-year strategic plan. Note: proposals are submitted to the

Office of Justice Programs, and approved by OJJDP and the Office of National Drug Control Policy.

Range/Average: to $100,000.

Activity: FY 03, 184 sites funded.

HQ: *(NOTE: CFDA 8/04 indicates that this program, formerly **16.729** was transferred to SAMHSA; as of January 2006, the CFDA web site still cites the following as the HQ contact.)* Demonstration Programs Division, OJJDP, OJP-DOJ, Washington, DC 20531. Phone: (202)307-5914. **Internet:** "www.usdoj.gov". (Note: no field offices for this program.)

93.279 DRUG ABUSE AND ADDICTION RESEARCH PROGRAMS

Assistance: project grants (100 percent/to 5 years).

Purposes: pursuant to PHSA as amended and SBRDEA, for epidemiologic, basic, clinical, and applied research on the etiology, treatment, prevention, and consequences of drug addiction, including HIV/AIDS. Research project grants support clearly defined projects or small groups of related research activities, and research conferences. Program project and center grants support large-scale, broad-based interdisciplinary research programs. Small grants (up to $50,000 per year for up to two years) support less experienced investigators, testing of new methods and techniques, small-scale exploratory and pilot studies or exploration of an unusual research opportunity. SBIR and STTR awards are available *(see Notes preceding **93.001**).*

Eligible applicants/beneficiaries: public, private, profit and nonprofit organizations; foreign or domestic agencies, including state, local or regional government agencies; IHEs; hospitals; academic or research institutions.

Range: $23,000 to $654,000. **Average:** $133,000.

Activity: FY 06 estimate, 2,124 grants.

HQ: National Institute on Drug Abuse, NIH-HHS, Neurosciences Bldg., 6001 Executive Bldg., Bethesda, MD 20892. Phone: Division of Basic Neurosciences and Behavioral Research, (301)443-1887; Division of Pharmacotherapies and Medical Consequences of Drug Abuse, (301)443-6173; Division of Epidemiology, Services and Prevention Research, (301)443-6504; Division of Clinical Neuroscience, Development and Behavioral Treatment, (301)443-4877; Center for Clinical Trials Network (301)443-6697; Coordinator of Research Training, SBIR, (301)443-6071. *Grants management information:* Grants Management Officer, National Institute on Drug Abuse, same address. Phone: (301)443-6710. **Internet:** "www.nih.gov"; "www.nida.nih.gov"; "www.drugabuse.gov". (Note: no field offices for this program.)

93.280 NATIONAL INSTITUTES OF HEALTH LOAN REPAYMENT PROGRAM FOR CLINICAL RESEARCHERS ("NIH LRP-CR")

Assistance: project grants (100 percent/from 2 years).

Purposes: pursuant to PHSA, to attract and retain health professionals to clinical research careers by offering extant educational loan repayment for participants agreeing to engage in clinical research at least half-time in a qualifying institution for at least two years. Research must be patient-oriented and conducted with human subjects in an out- or inpatient setting to clarify a problem in human physiology, pathophysiology or disease, or epidemiologic or behavioral studies, outcomes or health services research, or developing new technologies, therapeutic interventions, or clinical trials. Maximum annual benefit is $35,000 in loan repayment and $13,650 in federal tax reimbursement.

Eligible applicants/beneficiaries: U.S. citizens, nationals, or permanent residents with: a Ph.D., M.D., D.D.S., D.M.D., D.O., D.P.M., Pharm.D., D.C., N.D., or equivalent doctoral degree from an accredited institution; qualifying educational debt in excess of 20 percent of annual salary (half of which must be paid by program participant); a contract to conduct research supported by a nonprofit foundation, professional association, or other institution, or a U.S. or other state or local government agency. Full-time federal employees are ineligible.

Range: loan repayments per initial two-year contract period, $2,298 to $70,000; tax reimbursements, $1,040 to $32,000. **Average:** $49,000 including tax reimbursements.

Activity: new program listing in 2003. FY 06 estimate, 849 awards.

HQ: same as **93.220**. (Note: no field offices for this program.)

93.281 MENTAL HEALTH RESEARCH CAREER/SCIENTIST DEVELOPMENT AWARDS
("Research Career/Scientist Development Awards" - "'K' Awards")

Assistance: project grants (100 percent/to 5 years).

Purposes: pursuant to PHSA as amended, for research training in the problems of mental illness, behavioral disorders, and HIV/AIDS—through Mentored Research Scientist, Mentored Clinical Scientist, Mentored Scientist Development for New Minority Faculty, Mentored Patient-Oriented Career Development, Mid-career Investigator in Patient Oriented Research, Independent Scientist, and Senior Scientist Awards. Some research costs may be supported.

Eligible applicants/beneficiaries: same as for **93.271**.

Range: $50,000 to $311,000. **Average:** $141,000.

Activity: FY 06 estimate, 515 awards.

HQ same as **93.242**. (Note: no field offices for this program.)

93.282 MENTAL HEALTH NATIONAL RESEARCH SERVICE AWARDS FOR RESEARCH TRAINING

Assistance: project grants (100 percent/to 6 years).

Purposes: pursuant to PHSA as amended, for NRSA programs providing research training in mental health problems (*see Notes preceding* **93.001**). Included are: basic biomedical, clinical neuroscience, and behavioral research; epidemiology of mental disorders; etiology, description, diagnosis, and pathogenesis of mental disorders; treatment development, assessment, and evaluation; public health intervention and prevention approaches. Grants for up to six years are directed toward young scientists at the predoctoral or postdoctoral level for full-time work. Career Opportunities in Research (COR) Honors Undergraduate grants are available to minority trainees competing successfully for entry into Ph.D. degree programs. Postdoctoral students receiving support for less than 12 months must meet payback requirements through an equivalent period of research and/or teaching after training is completed.

Eligible applicants/beneficiaries: training grants—domestic public or private nonprofit organizations. Applicants for predoctoral support must have completed at least two years of graduate work and be enrolled in a doctoral degree program. Postdoctoral applicants must have a Ph.D., Psy.D., M.D., D.D.S., Sc.D., D.N.S., D.O., D.S.W., or equivalent degree. Applicants for individual awards must be U.S. citizens, nationals, or lawful permanent residents. COR Honors Undergraduate program awards—four-year IHEs or health professional schools whose enrollment is drawn substantially from ethnic groups.

Range: postdoctoral, $36,000 to $51,000; **Average:** predoctoral stipends, $21,000; COR honors undergraduate, $11,000.

Activity: FY 06 estimate, 324 individual, 187 institutional grants.

HQ: same as **93.242**. (Note: no field offices for this program.)

93.283 CENTERS FOR DISEASE CONTROL AND PREVENTION—INVESTIGATIONS AND TECHNICAL ASSISTANCE

Assistance: project grants (50-100 percent/1-3 years).

Purposes: pursuant to PHSA, Federal Mine Safety and Health Amendments Act of 1977 as amended, and Occupational Safety and Health Act of 1970, to strengthen state and local disease prevention and control programs, including communicable and chronic diseases such as tuberculosis, childhood immunization, tobacco use, diabetes, oral health, and sexually transmitted diseases. Services include investigations, epidemic aid, occupational safety and health programs, epidemiology, consultation, personnel training, responses to public health emergencies.

Eligible applicants/beneficiaries: states and their political subdivisions, local health authorities, and organizations with specialized health interests; IHES and research institutions; certain private, public nonprofit organizations.

Range: diabetes, $625,000 to $855,000 (only data provided).

Activity: not quantified specifically.

HQ: Extramural Program Teal Leader, National Center for Chronic Disease Prevention and Health Promotion, CDCP-HHS. Phone: (770)488-5549. Grants Management Branch, Procurement and Grants Office, CDCP-HHS, 2920 Brandywine Rd. - Rm.3000, Atlanta, GA 30341. Phone: (707)488-2700. **Internet:** "www.cdc.gov". (Note: no field offices for this program.)

93.284 INJURY PREVENTION PROGRAM FOR AMERICAN INDIANS AND ALASKAN NATIVES—COOPERATIVE AGREEMENTS

Assistance: project grants.

Purposes: pursuant to PHSA as amended, to provide injury prevention health services to American Indians and Alaska natives, through capacity building, implementation of interventions, and training.

Eligible applicants/beneficiaries: tribes, tribal organizations, urban Indian organizations, nonprofit organizations.

Range: capacity building, to $75,000; interventions, to $10,000.

Activity: FY 06 estimate, 33 grants.

HQ: Injury Prevention Program Manager, IHS-HHS, same address, web site as **93.123**. Phone: (301)443-1054. Grants management contact, address, web site: same as **93.123**. Phone: (301)443-5204.

93.285 NATIONAL INSTITUTES OF HEALTH PEDIATRIC RESEARCH LOAN REPAYMENT PROGRAM ("PR-LRP")

Assistance: project grants (100 percent/from 2 years).

Purposes: pursuant to PHSA as amended, to attract and retain health professionals to pediatric research careers by offering repayment of extant education loans for participants agreeing to engage in pediatric research for two years minimum in a qualifying nonprofit institution. Payments may be made up to $35,000 per year, plus $13,650 annually for tax reimbursements.

Eligible applicants/beneficiaries: same as for **93.220**, except that employment need not be at NIH.

Range: two-year contract repayment amounts, $2,916 to $70,000. **Average:** $51,000 including tax reimbursements.

Activity: new program listing in 2004. FY 06 estimate, 315.

HQ: same as **93.220**. (Note: no field offices for this program.)

93.286 DISCOVERY AND APPLIED RESEARCH FOR TECHNOLOGICAL INNOVATIONS TO IMPROVE HUMAN HEALTH

Assistance: project grants (100 percent/to 5 years).

Purposes: pursuant to PHSA, for hypothesis-, design-, technology- , or device-driven research relating to the discovery, design, development, validation, and applications of technologies in biomedical imaging and bioengineering. The program includes biomaterials, biosensors and biotransducers, nanotechnology, imaging device development, biomedical imaging technology development, image exploitation, contrast agents, informatics, and computer sciences—related to imaging, molecular and cellular imaging, bio-electrics/biomagnetics, organ and whole body imaging, screening for diseases and disorders, imaging technology assessment, and related disciplines. NRSAs, SBIR, and STTR awards are available (*see Notes preceding* **93.001**).

Eligible applicants/beneficiaries: corporations, public or private institutions, nonprofit or profit entities, individuals.

Range: $2,000 to $1,919,000. **Average:** $337,000.

Activity: FY 06 estimate, 721 awards.

HQ: National Institute of Biomedical Imaging and Bioengineering, NIH-HHS,

6707 Democracy Blvd., Bethesda, MD 20892. Phone: (301)496-9388, FAX (301)480-4973. *Business contact*: National Institute of Biomedical Imaging and Bioengineering, NIH-HHS, same address. Phone: (301)451-6773, FAX (301)480-4530. **Internet:** "www.nibib.nih.gov". (Note: no field offices for this program.)

93.288 NATIONAL HEALTH SERVICE CORPS SCHOLARSHIP PROGRAM ("NHSC Scholarship Program")

Assistance: project grants (100 percent/1-4 years).

Purposes: pursuant to PHSA, for scholarships to full-time students in the health professions. Disciplines include: allopathic and osteopathic medicine, and dentistry; family nurse practitioners; nurse midwifery; primary care physician assistants; and, other disciplines needed by the NHSC. Scholarship recipients must perform one year of service in a federally-designated health manpower shortage area for each year of support received, or a minimum of two years; however, service deferments may be granted to complete residencies in family practice, internal medicine, pediatrics, and OB/GYN. Service sites also may be located in the territories or possessions.

Eligible applicants/beneficiaries: U.S. citizens or nationals, enrolled or accepted in an accredited U.S. school.

Range: $1,128 monthly stipend plus tuition and other fees.

Activity: FY 06 estimate, 121 new, 78 continuation awards.

HQ: Division of NHSC, same address/phone, web site, grants management contact as **93.162**. (Note: no field offices for this program.)

93.289 PRESIDENT'S COUNCIL ON PHYSICAL FITNESS AND SPORTS

Assistance: advisory services/counseling.

Purposes: to provide professional assistance in the design, development, improvement, and implementation of physical fitness programs, as well as expanded exercise and sports participation opportunities for all age groups. This is accomplished through publications, media campaigns, and a web site, in coordination with school systems, government agencies, employee and industrial organizations, recreation and park departments, communications media, etc.—not with organizations with a commercial interest in physical fitness. No funding is provided.

Eligible applicants/beneficiaries: general public.

Activity: not quantified specifically.

HQ: Executive Director, President's Council on Physical Fitness and Sports, Office of Public Health and Science, OS-HHS, 200 Pennsylvania Ave. SW - Ste.738H, Washington, DC 20201-0004. Phone: (202)690-9000; Public Affairs Specialist, (202)690-5179, FAX (202)690-5211. **Internet:** "www.fitness.gov". (Note: no field offices for this program.)

93.290 NATIONAL COMMUNITY CENTERS OF EXCELLENCE IN WOMEN'S HEALTH ("CCOE")

Assistance: project grants (100 percent/to 5 years).

Purposes: for community-based programs integrating, coordinating, and strengthening linkages in women's health in the following components: comprehensive health service delivery; training for lay and professional health providers; community-based research; public education and outreach; leadership development for women as health care consumers and providers; technical assistance. Funds may be used for staffing, supplies, consultants, equipment, and travel.

Eligible applicants/beneficiaries: public or private nonprofit community-based hospitals or organizations, or community health centers serving underserved women. Note: existing programs and organizations in certain states and PR are ineligible.

Range/Average: to $150,000.

Activity: FY 04, 14 awards.

HQ: Office on Women's Health, OS-HHS, Parklawn Bldg. - Rm.16A-55, 5600 Fishers Lane, Rockville, MD 20857. Phone: (no number provided). *Grants management information*: same as **93.004**. **Internet:** "www.4woman.gov/owh/CCOE/index.htm". (Note: no field offices for this program.)

93.291 SURPLUS PROPERTY UTILIZATION
("Federal Property Assistance Program")

Assistance: sale, exchange, or donation of property and goods.

Purposes: pursuant to the Federal Property and Administrative Services Act of 1949 and SBMHAA as amended, to convey or lease surplus federal real properties needed and usable in health programs including research—e.g., land and buildings for use as hospitals, clinics, public health administration, water and sewer systems, rehabilitation programs, and facilities for the homeless. Discounts of up to 100 percent of value may be granted. Deed restrictions apply for 30 years for land, and lesser periods for improvements.

Eligible applicants/beneficiaries: states, political subdivisions and instrumentalities; tax-supported public and nonprofit health institutions.

Activity: N.A.

HQ: Director, Division of Property Management, Program Support Center, HHS, Parklawn Bldg. - Rm.5B-41, 5600 Fishers Lane, Rockville, MD 20857. Phone: (301)443-2265, FAX (202)443-0084. **Internet:** "www.psc.gov"; e-mail, "rpb@psc.gov". (Note: no field offices for this program.)

93.300 NATIONAL CENTER FOR HEALTH WORKFORCE ANALYSIS ("NCHWA")

Assistance: project grants (to 100 percent/to 5 years).

Purposes: pursuant to PHSA as amended and HPEPA, to develop information describing the health professions workforce and to analyze related issues, enabling decision-making on future directions in the field and in nursing programs in response to societal and professional needs. Funds may be used for targeted information collection and analysis, to develop a nonfederal analytic and research infrastructure, and for program evaluation and assessment.

Eligible applicants/beneficiaries: state and local governments, health professions schools, schools of nursing, academic health centers, community-based health facilities, and other public or private nonprofit entities.

Range: $50,000 to $400,000. **Average:** $250,000.

Activity: FY 06 estimate, 6 new awards.

HQ: NCHWA, Bureau of Health Professions, HRSA-HHS, 5600 Fishers Lane - Rm.9-105, Rockville, MD 20857. Phone: (301)443-5452, -6921. Grants management information, web site: same as **93.107**. (Note: no field offices for this program.)

93.301 SMALL RURAL HOSPITAL IMPROVEMENT GRANT PROGRAM

Assistance: project grants.

Purposes: pursuant to SSA, to implement "PPS"; to comply with legislative health improvement requirements; to reduce medical errors and support quality improvement.

Eligible applicants/beneficiaries: small rural hospitals, including in territories.

Range: $39,000 to $910,000. **Average:** $320,000.

Activity: FY 02-05, 1,500 awards through 46 state rural health offices.

HQ: Office of Rural Health Policy, same address/phone, grants management contact, web site as **93.155**. (Note: no field offices for this program.)

93.307 MINORITY HEALTH AND HEALTH DISPARITIES RESEARCH

Assistance: project grants (100 percent/1-5 years).

Purposes: pursuant to PHSA and SBRDEA, to support basic, clinical, social, and behavioral research; to promote research infrastructure and training; to foster emerging programs; to disseminate information—reaching out to minority and other health disparity communities. The Excellence in Partnerships for Community Outreach, Research on Health Disparities and Training Program ("Project EXPORT") provides funds to centers conducting interdisciplinary minority health and other health disparities research intervention activities. The Research Endowment Program grants provide income for: teaching programs in the biomedical and behavioral sciences and related areas; facilities; student and faculty recruitment and retention; instructional delivery systems and information technology; scholarships, tutoring and counseling programs, and student service programs. The Health Disparities Research-Loan Repayment Program (HDR-LRP) provides for repayment of existing educational loan debt incurred by health professionals engaged in research on minority health or other health disparity issues; recipients must contract for two-year periods minimum, with extensions available. The Research Infrastructure in Minority Institutions (RIMI) Program assists nondoctoral degree institutions in developing their research infrastructure through collaborations with research-intensive universities. SBIR and STIR funding also is available (*see Notes preceding* **93.001**).

Eligible applicants/beneficiaries: grants—individuals, public and private nonprofit and profit institutions. Endowment grants—"Section 736" health professions schools with net endowment assets less than 50 percent of the national average for similar institutions. HDR-LRP—U.S. citizens, nationals, or permanent residents, with qualifying outstanding educational loan debt equal to or less than 20 percentage of the applicant's annual salary, with no service obligations to federal, state, or other entities, nor judgment liens arising from federal debt.

Range: EXPORT, $100,000 to $1,629,000; endowment grants, $313,000 to $5,000,000; HDR-LRP, $3,841 to $106,000; RIMI, $406,000 to $972,000. **Average:** EXPORT, $782,000; endowment, $3,170,000; HDR-LRP, $41,000; RIMI, $862,000.

Activity: FY 06 estimates, 4 new EXPORT, 13 endowment, 150 HDR-LRP, 32 SBIR and STTR awards.

HQ: Director, Division of Research and Training Activities, National Center on Minority Health and Health Disparities (NCMHD), NIH-HHS, 6707 Democracy Blvd. - Ste.800, Bethesda, MD 20892-5465. Phone: (301)402-1366. *Grants management information*: same address/phone. **Internet:** "www.ncmhd.nih.gov". (Note: no field offices for this program.)

93.308 EXTRAMURAL LOAN REPAYMENT FOR INDIVIDUALS FROM DISADVANTAGED BACKGROUNDS CONDUCTING CLINICAL RESEARCH

Assistance: project grants (100 percent/2 to 4 years).

Purposes: pursuant to PHSA as amended, for repayment of existing educational loan debt incurred by health professionals from disadvantaged backgrounds, engaged in patient-oriented clinical research with human subjects, or research on the causes and consequences of disease in inpatient or outpatient settings. Recipients must contact for two-year periods minimum, with one-year extensions available.

Eligible applicants/beneficiaries: same as for **93.280**.

Range: for two-year period, $5,362 to $70,000 in loan repayments, plus $2,933 to $27,000 in tax reimbursements. **Average:** loans, $49,000 and $17,000 in tax payments.

Activity: FY 04 estimate, 44 awards.

HQ: NCMHD, same as **93.307**. (Note: no field offices for this program.)

93.342 HEALTH PROFESSIONS STUDENT LOANS, INCLUDING PRIMARY CARE LOANS/LOANS FOR DISADVANTAGED STUDENTS ("HPSL/PCL/LDS")

Assistance: direct loans (90 percent).

Purposes: pursuant to PHSA and HPEPA, to capitalize and administer student loan funds to provide long-term, low-interest loans to full-time students in financial need or from disadvantaged backgrounds, preparing for the health professions. Students may borrow amounts annually to cover reasonable living expenses, tuition, and educational expenses. Third- and fourth-year medical and osteopathic medicine students may borrow additional funds to repay earlier educational loans; they must agree to enter and complete a primary health care residency training program not later than four years after graduating, and to practice primary health care until the loan is paid in full. Payback service provisions apply. The loan interest rate is 5 percent.

Eligible applicants: accredited public or nonprofit private schools located in states, territories, or possessions, providing a course of study leading to a degree of doctor of medicine, dentistry, osteopathy, pharmacy, optometry, podiatry, or veterinary medicine, or B.S. in pharmacy—or an equivalent degree. For LDS, applicant schools must have student recruitment and retention programs, minority health issues curricula, clinic services for minority groups, and mentor programs.

Eligible beneficiaries: full-time students in need of a loan, enrolled or accepted in an eligible course of study—that are U.S. citizens, nationals, or permanent residents of a state or territories or possessions.

Range: $25,000 to $150,000. **Average:** $11,000.

Activity: FY 04 estimate, 12,000 students supported.

HQ: Division of Health Careers Diversity and Development, Bureau of Health Professions, HRSA-HHS, 5600 Fishers Lane - Rm.8-34, Rockville, MD 20857. Phone: (301)443-4776. **Internet:** "www.bhpr.hrsa.gov/dsa". (Note: no field offices for this program.)

93.358 ADVANCED EDUCATION NURSING TRAINEESHIPS

Assistance: project grants.

Purposes: pursuant to PHSA as amended and HPEPA, to provide financial support through traineeships for 36 months to nurses at the master's or doctoral level, preparing full-time for careers as nurse educators, clinical specialists, practitioners, administrators, midwives, public health nurses, and other approved specialties—and for nurse anesthetists for one year only.

Eligible applicants: schools of nursing, academic health centers, public or private nonprofit entities.

Eligible beneficiaries: U.S. citizens, nationals, or permanent residents licensed as registered nurses, enrolled full-time in graduate courses toward a master's degree or doctoral program.

Range: $1,000 to $235,000 **Average:** $45,000.

Activity: FY 04, 335 grants.

HQ: same as **93.247**. (Note: no field offices for this program.)

93.359 NURSE EDUCATION, PRACTICE AND RETENTION GRANTS ("NEPR")

Assistance: project grants (100 percent/to 5 years).

Purposes: pursuant to PHSA as amended and Nurse Reinvestment Act of 2002, to expand enrollment in baccalaureate nursing programs; to develop and implement internship and residency programs to encourage mentoring and the development of specialties; to provide education in new technologies including distance learning methodologies. Practice methodologies include: establishing or expanding nursing practice arrangements in non-institutional settings to demonstrate methods to improve access to primary health care in medically underserved areas; providing care for underserved populations and other high-risk groups such as the elderly, persons with HIV-AIDS, substance abusers, the homeless, and victims of domestic violence; providing managed care, quality improvement, and other skills needed to practice in existing and emerging organized health care systems; developing cultural competencies; promoting career mobility, cross training, or specialty training.

Eligible applicants/beneficiaries: collegiate schools of nursing, health care facilities, or partnerships involving academic health centers, state and local governments, and other public or private nonprofit or profit entities and community-based organizations.

Range: $25,000 to $400,000. **Average:** $250,000.

Activity: FY 05 estimate, 66 new, 103 continuation grants.

HQ: same address as **93.124**. Phone: (301)443-6193. Grants management contact, web site: same as **93.107**. (Note: no field offices for this program.)

93.361 NURSING RESEARCH

Assistance: project grants (100 percent/to 5 years).

Purposes: pursuant to PHSA as amended and SBRDEA, for clinical and basic research to establish a scientific basis for the care of individuals across the life span—from management of patients during illness and recovery to the reduction of risks for disease and disability and the promotion of healthy lifestyles, and extending to: patients, families, and care givers; special needs of at-risk and underserved populations; improving clinical care settings; translating scientific advances into cost-effective health care; bioethical issues. The Centers Program: promotes interdisciplinary research; supports research training and career development activities; concentrates research resources on selected research areas through Core Centers for Nursing Research. NRSA, SBIR, and STTR awards are available (*see Notes preceding* **93.001**).

Eligible applicants/beneficiaries: research—any corporation, public or private institution or agency, SBIR firm, or other legal entity whether profit or nonprofit; individuals. NRSA applicants must be registered professional nurses with a baccalaureate or master's degree in nursing or a related field.

Range: research, $2,000 to $748,000; NRSA, $2,352 to $514,000. **Average:** research, $339,000; NRSA, $37,000.

Activity: FY 05 estimate, 386 competing, 298 noncompeting awards.

HQ: National Institute of Nursing Research, NIH-HHS, 6707 Democracy Blvd. - Rm.710, Bethesda, MD 20817. Phone: (301)594-5962. *Grants management information*: Grants Management Officer, National Institute of Nursing Research, NIH-HHS, same address. Phone: (301)594-6869. **Internet:** "www.nih.gov/ninr". (Note: no field offices for this program.)

93.364 NURSING STUDENT LOANS ("NSL")

Assistance: direct loans (90 percent).

Purposes: pursuant to PHSA as amended and HPEPA, for nursing schools to make 5 percent interest, long-term loans to full- or half-time students with financial needs. The maximum loan in any one year is $2,500, except $4,000 for each of the final two years of study; the total borrowed may not exceed $13,000.

Eligible applicants/beneficiaries: accredited public and private nonprofit schools of nursing. Students must be U.S. citizens, nationals, or permanent residents.

Range/Average: $23,000.

Activity: FY 04, 143 nursing school awards; FY 05 no awards.

HQ: same address (Rm.8-42)/phone as **93.342**. Grants management contact, web site: same as **93.107**. (Note: no field offices for this program.)

93.389 NATIONAL CENTER FOR RESEARCH RESOURCES

Assistance: project grants (50-100 percent/1-5 years).

Purposes: pursuant to PHSA as amended and SBRDEA, for primary research to discover and develop critical resources, models, and technologies; to provide biomedical researchers with access to diverse instrumentation, technologies, basic and clinical research facilities, animal models, genetic stocks, biomaterials, and similar resources—enabling advances in biomedicine leading to lifesaving drugs, devices, and therapies. Awards are provided through program mechanisms including: Biomedical Technology Resource (BTR) grants; research project grants; Shared Instrumentation Grants (SIG); High End Instrumentation (HEI); Exploratory Grants. The Division of Clinical Research Resources helps translate scientific knowledge into effective patient care through General Clinical Research Centers (GCRC); such programs as Research Career Development, Mentored Clinical Research Scholar, National Gene Vector Laboratories (NGVL), Science Educational Partnership Award (SEPA); NRSA, SBIR, and STTR awards are available (*see Notes preceding* **93.001**). The Division of Comparative Medicine (DCM) supports National Primate Research Centers (NPRC), Biological Models and Materials Research (BMMR), and Laboratory Animal Science (LAS) programs. The Division of Research Infrastructure (DRI) supports enhancement of the research environment at minority institutions through grants supporting programs including: Research Centers in Minority Institutions (RCMI); Clinical Research Infrastructure Initiative (RCRII); Institutional Development Awards (IDeA); Animal Facilities Improvement; and, Research Facilities Improvement Program (RFIP).

Eligible applicants/beneficiaries: BTR grants—U.S. nonprofit health professional schools, other academic institutions, hospitals, state and local health agencies, research organizations. SIG and HEI awards—institutions only. GCRCs—schools, research hospitals, and other institutions. Research career development—public or private domestic, nonfederal organizations, and IHEs on behalf of candidates. SEPA—IHEs, professional organizations, school systems, scientific societies, science museums, and similar applicants. DCM—IHEs, hospitals, nonprofit and profit organizations. DRI programs—predominantly minority institutions, organizations with historically low success rate in obtaining NIH funding, and nonprofit and some profit organizations, depending on program.

Range: research projects, $100,000 to $1,103,000; research centers, $59,000 to $12,320,000; other research, $4,000 to $2,152,000; research training, $3,000 to $427,000; R&D, $5,000 to $4,147,000; construction, $1,350,000 to $7,000,000.

Activity: FY 06 estimate (representative), 126 research project, 106 clinical research center, 52 BTR, 55 CMC, 75 R&D awards.

HQ: National Center for Research Resources, NIH-HHS, Bethesda, MD 20892. Phone: BTR, (301)435-0755; Division of Clinical Research Resources, (301)435-0790; DCM, (301)435-0744; DRI, (301)435-0788. *Grants management information*: Grants Management Officer, Office of Grants and Contracts Management, National Center for Research Resources, NIH-HHS, Bethesda, MD 20892. Phone: (301)435-0844. **Internet:** "www.ncrr.nih.gov". (Note: no field offices for this program.)

93.390 ACADEMIC RESEARCH ENHANCEMENT AWARD ("AREA")

Assistance: project grants (100 percent/to 3 years).

Purposes: for small-scale health-related research projects, including feasibility or pilot studies, at educational institutions that are not major participants in other NIH programs.

Eligible applicants/beneficiaries: health professionals schools granting baccalaureate and higher degrees in the health sciences, that have not received NIH research grants totaling more than $3,000,000 per year in each of four or more of the last seven fiscal years; faculty at such schools with no active NIH research grants at the time of award.

Range/Average: $145,000.

Activity: FY 05 estimate, 214 grants.

HQ: Coordinator, Office of Extramural Programs, Office of Extramural Research, NIH-HHS, Rockledge I - Rm.3524, Bethesda, MD 20892-7910. Phone: (301)402-7989, FAX (301)480-0146. **Internet:** "www.nih.gov". (Note: no field offices for this program.)

93.392 CANCER CONSTRUCTION

Assistance: project grants (50 percent).

Purposes: pursuant to PHSA as amended, to renovate existing or build new cancer research facilities to meet basic research or clinical space requirements, or laboratory safety, biohazard containment, and animal care standards. Proposed facilities must be part of an existing or developing cancer research program, and used for grant purposes for at least 20 years.

Eligible applicants/beneficiaries: public or private nonprofit agencies, institutions, corporations, organizations, or associations—in the states, possessions, or territories.

Range/Average: $0.

Activity: FY 04-05, no awards. (Note: CFDA indicates that most funding for activities covered by this program have been obtained through **93.389**)

HQ: Associate Director/Space and Facilities Planning, Office of Management, National Cancer Institute, NIH-HHS, 6116 Executive Blvd., - Ste.600, Bethesda, MD 20892-8343. Phone: (301)496-8534. *Grants management information*: Grants Management Officer, National Cancer Institute (EPS-234), NIH-HHS, Bethesda, MD 20892. Phone: (301)496-7753. **Internet:** "www.nih.gov". (Note: no field offices for this program.)

93.393 CANCER CAUSE AND PREVENTION RESEARCH

Assistance: project grants (100 percent/to 5 years).

Purposes: pursuant to PHSA as amended and SBRDEA, for research into the causes of cancer and to develop prevention mechanisms. Programs include: epidemiology; chemical, physical, and biological carcinogenesis; nutrition; immunology; field studies and statistics; organ site. Grant funds may be used for personnel and consultants, equipment, patient costs, laboratory animals, alterations, and renovations. SBIR and STTR awards are made (*see Notes preceding* **93.001**).

Eligible applicants/beneficiaries: IHEs, hospitals, public agencies, nonprofit research institutions, or profit organizations.

Range: $36,000 to $5,024,000. **Average:** $401,000.

Activity: FY 06 estimate, 1,892 grants.

HQ: National Cancer Institute, NIH-HHS, 6130 Executive Blvd., Bethesda, MD 20892. Phone: Division of Cancer Control and Population Science (5113B), (301)496-9600; Division of Cancer Prevention (7309), (301)496-6616. **Internet:** "www.nih.gov"; "http://cancer.gov"; "http://cancercontrol.gov". (Note: no field offices for this program.)

93.394 CANCER DETECTION AND DIAGNOSIS RESEARCH

Assistance: project grants (100 percent/to 5 years).

Purposes: pursuant to PHSA as amended and SBRDEA, for research to improve cancer screening, early detection, and diagnostic techniques and methods. Grant funds may be used for patient costs, laboratory animals, equipment, renovations, alterations, personnel and consultant costs. SBIR and STTR awards are made (*see Notes preceding* **93.001**).

Eligible applicants/beneficiaries: same as for **93.393**.

Range: $60,000 to $3,826,000. **Average:** $439,000.

Activity: FY 06 estimate, 677 awards.

HQ: Associate Director, Cancer Diagnosis Program, Division of Cancer Treatment and Diagnosis, National Cancer Institute (EPN-6035A), NIH-HHS, 6130 Executive Blvd., Bethesda, MD 20892. Phone: (301)496-8639. Grants management contact, web site: same as **93.392**. (Note: no field offices for this program.)

93.395 CANCER TREATMENT RESEARCH

Assistance: project grants (100 percent/to 5 years).

Purposes: pursuant to PHSA as amended and SBRDEA, for fundamental, applied, and clinical cancer treatment research in all modes of therapy including surgery, radiotherapy, chemotherapy, and biological therapy. Supportive approaches include nutrition, stem cell and bone marrow transplantation, blood component replacement, toxicology, pharmacology. Grant funds may be used for patient costs, laboratory animals, alterations, renovations, personnel and consultant costs. SBIR and STTR awards are made (*see Notes preceding* **93.001**).

Eligible applicants/beneficiaries: same as for **93.393**.

Range: $59,000 to $6,243,000. **Average:** $468,000.

Activity: FY 06 estimate, 1,461 grants.

HQ: Division of Cancer Treatment and Diagnosis, National Cancer Institute, NIH-HHS, Bldg.31/3A44, 9000 Rockville Pike, Bethesda, MD 20892. Phone: (301)496-4291. *Grants management information*: same as **93.392**. **Internet:** "www.nci.nih.gov". (Note: no field offices for this program.)

93.396 CANCER BIOLOGY RESEARCH

Assistance: project grants (100 percent/to 5 years).

Purposes: pursuant to PHSA as amended and SBRDEA, for cancer biology research, including in the areas of nutrition, tumor biology, genetics, and immunology—toward the prevention, detection, diagnosis, and treatment of neoplastic diseases. Grant funds may be used for patient costs, laboratory animals, renovations, alterations, personnel and consultant costs. SBIR and STTR awards are made (*see Notes preceding* **93.001**).

Eligible applicants/beneficiaries: same as for **93.393**.

Range: $74,000 to $2,805,000. **Average:** $365,000.

Activity: FY 06 estimate, 1,605 grants.

HQ: Deputy Director, Division of Cancer Biology, National Cancer Institute (EPN-5050), NIH-HHS, 6130 Executive Blvd., Bethesda, MD 20892. Phone: (301)594-8782. Grants management contact, web site: same as **93.392**. (Note: no field offices for this program.)

93.397 CANCER CENTERS SUPPORT ("CCSG")

Assistance: project grants (100 percent/to 5 years).

Purposes: pursuant to PHSA as amended, to provide core funding for comprehensive and specialized cancer centers, supporting the coordination of interdisciplinary programs ranging from basic research to clinical investigation to population science. Funds may be used for professional staff, centralized shared resources and services, and recruitment. Generally, research projects are not supported as such; rather, grants enhance ongoing research.

Eligible applicants/beneficiaries: U.S. nonprofit institutions with a peer-reviewed cancer research base of $4,000,000.

Range: $16,000 to $10,371,000. **Average:** $2,903,000.

Activity: FY 06 estimate, 142 center awards.

HQ: Chief, Cancer Centers Branch, Office of Centers, Training and Resources,

NIH-HHS, 6116 Executive Blvd. - Ste.700, Bethesda, MD 20892. Phone: (301)496-8531. *Grants management information*: same address/phone as **93.392**. **Internet:** "www.nci.nih.gov/cancercenters". (Note: no field offices for this program.)

93.398 CANCER RESEARCH MANPOWER

Assistance: project grants (100 percent/to 5 years).

Purposes: pursuant to PHSA as amended, for biomedical training programs in basic, clinical, and cancer prevention research, and for fellowships to trainees under the NRSA program (*see Notes preceding* **93.001**). Cancer Education Grants are also available to promote cancer education programs. Various career awards provide short-term support for students.

Eligible applicants/beneficiaries: IHEs, hospitals, public agencies, or non-profit research institutions; U.S. citizens or permanent residents. Cancer Education Grants, career awards—profit organizations.

Range: $23,000 to $1,283,000. **Average:** $187,000.

Activity: FY 06 estimate, 995 awards.

HQ: Chief, Cancer Training Branch, National Cancer Institute, NIH-HHS, 6116 Executive Blvd. - Rm.7019, Bethesda, MD 20892. Phone: (301)496-8580. Grants management contact, web site: same as **93.392**. (Note: no field offices for this program.)

93.399 CANCER CONTROL

Assistance: project grants (100 percent/to 5 years).

Purposes: pursuant to PHSA as amended, for basic and applied research in cancer prevention and interventions. Programs include chemo-prevention; cancer communications; diet, nutrition, and physical activity; screening and early detection; biobehavioral mechanisms; tobacco control; special populations research; cancer survivorship; health services and outcomes research; surveillance research. Grant funds may be used for patient costs, renovations, alterations, personnel and consultant costs, and laboratory animals. SBIR and STTR awards are made (*see Notes preceding* **93.001**).

Eligible applicants/beneficiaries: same as for **93.393**.

Range: $15,000 to $14,905,000. **Average:** $1,078,000.

Activity: FY 06 estimate, 237 awards.

HQ: Director, Division of Cancer Prevention, National Cancer Institute, NIH-HHS, 6130 Executive Blvd, Rockville, MD 20852. Phone: (301)496-6616. Director, Division of Cancer Control and Population Science, National Cancer Institute, same address. Phone: (301)594-6776. *Grants management information*: same as **93.392**. **Internet:** same as **93.393**; *and,* "http://cancer.gov/prevention". (Note: no field offices for this program.)

93.441 INDIAN SELF-DETERMINATION
("Indian Self-Determination 638 Contracts")

Assistance: direct payments/specified use.

Purposes: pursuant to ISDEAA as amended, to provide funding for tribes to assume the management and operation of programs, functions, services, and activities for the delivery of health care to Indian people, transferred from IHS.

Eligible applicants/beneficiaries: recognized tribes.

Range: $32,000 to $25,951,000. **Average:** $1,723,000.

Activity: currently, contracts covering 3 hospitals, 97 health centers, 1 school health center, 65 health stations.

HQ: Director, Office of Tribal Programs, IHS-HHS, 801 Thompson Ave. - Ste.220, Rockville, MD 20852. Phone: (301)443-1104. **Internet:** same as **93.123**.

93.442 SPECIAL DIABETES PROGRAM FOR INDIANS (SDPI) COMPETITIVE GRANT PROGRAM ("SDPI")

Assistance: project grants (100 percent/5 years).

Purposes: for demonstration projects to implement and evaluate primary prevention of diabetes or prevention of cardiovascular disease in Indians with diabetes.

Eligible applicants/beneficiaries: IHS hospitals or clinics; tribes; Urban Indian Health Programs; consortia.

Range: $200,000 to $300,000 per year.

Activity: new program listing in 2004; 60 awards anticipated.

HQ: IHS National Diabetes Program, IHS-HHS, 5300 Homestead Rd. NE, Albuquerque, NM 87110. Phone: (505)248-4182, FAX (505)248-4188. *Grants management information*: same address as **93.123**. Phone: (301)443-5204. **Internet:** "www.ihs.gov/medicalprograms/diabetes". (Note: no field offices for this program.)

93.447 STATE HEALTH FRAUD TASK FORCE GRANTS

Assistance: project grants (100 percent).

Purposes: pursuant to PHSA, to assist and educate health professionals and persons with serious illnesses of the dangers and magnitude of health fraud; to assist law enforcement agencies in identifying and prosecuting health fraud perpetrators; to obtain and disseminate information on the use of fraudulent drugs and therapies, as well as on approved drugs and therapies; to provide health fraud information to all state health agencies and community-based organizations. Funds may be used: to hold conferences and workshops; to develop and disseminate publications; for travel.

Eligible applicants/beneficiaries: one existing state health fraud task force per state, with consideration to states in the process of organizing a task force.

Range/Average: $15,000.

Activity: new program in 2004 (CFDA on-line version).

HQ: Division of Federal-State Relations, Office of Regional Operations, Office of Regulatory Affairs, FDA-HHS (HFC-150), 5600 Fishers Lane - Rm.12-

07, Rockville, MD 20857. Phone: (301)827-2906, FAX (301)827-7107. Grants management address, web site: same as **93.103**. Phone: (301)827-7177, FAX (301)827-7101.

93.448 FOOD SAFETY AND SECURITY MONITORING PROJECT

Assistance: project grants (100 percent/1-3 years).

Purposes: pursuant to the Public Health Security and Bioterrorism Preparedness and Response Act of 2002, to expand participation in networks to enhance federal, state, tribal, and local food safety and security testing programs; to promote a continuing, reliable capability and capacity for laboratory sample analyses of foods and food products for the rapid detection and identification of toxic chemicals or toxins. Funding supports provision of supplies, personnel, facility upgrades, training, and participation in proficiency testing to establish additional reliable laboratory sample analysis capacity and analysis of surveillance samples.

Eligible applicants/beneficiaries: state, local, and tribal government food emergency response laboratories.

Range: to $350,000 annually.

Activity: new program in FY 05.

HQ: Division of Field Science, Office of Regulatory Affairs (HFC-140), FDA-HHS, 5600 Fishers Lane - Rm.1241, Rockville, MD 20857. Phone: (301)827-1026. *Grants management information*: Division of Contracts and Grants Management, FDA-HHS (HFA-500), 5600 Fishers Lane - Rm.2105, Rockville, MD 20857. Phone: (301)827-7180. **Internet:** "www.fda.gov/ora/fed_state/default.htm". (Note: contacts are with program headquarters; however, district offices are listed in Part IV for information purposes.)

93.449 RUMINANT FEED BAN SUPPORT PROJECT

Assistance: project grants (100 percent/to 3 years).

Purposes: pursuant to the Public Health Security and Bioterrorism Preparedness and Response Act of 2002, to increase surveillance throughout commercial feed channels to prevent the introduction or amplification of "BSE" in the U.S.A. Funds must supplement annual state program appropriations, and may be used for inspections or salvagers of food and feed and transporters of animal feed and ingredients, supplies, training, laboratory equipment for feed sample testing.

Eligible applicants/beneficiaries: state and tribal feed/BSE regulatory programs.

Range/Average: $250,000.

Activity: new program in FY 05.

HQ: Office of Surveillance and Compliance (HFV-235), Division of Compliance, Center for Veterinary Medicine, FDA-HHS, 7500 Standish Place - Rm.E441, Rockville, MD 20855. Phone: (301)827-0163. **Internet:** same as **93.448**. (Note: contacts are with program headquarters; however, district offices are listed in Part IV for information purposes.)

93.550 TRANSITIONAL LIVING FOR HOMELESS YOUTH

Assistance: project grants (90 percent/5 years).

Purposes: pursuant to the Runaway, Homeless, and Missing Children Protection Act of 2003, to establish and operate transitional living projects for homeless youth age 16-21, including pregnant and parenting youth—providing shelter, skills training, and support services to help them make a successful transition toward productive adulthood and self-sufficiency. Living accommodations may be provided as host family homes, agency-supervised apartments, or scattered-site units rented directly by young persons with agency support.

Eligible applicants/beneficiaries: states, localities, private nonprofit entities, and networks unless they are part of the justice system; tribal governments applying as private nonprofit agencies; community-based organizations.

Range: $100,000 to $200,000. **Average:** $195,000.

Activity: FY 06 estimate, 245 grants.

HQ: Associate Commissioner, Family and Youth Services Bureau, ACF-HHS, 330 C St, SW, Washington, DC 20447. Phone: (202)205-8102. **Internet:** "www.acf.hhs.gov/programs/fysb"; *related information,* National Clearinghouse on Families and Youth, "www.ncfy.com".

93.551 ABANDONED INFANTS

Assistance: project grants (90 percent/to 4 years).

Purposes: pursuant to the Abandoned Infants Assistance Act of 1988 as amended, for demonstration projects to prevent the abandonment of infants and young children, especially those exposed to HIV/AIDS or drug-affected, and to provide them and their families with appropriate services; to find homes for them, whether with their natural families or in foster care; to conduct residential programs; to provide respite care for families and care givers; to recruit and train service providers including foster parents, case management, and hospital staff; to provide technical assistance in planning, developing and operating projects.

Eligible applicants/beneficiaries: state, local, tribal governments; territories, possessions; nonprofit organizations; universities.

Range/Average: $100,000 to $450,000.

Activity: FY 06, 30 grants.

HQ: Children's Bureau, ACF-HHS, 330 C St. SW - Rm.2428, Washington, DC 20447. Phone: (202)205-8060. **Internet:** "www.acf.hhs.gov/programs/cb". (Note: no field offices for this program.)

93.556 PROMOTING SAFE AND STABLE FAMILIES

Assistance: formula grants (75 percent).

Purposes: pursuant to SSA as amended, Adoption and Safe Families Act of 1997, and Promoting Safe and Stable Families Amendments of 2001, for community-based family support services promoting the safety and well-being of children and families by enhancing family functioning and child development; for family preservation services for those at risk or in crisis, including reunification, adoption promotion and support, preplacement and prevention, follow-up after foster or respite care, and improving parenting skills; for infant safe haven programs.

Eligible applicants/beneficiaries: states, territories, and certain tribes.

Range: $194,000 to $48,000,000.

Activity: FY 06 estimate, 89 grants.

HQ: Deputy Associate Commissioner, Children's Bureau, ACF-HHS, 330 C St. SW, Washington, DC 20447. Phone: (202)205-8618. **Internet:** same as **93.551**.

93.557 EDUCATION AND PREVENTION GRANTS TO REDUCE SEXUAL ABUSE OF RUNAWAY, HOMELESS AND STREET YOUTH ("Street Outreach Program" - "SOP")

Assistance: project grants (90 percent/3 years).

Purposes: pursuant to VCCLEA and Runaway, Homeless, and Missing Children Protection Act of 2003, to provide street-based services to runaway, homeless, and "street youth" that have been subjected to or are at risk of sexual abuse, prostitution, or sexual exploitation—including education and outreach, emergency shelter, survival aid, case management, treatment and counseling, information and referral, crisis intervention, and follow-up support.

Eligible applicants/beneficiaries: private nonprofit agencies including non-federally recognized tribes and urban Indian organizations.

Range: $100,000 to $200,000 for three years. **Average:** $100,000.

Activity: FY 06 estimate, 128 grants.

HQ: same as **93.550**.

93.558 TEMPORARY ASSISTANCE FOR NEEDY FAMILIES ("TANF")

Assistance: formula grants.

Purposes: pursuant to SSA as amended and PRWORA, to provide cash grants, work opportunities, and other services to needy families so that their children can be cared for in their own homes; to reduce dependency by promoting job preparation, work, and marriage; to reduce and prevent out-of-wedlock pregnancies; and, to encourage the formation and maintenance of two-parent families. Permitted uses of funds are flexible, based on state plans developed in consultation with local governments and private organizations, including: assistance to low-income households in meeting home heating and cooling costs; uses permitted under the predecessor Aid to Families with Dependent Children (AFDC), Job Opportunities and Basic Skills Training (JOBS), and Emergency Assistance (EA) programs; transferring limited amounts to the Child Care and Development Block Grant (CCDBG) and Social Services Block Grant (SSBG) programs; to meet contingencies. "High Performance Bonus" and "Decrease in Illegitimacy Bonus" funds may be awarded to states meeting specific maintenance-of-effort requirements relating to superseded programs. Most families may receive assistance for no more than five years.

Eligible applicants/beneficiaries: states, tribes, specified Alaskan entities, territories.

Range: states, $21,781,000 to $3,733,818,000; tribes, $77,000 to $31,174,000.

Activity: FY 06 estimate, all states, DC, 3 territories, 65 tribal programs funded.

HQ: Director, Office of Family Assistance, ACF-HHS, Aerospace Bldg. - 5th floor, 370 L'Enfant Promenade SW, Washington, DC 20447. Phone: (no number provided). *Tribal grants,* Director, Office of Community Services, same address. Phone: (no number provided). **Internet:** "www.acf.dhhs.gov/program/ofa/"; Tribal TANF, "www.acf.dhhs.gov/programs/dts".

93.560 FAMILY SUPPORT PAYMENTS TO STATES—ASSISTANCE PAYMENTS ("Adult Programs in the Territories")

Assistance: formula grants (75 percent).

Purposes: to provide the federal share of assistance payments to aged, blind or disabled persons in Guam, PR, and VI—enabling recipients to pay for food, shelter, clothing, and other daily living needs.

Eligible applicants: Guam, PR, and VI

Eligible beneficiaries: needy aged, blind or disabled persons in Guam, PR, and VI.

Range: $700,000 to $21,000,000. **Average:** $7,700,000.

Activity: 3 awards annually.

HQ: same address, web site as **93.558**. Phone: (202)401-9275.

93.563 CHILD SUPPORT ENFORCEMENT

Assistance: formula grants (66-90 percent).

Purposes: pursuant to SSA, Title IV-D, as amended, to enforce the collection of child support obligations of absent parents, and to locate absent parents, establish paternity, and obtain child, spousal, and medical support.

Eligible applicants: state agencies, DC, PR, VI, and Guam; tribes.

Eligible beneficiaries: all TANF, foster care maintenance, and Medicaid payments applicants or recipients assigning support rights to the states; all ceasing to receive TANF payments; individuals authorizing the continuation of support enforcement services; other individuals applying for services.

Range/Average: $77,293,000.

Activity: annually, 54 grants. FY 06 estimated collections, $24 billion.

HQ: Director, Planning, Research and Evaluation Division, Office of Child Support Enforcement, ACF-HHS, 370 L'Enfant Promenade SW - 4th floor, Washington, DC 20447. Phone: (202)401-5374. **Internet:** "www.acf.dhhs.gov/programs/cse".

93.564 CHILD SUPPORT ENFORCEMENT RESEARCH

Assistance: project grants (to 95 percent/from 17 months).

Purposes: pursuant to SSA as amended, for innovative research and demonstration projects of regional and national significance to improve the administrative and services delivery aspects of child support payment enforcement programs.

Eligible applicants/beneficiaries: state agencies.

Range: $60,000 to $175,000.

Activity: FY 06 estimate, 8 new, 6 continuation grants.

HQ: Program Manager, CSE, same address/web site as **93.563**. Phone: (202) 401-3447.

93.566 REFUGEE AND ENTRANT ASSISTANCE—STATE ADMINISTERED PROGRAMS

Assistance: formula grants.

Purposes: pursuant to the Refugee Act of 1980 and Refugee Education Assistance Act of 1980 as amended, for resettlement assistance to eligible refugees from foreign countries including Cuban and Haitian entrants, asylees, victims of a severe form of trafficking, and certain Amerasians from Vietnam—including maintenance payments for up to eight months, medical and social services, English language training, case management, employment services. States may contract with other providers to offer such services.

Eligible applicants/beneficiaries: designated state agencies.

Range: $5,000 to $25,000,000; social services allocations, $75,000 to $15,000,000. **Average:** social services, $725,000.

Activity: FY 04-05, ceiling of 50,000 refugees; arrivals of 20,000 Cuban/Haitian entrants, 24,000 asylees, 500 victims of trafficking.

HQ: Office of Refugee Resettlement, ACF-HHS, 370 L'Enfant Promenade SW - 6th floor-west, Washington, DC 20447. Phone: (202)401-4579. **Internet:** "www.acf.hhs.gov/programs/orr". (Note: no field offices for this program.)

93.567 REFUGEE AND ENTRANT ASSISTANCE—VOLUNTARY AGENCY PROGRAMS

Assistance: project grants (67 percent/3 years).

Purposes: pursuant to the Refugee Act of 1980 as amended, to assist refugees in becoming self-supporting. Funds may be used for cash allowances, job training and development, English language training, case management, social services, and medical support. The federal share is up to $2,000 per refugee.

Eligible applicants/beneficiaries: private nonprofit agencies with a Reception and Placement Grant from the Department of State or DHS.

Range/Average: voluntary agencies, $6,000,000; local affiliates, $200,000.

Activity: FY 06, 9 agencies funded.

HQ: same address (8th floor-west), web site as **93.566**. Phone: (202)401-4559. (Note: no field offices for this program.)

93.568 LOW-INCOME HOME ENERGY ASSISTANCE ("LIHEAP")

Assistance: formula grants (100 percent).

Purposes: pursuant to the Community Opportunities, Accountability, Training, and Educational Services Act of 1998 (COATES), for Energy Assistance Block Grants to states, enabling them to make payments to or on behalf of eligible low-income households for their home energy costs, either heating or cooling. Recipients may also receive energy crisis and weatherization assistance. Funds may support training and technical assistance to state and other jurisdictions administering the program. Supplemental funds may be allocated to grantees that leverage nonfederal resources with their LIHEAP funds, under the Residential Energy Assistance Challenge Program (REACH).

Eligible applicants/beneficiaries: block grants—states, DC, tribal governments, specified territories. Training and technical assistance grants—states, tribes, tribal organizations, territories, public agencies, private nonprofit organizations, businesses applying jointly with private nonprofit organizations.

Range: $7,500 to $223,885,000. **Average:** $30,352,000.

Activity: FY 05 estimate, 5,000,000 households assisted.

HQ: Director, Division of Energy Assistance, Office of Community Services, ACF-HHS, 370 L'Enfant Promenade SW, Washington, DC 20447. Phone: (202)401-9351, FAX (202)401-5661. **Internet:** "www.acf.hhs.gov/programs/liheap". (Note: no field offices for this program.)

93.569 COMMUNITY SERVICES BLOCK GRANT ("CSBG")

Assistance: formula grants.

Purposes: pursuant to COATES, for anti-poverty programs and projects, conducted by local community action agencies and organizations, to eliminate the causes of poverty—including employment services, elderly services, housing, educational services, health care, emergency health and food assistance, services to migrant and seasonal farm workers, coordination of various governmental and private services.

Eligible applicants: states, territories, tribes, tribal organizations.

Eligible beneficiaries: locally-based nonprofit community anti-poverty agencies and other eligible entities providing services to low-income individuals and families.

Range: $3,342,000 to $51,752,000. **Average:** $2,545,000.

Activity: FY 05 estimate, 157 grants.

HQ: Division of State Assistance, Office of Community Services, ACF-HHS, 370 L'Enfant Promenade SW, Washington, DC 20447. Phone: (202)401-9343. **Internet:** "www.acf.hhs.gov/programs/ocs". (Note: no field offices for this program.)

93.570 COMMUNITY SERVICES BLOCK GRANT—DISCRETIONARY AWARDS ("Community Economic Development")

Assistance: project grants (100 percent/1-5 years).

Purposes: pursuant to COATES, for program activities to alleviate the causes of poverty in distressed communities. Eligible activities include those that: promote full-time permanent jobs for the poor; provide income or ownership opportunities for community members; address needs for rural water and waste-water treatment; provide character-building activities for youth, including sports and physical fitness; assist migrant and seasonal farm workers; promote electronic communication and access to program information. Special consideration is given to projects designated for Empowerment Zones or Enterprise Communities.

Eligible applicants/beneficiaries: economic development projects—private, locally initiated and governed nonprofit community development corporations.

Range: to $700,000.

Activity: FY 05 estimate, 48 awards.

HQ: Team Leader, Division of Community Discretionary Programs, Office of Community Services, ACF-HHS, 370 L'Enfant Promenade SW, Washington, DC 20447. Phone: (202)401-3446. **Internet:** same as **93.569**.

93.571 COMMUNITY SERVICES BLOCK GRANT FORMULA AND DISCRETIONARY AWARDS FOR COMMUNITY FOOD AND NUTRITION PROGRAMS

Assistance: formula grants (100 percent); direct payments/specified use (100 percent/to 17 months).

Purposes: pursuant to COATES, for community-based, local, statewide, and national food and nutrition initiatives to coordinate existing private and public resources for low-income populations. Funds must be subgranted to eligible agencies. Competitive grants may be awarded for innovative approaches, including outreach and public education activities to inform unserved or underserved target groups, including displaced workers, of available nutrition services.

Eligible applicants/beneficiaries: formula grants—states, territories, possessions. Direct grants—state and local public and private nonprofit agencies.

Range: formula grants, $715 to $363,000; direct grants, $50,000. **Average:** formula, $182,000.

Activity: FY 05 estimate, 104 grants.

HQ: same address, web site as **93.569**. Phone: *formula grants,* (202)401-9343; *direct grants,* Division of Community Discretionary Programs, (202)401-9352. (Note: no field offices for this program.)

93.575 CHILD CARE AND DEVELOPMENT BLOCK GRANT ("CCDF")

Assistance: formula grants.

Purposes: pursuant to the Child Care and Development Block Grant Act of 1990 and PRWORA, to develop and provide child care policies and fee-based services, mainly for working low-income families. Activities must include: comprehensive consumer education to parents and the public; increasing parental choice; resource and referral services; infant and toddler, and school-age services; implementation of state health, safety, licensing, and registration standards; staff training; research, demonstration, and evaluation projects; to improve resettlement services for refugees. Funds may not support any real estate or major construction costs:

Eligible applicants: states, territories, possessions; tribal governments and organizations, Alaska native and native Hawaiian organizations.

Eligible beneficiaries: children under age 13 (19 if disabled), residing with a family with income not above 85 percent of the state median, in which at least one parent has a job or attends a job training or educational program, or needing or receiving protective services.

Range: (including funding under **93.596**) states, DC, PR, $8,051,000 to $509,417,000; tribes, $23,000 to $12,445,000; territories, $1,594,000 to $4,191,000. **Average:** $90,000,000; tribes, $367,000; territories, $2,600,000.

Activity: FY 05 estimate, 321 grants.

HQ: Child Care Bureau, ACF-HHS, 330 C St. SW, Washington, DC 20447. Phone: (202)690-6782. **Internet:** "www.acf.dhhs.gov/programs/ccb".

93.576 REFUGEE AND ENTRANT ASSISTANCE—DISCRETIONARY GRANTS

Assistance: project grants (to 100 percent/1-5 years).

Purposes: pursuant to the Refugee Act of 1980 and Refugee Education Assistance Act of 1980 as amended, for projects promoting refugee self-sufficiency or addressing their special needs. Project examples: relocation from high welfare dependency areas to communities with favorable employment prospects; vocational training and employment services; microloans for start-up businesses.

Eligible applicants/beneficiaries: state and local governments, private non-profit organizations.

Range: $5,000 to $19,000,000.

Activity: FY 06, 260 discretionary, 49 targeted assistance grants.

HQ: same address, web site as **93.567**. Phone: *targeted assistance,* (202)401-4556; *discretionary,* (202)401-5363. (Note: no field offices for this program.)

93.577 EARLY LEARNING FUND
("Early Learning Opportunities Act" - "ELOA")

Assistance: project grants (75-85 percent/17 months).

Purposes: pursuant to the Early Learning Opportunities Act of 2001, to increase the availability of voluntary programs, services, and activities that support early childhood development, increase parent effectiveness, and promote the learning readiness of children to enter school ready to learn. Grant funds must be used to enhance early childhood literacy and for two or more of the following activities: (1) helping parents, caregivers, child care providers, and educators increase their capacity to facilitate the development of cognitive, language comprehension, expressive language, social-emotional, and motor skills, and promote learning readiness; (2) promoting effective parenting; (3) developing linkages among early learning programs and between early learning programs and health care services for young children; (4) increasing access to early learning opportunities for young children with special needs, including developmental delays, by facilitating coordination with other programs serving such young children; (5) increasing access to existing early learning programs by expanding the days or times that the young children are served, by expanding the number of young children served, or by improving the affordability of the programs for low-income families; (6) improving the quality of early learning through professional development and training activities, increased compensation, and recruitment and retention incentives; (7) removing barriers to early learning, including transportation difficulties and absence of programs during nontraditional work times.

Eligible applicants/beneficiaries: formula grants (if federal FY appropriation is at least $150,000,000)—states, for subgranting to eligible local councils designated by local governments, tribes, Alaska regional corporations, and native Hawaiian entities. Competitive grants (appropriations below $150,000,000)—local councils comprised of representatives of directly affected local agencies, educational resources and social services, parents, and key community leaders.

Range: $250,000 to $1,000,000. **Average:** $700,000.

Activity: FY 05 estimate, 55 awards. FY 06, no awards.

HQ: same address, web site as **93.575**. Phone: (202)690-6243.

93.579 U.S. REPATRIATION

Assistance: project grants (100 percent/5 years).

Purposes: pursuant to SSA, to provide temporary assistance, care, and treatment to citizens returning to the U.S. from foreign travel—required because of physical or mental illness, destitution, or because of war, threat of war, or a similar crisis. Assistance may include money, food, shelter, clothing, and transportation. Costs must be repaid to the federal government.

Eligible applicants/beneficiaries: international social service organizations.

Range/Average: one award, $834,000.

Activity: annual estimate, 175-200 citizens assisted.

HQ: same address, web site as **93.566**. Phone: (202)205-3589. (Note: no field offices for this program.)

93.581 IMPROVING THE CAPABILITY OF INDIAN TRIBAL GOVERNMENTS TO REGULATE ENVIRONMENTAL QUALITY

Assistance: project grants (80-100 percent/1-3 years).

Purposes: pursuant to the Native American Programs Act of 1974 as amended and Indian Environmental Regulatory Enhancement Act, to plan, develop, and implement tribal environmental regulatory programs pertaining to Indian lands, including: environmental protection regulations, ordinances, and laws; technical and operating capacity relating to both tribal and federal requirements; employee training and education; monitoring and enforcement; tribal court enforcement systems.

Eligible applicants/beneficiaries: tribes, incorporated nonfederally-recognized tribes, Alaska native villages, tribal governments, and consortia.

Range: $50,000 to $250,000.

Activity: FY 06 estimate, 16 grants.

HQ: Administration for Native Americans, ACF-HHS, 370 L'Enfant Promenade SW, Washington, DC 20447. Phone: (202)401-5590. **Internet:** "www.acf.dhhs.gov/programs/ana". (Note: no field offices for this program.)

93.582 MITIGATION OF ENVIRONMENTAL IMPACTS TO INDIAN LANDS DUE TO DEPARTMENT OF DEFENSE ACTIVITIES

Assistance: project grants (95-100 percent/1-3 years).

Purposes: pursuant to the Department of Defense Appropriations Act, to identify DOD environmental impacts to tribal lands and Alaska native villages, and to plan, develop, and implement mitigation programs.

Eligible applicants/beneficiaries: tribes; incorporated nonfederally-recognized and state-recognized tribes; Alaska native villages, tribes, or tribal governing bodies; nonprofit Alaska native regional associations or corporations or native organizations with village-specific projects; other tribal or village organizations or consortia.

Range/Average: N.A.

Activity: FY 05 estimate, 8-10 awards. FY 06 estimate, no grants.

HQ: same address, web site as **93.581**. Phone: (202)877-9262. (Note: no field offices for this program.)

93.583 REFUGEE AND ENTRANT ASSISTANCE—WILSON/FISH PROGRAMS ("Wilson/Fish Program"- "Fish/Wilson Program")

Assistance: project grants (100 percent/to 4 years).

Purposes: pursuant to the Refugee Act of 1980 and Refugee Education Assistance Act of 1980 as amended, for demonstration projects promoting early employment and self-sufficiency of refugees, including certain Amerasian immigrants, asylees, Cuban and Haitian entrants, and certified victims of a severe form of trafficking—developed as innovative approaches to the state-administered program (**93.566**), including the provision of integrated services, cash and medical assistance, social services, case management, and coordination among voluntary resettlement agencies and services providers.

Eligible applicants/beneficiaries: states, voluntary and other nonprofit resettlement organizations.

Range: $450,000 to $6,000,000. **Average:** $2,000,000

Activity: FY 06 estimate, 11 continuation projects funded.

HQ: same address, web site as **93.567**. Phone: (202)205-5933. (Note: no field offices for this program.)

93.584 REFUGEE AND ENTRANT ASSISTANCE—TARGETED ASSISTANCE GRANTS ("TAP"- "TAG")

Assistance: formula grants (100 percent/3 years).

Purposes: pursuant to the Immigration and Nationality Act, Refugee Assistance Extension Act of 1986, VTVPA, amendments, and related acts, for employment-related and other social services for refugees, asylees, Amerasians, victims of a severe form of trafficking, and entrants in areas of high concentrations and high welfare rates, including: job development and placement; on-the-job training; business and employer incentives; job-related and vocational English language training.

Eligible applicants: state agencies providing assistance to counties and similar areas.

Eligible beneficiaries: refugees admitted within last five years, Cuban and Haitian entrants, certain Amerasians from Vietnam and their accompanying family members, certified victims of a severe form of trafficking.

Range: $125,000 to $11,126,000.

Activity: FY 04, 53 counties in 28 states funded.

HQ: same as **93.566**. (Note: no field offices for this program.)

93.586 STATE COURT IMPROVEMENT PROGRAM

Assistance: formula grants (75 percent).

Purposes: to improve the performance of state courts in their role in the continuum of care provided for families and children at risk. Funds may be used to assess areas in need of correction or added attention and to implement reforms.

Eligible applicants/beneficiaries: the highest state court in each state, DC, and PR.

Range: $100,000 to $1,192,000. **Average:** $255,000.

Activity: annually, 52 grants.

HQ: Children's Bureau, ACF-HHS, 330 C St. SW, Washington, DC 20447. Phone: (202)205-8709. **Internet:** same as **93.551**.

93.587 PROMOTE THE SURVIVAL AND CONTINUING VITALITY OF NATIVE AMERICAN LANGUAGES

Assistance: project grants (80-100 percent/1-3 years).

Purposes: pursuant to the Native Americans Programs Act of 1974 as amended and Native Americans Languages Act of 1992, to plan and implement programs to assure the survival and continuing vitality of native American languages. Project examples: development of specialized school curricula; language training programs including language immersion camps and master/apprentice programs; compilation and transcription of oral narratives.

Eligible applicants/beneficiaries: same as for **93.582** and incorporated non-profit multipurpose community-based Indian organizations; urban Indian centers; public and private nonprofit agencies, tribally controlled community colleges, postsecondary vocational institutions, and IHEs serving native Hawaiians or native peoples from Guam, Samoa, Palau, or Northern Marianas; national or regional incorporated native American organizations.

Range: planning, to $105,000; implementation, to $175,000.

Activity: FY 06 estimate, 24 grants.

HQ: Program Operations Division, same address, web site as **93.581**. Phone: (202)690-5787. (Note: no field offices for this program.)

93.590 COMMUNITY-BASED CHILD ABUSE PREVENTION GRANTS

Assistance: formula grants.

Purposes: pursuant to the Child Abuse Prevention and Treatment Act as amended, to establish, operate, or expand statewide networks of community-based family resource programs to prevent child abuse and neglect.

Eligible applicants: states, some territories and possessions.

Eligible beneficiaries: children, families; organizations dealing with family resource programs.

Range: $175,000 to $4,000,000.

Activity: annually, 70 grants.

HQ: Office on Child Abuse and Neglect, ACF-HHS, 330 C St. SW, Washington, DC 20447. Phone: (202)205-2629. **Internet:** same as **93.551**; "www.friendsnrc.org". (Note: no field offices for this program.)

93.591 FAMILY VIOLENCE PREVENTION AND SERVICES/GRANTS FOR BATTERED WOMEN'S SHELTERS—GRANTS TO STATE DOMESTIC VIOLENCE COALITIONS

Assistance: formula grants (100 percent).

Purposes: pursuant to the Family Violence Prevention and Services Act, Child Abuse Prevention, Adoption and Family Services Act, VCCLEA, VTVPA, Child Abuse Prevention and Treatment Act, Keeping Children and Families Safe Act of 2003, amendments, and other acts, for prevention and intervention activities conducted by state domestic violence coalitions, including: program coordination with and technical assistance to local programs and services providers; encouraging appropriate responses to domestic violence cases; working with judicial and law enforcement officials to develop appropriate responses to child custody and visitation issues involving domestic violence; public education campaigns; training; related activities.

Eligible applicants/beneficiaries: statewide nonprofit coalitions in states, some territories and possessions.

Range/Average: states, $238,000.

Activity: annually, 53 grants.

HQ: Family and Youth Services Bureau, ACF-HHS, 330 C St. SW, Washington, DC 20447. Phone: (202)401-5529. **Internet:** "www.acf.hhs.gov/programs/fysb". (Note: no field offices for this program.)

93.592 FAMILY VIOLENCE PREVENTION AND SERVICES/GRANTS FOR BATTERED WOMEN'S SHELTERS—DISCRETIONARY GRANTS

Assistance: project grants (varying match/1-5 years).

Purposes: pursuant to the Family Violence Prevention and Services Act, Child Abuse Prevention, Adoption and Family Services Act, Child Abuse Prevention and Treatment Act, VCCLEA, VTVPA, Keeping Children and Families Safe Act of 2003, amendments, and other acts, to prevent family violence through projects and activities intended to improve the design, delivery, and coordination of services addressing the problem. Project activities may involve information gathering, research, demonstrations, evaluation, establishing specialized national resource centers, a national hotline, and public education.

Eligible applicants/beneficiaries: public and private nonprofit agencies, tribes, Alaska native villages or regional corporations.

Range: $30,000 to $1,495,000. **Average:** $260,000.

Activity: FY 06 estimate, 44 grants.

HQ: same as **93.591**. (Note: no field offices for this program.)

93.593 JOB OPPORTUNITIES FOR LOW-INCOME INDIVIDUALS ("JOLI Program")

Assistance: project grants (to 100 percent/to 3 years).

Purposes: pursuant to the Family Support Act as amended and PRWORA, to create new permanent employment and business opportunities for TANF recipients and others through: participant training, supportive, and follow-up activities; expansion of existing businesses through technical and financial assistance; self-employment and micro-enterprises; new business ventures; nontraditional employment initiatives leading to self-sufficiency. Projects must: involve cooperative relationships with local TANF agencies, involving supportive services and client referrals, with encouragement to establish partnerships with child support enforcement agencies; include a strong evaluation component.

Eligible applicants: nonprofit IRS Section 501(c) organizations including community development corporations and charitable and tribal organizations.

Eligible beneficiaries: TANF recipients and other low-income individuals.

Range to $500,000. **Average:** $437,000.

Activity: FY 05 estimate, 10 grants.

HQ: same address as **93.570**. Phone: (202)401-5483. **Internet:** "www.acf.hhs.gov/programs/ocs/index.html". (Note: no field offices for this program.)

93.594 TRIBAL WORK GRANTS ("Native Employment Works" - "NEW")

Assistance: formula grants.

Purposes: pursuant to SSA as amended, to allow tribes to operate programs to make work available to their members.

Eligible applicants/beneficiaries: tribes or Alaska native organizations that conducted JOBS programs in FY 95.

Range: $5,187 to $1,753,000. **Average:** $98,000.

Activity: FY 06 estimate, 78 grants.

HQ: Division of Tribal TANF Management, Office of Family Assistance, ACF-HHS, Aerospace Bldg. - 5th floor, 370 L'Enfant Promenade SW, Washington, DC 20447. Phone: (202)401-5308. **Internet:** "www.acf.hhs.gov/programs/".

93.595 WELFARE REFORM RESEARCH, EVALUATIONS AND NATIONAL STUDIES

Assistance: project grants (75 percent/1-5 years).

Purposes: pursuant to PRWORA, for research on the benefits, effects, and costs of various welfare reform interventions; for studies on the effects of different programs on welfare dependency, illegitimacy, teen pregnancy, employment rates, child well-being, and related areas; for demonstrations; for analyses and evaluations.

Eligible applicants/beneficiaries: governmental entities, IHEs, nonprofit and profit organizations.

Range: $10,000 to $6,000,000. **Average:** $500,000.

Activity: not quantified specifically.

HQ: Office of Planning, Research and Evaluation, ACF-HHS, Aerospace Bldg. - 7th floor, 370 L'Enfant Promenade SW, Washington, DC 20447. Phone: (202)401-4535, FAX (202)205-3598. **Internet:** "www.acf.hhs.gov/programs/opre".

93.596 CHILD CARE MANDATORY AND MATCHING FUNDS OF THE CHILD CARE AND DEVELOPMENT FUND
("Child Care and Development Fund" - "CCDF")

Assistance: formula grants (matching/2 years).

Purposes: pursuant to SSA, PRWORA, Child Care and Development Block Grant Act of 1990, and amendments, to assist low-income families with child care by: developing flexible child care programs and policies; promoting choices by working parents in selecting suitable child care; providing consumer education information to help parents make informed child care choices; implementing state health, safety, licensing, and registration standards. At least 70 percent of grant funds must be used to provide child care assistance to families: receiving assistance under a state TANF program; attempting to work to "transition" off temporary assistance programs through work activities, or at risk of becoming dependent on temporary assistance programs. The matching rate is the same as under the Medicaid program.

Eligible applicants: states, DC, tribal governments and organizations, Alaska native corporations.

Eligible beneficiaries: same as for **93.575**.

Range/Average: included in **93.575**.

Activity: FY 06 estimate, 302 grants.

HQ: same as **93.575**.

93.597 GRANTS TO STATES FOR ACCESS AND VISITATION PROGRAMS

Assistance: project grants (90 percent).

Purposes: pursuant to SSA, for programs that support and facilitate access and visitation by noncustodial parents with their children. Eligible project activities include mediation, counseling, education, development of parenting plans, visitation enforcement, and development of guidelines for visitation and alternative custody arrangements.

Eligible applicants/beneficiaries: states, DC, PR, VI, Guam.

Range/Average: N.A.

Activity: FY 06 estimate, 62 grants.

HQ: Director, Consumer Services, Office of Child Support Enforcement, same address, web site as **93.563**. Phone: (202)401-9373.

93.598 SERVICES TO VICTIMS OF A SEVERE FORM OF TRAFFICKING

Assistance: project grants.

Purposes: pursuant to VTVPA, to provide victims of a severe form of trafficking access to benefits and services to the same extent as refugees, including case management, referrals and funded cash, medical assistance, special mental health and other services, and community and local outreach.

Eligible applicants: state and local governments; private nonprofit organizations.

Eligible beneficiaries: adults and children certified by HHS as victims of a severe form of trafficking, in consultation with the Attorney General.

Range: $57,000 to $400,000.

Activity: FY 04, 500 victims certified as eligible for assistance.

HQ: same address, web site as **93.566**. Phone: (866)401-5510. (Note: no field offices for this program.)

93.599 CHAFEE EDUCATION AND TRAINING VOUCHERS PROGRAM ("Chafee ETV")

Assistance: formula grants (80 percent).

Purposes: pursuant to SSA, Chafee Foster Care Independence Act of 1999, and Promoting Safe and Stable Families Amendments of 2001, to make vouchers available for education and training, including postsecondary, to youths that have aged out of foster care or that have been adopted from the foster care system after age 16 until they reach age 23—as long as they are participating in the Chafee Foster Care Independence Program (program **93.674**) at age 21. Vouchers in amounts up to $5,000 per year may be used for the cost of attending an IHE.

Eligible applicants: state governments, DC, PR.

Eligible beneficiaries: youth otherwise eligible for services under program **93.674**, including those who have left foster care because they attained age 18 and not yet attained age 21; youth likely to remain in foster care until age 18.

Range: $70,000 to $9,000,000. **Average:** $847,000.

Activity: new program in FY 03. Annually, 52 grants.

HQ: Children's Bureau, ACF-HHS, 330 C St. SW, Washington, DC 20447. Phone: (202)205-8086. **Internet:** same as **93.551**.

93.600 HEAD START

Assistance: project grants (80-100 percent).

Purposes: pursuant to COATES, to promote school readiness through Head Start Programs offering comprehensive health, education, nutrition, social, and other services to economically disadvantaged preschool children, including children of migratory workers and on Indian reservations; to involve parents in the program. Training and technical assistance grants may be awarded to Head Start agencies and to agencies providing services. At least 90 percent of project enrollment must be from families with incomes below OMB poverty guidelines or receiving public assistance; at least 10 percent must be available for children with disabilities.

Eligible applicants: local governments, tribes, public or private nonprofit and profit agencies. Subcontracts with other agencies are permitted.

Eligible beneficiaries: children from birth until their entry into school systems.

Range: $134,000 to $207,974,000. **Average:** $4,075,000.

Activity: FY 06 estimate, 1,604 grants.

HQ: Head Start Bureau, ACF-HHS, 330 C St. SW, Washington, DC 20447. Phone: (202)205-8572. **Internet:** "www2.acf.dhhs.gov/programs/hsb".

93.601 CHILD SUPPORT ENFORCEMENT DEMONSTRATIONS AND SPECIAL PROJECTS

Assistance: project grants (100 percent/17 weeks).

Purposes: pursuant to SSA and PRWORA, for regional and national projects and demonstrations to improve the effectiveness of child support enforcement efforts on the regional and national levels, advancing the requirements of PRWORA.

Eligible applicants/beneficiaries: state human services umbrella and other state and local public agencies; nonprofit organizations; tribes and tribal organizations; consortia.

Range: $100,000 to $400,000. **Average:** $190,000.

Activity: FY 06 estimate, 12 grants.

HQ: Deputy Director, Division of State, Tribal, and Local Assistance, Office of Child Support Enforcement, ACF-HHS, 370 L'Enfant Promenade SW - 4th floor, Washington, DC 20447. Phone: (202)401-4849. **Internet:** same as **93.563**.

93.602 ASSETS FOR INDEPENDENCE DEMONSTRATION PROGRAM ("IDA Demonstration Program")

Assistance: project grants (50 percent/5 years).

Purposes: pursuant to the Assets for Independence Act and COATES as amended, for demonstration projects to establish and evaluate the social, civic, psychological, and economic effects of providing incentives to individuals and families with limited incomes to save a portion of their earned income to: obtain a postsecondary education; purchase first homes; capitalize small businesses; transfer assets to IDAs of family members. 85 percent of federal and matching funds must be used to match deposits in Individual Development Accounts (IDAs) by participants. The maximum federal contribution is $2,000 per individual and $4,000 per household.

Eligible applicants: national, state, regional, and community-based organizations; tax-exempt nonprofit organizations; state or local agencies; tribal governments applying jointly with nonprofit organizations; low-income credit unions; community development financial institutions collaborating with community-based organizations.

Eligible beneficiaries: individuals and members of households eligible for TANF or with adjusted incomes not exceeding the earned income amount specified in Section 32 of the Internal Revenue Code. Maximum net worth provisions apply.

Range: to $1,000,000. **Average:** $350,000.

Activity: FY 06 estimate, 55 grants.

HQ: Office of Community Services, ACF-HHS, 370 L'Enfant Promenade SW, Washington, DC 20447. Phone: (202)401-4626. **Internet:** "www.acf.hhs.gov/assetbuilding"; e-mail, "AFIProgram@acf.hhs.gov". (Note: no field offices for this program.)

93.603 ADOPTION INCENTIVE PAYMENTS

Assistance: formula grants.

Purposes: pursuant to SSA and Adoption Promotion Act of 2003, to provide incentives to states to increase the annual number of foster child, special needs, and older child adoptions. Funds may also be used for post-adoption services to children.

Eligible applicants/beneficiaries: states, DC, PR.

Range: $4,000 per foster child adoption, and $2,000 per special needs child adoption; states, $16,000 to $3,492,000. **Average:** $559,000.

Activity: FY 04, 32 grants.

HQ: Division of Program Implementation, Children's Bureau, ACF-HHS, 330 C St. SW, Washington, DC 20447. Phone: (202)205-8273. **Internet:** same as **93.551**.

93.604 ASSISTANCE FOR TORTURE VICTIMS ("Torture Victims")

Assistance: project grants.

Purposes: pursuant to the Torture Victims Relief Act of 1998 and amendments, to provide services and rehabilitation for victims of torture, with special emphasis on applicants for asylum. Eligible uses of funds include treatment, social and legal services, providing research and training for care providers.

Eligible applicants/beneficiaries: public or private organizations and institutions.

Range: $151,000 to $440,000.

Activity: FY 04-05, 27 grants serving 5,500 victims.

HQ: same address (8th floor), web site as **93.566**. Phone: (202)205-5933, FAX (202)401-5772. (Note: no field offices for this program.)

93.612 NATIVE AMERICAN PROGRAMS

Assistance: project grants (80-100 percent/1-3 years).

Purposes: pursuant to the Native American Programs Act of 1974, OAA, and amendments, to improve the social and economic conditions of native Americans within their communities. Funds may be used for such activities as: governance projects; economic and social development projects; financial assistance; training and technical assistance; research, demonstration, and evaluation.

Eligible applicants/beneficiaries: public and private nonprofit agencies including governing bodies of tribes on federal and state reservations, Alaska native villages and regional corporations, agencies serving Hawaii natives, organizations in urban or rural non-reservation areas, native American Pacific Islanders.

Range: tribal, urban grants, $50,000 to $500,000. **Average:** tribal, $125,000.

Activity: FY 06 estimate, 89 grants.

HQ: same as **93.587**. (Note: no field offices for this program.)

93.613 PRESIDENT'S COMMITTEE FOR PEOPLE WITH INTELLECTUAL DISABILITIES
("PCPID")

Assistance: advisory services/counseling.

Purposes: to advise and assist the President on matters pertaining to persons with intellectual disabilities, including mental retardation, through studies and coordination of federal, state, and local efforts; to provide public information; to mobilize support for related activities.

Eligible applicants/beneficiaries: general public.

Activity: not quantified specifically.

HQ: Executive Director, President's Committee for People with Intellectual Disabilities, ACF-HHS, Washington, DC 20447. Phone: (202)619-0634. **Internet:** "www.acf.dhhs.gov/programs/pcpid". (Note: no field offices for this program.)

93.616 MENTORING CHILDREN OF PRISONERS
("MCP")

Assistance: project grants (75 percent/3 years).

Purposes: pursuant to the Safe and Stable Families Act of 2001, to establish or expand and operate programs using a network of public and private entities to provide mentoring services for children of prisoners.

Eligible applicants/beneficiaries: state or local government units, tribes and tribal organizations, private nonprofit community groups—in areas with substantial numbers of children or prisoners.

Range: $100,000 to $1,000,000.

Activity: new program in FY 03. FY 05-06, 233 grants.

HQ: same as **93.550**. (Note: no field offices for this program.)

93.617 VOTING ACCESS FOR INDIVIDUALS WITH DISABILITIES—GRANTS TO STATES
("Election Assistance for Individuals with Disabilities-" - "EAID")

Assistance: formula grants.

Purposes: pursuant to the Help America Vote Act, to provide greater accessibility to polling places for persons with disabilities. Funds may be used to:

make polling places accessible, including the path of travel, entrances, exits, and voting areas of each polling place; provide opportunity for voting access and participation, including privacy and independence; train election officials, poll workers, and election volunteers in elections for federal office; provide appropriate information dissemination.

Eligible applicants/beneficiaries: states, territories and possessions.

Range: from $100,000.

Activity: N.A.

HQ: Administration on Developmental Disabilities, ACF-HHS, 200 Independence Ave. SW, Washington, DC 20201. Phone: (202)690-5962. **Internet:** "www.acf.hhs.gov/programs.add". (Note: no field offices for this program.)

93.618 VOTING ACCESS FOR INDIVIDUALS WITH DISABILITIES—GRANTS FOR PROTECTION AND ADVOCACY SYSTEMS

Assistance: formula grants; project grants.

Purposes: pursuant to the Help America Vote Act, to ensure full participation by persons with disabilities in the electoral process. Funds may be used to improve access and participation, and to provide training and technical assistance to protection and advocacy systems.

Eligible applicants/beneficiaries: states, territories and possessions with an approved Protection and Advocacy System in place.

Range: territories, from $35,000; states, from $70,000.

Activity: new program in FY 03.

HQ: same as **93.617**. (Note: no field offices for this program.)

93.623 BASIC CENTER GRANT ("BCP")

Assistance: project grants (to 90 percent/to 3 years).

Purposes: pursuant to the Runaway, Homeless, and Missing Children Protection Act of 2003, to establish or strengthen the operation of locally controlled, community-based centers for runaway and homeless youth and their families. Grants fund services must be delivered outside the law enforcement, child welfare, mental health, and juvenile justice systems. Centers provide services in residential settings normally accommodating no more than 20 youth, including activities such as individual and family counseling, temporary shelter for youth under age 18 for up to 15 days, food, clothing, transitional and after-care assistance. The program funds a national toll-free communication system, personnel training, research, demonstration, and service projects.

Eligible applicants/beneficiaries: states, localities, private entities, and coordinated networks of such agencies operating outside the law enforcement structure or juvenile justice system; Indian organizations.

Range: $100,000 to $200,000. **Average:** $128,000.

Activity: FY 06 estimate, 345 grants.

HQ: same as **93.550**.

93.630 DEVELOPMENTAL DISABILITIES BASIC SUPPORT AND ADVOCACY GRANTS
("State Councils on Developmental Disabilities and Protection and Advocacy Systems")

Assistance: formula grants (75-100 percent).

Purposes: pursuant to the Mental Retardation Facilities and Construction Act of 1963, Developmental Disabilities Assistance and Bill of Rights Act, and amendments, to plan and provide comprehensive and coordinated services to developmentally disabled persons, enabling them to reach their maximum potential in the community and to assure the protection of their legal and human rights. Funds may support state and local costs of planning and administration of services.

Eligible applicants: designated state agencies, territories and possessions.

Eligible beneficiaries: persons with developmental disabilities attributable to a mental and/or physical impairment manifested before age 22, resulting in functional limitations and reflecting lifelong need for services in at least three of seven functional areas—including self-care, receptive and expressive language, learning, mobility, self-direction, capacity for independent living, economic self-sufficiency; infants and children to age 9 showing high probability of a developmental disability.

Range/Average: basic support, $450,000; protection and advocacy, $200,000.

Activity: annually, 112 grants.

HQ: same address, web site as **93.617**. Phone: (202)401-6970.

93.631 DEVELOPMENTAL DISABILITIES PROJECTS OF NATIONAL SIGNIFICANCE

Assistance: project grants (varying match).

Purposes: pursuant to the Mental Retardation Facilities and Construction Act of 1963, Developmental Disabilities Assistance and Bill of Rights Act, and amendments, to increase and support the independence, productivity, and integration into communities of developmentally disabled persons. Grants support such activities as family support activities, education of policy makers, data collection and analysis, federal inter-agency initiatives, technical assistance including for developing information and referral systems, improved supportive services, services to minorities with disabilities, transitional services for youth, nationally significant projects.

Eligible applicants/beneficiaries: state, local, public, or private nonprofit agencies and organizations.

Range: $50,000 to $300,000.

Activity: FY 06 estimate, 53 grants.

HQ: same address, web site as **93.617**. Phone: (202)690-5985.

93.632 UNIVERSITY CENTERS FOR EXCELLENCE IN DEVELOPMENTAL DISABILITIES EDUCATION, RESEARCH, AND SERVICE ("UCEDD")

Assistance: project grants (75-90 percent/5 years).

Purposes: pursuant to the Mental Retardation Facilities and Construction Act of 1963, Developmental Disabilities Assistance and Bill of Rights Act, and amendments, to administer and operate university- or college-related programs for the developmentally disabled, including: interdisciplinary training for personnel; basic and applied research; information dissemination; community demonstration projects including direct services to developmentally disabled persons—e.g., family and individual support, educational, vocational, clinical, health and prevention services.

Eligible applicants/beneficiaries: public or nonprofit entities associated with or integral parts of IHEs.

Range/Average: $480,000.

Activity: FY 06 estimate, 64 grants.

HQ: same address, web site as **93.617**. Phone: (202)690-5982.

(Note: no field offices for this program.)

93.643 CHILDREN'S JUSTICE GRANTS TO STATES

Assistance: formula grants (100 percent/2 years).

Purposes: pursuant to the Child Abuse Prevention and Treatment Act, VOCA, and amendments, for improved response to, and investigation and prosecution of, child abuse and neglect cases, particularly cases of sexual abuse and exploitation—including experimental, model, and demonstration programs, and legal and procedural reforms. Projects must be designed to achieve reforms in such areas as: investigative, administrative, and judicial handling of cases; inter-jurisdictional matters, with emphasis on reducing trauma to victims and their families; performance of court-appointed attorneys and guardians.

Eligible applicants/beneficiaries: states, territories, possessions.

Range: $50,000 to $1,900,000.

Activity: FY 06 estimate, grants to 50 states, DC, 4 territorial governments.

HQ: same address **93.590**. Phone: (202)205-8714. **Internet:** same as **93.551**.

(Note: no field offices for this program.)

93.645 CHILD WELFARE SERVICES—STATE GRANTS

Assistance: formula grants (75 percent).

Purposes: pursuant to SSA as amended, for state, local, and tribal child welfare services to enable children in need of welfare services to remain in their own homes or to provide alternative permanent homes. Grants may cover costs of: personnel providing protective services; licensing and standard-setting for private child care organizations; return of runaway children; prevention and reunification services.

Eligible applicants/beneficiaries: state agencies, tribes, territories and possessions.

Range: $165,000 to $33,240,000.

Activity: annually, 194 grants awarded.

HQ: Children's Bureau, ACF-HHS, P.O. Box 1182, Washington, DC 20013. Phone: (202)401-0406. **Internet:** same as **93.551**.

93.647 SOCIAL SERVICES RESEARCH AND DEMONSTRATION

Assistance: project grants (75 percent/1-3 years).

Purposes: pursuant to SSA as amended, for innovative research projects to test, demonstrate, and evaluate new concepts in social services for children and families.

Eligible applicants/beneficiaries: governmental entities, IHEs, nonprofit or profit organizations.

Range: $10,000 to $6,000,000. **Average:** $500,000.

Activity: FY 06 estimate, 45 grant awards.

HQ: same address/phone, web site as **93.595**. *And:* Compassion Capital Fund, Office of Community Services, ACF-HHS, 370 L'Enfant Promenade SW, Washington, DC 20447. Phone: (202)260-2583.

93.648 CHILD WELFARE SERVICES TRAINING GRANTS

Assistance: project grants (to 100 percent).

Purposes: pursuant to SSA as amended, for programs to train current and prospective child welfare program personnel, including traineeship stipends. Previous projects examples include professional education for child welfare practices and cross-program training.

Eligible applicants/beneficiaries: IHEs.

Range: $75,000 to $350,000. **Average:** $155,000.

Activity: FY 06 estimate, 47 grants.

HQ: same address, web site as **93.551**. Phone: (202)205-8405.

93.652 ADOPTION OPPORTUNITIES

Assistance: project grants (to 100 percent/1-5 years).

Purposes: pursuant to the Child Abuse Prevention and Treatment and Adoption Reform Act of 1978 as amended, for projects to improve adoption practices including: adoption education and training; recruitment on the national level; child placement in kinship care arrangements, pre-adoptive, or adoptive homes; operation of national center for special needs adoption; minority recruitment, post-legal adoption services; improving the placement rate in foster care; barrier elimination across jurisdictional boundaries.

Eligible applicants/beneficiaries: state and local government entities, public and private nonprofit licensed agencies, community-based organizations, adoptive family groups, minority groups, sectarian institutions.

Range: $200,000 to $700,000. **Average:** $250,000.

Activity: FY 06 estimate, 54 grants.

HQ: same address, web site as **93.551**. Phone: (202)205-8354. (Note: no field offices for this program.)

93.658 FOSTER CARE—TITLE IV-E

Assistance: formula grants (50-83 percent).

Purposes: pursuant to SSA as amended, Title IV-E, for the operation of state and local foster child programs, including payments on behalf of the children, and training and administrative costs.

Eligible applicants/beneficiaries: states, DC, PR.

Range: $2,250,000 to $1,275,000,000.

Activity: annually, 54 grants, 233,000 children receiving monthly benefits.

HQ: same address, web site as **93.603**. Phone: (202)260-7684.

93.659 ADOPTION ASSISTANCE

Assistance: formula grants.

Purposes: pursuant to SSA as amended, Title IV-E, for adoption subsidy payments for adopted children with special needs. The subsidies are available from the time of adoption placement to age 18 (or older for certain handicaps).

Eligible applicants: states, DC, PR.

Eligible beneficiaries: children that are recipients of or eligible for AFDC, AFDC-FC, or SSI, and have special needs, e.g., a special factor or condition requiring adoption assistance for placement.

Range: $218,000 to $303,700,000.

Activity: annually, 52 grants; FY 06 estimate, 369,000 children assisted monthly.

HQ: same as **93.603**.

93.667 SOCIAL SERVICES BLOCK GRANT

Assistance: formula grants (100 percent).

Purposes: pursuant to SSA, Jobs Training Bill, Medicaid and Medicare Patient and Program Act of 1987, Family Support Act of 1988, and amendments, to provide social services to: prevent, reduce, or eliminate dependency; achieve or maintain self-sufficiency; prevent neglect, abuse, or exploitation of persons; prevent or reduce inappropriate institutional care; enable individuals to secure admission or referral for institutional care when other forms of care are inappropriate; supplement comprehensive community revitalization in designated Empowerment Zones and Enterprise Communities (EZ/EC). Funds may be used for activities relating to preventive health, mental health, substance abuse, and maternal and child health, as well as low-income home energy assistance. Ineligible uses include cash payments for subsistence or for room and board, medical care, health or prison facility social services, educational services, and most real estate costs—unless specifically approved by HHS.

Eligible applicants/beneficiaries: states, territories and possessions.

Range: $56,000 to $207,311,000. **Average:** $30,263,000.

Activity: annually, 57 grants.

HQ: same address as **93.569**. Phone: (202)401-2333. **Internet:** "www.acf.hhs.gov/programs/ocs/ssbg".

93.669 CHILD ABUSE AND NEGLECT STATE GRANTS

Assistance: formula grants (100 percent/to 5 years).

Purposes: pursuant to the Child Abuse Prevention, Adoption and Family Services Act of 1988, JJDPA, Child Abuse Prevention and Treatment Act,

Keeping Children and Families Safe Act of 2003, amendments, and other acts, to operate, improve, and augment state child protective systems, including such activities as: reporting, investigation, management, legal representation, and prosecution of cases of child abuse and neglect; research; treatment of and services to abused children and their families; personnel training; public education and information; community-based programs.

Eligible applicants/beneficiaries: same as for **93.667**.

Range: $55,000 to $3,367,000. **Average:** $369,000.

Activity: annually, 57 grants.

HQ: same as **93.586**.

93.670 CHILD ABUSE AND NEGLECT DISCRETIONARY ACTIVITIES

Assistance: project grants (varying match/to 5 years).

Purposes: pursuant to the Child Abuse Prevention and Treatment Act and Child Abuse Prevention, Adoption and Family Services Act of 1988 as amended, and Keeping Children and Families Safe Act of 2003, for research, demonstration service improvement, information dissemination, and technical assistance projects—toward the prevention, identification, assessment, and treatment of child abuse and neglect.

Eligible applicants/beneficiaries: states, local governments, public and private nonprofit agencies and organizations, tribes.

Range: $80,000 to $1,988,000. **Average:** $300,000.

Activity: FY 06 estimate, 50 grants.

HQ: same address, web site as **93.551**. Phone: (202)205-8172. (Note: no field offices for this program.)

93.671 FAMILY VIOLENCE PREVENTION AND SERVICES/GRANTS FOR BATTERED WOMEN'S SHELTERS—GRANTS TO STATES AND INDIAN TRIBES

Assistance: formula grants (65-80 percent).

Purposes: pursuant to the Family Violence Prevention and Services Act, Child Abuse Prevention, Adoption and Family Services Act of 1988, VCCLEA, VTVPA, Keeping Children and Families Safe Act of 2003, amendments, and other laws, for the prevention of family violence; to provide immediate shelter and other assistance to victims and their dependents. The program emphasizes community-based projects that provide shelter, counseling, advocacy, and self-help services to victims and their children—without income eligibility standards. Funds may not be used to make payments to victims.

Eligible applicants/beneficiaries: states, tribes, territories and possessions.

Range: states, $719,000 to $7,204,000; tribes, $20,000 to $2,013,000.

Activity: FY 06 estimate, 226 awards.

HQ: same as **93.591**. (Note: no field offices for this program.)

93.674 CHAFEE FOSTER CARE INDEPENDENCE PROGRAM ("CFCIP")

Assistance: formula grants (80 percent).

Purposes: pursuant to SSA as amended and Foster Care Independence Act of 1999, and Promoting Safe and Stable Families Amendments of 2001, for state and local programs designed to assist youth receiving foster care maintenance payments to make the transition to independent living. Funds may be used for skill development, mentoring activities, postsecondary education, supportive services, or training related to program purposes, including voucher payments.

Eligible applicants: states, DC, PR.

Eligible beneficiaries: youth age 18 and over, currently or formerly receiving foster care payments, until they reach age 21.

Range: $500,000 to $26,757,000. **Average:** $2,652,000.

Activity: annually, 53 grants.

HQ: same as **93.599**.

93.676 UNACCOMPANIED ALIEN CHILDREN PROGRAM

Assistance: project grants.

Purposes: pursuant to the Homeland Security Act of 2002, to develop plans and policies to coordinate and implement care and placement services for unaccompanied alien children in federal custody by reason of their immigration status.

Eligible applicants/beneficiaries: state and local governments, private non-profit and profit organizations.

Range: $235,000 to $5,300,000.

Activity: new program in FY 03. FY 06 estimate, 22 grants, 16 contracts, 5 interagency agreements.

HQ: Director, Division of Unaccompanied Children Services, same address (8th floor), web site as **93.566**. Phone: (202)401-5523. (Note: no field offices for this program.)

93.767 STATE CHILDREN'S INSURANCE PROGRAM ("CHIP" - "SCHIP")

Assistance: formula grants (to 85 percent).

Purposes: pursuant to the Medicare, Medicaid and State Children's Health Insurance Program Balanced Budget Refinement Act of 1999, Medicare, Medicaid, and State Children's Health Insurance Program Improvement Act of 2000, for states to initiate and expand child health assistance to uninsured low-income children, including under state Medicaid programs. Coverage may not discriminate on the basis of diagnosis nor pre-existing condition, and must be coordinated with other public and private programs. The cost of abortions may be covered only to save the life of the mother or if the pregnancy resulted from rape or incest.

Eligible applicants: states, possessions and territories with HHS-approved state plans.

Eligible beneficiaries: targeted low-income children whose family income exceeds Medicaid limits by no more than 50 percent, ineligible for Medicaid and not covered by other health insurance—not including families eligible for a state health benefits plan through employment with a state public agency.

Range: $468,000 (territories) to $667,444,000.

Activity: FY 04, 6,600,000 "unduplicated ever-enrolled enrollees".

HQ: Center for Medicaid and State Operations, Centers for Medicare & Medicaid Services-HHS, 7500 Security Blvd., Baltimore, MD 21244. Phone: (410)786-3870. **Internet:** "www.cms.hhs.gov".

93.768 MEDICAID INFRASTRUCTURE GRANTS TO SUPPORT THE COMPETITIVE EMPLOYMENT OF PEOPLE WITH DISABILITIES ("Ticket-to-Work Infrastructure Grants")

Assistance: project grants.

Purposes: pursuant to the Ticket-to-Work and Work Incentives Improvement Act of 1999, for states to enhance employment options for persons with disabilities, by creating health systems change through the Medicaid program and removing barriers to employment. Projects are expected to be designed to provide personal assistance services and Medicaid buy-ins to sustain adequate health coverage, even if relocation to another state is needed. Funds may not be used to provide direct services to clients except on a one-time, last resort, emergency basis to sustain competitive employment.

Eligible applicants: single state Medicaid agencies or partner agencies.

Eligible beneficiaries: employed persons with disabilities, age 16-65, and: meeting established income, asset, and resource standards; or, ceasing eligibility for Medicaid because of medical improvements but still with severe medically determined impairments.

Range: $500,000 to $2,750,000. **Average:** $500,000.

Activity: through FY 04, 48 states and DC approved for funding.

HQ: same address (zip code 21244-1850)/phone as **93.767**. **Internet:** "www.cms.hhs.gov/contracts/".

93.769 DEMONSTRATION TO MAINTAIN INDEPENDENCE AND EMPLOYMENT ("Ticket-to-Work Demonstrations")

Assistance: project grants.

Purposes: pursuant to the Ticket-to-Work and Work Incentives Improvement Act of 1999, for states to assist workers by providing the necessary medical assistance benefits and services they require to manage the progression of their conditions and remain employed. Projects are to provide benefits equivalent to those provided by Medicaid to the categorically needy and to workers with physical or mental impairments and, without medical assistance, will result in disabilities.

Eligible applicants: states.

Eligible beneficiaries: same as for **93.768**.

Range $284,000 to $3,980,000. **Average:** $2,132,000.

Activity: as of FY 04, 6 states and DC funded.

HQ: same as **93.768**.

93.770 MEDICARE—PRESCRIPTION DRUG COVERAGE ("Medicare Part D")

Assistance: direct payments/specified use.

Purposes: pursuant to SSA and Medicare Prescription Drug, Improvement and Modernization Act of 2003 (Medicare Modernization Act - "MMA"), to provide prescription drugs to Medicare beneficiaries through their voluntary participation in prescription drug plans, with a subsidy provided to low-income beneficiaries.

Eligible applicants: nongovernmental entities organized and licensed under state laws as risk-bearing entities to offer health insurance in state in which they offer plans.

Eligible beneficiaries: individuals entitled to Medicare benefits under Part A or enrolled in Part B, residing in an approved plan's service area, and not enrolled in a Medicare Advantage plan other than a Medicare savings account plan or private fee-for-service plan that does not provide qualified prescription drug coverage.

Range/Average: N.A.

Activity: new program listing in 2005. (Note: program began in 2006.)

HQ: CMS-HHS, 7500 Security Blvd., Baltimore, MD 21244-1850. Phone: *Eligibility, enrollment,* (410)786-9064; *benefits, beneficiary protections,* (410)767-6435; *plan bidding process,* (410)786-3198. **Internet:** same as **93.767**. (Note: no field offices for this program.)

93.773 MEDICARE—HOSPITAL INSURANCE

Assistance: direct payments/specified use.

Purposes: pursuant to SSA, Medicare, Medicaid, and State Children's Health Insurance Program Improvement Act of 2000, MMA, amendments, and other acts, to provide insurance coverage for treatment in hospitals and other care facilities for covered services to persons age 65 or over, to certain disabled persons, and to those with chronic renal disease. Benefits may be paid to participating and emergency hospitals, skilled nursing facilities, home health agencies, and hospice agencies—for inpatient hospital services and post-hospital extended care services incurred during a benefit period. For 2005, the beneficiary is responsible for a $912 inpatient hospital deductible, and varying coinsurance amounts according to the type and length of care received. Home health services are paid in full.

Eligible applicants/beneficiaries: persons age 65 or over and certain disabled persons. Nearly everyone that reached 65 before 1968 is eligible, including those ineligible for cash Social Security benefits. Those reaching age 65 in 1968 or after and ineligible need some work credit to qualify for hospital insurance benefits, the amount of which depends on their age. Hospital insurance is also available to persons age 65 or over and otherwise ineligible, through payment of a monthly premium. Certain federal, state, and local government employees are also eligible.

Range/Average: N.A.

Activity: FY 05 estimate, 41,677,000 persons insured.

HQ: no address provided (regional offices are listed in Part IV). Phone: (800)633-4227. **Internet:** "www.medicare.gov".

93.774 MEDICARE—SUPPLEMENTARY MEDICAL INSURANCE ("Medicare Part B")

Assistance: direct payments/specified use (50-100 percent).

Purposes: pursuant to SSA as amended, Medicare, Medicaid, and State Children's Health Insurance Program Improvement Act of 2000, MMA, amendments, and other acts, to provide medical insurance protection for covered services furnished by physicians and other suppliers of medical services to elderly or disabled persons and to those with chronic renal disease, including services provided by hospitals, skilled nursing facilities, and home health agencies. The beneficiary is responsible for an annual $110 deductible before benefits may begin, effective in FY 05; thereafter, Medicare pays a percentage of charges for covered services, varying from 50 to 100 percent. The enrollee pays a monthly premium ($78.20 in 2005). Some states and other third-parties pay the premium on behalf of qualifying individuals.

Eligible applicants/beneficiaries: all persons age 65 and over, and those under age 65 eligible for hospital insurance benefits (see **93.773**)—voluntarily enrolled for supplementary medical insurance. Eligibility is available to U.S. citizen-residents or lawful permanent residents residing in the U.S. continuously for the previous five years.

Range/Average: N.A.

Activity: FY 05 estimate, 39,237,000 enrollees.

HQ: Center for Beneficiary Choices, CMS-HHS, 7500 Security Blvd. Rm.C5-19-16, Baltimore, MD 21244. Phone: (301)786-3418. **Internet:** same as **93.767**.

93.775 STATE MEDICAID FRAUD CONTROL UNITS ("SMFCUs")

Assistance: formula grants (75-90 percent).

Purposes: pursuant to SSA as amended, to investigate and prosecute fraud and patient abuse in state Medicaid programs.

Eligible applicants/beneficiaries: specified state government entities.

Range: $253,000 to $30,562,000. **Average:** $2,939,000.

Activity: currently, 48 states, DC certified.

HQ: Director, Medicaid Fraud Unit Oversight Division, Office of Evaluation and Inspections, Office of Inspector General, OS-HHS, Cohen Bldg. - Rm.5656, 330 Independence Ave. SW, Washington, DC 20201. Phone: (202)260-3711. **Internet:** "www.dhhs.gov". (Note: no field offices for this program.)

93.777 STATE SURVEY AND CERTIFICATION OF HEALTH CARE PROVIDERS AND SUPPLIERS

Assistance: formula grants.

Purposes: pursuant to SSA as amended, to monitor health care providers and suppliers to assure their compliance with federal regulatory health and safety standards and conditions of participation in Medicare and Medicaid programs.

Eligible applicants/beneficiaries: designated state agencies.

Range: $15,000 to $28,027,000. **Average:** $4,517,000.

Activity: FY 06 estimate, 53 state and territorial agencies funded to provide monitoring of 55,000 certified providers and suppliers.

HQ: Director, Survey and Certification Group, CMS-HHS, 7500 Security Blvd., Baltimore, MD 21244. Phone: (410)786-9493. **Internet:** same as **93.768**.

93.778 MEDICAL ASSISTANCE PROGRAM ("Medicaid" - "Title XIX")

Assistance: formula grants (50-83 percent).

Purposes: pursuant to SSA as amended, for medical assistance payments on behalf of recipients of cash assistance, children, pregnant women, certain elderly, and other eligible groups. States must provide: hospital in- and outpatient care; rural health clinic services; federally qualified health center services; other laboratory and X-ray services; nursing facility services; home health services for persons over age 21; family planning services; early and periodic screening, diagnosis, and treatment for persons under age 21; pediatric or family nurse practitioner services; nurse-midwife services. States may use funds to pay for Medicare premiums, copayments, and deductible payments of eligible beneficiaries.

Eligible applicants: state and local welfare agencies.

Eligible beneficiaries: low-income persons over age 65 or blind or disabled, members of families with dependent children, low-income children and pregnant women; certain Medicare beneficiaries; in some states, medically-needy persons may apply to a state or local welfare agency for medical assistance.

Range: $2,380,000 to $26,504,617,000. **Average:** $3,493,341,000.

Activity: FY 04, 43,700,000 Medicaid enrollees.

HQ: same address/phone as **93.767**. **Internet:** same as **93.768**.

93.779 CENTERS FOR MEDICARE AND MEDICAID SERVICES (CMS) RESEARCH, DEMONSTRATIONS AND EVALUATIONS ("CMS Research")

Assistance: project grants (to 95 percent/to 2 years).

Purposes: pursuant to the SSA and Small Business Innovation Development Act of 1982 as amended, for analyses, experiments, demonstrations, and pilot projects to resolve major health care financing issues or to improve the administration of the Medicare and Medicaid programs. Funds may be provided as SBIR grants (*see Notes preceding* **93.001**), Hispanic health services grants, HBCU grants, IHE grants.

Eligible applicants/beneficiaries: private nonprofit or profit organizations; public agencies including state Medicaid agencies.

Range: $25,000 to $1,000,000. **Average:** $235,000.

Activity: FY 06 estimate, 37 new cooperative agreement, 23 new contract awards.

HQ: Director, Office of Research, Development, and Information, CMS-HHS, Central Bldg. - Rm.C3-20-11, 7500 Security Blvd., Baltimore, MD 21244-1850. Phone: (410)786-0948. **Internet:** same as **93.768**.

93.780 GRANTS TO STATES FOR OPERATION OF QUALIFIED HIGH-RISK POOLS

Assistance: formula grants.

Purposes: pursuant to the Trade Act of 2002, for the operation of qualified state high-risk health insurance pools by providing federal funding for up to 50 percent of losses incurred by the pool for a given state fiscal year.

Eligible applicants/beneficiaries: states that: (1) operate a qualified high-risk pool as defined in section 2744(c)(2) of PHSA; restrict premiums charged under the pool to no more than 150 percent of applicable standard risk rates for the state; offer a choice of two or more coverage options through the pool; have in effect a mechanism reasonably designed to ensure continued funding of losses after then end of FY 04; incurred losses in the state's FY 02, 03, or 04.

Range/Average: N.A.

Activity: new program listing in 2003.

HQ: Centers for Medicare and State Operations, CMS-HHS (MS S3-16-16), 7500 Security Blvd., Baltimore, MD 21244-1850. Phone: (401)786-9244. **Internet:** "http//:www.cms.hhs.gov/riskpool".

93.781 SEED GRANTS TO STATES FOR QUALIFIED HIGH-RISK POOLS

Assistance: project grants.

Purposes: pursuant to the Trade Act of 2002, to establish and for initial operation of qualified state high-risk health insurance pools for individuals who cannot purchase individual coverage because of pre-existing medical conditions.

Eligible applicants/beneficiaries: states that did not have qualified high-risk pools as of 6 August 2002.

Range: to $1,000,000.

Activity: new program in FY 03.

HQ: same as **93.780**.

93.782 MEDICARE TRANSITIONAL DRUG ASSISTANCE PROGRAM FOR TERRITORIES

Assistance: project grants (100 percent).

Purposes: pursuant to MMA, for transitional assistance in the provision of covered discount drugs for certain low-income Medicare beneficiaries.

Eligible applicants: commonwealths and territories.

Eligible beneficiaries: residents of commonwealth and territories, eligible for

Medicare benefits and with incomes below 135 percent of the federal poverty level.

Range/Average: N.A.

Activity: new program in FY 04; awards to each commonwealth or territory with an approved transition assistance plan.

HQ: Division of Financial Management, Center for Medicaid and State Operations, CMS-HHS, 7500 Security Blvd., Baltimore, MD 21244. Phone: (410)786-9291. **Internet:** same as **93.767**.

93.783 MEDICARE TRANSITIONAL DRUG ASSISTANCE PROGRAM FOR STATES

Assistance: direct payments/specified use.

Purposes: pursuant to MMA, for transitional assistance to certain low-income Medicare beneficiaries enabling them to purchase prescription drugs. Credits are provided to beneficiaries through private discount card sponsors.

Eligible applicants: nongovernmental, single legal entities doing business in the U.S., with three years of private sector experience in pharmacy benefit management, and serving at least 1,000,000 covered persons.

Eligible beneficiaries: Medicare beneficiaries with incomes not more than 135 percent of the poverty line, and not receiving outpatient coverage from other sources including Medicaid, TRICARE, group health insurance or federal employee health benefit plans unless the drug is covered through Part C Medicare+Choice plan or Medigap plan.

Range: to $600 per beneficiary.

Activity: new program in FY 04.

HQ: Health Plan Benefits Group, Center for Beneficiary Choices, CMS-HHS same address/web site as **93.782**. Phone: (410)786-1164. (Note: no field offices for this program.)

93.784 FEDERAL REIMBURSEMENT OF EMERGENCY HEALTH SERVICES FURNISHED TO UNDOCUMENTED ALIENS

Assistance: direct payments/specified use.

Purposes: pursuant to MMA, to reimburse providers for their otherwise unreimbursed costs associated with furnishing emergency health services required under the Emergency Medical Treatment and Active Labor Act (EMTALA), to undocumented and certain other aliens.

Eligible applicants: states.

Eligible beneficiaries: hospitals, certain physicians, ambulance services that provide emergency health care under EMTALA.

Range/Average: N.A.

Activity: new program in FY 05.

HQ: Hospital and Ambulatory Group, Center for Medicare Management, CMS-HHS, 7500 Security Blvd., Baltimore, MD 21244. Phone: (410)786-9317. **Internet:** (none). (Note: no field offices for this program.)

93.785 PILOT PROGRAM FOR NATIONAL AND STATE BACKGROUND CHECKS—DIRECT PATIENT ACCESS FOR LONG-TERM CARE

Assistance: project grants (100 percent).

Purposes: pursuant to MMA, for pilot programs to develop procedures to conduct background checks on prospective direct patient access employees.

Eligible applicants/beneficiaries: state agencies.

Range: $500,000 to $5,000,000.

Activity: new program in FY 04. FY 05, 7 grants.

HQ: Survey & Certification Group, same address as **93.767**. Phone: (301)786-6773. **Internet:** "www.cms.hhs.gov/medicaid/survey-cert/bsp.asp". (Note: no field offices for this program.)

93.786 STATE PHARMACEUTICAL ASSISTANCE PROGRAMS ("SPAPSs")

Assistance: formula grants.

Purposes: pursuant to MMA, for states with SPAPs to educate SPAP participants about Medicare Part D coverage, including technical assistance, phone support, and counseling in selecting and enrolling in Part D plans.

Eligible applicants/beneficiaries: states with CMS-approved transitional assistance grant applications (program **93.783**).

Range/Average: N.A.

Activity: new program in FY 05 (CFDA on-line).

HQ: same as **93.782**. (Note: no field offices for this program.)

93.822 HEALTH CAREERS OPPORTUNITY PROGRAM ("HCOP")

Assistance: project grants (100 percent/3 years).

Purposes: pursuant to PHSA as amended and HPEPA, to assist students from disadvantaged backgrounds to undertake education preparing them to enter a health or allied health professions schools, including graduate programs. Projects provide preparatory services, including recruitment, counseling, mentoring, preliminary education and health research training, information on financial aid, primary care exposure activities, and stipends.

Eligible applicants/beneficiaries: accredited schools of medicine, osteopathy, public health, dentistry, veterinary medicine, optometry, pharmacy, allied health, chiropractic, podiatry; public and private nonprofit schools with programs to train physician assistants or offering graduate programs in behavioral and mental health.

Range: $116,000 to $1,092,000. **Average:** $399,000.

Activity: FY 05 estimate, 40 continuation, 25 new awards. FY 06 estimate, no awards.

HQ: same as **93.157**. (Note: no field offices for this program.)

93.824 BASIC/CORE AREA HEALTH EDUCATION CENTERS ("AHEC")

Assistance: project grants (from 50-75 percent/3 years).

Purposes: pursuant to PHSA as amended and HPEPA, to improve the distribution, diversity, supply, and quality of health service delivery system personnel, by encouraging regionalization of health professions schools and involving students in grades 9-12 in health careers programs. Program funds may be used to plan, develop, and operate AHECs, linked with academic resources of university health sciences centers, to initiate education system incentives to attract and retain health care personnel in scarcity areas, emphasizing community-based training of primary care oriented students, residents, and providers—but not for construction, patient services, or stipends.

Eligible applicants/beneficiaries: public or nonprofit schools of medicine or osteopathy, consortia; accredited schools of nursing in states without AHECs.

Range: $401,000 to $3,123,000. **Average:** $1,014,000.

Activity: FY 04, 14 awards.

HQ: same as **93.107**. (Note: no field offices for this program.)

93.837 HEART AND VASCULAR DISEASES RESEARCH

Assistance: project grants (100 percent/1-5 years).

Purposes: pursuant to PHSA as amended and SBRDEA, for research and research training in prevention, education, and control activities related to heart and vascular diseases. Project funds may support salaries, equipment, and patient hospitalization costs required to perform the research effort. NRSA, SBIR, and STTR awards are available (*see Notes preceding* **93.001**).

Eligible applicants/beneficiaries: nonprofit and profit organizations engaged in biomedical research.

Range: $16,000 to $4,445,000. **Average:** $442,000.

Activity: FY 06 estimate, 3,117 research grants, 291 NRSAs.

HQ: Director, Division of Heart and Vascular Diseases, National Heart, Lung, and Blood Institute, NIH-HHS, Bethesda, MD 20892. Phone: (301)435-0466; SBIR, (301)435-0266. *Grants management information*: same address as **93.233**. Phone: (301)435-0166. **Internet:** "www.nih.gov" (Note: no field offices for this program.)

93.838 LUNG DISEASES RESEARCH

Assistance: project grants (100 percent/to 5 years).

Purposes: pursuant to PHSA as amended and SBRDEA, for research and research training concerning lung diseases, and to improve their prevention and treatment. Project funds may support salaries, equipment, and patient hospitalization costs required to perform the research effort. NRSA, SBIR, and STTR awards are available (*see Notes preceding* **93.001**).

Eligible applicants/beneficiaries: same as for **93.837**.

Range: $13,000 to $2,434,000. **Average:** $460,000.

Activity: FY 06 estimate, 1,108 research grants, 92 NRSAs.

HQ: Director, Division of Lung Diseases, National Heart, Lung, and Blood Institute, NIH-HHS, Bethesda, MD 20892. Phone: (301)435-0233. SBIR, grants management contact: same as **93.233**. **Internet:** same as **93.837**. (Note: no field offices for this program.)

93.839 BLOOD DISEASES AND RESOURCES RESEARCH

Assistance: project grants (100 percent/to 5 years).

Purposes: pursuant to PHSA as amended and SBRDEA, for research and research training toward the improved diagnosis, treatment, and prevention of nonmalignant blood diseases; for research on stem cell biology and transplantation; to improve the availability, safety, and use of blood and blood products. Project funds may support salaries, equipment, and patient hospitalization costs required to perform the research effort. NRSA, SBIR, and STTR awards are available *(see Notes preceding* **93.001**).

Eligible applicants/beneficiaries: same as for **93.837**.

Range: $68,000 to $2,900,000. **Average:** $471,000.

Activity: FY 06 estimate, 825 research grants, 72 NRSAs.

HQ: Director, Division of Blood Diseases and Resources, National Heart, Lung, and Blood Institute, NIH-HHS, Bethesda, MD 20892. Phone: (301) 435-0080. SBIR, grants management contact: same as **93.233**. **Internet:** "www.nhlbi.nih.gov". (Note: no field offices for this program.)

93.846 ARTHRITIS, MUSCULOSKELETAL AND SKIN DISEASES RESEARCH

Assistance: project grants (100 percent/to 5 years).

Purposes: pursuant to PHSA as amended and SBRDEA, for basic research, research training, and clinical investigations concerning all aspects and forms of arthritis and musculoskeletal and skin diseases, including a centers program for large-scale research. NRSA, SBIR, and STTR awards are available *(see Notes preceding* **93.001**).

Eligible applicants/beneficiaries: individuals, public and private nonprofit or profit institutions proposing to establish, expand, and improve research activities in health sciences and related fields.

Range: research, $5,000 to $3,100,000; NRSA, $19,000 to $362,000. **Average:** research, $300,000; NRSA, $107,000.

Activity: FY 06 estimate, 1,260 research grants including 52 SBIR, STTR awards; 280 NRSAs.

HQ: Director, Extramural Program, National Institute of Arthritis and Musculoskeletal and Skin Diseases, NIH-HHS, 6701 Democracy Blvd. - Ste.800, Bethesda, MD 20892. Phone: (301)594-2463. *SBIR and grants management information*: Grants Management Officer, Extramural Program, same address. Phone: (301)594-3278. **Internet:** "www.hhs.gov". (Note: no field offices for this program.)

93.847 DIABETES, ENDOCRINOLOGY AND METABOLISM RESEARCH

Assistance: project grants (100 percent/to 5 years).

Purposes: pursuant to PHSA as amended and SBRDEA, for basic and clinical biomedical research and research training in: diabetes and related complications, including its etiology, pathogenesis, prevention, diagnosis, and treatment; endocrinology, including the normal and abnormal functions of the pituitary, thyroid, parathyroid, adrenal, pineal, and thymus glands, as well as the action of hormones, hormone biosynthesis, secretion, metabolism, binding to protein carriers and subsequent release, and the kinetics of binding; metabolic processes of diseases such as membrane structure, function, and transport phenomena, as well as inherited disorders including cystic fybrosis, including their causes, prevention, and treatment. NRSA, SBIR, and STTR awards are available (*see Notes preceding* **93.001**).

Eligible applicants/beneficiaries: same as for **93.846**.

Range: research, $17,000 to $2,098,000; NRSA, $3,000 to $264,000. **Average:** research, $180,000; NRSA, $62,000.

Activity: FY 05 estimate, 1,443 research grants, 163 awards for 464 NRSAs, 65 SBIR grants.

HQ: Director, Division of Diabetes, Endocrinology, and Metabolic Diseases, National Institute of Diabetes and Digestive and Kidney Diseases, NIH-HHS, 6707 Democracy Blvd. - Rm.689, Bethesda, MD 20892-2560. Phone: (301)496-7349. *SBIR and grants management information*: Grants Management Officer, Division of Extramural Activities, National Institute of Diabetes and Digestive and Kidney Diseases, NIH-HHS, 6707 Democracy Plaza Blvd., Bethesda, MD 20892. Phone: (301)594-8854; SBIR, (301)594-8869. **Internet:** "www.niddk.nih.gov". (Note: no field offices for this program.)

93.848 DIGESTIVE DISEASES AND NUTRITION RESEARCH

Assistance: project grants (100 percent/to 5 years).

Purposes: pursuant to PHSA as amended and SBRDEA, for basic and clinical biomedical research and research training in digestive and liver diseases, nutrition, and obesity. Support is provided through investigator-initiated awards, cooperative agreements, contracts, centers. NRSA, SBIR, and STTR awards are available (*see Notes preceding* **93.001**).

Eligible applicants/beneficiaries: same as for **93.846**.

Range: research, $27,000 to $1,439,000; NRSA, $19,000 to $215,000. **Average:** research, $165,000; NRSA, $72,000.

Activity: FY 06 estimate, 1,207 research grants, 112 awards for 377 NRSAs, 44 SBIR awards.

HQ: Director, Division of Digestive Diseases and Nutrition, National Institute of Diabetes and Digestive and Kidney Diseases, same address (Rm.675) as **93.847**. Phone: (301)594-7680. Grants management contact, web site: same as **93.847**; SBIR phone, (301)594-8857. (Note: no field offices for this program.)

93.849 KIDNEY DISEASES, UROLOGY AND HEMATOLOGY RESEARCH

Assistance: project grants (100 percent/to 5 years).

Purposes: pursuant to PHSA as amended and SBRDEA, for basic and clinical biomedical research and research training concerning kidney diseases, urology, and hematology, and for the development of improved diagnostic tools and therapies. NRSA, SBIR, STTR awards are available (*see Notes preceding* **93.001**).

Eligible applicants/beneficiaries: same as for **93.846**.

Range: research, $15,000 to $1,647,000; NRSA, $9,168 to $220,000. **Average:** research, $171,000; NRSA, $74,000.

Activity: FY 06 estimate, 1,111 research awards, 98 awards for 319 NRSAs, 41 SBIR grants.

HQ: Director, Division of Kidney, Urologic and Hematologic Diseases, National Institute of Diabetes and Digestive and Kidney Diseases, same address (Rm.645) as **93.847**. Phone: (301)496-6325. SBIR, grants management contact, web site: same as **93.848**. (Note: no field offices for this program.)

93.853 EXTRAMURAL RESEARCH PROGRAMS IN THE NEUROSCIENCES AND NEUROLOGICAL DISORDERS

Assistance: project grants (100 percent/to 5 years).

Purposes: pursuant to PHSA as amended and SBRDEA, for clinical and basic research and research training concerning neurological disorders and stroke, and their diagnosis, prevention, epidemiology, and treatment through development of drugs and neural prostheses. Programs supported include research on stroke, traumatic brain and spinal cord injuries, Parkinson's and Alzheimer's diseases, brain tumors; cellular, molecular, and systems neuroscience, developmental neurobiology and disorders, and neurogenetics, epilepsy, multiple sceloris, AIDS, immune disorders, and sleep and pain disorders. Special programs include a number of career development awards (such as those cited within "Ranges", below), including Re-Entry into the Neurological Sciences awards for scientists that have been away from research for a least three years to re-establish their skills. NRSA, SBIR, and STTR awards are available (*see Notes preceding* **93.001**).

Eligible applicants/beneficiaries: research grants—any public or private nonprofit or profit institution. Career program awards—U.S. citizens or permanent residents nominated and sponsored by a public or private nonprofit institution.

Range: research, $51,000 to $7,382,000; Mentored Research Career Development Awards, $81,000 to $177,000; Independent Scientist Research Career Awards, $85,000 to $176,000; NRSA, $62,000 to $403,000. **Average:** research, $386,000; Mentored Career, $152,000; NRSA, $222,000.

Activity: FY 05 estimate, 140 competing research grants, 140 NRSAs.

HQ: National Institute of Neurological Disorders and Stroke, NIH-HHS, 6001 Executive Blvd., Bethesda, MD 20892. Phone: Director, Division of Extramural Research (Ste.3309), (301)496-9248; Repair and Plasticity (Ste. 2204), (301)496-1447; Neural Environment (Ste.2115), (301)496-1431; Neurodegeneration (Ste.2223), (301)496-5680; Systems & Cognitive Neuroscience (Ste.2113), (301)496-9964; Channels, Synapses & Circuits (Ste. 2142), (301)496-1917; Neurogenetics (Ste.2133), (301)496-5745; Clinical Trials (Ste.2216), (301)496-9135; Technology Development (Ste.2137), (301)496-1779; Office of Minority Health and Research, (Ste.2152), (301) 496-3102; Training, Career Development and Referral (Ste.2138), (301) 496-4188. *Grants management information*: Grants Management Branch, same address (Ste.3258). Phone: Grants Management Officer, (301)496-

9213; Contracts Management Officer (Ste.3280), (301)496-1813. **Internet:** "www.ninds.nih.gov". (Note: no field offices for this program.)

93.855 ALLERGY, IMMUNOLOGY AND TRANSPLANTATION RESEARCH

Assistance: project grants (100 percent/to 7 years).

Purposes: pursuant to PHSA as amended and SBRDEA, to establish, expand, and improve basic and clinical biomedical research and research training in allergic and immunologic diseases and related areas, including asthma, AIDS, transplantation biology, and related areas including genetics. Research Career Development Awards are available to institutions for up to five years, to train young scientists for independent research careers. NRSA, SBIR, and STTR awards are available (*see Notes preceding* **93.001**).

Eligible applicants/beneficiaries: IHEs, hospitals, laboratories, and other public or private, profit or nonprofit, institutions, state and local governments, small businesses, individuals.

Range: research projects, to $4,726,000; NRSA, $44,000 to $1,149,000. **Average:** projects, $373,000; NRSA, $168,000.

Activity: FY 06 estimate, 1,469 awards.

HQ: Director, Division of Extramural Activities, National Institute of Allergy and Infectious Diseases, NIH-HHS, Bethesda, MD 20892. Phone: (301)496-7291. *Grants management information*: Grants Management Officer, Grants Management Branch, same address. Phone: (301)496-7075. **Internet:** "www.niaid.nih.gov". (Note: no field offices for this program.)

93.856 MICROBIOLOGY AND INFECTIOUS DISEASES RESEARCH

Assistance: project grants (100 percent/to 7 years).

Purposes: pursuant to PHSA as amended and SBRDEA, for basic, applied, and clinical biomedical research and research training related to microbiology and infectious diseases. Program aims include the control of disease caused by infectious or parasitic agents, including AIDS, retroviruses, Reye's Syndrome. Studies are supported on the mechanisms of antibiotics, as well as epidemiological observations in hospitalized patients or community populations. Research Career Development Awards are available to institutions for up to five years, to train young scientists for careers in independent research. NRSA, SBIR, and STTR awards are available (*see Notes preceding* **93.001**).

Eligible applicants/beneficiaries: same as for **93.855**.

Range: research, $2,000 to $18,073,000; NRSA, $7,586 to $744,000. **Average:** research, $389,000; NRSA, $113,000.

Activity: FY 05 estimate, 3,559 grants.

HQ: same as **93.855**. (Note: no field offices for this program.)

93.859 BIOMEDICAL RESEARCH AND RESEARCH TRAINING

Assistance: project grants (100 percent/to 5 years).

Purposes: pursuant to PHSA as amended, for research and research training in basic biomedical sciences not targeted to specific diseases or disorders. Biomedical science fields supported include: cell biology and biophysics;

genetics and development biology; pharmacology, physiology, and biological chemistry; bio-informatics and computational biology. Special training programs include: Minority Access to Research Careers which supports research training at the undergraduate, graduate, and faculty levels; Minority Biomedical Research Support.

Eligible applicants/beneficiaries: U.S. citizens, non-citizen nationals, permanent residents.

Range: $20,000 to $7,500,000.

Activity: annually, approximately 4,500 grants.

HQ: National Institute of General Medical Sciences, 45 Center Drive, Bethesda, MD 20892-6200. Phone: Division of Cell Biology and Biophysics, (301)594-0828; Division of Genetics and Developmental Biology, (301) 594-0943; Division of Pharmacology, Physiology, and Biological Chemistry, (301)594-3827; Division of Minority Opportunities in Research, (301) 594-3900; Division of Extramural Activities, (301)594-3910; Center for Bioinformatics and Computational Biology, (301)451-6446. **Internet:** "www.nigms.nih.gov". (Note: no field offices for this program.)

93.865 CHILD HEALTH AND HUMAN DEVELOPMENT EXTRAMURAL RESEARCH

Assistance: project grants (100 percent/to 5 years).

Purposes: pursuant to PHSA as amended and SBRDEA, for fundamental and clinical, biomedical, and behavioral research and research training associated with growth and development biologic and reproductive functions, and population dynamics; also, to conduct research on the impact of disabilities, diseases, and defects, toward the restoration, increase, and maximization of the capabilities of persons so afflicted. NRSA, SBIR, and STTR awards are available (*see Notes preceding* **93.001**).

Eligible applicants/beneficiaries: IHEs; medical, dental, nursing, and public health schools; state and local health departments; hospitals; laboratories; other public or private profit or nonprofit organizations; individuals.

Range: research, $50,000 to $5,000,000. **Average:** research, $382,000; NRSA basic stipend first year beyond the doctoral degree, $36,000.

Activity: FY 06 estimate, 1,745 research grants, 843 NRSAs.

HQ: Director, Center for Research for Mothers and Children, National Institute of Child Health and Human Development, NIH-HHS, Bldg. 61E-Rm.4B05, Bethesda, MD 20892-7510. Phone: (301)496-5097, FAX (301)480-7773. *Grants management information*: Chief, Grants Management Branch, same address (Rm.8A01). Phone: (301)435-6975, FAX (301)402-0915. **Internet:** "www.nichd.nih.gov". (Note: no field offices for this program.)

93.866 AGING RESEARCH

Assistance: project grants (100 percent/to 5 years).

Purposes: pursuant to PHSA as amended and SBRDEA, for biomedical, social, and behavioral research and research training associated with the aging process and the diseases, special problems, and needs people as they age—

including geriatric research and research into genetic diseases and Alzheimer's, and social aspects of care and aging. NRSA, SBIR, and STTR awards are available (*see Notes preceding* **93.001**).

Eligible applicants/beneficiaries: same as for **93.865**.

Range: research, $40,000 to $8,000,000; institutional NRSA, $52,000 to $430,000. **Average**: research, $397,000; institutional NRSA, $211,000; individual NRSA, basic stipend first year beyond doctoral degree, $36,000.

Activity: FY 06 estimate, 390 competing research project grants, 103 competing NRSAs.

HQ: National Institute on Aging, NIH-HHS, Bethesda, MD 20892. Phone: *biology of aging*, (301)496-4996; *geriatrics and clinical research*, (301)496-6761; *behavioral and social research*, (301)496-3136; *neuroscience and neuro-psychology*, (301)496-9350; *SBIR information*, (301)496-9322. *Grants management information*: Grants Management Officer, Office of Extramural Affairs, National Institute on Aging, NIH-HHS, Bethesda, MD 20892. Phone: (301)496-1472. **Internet:** "www.nia.nih.gov". (Note: no field offices for this program.)

93.867 VISION RESEARCH

Assistance: project grants (100 percent/to 5 years.

Purposes: pursuant to PHSA as amended, SBRDEA, and other acts, for basic, clinical, and applied research and research training projects addressing the leading causes of blindness and impaired vision, including retinal and corneal diseases, diabetic retinopathy, macular degeneration, cataract, glaucoma, strabismus, and amblyopia; for related projects including enhancement of the rehabilitation, training, and quality of life of persons who are partially-sighted or blind. Conference grants, core grants, mentored clinical scientist development awards, clinical vision research development awards, clinical study planning grants, and small grants for data analysis may be offered. NRSA, SBIR, and STTR awards are available (*see Notes preceding* **93.001**).

Eligible applicants/beneficiaries: research grants, cooperative agreements, career development awards—IHEs, hospitals, laboratories, federal institutions; other public or private nonprofit and profit organizations including small businesses; state and local governments. Foreign institutions may apply for research grants only.

Range: research grants and cooperative agreements, $2,889 to $7,012,000; NRSA institutional, $19,000 to $521,000; NRSA individual, $25,000 to $56,000. **Average**: research, $333,000; institutional NRSA, $190,000; NRSA individual, $47,000.

Activity: FY 03 estimate, 1,460 grants including 267 NRSAs, 54 SBIR and STTR awards (latest data reported).

HQ: Research Resources Officer, National Eye Institute, NIH-HHS (EPS 350), 6120 Executive Blvd., Bethesda, MD 20892-7164. Phone: (301)451-2020. *Grants management information*: Chief, Grants Management Branch, same address/phone. **Internet:** "www.nei.nih/gov". (Note: no field offices for this program.)

93.879 MEDICAL LIBRARY ASSISTANCE

Assistance: project grants (100 percent/to 5 years).

Purposes: pursuant to PHSA as amended and SBRDEA, for training programs for professional medical library personnel; for fellowships; to expand or improve existing medical libraries; for biomedical publications; for research in medical informatics and related computer sciences; for similar uses, including computer and telecommunications technology. SBIR and STTR awards are made (*see Notes preceding* **93.001**).

Eligible applicants/beneficiaries: training grants—nonfederal public and nonprofit private institutions. Fellowships—pre- or postdoctoral candidates that are U.S. citizens, nationals, or lawful permanent residents. Other grants—depending on category, domestic public, private, nonprofit, profit health sciences institutions and organizations.

Range: $25,000 to $2,000,000. **Average:** $225,000.

Activity: FY 06 estimate, 211 grants.

HQ: Extramural Programs, National Library of Medicine, NIH-HHS, Bethesda, MD 20894. Phone: (301)496-4621, (301)594-4882. *Grants management information*: Grants Management Officer, same address. Phone: (301 496-4221; *grant review contact,* (301)496-4253. **Internet:** "www.nlm.nih/gov/ep". (Note: no field offices for this program.)

93.884 GRANTS FOR TRAINING IN PRIMARY CARE MEDICINE AND DENTISTRY
("Primary Care Training")

Assistance: project grants (100 percent/3 years).

Purposes: pursuant to PHSA as amended and HPEPA, for graduate education and residency programs leading to the practice of family medicine including geriatrics, general internal medicine, general pediatrics, general dentistry, or pediatric dentistry, as well as training of physician assistants in primary care. Grant funds may be used: to plan, develop, and operate or participate in approved programs; provide financial assistance to participants; for faculty development and improving academic administrative units to strengthen clinical instruction. Grants may not be used for construction or patient services.

Eligible applicants/beneficiaries: accredited public or private nonprofit schools of medicine or osteopathy, hospitals, or other entities.

Range: $27,000 to $657,000. **Average:** $179,000.

Activity: FY 05 estimate, family medicine—170 continuation awards; general internal medicine/pediatrics—32 continuation awards; general/pediatric dentistry, 24 continuation awards.

HQ: Primary Care Medical Education Branch, Division of Medicine and Dentistry, Bureau of Health Professions, HRSA-HHS, Parklawn Bldg. - Rm.9A-20, 5600 Fishers Lane, Rockville, MD 20857. Phone: (301)443-1467. Grants management contact, web site: same as **93.107**. (Note: no field offices for this program.)

93.887 HEALTH CARE AND OTHER FACILITIES ("Renovation or Construction Projects")

Assistance: project grants (100 percent/3-5 years).

Purposes: to construct, renovate, expand, repair, equip, or modernize health care facilities and other related facilities.

Eligible applicants/beneficiaries: state and local governments including their IHEs, quasi-governmental agencies, private IHEs, private profit and non-profit entities. Entities are eligible if specifically earmarked in Congressional appropriation.

Range: $45,000 to $24,945,000. **Average:** $1,164,000.

Activity: FY 04 estimate, 509 projects. FY 05 estimate, no awards.

HQ: Facilities Monitoring Branch, Division of Facilities Compliance and Recovery, Office of Special Programs, HRSA-HHS, Parklawn Bldg.- Rm. 16C-17, 5600 Fishers Lane, Rockville, MD 20857. Phone: (301)443-5656. *Grants management information*: Grants Management Specialist, Division of Grants Management Operations, HRSA-HHS, 4350 East-West Hwy. - 11th floor, Bethesda, MD 20814. Phone: (301)443-5906. **Internet:** "www.hrsa.gov/osp". (Note: no field offices for this program.)

93.888 SPECIALLY SELECTED HEALTH PROJECTS

Assistance: project grants (100 percent/3-5 years).

Purposes: for programs selected by the U.S. Congress as needed for improved health care.

Eligible applicants/beneficiaries: same as for **93.887**.

Range: $45,000 to $24,945,000. **Average:** $1,164,000.

Activity: new program in FY 04.

HQ: Division of Grants Policy, Office of Federal Assistance Management, 5600 Fishers Lane - Rm.11A-55, Rockville, MD 20857. Phone: (no number provided). **Internet:** same as **93.887**. (Note: no field offices for this program.)

93.889 NATIONAL BIOTERRORISM HOSPITAL PREPAREDNESS PROGRAM

Assistance: project grants.

Purposes: pursuant to the Public Health Security and Bioterrorism Preparedness and Response Act of 2002, for health care entities to upgrade their ability to deliver coordinated and effective care to victims of terrorism and other public health emergencies requiring mass immunization, treatment, isolation, and quarantine in the aftermath of bioterrorism or other outbreaks of infectious disease; for needs assessment updates; for continuation, refinement, and implementation of approved work plans.

Eligible applicants/beneficiaries: state health departments including territories and possessions; and, New York City, Chicago, and Los Angeles.

Range: $529,000 to $38,774,000.

Activity: new program listing in 2004 (CFDA on-line).

HQ: National Bioterrorism Hospital Preparedness Branch, Healthcare Systems Bureau, Division of Health Care Preparedness, HRSA-HHS, Parklawn Bldg. - Rm.13-103, 5600 Fishers Lane, Rockville, MD 20857. Phone: (301)443-0924. **Internet:** "www.hrsa.gov/bioterrorism.htm". Grants management contact, web site: same as **93.107**. (Note: no field offices for this program.)

93.890 HEALTHY COMMUNITIES ACCESS PROGRAM (HCAP) DEMONSTRATION AUTHORITY ("HCAP")

Assistance: project grants.

Purposes: pursuant to PHSA as amended, for Historically Black Health Professions Schools (HBHPSs) to: develop patient-based research infrastructure with HCAP providers; to establish joint and collaborative programs of medical research and data collection between HBHPSs and HCAPs whose goal is to improve the health status of medically underserved populations; support the related cost of patient care, data collection, and academic training resulting from affiliations with HCAP providers.

Eligible applicants/beneficiaries: HBHPSs affiliated with HCAPs.

Range: $707,000 to $933,000.

Activity: new program in FY 04 (CFDA on-line). FY 04, 4 grants.

HQ: same address (Rm.15C-04)/phone as **93.129**. Grants management contact, web site: same as **93.107**. (Note: no field offices for this program.)

93.891 ALCOHOL RESEARCH CENTER GRANTS

Assistance: project grants (100 percent/5 years).

Purposes: pursuant to PHSA as amended, for long-term, core support of alcohol research centers, focusing multi-disciplinary attention on the problems of alcohol use and alcoholism. The activities of investigators from biomedical, behavioral, and social sciences are coordinated at such centers.

Eligible applicants/beneficiaries: state and local governments; domestic public or private nonprofit institutions—for centers affiliated with an institution such as a university, medical center, or research center with resources to sustain long-term coordinated research programs, as well research and clinical training.

Range: $691,000 to $2,172,000. **Average:** $1,623,000.

Activity: FY 06 estimate, 20 grants.

HQ: same address/phones as **93.272**. *Grants management information*: same address/phone as **93.271**. **Internet** "www.niaa.nih.gov". (Note: no field offices for this program.)

93.894 RESOURCE AND MANPOWER DEVELOPMENT IN THE ENVIRONMENTAL HEALTH SCIENCES ("Core Centers and Research Training Program")

Assistance: project grants (100 percent/to 5 years).

Purposes: pursuant to PHSA as amended, for multidisciplinary research and research training on environmental health problems, at environmental health sciences centers and marine and freshwater biomedical sciences centers—consisting primarily of core support. NRSAs support individual pre- and postdoctoral training in environmental toxicology, pathology, mutagenesis, or epidemiology/biostatistics (*see Notes preceding* **93.001**).

Eligible applicants/beneficiaries: centers—university-based, nonprofit research institutions or profit organizations.

Range: centers, $365,000 to $1,715,000; NRSA, $12,000 to $1,056,000. **Average:** centers, $1,130,000; NRSA, $160,000.

Activity: FY 06 estimate, 38 center, 54 individual and 66 institutional NRSA awards.

HQ: same as **93.113**. (Note: no field offices for this program.)

93.908 NURSING EDUCATION LOAN REPAYMENT PROGRAM

Assistance: project grants (100 percent).

Purposes: pursuant to PHSA as amended and Nurse Reinvestment Act of 2002, to repay education loans on behalf of nurses entering full-time employment at IHS or native Hawaiian health centers, public hospitals, migrant or rural health clinics, or certain other health facilities with critical shortages of nurses. Repayment agreements are made for not less than two consecutive years of service; amounts range from 30 percent of the unpaid initial principal and interest of qualified loans in return for the first year of service, to 85 percent for three years.

Eligible applicants/beneficiaries: licensed or license-eligible registered nurses that: will have received a diploma or academic degree; will begin full-time employment (32 hours or more per week) for two or three years at an eligible health facility; have unpaid educational loans obtained for their nursing education; are U.S. citizens, nationals, or permanent legal residents.

Range: $3,54300 to $99,000.

Activity: FY 05 estimate, 860 contracts.

HQ: Chief, Diversity and Basic Nurse Education Branch, same as **93.124**. Phone: (301)443-6633. Grants management contact, web site: same as **93.107**. (Note: no field offices for this program.)

93.910 FAMILY AND COMMUNITY VIOLENCE PREVENTION PROGRAM ("Family Life Centers")

Assistance: project grants (100 percent/4 years).

Purposes: pursuant to PHSA as amended, to establish family life centers on the campuses of 24 minority IHEs, to prevent minority-related violence and to improve health and human services to minorities, through: assessments of, and coordination with, related local community resources; design and implementation of educational interventions addressing interpersonal family violence; outreach services to students from dysfunctional families. Funds may not be used to provide health care, nor for construction or demonstration projects

Eligible applicants/beneficiaries: an IHE representing four-year, primarily minority undergraduate institutions and a two-year tribal college.

Range/Average: one cooperative agreement award, $7,400,000.

Activity: FY 06 estimate, 1 continuation award representing 26 participating institutions.

HQ: same addresses/phones as **93.004**. **Internet:** "www.fcvp.gov". (Note: no field offices for this program.)

93.912 RURAL HEALTH CARE SERVICES OUTREACH AND RURAL HEALTH NETWORK DEVELOPMENT PROGRAM

Assistance: project grants (100 percent).

Purposes: pursuant to the Health Care Safety Net Amendment, to expand access to, coordinate, restrain the cost of, and improve essential rural health care services by developing integrated systems or networks in rural areas and regions—including mental health services, emergency services, prenatal care, free clinical services, prevention services, professionals training, and transportation services.

Eligible applicants/beneficiaries: rural public or private nonprofit entities that include three or more health care providers; organizations exclusively providing services to migrant and seasonal farm workers; tribal, quasi-tribal entities delivering services on reservations or tribal areas.

Range: outreach, to $150,000; network development, to $180,000.

Activity: FY 06 estimate—outreach, 60 new, 60 continuation grants; networks, 20 new, 13 continuation awards.

HQ: Outreach Program Coordinator *or* Network Development Program Coordinator, Office of Rural Health Policy, same address as **93.155**. Phone: (301)443-0835. Grants management contact, web site: same as **93.107**. (Note: no field offices for this program.)

93.913 GRANTS TO STATES FOR OPERATION OF OFFICES OF RURAL HEALTH

Assistance: project grants (to 75 percent/to 5 years).

Purposes: pursuant to PHSA as amended, to improve health care in rural areas by establishing state offices of rural health. Funds must support information clearinghouses, coordination of state and federal programs, technical assistance, health professionals recruitment activities.

Eligible applicants/beneficiaries: states.

Range: $100,000 to $150,000.

Activity: annually 50 continuation grants.

HQ: State Office of Rural Health Grant Program, Office of Rural Health Policy, same address/phone, grants management contact, web site as **93.155**. (Note: no field offices for this program.)

93.914 HIV EMERGENCY RELIEF PROJECT GRANTS

Assistance: project grants.

Purposes: pursuant to PHSA as amended and Ryan White Comprehensive AIDS Resources Emergency (CARE) Act Amendments of 2000, to assist areas most severely affected by the HIV epidemic, in developing, organizing, and operating programs providing a continuum of health and support services—including: HIV-related outpatient and ambulatory services; case management and comprehensive treatment services for patients and their families; substance abuse and mental health treatment; inpatient services to prevent unnecessary hospitalization or to expedite discharge; services to infants, women, and children with or exposed to HIV disease.

Eligible applicants/beneficiaries: metropolitan areas with populations of 500,000 or more, reporting more than 2,000 cases of AIDS during the most recent five years, per CDCP data.

Range: $875,000 to $118,000,000. **Average:** $11,518,000.

Activity: FY 06 estimate, 51 competing continuation grants.

HQ: Division of Service Systems, HIV/AIDS Bureau, HRSA-HHS, Parklawn Bldg. - Rm.7A-55, Rockville, MD 20857. Phone: (301)443-6745. Grants management contact, web site: same as **93.107**. (Note: no field offices for this program.)

93.917 HIV CARE FORMULA GRANTS

Assistance: formula grants (to 100 percent).

Purposes: pursuant to PHSA as amended and Ryan White Comprehensive AIDS Resources Emergency (CARE) Act Amendments of 2000, to improve the quality, availability, and organization of health care and support services for persons with HIV disease and their families. Funds may be used: to provide outpatient and ambulatory health and support services, including case management and comprehensive treatment services, substance abuse treatment, and mental health treatment; for inpatient case management services to prevent unnecessary hospitalization or to expedite discharge; to establish and operate consortia; to provide home and community-based care services; to assure the continuity of health insurance coverage; to provide therapeutics to treat individuals with HIV disease.

Eligible applicants/beneficiaries: states, territories and possessions.

Range: $50,000 to $171,787,000. **Average:** $17,964,000.

Activity: annually, 59 awards.

HQ: same as **93.914**. (Note: no field offices for this program.)

93.918 GRANTS TO PROVIDE OUTPATIENT EARLY INTERVENTION SERVICES WITH RESPECT TO HIV DISEASE

Assistance: project grants (100 percent/to 5 years).

Purposes: pursuant to PHSA as amended and the Ryan White Comprehensive AIDS Resources Emergency (CARE) Act Amendments of 2000, to improve the availability, accessibility, and organization of ambulatory services to persons infected with HIV or at high risk, and to offer early intervention services, including: counseling and testing; partner involvement in risk reduction; transmission prevention; primary care diagnosis and treatment; case management. Capacity building funding may be provided to develop new or expanded programs particularly in rural, underserved, and minority areas. Funds may not be used to acquire real property or to provide inpatient or residential care.

Eligible applicants/beneficiaries: public or private nonprofit: community health centers; family planning grantees under PHS Section 1001, other than states; comprehensive programs of primary health care; comprehensive hemophilia diagnostic and treatment centers.

Range: $100,000 to $650,000—planning, to $50,000; capacity building, to $150,000. **Average:** $350,000.

Activity: FY 04, 363 early intervention awards, 51 capacity building grants.

HQ: same address, grants management contact, web site as **93.153**. Phone: *early intervention services,* (301)443-7602; *capacity development* (301)443-1377. (Note: no field offices for this program.)

93.919 COOPERATIVE AGREEMENTS FOR STATE-BASED COMPREHENSIVE BREAST AND CERVICAL CANCER EARLY DETECTION PROGRAMS

Assistance: project grants (75 percent/1-5 years).

Purposes: pursuant to the Breast and Cervical Cancer Mortality Prevention Act of 1990, to develop comprehensive breast and cervical cancer early detection programs; to increase screening and follow-up among all groups of women, especially those that are low-income, uninsured, under-insured, minority, or native Americans. Funds may be used for public education and outreach, referrals services, staff training, project monitoring and evaluation—but not for treatment services.

Eligible applicants/beneficiaries: state health agencies, territories and possessions, tribes and tribal organizations.

Range: $145,000 to $8,400,000. **Average:** $2,100,000.

Activity: annually, 50 states, DC, 13 American Indian and Alaska native tribes, 4 territories funded.

HQ: Program Services Branch, Division of Cancer Prevention and Control, National Center for Chronic Disease Prevention and Health Promotion (K57), CDCP-HHS, 4770 Buford Hwy. NE, Atlanta, GA 30341. Phone: (404)488-4880. *Grants management information:* same address as **93.061**. Phone: (770)488-2722. **Internet:** "www.cdc.gov/cancer". (Note: no field offices for this program.)

93.923 DISADVANTAGED HEALTH PROFESSIONS FACULTY LOAN REPAYMENT AND MINORITY FACULTY FELLOWSHIP PROGRAM ("FLRP" - "MFFP")

Assistance: project grants (50-100 percent/to 3 years); direct payments/specified use.

Purposes: pursuant to PHSA as amended and HPEPA, to repay educational loans owed by health professionals from disadvantaged backgrounds, or to provide fellowships to minority faculty, serving for at least two years on the full-time or part-time faculty of a school of medicine, nursing, osteopathy, dentistry, pharmacy, podiatry, optometry, veterinary medicine, public health, allied health, or graduate programs in clinical psychology. Unless waived, schools are required to pay 50 percent of the repayment or fellowship amount due for each year of service.

Eligible applicants/beneficiaries: FLRP—health professionals from disadvantaged backgrounds with degrees or enrolled in approved graduate training programs, or enrolled as full-time students in their final course of study. MFFP—health professions schools with programs in the fields designated.

Range: loan repayments, $2,740 to $56,000 (including funds to cover tax liability); minority fellowships, $36,000 to $62,000. **Average:** loan repayments, $16,000; fellowships, $51,000.

Activity: FY 05 estimate, 48 awards total.

HQ: *faculty program,* same address (Rm.8-42)/phone as **93.342** *and* phone: (888)275-4772. *Minority faculty fellowship program,* Division of Health Careers, same address as **93.157**. Phone: (301)443-2100. Grants management contact, web site, same as **93.107**. (Note: no field offices for this program.)

93.924 RYAN WHITE HIV/AIDS DENTAL REIMBURSEMENTS/ COMMUNITY-BASED DENTAL PARTNERSHIP

Assistance: direct payments/specified use; project grants (to 5 years).

Purposes: pursuant to PHSA as amended and Ryan White CARE Act Amendments of 2000, to reimburse the uncompensated costs incurred for oral health services to patients with HIV/AIDS, by dental schools, and postdoctoral dental education and dental hygiene education programs; to increase access to oral health care services for HIV-positive individuals, while providing education and clinical training for dental and hygiene provided located in community-based settings through "dental partnerships."

Eligible applicants/beneficiaries: public or private nonprofit schools of dentistry and dental hygiene, and accredited postgraduate dental education programs in the states, territories, and possessions.

Range: reimbursements, $1,439 to $1,143,000; partnership projects, $185,000 to $403,000. **Average:** reimbursements, $155,000; projects, $278,000.

Activity: FY 04, 12 partnership programs funded. FY 06 estimate, 80 awards for oral health service reimbursements.

HQ: same address, grants management contact, web site as **93.153**. Phone: (301)443-1434. (Note: no field offices for this program.)

93.925 SCHOLARSHIPS FOR HEALTH PROFESSIONS STUDENTS FROM DISADVANTAGED BACKGROUNDS ("SDS")

Assistance: project grants.

Purposes: pursuant to PHSA as amended and HPEPA, for annual scholarships to full-time students from disadvantaged backgrounds, awarded by health professions schools that maintain special programs for enrollees, including recruiting and retaining students from disadvantaged backgrounds. At least 16 percent of funds must be allocated to schools providing scholarships only to nurses, and giving preference to former EFN and SDS recipients.

Eligible applicants: public or private nonprofit schools of medicine, nursing, osteopathy, dentistry, pharmacy, podiatry, optometry, veterinary medicine, chiropractic, allied health, or offering graduate programs in public health, behavioral and mental health, or physician assistants.

Eligible beneficiaries: U.S. citizens, nationals, or lawful permanent residents of states, territories, or possessions.

Range: $727 to $650,000. **Average:** $102,000.

Activity: FY 05 estimate, grants to 470 schools.

HQ: same address (Rm.8-42)/phone as **93.342**. Grants management contact, web site: same as **93.107**. (Note: no field offices for this program.)

93.926 HEALTHY START INITIATIVE

Assistance: project grants (100 percent/to 4 years).

Purposes: pursuant to PHSA, to eliminate disparities in perinatal and maternal health by enhancing community service systems and infrastructure, and state infrastructures, directing resources and interventions to improve access to, utilization, and full participation of comprehensive service projects for high-risk women and infants. Funds may be used to implement community-driven, multifaceted approaches integrating various health education, social and support services—including outreach, case management, screening and referral, peer mentoring by trained community members, and home visiting programs to promote access and use of preconceptional, perinatal, and inter-conceptional services. Projects must have a community-base consortium of individuals and organizations, including persons served, to collaborate with their state agency and to implement a local health system action plan.

Eligible applicants/beneficiaries: in urban and rural communities with significant disparities in perinatal health—public or private entities including community-based organizations, tribes, and tribal organizations; states needing to build their infrastructure and capacity to address and support eligible communities.

Range: $100,000 to $2,340,000. **Average:** $783,000.

Activity: FY 05 estimate, 101 projects.

HQ: Division of Perinatal Systems and Women's Health, Maternal and Child Health Bureau, HRSA-HHS, Parklawn Bldg. - Rm.18-12, 5600 Fishers Lane, Rockville, MD 20857. Phone: (301)443-0543. Grants management contact, web site: same as **93.107**. **Internet:** "www.mchb.hrsa.gov".

93.928 SPECIAL PROJECTS OF NATIONAL SIGNIFICANCE ("SPNS")

Assistance: project grants (100 percent/to 5 years).

Purposes: pursuant to PHSA as amended and Ryan White CARE Act Amendments of 2000, to advance knowledge and skills in the delivery of health and support services to persons with HIV disease. Funds support innovative projects: for which implementation, costs, utilization, and outcomes can be evaluated rigorously; providing models unlikely to exist without SPNS support; that extend the care model to previously underserved or unserved populations.

Eligible applicants/beneficiaries: public and private nonprofit entities including state or local health departments, hospitals, IHEs, community-based service organizations, IHEs; national service provider organizations.

Range: $75,000 to $600,000. **Average:** $283,000.

Activity: FY 06 estimate, 49 continuation, 15 new awards.

HQ: Chief, Demonstration Project Development and Evaluation Branch, Division of Science and Policy, HIV/AIDS Bureau, HRSA-HHS, 5600 Fishers Lane - Rm.7C-07, Rockville, MD 20857. Phone: (301)443-9976. Grants management contact, web site: same as **93.107**. (Note: no field offices for this program.)

93.932 NATIVE HAWAIIAN HEALTH SYSTEMS

Assistance: project grants (to 83.3 percent/to 3 years).

Purposes: pursuant to the Native Hawaiian Health Care Improvement Act, for programs raising the health status of native Hawaiians living in Hawaii, by providing comprehensive health promotion and disease prevention and primary health care services. Outreach, case management, and referral components should integrate traditional health concepts with western medicine, employing existing health resources as much as possible.

Eligible applicants/beneficiaries: Papa Ola Lokahi (a consortium of Hawaiian and native Hawaiian organizations); Native American Health Care Systems as specifically defined in Hawaii state laws.

Range: $1,222,000 to $2,093,000. **Average:** $1,746,000.

Activity: annually, 6 grants.

HQ: same address, grants management contact, web site as **93.224**. Phone: (301)594-4485. (Note: no field offices for this program.)

93.933 DEMONSTRATION PROJECTS FOR INDIAN HEALTH

Assistance: project grants (100 percent/to 5 years).

Purposes: pursuant to PHSA as amended, to promote improved health care among American Indians and Alaska natives, through research, studies, and demonstration projects addressing such issues as elder care, women's health care, and children and youth initiative.

Eligible applicants/beneficiaries: tribes, tribal organizations, nonprofit intertribal or urban Indian organizations contracting with IHS, public or private nonprofit health and education entities, state and local health agencies.

Range: $27,000 to $300,000. **Average:** $115,000.

Activity: FY 04 estimate, 49 projects.

HQ: *Elders health program,* Nashville Area Health Consultant, IHS-HHS, 45 Vernon St., Northampton, MA 01060. Phone: (413)584-0790. *Women's health demonstration,* Division of Nursing Services, IHS-HHS, 801 Thompson Ave. - Ste.300, Rockville, MD 20857. Phone: (301)443-1026. *Children & youth initiative,* Maternal and Child Health Coordinator, Office of Public Health, IHS-HHS, 801 Thompson Ave. - Ste.200, Rockville, MD 20857. Phone: (301)443-5070. Grants management contact address, web site: same as **93.123**. Phone: (301)443-5204. (Note: no other field offices for this program.)

93.936 NATIONAL INSTITUTES OF HEALTH ACQUIRED IMMUNODEFICIENCY SYNDROME RESEARCH LOAN REPAYMENT PROGRAM ("NIH AIDS Research LRP")

Assistance: project grants (100 percent/from 2 years).

Purposes: pursuant to PHSA as amended, for partial repayment of educational loans owed by physicians, registered nurses, and scientists employed by NIH in AIDS research. Recipients must have qualified educational debt exceeding 20 percent of their annual salary, and they must engage in research for a minimum of two years. Continuation contracts are available.

Eligible applicants/beneficiaries: NIH AIDS researchers with an M.D., Ph.D., D.D.S., D.O., D.M.D., D.V.M., D.P.M., A.D.N., B.S.N., or equivalent degree, that: are U.S. citizens, nationals, or permanent residents; have no existing service obligation to federal, state, or other entities.

Range: $4,000 to $70,000 (2 years); tax reimbursement, $1,977 to $35,000. **Average:** loan, $53,000 including tax reimbursement.

Activity: FY 06 estimate, 16 awards.

HQ: same as **93.220**. (Note: no field offices for this program.)

93.938 COOPERATIVE AGREEMENTS TO SUPPORT COMPREHENSIVE SCHOOL HEALTH PROGRAMS TO PREVENT THE SPREAD OF HIV AND OTHER IMPORTANT HEALTH PROBLEMS ("SHEPSA")

Assistance: project grants (100 percent/to 5 years).

Purposes: pursuant to PHSA as amended, to develop and implement health education programs for HIV and other health problems for school-age populations (elementary through college), parents, and school, health, and education personnel. Funds may support personnel salaries, training, data collection, monitoring, preparation and dissemination of information including audiovisuals, technical assistance; special outreach to minority, special needs, and high-risk youth. Funds may not be used for research, surveys, computer or office equipment purchases, office space costs, construction or renovation—unless specifically approved.

Eligible applicants/beneficiaries: states, territories and possessions; large urban school districts with high HIV-AIDS rates; national nongovernmental organizations.

Range: $87,000 to $650,000. **Average:** $299,000.

Activity: FY 04, 73 grants.

HQ: Program Development and Services Branch, Division of Adolescent and School Health, National Center for Chronic Disease Prevention and Health Promotion (K31), CDCP-HHS, 4770 Buford Hwy., Atlanta, GA 30341. Phone: (770)488-6130, FAX (770)488-6163. *Grants management information*: same as **93.135**. **Internet:** "www.cdc.gov/healthyyouth". (Note: no field offices for this program.)

93.939 HIV PREVENTION ACTIVITIES—NON-GOVERNMENTAL ORGANIZATION BASED

Assistance: project grants (to 100 percent/to 5 years).

Purposes: pursuant to PHSA as amended, to promote coordination for primary and secondary HIV prevention efforts among community-based organizations, HIV education and prevention service agencies, and national and regional nonprofit organizations. Project examples include street outreach, risk reduction, and community intervention programs.

Eligible applicants/beneficiaries: nongovernmental public and private nonprofit entities.

Range: $62,000 to $9,077,000. **Average:** $228,000.

Activity: FY 03 estimate, 341 awards.

HQ: same as **93.118**. (Note: no field offices for this program.)

93.940 HIV PREVENTION ACTIVITIES—HEALTH DEPARTMENT BASED

Assistance: project grants (to 100 percent/1-5 years).

Purposes: pursuant to PHSA as amended, for state and local health departments to develop, implement, and evaluate primary and secondary HIV prevention programs. Project activities may include: health education and risk reduction for drug users; public information; minority initiatives; counseling, testing, referral, and partner notification.

Eligible applicants/beneficiaries: states and, in consultation with state health authorities, political subdivisions, territories and possessions.

Range: $61,000 to $23,255,000. **Average:** $3,667,000.

Activity: annually, 88 awards.

HQ: same as **93.118**. (Note: no field offices for this program.)

93.941 HIV DEMONSTRATION, RESEARCH, PUBLIC AND PROFESSIONAL EDUCATION PROJECTS

Assistance: project grants (to 100 percent/1-5 years).

Purposes: pursuant to PHSA as amended, to develop, test, and disseminate improved HIV prevention strategies at the community level. Applicants are encouraged to involve research groups in the program.

Eligible applicants/beneficiaries: states and political subdivisions, other public and private nonprofit entities.

Range: $50,000 to $1,000,000. **Average:** $293,000.

Activity: annually, 91 awards.

HQ: same as **93.118**. (Note: no field offices for this program.)

93.942 RESEARCH, TREATMENT AND EDUCATION PROGRAMS ON LYME DISEASE IN THE UNITED STATES
("Lyme Disease")

Assistance: project grants (100 percent/to 3 years).

Purposes: pursuant to PHSA as amended, to develop and implement improved measures for the primary and secondary prevention of Lyme disease, including: surveillance activities; ecological and epidemiological studies; diagnostic tests; public education; use of primate models.

Eligible applicants/beneficiaries: public and private nonprofit organizations able to provide services in areas where Lyme disease is found, including IHEs, research institutions, state and local health departments.

Range: $100,000 to $700,000. **Average:** $350,000.

Activity: FY 06 estimate, 10 continuation grants.

HQ: Office of Extramural Research (C-19), National Center for Infectious Diseases, CDCP-HHS, 1600 Clifton Rd. NE, Atlanta, GA 30333. Phone: (404)639-0043; FAX (404)639-2469. Grants management contact address, web site: same as **93.061**. Phone: (770)488-2628; FAX (770)488-2777.

93.943 EPIDEMIOLOGIC RESEARCH STUDIES OF ACQUIRED IMMUNODEFICIENCY SYNDROME (AIDS) AND HUMAN IMMUNODEFICIENCY VIRUS (HIV) INFECTION IN SELECTED POPULATION GROUPS

Assistance: project grants (100 percent/1-3 years).

Purposes: pursuant to PHSA as amended, for research of HIV-related epidemiologic issues concerning risks of transmission, the natural history and transmission of the disease in certain populations, and development and evaluation of behavioral recommendations to reduce AIDS and HIV infection—particularly as they affect minority populations.

Eligible applicants/beneficiaries: states and their political subdivisions, agents, or instrumentalities; public or private nonprofit or profit organizations.

Range: $5,000 to $270,000. **Average:** $200,000.

Activity: FY 03 estimate, 32 cooperative agreements.

HQ: Epidemiology Branch, Division of HIV/AIDS Prevention/Surveillance and Epidemiology, National Center for HIV, STD, and TB Prevention (E-45), same address/phone, grants management contact, web site as **93.118**. (Note: no field offices for this program.)

93.944 HUMAN IMMUNODEFICIENCY VIRUS (HIV)/ACQUIRED IMMUNODEFICIENCY SYNDROME (AIDS) SURVEILLANCE

Assistance: project grants (100 percent/1-5 years).

Purposes: pursuant to PHSA as amended, to continue and strengthen HIV/AIDS surveillance programs; to effect, maintain, measure, and evaluate the extent of incidence and prevalence throughout the U.S. and its territories; to provide information for targeting and implementing prevention activities. Funds may support staffing costs, purchase of computer hardware and software, laboratory costs.

Eligible applicants/beneficiaries: state and local governments including territories and possessions currently receiving HIV/AIDS surveillance cooperative agreements.

Range: $20,000 to $3,000,000. **Average:** $706,000.

Activity: annually, 85 awards.

HQ: same as **93.118**. (Note: no field offices for this program.)

93.945 ASSISTANCE PROGRAM FOR CHRONIC DISEASE PREVENTION AND CONTROL
("State Cardiovascular Health Programs" - "CVH" - "Arthritis State-Based Program" - "National Arthritis Action Plan" - "Racial and Ethnic Approaches to Community Health" - "REACH")

Assistance: project grants (80-100 percent/3-5 years).

Purposes: pursuant to PHSA as amended, to prevent and control chronic diseases, including cardiovascular diseases and arthritis; to establish new chronic disease prevention programs such as Racial and Ethnic Approaches to Community Health (REACH) programs. Funds may support costs associated with planning, implementing, and evaluating programs—but not direct curative or rehabilitative services.

Eligible applicants/beneficiaries: *all programs,* health agencies of the states and U.S. territories and possessions. REACH—public and private community-based organizations.

Range: CVH core capacity building, $250,000 to $500,000; comprehensive, $262,000 to $360,000; basic implementation, $980,000 to $1,500,000; arthritis establishment, $40,000 to $80,000; planning, $120,000 to $150,000. REACH Phase I, $200,000 to $300,000; Phase II, $800,000 to $1,000,000. **Average:** CVH core, $300,000; comprehensive, $300,000; basic implementation, $1,250,000; arthritis, $60,000; planning, $130,000. REACH I, $250,000, REACH II, $900,000.

Activity: FY 06-07—CVH, 33 state programs funded; arthritis, 36 state establishment grants; REACH, 31 awards.

HQ: Deputy Director, Division of Adult and Community Health (K45), National Center for Chronic Disease Prevention and Health Promotion, CDCP-PHS-HHS, 4770 Buford Hwy., Atlanta, GA 30333. Phone: (770)488-5269. *Grants management information*: same as **93.135**. **Internet:** "www.cdc.gov/nccdphp". (Note: no field offices for this program.)

93.946 COOPERATIVE AGREEMENTS TO SUPPORT STATE-BASED SAFE MOTHERHOOD AND INFANT HEALTH INITIATIVE PROGRAMS
("Infant Health and Pre-term Delivery Initiative" - "Pregnancy Risk Assessment and Monitoring Systems" - "PRAMS" - "Maternal and Child Health Epidemiology Programs" - "MCHEP" - "Maternal Health Research")

Assistance: project grants (100 percent/to 5 years).

Purposes: pursuant to PHSA as amended, for: (1) Pregnancy Risk Assessment and Monitoring Systems (PRAMS), to establish and maintain state-specific, population-based surveillance of selected maternal behaviors that occur during pregnancy and early infancy, and to generate state-specific data for planning and assessing perinatal health programs; (2) Maternal and Child Health Epidemiology Programs (MCHEP) to develop state multidisciplinary teams to assist states in using epidemiological and surveillance data to address the health problems of women, infants, and children, related to pregnancy, in vitro fertilization, violence around pregnancy, pre-term delivery, and reproductive health complications. Funds also may support related other types of surveillance, research, and demonstration projects.

Eligible applicants/beneficiaries: state and territorial public health agencies designated as vital U.S. registration areas; New York City public health agency; tribal governments. Prevention research—public and private nonprofit agencies including universities.

Range: PRAMS, $100,000 to $150,000. **Average:** $125,000.

Activity: 30 ongoing PRAMS agreements.

HQ: Division of Reproductive Health, National Center for Chronic Disease Prevention and Health Promotion, CDCP-HHS, Atlanta, GA 30341. Phone: (770)488-5200. *Grants management information*: same as **93.135**. **Internet**: "www.cdc.gov". (Note: no field offices for this program.)

93.947 TUBERCULOSIS DEMONSTRATION, RESEARCH, PUBLIC AND PROFESSIONAL EDUCATION

Assistance: project grants (to 100 percent/3-5 years).

Purposes: pursuant to PHSA as amended, for research into the prevention and control of tuberculosis nationally and internationally; for demonstration projects; for public information and education programs; for education, training, and clinical skills improvement for health professionals including allied health personnel. Funds may not be used for inpatient care.

Eligible applicants/beneficiaries: states, political subdivisions; public and private nonprofit entities.

Range: $150,000 to $200,000. **Average:** $165,000.

Activity: FY 05 estimate, 3 awards.

HQ: same **93.116**. (Note: no field offices for this program.)

93.952 TRAUMA CARE SYSTEMS PLANNING AND DEVELOPMENT ("Rural EMS/Trauma Care")

Assistance: project grants (to 100 percent/to 3 years).

Purposes: pursuant to PHSA as amended, for research and demonstration projects designed to improve the availability and quality of emergency medical services in rural areas. Funds may be used to develop: innovative uses of communications technologies, or new technology; model curricula for training EMS personnel including first responders, emergency medical technicians, nurses, physicians, and paramedics—with respect to patient care as well as to management of EMS systems; making EMS training more accessible in rural areas through telecommunications, home studies, and other methods; innovative protocols and agreements to increase patient access to pre-hospital care and transportation equipment; evaluations of protocols.

Eligible applicants/beneficiaries: public or private nonprofit entities.

Range: $15,000 (territories) to $40,000 (states).

Activity: annually, 50 states, territories participating. (NOTE: program deleted from the CFDA in 1997, and reinstated in December 2001; CFDA 8/04 and 8/05 indicate "this program has been transferred to **93.953**;" however, **93.953** is deleted in CFDA 8/05.)

HQ: Trauma-EMS Branch, Healthcare Systems Bureau, same address as **93.889**. Phone: (no number provided). Grants management contact, web site: same as **93.107**. (Note: no field offices for this program.)

93.954 TRIBAL RECRUITMENT AND RETENTION OF HEALTH PROFESSIONALS INTO INDIAN HEALTH PROGRAMS

Assistance: project grants.

Purposes: pursuant to the Indian Health Care Improvement Act as amended, to establish and operate programs designed to recruit for and retain health professionals in Indian health programs and facilities, including those operated by IHS.

Eligible applicants/beneficiaries: tribes or Indian health organizations, with preference to proposed participants in the IHS Loan Repayment Program (**93.164**).

Range: $60,000 to $100,000. **Average:** $83,000.

Activity: annually, 6 continuation grants.

HQ: Leader, Health Professions Manager, IHS-HHS, 801 Thompson Ave. - Ste.120, Rockville, MD 20852. Phone: (301)443-5710. Grants management contact address, web site: same as **93.123**. Phone: (301)443-5204. (Note: no field offices for this program.)

93.958 BLOCK GRANTS FOR COMMUNITY MENTAL HEALTH SERVICES ("CMHS Block Grant")

Assistance: formula grants.

Purposes: pursuant to PHSA as amended, to provide comprehensive community mental health services to adults with a serious mental illness and to children with serious emotional disturbance; for program monitoring; for technical assistance in related planning and implementation. Services must be provided through qualified community programs including community mental health centers or child mental health, psycho-social rehabilitation, mental health peer-support, or mental health primary consumer-directed programs. Funds may not be used for inpatient services, cash payments to patients, most real estate or major equipment costs.

Eligible applicants/beneficiaries: state and territorial governments; tribal organizations.

Range: $50,000 to $54,955,000. **Average:** $27,503,000.

Activity: annually, 59 awards.

HQ: State Planning and System Development Branch, CMHS-SAMHSA-HHS, 1 Choke Cherry Rd., Rockville, MD 20857. Phone: (240)276-1736. Grants management contact, web site: same as **93.229**. (Note: no field offices for this program.)

93.959 BLOCK GRANTS FOR PREVENTION AND TREATMENT OF SUBSTANCE ABUSE
("Substance Abuse Prevention and Treatment Block Grant" - "SAPT")

Assistance: formula grants.

Purposes: pursuant to PHSA as amended, to develop and implement prevention, treatment, and rehabilitation activities directed to the diseases of alcohol and drug abuse. At least 20 percent of funds allocated must support education and counseling programs concerning alcohol and substance abuse and tobacco use, for persons not requiring treatment; at least 5 percent of funds must increase treatment services for pregnant women and women with dependent children. States must require treatment programs for intravenous drug abusers, stipulating prompt admittance of such individuals into treatment. States must provide tuberculosis services such as counseling, testing, treatment, and early intervention for substance abusers at risk for HIV disease—either directly or through public or nonprofit entities.

Eligible applicants/beneficiaries: state and territory governments; the Red Lake Band of Chippewa Indians.

Range: $111,000 to $252,450,000. **Average:** $126,286,000.

Activity: annually, 60 awards.

HQ: same address as **93.238**. Phone: (no number provided). Grants management contact, web site: same as **93.138**. (Note: no field offices for this program.)

93.962 HEALTH ADMINISTRATION TRAINEESHIPS PROGRAM

Assistance: project grants (100 percent/3 years).

Purposes: pursuant to PHSA as amended and HPEPA, for traineeships for graduate students enrolled in health program or hospital administration, or health policy analysis and planning; for programs to prepare students for employment with public or private nonprofit entities, such as practice-education linkages.

Eligible applicants: public or private nonprofit educational entities.

Eligible beneficiaries: enrolled U.S. citizens or permanent residents, with priority to students demonstrating a commitment to public or nonprofit employers.

Range: $12,000 to $112,000. **Average:** $34,000.

Activity: FY 05 estimate, 32 new awards.

HQ: Center for Public Health, same address as **93.117**. Phone: (301)443-3231. Grants management contact, web site: same as **93.107**. (Note: no field offices for this program.)

93.964 PUBLIC HEALTH TRAINEESHIPS

Assistance: formula grants (100 percent/to 3 years).

Purposes: pursuant to PHSA as amended and HPEPA, for traineeships for graduate students of public health. Training must be in: biostatistics; epidemiology; environmental health; toxicology; public health nutrition; maternal and child health.

Eligible applicants/beneficiaries: schools, programs of public health; other accredited public and private nonprofit institutions.

Range: $8,109 to $149,000. **Average:** $50,000.

Activity: FY 04, 34 awards.

HQ: same address as **93.117**. Phone: (301)443-1973. Grants management contact, web site: same as **93.107**. (Note: no field offices for this program.)

93.965 COAL MINERS RESPIRATORY IMPAIRMENT TREATMENT CLINICS AND SERVICES
("Black Lung Clinics")

Assistance: project grants.

Purposes: pursuant to the Federal Mine Safety and Health Act and Black Lung Benefits Act, for broad support of coal miners respiratory impairments treatment clinics and services, including patient and family member education to maximize the patient's ability for self-care.

Eligible applicants/beneficiaries: state, public or private entities.

Range: $120,000 to $1,240,000.

Activity: annually, 15 grants.

HQ: same as **93.224**. (Note: no field offices for this program.).

93.969 GERIATRIC EDUCATION CENTERS
("GECs")

Assistance: project grants (100 percent/5 years).

Purposes: pursuant to PHSA as amended and HPEPA, to develop collaborative arrangements among health professions schools and health care facilities, focusing on multi-disciplinary training of health professionals in geriatric health care, including faculty training and retraining; to provide students with clinical training in nursing homes, chronic and acute care hospitals, ambulatory care centers, and senior centers; to develop and disseminate pertinent curricula; provide continuing education for health professionals. Funds may not be used for trainee costs or for land acquisition or construction activities.

Eligible applicants/beneficiaries: accredited health professions schools; schools of allied health; physician assistant training programs.

Range: $47,000 to $432,000. **Average:** $317,000.

Activity: FY 04, 1 new, 46 continuation, 11 supplemental awards.

HQ: same address as **93.156**. Phone: (301)443-0908. Grants management contact, web site: same as **93.107**. (Note: no field offices for this program.)

93.970 HEALTH PROFESSIONS RECRUITMENT PROGRAM FOR INDIANS

Assistance: project grants (100 percent).

Purposes: pursuant to the Indian Health Care Improvement Act as amended, to establish and operate programs to recruit American Indians and Alaska natives into education or training programs at health or allied health professions schools; to increase the number of nurses, nurse midwives, nurse practitioners, and nurse anesthetists delivering health care services to Americans Indians and Alaska natives; to place health professional residents for short-term assignments at IHS facilities.

Eligible applicants/beneficiaries: public or private nonprofit health or educational entities, with preference to tribes and tribal or urban Indian health organizations.

Range: $300,000 to $500,000. **Average:** $225,000.

Activity: annually, 11 continuation projects.

HQ: *health professions, health residents recruitment,* same address/phone as **93.954**. *Nursing recruitment,* Nurse Consultant, Nursing Program, IHS-HHS, same address (Ste.300). Phone: (301)443-1026. Grants management contact, web site: same address as **93.123**. Phone: (301)443-5204. (Note: no field offices for this program.)

93.971 HEALTH PROFESSIONS PREPARATORY SCHOLARSHIP PROGRAM FOR INDIANS

Assistance: project grants.

Purposes: pursuant to the Indian Health Care Improvement Act as amended, for compensatory pre-professional health education scholarships to American Indians and Alaska natives, covering up to two years of full-time study. Eligible disciplines are pre-nursing, -pharmacy, -medical technology, -physical therapy, -engineering, and pre-sanitation.

Eligible applicants/beneficiaries: persons of American Indian or Alaska native descent, with high school completed and accepted into an eligible program.

Range: $18,000 to $26,000. **Average:** $17,000.

Activity: FY 06 estimate, 84 continuation awards.

HQ: Scholarship Branch, Division of Health Professions Support, same addresses/phones, web site as **93.123**.

93.972 HEALTH PROFESSIONS SCHOLARSHIP PROGRAM

Assistance: project grants (100 percent/to 4 years).

Purposes: pursuant to the Indian Health Care Amendments of 1988, for scholarships to American Indians and Alaska natives enrolling full- or part-time in health professions schools, to prepare them for careers serving Indians in: allopathic or osteopathic medicine; dentistry; baccalaureate or graduate nursing; graduate public health nutrition; graduate medical social work; graduate speech pathology/audiology; optometry; pharmacy; health care administration. Grantees must serve one year in the IHS or an Indian health organization for each year of support received through the program, with a minimum of two years—with deferments for certain types of advanced training.

Eligible applicants/beneficiaries: native American Indians or Alaskans enrolled as members of a tribe, accepted for study at a U.S. educational institution in a medical/health career education program deemed necessary by the IHS, and eligible for or holding an appointment to the PHS or for civil service in the IHS.

Range: $24,000 to $38,000. **Average:** $25,000.

Activity: FY 06 estimate, 58 new, 248 continuation awards.

HQ: same as **93.971**.

93.974 FAMILY PLANNING—SERVICE DELIVERY IMPROVEMENT RESEARCH GRANTS ("SDI")

Assistance: project grants (100 percent).

Purposes: pursuant to PHSA as amended and Family Planning Services and Population Research Acts, for research studies to improve family planning services delivery. Funds may not be used in programs where abortion is a method of family planning.

Eligible applicants/beneficiaries: public or private nonprofit entities, including in territories and possessions.

Range: $150,000 to $550,000.

Activity: FY 06 estimate, 15 continuation grants.

HQ: Office of Population Affairs, same addresses/phones, web site as **93.111**. (Note: no field offices for this program.)

93.977 PREVENTIVE HEALTH SERVICES—SEXUALLY TRANSMITTED DISEASES CONTROL GRANTS

Assistance: project grants (to 100 percent/1-5 years).

Purposes: pursuant to PHSA and amendments, for surveillance activities to prevent sexually transmitted disease, including reporting, screening, case follow-up including notification of sex partners; interstate epidemiological referral; personnel education and training; studies and demonstrations; development of control strategies and activities.

Eligible applicants/beneficiaries: any state, and in consultation with state authorities, political subdivisions.

Range: $19,000 to $5,100,000. **Average:** $850,000.

Activity: annually, 65 grants.

HQ: Division of STD Prevention (E-02), National Center for HIV, STD, and TB Prevention, CDCP-HHS, 1600 Clifton Rd. NE, Atlanta, GA 30333. Phone: (404)639-8259, FAX (404)639-8608. Grants management contact, web site: same as **93.116**. (Note: no field offices for this program.)

93.978 PREVENTIVE HEALTH SERVICES—SEXUALLY TRANSMITTED DISEASES RESEARCH, DEMONSTRATIONS, AND PUBLIC INFORMATION AND EDUCATION GRANTS

Assistance: project grants (100 percent/1-5 years).

Purposes: pursuant to PHSA and amendments, for applied research, demonstrations, personnel training activities, and public education activities concerning the prevention and control of sexually transmitted diseases. Participants in the applied research may receive reimbursements from grant funds.

Eligible applicants/beneficiaries: states, political subdivisions, public or private nonprofit institutions.

Range: $125,000 to $450,000. **Average:** $314,000.

Activity: annually, 10 prevention training center grants.

HQ: same as **93.977**. (Note: no field offices for this program.)

93.982 MENTAL HEALTH DISASTER ASSISTANCE AND EMERGENCY MENTAL HEALTH

Assistance: project grants (100 percent/9-12 months).

Purposes: pursuant to the Robert T. Stafford Disaster Relief and Emergency Assistance Act, for supplemental emergency mental health counseling services to victims of major disasters; to train workers to provide such counseling.

Eligible applicants/beneficiaries: state or local nonprofit agencies recommended by the state governor.

Range: $47,000 to $3,705,000. **Average:** $1,000,000.

Activity: FY 04, 10 grants. FY 05-06, no awards.

HQ: Emergency Services and Disaster Relief Branch, CMHS-SAMHSA-HHS, Rockville, MD 20857. Phone: (no number provided). *Grants management information*: same as **93.104**. **Internet:** "www.samhsa.gov".

93.988 COOPERATIVE AGREEMENTS FOR STATE-BASED DIABETES CONTROL PROGRAMS AND EVALUATION OF SURVEILLANCE SYSTEMS ("DCPs")

Assistance: project grants (80-84 percent/5 years).

Purposes: pursuant to PHSA as amended and Health Services and Centers Amendments Act of 1978, to plan, implement, and evaluate state-based diabetes control programs including: determining the size and nature diabetes-related problems; developing new strategies to prevention; establishing partnerships to prevent diabetes problems; increasing awareness of prevention and control opportunities among the public, health care and business communities, and diabetes patients; improving access to quality care. Direct curative or rehabilitative services to patients may not be provided with grant funds.

Eligible applicants/beneficiaries: official state and territorial health agencies.

Range: core capacity program, $75,000 to $350,000; implementation programs, $300,000 to $800,000. **Average:** core capacity, $250,000; implementation, $500,000.

Activity: estimate, capacity-building, 26 implementation awards.

HQ: Program Development Branch, Division of Diabetes Translation, National Center for Chronic Disease Prevention and Health Promotion, CDCP-HHS, 1600 Clifton Rd. NE, Atlanta, GA 30333. Phone: (770)488-5046. *Grants management information*: same as **93.135**. **Internet:** "www.cdc.gov". (Note: no field offices for this program.)

93.989 INTERNATIONAL RESEARCH AND RESEARCH TRAINING

Assistance: project grants (100 percent/to 5 years).

Purposes: pursuant to PHSA as amended, for research and research training to reduce disparities in global health and toward the international exchange of ideas and information. Research is supported in the basic biological, behavioral, and social sciences, including economics, demography, and ethics.

Grants may support stipends, foreign living allowances, travel, and minimal other costs required to perform research in a foreign country.

Eligible applicants/beneficiaries: IHEs, hospitals, laboratories, federal institutions, state and local governments, and other public or private nonprofit of profit institutions.

Range: regular research, education project, training grants, $100,000 to $1,300,000; career awards, $50,000 to $150,000; cooperative agreements, $300,000 to $700,000; small grants, $30,000 to $45,000. **Average:** regular, $400,000; career, $127,000; cooperative, $600,000; small, $41,000.

Activity: FY 04 (representative), 28 minority, 12 biodiversity, 11 maternal and child health, 1 health and economic development, 14 clinical-operational-health services, 13 environmental and occupational, 9 malaria research, 25 AIDS training and research, and 3 infectious diseases awards.

HQ: Fogarty International Center, NIH-HHS, Bldg. 31 - Rm.B2C39, Bethesda, MD 20892-2220. Phone: (301)496-1653. **Internet:** "www.fic.nih.gov"; "www.fic.nih.gov/programs/grants.html". (Note: no field offices for this program.)

93.990 NATIONAL HEALTH PROMOTION

Assistance: project grants (100 percent/to 3 years).

Purposes: pursuant to PHSA as amended, for national membership organizations from various sectors to participate in the National Health Promotion Program to educate the public about good health habits and programs designed to prevent disease and disability. Funds may be used to develop promotion programs and materials to be used by schools, medical treatment sites, work sites, and community health promotion programs; to identify the needs of special population groups; to fill gaps identified in the "Healthy People 2010: National Health Promotion and Disease Prevention Objectives."

Eligible applicants/beneficiaries: public or private nonprofit organizations.

Range: $50,000 to $75,000. **Average:** $65,000.

Activity: FY 05-06 estimate, no awards.

HQ: Office of Disease Prevention and Health Promotion, OS-HHS, 200 Independence Ave. SW, Washington, DC 20201. Phone: (202)401-6295. *Grants management information*: same as **93.004**. **Internet:** "www.health.gov/healthypeople". (Note: no field offices for this program.)

93.991 PREVENTIVE HEALTH AND HEALTH SERVICES BLOCK GRANT ("PHHS Block Grants")

Assistance: formula grants (100 percent/2 years).

Purposes: pursuant to PHSA, Health Omnibus Programs Extension Act of 1988, and amendments, for state preventive health service programs, including emergency medical services program improvement (but not program operations costs), health incentive activities, hypertension programs, rodent control, fluoridation programs, health education, risk reduction programs, home health services, services for victims of sex offenses including prevention of sex offenses, and other services related to the accomplishment of "Year 2000/2010" objectives.

Eligible applicants/beneficiaries: state and Pacific territorial governments, certain tribes.

Range: $29,000 to $9,430,000. **Average:** $2,118,000.

Activity: annually, all states and territories, two tribes funded.

HQ: Project Officer, National Center for Chronic Disease Prevention and Health Promotion (K30), CDCP-HHS, 4770 Buford Hwy. NE, Atlanta, GA 30341-3724. Phone: (404)488-5282. Grants management contact, web site: same as **93.988**. (Note: no field offices for this program.)

93.993 PUBLIC HEALTH RESEARCH ACCREDITATION PROJECT

Assistance: project grants (100 percent/to 3 years).

Purposes: pursuant to PHSA as amended, to develop pilot measures to assess the ability of the public health infrastructure to assess and monitor research involving human subjects. Projects will assess the role of accreditation of human research protection programs to enhance protections afforded to persons involved in public health research, including epidemiologic, health services, social and behavioral intervention, as well as traditional biomedical research and clinical trials.

Eligible applicants/beneficiaries: public or private, nonprofit or profit organizations actively engaged in accreditation of human research protection programs.

Range/Average: N.A.

Activity: new program listing in 2004.

HQ: Procurement and Grants Office, CDCP-HHS, 2920 Brandywine Rd., Atlanta, GA 30341-4146. Phone: *general questions,* Technical Information Management, (770)488-2700; *management, budget matters,* Contracts Specialist, (770)488-2736. *Program technical assistance,* Deputy Associate Director/Science, Office of Science Policy and Technology Transfer (D-50), CDCP-HHS, 1600 Clifton Rd. NE, Atlanta, GA 30333. Phone: (404)639-7262. **Internet:** "www.cdc.gov". (Note: no field offices for this program.)

93.994 MATERNAL AND CHILD HEALTH SERVICES BLOCK GRANT TO THE STATES
("MCH Block Grant")

Assistance: formula grants (57 percent).

Purposes: pursuant to SSA as amended, for a broad range of health and related services including preventive and primary care services to pregnant women, mothers, infants, and children including children with special health needs. Funds may support such costs as program planning, administration, education, and evaluation. Ineligible uses of funds are most inpatient services, cash payments for health services, major equipment purchases, construction costs, or research or training other than by public or nonprofit entities.

Eligible applicants/beneficiaries: states and insular areas.

Range: $159,000 to $48,442,000. **Average:** $9,981,000.

Activity: annually, 59 block grants.

HQ: Division of State and Community Health, Maternal and Child Health Bureau, HRSA-HHS, 5600 Fishers Lane - Rm.18-31, Rockville, MD 20857. Phone: (301)443-2204. Grants management contact, web site: same as **93.107**. (Note: no field offices for this program.)

93.995 ADOLESCENT FAMILY LIFE—DEMONSTRATION PROJECTS ("AFL")

Assistance: project grants (to 70 percent/to 5 years).

Purposes: pursuant to PHSA as amended, to establish innovative, comprehensive, and integrated approaches to the delivery of care services to pregnant and parenting adolescents, especially those under age 17; to promote abstinence from sexual relations through age-appropriate education on sexuality and decision making skills as the most effective method of preventing adolescent pregnancy and avoiding sexually transmitted diseases including HIV/AIDS. Funds may support costs of: care and prevention services; coordination of services among local providers; appropriate supplemental services.

Eligible applicants/beneficiaries: public organizations including city, county, regional, and state governments; private nonprofit organizations.

Range: $150,000 to $250,000.

Activity: FY 06 estimate, 100 continuation, 50 new grants.

HQ: same as **93.111**. (Note: no field offices for this program.)

93.996 BIOTERRORISM TRAINING AND CURRICULUM DEVELOPMENT PROGRAM ("BTCDP")

Assistance: project grants (100 percent/to 2 years).

Purposes: pursuant to the Public Health Security and Bioterrorism Preparedness and Response Act of 2002, to prepare a workforce of health care professionals to address the medical consequences of bioterrorism and other public health emergency preparedness and response issues. Funding may support multidisciplinary and collaborative: provision of continuing education for practicing providers; undergraduate and graduate curriculum development in health professions schools; drills, exercises, and simulations. Linkages and relationships must be demonstrated with such entities as awardees of the CDC Public Health Preparedness and Response for Bioterrorism Program and HRSA Bioterrorism Hospital Preparedness Programs, academic health centers, other service providers, and consumers.

Eligible applicants/beneficiaries: academic health centers, public and private nonprofit accredited or licensed health professions schools, multi-state or multi-institutional consortia, professional organizations and societies, and community-based organizations.

Range: continuing education projects, $488,000 to $1,771,000; curriculum development, $119,000 to $615,000. **Average:** continuing education, $1,771,000; curriculum, $330,000.

Activity: new program in FY 03. FY 05 estimate, 25-30 continuing education, 5 curriculum development awards.

HQ: same as **93.165**. (Note: no field offices for this program.)

CORPORATION FOR NATIONAL AND COMMUNITY SERVICE

94.002 RETIRED AND SENIOR VOLUNTEER PROGRAM ("RSVP")

Assistance: project grants (70-90 percent/3 years).

Purposes: pursuant to the Domestic Volunteer Service Act of 1973 as amended and National and Community Service Trust Act of 1993 (NCSA), for programs engaging retired persons as volunteers in community service projects—e.g., intergenerational activities, in-home care, consumer education, public safety, and health and human service activities. Grant funds cover program costs including staff salaries and reimbursements to volunteers for their out-of-pocket expenses, primarily for transportation. Technical assistance and materials toward establishing and operating programs are available.

Eligible applicants: public agencies including state and local government agencies, private nonprofit organizations.

Eligible beneficiaries: volunteers at least age 55.

Range: to $847,000. **Average:** $69,000.

Activity: 485,000 volunteers serving in 65,000 local organizations, contributing 77,000,000 hours of volunteer service.

HQ: National Senior Service Corps, RSVP, CNCS, 1201 New York Ave. NW, Washington, DC 20525. Phone: (202)606-5000; (800)424-8867. **Internet:** "www.nationalservice.org".

94.003 STATE COMMISSIONS

Assistance: project grants (cost sharing).

Purposes: pursuant to NCSA as amended, to operate independent, bipartisan state commissions to oversee funded AmeriCorps programs. Commissions generally include 15 to 25 members appointed by governors.

Eligible applicants/beneficiaries: state governments, DC, PR.

Range: $125,000 to $750,000.

Activity: N.A.

HQ: CNCS, 1201 New York Ave. NW, Washington, DC 20525. Phone: (202)606-5000, ext. 474. **Internet:** same as **94.002**.

94.004 LEARN AND SERVE AMERICA—SCHOOL AND COMMUNITY BASED PROGRAMS

Assistance: project grants (50-90 percent/to 5 years).

Purposes: pursuant to NCSA as amended, to encourage elementary and secondary schools and community-based agencies to establish, develop, and offer service-learning opportunities for school-age youth—in such areas as health, education, public safety, and environment; to educate teachers about service-learning and incorporate its concepts into classrooms; to coordinate adult volunteers serving in schools; to introduce young people to career opportunities. Funds may be used for: planning and capacity building; program operating costs including grants to local partnerships for service-learning projects; programs involving adult volunteers in educating students; teacher and staff training and technical assistance.

Eligible applicants/beneficiaries: SEAs, State Commissions on National Service, territories, tribes, public or private nonprofit entities.

Range: $20,000 to $2,376,000. **Average:** $299,000.

Activity: FY 02, 1,500,000 youth involved (latest data reported).

HQ: same address, web site as **94.003**. Phone: (202)606-5000, ext. 117.

94.005 LEARN AND SERVE AMERICA—HIGHER EDUCATION

Assistance: project grants (to 50 percent/to 3 years).

Purposes: pursuant to NCSA as amended and HEA of 1965, for service-learning projects engaging graduate and undergraduate college students and faculty members in meeting community needs, while enhancing student academic and civic learning; to build capacity and strengthen the service infrastructure of IHEs. Eligible project activities include tutoring, mentoring, health outreach and education, primary and preventive health care, conflict resolution, neighborhood clean-up and revitalization, and prevention of gang violence and substance abuse activities.

Eligible applicants/beneficiaries: IHEs, consortia of IHEs, and nonprofit organizations or public agencies including states in partnerships with IHEs.

Range: $40,000 to $320,000. **Average:** $189,000.

Activity: FY 03 estimate, 62 continuation grants supporting some 30,000 students participating at 300 IHEs.

HQ: same as **94.004**.

94.006 AMERICORPS

Assistance: project grants.

Purposes: pursuant to NCSA as amended, to plan or operate national and community service programs addressing community education, public safety, human, and environmental needs—by encouraging volunteers to serve part- or full-time. AmeriCorps members serve for one year, and receive education awards for postsecondary education or to pay off student loans. Examples include volunteers serving as mentors, tutors, teaching assistants, role models—in after-school, immunization, low-income housing renovation, "crime watch", environmental projects.

Eligible applicants/beneficiaries: states, tribes, territories, national nonprofit organizations, professional corps, and multi-state organizations.

Range: $200,000 (state programs) to $3,000,000 (national programs).

Activity: FY 01, 45,000 AmeriCorps members (latest data reported).

HQ: same as **94.003**.

94.007 PLANNING AND PROGRAM DEVELOPMENT GRANTS

Assistance: project grants.

Purposes: pursuant to NCSA as amended, for innovative demonstration projects that build the ethic of service among Americans of all ages and backgrounds—including through the AmeriCorps Education Award Program, AmeriCorps Promise Fellows Program, and Martin Luther King Day of Service Program, and Disability Outreach grants for programs ensuring participation of the disabled in national and community service.

Eligible applicants/beneficiaries: demonstration grants—state and local government agencies, nonprofit organizations. Disability grants—operating AmeriCorps programs, state commissions, national nonprofit organizations.

Range: demonstration grants, $25,000 to $500,000; Martin Luther King Day of Service grants, to $5,000.

Activity: no recent report.

HQ: same address, web site as **94.003**. Phone: (202)606-5000.

94.009 TRAINING AND TECHNICAL ASSISTANCE

Assistance: project grants.

Purposes: pursuant to the NCSA as amended, for training and technical assistance services to CNCS grantees in such areas as program and financial management, fund raising, sustainability, membership development and training, and program evaluation. Services are provided through national, regional, and state workshops, publications, on-site consultations.

Eligible applicants/beneficiaries: federal, state, and local agencies and other government units; tribes; IHEs; nonprofit and community-based organizations; some for-profit companies.

Range: $100,000 to $1,500,000.

Activity: no recent report.

HQ: same address, web site as **94.003**. Phone: (202)606-5000, ext. 139, FAX (202)208-4151.

94.011 FOSTER GRANDPARENT PROGRAM ("FGP")

Assistance: project grants (from 90 percent).

Purposes: pursuant to the Domestic Volunteer Service Act of 1973 as amended and National and Community Service Trust Act of 1993, to engage older volunteers with limited incomes in providing supportive services to infants, children, or youth with special or exceptional needs. Programs may be conducted in the children's homes or in residential or nonresidential facilities including preschools. Grant funds may be used: to pay stipends to low-income foster grandparents serving as volunteers, and to provide their transportation, physical exams, and meals; for staff salaries and travel, equipment, and space costs. Technical assistance and materials toward establishing and operating programs are available.

Eligible applicants: state and local government agencies, private nonprofit organizations.

Eligible beneficiaries: persons at least age 60, low-income, and physically, mentally, and emotionally capable of serving clients on a person-to-person basis; non-low-income individuals may serve as volunteers without stipends.

Range: to $1,949,000. **Average:** $318,000.

Activity: FY 01, 321 community-based projects funded, 23,000 volunteer service years provided by foster grandparents (latest data reported).

HQ: Foster Grandparent Program, National Senior Service Corps, CNCS, same address/phone, web site as **94.002**.

94.013 VOLUNTEERS IN SERVICE TO AMERICA ("AmeriCorps-VISTA")

Assistance: specialized services.

Purposes: pursuant to the Domestic Volunteer Service Act of 1973 as amended, to provide volunteers from all walks of life and age groups, working in projects addressing the problems of poverty such as health, illiteracy, substance abuse prevention and education, hunger, homelessness, housing, unemployment. Volunteers may be recruited locally or referred by CNCS; they serve full-time for one year, living at subsistence levels of support among the people they serve.

Eligible applicants/beneficiaries: federal, state, or local government agencies or private nonprofit organizations.

Activity: FY 01, 6,000 volunteers, 1,200 projects in 50 states, PR, DC (latest data reported).

HQ: Director, VISTA, CNCS, same address/phones/web site as **94.002**.

94.016 SENIOR COMPANION PROGRAM ("SCP")

Assistance: project grants (from 90 percent/3 years).

Purposes: pursuant to the Domestic Volunteer Service Act of 1973 as amended and National and Community Service Trust Act of 1993, for the operating costs of the Senior Companion Program, including stipends, transportation, physical exams, insurance, and meals for low-income older volunteers. SCP participants serve as companions to other adults, primarily older persons with special needs. Services to the adults may be provided in their homes or in residential or nonresidential facilities, including such activities as helping hospital patients during their recuperation, arranging for community social services, working with the terminally ill. Respite care services, including to Alzheimer's patients and their families, are also provided.

Eligible applicants/beneficiaries: same as for **94.011**.

Range: to $689,000. **Average:** $238,000.

Activity: FY 01, 9,375 service-years provided through 178 funded projects and 41 nonfunded projects supporting 3,700 volunteer service years, serving some 55,000 clients (latest data reported).

HQ: Senior Companion Program, CNCS, same address/phones (ext.189), web site as **94.002**.

SOCIAL SECURITY ADMINISTRATION

96.001 SOCIAL SECURITY—DISABILITY INSURANCE

Assistance: direct payments/unrestricted or specified use.

Purposes: pursuant to SSA as amended, to replace part of the earnings lost because of a physical or mental impairment preventing a person from working. Disability is defined as a medically determined physical or mental impairment that has lasted or is expected to last at least 12 months, or to result in death. There is a five-month waiting period. Costs of vocational rehabilitation for certain beneficiaries are eligible.

Eligible applicants/beneficiaries: disabled workers under full retirement age (66 for workers age 62 in 2005) if they have worked for a sufficient period of time under Social Security. Certain family members of disabled workers also are eligible for benefits, including: unmarried children under age 18, or 19 for full-time elementary and secondary students; disabled unmarried children under age 22; spouse caring for child under age 16 or disabled, receiving benefits on worker's Social Security record; spouses age 62 or over; divorced spouses age 62 or over, married to the worker for at least 10 years. Benefits are subject to an earnings test, and may be reduced by amounts received under other programs. Certain restrictions apply for impairments: based on drug addiction or alcoholism; based on felony- and confinement-related impairments. Coverage credits under the social security systems of certain foreign governments may be taken into account. Effective after 2003, lawfully admitted aliens may be eligible if they have a work-authorized Social Security Number. Applicants should contact local Social Security offices for additional details.

Range: 2005, to $2,099 monthly for a disabled worker; to $3,148.60 for a family. **Average:** FY 05, individual, $880; family, $1,496.

Activity: FY 05 estimate, 8,005,000 benefit recipients monthly (average).

HQ: Office of Public Inquiries, SSA, Annex - Rm.4100, Baltimore, MD 21235. Phone: (410)965-2736. **Internet:** "www.socialsecurity.gov".

96.002 SOCIAL SECURITY—RETIREMENT INSURANCE

Assistance: direct payments/unrestricted use.

Purposes: pursuant to SSA as amended, to pay monthly cash benefits to retired workers and their eligible auxiliaries.

Eligible applicants/beneficiaries: retired workers age 62 and over that have worked the required number of years under Social Security. Certain family members also are eligible for benefits (same as in **96.001**). Benefit payments to eligible workers applying before full-benefit retirement age (66 for workers age 62 in 2005) are reduced permanently. Benefit amounts may be reduced for a spouse receiving a government pension based on his or her work in non-covered employment. Coverage credits under the social security systems of certain foreign governments may be taken into account to meet eligibility requirements. Effective after 2003, lawfully admitted aliens may be eligible if they have a work-authorized Social Security Number. All applicants should contact local Social Security offices for additional details and restrictions.

Range: 2005, to $1,939 monthly for an individual retiring at full-retirement age; to $3,394.10 for a family receiving benefits. **Average**: as of 31 December 2004, individual, $942 monthly; retired worker and eligible spouse, $1,574 monthly.

Activity: FY 04, 32,709,000 monthly benefit recipients (average).

HQ: same as **96.001**.

96.003 SOCIAL SECURITY—SPECIAL BENEFITS FOR PERSONS AGED 72 AND OVER

Assistance: direct payments/unrestricted use.

Purposes: pursuant to the Tax Adjustment Act of 1966 as amended, to pay monthly cash benefits to persons age 72 and over who did not earn protection under the Social Security program during their working years. Payments are not made for any month during which payments are received under the Supplemental Security Income program (**96.006**); benefits are reduced by the amount of most other governmental pensions, retirement benefits, or annuities.

Eligible applicants/beneficiaries: persons that reached age 72 before 1968 need no work credits under Social Security. Those that reached age 72 in 1968-1971 need some work credits to be eligible. The amount of work credit needed increases gradually each year for persons reaching age 72 in 1968-1971.

Range/Average: as of December 2004, $237.70 monthly.

Activity: FY 04, monthly benefits to 9 persons.

HQ: same as **96.001**.

96.004 SOCIAL SECURITY—SURVIVORS INSURANCE

Assistance: direct payments/specified or unrestricted uses.

Purposes: pursuant to SSA as amended, to pay monthly cash benefits to a deceased worker's dependents if the deceased was insured for survivors' insurance protection.

Eligible applicants/beneficiaries: widows or widowers age 60 or over; surviving divorced spouses age 60 or over, married to the deceased worker for at least 10 years; survivors with a child in their care under age 16 or disabled; disabled widows, widowers, or divorced spouses age 50-59; unmarried children under age 18, or under 19 if in elementary or secondary school, or age 18 or older if disabled before age 22; dependent parents age 62 or over. Earnings tests and benefit limits apply, except for beneficiaries age 70 or over. Under certain conditions, a lump-sum death payment of $255 is payable to survivors. Benefits are subject to an earnings test, and may be reduced by amounts received under other programs. Benefit amounts are reduced for a spouse receiving a government pension based on his or her work in non-covered employment. Coverage credits under the social security systems of certain foreign governments may be taken into account to meet eligibility requirements. Effective after 2003, lawfully admitted aliens may be eligible if they have a work-authorized Social Security Number. Applicants should contact local Social Security offices for additional details.

Range: 2005, to $1,939 monthly. **Average:** for an aged widow or widower alone, $920 monthly; with two or more eligible children, $1,905 monthly.

Activity: FY 04, monthly benefits to 6,779,000 survivors (average).

HQ: same as **96.001**.

96.006 SUPPLEMENTAL SECURITY INCOME ("SSI")

Assistance: direct payments/unrestricted or specified uses.

Purposes: pursuant SSA as amended, to provide supplemental income to persons aged 65 and over and to blind or disabled persons with incomes and financial resources below specified levels.

Eligible applicants/beneficiaries: persons age 65 or over or blind or disabled, meeting U.S. citizenship or residence requirements, and with income and assets below certain levels.

Range: January 2005, to $579 monthly for individuals; to $869 for an individual with an eligible spouse. **Average:** $404 monthly.

Activity: FY 04, monthly benefits to 6,666,000 persons (average).

HQ: same as **96.002**.

96.007 SOCIAL SECURITY—RESEARCH AND DEMONSTRATION ("SSA Research and Demonstration")

Assistance: project grants (75-95 percent/3 months-5 years).

Purposes: pursuant to SSA as amended, for social, economic, and demographic research and demonstration projects and experiments to improve the management, administration, and effectiveness of facets of SSA programs.

Eligible applicants/beneficiaries: state and local governments, educational institutions, hospitals, public and private nonprofit and profit organizations.

Range: $100,000 to $1,750,000.

Activity: FY 05 estimate, 52 continuation awards.

HQ: Grants Management Officer, Office of Operations Contracts and Grants, Office of Acquisition and Grants, DCFAM, SSA, 6401 Security Blvd. - G-C-7 EHR, Baltimore, MD 21235. Phone: (410)965-9518. **Internet:** same as **96.001**. (Note: no field offices for this program.)

96.008 SOCIAL SECURITY—BENEFITS PLANNING, ASSISTANCE, AND OUTREACH PROGRAM

Assistance: project grants (75-95 percent/3 months-5 years).

Purposes: pursuant to SSA, Ticket-to-Work Incentives Improvement Act of 1999, Workforce Improvement Act of 1998, and other acts, for: statewide benefits planning and assistance programs, including information on the availability of protection and advocacy services, to all Social Security Disability Insurance and SSI beneficiaries; ongoing outreach to beneficiaries with disabilities and families eligible to participate in state or federal work incentives programs; to disseminate information to SSA beneficiaries with disabilities, including transition-to-work youth, about work incentives and related issues.

Eligible applicants/beneficiaries: state or local governments; public, private, profit or nonprofit organizations—including such organizations as centers for independent living, protection and advocacy organizations, tribal entities, client assistance programs, state vocational rehabilitation agencies, developmental disabilities councils, Workforce Investment Boards.

Range: $50,000 to $300,000.

Activity: annually, 56 cooperative agreements with all states and territories.

HQ: Project Officer, Office of Employment Support Programs, ODISP-SSA, 107 Altmeyer Bldg., 6401 Security Blvd., Baltimore, MD 21235. Phone: (410)966-8333. **Internet:** "www.socialsecurity.gov/oag/". (Note: no field offices for this program.)

96.009 SOCIAL SECURITY STATE GRANTS FOR WORK INCENTIVES ASSISTANCE TO DISABLED BENEFICIARIES

Assistance: project grants (formula based/3 months-5 five years).

Purposes: pursuant to SSA, Ticket-to-Work Incentives Improvement Act of 1999, Workforce Improvement Act of 1998, and other acts, to provide information, advice, and advocacy to disabled SSA beneficiaries, about obtaining vocational rehabilitation and other services to help them obtain or regain gainful employment.

Eligible applicants/beneficiaries: state protection and advocacy systems.

Range: $50,000 to $438,000. **Average:** $118,000.

Activity: not quantified specifically.

HQ: same address as **96.008**. Phone: (410)965-8658. **Internet:** "www.socialsecurity.gov/work/ServiceProviders/pafactsheet.html.". (Note: no field offices for this program.)

96.020 SPECIAL BENEFITS FOR CERTAIN WORLD WAR II VETERANS ("Special Veterans Benefits" - "SVB")

Assistance: direct payments/unrestricted use.

Purposes: pursuant to SSA and Foster Care Independence Act of 1999, to pay special benefits to certain World War II veterans that are eligible for SSI benefits and reside outside the U.S.

Eligible applicants/beneficiaries: World War II veterans age 65 or older as of December 14, 1999, residing outside the U.S. (including specific Filipino veterans), meeting length and dates of service requirements, and with other benefit income that is less than 75 percent of the SSI benefit rate.

Range: 2005, to $434.25 monthly. **Average:** $308.34.
Activity: currently, 2,550 beneficiaries residing in the Philippines.
HQ: same as **96.001**.

DEPARTMENT OF HOMELAND SECURITY

97.001 PILOT DEMONSTRATION OR EARMARKED PROJECTS ("Earmarked Projects" - "One-Time Funded Programs")

Assistance: project grants.

Purposes: pursuant to the Homeland Security Act and U.S.A. Patriot Act of 2001 (USAPA), for special programs or projects by entities specified in Congressional appropriations.

Eligible applicants/beneficiaries: nonfederal entities—e.g., state, local, tribal governments; private, public, profit, or nonprofit organizations, or individuals specified in Congressional appropriations.

Range/Average: N.A.

Activity: new program in FY 03.

HQ: Office of Grant Policy and Oversight-DHS, 245 Murray Lane - Rm.214, Washington, DC 20523. Phone: (202)205-9193. **Internet:** "www.dhs.gov/dhspublic/display/?theme=37&content-3608". (Note: no field offices for this program.)

97.002 RESEARCH PROJECTS ("Earmarked Research Projects" - "One-Time Funded Research Programs")

Assistance: project grants.

Purposes: pursuant to the Homeland Security Act and USAPA, for research programs or projects by entities specified in Congressional appropriations.

Eligible applicants/beneficiaries: same as for **97.001**.

Range/Average: N.A.

Activity: new program in FY 03.

HQ: same as **97.001**. (Note: no field offices for this program.)

97.004 STATE DOMESTIC PREPAREDNESS EQUIPMENT SUPPORT PROGRAM

Assistance: formula grants (100 percent/to 3 years).

Purposes: pursuant to USAPA, to enhance the capacity of state and local first responders to respond to Weapons of Mass Destruction (WMD) terrorist incidents involving nuclear, biological, chemical, incendiary, and explosive devices. Funds may be used to: conduct comprehensive threat and needs assessments; develop and implement Statewide Domestic Preparedness

Strategies; purchase equipment; plan and conduct of exercises. Program initially listed as a DOJ program, and transferred to DHS in CFDA 2003; CFDA 2005 indicates program has been renamed "State Homeland Security Grant Program, (**97.073**), and merged into "Homeland Security Grant Program (**97.067**); however, this program has not been deleted in CFDA 2005. (Note: re web site given under "HQ", below, CFDA 2005 cites web site as active.)

Eligible applicants/beneficiaries: states, territories, possessions.

Range/Average: N.A.

Activity: not quantified specifically.

HQ: Office of State and Local Government Coordination and Preparedness, Office for Domestic Preparedness-DHS, 245 Murray Lane - Bldg. 410, Washington, DC 20523. Phone: (800)368-6498. **Internet:** "www.ojp.usdoj.gov". (Note: no field offices for this program.)

97.005 STATE AND LOCAL HOMELAND SECURITY TRAINING PROGRAM

Assistance: project grants (100 percent/to 3 years).

Purposes: pursuant to USAPA, to develop and conduct training programs for state and local first responders to incidents involving WMD domestic terrorist incidents involving nuclear, biological, chemical, incendiary, and explosive devices—for personnel involved in fire-fighting, law enforcement, emergency medical services, emergency management, public works, and public health. (Note: re web site given under "HQ", below, program initially listed as a DOJ program, and transferred to DHS in CFDA 2003; however, CFDA 2005 cites web site as active.)

Eligible applicants: the National Domestic Preparedness Consortium. Others that may become eligible will be so notified.

Eligible beneficiaries: state and local government units.

Range: N.A.

Activity: not quantified specifically.

HQ: same address/phone as **97.004**. **Internet:** "www.ojp.usdoj.gov/odp". (Note: no field offices for this program.)

97.006 STATE AND LOCAL HOMELAND SECURITY EXERCISE SUPPORT

Assistance: project grants (100 percent/to 3 years).

Purposes: pursuant to the USAPA, to plan and conduct exercises for national, state, and local first responders to incidents of terrorism involving WMD including nuclear, biological, chemical, incendiary and explosive devices. (Note: program initially listed as a DOJ program, and transferred to DHS in CFDA 2003.)

Eligible applicants: public or private organizations with expertise and experience in providing program assistance.

Eligible beneficiaries: state and local units of government.

Range: N.A.

Activity: not quantified specifically.

HQ: same address/phone as **97.004**. **Internet:** "www.dhs.gov". (Note: no field offices for this program.)

97.007 HOMELAND SECURITY PREPAREDNESS TECHNICAL ASSISTANCE

Assistance: project grants (100 percent/to 3 years).

Purposes: pursuant to USAPA, to enhance the capacity of state and local first responders to respond to WMD terrorist incidents involving nuclear, biological, chemical, incendiary, and explosive devices. Funds may be used to develop, plan, and implement programs and to sustain and maintain specialized equipment.

Eligible applicants/beneficiaries: same as **97.006**.

Range: N.A.

Activity: not quantified specifically

HQ: same as **97.006**. (Note: no field offices for this program.)

97.008 URBAN AREAS SECURITY INITIATIVE

Assistance: project grants (100 percent/2.5 years).

Purposes: pursuant to USAPA, to address the unique needs of large urban areas and mass transit authorities to be prepared for and respond to threats of incidents of terrorism. Funds may be used for equipment, training, exercises, and planning.

Eligible applicants/beneficiaries: states containing selected cities.

Range/Average: N.A.

Activity: new program listing in 2003. Not quantified specifically.

HQ: same as **97.006**. (Note: no field offices for this program.)

97.009 CUBAN/HAITIAN ENTRANT PROGRAM

Assistance: project grants (100 percent/1-4 years).

Purposes: pursuant to the Refugee Education Assistance Act of 1980 as amended, for primary resettlement services to eligible Cubans and Haitians paroled into communities by DHS for humanitarian reasons; for Cuban and Haitian entrants living in south Florida and requiring secondary resettlement assistance. (Program initially listed as a DOJ program, and transferred to DHS in CFDA 2003.)

Eligible applicants/beneficiaries: public or private nonprofit organizations or agencies; certain profit organizations.

Range: to $4,500,000.

Activity: FY 04 estimate, 19,000 entrants served.

HQ: Parole and Humanitarian Assistance Branch, Immigration and Customs Enforcement, Office of International Affairs-DHS, 425 Eye St. NW, Washington, DC 20536. Phone: (no number provided). **Internet:** "www.dhs.gov".

97.010 CITIZENSHIP EDUCATION AND TRAINING

Assistance: technical information.

Purposes: pursuant to the Immigration and Nationality Act of 1952 as amended, to provide instruction and training materials in citizenship responsibilities for immigrants interested becoming U.S. citizens and in learning English and U.S. history and government. Free federal textbooks on citizenship at various reading levels are provided. (Program initially listed as a DOJ program, and transferred to DHS in CFDA 2003.)

Eligible applicants/beneficiaries: public schools or other educational groups conducting classes under supervision of public schools.

Activity: annually, 4,200 textbooks distributed.

HQ: Citizenship and Immigration Service-DHS, 20 Massachusetts Ave. NW, Washington, DC 20529. Phone: (202)272-1310. **Internet:** "www.uscis.gov".

97.011 BOATING SAFETY

Assistance: specialized services; technical information; training.

Purposes: for the Coast Guard Auxiliary to provide: boating safety education and training; Vessel Safety Checks; assistance in patrolling regattas and parades, and to boaters in distress; publications. (Program initially listed as a USCG-DOT program, and transferred to DHS in CFDA 2003.)

Eligible applicants/beneficiaries: U.S. citizens at least age 17 may apply for membership in the Auxiliary.

Activity: 112,000 vessel safety examinations; 220,000 public school students enrolled in courses; 2,256 regatta and 23,000 safety patrols, 3,733 public assists, 311 lives saved.

HQ: Commandant (G-OCX), U.S. Coast Guard-DHS, 2100 Second St. SW - Rm.3501, Washington, DC 20593-0001. Phone: (202)267-1001. **Internet:** "www.cgaux.org".

97.012 BOATING SAFETY FINANCIAL ASSISTANCE

Assistance: formula grants (50-100 percent/1 year).

Purposes: for states to develop and operate recreational boating safety programs. Funds may support: education, maintenance, and enforcement activities; costs of facilities acquisition and construction or repair of access sites; personnel training; administration. (Program initially listed as a USCG-DOT program, and transferred to DHS in CFDA 2003.)

Eligible applicants/beneficiaries: states, territories, and possessions with approved boating safety programs; national nonprofit service organizations.

Range: states, $346,000 to $3,959,000; organizations (100 percent funding), $7,000 to $439,000. **Average:** states, $1,038,000; organizations, $91,000.

Activity: 50 states, several territories and possessions, 16 national organizations funded.

HQ: Office of Boating Safety (G-OPB), U.S. Coast Guard-DHS, 2100 Second St. SW - Rm.3501, Washington, DC 20593. Phone: *states,* (202)267-0857; *nonprofits,* (202)267-0974. **Internet:** "www.uscboating.org"; "www.dhs.gov". (Note: no field offices for this program.)

97.013 STATE ACCESS TO THE OIL SPILL LIABILITY TRUST FUND

Assistance: project grants (100 percent).

Purposes: pursuant to the Oil Pollution Act of 1990, to reimburse states for costs incurred in responding to actual or threatened discharges of oil occurring after 18 August 1990. Eligible expenses include engaged state officials' salaries, personnel and materials transportation, equipment, and similar costs. (Program initially listed as a USCG-DOT program, and transferred to DHS in CFDA 2003.)

Eligible applicants/beneficiaries: governors of states, territories, and possessions.

Range: $250,000 maximum per incident.

Activity: N.A.

HQ: DHS, 245 Murray Dr. SW, Washington, DC 20528. Phone: (202)282-8000. **Internet:** "www.dhs.gov". (Note: no field offices for this program.)

97.014 BRIDGE ALTERATION ("Truman-Hobbs Act")

Assistance: direct payments/specified use.

Purposes: pursuant to the Rivers and Harbors Appropriations Act of 1899, Bridge Act of 1906 as amended, and Truman-Hobbs Act, for the alteration of obstructive bridges to render navigation reasonably free, easy, and unobstructed. Project funds may not be used for such activities as those providing special benefits to bridge owners, nor solely to achieve savings in repair or maintenance costs or to increase carrying capacity. (Program initially listed as a USCG-DOT program, and transferred to DHS in CFDA 2003.)

Eligible applicants/beneficiaries: any state, county, municipality, or other political subdivision, or any corporation, association, partnership, or individual—owning or jointly owning a lawful bridge over U.S. navigable waters used and operated to carry railroad or highway traffic.

Range: $14,740,000 to $42,800,000.

Activity: currently 9 projects under design and construction.

HQ: same as **97.013**.

97.015 SECRET SERVICE—TRAINING ACTIVITIES

Assistance: training.

Purposes: to acquaint local law enforcement officials with the functions of the Secret Service and the techniques used to detect counterfeit money and documents and to protect dignitaries. Bank tellers, department store cashiers, and other money handlers may be briefed in the detection of counterfeit currency and documents by Secret Service regional offices. (Program initially listed as a Department of the Treasury program, and transferred to DHS in CFDA 2003.)

Eligible applicants/beneficiaries: sworn members of police agencies.

Activity: annually, 3,200 participants.

HQ: U.S. Secret Service, DHS, same address/phone, web site as **97.013**.

97.016 REIMBURSEMENT FOR FIREFIGHTING ON FEDERAL PROPERTY

Assistance: direct payments/specified use.

Purposes: pursuant to the Federal Fire Prevention and Control Act of 1974 as amended, to reimburse fire service organizations for their direct expenses and losses from firefighting operations on federal property. (Program initially listed as a FEMA program, and transferred to DHS in CFDA 2003.)

Eligible applicants/beneficiaries: volunteer and paid fire departments of states, territories, possessions, and federal Indian lands.

Range/Average: to $500,000, with no stated limit.

Activity: FY 03, no claims approved.

HQ: FEMA-DHS, 245 Murray Lane - Bldg. 410, Washington, DC 20523. Phone: (no number provided). **Internet:** "www.dhs.gov". (Note: no field offices for this program.).

97.017 PRE-DISASTER MITIGATION (PDM) COMPETITIVE GRANTS ("PDM")

Assistance: project grants (75-90 percent/to 3 years).

Purposes: pursuant to the Robert T. Stafford Disaster Relief Act and Emergency Assistance Act ("Stafford Act") as amended by the Disaster Mitigation Act of 2000, for pre-disaster mitigation planning and projects primarily addressing natural hazards. Planning grants involve multi-hazard mitigation workshops and risk assessments, with two-year project periods. Mitigation project activities must be completed within three years, and may include: acquisition or relocation of hazard-prone property; structural retrofitting; minor structural hazard control or protection activities such as vegetation and storm-water management, shoreline or landslide stabilization, and localized flood control works.

Eligible applicants/beneficiaries: emergency management agencies of states, territories, possessions, and tribes participating in NFIP—which may award sub-grants to other agencies involved in emergency management, including other state-level agencies and local governments. Applicants and sub-applicants must be participants in the National Flood Insurance Program if they have special flood hazard areas.

Range: to $3,000,000.

Activity: new program listing in 2004.

HQ: Mitigation Division, Emergency Preparedness and Response Directorate, FEMA-DHS, same address as **97.016**. Phone: (202)646-3807, FAX (202) 646-3104. **Internet:** "www.fema.gov/fima/pdm/".

97.018 NATIONAL FIRE ACADEMY TRAINING ASSISTANCE ("Student Stipend Reimbursement Program")

Assistance: direct payments/specified use.

Purposes: pursuant to the Federal Fire Prevention and Control Act of 1974 as amended, for limited stipends, travel expenses, and lodging costs of attending resident or regional programs the National Fire Academy. (Program initially listed as a FEMA program, and transferred to DHS in CFDA 2003.)

Eligible applicants/beneficiaries: members of fire departments and others with significant responsibility for fire prevention and control. Federal and private industry employees and foreign students may attend courses, but are ineligible for payments.

Range/Average: resident courses, $330; regional, $112.

Activity: FY 03, 4,273 stipends paid.

HQ: Emergency Preparedness and Response, FEMA-DHS, same address, web site as **97.016**. Phone: (no number provided). (Note: no field offices for this program.)

97.019 NATIONAL FIRE ACADEMY EDUCATIONAL PROGRAM

Assistance: training.

Purposes: pursuant to the Federal Fire Prevention and Control Act of 1974 as amended, to increase the professional level of the fire service and others responsible for fire prevention and control through training at the National Fire Academy or at off-campus locations. Training is provided on specific subjects to specific audiences. (Program initially listed as a FEMA program, and transferred to DHS in CFDA 2003.)

Eligible applicants/beneficiaries: members of fire departments; others with significant responsibility for fire prevention and control.

Activity: 5,239 national facility, 787 regional, 2,872 "State Weekend," 60,000 train-the-trainer program participants.

HQ: same as **97.018**. (Note: no field offices for this program.)

97.020 HAZARDOUS MATERIALS TRAINING PROGRAM ("SARA Title III Training Program")

Assistance: project grants (80 percent/1 year).

Purposes: pursuant to CERCLA as amended and SARA, for education and training programs for tribal government personnel to improve emergency planning, preparedness, mitigation, response, and recovery capabilities—with emphasis on hazardous chemicals and related emergencies. (Program initially listed as a FEMA program, and transferred to DHS in CFDA 2003.)

Eligible applicants/beneficiaries: tribal governments.

Range: $2,000 to $251,000. **Average:** $84,000.

Activity: not quantified specifically.

HQ: same as **97.018**.

97.021 HAZARDOUS MATERIALS ASSISTANCE PROGRAM ("CERCLA Implementation")

Assistance: project grants.

Purposes: pursuant to CERCLA as amended and SARA, for planning, exercising, and educational projects enhancing emergency management capabilities for dealing with oil and hazardous materials releases. Limited funding is available for costs of certain training and equipment purchases. (Program initially listed as a FEMA program, and transferred to DHS in CFDA 2003.)

Eligible applicants/beneficiaries: states, locals, tribes, territories, State Emergency Response Committees, Local Emergency Planning Commissions.

Range: to $20,000.

Activity: N.A.
HQ: same as **97.018**.

97.022 FLOOD INSURANCE
("National Flood Insurance Program" - "NFIP")

Assistance: insurance.

Purposes: pursuant to the National Flood Insurance Act of 1968, to insure property owners against losses from floods, mudflow, and flood-caused erosion—at or below normal actuarial rates; to promote flood plain management practices. Flood insurance must be purchased as a condition of obtaining any form of federal financial assistance, including disaster assistance and mortgage loan insurance from VA, FmHA, and FHA, when projects are located within flood hazard areas where flood insurance is available. Special program provisions apply for properties within the Coastal Barrier Resource System. Maximum amounts of coverage and other requirements apply, according to type and location of structure; details are available from FEMA regional offices or responsible state offices. (Program initially listed as a FEMA program, and transferred to DHS in CFDA 2003.)

Eligible applicants: states and their political subdivisions that submit completed applications to FEMA consistent with program regulations.

Eligible beneficiaries: residential, business, and municipal property owners in states or political subdivisions that have enacted NFIP flood plain management measures.

Range: claims paid: $1 to $1,900,000. **Average:** $29,000.

Activity: as of FY 02, 19,706 communities participating; 4,365,000 policies in force, representing $597 billion in insurance.

HQ: same as **97.018**.

97.023 COMMUNITY ASSISTANCE PROGRAM—STATE SUPPORT SERVICES ELEMENT
("CAP-SSSE")

Assistance: project grants (75 percent).

Purposes: pursuant to the National Flood Insurance Act of 1968 and Flood Disaster Protection Act of 1973 as amended, to identify, prevent, and resolve flood plain management issues in communities participating in the NFIP, through the adoption of flood loss reduction measures. Project examples: community assistance visits, ordinance assistance, coordination meetings with FEMA regional offices, community rating system application assistance and review workshops. (Program initially listed as a FEMA program, and transferred to DHS in CFDA 2003.)

Eligible applicants/beneficiaries: states and through the states, NFIP communities and local governments.

Range: $50,000 to $350,000.

Activity: FY 04, 50 awards.

HQ: same as **97.018**.

97.024 EMERGENCY FOOD AND SHELTER NATIONAL BOARD PROGRAM

Assistance: formula grants.

Purposes: pursuant to SBMHAA as amended, to supplement and expand ongoing programs providing shelter, food, and supportive services for needy families and individuals; for projects to create more effective and innovative local programs; for minimum rehabilitation of existing mass shelter or feeding facilities, bringing them into compliance with local building codes. Eligible expenses include: costs of food and its transport, food preparation and serving equipment; mass shelter and other shelter, such as hotels and motels; rent or mortgage payments assistance for one month only; limited facility repairs; utility payments. Ineligible costs include such expenses as rental security or other deposits, cash payments to the homeless, major property improvements. (Program initially listed as a FEMA program, and transferred to DHS in CFDA 2003.)

Eligible applicants/beneficiaries: jurisdictions approved by the Emergency Food and Shelter Program National Board chaired by FEMA or State Set-Aside Committees, may award grants to: public or private nonprofit organizations, community action agencies, food banks, food pantries; specialized community groups such as domestic violence centers; native American organizations; organizations providing food and shelter to AIDS patients, handicapped persons, the elderly, teenage runaways, and others with emergency needs.

Range: $2,000 to $5,864,000.

Activity: assistance to 11,000 social service agencies in 2,500 jurisdictions, 10 training sessions with 700 participants.

HQ: same as **97.018**.

97.025 NATIONAL URBAN SEARCH AND RESCUE (US&R) RESPONSE SYSTEM ("US&R")

Assistance: project grants (50-100 percent).

Purposes: pursuant to the Earthquake Hazards Reduction Act of 1977 and Stafford Act as amended, to develop national immediately deployable urban search and rescue task forces to locate, extricate, and provide medical treatment to victims of structural collapse during a disaster. Funds may be used for training, exercises, and to acquire and maintain specialized equipment. (Program initially listed as a FEMA program, and transferred to DHS in CFDA 2003.)

Eligible applicants/beneficiaries: 28 jurisdictions designated by FEMA as members of the National Urban Search and Rescue Response System.

Range/Average: $150,000 per grantee.

Activity: 27 annual grants.

HQ: same as **97.013**. (Note: no field offices for this program.)

97.026 EMERGENCY MANAGEMENT INSTITUTE—TRAINING ASSISTANCE ("Student Stipend Reimbursement Program" - "SEP")

Assistance: direct payments/specified use.

Purposes: pursuant to the Stafford Act, National Security Act of 1947, Defense Production Act of 1950, Earthquake Hazards Reduction Act of 1977, and amendments, for emergency management personnel to obtain training at the Emergency Management Institute and selected other locations. Programs embody the Comprehensive Emergency Management System by unifying the elements of planning, preparedness, mitigation, response, and recovery. Travel and per diem costs are reimbursed for state and local participants. (Program initially listed as a FEMA program, and transferred to DHS in CFDA 2003.)

Eligible applicants/beneficiaries: state, local, and tribal emergency management personnel.

Range/Average: $380 stipend. (Students pay for their own meals.)

Activity: FY 03, 8,947 participants; 3,625 stipends paid.

HQ: same as **97.013**.

97.027 EMERGENCY MANAGEMENT INSTITUTE (EMI)—INDEPENDENT STUDY PROGRAM

Assistance: training.

Purposes: pursuant to the Stafford Act, National Security Act of 1947, Defense Production Act of 1950, Earthquake Hazards Reduction Act of 1977, and amendments, to offer home study courses in emergency management practices, of which 32 are available. Examples include: Emergency Program Manager; Radiological Emergency Management; A Citizen's Guide to Disaster Assistance; Building for the Earthquakes of Tomorrow: Engineering Principles and Practices for Retrofitting Flood Prone Residential Buildings; Animals in Disaster; and, refresher and other specialized courses. (Program initially listed as a FEMA program, and transferred to DHS in CFDA 2003.)

Eligible applicants/beneficiaries: general public, emergency management personnel, public officials. Some courses are restricted to certain audiences.

Activity: FY 04 estimate, 207,000 enrollments.

HQ: same as **97.018**.

97.028 EMERGENCY MANAGEMENT INSTITUTE (EMI)—RESIDENT EDUCATIONAL PROGRAM

Assistance: training.

Purposes: pursuant to the Stafford Act, National Security Act of 1947, Defense Production Act of 1950, Earthquake Hazards Reduction Act of 1977, and amendments, to provide training of federal, state, local, and tribal emergency management personnel involved in emergency and disaster response. Training emphasizes planning, mitigation, response, and recovery—embodied in the Comprehensive Emergency Management System. (Program initially listed as a FEMA program, and transferred to DHS in CFDA 2003.)

Eligible applicants/beneficiaries: official emergency management personnel.

Activity: FY 05 estimate, 8,947 participants.

HQ: same as **97.018**.

97.029 FLOOD MITIGATION ASSISTANCE ("FMA")

Assistance: project grants (base amount plus 75 percent/2 years).

Purposes: pursuant to the National Flood Insurance Reform Act of 1994, to implement measures that reduce or eliminate long-term risks of flood damage to buildings, manufactured homes, and other insurable structures under the NFIP. Funds may support planning, engineering and planning services, and such implementation activities as elevation or dry flood-proofing of structures, minor structural projects, beach nourishment. (Program initially listed as a FEMA program, and transferred to DHS in CFDA 2003.)

Eligible applicants/beneficiaries: planning and project grants—states and communities participating in the NFIP. Technical assistance grants—state agencies.

Range: N.A.

Activity: not quantified specifically.

HQ: same as **97.018**.

97.030 COMMUNITY DISASTER LOANS

Assistance: direct loans (generally, 5 years).

Purposes: pursuant to the Stafford Act, for local governments in declared disaster areas, suffering substantial loss of tax and other revenue and demonstrating a need for financial assistance. Funds may be used only to maintain existing municipal operating functions. (Program initially listed as a FEMA program, and transferred to DHS in CFDA 2003.)

Eligible applicants/beneficiaries: local governments in designated disaster areas.

Range: to 25 percent of the applicant's FY operating budget.

Activity: none.

HQ: same as **97.018**.

97.031 CORA BROWN FUND

Assistance: direct payments/specified use.

Purposes: pursuant to the Stafford Act as amended, to help victims of natural disasters that will not obtain assistance through other government or private programs. The fund was established by the late Cora C. Brown of Kansas City, Missouri, who left a portion of her estate to the U.S. government to help victims of natural disasters not caused by or attributed to war. (Program initially listed as a FEMA program, and transferred to DHS per CFDA 2003.)

Eligible applicants/beneficiaries: individuals, families, and groups in need of disaster-related home repair and rebuilding and other services.

Range/Average: N.A.

Activity: none.

HQ: same address, web site as **97.018**. Phone: (202)646-4528.

97.032 CRISIS COUNSELING

Assistance: project grants (100 percents/60 days).

Purposes: pursuant to the Stafford Act as amended and the Crisis Counseling Assistance and Training Act, to provide immediate crisis counseling services to victims of major natural disasters to relieve mental health problems, at no cost to the victims. Funding may support: such services as screening, diagnostic and counseling techniques, outreach, and public education; training of providers. (Program initially listed as a FEMA program, and transferred to DHS in CFDA 2003.)

Eligible applicants/beneficiaries: states or public or private agencies designated by the governor.

Range/Average: N.A.

Activity: FY 01, responses to 54 major disasters in 31 states or territories.

HQ: same as **97.031**.

97.034 DISASTER LEGAL SERVICES

Assistance: direct payments/specified use.

Purposes: pursuant to the Stafford Act as amended, to provide free legal services to persons affected by natural disasters, including legal advice, counseling, and representation in nonfee-generating cases. (Program initially listed as a FEMA program, and transferred to DHS per CFDA 2003.)

Eligible applicants/beneficiaries: low-income individuals, families, groups.

Range/Average: N.A.

Activity: N.A.

HQ: same as **97.031**.

97.034 DISASTER UNEMPLOYMENT ASSISTANCE ("DUA")

Assistance: direct payments/specified use (to 26 weeks); specialized services.

Purposes: pursuant to the Stafford Act as amended, to provide weekly unemployment benefits to persons left jobless by natural disasters and ineligible for regular unemployment insurance benefits. (Program initially listed as a FEMA program, and transferred to DHS in CFDA 2003.)

Eligible applicants/beneficiaries: disaster victims.

Range/Average: N.A.

Activity: N.A.

HQ: same as **97.031**.

97.036 PUBLIC ASSISTANCE GRANTS

Assistance: project grants (75 percent).

Purposes: pursuant to the Stafford Act, to provide supplemental assistance in alleviating suffering and hardship resulting from declared major disasters or emergencies. Eligible program costs include the removal of wreckage and debris on public and private lands, emergency protective measures, emergency transportation or communications, restoration of eligible facilities. (Program initially listed as a FEMA program, and transferred to DHS in CFDA 2003.)

Eligible applicants/beneficiaries: state and local governments, other state political subdivisions, territories and possessions, tribal governments, Alaska native villages or organizations, certain private nonprofit organizations.

Range: small projects, to $51,000.

Activity: N.A.

HQ: same as **97.031**.

97.039 HAZARD MITIGATION GRANT ("HMGP")

Assistance: project grants (75 percent/2 years).

Purposes: pursuant to the Stafford Act, for measures to permanently reduce or eliminate future damages and losses from natural hazards through safer building practices, improving existing structures, and supporting infrastructure. Funds may be used: to acquire, relocate, modify, or demolish structures; for seismic rehabilitation or retrofitting of structures; for initial implementation of vegetation management programs; to provide pertinent training to architects, engineers, building officials, and others; to bring structures into compliance with floodplain management requirements.

Eligible applicants/beneficiaries: state and local governments, other public entities, authorized tribal organizations, Alaska native villages or organizations, private nonprofit organizations.

Range/Average: N.A.

Activity: not quantified specifically. (Program initially listed as a FEMA program, and transferred to DHS per CFDA 2003.)

HQ: same as **97.018**.

97.040 CHEMICAL STOCKPILE EMERGENCY PREPAREDNESS PROGRAM ("CSEPP")

Assistance: projects grants.

Purposes: pursuant to the Department of Defense Authorization Act of 1986, to enhance emergency preparedness capabilities at the eight chemical agent stockpile facilities maintained by DOD. Funding has paid for operational siren systems, demographic surveys, dedicated radio and telephone systems, public training courses and exercises. (Program initially listed as a FEMA program, and transferred to DHS in CFDA 2003.)

Eligible applicants/beneficiaries: the states of Alabama, Arkansas, Colorado, Illinois, Indiana, Kentucky, Maryland, Oregon, Utah, and Washington. Local governments and tribes may receive subgrants.

Range: $60,000 to $13,000,000. **Average:** $8,100,000.

Activity: not quantified specifically.

HQ: same as **97.013**.

97.041 NATIONAL DAM SAFETY PROGRAM ("Dam Safety State Assistance Program")

Assistance: project grants (50 percent).

Purposes: pursuant to the Water Resources Development Act of 1996, to establish, improve, and maintain safety programs covering nonfederal dams.

States meeting specific criteria may use funds for such activities as permitting and approval of project plans, legislative modifications and regulations development, enforcement activities, emergency response, program staffing, public education, and training. (Program initially listed as a FEMA program, and transferred to DHS in CFDA 2003.)

Eligible applicants/beneficiaries: states, PR.

Range: $26,000 to $281,000.

Activity: N.A.

HQ: same as **97.018**.

97.042 EMERGENCY MANAGEMENT PERFORMANCE GRANTS ("EMPG")

Assistance: formula grants (to 50 percent/2.5 years).

Purposes: pursuant to the Stafford Act as amended, to develop, maintain, and improve comprehensive emergency management capabilities, by combining several funding streams into a consolidated grant. The key functional areas are: Laws and Authorities; Hazard Identification and Risk Assessment; Hazard Management; Resource Management; Planning; Direction, Control, and Coordination; Communications and Warning; Operations and Procedures; Logistics and Facilities; Training; Exercises; Public Education and Information; Finance and Administration. (Program initially listed as a FEMA program, and transferred to DHS in CFDA 2003.)

Eligible applicants/beneficiaries: states, territories, possessions.

Range: $410,000 to $10,600,000. **Average:** $2,377,000.

Activity: FY 02, all states and territories funded.

HQ: same as **97.006**.

97.043 STATE FIRE TRAINING SYSTEMS GRANTS ("National Fire Academy Training Grants")

Assistance: project grants.

Purposes: for state fire training systems to deliver National Fire Academy courses and programs. (Program initially listed as a FEMA program, and transferred to DHS in CFDA 2003.)

Eligible applicants/beneficiaries: 50 state fire training systems.

Range: $23,000 to $30,000 per state.

Activity: 50 grants annually.

HQ: same as **97.006**.

97.044 ASSISTANCE TO FIREFIGHTERS GRANT ("Fire Grants")

Assistance: project grants (70-90 percent).

Purposes: pursuant to the Federal Fire Prevention and Control Act of 1974 as amended by the Defense Authorization Bill of 2001, for direct assistance to fire departments for costs of firefighting operations and firefighter safety. Applicants must compete for grants which may be used for a broad range of eligible expenses including equipment and vehicles, training, public education, personnel, arson prevention, emergency medical services—with funding limits on certain categories. (Program initially listed as a FEMA program, and transferred to DHS in CFDA 2003.)

Eligible applicants/beneficiaries: fire departments in states, territories and possessions, local authorities, tribal nations—including their emergency medical services units.

Range: $900 to $700,000. **Average:** $51,000.

Activity: FY 03 estimate, 8,722 awards.

HQ: same as **97.006**.

97.045 COOPERATING TECHNICAL PARTNERS ("CTP")

Assistance: project grants (100 percent/1-2 years).

Purposes: pursuant to the National Flood Insurance Act of 1968 (Housing and Urban Development Acts of 1968 and 1969), Flood Disaster Protection Act of 1973, amendments, and National Flood Insurance Reform Act of 1994, to increase local involvement in and ownership of the development and maintenance of flood hazard maps produced for the NFIP. Project examples: Refinement of Zone A Boundaries; Digital Flood Insurance Rate Map Preparation. (Program initially listed as a FEMA program, and transferred to DHS in CFDA 2003.)

Eligible applicants/beneficiaries: states, territories, possessions, regional agencies, and communities participating in the NFIP.

Range: $35,000 to $6,000,000.

Activity: FY 04, 173 agreements as of 13 April 2004.

HQ: same as **97.016**, *and* **Internet:** "www.fema.gov/mit/tsd/ctp_news.htm".

97.046 FIRE MANAGEMENT ASSISTANCE GRANT

Assistance: project grants (75 percent); specialized services.

Purposes: pursuant to the Stafford Act, for the mitigation, management, and control of any fire on public (nonfederal) or privately owned forest or grassland that threatens to become a major disaster. (Program initially listed as a FEMA program, and transferred to DHS in CFDA 2003.)

Eligible applicants/beneficiaries: state and tribal governments.

Range/Average: N.A.

Activity: FY 01, 15 grants authorized.

HQ: same as **97.006**.

97.047 PRE-DISASTER MITIGATION ("PDM")

Assistance: project grants (75-90 percent/to 2 years).

Purposes: pursuant to the Stafford Act as amended by the Disaster Mitigation Act of 2000, for cost-affective hazard mitigation activities that are part of a comprehensive mitigation program and reduce injuries, fatalities, and property destruction. (Program initially listed as a FEMA program, and transferred to DHS in CFDA 2003.)

Eligible applicants/beneficiaries: states, territories, possessions, tribal governments. Subgrants may be awarded to local and tribal governments participating in the NFIP.

Range: from $500,000 per state.

Activity: N.A.

HQ: same as **97.013**.

97.048 FEDERAL ASSISTANCE TO INDIVIDUALS AND HOUSEHOLDS— HOUSING
("Individual and Household Housing")

Assistance: direct payments/specified use (75 percent/to 18 months).

Purposes: pursuant to the Stafford Act as amended, for individuals and households affected by disasters to enable them to: obtain temporary housing; make repairs to their primary residences; build replacement new permanent housing; meet such other needs as medical, dental, funeral, personal property, transportation costs. (Program initially listed as a FEMA program, and transferred to DHS in CFDA 2003.)

Eligible applicants/beneficiaries: U.S. citizens, noncitizen nationals, or qualified aliens whose primary residences: have been damaged or destroyed by declared major disasters; are not covered by insurance; are located in an insular area outside continental U.S. or in other remote locations where alternative housing resources are unavailable. (NOTE: states apply for funds under **94.050**.)

Range/Average: N.A.

Activity: N.A.

HQ: same address, web site as **97.016**. Phone: (202)646-3943.

97.049 FEDERAL ASSISTANCE TO INDIVIDUALS AND HOUSEHOLDS— DISASTER HOUSING OPERATIONS
("Individual and Household Housing Operations")

Assistance: direct payments/specified use (to 18 months).

Purposes: pursuant to the Stafford Act as amended, for individuals and households affected by disasters, who lack available housing resources and would be unable to rent alternative housing. (Program initially listed as a FEMA program, and transferred to DHS in CFDA 2003.)

Eligible applicants/beneficiaries: U.S. citizens, noncitizen nationals, or qualified aliens whose primary residences have been damaged or destroyed by declared major disasters and are not covered by insurance.

Range/Average: N.A.

Activity: N.A.

HQ: same as **97.048**.

97.050 FEDERAL ASSISTANCE TO INDIVIDUALS AND HOUSEHOLDS— OTHER NEEDS
("Individual and Household Other Needs")

Assistance: project grants (75 percent/to 18 months).

Purposes: pursuant to the Stafford Act as amended, for individuals and households affected by disasters to pay necessary expenses and address serious needs that cannot be met through other forms of assistance or through insurance. Assistance may be used to meet medical, dental, funeral, personal property, transportation needs. (Program initially listed as a FEMA program, and transferred to DHS in CFDA 2003.)

Eligible applicants/beneficiaries: states. (NOTE: if states do not apply, assistance to individuals is provided under **94.048**.)

Range/Average: N.A.

Activity: N.A.

HQ: same as **97.048**.

97.053 CITIZEN CORPS

Assistance: project grants (100 percent/2.5 years).

Purposes: pursuant to the Stafford Act, for Citizen Corps Council organization activities involving volunteer groups that enhance homeland security through outreach to individuals, communities, and families to increase their preparedness and strengthen homeland security. Funds may support: training, equipping, and maintaining Community Emergency Response Teams (CERTs); liability coverage for participants; public outreach and education activities. 75 percent of funds made available to states must be allocated to local governments.

Eligible applicants/beneficiaries: same as for **97.052**.

Range: $55,000 to $1,662,000. **Average:** $375,000.

Activity: new program listing in 2003.

HQ: same address as **97.004**. Phone: (202)646-3640. **Internet:** "www.citizenscorps.gov".

97.055 INTEROPERABLE COMMUNICATIONS EQUIPMENT

Assistance: project grants (75 percent/1 year).

Purposes: pursuant to the Homeland Security Act of 2002, Federal Fire Prevention and Control Act of 1974, and other acts, for demonstration projects on multidisciplinary and/or inter-juridictional uses of equipment and technologies to increase communications inter-operability among fire services, law enforcement, and emergency medical services. Funds may support purchases of equipment or services to participate in public safety, commercial, or other shared networks and portable gateway solutions.

Eligible applicants/beneficiaries: local governments nominated by state or territorial governments.

Range: $50,000 to $6,000,000.

Activity: new program in FY 03; 14 grants anticipated.

HQ: same address, web site as **97.051**. Phone: (202)646-3850, FAX (202)646-3061.

97.056 PORT SECURITY GRANT PROGRAM

Assistance: project grants (to 100 percent).

Purposes: for regulated seaports and terminals to enhance port security through: security assessments and mitigation strategies; enhanced facility and operational security—e.g., terminal and commuter or ferry vessels access control, and physical, cargo, and passenger security. Funds may support such costs as for planning, training, exercises, equipment, and administration.

Eligible applicants/beneficiaries: federally regulated public and private ports or terminals designated as "critical"; consortia of local stakeholder groups such as river groups, ports, and terminal associations.

Range: $650 to $3,278,000. **Average:** $321,000.

Activity: new program listing in 2003. 120 grants awarded for 154 projects.

HQ: Transportation Infrastructure Security Division, same address/phone as **97.004**. **Internet:** "www.portsecuritygrants.dottsa.net/". (Note: no field offices for this program.)

97.057 INTERCITY BUS SECURITY GRANTS

Assistance: project grants.

Purposes: to protect inter-city bus systems and the traveling public from terrorism, especially explosives and nonconventional threats. Funds may support such costs as for planning, training, exercises, equipment, and administration.

Eligible applicants/beneficiaries: not provided in CFDA 2005. (Previous edition listed "private or public operators of over-the-road buses including operators of regular route, charter, tour, and other services; bus associations; other associations related to the intercity bus industry—i.e., transportation industry organizations involved directly in training and providing technical assistance with an emphasis on security.")

Range/Average: $180,000.

Activity: new program listing in 2003. 80 projects funded.

HQ: same address/phone as **97.004**. **Internet:** "www.ojp.usdoj.gov/fundopps.htm". (Note: no field offices for this program.).

97.058 OPERATION SAFE COMMERCE (OSC) COOPERATIVE AGREEMENT PROGRAM ("OSC")

Assistance: project grants (100 percent/18 months).

Purposes: to explore commercially viable options to enhance Carlo security, including business processes and technology prototypes supporting containerized cargo supply chain security management while facilitating the flow of trade. Funds may support such costs as for personnel, equipment, supplies, services or consultants, facilities, and administration.

Eligible applicants/beneficiaries: load centers (defined as the Ports of Los Angeles/Long Beach, Seattle/Tacoma, and the Port Authority of New York/New Jersey.

Range: $5,200,000 to $6,700,000.

Activity: new program listing in 2003. 18 projects approved.

HQ: same address/phone as **97.004**. **Internet:** "www.tsa.gov/public/index.jsp". (Note: no field offices for this program.)

97.059 TRUCK SECURITY PROGRAM

Assistance: project grants.

Purposes: to promote security awareness among all segments of the commercial motor carriers and transportation community, by training drivers to observe and report any suspicious activities or items that may threaten the critical elements of the nation's highway transportation system. Funds may support such costs as for equipment, supplies, services or consultants, facilities, and administration.

Eligible applicants/beneficiaries: as directed by Congress.

Range/Average: N.A.

Activity: new program in FY 03. One award anticipated.

HQ: same as **97.057**. (Note: no field offices for this program.)

97.060 PORT SECURITY RESEARCH & DEVELOPMENT GRANT

Assistance: project grants (75 percent/to 18 months).

Purposes: pursuant to the Maritime Transportation Security Act of 2002 and Homeland Security Act of 2002, to identify technology solutions for port security through research and development to provide end products meeting or exceeding specific priorities: Cargo Information Action Center; Passengers and Vehicles Screening on Ferries; Transparency of Vessel Ownership; Operation Restore.

Eligible applicants/beneficiaries: national laboratories, private nonprofit organizations, IHEs, and others.

Range/Average: N.A.

Activity: new program listing in 2004.

HQ: Office of Acquisition (TSA-25), TSA-DHS, 701 S. 12th St., Arlington, VA 22202. Phone: (571)227-3056. **Internet:** "http://tsa.gov". (Note: no field offices for this program.)

97.061 CENTERS FOR HOMELAND SECURITY ("University- Based HS Centers")

Assistance: project grants (100 percent/to 3 years).

Purposes: pursuant to the Homeland Security Act of 2002 as amended and Emergency Wartime Supplemental Appropriation Act of 2003, to establish a coordinated, university-based system to enhance homeland security, complementing other DHS and other federal agency activities—to develop and deploy specific homeland security technologies and capabilities. Funds may be used for: targeted research area that leverage the multidisciplinary capabilities of universities; involve U.S. graduate and undergraduate students.

Eligible applicants/beneficiaries: IHEs.

Range: $1,000,000 to $6,000,000.

Activity: new program in FY 04. FY 05 estimate, 6 new awards anticipated.

HQ: University Programs, DHS, 245 Murray Lane - Bldg. 410, Washington,

DC 20523. Phone: (no number provided). **Internet:** "www.dhs.gov"; e-mail, "universityprograms@dhs.gov". (Note: no field offices for this program.)

97.062 SCHOLARS AND FELLOWS
("DHS Scholars and Fellows")

Assistance: direct payments/specified use.

Purposes: pursuant to the Homeland Security Act of 2002 as amended, to develop and increase the number of undergraduate and graduate students attaining advanced degrees and working in areas of importance to homeland security. Tuition and fee payments are paid to universities; students receive monthly stipends.

Eligible applicants/beneficiaries: U.S. citizens enrolled full-time as juniors, graduate students, or postdoctoral fellows in computer science, engineering, life or physical sciences, math, psychology, social sciences, DVM/PhD, and certain humanities.

Range: graduates, $2,300 monthly stipend; undergraduates, $1,000 monthly stipend. **Average:** graduates, $44,000 annually; undergraduates, $27,000 annually.

Activity: new program listing in 2004. 105 scholars and fellows.

HQ: same as **97.062**. (Note: no field offices for this program.)

97.064 DEBRIS REMOVAL INSURANCE

Assistance: project grants (100 percent/to 25 years).

Purposes: to incorporate a captive insurance company by the City of New York, N.Y. to insure the city and its contractors for claims arising from debris removal at the World Trade Center following the terrorist attacks of September 11, 2001.

Eligible applicants/beneficiaries: the State of New York to insure the City of New York and its debris removal contractors.

Range: $999,900,000.

Activity: new program in FY 04.

HQ: Recovery Division, same address as **97.063**. Phone: (202)646-3587. **Internet:** "www.fema.gov/rrr/pa".

97.065 HOMELAND SECURITY ADVANCED RESEARCH PROJECTS AGENCY ("HSARPA")

Assistance: project grants.

Purposes: pursuant to the Homeland Security Act of 2002 as amended, for basic and applied research and technology development projects in areas of science and technology supporting homeland security, including: development, testing, evaluation, and deployment of critical homeland security technologies; prototyping and deployment technologies addressing security vulnerabilities. SBIR contracts may be awarded.

Eligible applicants/beneficiaries: public, private, nonprofit, profit entities and organizations; federally funded R&D centers; universities, individuals, specialized groups.

Range/Average: N.A.

Activity: new program in FY 04.

HQ: HSARPA, S&T Directorate, DHS, 245 Murray Lane - Bldg. 410, Washington, DC 20528. Phone: (no number provided). **Internet:** "www.dhs.gov"; "www.hsarpabaa.com". (Note: no field offices for this program.)

97.066 HOMELAND SECURITY INFORMATION TECHNOLOGY AND EVALUATION PROGRAM ("ITEP")

Assistance: project grants.

Purposes: to foster and identify novel uses of existing "state-of-the-market" information technology that will remove barriers and improve information sharing and integration of state and local public safety interoperability communications.

Eligible applicants/beneficiaries: chief executive officers of states and territories.

Range/Average: $750,000.

Activity: new program in FY 04.

HQ: (no address provided). Phone: *ODP help line*, (800)368-6498. **Internet:** "www.dhs.gov". (Note: no field offices for this program.)

97.067 HOMELAND SECURITY GRANT PROGRAM ("HSGP")

Assistance: formula grants (100 percent/2.5 years).

Purposes: pursuant to the U.S.A. Patriot Act of 2001, to enhance the capacity of state and local emergency responders to prevent, respond to, and recover from a terrorism incident involving chemical, biological, radiological, nuclear, and explosive (CBRNE) devices and cyber attacks. The program encompasses: (1) State Homeland Security Program (SHSP); (2) Urban Areas Security Initiative (UASI); (3) Law Enforcement Terrorism Prevention Program (LETPP); (4) Citizen Corps Program (CCP); (5) Emergency Management Performance Grants; (6) Metropolitan Medical Response System. (See note in program description for **97.004**.)

Eligible applicants/beneficiaries: states, territories, possessions. Local government units may receive subgrants.

Range/Average: N.A.

Activity: new program in FY 04.

HQ: Office of State and Local Government Coordination and Preparedness, Office for Domestic Preparedness-DHS, 810 7th St. NW, Washington, DC 20531. Phone: (800)368-6498. **Internet:** "www.ojp.usdoj.gov/odp". (Note: no field offices for this program.)

97.068 COMPETITIVE TRAINING GRANTS

Assistance: project grants (100 percent/2 years).

Purposes: for training initiatives that prepare the nation to prevent, deter, respond to, and recover from terrorism incidents, covering a broad range of issues including: continuity of operations planning; increasing threat awareness among public officials, public health personnel and the medical community, and public safety and public works personnel; technicians and operating personnel training.

Eligible applicants/beneficiaries: state, local, tribal, and territorial governments; national public safety associations, IHEs, private corporations working with the nonprofit sector, nonprofit organizations.

Range/Average: N.A.

Activity: new program in FY 04.

HQ: same as **97.006**. (Note: no field offices for this program.)

97.069 AVIATION RESEARCH GRANTS

Assistance: project grants; use of property, facilities, and equipment.

Purposes: pursuant to the Federal Aviation Administration Research, Engineering and Development Authorization Act of 1990, Aviation Security Improvement Act of 1990, and Aviation Security Act of 2001, for innovative, advanced, and applied research and development in areas of potential benefit to the long-term growth of civil aviation security—specifically, in system security technology.

Eligible applicants/beneficiaries: public and private nonprofit organizations; IHEs; profit organizations.

Range: $25,000 to $5,000,000.

Activity: new program listing in 2004.

HQ: Aviation Research Grants Program (ACT-50), Hughes Technical Center, TSA-HHS, Atlantic City International Airport, NJ 08405. Phone: (609)485-4424, FAX (609)485-6509. **Internet:** "www.tsa.gov"; "www.its.tc.faa.gov/logistics/grants". (Note: the field office serves as headquarters for this program.)

97.070 MAP MODERNIZATION MANAGEMENT SUPPORT ("MMMS")

Assistance: project grants (100 percent/1-2 years).

Purposes: pursuant to the Housing and Urban Development Act of 1968 ("National Flood Insurance Act of 1968") as amended, Housing and Urban Development Act of 1969, Flood Disaster Protection Act of 1973 as amended, and National Flood Insurance Reform Act of 1994, to increase local involvement in and ownership of management of the development and maintenance of flood hazard maps produced for the National Flood Insurance Program ("NFIP").

Eligible applicants/beneficiaries: states, communities, territories, possessions participating in NFIP.

Range: from $25,000. **Average:** $35,000.

Activity: new program listing in 2004.

HQ: same as **97.016**.

97.071 METROPOLITAN MEDICAL RESPONSE SYSTEM ("MMRS")

Assistance: project grants (100 percent/2.5 years).

Purposes: pursuant to the National Defense Authorization Act of 1997 as amended by the Nunn-Lugar-Domenici Amendment, for the 124 highly populated jurisdictions (as of end-FY 03) to develop plans, conduct training and exercises, and acquire pharmaceuticals and personal protective equipment—to achieve the enhanced capability needed to respond to a mass casualty event caused by WMD with their locally controlled and operated resources until significant external resources arrive (e.g., from HRSA, CDC, and OSLGC programs). Key MMRS components require: activation and notification procedures; concept of operations plans; forward movement of patients, coordinated with the National Defense Medical System; hospital and health care system surge capacity management; provision of specially trained responders and equipment through exercises, drills, public information dissemination; coordinated response protocols; a bioterrorism plan including customized pharmaceuticals and plans for the prophylaxis of an affected population for up to 1,000 chemical and 10,000 biological victims.

Eligible applicants/beneficiaries: 124 highly populated jurisdictions.

Range: $250,000 to $700,000.

Activity: new program listing in 2004.

HQ: same as **97.005**. (Note: no field offices for this program.)

97.072 NATIONAL EXPLOSIVES DETECTION CANINE TEAM PROGRAM

Assistance: project grants (100 percent/5 years).

Purposes: pursuant to the Federal Aviation Reauthorization Act of 1996, Homeland Security Act of 2002, and Aviation and Transportation Security Act, for cooperative agreements to employ canine teams to deter and detect the introduction of explosives devices into the transportation system, including rail stations, airports, passenger terminals, seaports, surface carriers, and support facilities. The canine teams consist of a highly trained dog and trainer, with a three-team minimum.

Eligible applicants/beneficiaries: designated state and local law enforcement agencies.

Range: $121,000 to $801,000.

Activity: new program listing in 2004. Currently, 61 award recipients.

HQ: Director, National Explosives Detection Canine Team Program, TSA-DHS, 601 South 12th St. - Rm.5E210S, Arlington, VA 22202. Phone: (no number provided). **Internet:** "www.tsa.gov" (links: Security and Law Enforcement, Canine and Explosives Program). (Note: no field offices for this program.)

97.073 STATE HOMELAND SECURITY PROGRAM ("SHSP")

Assistance: formula grants (100 percent/30 months).

Purposes: pursuant to the U.S.A. Patriot Act, to enhance the capacity of state and local governments to prevent, respond to, and recover from a terrorism incident involving chemical, biological, radiological, nuclear, and explosive (CBRNE) devices and cyber attacks. The program supports costs of homeland security and emergency operations: planning; equipment purchases; CBRNE-related and cyber security training and exercises, and attendance at ODP-approved courses; management and administration; evaluations. (See note in program description for **97.004**.)

Eligible applicants/beneficiaries: state administrative agencies (SAAs), territories, and possessions. SAAs are obligated to allocated funds to local government units including authorities, commissions, tribes, special districts, and similar entities.

Range/Average: N.A.

Activity: new program listing in 2004 (CFDA on-line).

HQ: same as **97.005**. (Note: no field offices for this program.)

97.074 LAW ENFORCEMENT TERRORISM PREVENTION PROGRAM ("LETPP")

Assistance: formula grants (100 percent/30 months).

Purposes: pursuant to the U.S.A. Patriot Act, for prevention activities by state and local law enforcement communities, including: information sharing to preempt terrorist attacks; target hardening to reduce vulnerability of selected high-value targets; recognition and mapping of potential or developing threats; interoperable communications; interdiction of terrorists or terrorist intervention activities. Grant funds may be used for planning, organization, training, exercises, and equipment.

Eligible applicants/beneficiaries: same as for **97.073**.

Range/Average: N.A.

Activity: new program in FY 04 (CFDA on-line).

HQ: same as **97.005**. (Note: no field offices for this program.)

97.075 RAIL AND TRANSIT SECURITY GRANT PROGRAM

Assistance: project grants.

Purposes: pursuant to the U.S.A. Patriot Act, for rail and transit systems to develop a sustainable program to enhance their security and overall preparedness to prevent, respond to, and recover from acts of terrorism. Eligible uses of project funds include planning, organization, training, exercises, equipment, and limited management expenses.

Eligible applicants: state administrative agencies.

Eligible beneficiaries: rail and transit operators and industry associations.

Range/Average: N.A.

Activity: new program in FY 05 (CFDA on-line); 24 awards anticipated.

HQ: same as **97.057**. (Note: no field offices for this program.)

97.076 NATIONAL CENTER FOR MISSING AND EXPLOITED CHILDREN ("NCMEC")

Assistance: project grants.

Purposes: to prevent the abduction, abuse, and sexual exploitation of children through activities supporting investigative and forensics; to promote awareness of the child pornography tip line and Project Alert; to operate a national resource center and clearinghouse.

Eligible applicants/beneficiaries: a designated nonprofit organization.

Range/Average: N.A.

Activity: new program listing in 2005.

HQ: NCMEC, U.S. Secret Service-DHS, 245 Murray Lane - Bldg.410, Washington, DC 20523. Phone: Secret Service, (202)406-9277; Project Alert, ICE, (703)293-8006. **Internet:** "www.dhs.gov". (Note: no field offices for this program.)

97.077 HOMELAND SECURITY TESTING, EVALUATION, AND DEMONSTRATION OF TECHNOLOGIES

Assistance: project grants; use of property, facilities, and equipment; sale, exchange, donation of property and goods; technical information.

Purposes: pursuant to the Homeland Security Act of 2002, to provide funding and/or property to conduct testing, evaluation, and demonstration of homeland security technologies intended to identify, counter, or respond to terrorist threats.

Eligible applicants/beneficiaries: state, local, and tribal governments; private, public profit or nonprofit organizations; individuals.

Range/Average: N.A.

Activity: new program in FY 05.

HQ: Logistics and Property Manager, Science and Technology Directorate (no additional address provided in CFDA). Phone: (202)254-5667. **Internet:** same as **97.076**. (Note: no field offices for this program.)

97.078 BUFFER ZONE PROTECTION PLAN ("BZPP")

Assistance: project grants.

Purposes: to plan, equip, and manage protective actions toward the protection, securing, and reducing of vulnerabilities of identified critical infrastructure and key resource sites. State Administrative Agencies allocate funds to jurisdictions in which sites are located.

Eligible applicants: State Administrative Agencies, including in territories and possessions.

Eligible beneficiaries: responsible state and local governmental jurisdictions.

Range/Average: N.A.

Activity: new program in FY 05.

HQ: same address/phone, web site as **97.005** *and* **Internet:** "www.dhs.gov". (Note: no field offices for this program.)

97.079 PUBLIC ALERT RADIOS FOR SCHOOLS

Assistance: project grants.

Purposes: to disseminate public alerts and warnings by providing Public Alert Radios to K-12 schools designated by DHS.

Eligible applicants/beneficiaries: K-12 schools in locations identified by DHS.

Range/Average: N.A.

Activity: new program in FY 05.

HQ: Information Analysis and Infrastructure Protection Directorate-DHS, 245 Murray Lane - Bldg.410, Washington, DC 20528. Phone: (202)282-8396; alternate/NOAA, (301)713-1824. **Internet:** "www.dhs.gov/dhspublic/display?theme=52". (Note: no field offices for this program.)

97.080 INFORMATION ANALYSIS INFRASTRUCTURE PROTECTION (IAIP) PILOT PROJECTS ("IAIP")

Assistance: project grants.

Purposes: pursuant to the Department of Homeland Security Act, for pilot or demonstration projects to explore the feasibility and viability of commercially available protective measure technology to nonfederal entities.

Eligible applicants/beneficiaries: same as for **97.077**.

Range/Average: N.A.

Activity: new program in FY 05.

HQ: same address as **97.079**. Phone: (202)282-8753. **Internet:** "www.dhs.gov". (Note: no field offices for this program.)

97.081 LAW ENFORCEMENT TRAINING AND TECHNICAL ASSISTANCE

Assistance: specialized services; training.

Purposes: pursuant to OCCSSA as amended, to provide advanced and specialized training to state, local, tribal, and campus law enforcement agency personnel, either at the Federal Law Enforcement Training Center or at selected sites; to provide technical assistance to agencies on request. Participant expenses may be partially or wholly subsidized.

Eligible applicants/beneficiaries: state, local, tribal, and campus law enforcement, fire, and emergency management specialists; prosecutors and city attorneys; domestic violence advocates; certain applicants from private organizations sponsored by law enforcement or public safety agencies.

Range: 50 to 100 percent of tuition costs (FY 05).

Activity: new program listing in 2005.

HQ: Federal Law Enforcement Training Center, National Center for State and Local Law Enforcement Training, 1131 Chapel Crossing Rd. - Townhouse 393, Glynco, GA 31524. Phone: (800)74FLETC, FAX (912)267-2894. **Internet:** "www.fletc.gov.os"; e-mail, "stateandlocaltraining@dhs.gov". (Note: no field offices for this program.)

97.082 EARTHQUAKE CONSORTIUM

Assistance: project grants.

Purposes: pursuant to the Earthquake Hazards Reduction Act of 1977 as amended, to develop earthquake preparedness and response plans, prepare inventories, and conduct seismic safety inspection of critical structures and lifelines—including the development of multistate groups for such purposes. Project examples include education and training for community and state officials.

Eligible applicants/beneficiaries: restricted to Central U.S. Earthquake Consortium, Western States Seismic Policy Council, Northeast States Emergency Consortium, and Cascadia Region Earthquake Workgroup.

Range: $75,000 to $450,000.

Activity: new program listing in 2005.

HQ: Federal Insurance and Mitigation Directorate, FEMA-DHS, 245 Murray Lane - Bldg. 410. Washington, DC 20523. Phone: (202)646-2727. **Internet:** same as **97.051**. (Note: no field offices for this program.)

97.083 STAFFING FOR ADEQUATE FIRE AND EMERGENCY RESPONSE ("SAFER")

Assistance: project grants (to 90 percent/5 years).

Purposes: to recruit, hire, and retain firefighters in local communities, and help the communities meet industry minimum standards. Grant recipients may not use funds to supplant pre-existing local funding, and they must retain personnel under the program for at least one year beyond the grant period. Matching requirements increase from year to year.

Eligible applicants/beneficiaries: specific jurisdictions in states, possessions, and territories.

Range: $10,000 to $2,000,000 ($100,000 maximum per position). **Average:** $500,000.

Activity: new program in FY 05.

HQ: Fire Grants Program Office, Office for State and Local Government Coordination and Preparedness-DHS, 245 Murray Lane - Bldg. 410. Washington, DC 20523. Phone: (866)274-0960. **Internet:** "www.firegrantsupport.com/safer/sguidance.aspx"; e-mail, "firegrants@dhs.gov". (Note: no field offices for this program.)

97.084 HURRICANE KATRINA CASE MANAGEMENT INITIATIVE PROGRAM

Assistance: project grants (100 percent/2 years).

Purposes: pursuant to Homeland Security Act of 2002 and Stafford Act, to provide case management services for displaced persons from areas affected by Hurricane Katrina.

Eligible applicants/beneficiaries: National Case Management Consortium, consisting of 6-12 FEMA-designated private nonprofit organizations.

Range/Average: N.A.

Activity: new program in FY 06 (CFDA on-line).

HQ: Federal Coordinating Officer, FEMA-DHS, same address as **97.016**. Phone: (202)646-4395, FAX (202)646-2730. **Internet:** "www.fema.gov". (Note: no field offices for this program.)

97.085 HEROES STAMP PROGRAM

Assistance: direct payments/unrestricted use.

Purposes: pursuant to the 9/11 Heroes Stamp Act of 2001, to use the proceeds of the Hero postal stamp sales to provide assistance to personal representatives of emergency relief personnel killed or permanently physically disabled while serving in the line of duty in connection with the September 11, 2001 terrorist attacks. FEMA will distribute funds equally among eligible claimants until program funds have been liquidated.

Eligible applicants/beneficiaries: personal representatives of emergency relief personnel killed or permanently physically disabled while serving in the line of duty in connection with the September 11, 2001 terrorist attacks, at the World Trade Center, Pentagon, or Shanksville, PA. site.

Range/Average: approximately $10,000 per claimant.

Activity: new program in FY 06 (CFDA on-line).

HQ: Hero Stamp Program, U.S. Fire Administration, National Emergency Training Center, FEMA-DHS, 16825 S. Seton Ave., Emmitsburg, MD 21727. Phone: (866)887-9101. **Internet:** "www.fema.gov"; e-mail, "FEMA-HeroesStamp@dhs.gov". (Note: no field offices for this program.)

97.086 HOMELAND SECURITY OUTREACH, EDUCATION, AND TECHNICAL ASSISTANCE

Assistance: project grants; technical information.

Purposes: pursuant to the Homeland Security Act of 2002, for outreach, education, and technical assistance projects to increase public awareness of homeland security issues; to help communities forge partnerships across agencies and disciplines to address preparedness and response.

Eligible applicants/beneficiaries: state, local, tribal governments; private, public, profit, and nonprofit organizations; individuals.

Range/Average: N.A.

Activity: new program in FY 06 (CFDA on-line).

HQ: Director, Grants and Financial Assistance Division, Office of Procurement Operations, DHS, Washington, DC. Phone: (202)772-9826. **Internet:** "www.dhs.gov". (Note: no field offices for this program.)

97.088 DISASTER ASSISTANCE PROJECTS

Assistance: project grants.

Purposes: pursuant to the Homeland Security Act, Stafford Act, and Public Health Bioterrorism and Public Health Emergencies Act of 2002, for specified projects identified by Congress or a DHS program office.

Eligible applicants/beneficiaries: nonfederal entities invited to apply by DHS or specified in appropriation statute.

Range/Average: N.A.

Activity: new program listing in 2006 (CFDA on-line).

HQ: FEMA-DHS, 245 Murray Lane - Bldg. 410, Washington, DC 20523.

Phone: (202)646-4397. **Internet:** "www.fema.gov". (Note: no field offices for this program.)

97.089 REAL ID PROGRAM

Assistance: project grants.

Purposes: pursuant to the Homeland Security Act and Real ID Act, for projects integrating hardware, software, and information management systems to implement the Real ID Act, establishing national standards for issuing drivers licenses.

Eligible applicants/beneficiaries: state, territorial agencies responsible for issuing drivers licenses.

Range/Average: N.A.

Activity: new program listing in 2006 (CFDA on-line).

HQ: Office of Grants and Training, Preparedness Directorate, DHS, 245 Murray Lane - Bldg. 410, Washington, DC 20523. Phone: (800)368-6498. **Internet:** "www.ojp.usdoj.gov/odp". (Note: no field offices for this program.)

UNITED STATES AGENCY FOR INTERNATIONAL DEVELOPMENT

NOTE: *Although USAID programs have existed for several decades, they were included in the CFDA as "Domestic Assistance Programs" only as of 2004.*

98.001 USAID FOREIGN ASSISTANCE FOR PROGRAMS OVERSEAS

Assistance: project grants (to 5 years).

Purposes: pursuant to the Foreign Assistance Act of 1961 as amended, to advance U.S. foreign policy objectives by supporting economic growth, agriculture and trade, global health, democracy, conflict prevention, and humanitarian assistance projects. Funds usually are awarded competitively to U.S. nongovernmental and educational institutions, for projects conducted in developing countries virtually throughout the world.

Eligible applicants: any type of applicant.

Eligible beneficiaries: foreign governments, public or private institutions or organizations, or individuals.

Range/Average: N.A.

Activity: new program listing in 2004. Active projects under way in more than 100 countries.

HQ: USAID, 1300 Pennsylvania Ave. NW, Washington, DC 20523. Phone:

(202)712-4810. **Internet:** "www.usaid.gov"; e-mail, "pinquiries@usaid.gov". (Note: no field offices for this program.)

98.002 COOPERATIVE DEVELOPMENT PROGRAM ("CDP")

Assistance: project grants (3-5 years).

Purposes: pursuant to the Foreign Assistance Act of 1961 as amended, to support cooperative development organizations in the establishment and management of cooperatives worldwide. Funds may support feasibility studies and technical assistance or advisory services to cooperatives, private voluntary and other nongovernmental organizations, governments, and groups of individuals interested in developing new or existing cooperatives. Program emphasis is on developing, testing, and implementing solutions to major issues facing international cooperative development, including governance, modern management, cooperatives legislation and regulation, and achieving scale and salience.

Eligible applicants/beneficiaries: U.S. cooperatives and recognized cooperative development organizations.

Range: $1,000,000 to $5,000,000 over five years.

Activity: new program listing in 2004. FY 02, 8 continuation grants through FY 04.

HQ: Cooperative Coordinator, Office of Private and Voluntary Cooperation, Bureau for Democracy, Conflict and Humanitarian Assistance, USAID, Washington, DC 20523. Phone: (202)712-5226. **Internet:** "www.usaid.gov/hum_response/pvc/coop.html". (Note: no field offices for this program.)

98.003 OCEAN FREIGHT REIMBURSEMENT PROGRAM ("OFR")

Assistance: project grants (100 percent/2 years).

Purposes: pursuant to the Foreign Assistance Act of 1961, to pay transportation charges for overseas shipments of commodities used in privately funded development and humanitarian assistance programs for the relief and rehabilitation of friendly people. Shipments must consist only of approved commodities—e.g., medical and educational supplies, agricultural and building equipment—only to approved countries that receive shipments duty-free.

Eligible applicants/beneficiaries: U.S. private voluntary organizations registered with USAID, receiving at least 20 percent of their funding for international programs from nongovernment sources.

Range: $2,500 to $150,000 per year.

Activity: new program listing in 2004. FY 04, 59 grants awarded.

HQ: Ocean Freight Program Officer, same address as **98.002**. Phone: (202)712-4795. **Internet:** "www.usaid.gov"; keyword: ofr. (Note: no field offices for this program.)

98.004 NON-GOVERNMENTAL ORGANIZATION STRENGTHENING ("NGO")

Assistance: project grants (70 percent/to 5 years).

Purposes: pursuant to the Foreign Assistance Act of 1961 as amended, to improve the capacities of local indigenous nongovernmental organizations, networks, and intermediate service organizations in developing countries.

Eligible applicants: same as for **98.003**, and current matching grant recipients.

Eligible beneficiaries: foreign private institutions or organizations.

Range: $1,300,000 to $3,250,000. **Average:** $2,400,000.

Activity: new program listing in 2004. FY 03, 13 cooperative agreements awarded through FY 08.

HQ: (no address/phone provided). **Internet:** "www.usaid.gov/our_work/crosscutting_programs/private_voluntary_cooperation/ngo.html". (Note: no field offices for this program.)

98.005 INSTITUTIONAL CAPACITY BUILDING ("ICB")

Assistance: project grants (75-90 percent/to 5 years).

Purposes: pursuant to the Foreign Assistance Act of 1961 as amended, to strengthen the capacity of new and experienced "Food for Peace Title II Partners" to plan and implement food security programs, including in emergency situations. Funds may support establishing systems, training, food security assessments and aid logistics, and strengthening mechanisms.

Eligible applicants/beneficiaries: U.S. private voluntary organizations or cooperatives registered with USAID.

Range: to $3,500,000 per organization for 5 years.

Activity: new program listing in 2004.

HQ: Grants Manager, Program Operations Division, Office of Food for Peace, USAID, 1300 Pennsylvania Ave. NW, Washington, DC 20523. Phone: (no number provided). **Internet:** same web site as **98.001**. (Note: no field offices for this program.)

98.006 FOREIGN ASSISTANCE TO AMERICAN SCHOOLS AND HOSPITALS ABROAD ("ASHA")

Assistance: project grants (cost sharing/2-5 years).

Purposes: pursuant to the Foreign Assistance Act of 1961 as amended, to strengthen foreign schools and hospitals best demonstrating American ideas and practices. Project examples: upgrading of a training facility; construction and equipping of private health care ward; construction of telecommunication laboratory.

Eligible applicants/beneficiaries: U.S. nonprofit organizations demonstrating a continuing supportive relationship with overseas institutions.

Range/Average: N.A.

Activity: new program listing in 2004.

HQ: Office of American School and Hospitals Abroad, Bureau for Democracy, Conflict and Humanitarian Assistance, USAID, Washington, DC 20523.

Phone: (no number provided). **Internet:** same as **98.001**. (Note: no field offices for this program.)

98.007 FOOD FOR PEACE DEVELOPMENT ASSISTANCE PROGRAM ("DAP")

Assistance: project grants (cost sharing/to 5 years); sale, exchange, or donation of property and goods.

Purposes: pursuant to the Agriculture, Trade and Development Assistance Act of 1954 as amended, to improve access, availability, and utilization of food in food-insecure environments abroad. Program focus: improving household nutrition and health status, especially in children and mothers; increasing agricultural productivity including field production, post-harvest handling, transformation, and marketing. Applicants may request commodities and cash for program implementation.

Eligible applicants/beneficiaries: same as for **98.005**; registration with the Office of Food Peace also is required.

Range: $5,000,000 to $50,000,000 over 5-7 years.

Activity: new program listing in 2004.

HQ: Development Programs Division, Office of Food for Peace, USAID, 1300 Pennsylvania Ave. NW, Washington, DC 20523. Phone: (no number provided). **Internet:** same as **98.001**. (Note: no field offices for this program.)

98.008 FOOD FOR PEACE EMERGENCY PROGRAM ("EP")

Assistance: project grants; sale, exchange, or donation of property and goods.

Purposes: pursuant to the Agriculture, Trade and Development Assistance Act of 1954 as amended, to improve access, availability, and utilization of food in food-insecure environments abroad—especially in emergency situations in which hunger and malnutrition need to be prevented. Applicants may request commodities and cash for program implementation.

Eligible applicants/beneficiaries: same as for **98.007**.

Range/Average: N.A.

Activity: new program listing in 2004.

HQ: Emergency Programs Division, same address, web site as **98.007**. Phone: (no number provided). (Note: no field offices for this program.)

98.009 JOHN OGONOWSKI FARMER-TO-FARMER PROGRAM ("Development Assistance Program")

Assistance: project grants (5-10 years).

Purposes: pursuant to the Farm Security and Rural Investment Act of 2002 and Agriculture, Trade and Development Assistance Act of 1954, to improve global food production and marketing by transferring technical skills of the U.S. agricultural community to farmers in developing and middle-income countries, emerging markets, sub-Saharan African countries, and Caribbean Basin countries.

Eligible applicants/beneficiaries: agricultural producers, agriculturalists, IHEs and their foundations, private agribusinesses willing to waive profits and fees, private organizations—which must be registered with USAID.

Range: $1,500,000 to $16,000,000 covering 5-9 years.

Activity: new program listing in 2004. Currently, 8 participating private voluntary organizations.

HQ: Farmer-to-Farmer Program, USAID, Washington, DC 20523. Phone: Technical Advisor, (202)712-5837, FAX (202)216-3579; Program Analyst, (202)219-0476, FAX (202)219-0508. **Internet:** "www.usaid.gov/our_work/agriculture/farmer_to_farmer.html". (Note: no field offices for this program.)

98.010 DENTON PROGRAM

Assistance: specialized services.

Purposes: to use empty space on U.S. military carriers to transport eligible donated goods for humanitarian relief, at little or no cost to nongovernmental organizations. The program is jointly administered by USAID, Department of State, and DOD.

Eligible applicants/beneficiaries: U.S. private voluntary organizations, non-governmental organizations, or small organizations.

Activity: new program listing in 2004. FY 03, 25 shipments serving 13 countries.

HQ: Denton Program Officer, same address/phone, web site as **98.003**, *and,* **Internet:** "www.dentonfunded.ida.org". (Note: no field offices for this program.)

98.011 GLOBAL DEVELOPMENT ALLIANCE ("GDA")

Assistance: project grants (50 percent/to 5 years).

Purposes: pursuant to the Foreign Assistance Act of 1961 as amended, for activities by public-private alliances promoting such international objectives as: advancing the growth of democracy and good governance; strengthening world economic growth, development, and stability, while expanding opportunities for U.S. business; improving health, education, environmental conditions for the global population; minimizing the human costs of displacement, conflicts, and natural disasters.

Eligible applicants/beneficiaries: U.S. and non-U.S. nongovernmental organizations, private businesses, foundations, business and trade associations, international organizations, IHEs; U.S. cities and states, other federal agencies, host country parastals, individual and group philanthropies, other similar organizations.

Range: projects, $300,000 to $1,000,000.

Activity: new program listing in 2004. Currently, activities ongoing in more than 100 countries.

HQ: GDA Secretariat, USAID, Washington, DC 20523. Phone: (202)712-4272.

Internet: "www.usaid.gov/our_work/global_partnerships/gda/". (Note: no field offices for this program.)

98.012 USAID DEVELOPMENT PARTNERSHIPS FOR UNIVERSITY COOPERATION AND DEVELOPMENT

Assistance: project grants.

Purposes: for U.S. IHEs to collaborate with counterpart institutions in developing countries to conduct projects that address critical development needs in those countries.

Eligible applicants/beneficiaries: U.S. IHEs including community colleges.

Range/Average: N.A.

Activity: new program listing in 2005. To date, 226 partnerships financed in 59 countries.

HQ: Higher Education Community Liaison, USAID, 1300 Pennsylvania Ave. NW, Washington, DC 20523. Phone: (202)712-1531, FAX (202)216-3229. **Internet:** "www.usaid.gov"; *cooperative agreement information,* American Council on Education, Association Liaison Office, "www.aascu.org/alo/". (Note: no field offices for this program.)

PART III

Program Funding Levels

Summary Tables

Four tables are presented:

- *Table 1. Estimated Outlays/Credits for Domestic Assistance Programs, by Federal Administrative Entity* (FY 03, 04, 05, 06), beginning on page 689.
- *Table 2. Summary of Estimated Outlays/Credits, by Federal Department or Agency* (FY 03, 04, 05, 06), beginning on page 725.
- *Table 3. The Fifty Largest Domestic Assistance Programs in FY 2005, by Funds Outlayed and/or Credited* (page 729).
- *Table 4. The Fifty Smallest Domestic Assistance Programs in FY 2005, by Funds Outlayed and/or Credited* (page 730).

The tables are based on information in the *Catalog of Federal Domestic Assistance 2005* and prior editions. The tables offer a general perspective of government funding for specific programs and agencies, in relation to one another and to other federal activities. Such a perspective can be useful in several ways to persons or organizations interested in certain programs and in government assistance, including:

- Having identified programs meeting given needs, prospective applicants can use the tables to compare relative funding levels.
- Tables 1 and 2 show funding levels for four federal fiscal years. To our knowledge tables compiled specifically for the domestic assistance programs exist nowhere else—i.e., apart from the costs of other administering agency functions. Perhaps such a compilation adds a new dimension to perspectives of federal domestic assistance.
- Tables 3 and 4 answer some questions frequently posed to the editor.

Important Notes on the Tables, Footnotes

Certain inconsistencies in the source material cannot be corrected. Therefore, *the tables should be used only as a general guide to the availability of funding.*

In Table 2, the first two digits in the five-digit number preceding the name of the administering agency correspond to the program number series identifying programs in Part II—e.g., 11.000 preceding DEPARTMENT OF COMMERCE encompasses all department programs including administrative sub-units.

The following footnotes are employed:

amount shown is a "credit" rather than an actual cash outlay. In the tables, amounts loaned or insured by the government are classified as credits.

(a) funding for the program cannot be separately identified from other agency expenses.

e amount was estimated in the source material, the significance of which is discussed on page 21, following the heading **Range**.

\i includes funding for this and for one or more other programs; program descriptions in Part II explain such cases.

(n) program did not exist during the reported fiscal year.

(o) funding is included in an amount reported for another program, as noted in the Part II program descriptions.

\p includes value of property or goods awarded; such amounts are not necessarily appropriated funds.

\r program supports or is supported by a revolving fund.

\t program includes support from or is supported by a federal trust fund.

\u user charges, fees, or other nonfederal funds help support the program, including loan repayments; amounts shown are not necessarily or entirely appropriated funds.

Table 1. Estimated Outlays/Credits for All Domestic Assistance Programs, by Administrative Entity

Program number	ADMINISTRATIVE ENTITY/SUB-UNIT Program Title (abridged)	FY 2003 in $thousands	FY 2004 in $thousands	FY 2005 in $thousands	FY 2006 in $thousands
	DEPARTMENT OF AGRICULTURE				
10.001	Agricultural Research	17,997	17,997	15,411 e	15,411 e
10.025	Plant, Animal Disease, Pest Control \ t	169,057	197,398	177,018 e	167,945 e
10.028	Wildlife Services	363	363	365 e	365 e
10.029	Avian Influenza Indemnity Program	50,992	50,992	0 e	0 e
10.051	Commodity Loans, Deficiency Payments \ u	4,989,008 e	3,894,506 e	0 e	0 e
		9,691,206*	9,493,384*	9,493,384*e	9,493,384*e
10.053	Dairy Indemnity	982	600	600 e	600 e
10.054	Emergency Conservation	4,071,721	31,193	31,193 e	0 e
10.055	Direct, Counter-Cyclical Payments \ u	5,056,954	6,151,488	5,944,800 e	5,944,800 e
10.056	Farm Storage Facility Loans \ u	140,481*	25,037*	25,037*e	25,037*e
10.062	Water Bank Program	1	12	0 e	0 e
10.064	Forestry Incentives	1,877	2,409	0 e	0 e
10.066	Livestock Assistance Program \ u	429,867	130,621	475,000 e	250,000 e
10.069	Conservation Reserve Program	1,806,264	1,882,592	1,937,672 e	1,937,672 e
10.070	Colorado River Salinity Control	0	763	863 e	0 e
10.072	Wetlands Reserve	309,402	286,559	250,946 e	321,100 e
10.073	Crop Disaster Program	1,808,000	57,338	2,750,000 e	0 e
10.075	Special Apple Program	5,000*	0*	0*e	0*e
10.076	Emergency Loan for Seed Producers	35,000*	0*	0*e	0*e
10.077	Livestock Compensation Program	886,000	1,387,000	2,100 e	0 e
10.078	Bioenergy Program	150,000	150,000	150,000 e	150,000 e
10.079	Emerson Humanitarian Trust \ t	73,052	73,052	0 e	0 e
10.080	Milk Income Loss Contract	2,500,000	1,721,207 e	4,000 e	0 e
10.081	Lamb Meat Adjustment Assistance	10,000	32,700	13,000 e	0 e
10.082	Tree Assistance Program	(n)	9,700	33,500 e	0 e
10.083	Tobacco Loss Assistance Program \ r	340,000	129,000	5,500 e	0 e
10.084	Dairy Market Loss Assistance \ u	(n)	(n)	10,000 e	0 e
10.085	Tobacco Transition Payments \ u	(n)	(n)	10,000,000 e	10,000,000 e
10.153	Market News	29,797	30,297	30,595 e	31,844 e
10.155	Marketing Agreements and Orders	14,844	14,938	15,800 e	16,055 e
10.156	Federal-State Marketing Improvement	1,338	3,318	3,816 e	1,347 e
10.162	Inspection Grading, Standardization \ t	134,264	165,252	190,082 e	193,820 e
10.163	Market Protection and Promotion	31,986	31,419	31,651 e	42,045 e
10.164	Wholesale Farmers, Alternative Markets	2,654	2,724	2,736 e	2,810 e
10.165	Perishable Agricultural Commodities	10,005	9,678	9,397 e	9,578 e
10.167	Transportation Services	2,673	2,744	2,716 e	2,794 e
10.200	Agricultural Research, Special	104,961	116,067	126,457 e	17,173 e
10.202	Cooperative Forestry Research	20,686	20,556	20,979 e	10,479 e
10.203	Agricultural Experiment Stations	168,781	168,896	168,501 e	84,224 e
10.205	1890 Land-Grant Colleges	33,401	33,401	33,754 e	33,754 e
10.206	Agricultural Research—Competitive	112,514	150,890	165,013 e	240,000 e
10.207	Animal Health and Disease Research	4,705	4,705	4,205 e	4,205 e
10.210	Food, Sciences—Fellowships	3,093	3,093	2,768 e	2,768 e
10.212	Small Business Innovation Research	14,456	14,456	14,436 e	14,436 e
10.215	Sustainable Agriculture Research	12,786	11,440	11,606 e	8,639 e
10.216	1890 Institution Capacity Building	8,979	10,780	11,645 e	12,000 e
10.217	Higher Education Challenge Grants	4,166	4,166	4,692 e	4,665 e
10.219	Biotechnology Risk Assessment	636	636	697 e	624 e
10.220	Multicultural Scholars Program	952	952	947 e	947 e
10.221	Tribal Colleges Education Equity	1,689	1,679	2,232 e	2,250 e
10.222	Tribal Colleges Endowment	1,701	1,853	2,093 e	2,408 e
10.223	Hispanic Serving Institutions	3,910	3,910	4,460 e	4,460 e
10.224	FRA—Research, Education, Extension	0	0	0 e	0 e
10.225	Community Food Projects	4,800	4,800	4,800 e	0 e
10.226	Secondary Agriculture Education	954	854	952 e	960 e
10.227	1994 Institutions Research Program	1,023	1,017	1,009 e	958 e
10.228	Alaska, Hawaii Native Education	2,877	3,006	3,333 e	2,877 e
10.250	Agricultural, Rural Research	70,665	72,853	76,151 e	82,730 e
10.303	Integrated Programs	43,728	38,940	41,913 e	1,440 e

Please see "Important Notes on the Tables, Footnotes," page 688.

Table 1. (continued)

Program number	ADMINISTRATIVE ENTITY/SUB-UNIT Program Title (abridged)	FY 2003 in $thousands	FY 2004 in $thousands	FY 2005 in $thousands	FY 2006 in $thousands
10.304	Homeland Security-Agricultural	0	7,635	8,571 e	28,800 e
10.305	International Science, Education	477	477	859 e	952 e
10.306	Biodiesel	960	960	960 e	960 e
10.307	Organic Agriculture Research	(n)	0	2,880 e	2,880 e
10.308	Instruction/Insular Area Activities	(n)	(n)	476 e	0 e
10.350	Assistance/Cooperatives	(o)	(o)	(o)	(o)
10.352	Value-Added Producer Grants	(n)	13,200	14,300 e	15,500 e
10.404	Emergency Loans \ u	95,698*	65,000*	40,571*e	0*e
10.405	Farm Labor Housing \ r, u	4,382	17,651	17,000 e	14,000 e
		55,862*	36,063*	41,999*e	42,001*e
10.406	Farm Operating Loans \ u	1,974,658*	1,559,136*	2,050,000*e	0*e
10.407	Farm Ownership Loans \ u	1,448,170*	1,072,791*	1,600,000*e	0*e
10.410	Very Low/Moderate Income Housing \ u	4,124,628*	4,535,299*	1,102,500*e	4,474*e
10.411	Rural Site/Self-Help Loans \ u	2,144*	5,639*	15,045*e	10,048*e
10.415	Rural Rental Housing Loans \ u	115,857*	114,488*	99,200*e	27,027*e
10.417	Housing Repair Loans, Grants \ u	31,135	30,707	31,500 e	30,000 e
		31,036*	32,975*	35,000*e	35,969*e
10.420	Rural Self-Help Housing	35,729	35,306	34,000 e	34,000 e
10.421	Tribal Corporation Loans \ u	110*	2,000*	2,000*e	2,000*e
10.427	Rural Rental Assistance Payments	721,148	574,689	586,100 e	644,126 e
10.433	Rural Housing Preservation Grants	10,093	9,292	8,811 e	10,000 e
10.435	State Mediation Grants	3,000	4,000	3,000 e	0 e
10.437	Interest Assistance Program \ u	422,302*	271,219*	266,253*e	0*e
10.438	Section 538 Rural Rental Housing	101,751*	99,400*	99,200*e	200,000*e
10.441	Technical, Supervisory Assistance	1,113	2,038	1,000 e	1,000 e
10.442	Housing Application Packaging	78	145	0 e	0 e
10.443	Outreach/Farmers, Ranchers	3,331	5,697	5,698 e	0 e
10.444	Housing—Disaster Loans, Grants \ u	1,942	1,250	0 e	0 e
		410*	500*	0*e	0*e
10.445	Housing—Disaster Loans \ u	317*	140*	0*e	0*e
10.446	Rural Community Development \ u	6,000	6,537	6,299 e	0 e
10.449	Boll Weevil Eradication Loans	99,000*	100,000*	60,000 e	100,000*e
10.450	Crop Insurance \ u	2,041,680	2,041,680	2,043,929 e	2,153,908 e
		3,226,540*	3,226,540*	3,926,144*e	4,018,387*e
10.451	Noninsured Assistance \ u	176,500	160,000	314,184 e	0 e
10.452	Disaster Reserve Assistance	1,911,905 e	13,704 e	0 e	0 e
10.454	Dairy Options Pilot Program \ u	697	697	0 e	0 e
10.455	Community Outreach, Assistance \ u	4,576	4,576	4,000 e	4,000 e
10.456	Non-Insurance Risk Management \ u	9,700	9,700	10,000 e	4,000 e
10.457	Commodity Partnerships \ u	4,576	4,500	4,000 e	0 e
10.458	Crop Insurance Education \ u	4,539	4,539	4,500 e	4,500 e
10.459	Commodity Partnerships, Small \ u	(n)	(n)	500 e	0 e
10.475	Intrastate Meat, Poultry Inspection	43,396	43,477	44,254 e	45,424 e
10.477	Meat, Poultry and Egg Inspection \ t	697,672	745,729	776,166 e	807,621 e
10.500	Cooperative Extension Service	432,358	421,539	427,485 e	413,035 e
10.550	Food Donation \ p, u	237,620	237,620	166,575 e	186,876 e
10.551	Food Stamps	24,606,021	24,627,332	29,713,003 e	33,147,009 e
10.553	School Breakfast Program	1,674,236	1,786,906	1,910,822 e	2,030,357 e
10.555	School Lunch Program \ p	6,834,840	7,668,278	8,068,972 e	8,341,989 e
10.556	Special Milk Program	14,311	13,977	16,868 e	14,819 e
10.557	Nutrition/Women, Infants, Children	5,855,868 e	5,840,745 e	4,773,250 e	0 e
10.558	Child, Adult Care Food Program \ p	1,972,090 e	2,116,313 e	2,066,196 e	2,174,293 e
10.559	Summer Food Service \ p	268,231 e	268,177 e	283,226 e	298,364 e
10.560	State Expenses/Child Nutrition \ p	130,073	139,570	145,710 e	156,061 e
10.561	State Grants/Food Stamp Program	2,352,000	2,310,367	2,402,000 e	2,481,000 e
10.565	Commodity Supplemental Food \ p	113,756	(a)	(a)	(a)
10.566	Nutrition Assistance/Puerto Rico	1,395,396	1,413,370	1,495,346 e	1,516,280 e
10.567	Food Distribution/Indian \ p	82,165	81,023	82,200 e	76,500 e
10.568	Emergency Food—Administrative	49,675	49,675	49,705 e	50,000 e
10.569	Emergency Food—Commodities	140,000	140,000	140,000 e	140,000 e
10.572	WIC Farmers' Market Nutrition	15,000	27,952	23,524 e	20,000 e
10.574	Team Nutrition Grants	10,011	10,308	10,015 e	10,025 e
10.576	Senior Farmers Market Nutrition	(n)	0	0 e	20,000 e
10.578	WIC Grants to States	16,387	17,300	18,000 e	14,000 e

Please see "Important Notes on the Tables, Footnotes," page 688.

Table 1. (continued)

Program number	ADMINISTRATIVE ENTITY/SUB-UNIT Program Title (abridged)	FY 2003 in $thousands	FY 2004 in $thousands	FY 2005 in $thousands	FY 2006 in $thousands
10.579	Child Nutrition Discretionary \ p	(n)	0	920 e	15,000 e
10.580	Food Stamp Program Outreach	(n)	0	0 e	0 e
10.582	Fresh Fruit, Vegetable Program	(n)	(n)	9,000 e	9,000 e
10.600	Foreign Market Development \ u	34,500	34,500	34,500 e	34,500 e
10.601	Market Access Program \ u	110,000	125,000	140,000 e	200,000 e
10.603	Emerging Markets Program \ u	10,000	10,000	10,000 e	10,000 e
10.604	Assistance/Specialty Crops \ u	2,000	2,000	2,000 e	2,000 e
10.605	Quality Samples Program \ u	2,500	2,500	2,500 e	2,500 e
10.606	Food for Progress \ u	86,000	126,900	160,000 e	160,000 e
10.607	Section 416(B) \ u	332,275	156,600	78,700 e	78,700 e
10.608	Food for Education \ u	100,000	50,338	87,000 e	100,000 e
10.609	Trade Adjustment Assistance \ r	(n)	0 e	0 e	0 e
10.652	Forestry Research	13,762	13,762	14,000 e	14,000 e
10.664	Cooperative Forestry Assistance	38,270	38,270	38,107 e	40,069 e
10.665	Schools and Roads—States	359,277	359,277	366,463 e	0 e
10.666	Schools and Roads—Counties	5,655	5,655	6,038 e	6,287 e
10.670	Forest-Dependent Communities	3,642	3,642	9,000 e	0 e
10.671	Southeast Alaska Economic Disaster	10,000	10,000	12,000 e	0 e
10.672	Rural Development, Forestry	3,974	3,974	3,951 e	0 e
10.673	Wood in Transportation	478	478	416 e	0 e
10.674	Forest Products Lab: Technology Unit	1,700	0	4,431 e	0 e
10.675	Urban and Community Forestry	35,999	35,999	34,864 e	31,961 e
10.676	Forest Legacy	68,380	64,134	57,134 e	80,000 e
10.677	Forest Land Enhancement	20,000	20,000	0 e	0 e
10.678	Forest Stewardship	32,012	32,012	31,884 e	40,069 e
10.679	Collaborative Forest Restoration	(n)	4,101	4,101 e	4,101 e
10.680	Forest Health Protection	(n)	38,107	40,069 e	0 e
10.700	National Agricultural Library	23,895	23,763	22,413 e	23,329 e
10.760	Water, Waste Disposal Systems \ i, u	496,312	570,352	458,987 e	380,522 e
		767,174*	977,042*	1,067,000*e	1,075,000*e
10.761	Technical Assistance, Training	(o)	(o)	(o)	(o)
10.762	Solid Waste Management	3,361	3,440	3,472 e	3,500 e
10.763	Community Water Assistance	16,667	15,244	22,949 e	11,416 e
10.766	Community Facilities Loans, Grants \ u	18,487	17,453	17,000 e	17,000 e
		414,515*	705,301*	510,000*e	510,000*e
10.767	Intermediary Relending Program \ u	44,064*	39,764*	33,939*e	34,212*e
10.768	Business and Industry Loans \ u	956,502*e	963,180*e	609,689*e	898,800*e
10.769	Rural Business Enterprise Grants	51,403	45,960	39,828 e	0 e
10.770	Water, Waste Disposal	(o)	(o)	(o)	(o)
10.771	Rural Cooperative Development	6,332	5,000	4,464 e	5,000 e
10.772	Empowerment Zones Program	(o)	12,477	16,238 e	0 e
10.773	Rural Business Opportunity Grants	3,109	3,308	3,032 e	0 e
10.774	Sheep Industry Improvement \ r	(o)	(o)	(o)	(o)
10.775	Renewable Energy Systems	21,707*	22,864*	22,800*e	10,770*e
10.850	Rural Electrification Loans \ u	3,971,000*	3,831,803*	2,918,240*e	2,520,000*e
10.851	Rural Telephone Loans \ u	483,000*	513,468*	518,000*e	669,000*e
10.852	Rural Telephone Bank Loans \ u	168,000*	169,956*	175,000*e	0*e
10.853	Local Television Loan Guarantee	(n)*	0*	0*e	0*e
10.854	Rural Economic Development \ r, u	4,066	10,786	10,000 e	10,000 e
		3,176*	14,704*	24,803*e	25,002*e
10.855	Distance Learning, Telemedicine	33,507	24,871	25,000 e	25,000 e
		300,000*e	30,293*	50,000*e	0*e
10.856	1890 Land Grant Outreach	1,500	1,800	1,800 e	1,800 e
10.857	State Bulk Fuel Revolving Fund \ r	0	0	0 e	0 e
10.858	RUS Denali Commission	18,500	15,000	15,000 e	0 e
10.859	High Energy Cost Communities	0	16,104	36,000 e	0 e
10.860	Rural Business Investment	(n)	0	3,000 e	0 e
		(n)*	4,000*	60,000*e	0*e
10.861	Public Television Digital Transition	(n)	28,917	10,000 e	0 e
10.862	Household Water Well System	(n)	994	992 e	0 e
10.863	Community Connect Grant Program	33,000	0	17,900 e	0 e
10.864	Fund/Financing Water, Wastewater \ r	(n)	497	496 e	0 e
10.886	Rural Broadband Access Loans	(n)*	602,947*	2,157,000*e	359,000*e
10.900	Great Plains Conservation	97	173	0 e	0 e

Please see "Important Notes on the Tables, Footnotes," page 688.

Table 1. (continued)

Program number	ADMINISTRATIVE ENTITY/SUB-UNIT Program Title (abridged)		FY 2003 in $thousands	FY 2004 in $thousands	FY 2005 in $thousands	FY 2006 in $thousands
10.901	Resource Conservation, Development		50,057 e	53,880 e	52,446 e	25,600 e
10.902	Soil and Water Conservation		710,755	764,752	743,217 e	658,630 e
10.903	Soil Survey		79,222	88,120	88,884 e	88,149 e
10.904	Watershed Protection		122,446	102,769	80,268 e	0 e
10.905	Plant Materials for Conservation		10,255	11,615	15,046 e	10,547 e
10.906	Watershed Surveys and Planning		10,949	9,803	7,026 e	5,141 e
10.907	Snow Survey, Water Forecasting		5,991	9,702	10,658 e	10,457 e
10.910	Rural Abandoned Mine Program		70	45	34 e	0 e
10.912	Environmental Quality Incentives		199,942	902,802 e	994,709 e	1,000,000 e
10.913	Farm, Ranch Lands Protection		50,706	91,425	112,000 e	83,500 e
10.914	Wildlife Habitat Incentive		25,091	38,142	48,663 e	60,000 e
10.916	Watershed Rehabilitation		29,387	29,734	28,503 e	15,125 e
10.917	Agricultural Management Assistance		1,300	13,866	14,000 e	0 e
10.918	Water Conservation-Environmental		53,944	64,540	70,089 e	60,000 e
10.919	Klamath Basin-Environmental Quality		12,351	18,682	11,319 e	8,118 e
10.920	Grassland Reserve Program		38,184	56,796	84,001 e	0 e
10.921	Conservation Security Program		33	40,446	202,411 e	273,900 e
10.950	Agricultural Statistics Reports		155,887	155,887	151,329 e	159,172 e
10.960	Technical Agricultural Assistance		2,081	2,081	2,081 e	2,081 e
10.961	Scientific Cooperation and Research		2,500	2,500	2,500 e	2,500 e
10.962	International Training		5,090	5,090	5,340 e	5,340 e
10.994	Peanut Quota Buyout Program		(n)	259,600	259,600 e	259,600 e
10.995	Hard White Wheat Incentive \ u		(n)	15,208	4,792 e	0 e
	DEPARTMENT TOTAL:	OUTLAYS	78,982,129	72,716,321	83,351,853	78,546,076
		CREDITS*	28,699,308*	28,514,933*	27,002,804*	20,060,111*

DEPARTMENT OF COMMERCE

BUREAU OF THE CENSUS

11.001	Census Bureau Data Products		1,454	1,218	571 e	251 e
11.002	Census Customer Services		9	86	119 e	63 e
11.003	Census Geography		37,651	40,099	38,775 e	39,785 e
11.004	Intergovernmental Services		1,540	4,401	4,463 e	3,585 e
11.005	Census Special Tabulations		3,440	4,182	2,695 e	1,441 e
11.006	Personal Census Search		388	165	180 e	180 e
	Subtotal:	Outlays	44,482	50,151	46,803	45,305
		Credits*	0*	0*	0*	0*

ECONOMICS AND STATISTICS ADMINISTRATION

11.025	Measures and Analyses		64,344	67,101	72,615 e	81,250 e
11.026	National Trade Data Bank \ r, u		0	0	0	0
11.027	State of the Nation \ r, u		0	0	0	0
	Subtotal:	Outlays	64,344	67,101	72,615	81,250
		Credits*	0*	0*	0*	0*

INTERNATIONAL TRADE ADMINISTRATION

11.106	Antidumping Duty		33,622	69,105	61,741 e	64,134 e
11.108	Commercial Service		183,182	224,801	216,061 e	231,722 e
11.110	Manufacturing and Services		56,178	50,902	48,376 e	48,134 e
11.111	Foreign-Trade Zones/U.S.		956	1,088	1,130 e	1,026 e
11.112	Export Market Development		2,000	1,777	2,000 e	2,000 e
11.113	ITA Special Projects		14,000	14,000	13,319 e	14,000 e
11.114	American Business Internship		1,500	4,500	3,960 e	0 e
	Subtotal:	Outlays	291,438	366,173	346,587	361,016
		Credits*	0*	0*	0*	0*

BUREAU OF EXPORT ADMINISTRATION

11.150	Licensing Services, Information		226	1,841	1,689 e	1,723 e
	Subtotal:	Outlays	226	1,841	1,689	1,723
		Credits*	0*	0*	0*	0*

Please see "Important Notes on the Tables, Footnotes," page 688.

Table 1. (continued)

Program number	ADMINISTRATIVE ENTITY/SUB-UNIT Program Title (abridged)	FY 2003 in $thousands	FY 2004 in $thousands	FY 2005 in $thousands	FY 2006 in $thousands
	ECONOMIC DEVELOPMENT ADMINISTRATION				
11.300	Public Works, Economic Development	207,129	196,151	164,368 e	0 e
11.302	Support for Planning Organizations	24,003	23,747	23,667 e	0 e
11.303	Technical Assistance	9,229	8,346	8,322 e	0 e
11.307	Economic Adjustment Assistance	40,634	40,270	44,793 e	0 e
11.312	Research and Evaluation	457	495	488 e	0 e
11.313	Trade Adjustment Assistance	10,432	11,874	11,839 e	0 e
	Subtotal: Outlays	291,884	280,883	253,477	0
	Credits*	0*	0*	0*	0*
	NATIONAL OCEANIC AND ATMOSPHERIC ADMINISTRATION				
11.400	Geodetic Surveys and Services	7,797	11,187	15,738 e	16,642 e
11.405	Anadromous Fish Conservation	2,142	2,013	2,000 e	2,100 e
11.407	Interjurisdictional Fisheries	3,238	2,563	2,600 e	2,600 e
11.408	Fishermen's Contingency Fund	108	161	175 e	175 e
11.413	Fishery Products Inspection	0	15,799	17,069 e	17,923 e
11.415	Fisheries Finance Program \ u	62,300*	100,000*e	64,000*e	59,000*e
11.417	Sea Grant Support	64,046	57,837	57,800 e	58,148 e
11.419	Coastal Zone Management	114,082	140,200	129,500 e	71,500 e
11.420	Estuarine Research Reserves	39,467	29,900	24,200 e	22,500 e
11.426	Coastal Ocean Science	9,000	8,400	12,000 e	12,100 e
11.427	Fisheries Development	7,839	250	2,000 e	0 e
11.428	Intergovernmental Climate—NESDIS	890	0	0 e	0 e
11.429	Marine Sanctuary Program	9,371	7,169	19,626 e	5,930 e
11.430	Undersea Research	15,000	15,032	15,000 e	10,464 e
11.431	Climate, Atmospheric Research	45,168	46,000	46,000 e	36,000 e
11.432	Oceanic, Atmospheric Research	104,749	104,167	115,000 e	110,000 e
11.433	Marine Fisheries Initiative	2,361	2,500	3,400 e	2,500 e
11.434	Cooperative Fishery Statistics	5,309	5,733	6,000 e	6,000 e
11.435	Southeast Area Monitoring	1,111	1,391	1,400 e	1,400 e
11.436	Columbia River Fisheries	14,916	12,992	13,100 e	13,100 e
11.437	Pacific Fisheries	16,105	21,177	20,000 e	20,000 e
11.438	Pacific Coast Salmon Recovery	94,967	93,223	94,000 e	94,000 e
11.439	Marine Mammal Data Program	21,400	38,713 e	36,900 e	20,000 e
11.440	Environmental Sciences	6,221	19,157	20,000 e	20,500 e
11.441	Fishery Management Councils	21,397	22,458	24,000 e	26,000 e
11.443	Short Term Climate Fluctuations	0	0	0 e	0 e
11.444	Hawaii Fisheries/Aquaculture	581	503	503 e	503 e
11.445	Hawaii Stock Management	472	466	483 e	483 e
11.449	Independent Education and Science	9	0	0 e	0 e
11.450	Automated Flood Warning Systems	437	523	410 e	500 e
11.452	Unallied Industry Projects	60,189	21,545	4,000 e	2,000 e
11.454	Unallied Management Projects	17,323	8,628	10,000 e	10,000 e
11.455	Cooperative Science, Education	4,827	7,452	8,000 e	8,000 e
11.457	Chesapeake Bay Studies	7,721	12,673	13,000 e	13,000 e
11.459	Weather and Air Quality Research	0	0	0 e	0 e
11.460	Oceanic and Atmospheric Projects	16,600	22,600	23,500 e	1,500 e
11.462	Hydrologic Research	120	100	0 e	0 e
11.463	Habitat Conservation	30,260	42,635 e	43,000 e	40,000 e
11.467	Meteorologic, Hydrologic Projects	4,151	5,320	4,763 e	4,983 e
11.468	Applied Meteorological Research	2,033	6,444	5,512 e	1,544 e
11.469	Congressionally Identified Projects	0	0	0 e	0 e
11.472	Unallied Science Program	21,666	36,186	30,025 e	30,025 e
11.473	Coastal Services Center	17,500	31,000	36,000 e	30,000 e
11.474	Atlantic Coastal Fisheries	7,139	7,250	9,250 e	9,250 e
11.477	Fisheries Disaster Relief	669	109	0 e	100 e
11.478	Coastal Ocean Program	10,500	12,000	35,000 e	16,000 e
11.480	Ocean Service Intern Program	1,325	1,779	1,800 e	0 e
11.481	Educational Partnership Program	13,300	14,300	13,300 e	13,300 e
	Subtotal: Outlays	823,506	889,535	916,054	750,770
	Credits*	62,300*	100,000*	64,000*	59,000*

Please see "Important Notes on the Tables, Footnotes," page 688.

Table 1. (continued)

Program number	ADMINISTRATIVE ENTITY/SUB-UNIT Program Title (abridged)		FY 2003 in $thousands	FY 2004 in $thousands	FY 2005 in $thousands	FY 2006 in $thousands
	NATIONAL TELECOMMUNICATIONS AND INFORMATION ADMINISTRATION					
11.550	Public Telecommunications Facilities		43,493	24,550	19,988 e	0 e
11.552	Technology Opportunities Program		13,940	14,449	0 e	0 e
	Subtotal:	Outlays	57,433	38,999	19,988	0
		Credits*	0*	0*	0*	0*
	NATIONAL INSTITUTE OF STANDARDS AND TECHNOLOGY					
11.601	Calibration Program \ r		7,946	7,901	7,827 e	7,847 e
11.603	Standard Reference Data System \ r		4,746	4,880	4,652 e	4,732 e
11.604	Standard Reference Materials \ r		8,475	10,182	11,228 e	11,362 e
11.606	Weights and Measures Service \ r		4,791	4,364	4,482 e	4,482 e
11.609	Measurement, Engineering Research \ r		21,017	18,536	21,289 e	20,792 e
11.610	Standards and Certification \ r		700	700	700 e	700 e
11.611	Manufacturing Extension Partnership		92,704	33,258	93,000 e	39,730 e
11.612	Advanced Technology Program		155,390	148,916	102,957 e	0 e
11.617	Congressionally-Identified Projects		36,918	34,533	51,700 e	0 e
	Subtotal:	Outlays	332,687	263,270	297,835	89,645
		Credits*	0*	0*	0*	0*
	NATIONAL TECHNICAL INFORMATION SERVICE					
11.650	National Technical Information \ r, u		27,689	19,172	50,991 e	40,500 e
	Subtotal:	Outlays	27,689	19,172	50,991	40,500
		Credits*	0*	0*	0*	0*
	OFFICE OF THE SECRETARY					
11.702	Postsecondary Internships		1,159	1,156	1,200 e	1,200 e
	Subtotal:	Outlays	1,159	1,156	1,200	1,200
		Credits*	0*	0*	0*	0*
	MINORITY BUSINESS DEVELOPMENT AGENCY					
11.800	Minority Business Development		7,129	6,817	7,194 e	7,194 e
11.801	Native American Business Development		1,396	1,552	1,592 e	1,592 e
11.803	Minority Business Committee		1,497	1,633	1,633 e	1,633 e
	Subtotal:	Outlays	10,022	10,002	10,419	10,419
		Credits*	0*	0*	0*	0*
	PATENT AND TRADEMARK OFFICE					
11.900	Patent and Trademark Information		20,260	1,233,107	1,567,117 e	1,703,300 e
	Subtotal:	Outlays	20,260	1,233,107	1,567,117	1,703,300
		Credits*	0*	0*	0*	0*
	DEPARTMENT TOTAL:	OUTLAYS	1,965,130	3,221,390	3,584,775	3,085,128
		CREDITS*	62,300*	100,000*	64,000*	59,000*
	DEPARTMENT OF DEFENSE					
	DEFENSE LOGISTICS AGENCY					
12.002	Procurement Technical Assistance		12,000 e	12,000	12,000 e	0 e
	Subtotal:	Outlays	12,000	12,000	12,000	0
		Credits*	0*	0*	0*	0*
	DEPARTMENT OF THE ARMY, OFFICE OF THE CHIEF OF ENGINEERS					
12.100	Aquatic Plant Control		0 e	0	0 e	0 e
12.101	Beach Erosion Control Projects		2,500 e	2,800	2,500 e	0 e

Please see "Important Notes on the Tables, Footnotes," page 688.

Table 1. (continued)

Program number	ADMINISTRATIVE ENTITY/SUB-UNIT Program Title (abridged)		FY 2003 in $thousands	FY 2004 in $thousands	FY 2005 in $thousands	FY 2006 in $thousands
12.102	Emergency Flood Control Works		0 e	5,000	0 e	0 e
12.103	Emergency Flood Response		0 e	5,000	0 e	0 e
12.104	Flood Plain Management		9,000 e	8,500	9,000 e	0 e
12.105	Essential Highways, Public Works		9,000 e	13,000	9,000 e	0 e
12.106	Flood Control Projects		25,000 e	30,600	25,000 e	0 e
12.107	Navigation Projects		7,000 e	5,900	7,000 e	0 e
12.108	Snagging and Clearing		200 e	1,600	200 e	0 e
12.109	Protection, Clearing Channels		0 e	50	0 e	0 e
12.110	Planning Assistance to States		6,500 e	5,800	6,500 e	0 e
12.111	Flood Prevention		1,000 e	500	1,000 e	0 e
12.112	Payments to States/Taxes		0 e	5,000	0 e	0 e
12.113	Reimbursements/Technical Services		41,453 e	27,546	41,453 e	43,545 e
12.114	Collaborative Research, Development		5,306 e	4,660	5,306 e	6,000 e
12.116	DOD Appropriation Act of 2003		10,000 e	0	10,000 e	0 e
	Subtotal:	Outlays	116,959	115,956	116,959	49,545
		Credits*	0*	0*	0*	0*

DEPARTMENT OF THE NAVY, OFFICE OF NAVAL RESEARCH

12.300	Basic, Applied Scientific Research		480,000 e	470,000	480,000 e	480,000 e
	Subtotal:	Outlays	480,000	470,000	480,000	480,000
		Credits*	0*	0*	0*	0*

NATIONAL GUARD BUREAU

12.400	Military Construction		66,363 e	59,130	66,363 e	0 e
12.401	National Guard Operations		150,000 e	244,000	150,000 e	100,000 e
12.404	Civilian Youth Opportunities		62,500 e	62,300	62,500 e	62,500 e
	Subtotal:	Outlays	278,863	365,430	278,863	162,500
		Credits*	0*	0*	0*	0*

DEPARTMENT OF THE ARMY, U.S. ARMY MEDICAL COMMAND

12.420	Military Medical Research		56,530 e	137,380	56,530 e	140,000 e
	Subtotal:	Outlays	56,530	137,380	56,530	140,000
		Credits*	0*	0*	0*	0*

U.S. ARMY MATERIEL COMMAND

12.431	Basic Scientific Research		150,000 e	150,000	150,000 e	0 e
	Subtotal:	Outlays	150,000	150,000	150,000	0
		Credits*	0*	0*	0*	0*

ASSISTANT SECRETARY (STRATEGY AND REQUIREMENTS)

12.550	International Education \t		2,000 e	2,000	2,000 e	0 e
12.551	National Security—Scholarships \t		2,000 e	2,000	2,000 e	0 e
	Subtotal:	Outlays	4,000	4,000	4,000	0
		Credits*	0*	0*	0*	0*

ASSISTANT SECRETARY (ECONOMIC SECURITY)

12.600	Community Economic Adjustment \t		(a)	(a)	(a)	(a)
12.607	Community Economic Planning \t		3,000 e	1,171	3,000 e	0 e
12.610	Joint Land Use Studies \t		1,200 e	610	1,240 e	1,200 e
12.611	Community Planning Assistance		0 e	0	0 e	0 e
12.612	Community Base Reuse Plans		0 e	0	0 e	0 e
12.613	Growth Management Planning		0 e	0	0 e	0 e
12.614	Advance Planning \t		(n)	519	3,500 e	875 e
	Subtotal:	Outlays	4,200	2,300	7,740	2,075
		Credits*	0*	0*	0*	0*

Please see "Important Notes on the Tables, Footnotes," page 688.

696 GOVERNMENT ASSISTANCE ALMANAC 2006–07

Table 1. *(continued)*

Program number	ADMINISTRATIVE ENTITY/SUB-UNIT Program Title (abridged)		FY 2003 in $thousands	FY 2004 in $thousands	FY 2005 in $thousands	FY 2006 in $thousands
	OFFICE OF THE SECRETARY					
12.630	Research/Science, Engineering		220,000 e	224,196	220,000 e	215,000 e
	Subtotal:	Outlays	220,000	224,196	220,000	215,000
		Credits*	0*	0*	0*	0*
	SECRETARIES OF MILITARY DEPARTMENTS					
12.700	Obsolete DOD Property \ p		2,750 e	2,500	2,750 e	0 e
	Subtotal:	Outlays	2,750	2,500	2,750	0
		Credits*	0*	0*	0*	0*
	DEPARTMENT OF THE AIR FORCE, MATERIAL COMMAND					
12.800	Defense Research Sciences		260,000 e	263,000	260,000 e	275,000 e
	Subtotal:	Outlays	260,000	263,000	260,000	275,000
		Credits*	0*	0*	0*	0*
	NATIONAL SECURITY AGENCY					
12.900	Language Grant Program		50 e	50	50 e	0 e
12.901	Mathematical Sciences Grants		2,600 e	2,900	2,600 e	3,000 e
12.902	Information Security		1,000 e	1,400	1,000 e	2,000 e
	Subtotal:	Outlays	3,650	4,350	3,650	5,000
		Credits*	0*	0*	0*	0*
	ADVANCED RESEARCH PROJECTS AGENCY					
12.910	Research and Technology		80,000 e	80,000	80,000 e	0 e
	Subtotal:	Outlays	80,000	80,000	80,000	0
		Credits*	0*	0*	0*	0*
	DEPARTMENT TOTAL:	OUTLAYS	1,668,952	1,831,112	1,672,492	1,329,120
		CREDITS*	0*	0*	0*	0*
	DEPARTMENT OF HOUSING AND URBAN DEVELOPMENT					
14.103	Interest Reduction—Housing \ u		(a)	(a)	(a)	(a)
			(a)*	(a)*	(a)*	(a)*
14.108	Rehabilitation Mortgage Insurance \ u		687,855*	658,684*	632,184*e	589,151*e
14.110	Manufactured Home Loan Insurance \ i, u		73,427*	69,301*	109,608*e	109,608*e
14.112	Construction, Rehab/Condominiums \ u		(o)*	(o)*	(o)*	(o)*
14.117	Mortgage Insurance—Homes \ i, u		147,395,494*	107,698,993*	116,500,000*e	112,779,852*e
14.119	Homes for Disaster Victims \ u		(o)*	(o)*	(o)*	(o)*
14.122	Mortgage Insurance—Renewal Areas \ u		(o)*	(o)*	(o)*	(o)*
14.123	Mortgage Insurance—Declining Areas \ u		(o)*	(o)*	(o)*	(o)*
14.126	Mortgage Insurance—Cooperatives \ u		(o)*	(o)*	(o)*	(o)*
14.127	Manufactured Home Parks \ u		(o)*	(o)*	(o)*	(o)*
14.128	Mortgage Insurance—Hospitals \ u		284,887*	405,748*	450,000*e	600,000*e
14.129	Mortgage Insurance—Nursing Homes \ u		2,175,633*	1,556,000*	1,818,000*e	2,497,000*e
14.132	Sales/Cooperative Housing \ u		(o)*	(o)*	(o)*	(o)*
14.133	Mortgage Insurance—Condominiums \ i, u		14,145,183*	14,585,000*	11,189,619*e	10,817,855*e
14.134	Mortgage Insurance—Rental Housing \ u		(o)*	(o)*	(o)*	(o)*
14.135	Mortgage Insurance—Market Rate \ i, u		3,029,903*	3,913,117*	4,037,000*e	5,527,000*e
14.138	Mortgage Insurance—Elderly \ u		(o)*	(o)*	(o)*	(o)*
14.139	Rental Housing/Renewal Areas \ u		(o)*	(o)*	(o)*	(o)*
14.142	Property Improvement Loans \ u		61,241*	67,886*	98,768*e	98,768*e
14.149	Rent Supplements, Housing		(a)	(a)	(a)	(a)
14.151	Supplemental Loan Insurance \ u		6,331*	3,414*	7,500*e	10,300*e
14.155	Existing Multifamily Projects \ u		2,520,214*	2,980,875*	2,625,000*e	3,605,000*e
14.157	Supportive Housing/Elderly \ i, u		783,286	778,320	747,000 e	741,000 e
14.159	Graduated Payment Mortgage \ u		(o)*	(o)*	(o)*	(o)*

Please see "Important Notes on the Tables, Footnotes," page 688.

Table 1. (continued)

Program number	ADMINISTRATIVE ENTITY/SUB-UNIT Program Title (abridged)	FY 2003 in $thousands	FY 2004 in $thousands	FY 2005 in $thousands	FY 2006 in $thousands
14.162	Manufactured Home Lot Loans \ u	(o)*	(o)*	(o)*	(o)*
14.163	Single Family Cooperative Housing \ u	(o)*	(o)*	(o)*	(o)*
14.164	Operating Assistance/Multifamily \ u	2,151	0	0 e	0 e
14.165	Homes—Military Impacted Areas \ u	(o)*	(o)*	(o)*	(o)*
14.167	Operating Loss Loans \ u	3,820*	2,390*	3,000*e	4,120*e
14.168	Land Sales	323	422	350 e	350 e
14.169	Housing Counseling Assistance	39,740	39,764	41,664 e	39,700 e
14.171	Manufactured Home Standards \ t	9,041	9,036	13,000 e	13,000 e
14.172	Growing Equity Mortgages \ u	(o)*	(o)*	(o)*	(o)*
14.175	Adjustable Rate Mortgages \ u	(o)*	(o)*	(o)*	(o)*
14.181	Supportive Housing/Disabilities \ u	250,515	250,570	240,000 e	119,900 e
14.183	Home Equity Conversion Mortgages \ u	(o)*	(o)*	(o)*	(o)*
14.184	Mortgages/Single Room Occupancy \ u	(o)*	(o)*	(o)*	(o)*
14.188	HFA Risk Sharing Program \ u	254,646*	264,822*	50,000*e	68,667*e
14.189	QPE Risk Sharing \ u	16,579*	18,908*	37,500*e	51,500*e
14.191	Multifamily Housing Coordinators	(o)	(o)	(o)	(o)
14.195	Section 8—Special Allocations	4,718,248	4,615,110	6,326,435 e	4,830,729 e
14.197	Multifamily Housing Reform \ u	504,373	582,394	484,000 e	172,000 e
14.198	Officer Next Door Sales Program \ u	(o)	(o)	(o)	(o)
14.199	Multifamily Property Disposition \ p	3,234	1,000	0 e	3,000 e
14.218	CDBG/Entitlement	3,037,677	3,031,592	2,876,923 e	0 e
14.219	CDBG/Small Cities	5,889	6,138	5,858 e	0 e
14.225	CDBG/Insular Area	6,955	6,959	6,944 e	0 e
14.227	CDBG/Technical Assistance	(n)	1,491	1,389 e	0 e
14.228	CDBG/State	1,295,972	1,293,115	1,227,109 e	0 e
14.231	Emergency Shelter Grants	149,025	159,056	158,720 e	160,000 e
14.235	Supportive Housing Program	816,287	837,522	823,358 e	975,971 e
14.238	Shelter Plus Care	204,077	209,381	205,840 e	243,993 e
14.239	HOME Investment Partnerships	1,946,168	2,005,597	1,899,680 e	1,941,000 e
14.241	Housing/Persons with AIDS	290,102	294,751	281,778 e	268,000 e
14.243	Youthbuild Program	59,610	64,617	61,504 e	0 e
14.244	Empowerment Zones Program	29,805	14,912	9,920 e	0 e
14.246	CDBG/Economic Development	24,838	24,852	23,808 e	0 e
14.247	Self-Help Homeownership	25,086	26,841	24,800 e	30,000 e
14.248	CDBG—Section 108 Loans	333,683*	287,082*	287,082*e	0*e
14.249	Section 8—SRO	18,738	24,529	20,984 e	36,192 e
14.250	Rural Development	24,838	24,852	23,800 e	0 e
14.310	Teacher Next Door Initiative \ p, u	(o)	(o)	(o)	(o)
14.311	Single Family Property Disposition \ i, p	5,083,350	5,641,805	5,675,542 e	4,321,264 e
14.313	Dollar Home Sales \ p	(o)	(o)	(o)	(o)
14.314	Assisted Living Conversion	(o)	(o)	(o)	(o)
14.400	Equal Opportunity in Housing	(a)	(a)	(a)	(a)
14.401	FHAP—State, Local	25,482	27,587	26,288 e	22,700 e
14.402	Non-Discrimination/Age	(a)	(a)	(a)	(a)
14.404	Non-Discrimination/Disability	(a)	(a)	(a)	(a)
14.405	Non-Discrimination/Race, Color	(a)	(a)	(a)	(a)
14.406	Non-Discrimination/CDBG	(a)	(a)	(a)	(a)
14.407	Architectural Barriers	(a)	(a)	(a)	(a)
14.408	Fair Housing Initiatives	20,118	20,131	19,840 e	16,100 e
14.412	Employment/Lower Income	(a)	(a)	(a)	(a)
14.414	Non-Discrimination/Public Entities	(a)	(a)	(a)	(a)
14.415	Non-Discrimination/Sex	(a)	(a)	(a)	(a)
14.506	General Research and Technology	42,072	46,175	44,586 e	40,150 e
14.511	Community Outreach Partnership	6,955	6,959	6,646 e	5,979 e
14.512	CD Work-Study Program	2,981	2,982	2,877 e	2,562 e
14.514	Hispanic-Serving Institutions	6,458	6,959	6,646 e	5,979 e
14.515	Alaska/Hawaii Institutions	2,981	3,479	3,968 e	2,989 e
14.516	Doctoral Dissertation Research	400	400	400 e	400 e
14.517	Early Doctoral Student Research	147	147	150 e	150 e
14.519	Tribal Colleges and Universities	2,981	2,982	2,976 e	2,562 e
14.520	Historically Black Colleges	9,935	10,438	9,920 e	8,967 e
14.521	Universities Rebuilding America	(n)	(n)	(n)	2,000 e
14.850	Public and Indian Housing	3,616,858	3,580,984	2,440,936 e	3,407,000 e
14.856	Section 8 Moderate Rehabilitation	(a)	(a)	(a)	(a)

Please see "Important Notes on the Tables, Footnotes," page 688.

Table 1. (continued)

Program number	ADMINISTRATIVE ENTITY/SUB-UNIT Program Title (abridged)	FY 2003 in $thousands	FY 2004 in $thousands	FY 2005 in $thousands	FY 2006 in $thousands
14.862	Indian CDBG	43,747	71,575	68,448 e	0 e
14.865	Indian Housing Loans	40,305*	61,247*	145,345*e	98,967*e
14.866	Distressed Public Housing	595,144	548,219	164,621 e	0 e
14.867	Indian Housing Block Grants	663,840	663,435	621,984 e	582,600 e
14.869	Tribal Housing Activities	8,107*	10,203*	17,926*e	37,928*e
14.870	Residents—Supportive Services	53,339	33,553	119,943 e	24,000 e
14.871	Section 8 Housing Choice Vouchers	11,272,905	14,646,156	14,965,804 e	15,845,194 e
14.872	Public Housing Capital Fund	2,783,262	3,001,049	2,493,830 e	2,253,150 e
14.873	Hawaii Housing Block Grants	9,600	9,444	8,432 e	8,815 e
14.874	Native Hawaiian Housing	(n)*	0*	37,403*e	35,000*e
14.875	Public Housing Neighborhood Networks	(n)	8,492	38,039 e	0 e
14.900	Lead-Based Paint Hazards	95,376	95,434	92,851 e	92,555 e
14.901	Healthy Homes Demonstrations	5,900	6,710	5,000 e	5,000 e
14.902	Lead Technical Studies Grants	2,867	1,721	3,000 e	3,000 e
14.903	Operation Lead Elimination Action	6,500	8,947	7,936 e	8,815 e
14.904	Lead Outreach Grants	2,400	1,927	2,000 e	2,000 e
14.905	Lead Hazard Reduction Demonstration	49,675	48,209	48,120 e	0 e
14.906	Healthy Homes Technical Studies	2,009	2,683	2,000 e	2,000 e
	DEPARTMENT TOTAL: OUTLAYS	38,653,260	42,801,403	42,387,647 e	36,240,766
	CREDITS*	171,037,308*	132,583,670*	138,045,935*	136,930,716*
	DEPARTMENT OF THE INTERIOR				
15.020	Aid to Tribal Governments	36,298	35,426	35,492 e	38,670 e
15.021	Consolidated Tribal Government	64,846	64,901	64,629 e	62,268 e
15.022	Tribal Self-Governance	180,500	183,359	183,894 e	188,141 e
15.024	Indian Self-Determination	87,209	85,648	87,406 e	87,595 e
15.025	Children, Elderly, Families	21,352	20,952	20,855 e	21,175 e
15.026	Indian Adult Education	2,291	2,096	2,105 e	2,132 e
15.027	Tribally Controlled Colleges	39,294	48,933	53,493 e	43,739 e
15.028	Community College Endowments	975	965	947 e	947 e
15.029	Tribal Courts	7,625	9,445	9,358 e	9,441 e
15.030	Indian Law Enforcement	95,393	102,089	106,641 e	110,632 e
15.031	Indian Community Fire Protection	1,092	971	965 e	0 e
15.032	Indian Economic Development	1,640	1,608	2,000 e	1,834 e
15.033	Road Maintenance	7,471	7,392	7,281 e	7,226 e
15.034	Agriculture on Indian Lands	4,107	4,093	4,065 e	4,128 e
15.035	Forestry on Indian Lands	13,349	13,992	13,978 e	14,112 e
15.036	Indian Rights Protection	427	391	386 e	397 e
15.037	Water Resources on Indian Lands	8,397	8,342	8,166 e	6,583 e
15.038	Minerals, Mining/Indian Lands	624	990	979 e	996 e
15.039	Fish, Wildlife, Parks/Indian Lands	23,766	31,847	31,493 e	24,913 e
15.040	Real Estate Programs-Indian Lands	4,182	4,133	3,669 e	3,439 e
15.041	Environmental Management	6,429	6,416	6,326 e	6,449 e
15.042	Indian School Equalization	190,701	189,312	188,578 e	193,040 e
15.043	Indian Child and Family Education	9,616	9,831	9,674 e	7,654 e
15.044	Indian Schools—Transportation	24,644	24,394	25,244 e	25,521 e
15.045	Indian Children/Severe Disabilities	3,822	3,785	3,732 e	3,759 e
15.046	Administrative Costs/Indian Schools	46,065	46,065	49,182 e	52,000 e
15.047	Indian Education Facilities	41,535	41,116	40,303 e	40,785 e
15.048	BIA Facilities	1,404	1,388	1,202 e	1,429 e
15.049	Irrigation Operations, Maintenance	6,849	6,781	6,195 e	8,321 e
15.050	Indian Hunting, Fishing Rights	47	46	43 e	0 e
15.051	Endangered Species/Indian Lands	1,138	1,520	1,510 e	147 e
15.052	Litigation Support/Indian Rights	1,487	1,466	1,453 e	1,453 e
15.053	Attorney Fees-Indian Rights	993	1,146	1,131 e	978 e
15.055	Alaskan Indian Allotments	137	136	134 e	135 e
15.057	Navajo-Hopi Settlement	231	227	225 e	231 e
15.058	Indian Post Secondary Schools	(a)	(a)	(a)	(a)
15.059	Graduate Student Scholarships	1,328	1,508	1,731 e	2,231 e
15.060	United Tribes Technical College	2,980	2,963	3,451 e	0 e
15.061	United Sioux Tribes	348	444	444 e	0 e
15.062	Replacement, Repair—Schools	197,314	205,631	179,208 e	106,317 e
15.063	Improvement—Detention Facilities	1,417	1,399	3,600 e	7,556 e

Please see "Important Notes on the Tables, Footnotes," page 688.

Table 1. (continued)

Program number	ADMINISTRATIVE ENTITY/SUB-UNIT Program Title (abridged)	FY 2003 in $thousands	FY 2004 in $thousands	FY 2005 in $thousands	FY 2006 in $thousands
15.064	Fire Protection-BIA Facilities	556	549	541 e	541 e
15.065	Safety of Dams/Indian Lands	16,796	16,788	17,990 e	16,624 e
15.108	Indian Employment Assistance	7,787	7,458	7,367 e	7,329 e
15.113	Indian Social Services—Welfare	63,534	63,531	63,951 e	59,231 e
15.114	Indian—Higher Education	25,437	25,156	24,316 e	24,128 e
15.124	Indian Loans—Economic \ u	5,496*	6,417*	6,332*e	6,348*e
15.130	Indian Education—Schools	15,147	14,833	14,694 e	6,922 e
15.141	Indian Housing Assistance	16,482	16,271	16,017 e	16,053 e
15.144	Indian Child Welfare Act	11,122	10,774	10,300 e	10,322 e
15.146	Ironworker Training Program	518	515	508 e	0 e
15.147	Tribal Courts-Trust Reform	4,000	4,000	1,500 e	0 e
15.214	Disposals of Mineral Material \ p	(a)	(a)	(a)	(a)
15.222	Inspection Agreements	480	475	450 e	450 e
15.224	Cultural Resource Management	(a)	(a)	(a)	(a)
15.225	Recreation Resource Management	5,000	1,705	3,000 e	3,000 e
15.226	Payments in Lieu of Taxes	218,100	224,302	226,410 e	200,000 e
15.227	Receipts/State, Local Governments	183,928	184,071	290,936 e	301,432 e
15.228	Wildland Urban Fire Assistance	13,200	15,982	8,100 e	8,500 e
15.229	Wild Horse, Burro Resource Management	(n)	1,614	1,800 e	2,000 e
15.231	Fish, Wildlife, Plant Conservation	(n)	4,126	4,000 e	4,000 e
15.242	National Fire Plan—Rural Assistance	(n)	9,800	9,600 e	10,000 e
15.250	Surface Coal Mining	58,701	58,363	58,337 e	58,707 e
15.252	Abandoned Mine Land Reclamation	158,547	158,600	150,000 e	150,000 e
15.253	Not-for-Profit AMD Reclamation	2,740	2,740	2,000 e	1,000 e
15.254	Summer Watershed Intern	50	50	50 e	50 e
15.504	Water Reclamation and Reuse	36,040	28,700	22,300 e	10,229 e
15.506	Desalination Research, Development	3,800	3,800	100 e	0 e
15.507	Water 2025	(n)	4,000	10,000 e	20,000 e
15.508	Desert Terminal Lakes	(n)	4,030	11,500 e	7,000 e
15.602	Conservation Law Training	424	505	520 e	0 e
15.605	Sport Fish Restoration \ t	264,237	260,527	294,691 e	293,914 e
15.608	Fish and Wildlife Management	1,000	2,173	2,169 e	250 e
15.611	Wildlife Restoration	204,600	195,047	226,742 e	221,740 e
15.614	Coastal Wetlands \ t	12,201	16,813	12,440 e	13,136 e
15.615	Endangered Species Fund	80,474	81,596	80,462 e	80,000 e
15.616	Clean Vessel Act \ t	10,000	10,000	10,000 e	10,000 e
15.619	Rhinoceros, Tiger Conservation	1,100	1,274	1,399 e	1,020 e
15.620	African Elephant Conservation \ t	1,100	1,225	1,301 e	920 e
15.621	Asian Elephant Conservation	1,035	1,412	1,301 e	920 e
15.622	Sportfishing, Boating Safety \ t	8,000	8,000	8,000 e	8,000 e
15.623	Wetlands Conservation	36,777	59,142	61,552 e	75,899 e
15.626	Hunter Education and Safety	8,000	8,000	8,000 e	8,000 e
15.628	Multi-State Conservation Grants \ t	6,000	6,000	6,000 e	6,000 e
15.629	Great Apes Conservation	1,013	1,263	1,301 e	820 e
15.630	Coastal Program	11,000	10,000	11,400 e	0 e
15.631	Partners for Fish, Wildlife	28,000	31,000	35,000 e	0 e
15.632	Private Stewardship/Imperiled Species	65	7,408	6,903 e	10,000 e
15.633	Landowner Incentive	0	25,867	18,939 e	34,920 e
15.634	State Wildlife Grants	59,610	61,202	62,089 e	65,437 e
15.635	Neotropical Migratory Bird	2,981	4,685	3,923 e	3,880 e
15.636	Alaska Subsistence Management	5,000	5,913	5,915 e	5,915 e
15.637	Migratory Bird Joint Ventures	1,800	1,800	3,500 e	3,500 e
15.638	Tribal Landowner Incentive	(n)	2,874	2,104 e	1,776 e
15.639	Tribal Wildlife Grants	5,017	5,926	5,917 e	6,343 e
15.640	Wildlife—Latin America	675	650	454 e	430 e
15.641	Wildlife—Mexico	466	472	690 e	472 e
15.642	Challenge Cost Share	6,831	6,831	9,754 e	12,000 e
15.643	Alaska Migratory Bird Co-Management	(n)	261	221 e	221 e
15.644	Junior Duck Stamp Conservation \ p	(n)	215	119 e	164 e
15.645	Marine Turtle Conservation	(n)	(n)	90 e	220 e
15.647	Migratory Bird Conservation	(n)	64	64 e	64 e
15.805	State Water Resources Research	5,691	6,121	6,125 e	0 e
15.807	Earthquake Hazards Reduction	10,580	10,096	10,000 e	10,000 e
15.808	Geological Survey—Research, Data	25,750	49,518	50,000 e	50,000 e

Please see "Important Notes on the Tables, Footnotes," page 688.

Table 1. (continued)

Program number	ADMINISTRATIVE ENTITY/SUB-UNIT Program Title (abridged)	FY 2003 in $thousands	FY 2004 in $thousands	FY 2005 in $thousands	FY 2006 in $thousands
15.809	National Spatial Data	1,084	1,084	1,300 e	1,500 e
15.810	National Geologic Mapping Program	7,156	6,982	6,655 e	6,400 e
15.811	GAP Analysis Program	1,500	1,729	1,800 e	1,800 e
15.812	Cooperative Research Units Program	14,979	15,021	16,000 e	16,000 e
15.850	Indian Arts, Crafts Development	1,054	1,054	1,052 e	1,057 e
15.875	Economic, Social, Political Development	186,205	184,426	184,109 e	182,382 e
15.904	Historic Preservation	68,552	68,552	73,582 e	77,000 e
15.910	National Natural Landmarks	993	993	985 e	985 e
15.912	National Historic Landmarks	785	785	758 e	787 e
15.914	National Register/Historic Places	1,745	1,745	1,706 e	0 e
15.915	Technical Preservation Services	1,600	1,600	1,600 e	1,600 e
15.916	Outdoor Recreation	94,382	91,360	89,736 e	0 e
15.918	Federal Surplus Real Property	506	545	554 e	559 e
15.921	Rivers, Trails Conservation	8,174	8,172	8,185 e	7,835 e
15.922	Native American Graves Protection	2,451	2,451	2,437 e	2,451 e
15.923	Preservation Technology, Training	336	336	300 e	300 e
15.925	National Maritime Heritage	0	0	0 e	0 e
15.926	American Battlefield Protection	365	365	300 e	300 e
15.927	Hydropower Recreation Assistance	808	801	800 e	813 e
15.928	Civil War Battlefield Acquisition	6,000	6,000	0 e	0 e
15.929	Save America's Treasures	29,805	29,805	31,536 e	30,000 e
15.978	Upper Mississippi Monitoring	1,747	2,099	2,044 e	1,841 e
	DEPARTMENT TOTAL: OUTLAYS	3,210,942	3,345,165	3,491,459	3,263,463
	CREDITS*	5,496*	6,417*	6,332*	6,348*

DEPARTMENT OF JUSTICE

Program number	Program Title	FY 2003	FY 2004	FY 2005	FY 2006
16.001	Narcotics, Drugs—Laboratory	4,668	4,161	4,556 e	4,625 e
16.003	Narcotics, Drugs/Publications	13	2	2 e	2 e
16.004	Narcotics, Drugs Training	0	0	0 e	0 e
16.005	Public Education on Drug Abuse	796	760	778 e	0 e
16.012	ATF-Training Assistance	2,914	2,914	2,234 e	2,113 e
16.100	Desegregation of Public Education	4,631	4,793	5,780 e	5,646 e
16.101	Equal Employment Opportunity	7,797	8,042	9,680 e	9,545 e
16.103	Fair Housing and Equal Credit	14,278	14,594	14,492 e	13,660 e
16.104	Protection of Voting Rights	13,596	14,131	12,931 e	12,639 e
16.105	Institutionalized Persons	9,799	10,034	11,673 e	12,114 e
16.108	Disabilities Act Assistance	16,032	16,077	13,584 e	16,781 e
16.109	Civil Rights Prosecution	12,714	13,151	15,238 e	12,606 e
16.110	Education, Enforcement—Immigration	7,660	7,132	5,858 e	4,537 e
16.200	Community Relations Service	9,287	9,202	9,535 e	9,759 e
16.202	Offender Reentry Program	10,841	19,158	9,866 e	14,416 e
16.203	Sex Offender Management	4,937	5,632	4,356 e	4,362 e
16.300	FBI Advanced Police Training	14,679 e	15,072	15,464 e	15,866 e
16.301	FBI Crime Laboratory	133,225 e	173,180	167,192 e	174,298 e
16.302	FBI Field Police Training	9,699 e	10,051	10,352 e	10,663 e
16.303	FBI Fingerprint Identification	204,230 e	134,761	138,803 e	142,968 e
16.304	National Crime Information Center	36,024 e	23,452	24,156 e	24,881 e
16.305	Uniform Crime Reports	10,621 e	14,607	15,045 e	15,497 e
16.307	DNA Index System	9,993 e	7,165	7,947 e	7,947 e
16.308	Indian Country Investigations	1,000 e	1,000	1,185 e	1,113 e
16.309	Law Enforcement Assistance—NICS	67,462 e	23,452	24,156 e	24,881 e
16.320	Services for Trafficking Victims	9,866	5,409	9,866 e	0 e
16.321	Antiterrorism Emergency Reserve	17,241 e	8,000	0 e	7,000 e
16.523	Juvenile Accountability Incentives	161,633	78,457	54,265 e	0 e
16.524	Legal Assistance for Victims	39,480	38,051	39,209 e	39,220 e
16.525	Crimes Against Women/Campuses	10,809	9,465	9,052 e	9,054 e
16.526	Technical Assistance, Training	17,622	33,224	27,350 e	27,350 e
16.527	Supervised Visitation/Children	19,522	14,248	13,890 e	13,894 e
16.528	Elder Abuse, Neglect, Exploitation	4,853	7,288	7,153 e	7,155 e
16.529	Violence/Women with Disabilities	779	7,228	7,153 e	7,155 e
16.540	Juvenile Justice—States	78,415	90,833	82,878 e	88,653 e
16.541	Developing, Testing—New Programs	51,885	4,014	0 e	0 e
16.542	Research, Assistance, Training	47,564	6,589	0 e	0 e

Please see "Important Notes on the Tables, Footnotes," page 688.

Table 1. (continued)

Program number	ADMINISTRATIVE ENTITY/SUB-UNIT Program Title (abridged)	FY 2003 in $thousands	FY 2004 in $thousands	FY 2005 in $thousands	FY 2006 in $thousands
16.543	Missing Children's Assistance	38,461	36,359	46,274 e	34,914 e
16.544	Gang-Free Schools	17,822	310	0 e	0 e
16.547	Victims of Child Abuse	24,812	26,033	28,437 e	24,286 e
16.548	Delinquency Prevention Program	46,871	19,022	19,733 e	24,671 e
16.549	State Challenge Activities	14,038	77,372	100,812 e	4,768 e
16.550	State Justice Statistics Program	2,018	1,985	2,200 e	2,200 e
16.554	Criminal History Improvement	47,973	37,731	24,666 e	55,355 e
16.560	NIJ Research, Evaluation, Development	77,300	16,396	21,000 e	25,620 e
16.561	Visiting Fellowships	250	250	200 e	200 e
16.562	Graduate Research Fellowships	100	0	0 e	0 e
16.563	Corrections, Law Enforcement Support	1	2,780	1,973 e	0 e
16.564	Crime Laboratory Improvement—DNA	40,500	27,423	0 e	0 e
16.565	Counter-Terrorism Technology	6,000	103	0 e	0 e
16.566	Dubois Fellowship Program	150	79	0 e	0 e
16.571	Public Safety Officers' Benefits	55,622	42,690	66,621 e	53,332 e
16.575	Crime Victim Assistance	353,027	356,128	372,807 e	255,964 e
16.576	Crime Victim Compensation	164,933	186,149	169,653 e	255,964 e
16.577	Emergency Federal Law Enforcement	0	0	0 e	0 e
16.578	Federal Surplus Property Transfer	0	0	0 e	0 e
16.579	Byrne Formula Grant Program	486,626	474,922	0 e	0 e
16.580	Byrne Law Enforcement Assistance	192,615	192,680	167,756 e	0 e
16.582	Victim Assistance/Discretionary	28,141	30,226	29,867 e	26,945 e
16.583	Children's Justice/Indian	3,503	3,000	3,000 e	3,000 e
16.585	Drug Court Program	43,136	39,248	39,466 e	66,010 e
16.586	Violent Offender Incarceration	20,276	1,760	0 e	0 e
16.587	Violence Against Women/Indian	11,143	8,320	9,229 e	9,229 e
16.588	Violence Against Women	130,517	117,567	117,783 e	120,783 e
16.589	Rural Domestic Violence	39,554	37,306	39,155 e	39,166 e
16.590	Arrest Policies/Enforcement	63,422	60,986	62,643 e	62,660 e
16.592	Law Enforcement Block Grants	406,897	215,480	0 e	0 e
16.593	Substance Abuse Treatment/Prisoners	60,143	3,300	24,666 e	41,690 e
16.595	Community Capacity Development Office	69,092	59,308	69,971 e	62,720 e
16.596	Correctional Grant/Tribes	3,152	10,368	4,933 e	0 e
16.597	Motor Vehicle Theft Protection Act	2,174	145	99 e	0 e
16.601	Corrections—Training	4,857	5,678	5,750 e	5,000 e
16.602	Corrections—Research	2,085	2,314	1,750 e	1,750 e
16.603	Corrections—Technical Assistance	7,051	6,243	6,250 e	6,250 e
16.606	Criminal Alien Assistance	240,209	286,083	300,926 e	0 e
16.607	Bulletproof Vest Partnership	23,991	24,350	24,666 e	29,117 e
16.608	Tribal Court Assistance	15,449	8,435	7,893 e	0 e
16.609	Community Prosecution	5,982	51,083	0 e	70,719 e
16.610	Regional Information Sharing	28,857	29,654	39,466 e	43,296 e
16.611	Closed-Circuit TV/Child Abuse	236	47	970 e	970 e
16.612	National White Collar Crime Center	14,352	8,915	8,880 e	3,121 e
16.613	Scams Targeting the Elderly	2,174	0	1,973 e	0 e
16.614	Anti-Terrorism Training	0	0	0 e	0 e
16.615	Public Safety Educational Assistance	931	756	2,758 e	2,791 e
16.616	Indian Alcohol and Drug Prevention	11,736	5,851	4,933 e	0 e
16.710	Public Safety, Community Policing	1,117,201	747,016	568,747 e	88,600 e
16.712	Police Corps	37,052	12,408	14,800 e	0 e
16.726	Juvenile Mentoring Program	16,096	747	14,800 e	0 e
16.727	Enforcing Underage Drinking Laws	28,210	26,356	24,666 e	0 e
16.728	Drug Prevention Program	11,235	1,281	0 e	0 e
16.730	Safe Start	10,095	7,886	9,866 e	10,000 e
16.731	Tribal Youth Program	11,576	9,250	9,866 e	0 e
16.732	Safe Schools/Healthy Students	11,855	10,126	0 e	0 e
16.734	Special Data Collections	(a)	(a)	(a)	(a)
16.735	Protecting Inmates, Communities	(n)	22,944	36,506 e	9,322 e
16.736	Transitional Housing/Victims	(n)	1,909	12,333 e	15,000 e
16.737	Gang Resistance Education, Training	9,781	14,543	24,666 e	0 e
16.738	Byrne Memorial Justice Assistance	(n)	(n)	625,532 e	0 e
16.739	National Prison Rape Statistics	(n)	5,751	14,300 e	7,000 e
16.740	Victim Information Notification	(n)	(n)	7,393 e	0 e
16.741	Forensic DNA Capacity Enhancement	(n)	(n)	32,149 e	0 e

Please see "Important Notes on the Tables, Footnotes," page 688.

Table 1. (continued)

Program number	ADMINISTRATIVE ENTITY/SUB-UNIT Program Title (abridged)		FY 2003 in $thousands	FY 2004 in $thousands	FY 2005 in $thousands	FY 2006 in $thousands
16.742	Coverdell Forensic Sciences		(n)	9,598	13,773 e	0 e
16.743	Forensic DNA Backlog Reduction		(n)	(n)	21,022 e	0 e
	DEPARTMENT TOTAL:	OUTLAYS	5,127,845	4,219,979	4,035,257	2,202,813
		CREDITS*	0*	0*	0*	0*

DEPARTMENT OF LABOR

BUREAU OF LABOR STATISTICS

17.002	Labor Force Statistics		309,380	319,442	329,620 e	335,265 e
17.003	Prices and Cost of Living Data		159,545	166,212	169,370 e	174,779 e
17.004	Productivity and Technology Data		9,817	10,254	10,503 e	10,847 e
17.005	Compensation, Working Conditions		81,347	83,222	85,084 e	87,673 e
	Subtotal:	Outlays	560,089	579,130	594,577	608,564
		Credits*	0*	0*	0*	0*

EMPLOYEE BENEFITS SECURITY ADMINISTRATION

17.150	Employee Benefits Security		116,283	124,040	132,213 e	137,000 e
	Subtotal:	Outlays	116,283	124,040	132,213	137,000
		Credits*	0*	0*	0*	0*

EMPLOYMENT AND TRAINING ADMINISTRATION

17.201	Registered Apprenticeship, Training		20,699	20,760	21,136 e	21,655 e
17.202	Certification/Agricultural \ i		26,100	50,655	56,486 e	55,001 e
17.203	Certification/Alien Workers		(o)	(o)	(o)	(o)
17.207	Employment Service \ t		794,000	786,887	780,592 e	696,000 e
17.225	Unemployment Insurance \ t		46,258,487	45,518,202	38,573,138 e	40,018,445 e
17.235	Senior Community Service		442,305	438,650	436,678 e	436,678 e
17.245	Trade Adjustment Assistance		569,265	791,359	896,300 e	966,400 e
17.252	Attestations/Alien Specialty \ u		5,750	(o)	(o)	(o)
17.258	WIA Adult Program		893,909	893,195	896,618 e	865,736 e
17.259	WIA Youth Activities		989,123	995,059	986,288 e	0 e
17.260	WIA Dislocated Workers		1,418,412	1,445,939	1,476,064 e	1,343,584 e
17.261	Pilots, Demonstration, Research		42,935	57,751	85,962 e	30,000 e
17.262	ETA Evaluation		9,039	8,986	7,936 e	7,936 e
17.263	Youth Opportunity Grants		44,211	0	0 e	0 e
17.264	Migrant, Seasonal Farmworkers		72,214	76,874	76,259 e	0 e
17.265	Native American Employment		55,286	54,676	54,238 e	54,238 e
17.266	Work Incentives Grant		19,870	19,753	19,711 e	19,711 e
17.267	WIA Incentive Grants—Section 503		24,460	24,460	16,605 e	16,518 e
	Subtotal:	Outlays	51,686,065	51,183,206	44,384,011	44,531,902
		Credits*	0*	0*	0*	0*

EMPLOYMENT STANDARDS ADMINISTRATION

17.301	Federal, Construction Contractors		78,033	79,442	80,060 e	82,107 e
17.302	Longshore and Harbor Workers		3,000	150,000	148,000 e	151,000 e
17.303	Wage, Hour Standards \ i		155,867	160,096	164,494 e	167,359 e
17.306	Consumer Credit Protection		(o)	(o)	(o)	(o)
17.307	Coal Mine Workers' Compensation \ t		426,014	390,848	358,806 e	310,000 e
17.308	Farm Labor Contractors		(o)	(o)	(o)	(o)
17.309	Labor Organization Reports		34,279	38,580	41,681 e	48,799 e
	Subtotal:	Outlays	697,193	818,966	793,041	759,265
		Credits*	0*	0*	0*	0*

OCCUPATIONAL SAFETY AND HEALTH ADMINISTRATION

17.502	Susan Harwood Training	11,102	10,509	10,217 e	0 e
17.503	State Program	90,547	91,959	91,013 e	92,013 e
17.504	Consultation Agreements	53,204	52,211	53,362 e	53,896 e

Please see "Important Notes on the Tables, Footnotes," page 688.

Table 1. (continued)

Program number	ADMINISTRATIVE ENTITY/SUB-UNIT Program Title (abridged)		FY 2003 in $thousands	FY 2004 in $thousands	FY 2005 in $thousands	FY 2006 in $thousands
17.505	OSHA Data Initiative		1,640	1,607	1,436 e	1,436 e
	Subtotal:	Outlays	156,493	156,286	156,028	147,345
		Credits*	0*	0*	0*	0*

MINE SAFETY AND HEALTH ADMINISTRATION

17.600	Mine Health and Safety Grants		7,943	7,973	7,973 e	7,973 e
17.601	Mine Health, Safety Counseling		28,489	24,545	25,064 e	25,736 e
17.602	Mine Health, Safety Education		10,850	11,200	11,453 e	11,734 e
	Subtotal:	Outlays	47,282	43,718	44,490	45,443
		Credits*	0*	0*	0*	0*

OFFICE OF THE SECRETARY-WOMEN'S BUREAU

17.700	Women's Bureau		9,608	9,201	9,478 e	9,764 e
17.720	Disability Employment Policy		43,263	47,024	47,164 e	27,934 e
	Subtotal:	Outlays	52,871	56,225	56,642	37,698
		Credits*	0*	0*	0*	0*

ASSISTANT SECRETARY FOR VETERANS' EMPLOYMENT AND TRAINING

17.801	Disabled Veterans Outreach		81,615	81,615	81,207 e	82,831 e
17.802	Veterans Employment Program		7,800	7,505	8,482 e	7,500 e
17.803	Uniformed Services/Rights		(a)	(a)	(a)	(a)
17.804	Local Veterans Employment		77,280	77,253	78,254 e	79,584 e
17.805	Homeless Veterans Reintegration		18,131	18,888	20,832 e	22,000 e
17.806	Preference/Federal Employment		(a)	(a)	(a)	(a)
17.807	Transition Assistance Program		(n)	2,478	2,504 e	2,560 e
	Subtotal:	Outlays	184,826	187,739	191,279	194,475
		Credits*	0*	0*	0*	0*
	DEPARTMENT TOTAL:	OUTLAYS	53,501,102	53,149,310	46,352,281	46,461,692
		CREDITS*	0*	0*	0*	0*

DEPARTMENT OF STATE

BUREAU OF OCEANS & INTERNATIONAL ENVIRONMENTAL & SCIENTIFIC AFFAIRS

19.204	Fishermen's Guaranty Fund		0	0	0 e	500 e
	Subtotal:	Outlays	0	0	0	500
		Credits*	0*	0*	0*	0*

BUREAU OF INTELLIGENCE AND RESEARCH

19.300	Study/Eastern Europe		5,000	5,000	5,000 e	5,000 e
	Subtotal:	Outlays	5,000	5,000	5,000	5,000
		Credits*	0*	0*	0*	0*

BUREAU OF EDUCATIONAL AND CULTURAL AFFAIRS

19.400	Educational Exchange—Graduate	24,284	22,000	24,200 e	26,620 e
19.401	Lecturers and Research Scholars	27,557	31,000	34,100 e	37,510 e
19.402	International Visitors Program	60,095	10,612	11,012 e	12,007 e
19.403	Young Political Leaders	734	809	890 e	890 e
19.408	Exchange—Secondary, Postsecondary	6,407	8,878	10,250 e	10,500 e
19.409	Art Exchanges on International Issues	0	670	1,000 e	1,000 e
19.410	Exchange—Bundestag Youth	3,000	3,000	3,176 e	3,176 e
19.413	Cultural Exchange (Performing Arts)	160	160	0 e	0 e
19.415	Professional Exchanges	4,284	4,643	5,540 e	5,500 e
19.418	American Studies Institutes	2,600	2,600	2,600 e	2,600 e
19.421	English Language Fellow Program	3,887	5,640	4,973 e	6,000 e
19.423	English Language Specialist	534	641	600 e	600 e

Please see "Important Notes on the Tables, Footnotes," page 688.

Table 1. (continued)

Program number	ADMINISTRATIVE ENTITY/SUB-UNIT Program Title (abridged)		FY 2003 in $thousands	FY 2004 in $thousands	FY 2005 in $thousands	FY 2006 in $thousands
19.425	Gilman International Scholarship		1,575	1,600	2,600 e	4,600 e
19.430	International Education, Research		(n)	690	720 e	700 e
19.431	Scholar-In-Residence		(n)	1,000	1,000 e	1,250 e
19.432	Overseas Educational Advising		(n)	1,485	1,720 e	1,720 e
	Subtotal:	Outlays	135,117	95,428	104,381	114,673
		Credits*	0*	0*	0*	0*
	BUREAU OF NEAR EASTERN AFFAIRS					
19.500	Middle East Partnership Initiative		100,000	89,500	74,400 e	120 e
	Subtotal:	Outlays	100,000	89,500	74,400	120
		Credits*	0*	0*	0*	0*
	BUREAU OF POPULATION, REFUGEES, AND MIGRATION					
19.510	U.S. Refugee Admissions		45,309	55,145	50,700 e	74,000 e
19.511	Refugee Assistance/East Asia		(n)	20,750	21,280 e	21,500 e
19.517	Refugee Assistance/Africa		(n)	226,841	229,342 e	256,500 e
19.518	Refugee Assistance/Western Hemisphere		(n)	20,537	25,000 e	26,000 e
19.519	Refugee/Near East, South Asia		(n)	174,727	156,039 e	0 e
19.520	Refugee Assistance/Europe		(n)	58,965	50,000 e	44,720 e
19.522	Refugee/Strategic Global Priorities		(n)	62,637	61,705 e	62,000 e
	Subtotal:	Outlays	45,309	619,602	594,066	484,720
		Credits*	0*	0*	0*	0*
	DEPARTMENT TOTAL:	OUTLAYS	285,426	809,530	777,847	605,013
		CREDITS*	0*	0*	0*	0*

DEPARTMENT OF TRANSPORTATION

	FEDERAL AVIATION ADMINISTRATION					
20.100	Aviation Education		130	0	0 e	0 e
20.106	Airport Improvement Program \ t		3,400,000	3,400,000	3,500,000 e	3,600,000 e
20.108	Aviation Research \ t		30,000	30,000	30,000 e	30,000 e
20.109	Air Transportation Centers \ t		7,200	7,500	7,800 e	7,800 e
	Subtotal:	Outlays	3,437,330	3,437,500	3,537,800	3,637,800
		Credits*	0*	0*	0*	0*
	FEDERAL HIGHWAY ADMINISTRATION					
20.205	Highway Planning, Construction \ i, t		31,775,136	35,818,330	35,092,362 e	35,000,000
20.215	Highway Training, Education \ t		(o)	(o)	(o)	(o)
20.217	Motor Carrier Safety \ t		2,673	5,179	5,179 e	6,000 e
20.218	National Motor Carrier Safety \ t		163,928	168,002	167,648 e	172,000 e
20.219	Recreational Trails \ t		(o)	(o)	(o)	(o)
20.230	Crash Data Improvement Program \ t		(n)	1,762	4,800 e	4,800 e
20.232	Commercial Driver License State \ t		0	0	0	0
20.233	Border Enforcement Grants \ t		(n)	(n)	(n)	32,000 e
	Subtotal:	Outlays	31,941,737	35,993,273	35,269,989	35,214,800
		Credits*	0*	0*	0*	0*
	FEDERAL RAILROAD ADMINISTRATION					
20.303	Grants/Railroad Safety		0	0	0 e	0 e
20.312	High Speed Ground Transportation \ t		21,500	21,500	21,500 e	21,500 e
20.313	Railroad Research and Development		1,185	281	980 e	750 e
	Subtotal:	Outlays	22,685	21,781	22,480	22,250
		Credits*	0*	0*	0*	0*

Please see "Important Notes on the Tables, Footnotes," page 688.

Table 1. (continued)

Program number	ADMINISTRATIVE ENTITY/SUB-UNIT Program Title (abridged)	FY 2003 in $thousands	FY 2004 in $thousands	FY 2005 in $thousands	FY 2006 in $thousands
	FEDERAL TRANSIT ADMINISTRATION				
20.500	Capital Investment Grants \ t	3,082,964	4,064,415	3,421,571 e	1,565,699 e
20.505	Metropolitan Planning Grants \ t	115,697	35,640	59,902 e	123,211 e
20.507	Urbanized Area Formula Grants \ t	4,184,531	3,836,198	6,825,372 e	11,056,798 e
20.509	Nonurbanized Areas	256,841	242,521	490,702 e	294,480 e
20.513	Elderly, Persons with Disabilities \ t	92,901	173,455	94,526 e	95,093 e
20.514	Transit Planning, Research \ t	31,828	27,435	37,200 e	34,415 e
20.515	State Planning and Research \ t	18,211	9,718	12,513 e	25,730 e
20.516	Job Access—Reverse Commute \ t	135,618	86,030	123,489 e	123,211 e
20.518	Over-the-Road Bus Accessibility \ t	6,564	6,909	6,950 e	6,950 e
	Subtotal: Outlays	7,925,155	8,482,321	11,072,225	13,325,587
	Credits*	0*	0*	0*	0*
	NATIONAL HIGHWAY TRAFFIC SAFETY ADMINISTRATION				
20.600	State, Community Highway Safety \ t	163,000	160,000	160,000 e	167,000 e
20.601	Drunk Driving Prevention \ t	31,000	31,000	31,000 e	31,000 e
20.602	Occupant Protection \ t	25,700	25,700	25,700 e	25,000 e
20.603	Federal Highway Safety Data \ t	0	0	0 e	0 e
20.604	Safety Incentive/Seatbelts \ t	50,400	50,400	50,400 e	50,400 e
20.605	Safety Incentives/Intoxication \ t	85,000	85,000	85,000 e	85,000 e
20.607	Alcohol Open Container \ t	112,000	112,000	112,000 e	112,000 e
20.608	Penalties/Repeat Offenders \ t	173,000	173,000	173,000 e	173,000 e
	Subtotal: Outlays	640,100	637,100	637,100	643,400
	Credits*	0*	0*	0*	0*
	RESEARCH AND SPECIAL PROGRAMS ADMINISTRATION				
20.700	Pipeline Safety	19,000	19,209	19,209 e	19,209 e
20.703	Hazardous Materials Training	12,800	12,800	12,800 e	12,800 e
	Subtotal: Outlays	31,800	32,009	32,009	32,009
	Credits*	0*	0*	0*	0*
	MARITIME ADMINISTRATION				
20.801	Ports, Intermodal Transportation	138	141	143 e	145 e
20.802	Federal Ship Financing \ u	20,655*	11,315*	38,816*e	0*e
20.803	Maritime War Risk Insurance \ u	36	0	0 e	0 e
20.806	State Marine Schools	7,478	10,401	10,490 e	10,611 e
20.807	U.S. Merchant Marine Academy	47,822	55,703	559,469 e	63,854 e
20.808	Capital Construction Fund	136	139	141 e	143 e
20.810	Supplementary Training	195	195	195 e	195 e
20.812	Construction Reserve Fund	10	11	11 e	11 e
20.813	Maritime Security Fleet Program	98,058	98,707	101,335 e	156,000 e
	Subtotal: Outlays	153,873	165,297	671,784	230,959
	Credits*	20,655*	11,315*	38,816*	0*
	OFFICE OF THE SECRETARY				
20.900	Transportation—Consumer Affairs	1,490	1,748	1,825 e	1,870 e
20.901	Essential Air Services \ t	113,000	113,000	102,000 e	50,000 e
20.903	Support/Disadvantaged Businesses	1,100	1,080	900 e	1,100 e
20.905	Disadvantaged—Short-Term Lending	8,696*	8,000*	8,000*e	8,000*e
20.907	Minority Institutions	442	300	200 e	200 e
20.930	Small Community Air Service \ t	(n)	19,874	20,000 e	20,000 e
	Subtotal: Outlays	116,032	136,002	124,925	73,170
	Credits*	8,696*	8,000*	8,000*	8,000*
	DEPARTMENT TOTAL: OUTLAYS	44,268,712	48,905,283	51,368,312	53,179,975
	CREDITS*	29,351*	19,315*	46,816*	8,000*

Please see "Important Notes on the Tables, Footnotes," page 688.

Table 1. (continued)

Program number	ADMINISTRATIVE ENTITY/SUB-UNIT Program Title (abridged)		FY 2003 in $thousands	FY 2004 in $thousands	FY 2005 in $thousands	FY 2006 in $thousands
	DEPARTMENT OF THE TREASURY					
	INTERNAL REVENUE SERVICE					
21.003	Taxpayer Service		1,076,853	1,130,625	1,136,271 e	1,119,966 e
21.004	Federal Tax Information/States		0	0	0 e	0 e
21.006	Tax Counseling/Elderly		3,950	3,950	3,950 e	3,950 e
21.008	Low-Income Taxpayer Clinics		7,000	7,500	8,000 e	8,000 e
	Subtotal:	Outlays	1,087,803	1,142,075	1,148,221	1,131,916
		Credits*	0*	0*	0*	0*
	UNDER SECRETARY/DOMESTIC FINANCE					
21.020	Community Development Program		45,000	45,000	24,000 e	0 e
21.021	Bank Enterprise Award		13,882	17,000	10,000 e	0 e
	Subtotal:	Outlays	58,882	62,000	34,000	0
		Credits*	0*	0*	0*	0*
	DEPARTMENT TOTAL:	OUTLAYS	1,146,685	1,204,075	1,182,221	1,131,916
		CREDITS*	0*	0*	0*	0*
	APPALACHIAN REGIONAL COMMISSION					
23.001	Appalachian Regional Development		(o)	(o)	(o)	(o)
23.002	Appalachian Area Development		80,919	61,106	67,000 e	63,000 e
23.003	Highway System		446,545	484,830	530,000 e	530,000 e
23.009	Development District Assistance		6,275	6,100	5,357 e	5,400 e
23.011	Research, Technical Assistance		811	862	900 e	900 e
	DEPARTMENT TOTAL:	OUTLAYS	534,550	552,898	603,257	599,300
		CREDITS*	0*	0*	0*	0*
	OFFICE OF PERSONNEL MANAGEMENT					
27.001	Federal Civil Service		(a)	(a)	(a)	(a)
27.002	Employment Assistance/Veterans		(a)	(a)	(a)	(a)
27.003	Federal Student Employment		(a)	(a)	(a)	(a)
27.005	Federal Employment/Disabled		(a)	(a)	(a)	(a)
27.006	Federal Summer Employment		(a)	(a)	(a)	(a)
27.011	Intergovernmental Mobility		(a)	(a)	(a)	(a)
27.013	Presidential Management Intern \ r		(a)	(a)	(a)	(a)
	DEPARTMENT TOTAL:	OUTLAYS	0	0	0	0
		CREDITS*	0*	0*	0*	0*
	COMMISSION ON CIVIL RIGHTS					
29.001	Clearinghouse Services		8,500	8,740	8,740 e	8,740 e
	DEPARTMENT TOTAL:	OUTLAYS	8,500	8,740	8,740	8,740
		CREDITS*	0*	0*	0*	0*
	EQUAL EMPLOYMENT OPPORTUNITY COMMISSION					
30.001	Title VII/Civil Rights \ i		321,739	324,892	326,804 e	331,228 e
30.002	Fair Employment Agencies \ i		32,767	32,634	32,559 e	33,000 e
30.005	Private Bar Program		(a)	(a)	(a)	(a)
30.008	Age Discrimination		(o)	(o)	(o)	(o)
30.009	Indian Tribes		(o)	(o)	(o)	(o)
30.010	Discrimination Equal Pay Act		(o)	(o)	(o)	(o)
30.011	Title I ADA, Investigations		(o)	(o)	(o)	(o)
	DEPARTMENT TOTAL:	OUTLAYS	354,506	357,526	359,363	364,228
		CREDITS*	0*	0*	0*	0*

Please see "Important Notes on the Tables, Footnotes," page 688.

Table 1. (continued)

Program number	ADMINISTRATIVE ENTITY/SUB-UNIT Program Title (abridged)		FY 2003 in $thousands	FY 2004 in $thousands	FY 2005 in $thousands	FY 2006 in $thousands
	FEDERAL COMMUNICATIONS COMMISSION					
32.001	Information, Investigation		(a)	(a)	(a)	(a)
	DEPARTMENT TOTAL:	OUTLAYS	0	0	0	0
		CREDITS*	0*	0*	0*	0*
	FEDERAL MARITIME COMMISSION					
33.001	Shipping—Complaints		620	620	637 e	657 e
	DEPARTMENT TOTAL:	OUTLAYS	620	620	637	657
		CREDITS*	0*	0*	0*	0*
	FEDERAL MEDIATION AND CONCILIATION SERVICE					
34.001	Labor Mediation, Conciliation		41,155	43,129	43,438 e	42,331 e
34.002	Labor Management Cooperation		1,490	1,490	1,491 e	1,491 e
	DEPARTMENT TOTAL:	OUTLAYS	42,645	44,619	44,929	43,822
		CREDITS*	0*	0*	0*	0*
	FEDERAL TRADE COMMISSION					
36.001	Fair Competition Counseling		176,553 e	187,871	204,324 e	211,000 e
	DEPARTMENT TOTAL:	OUTLAYS	176,553	187,871	204,324	211,000
		CREDITS*	0*	0*	0*	0*
	GENERAL SERVICES ADMINISTRATION					
39.002	Real Property Disposal \ p		32,372	26,595	47,816 e	45,941 e
39.003	Personal Property Donation \ p		11,198	11,052	12,058 e	12,280 e
39.007	Personal Property Sale \ p, r		13,934	13,589	14,860 e	15,904 e
39.009	Federal Citizen Information Center \ r, u		12,017	16,716	21,649 e	24,990 e
	DEPARTMENT TOTAL:	OUTLAYS	69,521	67,952	96,383	99,115
		CREDITS*	0*	0*	0*	0*
	GOVERNMENT PRINTING OFFICE					
40.001	Depository Libraries		29,468	34,253	31,697 e	33,837 e
40.002	Government Publications Sales \ p, r		31,135	28,051	25,943 e	26,469 e
	DEPARTMENT TOTAL:	OUTLAYS	60,603	62,304	57,640	60,306
		CREDITS*	0*	0*	0*	0*
	LIBRARY OF CONGRESS					
42.001	Books for the Blind, Handicapped		48,777	48,777	51,401 e	53,937 e
42.002	Copyright Service \ i, u		43,572	44,286	53,182 e	58,191 e
42.008	Semiconductor Chip Protection \ u		(o)	(o)	(o)	(o)
42.009	Vessel Hull Design Protection \ u		(o)	(o)	(o)	(o)
	DEPARTMENT TOTAL:	OUTLAYS	92,349	93,063	104,583	112,128
		CREDITS*	0*	0*	0*	0*
	NATIONAL AERONAUTICS AND SPACE ADMINISTRATION					
43.001	Aerospace Education Services		10,569	9,737	10,300 e	10,240 e
43.002	Technology Transfer		46,988	78,572	51,300 e	42,100 e
	DEPARTMENT TOTAL:	OUTLAYS	57,557	88,309	61,600	52,340
		CREDITS*	0*	0*	0*	0*

Please see "Important Notes on the Tables, Footnotes," page 688.

Table 1. (continued)

Program number	ADMINISTRATIVE ENTITY/SUB-UNIT Program Title (abridged)		FY 2003 in $thousands	FY 2004 in $thousands	FY 2005 in $thousands	FY 2006 in $thousands
	NATIONAL CREDIT UNION ADMINISTRATION					
44.001	Credit Union Charter \ u		326,000*	274,000*	251,000*e	262,000*e
44.002	Revolving Loan Program \ u		2,000*e	8,981*	2,000*e	4,000*e
	DEPARTMENT TOTAL:	OUTLAYS	0	0	0	0
		CREDITS*	328,000*	282,981*	253,000*	266,000*
	NATIONAL FOUNDATION ON THE ARTS AND THE HUMANITIES					
	NATIONAL ENDOWMENT FOR THE ARTS					
45.024	Organizations and Individuals		64,252 e	64,412 e	59,671 e	58,884 e
45.025	Partnership Agreements		51,220 e	53,594 e	39,781 e	39,264 e
	Subtotal:	Outlays	115,472	118,006	99,452	98,148
		Credits*	0*	0*	0*	0*
	NATIONAL ENDOWMENT FOR THE HUMANITIES					
45.129	Federal-State Partnership		32,979	36,591	33,254 e	33,254 e
45.130	Challenge Grants		8,091	12,637	10,291 e	10,000 e
45.149	Preservation and Access		18,810	23,661	18,643 e	18,643 e
45.160	Fellowships and Stipends		7,543	8,146	8,041 e	8,041 e
45.161	Research		5,400 e	8,402	4,840 e	4,840 e
45.162	Teaching, Learning, Curriculum		3,296	3,296	4,002 e	4,500 e
45.163	Professional Development		8,024	8,024	12,283 e	13,075 e
45.164	Public Programs		11,670	11,670	12,952 e	13,114 e
45.168	We the People		10	9,876	11,217 e	11,217 e
	Subtotal:	Outlays	95,823	122,303	115,523	116,684
		Credits*	0*	0*	0*	0*
	FEDERAL COUNCIL ON THE ARTS AND THE HUMANITIES					
45.201	Arts and Artifacts Indemnity		0*	0*	0*e	0*e
	Subtotal:	Outlays	0	0	0	0
		Credits*	0*	0*	0*	0*
	INSTITUTE OF MUSEUM AND LIBRARY SERVICES					
45.301	Museum for America Grants		15,381	16,342	16,864 e	18,710 e
45.302	Museum Assessment Program		447	447	447 e	450 e
45.303	Conservation Project Support		2,792	2,782	2,788 e	2,810 e
45.304	Conservation Assessment Program		815	815	815 e	820 e
45.307	21st Century Museum Professionals		(n)	(n)	997	0 e
45.308	Native American/Hawaiian Museum		(n)	(n)	830	0 e
45.310	State Library Program		150,435	157,628	160,704 e	170,500 e
45.311	Native American, Hawaiian Library		3,055	3,206	3,472 e	3,675 e
45.312	National Leadership Grants		10,565	18,154	19,840 e	23,458 e
45.313	Librarians for the 21st Century		9,935	19,882	22,816 e	26,000 e
	Subtotal:	Outlays	193,425	219,256	229,573	246,423
		Credits*	0*	0*	0*	0*
	DEPARTMENT TOTAL:	OUTLAYS	404,720	459,565	444,548	461,255
		CREDITS*	0*	0*	0*	0*
	NATIONAL LABOR RELATIONS BOARD					
46.001	Labor-Management Relations \ u		238,982 e	242,526	249,959 e	252,367 e
	DEPARTMENT TOTAL:	OUTLAYS	238,982	242,526	249,959	252,367
		CREDITS*	0*	0*	0*	0*

Please see "Important Notes on the Tables, Footnotes," page 688.

Table 1. (continued)

Program number	ADMINISTRATIVE ENTITY/SUB-UNIT Program Title (abridged)		FY 2003 in $thousands	FY 2004 in $thousands	FY 2005 in $thousands	FY 2006 in $thousands
	NATIONAL SCIENCE FOUNDATION					
47.041	Engineering Grants		541,700	565,570	561,300 e	580,680 e
47.049	Mathematical, Physical Sciences		1,040,700	1,091,590	1,069,860 e	1,086,230 e
47.050	Geosciences		691,840	713,410	694,160 e	709,100 e
47.070	Computer, Information Science		589,290	605,350	613,720 e	620,560 e
47.074	Biological Sciences		570,490	587,050	576,610 e	581,790 e
47.075	Social, Behavioral, Economic		198,610	184,300	196,900 e	198,790 e
47.076	Education and Human Resources		934,880	944,100	841,420 e	737,000 e
47.078	Polar Programs		110,400	120,380	121,390 e	118,700 e
47.079	International Science, Engineering		(n)	29,840	33,730 e	34,510 e
	DEPARTMENT TOTAL:	OUTLAYS	4,677,910	4,841,590	4,709,090	4,667,360
		CREDITS*	0*	0*	0*	0*
	RAILROAD RETIREMENT BOARD					
57.001	Social Insurance/Railroad Workers \ t		9,063,000	9,105,000	9,383,000 e	9,597,000 e
	DEPARTMENT TOTAL:	OUTLAYS	9,063,000	9,105,000	9,383,000	9,597,000
		CREDITS*	0*	0*	0*	0*
	SECURITIES AND EXCHANGE COMMISSION					
58.001	Investigation of Complaints		619,322	755,012	888,000 e	888,000 e
	DEPARTMENT TOTAL:	OUTLAYS	619,322	755,012	888,000	888,000
		CREDITS*	0*	0*	0*	0*
	SMALL BUSINESS ADMINISTRATION					
59.002	Economic Injury Disaster Loans		100,565*	2,896*	0*e	0*e
59.005	Internet-Based Technical Assistance		14,226	6,825	6,789 e	7,342 e
59.006	8(a) Business Development		33,374	35,066	36,645 e	37,657 e
59.007	(7j) Technical Assistance		2,803	2,803	3,521 e	3,158 e
59.008	Physical Disaster Loans		7,339*	658*	0*e	0*e
59.009	Procurement Assistance		30,612	38,013	34,188 e	36,406 e
			0*	4,606,675*	3,250,000*e	3,000,000*e
59.011	Small Business Investment Companies		12,987*	12,987*	7,015*e	7,902*e
59.012	Small Business Loans		10,487,231*	162,718*	16,063,388*e	16,563,392*e
59.016	Bond Guarantees \ u		593,572*	598,487*	1,678,693*e	1,680,863*e
59.026	Service Corps of Retired Executives		11,284	17,209	18,831 e	19,048 e
59.037	Small Business Development Center		92,760	103,541	105,511 e	106,910 e
59.041	Certified Development Company Loans		0	28,668	29,347 e	31,535 e
			3,142,414*	3,966,133*	5,000,000*e	5,500,000*e
59.043	Women's Business Ownership		16,653	21,670	22,945 e	22,636 e
59.044	Veterans Entrepreneurial Training		1,729	3,167	2,968 e	3,012 e
59.046	Microloan Program		12,000 e	2,183	1,565 e	0 e
			41,714*e	29,075*	21,638*e	0*e
59.049	Disadvantaged Business Certification		4,750*	5,018*	5,206*e	5,323*e
59.050	Microenterprise Development Grants		14,899	16,039	15,232 e	0 e
59.051	Operational Assistance Grants		(a)	(a)	0	0 e
			12,626*	10,279*e	9,643*e	0*
59.052	Native American Economic Development		(n)	4,440	2,507 e	2,525 e
59.053	Ombudsman, Fairness Boards		(n)	1,469	1,270 e	1,407 e
59.054	7(a) Export Loans		(n)*	562,200*	600,000*e	0*e
	DEPARTMENT TOTAL:	OUTLAYS	230,340	281,093	281,319	271,636
		CREDITS*	14,403,198*	9,957,126*	26,635,583*	26,757,480*
	DEPARTMENT OF VETERANS AFFAIRS					
	VETERANS HEALTH ADMINISTRATION					
64.005	Construction/State Homes		101,564	146,610	113,907 e	12,339 e
64.007	Blind Rehabilitation Centers		59,820	60,215	61,247 e	62,220 e

Please see "Important Notes on the Tables, Footnotes," page 688.

Table 1. (continued)

Program number	ADMINISTRATIVE ENTITY/SUB-UNIT Program Title (abridged)		FY 2003 in $thousands	FY 2004 in $thousands	FY 2005 in $thousands	FY 2006 in $thousands
64.008	Veterans Domiciliary Care		437,808	372,866	409,770 e	434,796 e
64.009	Veterans Medical Care Benefits		18,907,752	28,301,366	29,984,283 e	31,019,242 e
64.010	Veterans Nursing Home Care		2,158,273	2,626,758	2,605,687 e	2,169,399 e
64.011	Veterans Dental Care		14,710	25,193	33,637 e	43,343 e
64.012	Veterans Prescription Service \ p		3,014,077	3,803,651	4,260,089 e	4,808,037 e
64.013	Veterans Prosthetic Appliances \ p		632,921	948,367	1,100,291 e	1,200,291 e
64.014	Veterans State Domiciliary Care		36,749	43,528	59,763 e	64,188 e
64.015	Veterans State Nursing Homes		322,289	394,433	400,828 e	167,001 e
64.016	Veterans State Hospital Care		5,605	4,471	4,051 e	4,327 e
64.018	Sharing Specialized Medical Resources		412,000	640,000	687,000 e	734,000 e
64.019	Alcohol and Drug Dependence		425,746	352,548	359,402 e	365,217 e
64.022	Home Based Primary Care		70,359	89,815	105,982 e	125,059 e
64.024	Homeless Providers Grants		22,431	62,965	86,000 e	99,000 e
64.026	State Adult Day Health Care		(n)	113	118 e	124 e
	Subtotal:	Outlays	26,622,104	37,872,899	40,272,055	41,308,583
		Credits*	0*	0*	0*	0*
	VETERANS BENEFITS ADMINISTRATION					
64.100	Automobiles, Adaptive Equipment		35,061	47,679	52,200 e	54,100 e
64.101	Burial Expenses Allowance		134,459	153,018	168,624 e	170,577 e
64.102	Compensation/Deaths		1,665	1,259	1,087 e	939 e
64.103	Life Insurance \ t, u		2,634,861	2,538,617	2,626,390 e	2,505,380 e
			74,635*	73,420*e	77,230*e	0*
64.104	Pension/Non-Service Connected		2,463,890	2,463,890	2,651,435 e	2,702,399 e
64.105	Pension/Survivors		700,140	722,175	736,397 e	745,227 e
64.106	Specially Adapted Housing		24,805	27,954	42,300 e	42,300 e
64.109	Service-Connected Disability		18,546,021	22,322,160	24,618,886 e	26,015,344 e
64.110	Dependency, Indemnity Compensation		3,793,106	4,006,267	4,268,410 e	4,463,171 e
64.114	Veterans Housing—Loans \ u		40,129,135*	44,130,601*	45,000,000*e	45,000,000*e
64.115	Veterans Information, Assistance		(a)	(a)	(a)	(a)
64.116	Vocational Rehabilitation \ u		486,888	552,111	589,728 e	634,130 e
			2,859*	3,117*	4,139*e	4,323*e
64.117	Dependents Educational Assistance		233,819	332,140	406,960 e	444,793 e
64.118	Housing—Disabled Veterans \ u		0*	0*	33*e	33*e
64.119	Manufactured Home Loans \ u		0*	0*	0*e	0*e
64.120	Post-Vietnam Era Educational \ t		8,659	3,480	3,395 e	9,654 e
64.124	All-Volunteer Force Educational		1,376,127	1,768,253	1,914,967 e	2,070,102 e
64.125	Vocational, Educational Counseling		6,000	5,581	6,000 e	6,000 e
64.126	Native American Direct Loan \ u		5,620*	5,870*	2,320*e	2,370*e
64.127	Allowance/Spina Bifida		16,845	16,073	17,148 e	17,922 e
64.128	Training/Spina Bifida		56	27	31 e	32 e
	Subtotal:	Outlays	30,462,402	34,960,684	38,103,958	39,882,070
		Credits*	40,212,249*	44,213,008*	45,083,722*	45,006,726*
	NATIONAL CEMETERY SYSTEM					
64.201	National Cemeteries		117,364	139,469	144,692 e	151,623 e
64.202	Headstones, Markers, Certificates		36,030	47,737	40,840 e	41,081 e
64.203	State Cemetery Grants		40,845	33,622	36,109 e	32,000 e
	Subtotal:	Outlays	194,239	220,828	221,641	224,704
		Credits*	0*	0*	0*	0*
	DEPARTMENT TOTAL:	OUTLAYS	57,278,745	73,054,411	78,597,654	81,415,357
		CREDITS*	40,212,249*	44,213,008*	45,083,722*	45,006,726*
	ENVIRONMENTAL PROTECTION AGENCY					
66.001	Air Pollution Control Support		180,575	78,456	172,759 e	177,118 e
66.032	State Indoor Radon Grants		8,158	6,813	7,000 e	8,000 e
66.033	Ozone Transport		649	650	635 e	635 e
66.034	Surveys, Studies/Clean Air Act		46,500	95,835	20,310 e	15,850 e
66.035	Community Action/Renewed Environment		(n)	(n)	1,650 e	9,000 e

Please see "Important Notes on the Tables, Footnotes," page 688.

Table 1. *(continued)*

Program number	ADMINISTRATIVE ENTITY/SUB-UNIT Program Title (abridged)	FY 2003 in $thousands	FY 2004 in $thousands	FY 2005 in $thousands	FY 2006 in $thousands
66.036	Clean School Bus USA	(n)	(n)	7,440 e	10,000 e
66.110	Healthy Communities Grant Program	(n)	(n)	0 e	0 e
66.111	Environmental Priority Projects	(n)	(n)	(n)	300 e
66.305	Compliance Assistance-Support	1,075	1,756	1,161 e	2,275 e
66.306	Environmental Justice Collaborative	1,500	1,500	1,500 e	1,500 e
66.307	Justice Training, Fellowship \ t	(n)	(n)	(n)	1,000
66.308	Justice Research Assistance \ t	(n)	(n)	(n)	1,000
66.309	Surveys, Studies, Investigations \ t	(n)	(n)	(n)	1,000
66.310	Compliance Assurance/Indian Country	(n)	1,450	1,450 e	1,450 e
66.418	Wastewater Treatment Works	9,393	0	7,500 e	7,000 e
66.419	Water Pollution Control	191,249	69,796	208,320 e	231,900 e
66.424	Surveys/Safe Drinking Water Act	3,200	7,172	1,200 e	1,600 e
66.432	Public Water System Supervision	92,495	101,995	105,100 e	105,100 e
66.433	Underground Water Source Protection	10,401	5,874	10,694 e	11,000 e
66.436	Surveys, Studies/Clean Water Act	11,907	34,078	15,000 e	15,000 e
66.437	Long Island Sound Program	2,990	7,317	2,332 e	477 e
66.439	Targeted Watershed Grants	14,903	7,435	17,856 e	15,000 e
66.454	Water Quality Management Planning	14,034	14,303	11,851 e	8,922 e
66.456	National Estuary Program	8,000	14,449	14,335 e	8,860 e
66.458	Clean Water State Revolving Funds \ r	1,250,000	1,327,225	1,091,200 e	730,000 e
66.460	Nonpoint Source Implementation	238,440	194,822	207,328 e	209,100 e
66.461	Regional Wetland Program Development	14,870	14,093	9,000 e	19,000 e
66.462	National Wetland Program Development	(n)	(n)	500 e	500 e
66.463	Water Quality Agreements	18,835	12,936	16,864 e	0 e
66.466	Chesapeake Bay Program	14,551	14,324	16,500 e	16,500 e
66.467	Wastewater Operator Training	1,200	1,973	1,488 e	0 e
66.468	Drinking Water/Revolving Fund \ r	844,475	846,220	843,200 e	850,000 e
66.469	Great Lakes Program	6,600	7,705	28,500 e	56,000 e
66.471	Small Water Systems	29,397	7,099	0 e	0 e
66.472	Beach Monitoring and Notification	9,935	7,905	9,920 e	10,000 e
66.473	Direct Implementation/Tribal	300	807	500 e	500 e
66.474	Water Protection Grants to States	4,968	3,870	4,960 e	5,000 e
66.475	Gulf of Mexico Program	1,800	1,859	2,100 e	2,000 e
66.478	Water Security Training, Assistance	3,200	0	1,000 e	0 e
66.479	Wetland Program Grants - State/Tribal	(n)	(n)	8,000 e	0 e
66.480	Assessment, Watershed Protection	(n)	222	900 e	900 e
66.481	Lake Champlain Basin Project	(n)	407	2,480 e	955 e
66.508	Senior Environmental Employment	54,562	62,121	55,000 e	55,000 e
66.509	Science to Achieve Results	79,773	50,884	61,900 e	57,400 e
66.510	Surveys, Studies/Office of Research	5,500	2,757	6,700 e	6,700 e
66.511	Consolidated Research, Training	48,000	30,950	50,000 e	50,000 e
66.512	REMAP Research Projects	(n)	646	1,694 e	1,991 e
66.513	Greater Opportunities Fellowship	1,090	0	1,500 e	1,500 e
66.514	STAR Fellowship Program	9,445	0	9,200 e	5,900 e
66.515	Greater Opportunities Research	1,152	0	1,100 e	1,200 e
66.516	Design Competition/Sustainability	(n)	647	500 e	300 e
66.518	State Senior Environmental Employment	(n)	(n)	500 e	500 e
66.600	Consolidated Grants—Program Support	(o)	(o)	(o)	(o)
66.604	Environmental Justice Small Grant \ t	920	884	750 e	750 e
66.605	Performance Partnership Grants	(o)	(o)	(o)	(o)
66.606	Surveys, Studies, Investigations	549,744	549,744	41,710 e	2,954 e
66.608	Information Exchange Network	20,000	1,650	19,344 e	20,000 e
66.609	Health Protection/Children, Elderly	700	679	1,400 e	1,000 e
66.610	Surveys/Office of Administrator	0	1,473	500 e	500 e
66.611	Environmental Policy, Innovation	1,444	2,227	700 e	500 e
66.700	Pesticide Enforcement	19,724	15,175	19,344 e	18,900 e
66.701	Toxic Substances Compliance	5,105	2,202	5,007 e	5,150 e
66.707	TSCA State Lead Grants	13,593	9,111	11,937 e	11,980 e
66.708	Pollution Prevention Grants	5,947	4,766	4,960 e	6,000 e
66.709	Multi-Media Capacity Building Grants	2,200	1,571	2,232 e	2,250 e
66.714	Pesticide Environmental Stewardship	494	30	470 e	470 e
66.715	Blood-Lead Screening/Tribal	1,094	175	1,200 e	1,210 e
66.716	Surveys, Studies, Training	2,359	4,455	1,295 e	1,295 e
66.717	Source Reduction Assistance	1,128	1,588	1,697 e	1,961 e

Please see "Important Notes on the Tables, Footnotes," page 688.

Table 1. (continued)

Program number	ADMINISTRATIVE ENTITY/SUB-UNIT Program Title (abridged)		FY 2003 in $thousands	FY 2004 in $thousands	FY 2005 in $thousands	FY 2006 in $thousands
66.801	Hazardous Waste Management		106,598	56,292	104,000 e	104,000 e
66.802	Superfund—Site Specific \ t		70,000	53,962	70,000 e	70,000 e
66.804	Underground Storage Tanks		11,841	7,937	11,904 e	11,950 e
66.805	Leaking Storage Tank Trust Fund\ t		58,193	58,742	57,421 e	61,241 e
66.806	TAG/Community Groups/NPL Sites		1,279	774	700 e	700 e
66.808	Solid Waste Management Assistance		4,000	4,108	4,000 e	4,000 e
66.809	Superfund/Core Program		14,800	10,112	12,000 e	12,000 e
66.810	CEPP Technical Assistance		130	256	80 e	0 e
66.812	Hazardous Waste Management/Tribes		298	536	298 e	298 e
66.813	Treatment Technology Research		7,200	442	350 e	350 e
66.814	Brownfields Agreements		2,576	2,576	3,000 e	3,000 e
66.815	Brownfield Job Training		2,400	2,400	2,000 e	2,000 e
66.816	Underground Storage Tanks \ t		0	175	125 e	125 e
66.817	State and Tribal Response		49,675	49,926	49,600 e	60,000 e
66.818	Brownfields Assessment, Cleanup		73,100	82,389	75,900 e	75,900 e
66.926	Indian Environmental GAP		57,096	47,812	61,504 e	57,500 e
66.931	International Financial Assistance		6,359	5,361	4,500 e	4,500 e
66.940	Environmental Policy, State Innovation		(n)	(n)	1,000 e	2,000 e
66.950	Environmental Education, Training		1,821	1,791	1,699 e	1,820 e
66.951	Environmental Education Grants		2,750	3,227	2,885 e	2,885 e
66.952	Environmental Management Fellowship		(n)	(n)	404	425 e
	DEPARTMENT TOTAL:	OUTLAYS	4,329,690	4,022,899	3,616,543	3,264,547
		CREDITS*	0*	0*	0*	0*

NATIONAL GALLERY OF ART

68.001	Art Extension Service		954 e	912	954 e	995 e
	DEPARTMENT TOTAL:	OUTLAYS	954	912	954	995
		CREDITS*	0*	0*	0*	0*

OVERSEAS PRIVATE INVESTMENT CORPORATION

70.002	Foreign Investment Financing \ u		19,000 e	0	0	0
			1,151,000*	1,851,000*	1,478,000*e	1,585,000*e
70.003	Foreign Investment Insurance \ u		1,733,000*	2,217,000*	2,100,000*e	2,200,000*e
	DEPARTMENT TOTAL:	OUTLAYS	19,000	0	0	0
		CREDITS*	2,884,000*	4,068,000*	3,578,000*	3,785,000*

COMMODITY FUTURES TRADING COMMISSION

78.004	Commodity Futures Reparations		67,850	67,850	70,400 e	70,400 e
	DEPARTMENT TOTAL:	OUTLAYS	67,850	67,850	70,400	70,400
		CREDITS*	0*	0*	0*	0*

DEPARTMENT OF ENERGY

81.003	Granting of Patent Licenses	(a)	(a)	(a)	(a)
81.022	Energy-Related Equipment \ p	(a)	(a)	(a)	(a)
81.036	Inventions and Innovations	2,633	1,633	1,600 e	1,600 e
81.039	National Energy Information Center	(a)	(a)	(a)	(a)
81.041	State Energy Program	44,568	43,706	44,000 e	45,000 e
81.042	Weatherization Assistance	223,538	227,166	228,160 e	230,000 e
81.049	Office of Science	515,000	830,000	830,000 e	830,000 e
81.057	University Coal Research	135,481	116,000	119,000 e	119,000 e
81.064	Scientific, Technical Information	6,900	7,700	8,800 e	8,800 e
81.065	Nuclear Waste Disposal Siting	11,451	19,460	15,268 e	16,518 e
81.079	Regional Biomass Programs	2,889	7,055	8,000 e	9,000 e
81.086	Conservation Research, Development	(a)	86,631	88,000 e	89,000 e
81.087	Renewable Energy Research	(a)	176,823	178,000 e	179,000 e
81.089	Fossil Energy Research, Development	247,991	247,991	220,000 e	200,000 e
81.104	Office of Environmental Cleanup	29,913	21,060	30,000 e	30,000 e
81.105	National Industrial Competitiveness	1,500	0	0 e	0 e

Please see "Important Notes on the Tables, Footnotes," page 688.

Table 1. (continued)

Program number	ADMINISTRATIVE ENTITY/SUB-UNIT Program Title (abridged)	FY 2003 in $thousands	FY 2004 in $thousands	FY 2005 in $thousands	FY 2006 in $thousands
81.106	Transport/Transuranic Waste	1,009	5,163	5,832 e	5,882 e
81.108	Epidemiology, Health Studies	18,000	12,000	18,000 e	18,000 e
81.112	Stewardship Science	10,949	17,000	9,834 e	13,000 e
81.113	Nuclear Nonproliferation Research	4,000	11,707	12,000 e	11,000 e
81.114	University Reactor Infrastructure	18,500	23,000	23,800 e	24,000 e
81.117	Energy Efficiency—Renewable	0	24,004	25,000 e	26,000 e
81.119	State Energy Special Projects	17,320	16,331	17,000 e	17,500 e
81.121	Nuclear Energy Research, Development	(a)	10,900	83,900 e	80,000 e
81.122	Electricity Delivery, Reliability	(n)	(n)	4,200 e	4,200 e
81.123	HBCU Program	(n)	(n)	8,200	0 e
	DEPARTMENT TOTAL: OUTLAYS	1,291,642	1,905,330	1,978,594	1,957,500
	CREDITS*	0*	0*	0*	0*

DEPARTMENT OF EDUCATION

84.002	Adult Education—State Grant	571,262	574,372	569,672 e	200,000 e
84.004	Civil Rights Training	7,286	7,243	7,185 e	7,185 e
84.007	Educational Opportunity Grants	760,028	770,455	778,720 e	778,720 e
84.010	Title I Grants	11,688,664	12,342,309	12,739,571 e	13,342,309 e
84.011	Migrant Education	386,000	383,577	380,428 e	380,428 e
84.013	Neglected and Delinquent Children	48,682	48,395	49,600 e	49,600 e
84.015	Language, Area Studies	59,122	58,675	56,919 e	58,130 e
84.016	Undergraduate International Studies	4,600	4,490	4,490 e	4,500 e
84.017	International Research and Studies	5,705	5,791	5,893 e	6,000 e
84.018	Overseas—Bilateral Projects	1,942	2,172	2,016 e	2,166 e
84.019	Overseas—Faculty Research Abroad	1,608	1,386	1,395 e	1,395 e
84.021	Overseas—Group Projects Abroad	4,350	4,312	4,348 e	4,273 e
84.022	Overseas—Doctoral Dissertation	4,823	4,441	4,400 e	4,400 e
84.027	Special Education—State Grants	8,874,398	10,068,106	10,589,746 e	11,097,746 e
84.031	Higher Education—Institutional Aid	388,869	399,961	421,476 e	418,464 e
84.032	Family Education Loans	103,661,000*	104,673,000*	99,320,000*e	89,963,000*e
84.033	Work-Study Program	1,004,428	998,502	990,257 e	990,257 e
84.037	Perkins Loan Cancellations	67,061	66,665	66,132 e	66,132 e
84.038	Perkins Loans	99,350*	98,764*	0*e	0*e
84.040	Impact Aid—Facilities Maintenance	7,948	7,901	7,838 e	7,838 e
84.041	Impact Aid	1,025,292	1,063,687	1,075,018 e	1,075,018 e
84.042	TRIO—Student Support Services	263,650	263,031	274,858 e	274,858 e
84.044	TRIO—Talent Search	144,811	144,230	144,887 e	0 e
84.047	TRIO—Upward Bound	312,562	312,451	312,556 e	0 e
84.048	Vocational Education—States	1,165,495	1,168,239	1,167,578 e	0 e
84.051	Vocational Education—National	11,922	11,852	11,757 e	0 e
84.060	Indian Education—LEAs	96,502	95,933	95,165 e	96,294 e
84.063	Pell Grant Program	11,364,646	12,006,738	12,364,997 e	17,952,821 e
84.066	TRIO—Educational Opportunity	47,695	48,972	48,972 e	48,972 e
84.069	Leveraging Educational Assistance	66,565	66,172	65,643 e	0 e
84.083	Women's Educational Equity	2,980	2,962	2,956 e	0 e
84.101	Vocational Education—Indians	14,903	14,938	14,929 e	0 e
84.103	TRIO Staff Training Program	7,500	5,299	5,299 e	2,500 e
84.116	Fund/Postsecondary Education	171,068	156,905	162,108 e	22,211 e
84.120	Minority Science, Engineering	8,942	8,889	8,818 e	8,818 e
84.126	Rehabilitation Services—State	2,533,492	2,553,362	2,603,845 e	2,687,168 e
84.128	Rehabilitation Services—Projects	4,914	4,885	4,845 e	0 e
84.129	Rehabilitation Training	25,000	25,000	25,000 e	25,000 e
84.132	Centers for Independent Living	69,545	73,563	75,392 e	75,392 e
84.133	Disability, Rehabilitation Research	109,285	106,652	107,783 e	107,783 e
84.141	Migrant Education—High School	23,347	18,888	18,737 e	18,737 e
84.144	Migrant Education—Coordination	9,413	10,000	10,000 e	10,000 e
84.145	Federal Real Property Assistance \ p	(a)	(a)	(a)	(a)
84.149	Migrant Education—College	15,399	15,657	15,532 e	15,532 e
84.153	Business, International Education	4,634	4,491	4,491 e	4,500 e
84.160	Training Interpreters for Deaf	2,100	2,100	2,100 e	2,100 e
84.161	Rehabilitation—Client Assistance	12,068	11,997	11,901 e	11,901 e
84.165	Magnet Schools	109,285	108,640	107,771 e	107,771 e
84.169	Independent Living	22,151	22,020	22,816 e	22,816 e

Please see "Important Notes on the Tables, Footnotes," page 688.

Table 1. (continued)

Program number	ADMINISTRATIVE ENTITY/SUB-UNIT Program Title (abridged)	FY 2003 in $thousands	FY 2004 in $thousands	FY 2005 in $thousands	FY 2006 in $thousands
84.170	Javits Fellowships	9,935	9,876	9,797 e	9,797 e
84.173	Special Education—Preschool	387,465	387,699	384,597 e	384,597 e
84.177	Rehabilitation Services—Blind	27,818	31,811	33,227 e	33,227 e
84.181	Infants, Families/Disabilities	434,159	444,363	440,808 e	440,808 e
84.184	Drug-Free Schools—National	197,404	233,295	234,580 e	317,274 e
84.185	Byrd Honors Scholarships	40,734	40,758	40,672 e	0 e
84.186	Safe/Drug-Free Schools—State	468,949	440,908	437,381 e	0 e
84.187	Supported Employment	37,904	37,680	37,379 e	0 e
84.191	Adult Education—National Leadership	9,438	9,169	9,096 e	9,096 e
84.196	Homeless Children, Youth	54,642	59,646	62,496 e	62,496 e
84.200	Graduate Assistance/National Need	30,798	30,616	30,371 e	30,371 e
84.203	Star Schools	27,341	20,362	20,832 e	0 e
84.206	Javits Gifted/Talented Students	11,177	11,111	11,022 e	0 e
84.213	Even Start—State	224,021	222,688	202,836 e	0 e
84.214	Even Start—Migrant	8,693	8,642	7,878 e	0 e
84.215	Improvement of Education	318,630	280,453	257,114 e	29,000 e
84.217	TRIO/Post-Baccalaureate	41,886	42,093	41,935 e	41,935 e
84.220	International Business Education	11,100	10,700	10,700 e	10,800 e
84.224	Assistive Technology	26,227	20,289	20,289 e	0 e
84.229	Language Resource Centers	5,100	4,850	4,850 e	4,950 e
84.234	Projects with Industry	21,928	21,799	21,625 e	0 e
84.235	Rehabilitation Services/Training	21,392	24,286	25,607 e	6,577 e
84.240	Protection and Advocacy	16,890	16,790	16,656 e	16,656 e
84.243	Tech-Prep Education	107,298	106,665	105,812 e	0 e
84.245	Tribal Vocational/Technical	6,955	7,185	7,440 e	7,440 e
84.246	Rehabilitation Short-Term Training	500	500	500 e	500 e
84.250	Rehabilitation—Indians/Disabilities	28,436	30,800	32,000 e	33,024 e
84.255	Literacy for Prisoners	4,968	4,971	4,980 e	0 e
84.256	Freely Associated States—Education	5,000	5,000	5,000 e	5,000 e
84.257	Institute for Literacy	4,018	4,220	4,156 e	4,106 e
84.258	Even Start—Indian	4,968	4,938	4,502 e	0 e
84.259	Hawaiian Vocational Education	2,980	2,988	2,986 e	0 e
84.263	Rehabilitation Training—Innovative	500	500	500 e	500 e
84.264	Rehabilitation Training—Continuing	10,000	10,000	10,000 e	10,000 e
84.265	Rehabilitation Training—State Unit	6,000	6,000	6,000 e	6,000 e
84.268	Federal Direct Student Loans	25,283,000*	20,622,000*	22,896,000*e	22,808,000*e
84.269	International Public Policy	1,639	1,629	1,616 e	1,616 e
84.274	Overseas Research Centers	1,000	1,000	1,000 e	1,000 e
84.275	Rehabilitation Training—General	300	300	300 e	300 e
84.282	Charter Schools	198,700	218,702	216,952 e	218,702 e
84.283	Comprehensive Centers	27,818	27,654	56,825 e	56,825 e
84.286	Ready to Teach	14,406	14,321	14,291 e	0 e
84.287	Community Learning Centers	993,500	999,070	991,077 e	991,077 e
84.293	Foreign Language Assistance	16,144	16,546	17,856 e	0 e
84.295	Ready-To-Learn TV	22,850	22,864	23,312 e	23,312 e
84.298	State Grants/Innovative Programs	382,498	296,549	198,400 e	100,000 e
84.304	Civic Education—Exchange	11,922	11,852	12,194 e	0 e
84.305	Education Research, Development	139,090	165,518	164,194 e	164,194 e
84.310	Parental Assistance Centers	42,224	41,975	41,866 e	0 e
84.315	Capacity Building	2,445	2,552	2,597 e	2,846 e
84.318	Education Technology State Grants	695,947	691,841	691,841 e	0 e
84.319	Eisenhower Math, Science Consortia	14,902	14,902	14,814 e	0 e
84.323	State Personnel Development	51,364	51,061	50,653 e	50,653 e
84.324	Research in Special Education	76,713	78,125	83,104 e	72,566 e
84.325	Personnel/Children with Disabilities	91,899	91,357	90,626 e	90,626 e
84.326	Technical/Children with Disabilities	53,133	52,819	52,936 e	49,397 e
84.327	Technology/Individuals/Disabilities	37,961	39,129	38,816 e	31,992 e
84.328	Parent Information Centers	26,328	26,173	25,964 e	25,964 e
84.329	Studies, Evaluations	15,950	16,000	0 e	10,000 e
84.330	Advanced Placement Program	23,347	23,534	29,760 e	51,500 e
84.331	Incarcerated Youth Offenders	18,380	19,882	21,824 e	0 e
84.332	Comprehensive School Reform	233,473	233,613	205,344 e	0 e
84.333	Disabilities—Higher Education	6,954	6,913	6,944 e	0 e
84.334	Awareness, Readiness—Undergraduate	293,082	298,230	306,488 e	0 e

Please see "Important Notes on the Tables, Footnotes," page 688.

Table 1. (continued)

Program number	ADMINISTRATIVE ENTITY/SUB-UNIT Program Title (abridged)	FY 2003 in $thousands	FY 2004 in $thousands	FY 2005 in $thousands	FY 2006 in $thousands
84.335	Child Care/Parents in School	16,194	16,099	15,970 e	15,970 e
84.336	Teacher Quality Enhancement Grants	89,415	88,888	68,337 e	0 e
84.337	Education—Technology/Foreign Access	1,700	1,700	1,700 e	1,700 e
84.341	Community Technology Centers	32,264	9,941	4,690 e	0 e
84.343	Assistive Technology/Protection	4,573	4,421	4,385 e	0 e
84.344	TRIO—Dissemination Partnership	4,374	4,386	4,386 e	0 e
84.345	Underground Railroad Education	2,235	2,222	2,204 e	0 e
84.346	Occupational, Employment Information	9,438	9,382	9,307 e	0 e
84.349	Early Childhood Educator	14,902	14,814	14,696 e	14,696 e
84.350	Transition to Teaching	41,727	45,295	44,933 e	44,933 e
84.351	Arts in Education	33,779	35,071	35,633 e	0 e
84.353	Tech-Prep Demonstration Grants	4,968	4,939	4,900 e	0 e
84.354	Credit Enhancement/Charter School	24,838	37,279	36,981 e	36,981 e
84.356	Alaska Native Educational Programs	30,798	33,302	34,224 e	31,224 e
84.357	Reading First State Grants	993,500	1,023,923	1,041,600 e	1,041,600 e
84.358	Rural Education	167,653	167,831	170,624 e	170,624 e
84.359	Early Reading First	74,512	94,440	104,160 e	104,160 e
84.360	Dropout Prevention Programs	10,929	4,971	4,930 e	0 e
84.361	Voluntary Public School Choice	25,831	26,757	26,543 e	26,543 e
84.362	Native Hawaiian Education	30,798	33,302	34,224 e	32,624 e
84.363	School Leadership	12,419	12,346	14,880 e	0 e
84.364	Literacy through School Libraries	12,419	19,842	19,683 e	19,683 e
84.365	English Language Acquisition	530,032	597,374	631,124 e	675,765 e
84.366	Mathematics, Science Partnerships	100,344	149,115	178,560 e	269,000 e
84.367	Improving Teacher Quality	2,930,825	2,930,126	2,916,605 e	2,916,605 e
84.369	State Assessments, Activities	384,484	390,000	411,680 e	411,680 e
84.370	DC School Choice Incentive Program	(n)	14,000	14,000 e	14,000 e
	DEPARTMENT TOTAL: OUTLAYS	53,226,116	55,905,834	57,204,017	59,224,247
	CREDITS*	129,043,350*	125,393,764*	122,216,000*	112,771,000*

SCHOLARSHIP AND FELLOWSHIP FOUNDATIONS

HARRY S TRUMAN SCHOLARSHIP FOUNDATION

85.001	Truman Scholarship Program \ t		2,000	2,000	2,000 e	2,000 e
	Subtotal:	Outlays	2,000	2,000	2,000	2,000
		Credits*	0*	0*	0*	0*

CHRISTOPHER COLUMBUS FELLOWSHIP FOUNDATION

85.100	Columbus Fellowship Program \ t		649	577	622 e	650 e
	Subtotal:	Outlays	649	577	622	650
		Credits*	0*	0*	0*	0*

BARRY M. GOLDWATER SCHOLARSHIP AND EXCELLENCE IN EDUCATION FOUNDATION

85.200	Goldwater Scholarship Program \ t		3,000 e	2,800	3,000 e	0 e
	Subtotal:	Outlays	3,000	2,800	3,000	0
		Credits*	0*	0*	0*	0*

WOODROW WILSON INTERNATIONAL CENTER FOR SCHOLARS

85.300	Wilson Fellowships		1,121 e	1,208	1,355 e	1,405 e
	Subtotal:	Outlays	1,121	1,208	1,355	1,405
		Credits*	0*	0*	0*	0*

MORRIS K. UDALL SCHOLARSHIP FOUNDATION

85.400	Udall Scholarship Program		400	400	400 e	400 e
85.401	Udall Fellowship Program		48	48	48 e	48 e
85.402	Udall Congressional Internships		140	140	140 e	170 e
	Subtotal:	Outlays	588	588	588	618
		Credits*	0*	0*	0*	0*

Please see "Important Notes on the Tables, Footnotes," page 688.

Table 1. (continued)

Program number	ADMINISTRATIVE ENTITY/SUB-UNIT Program Title (abridged)		FY 2003 in $thousands	FY 2004 in $thousands	FY 2005 in $thousands	FY 2006 in $thousands
	JAMES MADISON MEMORIAL FELLOWSHIP FOUNDATION					
85.500	Madison Fellowship Program \t		1,026	1,120	1,195 e	1,210 e
	Subtotal:	Outlays	1,026	1,120	1,195	1,210
		Credits*	0*	0*	0*	0*
	SMITHSONIAN INSTITUTION					
85.601	Smithsonian Institution Fellowship		(n)	(n)	850 e	1,000 e
	Subtotal:	Outlays	0	0	850	1,000
		Credits*	0*	0*	0*	0*
	DEPARTMENT TOTAL:	OUTLAYS	8,384	8,293	9,610	6,883
		CREDITS*	0*	0*	0*	0*
	PENSION BENEFIT GUARANTY CORPORATION					
86.001	Pension Plan Termination Insurance \u		2,277,000	2,971,713	3,273,000 e	5,192,000 e
	DEPARTMENT TOTAL:	OUTLAYS	2,277,000	2,971,713	3,273,000	5,192,000
		CREDITS*	0*	0*	0*	0*
	ARCHITECTURAL AND TRANSPORTATION BARRIERS COMPLIANCE BOARD					
88.001	Compliance Board		5,013	5,160	5,369 e	5,686 e
	DEPARTMENT TOTAL:	OUTLAYS	5,013	5,160	5,369	5,686
		CREDITS*	0*	0*	0*	0*
	NATIONAL ARCHIVES AND RECORDS ADMINISTRATION					
89.001	Historical Research		47,489 e	80,262	81,217 e	83,921 e
89.003	National Historical Publications		6,458 e	9,563	4,960 e	0 e
	DEPARTMENT TOTAL:	OUTLAYS	53,947	89,825	86,177	83,921
		CREDITS*	0*	0*	0*	0*
	INDEPENDENT BOARDS AND COMMISSIONS					
	DENALI COMMISSION					
90.100	Denali Commission Program \t		49,000	110,000	120,000 e	50,000 e
	Subtotal:	Outlays	49,000	110,000	120,000	50,000
		Credits*	0*	0*	0*	0*
	DELTA REGIONAL AUTHORITY					
90.200	Delta Regional Development		(a)	(a)	(a)	(a)
90.201	Delta Area Economic Development		7,576	7,576	3,595 e	4,200 e
90.202	Delta Local Development District		1,440	360	396 e	0 e
	Subtotal:	Outlays	9,016	7,936	3,991	4,200
		Credits*	0*	0*	0*	0*
	JAPAN-U.S. FRIENDSHIP COMMISSION					
90.300	Japan-US Friendship Grants		2,655	2,655	2,655 e	2,655 e
	Subtotal:	Outlays	2,655	2,655	2,655	2,655
		Credits*	0*	0*	0*	0*

Please see "Important Notes on the Tables, Footnotes," page 688.

Table 1. (continued)

Program number	ADMINISTRATIVE ENTITY/SUB-UNIT Program Title (abridged)		FY 2003 in $thousands	FY 2004 in $thousands	FY 2005 in $thousands	FY 2006 in $thousands
	ELECTIONS ASSISTANCE COMMISSION					
90.400	Help America Vote—Pollworker		(n)	645,750	0 e	0 e
90.401	Help America Vote Act Requirements		(n)	1,489,361	0 e	0 e
	Subtotal:	Outlays	0	2,135,111	0	0
		Credits*	0*	0*	0*	0*
	DEPARTMENT TOTAL:	OUTLAYS	60,671	2,255,702	126,646	56,855
		CREDITS*	0*	0*	0*	0*
	UNITED STATES INSTITUTE OF PEACE					
91.001	Unsolicited Grant Program		1,705	1,705	2,000 e	2,500 e
91.002	Solicited Grant Program		1,070	1,386	1,500 e	2,000 e
	DEPARTMENT TOTAL:	OUTLAYS	2,775	3,091	3,500	4,500
		CREDITS*	0*	0*	0*	0*
	DEPARTMENT OF HEALTH AND HUMAN SERVICES					
93.001	Civil Rights, Privacy Rule		32,972	33,902	35,014 e	34,996 e
93.003	Health, Social Services Emergency		2,168	2,168	0 e	0 e
93.004	Health Status/Minority Populations		5,224	5,224	5,224 e	2,000 e
93.006	Minority HIV/AIDS Demonstration		9,044	7,050	2,000 e	2,000 e
93.007	Public Awareness/Embryo Adoption		950	950	950 e	950 e
93.008	Medical Reserve Corps		8,350	8,350	8,350 e	8,350 e
93.009	Compassion Capital Fund		34,773	47,702	54,549 e	100,000 e
93.010	Community-Based Abstinence Education		(n)	74,549	103,698 e	142,545 e
93.012	Heart Health Care/High-Risk Women		(n)	(n)	750 e	0 e
93.041	Aging—Prevention of Abuse, Neglect		5,198	5,167	5,127 e	5,198 e
93.042	Aging—Long-Term Care Ombudsman		13,362	14,276	14,162 e	14,162 e
93.043	Aging—Disease Prevention		21,919	21,790	21,616 e	21,616 e
93.044	Aging—Senior Centers		355,673	353,889	354,136 e	354,136 e
93.045	Aging—Nutrition Services		565,577	566,270	570,101 e	570,100 e
93.047	Aging—Indian, Native Hawaiian		33,704	31,771	32,702 e	32,702 e
93.048	Aging—Discretionary Projects		42,621	46,803	56,552 e	37,109 e
93.051	Alzheimer's Disease Demonstration		13,412	11,883	11,796 e	11,786 e
93.052	National Family Caregiver Support		155,234	159,056	162,048 e	162,048 e
93.053	Nutrition Services Incentive		148,697	148,191	148,596 e	148,596 e
93.061	Applied Public Health Research		(n)	21,700	29,700 e	21,700 e
93.063	Centers/Genomics,Public Health		(n)	2,500	600 e	600 e
93.064	Laboratory Training, Evaluation		(n)	425	425 e	425 e
93.065	Improving Public Health Laboratory		(n)	4,758	4,739 e	4,905 e
93.066	Vital Statistics Re-Engineering		172	172	172 e	172 e
93.067	Global Aids		(n)	(n)	375 e	375 e
93.068	Research, Control, Prevention		(n)	(n)	2,000	6,000 e
93.100	Health Disparities/Minority		1,000	1,000	1,000 e	0 e
93.103	FDA—Research		28,540	29,452	23,109 e	25,276 e
93.104	CMHS/Serious Emotional Disturbances		53,260	15,396	4,383 e	3,700 e
93.105	Bilingual/Bicultural Service		2,950	2,950	2,950 e	0 e
93.107	Model Area Health Education Centers		15,635	13,700	14,000 e	0 e
93.110	Maternal, Child Health Programs		110,655	115,794	114,314 e	113,398 e
93.111	Adolescent Family Life Research		1,000	1,000	1,000 e	1,000 e
93.113	Biological Response/Health Hazards		171,843	170,338	167,932 e	164,571 e
93.114	Toxicological Research, Testing		30,000	32,291	34,000 e	34,500 e
93.115	Biometry, Risk/Environmental		44,500	45,500	46,000 e	46,500 e
93.116	Tuberculosis Control Programs		103,277	102,632	109,807 e	109,807 e
93.117	Preventive Medicine		1,816	1,400	1,400 e	0 e
93.118	AIDS Activity		5,565	5,565	2,164 e	2,164 e
93.121	Oral Diseases/Disorders Research		269,915	269,915	291,766 e	300,238 e
93.123	Pregraduate Scholarship/Indians		1,965	638	638 e	638 e
93.124	Nurse Anesthetist Traineeships		1,000	1,250	1,250 e	500 e
93.127	Emergency Medical Services/Children		13,978	13,875	14,177 e	0 e
93.129	Assistance to Health Centers		25,000	25,000	29,000 e	29,000 e

Please see "Important Notes on the Tables, Footnotes," page 688.

Table 1. (continued)

Program number	ADMINISTRATIVE ENTITY/SUB-UNIT Program Title (abridged)	FY 2003 in $thousands	FY 2004 in $thousands	FY 2005 in $thousands	FY 2006 in $thousands
93.130	State Primary Care Offices	9,644	10,205	10,205 e	10,205 e
93.134	Organ Donations	13,712	11,279	7,127 e	4,982 e
93.135	Centers/Health Promotion	24,300	22,200	25,300 e	25,300 e
93.136	Injury Prevention, Control Research	109,390	111,766	111,766 e	111,766 e
93.137	Community Minority Health	6,500	6,500	6,500 e	6,500 e
93.138	Advocacy/Mental Illness	33,103	33,103	33,928 e	33,928 e
93.140	Intramural Research Training	40,850	44,935	49,428 e	49,428 e
93.142	Hazardous Waste Worker Training	25,785	26,641	27,356 e	27,504 e
93.143	Hazardous Substances Research	47,408	47,324	47,819 e	48,085 e
93.145	AIDS Education, Training Centers	34,135	33,866	33,538 e	33,500 e
93.150	Transition from Homelessness	41,306	41,306	47,670 e	52,929 e
93.153	Research/Women, Infants, Youth	61,441	69,726	69,726 e	69,726 e
93.155	Rural Health Research Centers	4,500	3,960	5,000 e	5,000 e
93.156	Geriatric Fellowships	5,840	4,869	6,500 e	0 e
93.157	Centers of Excellence	34,311	31,509	31,509 e	0 e
93.161	Toxic Substances, Disease Registry	7,684	6,662	6,662 e	6,662 e
93.162	NHSC Loan Repayment	91,878	85,035	59,800 e	59,400 e
93.164	IHS Loan Repayment	17,111	16,817	16,536 e	16,924 e
93.165	State Loan Repayment	6,844	6,317	7,000 e	7,000 e
93.172	Human Genome Research	348,135	348,135	351,688 e	366,859 e
93.173	Deafness, Communication Disorders	370,330	381,888	394,260 e	397,432 e
93.178	Nursing Workforce Diversity	10,000	15,600	15,000 e	18,500 e
93.181	Podiatric Residency Training	610	492	418 e	0 e
93.184	Disabilities Prevention	13,590	13,500	13,500 e	14,500 e
93.185	Immunization Research, Demonstration	9,500	7,435	7,435 e	7,435 e
93.186	NRSA/Primary Care	7,158	7,404	7,638 e	7,737 e
93.187	Undergraduate Scholarships	793	838	800 e	852 e
93.189	Health Education, Training Centers	4,007	3,599	3,734 e	0 e
93.191	Allied Health Special Projects	4,100	4,413	5,040 e	0 e
93.192	Rural Interdisciplinary Training	5,972	5,752	6,066 e	0 e
93.193	Urban Indian Health Services	7,135	8,486	7,662 e	7,662 e
93.197	Childhood Lead Poisoning Prevention	32,254	31,000	31,000 e	31,000 e
93.202	Capacity Building/Indian Tribes	200	100	100 e	100 e
93.204	Hazardous Substance Emergency	0	2,000	2,000 e	2,000 e
93.206	Health Studies/Research	2,830	1,930	1,930 e	1,930 e
93.208	Great Lakes Health Effects	1,473	1,260	1,260 e	1,260 e
93.209	Contraception, Infertility LRP	700	1,045	1,000 e	1,000 e
93.210	Tribal Self-Governance	898,830	898,830	910,720 e	910,720 e
93.211	Telehealth Network Grants	3,742	3,743	3,750 e	3,750 e
93.212	Chiropractic Demonstration Projects	1,023	1,159	1,308 e	0 e
93.213	Complementary/Alternative Medicine	84,659	85,891	87,639 e	87,501 e
93.217	Family Planning—Services	238,410	238,410	238,410 e	238,410 e
93.219	Scholarships/Indians	328	328	328 e	328 e
93.220	Loan Repayment/Disadvantaged	638	551	725 e	759 e
93.223	Rural Health Services	900	900	771 e	771 e
93.224	Consolidated Health Centers	300,200	1,577,105	1,600,000 e	1,600,000 e
93.225	Health Services Research Training	7,732	7,400	7,615 e	7,400 e
93.226	Research/Healthcare Cost, Quality	141,852	128,891	104,772 e	102,996 e
93.228	IHS—Health Management	6,033	6,019	5,343 e	5,430 e
93.229	Criminal Justice Treatment	1,000	1,000	1,000 e	1,000 e
93.230	Knowledge Development, Application	188,804	25,769	43,758 e	20,503 e
93.231	Epidemiology Agreements	3,250	3,250	3,250 e	4,826 e
93.232	Loan Repayment/General Research	4,596	4,875	4,906 e	5,157 e
93.233	Sleep Disorders Research	47,515	50,229	43,593 e	43,686 e
93.234	Traumatic Brain Injury	4,592	5,180	2,225 e	0 e
93.235	Abstinence Education	43,944	40,895	50,000 e	50,000 e
93.236	Dental Public Health Training	641	516	749 e	0 e
93.237	Special Diabetes Program/Indians	100,200	100,200	105,100 e	105,100 e
93.238	Treatment Outcomes Studies	1,600	1,973	0 e	0 e
93.239	Policy Research	2,500	2,381	2,300 e	0 e
93.240	State Capacity Building	10,037	14,748	8,783 e	8,783 e
93.241	State Rural Hospital Flexibility	22,300	22,300	24,283 e	24,000 e
93.242	Mental Health Research	916,464	957,603	979,495 e	982,563 e
93.243	Substance Abuse, Mental Health	163,662	122,770	134,137 e	116,204 e

Please see "Important Notes on the Tables, Footnotes," page 688.

Table 1. (continued)

Program number	ADMINISTRATIVE ENTITY/SUB-UNIT Program Title (abridged)	FY 2003 in $thousands	FY 2004 in $thousands	FY 2005 in $thousands	FY 2006 in $thousands
93.244	Mental Health Clinical, AIDS	2,000	3,200	3,200 e	3,200 e
93.247	Advanced Education Nursing	8,480	38,287	37,900 e	30,300 e
93.249	Public Health Training Centers	5,500	4,900	4,500 e	0 e
93.250	Geriatric Academic Career Awards	4,115	5,460	5,800 e	0 e
93.251	Universal Newborn Hearing Screening	8,902	8,856	8,584 e	0 e
93.252	Healthy Communities Access Program	105,000	85,000	85,000 e	0 e
93.253	Poison Control Centers	18,461	19,541	19,043 e	19,043 e
93.254	Infant Adoption Awareness Training	12,823	12,785	12,802 e	12,802 e
93.255	Children's Hospitals Education	292,000	303,000	300,000 e	200,000 e
93.256	Health Care Access/Uninsured	10,300	0	9,500 e	0 e
93.257	Radiogenic Cancers, Diseases	2,000	2,000	2,000 e	2,000 e
93.259	Rural Access/Emergency Devices	12,500	10,000	7,300 e	7,300 e
93.260	Family Planning—Personnel	8,442	8,442	8,442 e	8,442 e
93.262	Occupational Safety, Health Program	32,146	101,673	102,898 e	102,898 e
93.264	Nurse Faculty Loan Program	2,800*	4,686*	4,600*e	4,600*e
93.265	Comprehensive Geriatric Education	2,670	3,260	3,250 e	3,200 e
93.266	Global AIDS Relief	(n)	42,000	63,817 e	75,000 e
93.267	Protection, Advocacy Services	2,970	3,000	2,976 e	0 e
93.268	Immunization Grants	1,389,500	1,401,492	1,582,000 e	1,694,000 e
93.271	Alcohol Research Career Awards	9,429	9,874	11,268 e	11,440 e
93.272	Alcohol Research Training	10,440	11,417	11,420 e	11,361 e
93.273	Alcohol Research Programs	252,511	260,939	261,911 e	262,844 e
93.275	Mental Health—Access to Recovery	100,000	15,182	99,410 e	99,410 e
93.276	Drug-Free Communities Support	53,495	54,562	0 e	0 e
93.279	Drug Abuse, Addiction Research	727,140	32,418	34,886 e	35,278 e
93.280	NIH Loan Repayment/Researchers	38,200	40,631	42,626 e	42,631 e
93.281	Mental Health/Development Awards	67,397	73,769	74,615 e	75,170 e
93.282	Mental Health Research Training	58,737	59,726	60,072 e	59,980 e
93.283	Disease Control—Investigations	10,062 e	235,239	242,700 e	241,133 e
93.284	Injury Prevention—Indians/Alaskans	1,475	1,475	1,475 e	1,475 e
93.285	NIH Pediatric Research LRP	15,300	15,914	15,990 e	15,990 e
93.286	Discovery and Applied Research	111,740 e	286,684	298,209 e	299,808 e
93.288	NHSC Scholarship	22,888	29,299	17,400 e	17,600 e
93.289	Physical Fitness and Sports	1,215	1,215	1,185 e	1,185 e
93.290	Centers/Women's Health	600	600	0 e	0 e
93.291	Surplus Property Utilization	731	731	703 e	717 e
93.300	Health Workforce Analysis	2,200	1,500	1,500 e	1,500 e
93.301	Small Rural Hospital Improvement	14,800	14,700	14,700 e	14,700 e
93.307	Minority Health, Disparities Research	113,551	129,321	150,969 e	153,962 e
93.308	Loan Repayment/Clinical Research	2,020	1,672	2,231 e	2,244 e
93.342	Health Professions Student Loans	22,000*	22,000*	26,000*e	24,000*e
93.358	Advanced Nursing Traineeships	15,000	16,000	16,000 e	9,000 e
93.359	Nurse Education, Practice, Retention	27,000	24,202	33,900 e	41,000 e
93.361	Nursing Research	108,152	106,860	107,772 e	107,128 e
93.364	Nursing Student Loans \ r	5,300*	3,296*	0*e	0*e
93.389	National Center/Research Resources	1,115,510	1,166,470	1,089,072 e	1,071,801 e
93.390	Academic Research Enhancement	31,055	38,327	39,055 e	39,250 e
93.392	Cancer Construction	3,000	0	0 e	0 e
93.393	Cancer Cause, Prevention	659,705	705,496	678,244 e	713,738 e
93.394	Cancer Detection, Diagnosis	245,979	259,590	255,021 e	263,164 e
93.395	Cancer Treatment Research	538,555	619,456	635,685 e	654,657 e
93.396	Cancer Biology Research	555,873	576,820	659,190 e	604,974 e
93.397	Cancer Centers Support	378,079	409,288	407,984 e	434,422 e
93.398	Cancer Research Manpower	167,736	172,683	180,519 e	181,739 e
93.399	Cancer Control	221,620	214,964	216,197 e	216,197 e
93.441	Indian Self-Determination	490,000	490,000	509,600 e	509,600 e
93.442	Special Diabetes Program/Indians	23,300	23,300	23,300 e	23,300 e
93.447	State Health Fraud Task Force	(n)	150	150 e	150 e
93.448	Food Safety, Security Monitoring	(n)	(n)	2,100 e	2,100 e
93.449	Ruminant Feed Ban Support Project	(n)	(n)	1,500 e	1,500 e
93.550	Transitional Living/Homeless Youth	40,504	40,260	39,938 e	49,941 e
93.551	Abandoned Infants	12,125	12,052	11,955 e	11,955 e
93.556	Promoting Safe and Stable Families	391,071	404,383	403,586 e	410,000 e
93.557	Street Outreach Program	15,399	15,302	15,178 e	15,179 e

Please see "Important Notes on the Tables, Footnotes," page 688.

Table 1. (continued)

Program number	ADMINISTRATIVE ENTITY/SUB-UNIT Program Title (abridged)	FY 2003 in $thousands	FY 2004 in $thousands	FY 2005 in $thousands	FY 2006 in $thousands
93.558	Temporary Assistance/Families	17,608,626	17,408,551 e	19,248,581 e	17,248,581 e
93.560	Family Support Payments	23,000	23,000	33,000 e	33,000 e
93.563	Child Support Enforcement	4,053,186	3,994,187	4,056,465 e	4,173,816 e
93.564	Child Support Enforcement Research	1,800	1,800	1,800 e	1,800 e
93.566	Refugee and Entrant Assistance	229,788	169,000	192,000 e	264,000 e
93.567	Refugees, Entrants—Agencies	53,000	50,400	50,000 e	50,000 e
93.568	Low-Income Home Energy Assistance	1,788,290	1,888,759	2,134,788 e	1,799,988 e
93.569	Community Services Block Grant	645,687	641,911	636,793 e	0 e
93.570	CSBG—Discretionary	51,175	51,984	52,391 e	0 e
93.571	CSBG—Community Food, Nutrition	7,281	7,188	7,180 e	0 e
93.575	Child Care, Development Block Grant	2,086,344	2,087,310	2,082,921 e	2,082,910 e
93.576	Refugee, Entrant—Discretionary	84,836	71,500	86,500 e	72,300 e
93.577	Early Learning Fund	32,506	33,580	35,712 e	0 e
93.579	U.S. Repatriation Program	1,000*	1,000*	1,000*e	1,300*e
93.581	Indian/Environmental Quality	2,499	1,416	3,000 e	3,000 e
93.582	Environmental Impacts/Indian Lands	1,196	0	1,200 e	0 e
93.583	Refugee, Entrant Assistance-Wilson	12,707	18,700	19,000 e	20,000 e
93.584	Refugee, Entrant Assistance—Targeted	44,240	44,000	44,000 e	44,000 e
93.586	State Court Improvement	13,279	13,280	13,253 e	13,465 e
93.587	Native American Languages	2,559	3,968	4,000 e	4,000 e
93.590	Community-Based Child Abuse Prevention	33,188	33,205	42,858 e	42,859 e
93.591	Domestic Violence Coalitions	12,640	12,565	12,563 e	12,599 e
93.592	Family Violence—Discretionary	10,591	14,362	14,417 e	14,221 e
93.593	Job Opportunities/Low-Income	4,407	5,432	5,436 e	0 e
93.594	Tribal Work Grants	7,633	7,558	7,558 e	7,558 e
93.595	Welfare Reform Research \ i	69,500	87,900	107,269 e	127,000 e
93.596	Child Care, Development	2,723,793 e	2,717,000	2,717,000 e	2,717,000 e
93.597	Access and Visitation Programs	10,000	10,000	10,000 e	12,000 e
93.598	Victims of Trafficking	6,661	9,863	9,920 e	9,915 e
93.599	Chafee Vouchers	41,725	44,730	46,623 e	59,999 e
93.600	Head Start	6,667,533	6,774,848	6,843,114 e	6,888,136 e
93.601	Child Support Enforcement	2,082	1,551	1,800 e	1,000 e
93.602	Assets/Independence Demonstration	22,325	24,675	24,704 e	24,699 e
93.603	Adoption Incentive Payments	14,927	17,896	31,846 e	31,846 e
93.604	Assistance for Torture Victims	9,935	9,900	9,900 e	9,900 e
93.612	Native American Programs	32,199	37,353	35,000 e	35,000 e
93.613	President's Committee/Disabilities	522	(a)	(a)	(a)
93.616	Mentoring Children of Prisoners	9,935	49,692	49,598 e	49,993 e
93.617	Voting/Individuals with Disabilities	13,000	9,941	9,919 e	9,919 e
93.618	Voting/P & A Systems	2,140	4,796	4,784 e	4,784 e
93.623	Basic Center Grant	49,473	49,165	49,786 e	48,787 e
93.630	Developmental Disabilities/Basic	107,355	111,493	109,840 e	109,840 e
93.631	Developmental Disabilities/Projects	12,079	11,562	11,542 e	11,529 e
93.632	Developmental Disabilities/University	24,962	26,803 e	31,549 e	31,548 e
93.643	Children's Justice Grants	17,000	17,000	17,000 e	17,000 e
93.645	Child Welfare Services	290,088	289,320	289,650 e	289,650 e
93.647	Social Services Research	(o)	(o)	(o)	(o)
93.648	Child Welfare Services Training	7,449	7,411	7,409 e	7,409 e
93.652	Adoption Opportunities	27,227	27,103	27,116 e	27,119 e
93.658	Foster Care	4,573,318	4,714,290	4,627,000 e	4,643,000 e
93.659	Adoption Assistance	1,481,956	1,544,634	1,703,000 e	1,797,000 e
93.667	Social Services Block Grant	1,700,000	1,700,000	1,700,000 e	1,700,000 e
93.669	Child Abuse, Neglect State Grants	21,870	21,883	27,280 e	27,280 e
93.670	Child Abuse, Neglect Discretionary	33,264	34,386	31,640 e	31,645 e
93.671	Family Violence/States, Indians	103,172	100,520	100,504 e	100,793 e
93.674	Chafee Foster Care Independence	139,962	184,692	186,623 e	199,999 e
93.676	Unaccompanied Alien Children	15,867	41,000	44,400 e	49,900 e
93.767	State Children's Insurance Program	5,381,640	4,924,221	4,725,018 e	4,082,400 e
93.768	Medicaid Infrastructure/Disabled	19,727	17,945	22,000 e	22,000 e
93.769	Independence, Employment	0	8,619	40,000 e	49,900 e
93.770	Medicare Prescription Drugs \ t	(n)	935,000	73,000 e	59,268,000 e
93.773	Medicare—Hospital Insurance \ t	150,970,000	163,764,336	178,889,000 e	182,624,000 e
93.774	Medicare—Supplementary \ t	121,628,633	131,546,451	146,565,000 e	152,548,000 e
93.775	Medicaid Fraud Control	120,300	131,500	149,400 e	161,600 e

Please see "Important Notes on the Tables, Footnotes," page 688.

Table 1. (continued)

Program number	ADMINISTRATIVE ENTITY/SUB-UNIT Program Title (abridged)	FY 2003 in $thousands	FY 2004 in $thousands	FY 2005 in $thousands	FY 2006 in $thousands
93.777	State Survey/Providers, Suppliers	399,398	401,569	486,839 e	495,515 e
93.778	Medicaid	169,105,405	184,381,051	188,535,007 e	215,570,809 e
93.779	Medicare, Medicaid Research	73,570	77,664	77,494 e	45,194 e
93.780	Grants to States/High-Risk Pools	0	40,000	40,000 e	0 e
93.781	Seed Grants/High-Risk Pools	690	3,513	0 e	0 e
93.782	Medicare Drug Assistance/Territories	(n)	35,000	0 e	0 e
93.783	Medicare Drug Assistance/States \ t	(n)	0	2,286,000 e	2,792,000 e
93.784	Reimbursement/Undocumented Aliens	(n)	0	250,000 e	250,000 e
93.785	Background Checks—Long-Term Care	(n)	2,298	11,702 e	11,000 e
93.786	State Pharmaceutical Assistance	(n)	0	62,500 e	62,500 e
93.822	Health Careers Opportunity Program	36,389	33,995	35,935 e	0 e
93.824	Area Health Education Centers	12,169	14,200	14,000 e	0 e
93.837	Heart, Vascular Diseases Research	1,230,551	1,309,557	1,243,088 e	1,245,746 e
93.838	Lung Diseases Research	509,239	508,457	429,979 e	430,899 e
93.839	Blood Diseases, Resources Research	385,009	388,910	336,193 e	336,912 e
93.846	Arthritis/Skin Diseases Research	388,743	407,411	412,180 e	410,469 e
93.847	Diabetes, Endocrinology, Metabolism	499,327 e	499,327	531,925 e	548,512 e
93.848	Digestive Diseases, Nutrition	386,689	386,689	411,931 e	424,774 e
93.849	Kidney Diseases, Urology, Hematology	373,654	373,654	398,070 e	410,492 e
93.853	Neuroscience, Neurological Disorders	1,277,300	1,317,606	1,348,338 e	1,354,250 e
93.855	Allergy, Immunology, Transplantation	468,468	574,861	599,163 e	607,771 e
93.856	Microbiology, Infectious Diseases	1,801,042	1,895,802	2,122,821 e	2,033,501 e
93.859	Biomedical Research, Training	1,760	1,849,215	1,574,716 e	1,882,780 e
93.865	Child Health, Development Research	918,577	928,032	935,688 e	940,266 e
93.866	Aging Research	802,431	832,176	849,232 e	852,578 e
93.867	Vision Research	523,968	523,968	541,980 e	555,563 e
93.879	Medical Library Assistance	64,073	66,321	66,619 e	65,777 e
93.884	Primary Care Medicine, Dentistry	82,439	75,634	83,535 e	0 e
93.887	Renovation/Health Care Facilities	298,049	298,048	308,972 e	0 e
93.888	Specially Selected Health Projects	(n)	56,136	0 e	0 e
93.889	Bioterrorism Hospital Preparedness	(n)	497,000	466,000 e	458,000 e
93.890	Healthy Communities Access Program	(n)	3,200	3,200 e	0 e
93.891	Alcohol Research Center Grants	26,171	29,893	31,876 e	32,468 e
93.894	Environmental Health Sciences	59,606	61,168	63,064 e	63,929 e
93.908	Nursing Education Loan Repayment	15,000	17,607	17,600 e	17,600 e
93.910	Family Life Centers	7,400	7,400	7,400 e	7,400 e
93.912	Rural Health Outreach, Development	28,913	29,913	27,710 e	28,900 e
93.913	Offices of Rural Health	6,975	6,900	7,400 e	7,400 e
93.914	HIV Emergency Relief Project Grants	597,256	595,342	587,426 e	587,426 e
93.917	HIV Care Formula Grants	999,308	1,030,309	1,059,875 e	1,059,875 e
93.918	Outpatient Early Intervention/HIV	174,729	184,104 e	186,656 e	186,994 e
93.919	Breast, Cervical Cancer Detection	192,598	167,280	174,280 e	174,280 e
93.923	Disadvantaged Health Faculty Loan	1,248	1,273	1,108 e	0 e
93.924	HIV/AIDS Dental Reimbursements	9,702	12,787	13,033 e	13,033 e
93.925	Health Professions Scholarships	46,000	45,496	45,000 e	9,000 e
93.926	Healthy Start Initiative	92,923	92,393	95,162 e	90,362 e
93.928	Projects of National Significance	25,000	25,000	25,000 e	25,000 e
93.932	Hawaiian Health Systems	6,920	10,474	12,285 e	12,285 e
93.933	Demonstration Projects/Indian Health	7,668	9,576	9,576 e	9,576 e
93.936	AIDS Research Loan Repayment	1,150	271	610 e	610 e
93.938	School Health Programs/HIV	1,451	34,059	34,059 e	35,594 e
93.939	HIV Prevention—Non-Governmental	72,457	72,457	65,351 e	65,351 e
93.940	HIV Prevention—Health Department	320,883	320,883	313,219 e	313,219 e
93.941	HIV Demonstration, Research	71,419	145,419	15,136 e	15,136 e
93.942	Research, Treatment/Lyme Disease	3,830	3,522	3,490 e	3,400 e
93.943	Epidemiologic Research/AIDS, HIV	23,445	23,445	38,785 e	38,785 e
93.944	HIV/AIDS Surveillance	47,532	47,532	61,171 e	61,171 e
93.945	Chronic Disease Prevention, Control	62,809	71,800	75,400 e	75,400 e
93.946	Motherhood, Infant Health Initiative	4,500	4,600	4,600 e	4,610 e
93.947	Tuberculosis Demonstration	501	508	1,416 e	1,416 e
93.952	Trauma Care	(a)	1,768	2,000 e	2,000 e
93.954	Tribal Recruitment/Health	580	580	580 e	580 e
93.958	Block Grants/Mental Health	415,283	412,840	410,953 e	410,953 e
93.959	Block Grants/Substance Abuse	1,666,235	1,690,189	1,686,777 e	1,686,777 e

Please see "Important Notes on the Tables, Footnotes," page 688.

Table 1. (continued)

Program number	ADMINISTRATIVE ENTITY/SUB-UNIT Program Title (abridged)	FY 2003 in $thousands	FY 2004 in $thousands	FY 2005 in $thousands	FY 2006 in $thousands
93.962	Health Administration Traineeships	1,099	1,045	1,035 e	1,035 e
93.964	Public Health Traineeships	1,705	1,501	1,501 e	0 e
93.965	Coal Miners Respiratory Impairment	6,000	5,800	5,800 e	5,800 e
93.969	Geriatric Education Centers	15,705	18,383	15,923 e	0 e
93.970	Health Professions/Indians	3,520	3,520	3,520 e	3,520 e
93.971	Health Preparatory/Indians	2,573	2,018	2,018 e	2,018 e
93.972	Health Professions Scholarship	9,259	9,287	9,287 e	9,287 e
93.974	Family Planning—Service Research	4,800	4,800	4,800 e	4,800 e
93.977	STD Control	5,175	5,184	5,184 e	5,651 e
93.978	STD Research	131,926	132,084	112,287 e	112,287 e
93.982	Mental Health Disaster Assistance	163,662	5,811	0 e	0 e
93.988	Diabetes Control Programs	27,352	28,576	29,071 e	29,911 e
93.989	International Research, Training	48,286	50,894	51,000 e	51,000 e
93.990	National Health Promotion	4,000	0	4,000 e	4,000 e
93.991	Health Services Block Grant	129,179	128,700	106,100 e	0 e
93.993	Public Health Research Accreditation	100	100	100 e	0 e
93.994	Maternal, Child Health Block Grant	593,482	589,399	585,970 e	596,702 e
93.995	Adolescent Family Life	25,000	25,000	25,000 e	25,000 e
93.996	Bioterrorism Training, Curriculum	27,753	26,600	26,000 e	26,000 e
	DEPARTMENT TOTAL: OUTLAYS	524,523,418	567,363,341	605,875,712	698,525,800
	CREDITS*	31,100*	30,982*	31,600*	29,900*

CORPORATION FOR NATIONAL AND COMMUNITY SERVICE

Program number	Program Title	FY 2003	FY 2004	FY 2005	FY 2006
94.002	Retired, Senior Volunteer Program	56,435	58,156	58,528 e	60,288 e
94.003	State Commissions	12,600	11,929	11,904 e	12,642 e
94.004	Learn and Serve/School, Community	32,250	32,060	32,300 e	32,300 e
94.005	Learn and Serve/Higher Education	10,665	10,687	10,750 e	10,750 e
94.006	AmeriCorps	162,863	312,147	287,680 e	275,000 e
94.007	Planning, Program Development	19,717	11,159	13,227 e	9,945 e
94.009	Training, Technical Assistance	13,500	13,500	13,500 e	13,500 e
94.011	Foster Grandparent Program	108,897	110,212	111,424 e	112,058 e
94.013	Volunteers in Service to America	96,674	93,731	94,240 e	96,428 e
94.016	Senior Companion Program	45,255	45,987	45,905 e	47,438 e
	DEPARTMENT TOTAL: OUTLAYS	558,856	699,568	679,458	670,349
	CREDITS*	0*	0*	0*	0*

SOCIAL SECURITY ADMINISTRATION

Program number	Program Title	FY 2003	FY 2004	FY 2005	FY 2006
96.001	Social Security—Disability \t	69,788,000	76,212,000	81,749,000 e	87,608,000 e
96.002	Social Security—Retirement \t	330,606,100	343,652,000	358,737,000 e	375,580,000 e
96.003	Special Benefits/Age 72, Over \t	50	29	15 e	0 e
96.004	Survivors Insurance \t	63,519,500	64,184,000	66,167,000 e	68,248,000 e
96.006	Supplemental Security Income	32,535,000	33,661,000	38,611,000 e	38,203,000 e
96.007	Research and Demonstration \t	14,868	22,690	18,285 e	16,338 e
96.008	Benefits Planning, Outreach \t	23,000	23,000	23,000 e	23,000 e
96.009	Incentives/Disabled Beneficiaries \t	7,000	7,000	7,000 e	7,000 e
96.020	Benefits/World War II Veterans	9,238	9,544	10,000 e	11,000 e
	DEPARTMENT TOTAL: OUTLAYS	496,502,756	517,771,263	545,322,300	569,696,338
	CREDITS*	0*	0*	0*	0*

DEPARTMENT OF HOMELAND SECURITY

Program number	Program Title	FY 2003	FY 2004	FY 2005	FY 2006
97.001	Earmarked Projects	(a)	(a)	(a)	(a)
97.002	Research Projects	(a)	(a)	(a)	(a)
97.004	State Domestic Preparedness	325,639	(o)	(o)	(o)
97.005	State, Local Training Program	233,000	135,000	160,000 e	0 e
97.006	State, Local Exercise Support	112,000	0	50,000 e	0 e
97.007	Preparedness Technical Assistance	88,000	34,625	51,081 e	7,600 e
97.008	Urban Areas Security Initiative	97,000	854,035	854,657 e	1,020,000 e
97.009	Cuban/Haitian Entrant Program	7,500	11,990	9,000 e	9,000 e
97.010	Citizenship Education, Training	30	30	30 e	30 e

Please see "Important Notes on the Tables, Footnotes," page 688.

Program Funding Levels—Summary Tables 723

97.011	Boating Safety	14,187	17,500	17,750 e	17,750 e
97.012	Boating Safety Financial \ t	60,005	60,000	64,000 e	64,000 e
97.013	Oil Spill Trust Fund \ t	0	0	0 e	0 e
97.014	Bridge Alteration	0	19,250	0 e	0 e
97.015	Secret Service—Training Activities	571	0	0 e	0 e
97.016	Firefighting/Federal Property	0	85	0 e	0 e
97.017	Pre-Disaster Mitigation Grants	13,434	63,162	132,585 e	132,585 e
97.018	National Fire Academy Training	1,400	1,400	0 e	0 e
97.019	Fire Academy Educational Program	7,875	1,505	0 e	0 e
97.020	Hazardous Materials Training	188	159	181 e	181 e
97.021	Hazardous Materials Assistance	304	79	123 e	123 e
97.022	Flood Insurance \ r	109,343*	110,472*	112,593*e	112,593*e
97.023	Community Assistance Program \ r	6,083	1,326	8,901 e	8,901 e
97.024	Emergency Food, Shelter	152,000	152,097	153,000 e	153,000 e
97.025	National Urban Search, Rescue	52,575	51,716	7,000 e	7,000 e
97.026	EMI—Training Assistance	1,379	1,436	1,300 e	0 e
97.027	EMI—Independent Study	(a)	1,405	422 e	422 e
97.028	EMI—Resident Education	4,860	4,860	0 e	0 e
97.029	Flood Mitigation Assistance	10,235	1,867	18,000 e	18,000 e
97.030	Community Disaster Loans	35*	129*	567*e	567*e
97.031	Cora Brown Fund \ t	49	200	0 e	0 e
97.032	Crisis Counseling	92,516	9,522	41,193 e	0 e
97.033	Disaster Legal Services	91	43	124 e	0 e
97.034	Disaster Unemployment Assistance	19,043	72,681	27,036 e	0 e
97.036	Disaster Grants—Public Assistance	4,112,096	287,130	2,475,684 e	2,475,684 e
97.039	Hazard Mitigation Grant	647,580	114,599	0 e	0 e
97.040	Chemical Stockpile Emergency	84,473	56,746	54,871 e	54,873 e
97.041	Dam Safety	3,509	2,865	3,404 e	3,040 e
97.042	Emergency Management Performance	166,180	178,277	178,828 e	170,000 e
97.043	State Fire Training Systems Grants	1,400	1,400	1,400 e	1,400 e
97.044	Assistance to Firefighters Grant	345,000	720,000	633,500 e	500,000 e
97.045	Cooperating Technical Partners	10,391	46,981	40,000 e	40,000 e
97.046	Fire Management Assistance	70,581	49,460	60,435 e	60,435 e
97.047	Pre-Disaster Mitigation	25,000	148,810	150,000 e	0 e
97.048	Individual, Household Housing	202,759	1,260,676	0 e	0 e
97.049	Disaster Housing Operations	0 e	240,073	2,375,545 e	0 e
97.050	Individuals, Households/Other	0	30,667	66,189 e	0 e
97.053	Citizen Corps	25,000	39,763	13,486 e	0 e
97.055	Interoperable Communications	79,750	79,750	0 e	0 e
97.056	Port Security Grant Program	170,000	179,000	150,000 e	0 e
97.057	Intercity Bus Security	5,000	10,000	10,000 e	0 e
97.058	Operation Safe Commerce	30,000	17,000	0 e	0 e
97.059	Truck Security	19,700	22,000	5,000 e	0 e
97.060	Port Security Research, Development	9,200	0	0 e	0 e
97.061	Centers for Homeland Security	(n)	16,000	31,000 e	38,500 e
97.062	Scholars and Fellows	2,500	3,750	10,900 e	16,800 e
97.064	Debris Removal Insurance	(n)	999,900	0 e	0 e
97.065	Advanced Research Projects Agency	(n)	1,300	4,000 e	4,000 e
97.066	Information Technology, Evaluation	(n)	9,000	24,000 e	0 e
97.067	Homeland Security Grant Program \ i	(n)	2,220,000	2,610,000 e	2,090 e
97.068	Competitive Training Grants	(n)	33,600	30,000 e	0 e
97.069	Aviation Research Grants	15,000	42,371	15,535 e	23,721 e
97.070	Map Modernization Management Support	1,890	4,754	7,755 e	7,755 e
97.071	Metropolitan Medical Response System	49,100	50,000	22,281,408 e	0 e
97.072	Explosives Detection Canine Team	10,101	17,200	20,000 e	20,000 e
97.073	State Homeland Security Program	(n)	1,669,419	1,062,285 e	1,020,000 e
97.074	Law Enforcement Terrorism Prevention	(n)	497,050	386,286 e	0 e
97.075	Rail and Transit Security	(n)	0	150,000 e	0 e
97.076	Center/Missing, Exploited Children	(n)	4,970	5,200 e	5,000 e
97.077	Testing, Evaluation, Demonstration \ p	(n)	(n)	1,000 e	1,000 e
97.078	Buffer Zone Protection Plan	(n)	(n)	92,000 e	50,000 e
97.079	Public Alert Radios for Schools	(n)	(n)	500 e	1,500 e
97.080	IAIP Pilot Projects	(n)	(n)	60,000 e	60,000 e
97.081	Law Enforcement Training, Technical	(n)	1,415	1,622 e	1,622 e
97.082	Earthquake Consortium	(n)	750	810 e	800 e
97.083	Staffing/Fire, Emergency	(n)	(n)	65,000 e	0 e
97.084	Hurricane Katrina Case Management \ t	(n)	(n)	(n)	66,000 e
97.085	9/11 Heroes Stamp Program \ t	(n)	(n)	(n)	10,565 e

Please see "Important Notes on the Tables, Footnotes," page 688.

97.086	Outreach, Education, Technical		(n)	(n)	(n)	2,500 e
97.088	Disaster Assistance Projects		(n)	0 e	0 e	0 e
97.089	Real ID Program		(n)	(n)	0 e	6,000 e
	DEPARTMENT TOTAL:	OUTLAYS	7,386,174	10,552,649	34,674,026	6,081,877
		CREDITS*	109,378*	110,601*	113,160*	113,160*

UNITED STATES AGENCY FOR INTERNATIONAL DEVELOPMENT

98.001	Foreign Assistance Programs		2,877	4,374	4,267 e	4,078 e
98.002	Cooperative Development Program		5,500	5,500	5,500 e	5,500 e
98.003	Ocean Freight Reimbursement		2,800	2,700	2,700 e	2,700 e
98.004	NGO Strengthening		3,801	6,139	6,159 e	6,159 e
98.005	Institutional Capacity Building		5,000	5,000	5,000 e	0 e
98.006	American Schools, Hospitals Abroad		16,951	18,890	19,089 e	19,800 e
98.007	Food for Peace DAP \ p		172,271	377,362	360,997 e	464,000 e
98.008	Food for Peace Emergency Program \ p		363,619	293,074	226,140 e	0 e
98.009	John Ogonowski Farmer-to-Farmer		10,587	10,702	10,656 e	10,661 e
98.010	Denton Program		50	50	50 e	50 e
98.011	Global Development Alliance		273,000	342,000	359,000 e	377,000 e
98.012	USAID/University Partnerships		(n)	14,297	22,500 e	31,000 e
	DEPARTMENT TOTAL:	OUTLAYS	856,456	1,080,088	1,022,058	920,948
		CREDITS*	0*	0*	0*	0*
	GRAND TOTAL:	OUTLAYS	1,393,891,308	1,487,110,185	1,588,247,534	1,670,913,419
		CREDITS*	386,845,038*	345,280,797*	363,076,952*	345,793,441*
	GRAND TOTAL: OUTLAYS + CREDITS		1,780,736,346	1,832,390,982	1,951,324,486	2,016,706,860

Please see "Important Notes on the Tables, Footnotes," page 688.

Table 2. Summary of Estimated Outlays/Credits, by Federal Department or Agency (FY 03, 04, 05, 06)

Program Series	DEPARTMENT OR AGENCY	FY 2003 in $thousands	FY 2004 in $thousands	FY 2005 in $thousands	FY 2006 in $thousands
10.000	**DEPARTMENT OF AGRICULTURE**				
	Total Outlays	78,982,129	72,716,321	83,351,853	78,546,076
	Total Credits	28,699,308	28,514,933	27,002,804	20,060,111
	TOTAL OUTLAYS + CREDITS	107,681,437	101,231,254	110,354,657	98,606,187
11.000	**DEPARTMENT OF COMMERCE**				
	Total Outlays	1,965,130	3,221,390	3,584,775	3,085,128
	Total Credits	62,300	100,000	64,000	59,000
	TOTAL OUTLAYS + CREDITS	2,027,430	3,321,390	3,648,775	3,144,128
12.000	**DEPARTMENT OF DEFENSE**				
	Total Outlays	1,668,952	1,831,112	1,672,492	1,329,120
	Total Credits	0	0	0	0
	TOTAL OUTLAYS + CREDITS	1,668,952	1,831,112	1,672,492	1,329,120
14.000	**DEPARTMENT OF HOUSING AND URBAN DEVELOPMENT**				
	Total Outlays	38,653,260	42,801,403	42,387,647	36,240,766
	Total Credits	171,037,308	132,583,670	138,045,935	136,930,716
	TOTAL OUTLAYS + CREDITS	209,690,568	175,385,073	180,433,582	173,171,482
15.000	**DEPARTMENT OF THE INTERIOR**				
	Total Outlays	3,210,942	3,345,165	3,491,459	3,263,463
	Total Credits	5,496	6,417	6,332	6,348
	TOTAL OUTLAYS + CREDITS	3,216,438	3,351,582	3,497,791	3,269,811
16.000	**DEPARTMENT OF JUSTICE**				
	Total Outlays	5,127,845	4,219,979	4,035,257	2,202,813
	Total Credits	0	0	0	0
	TOTAL OUTLAYS + CREDITS	5,127,845	4,219,979	4,035,257	2,202,813
17.000	**DEPARTMENT OF LABOR**				
	Total Outlays	53,501,102	53,149,310	46,352,281	46,461,692
	Total Credits	0	0	0	0
	TOTAL OUTLAYS + CREDITS	53,501,102	53,149,310	46,352,281	46,461,692
19.000	**DEPARTMENT OF STATE**				
	Total Outlays	285,426	809,530	777,847	605,013
	Total Credits	0	0	0	0
	TOTAL OUTLAYS + CREDITS	285,426	809,530	777,847	605,013
20.000	**DEPARTMENT OF TRANSPORTATION**				
	Total Outlays	44,268,712	48,905,283	51,368,312	53,179,975
	Total Credits	29,351	19,315	46,816	8,000
	TOTAL OUTLAYS + CREDITS	44,298,063	48,924,598	51,415,128	53,187,975
21.000	**DEPARTMENT OF THE TREASURY**				
	Total Outlays	1,146,685	1,204,075	1,182,221	1,131,916
	Total Credits	0	0	0	0
	TOTAL OUTLAYS + CREDITS	1,146,685	1,204,075	1,182,221	1,131,916
23.000	**APPALACHIAN REGIONAL COMMISSION**				
	Total Outlays	534,550	552,898	603,257	599,300
	Total Credits	0	0	0	0
	TOTAL OUTLAYS + CREDITS	534,550	552,898	603,257	599,300
27.000	**OFFICE OF PERSONNEL MANAGEMENT**				
	Total Outlays	0	0	0	0
	Total Credits	0	0	0	0
	TOTAL OUTLAYS + CREDITS	0	0	0	0

Please see "Important Notes on the Tables, Footnotes," page 688.

Table 2. (continued)

Program Series	DEPARTMENT OR AGENCY	FY 2003 in $thousands	FY 2004 in $thousands	FY 2005 in $thousands	FY 2006 in $thousands
29.000	**COMMISSION ON CIVIL RIGHTS**				
	Total Outlays	8,500	8,740	8,740	8,740
	Total Credits	0	0	0	0
	TOTAL OUTLAYS + CREDITS	8,500	8,740	8,740	8,740
30.000	**EQUAL EMPLOYMENT OPPORTUNITY COMMISSION**				
	Total Outlays	354,506	357,526	359,363	364,228
	Total Credits	0	0	0	0
	TOTAL OUTLAYS + CREDITS	354,506	357,526	359,363	364,228
32.000	**FEDERAL COMMUNICATIONS COMMISSION**				
	Total Outlays	0	0	0	0
	Total Credits	0	0	0	0
	TOTAL OUTLAYS + CREDITS	0	0	0	0
33.000	**FEDERAL MARITIME COMMISSION**				
	Total Outlays	620	620	637	657
	Total Credits	0	0	0	0
	TOTAL OUTLAYS + CREDITS	620	620	637	657
34.000	**FEDERAL MEDIATION AND CONCILIATION SERVICE**				
	Total Outlays	42,645	44,619	44,929	43,822
	Total Credits	0	0	0	0
	TOTAL OUTLAYS + CREDITS	42,645	44,619	44,929	43,822
36.000	**FEDERAL TRADE COMMISSION**				
	Total Outlays	176,553	187,871	204,324	211,000
	Total Credits	0	0	0	0
	TOTAL OUTLAYS + CREDITS	176,553	187,871	204,324	211,000
39.000	**GENERAL SERVICES ADMINISTRATION**				
	Total Outlays	69,521	67,952	96,383	99,115
	Total Credits	0	0	0	0
	TOTAL OUTLAYS + CREDITS	69,521	67,952	96,383	99,115
40.000	**GOVERNMENT PRINTING OFFICE**				
	Total Outlays	60,603	62,304	57,640	60,306
	Total Credits	0	0	0	0
	TOTAL OUTLAYS + CREDITS	60,603	62,304	57,640	60,306
42.000	**LIBRARY OF CONGRESS**				
	Total Outlays	92,349	93,063	104,583	112,128
	Total Credits	0	0	0	0
	TOTAL OUTLAYS + CREDITS	92,349	93,063	104,583	112,128
43.000	**NATIONAL AERONAUTICS AND SPACE ADMINISTRATION**				
	Total Outlays	57,557	88,309	61,600	52,340
	Total Credits	0	0	0	0
	TOTAL OUTLAYS + CREDITS	57,557	88,309	61,600	52,340
44.000	**NATIONAL CREDIT UNION ADMINISTRATION**				
	Total Outlays	0	0	0	0
	Total Credits	328,000	282,981	253,000	266,000
	TOTAL OUTLAYS + CREDITS	328,000	282,981	253,000	266,000
45.000	**NATIONAL FOUNDATION ON THE ARTS AND THE HUMANITIES**				
	Total Outlays	404,720	459,565	444,548	461,255
	Total Credits	0	0	0	0
	TOTAL OUTLAYS + CREDITS	404,720	459,565	444,548	461,255
46.000	**NATIONAL LABOR RELATIONS BOARD**				
	Total Outlays	238,982	242,526	249,959	252,367
	Total Credits	0	0	0	0
	TOTAL OUTLAYS + CREDITS	238,982	242,526	249,959	252,367

Please see "Important Notes on the Tables, Footnotes," page 688.

Table 2. (continued)

Program Series	DEPARTMENT OR AGENCY	FY 2003 in $thousands	FY 2004 in $thousands	FY 2005 in $thousands	FY 2006 in $thousands
47.000	**NATIONAL SCIENCE FOUNDATION**				
	Total Outlays	4,677,910	4,841,590	4,709,090	4,667,360
	Total Credits	0	0	0	0
	TOTAL OUTLAYS + CREDITS	4,677,910	4,841,590	4,709,090	4,667,360
57.000	**RAILROAD RETIREMENT BOARD**				
	Total Outlays	9,063,000	9,105,000	9,383,000	9,597,000
	Total Credits	0	0	0	0
	TOTAL OUTLAYS + CREDITS	9,063,000	9,105,000	9,383,000	9,597,000
58.000	**SECURITIES AND EXCHANGE COMMISSION**				
	Total Outlays	619,322	755,012	888,000	888,000
	Total Credits	0	0	0	0
	TOTAL OUTLAYS + CREDITS	619,322	755,012	888,000	888,000
59.000	**SMALL BUSINESS ADMINISTRATION**				
	Total Outlays	230,340	281,093	281,319	271,636
	Total Credits	14,403,198	9,957,126	26,635,583	26,757,480
	TOTAL OUTLAYS + CREDITS	14,633,538	10,238,219	26,916,902	27,029,116
64.000	**DEPARTMENT OF VETERANS AFFAIRS**				
	Total Outlays	57,278,745	73,054,411	78,597,654	81,415,357
	Total Credits	40,212,249	44,213,008	45,083,722	45,006,726
	TOTAL OUTLAYS + CREDITS	97,490,994	117,267,419	123,681,376	126,422,083
66.000	**ENVIRONMENTAL PROTECTION AGENCY**				
	Total Outlays	4,329,690	4,022,899	3,616,543	3,264,547
	Total Credits	0	0	0	0
	TOTAL OUTLAYS + CREDITS	4,329,690	4,022,899	3,616,543	3,264,547
68.000	**NATIONAL GALLERY OF ART**				
	Total Outlays	954	912	954	995
	Total Credits	0	0	0	0
	TOTAL OUTLAYS + CREDITS	954	912	954	995
70.000	**OVERSEAS PRIVATE INVESTMENT CORPORATION**				
	Total Outlays	19,000	0	0	0
	Total Credits	2,884,000	4,068,000	3,578,000	3,785,000
	TOTAL OUTLAYS + CREDITS	2,903,000	4,068,000	3,578,000	3,785,000
78.000	**COMMODITY FUTURES TRADING COMMISSION**				
	Total Outlays	67,850	67,850	70,400	70,400
	Total Credits	0	0	0	0
	TOTAL OUTLAYS + CREDITS	67,850	67,850	70,400	70,400
81.000	**DEPARTMENT OF ENERGY**				
	Total Outlays	1,291,642	1,905,330	1,978,594	1,957,500
	Total Credits	0	0	0	0
	TOTAL OUTLAYS + CREDITS	1,291,642	1,905,330	1,978,594	1,957,500
84.000	**DEPARTMENT OF EDUCATION**				
	Total Outlays	53,226,116	55,905,834	57,204,017	59,224,247
	Total Credits	129,043,350	125,393,764	122,216,000	112,771,000
	TOTAL OUTLAYS + CREDITS	182,269,466	181,299,598	179,420,017	171,995,247
85.000	**SCHOLARSHIP AND FELLOWSHIP FOUNDATIONS**				
	Total Outlays	8,384	8,293	9,610	6,883
	Total Credits	0	0	0	0
	TOTAL OUTLAYS + CREDITS	8,384	8,293	9,610	6,883
86.000	**PENSION BENEFIT GUARANTY CORPORATION**				
	Total Outlays	2,277,000	2,971,713	3,273,000	5,192,000
	Total Credits	0	0	0	0
	TOTAL OUTLAYS + CREDITS	2,277,000	2,971,713	3,273,000	5,192,000

Please see "Important Notes on the Tables, Footnotes," page 688.

Table 2. (continued)

Program Series	DEPARTMENT OR AGENCY	FY 2003 in $thousands	FY 2004 in $thousands	FY 2005 in $thousands	FY 2006 in $thousands
88.000	**ARCHITECTURAL AND TRANSPORTATION BARRIERS COMPLIANCE BOARD**				
	Total Outlays	5,013	5,160	5,369	5,686
	Total Credits	0	0	0	0
	TOTAL OUTLAYS + CREDITS	5,013	5,160	5,369	5,686
89.000	**NATIONAL ARCHIVES AND RECORDS ADMINISTRATION**				
	Total Outlays	53,947	89,825	86,177	83,921
	Total Credits	0	0	0	0
	TOTAL OUTLAYS + CREDITS	53,947	89,825	86,177	83,921
90.000	**INDEPENDENT BOARDS AND COMMISSIONS**				
	Total Outlays	60,671	2,255,702	126,646	56,855
	Total Credits	0	0	0	0
	TOTAL OUTLAYS + CREDITS	60,671	2,255,702	126,646	56,855
91.000	**UNITED STATES INSTITUTE OF PEACE**				
	Total Outlays	2,775	3,091	3,500	4,500
	Total Credits	0	0	0	0
	TOTAL OUTLAYS + CREDITS	2,775	3,091	3,500	4,500
93.000	**DEPARTMENT OF HEALTH AND HUMAN SERVICES**				
	Total Outlays	524,523,418	567,363,341	605,875,712	698,525,800
	Total Credits	31,100	30,982	31,600	29,900
	TOTAL OUTLAYS + CREDITS	524,554,518	567,394,323	605,907,312	698,555,700
94.000	**CORPORATION FOR NATIONAL AND COMMUNITY SERVICE**				
	Total Outlays	558,856	699,568	679,458	670,349
	Total Credits	0	0	0	0
	TOTAL OUTLAYS + CREDITS	558,856	699,568	679,458	670,349
96.000	**SOCIAL SECURITY ADMINISTRATION**				
	Total Outlays	496,502,756	517,771,263	545,322,300	569,696,338
	Total Credits	0	0	0	0
	TOTAL OUTLAYS + CREDITS	496,502,756	517,771,263	545,322,300	569,696,338
97.000	**DEPARTMENT OF HOMELAND SECURITY**				
	Total Outlays	7,386,174	10,552,649	34,674,026	6,081,877
	Total Credits	109,378	110,601	113,160	113,160
	TOTAL OUTLAYS + CREDITS	7,495,552	10,663,250	34,787,186	6,195,037
98.000	**UNITED STATES AGENCY FOR INTERNATIONAL DEVELOPMENT**				
	Total Outlays	856,456	1,080,088	1,022,058	920,948
	Total Credits	0	0	0	0
	TOTAL OUTLAYS + CREDITS	856,456	1,080,088	1,022,058	920,948
	GRAND TOTAL: OUTLAYS	1,393,891,308	1,487,110,185	1,588,247,534	1,670,913,419
	CREDITS	386,845,038	345,280,797	363,076,952	345,793,441
	GRAND TOTAL: OUTLAYS + CREDITS	1,780,736,346	1,832,390,982	1,951,324,486	2,016,706,860

Please see "Important Notes on the Tables, Footnotes," page 688.

Table 3. The Fifty Largest Domestic Assistance Programs in FY 2005, by Funds Outlayed or Credited

Program number	PROGRAM TITLE (abridged)	Outlays in $thousands	Credits in $thousands	Totals in $thousands	Rank
96.002	Social Security—Retirement \ t	358,737,000	0	358,737,000	1
93.778	Medicaid	188,535,007	0	188,535,007	2
93.773	Medicare—Hospital Insurance \ t	178,889,000	0	178,889,000	3
93.774	Medicare—Supplementary \ t	146,565,000	0	146,565,000	4
14.117	Mortgage Insurance—Homes \ i, u	0	116,500,000	116,500,000	5
84.032	Family Education Loans	0	99,320,000	99,320,000	6
96.001	Social Security—Disability \ t	81,749,000	0	81,749,000	7
96.004	Survivors Insurance \ t	66,167,000	0	66,167,000	8
64.114	Veterans Housing—Loans \ u	0	45,000,000	45,000,000	9
96.006	Supplemental Security Income	38,611,000	0	38,611,000	10
17.225	Unemployment Insurance \ t	38,573,138	0	38,573,138	11
20.205	Highway Planning, Construction \ i, t	35,092,362	0	35,092,362	12
64.009	Veterans Medical Care Benefits	29,984,283	0	29,984,283	13
10.551	Food Stamps	29,713,003	0	29,713,003	14
64.109	Service-Connected Disability	24,618,886	0	24,618,886	15
84.268	Federal Direct Student Loans	0	22,896,000	22,896,000	16
97.071	Metropolitan Medical Response System	22,281,408	0	22,281,408	17
93.558	Temporary Assistance/Families	19,248,581	0	19,248,581	18
59.012	Small Business Loans	0	16,063,388	16,063,388	19
14.871	Section 8 Housing Choice Vouchers	14,965,804	0	14,965,804	20
84.010	Title I Grants	12,739,571	0	12,739,571	21
84.063	Pell Grant Program	12,364,997	0	12,364,997	22
14.133	Mortgage Insurance—Condominiums \ i, u	0	11,189,619	11,189,619	23
84.027	Special Education—State Grants	10,589,746	0	10,589,746	24
10.085	Tobacco Transition Payments \ u	10,000,000	0	10,000,000	25
10.051	Commodity Loans, Deficiency Payments \ u	0	9,493,384	9,493,384	26
57.001	Social Insurance/Railroad Workers \ t	9,383,000	0	9,383,000	27
10.555	School Lunch Program \ p	8,068,972	0	8,068,972	28
93.600	Head Start	6,843,114	0	6,843,114	29
20.507	Urbanized Area Formula Grants \ t	6,825,372	0	6,825,372	30
14.195	Section 8—Special Allocations	6,326,435	0	6,326,435	31
10.450	Crop Insurance \ u	2,043,929	3,926,144	5,970,073	32
10.055	Direct, Counter-Cyclical Payments \ u	5,944,800	0	5,944,800	33
14.311	Single Family Property Disposition \ i, p	5,675,542	0	5,675,542	34
59.041	Certified Development Company Loans	29,347	5,000,000	5,029,347	35
10.557	Nutrition/Women, Infants, Children	4,773,250	0	4,773,250	36
93.767	State Children's Insurance Program	4,725,018	0	4,725,018	37
93.658	Foster Care	4,627,000	0	4,627,000	38
64.110	Dependency, Indemnity Compensation	4,268,410	0	4,268,410	39
64.012	Veterans Prescription Service \ p	4,260,089	0	4,260,089	40
93.563	Child Support Enforcement	4,056,465	0	4,056,465	41
14.135	Mortgage Insurance—Market Rate \ i, u	0	4,037,000	4,037,000	42
20.106	Airport Improvement Program \ t	3,500,000	0	3,500,000	43
20.500	Capital Investment Grants \ t	3,421,571	0	3,421,571	44
59.009	Procurement Assistance	34,188	3,250,000	3,284,188	45
86.001	Pension Plan Termination Insurance \ u	3,273,000	0	3,273,000	46
10.850	Rural Electrification Loans \ u	0	2,918,240	2,918,240	47
84.367	Improving Teacher Quality	2,916,605	0	2,916,605	48
14.218	CDBG/Entitlement	2,876,923	0	2,876,923	49
10.073	Crop Disaster Program	2,750,000	0	2,750,000	50

Please see "Important Notes on the Tables, Footnotes," page 688.

Table 4. The Fifty Smallest Domestic Assistance Programs in FY 2005, by Funds Outlayed or Credited *

Program number	PROGRAM TITLE (abridged)	Outlays in $actual	Credits in $actual	Totals in $actual	Rank
16.003	Narcotics, Drugs/Publications	1,600	0	1,600	1
20.812	Construction Reserve Fund	10,715	0	10,715	2
96.003	Special Benefits/Age 72, Over \ t	15,000	0	15,000	3
97.010	Citizenship Education, Training	30,000	0	30,000	4
64.128	Training/Spina Bifida	31,000	0	31,000	5
64.118	Housing—Disabled Veterans \ u	0	33,000	33,000	6
10.910	Rural Abandoned Mine Program	34,251	0	34,251	7
15.050	Indian Hunting, Fishing Rights	43,000	0	43,000	8
85.401	Udall Fellowship Program	48,000	0	48,000	9
12.900	Language Grant Program	50,000	0	50,000	10
15.254	Summer Watershed Intern	50,000	0	50,000	11
98.010	Denton Program	50,000	0	50,000	12
15.647	Migratory Bird Conservation	63,500	0	63,500	13
66.810	CEPP Technical Assistance	80,000	0	80,000	14
15.645	Marine Turtle Conservation	89,610	0	89,610	15
16.597	Motor Vehicle Theft Protection Act	98,664	0	98,664	16
15.506	Desalination Research, Development	100,000	0	100,000	17
93.202	Capacity Building/Indian Tribes	100,000	0	100,000	18
93.993	Public Health Research Accreditation	100,000	0	100,000	19
64.026	State Adult Day Health Care	118,362	0	118,362	20
11.002	Census Customer Services	118,500	0	118,500	21
15.644	Junior Duck Stamp Conservation \ p	119,000	0	119,000	22
97.021	Hazardous Materials Assistance	123,000	0	123,000	23
97.033	Disaster Legal Services	124,000	0	124,000	24
66.816	Underground Storage Tanks \ t	125,000	0	125,000	25
15.055	Alaskan Indian Allotments	134,000	0	134,000	26
85.402	Udall Congressional Internships	140,000	0	140,000	27
20.808	Capital Construction Fund	140,612	0	140,612	28
20.801	Ports, Intermodal Transportation	143,125	0	143,125	29
14.517	Early Doctoral Student Research	150,000	0	150,000	30
93.447	State Health Fraud Task Force	150,000	0	150,000	31
93.066	Vital Statistics Re-Engineering	171,500	0	171,500	32
11.408	Fishermen's Contingency Fund	175,000	0	175,000	33
11.006	Personal Census Search	180,000	0	180,000	34
97.020	Hazardous Materials Training	181,000	0	181,000	35
20.810	Supplementary Training	195,000	0	195,000	36
12.108	Snagging and Clearing	200,000	0	200,000	37
16.561	Visiting Fellowships	200,000	0	200,000	38
20.907	Minority Institutions	200,000	0	200,000	39
15.643	Alaska Migratory Bird Co-Management	221,000	0	221,000	40
15.057	Navajo-Hopi Settlement	225,000	0	225,000	41
66.812	Hazardous Waste Management/Tribes	297,600	0	297,600	42
15.926	American Battlefield Protection	300,000	0	300,000	43
84.275	Rehabilitation Training—General	300,000	0	300,000	44
15.923	Preservation Technology, Training	300,130	0	300,130	45
93.219	Scholarships/Indians	328,170	0	328,170	46
14.168	Land Sales	350,000	0	350,000	47
66.813	Treatment Technology Research	350,000	0	350,000	48
10.028	Wildlife Services	365,000	0	365,000	49
93.067	Global Aids	375,000	0	375,000	50

* Excluding programs without allocations when data were compiled

Please see "Important Notes on the Tables, Footnotes," page 688.

PART IV

Field Office Contacts

NOTE: Field offices manage specific programs, or they may provide information about programs. However, if the program description in Part II states "Note: no field offices for this program," contacts should be with the headquarters office. "PART I - Obtaining Federal Assistance" offers observations concerning field office contacts, especially in the discussion of the entry heading "⑩ *Program headquarters address and phone number*" on pages 22-23.

DEPARTMENT OF AGRICULTURE

AGRICULTURAL RESEARCH SERVICE

10.001 **REGIONAL OFFICES**

BELTSVILLE—Bldg. 003 - Rm.203, BARC-West, Beltsville, MD 20705. Phone: FTS (301)504-7019.

MIDSOUTH—Delta States Research Center, P.O. Box 225, Stoneville, MS 38776. Phone: FTS (601)686-5345.

MIDWEST—Northern Regional Research Center, 1815 N. University St., Peoria, IL 61604. Phone: FTS (700)360-4618.

NORTH ATLANTIC—Eastern Regional Research Center, 600 E. Mermaid Lane, Philadelphia, PA 19118. Phone: FTS (215)233-6551.

NORTHERN PLAINS—National Resources Research Center, Bldg.D - Ste.310, 2150 Centre Ave., Ft. Collins, CO 80525-5526. Phone: FTS (303)229-5513.

PACIFIC WEST—Western Regional Research Center, 800 Buchanan St., Albany, CA 94710. Phone: FTS (510)559-6016.

SOUTH ATLANTIC—Russell Research Center, College Station Rd., Athens, GA 30604-5677. Phone: FTS (706)546-3532.

SOUTHERN PLAINS—7607 Eastmark Dr. - Ste.230, College Station, TX 77840. Phone: FTS (979)960-9444.

ANIMAL AND PLANT HEALTH INSPECTION SERVICE

10.025 and 10.028 **REGIONAL OFFICES**

Plant Protection and Quarantine

CENTRAL *(Arkansas, Iowa, Kansas, Louisiana, Missouri, Nebraska, North Dakota, Oklahoma, South Dakota, Texas)*—3505 Boca Chica Blvd. - Ste.360, Brownsville, TX 78521-4065. Phone: (956)504-4150.

**10.025
and
10.028
(cont.)**

EASTERN *(Connecticut, Delaware, District of Columbia, Illinois, Indiana, Maine, Maryland, Massachusetts, Michigan, Minnesota, New Hampshire, New Jersey, New York, Ohio, Pennsylvania, Rhode Island, Vermont, Virginia, West Virginia, Wisconsin)*—Blason II - 2nd fl., 505 S. Lenola Rd., Moorestown, NJ 08057-1549. Phone: (609)968-4970.

SOUTHEAST *(Alabama, Florida, Georgia, Kentucky, Mississippi, North Carolina, Puerto Rico, South Carolina, Tennessee, Virgin Islands)*—Bldg. 1, 3505 25th Ave., Gulfport, MS 39501. Phone: (601)863-1813.

WESTERN *(Alaska, Arizona, California, Colorado, Guam, Hawaii, Idaho, Montana, Nevada, New Mexico, Oregon, Utah, Washington, Wyoming)*—9580 Micron Ave. - Ste.1, Sacramento, CA 95827. Phone: (916)857-6065.

Veterinary Services

CENTRAL *(Arkansas, Iowa, Kansas, Louisiana, Missouri, Nebraska, North Dakota, Oklahoma, South Dakota, Texas)*—100 W. Pioneer Pkwy. - Ste.100, Arlington, TX 76010. Phone: (817)276-2201.

NORTHERN *(Illinois, Indiana, Maryland, Massachusetts, Michigan, Minnesota, New Jersey, New York, Ohio, Pennsylvania, Virginia, West Virginia, Wisconsin)*—1 Winner's Circle - Ste.100, Albany, NY 12205. Phone (518)453-0103.

SOUTHEAST *(Alabama, Florida, Georgia, Kentucky, Mississippi, North Carolina, Puerto Rico, South Carolina, Tennessee)*—500 E. Zack St. - Ste.410, Tampa, FL 33602-3945. Phone: (813)228-2952.

WESTERN *(Alaska, Arizona, California, Colorado, Hawaii, Idaho, Montana, Nevada, New Mexico, Oregon, Utah, Washington, Wyoming)*—384 Inverness Dr. S. - Ste.150, Englewood, CO 80112. Phone (303)784-6202.

Wildlife Service

EASTERN *(Alabama, Arkansas, Connecticut, Delaware, District of Columbia, Florida, Georgia, Illinois, Indiana, Iowa, Louisiana, Kentucky, Maine, Maryland, Massachusetts, Michigan, Minnesota, Mississippi, Missouri, New Hampshire, New Jersey, New York, North Carolina, Ohio, Pennsylvania, Puerto Rico, Rhode Island, South Carolina, Tennessee, Vermont, Virginia, Virgin Islands, West Virginia, Wisconsin)*—3322 West End Ave. - Ste.301, Nashville, TN 37203. Phone: (615)736-2007.

WESTERN *(Alaska, Arizona, California, Colorado, Guam, Hawaii, Idaho, Kansas, Montana, Nebraska, Nevada, New Mexico, North Dakota, Oklahoma, Oregon, South Dakota, Texas, Utah, Washington, Wyoming)*—12345 W. Alameda Pkwy. - Ste.204, Lakewood, CO 80228. Phone: (303)969-6560.

■ National Wildlife Research Center, 1201 Oakridge Dr., Ft. Collins, CO 80525. Phone: (970)223-1588.

10.029 Applicants may obtain information about assistance from county offices by contacting those listed under **10.051**.

FARM SERVICE AGENCY

**10.051
thru
10.056**

STATE OFFICES

Alabama—4121 Carmichael Rd. - Ste.600, Montgomery, AL 36106-5013. Phone: (334)279-3500. *For mail:* P.O. Box 235013.

Alaska—800 W. Evergreen -Ste.216, Palmer, AK 99645-6389. Phone: (907)745-7982.

Arizona—77 E. Thomas Rd. - Ste.240, Phoenix, AZ 85012-3318. Phone: (602)640-5200.

FIELD OFFICE CONTACTS   733

Arkansas—Federal Bldg. - Rm.5416, 700 W. Capitol Ave., Little Rock, AR 72201-3225. Phone: (501)301-3000.

California—430 G St. - Ste.4161, Davis, CA 95616-4161. Phone: (530)792-5538.

Caribbean Area—Fernandez Junzos Station, Cobian's Plaza - Ste.309,P.O. Box 11188, 1607 Ponce DeLeon Ave., Santurce, PR 00909-0001. Phone: (809)729-6872.

Colorado—655 Parfet St. - Ste.E-305, Lakewood, CO 80215-5517. Phone: (303)236-2866.

Connecticut—88 Day Hill Rd., Windsor, CT 06095. Phone: (860)285-8483.

Delaware—1201 College Park Dr. - Ste.101, Dover, DE 19904-8713. Phone: (302)678-2547.

Florida—440 NW 25th Place - Ste.1, Gainesville, FL 32606. Phone: (352)379-4500.

Georgia—Federal Bldg. - Rm.102, 355 E. Hancock Ave., Athens, GA 30603-1907. Phone: (706)546-2266.

Hawaii—300 Ala Moana Blvd. - Rm.5106, P.O. Box 50008, Honolulu, HI 96850. Phone: (808)541-2644.

Idaho—9173 W. Barners - Ste.B, Boise, ID 83705-1511. Phone: (208)378-5650.

Illinois—3500 W Avenue, P.O. Box 19273, Springfield, IL 62794-9273. Phone: (217)241-6600.

Indiana—5981 Lakeside Blvd., Indianapolis, IN 46278. Phone: (317)290-3030, ext. 317.

Iowa—10500 Buena Vista Ct., Des Moines, IA 50322. Phone: (515)254-1540, ext.600.

Kansas—3600 Anderson Ave., Manhattan, KS 66502-2511. Phone: (785)539-3531.

Kentucky—771 Corporate Dr. - Ste.100, Lexington, KY 40503-5478. Phone: (606)224-7601.

Louisiana—3737 Government St., Alexandria, LA 71302-3395. Phone: (318)473-7721.

Maine—444 Stillwater Ave. - Ste.1, Bangor, ME 04402-0406. Phone: (207)990-9140.

Maryland—River Center - Ste.E, 8335 Guilford Rd., Columbia, MD 21046. Phone: (410)381-4550.

Massachusetts—445 West St., Amherst, MA 01002-2957. Phone: (413)256-0232.

Michigan—3001 Coolidge Rd. - Ste.100, East Lansing, MI 48823-6321. Phone: (517)337-6659, ext.1201.

Minnesota—400 Farm Credit Service Bldg., 375 Jackson St., St. Paul, MN 55101-1852. Phone: (612)602-7700.

Mississippi—6310 I-55 North, P.O. Box 14995, Jackson, MS 39211. Phone: (601)965-4300.

Missouri—Parkade Plaza, 601 Business Loop 70 West - Ste.225, Columbia, MO 65203. Phone: (573)876-0925.

Montana—10 E. Babcock - Rm.557, P.O. Box 670, Bozeman, MT 59715. Phone: (406)587-6872.

Nebraska—7131 A St., P.O. Box 57975, Lincoln, NE 68510-7975. Phone: (402)437-5581.

Nevada—1755 E. Plumb Lane - Ste.202, Reno, NV 89502-3207. Phone: (702)784-5411.

New Hampshire—22 Bridge St. - 4th fl., P.O. Box 1388, Concord, NH 03302-1338. Phone: (603)224-7941.

New Jersey—Mastoris Professional Plaza, Bldg. 2 - Ste.E, 163 Rt. 130, Bordentown, NJ 08505-2249. Phone: (609)298-3446.

New Mexico—6200 Jefferson St. NE, Albuquerque, NM 87109. Phone: (505)761-4900.

New York—441 S. Salina St. - (5th fl.) Ste.356, Syracuse, NY 13202-2455. Phone: (315)477-6303.

10.051 thru 10.056 (cont.)

North Carolina—4407 Bland Rd. - Ste.175, Raleigh, NC 27609-6296. Phone: (919) 875-4800.

North Dakota—1025 28th St. SW, P.O. Box 3046, Fargo, ND 58108. Phone: (701)239-5205.

Ohio—Federal Bldg. - Rm.540, 200 N. High St., Columbus, OH 43215. Phone: (614)469-6735.

Oklahoma—100 USDA - Ste.102, Farm Rd. and McFarland St., Stillwater, OK 74074-2653. Phone: (405)742-1130.

Oregon—7620 SW Mohawk, P.O. Box 1300, Tualatin, OR 97062-8121. Phone: (503) 692-6830.

Pennsylvania—One Credit Union Pl. - Ste.320, Harrisburg, PA 17110-2994. Phone: (717)237-2113.

Rhode Island—West Bay Office Complex - Rm.40, 60 Quaker Lane, Warwick, RI 02886-0111. Phone: (401)828-8232.

South Carolina—1927 Thurmond Mall - Ste.100, Columbia, SC 29201-2375. Phone: (803)806-3830.

South Dakota—Federal Bldg. - Rm.308, 200 4th St. SW, Huron, SD 57350-2478. Phone: (605)352-1160.

Tennessee—U.S. Courthouse - Rm.579, 801 Broadway, Nashville, TN 37203-3816. Phone: (615)736-5555.

Texas—Commerce National Bank Bldg. - 2nd fl., 2405 Texas Ave. S., College Station, TX 77840. Phone: (409)260-9207. *For mail:* P.O. Box 2900, College Station, TX 77841-0001.

Utah—125 S. State St. - Rm.4239, P.O. Box 11350, Salt Lake City, UT 84147-0350. Phone: (801)524-5013.

Vermont—Executive Square Office Bldg., 346 Shelburne St., Burlington, VT 05401-4995. Phone: (802)658-2803.

Virginia—Culpeper Bldg. - Ste.138, 1606 Santa Rosa Rd., Richmond, VA 23229. Phone: (804)287-1500.

Washington—Rock Pointe Tower - Ste.568, 316 W. Boone Ave., Spokane, WA 99201-2350. Phone: (509)323-3000.

West Virginia—New Federal Bldg. - Rm.239, 75 High St., P.O. Box 1049, Morgantown, WV 26507-1049. Phone: (304)291-4351.

Wisconsin—6515 Watts Rd. - Rm.100, Madison, WI 53719-2797. Phone: (608)276-8732, ext.100.

Wyoming—951 Werner Ct. - Ste.130, Casper, WY 82601-1307. Phone: (307)261-5231.

10.062 and 10.064 Listed under **10.900**.

10.066 and 10.069 Listed under **10.051**.

10.070 and 10.072 Listed under **10.900**.

10.073 thru 10.077 Listed under **10.051**.

10.080 thru 10.085 Liseted under **10.051**.

AGRICULTURAL MARKETING SERVICE

10.153 thru 10.163

COTTON DIVISION

Grading, Marketing Services (including Market News)

3275 Appling Rd., Memphis, TN 38133. Phone: (901)384-3000.

Standardization and Quality Assurance Branch

3275 Appling Rd., Memphis, TN 38133. Phone: (901)384-3015.

DAIRY DIVISION

Dairy Inspection, Grading Branch and Laboratory

Bldg. A - Ste.370, 800 Roosevelt Rd., Glen Ellyn, IL 60137. Phone: (708)790-6920.

Market News Service

2811 Agricultural Dr., Madison, WI 53704-6777. Phone: (608)224-5080.

FRUIT AND VEGETABLE DIVISION

Fresh and Processed Products

Alabama—1557 Reeves St., P.O. Box 1368, Dothan, AL 36302. Phone: (334)792-5185.

Arizona—1688 W. Adams - Rm.415, Phoenix, AZ 85007. Phone: (602)542-0880.

California—1320 E. Olympic Ave. - Rm.212, Los Angeles, CA 90021. Phones: (213) 894-2489, -6553.

- 1220 N St. - Rm.A-270, P.O. Box 942871, Sacramento, CA 94271-0001. Phones: (916)654-0810, -0813, -0815.

Colorado—2331 W. 31st Ave., Denver, CO 80211. Phones: (303)844-4570, 477-0093.

Connecticut—Connecticut Regional Market, 101 Reserve Rd. - Rm.5, Hartford, CT 06114. Phone: (860)240-3446.

Delaware—2320 S. DuPont Hwy., Dover, DE 19901. Phone: (302)736-4811.

District of Columbia/Maryland—Baltimore-Washington Terminal Market Office, 8610 Baltimore-Washington Blvd. - Ste.212, Jessup, MD 20794. Phones: (301)317-4387, -4587.

Florida—Techniport Bldg. - Rm.556, 5600 NW 36th St., Miami, FL 33122. Phone: (305)870-9542.

Georgia—Administration Bldg. - Rm.205, 16 Forest Pkwy., Forest Park, GA 30050. Phone: (404)366-7522.

Hawaii—1428 S. King St., P.O. Box 22159, Honolulu, HI 96823-2159. Phone: (808) 973-9566.

Idaho—2270 Old Penitentiary Rd., Boise, ID 83712. Phone: (208)332-8670.

Indiana—Greenfield, IN 46140-0427. Phone: (317)462-5897.

Kentucky—No. 1 Produce Terminal, Louisville, KY 40218. Phones: (502)595-4266, -4278.

Louisiana—U.S. Postal Service Bldg. - Rm.11036, 701 Loyola Ave., New Orleans, LA 70113. Phones: (504)589-6741, -6742.

Maine—744 Main St. - Ste.4, P.O. Box 1058, Presque Isle, ME 04769. Phone: (207)764-2100.

Massachusetts—Boston Market Terminal Bldg. - Rm.1, 34 Market St., Everett, MA 02149. Phones: (617)389-2480, -2481.

10.153 thru 10.163 (cont.)

Michigan—90 Detroit Union Produce Union Terminal, 7201 W. Fort St., Detroit, MI 48209. Phones:(313)226-6059, -6225.

Minnesota—90 W. Plato Blvd., St. Paul, MN 55107. Phones: (612)296-8557, -0593.

Missouri—Gumble Bldg. - Rm.502, 801 Walnut St., Kansas City, MO 64106. Phone: (816)374-6273.

- Unit 1 Produce Row - (1st fl.) Rm.100, St. Louis, MO 63102. Phone: (314)425-4514, -4515.

New Jersey—Federal Bldg. - Rm.1430, 970 Broad St., Newark, NJ 07102. Phone: (201)645-2636.

New York—Division of Food Safety and Inspection Service, Capital Plaza - Bldg. 2 (2nd fl.), 1 Winners Circle, Albany, NY 12235. Phones: (518)457-1211, -2090, -1982.

- 465B Hunts Point Market, Bronx, NY 10474. Phones: (718)991-7665, -7669.

Ohio—3716 Croton Ave., Cleveland, OH 44115. Phone: (216)522-2135.

- Division of Food, Dairy and Drugs, Bldg. 2, 8995 E. Main St., Reynoldsburg, OH 43068. Phone: (614)728-6350.

Oklahoma—2800 N. Lincoln Blvd., Oklahoma City, OK 73105. Phone: (405)521-3864.

Oregon—635 Capitol St. NE, Salem, OR 97310-0110. Phone: (503)986-4629.

Pennsylvania—2301 N. Cameron St. - Rm.112, Harrisburg, PA 17110. Phones: (717) 787-5107, -5108.

- 210 Produce Bldg., 3301 S. Galloway St., Philadelphia, PA 19148. Phones: (215)336-0845, -0846.
- Pittsburgh Produce Terminal Bldg. - Rm.206, 2100 Smallman St., Pittsburgh, PA 15222. Phones: (412)261-6435.

Puerto Rico—Federal-State Inspection, GSA Service Center, 651 Federal Dr. - Ste.103-05, Guaynabo, PR 00965. Phones: (787)783-2230, -4116.

Tennessee—3211 Alcoa Hwy., Knoxville, TN 37920. Phone: (423)577-2633.

- Melrose Station, P.O. Box 40627, Nashville, TN 37204. Phone: (615)360-0169.

Texas—1406 Parker St. - Ste.203, Dallas, TX 75215. Phones: (214)767-5337, -5338.

- 8001 E N. Mesa - Ste.303, El Paso, TX 79932. Phone: (505)589-3753.
- 3100 Produce Row - Rm.1A, Houston, TX 77023. Phones: (713)923-2557, -2558.
- Administration Bldg. - Rm.244, 1500 S. Zarzamora St., San Antonio, TX 78207. Phone: (210)222-2751.
- 1301 W. Expressway, P.O. Box 107, San Juan,TX 78589. Phones: (210)787-4091, -6881.

Utah—350 N. Redwood Rd. - Rm.217, Salt Lake City, UT 84116. Phone: (801)538-7187.

Washington—National Resources Bldg. - 2nd fl., 1111 Washington St., Olympia, WA 98504-2560. Phone: (360)902-1831.

Market News Branch

Arizona—522 N. Central Ave. - Rm.106, Phoenix, AZ 85004. Phone: (602)379-3066.

California—2202 Monterey St. - Ste.104-A, Fresno, CA 93721. Phone: (209)487-5178.

- 1320 E. Olympic Blvd. - Ste.212, Los Angeles, CA 90021-1907. Phone: (213)894-3077.
- 630 Sansome St. - Rm.727, San Francisco, CA 94111. Phone: (415)705-1300.

Colorado—Greeley Producers Bldg., 711 "O" St., Greeley, CO 80631. Phones: (970) 351-7097, -8256.

Florida—Brickell Plaza Bldg. - Ste.424, 909 SE 1st Ave., Miami, FL 33131. Phone: (305)373-2955.

- (*Seasonal*)775 Warner Ln., Orlando, FL 32803. Phone: (407)897-5950.

Georgia—203 Administration Bldg., 16 Forest Pkwy., Forest Park, GA 30050. Phones: (404)763-7297, 361-1376.

- Georgia State Farmers Market - Stall 39, 502 Smith Ave., U.S. Hwy. 84, P.O. Box 1447, Thomasville, GA 31799. Phone: (912)228-1208.

Idaho—1820 E. 17th St. - Ste.130, Idaho Falls, ID 83404. Phone: (208)526-0166.

Illinois—Kluczynski Bldg. - Rm.512, 230 S. Dearborn St., Chicago, IL 60604. Phone: (312)353-0111.

Maryland—Maryland Wholesale Produce Market, Bldg. B - Rm.101, 7460 Conowingo Ave., Jessup, MD 20794. Phones: (410)799-4840, -4841; Washington DC only: (301)621-1261.

Massachusetts—Boston Market Terminal - Rm.10, 34 Market St., Everett, MA 02149. Phones: (617)387-4498, -4615, -4681.

Michigan—Federal Bldg. - Rm.201, 175 Territorial Rd., P.O. Box 1204, Benton Harbor, MI 49023. Phones: (616)925-3270, -3271.

- Union Produce Terminal - Rm.53, 7201 W. Fort St., Detroit, MI 48209. Phone: (313)841-1111.

Missouri—Unit 1, Produce Row - Rm.101, St. Louis, MO 63102-1418. Phone: (314)425-4520.

New York—5A NYC Terminal Market, Halleck St. at Edgewater Rd., Bronx, NY 10474-7355. Phone: (718)542-2225.

Pennsylvania—3301 S. Galloway St. - Rm.261, Philadelphia, PA 19148. Phone: (215)597-4536.

- 2100 Smallman St. - Rm.207, Pittsburgh, PA 15222. Phone: (412)644-5847.

Texas—1406 Parker - Rm.201, Dallas, TX 75215. Phones: (214)767-5375, -5376, -5377.

Washington—Interwest Savings Bank - Ste.302, 15111 8th Ave. SW, Seattle, WA 98148-0099. Phones: (206)764-3753, -3804.

- Agricultural Service Center - Rm.4, 2015 S. 1st St., Yakima, WA 98903. Phones: (509)575-2492, -2493.

Marketing Field Service

California—2202 Monterey St. - Ste.102-B, Fresno, CA 93721. Phone: (209)487-5901.

Florida—301 3rd St. NW - Ste.206, P.O. Box 2276, Winterhaven, FL 33881. Phones: (941)299-4770, -4886.

Oregon—1220 SW 3rd Ave. - Rm.369, Portland, OR 97204. Phones: (503)326-2724, -2725.

Texas—1313 E. Hackberry, McAllen, TX 78501. Phone: (956)682-2833.

Processed Products Branch

EASTERN—Regional Director, Bldg. A - Ste.380, 800 Roosevelt Rd., Glen Ellyn, IL 60137-5875. Phone: (630)790-6957.

Florida—6966 NW 36th Ave., Miami, FL 33147-6506. Phone: (305)835-7626.

- 98 3rd St. SW, Winter Haven, FL 33880-2909. Phone: (941)294-7416.

Georgia—1555 St. Joseph Ave., East Point, GA 30344-2591. Phone: (404)763-7495.

Indiana—4318 Technology Dr., South Bend, IN 46628-9752. Phone: (219)287-5407.

Louisiana (*Inspection Point of East Point, GA*)—Commerce Bldg. - Ste.3, 1942 Williams Blvd., Kenner, LA 70062-6285. Phone: (504)466-0343.

Maine—165 Lancaster St., Portland, ME 04101-2499. Phone: (207)772-1588.

Maryland (*Inspection Point of Hunt Valley, MD*)—102 Maryland Ave., Easton, MD 21601-3409. Phone: (410)822-3383.

10.153 thru 10.163 (cont.)

- Hunt Valley Professional Bldg., 9 Schilling Rd., Hunt Valley, MD 21031-1106. Phone: (410)962-4946.

Michigan (*Inspection Point of South Bend, IN*)—c/o Vroom Cold Storage, Russell Rd., Hart, MI 49420-0113. Phone: (616)873-5654.

Minnesota (*Inspection Point of Ripon, WI*)—2126 Hoffman Rd., Mankato, MN 56001-5863. Phone: (507)387-6101.

New Jersey—Park Plaza, Professional Bldg. - Ste.304, 622 Georges Rd., North Brunswick, NJ 08902-3313. Phone: (908)545-0939.

New York (*Inspection Point of North Brunswick, NJ*)—Genesee Valley Regional Market, 900 Jefferson Rd. - Rm.110, Rochester, NY 14623-3289. Phones: (716)424-2092, -2096.

Oklahoma (*Inspection Point of Weslaco, TX*)—716 S. 2nd St. - Ste.106, Stillwater, OK 74960-4806. Phone: (918)696-6333.

Puerto Rico—Federal State Inspection Service, GSA Center - Ste.103-05, 651 Federal Dr., Guaynabo, PR 00965-1030. Phones: (809)783-2230, -4116.

Texas—Federal Bldg. - Rm.1011, 2320 La Branch St., Houston, TX 77004-1036. Phone: (713)659-3836.

- (*Inspection Point of Weslaco, TX*)—319 Market St., Laredo, TX 78040-8529. Phone: (210)726-2258.

- 117 S. Westgate, Weslaco, TX 78596-2701. Phones: (210)968-2772, -2126.

Virginia—No.1 N. 14th St. - Rm.332, Richmond, VA 23219-3691. Phone: (804)786-0930.

Wisconsin—742 E. Fond du Lac St., Ripon, WI 54971-9555. Phone: (414)748-2287.

WESTERN—Regional Director, 2202 Monterey St. - Ste.102-C, Fresno, CA 93721-3175. Phone: (209)487-5891.

California—2202 Monterey St. - Ste.102-A, Fresno, CA 93721-3129. Phone: (209)487-5210.

- (*Inspection Point of Fresno*)—45-116 Commerce St. - Ste.15, Indio, CA 92201-3440. Phone: (619)347-1057.

- 1320 E. Olympic Rd. - Rm.212, Los Angeles, CA 90021-1948. Phone: (213)894-3173.

Hawaii—State of Hawaii Department of Agriculture, 1428 S. King St., P.O. Box 22159, Honolulu, HI 96823-2159. Phone: (808)973-9566.

Oregon (*Inspection Point of Yakima, WA*)—111 S. Main St., Milton-Freewater, OR 97862-1342. Phone: (541)938-3251.

- 340 High St. NE, Salem, OR 97301-3631. Phone: (503)399-5761.

Washington—32 N. 3rd St. - Rm.212, Yakima, WA 98901-2791. Phone: (509)575-5869.

LIVESTOCK DIVISION

Livestock and Grain Market News Branch

Alabama—1445 Federal Dr. - Rm.107, P.O. Box 3336, Montgomery, AL 36109-0336. Phone: (334)223-7488.

Arizona—Stockyards Bldg. - Rm.102, 5001 E. Washington St., Phoenix, AZ 85034-2010. Phone: (602)379-4376.

Arkansas—2301 S. University - Rm.110-B, Little Rock, AR 72203-3910. Phone: (501)671-2203.

Colorado—711 "O" St., Greeley, CO 80631-9540. Phone: (970)353-9750.

Florida—775 Warner Lane, Orlando, FL 32803. Phone: (407)897-2708.

FIELD OFFICE CONTACTS   739

Georgia—Georgia State Farmers Market, 502 Smith Ave. - Stall 38, Thomasville, GA 31792-0086. Phone: (912)226-2198.

Illinois—Illinois Department of Agriculture, Division of Marketing, State Fairgrounds, P.O. Box 19281, Springfield, IL 62794-9281. Phone: (217)782-4925.

Iowa—210 Walnut St. - Rm.767, Des Moines, IA 50309-2106. Phone: (515)284-4460.

- 800 Cunningham Dr. - Rm.225, Sioux City, IA 51107-2437. Phone: (712)252-3286.

Kansas—100 Military Ave. - Ste.217, Dodge City, KS 67801-4945. Phone: (316)227-8881.

Kentucky—1321 Story Ave., Louisville, KY 40206-1884. Phone: (502)582-5287.

Louisiana—Capitol Station, 5825 Florida Blvd., Baton Rouge, LA 70821-3334. Phone: (504)922-1328.

Minnesota—New Livestock Exchange Bldg. - Ste.208, S. St. Paul, MN 55075-5598. Phone: (612)451-1565.

Missouri—601 Illinois Ave. - Rm.210, St. Joseph, MO 64504-1396. Phone: (816)238-0678.

Montana—Public Auction Yards Bldg. - Rm.206, 112 S. 18th and Minnesota Ave., Billings, MT 59103-1191. Phone: (406)657-6285.

Nebraska—213 Livestock Exchange Bldg., 29th and O St., Omaha, NE 68107-2603. Phone: (402)731-4520.

New Mexico—2507 N. Telshor Blvd. - Ste.4, Las Cruces, NM 88001. Phone: (505)521-4928.

Oklahoma—Livestock Exchange Bldg. - Rm.140, 2501 Exchange Ave., Oklahoma City, OK 73108-2477. Phone: (405)232-5425.

Oregon—1220 SW 3rd Ave. - Rm.1772, Portland, OR 97204-2899. Phone: (503)326-2237.

Pennsylvania—c/o New Holland Sales Stables, 101 W. Fulton St., P.O. Box 155, New Holland, PA 17557. Phone: (717)354-2391.

South Carolina—Youngblood Bldg., 1001 Bluff Rd., Columbia, SC 29201-3405. Phone: (803)737-4491.

South Dakota—803 E. Rice St. - Rm.103, Sioux Falls, SD 57103-0193. Phone: (605)338-4061.

Tennessee—Melrose Station, Ellington Agriculture Center, Hogan Rd., Nashville, TN 37204-0627. Phone: (615)781-5406.

Texas—Livestock Exchange Bldg. - 1st fl., 101 S. Manhattan St., P.O. Box 30217, Amarillo, TX 79104-0217. Phone: (806)372-6361.

- Producers Livestock Auction Bldg., San Angelo, TX 76903-0160. Phone: (915)653-1778.

Washington—988 Juniper St., Moses Lake, WA 98837-2250. Phone: (509)765-3611.

Wyoming—1834 E. A St., Torrington, WY 82240-1813. Phone: (307)532-4146.

Meat Grading and Certification

Colorado—400 Livestock Exchange Bldg., Denver, CO 80216-2139. Phone: (303)294-7676.

Illinois—Bldg. A - Ste.330, 800 Roosevelt Rd., Glen Ellyn, IL 60137-5832. Phone: (708)790-6905.

Iowa—210 Walnut St. - Rm.575-A, Des Moines, IA 50309-2106. Phone: (515)284-7166.

Nebraska—204 Livestock Exchange Bldg., 29th and O St., Omaha, NE 68107-2603. Phone: (402)733-4833.

Texas—Livestock Exchange Bldg., 101 S. Manhattan St., P.O. Box 30217, Amarillo, TX 79104. Phone: (806)373-7111.

10.153 thru 10.163 (cont.)

POULTRY DIVISION

Poultry Grading Branch

EAST MIDWEST *(Alabama, Arkansas, Louisiana, Mississippi, Oklahoma, Tennessee, Texas)*—1 Natural Resources Dr. - Rm.110, Little Rock, AR 72215-8521. Phone: (501)324-5955.

EASTERN *(Connecticut, Delaware, District of Columbia, Florida, Georgia, Maine, Maryland, Massachusetts, New Hampshire, New Jersey, New York, North Carolina, Pennsylvania, Puerto Rico, Rhode Island, South Carolina, Vermont, Virgin Islands, Virginia, West Virginia)*—635 Cox Rd. - Ste.G, Gastonia, NC 28054-3441. Phone: (704)867-3871.

WEST MIDWEST *(Illinois, Indiana, Iowa, Kansas, Kentucky, Michigan, Minnesota, Missouri, Nebraska, North Dakota, Ohio, South Dakota, Wisconsin)*—Federal Bldg. - Rm.777, 210 Walnut St., Des Moines, IA 50309-2100. Phone: (515)284-4581.

WESTERN *(Alaska, Arizona, California, Colorado, Hawaii, Idaho, Montana, New Mexico, Nevada, Oregon, Utah, Washington, Wyoming)*—2909 Coffee Rd. - Ste.4, Modesto, CA 95355-3188. Phone: (209)522-5251.

Poultry Market News Branch

California—Bldg. 6 - Section E, 5600 Rickenbacker Rd., Bell, CA 90201-6418. Phones: (213)269-4154; *Recorded messages 24 hrs./day*: (213)260-4676.

Connecticut—Connecticut Department of Agriculture, Marketing Division, State Office Bldg. - Rm.263, 165 Capital Ave., Hartford, CT 06106-1688. Phone: (860)566-3671.

District of Columbia—AMS, PY Division, USDA National Poultry Supervisor/National Egg Supervisor, South Bldg. - Rm.3960, Washington, DC 20090-6456. Phone: (202)720-6911.

Georgia—60 Forsyth St. SW - Rm.6M80, Atlanta, GA 30303. Phones: FTS (404)562-5830, -5856.

Iowa—210 Walnut St. - Rm.951, Des Moines, IA 50309-2103. Phone: (515)284-4545 *(recorded messages 24 hrs./day)*.

Louisiana—Louisiana Department of Agriculture, Wilson Bldg., Baton Rouge, LA 70821-3334. Phone: (504)922-1328.

Mississippi—352 E. Woodrow Wilson, Jackson, MS 39296-4629. Phone: (601)965-4662.

North Carolina—North Carolina Department of Agriculture, State Agriculture Bldg. - Rm.402, 2 W. Edenton St., P.O. Box 27647, Raleigh, NC 27611-7647. Phone: (919)733-7252.

Texas—Texas Department of Agriculture, Capitol Station, 1700 N. Congress Ave., Austin, TX 78711-2847. Phones: (512)463-7628; (toll-free within state, 1-800-252-3407).

Virginia—Virginia Department of Agriculture and Consumer Services, 116 Reservoir St., Harrisonburg, VA 22801-4232. Phone: (540)434-0779.

SCIENCE DIVISION

Alabama—Supervisory Chemist, Aflatoxin Laboratories, 3119 Wesley Way, Dothan, AL 36301-2020. Phone: (334)794-5070.

▪ Laboratory Supervisor, 1557 Reeves St., P.O. Box 1368, Dothan, AL 36302. Phone: (334)792-5185.

Florida—Supervisory Chemist, Eastern Laboratories, 98 3rd St. SW - Ste.211, Winter Haven, FL 33880-2909. Phone: (941)299-7958.

Georgia—Laboratory Supervisor, 1211 Schley Ave., Albany, GA 31707. Phone: (912)430-8490.

FIELD OFFICE CONTACTS

- Laboratory Supervisor, P.O. Box 488, Ashburn, GA 31714. Phone: (912)567-3703.
- Laboratory Supervisor, 610 N. Main St., Blakely, GA 31723. Phone: (912)723-4570.
- Laboratory Supervisor, P.O. Box 272, Dawson, GA 31742. Phone: (912)995-7257.

Illinois—Laboratory Director, Midwestern Laboratory, 3570 N. Avondale Ave., Chicago, IL 60618-5391. Phone: (312)353-6525.

North Carolina—Laboratory Supervisor, 301 W. Pearl St., P.O. Box 279, Aulander, NC 27805. Phone: (919)345-1661, ext.156.

- Laboratory Director, Eastern Laboratory, 2311-B Aberdeen Blvd., Gastonia, NC 28054-0614. Phone: (704)867-3873.
- Laboratory Address, 645 Cox Rd., Gastonia, NC 28054-0614. Phone: (704)867-1882.

Oklahoma—Laboratory Supervisor, 107 S. 4th St., Madill, OK. 73446. Phone: (405) 795-5615.

Virginia—Pesticide Records Branch, 8700 Centreville Rd. - Ste.200, Manassas, VA 22110-0031, Phones: (703)330-7826; Residue Branch, (703)330-2300.

- Laboratory Supervisor, 308 Culloden St., P.O. Box 1130, Suffolk, VA 23434. Phone: (757)925-2286.

TOBACCO DIVISION

Tobacco Inspection and Market News

LEXINGTON REGION *(Indiana, Kentucky, Maryland, Missouri, North Carolina, Ohio, Tennessee, Virginia, West Virginia (burley), and Connecticut, Massachusetts, Pennsylvania, Wisconsin cigar areas)*—771 Corporate Dr. - Ste.500, Lexington, KY 40503. Phone: (606)224-1088.

RALEIGH REGION *(Alabama, Florida, Georgia, North Carolina, South Carolina, Virginia(Flue-cured, Tobacco and Naval Stores Inspection))*—1306 Annapolis Dr. - Rm.205, Raleigh, NC 27608-0001. Phone: (919)856-4584.

10.165 REGULATORY BRANCH REGIONAL OFFICES (Perishable Agricultural Commodities Act)

Arizona—Federal Bldg. - Rm.7, 300 W. Congress St., P.O. Box FB30, Tucson, AZ 85701-1319. Phone: (520)670-4793.

Illinois—Bldg. A - Ste.360, 800 Roosevelt Rd., Glen Ellyn, IL 60137-5832. Phone: (630)790-6929.

New Jersey—622 Georges Rd. - Ste.303, North Brunswick, NJ 08902-3303. Phone: (908)846-8222.

Texas—1200 E. Copeland Rd. - Ste.404, Arlington, TX 76011-4938. Phone: (817)885-7805.

Virginia—8700 Centerville Rd. - Ste.206, Manassas, VA 22110. Phone: (703)330-4455.

10.352 Listed under **10.405**.

10.404 Listed under **10.051**.

RURAL DEVELOPMENT
(Rural Housing Service -
Rural Business-Cooperative Service)

10.405 STATE OFFICES

Alabama—Sterling Center - Ste.601, 4121 Carmichael Rd., Montgomery, AL 36106-3683. Phone: (334)279-3400.

10.405 (cont.)

Alaska—800 W. Evergreen - Ste.201, Palmer, AK 99645-6539. Phone: (907)745-2176.

Arizona—3003 N. Central Ave. - Ste.900, Phoenix, AZ 85012-2906. Phone: (602)280-8700.

Arkansas—700 W. Capitol Ave. - Rm.3416, P.O. Box 2778, Little Rock, AR 72201-3325. Phone: (501)301-3200.

California—430 G St. - Agency 4169, Davis, CA 95616-4169. Phone: (530)792-5800.

Colorado—655 Parfet St. - Rm.E-100, Lakewood, CO 80215. Phone: (303)236-2801.

Connecticut—*See* **Massachusetts**.

Delaware *(Delaware, Maryland)*—5201 S. Dupont Hwy., P.O. Box 400, Camden, DE 19934-9998. Phone: (302)697-4300.

Florida *(Florida, Virgin Islands)*—Federal Bldg., 4440 NW 25th Place, Gainesville, FL 32614-7010. Phone: (352)338-3400.

Georgia—Stephens Federal Bldg., 355 E. Hancock Ave., Athens, GA 30601-2768. Phone: (706)546-2162.

Hawaii—Federal Bldg. - Rm.311, 154 Waianuenue Ave., Hilo, HI 96720. Phone: (808)933-3000.

Idaho—9173 W. Barnes Dr. - Ste.A1, Boise, ID 83709. Phone: (208)378-5600.

Illinois—Illini Plaza - Ste.103, 1817 S. Neil St., Champaign, IL 61820. Phone: (217)398-5235.

Indiana—5975 Lakeside Blvd., Indianapolis, IN 46278. Phone: (317)290-3100.

Iowa—Federal Bldg. - Rm.873, 210 Walnut St., Des Moines, IA 50309. Phone: (515)284-4663.

Kansas—1200 SW Executive Dr., P.O. Box 4653, Topeka, KS 66605. Phone: (785)271-2700.

Kentucky—771 Corporate Plaza - Ste.200, Lexington, KY 40503. Phone: (606)224-7300.

Louisiana—3727 Government St., Alexandria, LA 71302. Phone: (318)473-7920.

Maine—444 Stillwater Ave. - Ste.2, Bangor, ME 04402-0405. Phone: (207)990-9106.

Maryland—*See* **Delaware**.

Massachusetts *(Connecticut, Massachusetts, Rhode Island)*—451 West St., Amherst, MA 01002. Phone: (413)253-4300.

Michigan—3001 Coolidge Rd. - Ste.200, East Lansing, MI 48823. Phone: (517)337-6635.

Minnesota—410 Agribank Bldg., 375 Jackson St., St. Paul, MN 55101-1853. Phone: (651)602-7800.

Mississippi—Federal Bldg. - Ste.831, 100 W. Capitol St., Jackson, MS 39269. Phone: (601)965-4316.

Missouri—Parkade Center - Ste.235, 601 Business Loop - 70 West, Columbia, MO 65203. Phone: (573)876-0976.

Montana—900 Technology Blvd. - (Unit 1) Ste.B, P.O. Box 850, Bozeman, MT 59715. Phone: (406)585-2580.

Nebraska—Federal Bldg. - Rm.152, 100 Centennial Mall North, Lincoln, NE 68508. Phone: (402)437-5551.

Nevada—1390 S. Curry St., Carson City, NV 89703-9910. Phone: (702)887-1222.

New Hampshire—*See* **Vermont**.

New Jersey—Tarnsfield Plaza - Ste.22, 790 Woodland Rd., Mt. Holly, NJ 08060. Phone: (609)265-3600.

FIELD OFFICE CONTACTS   743

New Mexico—6200 Jefferson St. NE - Rm.255, Albuquerque, NM 87109. Phone: (505)761-4950.

New York—The Galleries of Syracuse, 441 S. Salina St. - Ste.357, Syracuse, NY 13202-2541. Phone: (315)477-6400.

North Carolina—4405 Bland Rd. - Ste.260, Raleigh, NC 27609. Phone: (919)873-2000.

North Dakota—Federal Bldg. - Rm.208, 220 E. Rosser, Bismarck, ND 58502-1737. Phone: (701)250-4781.

Ohio—Federal Bldg. - Rm.507, 200 N. High St., Columbus, OH 43215-2477. Phone: (614)469-5606.

Oklahoma—100 USDA - Ste.108, Stillwater, OK 74074-2654. P*hone: (405)742-1000.

Oregon—101 SW Main St. - Ste.1410, Portland, OR 97204-3222. Phone: (503)414-3300.

Pennsylvania—One Credit Union Pl. - Ste.330, Harrisburg, PA 17110-2996. Phone: (717)237-2299.

Puerto Rico—New San Juan Office Bldg. - Rm.501, 159 Carlos E. Chardon St., Hato Rey, PR 00918-5481. Phone: (787)766-5095.

Rhode Island— *See* **Massachusetts**.

South Carolina—Thurmond Federal Bldg. - Rm.1007, 1835 Assembly St., Columbia, SC 29201. Phone: (803)765-5163.

South Dakota—Huron Federal Bldg. - Rm.210, 200 4th St. SW, Huron, SD 57350. Phone: (605)352-1100.

Tennessee—3322 West End Ave. - Ste.300, Nashville, TN 37203-1084. Phone: (615)783-1300.

Texas—Federal Bldg. - Ste.102, 101 S. Main, Temple, TX 76501. Phone: (254)742-9700.

Utah—Federal Bldg. - Rm.4311, 125 S. State St., P.O. Box 11350, Salt Lake City, UT 84147-0350. Phone: (801)524-4063.

Vermont *(New Hampshire, Vermont)*—City Center - 3rd fl., 89 Main St., Montpelier, VT 05602. Phone: (802)828-6010.

Virgin Islands— *See* **Florida**.

Virginia—Culpeper Bldg. - Ste.238, 1606 Santa Rosa Rd., Richmond, VA 23229. Phone: (804)287-1550.

Washington—1835 Black Lake Blvd. SW - Ste.B, Olympia, WA 98512-5715. Phone: (360)704-7740.

West Virginia—Federal Bldg. - Rm.320, 75 High St., Morgantown, WV 26505-7500. Phone: (304)291-4791.

Wisconsin—4949 Kirschling Court, Stevens Point, WI 54481. Phone: (715)345-7600.

Wyoming—Federal Bldg. - Rm.1005, 100 E. B St., P.O. Box 820, Casper, WY 82602. Phone: (307)261-6300.

10.406 and 10.407	Listed under **10.051**.
10.410 thru 10.420	Listed under **10.405**.
10.421	Listed under **10.051**.
10.427 and 10.433	Listed under **10.405**.

10.437	Listed under **10.051**.
10.438 thru 10.442	Listed under **10.405**.
10.443	Contact appropriate office listed under **10.051**, **10.405**, or **10.900**.
10.444 thru 10.446	Listed under **10.405**.

RISK MANAGEMENT AGENCY

10.450 **REGIONAL SERVICE OFFICES**

REGION 1 *(Connecticut, Delaware, Maine, Maryland, Massachusetts, New Hampshire, New Jersey, New York, North Carolina, Pennsylvania, Rhode Island, Vermont, Virginia, West Virginia)*—4407 Bland Rd. - Ste.160, Raleigh, NC 27609. Phone: (919)875-4880.

REGION 2 *(Alabama, Florida, Georgia, Puerto Rico, South Carolina, Virgin Islands)*—106 S. Patterson St. - Ste.250, Valdosta, GA 31601-5609. Phone: (912)242-3044.

REGION 3 *(Arkansas, Kentucky, Louisiana, Mississippi, Tennessee)*—8 River Bend Place, Jackson, MS 39208. Phone: (601)965-4771.

REGION 4 *(Illinois, Indiana, Michigan, Ohio)*—3500 W. Wabash - Ste.B, Springfield, IL 62707. Phone: (217)241-6601.

REGION 5 *(Iowa, Minnesota, Wisconsin)*—Minnesota World Trade Center, 30 E. 7th St. - Ste.910, St. Paul, MN 55101-4901. Phone: (651)290-3304.

REGION 6 *(Montana, North Dakota, South Dakota, Wyoming)*—3490 Gabel Rd. - Ste.100, Billings, MT 59102-6440. Phone: (406)657-6447.

REGION 7 *(Colorado, Kansas, Missouri, Nebraska)*—3401 SW Van Buren St., Topeka, KS 66611-2227. Phone: (785)266-0248.

REGION 8 *(New Mexico, Oklahoma, Texas)*—205 NW 63rd St. - Ste.170, Oklahoma City, OK 73116-8209. Phone: (405)879-2700.

REGION 9 *(Arizona, California, Hawaii, Nevada, Utah)*—430 G St. - Ste.4168, Davis, CA 95616-4168. Phone: (530)792-5870.

REGION 10 *(Alaska, Idaho, Oregon, Washington)*—112 N. University Rd. - Ste.205, Spokane, WA 99206-5295. Phone: (509)353-2147.

COMPLIANCE FIELD OFFICES

CENTRAL *(Colorado, Kansas, Missouri, Nebraska)*—6501 Beacon Dr., Kansas City, MO 64131. Phone: (816)926-7963.

EASTERN *(Alabama, Connecticut, Delaware, Florida, Georgia, Maine, Maryland, Massachusetts, New Hampshire, New Jersey, New York, North Carolina, Pennsylvania, Puerto Rico, Rhode Island, South Carolina, Vermont, Virginia, West Virginia)*—4407 Bland Rd. - Ste.280, Raleigh, NC 27609. Phone: (919)875-4930.

MIDWEST *(Illinois, Indiana, Ohio, Michigan)*—6045 Lakeside Blvd., Indianapolis, IN 46278. Phone: (317)290-3050.

NORTHERN *(Iowa, Minnesota, Montana, North Dakota, South Dakota, Wisconsin, Wyoming)*—3440 Federal Dr. - Ste.200, Eagan, MN 55122-1301. Phone: (612)725-3730.

SOUTHERN *(Kentucky, Louisiana, Mississippi, New Mexico, Oklahoma, Tennessee, Texas)*—1111 W. Mockingbird Lane - Ste. 280, Dallas, TX 75247-5016. Phone: (214)767-7700.

	WESTERN *(Alaska, Arizona, California, Hawaii, Idaho, Nevada, Oregon, Utah, Washington)*—430 G St. - Ste.4167, Davis, CA 95616-4167. Phone: (530)792-5850.
10.451 and 10.452	Listed under **10.051**.
10.455	Listed under **10.450**.
10.456	Risk Management Agency, Research and Evaluation Division, 6501 Beacon Dr., Stop 0813, Kansas City, MO 64133-4676. Phones: (816)926-6343; FAX (816)926-7343. **Internet:** e-mail,"www.RMARED.Applications@rma.usda.gov".
10.457 thru 10.459	Listed under **10.450**.

FOOD SAFETY AND INSPECTION SERVICE

Meat, Poultry, and Egg Products Inspection

10.475 and 10.477

DISTRICT OFFICES

Arkansas *(DISTRICT 35: Arkansas, Louisiana, Oklahoma)*—Country Club Center - Ste.201, 4700 S. Thompson Bldg. B, Springdale, AR 72764. Phone: (501)751-8412.

California *(DISTRICT 5: California)*—Bldg. 2C, 620 Central Ave., Alameda, CA 94501. Phone: (510)337-5000.

Colorado *(DISTRICT 15: Arizona, Colorado, New Mexico, Nevada, Utah)*—665 S. Broadway - Ste.B, Boulder, CO 80303. Phone: (303)497-5411.

Georgia *(DISTRICT 85: Florida, Georgia, Puerto Rico, Virgin Islands)*—Bldg. 1924 - Ste.3R90, 100 Alabama St. SW, Atlanta, GA 30303. Phone: (404)562-5900.

Illinois *(DISTRICT 50: Illinois, Indiana, Ohio)*—1919 S. Highland Ave. - Ste.115C, Lombard, IL 60148. Phone: (630)620-7474.

Iowa *(DISTRICT 25: Iowa, Nebraska)*—Federal Bldg. - Rm.985, 210 Walnut St., Des Moines, IA 50309. Phone: (515)727-8960.

Kansas *(DISTRICT 30: Kansas, Missouri)*—4920 Bob Billings Pkwy, Lawrence, KS 66049. Phone: (785)841-5600.

Maryland *(DISTRICT 75: Delaware, Maryland, Virginia, Washington D.C., West Virginia)*—5601 Sunnyside Ave. - Ste.1-2288B, Beltsville, MD 20705-5200. Phone: (301)504-2136.

Minnesota *(DISTRICT 20: Minnesota, Montana, North Dakota, South Dakota, Wyoming)*—Butler Square West - Ste.989C, 100 N. 6th St., Minneapolis, MN 55403. Phone: (612)370-2400.

Mississippi *(DISTRICT 90: Alabama, Mississippi, Tennessee)*—715 S. Pear Orchard Rd. - Ste.101, Ridgeland, MS 39157. Phone: (601)965-4312.

New York *(DISTRICT 65: Connecticut, Maine, Massachusetts, New Hampshire, New York, Rhode Island, Vermont)*—230 Washington Ave., Albany, NY 12203-6870. Phone: (518)452-6870.

North Carolina *(DISTRICT 80: Kentucky, North Carolina, South Carolina)*—6020 Six Forks Rd., Raleigh, NC 27609. Phone: (919)844-8400.

Oregon *(DISTRICT 10: Alaska, American Samoa, Guam, Hawaii, Idaho, Northern Mariana Islands, Oregon, Washington)*—530 Center St. NW, Salem, OR 97301. Phone: (503)399-5831.

Pennsylvania *(DISTRICT 60: New Jersey, Pennsylvania)*—Mellon Independence Center - Ste.4100-A, 701 Market St., Philadelphia, PA 19106-1576. Phone: (215)597-4219, ext.106.

10.475 and 10.477 (cont.)

Texas *(DISTRICT 40: Texas)*—1100 Commerce - Rm.516, Dallas, TX 75242-0598. Phone: (214)767-9116.

Wisconsin *(DISTRICT 45: Michigan, Wisconsin)*—2810 Crossroads Dr. - Ste.3500, Madison, WI 53718-7969. Phone: (608)240-4080.

FOOD AND NUTRITION SERVICE

10.550 thru 10.580

REGIONAL OFFICES

MID-ATLANTIC *(Delaware, District of Columbia, Maryland, New Jersey, Pennsylvania, Puerto Rico, Virgin Islands, Virginia, West Virginia)*—Mercer Corporate Park, 300 Corporate Blvd., Robinsville, NJ 08691. Phone: (609)259-5025.

MIDWEST *(Illinois, Indiana, Michigan, Minnesota, Ohio, Wisconsin)*—77 W. Jackson Blvd - 20th fl., Chicago, IL 60604-3507. Phone: (312)353-6664.

MOUNTAIN PLAINS *(Colorado, Iowa, Kansas, Missouri, Montana, Nebraska, North Dakota, South Dakota, Utah, Wyoming)*—1244 Speer Blvd. - Ste.903, Denver, CO 80204. Phone: (303)844-0300.

NORTHEAST *(Connecticut, Maine, Massachusetts, New Hampshire, New York, Rhode Island, Vermont)*—10 Causeway St. - Rm.501, Boston MA 02222-1068. Phone: (617)565-6370.

SOUTHEAST *(Alabama, Florida, Georgia, Kentucky, Mississippi, North Carolina, South Carolina, Tennessee)*—Martin Luther King, Jr. Federal Annex - (1st fl.) Rm.8T36, 61 Forsythe St. SW, Atlanta, GA 30303. Phone: (404)562-1801, -1802

SOUTHWEST *(Arkansas, Louisiana, New Mexico, Oklahoma, Texas)*—1100 Commerce St. - Rm.555, Dallas, TX 75242. Phone: (214)290-9800.

WESTERN *(Alaska, American Samoa, Arizona, California, Guam, Hawaii, Idaho, Nevada, Northern Marianas, Oregon, Washington, Freely Associated States of the Pacific)*—550 Kearny St. - Rm.400, San Francisco, CA 94108. Phone: (415)705-1310.

10.609 Consult local phone directory for nearest county FSA office or state offices listed under **10.051** or via: **Internet:** "www.fsa.usda.gov/edso/statedefault.htm".

FOREST SERVICE

10.652 **RESEARCH HEADQUARTERS - Forest and Range Experiment Stations**

INTERMOUNTAIN *(Idaho, Montana, Nevada, Utah, Wyoming-western one-third)*—324 25th St., Ogden, UT 84401. Phone: (801)625-5421.

NORTH CENTRAL *(Illinois, Indiana, Iowa, Michigan, Minnesota, Missouri, Wisconsin)*—1992 Folwell Ave., St. Paul, MN 55108. Phone: (612)649-5252.

NORTHEASTERN *(Connecticut, Kentucky, Maine, Massachusetts, New Hampshire, New Jersey, New York, Ohio, Pennsylvania, Vermont, West Virginia)*—5 Radnor Corporate Center - Ste.200, Radnor, PA 19087-4585. Phone: (610)975-4207.

PACIFIC NORTHWEST *(Alaska, Oregon, Washington)*—Portland, OR 97208-3890. Phone: (503)326-5644.

PACIFIC SOUTHWEST *(California, Hawaii)*—Berkeley, CA 94701-0245. Phone: (510)559-6317.

ROCKY MOUNTAIN *(Arizona, Colorado, Kansas, Nebraska, New Mexico, North Dakota, Panhandle, South Dakota, Texas-western, Wyoming-eastern two-thirds)*—240 W. Prospect Rd., Ft. Collins, CO 80526-2098. Phone: (970)498-1139.

SOUTHERN *((Alabama, Arkansas, Florida, Georgia, Louisiana, Mississippi, North Carolina, Oklahoma-except Panhandle, Puerto Rico, South Carolina, Tennessee,*

FIELD OFFICE CONTACTS   747

Texas-eastern, Virginia)—200 Weaver Blvd., P.O. Box 2680, Asheville, NC 28802. Phone: (704)257-4301.

Forest Products Laboratory: One Gifford Pinchot Dr., Madison, WI 53705-2398. Phone: (608)231-9315.

10.664 thru 10.674

REGIONAL OFFICES

Note: to contact local Forest Supervisor or Ranger District Offices, consult phone directory under USDA, or the appropriate regional office, following.

REGION 1 *(Idaho-northern, Montana, North Dakota, South Dakota-northwestern corner)*—Federal Bldg., P.O. Box 7669, Missoula, MT 59807. Phone: (406)329-3280.

REGION 2 *(Colorado, Kansas, Nebraska, South Dakota-except northwestern corner, Wyoming-eastern two-thirds)*—740 Simms St., P.O. Box 25127, Lakewood, CO 80255. Phone: (303)275-5741.

REGION 3 *(Arizona, New Mexico)*—P.O. Box 1689, Santa Fe, NM 87504. Phone: (505)842-3344.

REGION 4 *(Idaho-southern, Nevada, Utah, Wyoming-western one-third)*—Federal Office Bldg., 324 25th St., Ogden, UT 84401. Phone: (801)625-5239.

REGION 5 *(California, Hawaii)*—1323 Club Dr., Vallejo, CA 94592. Phone: (707)562-8910.

REGION 6 *(Oregon, Washington)*—333 SW 1st St., Portland, OR 97208-3623. Phone: (503)808-2355, -2348.

REGION 8 *(Alabama, Arkansas, Florida, Georgia, Kentucky, Louisiana, Mississippi, North Carolina, Oklahoma, Puerto Rico, South Carolina, Tennessee, Texas, Virginia, Virgin Islands)*—1720 Peachtree Rd. NW, Atlanta, GA 30367. Phone: (404)347-7486.

REGION 9 *(Connecticut, Delaware, Illinois, Indiana, Iowa, Maine, Maryland, Massachusetts, Michigan, Minnesota, Missouri, New Hampshire, New Jersey, New York, Ohio, Pennsylvania, Rhode Island, Vermont, West Virginia, Wisconsin)*—5 Radnor Corporate Center - Ste.200, P.O. Box 6775, Radnor, PA 19087-4555. Phone: (610) 975-4103.

REGION 10 *(Alaska)*—3301 C St. - Ste.522, Anchorage, AK 99503-3956. Phone: (907)271-2519.

State and Private Forestry Areas

NORTHEASTERN AREA *(Covers states listed under Region 9, foregoing)*—5 Radnor Corporate Center, P.O. Box 6775, Radnor, PA 19087-8775. Phone: (610)975-4103.

10.675   Contact the State and Private Forestry office addresses and phone numbers via: **Internet:** "www.fs.fed.us/ucf/Regional_Offices.htm".

10.676   Contacts for the Regional and Area State and Private Forestry offices and for addresses and phone numbers of Regional Foresters and Area Director of the Forest Service can be found via: **Internet:** "www.fs.fed.us/spf/coop/library/flp_region_coord.shtml".

10.677   Same as **10.676** via **Internet:** "http://www.fs.fed.us/contactus/regions.shtml".

10.678   ## FOREST STEWARDSHIP

ALASKA *(Alaska)*—3301 C St. - Ste.522, Anchorage, AK 99503. Phones: (907)271-2550; FAX (907)271-2897.

INTERMOUNTAIN *(Idaho, Montana, North Dakota, Nevada, Utah)*—Federal Bldg., 324 25th St., Ogden, UT 84401. Phones: (801)625-5189; FAX (801)625-5127.

NORTHEASTERN *(Connecticut, Delaware, Illinois, Indiana, Iowa, Massachusetts, Maryland, Maine, Michigan, Minnesota, Missouri, New Jersey, New Hampshire,*

748   GOVERNMENT ASSISTANCE ALMANAC 2006–07

10.678 *New York, Ohio, Pennsylvania, Rhode Island, Vermont, Wisconsin, West Virginia)—*
(cont.) 11 Campus Blvd. - Ste.200, Newtown Square, PA 19073. Phones: (610)557-4029; FAX (610)557-4136.

PACIFIC NORTHWEST *(Oregon, Washington)*—333 SW 1st Ave., P.O. Box 3623, Portland, OR 97208. Phones: (503)808-2355; FAX (503)808-2339.

PACIFIC SOUTHWEST *(California, Hawaii)*—1323 Club Drive, Vallejo, CA 94592. Phones: (707)562-8918; FAX (707)562-9054.

ROCKY MOUNTAIN *(Colorado, Kansas, Nebraska, South Dakota, Wyoming)*—P.O. Box 25127, Lakewood, CO 80225. Phones: (303)275-5239; FAX (303)275-5754.

SOUTHERN *(Alabama, Arkansas, Florida, Georgia, Kentucky, Louisiana, Mississippi, North Carolina, Oklahoma, South Carolina, Tennessee, Texas, Virginia)*—1720 Peachtree Rd. NW - Ste.8508, Atlanta, GA 30367. Phones: (404)347-1649; FAX (404)347-2776.

SOUTHWESTERN *(Arizona, New Mexico)*—517 Gold Ave. SW, Albuquerque, NM 87102. Phones: (505)842-3229; FAX (505)842-3800.

10.679 Listed under **10.664**.
and
10.680

10.760 Listed under **10.405**.
thru
10.773

10.775 *Obtain information contacts for each state from headquarters office.*

10.854 Listed under **10.405**.

10.856 Listed under **10.405** or via **Internet:** e-mail,"CSGrants@usda.gov".

10.860 Listed under **10.405**
and
10.862

10.864 Listed under **10.405**.

NATURAL RESOURCES CONSERVATION SERVICE

10.900 **REGIONAL OFFICES**
thru
10.950 **EAST**—1400 Wilson Blvd. - Ste.1100, Arlington, VA 22209. Phone: (703)312-7282.

MIDWEST—One Gifford Pinchot Dr. - Rm.204, Madison, WI 53705-3210. Phone: (608)264-5281.

NORTHERN PLAINS—100 Centennial Mall North - Rm.152, Lincoln, NE 68508. Phone: (402)437-5315.

SOUTH CENTRAL—Bldg. 23, 501 W. Felix St., P.O. Box 6459, Ft. Worth, TX 76115. Phone: (817)334-5224, ext.3700.

SOUTHEAST—1720 Peachtree Rd. NW - Ste.716-N, Atlanta, GA 30367. Phone: (404)347-6105.

WEST—650 Capitol Mall - Rm.6072, Sacramento, CA 95814. Phone: (916)498-5284.

STATE OFFICES

Alabama—3381 Skyway Dr., Auburn, AL 36830. Phone: (334)887-4500.

Alaska—949 E. 36 Ave. - Ste.400, Anchorage, AK 99508-4302. Phone: (907)271-2424.

Arizona—3003 N. Central Ave. - Ste.800, Phoenix, AZ 85012-2945. Phone: (602)280-8808.

Arkansas—Federal Bldg. - Rm.5404, 700 W. Capitol Ave., P.O. Box 2323, Little Rock, AR 72201-3228. Phone: (501)324-5445.

California—2121-C 2nd St. - Ste.102, Davis, CA 95616-5475. Phone: (916)757-8215.

Colorado—655 Parfet St. - Rm.E200C, Lakewood, CO 80215-5517. Phone: (303)236-2886, ext.202.

Connecticut—16 Professional Park Rd., Storrs, CT 06268-1299. Phone: (203)487-4014.

Delaware—1203 College Park Dr. - Ste.101, Dover, DE 19904-8713. Phone: (302)678-4160.

Florida—2614 NW 43rd St., Box 141510, Gainesville, FL 32606-6611. Phone: (904)338-9500.

Georgia—Federal Bldg., 355 E. Hancock Ave., P.O. Box 13, Athens, GA 30601-2769. Phone: (706)546-2272.

Hawaii—300 Ala Moana Blvd. - Rm.4316, P.O. Box 50004, Honolulu, HI 96850-0002. Phone: (808)541-2601.

Idaho—3244 Elder St. - Rm.124, Boise, ID 83705-4711. Phone: (208)378-5700.

Illinois—1902 Fox Dr., Champaign, IL 61820-7335. Phone: (217)398-5267.

Indiana—6013 Lakeside Blvd., Indianapolis, IN 46278-2933. Phone: (317)290-3200.

Iowa—Federal Bldg. - Ste.693, 210 Walnut St., Des Moines, IA 50309-2180. Phone: (515)284-6655.

Kansas—760 S. Broadway, Salina, KS 67401. Phone: (913)823-4565.

Kentucky—771 Corporate Dr. - Ste.110, Lexington, KY 40503-5479. Phone: (606)224-7350.

Louisiana—3737 Government St., Alexandria, LA 71302-3727. Phone: (318)473-7751.

Maine—5 Godfrey Dr., Orono, ME 04473. Phone: (207)866-7241.

Maryland—John Hansen Business Center - Ste.301, 339 Busch's Frontage Rd., Annapolis, MD 21401-5534. Phone: (410)757-0861.

Massachusetts—451 West St., Amherst, MA 01002-2995. Phone: (413)253-4351.

Michigan—1405 S. Harrison Rd. - Rm.101, East Lansing, MI 48823-5243. Phone: (517)337-6701, ext.1201.

Minnesota—600 Farm Credit Bldg., 375 Jackson St., St. Paul, MN 55101-1854. Phone: (612)290-3675.

Mississippi—Federal Bldg. - Ste.1321, 100 W. Capital St., Jackson, MS 39269-1399. Phone: (601)965-5205.

Missouri—Parkade Center - Ste.250, 601 Business Loop - 70 West, Columbia, MO 65203-2546. Phone: (573)876-0901.

Montana—Federal Bldg. - Rm.443, 10 E. Babcock St., Bozeman, MT 59715-4704. Phone: (406)587-6813.

Nebraska—Federal Bldg. - Rm.152, 100 Centennial Mall N., Lincoln, NE 68508-3866. Phone: (402)437-5327.

Nevada—Bldg. F - Ste.201, 5301 Longley Lane, Reno, NV 89511-1805. Phone: (702)784-5863.

New Hampshire—Federal Bldg., 2 Madbury Rd., Durham, NH 03824-1499. Phone: (603)433-0505.

New Jersey—1370 Hamilton St., Somerset, NJ 08873-3157. Phone: (908)246-1205.

New Mexico—6200 Jefferson NE - Rm.305, Albuquerque, NM 87109-3734. Phone: (505)761-4400.

New York—441 S. Salina St. - (Ste.354) Rm.520, Syracuse, NY 13202-2450. Phone: (315)477-6504.

North Carolina—4405 Bland Rd. - Ste.205, Raleigh, NC 27609-6293. Phone: (919)873-2102.

10.900 thru 10.950 (cont.)	**North Dakota**—Federal Bldg. - Rm.270, 220 E. Rosser Ave. and 3rd St., Bismarck, ND 58502-1458. Phone: (701)250-4421.
Ohio—Federal Bldg. - Rm.522, 200 N. High St., Columbus, OH 43215-2478. Phone: (614)469-6962.
Oklahoma—100 USDA - Ste.203, Stillwater, OK 74074-2624. Phone: (405)742-1204.
Oregon—Federal Bldg. - (16th fl.) Ste.1300, 101 SW Main St., Portland, OR 97204-3221. Phone: (503)414-3201.
Pacific Basin Area—FHB Bldg. - Ste.301, 400 Route 9, Guam 96927. Phone: (9-011-671)472-7490.
Pennsylvania—One Credit Union Place - Ste.340, Harrisburg, PA 17110-2993. Phone: (717)782-2202.
Puerto Rico—IBM Bldg. - Ste.604, 654 Munoz Rivera Ave., Hato Rey, PR 00918-4123. Phone: (no number provided).
Rhode Island—60 Quaker Lane - Ste.46, Warwick, RI 02886-0111. Phone: (401)828-1300.
South Carolina—Thurmond Federal Bldg. - Rm.950, 1835 Assembly St., Columbia, SC 29201-2489. Phone: (803)765-5681.
South Dakota—Federal Bldg., 200 4th St. SW, Huron, SD 57350-2475. Phone: (605)352-1200.
Tennessee—675 U.S. Courthouse, 801 Broadway, Nashville, TN 37203-3878. Phone: (615)736-5471.
Texas—Poage Federal Bldg., 101 S. Main St., Temple, TX 76501-7682. Phone: (817)774-1214.
Utah—Bennett Federal Bldg. - Rm.4402, 125 S. State St., Salt Lake City, UT 84147. Phone: (801)524-5050.
Vermont—69 Union St., Winooski, VT 05404-1999. Phone: (802)951-6795.
Virginia—Culpeper Bldg. - Ste.209, 1606 Santa Rosa Rd., Richmond, VA 23229-5014. Phone: (804)287-1691.
Washington—W. 316 Boone Ave. - Ste.450, Spokane, WA 99201-2348. Phone: (509)323-2900.
West Virginia—75 High St. - Rm.301, Morgantown, WV 26505. Phone: (304)291-4153.
Wisconsin—6515 Watts Rd. - Ste.200, Madison, WI 53719-2726. Phone: (608)264-5577.
Wyoming—Federal Office Bldg. - Rm.3124, 100 E. B St., Casper, WY 82601. Phones: (307)261-5201, -1911.
10.994 and 10.995	Listed under **10.051**.

DEPARTMENT OF COMMERCE

BUREAU OF THE CENSUS

11.001 thru 11.005	**REGIONAL OFFICES**
California—15350 Sherman Way - Ste.300, Van Nuys, CA 91406-4224. Phones: (818)904-6393, -6427.

FIELD OFFICE CONTACTS   751

Colorado—6900 W. Jefferson Ave. - Ste.100, Denver, CO 80235-2032. Phones: (303)969-6750, -6777.

Georgia—101 Marietta St. NW - Ste.3200, Atlanta, GA 30303-2700. Phones: (404)730-3832, -3835.

Illinois—2255 Enterprise Dr. - Ste.5501, Westchester, IL 60154-5800. Phones: (708)562-1377, -1788.

Kansas—1211 N. 8th St., Kansas City, KS 66101-2129. Phones: (913)551-6728, -6789.

Massachusetts—4 Copley Place - Ste.301, Boston, MA 02117-9108. Phones: (617)424-4501, -0547.

Michigan—1395 Brewery Park Blvd. - Ste.100, Detroit, MI 48207-2635. Phones: (313)259-1158, -5045.

New York—395 Hudson St. - Ste.800, New York, NY 10014. Phones: (212)584-3400, 478-4800.

North Carolina—901 Center Park Dr. - Ste.106, Charlotte, NC 28217-2935. Phones: (704)424-6400, 344-6444.

Pennsylvania—833 Chestnut St.- Ste.504, Philadelphia, PA 19103-2395. Phones: (215)717-1800, -0755.

Texas—8585 N. Stemmons Fwy. - Ste.800S, Dallas, TX 75247-3841. Phones: (214)253-4401, 655-5362.

Washington—Key Tower - Ste.5100, 700 5th Ave., Seattle, WA 98104-5018. Phones: (206)553-5837, -5857.

11.006 **Personal Census Records Service**—Technical Services Supervisor, Personal Census Search Unit, U.S Census Bureau, P.O. Box 1545, Jeffersonville, IN 47131. Phone: (812)218-3046.

INTERNATIONAL TRADE ADMINISTRATION (including Export Assistance Centers)

11.108 thru 11.112

Alabama—Medical Forum Bldg. - Rm.707, 950 22nd St. N., Birmingham, AL 35203. Phones: (205)731-1331; FAX (205)731-0076.

Alaska—431 W. 7th Ave. - Ste.108, Anchorage, AK 99501. Phones: (907)271-6237; FAX (907)271-6242.

Arizona—2901 N. Central Ave. - Ste.970, Phoenix, AZ 85012. Phones: (602)640-2513; FAX (602)640-2518.

- 255 W. Alameda - 3rd fl., Tucson, AZ 85701. Phones: (520)670-5540; FAX (520)791-5413.

Arkansas—425 W. Capitol Ave. - Ste.700, Little Rock, AR 72201. Phones: (501)324-5794; FAX (501)324-7380.

California—390-B Fir Ave., Clovis, CA 93611. Phones: (559)325-1619; FAX (559)325-1647.

- 550 Shaw Ave., Fresno, CA 93710. Phones: (559)325-1619; FAX (559)325-1647.

- One World Trade Center - Ste.1670, Long Beach, CA 90831. Phones: (562)980-4550; FAX (562)980-4561.

- 11150 Olympic Blvd. - Ste.975, Los Angeles, CA 90064. Phones: (310)235-7104; FAX (310)235-7220.

- c/o Monterey Institute of International Studies, 411 Pacific St. - Ste.316A, Monterey, CA 93940. Phones: (831)641-9850; FAX (831)641-9849.

- Orange County Export Assistance Center, 3300 Irvine Ave. - Ste.305, Newport Beach, CA 92660. Phones: (949)660-1688; FAX (949)660-8039.

11.108 thru 11.112 (cont.)

- 530 Water St. - Ste.740, Oakland, CA 94607. Phones: (510)273-7350; FAX (510)251-7352.
- Inland Empire Export Assistance Center, 2940 Inland Empire Blvd. - Ste.121, Ontario, CA 91764. Phones: (909)466-4134; FAX (909)466-4140.
- 917 7th St. - 2nd fl., Sacramento, CA 95814. Phones: (916)498-5155; FAX (916)498-5923.
- 6363 Greenwich Dr. - Ste.230, San Diego, CA 92122. Phones: (619)557-5395; FAX (619)557-6176.
- 250 Montgomery St. - 14th fl., San Francisco, CA 94104. Phones: (415)705-2300; FAX (415)705-2297.
- 101 Park Center Plaza - Ste.1001, San Jose, CA 95113. Phones: (408)271-7300; FAX (408)271-7307.
- 4040 Civic Center Dr. - Ste.200, San Rafael, CA 94903. Phones: (415)883-1966; FAX (415)883-2711.
- 5201 Great American Pkwy. - Ste.456, Santa Clara, CA 95054. Phones: (408)970-4610; FAX (408)970-4618.

Colorado—1625 Broadway - Ste.680, Denver, CO 80202. Phones: (303)844-6623; FAX (303)844-5651.

Connecticut—213 Court St. - Rm.903, Middletown, CT 06457-3346. Phones: (860) 638-6950; FAX (860)638-6970.

Delaware—*See* **Pennsylvania**, Philadelphia office.

Florida—14010 Roosevelt Blvd. - Ste.704, Clearwater, FL 33762. Phones: (727)893-3738; FAX (727)449-2889.

- 200 E. Las Olas Blvd. - Ste.1600, Ft. Lauderdale, FL 33301. Phones: (954)356-6640; FAX (954)356-6644.
- 777 NW 72nd Ave - Mailbox 3L2, Miami, FL 33126-3009. Phones: (305)526-7425; FAX (305)526-7434.
- Eola Park Centre - Ste.1270, 200 E. Robinson St., Orlando, FL 32801. Phones: (407)648-6235; FAX (407)648-6756.
- 325 John Knox Rd. - Ste.201 Tallahassee, FL 32303. Phones: (850)942-9635; FAX (850)922-9595.

Georgia—Centergy One Bldg. - Ste.1055, 75 5th St., NW, Atlanta, GA 30308. Phones: (912)652-4204; FAX (912)652-4241.

- 111 E. Liberty St. - Ste.202, Savannah, GA 31401. Phones: (404)657-1900; FAX (404)657-1970.

Hawaii—521 Ala Moana Blvd. - Rm.214, Honolulu, HI 96813. Phones: (808)522-8040; FAX (808)522-8045.

Idaho (*Portland, OR district*)—700 W. State St. - 2nd fl., Boise, ID 83720. Phones: (208)334-3857; FAX (208)334-2783.

Illinois—200 W. Adams St. - Ste.2450, Chicago, IL 60603. Phones: (312)353-8045; FAX (312)353-8120.

- 610 Central Ave. - Ste.150, Highland Park, IL 60035. Phones: (847)681-8010; FAX (847)681-8012.
- 515 N. Court St., P.O. Box 1747, Rockford, IL 61103. Phones: (815)987-8123; FAX (815)963-7943.

Indiana—Indianapolis Export Assistance Center, Pennwood One - Ste.106, 11405 N. Pennsylvania St., Carmel, IN 46032. Phones: (317)582-2300; FAX (317)582-2301.

Iowa—700 Locust St. - Ste.100, Des Moines, IA 50309-3739. Phones: (515)288-8614; FAX (515)288-1437.

Kansas (*Kansas City, MO district*)—209 E. William - Ste.300, Wichita, KS 67202-4012. Phones: (316)263-4067; FAX (316)263-8306.

Kentucky—601 W. Broadway - Rm.634B, Louisville, KY 40202. Phones: (502)582-5066; FAX (502)582-6573.

FIELD OFFICE CONTACTS 753

- 140 E. Main St., Lexington, KY 40507. Phones: (606)677-6160; FAX (606)677-6161.

Louisiana—Delta Export Assistance Center, 2 Canal St. - Ste.2710, New Orleans, LA 70130. Phones: (504)589-6546; FAX (504)589-2337.

- Business Education Bldg.- 119H, One University Place, Shreveport, LA 71129. Phones: (318)676-3064; FAX (318)676-3063.

Maine (*Boston, MA District*)—511 Congress St., Portland, ME 04101. Phones: (207) 541-7400; FAX (207)541-7420.

Maryland—World Trade Center - Ste.2432, 401 E. Pratt St., Baltimore, MD 21202. Phones: (410)962-4539; FAX (410)962-4529.

Massachusetts—World Trade Center - Ste.307, 164 Northern Ave., Boston, MA 02210-2071. Phones: (617)424-5990; FAX (617)424-5992.

Michigan—425 S. Main St. - Ste.103, Ann Arbor, MI 48104. Phones: (734)741-2430; FAX (734)741-2432.

- 211 W. Fort St. - Ste.2220, Detroit, MI 48226. Phones: (313)226-3650; FAX (313) 226-3657.
- 301 W. Fulton St. - Ste.718-S, Grand Rapids, MI 49504. Phones: (616)458-3564; FAX (616)458-3872.
- Oakland Pointe Office Bldg. - Ste.1300 West, 250 Elizabeth Lake Rd., Pontiac, MI 48341. Phones: (248)975-9600; FAX (248)975-9606.

Minnesota—45 S. 7th St. - Ste.2240, Minneapolis, MN 55402. Phones: (612)348-1638; FAX (612)348-1650.

Mississippi—704 E. Main St., Raymond, MS 39154. Phones: (601)857-0128; FAX (601)857-0026.

Missouri—2345 Grand - Ste.650, Kansas City, MO 64108. Phones: (816)410-9201; FAX (816)410-9208.

- 8182 Maryland Ave. - Ste.303, St. Louis, MO 63105. Phones: (314)425-3302; FAX (314)425-3381.

Montana—c/o Montana World Trade Center - Ste.257, Gallagher Business Bldg., Missoula, MT 59812. Phones: (406)243-2098; FAX (406)243-5259.

Nebraska—11135 "O" St., Omaha, NE 68137. Phones: (402)221-3664; FAX (402)221-3668.

Nevada—1755 E. Plumb Lane - Ste.152, Reno, NV 89502. Phones: (702)784-5203; FAX (702)784-5343.

New Hampshire *(Boston, MA district)*—17 New Hampshire Ave., Portsmouth, NH 03801-2838. Phones: (603)334-6074; FAX (603)334-6110.

New Jersey—One Gateway Center - 9th fl., Newark, NJ 07102. Phones: (973)645-4682; FAX (973)645-4783.

- Bldg.4 - Ste.105, 3131 Princeton Pike, Trenton, NJ 08648. Phones: (609)989-2100; FAX (609)989-2395.

New Mexico *(Dallas, TX District)*—c/o New Mexico Department of Economic Development, 1100 St. Francis Dr., Santa Fe, NM 87503. Phones: (505)827-0350; FAX (505)827-0263.

New York—111 W. Huron St. - Rm.1304, Buffalo, NY 14202. Phones: (716)551-4191; FAX (716)551-5290.

- Long Island Export Assistance Center, 1550 Franklin Ave. - Rm.207, Mineola, NY 11501. Phones: (516)739-1765; FAX (516)739-3310.
- Harlem Export Assistance Center, 163 W. 125th St. - Ste.904, New York, NY 10027. Phones: (212)860-6200; FAX (212)860-6203.
- 6 World Trade Center - Rm.635, New York, NY 10048. Phones: (212)466-5222; FAX (212)264-1356.
- Westchester Export Assistance Center, 707 W. Chester Ave. - Ste.209, White Plains, NY 10604. Phones: (914)682-6712; FAX (914)682-6698.

11.108 thru 11.112 (cont.)

North Carolina—521 E. Morehead St. - Ste.435, Charlotte, NC 28202. Phones: (704)333-4886; FAX (704)332-2681.
- 400 W. Market St. - Ste.102, Greensboro, NC 27401. Phones: (336)333-5345; FAX (336)333-5158.

North Dakota—*See* **Minneapolis, MN** Export Assistance Center.

Ohio—36 E. 7th St. - Ste.2650, Cincinnati, OH 45202. Phones: (513)684-2944; FAX (513)684-3227.
- Bank One Center - Ste.700, 600 Superior Ave. E., Cleveland, OH 44114. Phones: (216)522-4750; FAX (216)522-2235.
- Two Nationwide Plaza - Ste.1400, Columbus, OH 43215. Phones: (614)365-9510; FAX (614)365-9598.
- 300 Madison Ave., Toledo, OH 43604. Phones: (419)241-0683; FAX (419)241-0684.

Oklahoma—301 NW 63rd St. - Ste.330, Oklahoma City, OK 73116. Phones: (405)608-5302; FAX (405)608-4211.
- 700 N. Greenwood Ave. - Ste.1400, Tulsa, OK 74106. Phones: (918)581-7650; FAX (918)581-6263.

Oregon—1401 Willamette St., Eugene, OR 97401-4003. Phones: (541)465-6575; FAX (541)465-6704.
- One World Trade Center - Ste.242, 121 SW Salmon St., Portland, OR 97204. Phones: (503)326-3001; FAX (503)326-6351.

Pennsylvania—One Commerce Square, 228 Walnut St. - Ste.850, P.O. Box 11698, Harrisburg, PA 17108-1698. Phones: (717)221-4510; FAX (717)221-4505.
- The Curtis Center - Ste.580W, Independence Square West, Philadelphia, PA 19106. Phones: (215)597-6101; FAX (215)597-6123.
- Federal Bldg. - Rm.2002, 1000 Liberty Ave., Pittsburgh, PA 15222. Phones: (412)395-5050; FAX (412)395-4875.

Puerto Rico *(Hato Rey)*—525 F.D. Roosevelt Ave. - Ste.905, San Juan, PR 00918. Phones: (787)766-5555; FAX (787)766-5692.

Rhode Island *(Hartford, CT district)*—One West Exchange St., Providence, RI 02903. Phones: (401)528-5104; FAX (401)528-5067.

South Carolina—5300 International Blvd. - Ste.201-C, North Charleston, SC 29418. Phones: (843)760-3794; FAX (843)760-3798.
- Thurmond Federal Bldg. - Ste.172, 1835 Assembly St., Columbia, SC 29201. Phones: (803)765-5345; FAX (803)253-3614.
- Upstate Export Assistance Center, Park Central Office Park - Bldg. 1 (Ste.109), 555 N. Pleasantburg Dr., Greenville, SC 29607. Phones: (864)271-1976; FAX (864)271-4171.

South Dakota—Siouxland Export Assistance Center, Augustana College - Rm.122, 2001 S. Summit Ave. Sioux Falls, SD 57197. Phones: (605)330-4264; FAX (605)330-4266.

Tennessee—c/o Centre for Enterprise, Buckman Hall - 3rd fl.(Ste.348), 650 E. Parkway S., Memphis, TN 38104. Phones: (901)323-1543; FAX (901)320-9128.
- Old Historic City Hall - Ste.300, 600 W. Summit Hill Dr., Knoxville, TN 37902-2011. Phones: (865)545-4637; FAX (865)545-4435.
- 211 Commerce St. - Ste.100(3rd fl.), Nashville, TN 37201. Phones: (615)736-5161; FAX (615)736-2454.

Texas—1700 Congress - 2nd fl., Austin, TX 78701. Phones: (512)916-5939; FAX (512)916-5940. *For mail:* P.O. Box 12728, Austin, TX 78711.
- 2050 N. Stemmons Fwy. - Ste.170, Dallas, TX 75207. Phones: (214)767-0542; FAX (214)767-8240. *For mail:* Dallas, TX 75342-0069.
- 711 Houston St., Ft. Worth, TX 76102. Phones: (817)212-2673; FAX (817)978-0178.
- 500 Dallas - Ste.1160, Houston, TX 77002. Phones: (713)718-3062; FAX (713)718-3060.

FIELD OFFICE CONTACTS

- 203 S. St. Mary St. - Ste.360, San Antonio, TX 78205. Phones: (210)228-9878; FAX (210)228-9874.

Utah—324 S. State St. - Ste.221, Salt Lake City, UT 84111. Phones: (801)524-5116; FAX (801)524-5886.

Vermont—National Life Bldg. - 6th fl., Drawer 20, Montpelier, VT 05620-0501. Phones: (802)828-4508; FAX (802)828-3258.

Virginia—1911 N. Ft. Myer Dr. - Ste.601, Arlington, VA 22209. Phones: (703)524-2885; FAX (703)524-2649.

- 400 N. 8th St. - Ste.540, P.O. Box 10026, Richmond, VA 23240. Phones: (804)771-2246; FAX (804)771-2390.

Washington—2001 6th Ave. - Ste.650, Seattle, WA 98121. Phones: (206)553-5615; FAX (206)553-7253.

- 801 W. Riverside Ave. - Ste.400, Spokane, WA 99201. Phones: (509)353-2625; FAX (509)353-2449.

- 950 Pacific Ave. - Ste.410, Tacoma, WA 98402. Phones: (253)593-6736; FAX (253)383-4676.

West Virginia—405 Capitol St. - Ste.807, Charleston, WV 25301. Phones: (304)347-5123; FAX (304)347-5408.

- Wheeling Jesuit University/NTTC, 316 Washington Ave., Wheeling, WV 26003. Phones: (304)243-5493; FAX (304)243-5494.

Wisconsin—517 E. Wisconsin Ave. - Rm.596, Milwaukee, WI 53202. Phones: (414)297-3473; FAX (414)297-3470.

Wyoming—*See* **Denver, Colorado** Export Assistance Center.

11.150 Bureau of Export Administration

Western—3300 Irvine Ave. - Ste.345, Newport Beach, CA 92660-3198. Phone: (714)660-0144.

- 101 Park Center Plaza - Ste.1001, San Jose, CA 95113. Phone: (408)998-7402.

ECONOMIC DEVELOPMENT ADMINISTRATION

11.300 thru 11.313 REGIONAL OFFICES

Atlanta *(Alabama, Florida, Georgia, Kentucky, Mississippi, North Carolina, South Carolina, Tennessee)*—401 W. Peachtree St. NW - Ste.1820, Atlanta, GA 30308-3510. Phone: (404)730-3002.

Austin *(Arkansas, Louisiana, New Mexico, Oklahoma, Texas)*—327 Congress Ave. - Ste.200, Austin, TX 78701-5595. Phone: (512)381-8144.

Chicago *(Illinois, Indiana, Michigan, Minnesota, Ohio, Wisconsin)*—111 N. Canal St. - Ste.855, Chicago, IL 60606-7204. Phone: (312)353-8143.

Denver *(Colorado, Iowa, Kansas, Missouri, Montana, Nebraska, North Dakota, South Dakota, Utah, Wyoming)*—1244 Speer Blvd. - Rm.670, Denver, CO 80204. Phone: (303)844-4715.

Philadelphia *(Connecticut, Delaware, District of Columbia, Maine, Maryland, Massachusetts, New Hampshire, New Jersey, New York, Pennsylvania, Puerto Rico, Rhode Island, Vermont, Virgin Islands, Virginia, West Virginia)*—Curtis Center, Independence Square West - Ste.140 South, Philadelphia, PA 19106. Phone: (215)597-4603.

Seattle *(Alaska, American Samoa, Arizona, California, Guam, Hawaii, Idaho, Marshall Islands, Micronesia, Nevada, Northern Mariana Islands, Oregon, Washington)*—Jackson Federal Bldg. - Ste.1856, 915 2nd Ave., Seattle, WA 98174. Phone: (206)220-7660.

NATIONAL OCEANIC AND ATMOSPHERIC ADMINISTRATION

11.405 thru 11.427

REGIONAL OFFICES

ALASKA—Juneau, AK 99802-1668. Phone: (907)586-7221.

NORTHEAST—One Blackburn Dr., Gloucester, MA 01930. Phone: (978)281-9250.

NORTHWEST—7600 Sand Point Way NE, Seattle, WA 98115. Phone: (206)526-6150.

SOUTHEAST—9721 Executive Center Dr. N. - Ste.201, St. Petersburg, FL 33702. Phone: (727)570-5301.

SOUTHWEST—501 W. Ocean Blvd. - Ste.4200, Long Beach, CA 90802-4213. Phone: (562)980-4001.

- Southwest Fisheries Science Center, La Jolla, CA 92038-0271. Phone: (619)546-7081.

FIELD AREAS

Virginia—Atlantic Marine Center, 439 W. York St., Norfolk, VA 23510-1114. Phone: (757)441-6776.

Washington—Pacific Marine Center, 1801 Fairview Ave. E., Seattle, WA 98102. Phone: (206)553-7656.

11.433
NORTHEAST—NMFS, One Blackburn Dr., Gloucester, MA 01930. Phone: (978)281-9267. **Internet:** e-mail, "Grants.Information@noaa.gov".

SOUTHEAST—State/Federal Liaison Office, NMFS, 263 13th Ave. S., St. Petersburg, FL 33701. Phone: (727)824-5324.

11.434
SOUTHEAST—Federal Program Officer, State/Federal Liaison Office, 263 13th Ave. S., St. Petersburg, FL 33701. Phones: (727)824-5324; FAX (727)824-5364.

11.435
SOUTHEAST—Federal Program Officer, State/Federal Liaison Branch, 263 13th Ave. S., St. Petersburg, FL 33701. Phones: (727)824-5324; FAX (727)824-5364.

11.436
NORTHWEST—Columbia River Fisheries Development Program, NMFS-NOAA, Salmon Recovery Division, Hatcheries and Inland Fisheries Branch, 1201 NE Lloyd Blvd., Portland, OR 97232-1274. Phones: (503)231-2009; FAX (503)872-2737.

Northwest Fisheries Science Center, NOAA-NMFS, 2725 Montlake Blvd. E., Seattle, WA 98112-2097. Phones: (206)860-3234; FAX (206)860-3467.

11.437
ALASKA—NMFS, Federal Program Officer, Juneau, AK 99802-1668. Phones: (907) 586-7255; FAX (907)586-7255.

11.438
ALASKA—Pacific Coast Salmon Recovery Program, NMFS, Juneau, AK 99802-1668. Phone: (907)586-7280.

NORTHWEST—Pacific Salmon Treaty, NOAA-NMFS, 7600 Sand Point Way NE, Seattle, WA 98115. Phones: (206)526-4140; FAX (206)526-6534.

- NOAA-NMFS, 7600 Sand Point Way NE, Seattle, WA 98115. Phones: (206)526-6150; FAX (206)526-6426.

11.439
Discretionary: Stranding Network Contacts

ALASKA—NMFS, Federal Bldg. - 14th fl., 709 W. 9th St., Juneau, AK 99802-1668. Phone: (907)586-7824.

NORTHEAST—NMFS, One Blackburn Dr., Gloucester, MA 01930-2298. Phone: (978)281-9328.

NORTHWEST—NMFS, Bldg. 1, 7600 Sand Point Way, NE, Seattle, WA 98115. Phone: (206)526-6733.

SOUTHEAST—NMFS, 263 13th Ave. S., St. Petersburg, FL 33701. Phone: (727)824-5312.

SOUTHWEST—NMFS, 501 W. Ocean Blvd. - Ste.4200, Long Beach, CA 90802-4213. Phone: (562)980-4017.

Nondiscretionary:

ALASKA—NOAA/NMFS, Juneau, AK 99802-1668. Phone: (907)586-7273.

NORTHWEST—NOAA/NMFS, 7600 Sand Point Way NE, Seattle, WA 98115. Phones: (206)526-6150; FAX (206)526-6426.

PACIFIC ISLANDS—NMFS, 1601 Kapiolani Blvd. - Ste.1110, Honolulu, HI 96814-4700. Phone: (808)973-2935.

11.441 Listed under **11.405**.

11.444 and 11.445 PACIFIC ISLANDS—Pacific Islands Fisheries Science Center, NMFS, 2570 Dole St., Honolulu, HI 96822. Phones: (808)983-5374; FAX (808)983-2902.

11.449 NOAA/OAR, Bldg. 22, 325 Broadway, Boulder, CO 80303. Phone: (303)497-6731.

11.450 AFWS Operations Manager, Hydrologic Services Division, National Weather Service Eastern Region (W/ER2), Airport Corporate Center, 630 Johnson Ave., Bohemia, NY 11716. Phone: (631)244-0112.

11.452 ALASKA—NMFS, P.O. Box 12668, Juneau, AK 99802. Phone: (907)586-7280.

NORTHEAST—Director, State, Federal and Constituent Programs Office, NMFS, One Blackburn Dr., Gloucester, MA 01930-2298. Phones: (978)281-9243; FAX (978)281-9117. **Internet:** e-mail, "Grants.Information@noaa.gov".

NORTHWEST—NMFS, 7600 Sand Point Way NE, Seattle, WA 98115. Phones: (206)526-6115; FAX (206)526-4461.

SOUTHEAST—State/Federal Liaison Branch, 263 13th Ave. S., St. Petersburg, FL 33701. Phones: (727)824-5364; FAX (727)824-5364.

SOUTHWEST—Federal Programs Officer, 501 W. Ocean Blvd. - Ste.4200, Long Beach, CA 90802. Phones: (562)980-4033; FAX (562)980-4047.

PACIFIC ISLANDS AREA OFFICE—Program Analyst, 1601 Kapiolani Blvd. - Ste.1110, Honolulu, HI 96814. Phones: (808)973-2935, ext.213; FAX (808)973-2941.

11.454 ALASKA—NMFS, Juneau, AK 99802-1668. Phone: (907)586-7845.

NORTHEAST—State, Federal and Constituent Programs Office, NMFS, One Blackburn Dr., Gloucester, MA 01930-2298. Phones: (978)281-9243; FAX (978)281-9117. **Internet:** e-mail, "Grants.Information@noaa.gov".

NORTHWEST—NMFS, 7600 Sand Point Way NE, Seattle, WA 98115. Phones: (206)526-6150; FAX (206)526-6426.

SOUTHEAST—Federal Program Officer, State/Federal Liaison Branch, 263 13th Ave. S., St. Petersburg, FL 33701. Phones: (727)824-5324; FAX (727)824-5364.

SOUTHWEST—Federal Program Officer, 501 W. Ocean Blvd. - Ste.4200, Long Beach, CA 90802-4213. Phones: (562)980-4033; FAX (562)980-4047.

11.455 ALASKA—Director, Alaska Fisheries Science Center - Bldg. 4, 7600 Sand Point Way NE, Seattle, WA 98115-6349. Phones: (206)526-4000; FAX (206)526-4004.

NORTHEAST—Chief/Office of Marine Ecosystem Studies, Northeast Fisheries Science Center, 28 Tarzwell Dr., Narragansett, RI 02882. Phones: (401)782-3211; FAX (401)782-3201.

NORTHWEST—Deputy Director, Northwest Fisheries Science Center, 2725 Montlake Blvd. E., Seattle, WA 98112-2097. Phones: (206)860-3200; FAX (206)860-3217.

SOUTHEAST—Federal Program Officer, State/Federal Liaison Branch, 263 13th Ave. S., St. Petersburg, FL 33701. Phones: (727)824-5324; FAX (727)824-5364.

SOUTHWEST—Deputy Science Director, Southwest Fisheries Science Center, 8604

11.455 (cont.)	La Jolla Shores Drive, La Jolla, CA 92038-1508. Phones: (858)546-7066; (858)546-7003.
11.457	Chesapeake Bay Office, NMFS-NOAA, 410 Severn Ave. - Ste.107A, Annapolis, MD 21403. Phones: (410)267-5660; FAX (410)267-5666.
11.463	Listed under **11.405**
11.472	**ALASKA**—NMFS, Juneau, AK 99802-1668. Phones: (907)586-7845; FAX (907)586-7255.
	NORTHEAST—Director, State, Federal and Constituent Programs Office, NMFS, One Blackburn Drive, Gloucester, MA 01930-2298. Phones: (978)281-9243; (978) 281-9117. **Internet:** e-mail, "Grants.Information@noaa.gov".
	NORTHWEST—NMFS, 7600 Sand Point Way NE, Seattle, WA 98115. Phones: (206)526-6115; FAX (206)526-4461.
	SOUTHEAST—State/Federal Liaison Staff, 9721 Executive Center Drive N., St. Petersburg, FL 33702-2432. Phones: (727)570-5324; FAX (727)570-5364.
	SOUTHWEST—Federal Program Officer, 501 W. Ocean Blvd. - Ste.4200, Long Beach, CA 90802-4213. Phones: (562)980-4033; (562)980-4047.
11.473	Director, NOAA Coastal Services Center, 2234 S. Hobson Ave., Charleston, SC 29405-2413. Phone: (843)740-1200.
11.474	**NORTHEAST**—State, Federal and Constituent Programs Division, NMFS, One Blackburn Dr., Gloucester, MA 01930. Phones: (978)281-9243; FAX (978)281-9117. **Internet:** e-mail, "Grants.Information@noaa.gov".
	SOUTHEAST—Federal Program Officer, State/Federal Liaison Branch, 263 13th Ave. S., St. Petersburg, FL 33701. Phones: (727)824-5324; FAX (727)824-5364.
11.477	**ALASKA**—NMFS, Juneau, AK 99802-1668. Phones: (907)586-7845; FAX (907)586-7255.
	NORTHEAST—Director, State,Federal and Constituent Programs Office, NMFS, One Blackburn Dr., Gloucester, MA 01930-2298. Phones: (978)281-9243; FAX (978) 281-9117. **Internet:** e-mail, "Grants.Information@noaa.gov".
	NORTHWEST—NMFS, Sustainable Fisheries Division, 7600 Sand Point Way NE, Seattle, WA 98115. Phones: (206)526-6113; FAX (206)526-4461.
	SOUTHEAST—State/Federal Liaison Staff, 263 13th Ave. S., St. Petersburg, FL 33702-2432. Phones: (727)570-5324; FAX (727)570-5364.
	SOUTHWEST—Federal Program Officer, 501 W. Ocean Blvd., Long Beach, CA 90802-4213. Phones: (562)980-4239; FAX (562)980-4047.

NATIONAL INSTITUTE OF STANDARDS AND TECHNOLOGY

11.603 and 11.604	Listed under **11.108**.

MINORITY BUSINESS DEVELOPMENT AGENCY

11.800 thru 11.803	**REGIONAL AND DISTRICT OFFICES**
	REGIONS I, II, AND III *(Connecticut, Delaware, District of Columbia, Maine, Maryland, Massachusetts, New Hampshire, New Jersey, New York, Pennsylvania, Puerto Rico, Rhode Island, Vermont, Virgin Islands, West Virginia)*—26 Federal Plaza - Rm.3720, New York, NY 10278. Phone: (212)264-3262.

Massachusetts—10 Causeway St. - Rm.418., Boston, MA 02222-1041. Phone: (617) 565-6850.

Pennsylvania—Federal Office Bldg. - Rm.10128, 600 Arch St., Philadelphia, PA 19106. Phone: (215)597-9236.

REGION IV *(Alabama, Florida, Georgia, Kentucky, Mississippi, North Carolina, South Carolina, Tennessee)*—401 W. Peachtree St. NW - Rm.1715, Atlanta, GA 30308-3516. Phone: (404)730-3300.

Florida—Federal Bldg. - Rm.1314, 51 SW 1st Ave., P.O. Box 25, Miami, FL 33130. Phone: (305)536-5054.

REGIONS V AND VII *(Illinois, Indiana, Iowa, Kansas, Michigan, Minnesota, Missouri, Nebraska, Ohio, Wisconsin)*—55 E. Monroe St. - Ste.1406, Chicago, IL 60603. Phone: (312)353-0182.

REGIONS VI AND VIII *(Arkansas, Colorado, Louisiana, Montana, New Mexico, North Dakota, Oklahoma, South Dakota, Texas, Utah, Wyoming)*—1100 Commerce St. - Rm.7B23, Dallas, TX 75242. Phone: (214)767-8001.

REGIONS IX AND X *(Alaska, American Samoa, Arizona, California, Guam, Hawaii, Idaho, Nevada, Oregon, Washington)*—221 Main St. - Rm.1280, San Francisco, CA 94105. Phone: (415)744-3001.

California—9660 Flair Dr. - Ste.455, El Monte, CA 91731. Phone: (818)453-8636.

PATENT AND TRADEMARK OFFICE

11.900   Listed under **11.108**.

DEPARTMENT OF DEFENSE

DEPARTMENT OF THE ARMY, CORPS OF ENGINEERS

12.100 thru 12.111

Alabama *(Mobile District)*—P.O. Box 2288, Mobile, AL 36628. Phone: (205)690-2511.

Alaska *(Alaska District)*—P.O. Box 898, Anchorage, AK 99506. Phone: (907)752-5233.

Arkansas *(Little Rock District)*—P.O. Box 867, Little Rock, AR 72203. Phone: (501) 378-5531.

California *(Los Angeles District)*—P.O. Box 2711, Los Angeles, CA 90053. Phone: (213)688-5300.

- *(Sacramento District)*—650 Capitol Mall, Sacramento, CA 95814. Phone: (916)448-2232.

- *(San Francisco District)*—211 Main St., San Francisco, CA 94105. Phone: (415)974-0358.

- *(South Pacific Division)*—630 Sansome St. - Rm.720, San Francisco, CA 94111. Phone: (415)556-0914.

District of Columbia—CDR, USACA/CEMP-RI, 20 Massachusetts Ave. NW, Washington, DC 20314. Phone: (202)504-4950.

Florida *(Jacksonville District)*—P.O. Box 4970, Jacksonville, FL 32232. Phone: (904) 791-2241.

Georgia *(Savannah District)*—P.O. Box 889, Savannah, GA 31402. Phone: (912)944-5224, ext.224.

12.100 thru 12.111 (cont.)

- *(South Atlantic Division)*—510 Title Bldg., 30 Pryor St. SW, Atlanta, GA 30335. Phone: (404)221-6711.

Hawaii *(Pacific Ocean Division)*—Ft. Shafter, HI 96858. Phone: (808)438-1500.

Illinois *(Chicago District)*—219 S. Dearborn St., Chicago, IL 60604. Phone: (312)353-6400.

- *(North Central Division)*—536 S. Clark St., Chicago, IL 60605. Phone: (312)353-6310.
- *(Rock Island District)*—Clock Tower Bldg., P.O. Box 2004, Rock Island, IL 61204. Phone: (309)788-6361.
- Constitution Engineering Research Laboratory, Champaign, IL 61820-1305. Phone: (217)373-6789.

Kentucky *(Louisville District)*—P.O. Box 59, Louisville, KY 40201. Phone: (502)582-5601.

Louisiana *(New Orleans District)*—P.O. Box 60267, New Orleans, LA 70160. Phone: (504)838-1121.

Maryland *(Baltimore District)*—P.O. Box 1715, Baltimore, MD 21203. Phone: (301)962-4545.

Massachusetts *(New England Division)*—424 Trapelo Rd., Waltham, MA 02254. Phone: (617)647-8220.

Michigan *(Detroit District)*—P.O. Box 1027, Detroit, MI 48231. Phone: (313)226-6762.

Minnesota *(St. Paul District)*—1135 USPO and Custom House, St. Paul, MN 55101. Phone: (612)725-7501.

Mississippi *(Lower Mississippi Valley Division)*—P.O. Box 80, Vicksburg, MS 39180. Phone: (601)634-5750.

- *(Vicksburg District)*—P.O. Box 60, Vicksburg, MS 39180. Phone: (601)634-5010.
- Waterways Experiment Station, Vicksburg, MS 39180-0631. Phone: (601)634-2424.

Missouri *(Kansas City District)*—700 Federal Bldg., Kansas City, MO 64106. Phone: (816)374-3201.

- *(St. Louis District)*—210 N. Tucker Blvd., St. Louis, MO 63101. Phone: (314)263-5660.

Nebraska *(Missouri River Division)*—Downtown Station, P.O. Box 103, Omaha, NE 68101. Phone: (402)221-7201.

- *(Omaha District)*—USPO and Courthouse - Rm.6014, Omaha, NE 68102. Phone: (402)221-3900.

New Hampshire—Cold Regions Research and Engineering Laboratory, Hanover, NH 03755-1290. Phone: (603)646-4390.

New Mexico *(Albuquerque District)*—P.O. Box 1580, Albuquerque, NM 87103. Phone: (505)766-2732.

New York *(Buffalo District)*—1776 Niagara St., Buffalo, NY 14207. Phone: (716)876-5454, ext.2200.

- *(New York District)*—26 Federal Plaza, New York, NY 10278. Phone: (212)264-0100.
- *(North Atlantic Division)*—90 Church St., New York, NY 10007. Phone: (212)264-7101.

North Carolina *(Wilmington District)*—P.O. Box 1890, Wilmington, NC 28402. Phone: (919)343-4501.

Ohio *(Ohio River Division)*—P.O. Box 1159, Cincinnati, OH 45201. Phone: (513)221-6000.

Oklahoma *(Tulsa District)*—P.O. Box 61, Tulsa, OK 74121. Phone: (918)581-7311.

FIELD OFFICE CONTACTS

Oregon *(North Pacific Division)*—P.O. Box 2870, Portland, OR 97208. Phone: (503)221-3700.
- *(Portland District)*—P.O. Box 2946, Portland, OR 97208. Phone: (503)221-6000.

Pennsylvania *(Philadelphia District)*—U.S. Custom House, 2nd and Chestnut St., Philadelphia, PA 19106. Phone: (215)597-4848.
- *(Pittsburgh District)*—Federal Bldg., 1000 Liberty Ave., Pittsburgh, PA 15222. Phone: (412)644-6800.

South Carolina *(Charleston District)*—P.O. Box 919, Charleston, SC 29402. Phone: (803)724-4229.

Tennessee *(Memphis District)*—B-202 Clifford Davis Federal Bldg., Memphis, TN 38103. Phone: (901)521-3221.
- *(Nashville District)*—P.O. Box 1070, Nashville, TN 37202. Phone: (615)251-5626.

Texas *(Ft. Worth District)*—P.O. Box 17300, Ft. Worth, TX 76102. Phone: (817)334-2300.
- *(Galveston District)*—P.O. Box 1229, Galveston, TX 77553. Phone: (409)766-3006.
- *(Southwestern Division)*—1114 Commerce St., Dallas, TX 75242. Phone: (214)767-2500.

Virginia *(Norfolk District)*—803 Front St., Norfolk, VA 23510. Phone: (804)441-3601.
- Humphreys Engineer Center Support Activity, Ft. Belvoir, VA 22060-5580. Phone: (202)355-2153.
- Topographic Engineering Center, Ft. Belvoir, VA 22060-5546. Phone: (202)355-2659.

Washington *(Seattle District)*—P.O. Box C-3755, Seattle, WA 98124. Phone: (206)764-3690.
- *(Walla Walla District)*—City-County Airport - Bldg. 602, Walla Walla, WA 99362. Phone: (509)522-6506.

West Virginia *(Huntington District)*—502 8th St., Huntington, WV 25721. Phone: (304)529-5395.

12.114 and 12.116 **Research and Development Laboratories**

USAE Hydrologic Engineering Center, 609 2nd St., Davis, CA 95616-4887. Phone: (916)756-1104.

USA Construction Engineering Research Laboratory, 2902 Newmark Dr., Champaign, IL 61821-1075. Phones: (800)872-2375, (800)252-7122.

USAE Waterways Experiment Station, 3909 Falls Ferry Rd., Vicksburg, MS 39180-6199. Phones: (601)634-2512, (800)522-6937.

USA Cold Regions Research and Engineering Laboratory, 72 Lynn Rd., Hanover, NH 03755-1290. Phone: (603)646-4445.

USA Topographic Engineering Center, Cude Bldg. No. 2592, Ft. Belvoir, VA 22060-5546. Phone: (703)355-3133.

USAE Institute for Water Resources, Casey Bldg. No. 2594, Ft. Belvoir, VA 22060-5586. Phone: (703)355-3084.

DEPARTMENT OF THE ARMY, U.S. ARMY MEDICAL COMMAND

12.420 Commander, Army Medical Research Acquisition Activity, Attn: SGRD-RMA-RC, Ft. Detrick, Frederick, MD 21702-5014. Phone: (301)619-2036.

OFFICE OF THE SECRETARY (ECONOMIC SECURITY)

12.600 thru 12.614 WESTERN REGION—Office of Economic Adjustment, OASD(FM&P), 1325 J St. - Ste.1500, Sacramento, CA 95814. Phone: (916)567-7365.

SECRETARIES OF MILITARY DEPARTMENTS

12.700 *Contact nearest military installation. Consult local phone directory.*

DEPARTMENT OF THE AIR FORCE, MATERIAL COMMAND

12.800 Air Force Office of Scientific Research, Bolling AFB - Ste.B115, 110 Duncan Ave., Washington, DC 20332-4990. Phone: (no number provided).

Armstrong Laboratory, 8005 9th St., Brooks AFB, TX 78235-5353. Phone: (no number provided).

Phillips Laboratory, 3651 Lowry Ave. SE, Kirkland AFB, NM 87117-5777. Phone: (505)846-4979.

Rome Laboratory, 26 Electronics Pkwy., Griffins AFB, NY 13441-4514. Phone: (315) 330-7746.

Wright Laboratory, Bldg. 7, 2530 C St., Wright-Patterson AFB, OH 45433-7607. Phone: (513)255-4813.

DEPARTMENT OF HOUSING AND URBAN DEVELOPMENT

HOUSING - FEDERAL HOUSING COMMISSIONER

14.103 thru 14.195 **FIELD OFFICES**

Alabama—950 22nd St. N. - Ste.900, Birmingham, AL 35203-5302. Phones: (205)731-2617; FAX (205)731-2593.

Alaska—3000 C St. - Ste.401, Anchorage, AK 99503. Phones: (907)677-9800; FAX (907)677-9803.

Arizona—1 N. Central Ave. - Ste.600, Phoenix, AZ 85004. Phones: (602)379-7100; FAX (602)379-3985.

▪ 160 N. Stone Ave., Tucson, AZ 85701-1467. Phones: (602)670-6000; FAX (602)670-6207.

Arkansas—TCBY Tower, 425 W. Capitol Ave. - Ste.900, Little Rock, AR 72201-3488. Phones: (501)324-5931; FAX (501)324-6142.

California—2135 Fresno St. - Ste.100, Fresno, CA 93721-1718. Phones: (559)487-5033, ext.232; FAX (559)487-5191.

▪ AT&T Center - Ste.800, 611 W. 6th St., Los Angeles, CA 90017-3127. Phones: (213)894-8007; FAX (213)894-8110.

FIELD OFFICE CONTACTS 763

- 925 L St., Sacramento, CA 95814-2601. Phones: (916)498-5220, ext.322; FAX (916)498-5262.
- Symphony Towers - Ste.1600, 750 B St., San Diego, CA 92101-8131. Phones: (619)557-5310; FAX (619)557-5312.
- 600 Harrison St. - 3rd fl., San Francisco, CA 94107-1300. Phones: (415)489-6400; FAX (415)489-6419.
- World Trade Tower, 1600 N. Broadway - Ste.101, Santa Ana, CA 92706-3927. Phones: (714)796-5577; FAX (714)796-1285.

Colorado—1670 Broadway 23rd fl.,, Denver, CO 80202. Phones: (303)672-5440; FAX (303)672-5004.

Connecticut—One Corporate Center - 19th fl., 20 Church St., Hartford, CT 06103-3220. Phones: (860)240-4800; FAX (860)240-4850.

Delaware—One Rodney Square - Ste.404, 920 King St., Wilmington, DE 19801. Phones: (302)573-6300; FAX (302)573-6259.

District of Columbia—820 1st St. NE - Ste.300, Washington, DC 20002-4205. Phones: (202)275-9200; FAX (202)523-9212.

Florida—Southern Bell Tower - Ste.2200, 301 W. Bay St., Jacksonville, FL 32202-5121. Phones: (904)232-2627; FAX (904)232-3759.

- Brickell Plaza Bldg., 909 SE 1st Ave., Miami, FL 33131-3028. Phones: (305)536-4456; FAX (305)536-5765.
- Langley Bldg. - Ste.270, 3751 Maguire Blvd., Orlando, FL 32803-3032. Phones: (407)648-6441; FAX (407)648-6310.
- Timberlake Federal Bldg. Annex - Ste.402, 501 E. Zack St., Tampa, FL 33602-3945. Phones: (813)228-2026; FAX (813)228-2431.

Georgia—Five Points Plaza, 40 Marietta St., Atlanta, GA 30303-2806. Phones: (404)331-4111; FAX (404)730-2392.

Hawaii—3 Waterfront Plaza - Ste.3A, 500 Ala Moana Blvd., Honolulu, HI 96813-4918. Phones: (808)522-8175, ext.256 or 259; FAX (808)522-8194.

Idaho—Plaza IV - Ste.220, 800 Park Blvd., Boise, ID 83712-7743. Phones: (208)334-1990, ext.3007; FAX (208)334-9648.

Illinois—Metcalfe Federal Bldg., 77 W. Jackson Blvd., Chicago, IL 60604-3507. Phones: (312)353-5680; FAX (312)886-2729.

- 500 W. Monroe St. - Ste.1SW, Springfield, IL 62704. Phones: (217)492-4120; FAX (217)492-4154.

Indiana—151 N. Delaware St. - Ste.1200, Indianapolis, IN 46204-2526. Phones: (317)226-6303; FAX (317)226-6317.

Iowa—Federal Bldg.- Rm.239, 210 Walnut St., Des Moines, IA 50309-2155. Phones: (515)284-4512; FAX (515)284-4743.

Kansas—Gateway Tower II, 400 State Ave. - Rm.200, Kansas City, KS 66101-2406. Phones: (913)551-5462, ext.4; FAX (913)551-5469.

Kentucky—601 W. Broadway, Louisville, KY 40202. Phones: (502)582-5251; FAX (502)582-6074.

Louisiana—Boggs Federal Bldg. - 9th fl., 501 Magazine St., New Orleans, LA 70130-3099. Phones: (504)589-7201; FAX (504)589-6619.

- 401 Edwards St. - Ste.1510, Shreveport, LA 71101-5513. Phones: (318)676-3440; FAX (318)676-3407.

Maine—Smith Federal Bldg. - Rm.101, 202 Harlow St., Bangor, ME 04401-4919. Phones: (207)945-0467; FAX (207)945-0533.

Maryland—City Crescent Bldg. - 5th fl., 10 S. Howard St., Baltimore, MD 21201-2505. Phones: (410)962-2520, ext.3474; FAX (410)962-1849.

Massachusetts—O'Neill Jr. Federal Office Bldg. - Rm.301, 10 Causeway St., Boston, MA 02222-1092. Phones: (617)994-8200; FAX (617)565-5257.

**14.103
thru
14.195
(cont.)**

Michigan—McNamara Federal Bldg., 477 Michigan Ave., Detroit, MI 48226-2592. Phones: (313)226-7900; FAX (313)226-5611.

• Phoenix Bldg., 801 S. Saginaw St., Flint, MI 48502. Phones: (810)766-5112; FAX (810)766-5122.

• Trade Center Bldg., 50 Louis St. NW, Grand Rapids, MI 49503-2633. Phones: (616)456-2100; FAX (616)456-2114.

Minnesota—Kinnard Financial Center, 920 Second St. S., Minneapolis, MN 55402. Phones: (612)370-3000, ext.2045; FAX (612)370-3220.

Mississippi—McCoy Federal Bldg. - Rm.910, 100 W. Capitol St., Jackson, MS 39269-1096. Phones: (601)965-4757; FAX (601)965-4773.

Missouri—Young Federal Bldg. - Ste.3207, 1222 Spruce St., St. Louis, MO 63103-2836. Phones: (314)539-6583; FAX (314)539-6384.

Montana—Power Block Bldg., 7 W. 6th Ave., Helena, MT 59601. Phones: (406)449-5050; FAX (406)449-4052.

Nebraska—Executive Tower Centre - Ste.100, 10909 Mill Valley Rd., Omaha, NE 68154-3955. Phones: (402)492-3101; FAX (402)492-3150.

Nevada—300 S. Las Vegas Blvd. - Ste.2900, Las Vegas, NV 89101-5833. Phones: (702)366-2100; FAX (702)388-6244.

• 3702 S. Virginia Ave., Reno, NV 89502-6581. Phones: (775)784-5383; FAX (775)784-5005.

New Hampshire—1000 Elm St. - 8th fl., Manchester, NH 03101-1730. Phones: (603)666-7510; FAX (603)666-7667.

New Jersey—Hudson Bldg. - 2nd fl., 800 Hudson Square, Camden, NJ 08102-1156. Phones: (856)757-5081; FAX (856)757-5373.

• One Newark Center - 13th fl., Newark, NJ 07102-5260. Phones: (973)622-7900; FAX (973)645-2323.

New Mexico—625 Silver Ave. SW - Ste.100, Albuquerque, NM 87102-3185. Phones: (505)346-6463, ext.7332; FAX (505)346-6704.

New York—52 Corporate Circle, Albany, NY 12203-5121. Phones: (518)464-4200, ext.4204; FAX (518)464-4300.

• Lafayette Court - 5th fl., 465 Main St., Buffalo, NY 14203-1780. Phones: (716)551-5755, ext.5000; FAX (716)551-5752.

• 26 Federal Plaza - Ste.3541, New York, NY 10278-0068. Phones: (212)264-8000; FAX (212)264-3068.

• 128 Jefferson St., Syracuse, NY 13202. Phones: (315)477-0616; FAX (315)477-0196.

North Carolina—Asheville Bldg. - Ste.401, 1500 Pinecroft Rd., Greensboro, NC 27407-3838. Phones: (336)547-4001; FAX (336)547-4138.

North Dakota—Federal Bldg. - Rm.366, 657 2nd Ave., Fargo, ND 58108-2483. Phones: (701)239-5136; FAX (701)239-5249.

Ohio—15 E. 7th St., Cincinnati, OH 45202-2401. Phones: (513)684-3451; FAX (513)684-6224.

• Renaissance Bldg. - Ste.500, 1350 Euclid Ave., Cleveland, OH 44115-1815. Phones: (216)522-4058, ext.7102; FAX (216)522-4067.

• 200 N. High St., Columbus, OH 43215-2463. Phones: (614)469-2540; FAX (614)469-2432.

Oklahoma—301 NW 6th St. - Ste.200, Oklahoma City, OK 73102. Phones: (405)609-8509; FAX (405)609-8588.

• 1516 S. Boston St. - Ste.100, Tulsa, OK 74119-4030. Phones: (918)581-7434; FAX (918)581-7440.

Oregon—400 SW 6th Ave. - Ste.700, Portland, OR 97204-1632. Phones: (503)326-2561; FAX (503)326-2568.

Pennsylvania—The Wanamaker Bldg., 100 Penn Square East, Philadelphia, PA 19107-3380. Phones: (215)656-0600; FAX (215)656-3445.
- 339 6th Ave. - 6th fl., Pittsburgh, PA 15222-2515. Phones: (412)644-6428; FAX (412)644-4240.

Puerto Rico—New San Juan Office Bldg., 171 Carlos E. Chardon Ave., San Juan, PR 00918-0903. Phones: (787)766-5201; FAX (787)766-5995.

Rhode Island—10 Weybosset St. - 6th fl., Providence, RI 02903-2818. Phones: (401) 528-5230; FAX (401)528-5312.

South Carolina—Thurmond Federal Bldg. - 13th fl., 1835 Assembly St., Columbia, SC 29201-2480. Phones: (803)765-5592; FAX (803)253-3043.

South Dakota—2400 W. 49th St. - Ste.I-201, Sioux Falls, SD 57105-6558. Phones: (605)330-4223; FAX (605)330-4428.

Tennessee—Duncan Federal Bldg. - 3rd fl., 710 Locust St., Knoxville, TN 37902-2526. Phones: (865)545-4384; FAX (865)545-4569.
- One Memphis Place - Ste.1200, 200 Jefferson Ave., Memphis, TN 38103-2389. Phones: (901)544-3367; FAX (901)544-3697.
- 235 Cumberland Bend Dr. - Ste.200, Nashville, TN 37228-1803. Phones: (615)736-5213, ext.7120; FAX (615)736-7848.

Texas—525 Griffin St. - Rm.860, Dallas, TX 75202-5007. Phones: (214)767-8300; FAX (214)767-8973.
- 801 Cherry St., Ft. Worth, TX 76113-2905. Phones: (817)978-5965; FAX (817)978-5567.
- 1301 Fannin - Ste.2200, Houston, TX 77002. Phones: (713)718-3199; FAX (713)313-2319.
- Mahon Federal Bldg. and U.S. Courthouse - Rm.511, 1205 Texas Ave., Lubbock, TX 79401-4093. Phones: (806)472-7265, ext.3030; FAX (806)472-7275.
- One Alamo Center, 106 S. St. Mary's St, Antonio, TX 78205. Phones: (210)475-6806; FAX (210)472-6804.

Utah—125 S. State St. - Ste.3001, Salt Lake City, UT 84138. Phones: (801)524-6070; FAX (801)524-3439.

Vermont—159 Bank St. - 2nd fl., Burlington, VT 05401-4410. Phones: (802)951-6290; FAX (802)951-6298.

Virginia—The 3600 Centre, 600 E. Broad St. - 3rd fl., Richmond, VA 23219-4920. Phones: (804)771-2100; FAX (804)771-2090.

Washington—Seattle Federal Office Bldg. - Ste.200, 909 1st Ave., Seattle, WA 98104-1000. Phones: (206)220-5101; FAX (206)220-5108.
- US Courthouse Bldg. - Rm.588, 920 W. Riverside, Spokane, WA 99201-1010. Phones: (509)353-0674; FAX (509)353-0682.

West Virginia—Kanawha Valley Bldg. - Ste.708, 405 Capitol St., Charleston, WV 25301-1795. Phones: (304)347-7000, ext.101; FAX (304)347-7050.

Wisconsin—Reuss Federal Plaza - Ste.1380, 310 W. Wisconsin Ave., Milwaukee, WI 53203-2289. Phones: (414)297-3214, ext.8001; FAX (414)297-3947.

Wyoming—Federal Bldg. - Rm.1010, 100 E. B St., Casper, WY 82601-1969. Phones: (307)261-6250; FAX (307)261-6245.

OFFICE OF NATIVE AMERICAN PROGRAMS

Alaska—3000 C St. - Ste.401, Anchorage, AK 99503. Phones: (907)677-9800; FAX (907)667-9807.

Eastern/Woodlands (*Iowa, all states east of Mississippi River*)—77 W. Jackson Blvd. - Rm.2404, Chicago, IL 60604-3507. Phones: (800)735-3239; FAX (312)353-8936.

Northern Plains (*Colorado, Montana, Nebraska, North Dakota, South Dakota, Utah,*

14.103 thru 14.195 (cont.)	*Wyoming*)—UMB Plaza - 22nd fl., 1670 Broadway, Denver, CO 80202-4801. Phones: (303)672-5465; FAX (303)672-5003.
	Northwest (*Idaho, Oregon, Washington*)—Seattle Federal Office Bldg. - Ste.300, 909 1st Ave., Seattle, WA 98104-1000. Phones: (206)220-5270; FAX (206)220-5234.
	Southern Plains (*Arkansas, Kansas, Louisiana, Missouri, Oklahoma,Texas*)—301 NW 6th St. - Ste.200., Oklahoma City, OK 73102. Phones: (405)609-8532; FAX (405) 609-8403.
	Southwest (*Arizona, California, Nevada, New Mexico*)—1 N. Central Ave. - Ste.600, Phoenix, AZ 85004-2361. Phones: (602)379-7200; FAX (602)379-3101.
14.197	Office of Multifamily Housing Assistance Restructuring:
	▪ **Chicago**—Metcalfe Federal Bldg. - Rm.2301, 77 W. Jackson Blvd., Chicago, IL 60604. Phone: (312)886-4133, ext.2371.
	▪ **District of Columbia**—The Portals Bldg. - Ste.380, 1280 Maryland Ave. SW, Washington, DC 20024. Phone: (202)260-2746, ext.3768.
14.198	Listed under **14.103**.
14.199	Contact Multifamily Property Disposition Centers in the Atlanta and Fort Worth HUD offices listed under **14.103**.

COMMUNITY PLANNING AND DEVELOPMENT

14.218 thru 14.250	Office of Community Planning and Development. Addresses are listed under **14.103**.
14.310 thru 14.314	Listed under **14.103**.

FAIR HOUSING AND EQUAL OPPORTUNITY

14.400 thru 14.415	Director, Office of Fair Housing and Equal Opportunity, HUD Regional Office. Addresses are listed under **14.103**.

POLICY DEVELOPMENT AND RESEARCH

14.520	Listed under **14.103**.

PUBLIC AND INDIAN HOUSING

14.850 thru 14.867	Office of Public Housing *or* Office of Native American Programs. Addresses are listed under **14.103**.
14.870 thru 14.872	Listed under **14.103**.

… FIELD OFFICE CONTACTS 767

DEPARTMENT OF THE INTERIOR

BUREAU OF INDIAN AFFAIRS

15.020 thru 15.025

AREA OFFICES

Alaska—Alaska Regional Office, Juneau, AK 99802-5520. Phone: (907)586-7177.

Arizona—Western Regional Office, (MS 100), Two Arizona Center - 12th fl., Phoenix, AZ 85001-0010. Phone: (602)379-6600.

California—Pacific Regional Office, Federal Office Bldg., 2800 Cottage Way, Sacramento, CA 95825-1846. Phone: (916)979-2600. *See also* **Arizona**.

District of Columbia—Deputy Commissioner of Indian Affairs, (MS 4140 MIB), 1849 C St. NW, Washington, DC 20240. Phone: (202)208-5116.

Minnesota—Midwest Regional Office, One Federal Dr. - Rm.550, St. Snelling, MN 55111. Phone: (612)713-4400, ext.1020.

Montana—Rocky Mountain Regional Office, 316 N. 26th St., Billings, MT 59101-1397. Phone: (406)247-7943.

New Mexico—Southwest Regional Office, 615 1st St. NW, P.O. Box 26567, Albuquerque, NM 87125-6567. Phone: (505)346-7590. *See also* **Arizona**.

- Navajo Regional Office, P.O. Box 1060, Gallup, NM 87305. Phone: (505)863-8314.

New York—*See* **Virginia**—Eastern Regional Office.

North Carolina—*See* **Virginia**—Eastern Regional Office.

North Dakota—*See* **South Dakota**.

Oklahoma—Southern Plains Office, Anadarko, OK 73005-0368. Phone: (405)247-6673, ext.257.

- Eastern Oklahoma Regional Office, 101 N. 5th St., Muskogee, OK 74401-6206. Phone: (918)687-2295.

Oregon——Northwest Regional Office, 911 NE 11th Ave., Portland, OR 97232-4169. Phone: (503)231-6702. *See also* **Arizona**.

South Dakota—Great Plains Regional Office, 115 4th Ave. SE, Aberdeen, SD 57401-4382. Phone: (605)226-7343.

Utah—*See* **Arizona, New Mexico(Navajo), and Oregon.**

Virginia—Eastern Regional Office, 3701 N. Fairfax Dr. - Ste.260, Arlington, VA 22203. Phone: (703)235-3006.

Washington—*See* **Oregon**.

Wisconsin—*See* **Minnesota**.

Wyoming—*See* **Montana**.

FIELD AGENCIES

Alaska—Anchorage Field Office, 1675 C St. - Ste.211, Anchorage, AK 99501-5198. Phone: (907)271-4088.

- Bethel Field Office, 1675 C St. - Ste.279, Anchorage, AK 99501-5198. Phone: (907)271-4086.
- Fairbanks Agency, 101 12th Ave. - Rm.16, Fairbanks, AK 99701-6270. Phone: (907)456-0222.
- Metlakatla Field Office, P.O. Box 450, Metlakatla, AK 99926. Phone: (907)886-3791.

Arizona—Chinle Agency, P.O. Box 7-H, Chinle, AZ 86503. Phone: (520)674-5100.

- Colorado River Agency, Rt.1 - Box 9-C, Parker, AZ 85344. Phone: (520)669-7111.

15.020 thru 15.025 (cont.)

- Ft. Apache Agency, P.O. Box 560, Whiteriver, AZ 85941. Phone: (520)338-5353.
- Ft. Defiance Agency, P.O. Box 619, Ft. Defiance, AZ 86504. Phone: (520)729-7217, -7218.
- Ft. Yuma Field Office, P.O. Box 11000, Yuma, AZ 85366-1000. Phone: (760)572-0248.
- Hopi Agency, P.O. Box 158, Keams Canyon, AZ 86034. Phone: (520)738-2228.
- Papago Agency, P.O. Box 578, Sells, AZ 85634. Phone: (520)383-3286.
- Pima Agency, P.O. Box 8, Sacaton, AZ 85247. Phone: (520)562-3326.
- Salt River Field Office, 10000 E. McDowell Rd., Scottsdale, AZ 85256. Phone: (602)640-2168.
- San Carlos Agency, P.O. Box 209, San Carlos, AZ 85550. Phone: (520)475-2321.
- Truxton Canon Field Office, P.O. Box 37, Valentine, AZ 86437. Phone: (520)769-2286.
- Western Navajo Agency, P.O. Box 127, Tuba City, AZ 86045. Phone: (520)283-2254, -2252.

California—Central California Agency, 1824 Tribute Rd. - Ste.J, Sacramento, CA 95815. Phone: (916)566-7121.

- Northern California Field Office, 1900 Churn Creek Rd. - Ste.300, Redding, CA 96002. Phone: (530)246-5141.
- Palm Springs Field Office, 650 E. Tahquitz Canyon Way - Ste.A, P.O. Box 2245, Palm Springs, CA 92262. Phone: (760)416-2133.
- Southern California Agency, 2038 Iowa Ave. - Ste.101, Riverside, CA 92507-0001. Phone: (909)276-6624.

Colorado—Southern Ute Agency, P.O. Box 315, Ignacio, CO 81137. Phone: (970)563-4511.

- Ute Mountain Ute Field Office, P.O. Box KK, Towaoc, CO 81334. Phone: (970)565-8473.

Florida—Seminole Agency, 6075 Sterling Rd., Hollywood, FL 33024. Phone: (954)356-7288.

Idaho—Ft. Hall Agency, P.O. Box 220, Ft. Hall, ID 83203. Phone: (208)238-2301.

- Northern Idaho Agency, P.O. Drawer 277, Lapwai, ID 83540. Phone: (208)843-2300.
- Plummer Subagency, 850 A St., P.O. Box 408, Plummer, ID 83851. Phone: (208)686-1887.

Kansas—Haskell Indian Nations University, 155 Indian Ave., Lawrence, KS 66046. Phone: (785)749-8404.

- Horton Field Office, P.O. Box 31, Horton, KS 66439. Phone: (785)486-2161.

Michigan—Michigan Field Office, 2901.5 I-75 Business Spur, Sault Ste. Marie, MI 49783. Phone: (906)632-6809.

Minnesota—Minnesota Agency, Federal Bldg. - Rm.418, 522 Minnesota Ave. NW, Bemidgi, MN 56601-3062. Phone: (218)751-2011.

- Red Lake Field Office, Red Lake, MN 56671. Phone: (218)679-3361.

Mississippi—Choctaw Field Office, 421 Powell St., Philadelphia, MS 39350. Phone: (601)656-1522.

Montana—Blackfeet Agency, P.O. Box 880, Browning, MT 59417. Phone: (406)338-7544.

- Crow Agency, P.O. Box 69, Crow Agency, MT 59022. Phone: (406)638-2672.
- Flathead Field Office, P.O. Box 40, Pablo, MT 59855-5555. Phone: (406)675-0242.
- Ft. Belknap Agency, R.R. 1 - P.O. Box 980, Harlem, MT 59526. Phone: (406)353-2901, ext.23.
- Ft. Peck Agency, P.O. Box 637, Poplar, MT 59255. Phone: (406)768-5312.
- Northern Cheyenne Agency, P.O. Box 40, Lame Deer, MT 59043. Phone: (406)477-8242.

FIELD OFFICE CONTACTS   769

- Rocky Boy's Field Office, R.R. 1 - P.O. Box 542, Box Elder, MT 59521. Phone: (406)395-4476.

Nebraska—Winnebago Agency, P.O. Box 18, Winnebago, NE 68071. Phone: (402) 878-2502.

Nevada—Eastern Nevada Field Office, 1555 Shoshone Circle, Elko, NV 89801. Phone: (775)738-0569.
- Western Nevada Agency, 1677 Hot Springs Rd., Carson City, NV 89706. Phone: (775)887-3500.

New Mexico—Eastern Navajo Agency, P.O. Box 328, Crownpoint, NM 87313. Phone: (505)786-6100.
- Jicarilla Agency, P.O. Box 167, Dulce, NM 87528. Phone: (505)759-3951.
- Laguna Agency, P.O. Box 1448, Laguna, NM 87026. Phone: (505)552-6001.
- Mescalero Agency, P.O. Box 189, Mescalero, NM 88340. Phone: (505)671-4423.
- Northern Pueblos Agency, Fairview Station, P.O. Box 4269, Espanola, NM 87533. Phone: (505)753-1400.
- Ramah-Navajo Agency, Rt.2 - Box 14, Ramah, NM 87321. Phone: (505)775-3235.
- Shiprock Agency, P.O. Box 966, Shiprock, NM 87420. Phone: (505)368-3300.
- Southern Pueblos Agency, P.O. Box 1667, Albuquerque, NM 87103. Phone: (505) 346-2424.
- Zuni Agency, P.O. Box 369, Zuni, NM 87327. Phone: (505)782-5591.

New York—New York Field Office, Syracuse, NY 13261-7366. Phone: (315)448-0620.

North Carolina—Cherokee Agency, Cherokee, NC 28719. Phone: (704)497-9131.

North Dakota—Ft. Berthold Agency, P.O. Box 370, New Town, ND 58763. Phone: (701)627-4707.
- Ft. Totten Agency, P.O. Box 270, Ft. Totten, ND 58335. Phone: (701)766-4545.
- Standing Rock Agency, P.O. Box E, Ft. Yates, ND 58538. Phone: (701)854-3433.
- Turtle Mountain Agency, P.O. Box 60, Belcourt, ND 58316. Phone: (701)477-3191.

Oklahoma—Anadarko Agency, P.O. Box 309, Anadarko, OK 73005. Phone: (405)247-6677.
- Chickasaw Agency, 1500 N. Country Club Rd., P.O. Box 2240, Ada, OK 74821. Phone: (580)436-0784.
- Concho Field Office, El Reno, OK 73036-0068. Phone: (405)262-7481.
- Okmulgee Field Office, P.O. Box 370, Okmulgee, OK 74447. Phone: (918)756-3950.
- Osage Agency, P.O. Box 1539, Pawhuska, OK 74056. Phone: (918)287-1032.
- Miami Field Office, P.O. Box 391, Miami, OK 74355. Phone: (918)542-3396.
- Pawnee Agency, Pawnee, OK 74058-0440. Phone: (918)762-2585.
- Shawnee Field Office, 624 W. Independence - Ste.114, Shawnee, OK 74801. Phone: (405)273-0317.
- Talihina Office, Drawer H, Talihina, OK 74571. Phone: (918)567-2207.
- Wewoka Agency, P.O. Box 1060, Wewoka, OK 74884. Phone: (405)257-6259.

Oregon—Siletz Field Office, P.O. Box 569, Siletz, OR 97380. Phone: (541)444-2679.
- Umatilla Agency, P.O. Box 520, Pendleton, OR 97801. Phone: (541)278-3786.
- Warm Springs Agency, P.O. Box 1239, Warm Springs, OR 97761. Phone: (541)553-2411.

South Dakota—Cheyenne River Agency, P.O. Box 325, Eagle Butte, SD 57625. Phone: (605)964-6611.
- Crow Creek Agency, P.O. Box 139, Ft. Thompson, SD 57339. Phone: (605)245-2311.
- Lower Brule Agency, P.O. Box 190, Lower Brule, SD 57548. Phone: (605)473-5512.
- Pine Ridge Agency, P.O. Box 1203, Pine Ridge, SD 57770. Phone: (605)867-5125.
- Rosebud Agency, P.O.Box 550, Rosebud, SD 57570. Phone: (605)747-2224.
- Sisseton Agency, P.O. Box 688, Agency Village, SD 57262. Phone: (605)698-3001.

15.020 thru 15.025 (cont.)

- Yankton Agency, P.O. Box 577, Wagner, SD 57380. Phone: (605)384-3651.

Utah—Uintah and Ouray Agency, P.O. Box 130, Ft. Duchesne, UT 84026. Phone: (435)722-4300.

- Southern Paiute Field Office, P.O. Box 720, St. George, UT 84771. Phone: (435)674-9720.

Washington—Colville Agency, Nespelem, WA 99155-0111. Phone: (509)634-2316.

- Makah Field Office, P.O. Box 115, Neah Bay, WA 98357. Phone: (360)645-3232.
- Olympic Peninsula Agency, P.O. Box 48, Aberdeen, WA 98520. Phone: (360)533-9100.
- Puget Sound Field Office, 2707 Colby Ave. - Ste.1101, Everett, WA 98201. Phone: (425)258-2651.
- Spokane Agency, P.O. Box 389, Wellpinit, WA 99040. Phone: (509)258-4561.
- Yakima Agency, P.O. Box 632(BIA) - P.O. Box 151(Tribal), Toppenish, WA 98948. Phone: (509)865-5121.

Wisconsin—Great Lakes Agency, 615 Main St. W., Ashland, WI 54806-0273. Phone: (715)682-4527.

Wyoming—Wind River Agency, P.O. Box 158, Ft. Washakie, WY 82514. Phone: (307)332-7810.

15.026 thru 15.028 EDUCATION LINE OFFICES

Alaska—Anchorage Education Field Office, 1675 C St., Anchorage, AK 99501. Phone: (907)271-4115.

Arizona—Chinle Agency-Education, Navajo Rt. 7, P.O. Box 6003, Chinle, AZ 86503. Phone: (520)674-5130, ext.201.

- Ft. Apache Agency-Education, Hwy. 73 and Elm St., P.O. Box 920, White River, AZ 85941. Phone: (520)338-5441.
- Ft. Defiance Agency-Education, Bldg. 38, Blue Canyon Hwy., Ft. Defiance, AZ 86504-0110. Phone: (520)729-7251.
- Hopi Agency-Education, Hwy. 264, P.O. Box 568, Keams Canyon, AZ 86034. Phone: (520)738-2262.
- Papago Agency-Education, South Bldg. 49, P.O. Box 38, Sells, AZ 85634. Phone: (520)383-3292.
- Pima Agency-Education, 400 N. 5th St., P.O. Box 10, Phoenix, AZ 85001. Phone: (602)379-3944.
- Western Navajo Agency-Education, Bldg. 407, Hwy. 160 and Warrior Dr., P.O. Box 746, Tuba City, AZ 86045. Phone: (520)283-2218.

California—Sacramento Area Education Office, 2800 Cottage Way, Sacramento, CA 95825. Phone: (916)979-2560, ext.234.

Kansas—Haskell Indian Nations University, 155 Indian Ave. - #1305, Lawrence, KS 66046-4800. Phone: (785)749-8404.

Minnesota—Minneapolis Area Education Office, 331 S. 2nd Ave., Minneapolis, MN 55401-2241. Phone: (612)373-1000, ext.1090.

Montana—Billings Area Education Office, 316 N. 26th St., Billings, MT 59101-1397. Phone: (406)247-7953.

New Mexico—Eastern Navajo Agency Education, Bldg. 222, 1 Main St., P.O. Box 328, Crownpoint, NM 87313. Phone: (505)786-6150.

- Northern Pueblos Agency-Education, Fairview Station, 1 Mile N. of Espanola - Hwy. 68, P.O. Box 4269, Espanola, NM 87533. Phone: (505)753-1465.
- Shiprock Agency-Education, Hwy. 666N, Shiprock, NM 87420-3239. Phone: (505) 368-4427, ext.360.
- Southern Pueblos Agency-Education, 1000 Indian School Rd. NW, P.O. Box 1667, Albuquerque, NM 87103. Phone: (505)346-2431.

- Southwestern Indian Polytechnic Institute, 9169 Coors Rd. NW, P.O. Box 10146-9196, Albuquerque, NM 87184. Phone: (505)346-2343.

North Dakota—Standing Rock Agency-Education, Main St. off Hwy. 106, Agency Ave., P.O. Box E, Ft. Yates, ND 58538. Phone: (701)854-3497.
- Turtle Mountain Agency-Education, School St., P.O. Box 30, Belcourt, ND 58316. Phone: (701)477-6471, ext.211.

Oklahoma—Oklahoma Education Office, 4149 Highline Blvd. - Ste.380, Oklahoma City, OK 73108. Phone: (605)945-6051, ext.301, (405)605-6057.

Oregon—Portland Area Education Office, 911 NE 11th Ave., Portland, OR 97232-4169. Phone: (503)872-2743.

South Dakota—Cheyenne River Agency-Education, 100 N. Main, P.O. Box 2020, Eagle Butte, SD 51625. Phone: (605)964-8722.
- Crow Creek/Lower Brule Agency-Education, 140 Education Ave., P.O. Box 139, Ft. Thompson, SD 57339. Phone: (605)245-2398.
- Pine Ridge Agency-Education, 101 Main St., P.O. Box 333, Pine Ridge, SD 57770. Phone: (605)867-1306.
- Rosebud Agency-Education, 1001 Ave. D, P.O. Box 669, Mission, SD 57555. Phone: (605)856-4478, ext.261.

Virginia—South and Eastern States Agency-Education, 3701 N. Fairfax Dr. - Ste.260, Arlington, VA 22203. Phone: (703)235-3233.

15.029 Listed under **15.020**.

15.030 **LAW ENFORCEMENT DISTRICTS**

(No phone numbers provided).

DISTRICT I *(All Indian reservations in Michigan, Minnesota, Nebraska, North Dakota, South Dakota, Wisconsin)*—Office of Law Enforcement, Bureau of Indian Affairs, 115 4th Ave. SE, (MC 302), Aberdeen, SD 57401.

DISTRICT II *(All Indian reservations in Kansas and western Oklahoma, all Indian tribes in eastern Oklahoma)*—Office of Law Enforcement, Bureau of Indian Affairs, 101 N. 5th St., Muskogee, OK 74401.

DISTRICT III *(All Indian reservations in Arizona, northern California, Nevada, Utah (excluding Navajo))*—Office of Law Enforcement, Bureau of Indian Affairs, Bldg. 2 - N. 5th St., Phoenix, AZ 85004. *For mail:* P.O. Box 10, Phoenix, AZ 85001.

DISTRICT IV *(All Indian reservations in southern Colorado, New Mexico, and all Navajo Indian reservations in Arizona, New Mexico, Utah)*—Office of Law Enforcement, Bureau of Indian Affairs, P.O. Box 26567, Albuquerque, NM 87125-6567.

DISTRICT V *(All Indian reservations in Alaska, Idaho, Montana, Oregon, Washington, Wyoming)*—Office of Law Enforcement, Bureau of Indian Affairs, 316 N. 26th St., Billings, MT 59101.

DISTRICT VI *(All Indian reservations in Alabama, Connecticut, Florida, Louisiana, Maine, Mississippi, New York, North Carolina, Rhode Island)*—Office of Law Enforcement, Bureau of Indian Affairs, 1849 C St. NW, (MS 4550 MIB), Washington, DC 20240-0001.

15.031 thru 15.041 Listed under **15.020**.

15.042 thru 15.046 Listed under **15.026**.

15.047 thru 15.058 Listed under **15.020**.

15.060	Contact BIA agency office listed under **15.020**, *or* United Tribes Technical College, 3315 University Dr., Bismarck, ND 58504. Phone: (701)255-3285, ext.334.
15.061	United Sioux Tribes Development Corporation, 1830 Lombardy Dr., Rapid City, SD 57701. Phone: (605)226-7426.
15.062 thru 15.113	Listed under **15.020**.
15.114	Listed under **15.026**.
15.124	Listed under **15.020**.
15.130	Listed under **15.026**.
15.141 and 15.144	Listed under **15.020**.
15.146	Contact BIA agency office listed under **15.020**, *or* Director, National Ironworkers Training Program for American Indians, 1819 Beach St., Broadview, IL 60153. Phone: (708)345-2344.
15.147	Listed under **15.020**.

BUREAU OF LAND MANAGEMENT

15.214 thru 15.242 **STATE OFFICES**

Alaska—6881 Abbott Loop Rd., Anchorage, AK 99507. Phone: (907)267-1323.

Arizona—222 N. Central Ave., P.O. Box 16563, Phoenix, AZ 95004-2203. Phone: (602)417-9266.

California—2800 Cottage Way - Ste.W-1834, Sacramento, CA 95825-1886. Phone: (916)978-4527.

Colorado—2850 Youngfield St., Lakewood, CO 80215-7076. Phone: (303)239-3677.

District of Columbia - Branch of Procurement Management *(For bureauwide inquiries)*—1849 C St. NW, (MS 1075-LS), Washington, DC 20240. Phone: (202) 452-5170.

Idaho—1387 S. Vinnell Way, Boise, ID 83709-1657. Phone: (208)373-3909.

Montana—5001 Southgate Dr., P.O. Box 36800, Billings, MT 59107-6800. Phone: (406)896-5205.

Nevada—1340 Financial Blvd, P.O. Box 12000, Reno, NV 89520-0006. Phone: (702) 861-6417.

New Mexico—435 Montano NE, Albuquerque, NM 87107. Phone: (505)761-8994.

Oregon—1515 SW 5th Ave., P.O. Box 2965, Portland, OR 97208. Phone: (503)952-6220.

Utah—324 S. State St. - Ste.301, Salt Lake City, UT 84111-2303. Phone: (801)539-4172.

Virginia-Eastern States Office—7450 Boston Blvd., Springfield, VA 22153. Phone: (703)440-1596.

Wyoming—5353 Yellowstone Rd., P.O. Box 1828, Cheyenne, WY 82005. Phone: (307)775-6058.

OFFICE OF SURFACE MINING RECLAMATION AND ENFORCEMENT

15.250 thru 15.254

FIELD OFFICES

Alabama—135 Gemini Circle - Ste.215, Homewood, AL 35209. Phone: (205)290-7282.

District of Columbia—1951 Constitution Ave. NW, Washington, DC 20240. Phone: (202)208-4006.

Indiana—575 N. Pennsylvania St. - Rm.301, Indianapolis, IN 46204. Phone: (317)226-6700.

Kentucky—2675 Regency Rd., Lexington, KY 40503-2922. Phone: (859)233-2494.

New Mexico—505 Marquette Ave. NW - Ste.1200, Albuquerque, NM 87102. Phone: (505)248-5070.

Oklahoma—5100 E. Skelly Dr. - Ste.470, Tulsa, OK 74135. Phone: (918)581-6431.

Pennsylvania—Harrisburg Transportation Center - Ste.3C, 415 Market St., Harrisburg, PA 17101. Phone: (717)782-4036.

Tennessee—530 Gay St. SW - Ste.500, Knoxville, TN 37902. Phone: (423)545-4103.

Virginia—Powell Valley Square Shopping Center, 1941 Neeley Rd. - Ste.201 (Compartment 116), Big Stone Gap, VA 24219. Phone: (540)523-4303.

West Virginia—1027 Virginia St. E., Charleston, WV 25301. Phone: (304)347-7162.

Wyoming—Federal Bldg. - Rm.2128, 100 E. "B" St., Casper, WY 82601-1918. Phone: (307)261-6555.

REGIONAL COORDINATING CENTERS

APPALACHIAN REGION—Three Parkway Center, Pittsburgh, PA 15220. Phone: (412)937-2828.

MID-CONTINENT REGION—Alton Federal Bldg., 501 Belle St. - Rm.216, Alton, IL 62002. Phone: (618)463-6460.

WESTERN REGION—1999 Broadway - Ste.3320, Denver, CO 80202-5733. Phone: (303)844-1401.

BUREAU OF RECLAMATION

15.504

REGIONAL OFFICES

COMMISSIONER'S OFFICE—Denver Federal Center, P.O. Box 25007, Denver, CO 80225-0007. Phone: (303)445-2692.

GREAT PLAINS—P.O. Box 36900, Billings, MT 59107-6900. Phone: (406)247-7600.

LOWER COLORADO—Boulder City, NV 89006-1470. Phone: (702)293-8411.

MID-PACIFIC—Federal Office Bldg., 2800 Cottage Way, Sacramento, CA 95825-1898. Phone: (916)978-5000.

PACIFIC NORTHWEST—1150 N. Curtis Rd. - Ste.100, Boise, ID 83706-1234. Phone: (208)378-5012.

UPPER COLORADO—125 S. State St. - Rm.6107, Salt Lake City, UT 84138-1102. Phone: (801)524-3600.

15.508   *Technical/Program Information:*
Bureau of Reclamation, Lahontan Basin Area Office, 705 N. Plaza St. - Rm.320, Carson City, NV 89701-4015. Phones: (775)882-3436; FAX (775)882-7592.

Acquistion Office:

Bureau of Reclamation, Mid-Pacific Regional Office, Acquisition Services, 2800 Cottage Way - Rm.E-1815, Sacramento, CA 95825-1898. Phones: (916)978-5130; FAX (916)978-5175, -5182. **Internet:** e-mail, "2WG4@mp.usbr.gov".

U.S. FISH AND WILDLIFE SERVICE

15.602   Federal Law Enforcement Training Center, Bldg. 69 - Rm.100, Glynco, GA 31524. Phone: (912)267-2370.

15.605 thru 15.634   **REGIONAL OFFICES**

REGION I *(California, Hawaii, Idaho, Nevada, Oregon, Washington)*—911 NE 11th Ave., Portland, OR 97232-4181. Phones: (503)872-2716; FAX (503)231-6118.

REGION II *(Arizona, New Mexico, Oklahoma, Texas)*—500 Gold Ave. SW - Rm.3018, P.O. Box 1306, Albuquerque, NM 87103. Phones: (505)248-6910; FAX (505)248-6282.

REGION III *(Illinois, Indiana, Iowa, Michigan, Minnesota, Missouri, Ohio, Wisconsin)*—Federal Bldg., 1 Federal Dr., Ft. Snelling, MN 55111. Phones: (612)713-5284; FAX (612)713-5301.

REGION IV *(Alabama, Arkansas, Florida, Georgia, Kentucky, Louisiana, Mississippi, North Carolina, Puerto Rico, South Carolina, Tennessee, Virgin Islands)*—1875 Century Blvd., Atlanta, GA 30345. Phones: (404)679-4006; FAX (404)679-4000.

REGION V *(Connecticut, Delaware, District of Columbia, Maine, Maryland, Massachusetts, New Hampshire, New Jersey, New York, Pennsylvania, Rhode Island, Vermont, Virginia, West Virginia)*—300 Westgate Center Dr., Hadley, MA 01035. Phones: (413)253-8308; FAX (413)253-8300.

REGION VI *(Colorado, Kansas, Montana, Nebraska, North Dakota, South Dakota, Utah, Wyoming)*—Denver Federal Center, P.O. Box 25486, Denver, CO 80025. Phones: (303)236-7920; FAX (303)236-8295.

REGION VII *(Alaska)*—1011 E. Tudor Rd., Anchorage, AK 99503. Phones: (907)786-3306; FAX (907)786-3542.

15.637 thru 15.643   Listed under **15.605**

15.644   **REGIONAL OFFICES**
(Junior Duck Stamp Conservation and Design)

Alabama—Wheeler NWR, 2700 Refuge Hdqtrs. Rd., Decatur, AL 35603. Phone: (256)350-6639.

Alaska—Yukon Flats NWR, 101 12th Ave., Rte.264 - Box 14, Fairbanks, AK 99701. Phone: (907)456-0440. **Internet:** e-mail, "Education_Specialist@fws.gov".

American Samoa—USFWS, 911 NE 11th Ave., Portland, OR 97232. Phone: (503)231-6164.

Arizona—Cabeza Prieta NWR, 1611 N. 2nd Ave., Ajo, AZ 85321. Phone: (520)387-6483.

Arkansas—One 4H Way, Little Rock, AR 72223. Phone: (501)821-6884.

California—Sacramento NWR Complex, 752 County Rd. 99W, Willows, CA 95988. Phone: (530)934-2801.

Colorado—Alamosa/Monte Vista NWR, 9383 El Rancho Lane, Alamosa, CO 81101. Phone: (719)589-4021.

Field Office Contacts

Connecticut—CN Waterfowl Association, 29 Bowers Hill Rd., Oxford, CT 06478. Phone: (no number provided).

Delaware—DE Division/Fish and Wildlife, 4876 Hay Point Landing Rd., Smyrna, DE 19977. Phone: (302)653-2882, ext.104.

District of Columbia—DC Fish and Wildlife Division, 51 N. St. NE - Rm.5002, Washington, DC 20002. Phone: (202)535-2266.

Florida—J.N. Ding Darling NWR, 1 Wildlife Drive, Sanibel, FL 33957. Phone: (239)472-1100.

Georgia—GA Ecological Services, 247 S. Milledge, Athens, GA 30605. Phone: (706) 613-9493.

Hawaii—USFWS, Pacific Islands Office, Rm.5-311 - Box 50187, 300 Ala Moana Blvd., Honolulu, HI 96850. Phone: (808)792-9530.

Idaho—Deer Flat NWR, 13751 Upper Embankment Rd., Nampa, ID 83686. Phone: (208)467-9378, -9379.

Illinois—IL DNR, Division of Education, 1 Natural Resources Way, Springfield, IL 62702. Phone: (217)524-4126.

Indiana—Muscatatuck NWR, 12985 E. US Hwy. 50, Seymour, IN 47274. Phone: (812)522-4352.

Iowa—Neal Smith NWR, 9981 Pacific St., P.O. Box 399, Prairie City, IA 50228. Phone: (515)994-3400.

Kansas—Great Plains Nature Center, 6232 E. 29th N., Wichita, KS 67220. Phone: (316)683-5499, ext.108.

Kentucky—KY Department of Fish and Wildlife, #1 Game Farm Rd., Frankfort, KY 40601. Phone: (502)564-3400.

Louisiana—Natchitoches NFH, 615 South Dr., Natchitoches, LA 71457. Phone: (318) 352-5324.

Maine—Rachel Carson NWR, 321 Port Rd., Wells, ME 04090. Phone: (207)646-9226.

Maryland—Patuxent Research Refuge, 10901 Scarlet Tanager Loop, Laurel, MD 20708-4027. Phone: (301)497-5761.

Massachusetts—MA Wildlife Federation, One Rabbit Hill Rd., Westboro, MA 01581. Phone: (508)792-7270, ext.110.

Michigan—MI Duck Hunter Tournament, 3517 Anna, Trenton, MI 48183. Phone: (734)676-1995.

Minnesota—MN Valley NWR, 3815 American Blvd. E., Bloomington, MN 55425. Phone: (952)858-0710.

Mississippi—MS Museum of Natural Science, 2148 Riverside Dr., Jackson, MS 39202. Phone: (601)354-7303.

Missouri—Big Muddy NWR, 4200 New Haven Dr., Columbia, MO 65102. Phone: (573)441-2799.

Montana—Lee Metcalf NWR, Outdoor Recreation Planner, P.O. Box 247, Stevensville, MT 59870. Phone: (406)777-5552.

Nebraska—Crescent Lake NWR Complex, 115 Railway, Scottsbluff, NE 69361. Phone: (308)635-7851.

Nevada—Stillwater NWR, 1000 Auction Rd., Fallon, NV 89406. Phone: (775)423-5128.

New Hampshire—NH Fish and Game Department, 11 Hazen Dr., Concord, NH 03301. Phone: (603)271-3211.

New Jersey—The Wetlands Institute, 1075 Stone Harbor Blvd., Stone Harbor, NJ 08247. Phone: (609)368-1211.

New Mexico—Bitter Lake NWR, 4065 Bitter Lakes Rd., Roswell, NM 88201. Phone: (505)622-6755, ext.29.

15.644 (cont.)	**New York**—Wertheim NWR, P.O. Box 21, 360 Smith Rd., Shirley, NY 11967. Phone: (631)874-4814.
	North Carolina—USFWS Ecological Survey, 551 E. Pylon Dr., Raleigh, NC 27606. Phone: (919)856-4520, ext.25.
	North Dakota—Tewaukon NWR, 9754 143 1/2 Ave. SE, Cayuga, ND 58013. Phone: (701)724-3598.
	Ohio—Ottawa NWR, 14000 W. State Rte.2, Oak Harbor, OH 43449. Phone: (419)898-0014.
	Oklahoma—Wichita Mountains Wildlife Refuge, Rte.1 - Box 448, Indiahoma, OK 73552. Phone: (580)429-3221.
	Oregon—OR Coast NWR Complex, 2127 SE Marine Science Dr., Newport, OR 97365. Phone: (541)867-4550.
	Pennsylvania—Erie NWR, 11296 Wood Duck Lane, Guys Mills, PA 16327. Phone: (814)789-3585.
	Rhode Island—USFWS Division of Migratory Birds-R5, 300 Westgate Center Dr., Hadley, MA 01035. Phone: (413)253-8643.
	South Carolina—SC Dept. of Natural Resources, 1000 Assembly St. #209, Columbia, SC 29202. Phone: (803)734-3885.
	South Dakota—USFWS, Federal Bldg. - Rm.309, 200 4th St. SW, Huron, SD 57350. Phone: (605)352-5894.
	Tennessee—Tennessee NWR, 3006 Dinkins Lane, Paris, TN 38242. Phone: (731)642-2091.
	Texas—Santa Ana NWR, RR-2 - Box 202A, Alamo, TX 78516. Phone: (956)787-7630.
	Utah—Bear River Bird Refuge, 58 S. 950 West, Brigham City, UT 84302. Phone: (435)723-5887, ext.16.
	Vermont—Missisquoi NWR, 371 N. River St., Swanton, VT 05488. Phone: (802)868-4781.
	Virginia—USFWS Division of Migratory Birds-R5, 300 Westgate Center Dr., Hadley, MA 01035. Phone: (413)253-8643.
	Virgin Islands—VI Division of Fish and Wildlife, 45 Mars Hill, Frederiksted, VI 00840. Phone: (340)713-2422.
	Washington—Nisqually NWR, 100 Brown Farm Rd., Olympia, WA 98516. Phone: (360)753-9467.
	West Virginia—Ohio River Islands NWR, P.O. Box 1811, 3004 7th St., Parkersburg, WV 26102. Phone: (304)422-0752.
	Wisconsin—Necedah NWR, W7996 20th St. W., Necedah, WI 54646. Phone: (608)565-2551.
	Wyoming—National Museum of Wildlife Art, P.O. Box 6825, 2820 Rungius Rd., Jackson, WY 83002. Phone: (307)733-5771.
15.645	USFWS, University of West Georgia, Department of Biology, Carrollton, GA 30118-6300. Phones: (770)214-9293; FAX (678)839-6548.
15.647	Division of Migratory Birds, USFWS, 1 Federal Dr., Fort Snelling, MN 55111-4056. Phones: (612)713-5473, 5470; FAX (612)713-5393.

U.S. GEOLOGICAL SURVEY

15.808   **REGIONAL OFFICES**

Biological Resources Division

CENTRAL *(Arkansas, Colorado, Iowa, Kansas, Louisiana, Minnesota, Missouri, Montana, Nebraska, New Mexico, North Dakota, Oklahoma, South Dakota, Texas,*

Wyoming)—Regional Chief Biologist, Denver Federal Center Bldg, 020 - Rm. A1419, (MS 300), Denver, CO 80225. Phone: (303)236-2739, ext.238.

EASTERN *(Alabama, Connecticut, District of Columbia, Florida, Georgia, Illinois, Indiana, Kentucky, Maine, Maryland, Massachusetts, Michigan, Mississippi, New Hampshire, New Jersey, New York, North Carolina, Ohio, Pennsylvania, Puerto Rico, Rhode Island, South Carolina, Tennessee, Vermont, Virginia, West Virginia, Wisconsin)*—Acting Regional Chief Biologist, National Center - Rm.4A100, (MS 300), 12201 Sunrise Valley Dr., Reston, VA 20192. Phone: (703)648-4060.

WESTERN *(Alaska, Arizona, California, Hawaii, Idaho, Nevada, Oregon, Utah, Washington)*—Regional Chief Biologist, 909 1st Ave. - Ste.800, Seattle, WA 98104. Phone: (206)220-4600.

Geologic Division

CENTRAL—Federal Center, (MS 911), Denver, CO 80225. Phone: (303)236-5435.

EASTERN—953 National Center, Reston, VA 20192. Phone: (703)648-6662.

WESTERN—345 Middlefield Rd., (MS 919), Menlo Park, CA 94025. Phone: (415) 650-5102.

National Mapping Division

Mapping Application Center—National Center, (MS 567), Reston, VA 20192. Phone: (703)648-6002.

Midcontinent Mapping Center—1400 Independence Rd., (MS 300), Rolla, MO 65401. Phone: (573)308-3800.

Rocky Mountain Mapping Center—Denver Federal Center, (MS 508), Bldg. 810, Box 25046, Denver, CO 80225-0046. Phone: (303)202-4040.

South Dakota - Earth Resources Observation Systems Data Center—Mundt Federal Bldg., Sioux Falls, SD 57198. Phone: (605)594-6123.

Western Mapping Center—345 Middlefield Rd., (MS 531), Menlo Park, CA 94025-3591. Phone: (415)329-4254.

Water Resources Division

CENTRAL *(Colorado, Iowa, Kansas, Minnesota, Montana, Nebraska, New Mexico, North Dakota, Oklahoma, South Dakota, Texas, Wyoming)*—Regional Hydrologist, (MS 406), Denver Federal Center, Bldg. 25, Box 25046, Lakewood, CO 80225-0046. Phone: (303)236-5950, ext.0.

NORTHEAST *(Connecticut, Delaware, Illinois, Indiana, Kentucky, Maine, Maryland, Massachusetts, Michigan, New Hampshire, New Jersey, New York, Ohio, Pennsylvania, Rhode Island, Vermont, Virginia, West Virginia, Wisconsin)*—Regional Hydrologist, (MS 433), 433 National Center, Reston, VA 22092. Phone: (703)648-5813.

SOUTHEAST *(Alabama, Arkansas, Florida, Georgia, Louisiana, Mississippi, Missouri, North Carolina, Puerto Rico, South Carolina, Tennessee, Virgin Islands)*—Regional Hydrologist, Spalding Woods Office Park - Ste.160, 3850 Holcomb Bridge Rd., Norcross, GA 30092-2202. Phone: (404)409-7701.

WESTERN *(Alaska, American Samoa, Arizona, California, Guam, Hawaii, Idaho, Nevada, Oregon, other Pacific Islands, Utah, Washington)*—Regional Hydrologist, (MS 470), 345 Middlefield Rd., Menlo Park, CA 94025-3591. Phone: (415)329-4414.

NATIONAL PARK SERVICE

For financial assistance information contact the State Historic Preservation Officer in your state, and the appropriate regional office for subgrant eligibility information, following.

15.904 thru 15.921 NATIONAL HEADQUARTERS

National Park Service—Professional Services, 1849 C St. NW, Washington, DC 20240. Phone: (202)208-3264.

REGIONAL OFFICES

ALASKA—2525 Gambell St., Anchorage, AK 99503-2892. Phone: (907)257-2690.

INTERMOUNTAIN—12795 W. Alameda Pkwy., Denver, CO 80225-0287. Phone: (303)969-2503.

MIDWEST—Professional Services and Legislation, 1709 Jackson St., Omaha, NE 68102. Phone: (402)221-3084.

NATIONAL CAPITAL—Finance Management Officer, 1100 Ohio Dr. SW, Washington, DC 20242. Phone: (202)619-7160.

NORTHEAST—U.S. Custom House, 200 Chestnut St. - 3rd fl., Philadelphia, PA 19106. Phone: (215)597-7013.

SOUTHEAST—Atlanta Federal Center - 1924 Building, 100 Alabama St. SW, Atlanta, GA 30303. Phone: (404)562-3100.

PACIFIC WEST—Resources, Stewardship and Partnership, 111 Jackson St. - Ste.700, Oakland, CA 94607. Phone: (415)427-1321.

SERVICE CENTERS

Denver Service Center—P.O. Box 25287, Denver, CO 80225. Phone: (303)969-2100.

Harpers Ferry Center—Harpers Ferry, WV 25425-0050. Phone: (304)535-6211.

15.923 PTT Grants, NCPTT, 645 College Ave., Natchitoches, LA 71457. Phones: (318)356-7444; FAX (318)356-9119. **Internet:** e-mail, "ncptt@ncptt.nps.gov".

15.927 Listed under **15.904**.

DEPARTMENT OF JUSTICE

DRUG ENFORCEMENT ADMINISTRATION

FIELD OFFICES

16.001 thru 16.005

(No phone numbers provided)

Atlanta—75 Spring St. SW - Rm.740, A53, Atlanta, GA 30303.

Boston—JFK Federal Bldg. - Rm.E-400, 15 Sudbury St., Boston, MA 02203-0402.

Caribbean—Metro Office Park - Bldg.17, Guayanabo, PR 00968.

Chicago—230 S. Dearborn St. - Ste.1200, Chicago, IL 60604.

Dallas—10160 Technology Blvd., East Dallas, TX 75220-4343.

Denver—115 Inverness Dr. E., Englewood, CO 80112-5116.

Detroit—431 Howard St., Detroit, MI 48226.

El Paso—DEA/EPIC, SSG Sims St., El Paso, TX 79908-8098.

▪ 600 S. Mesa Hills Dr., El Paso, TX 79912.

Houston—1433 W. Loop South - Ste.600, Houston, TX 77027-9506.

Los Angeles—Royal Federal Bldg. - 20th fl., 255 E. Temple St., Los Angeles, CA 90012.

Miami—8400 NW 53rd St., Miami, FL 33166.

Newark—80 Mulberry St. - 2nd fl., Newark, NJ 07102-4206.

New Orleans—Three Lakeway Center - Ste.1800, 3838 N. Causeway Blvd., Metairie, LA 70002.
New York—99 10th Ave., New York, NY 10011.
Philadelphia—600 Arch St. - Rm.10224, Philadelphia, PA 19106.
Phoenix—3010 N. 2nd St. - Ste.301, Phoenix, AZ 85012.
San Diego—4560 Viewridge Ave., San Diego, CA 92123-1672.
San Francisco—450 Golden Gate Ave., San Francisco, CA 94102.
Seattle—400 2nd Ave. W, Seattle, WA 98119-4140.
St. Louis—7911 Forsythe Blvd. - Ste.500, St. Louis, MO 63105.
Washington, D.C.—801 K St. NW - Ste.500, Washington, DC 20001.

Laboratories

MID-ATLANTIC—460 New York Ave. NW, Washington, DC 20532-0001.
NORTH CENTRAL—536 S. Clark St. - Rm.800, Chicago, IL 60605,
NORTHEAST—99 Tenth Ave. - Rm.721, New York, NY 10011.
SOUTH CENTRAL—1880 Regal Row, Dallas, TX 75235.
SOUTHEAST—5205 NW 84th Ave., Miami, FL 33166.
SOUTHWEST—410 W.35th St., National City, CA 91950.
SPECIAL TESTING AND RESEARCH—3650 Concorde Pkwy. - Ste.200, Chantilly, VA 20151.
WESTERN—390 Main St. - Rm.700, San Francisco, CA 94105.

Office of Training

Drug Enforcement Administration, FBI Academy, Quantico, VA 22134-1475.

CIVIL RIGHTS DIVISION

CRIMINAL SECTION

16.109 Contact local U.S. Attorney's Office, or FBI (addresses listed under **16.300**).

COMMUNITY RELATIONS SERVICE

16.200 ### REGIONAL OFFICES

REGION I *(Connecticut, Maine, Massachusetts, New Hampshire, Rhode Island, Vermont)*—408 Atlantic Ave. - Ste.222, Boston, MA 02110. Phone: (617)424-5715.

REGION II *(New Jersey, New York, Puerto Rico, Virgin Islands)*—26 Federal Plaza - Rm.36-118, New York, NY 10278. Phone: (212)264-0700.

REGION III *(Delaware, District of Columbia, Maryland, Pennsylvania, Virginia, West Virginia)*—2nd and Chestnut St. - Rm.208, Philadelphia, PA 19106. Phone: (215)597-2344.

REGION IV *(Alabama, Florida, Georgia, Kentucky, Mississippi, North Carolina, South Carolina, Tennessee)*—75 Piedmont Ave. NE - Rm.900, Atlanta, GA 30303. Phone: (404)331-6883.

REGION V *(Illinois, Indiana, Michigan, Minnesota, Ohio, Wisconsin)*—55 W. Monroe St. - Rm.420, Chicago, IL 60603. Phone: (312)353-4391.

REGION VI *(Arkansas, Louisiana, New Mexico, Oklahoma, Texas)*—1420 Mockingbird Ln. - Ste.250, Dallas, TX 75247. Phone: (214)655-8175.

16.200
(cont.)

REGION VII *(Iowa, Kansas, Missouri, Nebraska)*—1100 Main St. - Ste.1320, Kansas City, MO 64105. Phone: (816)426-7434.

REGION VIII *(Colorado, Montana, North Dakota, South Dakota, Utah, Wyoming)*—1244 Speer Blvd. - Ste.650, Denver, CO 80204-3584. Phone: (303)844-2973.

REGION IX *(Arizona, California, Guam, Hawaii, Nevada)*—888 S. Figueroa St. - Ste.1880, Los Angeles, CA 90017. Phone: (213)894-2941.

REGION X *(Alaska, Idaho, Oregon, Washington)*—915 2nd Ave. - Rm.1808, Seattle, WA 98174. Phone: (206)220-6700.

FIELD OFFICES

Detroit—211 W. Fort St. - Rm.1404, Detroit, MI 48226. Phone: (313)226-4010.

Houston—515 Rusk Ave. - Rm.12605, Houston, TX 77002. Phone: (713)718-4861.

Miami—51 SW 1st Ave. - Rm.624, Miami, FL 33130. Phone: (305)536-5206.

San Francisco—120 Howard St. - Ste.790, San Francisco, CA 94105. Phone: (415)744-6565.

FEDERAL BUREAU OF INVESTIGATION

16.300 thru 16.303

FIELD OFFICES (Special Agent in Charge)

REGION I *(Connecticut, Maine, Massachusetts, New Hampshire, Rhode Island, Vermont)*:

- Federal Office Bldg., 600 State St., New Haven, CT 06510-2020. Phones: (203)503-5000, 786-7000.
- 1 Center Plaza - Ste.600, Boston, MA 02108-1801. Phones: (617)742-5533, 223-6000.

REGION II *(New Jersey, New York, Puerto Rico, Virgin Islands)*:

- One Gateway Center - 22nd fl., Newark, NJ 07102-9889. Phone: (973)792-3000.
- Foley Bldg., 200 McCarty Ave., Albany, NY 12209-2095. Phones: (518)465-7551, 431-7200.
- One FBI Plaza, Buffalo, NY 14202-2698. Phones: (716)856-7800, 843-4300.
- Javits Federal Office Bldg., 26 Federal Plaza, New York, NY 10278-0004. Phone: (212)384-1000.
- U.S. Federal Office Bldg. - Rm.526, 150 Carlos Chardon, Hato Rey, PR 00918-1716. Phones: (787)754-6000, -3292.

REGION III *(Delaware, District of Columbia, Maryland, Pennsylvania, Virginia, West Virginia)*:

- Washington Metropolitan Field Office, 601 4th St. NW, Washington, DC 20535-0002. Phone: (202)278-2000.
- 7142 Ambassador Rd., Baltimore, MD 21244-2754. Phones: (410)265-8080, 281-0198.
- Federal Office Bldg. - 8th fl., 600 Arch St., Philadelphia, PA 19106-1675. Phones: (215)418-4500, -4000.
- U.S. Post Office - Ste.300, 700 Grant St., Pittsburgh, PA 15219-1906. Phones: (412)471-2000, 456-9100.
- 150 Corporate Blvd., Norfolk, VA 23502-4999. Phones: (757)455-0100, -0123.
- 111 Greencourt Rd., Richmond, VA 23228-4948. Phones: (804)261-1044, (700)923-2000.

REGION IV *(Alabama, Florida, Georgia, Kentucky, Mississippi, North Carolina, South Carolina, Tennessee)*:

- 2121 8th Ave. N. - Rm.1400, Birmingham, AL 35203-2396. Phones: FTS (205)715-0300; FAX (205)326-6166.

Field Office Contacts 781

- St. Louis Centre - 3rd fl., 1 St. Louis St., Mobile, AL 36602-3930. Phones: (334)438-3674, (334)219-3555.
- 7820 Arlington Expressway - Ste.200, Jacksonville, FL 32211-7499. Phones: (904)721-1211.
- 16320 NW 2nd Ave., North Miami Beach, FL 33169-6508. Phones: (305)944-9101, 787-6100.
- Federal Office Bldg. - Rm.610, 500 E. Zack St., Tampa, FL 33602-3917. Phones: (813)273-4566, 272-8000.
- 2635 Century Pkwy. NE - Ste.400, Atlanta, GA 30345-3112. Phones: (404)679-9000, -6100.
- Federal Office Bldg. - Ste.500, 600 Martin Luther King Place, Louisville, KY 40202-2231. Phones: (502)583-3941.
- Federal Office Bldg. - Ste.1553, 100 W. Capitol St., Jackson, MS 39269-1601. Phones: (601)948-5000, 360-7550.
- Wachovia Bldg. - Ste.900, 400 S. Tyron, Charlotte, NC 28285-0001. Phone: (704)377-9200, 331-4500.
- 151 W. Park Blvd., Columbia, SC 29210-3857. Phones: (803)551-4200, 551-4209.
- 710 Locust St. - Ste.600, Knoxville, TN 37902-2537. Phones: (865)544-0751, 544-3500.
- Eaglecrest Bldg. - Ste.3000, 225 N. Humphreys Blvd., Memphis, TN 38120-2107. Phones: (901)747-4300, -9739.

REGION V *(Illinois, Indiana, Michigan, Minnesota, Ohio, Wisconsin)*:
- Dirksen Federal Office Bldg. - Rm.905, 219 S. Dearborn St., Chicago, IL 60604-1702. Phones: (312)431-1333, 786-2500.
- 400 W. Monroe St. - Ste.400, Springfield, IL 62704-1800. Phones: (217)522-9675, 535-4400.
- Federal Office Bldg. - Rm.679, 575 N. Pennsylvania St., Indianapolis, IN 46204-1585. Phones: (317)639-3301, 321-6100.
- McNamara Federal Office Bldg. - 26th fl., 477 Michigan Ave., Detroit, MI 48226-2598. Phones: (313)965-2323, 237-4355.
- 111 Washington Ave. S. - Ste.1100, Minneapolis, MN 55401-2176. Phones: (612)376-3200.
- Federal Office Bldg. - Rm.9000, 550 Main St., Cincinnati, OH 45202-8501. Phones: (513)421-4310, 562-5600.
- Federal Office Bldg. - Rm.3005, 1240 E. 9th St., Cleveland, OH 44199-9912. Phones: (216)522-1400, 622-6600.
- 330 E. Kilbourn Ave. - Ste.600, Milwaukee, WI 53202-6627. Phones: (414)276-4684, 291-4899.

REGION VI *(Arkansas, Louisiana, New Mexico, Oklahoma, Texas)*:
- Two Financial Centre - Ste.200, 10825 Financial Centre Pkwy., Little Rock, AR 72211-3552. Phones: (501)221-9100, 228-8400.
- 2901 Leon C. Simon Blvd., New Orleans, LA 70126-1061. Phones: (504)816-3000.
- 415 Silver Ave. SW - Ste.300, Albuquerque, NM 87102. Phone: (505)224-2000.
- 3301 W. Memorial Rd., Oklahoma City, OK 73134. Phones: (405)290-7770, -3875.
- 1801 N. Lamar - Ste.300, Dallas, TX 75202-1795. Phones: (214)720-2200, 922-7475.
- 600 S. Mesa Hills Dr. - Ste.3000, El Paso, TX 79912-5533. Phone: (915)832-5000.
- 2500 E. T.C. Jester, Houston, TX 77008-1300. Phones: (713)693-5000, -3800.
- U.S. Post Office and Courthouse Bldg. - Ste.200, 615 E. Houston St., San Antonio, TX 78205-9998. Phones: (210)225-6741, 978-5400.

REGION VII *(Iowa, Kansas, Missouri, Nebraska)*:
- U.S. Courthouse - Rm.300, 1300 Summit, Kansas City, MO 64105-1362. Phones: (816)221-6100, 512-8200.

16.300 thru 16.303 (cont.)

- 2222 Market St. - Rm.2704, St. Louis, MO 63103-2516. Phones: (314)231-4324, 589-2500.
- Federal Office Bldg., 10755 Burt St., Omaha, NE 68114-2000. Phones: (402)493-8688, 492-3700.

REGION VIII *(Colorado, North Dakota, South Dakota, Utah, Wyoming)*:

- Federal Office Bldg. - Ste.1823 (18th fl.), 1961 Stout St., Denver, CO 80294-1823. Phones: (303)629-7171, 628-3000.
- 257 Towers Bldg. - Ste.1200, 257 E. 200 S., Salt Lake City, UT 84111-2048. Phones: (801)579-1400, -4400.

REGION IX *(American Samoa, Arizona, California, Guam, Hawaii, Nevada)*:

- Midtowne Business Centre II - Ste.400, 201 E. Indianola Ave., Phoenix, AZ 85012-2080. Phones: (602)279-5511, 650-3300.
- Federal Office Bldg. - Ste.1700, 11000 Wilshire Blvd., Los Angeles, CA 90024-3672. Phones: (858)565-1255, 514-5500.
- 4500 Orange Grove Ave., Sacramento, CA 95841-4205. Phones: (916)481-9110, 977-2200.
- Federal Office Bldg., 9797 Aero Dr., San Diego, CA 92123-1800. Phones: (619)565-1255, 514-5500.
- 450 Golden Gate Ave. - 13th fl., San Francisco, CA 94102-9523. Phones: (415)553-7400, -2000.
- Kalanianaole Federal Office Bldg. - Rm.4-230, 300 Ala Moana Blvd., Honolulu, HI 96850-0053. Phone: (808)566-4300.
- John Lawrence Bailey Bldg., 700 E. Charleston Blvd., Las Vegas, NV 89101-1545. Phones: (702)385-1281, (700)545-0110.

REGION X *(Alaska, Idaho, Oregon, Washington)*:

- 101 E. 6th Ave., Anchorage, AK 99501-2523. Phones: (907)258-5322, 276-4441.
- Crown Plaza Bldg. - Ste.400, 1500 SW 1st Ave., Portland, OR 97201-5828. Phones: (503)224-4181, 552-5200.
- Federal Office Bldg. - Rm.710, 915 2nd Ave., Seattle, WA 98101. Phones: (206)262-2000, (700)391-8760.

Office of the Inspector General

FIELD INSTALLATIONS

Arizona—*Investigations,* 10 E. Broadway - Ste.105, Tucson, AZ 85701. Phones: (520)670-5243; FAX (520)670-5246. *For mail:* Tucson, AZ 85702-0471.

California—*Investigations,* 321 S. Waterman Ave. - Rm.108, El Centro, CA 92243. Phones: (760)335-3549; FAX (760)335-3534.

- *Investigations,* 330 N. Brand St. - Ste.655, Glendale, CA 91203. Phones: (818)543-1172; FAX (818)637-5082.
- 1200 Bayhill Dr. - Stes.220/201, San Bruno, CA 94066. Phones: *audits,* (650)876-9220; FAX (650)876-0902; *investigations,* (650)876-9058; FAX (650)876-9083.
- *Investigations,* 701 "B" St. - Ste.560, San Diego, CA 92101. Phones: (619)557-5970; FAX(619)557-6518.

Colorado—*Investigations,* Plaza of the Rockies, 111 S. Tejon St. - Ste.312, Colorado Springs, CO 80903. Phones: (719)635-2366; FAX (719)635-4769.

- *Audits,* The Chancery Bldg. - Ste.1603, 1120 Lincoln St., Denver, CO 80203. Phones: (303)864-2000; FAX (303)864-2004.

District of Columbia—1425 New York Ave. NW - Stes.6100/7100, Washington, DC 20530. Phones: *audits,* (202)616-4688; FAX (202)616-4581; *investigations and fraud detection unit,* (202)616-4760; FAX (202)616-9881. *For mail(investigations):* P.O. Box 27718, Washington, DC 20038-7718.

Florida—*Investigations,* 3800 Inverrary Blvd. - Ste.312, Ft. Lauderdale, FL 33319. Phones: (954)535-2859; FAX (954)535-5436.

Georgia—*Audits,* Russell Federal Bldg. - Ste.1130, 75 Spring St., Atlanta, GA 30303. Phones: (404)331-5928; FAX (404)331-5046.

- *Investigations,* 60 Forsyth St. SW - Ste.8M45, Atlanta, GA 30303. Phones: (404)562-1980; FAX (404)562-1960.

Illinois—Citicorp Center, 500 W. Madison Blvd. - Stes.3510/3510B, Chicago, IL 60661. Phones: *audits,* (312)353-1203; FAX (312)886-0513; *investigations,* (312) 886-7050; FAX (312)886-7065. *For mail (investigations):* Chicago, IL 60690-1802.

Massachusetts—*Investigations,* 1 Courthouse Way - Rm.9200, Boston, MA 02210. Phones: (617)748-3218; FAX (617)748-3965. *For Mail:* Boston, MA 02106-2134.

New York—*Investigations,* JFK Airport, Bldg. 77 - Penthouse no. 2, N. Boundary Rd., Jamaica, NY 11430. Phones: FTS (718)553-7520; FAX (718)553-7533. *For mail:* JFK Airport, Jamaica, NY 11430-0999.

Pennsylvania—*Audits,* 701 Market St. - Ste.201, Philadelphia, PA 19106. Phones: (215)580-2111; FAX (215)597-1348.

Texas—207 S. Houston St. - *(audits)* Rm.575 (Box 4), *(investigations)* Rm.551 (Box 5), Dallas, TX 75202-4724. Phones: *audits,* (214)655-5000; FAX (214)655-5025; *investigations.* (214)655-5076; FAX (214)655-5071.

- *Investigations,* 4050 Rio Bravo - Ste.200, El Paso, TX 79902. Phones: (915)577-0102; FAX (915)577-9012.

- *Investigations,* Casey Federal Courthouse - Ste.3307, 515 Rusk Ave., Houston, TX 77002. Phones: (713)718-4888; FAX (713)718-4706. *For mail:* P.O. Box 610071, Houston, TX 77208-9998.

- *Investigations,* Texas Commerce Center, Bentsen Tower - Ste.510, 1701 W. Business Hwy.83, McAllen, TX 78501. Phones: (956)618-8145; FAX (956)618-8151.

Washington—*Investigations,* 620 Kirkland Way - Ste.104, Kirkland, WA 98033-6021. Phones: (425)828-3998; FAX (425)827-2183.

NATIONAL INSTITUTE OF CORRECTIONS

16.601 thru 16.603 NIC Academy Division *or* Jails Division, 1960 Industrial Circle - Ste.A, Longmont, CO 80501. Phones: (303)682-0382, (800)995-6429; FAX (303)682-0469.

BUREAU OF JUSTICE ASSISTANCE

16.737 G.R.E.A.T program regional offices:

MIDWEST—La Crosse Police Dept., 400 La Crosse St., La Crosse, WI 54601. Phone: (608)789-8202.

NORTHEAST—Philadelphia Police Department, Community Relations Division, 1328 Race. St. - 2nd fl., Philadelphia, PA 19107. Phone: (215)686-1477.

NORTHWEST—Portland Police Bureau, 449 NE Emerson, Portland, OR 97211. Phone: (503)823-2111.

SOUTHEAST—Orange County Sheriff's Office, 2500 W. Colonial Dr. - 2nd fl., Orlando, FL 32804. Phone: (407)254-7369.

SOUTHWEST—Phoenix Police Dept., 620 W. Washington St., Phoenix, AZ 85003. Phone: (602)495-0432.

DEPARTMENT OF LABOR

BUREAU OF LABOR STATISTICS

17.002 thru 17.005 **REGIONAL OFFICES**

ATLANTA *(Alabama, Florida, Georgia, Kentucky, Mississippi, North Carolina, South Carolina, Tennessee)*—AFC - Rm.7T50, 61 Forsyth St. SW, Atlanta, GA 30303. Phone: (404)331-3446.

BOSTON/NEW YORK *(Connecticut, Maine, Massachusetts, New Hampshire, New York, Puerto Rico, Virgin Islands, Rhode Island, Vermont)*—JFK Federal Bldg. - E310, Boston, MA 02203. Phone: (617)565-2324.

• 201 Varick St. - Rm.808, New York, NY 10014-4811. Phone: (212)337-2420.

CHICAGO *Illinois, Indiana, Iowa, Michigan, Minnesota, Nebraska, North Dakota, Ohio, South Dakota, Wisconsin)*—Federal Office Bldg. - 9th fl., 230 S. Dearborn St., Chicago, IL 60604-1595. Phone: (312)353-7200, ext.229.

DALLAS/KANSAS CITY *(Arkansas, Colorado, Kansas, Louisiana, Missouri, Montana, New Mexico, Oklahoma, Texas, Utah, Wyoming)*—A. Maceo Federal Bldg. - Ste.221, 525 Griffin St., Dallas, TX 75202-5028. Phone: (214)767-9379.

• City Center Square - Ste.600, 1100 Main St., Kansas City, MO 64105-2112. Phone: (816)426-3176.

PHILADELPHIA *(Delaware, District of Columbia, Maryland, Pennsylvania, New Jersey, Virginia, West Virginia)*—The Curtis Center - Ste.610 E., 170 S. Independence Mall W., Philadelphia, PA 19106-3305. Phone: (215)861-5603.

SAN FRANCISCO *(Alaska, American Samoa, Arizona, California, Guam, Hawaii, Idaho, Nevada, Oregon, Washington, Trust Territory of the Pacific Islands)*—71 Stevenson St. - 6th fl., San Francisco, CA 94105. Phone: (415)975-4403. *For mail:* San Francisco, CA 94119-3766.

EMPLOYEE BENEFITS SECURITY ADMINISTRATION

17.150 **FIELD OFFICES**

California—1055 E. Colorado Blvd. - Ste.200, Pasadena, CA 91106. Phones: (626)229-1000; FAX (626)229-1098.

• 71 Stevenson St. - Ste.915, San Francisco, CA 94105. Phones: (415)975-4600; FAX (415)975-4589.

District of Columbia—1335 East-West Hwy. - Ste.200, Silver Spring, MD 20910-3225. Phones: (301)713-2000; FAX (301)713-2008.

Florida—Bldg. H - Site 104, 8040 Peters Rd., Plantation, FL 33324. Phones: (954)424-4022; FAX (954)424-0548.

Georgia—61 Forsyth St. SW - Ste.7B54, Atlanta, GA 30303. Phones: (404)562-2156; FAX (404)562-2168.

Illinois—200 W. Adams St. - Ste.1600, Chicago, IL 60606. Phones: (312)353-0900; FAX (312)353-1023.

Kentucky—1885 Dixie Hwy. - Ste.210, Ft. Wright, KY 41011-2664. Phones: (859)578-4680; FAX (859)578-4688.

Massachusetts—JFK Bldg. - Rm.575, Boston, MA 02203. Phones: (617)565-9600; FAX (617)565-9666.

Michigan—211 W. Fort St. - Ste.1310, Detroit, MI 48226-3211. Phones: (313)226-7450; FAX (313)226-4257.

Missouri—1100 Main St. - Ste.1200, Kansas City, MO 64105-5148. Phones: (816)426-5131; FAX (816)426-5511.

- Young Federal Bldg. - Rm.6310, 1222 Spruce St., St. Louis, MO 63101-2818. Phones: (314)539-2693; FAX (314)539-2697.

New York—33 Whitehall St. - Ste.1200(12th fl.), New York, NY 10004. Phones: (212)607-8600; FAX (212)607-8681.

Pennsylvania—170 S. Independence Mall W. - Ste.870 West, Philadelphia, PA 19106-3317. Phones: (215)861-5300; FAX (215)861-5347.

Texas—525 Griffin St. - Rm.900, Dallas, TX 75202-5025. Phones: (214)767-6831; FAX (214)767-1055.

Washington—1111 3rd Ave. - Ste.860, Seattle, WA 98101-3212. Phones: (206)553-4244; FAX (206)553-0913.

EMPLOYMENT AND TRAINING ADMINISTRATION

BUREAU OF APPRENTICESHIP AND TRAINING (BAT)

17.201 REGIONAL OFFICES

Apprenticeship Training, Employer and Labor Services Director:

REGION I *(Connecticut, Maine, Massachusetts, New Hampshire, Rhode Island, Vermont)*—JFK Federal Bldg. - Rm.E-370, Boston, MA 02203. Phones: (617)565-2288; FAX (617)565-9171.

REGION II *(New Jersey, New York, Puerto Rico, Virgin Islands)*—201 Varick St. - Rm.602, New York, NY 10014. Phones: (212)337-2313; FAX (212)337-2317.

REGION III *(Delaware, Maryland, Pennsylvania, Virginia, West Virginia)*—3535 Market St. - Rm.13240, Philadelphia, PA 19104. Phones: (215)596-6417; FAX (215)596-0192.

REGION IV *(Alabama, Florida, Georgia, Kentucky, Mississippi, North Carolina, South Carolina, Tennessee)*—61 Forsyth St. NW - Rm.6T71, Atlanta, GA 30303. Phones: (404)562-2335; FAX (404)562-2329.

REGION V *(Illinois, Indiana, Michigan, Minnesota, Ohio, Wisconsin)*—230 S. Dearborn St. - Rm.708, Chicago, IL 60604. Phones: (312)353-7205; FAX (312)353-5506.

REGION VI *(Arkansas, Louisiana, New Mexico, Oklahoma, Texas)*—Federal Bldg. - Rm.311, 525 Griffin St. Dallas, TX 75202. Phones: (214)767-4993; FAX (214)767-4995.

REGION VII *(Iowa, Kansas, Missouri, Nebraska)*—1100 Main St. - Ste.1040, Kansas City, MO 64105-2112. Phones: (816)426-3856; FAX (816)426-3664.

REGION VIII *(Colorado, Montana, North Dakota, South Dakota, Utah, Wyoming)*—U.S. Custom House - Rm.465, 721 19th St., Denver, CO 80202. Phones: (303)844-4791; FAX (303)844-4701.

REGION IX *(Arizona, California, Hawaii, Nevada)*—Federal Bldg. - Rm.815, 71 Stevenson St., San Francisco, CA 94105. Phones: (415)975-4007; FAX (415)975-4010.

REGION X *(Alaska, Idaho, Oregon, Washington)*—1111 3rd Ave. - Rm.925, Seattle, WA 98101-3212. Phones: (206)553-5286; FAX (206)553-1689.

17.202 thru 17.266 **ETA REGIONAL OFFICES**

Contact the nearest office of the state employment service in your area, or the appropriate regional office following:

REGION I *(Connecticut, Maine, Massachusetts, New Hampshire, Rhode Island, Vermont)*—JFK Federal Bldg. - Rm.E-350, Boston, MA 02203. Phones: (617)565-3630; FAX (617)565-2229.

REGION II *(Canal Zone, New Jersey, New York, Puerto Rico, Virgin Islands)*—201 Varick St. - Rm.755, New York, NY 10014. Phones: (212)337-2139; FAX (212)337-2144.

REGION III *(Delaware, District of Columbia, Maryland, Pennsylvania, Virginia, West Virginia)*—The Curtis Center- Ste.825E, 170 S. Independence Mall West, Philadelphia, PA 19106-3315. Phones: (215)861-5205; FAX (215)861-5260.

REGION IV *(Alabama, Florida, Georgia, Kentucky, Mississippi, North Carolina, South Carolina, Tennessee)*—Atlanta Federal Center - Rm.6M12, 61 Forsyth St. SW, Atlanta, GA 30303. Phones: (404)562-2092; FAX (404)562-2149.

REGION V *(Arkansas, Colorado, Louisiana, Montana, New Mexico, North Dakota, Oklahoma, South Dakota, Texas, Utah, Wyoming)*—525 Griffin St. - Rm.317, Dallas, TX 75202. Phones: (214)767-8263; FAX (214)767-5113.

REGION VI *(Illinois, Indiana, Iowa, Kansas, Michigan, Minnesota, Missouri, Nebraska, Ohio, Wisconsin)*—230 S. Dearborn St. - Rm.628, Chicago, IL 60604. Phones: (312)353-0313; FAX (312)353-4474.

REGION VII *(Alaska, American Samoa, Arizona, California, Guam, Hawaii, Idaho, Micronesia, Nevada, Northern Mariana Islands, Oregon, Republic of Palau, Washington)*—71 Stevenson St. - Rm.830, San Francisco, CA 94119-3767. Phones: (415)975-4610; FAX (415)975-4612.

EMPLOYMENT STANDARDS ADMINISTRATION

17.301 **OFFICE OF FEDERAL CONTRACT COMPLIANCE PROGRAMS**

REGIONAL OFFICES

REGION I *(Connecticut, Maine, Massachusetts, New Hampshire, Rhode Island, Vermont)*—JFK Federal Bldg. - Rm.E-235, One Congress St., Boston, MA 02203. Phone: (617)565-2055.

REGION II *(New Jersey, New York, Puerto Rico, Virgin Islands)*—201 Varick St. - Rm.750, New York, NY 10014. Phone: (212)337-2007.

REGION III *(Delaware, District of Columbia, Maryland, Pennsylvania, Virginia, West Virginia)*—Curtis Center - Ste.750W, 170 S. Independence Mall W., Philadelphia, PA 19106-3309 Phone: (215)861-5763.

REGION IV *(Alabama, Florida, Georgia, Kentucky, Mississippi, North Carolina, South Carolina, Tennessee)*—Atlanta Federal Center - Rm.7B75, 61 Forsyth St. SW, Atlanta, GA 30303. Phone: (404)562-2424.

REGION V *(Illinois, Indiana, Iowa, Kansas, Michigan, Minnesota, Missouri, Nebraska, Ohio, Wisconsin)*—Kluczynski Federal Bldg. - Rm.570, 230 S. Dearborn St., Chicago, IL 60604. Phone: (312)596-7010.

REGION VI *(Arkansas, Colorado, Louisiana, Montana, New Mexico, North Dakota, Oklahoma, South Dakota, Texas, Utah, Wyoming)*—Federal Bldg. - Ste.840, 525 S. Griffin St., Dallas, TX 75202. Phone: (214)767-2804.

REGION IX *(Arizona, California, Guam, Hawaii, Nevada)*—71 Stevenson St. - Ste. 1700, San Francisco, CA 94105. Phone: (415)975-4720.

FIELD OFFICE CONTACTS 787

REGION X *(Alaska, Idaho, Oregon, Washington)*—1111 3rd Ave. - Ste.745, Seattle, WA 98101. Phone: (206)553-7182.

DISTRICT AND AREA OFFICES

Alabama—Medical Forum Bldg. - Ste.660, 950 22nd St. N., Birmingham, AL 35203. Phone: (205)731-0820.

Arizona—3221 N. 16th St. - Ste.303, Phoenix, AZ 85016. Phone: (602)640-2960.

Arkansas—TCBY Tower - Ste.735, 425 W. Capitol Ave., Little Rock, AR 72201. Phone: (501)324-5436.

California—Federal Bldg. - Ste.8103, 11000 Wilshire Blvd., Los Angeles, CA 90024. Phone: (310)235-6800.

- 1301 Clay St. - Ste.1080N, Oakland, CA 94612. Phone: (510)637-2938.
- 5675 Ruffin Rd. - Ste.320, San Diego, CA 92123. Phone: (619)557-6489.
- 60 S. Market St. - Ste.410, San Jose, CA 95113. Phone: (408)291-7384.
- 34 Civic Center Plaza - Ste.406, P.O. Box 12800, Santa Ana, CA 92712. Phone: (714)836-2784.

Colorado—1244 Spee Blvd. - Rm.620, Denver, CO 80204-3584. Phone: (303)844-4481.

Connecticut—135 High St. - Rm.311, Hartford, CT 06103. Phone: (860)240-4277.

District of Columbia—Riddell Bldg. - Ste.422, 1730 K St. NW, Washington, DC 20006. Phone: (202)254-2501.

Florida—1851 Executive Center Dr. - Ste.200, Jacksonville, FL 32207. Phone: (904) 232-3073.

- Brickell Plaza Federal Bldg. - Ste.722, 909 SE 1st Ave., Miami, FL 33131. Phone: (305)536-5670.
- Commodore Bldg. - Ste.160, 3444 McCrory Pl., Orlando, FL 32803. Phone: (407)648-6181.

Georgia—61 Forsyth St. - Rm.7B65, Atlanta, GA 30303. Phone: (404)562-2444.

Hawaii—300 Ala Moana Blvd. - Rm.7326, P.O. Box 50149, Honolulu, HI 96850. Phone: (808)541-2933.

Illinois—230 S. Dearborn St. - Rm.434, Chicago, IL 60604. Phone: (312)596-7046.

Indiana—429 N. Pennsylvania St. - Rm.308, Indianapolis, IN 46204. Phones: (317)226-5860.

Kentucky—Mazzoli Federal Bldg. - Rm.185, 600 Martin Luther King Place, Louisville, KY 40202. Phone: (502)582-6275.

Louisiana—701 Loyola Ave. - Rm.13029, New Orleans, LA 70113. Phone: (504)589-6575.

Maryland—Appraiser's Store Bldg. - Rm.202, 103 S. Gay St., Baltimore, MD 21202. Phone: (410)962-3572.

Massachusetts—JFK Federal Bldg. - Rm.E-235, Boston, MA 02203. Phone: (617)565-2055.

Michigan—McNamara Federal Bldg. - Rm.1320, 211 W. Fort St., Detroit, MI 48226. Phone: (313)226-3728.

- 50 Louis St. NW - 2nd fl.(NW-c/o), Ste.300-HUD, Grand Rapids, MI 49503. Phone: (616)456-2144.

Minnesota—Bridgeplace Bldg. - Rm.102, 220 2nd St. S., Minneapolis, MN 55401. Phone: (612)370-3177.

Mississippi—Millsaps Bldg. - Ste.700, 201 W. Capitol St., Jackson, MS 39201. Phone: (601)965-4668.

Missouri—1100 Main St. - Rm.860, Kansas City, MO 64105. Phone: (816)426-3860.

- 1222 Spruce St. - Rm.10207, St. Louis, MO 63103. Phone: (314)539-6394.

17.301
(cont.)

Nebraska—106 S. 15th St. - Rm.808, Omaha, NE 68116. Phone: (402)221-3381.

New Jersey—Bldg. 5 - Rm.203, 3131 Princeton Pike, Lawrenceville, NJ 08648. Phone: (609)989-2380.

- Diamond Head Bldg. - Rm.102, 200 Sheffield Dr., Mountainside, NJ 07092. Phone: (201)645-6104.

New Mexico—505 Marquette Ave. NW - Ste.810, Albuquerque, NM 87102. Phone: (505)248-5015.

New York—O'Brien Federal Bldg. - Rm.740, 19 Aviation Rd., Albany, NY 12205. Phone: (518)435-0326.

- Six Fountain Plaza - Ste.300, Buffalo. NY 14202. Phone: (716)551-5065.
- 26 Federal Plaza - Rm.36-116, New York, NY 10278. Phone: (212)264-7742.

North Carolina—Mart Office Bldg. - Rm.BB-401, 800 Briar Creek Rd., Charlotte, NC 28205. Phone: (704)344-6113.

- 300 Fayetteville Street Mall - Ste.121, Raleigh, NC 27601. Phone: (919)856-4058.

Ohio—55 Rennaissance Center - Ste.350, 1350 Euclid St. - Ste.350, Cleveland, OH 44114. Phone: (216)522-7472.

- 200 N. High St. - Rm.409, Columbus, OH 43215. Phone: (614)469-5831.

Oklahoma—51 Yale Bldg. - Rm.304, 5110 S. Yale, Tulsa, OK 74135. Phone: (918)496-6772.

Oregon—Federal Office Bldg. - Ste.1030, 1515 SW 5th Ave., Portland, OR 97201. Phone: (503)326-4112.

Pennsylvania—Nix Federal Bldg. - Rm.311, 9th and Market St., Philadelphia, PA 19107. Phone: (215)597-4122.

- Federal Bldg. - Rm.1132, 1000 Liberty Ave., Pittsburgh, PA 15222. Phone: (412)395-6330.

Puerto Rico—San Patricio Office Center - 4th fl., 7 Tabonuco St., Guaynabo, PR 00968. Phone: (787)775-1901.

South Carolina—Thurmond Federal Bldg. - Ste.608, 1835 Assembly St., Columbia, SC 29201. Phone: (803)765-5244.

Tennessee—167 N. Main St. - Ste.201, Memphis, TN 38103. Phone: (901)544-3458.

- 1321 Murfreesboro Rd., Ste.301, Nashville, TN 37217. Phone: (615)781-5395.

Texas—Federal Office Bldg. - Rm.512, 525 Griffin St., Dallas, TX 75202. Phone: (214)767-2911.

- 2320 La Branch St. - Rm.1103, Houston, TX 77004. Phone: (713)718-3800.
- 800 Dolorosa St. - Rm.200, San Antonio, TX 78207. Phone: (210)472-5835.

Utah—Gateway Tower East - Ste.1690, 10 E. South Temple, Salt Lake City, UT 84101. Phone: (801)524-4470.

Virginia—400 N. 8th St. - Rm.552, Richmond, VA 23240. Phone: (804)771-2136.

Washington—Federal Office Bldg. - Ste.745, 1111 3rd Ave., Seattle, WA 98101. Phone: (206)553-7182.

Wisconsin—Federal Bldg. - Ste.1115, 310 W. Wisconsin Ave., Milwaukee, WI 53203. Phone: (414)297-3821.

OFFICE OF WORKERS' COMPENSATION PROGRAMS

REGIONAL OFFICES

California—71 Stevenson St. - Ste.1705, San Francisco, CA 94105. Phone: (415)975-4160.

Colorado—1801 California St. - Ste.920, Denver, CO 80202-2614. Phone: (720)264-3160.

Florida—214 N. Hogan St. - Ste.1026, Jacksonville, FL 32202. Phone: (904)357-4725.

Illinois—230 S. Dearborn St. - Rm.800, Chicago, IL 60604. Phone: (312)596-7131.

Massachusetts—JFK Federal Bldg. - Rm.E-260, Boston, MA 02203. Phone: (617)565-2130.

Missouri—City Center Square - Ste.750, 1100 Main St., Kansas City, MO 64105. Phone: (816)426-2196.

New York—201 Varick St. - Rm.750, New York, NY 10014. Phone: (212)337-2033.

Pennsylvania—Curtis Center - Ste.780 W., 170 S. Independence Mall W., Philadelphia, PA 19106-3313. Phone: (215)861-5406.

Texas—525 S. Griffin St. - Rm.407, Dallas, TX 75202. Phone: (214)767-4713.

Washington—1111 3rd Ave. - Ste.615, Seattle, WA 98101-3212. Phone: (206)553-5508.

17.302 Longshore and Harbor Workers' Compensation

DISTRICT OFFICES

DISTRICT 1 *(Connecticut, Maine, Massachusetts, New Hampshire, Rhode Island, Vermont)*—JFK Federal Bldg. - Rm.E-260, Boston, MA 02203. Phone: (617)565-2103.

DISTRICT 2 *(New Jersey, New York, Puerto Rico, Virgin Islands)*—201 Varick St. - Rm.750, New York, NY 10014-0249. Phone: (212)337-2030.

DISTRICT 3 *(Delaware, Pennsylvania, West Virginia)*—Curtis Center - Ste.790 W., 170 S. Independence Mall W., Philadelphia, PA 19106-3313. Phone: (215)861-5459.

DISTRICT 4 *(District of Columbia, Maryland)*—31 Hopkins Plaza - Rm.410-B, Baltimore, MD 21201. Phone: (410)962-3577.

DISTRICT 5 *(Virginia)*—200 Granby Mall - Rm.212, Norfolk, VA 23510. Phone: (757)441-3071.

DISTRICT 6 *(Alabama, Florida, Georgia, Kentucky, Mississippi, North Carolina, South Carolina, Tennessee)*—214 N. Hogan St. - Ste.1040, Jacksonville, FL 32202. Phone: (904)357-4757.

DISTRICT 7 *(Arkansas, Louisiana)*—701 Loyola Ave. - Rm.13032, New Orleans, LA 70113. Phone: (504)589-2671.

DISTRICT 8 *(Oklahoma, New Mexico, Texas)*—8866 Gulf Freeway - Ste.140, Houston, TX 77017. Phone: (713)943-1605.

DISTRICT 10 *(Illinois, Indiana, Iowa, Kansas, Michigan, Minnesota, Missouri, Nebraska, Ohio, Wisconsin)*—230 S. Dearborn St. - Rm.578, Chicago, IL 60604. Phone: (312)596-7153.

DISTRICT 13 *(Arizona, California-northern, Nevada)*—71 Stevenson St. - Rm.1705, San Francisco, CA 94119-3770. Phone: (415)975-4274.

DISTRICT 14 *(Alaska, Colorado, Idaho, Montana, Oregon, North Dakota, South Dakota, Utah, Washington, Wyoming)*—1111 3rd Ave. - Ste.620, Seattle, WA 98101-3212. Phone: (206)553-4471.

DISTRICT 15 *(Hawaii, Pacific Area to 60 east longitude)*—300 Ala Moana Blvd. - Rm.5-135, P.O. Box 50209, Honolulu, HI 96850 *(via air mail)*. Phone: (808)541-1983.

DISTRICT 18 *(Southern California)*—401 E. Ocean Blvd. - Ste.720, Long Beach, CA 90802. Phone: (562)980-3578.

17.303 and 17.306 Wage and Hour Division

REGIONAL OFFICES

MIDWEST—230 S. Dearborn St. - Rm.820, Chicago, IL 60604-1591. Phone: (312)596-7180.

**17.303
and
17.306
(cont.)**

NORTHEAST—The Curtis Center - Ste.850 West, 170 Independence Mall W., Philadelphia, PA 19107-3317. Phone: (215)861-5800.

SOUTHEAST—Atlanta Federal Center - Rm.7M40, 61 Forsyth St. SW, Atlanta, GA 30303. Phone: (404)562-2202.

SOUTHWEST—Federal Bldg. - Rm.800, 525 S. Griffin St., Dallas, TX 75202-5007. Phone: (214)767-6895.

WESTERN—71 Stevenson St. - Ste.930, San Francisco, CA 94105. Phone: (415)975-4510.

DISTRICT OFFICES

Alabama—Aronov Bldg. - Rm.708, 474 S. Court St., Montgomery, AL 36104-4158. Phone: (304)223-7641.

Arizona—3221 N. 16th St. - Ste.301, Phoenix, AZ 85016-7161. Phone: (602)640-2990.

Arkansas—TCBY Tower - Ste.725, 425 W. Capitol Ave., Little Rock, AR 72201. Phones: (501)324-5377.

California-Los Angelos—300 S. Glendale Ave. - Ste.400, Glendale, CA 91205-1752. Phones: (213)894-6375.

- 2800 Cottage Way - Rm.W-1836, Sacramento, CA 95825. Phone: (916)978-6120.
- 5675 Ruffin Rd. - Ste.320, San Diego, CA 92123-1362. Phone: (619)557-5606.
- 455 Market St. - Ste.800, San Francisco, CA 94105. Phone: (415)744-5590.

Colorado—1999 Broadway - Ste.2445, P.O. Drawer 3505, Denver, CO 80202. Phone: (720)264-3250.

Connecticut—135 High St. - Rm.310, Hartford, CT 06103-1595. Phone: (860)240-4160.

Florida—Federal Bldg. - Rm.408, 299 E. Broward Blvd., Ft. Lauderdale, FL 33301-1976. Phone: (954)356-6896.

- 3728 Phillips Hwy. - Ste.219, Jacksonville, FL 32207. Phone: (904)232-2489.
- Sunset Center - Rm.255, 10300 SW Sunset Dr., Miami, FL 33173-3038. Phones: (305)598-6607; FAX (305)279-8393.
- Austin Laurel Bldg. - Ste.300, 4905 W. Laurel Ave., Tampa, FL 33607-3838. Phone: (813)288-1242.

Georgia—Atlanta Federal Center - Rm.7M10, 61 Forsyth St. SW, Atlanta, GA 30303. Phone: (404)562-2201.

- Low Federal Bldg. Complex - Ste.B-210, 124 Barnard St., Savannah, GA 31401-3648. Phones: (912)652-4221, -4229.

Illinois—230 S. Dearborn - Rm.412, Chicago, IL 60604-1595. Phone: (312)596-7182.

- 509 W. Capitol Ave. - Ste.205, Springfield, IL 62704-1929. Phone: (217)492-4060.

Indiana—429 N. Pennsylvania St. - Rm.403, Indianapolis, IN 46204-1873. Phone: (317)226-6801.

- River Glen Plaza - Ste.160, 501 E. Monroe St., South Bend, IN 46601-1615. Phones:(219)236-8331, -8332.

Iowa—Federal Bldg. - Rm.643, 210 Walnut St., Des Moines, IA 50309. Phone: (515)284-4625.

Kansas—Gateway Tower II - Ste.1010, 400 State Ave., Kansas City, KS 66101. Phone: (913)551-5721.

Kentucky—Snyder U.S. Courthouse and Custom House - Rm.31, 601 W. Broadway, Louisville, KY 40202-9570. Phone: (502)582-5226.

Louisiana—701 Loyola Ave. - Rm.13028, New Orleans, LA 70113-1931. Phone: (504)589-6171.

Maryland—207 Appraisers Stores Bldg., 103 S. Gay St., Baltimore, MD 21201-4061. Phone:(410)962-4984.

FIELD OFFICE CONTACTS 791

Massachusetts—Kennedy Federal Bldg. - Rm.525, Boston, MA 02203. Phone: (617) 565-2066.

Michigan—211 Fort St. - Rm.1317, Detroit, MI 18226-2799. Phone: (313)226-7447.

- 2920 Fuller Ave. NE - Ste.100, Grand Rapids, MI 49505-3409. Phone: (616)456-2004.

Minnesota—Midland Square - Ste.920, 331 2nd Ave S., Minneapolis, MN 55401-2233. Phone: (612)370-3371.

Mississippi—One Jackson Place - Ste.1020, 188 E. Capitol St., Jackson, MS 39201-2126. Phones: (601)965-4347, -4348.

Missouri—1222 Spruce St. - Rm.9102-B, St. Louis, MO 63103. Phones: (314)539-2706, -3014.

Nebraska—Federal Bldg. - Rm.715, 106 S. 15th St., Omaha, NE 68102. Phone: (402)221-4682.

New Hampshire—2 Wall St. - 1st fl., Manchester, NH 03101. Phones: (603)666-7716; FAX (603)666-7600.

New Jersey—Bldg. 5 - Rm.216, 3131 Princeton Pike, Lawrenceville, NJ 08648. Phones: (609)989-2247, -2368.

- 200 Sheffield St. - Ste.102, Mountainside, NJ 07092. Phone: (973)645-2279.

New Mexico—Western Bank Bldg. - Ste.840, 505 Marquette NW, Albuquerque, NM 87102-2160. Phone: (505)248-5115.

New York—O'Brien Federal Bldg. - Rm.822, Albany, NY 12207. Phone: (518)431-4279.

- 26 Federal Plaza - Rm.3700, New York, NY 10278. Phone: (212)264-8185.
- 1400 Old Country Rd. - Ste.410, Westbury, NY 11590-5119. Phone: (516)338-1890.

North Carolina—800 Briar Creek Rd. - Ste.CC-412, Charlotte, NC 28205-6903. Phone: (704)344-6298.

- Somerset Park Bldg. - Ste.260, 4407 Bland Rd., Raleigh, NC 27609-6296. Phones: (919)790-2741, -2742.

Ohio—525 Vine St. - Ste.880, Cincinnati, OH 45202-3268. Phone: (513)684-2908.

- Federal Bldg. - Rm.817, 1240 E. 9th St., Cleveland, OH 44199-2054 Phones: (216)522-3892, -3893.
- 646 Federal Bldg., 200 N. High St., Columbus, OH 43215-2475. Phones: (614)469-5678; FAX (614)469-5428.

Oregon—1515 SW 5th Ave. - Ste.1040, Portland, OR 97201-5445. Phone: (503)326-3057.

Pennsylvania—U.S. Customs House - Rm.400, 2nd and Chestnut St., Philadelphia, PA 19106. Phone: (215)597-4950.

- Federal Bldg. - Rm.313, 1000 Liberty Ave., Pittsburgh, PA 15222. Phone: (412)395-4996.
- Stegmaier Bldg. - Ste.373-M, 7 N. Wilkes-Barre Blvd., Wilkes-Barre, PA 18702-3594. Phone: (570)826-6316.

Puerto Rico—San Patricio Office Center - 4th fl., 7 Tabonuco St., Guaynabo, PR 00968. Phone: (787)775-1924.

South Carolina—Federal Bldg. - Rm.1072, 1835 Assembly St., Columbia, SC 29201-9863. Phone: (803)765-5981.

Tennessee—Executive Plaza - Bldg.511, 1321 Murfreesboro Rd., Nashville, TN 37217-2626. Phones: (615)781-5343, -5345.

Texas—Smith Federal Bldg. - Rm.507, 525 S. Griffin St., Dallas, TX 75202-5007. Phone: (214)767-6294.

- South Bldg. - Ste.202, 9990 Richmond Ave., Houston, TX 77042-4546. Phone: (713)339-5575.

17.303 and 17.306 (cont.)

- Northchase I Office Bldg. - Ste.140, 10127 Morocco St., San Antonio, TX 78216. Phone: (210)308-4515.

Utah—10 E. South Temple - Ste.1680, Salt Lake City, UT 84133. Phone: (801)524-5706.

Virginia—Federal Bldg. - Ste.416, 400 N. 8th St., Richmond, VA 23240. Phone: (804)771-2995.

Washington—1111 3rd Ave. - Ste.755, Seattle, WA 98101-3212. Phone: (206)553-4482.

West Virginia—500 Quarrier St. - Ste.720, Charleston, WV 25301. Phone: (304)347-5206.

Wisconsin—740 Regent St. - Ste.102, Madison, WI 53715. Phone: (608)264-5221.

17.307 Division of Coal Mine Workers' Compensation

DISTRICT OFFICES

Contact nearest Social Security office or appropriate CMWC office, following.

Colorado *(Western United States)*—1801 California St. - Ste.925, Denver, CO 80202-2614. Phone: (720)264-3100.

Kentucky *(Kentucky)*—334 Main St. - 5th fl., Pikeville, KY 41501. Phone: (1-800-366-4599).

- *(Alabama, Florida, Georgia, Mississippi, North Carolina, South Carolina, Tennessee)*—402 Campbell Way, Spring St., Mt. Sterling, KY 40353. Phone: (1-800-366-4628).

Ohio *(Illinois, Indiana, Michigan, Minnesota, Ohio, Wisconsin)*—1160 Dublin Rd. - Ste.300, Columbus, OH 43215. Phone: (1-800-347-3771).

Pennsylvania *(Connecticut, Delaware, District of Columbia, Maine, Massachusetts, New Hampshire, New Jersey, New York, Pennsylvania-eastern, Rhode Island, Vermont)*—S. Main Towers, 105 N. Main St. - Ste.100, Wilkes-Barre, PA 18701. Phone: (1-800-347-3755).

- *(Maryland, Pennsylvania-western)*—Wellington Square - Ste.405, 1225 S. Main St., Greensburg, PA 15601. Phone: (1-800-347-3753).

- *(Pennsylvania-central, Virginia)*—Penn Traffic Bldg. - 2nd fl., 319 Washington St., Johnstown, PA 15901. Phone: (1-800-347-3754).

West Virginia *(West Virginia-northern)*—Federal Bldg. - Ste.3116, 425 Juliana St., Parkersburg, WV 26101. Phone: (1-800-347-3751).

- *(West Virginia-southern)*—Charleston Federal Center - Ste.110, 500 Quarrier St., Charleston, WV 25301. Phone: (1-800-347-3749).

17.308 Contact the nearest office of the state employment service in your area, or nearest Wage and Hour Division Office listed under **17.303**.

OFFICE OF LABOR-MANAGEMENT STANDARDS

17.309 FIELD OFFICES

California—3660 Wilshire Blvd. - Ste.708, Los Angeles, CA 90010-2713. Phone: (213)252-7508.

- 71 Stevenson Pl. - Ste.725, San Francisco, CA 94105-2997. Phone: (415)975-4020.

Colorado—1999 Broadway St. - Rm.2435, P.O. Box 46550, Denver, CO 80201-6550. Phone: (720)264-3231.

District of Columbia—Riddell Bldg. - Ste.558, 1730 K St. NW, Washington, DC 20006. Phone: (202)254-6510.

FIELD OFFICE CONTACTS   793

Georgia—61 Forsyth St. SW - Rm.8B85, Atlanta, GA 30303-2219. Phone: (404)562-2083.

Illinois—Federal Office Bldg. - Ste.774, 230 S. Dearborn St., Chicago, IL 60604-1505. Phone: (312)596-7160.

Louisiana—701 Loyola Ave. - Ste.13009, New Orleans, LA 70113- 1912. Phone: (504)589-6174.

Massachusetts—JFK Federal Bldg. - Rm.E-365, Boston, MA 02203- 0002. Phone: (617)565-9880.

Michigan—211 W. Fort St. - Ste.1313, Detroit, MI 48226-3237. Phone: (313)226-6200.

Missouri—1222 Spruce St. - Ste.9.109E, St. Louis, MO 63103- 2830. Phone: (314)539-2667.

New York—Federal Bldg. - Ste.1310, 111 W. Huron St., Buffalo, NY 14202-2379. Phone: (716)551-4976.

- 201 Varick St. - Ste.878,, New York, NY 10014-4811. Phone: (212)337-2580.

Ohio—525 Vine St. - Ste.950, Cincinnati, OH 45202-3168. Phone: (513)684-6840.

- Federal Office Bldg. - Ste.831, 1240 E. 9th St., Cleveland, OH 44199-2053. Phone: (216)522-3855.

Pennsylvania—The Curtis Center - Rm.760W, 170 S. Independence Mall West, Philadelphia, PA 19106-3310. Phone: (215)861-4818.

- Federal Office Bldg. - Ste.801, 1000 Liberty Ave., Pittsburgh, PA 15222-4004. Phone: (412)395-6925.

Tennessee—233 Cumberland Bend Dr. - Ste.110, Nashville, TN 37228-1809. Phone: (615)736-5906.

Texas—Maceo Smith Federal Bldg. - Ste.300, 525 Griffin St., Dallas, TX 75202-5007. Phone: (214)767-6834.

Washington—Federal Office Bldg. - Ste.605, 1111 3rd Ave., Seattle, WA 98101-3212. Phone: (206)553-5216.

Wisconsin—517 E. Wisconsin Ave. - Ste.118, Milwaukee, WI 53202-4504. Phone: (414)297-1501.

OCCUPATIONAL SAFETY AND HEALTH ADMINISTRATION

17.502 thru 17.505

REGIONAL OFFICES

REGION I *(Connecticut, Maine, Massachusetts, New Hampshire, Rhode Island, Vermont)*—JFK Federal Bldg. - Low Rise Bldg. (Rm.E-340), Boston, MA 02114. Phone: (617)565-9860.

REGION II *(New Jersey, New York, Puerto Rico)*—201 Varick St. - Ste.670, New York, NY 10014. Phone: (212)337-2378.

REGION III *(Delaware, District of Columbia, Maryland, Pennsylvania, Virginia, West Virginia)*—The Curtis Center - Ste.740 West, 170 Independence Mall W., Philadelphia, PA 19106- 3309. Phone: (215)861-4900.

REGION IV *(Alabama, Florida, Georgia, Kentucky, Mississippi, North Carolina, South Carolina, Tennessee)*—61 Forsyth St. SW - Rm.6T50, Atlanta, GA 30303. Phone: (404)562-2300.

REGION V *(Illinois, Indiana, Minnesota, Michigan, Ohio, Wisconsin)*—230 S. Dearborn St. - 32nd fl. (Rm.3244), Chicago, IL 60604. Phone: (312)353-2220.

REGION VI *(Arkansas, Louisiana, New Mexico, Oklahoma, Texas)*—525 Griffin Square Bldg. - Rm.602, Dallas, TX 75202. Phone: (214)767-4731.

794 GOVERNMENT ASSISTANCE ALMANAC 2006-07

17.502 thru 17.505 (cont.)

REGION VII *(Iowa, Kansas, Missouri, Nebraska)*—City Center Square - Ste.800, 1100 Main St., Kansas City, MO 64105. Phone: (816)426-5861.

REGION VIII *(Colorado, Montana, North Dakota, South Dakota, Utah, Wyoming)*— 1999 Broadway St. - Rm.1690, Denver, CO 80202-5716. Phone: (720)264-6550.

REGION IX *(American Samoa, Arizona, California, Guam, Hawaii, Nevada, Trust Territory of the Pacific Islands)*—71 Stevenson St. - Rm.420, San Francisco, CA 94105. Phone: (415)975- 4310.

REGION X *(Alaska, Idaho, Oregon, Washington)*—1111 3rd Ave. - Ste.715, Seattle, WA 98101-3212. Phone: (206)553-5930.

AREA OFFICES

Alabama—Todd Mall, 2047 Canyon Rd., Birmingham, AL 35216- 1981. Phone: (205)731-1534, ext.133.
- 3737 Government Blvd. - Ste.100, Mobile, AL 36693-4309. Phone: (251)441-6131.

Alaska—301 W. Northern Lights Blvd. - Rm.407, Anchorage, AK 99503-7571. Phone: (907)271-5152.

Arizona—3221 N. 16th St. - Ste.100, Phoenix, AZ 85016. Phone: (602)640-2007.

Arkansas—TCBY Bldg. - Ste.450., 425 W. Capitol Ave., Little Rock, AR 72201. Phone: (501)324-6291.

California—Resource Center - Ste.105, 101 El Camino Blvd., Sacramento, CA 95815. Phone: (916)566-7470.
- Resource Center, 5675 Ruffin Rd. - Ste.330, San Diego, CA 92123. Phone: (619)557-5904.
- Resource Center, 71 Stevenson St. - Ste.420, San Francisco, CA 94105. Phone: (415)975-4316.

Colorado—1391 Speer Blvd. - Ste.210, Denver, CO 80204-2552. Phone: (303)844-5285.
- 7935 E. Prentice Ave. - Ste.209, Englewood, CO 80111- 2714. Phone: (303)843-4500.

Connecticut—Clark Bldg. - 4th fl., 1057 Broad St., Bridgeport, CT 06604. Phone: (203)579-5581.
- Federal Bldg. - Rm.613, 450 Main St., Hartford, CT 06103. Phone: (860)240-3152.

Delaware—Caleb Boggs Federal Bldg. - Rm.2209, 844 King St., Wilmington, DE 19801. Phone: (302)573-6518.

Florida—Bldg. H100, 8040 Peters Rd., Ft. Lauderdale, FL 33324. Phone: (954)424-0242.
- Ribault Bldg. - Ste.227, 1851 Executive Center Dr., Jacksonville, FL 32207. Phone: (904)232-2895.
- 5807 Breckenridge Pkwy. - Ste.A, Tampa, FL 33610. Phone: (813)626-1177.

Georgia—450 Mall Blvd. - Ste.J, Savannah, GA 31406-1418. Phone: (912)652-4393.
- 2400 Herodian Way - Ste.250, Smyrna, GA 30080-2968. Phone: (770)984-8700.
- La Vista Perimeter Office Park, Bldg. 7 - Ste.110,, 2183 N. Lake Pkwy., Tucker, GA 30084-4154. Phone: (770)493-6644.

Hawaii—Resource Center - Ste.5-146, 300 Ala Moana Blvd., Honolulu, HI 96850. Phone: (808)541-2685.

Idaho—1150 N. Curtis Rd. - Ste.201, Boise, ID 83703. Phone: (208)321-2960.

Illinois—1600 167th St. - Ste.12, Calumet City, IL 60409. Phone: (708)891-3800.
- 701 Lee St. - Ste.950, Des Plaines, IL 60016. Phone: (847)803-4800.
- 11 Executive Dr. - Ste.11, Fairview Heights, IL 62208. Phone: (618)632-8612.
- 365 Smoke Tree Plaza, North Aurora, IL 60542. Phone: (630)896-8700.
- 2918 W. Willow Knolls Rd., Peoria, IL 61614. Phone: (309)671-7033.

FIELD OFFICE CONTACTS 795

Indiana—U.S. Post Office and Courthouse - Rm.423, 46 E. Ohio St., Indianapolis, IN 46204. Phone: (317)226-7290.

Iowa—210 Walnut St. - Rm.815, Des Moines, IA 50309. Phone: (515)284-4794.

Kansas—8600 Farley - Ste.105, Overland Park, KS 66212-4677. Phone: (913)385-7380.

- 271 W. 3rd St. N. - Rm.400, Wichita, KS 67202. Phone: (316)269-6644.

Kentucky—Watts Federal Bldg. - Rm.108, 330 W. Broadway, Frankfort, KY 40601-1922. Phone: (502)227-7024.

Louisiana—9100 Bluebonnet Centre Blvd. - Ste.201, Baton Rouge, LA 70809. Phone: (225)389-0474.

Maine—Muskie Federal Bldg. - Rm.G26, 40 Western Ave., Augusta, ME 04330. Phone: (207)626-9160.

- 202 Harlow St. - Rm.211, Bangor, ME 04401-4906. Phone: (207)941-8177.

Maryland—1099 Winterson Rd. - Ste.140, Linthicum, MD 21090. Phones: (410)865-2055, -2056.

Massachusetts—639 Granite St. - 4th fl., Braintree, MA 02184. Phone: (617)565-6924.

- Valley Office Park - 1st fl., 13 Branch St., Methuen, MA 01844. Phone: (617)565-8110.
- 1441 Main St. - Rm.550, Springfield, MA 01103-1493. Phone: (413)785-0123.

Michigan—801 S. Waverly Rd. - Ste.306, Lansing, MI 48917- 4200. Phone: (517)327-0904.

Minnesota—330 S. 4th St. - Ste.1205, Minneapolis, MN 55415. Phone: (612)664-5460.

Mississippi—3780 I-55N. - Ste.210., Jackson, MS 39211-6323. Phone: (601)965-4606.

Missouri—6200 Connecticut Ave. - Ste.100, Kansas City, MO 64120. Phone: (816)483-9531.

- 911 Washington Ave. - Rm.420, St. Louis, MO 63101. Phone: (314)425-4249.

Montana—2900 4th Ave. N. - Ste.303, Billings, MT 59101. Phone: (406)247-7494.

Nebraska—Overland-Wolf Bldg. - Rm.100, 6910 Pacific St., Omaha, NE 68106. Phone: (402)221-3182.

Nevada—Federal Bldg. - Rm.204, Resource Center, 705 North Plaza, Carson City, NV 89701. Phone: (702)885-6963.

New Hampshire—55 Pleasant St. - Rm.3901, Concord, NH 03301. Phone: (603)225-1629.

New Jersey—Plaza 35 - Ste.205, 1030 St. Georges Ave., Avenel, NJ 07001 Phone: (732)750-3270.

- 500 Rt. 17 S. - 2nd fl., Hasbrouck Heights, NJ 07604. Phone: (201)288-1700.
- Marlton Executive Park, South Bldg. 2 - Ste.120, 701 Rt. 73, Marlton, NJ 08053. Phone: (856)757-5181.
- 299 Cherry Hill Rd.- Ste.304, Parsippany, NJ 07054. Phone: (973)263-1003.

New Mexico—Western Bank Bldg. - Ste.820, 505 Marquette Ave. NW, Albuquerque, NM 87102. Phone: (505)248-5302.

New York—Tomich Federal Bldg. - Ste.300, 401 New Karner Rd., Albany, NY 12205-3809. Phone: (518)464-4338.

- 42-40 Bell Blvd., Bayside, NY 11361. Phone: (718)279- 9060.
- 5360 Genessee St., Bowmansville, NY 14026. Phone: (716)684-3891.
- 201 Varick St. - Rm.905, New York, NY 10014. Phone: (212)620-3200.
- 3300 Vickery Rd., North Syracuse, NY 13212. Phone: (315)451-0808.
- 660 White Plains Rd. - 4th fl., Tarrytown, NY 10591- 5107. Phone: (914)524-7510.
- 1400 Old Country Rd. - Ste.208, Westbury, NY 11590. Phone: (516)334-3344.

**17.502
thru
17.505
(cont.)**

North Carolina—Century Station, Federal Bldg. - Rm.438, 300 Fayetteville Mall, Raleigh, NC 27601-9998. Phone: (919)856-4770.

North Dakota—Federal Office Bldg., 1640 E. Capitol Ave., Bismarck, ND 58501. Phone: (701)250-4521.

Ohio—Federal Bldg. - Rm.4028, 36 Triangle Park Dr., Cincinnati, OH 45246. Phone: (513)841-4132.

- Federal Bldg. - Rm.899, 1240 E. 9th St., Cleveland, OH 44199. Phone: (216)522-3818.
- Federal Office Bldg. - Rm.620, 200 N. High St, Columbus, OH 43215. Phone: (614)469-5582.
- Ohio Bldg. - Ste.600, 420 Madison Ave., Toledo, OH 43604. Phone: (419)259-7542.

Oklahoma—55 N. Robinson - Ste.315, Oklahoma City, OK 73102. Phone: (405)278-9560.

Oregon—1220 SW 3rd St. - Rm.640, Portland, OR 97204. Phone: (503)326-2251.

Pennsylvania—850 N. 5th St., Allentown, PA 18102. Phone: (610)776-0592.

- 3939 W. Ridge Rd. - Ste.B-12, Erie, PA 16506. Phone: (814)833-5758.
- Progress Plaza, 49 N. Progress Ave., Harrisburg, PA 17109. Phone: (717)782-3902.
- U.S. Customs House - Rm.242, 2nd and Chestnut St., Philadelphia, PA 19106. Phone: (215)597-4955.
- Federal Bldg. - Rm.1428, 1000 Liberty Ave., Pittsburgh, PA 15522-4101. Phone: (412)395-4903.
- 7 N. Wilkes-Barre Blvd. - Ste.410, Wilkes-Barre, PA 18702. Phone: (570)826-6538.

Puerto Rico—BBV Plaza Bldg. - Ste.5B, 1510 F.D. Roosevelt Ave., Guaynabo, PR 00968. Phone: (787)277-1560.

Rhode Island—380 Westminster Mall - Rm.243, Providence, RI 02903. Phone: (401)528-4669.

South Carolina—1835 Assembly St. - Rm.1468, Columbia, SC 29201. Phone: (803)765-5904.

Tennessee—2002 Richard Jones Rd. - Ste.C-205, Nashville, TN 37215-2809. Phone: (615)781-5423.

Texas—903 San Jacinto Blvd. - Ste.319, Austin, TX 78701. Phone: (512)916-5783.

- Wilson Plaza West - Ste.700, 606 N. Carancahua, Corpus Christi, TX 78476. Phone: (361)888-3420.
- 8344 East R.L. Thornton Fwy. - Ste.420, Dallas, TX 75228. Phone: (214)320-2400.
- 700 E. San Antonio - Rm.C-408, El Paso, TX 79901. Phone: (915)534-6251.
- North Star II - Ste.302, 8713 Airport Fwy., Ft. Worth, TX 76180-7610. Phone: (817)428-2470.
- 17625 El Camino Real - Ste.400, Houston, TX 77058. Phone: (281)286-0583.
- 507 N. Sam Houston Pkwy. E. - Ste.400, Houston, TX 77060. Phone: (281)591-2438.
- Federal Bldg. - Rm.806, 1205 Texas Ave., Lubbock, TX 79401. Phone: (806)472-7681.

Utah—1781 South 300 W., P.O. Box 65200, Salt Lake City, UT 84165-0200. Phone: (801)487-0521.

Virginia—200 Granby Mall - Rm.614, Norfolk, VA 23510. Phone: (757)441-3820.

Washington—505 106th Ave. NE - Ste.302, Bellevue, WA 98004. Phone: (206)553-7520.

West Virginia—405 Capitol St. - Ste.407, Charleston, WV 25301. Phone: (304)347-5937.

Wisconsin—1648 Tri Park Way, Appleton, WI 54914. Phone: (920)734-4521.

- 1310 W. Clairmont Ave., Eau Claire, WI 54701. Phone: (715)832-9019.
- 4802 E. Broadway, Madison, WI 53716. Phone: (608)441-5388.

- Reuss Bldg. - Ste.1180, 310 Wisconsin Ave., Milwaukee, WI 53203. Phone: (414) 297-3315.

MINE SAFETY AND HEALTH ADMINISTRATION

17.601 and 17.602

Coal Mine Safety and Health

DISTRICT OFFICES

DISTRICT NO. 1 *(Connecticut, Delaware, Maine, Massachusetts, New Hampshire, New Jersey, New York, Pennsylvania (counties east of and including Susquehanna, Sullivan, Columbia, Montour, Northumberland, Dauphin, York), Rhode Island, Vermont)*—Stegmaier Bldg. - Ste.034, 7 N. Wilkes-Barre Blvd., Wilkes-Barre, PA 18702. Phone: (570)826-6321.

DISTRICT NO. 2 *(Pennsylvania counties west of and including Bradford, Lycoming, Union, Snyder, Juniata, Perry, Cumberland, Adams)*—Rural Rt.1 - Box 736, Hunter, PA 15639. Phone: (412)925-5150, ext.111.

DISTRICT NO. 3 *(Maryland, Ohio, West Virginia counties north of and including Jackson, Roane, Calhoun, Braxton, Randolph, Pendleton)*—5012 Mountaineer Mall, Morgantown, WV 26505. Phone: (304)291-4277.

DISTRICT NO. 4 *(West Virginia counties south of and including Mason, Putnam, Kanawha, Clay, Nicholas, Webster, Greenbrier, Pocahontas)*—100 Bluestone Rd., Mt. Hope, WV 25880. Phone: (304)877-3900, ext.125.

DISTRICT NO. 5 *(Virginia)*—P.O. Box 560, Norton, VA 24273. Phone: (540)679-0230.

DISTRICT NO. 6 *(Kentucky counties east of and including Mason, Robertson, Fleming, Rowan, Menifee, Morgan, Magoffin, Floyd, Pike, Letcher)*—159 N. Mayo Trail, Pikeville, KY 41501-3249. Phone: (606)432-0943, ext.116.

DISTRICT NO. 7 *(Alabama (counties north and east of, and including, Jackson, Marshall, Etowah, Cherokee), Georgia (counties north of, and including, Polk, Bartow, Cherokee, Forsyth, Hall, Jackson, Madison, Elbert), Kentucky (counties east of and including Boone, Grant, Scott, Woodford, Jessamine, Garrard, Lincoln, Pulaski, Clinton up to District 6 boundary), North Carolina, South Carolina, Tennessee)*—HC 66-Box 1699, Barbourville, KY 40906. Phone: (606)546-5123.

DISTRICT NO. 8 *(Illinois, Indiana, Iowa, Michigan, Minnesota, Missouri counties north of the Missouri River, Wisconsin)*—2300 Old Decker Rd. - Ste.200, Vincennes, IN 47591. Phone: (812)882-7617.

DISTRICT NO. 9 *(All states west of the Mississippi River including Alaska and Hawaii, except Minnesota, Iowa and all counties of Missouri south of the Missouri River)*—Denver Federal Center, Denver, CO 80225-0367. Phone: (303)231-5458.

DISTRICT NO. 10 *(Kentucky counties west of and including Gallatin, Owen, Franklin, Anderson, Mercer, Boyle, Casey, Russell, Cumberland)*—100 YMCA Dr., Madisonville, KY 42431- 9019. Phone: (270)821-4180.

DISTRICT NO. 11 *(Alabama and Georgia (counties south and west of the District 7 boundary) Florida, Mississippi, Puerto Rico, Virgin Islands)*—135 Gemini Circle - Ste.213, Birmingham, AL 35209. Phone: (205)290-7300.

Metal and Nonmetal Mine Safety and Health

DISTRICT OFFICES

Alabama *(Southeastern: Alabama, Florida, Georgia, Kentucky, Mississippi, North Carolina, Puerto Rico, South Carolina, Tennessee, Virgin Islands)*—135 Gemini Circle - Ste.212, Birmingham, AL 35209. Phone: (205)290-7294.

California *(Western: Alaska, California, Hawaii, Idaho, Nevada, Oregon, Washing-*

17.601 and 17.602 (cont.)

ton)—2060 Peabody Rd. - Ste.610, Vacaville, CA 95687-6696. Phone: (707)447-9844.

Colorado *(Rocky Mountain: Arizona, Colorado, Kansas, Montana, Nebraska, North Dakota, South Dakota, Utah, Wyoming)*—Denver, CO 80225-0367. Phone: (303)231-5465.

Minnesota *(North Central: Illinois, Indiana, Iowa, Michigan, Minnesota, Ohio, Wisconsin)*—515 W. 1st St. - #333, Duluth, MN 55802-1302. Phone: (218)720-5448.

Pennsylvania *(Northeastern: Connecticut, Delaware, District of Columbia, Maine, Maryland, Massachusetts, New Hampshire, New Jersey, New York, Pennsylvania, Rhode Island, Vermont, Virginia, West Virginia)*—230 Executive Dr. - Ste.2, Cranberry Township, PA 16066-6415. Phone: (724)772-2333.

Texas *(South Central: Arkansas, Louisiana, Missouri, New Mexico, Oklahoma, Texas)*—1100 Commerce St. - Rm.4C50, Dallas, TX 75242-0499. Phone: (214)767-8401.

TECHNICAL SUPPORT FIELD CENTERS

Pennsylvania—Safety and Health Technology Center, Cochrans Mill Rd., P.O. Box 18233, Pittsburgh, PA 15236. Phone: (412)386- 6902.

West Virginia—Approval and Certification Center, Industrial Park Rd., Rural Rt. 1 - Box 251, Triadelphia, WV 26059. Phone: (304)547-2029.

National Mine Health and Safety Academy

1301 Airport Rd., Beaver, WV 25813-9426. Phone: (304)256-3200.

OFFICE OF THE SECRETARY, WOMEN'S BUREAU

17.700 REGIONAL OFFICES

REGION I *(Connecticut, Maine, Massachusetts, New Hampshire, Rhode Island, Vermont)*—JFK Federal Bldg. - Rm.E-270, One Congress St., Boston, MA 02114. Phones: (617)565-1988, 1-800-518- 3585..

REGION II *(New Jersey, New York, Puerto Rico, Virgin Islands)*—201 Varick St. - Rm.601, New York, NY 10014. Phone: (212)337-2389.

REGION III *(Delaware, District of Columbia, Maryland, Pennsylvania, Virginia, West Virginia)*—The Curtis Center - Ste.880 West, 170 S. Independence Mall W., Philadelphia, PA 19104. Phones: (215)861-4860, 1-800-379-9042.

REGION IV *(Alabama, Florida, Georgia, Kentucky, Mississippi, North Carolina, South Carolina, Tennessee)*—61 Forsyth St. SW - Ste.7T95, Atlanta, GA 30367. Phones: (404)562-2336, 1-800- 672-8356.

REGION V *(Illinois, Indiana, Michigan, Minnesota, Ohio, Wisconsin)*—230 S. Dearborn St. - Rm.1022, Chicago, IL 60604. Phones: (312)353-6985, 1-800-648-8183.

REGION VI *(Arkansas, Louisiana, New Mexico, Oklahoma, Texas)*—Federal Bldg. - Ste.735, 525 Griffin St., Dallas, TX 75202. Phones: (214)767-6985, 1-800-887-6794.

REGION VII *(Iowa, Kansas, Missouri, Nebraska)*—City Center City Square - Ste.845, 1100 Main St., Kansas City, MO 64106. Phones: (816)426-6108, 1-800-252-4706.

REGION VIII *(Colorado, Montana, North Dakota, South Dakota, Utah, Wyoming)*—Federal Office Bldg. - Ste.905, 1801 California St., Denver, CO 80202-2614. Phones: (303)844-1286, 1- 800-299-0886.

REGION IX *(Arizona, California, Hawaii, Nevada)*—71 Stevenson St. - Rm.927, San Francisco, CA 94105. Phone: (415)975- 4750.

REGION X *(Alaska, Idaho, Oregon, Washington)*—1111 3rd Ave. - Rm.925, Seattle, WA 98101-3211. Phones: (206)553-1534, 1- 888-296-7011.

OFFICE OF THE ASSISTANT SECRETARY FOR VETERANS' EMPLOYMENT AND TRAINING

17.801 thru 17.806 REGIONAL AND STATE OFFICES

REGION I *(Connecticut, Maine, Massachusetts, New Hampshire, Rhode Island, Vermont, Virgin Islands)*—Connecticut Department of Labor Bldg., 200 Folly Brook Blvd., Wethersfield, CT 06109. Phone: (860)263-6490.

- JFK Federal Bldg. - Government Center (Rm.E-315), Boston, MA 02203. Phone: (617)565-2080.
- Hurley Bldg. - 2nd fl., ES Operations Section, 19 Staniford St., Boston, MA 02114. Phone: (617)626-6699.
- 5 Mollison Way, P.O. Box 3106, Lewiston, ME 04243. Phone: (207)753-9090.
- 143 N. Main St. - Rm.208, Concord, NH 03301. Phone: (603)225-1424.
- 57 Spruce St., Westerly, RI 02891. Phone: (401)528- 5134.
- Post Office Bldg. - Rm.303, 87 State St., P.O. Box 603, Montpelier, VT 05602. Phone: (802)828-4441.

REGION II *(New Jersey, New York, Puerto Rico, Virgin Islands)*—Labor Bldg. - 11th fl. (CN058), Trenton, NJ 08625. Phone: (609)292-2930.

- Harriman State Campus - Bldg. 12 (Rm.518), Albany, NY 12240-0099. Phone: (518)457-7465.
- 201 Varick St. - Rm.766, New York, NY 10014. Phone: (212)337-2211.
- 198 Calle Guayama - 20th fl., Hato Rey, PR 00917. Phone: (787)754-5391.

REGION III *(Delaware, District of Columbia, Maryland, Pennsylvania, Virginia, West Virginia)*—500 C St. NW - Rm.108, Washington, DC 20001. Phone: (202)724-7005.

- 4425 N. Market St. - Rm.420, Wilmington, DE 19809-0828. Phone: (302)761-8138.
- 1100 N. Eutaw St. - Rm.210, Baltimore, MD 21201. Phone: (410)767-2110.
- Labor and Industry Bldg. - Rm.1108,, 7th and Forster St., Harrisburg, PA 17121. Phone: (717)787-5834.
- The Curtis Center - Ste.770W, 170 S. Independence Mall West, Philadelphia, PA 19106. Phone: (215)861-5390.
- 703 E. Main St. - Rm.118, Richmond, VA 23219. Phone: (804)786-7269.
- Capitol Complex - Rm.204, 112 California Ave., Charleston, WV 25305-0112. Phone: (304)558-4001.

REGION IV *(Alabama, Florida, Georgia, Kentucky, Mississippi, North Carolina, South Carolina, Tennessee)*—649 Monroe St. - Rm.543, Montgomery, AL 36131-6300. Phone: (334)223-7677.

- Tallahassee, FL 32302-1527. Phone: (850)942-8800.
- Nunn Atlanta Federal Center - Rm.6-T85, 61 Forsyth St. SW, Atlanta, GA 30303. Phone: (404)562-2305.
- Sussex Place - Ste.504, 148 International Blvd. NE, Atlanta, GA 30303-1751. Phone: (404)656-3127.
- c/o Department for Employment Services, 275 E. Main St., Frankfort, KY 40621-2339. Phone: (502)564-7062.
- 1520 W. Capitol St., Jackson, MS 39215-1699. Phone: (601)965-4204.
- P.O. Box 27625, Raleigh, NC 27611-7625. Phones: (919)733-7402, -7407.
- Columbia, SC 29202-1755. Phone: (803)765-5195.

17.801 thru 17.806 (cont.)

- 915 8th Ave. N., Nashville, TN 37219-3795. Phone (615)736-7680.

REGION V *(Illinois, Indiana, Michigan, Minnesota, Ohio, Wisconsin)*—230 S. Dearborn - Rm.1064, Chicago, IL 60604. Phone: (312)353-0970.

- 401 S. State St. - 744 North, Chicago, IL 60605. Phone: (312)793-3433.
- 10 N. Senate Ave. - Rm.SE-103, Indianapolis, IN 46204. Phone: (317)232-6804.
- 7310 Woodward Ave. - Ste.407, Detroit, MI 48202. Phone: (313)876-5613.
- 390 Robert St. N. - 1st fl., St. Paul, MN 55101. Phone: (651)296-3665.
- P.O. Box 1618, Columbus, OH 43216. Phone: (614)644- 3688.
- Madison, WI 53708-8310. Phone: (608)266-3110.

REGION VI *(Arkansas, Louisiana, New Mexico, Oklahoma, Texas)*—P.O. Box 128, Little Rock, AR 72203. Phone: (501)682-3786.

- P.O. Box 94094, Rm.184, Baton Rouge, LA 70804-9094. Phone: (225)389-0339.
- P.O. Box 25085, Albuquerque, NM 87125-5085. Phone: (505)346-7502.
- 201 N. Lincoln Blvd., P.O. Box 52003, Oklahoma City, OK 73152-2003. Phone: (405)231-5088.
- P.O. Box 1468, Austin, TX 78767. Phone: (512)463-2814.
- 525 Griffin St. - Rm.858, Dallas, TX 75202. Phone: (214)767-4987.

REGION VII *(Iowa, Kansas, Missouri, Nebraska)*—150 Des Moines St., Des Moines, IA 50309-5563. Phone: (515)281-9061.

- 401 Topeka Blvd., Topeka, KS 66603-3182. Phone: (913)296-5032.
- 421 E. Dunklin St., Jefferson City, MO 65102-1087. Phone: (573)751-3921.
- City Center Square - Ste.850, 1100 Main St., Kansas City, MO 64105-2112. Phone: (816)426-7151.
- 550 S. 16th St., P.O. Box 94600, Lincoln, NE 68508. Phone: (402)437-5289.

REGION VIII *(Colorado, Montana, North Dakota, South Dakota, Utah, Wyoming)*— 1999 Broadway - Ste.1730, Denver, CO 80202- 2614. Phone: (303)844-1175.

- 2 Park Central - Ste.400, 1515 Arapahoe St., Denver, CO 80202-2117. Phone: (303)844-2151.
- 1215 8th Ave., Helena, MT 59601-4144. Phone: (406)449- 5431.
- 1000 E. Divide Ave., Bismarck, ND 58502-1632. Phone: (701)328-2865.
- 420 S. Roosevelt St., Aberdeen, SD 57402-4730. Phone: (605)626-2325.
- 140 E. 300 South, Salt Lake City, UT 84111-2333. Phone: (801)524-5703.
- 100 W. Midwest Ave., Casper, WY 82602-2760. Phone: (307)261-5454.

REGION IX *(Arizona, California, Hawaii, Nevada)*—1400 W. Washington St., P.O. Box 6123-SC760E, Phoenix, AZ 85005. Phone: (602)379-4961.

- 800 Capitol Mall - Rm.W-1142, P.O. Box 826880, Sacramento, CA 94280-0001. Phone: (916)654-8178.
- 71 Stevenson St. - Ste.705, San Francisco, CA 94105. Phone: (415)975-4700.
- P.O. Box 3680, Honolulu, HI 96811. Phone: (808)522- 8216.
- 1923 N. Carson St. - Rm.205, Carson City, NV 89702. Phone: (702)687-4632.

REGION X *(Alaska, Idaho, Oregon and Washington)*—1111 W. 8th St., Juneau, AK 99802-5509. Phone: (907)465-2723.

- P.O. Box 2697, Boise, ID 83701. Phone: (208)334-6163.
- 312 Employment Division Bldg. - Rm.108, 875 Union St. NE, Salem, OR 97311-0100. Phone: (503)947-1490.
- Olympia, WA 98507-0165. Phone: (360)438-4600.
- 1111 3rd Ave. - Ste.900, Seattle, WA 98101-3212. Phone: (206)553-4831.

DEPARTMENT OF STATE

BUREAU OF EDUCATIONAL AND CULTURAL AFFAIRS

19.400 *Contact Fulbright program advisor at local college, or contact the Institute of International Education: 809 United Nations Plaza, New York, NY 10017, or via **Internet:** "www.iie.org".*

19.403 American Council of Young Political Leaders, 1612 K St. NW - Ste.300, Washington, DC 20006. Phone: (202)857-0999.

19.410 *Young Professionals Component:*

CDS International, 330 7th Ave., New York, NY 10001. Phone: (212)497-3509.

Vocational Component:

Nacel/Open Door, 3410 Federal Dr. - Ste.101, St. Paul, MN 55122. Phone: (651)686-0080.

19.430 *International Education Training:*

NAFSA, Association of International Educators, 1307 New York Ave. NW - 8th fl., Washington, DC 20005-4701. Phones:(202)737-3699; FAX (202)737-3657.

Research:

Institute of International Education, 809 United Nations Plaza, New York, NY 10017. Phone: (212)984-5331.

19.500 MEPI Regional Offices will open in Tunis, Tunisia and Abu Dhabi, UAE in summer 2004.

19.522 Office Director/MCE: (202)663-1075.

Refugee Children: (202)663-1713.

Refugee Women and GBV/NGO Liaison: (202)663-1481.

Office Director/PRP: (202)663-3954.

Program Officer, Policy Office: (202)663-3881, -3104.

DEPARTMENT OF TRANSPORTATION

FEDERAL AVIATION ADMINISTRATION

20.100 Aviation Information Distribution Program

REGIONAL OFFICES

Aviation Education:

ALASKA—(AHT-200/AAL-17), 222 W. 7th Ave., Box 14, Anchorage, AK 99513-7587. Phones: (202)267-3436, (907)271-5377.

CENTRAL—(ACE-4), 601 E. 12th St., Kansas City, M0 64106-2808. Phone: (816) 329-2420.

EASTERN—(ACH-1), Technical Center, Atlantic City International Airport, Atlantic City, NJ 08405. Phone: (605)485-6515.

- (AEA-60), JFK International Airport, Federal Bldg. - Rm.111, Jamaica, NY 11430. Phone: (718)553-3363.

20.100
(cont.)
GREAT LAKES—(AGL-4), O'Hare Lake Office Center, 2300 E. Devon Ave., Des Plaines, IL 60018. Phone: (847)294-7106.

NEW ENGLAND—(ANE-40), 12 New England Executive Park, Burlington, MA 01803-5299. Phone: (781)238-7378.

NORTHWEST MOUNTAIN—(ANM-4CL), 1601 Lind Ave. SW, Renton, WA 98055-4056. Phone: (425)227-1725.

SOUTHERN—(ASO-1), 1701 Columbia Ave., P.O. Box 20636, Atlanta, GA 30320-0631. Phone: (425)227-1725.

SOUTHWEST—(AMC-3), Aeronautical Center, P.O. Box 25082, Oklahoma City, OK 73135. Phone: (405)954-5332.

▪ (ASW-18B), 2601 Meacham Blvd., Ft. Worth, TX 76137-4298. Phone: (817)222-5833.

WESTERN PACIFIC—(AWP-4), Worldway Postal Center, P.O. Box 92007, Los Angeles, CA 90009-2007. Phone:(310)725-3802.

20.106 **REGIONAL OFFICES**

Same addresses as **20.100**.

ALASKA—Phone: (907)271-5438.

CENTRAL—(ACE-600), Phone: (816)426-4698.

EASTERN—(AEA-600), Phone: (718)553-3331.

GREAT LAKES—(AGL-600), Phone: (847)294-7272.

NEW ENGLAND—(ANE-600), Phone: (617)238-7600.

NORTHWEST MOUNTAIN—(ANM-600), Phone: (206)227-2600.

SOUTHERN—(ASO-600), Phone: (404)305-6700.

SOUTHWEST—(ASW-600), Phone: (817)222-5600.

WESTERN PACIFIC—(AWP), Phone: (310)725-3600.

FEDERAL HIGHWAY ADMINISTRATION

20.205
thru
20.217
DIVISION OFFICES

Alabama—500 Eastern Blvd. - Ste.200, Montgomery, AL 36117-2018. Phone: (334)223-7370.

Alaska—709 W. 9th St. - Rm.851, Juneau, AK 99802-1648. Phone: (907)586-7180.

Arizona—234 N. Central Ave. - Ste.330, Phoenix, AZ 85004-2220. Phone: (602)379-3646.

Arkansas—700 W. Capitol Ave. - Rm.3130, Little Rock, AR 72201-3298. Phone: (501)324-5625.

California—980 9th St. - Ste.400, Sacramento, CA 95814-2724. Phone: (916)498-5001.

Colorado—555 Zang St. - Rm.250, Lakewood, CO 80228-1097. Phone: (303)969-6730, ext.3.

Connecticut—628-2 Hebron Ave. - Ste.303, Glastonbury, CT 06033-5007. Phone: (860)659-6703, ext.3009.

Delaware—300 S. New St. - Rm.2101, Dover, DE 19904-0726. Phone: (302)734-5323.

District of Columbia—Union Center Plaza - Ste.750, 820 1st St. NE, Washington, DC 20002-4205. Phone: (202)523-0163.

Florida—227 N. Bronough St. - Rm.2015, Tallahassee, FL 32301-1330. Phone: (850)942-9650.

FIELD OFFICE CONTACTS 803

Georgia—61 Forsyth St. SW - Ste.17T100, Atlanta, GA 30303-3104. Phone: (404)562-3630.

Hawaii—Kalanianaole Federal Bldg. - Rm.3-306, 300 Ala Moana Blvd., P.O. Box 50206, Honolulu, HI 96850-5000. Phone: (808)541-2700, ext.312.

Idaho—3050 Lakeharbor Lane - Ste.126, Boise, ID 83703-6243. Phone: (208)334-9180.

Illinois—3250 Executive Park Dr., Springfield, IL 62703-4514. Phone: (217)492-4640.

Indiana—575 N. Pennsylvania St. - Rm.254, Indianapolis, IN 46204-1576. Phone: (317)226-7475.

Iowa—105 6th St., Ames, IA 50010-6337. Phone: (515)233-7300.

Kansas—3300 S. Topeka Blvd. - Ste.1, Topeka, KS 66611-2237. Phone: (785)267-7281.

Kentucky—330 W. Broadway, Frankfort, KY 40601-1922. Phone: (502)223-6720.

Louisiana—5304 Flanders Dr. - Ste.A, Baton Rouge, LA 70808-4348. Phone: (225) 757-7600.

Maine—Muskie Federal Bldg. - Rm.614, 40 Western Ave., Augusta, ME 04330-6394. Phone: (207)622-8487, ext.19.

Maryland—711 W. 40th St. - Ste.220, Baltimore, MD 21211-2108. Phone: (410)962-4440.

Massachusetts—55 Broadway - 10th fl., Cambridge, MA 02142-1093. Phone: (617) 494-3657.

Michigan—315 W. Allegan St. - Rm.207, Lansing, MI 48933-1528. Phone: (517)377-1844.

Minnesota—Galtier Plaza - Ste.500 (Box 75), 380 Jackson St., St. Paul, MN 55101-2904. Phone: (651)291-6100.

Mississippi—666 North St. - Ste.105, Jackson, MS 39202-3199. Phone: (601)965-4215.

Missouri—209 Adams St., Jefferson City, MO 65101-3203. Phone: (573)636-7104.

Montana—2880 Skyway Dr., Helena, MT 59602-1230. Phone: (406)449-5303, ext. 235.

Nebraska—Federal Bldg. - Rm.220, 100 Centennial Mall N., Lincoln, NE 68508-3851. Phone: (402)437-5765.

Nevada—705 N. Plaza St. - Ste.220, Carson City, NV 89701-0602. Phone: (775)687-1204.

New Hampshire—279 Pleasant St. Ste.204, Concord, NH 03301-7502. Phone: (603) 228-0417.

New Jersey—840 Bear Tavern Rd. - Ste.310, West Trenton, NJ 08628-1019. Phone: (609)637-4200.

New Mexico—604 W. San Mateo Rd., Santa Fe, NM 87505-3920. Phone: (505)820-2021.

New York—O'Brien Federal Bldg. - Rm.719., Clinton Ave. and N. Pearl St., Albany, NY 12207. Phone: (518)431-4125.

North Carolina—310 New Bern Ave - Ste.410, Raleigh, NC 27601-1441. Phone: (919)856-4346.

North Dakota—1471 Interstate Loop, Bismarck, ND 58501-0567. Phone: (701)250-4204.

Ohio—200 N. High St. - Rm.328, Columbus, OH 43215. Phone: (614)280-6896.

Oklahoma—300 N. Meridan - Ste.105S, Oklahoma City, OK 73107-6560. Phone: (405)605-6011.

Oregon—The Equitable Center - Ste.100, 530 Center St. NE, Salem, OR 97301-3740. Phone: (503)399-5749.

20.205 thru 20.217 (cont.)

Pennsylvania—228 Walnut St. - Rm.558, Harrisburg, PA 17101-1720. Phone: (717) 221-3461.

Puerto Rico—Degetau Federal Bldg. - Rm.210, 330 Carlos Chardon Ave., San Juan, PR 00916. Phone:(787)766-5600, ext.223.

Rhode Island—380 Westminster Mall - 5th fl., Providence, RI 02903-3246. Phone: (401)528-4560.

South Carolina—1835 Assembly St. - Ste.1270, Columbia, SC 29201-2483. Phone: (803)765-5411.

South Dakota—116 E. Dakota Ave., Pierre, SD 57501-3110. Phone: (605)224-8033.

Tennessee—640 Grassmere Park Rd. - Ste.112, Nashville, TN 37211-3658. Phone: (615)781-5770.

Texas—Federal Office Bldg. - Rm.826, 300 E. 8th St., Austin, TX 78701-3233. Phone: (512)536-5900.

Utah—2520 W. 4700 S. - Ste.9A, Salt Lake City, UT 84118-1847. Phone: (801)963-0182.

Vermont—Federal Bldg., 87 State St., Montpelier, VT 05601-0568. Phone: (802)828-4423.

Virginia—400 N. 8th St. - Rm.750, P.O. Box 10249, Richmond, VA 23240-0249. Phone: (804)775-3320.

Washington—Evergreen Plaza, - Ste.501, 711 S. Capitol Way, Olympia, WA 98501-1284. Phone: (360)753-9480.

West Virginia—Geary Plaza - Ste.200, 700 Washington St. E., Charleston, WV 25301-1604. Phone: (304)347-5928.

Wisconsin—Highpoint Office Park, 567 D'Onofrio Dr., Madison, WI 53719-2814. Phone: (608)829-7500.

Wyoming—2617 E. Lincolnway - Ste.D, Cheyenne, WY 82001-5662. Phone: (307) 772-2101, ext.40.

Federal Lands Highway Division Offices

CENTRAL—555 Zang St., Lakewood, CO 80228-1010. Phone: (303)716-2000.

EASTERN—Loudoun Technical Center, 21400 Ridgetop Circle, Sterling, VA 20166-6511. Phone: (703)404-6201.

WESTERN—610 E. 5th St., Vancouver, WA 98661-3801. Phone: (360)619-7700.

FEDERAL MOTOR CARRIER SAFETY ADMINISTRATION

20.218 DIVISION OFFICES

(Other addresses same as **20.205**.)

Alabama—Phone: (334)223-7244.

Alaska—Historic Federal Bldg. - Rm.429, 605 W. 4th Ave., Anchorage, AK 99501. Phone: (907)271-4068.

Arizona—234 N. Central Ave. - Ste.305, Phoenix, AZ 85004-2002. Phone: (602)379-6851.

Arkansas—Phone: (501)324-5050.

California—980 9th St., Sacramento, CA 95814-2724. Phone: (916)498-5050.

Colorado—555 Zang St. - Rm.264, Lakewood, CO 80228-1097. Phone: (303)969-6748.

Connecticut—Phone: (860)659-6700.

Delaware—Phone: (302)734-8173.

District of Columbia—Phone:(202)523-0178.

Florida—227 N. Bronough St. - Rm.2060, Tallahassee, FL 32301-1330. Phone: (850) 942-9338.

Georgia—61 Forsyth St. SW - Ste.17T85, Atlanta, GA 30303-3104. Phone: (404)562-3620.

Hawaii—Kalanianaole Federal Bldg. - Rm.3-243, 300 Ala Moana Blvd., P.O. Box 50206, Honolulu, HI 96850-5000. Phone: (808)541-2700.

Idaho—Phone: (208)334-1842.

Illinois—Phone: (217)492-4608.

Indiana—575 N. Pennsylvania St. - Rm.261, Indianapolis, IN 46204-1570. Phone: (317)226-7474.

Iowa—Phone: (515)233-7400.

Kansas—Phone: (785)267-7288.

Kentucky—Phone: (502)223-6779.

Louisiana—Phone: (225)757-7640.

Maine—Muskie Federal Bldg. - Rm.601, 40 Western Ave., Augusta, ME 04330-6394. Phone: (207)622-8358.

Maryland—711 W. 40th St. - Ste.220, Baltimore, MD 21211-2100. Phone: (410)962-2889.

Massachusetts—55 Broadway - Rm.I-35, Cambridge, MA 02142-1093. Phone: (617) 494-2770.

Michigan—315 W. Allegan St. - Rm.205, Lansing, MI 48933-1528. Phone: (517)377-1866.

Minnesota—Galtier Plaza - Box 75(Ste.500), 175 E. 5th St., St. Paul, MN 55101-2904. Phone: (651)291-6150.

Mississippi—666 North St. - Ste.103, Jackson, MS 39202-3199. Phone: (601)965-4219.

Missouri—Phone: (573)636-3246.

Montana—Phone: (406)449-4304.

Nebraska—Phone: (402)437-5986.

Nevada—Phone: (775)687-5335.

New Hampshire—Federal Bldg. - Rm.202, 279 Pleasant St., Concord NH 03301-7502. Phone: (603)228-3112.

New Jersey—Phone: (609)637-4222.

New Mexico—2400 Louisiana Blvd. NE - Ste.520, AFC-5, Albuquerque, NM 87110. Phone: (505)346-7858.

New York—Phone: (518)431-4145.

North Carolina—310 New Bern Ave. - Ste.468, Raleigh, NC 27601-1441. Phone: (919)856-4378.

North Dakota—Phone: (701)250-4346.

Ohio—Phone: (614)280-5657.

Oklahoma—300 N. Meridian - Ste.106-S, Oklahoma City, OK 73107-6560. Phone: (405)605-6047.

Oregon—Phone: (503)399-5775.

Pennsylvania—228 Walnut St. - Rm.536, Harrisburg, PA 17101-1720. Phone: (717) 221-4443.

Puerto Rico—US Courthouse and Federal Bldg. - Rm.329, Carlos Chardon St., Hato Rey, PR 00918. Phone: (787)766-5985.

Rhode Island—380 Westminster Mall - Rm.547, Providence, RI 02903-3246. Phone: (401)528-4578.

20.218
(cont.)
South Carolina—1835 Assembly St. - Ste.1253, Columbia, SC 29201-2430. Phone: (803)765-5414.

South Dakota—Phone: (605)224-8202.

Tennessee—640 Grassmere Park Rd. - Ste.111, Nashville, TN 37211. Phone: (615)781-5781.

Texas—Phone: (512)536-5980.

Utah—2520 W. 4700 S. - Ste.9B, Salt Lake City, UT 84118-1847. Phone: (801)963-0096.

Vermont—87 State St. - Rm.216, Montpelier, VT 05602-2954. Phone: (802)828-4480.

Virginia—400 N. 8th St. - Rm.750, Richmond, VA 23240. Phone: (804)775-3322.

Washington—Phone: (360)753-9875.

West Virginia—700 Washington St. E. - Ste.205, Charleston, WV 25301-1604. Phone: (304)347-5935.

Wisconsin—567 D'Onofrio Dr. - Ste.101, Madison WI 53719-2814. Phone: (608)829-7534.

Wyoming—1916 Evans Ave., Cheyenne, WY 82001-3764. Phone: (307)772-2305.

20.219 Listed under **20.205**.

20.232 and 20.233 Listed under **20.218**.

FEDERAL RAILROAD ADMINISTRATION

20.303 **REGIONAL OFFICES**

Regional Director/Railroad Safety:

REGION I - Northeastern *(Connecticut, Maine, Massachusetts, New Hampshire, New Jersey, New York, Rhode Island, Vermont)*—55 Broadway - Rm.1077, Cambridge, MA 02142. Phone: (617)494-2302.

REGION II - Eastern *(Delaware, District of Columbia, Pennsylvania, Maryland, Virginia, West Virginia, Ohio)*—2 International Plaza - Ste.550, Philadelphia, PA 19113. Phone: (610)521-8200.

REGION III - Southern *(Alabama, Florida, Georgia, Kentucky, Mississippi, North Carolina, South Carolina, Tennessee)*—Atlanta Federal Center - Ste.16T20, 61 Forsyth St. SW, Atlanta, GA 30303-3104. Phone: (404)562-3800.

REGION IV - Central *(Illinois, Indiana, Michigan, Minnesota, Wisconsin)*—200 W. Adams St. - Ste.310, Chicago, IL 60606. Phone: (312)353-6203.

REGION V - Southwestern *(Arkansas, Louisiana, New Mexico, Oklahoma, Texas)*—4100 International Plaza - Ste.450, Ft. Worth, TX 76109. Phone: (817)862-2200.

REGION VI - Midwestern *(Colorado, Iowa, Kansas, Missouri, Nebraska)*—DOT Bldg. - Ste.464, 901 Locust St., Kansas City, MO 64106-2095. Phone: (816)426-2497.

REGION VII - Western *(Arizona, California, Nevada, Utah)*—801 "I" St. - Ste.466, Sacramento, CA 95814-2559. Phone: (916)498-6540.

REGION VIII - Northwestern *(Alaska, Idaho, Montana, North Dakota, Oregon, South Dakota, Washington, Wyoming)*—Murdock Executive Plaza - Ste.650, 703 Broadway, Vancouver, WA 98660. Phone: (360)696-7536.

FEDERAL TRANSIT ADMINISTRATION

20.500 thru 20.518

REGIONAL OFFICES

REGION I *(Connecticut, Maine, Massachusetts, New Hampshire, Rhode Island, Vermont)*—c/o Volpe National, Transportation Systems Center, Kendall Square - Ste. 920, 55 Broadway, Cambridge, MA 02142-1093. Phone: (617)494-2055.

REGION II *(New Jersey, New York, Virgin Islands)*—Metropolitan Office - Ste.429, One Bowling Green, New York, NY 10004-1415. Phone: (212)668-2170.

REGION III *(Delaware, District of Columbia, Maryland, Pennsylvania, Virginia, West Virginia)*—1760 Market St. - Ste.500, Philadelphia, PA 19103-4124. Phone: (215) 656-7100.

REGION IV *(Alabama, Florida, Georgia, Kentucky, Mississippi, North Carolina, Puerto Rico, South Carolina, Tennessee)*—61 Forsyth St. SW - Ste.17T50, Atlanta, GA 30303-8917. Phone: (404)562-3000.

REGION V *(Illinois, Indiana, Michigan, Minnesota, Ohio, Wisconsin)*—200 W. Adams St. - Ste.2410, Chicago, IL 60606-5232. Phone: (312)353-2789.

REGION VI *(Arkansas, Louisiana, New Mexico, Oklahoma, Texas)*—Lanham Federal Bldg. - Ste.8A36, 819 Taylor St., Ft. Worth, TX 76102. Phone: (817)978-0550.

REGION VII *(Iowa, Kansas, Missouri, Nebraska)*—901 Locust St. - Rm.404, Kansas City, MO 64106. Phone: (816)329-3920.

REGION VIII *(Note: grant making activity for Arizona and Nevada falls under Region VIII) (Colorado, Montana, North Dakota, South Dakota, Utah, Wyoming)*—216 16th St. - Ste.650, Denver, CO 80202-5120. Phone: (303)844-3242.

REGION IX *(American Samoa, Arizona, California, Guam, Hawaii, Nevada)*—201 Mission St. - Ste.2210, San Francisco, CA 94105-1926. Phone: (415)744-3133.

REGION X *(Alaska, Idaho, Oregon, Washington)*—Jackson Federal Bldg. - Ste.3142, 915 2nd Ave., Seattle, WA 98174-1002. Phone: (206)220-7954.

NATIONAL HIGHWAY TRAFFIC SAFETY ADMINISTRATION

20.600 thru 20.608

REGIONAL OFFICES

REGION I *(Connecticut, Maine, Massachusetts, New Hampshire, Rhode Island, Vermont)*—Transportation System Center, Kendall Square (Code 903), Cambridge, MA 02142. Phone: (617)494-3427.

REGION II *(New Jersey, New York, Puerto Rico, Virgin Islands)*—222 Mamaroneck Ave. - Ste.204, White Plains, NY 10605. Phone: (914)682-6162.

REGION III *(Delaware, District of Columbia, Maryland, Pennsylvania, Virginia, West Virginia)*—Crescent Bldg. - Ste.4000, 10 S. Howard St., Baltimore, MD 21201. Phone: (410)962-0077.

REGION IV *(Alabama, Florida, Georgia, Kentucky, Mississippi, North Carolina, South Carolina, Tennessee)*—61 Forsyth St. SW - Ste.17T30, Atlanta, GA 30303-3104. Phone: (404)562-3739.

REGION V *(Illinois, Indiana, Michigan, Minnesota, Ohio, Wisconsin)*—19900 Governors Dr. - Ste.201, Olympia Fields, IL 60461. Phone: (708)503-8822.

REGION VI *(Arkansas, Indian Nations, Louisiana, New Mexico, Oklahoma, Texas)*— 819 Taylor St. - Rm.8A38, Ft. Worth, TX 76102-6177. Phone: (817)978-3653.

| 20.600 thru 20.608 (cont.) | **REGION VII** *(Iowa, Kansas, Missouri, Nebraska)*—P.O. Box 412515, Kansas City, MO 64141. Phone: (816)822-7233.

REGION VIII *(Colorado, Montana, North Dakota, South Dakota, Utah, Wyoming)*—555 Zang St. - Rm.430, Denver, CO 80228. Phone: (303)969-6917.

REGION IX *(American Samoa, Arizona, California, Guam, Hawaii, Mariana Islands, Nevada)*—201 Mission St. - Ste.2230, San Francisco, CA 94105. Phone: (415)744-3089.

REGION X *(Alaska, Idaho, Oregon, Washington)*—3140 Jackson Federal Bldg., 915 2nd Ave., Seattle, WA 98174. Phone: (206)220-7640. |

RESEARCH AND SPECIAL PROGRAMS ADMINISTRATION

| 20.700 | **REGIONAL OFFICES**

CENTRAL *(Illinois, Indiana, Iowa, Kansas, Michigan, Minnesota, Missouri, Nebraska, North Dakota, Ohio, South Dakota, Wisconsin)*—1900 Locust St. - Rm.462, Kansas City, MO 64106. Phones: (816)329-3800; FAX (816)329-3831.

EASTERN *(Connecticut, Delaware, District of Columbia, Maine, Maryland, Massachusetts, New Hampshire, New Jersey, New York, Pennsylvania, Rhode Island, Vermont, Virginia, West Virginia)*—400 7th St. SW - Rm.7130, Washington, DC 20590. Phones: (202)366-4580; FAX (202)366-3274.

SOUTHERN *(Alabama, Arkansas, Florida, Georgia, Kentucky, Mississippi, North Carolina, Puerto Rico, South Carolina, Tennessee)*—61 Forsyth St. - Ste.16T15, Atlanta, GA 30303. Phones: (404)562-3530; FAX (404)562-3569.

SOUTHWEST *(Arizona, Louisiana, New Mexico, Oklahoma, Texas)*—2320 La Branch - Rm.2100, Houston, TX 77004. Phones: (713)718-3746; FAX (713)718-3724.

WESTERN *(Alaska, California, Colorado, Hawaii, Idaho, Montana, Nevada, Oregon, Utah, Washington, Wyoming)*—Golden Hills Centre - Ste.A250, 12600 W. Colfax Ave., Lakewood, CO 80215. Phones: (303)231-5701; FAX (303)231-5711. |

MARITIME ADMINISTRATION

| 20.801 and 20.802 | **REGIONAL OFFICES**

CENTRAL *(Alabama, Arkansas, Colorado, Florida (western half), Louisiana, Mississippi, New Mexico, Oklahoma, Tennessee, Texas)*—501 Magazine St. - Rm.1223, New Orleans, LA 70130-3394. Phone: (504)589-2000.

GREAT LAKES *(Illinois, Indiana, Iowa, Kansas, Kentucky, Michigan, Minnesota, Missouri, Nebraska, New York (lake coastal area), North Dakota, Ohio, Pennsylvania (lake coastal area), South Dakota, West Virginia (western third), Wisconsin)*—2860 South River Road - Ste.185, Des Plaines, IL 60018-2413. Phone: (847)298-4535.

NORTH ATLANTIC *(Connecticut, Delaware, Maine, Maryland, Massachusetts, New Hampshire, New Jersey, New York (except lake coastal area), Pennsylvania (except lake coastal area), Rhode Island, Vermont)*—26 Federal Plaza - Rm.3737, New York, NY 10278. Phone: (212)264-1300.

SOUTH ATLANTIC *(Florida (eastern half), Georgia, North Carolina, Puerto Rico, South Carolina, Virginia, West Virginia (eastern two-thirds)*—Bldg. 4D - Rm.211, 7737 Hampton Blvd., Norfolk, VA 23505. Phone: (757)441-6393.

WESTERN *(Alaska, Arizona, California, Hawaii, Idaho, Montana, Nevada, Oregon, Utah, Washington, Wyoming)*—201 Mission St. - Ste.2200, San Francisco, CA 94105. Phone: (415)744-3125. |

FIELD OFFICE

New York—U.S. Merchant Marine Academy, Kings Point, NY 11024-1699. Phone: (516)773-5000.

20.803 American War Risk Agency, 30 Broad St. - 7th fl., New York, NY 10004. Phone: (212)405-2814.

20.806 No field offices. Direct contact with HQ. See main entry. *Information for prospective students may be obtained from:*
- California Maritime Academy, Vallejo, CA 94591.
- Great Lakes Maritime Academy, Traverse City, MI 49684.
- Maine Maritime Academy, Castine, ME 04421.
- Massachusetts Maritime Academy, Buzzards Bay, MA 02532.
- State University of New York Maritime College, Ft. Schuyler, NY 10465.
- Texas State Maritime Program, Galveston, TX 77550.

20.807 thru 20.812 Listed under **20.801**.

OFFICE OF THE SECRETARY

20.900 Alaska Aviation Statistics Field Office, DOT, 801 B St. - Rm.506, Anchorage, AK 99501-23657. Phone: (907)271-5147.

DEPARTMENT OF THE TREASURY

INTERNAL REVENUE SERVICE

21.003 *Consult local phone directory under "U.S. Government - Internal Revenue Service."* Toll-free phones: Taxpayer Assistance Centers,(800)829-3676; Taxpayer Advocate's Help Line, (877)777-4778; hearing impaired, (800)829-4059.

21.004 *Contact:* District Director, Attn: Disclosure Officer, in local IRS offices or via **Internet:** "www.irs.gov/foia/article/0,,id=120681,00.html". *Consult local phone directory under "U.S. Government - Internal Revenue Service."*

APPALACHIAN REGIONAL COMMISSION

23.001 thru 23.011 **STATE ALTERNATES OFFICES**

Alabama—Director, Department of Economic and Community Affairs, 401 Adams Ave., Montgomery, AL 36104-5690. Phone: (334)242-8672.

Georgia—Director, Intergovernmental Relations, Office of the Governor, State Capital - Rm.131, Atlanta, GA 30334. Phone: (404)463-7775.

Kentucky—Community Holding Company, 220 Main St., P.O. Box 331, Inez, KY 41224. Phone: (606)298-3510.

23.001 **thru** **23.011** *(cont.)*	**Maryland**—Director, Maryland Office of Planning, 301 W. Preston St. - Rm.1101, Baltimore, MD 21201. Phone: (410)767-4510. **Mississippi**—Community Assistance, Mississippi Development Authority, Jackson, MS 39205-0849. Phone: (601)359-6622. **New York**—Secretary of State, 41 State St., Albany, NY 12231. Phone: (518)486-9844. **North Carolina**—Director, North Carolina Washington Office, 441 N. Capitol St. - Ste.332, Washington DC 20001-1512. Phone: (202)624-5833. **Ohio**—Director, Governor's Office of Appalachia, 77 S. High St. - 28th fl., Columbus, OH 43266-1001. Phone: (614)644-9228. **Pennsylvania**—Deputy Secretary/Community Affairs and Development, Department of Community and Economic Development, Commonwealth Keystone Bldg. - 4th fl., 400 North St., Harrisburg, PA 17120. Phone: (717)787-3003. **South Carolina**—Policy Advisor to the Governor, Office of the Governor, P.O. Box 12267, Columbia, SC 29211. Phone: (803)734-5166. **Tennessee**—Commissioner, Department of Economic and Community Development, William R. Snodgrass Tennessee - 11th fl., 312 8th Ave. N., Nashville, TN 37243-0405. Phone: (615)741-1888. **Virginia**—Department of Housing and Community Development, Jackson Center, 501 N. 2nd St., Richmond, VA 23219. Phone: (804)371-7002 **West Virginia**—Director/Community Development Division, West Virginia Development Office, State Capitol Complex - Bldg. 6 (Rm.553), Charleston, WV 25305. Phone: (304)558-4010.

OFFICE OF PERSONNEL MANAGEMENT

27.001 **thru** **27.006**	*Contact should be made directly with personnel offices of federal agencies of interest, or through national job information sources listed under the Headquarters office.*
27.011	**SERVICE CENTERS** **REGION I** *(Connecticut, Delaware, Maine, Maryland, Massachusetts, New Hampshire, New Jersey, New York, Pennsylvania, Rhode Island, Vermont)*—Green Federal Bldg. - Rm.3400, 600 Arch St., Philadelphia, PA 19106-1596. Phone: (215)597-7670. *(Puerto Rico)*—Plaza Laz American Tower - Rm.1100, 525 Roosevelt Ave., Hato Rey, PR 00918. Phone: (809)766-5620. **REGION II** *(Alabama, Arkansas, Mississippi, Tennessee)*—520 Wynn Dr. NW, Huntsville, AL 35816-3426. Phone: (205)837-1271. *(Florida, Georgia)*—Russell Federal Bldg. - Ste.956, 75 Spring St. SW, Atlanta, GA 30303-3109. Phone: (404)331-4588. *(North Carolina, South Carolina)*—Somerset Park - Ste.200, 4407 Bland Rd., Raleigh, NC 27609-6296. Phone: (919)790-2817. *(Virginia)*—Federal Bldg. - Rm.500, 200 Granby St., Norfolk, VA 23510-1886. Phone: (804)441-3373. **REGION III** *(Illinois)*—Kluzynski Federal Bldg. - DPN30-3, 230 S. Dearborn St., Chicago, IL 60604-1687. Phone: (312)353-6234. *(Indiana, Kentucky, Michigan, northern Ohio)*—477 Michigan Ave. - Rm.594, Detroit, MI 48226-2574. Phone: (313)226-2095.

(Iowa, Kansas, Missouri, Nebraska)—Federal Bldg. - Rm.131, 601 E. 12th St., Kansas City, MO 64106-2826. Phone: (816)426-5706.

(Minnesota, North Dakota, South Dakota, Wisconsin)—Whipple Federal Bldg. - Rm. 503, One Federal Dr., Ft. Snelling, MN 55111-4007. Phone: (612)725-3437.

(Ohio, Indiana, Kentucky, West Virginia)—U.S. Courthouse and Federal Bldg. - Rm. 507, 200 W. 2nd St., Dayton, OH 45402-0001. Phone: (513)225-2576.

REGION IV *(Arizona, Colorado, Montana, New Mexico, Utah, Wyoming)*—12345 W. Alameda Pkwy. - Rm.316, P.O. Box 25167, Denver, CO 80225-0001. Phone: (303)969-6931.

(Arkansas, Louisiana, Nevada, Oklahoma, Texas)—8610 N. Broadway - Rm.305, San Antonio, TX 78217-0001. Phone: (210)805-2423.

REGION V*(California, Nevada)*—20 Howard St. - Rm.735, San Francisco, CA 94105-0001. Phone: (415)281-7074.

(Alaska, Hawaii (Honolulu and Island of Oahu), Pacific Overseas)—Federal Bldg., 300 Ala Moana Blvd., P.O. Box 50028, Honolulu, HI 96850-0001. Phone: (808)541-2795.

(Idaho, Oregon, Washington)—700 5th Ave. - Ste.5950, Seattle, WA 98104-5012. Phone: (206)553-0870.

27.013 Students may obtain information from their college career guidance office, or via phone by contacting the Career America Connection at (912)757-3000. **Internet:** "www.opm.gov", under Presidential Management Intern Program.

COMMISSION ON CIVIL RIGHTS

29.001 **REGIONAL OFFICES**

CENTRAL—Gateway Tower II - Ste.908, 400 State Ave., Kansas City, KS 66101. Phones: (913)551-1400, TDD (913)551-1414.

EASTERN—624 9th St. NW - Ste.500, Washington, DC 20425. Phones: (202)376-7533, TDD (202)376-8116.

MIDWESTERN—55 W. Monroe St. - Ste.410, Chicago, IL 60603. Phones: (312)353-8311, TDD (312)353-8362.

ROCKY MOUNTAIN—1700 Broadway - Ste.710, Denver, CO 80290. Phones: (303)866-1040, TDD (303)866-1049.

SOUTHERN—61 Alabama St. SW - Ste.1840T, Atlanta, GA 30303. Phones: (404)562-7000, TDD (404)562-7004.

WESTERN—3660 Wilshire Blvd. - Ste.810, Los Angeles, CA 90010. Phones: (213)894-3437, TDD (213)894-3435.

EQUAL EMPLOYMENT OPPORTUNITY COMMISSION

30.001 thru 30.011 **DISTRICT OFFICES**

Alabama—1130 22nd St. S. - Ste.200, Birmingham, AL 35205-2397. Phone: (205)212-2100.

30.001 thru 30.011 (cont.)

Arizona—Norwest Tower - Ste.690, 3300 N. Central Ave., Phoenix, AZ 85012-2504. Phone: (602)640-5000.

California—255 E. Temple Ave. - 4th fl., Los Angeles, CA 90012. Phone: (213)894-5980.

- 350 Embarcadero - Ste.500, San Francisco, CA 94105-1687. Phone: (415)625-5600.

Colorado—303 E. 17th Ave. - Ste.510, Denver, CO 80203-9634. Phone: (303)866-1300.

District of Columbia—1801 L St. NW - Ste.200, Washington, DC 20507. Phone: (202)275-7377.

Florida—One Biscayne Tower, 2 S. Biscayne Blvd. - Ste.2700, Miami, FL 33131. Phone: (305)536-4491.

Georgia—100 Alabama St. - Ste.4R30., Atlanta, GA 30303. Phone: (404)562-6930.

Illinois—500 W. Madison St. - Ste.2800, Chicago, IL 60661. Phone: (312)353-2713.

Indiana—Federal Bldg. - Ste.1900, 101 W. Ohio St., Indianapolis, IN 46204-4203. Phone: (317)226-7212.

Louisiana—701 Loyola Ave. - Ste.600, New Orleans, LA 70113-9936. Phone: (504)589-2329.

Maryland—City Crescent Bldg. - 3rd fl., 10 S. Howard St., Baltimore, MD 21201. Phone: (410)962-3932.

Michigan—McNamara Federal Bldg. - Ste.865, 477 Michigan Ave., Detroit, MI 48226-9704. Phone: (313)226-4600.

Missouri—1222 Spruce St. - Rm.8100, St. Louis, MO 63103. Phone: (314)539-7800.

New York—33 Whitehall St. - 5th fl., New York, NY 10004-2112. Phone: (212)336-3620.

North Carolina—129 W. Trade St. - Ste.400, Charlotte, NC 28202. Phone: (704)344-6682.

Ohio—Tower City, Skylight Office Tower - Ste.850,, 1660 W. 2nd St., Cleveland, OH 44113-1454. Phone: (216)522-2001.

Pennsylvania—Bourse Bldg. - Ste.400, 21 S. 5th St., Philadelphia, PA 19106-2515. Phone: (215)440-2623.

Tennessee—1407 Union Ave. - Ste.621, Memphis, TN 38104. Phone: (901)544-0115.

Texas—207 S. Houston St. - 3rd fl., Dallas, TX 75202-4726. Phone: (214)253-2700.

- Leland Bldg. - 7th fl., 1919 Smith St., Houston, TX 77002. Phone: (713)209-3320.

- Mockingbird Plaza II - Ste.200, 5410 Fredericksburg Rd., San Antonio, TX 78229-3555. Phone: (210)281-7600.

Washington—Federal Office Bldg. - Ste.400, 909 1st Ave., Seattle, WA 98104-1061. Phone: (206)220-6883.

Wisconsin—Reuss Federal Plaza - Ste.800, 310 W. Wisconsin Ave., Milwaukee, WI 53203-2292. Phone: (414)297-1111.

AREA OFFICES

Arkansas—820 Louisiana St. - Ste.200, Little Rock, AR 72201. Phone: (501)324-5060.

California—410 B St. - Ste.1550, San Diego, CA 92101. Phone: (619)557-7235.

Florida—501 E. Polk St. - Rm.1000, Tampa, FL 33602. Phone: (813)228-2310.

Kansas—400 State Ave. - Ste.905, Kansas City, KS 66101. Phone: (913)551-5655.

Kentucky—U.S. Post Office and Courthouse - Rm.268, 600 Martin Luther King Jr. Place, Louisville, KY 40202. Phone: (502)582-6082.

Massachusetts—Kennedy Federal Bldg. - Rm.475, One Congress St., Boston, MA 02203-0506. Phone: (617)565-3200.

FIELD OFFICE CONTACTS   813

Minnesota—330 S. 2nd Ave. - Ste.430, Minneapolis, MN 55401-2224. Phone: (612) 335-4040.

Mississippi—100 W. Capitol St. - Ste.207, Jackson, MS 39269. Phone: (601)965-4537.

New Jersey—One Newark Center - 21st fl., Newark, NJ 07102-5233. Phone: (973)645-6383.

New Mexico—505 Marquette Ave. NW - Ste.900, Albuquerque, NM 87102-2189. Phone: (505)248-5201.

North Carolina—1309 Annapolis Dr., Raleigh, NC 27608-2129. Phone: (919)856-4064.

Ohio—Peck Federal Office Bldg. - Ste.10-019, 550 Main St., Cincinnati, OH 45202-3122. Phone: (513)684-2851.

Oklahoma—Oklahoma Tower - Ste.1350, 210 Park Ave., Oklahoma City, OK 73102-2265. Phone: (405)231-4911.

Pennsylvania—Federal Bldg. - Ste.300, 1000 Liberty Ave., Pittsburgh, PA 15222-4187. Phone: (412)644-3444.

Puerto Rico—Plaza Las Americas - Ste.120L, 525 F.D Roosevelt Ave., San Juan PR 00918-8001. Phone: (787)771-1464.

Tennessee—50 Vantage Way - Ste.202, Nashville, TN 37228. Phone: (615)736-5820.

Texas—300 E. Main St. - Ste.500, El Paso, TX 79901. Phone: (915)534-6700.

Virginia—Federal Bldg. - Ste.739, 200 Granby St., Norfolk, VA 23510. Phone: (757) 441-3470.

▪ 830 E. Main St. - Ste.600, Richmond, VA 23219. Phone: (804)771-2200.

LOCAL OFFICES

California—1265 W. Shaw Ave. - Ste.103, Fresno, CA 93711. Phone: (559)487-5793.

▪ 1301 Clay St. - Ste.1170-N, Oakland, CA 94612-5217. Phone: (510)637-3230.

▪ 96 N. 3rd St. - Ste.200, San Jose, CA 95112. Phone: (408)291-7353.

Georgia—410 Mall Blvd. - Ste.G, Savannah, GA 31406-4821. Phone: (912)652-4234.

Hawaii—300 Ala Moana Blvd. - Ste.7-127, P.O. Box 50082, Honolulu, HI 96850-0051. Phone: (808)541-3120.

New York—6 Fountain Plaza - Ste.350, Buffalo, NY 14202. Phone: (716)551-4441.

North Carolina—2303 W. Meadowview Dr. - Ste.201, Greensboro, NC 27407. Phone: (336)547-4188.

South Carolina—301 N. Main St. - Ste.1402, Greenville, SC 29601. Phone: (803)241-4400.

FEDERAL COMMUNICATIONS COMMISSION

32.001 **REGIONAL OFFICES**

Regional Directors:

California—3777 Depot Rd. - Rm.420, Hayward, CA 94545-2756. Phone: (510)732-9046.

Illinois—Park Ridge Office Center - Rm.306, 1550 Northwest Hwy., Park Ridge, IL 60608-1460. Phone: (708)298-5405.

32.001
(cont.)

Missouri—Brywood Office Tower - Rm.320, 8800 E. 63rd St., Kansas City, MO 64133-4895. Phone: (816)353-9035.

DISTRICT OFFICES

Alaska—6721 Raspberry Rd., Anchorage, AK 99502-1896. Phone: (907)243-2153.

California—18000 Studebaker Rd. - Rm.660, Cerritos, CA 90701-3684. Phones: (310) 809-2096, (310)865-0598.

- 3777 Depot Rd. - Rm.420, Hayward, CA 94545-2725. Phone: (510)732-9046.

- Interstate Office Park, 4542 Ruffner St. - Rm.370, San Diego, CA 92111-2216. Phone: (619)467-0549.

Colorado—165 S. Union Blvd. - Ste.860, Lakewood, CO 80228-2213. Phones: (303) 969-6497, 776-8026.

Florida—Rochester Bldg. - Rm.310, 8390 NW 53rd St., Miami, FL 33166-4668. Phone: (305)526-7420.

- 2203 N. Lois Ave. - Rm.1215, Tampa, FL 33607-2356. Phone: (813)348-1502.

Georgia—Koger Center-Gwinnett - Rm.320, 3575 Koger Blvd., Duluth, GA 30136-4958. Phone: (404)279-4621.

- Powder Springs, GA 30073-0085. Phones: (770)943-5420, 242-0165.

Hawaii—Waipahu, HI 96797-1030. Phone: (808)677-3318.

Illinois—Park Ridge Office Center - Rm.306, 1550 Northwest Hwy., Park Ridge, IL 60068-1460. Phones: (708)298-5401, -5402.

Louisiana—800 W. Commerce St. - Rm.505, New Orleans, LA 70123-3333. Phone: (504)589-2095.

Maine—Belfast, ME 04915-0470. Phone: (207)338-4088.

Maryland—P.O. Box 250, Columbia, MD 21045-9998. Phone: (301)725-3474.

Massachusetts—One Batterymarch Park, Quincy, MA 02169-7495. Phone: (617)770-4023.

Michigan—P.O. Box 89, Allegan, MI 49010-9437. Phone: (616)673-2063.

- 24897 Hathaway St., Farmington Hills, MI 48335-1552. Phones: (810)471-5605; *recorded information,* 471-0052.

Minnesota—2025 Sloan Pl. - Ste.31, Maplewood, MN 55117-2058. Phone: (612)774-5175.

Missouri—Brywood Office Tower - Rm.320, 8800 E. 63rd St., Kansas City, MO 64133-4895. Phone: (816)353-3773.

Nebraska—Grand Island, NE 68802-1588. Phone: (308)382-4296 (*recorded information at night*).

New York—1307 Federal Bldg., 111 W. Huron St., Buffalo, NY 14202-2398. Phone: *recorded information,* (716)551-4511.

- 201 Varick St., New York, NY 10014-4870. Phones: (212)620-3437, -3438, 660-3437; *recorded information,* (212)620-3435, 660-3436.

Oregon—1782 Federal Bldg., 1220 SW 3rd Ave., Portland, OR 97204-2898. Phones: (503)326-4114, -4115.

Puerto Rico—San Juan Field Office, Federal Bldg. - Rm.747, Hato Rey, PR 00918-1731. Phone: (809)766-5567.

Texas—Kingsville, TX 78363-0632. Phone: (512)592-2531.

Washington—11410 NE 122nd Way - Ste.312, Kirkland, WA 98034-6927. Phone: (206)821-9037.

Equipment Construction and Installation Branch

3600 Hiram-Lithia Spring Rd. SW, P.O. Box 65, Powder Springs, GA 30073. Phone: (404)943-6425.

FOB Monitoring Assistance

Watch Officer, Signal Analysis Branch, Enforcement Division, 1919 M St. NW - Rm.749, Washington, DC 20554. Phone: (202)418-1180.

Field Operations Bureau

Chief, 1919 M St. NW - Rm.734, Washington, DC 20554-0001. Phone: (202)418-1100.

FEDERAL MARITIME COMMISSION

33.001 DISTRICT OFFICES

Los Angeles—Los Angeles Area Representative, U.S. Customs House Bldg. - Rm.320, 839 S. Beacon St., San Pedro, CA 90733-0230. Phones: (310)514-4905; FAX (310)514-3931.

Miami—South Florida Area Representative, Federal Maritime Commission, Hollywood, FL 33081-3609. Phones: (305)963-5362; FAX (305)963-5630.

New Orleans—New Orleans Area Representative, U.S. Customs House - Rm.309B, 423 Canal St., New Orleans, LA 70130. Phones: (504)589-6662; FAX (504)589-6663.

New York—New York Area Representative, JFK International Airport, Bldg. 75 - Rm.205-B, Jamaica, NY 11430. Phone: (718)553-2228; FAX (718)553-2229.

Seattle—Seattle Area Representative, c/o U.S. Customs, 7 S. Nevada St. - Ste.100, Seattle, WA 98134. Phones: (206)553-0221; FAX (206)553-0222.

FEDERAL MEDIATION AND CONCILIATION SERVICE

34.001 REGIONAL OFFICES

MIDWESTERN—6161 Oak Tree Blvd. - Ste.100, Independence, OH 44131. Phones: (216)522-4805; FAX (216)522-7541.

NORTHEASTERN—One Newark Center - 16th fl., Newark, NJ 17102. Phones: (973)645-2200; FAX (973)297-4860.

SOUTHERN—401 W. Peachtree St. NW - Ste.472, Atlanta, GA 30308. Phones: (404)331-3995; FAX (404)331-4017.

UPPER MIDWESTERN—Broadway Place West - Ste.3950, 1300 Godward St., Minneapolis, MN 55413. Phones: (612)370-3300; FAX (612)370-3104.

WESTERN—Westin Bldg. - Ste.11000, 2001 6th Ave., Seattle, WA 98121. Phones: (206)553-5800: FAX (206)553-6653.

FEDERAL TRADE COMMISSION

36.001 REGIONAL OFFICES

California—10877 Wilshire Blvd. - Ste.700, Los Angeles, CA 90024. Phone: (310)824-4343.

• 901 Market St. - Ste.570, San Francisco, CA 94103. Phone: (415)848-5100.

Georgia—225 Peachtree St. NE - Ste.1500, Atlanta, GA 30303. Phone: (404)656-1390.

Illinois—55 E. Monroe St. - Ste.1860, Chicago, IL 60603-5713. Phone: (312)960-5634.

New York—One Bowling Green - Ste.318, New York, NY 10004. Phone: (212)607-2829.

Ohio—Eaton Center - Ste.200, 1111 Superior Ave., Cleveland, OH 44114-2507. Phone: (216)263-3455.

Texas—1999 Bryan St. - Ste.2150, Dallas, TX 75201-6808. Phone: (214)979-9350.

Washington—915 2nd Ave. - Ste.2896, Seattle, WA 98174. Phone: (206)220-6350.

GENERAL SERVICES ADMINISTRATION

39.002 Offices of Property Sales

NATIONAL CAPITOL REGION *(District of Columbia and the DC, Metropolitan area: In Maryland: Montgomery and Prince Georges counties. In Virginia: Arlington, Fairfax, Loudoun and Prince Williams counties)*—7th and D Sts. SW, Washington, DC 20407. Phone: (202)260-6438.

REGION I *(Connecticut, Illinois, Indiana, Maine, Massachusetts, Michigan, Minnesota, New Hampshire, New Jersey, New York, Ohio, Puerto Rico, Rhode Island, Vermont, Virgin Islands, Wisconsin)*—10 Causeway St., Boston, MA 02222. Phone: (617)565-5700.

REGION IV *(Alabama, Delaware, District of Columbia, Florida, Georgia, Kentucky, Maryland, Mississippi, North Carolina, Pennsylvania, South Carolina, Tennessee, Virginia, West Virginia)*—401 W. Peachtree St., Atlanta, GA 30365-2550. Phone: (404)331-5133.

REGION VII *(Arkansas, Colorado, Iowa, Kansas, Louisiana, Missouri, Montana, Nebraska, New Mexico, North Dakota, Oklahoma, South Dakota, Texas, Utah)*—819 Taylor St., Ft. Worth, TX 76102. Phone: (817)978-2331.

REGION IX *(American Samoa, Alaska, Arizona, California, Guam, Hawaii, Idaho, Oregon, Nevada, Trust Territory of the Pacific Islands, Washington)*—450 Golden Gate Ave. - 4th fl. E., San Francisco, CA 94102-3429. Phone: (415)522-3429.

39.003 Federal Supply Service/Property Management Offices

GREAT LAKES REGION *(Illinois, Indiana, Michigan, Minnesota, Ohio, Wisconsin)*—230 S. Dearborn St. - Rm.3430, (MS 34-6),Chicago, IL 60604-1696. Phone: (312)886-8996.

GREATER SOUTHWEST REGION *(Arkansas, Louisiana, New Mexico, Oklahoma, Texas)*—819 Taylor St. - Rm.3A05, Ft. Worth, TX 76102-6105. Phone: (817)978-3794.

FIELD OFFICE CONTACTS   817

HEARTLAND REGION *(Iowa, Kansas, Missouri, Nebraska)*—1500 E. Bannister Rd. - Rm.1102, Kansas City, MO 64131. Phone: (816)823-3700.

MID-ATLANTIC REGION *(Delaware, Maryland, Virginia, Pennsylvania, West Virginia (except those areas in the National Capital Region))*—Strawbridge's Bldg. - 10th fl., 20 N. 8th St., Philadelphia, PA 19107-3191. Phone: (215)446-5065.

NATIONAL CAPITAL REGION *(District of Columbia, the counties of Montgomery and Prince Georges in Maryland, the cities of Alexandria, Fairfax, and Falls Church and the counties of Arlington, Fairfax, Loudoun, and Prince William in Virginia)*—470 L'Enfant Plaza East SW - Ste.8100, Washington, DC 20407. Phone: (202)619-8975.

- Central Office, GSA-FSS, 1901 S. Bell St. - Rm.804, Arlington, VA 22202. Phone: (703)605-5610.

NEW ENGLAND REGION *(Connecticut, Maine, Massachusetts, New Hampshire, Rhode Island, Vermont)*—O'Neill Jr. Federal Bldg. - Rm.347 (3rd fl.), 10 Causeway St., Boston, MA 02222. Phone: (617)565-7319.

NORTHEAST AND CARIBBEAN REGION *(New Jersey, New York, Puerto Rico, U.S. Virgin Islands)*—26 Federal Plaza - Rm.20-112, New York, NY 10278. Phone: (212)264-3300.

NORTHWEST/ARCTIC REGION *(Alaska, Idaho, Oregon, Washington)*—400 15th St. SW, Auburn, WA 98001-6599. Phone: (253)931-7934.

PACIFIC RIM REGION *(American Samoa, Arizona, California, Guam, Hawaii, Nevada, Northern Mariana Islands)*—450 Golden Gate Ave., San Francisco, CA 94102-3434. Phone: (415)522-3029.

ROCKY MOUNTAIN REGION *(Colorado, Montana, North Dakota, South Dakota, Utah, Wyoming)*—Denver Federal Center - Bldg. 41, P.O. Box 25506, Denver, CO 80225-0506. Phone: (303)236-7700.

SOUTHEAST SUNBELT REGION *(Alabama, Florida, Georgia, Kentucky, Mississippi, North Carolina, South Carolina, Tennessee)*—401 W. Peachtree St. - Rm.2600, Atlanta, GA 30365. Phone: (404)331-0040.

39.007 *Contact offices listed under* **39.003**, *or for DOD surplus property, contact:* Defense Reutilization and Marketing Service, National Sales Office, 74 Washington Ave. N, Battle Creek, MI 49017-3092. Phone: (no number provided). **Internet:** "www.gsa.gov".

GOVERNMENT PRINTING OFFICE

40.001 *No field offices. There are 1,270 depository libraries in the U.S., with GPO publications on file; consult local phone directory or local librarian for the nearest depository library.*

40.002 **GPO Bookstore** - Direct purchases of publications carried in stock may be made from the following GPO bookstores or via **Internet:** *(online bookstore,)* "www.bookstore.gpo.gov".

District of Columbia—Government Printing Office, 710 N. Capitol St. NW, Washington, DC 20401. Phone: (202)512-0132.

Maryland—Retail Sales Branch, 8660 Cherry Lane, Laurel, MD 20707. Phone: (301) 953-7974.

LIBRARY OF CONGRESS

42.001 *There are 57 regional and 77 subregional libraries in the U.S. Each state has an agency that distributes talking book machines. Local public libraries have information available. Consult local phone directories. Otherwise, contact headquarters office.*

NATIONAL AERONAUTICS AND SPACE ADMINISTRATION

43.001 FIELD CENTERS

Education Officer:

Alabama—Marshall Space Flight Center, Huntsville, AL 35812.

California—Ames Research Center, Moffett Field, CA 94035.

• Dryden Flight Research Center, Edwards, CA 93523.

Florida—John F. Kennedy Space Center, Kennedy Space Center, FL 32899.

Maryland—Goddard Space Flight Center, Greenbelt, MD 20771.

Mississippi—Stennis Space Center, Stennis Space Center, MS 39529.

Ohio—Glenn Research Center, 21000 Brookpark Rd., Cleveland, Ohio 44135.

Texas—Johnson Space Center, Houston, TX 77058.

Virginia—Langley Research Center, Langley Station, Hampton, VA 23365.

43.002 TECHNOLOGY UTILIZATION CENTERS

Technology Transfer Officer:

Alabama—Marshall Space Flight Center, (MS CD30), Marshall Space Flight Center, AL 35812. Phone: (205)544-4266.

California—Ames Research Center, (MS 202A-3), Moffett Field, CA 94035-1000. Phone: (650)604-1754.

• Dryden Flight Research Center, (MS 4839), Edwards, CA 93253-0273. Phone: (661)276-3689.

• NASA Management Office-JPL, (MS 301-350), 4800 Oak Grove Dr., Pasadena, CA 91109-8099. Phone: (818)354-3480.

District of Columbia—NASA Headquarters, Office of Exploration Systems, Washington, DC 20546-0001. Phone: (202)358-2320.

Florida—Kennedy Space Center, (MS YA-C1), Kennedy Space Center, FL 32899-0001. Phone: (407)867-6624.

Maryland—Goddard Space Flight Center, (MS 504), Greenbelt, MD 20771-0001. Phone: (301)286-5810.

Mississippi—Stennis Space Center, (MS JAOO), Stennis Space Center, MS 39529-6000. Phone: (601)688-1914.

Ohio—Glenn Research Center, (MS 3-7), 21000 Brookpark Rd., Cleveland, OH 44135. Phone: (216)433-5398.

Texas—Johnson Space Center, (MS HA), 2101 NASA Road 1, Houston, TX 77058-3696. Phone: (281)483-0474.

Virginia—Langley Research Center, (MS 118), 11 Langley Blvd., Hampton, VA 23681-0001. Phone: (757)864-6005.

REGIONAL TECHNOLOGY TRANSFER CENTERS

Persons or organizations desiring comprehensive technical information may contact the Central Network at (800)642-2872) or regional affiliates, following:

FAR WEST—3716 S. Hope St. - Ste.200, Los Angeles, CA 90007-4344. Phone: (213)743-2353.

- Montana State University Techlink Center - Ste.A, 900 Technology Blvd., Bozeman, MT 59718. Phone: (406)994-7700.

MID-ATLANTIC—Technology Commercialization Center, Inc., 12050 Jefferson Ave. - Ste.350, Newport News, VA 23606. Phone: (757)269-0025.

- Research Triangle Institute Center for Technology Applications, P.O. Box 12194, Research Triangle Park, NC 27709. Phone: (919)541-7205.

MID-CONTINENT—Texas Engineering Extension Service, Texas A and M University System, 301 Tarrow, College Station, TX 77843-8000. Phone: (979)845-8762.

MIDWEST—Great Lakes Industrial Technology Center, Battelle Memorial Institute, 25000 Great Northern Corporate Center - Ste.260, Cleveland, OH 44070-5310. Phone: (440)734-0094.

NATIONAL RTTC—Wheeling Jesuit College, 316 Washington Ave., Wheeling, WV 26003. Phone: (800)678-6882.

NORTHEAST—Center for Technology Commercialization, Westborough, MA 01581. Phone: (508)870-0042.

SOUTHEAST—Georgia Tech Research Corp., Georgia Institute of Technology, Office of Sponsored Programs, Atlanta, GA 30332. Phone: (404)894-6786.

NATIONAL CREDIT UNION ADMINISTRATION

44.001 REGIONAL OFFICES

Arizona—1230 W. Washington St. - Ste.301, Tempe, AZ 85281. Phone: (602)302-6000.

Georgia—7000 Central Pkwy. - Ste.1600, Atlanta, GA 30328. Phone: (678)443-3000.

New York—9 Washington Square, Washington Ave. Extension, Albany, NY 12205. Phone: (518)862-7400.

Texas—4807 Spicewood Springs Rd. - Ste.5200, Austin, TX 78759-8490. Phone: (512)342-5600.

Virginia—1775 Duke St. - Ste.4206, Alexandria, VA 22314-3437. Phone: (703)519-6400.

Asset Management Assistance Center

4807 Spicewood Springs Rd. - Ste.5100, Austin, TX 78759-8490. Phone: (512)231-7900.

NATIONAL LABOR RELATIONS BOARD

46.001   REGIONAL, SUBREGIONAL, AND RESIDENT OFFICES

Information Officer:

Alabama—Massey Bldg. - 3rd fl., 1900 3rd Ave., Birmingham, AL 35203-3502. Phone: (205)731-1492.

Alaska—Federal Office Bldg. - Ste.21, 222 W. 7th Ave., Anchorage, AK 99513-3546. Phone: (907)271-5015.

Arizona—234 N. Central Ave. - Ste.440, Phoenix, AZ 85004-2212. Phone: (602)379-3361.

Arkansas—425 W. Capitol St. - Ste.375, Little Rock, AR 72201-3489. Phone: (501) 324-6311.

California—888 Figueroa St. - 9th fl., Los Angeles, CA 90017-5455. Phone: (213)894-5200.

- 11150 W. Olympic Blvd. - Ste.700, Los Angeles, CA 90064-1824. Phone: (310)575-7351.
- 1301 Day St. - Rm.300-N, Oakland, CA 94612-5211. Phone: (510)637-3000.
- 555 W. Beech St. - Ste.418, San Diego, CA 92101-2939. Phone: (619)557-6184.
- 901 Market St. - Ste.400, San Francisco, CA 94103-1735. Phone: (415)356-5130.

Colorado—North Tower - 7th fl., 600 17th St., Denver, CO 80202-5433. Phone: (303)844-3551.

Connecticut—One Commercial Plaza - 21st fl., Hartford, CT 06103-3503. Phone: (203)240-3522.

District of Columbia—1099 14th St. NW - Ste.5530, Washington, DC 20570-0001. Phone: (202)208-3000.

Florida—550 Water St. - Rm.340, Jacksonville, FL 32202-5177. Phone: (904)232-3768.

- Federal Bldg. - Rm.1320, 51 SW 1st Ave., Miami, FL 33130-1608. Phone: (305)536-5391.
- 201 E. Kennedy Blvd. - Ste.530, Tampa, FL 33602-5824. Phone: (813)228-2641.

Georgia—233 Peachtree St. NE - Ste.1000, Atlanta, GA 30303-1504. Phone: (404)331-2896.

Hawaii—300 Ala Moana Blvd. - Rm.7318, Honolulu, HI 96850-4980. Phone: (808)541-2814.

Illinois—200 W. Adams St. - Ste.800, Chicago, IL 60606-5208. Phone: (312)353-7570.

- 300 Hamilton Blvd. - Ste.200, Peoria, IL 61602-1246. Phone: (309)671-7080.

Indiana—575 N. Pennsylvania St. - Rm.238, Indianapolis, IN 46204-1577. Phone: (317)226-7382.

Iowa—210 Walnut St. - Ste.439, Des Moines, IA 50309-2103. Phone: (515)284-4391.

Kansas—8600 Farley St. - Ste.100, Overland Park, KS 66212-4677. Phone: (913)967-3000.

Louisiana—1515 Poydras St. - Rm.610, New Orleans, LA 70112-3723. Phone: (504) 589-6361.

Maryland—103 S. Gay St. - 8th fl., Baltimore, MD 21202-4061. Phone: (410)962-2822.

Massachusetts—10 Causeway, St. - 6th fl., Boston, MA 02222-1072. Phone: (617)565-6700.

FIELD OFFICE CONTACTS   821

Michigan—477 Michigan Ave. - Rm.300, Detroit, MI 48226-2569. Phone: (313)226-3200.
- 82 Ionia NW - Rm.330, Grand Rapids, MI 49503-3022. Phone: (616)456-2679.

Minnesota—330 2nd Ave. S. - Ste.790, Minneapolis, MN 55401-2221. Phone: (612)348-1757.

Missouri—611 N. 10th St. - Ste.400, St. Louis, MO 63101-1214. Phone: (314)425-4167.

Nevada—600 Las Vegas Blvd. S. - Ste.400, Las Vegas, NV 89101-6637. Phone: (702)388-6416.

New Jersey—20 Washington Place - 5th fl., Newark, NJ 07102-3110. Phone: (973)645-2100.

New Mexico—505 Marquette Ave. NW - Rm.1820, Albuquerque, NM 87102-2181. Phone: (505)248-5125.

New York—Clinton Ave. at N. Pearl St. - Rm.342, Albany, NY 12207-2350. Phone: (518)431-4156.
- Jay St. and Myrtle Ave. - 10th fl., Brooklyn, NY 11201-4201. Phone: (718)330-7713.
- 111 W. Huron St. - Rm.901, Buffalo, NY 14202-2387. Phone: (716)551-4931.
- 26 Federal Plaza - Rm.3614, New York, NY 10278-0104. Phone: (212)264-0300.

North Carolina—4035 University Pkwy. - Ste.200, Winston-Salem, NC 27106-3325. Phone: (919)631-5201.

Ohio—550 Main St. - Rm.3003, Cincinnati, OH 45202-3271. Phone: (513)684-3686.
- 1240 E. 9th St. - Rm.1695, Cleveland, OH 44199-2086. Phone: (216)522-3715.

Oklahoma—224 S. Boulder Ave. - Rm.318, Tulsa, OK 74103-4214. Phone: (918)581-7951.

Oregon—601 SW 2nd Ave. - Ste.1910, Portland, OR 97204. Phone: (503)326-3085.

Pennsylvania—615 Chestnut St. - 7th fl., Philadelphia, PA 19016-4404. Phone: (215)597-7601.
- 1000 Liberty Ave. - Rm.1501, Pittsburgh, PA 15222-4173. Phone: (412)395-4400.

Puerto Rico—525 F.D. Roosevelt Ave. - Ste.1002, Hato Rey, PR 00918-1002. Phone: (809)766-5347.

Tennessee—1407 Union Ave. - Ste.800, Memphis, TN 38104-3627. Phone: (901)544-0018.
- 810 Broadway - Ste.320., Nashville, TN 37203-3859. Phone: (615)736-5921.

Texas—700 E. San Antonio Ave. - Ste.C403, El Paso, TX 79901-7020. Phone: (915)534-6434.
- 819 Taylor St. - Rm.8-A-24, Ft. Worth, TX 76102-6178. Phone: (817)978-2921.
- 1919 Smith St. - Ste.1545, Houston, TX 77002-2649. Phone: (713)209-4888.
- Travis Park Plaza Bldg. - Ste.705, 711 Navarro St., San Antonio, TX 78205-1711. Phone: (210)472-6140.

Washington—915 2nd Ave. - Rm.2948, Seattle, WA 98174-1078. Phone: (206)220-6300.

Wisconsin—310 W. Wisconsin Ave. - Ste.700, Milwaukee, WI 53203-2211. Phone: (414)297-3861.

RAILROAD RETIREMENT BOARD

57.001   REGIONAL OFFICES

Colorado—1999 Broadway - Ste.3300 (Box 7), Denver CO 80202-5737. Phone: (303)844-0800.

57.001
(cont.)

Georgia—401 W. Peachtree St. - Ste.1703, Atlanta, GA 30308-3519. Phone: (404)331-2691.

Pennsylvania—NIX Federal Bldg. - Ste.304, 900 Market St., Philadelphia, PA 19107-4228. Phone: (215)597-2647.

SECURITIES AND EXCHANGE COMMISSION

58.001   REGIONAL OFFICES

California—5670 Wilshire Blvd. - 11th fl., Los Angeles, CA 90036-3648. Phone: (213)965-3998.

Colorado—1801 California St. - Ste.4800, Denver, CO 80202-2648. Phone: (303)844-1000.

Florida—801 Brickell Ave. - Ste.1800, Miami, FL 33131. Phone: (305)982-6300.

Illinois—175 W. Jackson Blvd. - Ste.900, Chicago, IL 60604. Phone: (312)353-7390.

New York—The Woolworth Bldg., 233 Broadway, New York, NY 10279. Phone: (646)428-1500.

DISTRICT OFFICES

California—44 Montgomery St. - Ste.2600, San Francisco, CA 94104. Phone: (415)705-2500.

Georgia—3475 Lenox Rd. NE - Ste.1000, Atlanta, GA 30326-1232. Phone: (404)842-7600.

Massachusetts—73 Tremont St., Boston, MA 02108-3912. Phone: (617)573-8900.

Pennsylvania—Mellon Independence Center, 701 Market St., Philadelphia, PA 19106-1532. Phone: (215)597-3100.

Texas—801 Cherry St. - Ste.800, Ft. Worth, TX 76102. Phone: (817)978-6465.

Utah—15 W. South Temple St. - Ste.1800, Salt Lake City, UT. 84101. Phone: (801)524-5796.

SMALL BUSINESS ADMINISTRATION

59.002   DISASTER AREA OFFICES

AREA 1 (Regions I and II)—130 S. Elmwood St., Buffalo, NY 14202-1192. Phone: (716)843-4100.

AREA 2 (Regions III, IV, and V)—One Baltimore Place - Ste.300, Atlanta, GA 30308. Phone: (404)347-3771.

AREA 3 (Regions VI and VII)—14925 Kingsport Rd., Ft. Worth, TX 76155-2243. Phone: (817)868-2300.

AREA 4 (Regions VIII, IX, and X)—6501 Sylvan Rd., Citrus Heights, CA 95610. Phone: (916)735-1500.

59.005 thru 59.007 REGIONAL AND DISTRICT OFFICES

REGION I *(Connecticut, Maine, Massachusetts, New Hampshire, Rhode Island, Vermont)*—10 Causeway St. - Ste.812, Boston, MA 02222. Phone: (617)565-8415.

Connecticut—Federal Bldg., 330 Main St. - 2nd fl., Hartford, CT 06106. Phone: (203)240-4700.

Maine—Federal Bldg. - Rm.512, 68 Sewall St., Augusta, ME 04330. Phone: (207)622-8274, ext.386.

Massachusetts—10 Causeway St. - Rm.265, Boston, MA 02222-1093. Phone: (617) 565-5561.

- One Federal St. - Bldg.101-R, Springfield, MA 01105. Phone: (413)785-0484.

New Hampshire—55 Pleasant St. - Ste.3101, Concord, NH 03301-1257. Phone: (603)225-1400.

Rhode Island—380 Westminster Mall - 5th fl., Providence, RI 02903. Phone: (401)528-4561.

Vermont—Federal Bldg. - Rm.205, 87 State St., Montpelier, VT 05602. Phone: (802)828-4422.

REGION II *(New Jersey, New York, Puerto Rico, Virgin Islands)*—26 Federal Plaza - Ste.3108, New York, NY 10278. Phone: (212)264-1450.

New Jersey—2 Gateway Center - 15th fl., Newark, NJ 07102. Phone: (973)645-3680.

New York—Federal Bldg. - Rm.1311, 111 W. Huron St., Buffalo, NY 14202. Phone: (716)551-4305.

- 333 E. Water St. - 4th fl., Elmira, NY 14901. Phone: (607)734-1571.
- 35 Pinelawn Rd. - Ste.207W, Melville, NY 11747. Phone: (516)454-0750.
- 26 Federal Plaza - Rm.31-00, New York, NY 10278. Phone: (212)264-1318.
- 100 State St. - Ste.410, Rochester, NY 14614. Phone: (716)263-6700.
- 401 S. Salina St. - 5th fl., Syracuse, NY 13202. Phone: (315)471-9393.

Puerto Rico and U.S. Virgin Islands—Degatau Federal Bldg. - Ste.201, 252 Ponce DeLeon Blvd., San Juan, PR 00918. Phone: (787)766-5002.

REGION III *(Delaware, District of Columbia, Maryland, Pennsylvania, Virginia, West Virginia)*—900 Market St. - 5th fl., Philadelphia, PA 19107. Phone: (215)580-2SBA.

Delaware Branch Office—1007 N. Orange St. - Ste.1120, Wilmington, DE 19801. Phone: (302)573-6294.

District of Columbia—740 15th St. - 3rd fl., Washington, DC 20005. Phone: (202)272-0340.

Maryland—10 S. Howard St. - Ste.6220, Baltimore, MD 21201-2565. Phone: (410) 962-6195.

Pennsylvania—100 Chestnut St. - Rm.107, Harrisburg, PA 17101. Phone: (717)782-3840.

- 900 Market St. - 5th fl., Philadelphia, PA 19406. Phone: (215)580-2700.
- 411 7th Ave. - Ste.1450, Pittsburgh, PA 15219. Phone: (412)395-6560.
- 7 N. Wilkes-Barre Blvd., Wilkes-Barre, PA 18702. Phone: (570)826-6497.

Virginia—400 N. 8th St. - Ste.1150, Richmond, VA 23240-0126. Phone: (804)771-2400.

West Virginia—320 W. Pike St., Clarksburg, WV 26301. Phone: (304)623-5631.

REGION IV *(Alabama, Florida, Georgia, Kentucky, Mississippi, North Carolina, South Carolina, Tennessee)*—1720 Peachtree St. NW - Ste.496, Atlanta, GA 30309-2482. Phone: (404)347-4999.

Alabama—801 Tom Martin Dr. - Ste.201, Birmingham, AL 35203-2398. Phone: (205)290-7101.

59.005 thru 59.007 (cont.)

Florida—7825 Baymeadows Way - Ste.100-B, Jacksonville, FL 32256-7504. Phone: (904)443-1900.
- 100 S. Biscayne Blvd. - 7th fl., Miami FL 33131. Phone: (305)536-5521.

Georgia—233 Peachtree St., NE, Atlanta, GA 30303. Phone: (404)331-0100.

Kentucky—Federal Bldg. - Rm.188, 600 Martin Luther King Jr. Pl., Louisville, KY 40202. Phone: (502)582-5971.

Mississippi—2510 14th St. - Ste.101, Gulfport, MS 39501. Phone: (228)863-4449.
- 210 E. Capital St. - 210E, Jackson, MS 39201. Phone: (601)965-4378.

North Carolina—6302 Fairview Rd. - Ste.300, Charlotte, NC 28210-2227. Phone: (704)344-6563.

South Carolina—1835 Assembly St. - Rm.358, Columbia, SC 29201. Phone: (803)765-5377.

Tennessee—50 Vantage Way - Ste.201, Nashville, TN 37228-1500. Phone: (615)736-5850.

REGION V *(Illinois, Indiana, Michigan, Minnesota, Ohio, Wisconsin)*—Federal Bldg. - Ste.1250, 500 W. Madison St., Chicago, IL 60661-2511. Phone: (312)353-4493.

Illinois—500 W. Madison St. - Rm.1250, Chicago, IL 60661-2511. Phone: (312)353-4508.
- 511 W. Capitol Ave. - Ste.302, Springfield, IL 62704. Phone: (217)492-4416.

Indiana—429 N. Pennsylvania St. - Ste.100, Indianapolis, IN 46204-1873. Phone: (317)226-7272.

Minnesota—100 N. 6th St. - Ste.210C, Minneapolis, MN 55403-1563. Phone: (612)370-2306.

Michigan—477 Michigan Ave. - Rm.515, Detroit, MI 48226. Phone: (313)226-7204.
- 501 S. Front St., Marquette, MI 49885. Phone: (906)225-1108.

Ohio—1350 Euclid St. - Ste.211, Cleveland, OH 44115. Phone: (216)522-4180.
- 525 Vine St. - Ste.870, Cincinnati, OH 45202. Phone: (513)684-2814.
- 2 Nationwide Plaza - Ste.1400, Columbus, OH 43215-2592. Phone: (614)469-6860.

Wisconsin—740 Regent St. - Ste.100, Madison, WI 53715. Phone: (608)264-5263.
- 310 W. Wisconsin Ave. - Ste.400, Milwaukee, WI 53202. Phone: (414)297-3941.

REGION VI *(Arkansas, Louisiana, New Mexico, Oklahoma, Texas)*—4300 Amon Carter Blvd. - Ste.108, Ft. Worth, TX 76155. Phone: (817)684-5581.

Arkansas—2120 Riverfront Dr. - Ste.100, Little Rock, AR 72202. Phone: (501)324-5871.

Louisiana—365 Canal St. - Ste.2250, New Orleans, LA 70130. Phone: (504)589-6685.

New Mexico—625 Silver Ave. SW, - Ste.320, Albuquerque, NM 87102. Phone: (505)346-7909.

Oklahoma—301 N. 6th St. - Ste.116, Oklahoma City, OK 73102. Phone: (405)609-8000.

Texas—3649 Leopard St. - Ste.411, Corpus Christi, TX 78408. Phone: (361)879-0017.
- 10737 Gateway West - Ste.320, El Paso, TX 79935. Phone: (915)633-7001.
- 4300 Amon Center Blvd. - Ste.114, Ft. Worth, TX 76155. Phone: (817)885-6500.
- Lower Rio Grande Valley District Office, 222 E. Van Buren St. - Rm.500, Harlingen, TX 78550. Phone: (956)427-8533.
- 8701 S. Gessner Dr. - Ste.1200, Houston, TX 77074. Phone: (713)773-6500.
- 1205 Texas Ave. - Rm.408, Lubbock, TX 79401-2693. Phone: (806)472-7462.
- 7319 San Pedro Bldg.2 - Ste.200, San Antonio, TX 78232. Phone: (210)403-5904.

REGION VII *(Iowa, Kansas, Missouri, Nebraska)*—323 W. 8th St. - Ste.307, Kansas City, MO 64105-1500. Phone: (816)374-6380.

FIELD OFFICE CONTACTS   825

Iowa—215 4th Ave. SE - Ste.200, Cedar Rapids, IA 52401-1806. Phone: (319)362-6405.
- New Federal Bldg. - Rm.749, 210 Walnut St., Des Moines, IA 50309. Phone: (515)284-4026.

Kansas—271 W. 3rd St. N. - Ste.2500, Wichita, KS 67202. Phone: (316)269-6566.

Missouri—323 W. 8th St. - Ste.501, Kansas City, MO 64105. Phone: (816)374-6708.
- 830 E. Primrose - Ste.101, Springfield, MO 65807. Phone: (417)890-8501.
- 200 N. Broadway - Ste.1500, St. Louis, MO 63102. Phone: (314)539-6600.

Nebraska—11145 Mill Valley Rd., Omaha, NE 68154. Phone: (402)221-4691.

REGION VIII *(Colorado, Montana, North Dakota, South Dakota, Utah, Wyoming)*—721 19th St. - Ste.400, Denver, CO 80202-2599. Phone: (303)844-0500.

Colorado—721 19th St. - Rm.426, Denver, CO 80202-2599. Phone: (303)844-2607.

Montana—301 S. Park Ave. - Rm.334, Helena, MT 59626. Phone: (406)441-1081.

North Dakota—Federal Bldg. - Rm.219, 657 2nd Ave. N., Fargo, ND 58108-3086. Phone: (701)239-5131.

South Dakota—110 S. Phillips Ave. - Ste.200, Sioux Falls, SD 57104-6727. Phone: (605)330-4243.

Utah—Federal Bldg. - Rm.2231, 125 S. State St., Salt Lake City, UT 84138-1195. Phone: (801)524-5804.

Wyoming—Federal Bldg. - Rm.4001, 100 E. "B" St., Casper, WY 82602-2839. Phone: (307)261-6500.

REGION IX *(Arizona, California, Hawaii, Nevada, Pacific Islands)*—330 N. Brand Blvd. - Ste.1200, Glendale, CA 91203. Phone: (818)552-3436.

Arizona—2828 N. Central Ave. - Ste.800, Phoenix, AZ 85004-1093. Phone: (602)745-7200.

California—2719 N. Air Fresno Dr. - Ste.200, Fresno, CA 93727-1547. Phone: (559)487-5791.
- 330 N. Brand Blvd. - Ste.1200, Glendale, CA 91203-2304. Phone: (818)552-3210.
- 650 Capital Mall - Ste.7-5000, Sacramento, CA 95814. Phone: (916)930-3700.
- 500 W. C St. - Ste.550, San Diego, CA 92101-3540. Phone: (619)557-7250.
- 455 Market St. - 6th fl., San Francisco, CA 94105. Phone: (415)744-6801.
- 200 W. Santa Ana Blvd. - Ste.700, Santa Ana, CA 92701. Phone: (714)550-7420.

Hawaii—300 Ala Moana Blvd. - Rm.2-235, Honolulu, HI 96850-4981. Phone: (808)541-2990.

Guam—400 Route 8 - Ste.302, Hagatna, GU 96910-2003. Phone: (671)471-7419.

Nevada—400 S. 4th St. - Ste.250, Las Vegas, NV 89101. Phone: (702)388-6611.

REGION X *(Alaska, Idaho, Oregon, Washington)*—1200 6th Ave. - Ste.1805, Seattle, WA 98101-1128. Phone: (206)553-5676.

Alaska—222 W. 8th Ave. - Rm.A36, Anchorage, AK 99513-7559. Phone: (907)271-4022.

Idaho—1020 Main St. - Ste.290, Boise, ID 83702-5745. Phone: (208)334-1696.

Oregon—1515 SW 5th Ave. - Ste.1050, Portland, OR 97201-5494. Phone: (503)326-2682.

Washington—1200 6th Ave. - Ste.1700, Seattle, WA 98101-1128. Phone: (206)553-7310.
- 801 W. Riverside Ave. - Ste.200., Spokane, WA 99201-0901. Phone: (509)353-2809.

59.008   Listed under **59.002**
59.009 thru 59.046   Listed under **59.005**

59.054 U.S Export Assistance Service Centers

California—3300 Irvine Ave. - #307, Newport Beach, CA 92660. Phone: (949)660-1688, ext.307.

Colorado—1625 Broadway Ave. - Ste.680, Denver, CO 80202. Phone: (303)844-6622, ext.18.

Florida—5835 Blue Lagoon Dr. - Ste.203, Miami, FL 33126. Phone: (305)526-7429, ext.21.

Georgia—75 5th St. NW - Ste.1055, Atlanta, GA 30308. Phone: (404)897-6090.

Illinois—55 W. Monroe St. - Ste.2440, Chicago, IL 60603. Phone: (312)353-8065.

Maryland—401 E. Pratt St. - Ste.2432, Baltimore, MD 21202. Phone: (410)962-4539.

Massachusetts—World Trade Center - Ste.307, Boston, MA 02210. Phone: (617)424-5953.

Michigan—211 W. Fort St. - Ste.1104, Detroit, MI 48226. Phone: (313)226-3670.

Minnesota—Plaza VSS Tower - Ste.2240, 45 S. 7th St., Minneapolis, MN 55403. Phone: (612)348-1642.

Missouri—8235 Forsyth Blvd. - Ste.520, St. Louis, MO 63105. Phone: (314)425-3304.

North Carolina—521 E. Morehead St. - Ste.435, Charlotte, NC 28202. Phone: (704)333-2130.

Ohio—600 Superior Ave. - Ste.700, Cleveland, OH 44114. Phone: (216)522-4731.

Oregon—One World Trade Center - Ste.242, 121 SW Salmon St., Portland, OR 97204. Phone: (503)326-5498.

Pennsylvania—The Curtis Center - Ste.580 W., 601 Walnut St., Philadelphia, PA 19106. Phone: (215)597-6101.

Texas—2000 E. Lamar Blvd. - Ste.430, Arlington, TX 76006. Phone: (817)310-3749.

Washington—4th and Vine Blvd., 2601 4th Ave. - Ste.320, Seattle, WA 98121. Phone: (206)553-0051.

DEPARTMENT OF VETERANS AFFAIRS

VETERANS HEALTH ADMINISTRATION

64.007 thru 64.026 VETERANS MEDICAL FACILITIES

Alabama—700 S. 19th St., Birmingham, AL 35233. Phone: (205)933-8101.
- 215 Perry Hill Rd., Montgomery, AL 36109-3798. Phone: (334)272-4670.
- Tuscaloosa, AL 35404. Phone: (205)554-2000.
- Tuskegee, AL 36083. Phone: (304)727-0550.

Alaska—Medical/Regional Office Center, 235 E. 8th Ave., Anchorage, AK 99508-2989. Phone: (907)257-4700.

Arizona—7th St. at Indian School Rd., Phoenix, AZ 85012. Phone: (602)277-5551.
- Prescott, AZ 86313-5000. Phone: (520)445-4860.
- Tucson, AZ 85723-0001. Phone: (520)792-1450.

Arkansas—Fayetteville, AR 72703. Phone: (501)443-4301.
- 300 E. Roosevelt Rd., Little Rock, AR 72205. Phone: (501)660-1202.

California—2615 E. Clinton Ave., Fresno, CA 93703-2223. Phone: (209)225-6100.
- Livermore, CA 94550. Phone: (510)447-2560.

FIELD OFFICE CONTACTS

- 11201 Benton St., Loma Linda, CA 90822-5201. Phone: (909)825-7084.
- 5901 E. 7th St., Long Beach, CA 90822-5201. Phone: (310)494-2611.
- 3801 Miranda Ave., Palo Alto, CA 94304-1207. Phone: (415)493-5000.
- 2800 Contra Costa Blvd., Pleasant Hill, CA 94523-3961. Phone: (510)372-2000.
- 3350 La Jolla Village Dr., San Diego, CA 92161-0001. Phone: (619)552-8585.
- 4150 Clement St., San Francisco, CA 94121-1598. Phone: (415)221-4810.
- Sepulveda, CA 91343-2099. Phone: (818)891-7711.
- 11301 Wilshire Blvd., West Los Angeles, CA 90073-1002. Phone: (310)478-3711.

Colorado—1055 Clermont St., Denver, CO 80220-0166. Phone: (303)399-8020.
- Ft. Lyon, CO 81038-5000. Phone: (719)384-3100.
- Grand Junction, CO 81501-6499. Phone: (303)242-0731.

Connecticut—55 Willard Ave., Newington, CT 06111. Phone: (860)666-6951.
- West Spring St., West Haven, CT 06516. Phone: (203)932-5711.

Delaware—1601 Kirkwood Hwy., Wilmington, DE 19805. Phone: (302)994-2511.

District of Columbia—50 Irving St. NW, Washington, DC 20422. Phone: (202)745-8000.

Florida—Bay Pines, FL 33744. Phone: (813)398-6661.
- Archer Rd., Gainesville, FL 32608-1197. Phone: (325)376-1611.
- Lake City, FL 32055-5898. Phone: (904)755-3016.
- 1201 NW 16th St., Miami, FL 33125. Phone: (305)324-4455.
- Bruce B. Downs Blvd., Tampa, FL 33612. Phone: (813)972-2000.
- West Palm Beach, FL 33420-3207. Phone: (561)882-6700.

Georgia—1670 Clairmont Rd., Atlanta, GA 30033. Phone: (404)321-6111.
- 2460 Wrightsboro Rd., Augusta, GA 30904-6285. Phone: (706)733-0188.
- 2460 Wrightsboro Rd., Dublin, GA 31021. Phone: (912)272-1210.

Idaho—5th and Fort St., Boise, ID 83702-4598. Phone: (208)336-5100.

Illinois—333 E. Huron St., Chicago, IL 60611. Phone: (312)943-6600.
- 820 S. Damen Ave., Chicago, IL 60612. Phone: (312)666-6500.
- Danville, IL 61832-5198. Phone: (217)442-8000.
- Hines, IL 60141-5000. Phone: (708)343-7200.
- 2401 W. Main St., Marion, IL 62959. Phone: (618)997-5311.
- North Chicago, IL 60064. Phone: (847)688-1900.

Indiana—1600 Randallia Dr., Ft. Wayne, IN 46805-5100. Phone: (219)426-5431.
- 1481 W. 10th St., Indianapolis, IN 46202-2884. Phone: (317)635-7401.
- 46952 E. 38th St., Marion, IN 46953-4589. Phone: (317)674-3321.

Iowa—30th and Euclid Ave., Des Moines, IA 50310-5774. Phone: (515)699-5999.
- Highway 6 W., Iowa City, IA 52246-2208. Phone: (319)338-0581.
- 1515 W. Pleasant St., Knoxville, IA 50138-3399. Phone: (515)842-3101.

Kansas—4201 S. 4th St. Traffic Way, Leavenworth, KS 66048. Phone: (913)682-2000.
- 2200 Gage Blvd., Topeka, KS 66622. Phone: (913)272-3111.
- 5500 E. Kellogg, Wichita, KS 67218. Phone: (316)685-2221.

Kentucky—Leestown Rd., Lexington, KY 40511-1093. Phone: (606)233-4511.
- 800 Zorn Ave., Louisville, KY 40206-1499. Phone: (502)895-3401.

Louisiana—Shreveport Hwy., Alexandria, LA 71301. Phone: (318)473-0010.
- 1601 Perdido St., New Orleans, LA 70146. Phone: (504)568-0811.
- 510 E. Stoner Ave., Shreveport, LA 71101-4295. Phone: (318)221-8411.

Maine—Rt. 17 E., Togus, ME 04330. Phone: (207)623-8411.

Maryland—Baltimore, Ft. Howard and Perry Point Divisions, 3900 Lock Raven Blvd., Baltimore, MD 21201. Phone: (410)605-7000.

**64.007
thru
64.026
(cont.)**

Massachusetts—200 Spring Rd., Bedford, MA 01730. Phone: (617)275-7500.
- 150 S. Huntington Ave., Boston, MA 02130. Phone: (617)232-9500.
- 940 Belmont St., Brockton, MA 02401. Phone: (508)583-4500.
- N. Main St., Northampton, MA 01060-1288. Phone: (413)584-4040.
- 1400 Veterans of Foreign Wars Pkwy., West Roxbury, MA 02401. Phone: (508)583-4500.

Michigan—2215 Fuller Rd., Ann Arbor, MI 48105-2300. Phone: (313)769-7100.
- 5500 Armstrong Rd., Battle Creek, MI 49016-0544. Phone: (616)966-5600.
- Detroit, MI 48201-1932. Phone: (313)576-1000.
- Iron Mountain, MI 49801. Phone: (906)779-3150.
- 1500 Weiss St., Saginaw, MI 48602-5298. Phone: (517)793-2340.

Minnesota—54th St. and 48th Ave. S., Minneapolis, MN 55417. Phone: (612)725-2000.
- 8th St., N. 44th Ave., St. Cloud, MN 56303. Phone: (612)252-1670.

Mississippi—Pass Rd., Biloxi, MS 39531. Phone: (601)388-5541.
- 1500 E. Woodrow Wilson Dr., Jackson, MS 39216. Phone: (601)362-4471.

Missouri—800 Stadium Rd., Columbia, MO 65201. Phone: (573)443-2511.
- 4801 Linwood Blvd., Kansas City, MO 64128. Phone: (816)861-4700.
- Hwy. 67 N., Poplar Bluff, MO 63901. Phone: (573)686-4151.
- Jefferson Barracks, St. Louis, MO 63125. Phone: (314)487-0400.
- 915 N. Grand Blvd., St. Louis, MO 63106. Phone: (314)652-4100.

Montana—William St. and Hwy. 12 W., Ft. Harrison, MT 59636-1500. Phone: (406)447-7900
- 210 S. Winchester, Miles City, MT 59301-4798. Phone: (406)232-3060.

Nebraska—2201 N. Broad Well, Grand Island, NE 68803-2153. Phone: (308)382-3660.
- 600 S. 70th St., Lincoln, NE 68510-2493. Phone: (402)489-3802.
- 4101 Woolworth Ave., Omaha, NE 68105-1873. Phone: (402)346-8800.

Nevada—1703 Charleston Blvd., Las Vegas, NV 89102-2395. Phone: (702)385-3700.
- 1000 Locust St., Reno, NV 89520-0111. Phone: (702)786-7200.

New Hampshire—718 Smyth Rd., Manchester, NH 02104. Phone: (603)624-4366.

New Jersey—Tremont Ave. and S. Center, East Orange, NJ 07018. Phone: (201)676-1000.
- Valley and Knollcroft Rd., Lyons, NJ 07939. Phone: (201)647-0180.

New Mexico—2100 Ridgecrest Dr. SE, Albuquerque, NM 87108-5138. Phone: (505)256-2843.

New York—113 Holland Ave., Albany, NY 12208. Phone: (518)462-3311.
- Redfield Pkwy., Batavia, NY 14020. Phone: (716)343-7500.
- Medical Center, Argonne Ave., Bath, NY 14810. Phone: (607)776-2111.
- 130 W. Kingsbridge Rd., Bronx, NY 10468. Phone: (718)584-9000.
- 800 Poly Pl., Brooklyn, NY 11209. Phone: (718)630-3521.
- 3495 Bailey Ave., Buffalo, NY 14215. Phone: (716)834-9200.
- Ft. Hill Ave., Canandaigua, NY 14424. Phone: (716)394-2000.
- Castle Point, NY 12511. Phone: (914)831-2000.
- Old Albany Post Rd., Montrose, NY 10548. Phone: (914)737-1216.
- 1st Ave. at E. 24th St., New York, NY 10010. Phone: (212)951-5959.
- Long Island-Middleville Rd., Northport, NY 11768. Phone: (516)261-4400.
- Irving Ave. at University Place, Syracuse, NY 13210. Phone: (315)477-7461.

North Carolina—Asheville, NC 28805. Phone: (704)299-7431.
- 508 Fulton St., Durham, NC 27705. Phone: (919)286-0411.

FIELD OFFICE CONTACTS 829

- 2300 Ramsey St., Fayetteville, NC 28301. Phone: (910)822-7059.
- 1601 Brenner Ave., Salisbury, NC 28144. Phone: (704)638-9000.

North Dakota—2101 Elm St., Fargo, ND 58102. Phone: (701)232-3241.

Ohio—17273 State Rt. 104, Chillicothe, OH 45601. Phone: (614)773-1141.
- 3200 Vine St., Cincinnati, OH 45220. Phone: (513)475-6300.
- 10701 East Blvd., Cleveland, OH 44106-3800. Phone: (216)791-3800.
- Medical Center Nursing Home and Domiciliary, 4100 W. 3rd St., Dayton, OH 45428. Phone: (513)262-2170.

Oklahoma—125 S. Main St., Muskogee, OK 74401. Phone: (918)683-3261.
- 921 NE 13th St., Oklahoma City, OK 73104. Phone: (405)270-0501.

Oregon—3710 SW U.S. Veterans Hospital Rd., Portland, OR 97207-1034. Phone: (503)220-8262.
- New Garden Valley Blvd., Roseburg, OR 97470-6153. Phone: (541)440-1000.
- Domiciliary, White City, OR 97503-3207. Phone: (541)826-2111.

Pennsylvania—Pleasant Valley Blvd., Altoona, PA 16602-4377. Phone: (814)943-8164.
- New Castle Rd., Butler, PA 16001-2480. Phone: (412)287-4781.
- Coatesville, PA 19320. Phone: (610)384-7711.
- 135 E. 38th St., Erie, PA 16504. Phone: (814)868-8661.
- S. Lincoln Ave., Lebanon, PA 17042. Phone: (717)272-6621.
- University and Woodland Ave., Philadelphia, PA 19104. Phone: (215)823-5800.
- Highland Dr., Pittsburgh, PA 15206. Phone: (412)363-4900.
- University Dr., Pittsburgh, PA 15240. Phone: (412)688-6000.
- 1111 East End Blvd., Wilkes-Barre, PA 18711-0026. Phone: (717)824-3521.

Puerto Rico—Barrio Monacillos, Rio Piedras, PR 00927-5800. Phone: (787)758-7575.

Rhode Island—380 Westminster Mall, Providence, RI 02908-4799. Phone: (401)273-7100.

South Carolina—109 Bee St., Charleston, SC 29401-5799. Phone: (803)577-5011.
- 1801 Assembly St., Columbia, SC 29201-1639. Phone: (803)776-4000.

South Dakota—I-90 and Hwy. 34, Ft. Meade, SD 57741. Phone: (605)745-2000.
- 5th St., Hot Springs, SD 57757. Phone: (605)745-2000.
- 2501 W. 22nd St., Sioux Falls, SD 57117. Phone: (605)336-3230.

Tennessee—1030 Jefferson Ave., Memphis, TN 38104-2193. Phone: (901)523-8990.
- Mountain Home, TN 37684. Phone: (423)926-1171.
- 3400 Lebanon Rd., Murfreesboro, TN 37129-1236. Phone: (615)893-1360.
- 1310 24th Ave. S., Nashville, TN 37212-2637. Phone: (615)327-4751.

Texas—6010 Amarillo Blvd. W., Amarillo, TX 79106. Phone: (806)355-9703.
- 2400 S. Gregg St., Big Spring, TX 79720. Phone: (915)263-7361.
- Sam Rayburn Memorial Veterans Center, Bonham, TX 75418. Phone: (903)583-2111.
- 4500 S. Lancaster Rd., Dallas, TX 75216. Phone: (214)376-5451.
- 5919 Brook Hollow Dr., El Paso, TX 79925. Phone: (915)564-6100.
- 2002 Holcombe Blvd., Houston, TX 77030. Phone: (713)479-1414.
- Memorial Blvd., Kerrville, TX 78028. Phone: (210)896-2020.
- 1016 Ward St., Marlin, TX 76661. Phone: (817)883-3511.
- 7400 Merton Minter Blvd., San Antonio, TX 78284. Phone: (210)617-5300.
- 1901 S. 1st St., Temple, TX 76504. Phone: (817)778-4811.
- 4800 Memorial Dr., Waco, TX 76711. Phone: (817)752-6581.

Utah—500 Foothill Blvd., Salt Lake City, UT 84148-0001. Phone: (801)582-1565.

Vermont—White River Junction, VT 05001-0001. Phone: (802)295-9363.

**64.007
thru
64.019
(cont.)**

Virginia—Emancipation Dr., Hampton, VA 23667. Phone: (804)722-9961.
- 1201 Broad Rock Rd., Richmond, VA 23249. Phone: (804)230-0001.
- 1970 Roanoke Blvd., Salem, VA 24153. Phone: (540)982- 2463.

Washington—American Lake, WA 98493. Phone: (206)762-1010.
- 1660 S. Columbian Way, Seattle, WA 98108. Phone: (206)762-1010.
- North 4816 Assembly St., Spokane, WA 99205-6197. Phone: (509)328-4521.
- 77 Wainwright Dr., Walla Walla, WA 99362-3975. Phone: (509)525-5200.

West Virginia—200 Veterans Ave., Beckley, WV 25801. Phone: (304)255-2121.
- Milford and Chestnut St., Clarksburg, WV 26301. Phone: (304)623-3461.
- 1540 Spring Valley Dr., Huntington, WV 25704. Phone: (304)429-6741.
- Rt. 9, Martinsburg, WV 25401-9809. Phone: (304)263- 0811.

Wisconsin—2500 Overlook Terrace, Madison, WI 53705. Phone: (608)256-1901.
- 5000 W. National Ave., Milwaukee, WI 53295. Phone: (414)384-2000.
- Tomah, WI 54660. Phone: (608)372-3971.

Wyoming—2360 W. Pershing Blvd., Cheyenne, WY 82001-5392. Phone: (307)778-7300.
- Fort Rd., Sheridan, WY 82801-8320. Phone: (307)672- 1675.

VETERANS BENEFITS ADMINISTRATION

**64.100
thru
64.128**

FIELD OFFICES

Note: DVA provides toll-free phone service throughout the 50 states, Washington DC, and Puerto Rico: (800)827-1000.

Alabama—345 Perry Hill Rd., Montgomery, AL 36109-3798.

Alaska—2925 DeBarr Rd., Anchorage, AK 99508-2989.

Arizona—3225 N. Central Ave., Phoenix, AZ 85012-2405.

Arkansas—Ft. Roots - Bldg. 65, North Little Rock, AR 72115- 1280.

California—Federal Bldg., 11000 Wilshire Blvd., Los Angeles, CA 90024-3602.
- Oakland Federal Bldg., 1301 Clay St., Oakland, CA 94612-5209.
- 8810 Rio San Diego Dr., San Diego, CA 92108-1508.

Colorado—155 Van Gordon St., Lakewood, CO 80228-1709.

Connecticut—450 Main St., Hartford, CT 06103-3077.

Delaware—1601 Kirkwood Hwy., Wilmington, DE 19805-4988.

District of Columbia—1120 Vermont Ave. NW, Washington, DC 20421-1111.

Florida—1833 Blvd. - Rm.3109, Jacksonville, FL 32206.
- Federal Bldg. - Rm.120, 51 SW 1st Ave., Miami, FL 33130.
- 5201 Raymond St. - Rm.1704, Orlando, FL 32806.
- 312 Kenmore Rd. - Rm.IG250, Pensacola, FL 32503-7492.
- 9500 Bay Pines Blvd., P.O. Box 1437, St. Petersburg, FL 33708.

Georgia—1700 Clairmont Rd., Decatur, GA 30033-4032.

Hawaii—PJKK Federal Bldg., 300 Ala Moana Blvd., P.O. Box 50188, Honolulu, HI 96850.

Idaho—805 W. Franklin St., Boise, ID 83702-5560.

Illinois—536 S. Clark St., P.O. Box 8136, Chicago, IL 60605- 1523.

Indiana—575 N. Pennsylvania St., Indianapolis, IN 46204-1526.

Iowa—210 Walnut St. - Rm.1063, Des Moines, IA 50309-9825.

Kansas—5500 E. Kellogg, Wichita, KS 67218-1698.

Field Office Contacts

Kentucky—545 S. 3rd St., Louisville, KY 40202-3835.
Louisiana—701 Loyola Ave. - Rm.4210, New Orleans, LA 70113-1912.
Maine—Bldg. 428 - Rm.103, 475 Stevens Ave., Portland, ME 04103.
- 1 VA Center, Togus, ME 04330-6795.

Maryland—Federal Bldg. - Rm.233, 31 Hopkins Plaza, Baltimore, MD 21201-0001.
Massachusetts—JFK Federal Bldg., Government Center - Rm.1265, Boston, MA 02203-0393.
Michigan—McNamara Federal Bldg. - Rm.1400, 477 Michigan Ave., Detroit, MI 48226-2591.
Minnesota—Federal Bldg., Ft. Snelling, St. Paul, MN 55111-4050.
Mississippi—1600 E. Woodrow Wilson Ave., Jackson, MS 39216-5102.
Missouri—601 E. 12th St. - Rm.120, Kansas City, MO 64106-0199.
- 400 S. 18th St., St. Louis, MO 63103-2676.

Montana—Williams St., Ft. Harrison, MT 59636-9999.
Nebraska—5631 S. 48th St., Lincoln, NE 68516-4198.
Nevada—1201 Terminal Way, Reno, NV 89520-0118.
New Hampshire—Cotton Federal Bldg., 275 Chestnut St., Manchester, NH 03101-2489.
New Jersey—20 Washington Pl., Newark, NJ 07102-3174.
New Mexico—Chavez Federal Bldg. and U.S. Courthouse, 500 Gold Ave. SW, Albuquerque, NM 87102-3118.
New York—O'Brien Federal Bldg., Clinton Ave. and N. Pearl St., Albany, NY 12207.
- Federal Bldg., 111 W. Huron St., Buffalo, NY 14202-2368.
- 245 W. Houston St., New York, NY 10014-4805.
- Federal Office Bldg. and Courthouse, 100 State St., Rochester, NY 14614. Phone: (800)827-0619.
- 344 W. Genesee St., Syracuse, NY 13202.

North Carolina—Federal Bldg., 251 N. Main St., Winston-Salem, NC 27155-1000.
North Dakota—2101 Elm St., Fargo, ND 58102-2417.
Ohio—801-B W. 8th St., Cincinnati, OH 45203-2001.
- 1240 E. 9th St., Cleveland, OH 44199-2001.
- Federal Bldg. - Rm.309, 200 N. High St., Columbus, OH 43215.

Oklahoma—Federal Bldg., 125 S. Main St., Muskogee, OK 74401-7025.
- 215 Dean A. McGee Ave. - Rm.276, Oklahoma City, OK 73102.

Oregon—Federal Bldg. - Rm.1217, 1220 SW 3rd Ave., Portland, OR 97204-2825.
Pennsylvania—5000 Wissahickon Ave., Philadelphia, PA 19101-8079.
- 1000 Liberty Ave., Pittsburgh, PA 15222-4004.
- 1111 East End Blvd., Wilkes-Barre, PA 18711.

Philippines—Manila Regional Office and Outpatient Clinic, FPO AP 96515-1100.
Puerto Rico—U.S. Courthouse and Federal Bldg., Carlos E. Chardon St., Hato Rey, San Juan, PR 00936-4867. Phone: (809)766-5510.
Rhode Island—380 Westminster Mall, Providence, RI 02903-3246.
South Carolina—1801 Assembly St., Columbia, SC 29201-2495.
South Dakota—2501 W. 22nd St., Sioux Falls, SD 57117-5046.
Tennessee—U.S. Courthouse Federal Office Bldg., 110 9th Ave. S., Nashville, TN 37203-3817.
Texas—U.S. Courthouse and Federal Office Bldg., 1114 Commerce St., Dallas, TX 75242.

64.100 thru 64.128 (cont.)

- 6900 Almeda Rd., Houston, TX 77030-4200.
- 4902 34th St. - Ste.10 (Rm.134), Lubbock, TX 79410- 0001.
- 3601 Bluemel Rd., San Antonio, TX 78229-2041.
- One Veteran Plaza, 701 Clay Ave., Waco, TX 76799-0001.

Utah—Federal Bldg., 125 S. State St., P.O. Box 11500, Salt Lake City, UT 84147-0500.
Vermont—215 Main St., White River Junction, VT 05009-0001.
Virginia—210 Franklin Rd. SW, Roanoke, VA 24011-2204.
Washington—Federal Bldg., 915 2nd Ave., Seattle, WA 98174- 1060.
West Virginia—640 4th Ave., Huntington, WV 25701-1340.
Wisconsin—Bldg. 6, 5000 W. National Ave., Milwaukee, WI 53295-0006.
Wyoming—2360 E. Pershing Blvd., Cheyenne, WY 82001-5356.

NATIONAL CEMETERY ADMINISTRATION

64.201   AREA OFFICES

California—1301 Clay St. - 1230 North, Oakland, CA 94612- 5209. Phone: (510)637-6270.

Colorado—P.O. Box 25126, Denver, CO 80225. Phone: (303)914- 5700.

Georgia—1700 Clairmont Rd. - 4th fl., Decatur, GA 30333-4032. Phone: (404)929-5899.

Indiana—575 N. Pennsylvania St., Indianapolis, IN 46204. Phone: (317)226-0205.

Pennsylvania—5000 Wissahickon Ave., Philadelphia, PA 19144. Phone: (215)381-3787.

64.202   Memorial Programs Processing Sites

Kansas—Ft. Leavenworth National Cemetery, 395 Biddle Blvd., Ft. Leavenworth, KS 66027-2307. Phones: Toll free, 1-888-460- 9709, (913)758-1805; FAX (913)758-1839.

Pennsylvania—Lebanon VA Medical Center - Bldg.27, 1700 S. Lincoln Ave., Lebanon, PA 17042. Phones: Toll free, 1-888-574- 9107, (717)270-9424; FAX (717)270-9428.

Tennessee—Nashville Processing Site, 220 Athens Way - Ste. 102, Nashville, TN 37228-1346. Phones: Toll free, 1-888-367-1330, (615)736-2841, ext.228; FAX(615) 736-2026.

Virginia—Logistics Management Service, 5105 Russell Rd., Quantico, VA 22134. Phone: (703)441-4014.

- 5109 Russell Road, Quantico, VA 22134. Phones: *Program Support Unit*, (202)501-3028; *Applicant Assistance Unit*, (202)501-3078; *Presidential Certificate Program*, (202)565-4259.

ENVIRONMENTAL PROTECTION AGENCY

66.001   Regional Grants Management Contacts

REGION I *(Connecticut, Maine, Massachusetts, New Hampshire, Rhode Island, Vermont)*—One Congress St. - Ste.1100, (MC MGM), Boston, MA 02114-2023. Phones: (617)918-1972; FAX (617)918- 1929.

FIELD OFFICE CONTACTS   833

REGION II *(New Jersey, New York, Puerto Rico, Virgin Islands)*—Grants Administration Branch, (OPM-GRA), 290 Broadway, New York, NY 10007-1866. Phones: (212)637-3402; FAX (212)637-3518.

REGION III *(Delaware, District of Columbia, Maryland, Pennsylvania, Virginia, West Virginia)*—Grants Management Section, Office of the Comptroller, (3PM70), 1650 Arch St., Philadelphia, PA 19103-2029. Phones: (215)814-5410; FAX (215)814-5271.

REGION IV *(Alabama, Florida, Georgia, Kentucky, Mississippi, North Carolina, South Carolina, Tennessee)*—Grants and Contracts Administration Section, Management Division, 61 Forsyth St. SW, Atlanta, GA 30303-8960. Phones: (404)562-8371; FAX (404)562-8370.

REGION V *(Illinois, Indiana, Michigan, Minnesota, Ohio, Wisconsin)*—Acquisition and Assistance Branch, (MC 10J), 77 W. Jackson Blvd., Chicago, IL 60604-3507. Phones: (312)886-2400; FAX (312)353-9096.

REGION VI *(Arkansas, Louisiana, New Mexico, Oklahoma, Texas)*—Grants Audit Section, (6M-PG), Management Division, First International Bldg., 1445 Ross Ave., Dallas, TX 75202-2733. Phones: (214)665-6510; FAX (214)665-7284.

REGION VII *(Iowa, Kansas, Missouri, Nebraska)*—Grants Administration Branch, 901 N. 5th St., Kansas City, KS 66101. Phones: (913)551-7346; FAX (913)551-7579.

REGION VIII *(Colorado, Montana, North Dakota, South Dakota, Utah, Wyoming)*—Grants Administration Branch, (8PM-GFM), 999 18th St. - Ste.500, Denver, CO 80202-2466. Phones: (303)312-6305; FAX (303)312-6685.

REGION IX *(American Samoa, Arizona, California, Guam, Hawaii, Nevada, Trust Territories of Pacific Islands, Wake Island)*—Grants and Finance Branch, 75 Hawthorne St., San Francisco, CA 94105. Phones: (415)744-1693; FAX (415)744-1678.

REGION X *(Alaska, Idaho, Oregon, Washington)*—Grants Administration Unit, 1200 6th Ave., Seattle, WA 98101. Phones: (206)553-2722; FAX (206)553-4957.

Chemical Emergency Preparedness and Prevention Office (CEPP)
REGIONAL OFFICES

REGION I—One Congress St. - Ste.1100, (MC SEP), Boston, MA 02114-2023. Phone: (617)918-1804.

REGION II—Bldg. 209, 2890 Woodbridge Ave., Edison, NJ 08837-3679. Phone: (732)906-6194.

REGION III—1650 Arch St., (MC 3HS33), Philadelphia, PA 19103. Phone: (215)814-3273.

REGION IV—Air Division - 12th fl., 61 Forsyth St. SW, Atlanta, GA 30303. Phone: (404)562-9085.

REGION V—77 W. Jackson Blvd., (MC SC-6J), Chicago, IL 60604. Phone: (312)353-9045.

REGION VI—1445 Ross Ave., (MC 6SF-RO), Dallas, TX 75202-2733. Phone: (214)665-2270.

REGION VII—901 N. 5th St., (MC ATRDCRIB), Kansas City, KS 66101. Phone: (913)551-7540.

REGION VIII—One Denver Place, (MC EPR-SA), 999 18th St. - Ste.300, Denver, CO 80202-2405. Phone: (303)312-6760.

REGION IX—75 Hawthorne St., (MC SFD 9-3), San Francisco, CA 94105. Phone: (415)972-3039.

REGION X—1200 6th Ave., (MC ECL-116), Seattle, WA 99101. Phone: (206)553-8414.

66.001 Municipal Solid Waste Primary Contacts
(cont.)

REGION I—One Congress St. - Ste.1100, (MC SPP-SPP), Boston, MA 02114-2023. Phones: (617)918-1813; FAX (617)918-1810.

REGION II—290 Broadway, (MC 2DEPP-RPB), New York, NY 10007- 1866. Phones: (212)637-4125; FAX (212)637-4437.

REGION III—1650 Arch St., (MC 3WC21/3HW60), Philadelphia, PA 19103. Phones: (215)814-3298; FAX (215)814-3163.

REGION IV—Atlanta Federal Center, (MC 4WD-RPB/RSS), 61 Forsyth St., Atlanta, GA 30303-3104. Phones: (404)562-8449; FAX (404)562-8439.

REGION V—77 W. Jackson Blvd., (MC DRP-8J), Chicago, IL 60604- 3590. Phones: (312)886-0976; FAX (312)353-4788.

REGION VI—1445 Ross Ave., (MC 6PD-U), Dallas, TX 75202-2733. Phones: (214) 665-6760; FAX (214)665-7263.

REGION VII—901 N. 5th St., (MC ARTD/SWPP), Kansas City, KS 66101. Phones: (913)551-7523; FAX (913)551-7947.

REGION VIII—999 18th St. - Ste.500, (MC 8P-P3T), Denver, CO 80202-2466. Phones: (303)312-6099; FAX (303)312-6044.

REGION IX—75 Hawthorne St., (MC WST-7), San Francisco, CA 94105. Phones: (415)744-1284; FAX (415)744-1044.

REGION X—1200 6th Ave., (MC WCM-128), Seattle, WA 98101. Phones: (206)553-6117; FAX (206)553-8509.

Pollution Prevention Contacts

REGION I—JFK Federal Bldg. - Rm.2203 (SPN), Boston, MA 02203. Phones: (617) 918-1817; FAX (617)918-4939.

REGION II—290 Broadway - 25th fl. (2-OPM-PPI), DEPP, New York, NY 10007-1866. Phones: (212)637-3742; FAX (212)637-3771.

REGION III—1650 Arch St. (3RA20), Philadelphia, PA 19103- 2029. Phones: (215) 814-2761; FAX (215)566-2782.

REGION IV—Air and Pesticide Center, 61 Forsyth St. SW, Atlanta, GA 30303. Phones: (404)562-9430; FAX (404)562-9066.

REGION V—Waste, Pesticide and Toxics Division, 77 W. Jackson Blvd. (DRP-8J), Chicago, IL 60604-3590. Phones: (312)353-4669; FAX (312)353-4788.

REGION VI—Compliance Assurance and Enforcement Division, 1445 Ross Ave. - Ste.1200 (6EN-XP), Dallas, TX 75202. Phones: (214)665-2119; FAX (214)665-7446.

REGION VII—Air, RCRA and Toxics Division, 726 Minnesota Ave., (ARTD/TSPP), Kansas City, KS 66101. Phones: (913)551-7517; FAX (913)551-7065.

REGION VIII—Office of P2, State and Tribal Assistance, 999 18th St.- Ste.500 (8P2-P2), Denver, CO 80202-2466. Phones: (303)312-6385; FAX (303)312-6339.

REGION IX—Waste Division, 75 Hawthorne St. (WST-1-1), San Francisco, CA 94105. Phones: (415)744-2192; FAX (415)744-1796.

REGION X—Office of Innovation, 1200 6th Ave., Seattle, WA 98101. Phones: (206) 553-4072; FAX (206)553-6647.

RCRA and Superfund

REGION I—Office of Ecosystem Protection, (MC HHA) and/or Office of Site Remediation and Restoration, One Congress St., Boston, MA 02114-2023. Phones: (617) 918-1501, -1201.

FIELD OFFICE CONTACTS   835

REGION II—Division of Environmental Planning and Protection, 26 Federal Plaza - Rm.1000 (2AWM-SW), New York, NY 10278. Phone: (212)637-3772.
- Emergency and Remedial Response Division, 290 Broadway, New York, NY 10007. Phones: (212)637-4390.

REGION III—Waste Chemical Management Division, 841 Chestnut Bldg. (3HWOO), Philadelphia, PA 19107. Phones: (215)814-2005.
- Hazardous Site Cleanup Division, 1650 Arch St., Philadelphia, PA 19106. Phone: (215)813-3143.

REGION IV—Waste Management Division, 61 Forsyth St., Atlanta, GA 30303. Phones: (404)562-8651.

REGION V—Waste, Pesticides and Toxics Division, 77 W. Jackson Blvd., Chicago, IL 60604-3507. Phones: (312)353-2024.
- Superfund Division, Metcalfe Federal Bldg., 77 W. Jackson Blvd., Chicago, IL 60604. Phone: (312)353-9773.

REGION VI—Multimedia Planning and Permitting Division and/or Superfund Division, Fountain Place - Ste.1200, 1445 Ross Ave., Dallas, TX 75202-2733. Phones: (214)665-7200, -6701.

REGION VII—Air/RCRA Toxics Division and/or Superfund Division, 901 N. 5th St., Kansas City, KS 66101. Phones: (913)551-7020, -7664.

REGION VIII—Hazardous Waste Program, (MC 8P2-SA), Denver Place - Ste.500, 999 18th St., Denver, CO 80202-2466. Phones: (303)312-7081.
- Office of Ecosystems Protection and Remediation, 999 18th St. - Ste.500, Denver, CO 80202. Phone: (303)312-6598.

REGION IX—Waste Division and/or Hazardous Waste Management Division, 75 Hawthorne St., San Francisco, CA 94105. Phones: (415)744-2138, -1730.

REGION X—Office of Waste and Chemical Management and/or Office of Environmental Cleanup, 1200 6th Ave., Seattle, WA 98101. Phones: (206)553-4198, -7151.

66.032 **Radon Regional Program Office Contacts**

(No phone numbers provided.)

REGION I—JFK Federal Bldg. - Ste.1100, One Congress St., (MC CPT), Boston, MA 02114-2023.

REGION II—290 Broadway - 28th fl., (MC R2DEPDIV), New York, NY 10007-1866.

REGION III—1650 Arch St., (MC 3AP23), Philadelphia, PA 19103- 2029.

REGION IV—61 Forsyth St. SW, Atlanta, GA 30303-3104..

REGION V—77 W. Jackson Blvd., (MC AE-17J), Chicago, IL 60604- 3590.

REGION VI—1445 Ross Ave., Dallas, TX 75202-2733.

REGION VII—901 N. 5th St., (MC ARTD/RALI), Kansas City, KS 66101.

REGION VIII—999 18th St. - Ste.500, (MC 8P-AR), Denver, CO 80202-2466.

REGION IX—75 Hawthorne St., (MC Air-6), San Francisco, CA 94105.

REGION X—1200 6th Ave., (MC OAQ-107), Seattle, WA 98101-9797.

66.033 thru 66.036   Listed under **66.001**.

66.110   One Congress St. - Ste.1100, CPT, Boston, MA 02114. Phone: (617)918-1797.

66.111   EPA Region 7, 901 N 5th St., Kansas City, KS 66101. Phones: (913)551-7782, 7193; FAX (913)551-9782, -9193.

66.306   Listed under **66.001**.

Office of Enforcement and Compliance Assurance

66.310 Contact the EPA Regional Offices listed under **66.001** and the following telephone numbers:

REGION I—Phone: (617)918-1703.
REGION II—Phone: (212)637-3949.
REGION IV—Phone: (404)562-8425.
REGION V—Phone: (312)353-9681.
REGION VI—Phone: (214)665-6431.
REGION VII—Phone: (913)551-7381.
REGION VIII—Phone: (303)312-6974.
REGION IX—Phone: (415)947-4262.
REGION X—Phone: (206)553-8257.

66.418 thru 66.436 Listed under **66.001**.

66.437 USEPA Long Island Sound Office, Government Center - Ste.6-5, 888 Washington Blvd., Stamford, CT 06904. Phones: (203)977-1541; FAX (203)977-1546.

66.439 ### Targeted Watershed Offices

REGION I—Phone: (617)918-1035, -1601.
REGION II—Phone: (212)637-3844.
REGION III—Phone: (215)814-2718.
REGION IV—Phone: (404)562-9351.
REGION V—Phone: (312)886-7742.
REGION VI—Phone: (214)665-6683.
REGION VII—Phone: (417)575-8028.
REGION VIII—Phone: (303)312-6215.
REGION IX—Phone: (415)972-3399.
REGION X—Phone: (206)553-1566.

66.454 Listed under **66.001**.

66.456 ### National Estuary Program Offices

REGION I—Water Quality Policy Division, Boston, MA 02114-2023. Phone: (617) 918-1511.

REGION II—Environmental Planning and Protection Division, 290 Broadway, New York, NY 10007-1866. Phone: (212)637-3724.

REGION III—Environmental Services Division, 1650 Arch St., Philadelphia, PA 19103-2029. Phone: (215)814-2989.

REGION IV—Water Management Division, 61 Forsyth St. SW, Atlanta, GA 30303. Phone: (404)562-9345.

REGION VI—Water Quality Protection Division, 1445 Ross Ave., Dallas, TX 75202-2733. Phone: (214)655-7101.

REGION IX—Water Management Division, 75 Hawthorne St., San Francisco, CA 94105. Phone: (415)744-1860.

REGION X—Office of Ecosystems and Communities, 1200 6th Ave., Seattle, WA 98101. Phone: (206)553-4181.

66.458 and 66.460 Listed under **66.001**.

FIELD OFFICE CONTACTS 837

66.461 **Wetland Program Offices**

REGION I—One Congress St. - Ste.100, (MC CSP), Boston, MA 02114. Phone: (617)918-1669.

REGION II—290 Broadway, New York, NY 10007. Phone: (212)637-3817.

REGION III—1650 Arch St., (MC 3EA30), Philadelphia, PA. 19103. Phone: (215)814-2715.

REGION IV—61 Forsyth St. SW, Atlanta, GA 30303. Phone: (404)562-9269.

REGION V—77 W. Jackson Blvd., (MC WW16J), Chicago, IL 60604. Phone: (312) 886-0241.

REGION VI—1445 Ross Ave., (MC 6WQ-AT), Dallas, TX 75202. Phone: (214)665-7375.

REGION VII—901 N 5th St., Kansas City, KS 66101. Phone: (913)551-7297, -7542.

REGION VIII—999 18th St. - Ste.300, Denver, CO 80202. Phone: (303)312-6235.

REGION IX—75 Hawthorne St., San Francisco, CA 94105. Phone: (415)972-3415, -3468.

REGION X—1200 6th Ave., Seattle, WA 98101. Phone: (206)553-6219.

66.463 Use general addresses listed under **66.001** or the Regional WCQA Coordinator shown via **Internet:** "http://epa.gov/owm/mab/indian/104coord.htm".

66.466 Chesapeake Bay Program Office, EPA, 410 Severn Ave. - Ste.109, Annapolis, MD 21403. Phone: (410)267-5743.

66.467 thru 66.471 Listed under **66.001**.

66.472 **Beach Monitoring**

REGION I *(Connecticut, Maine, Massachusetts, New Hampshire, Rhode Island)*—One Congress St. - Ste.1110, (CWQ), Boston, MA 02114-2023. Phones: (617)918-1626; FAX (617)918-1505.

REGION II *(New Jersey, New York, Puerto Rico, U.S. Virgin Islands)*—2890 Woodbridge Ave., (MS 220), Edison, NJ 08837-3679. Phones: (732)321-6797; FAX (732)321-6616.

REGION III *(Delaware, Maryland, Pennsylvania, Virginia)*—1650 Arch St., (3ES10), Philadelphia, PA 19103-2029. Phones: (215)814-5776; FAX (215)814-2729.

REGION IV *(Alabama, Florida, Georgia, Mississippi, North Carolina, South Carolina)*—61 Forsyth St. - 15th fl., Atlanta, GA 30303-3415. Phones: (404)562-9274; FAX (404)562-9224.

REGION V *(Illinois, Indiana, Michigan, Minnesota, Ohio, Wisconsin)*—77 W. Jackson Blvd., (WT-16J), Chicago, IL 60604-3507. Phones: (312)353-6704; FAX (312)886-0168.

REGION VI *(Louisiana, Texas)*—1445 Ross Ave., (6WQ-EW), Dallas, TX 75202-2733. Phones: (214)665-7314; FAX (214)665-6689.

REGION IX *(American Samoa, California, Commonwealth of the Mariana Islands, Guam, Hawaii)*—75 Hawthorne St., (WtR-2), San Francisco, CA 94105. Phones: (415)744-1939; FAX (415)744-1078.

REGION X *(Alaska, Oregon, Washington)*—120 6th Ave., (OW-134), Seattle, WA 98101. Phones: (206)553-1646; FAX (206)553-0165.

66.474 Listed under **66.001**.

66.475 Contact the EPA Region 4 Office listed under **66.001**.

66.478 Listed under **66.001**.

66.479 Same as **66.461**.

66.480	Listed under **66.001**.
66.481	One Congress St. - Ste.1100-CWN, Boston, MA 02114-2023. Phones: (617)918-1606; FAX (617)918-0606.
	290 Broadway - 24th fl., New York, NY 10007-1866. Phones: (212)637-3779; FAX (212)637-3889.
66.509 thru 66.516	Listed under **66.001**.
66.600	Contact the EPA Region 2 and 9 Offices listed under **66.001**.

66.604 Environmental Justice

REGION I—One Congress St. - Ste.1100 (RAA), Boston, MA 02203- 0001. Phones: (617)918-1343, -1020.

REGION II—290 Broadway - 26th fl., New York, NY 10007. Phones: (212)637-5027, -3861.

REGION III—1650 Arch St. (3DA00), Philadelphia, PA 19103- 2029. Phone: (215) 814-2988.

REGION IV—61 Forsyth St., Atlanta, GA 30303-8960. Phones: (404)562-8407, -9650, -8316.

REGION V—77 W. Jackson Blvd. (DM7J), Chicago, IL 60604-3507. Phones: (312) 353-1440, 886-5993.

REGION VI—Fountain Place - 13th fl., 1445 Ross Ave. (RA-D), Dallas, TX 75202-2733. Phones: (214)665-2713, -2209.

REGION VII—901 N. 5th St. (RGAD/ECO), Kansas City, KS 66101. Phones: (913) 551-7649, -7058.

REGION VIII—999 18th St. - Ste.300, (8ENF-EJ), Denver, CO 80202-2466. Phones: (303)312-6040, -6556.

REGION IX—75 Hawthorne St. (CMD -1), San Francisco, CA 94105. Phones: (415) 972-3795, -3839.

REGION X—1200 6th Ave. (OMP-143), Seattle, WA 98101. Phones: (206)553-1107, -8580.

66.605 and 66.606	Listed under **66.001**.
66.611 thru 66.707	Listed under **66.001**.

66.708 Pollution Prevention Information Network

REGION I—One Congress St. - Ste.1100(Rm.2203), (MC SPP), Boston, MA 02114-2023. Phones: (617)918-1814; FAX (617)918-1810.

REGION II—290 Broadway - 25th fl., (MC SPMMB), New York, NY 10007-1866. Phones: (212)637-3753; FAX (212)637-3771.

REGION III—1650 Arch St., (MC 3E100), Philadelphia, PA 19103- 2029. Phones: (215)814-5415, -3299; FAX (215)814-3274.

REGION IV—Atlanta Federal Center, 61 Forsyth St. SW, Atlanta, GA 30303. Phones: (404)562-9028; FAX (404)562-9066.

REGION V—77 W. Jackson Blvd., (MC DW-8J), Chicago, IL 60604- 3590. Phones: (312)866-4669; FAX (312)353-4788.

REGION VI—1445 Ross Ave. - Ste. 1200, (MC 6EN-XP), Dallas, TX 75202. Phones: (214)665-2119, -7261; FAX (214)665-7446.

REGION VII—901 N. 5th St., (MC ARTD/TSPP), Kansas City, KS 66101. Phones: (913)551-7097; FAX (913)551-7065.
REGION VIII—999 18th St. - Ste.300, (MC 8P-P3T). Denver, CO 80202-2466. Phones: (303)312-6385; FAX (303)312-6044.
REGION IX—75 Hawthorne St., (MC WST-7), San Francisco, CA 94105. Phones: (415)972-3283, -3288; FAX (415)947-3530.
REGION X—1200 6th Ave., (MC 01-085), Seattle, WA 98101. Phones: (206)553-4072, -4803; FAX (206)553-8338.

66.709 Listed under **66.001**.

Pesticide Environmental Stewardship Program

66.714 Regional PESP Coordinator:
REGION I—One Congress St. - Ste.1100 (CPT), Boston, MA 02114- 2023. Phone: (617)918-1198.
REGION II—2890 Woodbridge Ave., (MS 500), Edison, NJ 08837- 3679. Phone: (732)906-6183.
REGION III—1650 Arch St. (3WC32), Philadelphia, PA 19103- 2029. Phone: (215) 814-2129.
REGION IV—61 Forsyth St. SW, Atlanta, GA 30303-8960. Phone: (404)562-9014.
REGION V—77 W. Jackson Blvd. (DT-8J), Chicago, IL 60604-3507. Phone: (312) 886-3572.
REGION VI—1445 Ross Ave. - Ste.1200 (6PD-P), Dallas, TX 75202-2733. Phone: (214)665-7562.
REGION VII—901 N. 5th St. (WWPDPEST), Kansas City, KS 66101. Phone: (913) 551-7137.
REGION VIII—999 18th St. - Ste.300 (8P-P3T), Denver, CO 80202-2466. Phone: (303)312-6286.
REGION IX—75 Hawthorne St. (CMD-1), San Francisco, CA 94105. Phone: (415) 947-4240.
REGION X—24106 N.Bunn Rd. (WSU-IAREC), Prosser, WA 99350. Phone: (509) 786-9225.

66.715 and 66.716 Listed under **66.001**

66.717 Listed under **66.708**.

66.801 Listed under **66.001**.

66.802 Superfund Regional Administrators

REGION I—Office of Site Remediation and Restoration, One Congress St., (MC HBS), Boston, MA 02114-2023. Phones: Toll Free, 1-888-372-7341, (617)918-1421; FAX (617)918-1291.
REGION II—Grants and Contracts Management Branch, Office of Policy and Management, 290 Broadway - 27th fl., (MC 2 OPM-GCMB), New York, NY 10007-1866. Phones: (212)637-3420; FAX (212)637- 3518.
REGION III—1650 Arch St., (MC 3HS52), Philadelphia, PA 19103. Phones: Toll Free, 1-800-553-2509, (215)814-5522; FAX (215)814- 5518.
REGION IV—Waste Management Division, Program Services Branch, Atlanta Federal Center, 61 Forsyth St., (MC WDCSB), Atlanta, GA 30303. Phones: Toll Free, 1-800-564-7577, (404)562-8866(DB), -8867(RF); FAX (404)562-8842.
REGION V—Office of Public Affairs and Community Involvement Section (MC P-19J), Superfund Division and Contracts and Assistance Agreements Section (MC

66.802
(cont.)
SM-5J), 77 W. Jackson Blvd., Chicago, IL 60604-3507. Phones: Toll Free, 1-800-621-8431, (312)353-1325, 886-6044; FAX (312)353-1155, 886-0186.

REGION VI—Wells Fargo Bank, Tower at Fountain Place - Ste.1200, 1445 Ross Ave., (MC 6SF-PO), Dallas, TX 75202-2733. Phones: Toll Free, 1-800-533-3508, (214) 665-8157, -8163; FAX (214)665-6660.

REGION VII—Office of External Programs, 901 N. 5th St., (MC PBAF), Kansas City, KS 66101. Phones: Toll Free, 1-800-223-0425, (913)551-7762; FAX (913)551-7066.

REGION VIII—Office of Communications and Public Involvement, 999 18th St. - Ste.300, (MC 8EPR-PS), Denver, CO 80202-2466. Phones: Toll Free, 1-800-227-8917, (303)312-6696; FAX (303)312-6065.

REGION IX—Office of Community Involvement, 75 Hawthorne St., (MC SFD-3), San Francisco, CA 94105. Phones: Toll Free, 1-800-231-3075, (415)972-3237; FAX (415)947-3528.

REGION X—Community Involvement and Outreach Unit, 1200 6th Ave., (MC ECO-081), Seattle, WA 98101. Phones: Toll Free, 1-800- 424-4372, (206)553-0247, -1237; FAX (206)553-2955.

HEADQUARTERS—Community Involvement and Outreach Branch, Ariel Rios Bldg., 1200 Pennsylvania Ave., NW, (MC 5204G), Washington DC 20460. Phones: (703)603-8889; FAX (703)603-9100.

66.804
and
66.805
Underground Storage Tank Regional Program Managers

REGION I—One Congress St. - Ste.1100, Boston, MA 02114-2023. Phone: (617)918-1311.

REGION II—Water Compliance Branch (2DECA-WCB-GWCS), 290 Broadway, New York, NY 10007-1866. Phone: (212)637-4232.

REGION III—State Programs Branch (3WC21), 1650 Arch St., Philadelphia, PA 19103. Phone: (215)814-3231.

REGION IV—Atlanta Federal Center, 61 Forsyth St. SW, (MC GW- PB-15), Atlanta, GA 30303-3104. Phone: (404)562-9441.

REGION V—Underground Storage Tanks (DRU-7J), 77 W. Jackson Blvd., Chicago, IL 60604-3590. Phone: (312)886-6136.

REGION VI—1st Interstate Bank Tower - Ste.1200. (6PD-U), 1445 Ross Ave., Dallas, TX 75202-2733. Phone: (214)665-6760.

REGION VII—901 N. 5th St., Kansas City, KS 66101. Phone: (913)551-7547.

REGION VIII—999 18th St. - Ste.500 (8P2-W-GW), Denver, CO 80202-2466. Phone: (303)312-6137.

REGION IX—75 Hawthorne St. - 10th fl. (H-W-4), San Francisco, CA 94105. Phone: (415)744-2079.

REGION X—1200 6th Ave. (WD-133), Seattle, WA 98101. Phone: (206)553-1563.

66.806 Contact TAG coordinators listed under **66.802**.
66.808
and
66.809
Listed under **66.001**.

66.810 ## CEPP TECHNICAL ASSISTANCE

REGION I—One Congress St. - Ste.1100, (MC SEP), Boston, MA 02114-2023. Phone: (617)918-1804.

REGION II—Bldg. 209, 2890 Woodbridge Ave., Edison, NJ 08837- 3679. Phone: (732)906-6194.

REGION III—1650 Arch St., (MC 3HS33), Philadelphia, PA 19103. Phone: (215)814-3273.

REGION IV—Air Division - 12th fl., 61 Forsyth St. SW, Atlanta, GA 30303. Phone: (404)562-9085.

REGION V—77 W. Jackson Blvd., (MC SC-6J), Chicago, IL 60604. Phone: (312)353-9045.

REGION VI—1445 Ross Ave., (MC 6SF-RO), Dallas, TX 75202-2733. Phone: (214)665-2270.

REGION VII—901 5th St., (MC ATRDCRIB), Kansas City, KS 66101. Phone: (913)551-7540.

REGION VIII—One Denver Place - Ste.300, 999 18th St., (MC EPR-SA), Denver, CO 80202-2405. Phone: (303)312-6760.

REGION IX—75 Hawthorne St., (MC SFD 9-3), San Francisco, CA 94105. Phone: (415)972-3039.

REGION X—1200 6th Ave., (MC ECL-116), Seattle, WA 98101. Phone: (206)553-8414.

66.812 **Hazardous Waste Management for Tribes**

REGION I—Phones: (617)918-1554; FAX (617)918-1505.

REGION II—Phones: (212)637-4099; FAX (212)637-4437.

REGION IV—Phones: (404)562-8457; FAX (404)562-8439.

REGION V—Phones: (312)353-1440; FAX (312)353-6519.

REGION VI—Phones: (214)665-7226, -7216; FAX (214)665-7263, -6762.

REGION VII—Phones: (913)551-7669; FAX (913)551-9669.

REGION VIII—Phones: (303)312-6149; FAX (303)312-6064.

REGION IX—Phones: (415)972-3378; FAX (415)947-3530.

REGION X—Phones: (206)553-6502; FAX (206)553-8509.

66.813 and 66.815 Listed under **66.001**.

66.816 Listed under **66.804** or via **Internet:** "http://www.epa.gov/OUST/regions/index.htm".

OFFICE OF SOLID WASTE AND EMERGENCY RESPONSE

66.817 and 66.818 Regional Brownfields Coordinator:

REGION I—One Congress St. (HBT), Boston, MA 02114-2023. Phones: (617)918-1221; FAX (617)918-1291.

REGION II—290 Broadway - 18th fl., New York, NY 10007. Phones: (212)637-4314; FAX (212)637-4360.

REGION III—1650 Arch St., Philadelphia, PA 19103. Phones: (215)814-3129; FAX (215)814-5518.

REGION IV—Nunn Atlanta Federal Center, 61 Forsyth St., Atlanta, GA 30303. Phones: (404)562-8684; FAX (404)562-8566.

REGION V—77 W. Jackson Blvd., Chicago, IL 60604-3507. Phones: (312)886-7576; FAX (312)886-7190.

REGION VI—First Interstate Bank Tower at Fountain Place - Ste.1200, 1445 Ross Avenue, Dallas, TX 75202-2733. Phones: (214)665-6737; FAX (214)665-6660.

REGION VII—901 N. 5th St., Kansas City, KS 66101. Phones: (913)551-7646, -7786; FAX (913)551-7063.

66.817 thru 66.818 (cont.)	**REGION VIII**—999 18th St. - Ste.300 (EPR), Denver, CO 80202-2406. Phones: (303)312-6803; FAX (303)312-6067. **REGION IX**—75 Hawthorne St. (SFD-1-1), San Francisco, CA 94105. Phones: (415) 972-3188; FAX (415)947-3528. **REGION X**—1200 6th Ave., Seattle, WA 98101. Phones: (206)553-2100; FAX (206) 553-0124.

American Indian Environmental Office

66.926	Regional Indian Program Coordinator: **REGION I**—JFK Federal Bldg., One Congress St. - Ste.1100, Boston, MA 02114-2023. Phone: (617)918-1672. **REGION II**—26 Federal Plaza, New York, NY 10278. Phone: (212)637-3564. **REGION IV**—345 Courtland St. NE, Atlanta, GA 30365. Phone: (404)562-9639. **REGION V**—77 W. Jackson Blvd., Chicago, IL 60604-3507. Phone: (312)353-1394. **REGION VI**—1445 Ross Ave.- Ste.1200, Dallas, TX 75202-2733. Phone: (214)665-7454. **REGION VII**—726 Minnesota Ave., Kansas City, KS 66101. Phone: (913)551-7539. **REGION VIII**—999 18th St. - Ste.500, Denver, CO 80202-2405. Phone: (303)312-6343. **REGION IX**—75 Hawthorne St., San Francisco, CA 94105. Phone: (415)744-1607. **REGION X**—1200 6th Ave., Seattle, WA 98101. Phone: (206)553-6200.

OFFICE OF POLICY, ECONOMICS AND INNOVATIONS

66.940	Listed under **66.001**.

OFFICE OF ENVIRONMENTAL EDUCATION

66.950 and 66.951	Listed under **66.001**.

COMMODITY FUTURES TRADING COMMISSION

78.004	**REGIONAL OFFICES** **CENTRAL**—300 S. Riverside Plaza. - Ste.1600 N., Chicago, IL 60606. Phone: (312) 353-9000. ▪ 510 Grain Exchange Bldg., Minneapolis, MN 55415. Phone: (612)370-3255. **EASTERN**—One World Trade Center - Ste.3747, New York, NY 10048. Phone: (212)466-2071. **SOUTHWESTERN**—4900 Main St. - Ste.721, Kansas City, MO 64112. Phone: (816)931-7600. **WESTERN**—10900 Wilshire Blvd. - Ste.400, Los Angeles, CA 90024. Phone: (310) 235-6783.

DEPARTMENT OF ENERGY

81.022 **FIELD OFFICES - OPERATIONS**

California—Oakland Operations Office, 1301 Clay St., Oakland, CA 94612-5208. Phone: (510)637-1802.

Colorado—Rocky Flats Office, Golden, CO 80402-0928. Phone: (303)966-7000.

Idaho—Idaho Operations Office, 850 Energy Dr., (MS 1221), Idaho Falls, ID 83401-1563. Phone: (208)526-0111.

Illinois—Chicago Operations Office, 9800 S. Cass Ave., Argonne, IL 60439-4899. Phone: (630)252-2001.

New Mexico—Albuquerque Operations Office, Albuquerque, NM 87185-5400. Phone: (505)845-6049.

Nevada—Nevada Operations Office, P.O. Box 98518, Las Vegas, NV 89193-8518. Phone: (702)295-1000.

Ohio—Miamisburg, OH 45343-0066. Phone: (937)865-4020.

Pennsylvania—National Energy Technology Laboratory, 626 Cochrans Mills Rd., P.O. Box 10940, Pittsburgh, PA 15236-0940. Phone: (412)386-6000.

South Carolina—Savannah River Operations Office, P.O. Box A, Aiken, SC 29801. Phone: (803)725-6211.

Tennessee—Oak Ridge Operations Office, P.O. Box 2001, Oak Ridge, TN 37831. Phone: (865)574-1000.

Washington—Richland Operations Office, 825 Jadwin Ave., P.O. Box 550, Richland, WA 99352. Phone: (509)376-7411.

West Virginia—National Energy Technology Laboratory, 3610 Collins Ferry Rd., Morgantown, WV 26507-0880. Phone: (304)285-4764.

81.036 **OFFICE OF ENERGY EFFICIENCY AND RENEWABLE ENERGY**

REGIONAL OFFICES

CENTRAL—1617 Cole Blvd., (MS 1521), Golden, CO 80401. Phone: (303)275-4785.

MID-ATLANTIC—The Wanamaker Bldg. - Ste.890 South, 100 Penn Square E., Philadelphia, PA 19107. Phone: (215)656-6954.

MIDWEST—One S. Whacker Dr. - Ste.2380, Chicago, IL 60606-4616. Phone: (312)886-8588.

NORTHEAST—JFK Federal Bldg. - Rm.675, Boston, MA 02203. Phone: (617)565-9708.

SOUTHEAST—75 Spring St. SW - Ste.200, Atlanta, GA 30303. Phone: (404)562-0599.

WESTERN—800 5th Ave. - Ste.3950, Seattle, WA 98104-3122. Phone: (206)553-2875.

81.041 Listed under **81.022**.

81.042 *Contact may be made at the following phone numbers:*

CENTRAL—Phone: (303)275-4785.

MID-ATLANTIC—Phone: (215)656-6954.

MIDWEST—Phone: (312)886-8588.

NORTHEAST—Phone: (617)565-9708.

SOUTHEAST—Phone: (404)562-0599.

WESTERN—Phone: (206)553-2875.

81.049	Listed under **81.022**.
81.057	Project Office, National Energy Technology Laboratory, P.O. Box 10940, Pittsburgh, PA 15236. Phone: (412)386-4781.
81.065	Office of Repository Development, Las Vegas, NV. Phone: (702)794-1368.
81.079	**Regional Biomass Energy Program Offices**

GREAT LAKES—25 E. Wacker Dr., Chicago, IL 60601. Phone: (312)407-0177.

NORTHEAST—400 N. Capitol St. NW, Washington, DC 20001. Phone: (202)624-8454.

NORTHWEST—800 5th Ave. - Ste.3950, Seattle, WA 98104. Phone: (206)553-2079.

SOUTHEAST—Southern States Energy Board, Norcross, GA 30092. Phone: (770) 242-7712.

WESTERN—1200 N. St., Lincoln, NE 68508. Phone: (402)471-3218.

81.089	National Energy Technology Laboratory (MS 921-107)/ (FE-UPC/AD21), P.O. Box 10940, 626 Cochrans Mill Rd., Pittsburgh, PA 15276. Phone: (412)386-4524.
81.105	**SUPPORT OFFICES**

Colorado—DOE, Denver Regional Support Office, 1617 Cole Blvd. - Bldg.17-2, Golden, CO 80401. Phone: (303)275-4816.

▪ DOE, Golden Field Office, 1617 Cole Blvd, Golden, CO 80401. Phones: (303)275-4737; FAX (303)275-4788.

Georgia—DOE, 75 Spring St. SW - Ste.200, Atlanta, GA 30303. Phone: (404)562-0556.

Illinois—DOE, One S. Wacker Dr. - Ste.2380, Chicago, IL 60606-4616. Phone: (312) 886-8571.

Massachusetts—DOE, JFK Federal Bldg. - Rm.675, Boston, MA 02203.Phone: (617) 565-9700.

Pennsylvania—DOE, 1880 JFK Blvd. - 5th fl., Philadelphia, PA 19102. Phone: (215) 656-6964.

Washington—DOE, 800 5th Ave. - Ste.3950, Seattle, WA. 98104-3122. Phone: (206) 553-1004.

81.106	Institutional Relations Manager, Area Office, DOE, Carlsbad, NM 88221-3090. Phone: (505)234-7335.
81.112	Listed under **81.022**.
81.114	Idaho Operations Office Program Manager: Phone: (208)526-4169
81.119	Listed under **81.022**.
81.121	Research and Development Division, Idaho Operations Office, 1955 Fremont Ave., Idaho Falls, ID 83401. Phone: (208)526-2176.

DEPARTMENT OF EDUCATION

84.007	**REGIONAL ADMINISTRATORS/STUDENT FINANCIAL AID**

Students should contact their educational institution. Educational institutions should contact:

REGION I—McCormack Post Office and Courthouse - Rm.502, 5 Post Office Square, (MS 01-0070), Boston, MA 02109. Phone: (617)223-9328.

FIELD OFFICE CONTACTS   845

REGION II—Institutional Review Branch, 75 Park Place - 12th fl., New York, NY 10007. Phone: (212)637-6423.

REGION III—3535 Market St. - Rm.16200, (MS 03-2080), Philadelphia, PA 19104. Phone: (215)596-1018.

REGION IV—P.O. Box 1692, Atlanta, GA 30301. Phone: (404)331-0556.

REGION V—401 S. State St. - Rm.700-D, (MS 05-4080), Chicago, IL 60605. Phone: (312)353-0375.

REGION VI—1200 Main Tower Bldg. - Rm.2150, (MS 06-5080), Dallas, TX 75202. Phone: (214)767-3811.

REGION VII—Institutional Review Branch, 10220 N. Executive Hills Blvd. - 9th fl., Kansas City, MO 64153. Phone: (816)880-4054.

REGION VIII—Institutional Review Branch, 1244 Speer Blvd. - Rm.322, Denver, CO 80204. Phone: (303)844-3676.

REGION IX—50 United Nations Plaza - Rm.227, (MS 09-8080), San Francisco, CA 94102-4987. Phone: (415)556-8382.

REGION X—1000 2nd Ave. - Rm.1200, Seattle, WA 98174-1099. Phone: (206)287-1770.

84.027 *Potential applicants should contact their state department of education.*

84.032 Listed under **84.007**. *(Each state with an operating guarantee agency maintains an office; obtain list from headquarters office.)*

84.033 thru 84.038 *Students should contact their educational institution. Public and private nonprofit organizations should contact grantee educational institutions. Educational institutions should contact the appropriate Regional Office, listed under* **84.007**.

84.042 and 84.047

SECRETARY'S REGIONAL REPRESENTATIVES

REGION I—McCormack Post Office and Courthouse - Rm.540, Boston, MA 02109. Phone: (617)223-9317.

REGION II—75 Park Place - 12th fl., New York, NY 10007. Phone: (212)637-6283.

REGION III—100 Penn Square E. - Ste.505, Philadelphia, PA 19107. Phone: (215)656-6010.

REGION IV—61 Forsyth St. SW - Rm.19T40, Atlanta, GA 30303. Phone: (404)562-6225.

REGION V—111 N. Canal St. - Rm.1094, Chicago, IL 60606. Phone: (312)553-8192.

REGION VI—1999 Bryan St. - Ste.2700, Dallas, TX 75201-6817. Phone: (214)880-3011.

REGION VII—10220 N. Executive Hills Blvd. - Ste.720, Kansas City, MO 64153-1367. Phone: (816)880-4000.

REGION VIII—Federal Regional Office Bldg. - Rm.310, 1244 Speer Blvd., Denver, CO 80204-3582. Phone: (303)844-3544.

REGION IX—50 United Nations Plaza - Rm.205, San Francisco, CA 94102-4987. Phone: (415)437-7520.

REGION X—915 2nd Ave. - Rm.3362, Seattle, WA 98174-1099. Phone: (206)220-7800.

84.063 Federal Student Aid Information Center. Phone: (800)433-3243. *Or, contact the director of student financial aid at the institution the student wishes to attend, high school guidance counselors, directors of state agencies, or regional office listed under* **84.007**.

84.069 *List of state student scholarship or assistance agencies available in the Regional Offices listed under* **84.007**. *Program administered from headquarters.*

84.126 thru 84.132

REGIONAL COMMISSIONERS/REHABILITATIVE SERVICES

REGION I—McCormack Post Office and Courthouse - Rm.232, Boston, MA 02109-4557. Phone: (617)223-4085.

84.126 thru 84.132 (cont.)	**REGION II**—75 Park Place - 12th fl., New York, NY 10007. Phone: (212)264-4016. **REGION III**—100 Penn Square E. - Ste.512, Philadelphia, PA 19107. Phone: (215)656-8531. **REGION IV**—61 Forsyth St. SW - Rm.18T91, Atlanta, GA 30303. Phone: (404)562-6330. **REGION V**—10220 N. Executive Hills Blvd., Kansas City, MO 64153-1367. Phone: (816)880-4107. **REGION VI**—1999 Bryan St. - Rm.2740, Dallas, TX 75202. Phone: (214)808-4927. **REGION VII**—111 N. Canal St. - Ste.510, Chicago, IL 60606. Phone: (816)880-4107. **REGION VIII**—Harwood Center, 1999 Bryan St., Dallas, TX 75201-6817. Phone: (214)880-4927. **REGION IX**—Federal Office Bldg. - Rm.215, 50 United Nations Plaza, San Francisco, CA 94102. Phone: (415)437-7840. **REGION X**—915 2nd Ave. - Rm.2848, Seattle, WA 98174-1099. Phone: (206)220-7840.
84.145	**FEDERAL REAL PROPERTY ASSISTANCE PROGRAM** **REGIONAL OFFICES** **EASTERN ZONE (Regions I, II, III, IV, V)**—Director, Office of Administrator/Management Services, McCormack Post Office and Courthouse - Rm.536, Boston, MA 02109-4557. Phone: (617)223-9321. **WESTERN ZONE (Regions VI, VII, XIII, IX, X)**—Director, Office of Administrator/Management Services, 400 Maryland Ave. SW - Rm.2C107, Washington, DC 20202. Phone: (202)401-0506.
84.161 and 84.169	Listed under **84.126**.
84.173	*Contact the state educational agency.*
84.177 thru 84.250	Listed under **84.126**.
84.256	Contact Pacific Resources for Education and Learning, Honolulu, HI. Phone: (no number provided).
84.263 thru 84.265	Listed under **84.126**.
84.268	Listed under **84.007**.
84.275	Listed under **84.126**.
84.315	Listed under **84.126**.

PENSION BENEFIT GUARANTY CORPORATION

86.001	*Contact the Employee Benefits Security Administration (Department of Labor) office listed under* **17.150**.

NATIONAL ARCHIVES AND RECORDS ADMINISTRATION

89.001 **PRESIDENTIAL LIBRARIES**

Arkansas—Clinton Presidential Material Project, 1000 Laharpe Blvd., Little Rock, AR 72201. Phone: (501)254-6866.

California—Ronald Reagan Library, 40 Presidential Dr., Simi Valley, CA 93065-0600. Phone: (800)410-8354.

District of Columbia—Presidential Materials Staff, 700 Pennsylvania Ave. NW, Washington DC 20408-0001. Phone: (202)501-5705.

Georgia—Jimmy Carter Library, 441 Freedom Pkwy., Atlanta, GA 30307-1498. Phone: (404)331-3942.

Iowa—Herbert Hoover Library, 210 Parkside Dr., West Branch, IA 52358-0488. Phone: (319)643-5301.

Kansas—Dwight D. Eisenhower Library, 200 SE 4th St., Abilene, KS 67410-2900. Phone: (785)263-4751.

Maryland—Nixon Presidential Materials Staff, National Archives at College Park, College Park, MD 20740-6001. Phone: (301)713-6950.

Massachusetts—John F. Kennedy Library, Columbia Point, Boston, MA 02125-3398. Phone: (617)929-4500.

Michigan—Gerald R. Ford Museum, 303 Pearl St. NW, Grand Rapids, MI 49504-5353. Phone (616)451-9263.

- Gerald R. Ford Library, 1000 Beal Ave., Ann Arbor, MI 48109-2114. Phone: (734)741-2218.

Missouri—Harry S. Truman Library, 500 W. U.S. Hwy. 24, Independence, MO 64050-1798. Phone: (816)833-1400.

New York—Franklin D. Roosevelt Library, 511 Albany Post Rd., Hyde Park, NY 12538-1999. Phone: (914)229-8114.

Texas—Lyndon B. Johnson Library, 2313 Red River St., Austin, TX 78705-5702. Phone: (512)916-5137.

- George Bush Library, 1000 George Bush Dr. W., College Station, TX 77845. Phone: (409)260-9554.

OFFICE OF REGIONAL RECORDS SERVICES

CENTRAL PLAINS REGION—200 Space Center Dr., Lee's Summit, MO 64064-1182. Phones: (816)478-7079; FAX (816)478-7623.

- 2312 E. Bannister Rd., Kansas City, MO 64131-3011. Phones: (816)926-6920; FAX (816)926-6982. **Internet:** e-mail, "kansascity.archives@nara.gov".
- (Military Records) 9700 Page Ave., St. Louis, MO 63132-5100. Phones: (314)538-4247; FAX (314)538-4005. **Internet:** e-mail, "center@stlouis.nara.gov".
- (Civilian Records) 111 Winnebago St., St. Louis, MO 63118-4199. Phones: (314)425-5722; FAX (314)425-5719. **Internet:** e-mail, "center@cpr.nara.gov".

DISTRICT OF COLUMBIA—Washington National Records Center, Reference Service Branch, Washington, DC 20409-0002. Phone: (301)457-7000.

- Archives I - Research Room Support Branch, 700 Pennsylvania Ave. NW, Washington, DC 20408. Phone: (202)501-5403.

GREAT LAKES REGION—7358 S. Pulaski Rd., Chicago, IL 60629-5898. Phones:

89.001 (cont.) (773)581-9688; FAX (312)886-7883. **Internet:** e-mail, "chicago.archives@nara.gov".

- 3150 Springboro Rd., Dayton, OH 45439-1883. Phones: (937)225-2878; FAX (937)225-7236. **Internet:** e-mail, "center@dayton.nara.gov".

MARYLAND—Archives II - Research Room Support Branch, College Park, MD 20740-6001. Phone: (301)713-6800.

MID ATLANTIC REGION—900 Market St., Philadelphia, PA 19107-4292. Phones: (215)597-3000, -9752; FAX (215)597-2303. **Internet:** e-mail, "archives@philarch.nara.gov".

- 14700 Townsend Rd., Philadelphia, PA 19154-1096. Phones: (215)671-8005; FAX (215)671-8001.

NORTHEAST REGION—10 Conte Dr., Pittsfield, MA 01201-8230. Phones: (413)445-6885; FAX (413)445-7305.

- 380 Trapelo Rd., Waltham, MA 02154-6399. Phones: (617)647-8108; FAX (617)647-8008. **Internet:** e-mail, "waltham.archives@nara.gov".
- 201 Varick St., New York, NY 10014-4811. Phones: (212)337-1300; FAX (212)337-1306. **Internet:** e-mail, "newyork.archives@nara.gov".

PACIFIC REGION—654 W. 3rd Ave., Anchorage, AK 99501-2145. Phones: (907)271-2443; FAX (907)271-2442. **Internet:** e-mail, "alaska.archives@nara.gov".

- 24000 Avila Rd. - 1st fl. (east entrance), Laguna Niguel, CA 92607-6719. Phones: (949)360-2618; FAX (949)360-2624. **Internet:** e-mail, "laguna.archives@nara.gov"
- 1000 Commodore Dr., San Bruno, CA 94066-2350. Phones: (650)876-9249; FAX (650)876-9233. **Internet:** e-mail, "sanbruno.archives@nara.gov".

ROCKY MOUNTAIN REGION—Denver Federal Center - Bldg. 48, Denver, CO 80225-0307. Phones: (303)236-0801; FAX (303)236-9297. **Internet:** e-mail, "denver.archives@nara.gov".

SOUTHEAST REGION—1557 St. Joseph Ave., East Point, GA 30344-2593. Phones: (404)763-7438; FAX (404)763-7059. **Internet:** e-mail, "atlanta.archives@nara.gov".

SOUTHWEST REGION—Bldg. 1, 501 W. Felix St., Ft. Worth, TX 76115-3405. *For mail:* P.O. Box 6216, Ft. Worth, TX 76115-0216. Phones: (817)334-5736; FAX (817)334-5621. **Internet:** e-mail, "ftworth.archives@nara.gov".

DEPARTMENT OF HEALTH AND HUMAN SERVICES

OFFICE OF THE SECRETARY

93.001 HHS REGIONAL OFFICES

Regional Managers, Office for Civil Rights:

REGION I—JFK Federal Bldg. - Rm.1875, Boston, MA 02203. Phones: (617)565-1340; TDD (617)565-1343; FAX (617)565-3809.

REGION II—Javits Federal Bldg. - Ste.3313, 26 Federal Plaza, New York, NY 10278. Phones: (212)264-3313; TDD (212)264-2355; FAX (212)264-3039.

FIELD OFFICE CONTACTS 849

REGION III—150 S. Independence Mall - Ste.372, Philadelphia, PA 19106-3499. Phones: (215)861-4441; TDD (215)861-4440; FAX (215)861-4431.

REGION IV—61 Forsyth St. SW - Ste.3B70, Atlanta, GA 30323. Phones: (404)562-7886; TDD (404)562-7884; FAX (404)562-7881.

REGION V—233 N. Michigan Ave. - Ste.240, Chicago, IL 60601. Phones: (312)886-2359; TDD (312)353-5693; FAX (312)886-1807.

REGION VI—1301 Young St. - Ste.1169, Dallas, TX 75202. Phones: (214)767-4056; TDD (214)767-8940; FAX (214)767-0432.

REGION VII—601 E. 12th St. - Rm.248, Kansas City, MO 64106. Phones: (816)426-7278; TDD (816)426-7065; FAX (816)426-3686.

REGION VIII—1961 Stout St. - Rm.1426, Denver, CO 80294. Phones: (303)844-2024; TDD (303)844-3439; FAX (303)844-2025.

REGION IX—50 United Nations Plaza - Rm.322, San Francisco, CA 94103. Phones: (415)437-8310; TDD (415)437-8311; FAX (415)437-8329.

REGION X—2201 6th Ave. - Ste.900, Seattle, WA 98121. Phones: (206)615-2290; TDD (206)615-2296; FAX (206)615-2297.

ADMINISTRATION ON AGING

REGIONAL OFFICES

93.041 thru 93.053

Regional Administrator, Administration on Aging:

REGION I *(Connecticut, Maine, Massachusetts, New Hampshire, Rhode Island, Vermont)*—JFK Federal Bldg. - Rm.2100, Government Center, Boston, MA 02203. Phone: (617)565-1500.

REGION II *(New York, New Jersey, Puerto Rico, Virgin Islands)*—26 Federal Plaza - Rm.3835, New York, NY 10278. Phone: (212)264-4600.

REGION III *(Delaware, District of Columbia, Maryland, Pennsylvania, Virginia, West Virginia)*—Gateway Bldg. - Rm.11480, 3535 Market St., Philadelphia, PA 19104. Phone: (215)596-6492.

REGION IV *(Alabama, Florida, Georgia, Kentucky, Mississippi, North Carolina, South Carolina, Tennessee)*—101 Marietta Tower Bldg. - Ste.1515, Atlanta, GA 30323. Phone: (404)331-2442.

REGION V *(Illinois, Indiana, Michigan, Minnesota, Ohio, Wisconsin)*—105 W. Adams - 23rd fl., Chicago, IL 60603. Phone: (312)353-5160.

REGION VI *(Arkansas, Louisiana, New Mexico, Oklahoma, Texas)*—1301 Young St. - Ste.1124, Dallas, TX 75202. Phone: (214)767-3301.

REGION VII *(Iowa, Kansas, Missouri, Nebraska)*—601 E. 12th St. - Rm.210, Kansas City, MO 64106. Phone: (816)426-2821.

REGION VIII *(Colorado, Montana, North Dakota, South Dakota, Utah, Wyoming)*—Federal Bldg. - Rm.325, 1961 Stout St., Denver, CO 80294-3538. Phone: (303)844-3372.

REGION IX *(American Samoa, Arizona, California, Guam, Hawaii, Nevada, Northern Mariana Islands, Trust Territories of the Pacific Islands)*—Federal Office Bldg. - Rm.431, 50 United Nations Plaza, San Francisco, CA 94102. Phone: (415)437-8500.

REGION X *(Alaska, Idaho, Oregon, Washington)*—2201 6th Ave. - Rm.1208, Seattle, WA 98121. Phone: (206)615-2010.

93.066 Technical Information Management Section, CDC Procurement and Grants Office, 2920 Brandywine Rd., Atlanta, GA 30341. Phone: (770)488-2700.

93.067 Lead Contract Specialist, International Branch, 2920 Brandywine Rd., Atlanta, GA 30341. Phone: (770)488-2632.

FOOD AND DRUG ADMINISTRATION

93.103 DISTRICT OFFICES

No field offices. Direct contact with HQ concerning grants. See main entry. However, for general information concerning Food and Drug Administration activities contact the nearest district office, following:

California—1431 Harbor Bay Pkwy., Alameda, CA 94502-7070. Phone: (510)337-6783.

- 19900 McArthur Blvd. - Ste.300, Irvine, CA 92715-2445. Phone: (714)798-7714.

Colorado—Denver Federal Center, 6th and Kipling St., Denver, CO 80225-0087. Phone: (303)236-3016.

Florida—7200 Lake Ellenor Dr. - Ste.120, Orlando, FL 32809. Phone: (407)648-6995.

Georgia—60 8th St. NE, Atlanta, GA 30309. Phone: (404)347-4344.

Illinois—300 S. Riverside Plaza - Ste.550 S., Chicago, IL 60606. Phone: (312)353-7379.

Kansas—11630 W. 80th St., Lenexa, KS 66285-5905. Phone: (913)752-2144.

Louisiana—4298 Elysian Fields Ave., New Orleans, LA 70122. Phone: (504)589-2401, ext.124.

Maryland—900 Madison Ave., Baltimore, MD 21201. Phone: (410)962-4012.

Massachusetts—One Montvale Ave. - 4th fl., Stoneham, MA 02180. Phone: (617)279-1675, ext.155.

Michigan—1560 E. Jefferson Ave., Detroit, MI 48207. Phone: (313)226-6260, ext.101.

Minnesota—240 Hennepin Ave., Minneapolis, MN 55401-1912. Phone: (612)334-4100, ext.121.

New Jersey—Waterview Corporate Center - 3rd fl., 10 Waterview Blvd., Parsippany, NJ 07054. Phone: (973)331-2901.

New York—850 3rd Ave., Brooklyn, NY 11232-1593. Phone: (718)340-7000, ext.5301.

- 599 Delaware Ave., Buffalo, NY 14202. Phone: (716)551-4461.

Ohio—1141 Central Pkwy., Cincinnati, OH 45202-1097. Phone: (513)684-3504.

Pennsylvania—U.S. Customhouse - Rm.900, 2nd & Chestnut St., Philadelphia, PA 19106. Phone: (215)597-4390, ext.4200.

Puerto Rico—466 Fernandez Juncos Ave., San Juan, PR 00901-3223. Phone: (787)729-6842.

Tennessee—297 Plus Park Blvd., Nashville, TN 37217. Phone: (615)781-5392, ext.128.

Texas—3310 Live Oak St., Dallas, TX 75204. Phone: (214)655-5315, ext.302.

Washington—Federal Office Bldg., 22201 23rd Dr. SE, Bothell, WA 98041-3012. Phone: (425)483-4950.

INDIAN HEALTH SERVICE

93.164 AREA OFFICES

Alaska Area *(Alaska)*—4141 Ambassador Dr., Anchorage, AK 99508-5928. Phone: (907)257-3686.

Arizona: Navajo Area *(Arizona, Colorado, New Mexico, Utah)*—Window Rock, AZ 86515-9020. Phone: (520)871-5811.

- **Phoenix Area** *(Arizona, Nevada, Utah)*—3738 N. 16th St. - Ste.A, Phoenix, AZ 85016-5981. Phone: (602)640-2052.
- **Tucson Area** *(Arizona)*—OHPRD, 7900 S. "J" Stock Rd., Tucson, AZ 85746-9352. Phone: (520)295-2406.

California Area *(California)*—1825 Bell St. - Ste.200, Sacramento, CA 95825-1097. Phone: (916)566-7101.

Maryland: Headquarters Office—5600 Fishers Ln. - Rm.6-05, Rockville, MD 20857. Phone: (301)443-1083.

Minnesota: Bemidji Area *(Michigan, Minnesota, Wisconsin)*—127 Federal Bldg., Bemidji, MN 56601. Phone: (218)759-3412.

Montana: Billings Area *(Montana, Wyoming)*—2900 4th Genuire N. - P.O. Box 2143, Billings, MT 59103. Phone: (406)247-7107.

New Mexico: Albuquerque Area *(Colorado, New Mexico)*—505 Marquette NW - Ste.1502, Albuquerque, NM 87102-2163. Phone: (505)248-4500.
- **Headquarters West Office**—5300 Homestead Rd. NE, Albuquerque, NM 87110. Phone: (505)248-4102.

Oklahoma: Oklahoma City Area *(Kansas, Oklahoma)*—5 Corporate Plaza, 3625 NW 56th St., Oklahoma City, OK 73112. Phone: (405)951-3768.

Oregon: Portland Area *(Idaho, Oregon, Washington)*—1220 SW 3rd Ave. - Rm.476, Portland, OR 97204-2892. Phone: (503)326-2020.

South Dakota: Aberdeen Area *(Iowa, Nebraska, North Dakota, South Dakota)*—Federal Bldg., 115 4th Ave. SE, Aberdeen, SD 57401. Phone: (605)226-7581.

Tennessee: Nashville Area *(Alabama, Arkansas, Connecticut, Delaware, Florida, Georgia, Illinois, Indiana, Kentucky, Louisiana, Maine, Maryland, Massachusetts, Mississippi, Missouri, New Hampshire, New Jersey, New York, North Carolina, Ohio, Pennsylvania, Rhode Island, South Carolina, Tennessee, Texas, Vermont, Virginia, West Virginia)*—711 Stewarts Ferry Pike, Nashville, TN 37214-2634. Phone: (615) 736-2400.

93.217	Listed under **93.001**.
93.228	Listed under **93.164**.
93.260	Listed under **93.001**.
93.284	Listed under **93.164**.
93.441	Listed under **93.164**.
93.447 thru **93.449**	Regional office information will be provided in the application packet, if applicable.

ADMINISTRATION FOR CHILDREN AND FAMILIES

93.550 thru **93.674** — Regional Administrator, ACF, HHS Regional Office. *Use addresses listed under* **93.041**.

CENTERS FOR MEDICARE AND MEDICAID SERVICES

93.767 thru **93.778** — Regional Administrator, CMS, HHS Regional Office. *Use addresses listed under* **93.041**.

93.779 thru **93.781** — Same as **93.767**

93.782 Contacts may be made at the following regional offices:
- New York, NY. Phone: (212)264-3904.
- San Francisco, CA. Phone: (415)744-3598.

93.945 Listed under **93.041**.

93.971 and 93.972 Same as **93.164**.

93.982 Regional Director, FEMA Regional Office. *See addresses listed under* **97.017**.

CORPORATION FOR NATIONAL AND COMMUNITY SERVICE

94.002 thru 94.016

ATLANTIC CLUSTER OFFICES

CLUSTER DIRECTOR—801 Arch St. - Ste.103, Philadelphia, PA 19107-2416. Phones: (215)597-9972; FAX (215)597-4933.

Connecticut—One Commercial Plaza - 21st fl., Hartford, CT 06103-3510. Phones: (860)240-3237; FAX (860)240-3238.

Delaware—*see* **Maryland**.

Maine—*see* **New Hampshire**.

Maryland—Fallon Federal Bldg. - Ste.400B, 31 Hopkins Plaza, Baltimore, MD 21201-3418. Phones: (410)962-4443; FAX (410)962-3201.

Massachusetts—10 Causeway St. - Rm.473, Boston, MA 02222-1038. Phones: (617) 565-7000; FAX (617)565-7011.

New Hampshire—1 Pillsbury St. - Ste.201, Concord, NH 03301-3556. Phones: (603) 225-1450; FAX (603)225-1459.

New Jersey—44 S. Clinton Ave. - Ste.702, Trenton, NJ 08609-1507. Phones: (609)989-2243; FAX (609)989-2304.

New York—O'Brien Federal Bldg. - Rm.818, Clinton Ave. and Pearl St., Albany, NY 12207. Phones: (518)431-4150; FAX (518)431-4154.

Pennsylvania—Nix Federal Bldg. - Ste.229, 900 Market St., Philadelphia, PA 19107. Phones: (215)597-2806; FAX (215)597-2807.

Puerto Rico - Virgin Islands—Federal Bldg. - Ste.662, 150 Carlos Chardon Ave., Hato Rey, PR 00918-1737. Phones: (787)766-5314; FAX (787)766-5189.

Rhode Island—400 Westminster St. - Rm.203, Providence, RI 02903. Phones: (401) 528-5424; FAX (401)528-5220.

Vermont—*See* **New Hampshire**.

NORTH CENTRAL CLUSTER OFFICES

CLUSTER DIRECTOR—77 W. Jackson Blvd. - Ste.442, Chicago, IL 60604-3511. Phones: (312)353-7705; FAX (312)353-5343.

Illinois—77 W. Jackson Blvd. - Ste.442, Chicago, IL 60604-3511. Phones: (312)353-3622; FAX (312)353-5343.

Indiana—46 E. Ohio St. - Rm.457, Indianapolis, IN 46204-1922. Phones: (317)226-6724; FAX (317)226-5437.

Iowa—Federal Bldg. - Rm.917, 210 Walnut St., Des Moines, IA 50309-2195. Phones: (515)284-4816; FAX (515)284-6640.

Michigan—211 W. Fort St. - Ste.1408, Detroit, MI 48226-2799. Phones: (313)226-7848; FAX (313)226-2557.

Minnesota—431 S. 7th St. - Ste.2480, Minneapolis, MN 55415-1854. Phones: (612)334-4083; FAX (612)334-4084.

Nebraska—Federal Bldg. - Rm.156, 100 Centennial Mall N., Lincoln, NE 68508-3896. Phones: (402)437-5493; FAX (402)437-5495.

North Dakota - South Dakota—Federal Bldg. - Rm.225, 225 S. Pierre St., Pierre, SD 57501-2452. Phones: (605)224-5996; FAX (605)224-9201.

Ohio—51 N. High St. - Ste.451, Columbus, OH 43215. Phones: (614)469-7441; FAX (614)469-2125.

Wisconsin—Reuss Federal Plaza - Rm.1240, 310 W. Wisconsin Ave., Milwaukee, WI 53203-2211. Phones: (414)297-1118; FAX (414)297-1863.

PACIFIC CLUSTER OFFICES

CLUSTER DIRECTOR—P.O. Box 29996, Presidio of San Francisco, CA 94129-0996. Phones: (415)561-5960; FAX (415)561-5970.

Alaska—*See* **Washington**. Phones: (206)220-7736; FAX (206)553-4415.

California—11150 W. Olympia Blvd. - Ste.170, Los Angeles, CA 90064. Phones: (310)235-7421; FAX (310)235-7422.

Hawaii, Guam, American Samoa—Federal Bldg. - Rm.6213, 300 Ala Moana Blvd., Honolulu, HI 96850-0001. Phones: (808)541-2832; FAX (808)541-3603.

Idaho—304 N. 8th St. - Rm.344, Boise, ID 83702-5835. Phones: (208)334-1707; FAX (208)334-1421.

Montana—Capitol One Center - Ste.206, 208 N. Montana Ave. Helena, MT 59601-3837. Phones: (406)449-5404; FAX (406)449-5412.

Nevada—4600 Kietzke Ln. - Ste.E-141, Reno, NV 89502-5033. Phones: (702)784-5314; FAX (702)784-5026.

Oregon—2010 Lloyd Center, Portland, OR 97232. Phones: (503)231-2103; FAX (503)231-2106.

Utah—350 S. Main St. - Rm.504, Salt Lake City, UT 84101-2198. Phones: (801)524-5411; FAX (801)524-3599.

Washington—Jackson Federal Bldg. - Ste.3190, 915 2nd Ave., Seattle, WA 98174-1103. Phones: (206)220-7745; FAX (206)553-4415.

Wyoming—Federal Bldg. - Rm.1110, 2120 Capitol Ave., Cheyenne, WY 82001-3649. Phones: (307)772-2385; FAX (307)772-2389.

SOUTHERN CLUSTER OFFICES

CLUSTER DIRECTOR—60 Forsyth St. SW, - Ste.3M40, Atlanta, GA 30323-2301. Phones: (404)562-4055; FAX (404)562-4071.

Alabama—Medical Forum - Ste.428, 950 22nd St. N., Birmingham, AL 35203. Phones: (205)731-0027; FAX(205)731-0031.

District of Columbia—*See* **Virginia**.

Florida—3165 McCrory St. - Ste.115, Orlando, FL 32803-3750. Phones: (407)648-6117; FAX (407)648-6116.

Georgia—75 Piedmont Ave. NE - Ste.982, Atlanta, GA 30303-2587. Phones: (404)331-4646; FAX (404)331-2898.

Kentucky—Federal Bldg. - Rm.372-D, 600 Martin Luther King Place, Louisville, KY 40202-2230. Phones: (502)582-6384; FAX (502)582-6386.

Mississippi—100 W. Capitol St. - Rm.1005A, Jackson, MS 39269-1092. Phones: (601)965-5664; FAX (601)965-4617.

North Carolina—300 Fayetteville St. Mall - Rm.131, Raleigh, NC 27601-1739. Phones: (919)856-4731; FAX (919)856-4738.

94.002
thru
94.016
(cont.)

South Carolina—1835 Assembly St. - Ste.872, Columbia, SC 29201-2430. Phones: (803)765-5771; FAX (803)765-5777.

Tennessee—265 Cumberland Bend Dr., Nashville, TN 37228. Phones: (615)736-5561; FAX (615)736-7937.

Virginia—400 N. 8th St. - Ste.446, P.O. Box 10066, Richmond, VA 23240-1832. Phones: (804)771-2197; FAX (804)771-2157.

West Virginia—10 Hale St. - Ste.203, Charleston, WV 25301-1409. Phones: (304)347-5246; FAX (304)347-5464.

SOUTHWEST CLUSTER OFFICES

CLUSTER DIRECTOR—1999 Bryan St. - Rm.2050, Dallas, TX 75201. Phones: (214)880-7050; FAX (214)880-7074.

Arizona—522 N. Central - Rm.205A, Phoenix, AZ 85004-2190. Phones: (602)379-4825; FAX (602)379-4030.

Arkansas—Federal Bldg. - Rm.2506, 700 W. Capitol St., Little Rock, AR 72201. Phones: (501)324-5234; FAX (501)324-6949.

Colorado—999 18th St. - Ste.1440 South, Denver, CO 80202. Phones: (303)312-7950; FAX (303)312-7954.

Kansas—444 SE Quincy - Rm.260, Topeka, KS 66683-3572. Phones: (785)295-2540; FAX (785)295-2596.

Louisiana—707 Florida St. - Ste.316, Baton Rouge, LA 70801-1910. Phones: (504)389-0473; FAX (504)389-0510.

Missouri—801 Walnut St. - Ste.504, Kansas City, MO 64106-2009. Phones: (816)347-6300; FAX (816)347-6305.

New Mexico—120 S. Federal Place - Rm.315, Santa Fe, NM 87501-2026. Phones: (505)988-6577; FAX (505)988-6661.

Oklahoma—215 Dean A. McGee - Ste.324, Oklahoma City, OK 73102. Phones: (405)231-5201; FAX (405)231-4329.

Texas—903 San Jacinto St. - Ste.130, Austin, TX 78701-3747. Phones: (512)916-5671; FAX (512)916-5806.

SOCIAL SECURITY ADMINISTRATION

96.001
thru
96.020

There are 1,296 district and branch SSA offices located in cities and towns throughout the U.S. Consult the local phone directory under "Social Security Administration" or "U.S. Government" or ask for address at local U.S. Post Office.

DEPARTMENT OF HOMELAND SECURITY

IMMIGRATION AND CUSTOMS ENFORCEMENT

97.009   DHS,ICE, OIA, PHAB Miami Office, 51 SW 1st Ave. - Rm.220, Miami, FL 33130. Phone:(305)536-4261.

97.010 FIELD OFFICES

Alabama—Mobile Border Patrol, P.O. Box 1526, Mobile, AL 36633. Phones: (334) 441-6139.
- Mobile Port of Entry, P.O. Box 1526, Mobile, AL 36601. Phones: (334)441-5135.

Alaska—Anchorage District Office, 620 E. 10th Ave. - Ste.102, Anchorage, AK 99501-3701. Phone: (907)271-3524.
- Anchorage International Airport, 4601 Satellite Dr., P.O. Box 19068, Anchorage, AK 99519-0688. Phone: (907)243-1400.
- Dutch Harbor Port of Entry, 2315 Airport Beach Rd. - Rm.205, P.O. Box 750, Dutch Harbor, AK 99692. Phone: (907)581-4114.
- Eagle Port of Entry, c/o Postmaster -Box 1, Eagle, AK 99738. Phone: (907)547-2211.
- Fairbanks Port of Entry, 6450 Old Airport Way, Fairbanks, AK 99709. Phone: (907)474-0307.
- Gambell Port of Entry, P.O. Box 1, Gambell, AK 99742. Phone: (907)985-5211.
- Dalton's Cache Port of Entry, Haines Hwy. - Mile 40, Haines, AK 99827-1509. Phone: (907)767-5580.
- Ketchikan Port of Entry, 111 Main St., Ketchikan, AK 99840. Phone: (907)225-2380.
- Alaska Marine Hwy. Terminal, Prince Rupert, BC Canada, c/o 111 Main St., Ketchikan, AK 99840. Phone: (604)624-3833.
- Nome Port of Entry, P.O. Box 281, Nome, AK 99762. Phone: (907)443-2065.
- Skagaway Port of Entry, Klondike Hwy. Border Station, Skagaway, AK 99840-0475. Phone: (907)983-3144.
- Turner Port of Entry, P.O. Box 1221, Tok, AK 99780. Phone: (907)774-2242.

Arizona—Ajo Border Patrol, 850 N. Tucson - Ajo Hwy. 86, P.O. Drawer J, Ajo/Highway, AZ 85321. Phone: (520)387-7002.
- Casa Grande Border Patrol, 396 Camino Mercado, Casa Grande, AZ 85222. Phone: (520)836-7812.
- Douglas Border Patrol, 1051 Lawrence St., P.O. Box 1175, Douglas, AZ 85608. Phone: (520)364-3991.
- Douglas Port of Entry, Pan American Ave. and 1st St., Douglas, AZ 85607. Phones: (520)364-5532, -6479.
- Eloy Processing Center, 4465 E. Hanna Rd. - Ste.343, Eloy, AZ 85231. Phone: (520)466-2000.
- Florence Processing Center, 3250 N. Pinal Pkwy. Ave., Florence, AZ 85232. Phone: (520)868-5862.
- Lukeville Port of Entry, Highway 85, P.O. Box D, Lukeville, AZ 85341. Phone: (520)387-6047.
- Naco Border Patrol, 2136 Naco Hwy., Bisbee, AZ 85603. Phone: (520)432-5121.
- Naco Port of Entry, 106 "D" St., P.O. Box 277, Naco, AZ 85620. Phones: (520)432-3111, -2791.
- Nogales Border Patrol, 1500 W. La Quinta Rd., Nogales, AZ 85621. Phone: (520)377-6000.
- Phoenix Border Patrol, 3006 W. Claredon Ave., Phoenix, AZ 85017. Phone: (520)670-6865.
- Phoenix Sky Harbor Airport, P.O. Box 63673, Phoenix, AZ 85082-2673. Phones: (602)275-7745, -7763, -7785.
- Phoenix District Office, 2035 N. Central Ave., Phoenix, AZ 85004-1548. Phone: (602)514-7799.
- San Luis Port of Entry, Hwy. 95, P.O. Box 448, San Luis, AZ 85349. Phone: (520)627-3591.

97.010
(cont.)

- Sasabe Port of Entry, Federal Inspection Bldg., Sasabe, AZ 85633-0326. Phone: (520)823-4230.
- Sonoita Border Patrol, Hwy. 82 and 83, Sonoita, AZ 85637-0037. Phone: (520)455-5051.
- Tucson Border Patrol, 2010 Ajo Way, Tucson, AZ 85713. Phone: (520)670-6865.
- Tucson Border Patrol Sector Hdqtrs., 1970 W. Ajo Way, Tucson, AZ 85713. Phones: (520)670-6871, -6880.
- Wellton Border Patrol, 29820 Frontage Rd., P.O. Box 128, Wellton, AZ 85356. Phone: (520)785-9364.
- Willcox Border Patrol, 200 W. Downen St., Willcox, AZ 85644-0909. Phone: (520)384-2412.
- Yuma Border Patrol, 12122 S. Ave. A, Yuma, AZ 85366-2708. Phone: (520)726-8731.
- Yuma Border Patrol Sector Hdqtrs., 350 W. 1st St., Yuma, AZ 85366-2708. Phone: (520)782-9548.

Bahamas—Freeport Bahamas Sub-Office, P.O. Box F-2664, Freeport, Grand Bahama, BAHAMAS. Phone:(242)352-5586.
- Nassau, Bahamas Sub-Office, U.S. Immigration, Miami, FL 33159-9009. Phone: (242)377-7125.

California—Bakersfield Processing Center, 17635 Industrial Farm Rd., P.O. Box 81143, Bakersfield, CA 93380. Phone: (805)861-4465.
- Bakersfield Satellite Investigations, 800 Truxton Ave. - Rm.317, Bakersfield, CA 93301. Phone: (805)861-4478.
- Western Form Center, Bldg. 701 - Bay A, 5600 Rickenbacker Rd., Bell, CA 90201. Phone: (213)526-7404.
- Blythe Border Patrol, 16870 W. Hobsonway, P.O. Box 836, Blythe, CA 92226. Phone: (619)922-6715.
- Boulevard Border Patrol, 39701 Avenue de Robles Verde, P.O. Box 1320, Boulevard, CA 92005. Phone: (619)766-4542.
- Calexico Port of Entry, 200 E. 1st St., P.O. Box 1780, Calexico, CA 92231. Phones: (619)357-1189, -7968, -1143.
- Calexico East Port of Entry, 1699 E. Carr Rd., Calexico, CA 92231. Phone: (619)768-2450.
- Oxnard Border Patrol, 275 Skyway Dr., P.O. Box 88, Camarillo, CA 93011. Phone: (805)482-8997.
- Campo Border Patrol, 3 Forest Gate Rd., P.O. Box 68, Campo, CA 91906. Phone: (619)557-6144.
- Livermore Border Patrol Station and Sector Hdqtrs., 6102 9th St., Dublin, CA 94568. Phones: (925)828-3770, (925)828-0371.
- El Cajon Border Patrol, 225 Kenney St., El Cajon, CA 92020. Phone: (619)557-5072.
- El Centro Processing Center, 1115 N. Imperial Ave., El Centro, CA 92243-1739. Phone: (619)353-2170.
- El Centro Border Patrol Sector Hdqtrs., 1111 N. Imperial Ave., El Centro, CA 92243-1795. Phone: (619)352-3241.
- El Centro Border Patrol Station, 1081 N. Imperial Ave., El Centro, CA 92243. Phone: (760)353-0541.
- Fresno Border Patrol Station, 4367 N. Golden State Blvd., Fresno, CA 93722. Phone: (209)487-5506.
- Fresno Sub-Office, 865 Fulton Mall, Fresno, CA 93721-2816. Phone: (209)487-5126.
- Imperial Beach Border Patrol, 1802 Saturn Way, Imperial Beach Beach, CA 91933-0068. Phone: (619)662-7149.
- Indio Border Patrol, 45-620 Commerce St., Indio, CA 92201. Phone: (760)347-3658.
- Western Operations Region, 24000 Avila Rd., P.O. Box 30080, Laguna Niguel, CA 92607-0080. Phone: (714)643-4236.

- Long Beach Seaport Unit, 501 W. Ocean Blvd. - Ste.6300, Long Beach, CA 90802. Phone: (310)980-3400.
- Los Angeles District Office, 300 N. Los Angeles St., Los Angeles, CA 90012. Phone: (213)894-4627.
- Los Angeles International Airport, Tom Bradley International Terminal - Lower Level, 380 Worldway, P.O. Box N-20, Los Angeles, CA 90045. Phones: (310)215-2104, ext.107; (310)215-2101, ext.103.
- Oakland International Airport, International Terminal, 1 Airport Dr., Oakland, CA 94621. Phone: (510)273-7390.
- Ontario Airport, 222 E. Airport Dr., Ontario, CA 91761. Phones: (909)395-8668, -8673.
- Riverside Border Patrol, 2060 Chicago Ave. - Ste.A2, Riverside, CA 92507. Phone: (909)686-4100.
- Sacramento Border Patrol Station, Bldg. 500 - Ste.575, 7000 Franklin Blvd., Sacramento, CA 95823. Phone: (916)391-9087.
- Sacramento Sub-Office, 650 Capital Mall, Sacramento, CA 95814. Phone: (916)498-6460.
- Salinas Border Patrol, 1636 E. Alisal St., P.O. Box 218, Salinas, CA 93902. Phone: (408)754-0633.
- San Clemente Border Patrol, I-5 Northbound Traffic Checkpoint, P.O. Box 3188, San Clemente, CA 92674. Phone: (619)557-5272.
- San Diego District Office, 880 Front St. - Ste.1234, San Diego, CA 92101-8834. Phone: (619)557-5645.
- Brown Field Border Patrol, 7560 Britannia St., San Diego, CA 92173. Phone: (619)661-3154.
- Ota Mesa Port of Entry, 2500 Paseo International, San Diego, CA 92143-9018. Phones: (619)661-3249, -3231.
- San Diego International Airport, Lindbergh Field Airport, 3665 N. Harbor Dr., San Diego, CA 92101. Phone: (619)298-2612.
- San Ysidro Port of Entry, 720 San Ysidro Blvd., San Diego, CA 92143-9018. Phones: (619)662-7314, -7240.
- San Francisco International Airport, Central Terminal - Lower Level, Customs Area, P.O. Box 280551, San Francisco, CA 94128. Phone: (415)876-2876.
- San Francisco District Office, 630 Sansome St., San Francisco, CA 94111-2280. Phone: (415)705-3102.
- San Jose International Airport, c/o P.O. Box 280551, Central Terminal - Lower Level, Customs Area, San Jose, CA 95110. Phone: (408)291-7209.
- San Jose Sub-Office, 280 S. 1st St. - Rm.1150, San Jose, CA 95113. Phone: (408)535-5174.
- San Luis Obispo Border Patrol Station, 1170 Calle Joaquin, P.O. Box 1486, San Luis Obispo, CA 93406. Phone: (805)543-9490.
- San Marcos Border Patrol, 126 S. Pacific, P.O. Box 5099, San Marcos, CA 92069. Phone: (619)557-5589.
- San Pedro Processing Center, Terminal Island, 2001 Seaside Ave., San Pedro, CA 90731. Phone: (310)732-0777.
- Stockton Border Patrol, P.O. Box 2047, Stockton, CA 95201. Phones: (209)946-6211, -6284.
- Tecate Port of Entry, Tecate, CA 92080-0219. Phone: (619)478-5029.
- Temecula Border Patrol, 43136 Rancho Way, P.O. Box 38, Temecula, CA 92593. Phone: (909)694-6871.
- Andrade Port of Entry, 235 Andrade Rd., Winterhaven, CA 92283. Phones: (619)572-5350, -5184.

Colorado—Denver District Office, Albrook Center, 4730 Paris St., Denver, CO 80239-2804. Phone: (303)371-6213.

97.010
(cont.)
- Grand Junction Port of Entry, 255 Main St., Grand Junction, CO 81501. Phone: (303)243-5141.
- Pueblo Port of Entry, P.O. Box 1879, Pueblo, CO 81002. Phone: (719)544-9369.

Connecticut—Hartford Sub-Office, Ribicoff Federal Bldg., 450 Main St., Hartford, CT 06103-3060. Phone: (203)240-3052.

District of Columbia—Dulles International Airport, P.O. Box 17775, Washington, DC 20041. Phone: (703)661-5100.
- INS Headquarters, 425 I St. NW, Washington, DC 20536. Phone: (202)514-4316.

Florida—Jacksonville Port of Entry, Federal Bldg - Rm.G-18, 400 W. Bay St., Jacksonville, FL 32202. Phone: (904)232-2164.
- Key West Port of Entry and Sub-Office, Federal Bldg. - Rm.201, 301 Simontown St., Key West, FL 33040. Phones: (305)293-9150, 296-2233. *For mail:* P.O. Box 86, Key West, FL 33041.
- Miami International Airport - Concourse E (3rd fl.), Miami, FL 33299-7895. Phones: (305)526-2612, -2626, -2851, -2930.
- Krome North Service Processing Center, Snapper Creek Station, 18201 SW 12th St., P.O. Box 160327, Miami, FL 33194. Phone: (305)552-1845.
- Miami District Office, 7880 Biscayne Blvd., Miami, FL 33138. Phone: (305)762-3405.
- Miami Border Patrol Sector Hdqtrs., 7201 Pembroke Rd., Pembroke Pines, FL 33023. Phone: (954)963-9807.
- West Palm Beach Port of Entry, 4 E. Port Rd. - Rm.410, Riviera Beach, FL 33419. Phone: (407)845-6898.
- West Palm Beach Sub-Office, 301 N. Broadway, Riviera Beach, FL 33404. Phone: (561)841-0498.
- Tampa Border Patrol, 1821B E. Sahlman Dr., Tampa, FL 33605. Phones: (813)228-2156, -2160.
- Orlando Border Patrol, Winter Park, FL 32790-0440. Phone: (407)648-6081.

Georgia—Atlanta District Office, 77 Forsyth St. SW, Atlanta, GA 30303-0253. Phone: (404)331-0253.
- Hartsfield International Airport Port of Entry, P.O. Box 45527, Atlanta, GA 30320. Phone: (404)763-7816.
- Savannah International Airport, 33 Bull St. - Ste.505, Savannah, GA 31401. Phone: (912)652-4460.

Guam—Guam International Airport, Sirena Plaza - Ste.100, 108 Hernan Cortez Ave., Agana, GU 96910. Phone: (671)642-7611.

Hawaii—Honolulu District Office, 595 Ala Moana Blvd., Honolulu, HI 96813. Phones: (808)532-3748, -3746.
- Honolulu International Airport, 300 Rodgers Blvd., Terminal Box 50, Honolulu, HI 96819. Phones: (808)861-8401, -8406, -8400, -8409.

Idaho—4620 Overland Rd. - Rm.108, Boise, ID 83705. Phone: (208)334-1822.
- Eastport Port of Entry, Hwy. 95, P.O. Box 8, Eastport, ID 83826. Phones: (208)267-2183, -3745.
- Porthill Port of Entry, P.O. Box 40, Porthill, ID 83853. Phone: (208)267-5309.

Illinois—Chicago District Office, 10 W. Jackson Blvd. - Ste.600, Chicago, IL 60604. Phone: (312)385-1900.

Indiana—Indianapolis Sub-Office, Gateway Plaza - Rm.400, 950 N. Meridan St., Indianapolis, IN 46204. Phone: (217)226-6181.

Kansas—Garden City Port of Entry, 1404 E. Fulton, Box 1239, Garden City, KS 67846. Phone: (316)275-1054.
- Wichita Port of Entry, 625 N. Winterset, Wichita, KS 67212. Phone: (316)945-9741.

FIELD OFFICE CONTACTS   859

Kentucky—Louisville Sub-Office, Snyder Courthouse - Rm.604, 601 W. Broadway, Louisville, KY 40202. Phone: (502)582-6526.

Louisiana—Baton Rouge Border Patrol, 9522 Brookline Dr., P.O. Box 338, Baton Rouge, LA 70821. Phone: (504)389-0231.

- New Orleans International Airport, 900 Airline Hwy., Kenner, LA 70062. Phone: (504)589-3949.
- Lake Charles Border Patrol, P.O. Box 868, Lake Charles, LA 70601. Phone: (318)477-9245.
- New Orleans District Office, Postal Services Bldg. - Rm.T-8011, 701 Loyola Ave., New Orleans, LA 70113. Phone: (504)589-6521.
- New Orleans Border Patrol Sector Hdqtrs., 3819 Patterson Dr., P.O. Box 6218, New Orleans, LA 70174. Phone: (504)589-6107.
- Oakdale Processing Center, 207 E. 5th Ave., P.O. Box 5095, Oakdale, LA 71463. Phone: (318)335-0713.

Maine—Bangor Port of Entry, 267A Godfrey Blvd., Bangor, ME 04402-0677. Phone: (207)945-0334.

- Bar Harbor Port of Entry, Marine Atlantic Ferry Terminal, Eden St., Bar Harbor, ME 04609. Phone: (207)288-4675.
- Bridgewater Port of Entry, RFD Rt. 1 - Box 42, Boundary Line Rd., Bridgewater, ME 04735. Phone: (207)425-4502.
- Calais Border Patrol, One Main St., P.O. Box 245, Calais, ME 04619. Phone: (207)454-3613.
- Calais Port of Entry, Border Inspection Station, One Main St. - P.O. Drawer 421, Calais, ME 04619. Phone: (207)454-2546.
- Coburn Gore Port of Entry, Star Rt. 73, P.O. Box 35, Eustis, ME 04936. Phone: (207)297-2771.
- Ft. Fairfield Border Patrol, 205 Main St., P.O. Box 410, Ft. Fairfield, ME 04742. Phone: (207)472-5041.
- Ft. Fairfield Port of Entry, Rural Rt. 1 - Box 217, Ft. Fairfield, ME 04742. Phone: (207)473-7396.
- Ft. Kent Port of Entry, 98 W. Main St., Ft. Kent, ME 04743-1016. Phone: (207)834-3223.
- Houlton Border Patrol Sector Hdqtrs. and Border Station, Rt. 1 - Calais Rd., P.O. Box 706, Houlton, ME 04730. Phones: (207)532-9061, -6521, -6522 (24 hours).
- Houlton Port of Entry, Interstate 95, P.O. Box 189, Houlton, ME 04730. Phone: (207)532-2906.
- Jackman Border Patrol, Nickels Rd., P.O. Box 608, Jackman, ME 04945. Phone: (207)668-3151 (24 hours).
- Jackman Port of Entry, Star Rt. 76 - Box 629, Jackman, ME 04945. Phone: (207)668-3771.
- Limestone Port of Entry, R.F.D. 1, Box 258, Limestone, ME 04750-9729. Phone: (207)325-4760.
- Lubec Port of Entry, Federal Bldg., U.S. Post Office and Border Station, Washington St. and Campobello Bridge, Lubec, ME 04652. Phone: (207)733-4960.
- Madawaska Port of Entry, 2 Bridge St., Madawaska, ME 04756-1230. Phone: (207)728-4565.
- Vanceboro Port of Entry, USINS, Water St., P.O. Box C, Vanceboro, ME 04491. Phone: (207)788-7813.
- Van Buren Port of Entry, International Bridge, Bridge St., P.O. Box 116, Van Buren, ME 04785. Phones: (207)868-2202, -3900.
- Van Buren Border Patrol, Main St., P.O. Box 26, Van Buren, ME 04785. Phone: (207)868-3900.
- Hamlin Port of Entry, H.C. 62 - Box 63, Van Buren, ME 04785. Phone: (207)868-0966.

97.010
(cont.)

Maryland—Baltimore District Office, Fallen Federal Bldg., 31 Hopkins Plaza, Baltimore, MD 21201. Phone: (410)962-2010.

Massachusetts—Boston District Office, Kennedy Federal Bldg. - Rm.1700, Government Center, Boston, MA 02203. Phone: (617)565-4214.

- Boston Service Processing Center, 427 Commercial St., Boston, MA 02109. Phones: (617)223-3090, -3089, -3088.

Michigan—Algonac Port of Entry, 202 Fruit St., Algonac, MI 48001. Phone: (810)794-3321.

- District/Canada Tunnel, 150 E. Jefferson Ave., Detroit, MI 48226. Phone: (313)568-6019.
- Detroit International Bridge, 3033 Porter, Detroit, MI 48216. Phone: (313)963-4408.
- Detroit City Airport, 11499 Conner - Rm.138C, Detroit, MI 48213. Phone: (313)521-8430.
- Grand Rapids Border Patrol, 100 W. 7th St., Holland, MI 49422-1678. Phone: (616)392-4070.
- Port Huron Border Patrol, 2112 River Rd., Marysville, MI 48040. Phone: (810)364-6041.
- Port Huron Port of Entry, 2321 Pinegrove Ave., Port Huron, MI 48060. Phone: (810)942-0493.
- Detroit Metro Airport, International Terminal, Romulus, MI 48242. Phone: (313)955-6293.
- Sault Ste. Marie Port of Entry and Border Patrol, International Bridge Plaza, P.O. Box 141, Sault Ste. Marie, MI 49783. Phones: (906)632-3383, -8822.
- Trenton Border Patrol, 23100 W. Rd., P.O. Box 206, Trenton, MI 48183. Phone: (313)676-2972.

Minnesota—Baudette Port of Entry, International Bridge, P.O. Box 487, Baudette, MN 56623. Phone: (218)634-2661.

- St. Paul District Office, 2901 Metro Dr. - Ste.100, Bloomington, MN 55425. Phone: (612)335-2211.
- Crane Lake Port of Entry, 7544 Gold Coast Rd., Crane Lake, MN 55725. Phone: (218)993-2321.
- Duluth Port of Entry and Border Patrol, U.S. Courthouse and Custom House, 114 Federal Bldg., 515 W. 1st St., Duluth, MN 55802. Phones: (218)720-5207, -5465.
- Ely Port of Entry, P.O. Box 28, Ely, MN 55731. Phone: (218)365-3262.
- Grand Marais Border Patrol, Hwy. 61 East - P.O. Box 685, Grand Marais, MN 55604. Phone: (218)387-1770.
- Grand Portage Port of Entry, Hwy. 61, Grand Portage, MN 55605. Phone: (218)475-2494.
- International Falls Border Patrol, 1412 Hwy. 11-71 West, International Falls, MN 56649. Phone: (218)283-2461.
- No.2 2nd Ave., International Falls, MN 56649-2328. Phone: (218)283-8611.
- Lancaster Port of Entry, Rt. 1 Box 138 - Hwy. 59, Lancaster, MN 56735. Phone: (218)762-4100.
- Noyes Port of Entry, Rural Rt. 1 - Box 110, Noyes, MN 56740. Phone: (218)823-6291.
- Pembina Border Patrol, Rural Rt. 1 - P.O. Box 106, Noyes, MN 56740. Phones: (218)823-6528, -6594.
- Pine Creek Port of Entry, Hwy. 89, Star Rt. 5, Roseau, MN 56751. Phone: (218)463-1952.
- Roseau Port of Entry, Rt. 1 Box 31 - Hwy. 310 N., Roseau, MN 56751. Phone: (218)463-2054.
- Warroad Port of Entry, H.C. 02, P.O. Box 245, Warroad, MN 56763. Phone: (218)386-1676.

FIELD OFFICE CONTACTS   861

- Warroad Border Patrol, P.O. Box 24, Hwy. 11, Warroad, MN 56763. Phone: (218) 386-1802.

Mississippi—Gulfport Border Patrol, P.O. Box 4273, Gulfport, MS 39502. Phone: (228)863-3582.

- Gulfport Port of Entry, P.O. Box 1120, Gulfport, MS 39501. Phone: (601)864-3029.

Missouri—Kansas City District Office, 9747 N. Conant Ave., Kansas City, MO 64153. Phone: (816)891-0864.

- St. Louis Sub-Office, Young Federal Bldg. - Rm.100, 1222 Spruce St., St. Louis, MO 63103-2815. Phone: (314)539-2516.
- St. Louis International Airport, Lambert Field, P.O. Box 10406, St. Louis, MO 63145. Phone: (314)425-7179.

Montana—Piegan Port of Entry, P.O. Box 109, Babb, MT 59411. Phone: (406)732-9297.

- Chief Mountain Port of Entry, P.O. Box 376, Chief Mountain, MT 59411 via Babb, MT 59411. Phone: (406)732-4576.
- Billings Border Patrol, 2601 1st Ave. N., P.O. Box 2298, Billings, MT 59103. Phone: (406)247-7563.
- Del Bonita Port of Entry, Del Bonita Star Rt., Cut Bank, MT 59427. Phone: (406) 336-2130.
- Eureka Border Patrol, Hwy. 93 (JB Shopping Center), P.O. Box 909, Eureka, MT 59917. Phone: (406)296-2938.
- Roosville Port of Entry, 8395 Hwy. 93 N., Eureka, MT 59917-9331. Phone: (406)889-3737.
- Havre Border Patrol Sector Hdqtrs., 2605 5th Ave. SE, P.O. Box 112, Havre, MT 59501. Phone: (406)265-6781.
- Wild Horse Port of Entry, Havre, MT 59501. Phone: (406)394-2371.
- Willow Creek Port of Entry, Simpson Rt., Havre, MT 59501. Phone: (406)398-5512.
- Havre Port of Entry, Simpson Rt., Willow Creek Station, Havre, MT 59501. Phone: (406)265-6781.
- Loring Port of Entry, Port of Morgan, HC82 - Box 9250, Loring, MT 59537-9600. Phone: (406)674-5248.
- Malta Border Patrol, P.O. Box 36, Malta, MT 59538. Phone: (406)654-2711.
- Opheim Port of Entry, P.O. Box 317, Opheim, MT 59250. Phone: (406)724-3212.
- Plentywood Border Patrol, P.O. Box 434, Plentywood, MT 59254. Phone: (406)765-1852.
- Raymond Border Patrol, P.O. Box 158, Raymond, MT 59256. Phone: (406)895-2620.
- Scobey Border Patrol, P.O. Box 820, Scobey, MT 59263. Phone: (406)487-2621.
- Scobey Port of Entry, P.O. Box 2300, Scobey, MT 59263. Phone: (406)783-5372.
- Shelby Border Patrol, 906 Oilfield Ave., P.O. Box 653, Shelby, MT 59474. Phone: (406)434-5588.
- Sweetgrass Port of Entry, P.O. Box 165 - Interstate 15, Sweetgrass, MT 59484. Phone: (406)335-2911.
- Whitetail Port of Entry, U.S. Border Inspection Station, P.O. Box 38, Whitetail, MT 59276. Phone: (406)779-3531.

Nebraska—Nebraska Service Center, 850 S. St., P.O. Box 82521, Lincoln, NE 68501-2521. Phone: (402)437-5464.

- Omaha District Office, 3736 S. 132nd St., Omaha, NE 68144. Phone: (402)697-9152.

Nevada—Boulder City Border Patrol, Boulder City, NV 89006-0928. Phone: (702)293-8507.

- Las Vegas Sub-Office, 3373 Pepper Lane, Las Vegas, NV 89120. Phone: (702)388-6640.
- Las Vegas Mecarren International Airport, 5757 Wayne Newton Blvd., Las Vegas, NV 89111. Phone: (702)388-6024.

97.010
(cont.)

- Reno Sub-Office, 1351 Corporate Blvd., Reno, NV 89502. Phone: (702)784-5186.

New Hampshire—Pittsburg Port of Entry, Rt. 3, P.O. Box 277, Pittsburg, NH 03592. Phone: (819)656-2261.

New Jersey—Newark District Office, Federal Bldg., 970 Broad St., Newark, NJ 07102. Phone: (201)645-2298.

- Newark International Airport, Terminal B (SAT 3), Newark, NJ 07114. Phone: (201)645-6589.

New Mexico—Alamagordo Border Patrol, 1997 Hwy. 54 S., Alamagordo, NM 88310-7377. Phone: (505)437-6960.

- Albuquerque Sub-Office, 517 Gold Ave. SW - Rm.1010, P.O. Box 567, Albuquerque, NM 87103. Phone: (505)248-7357.
- Columbus Port of Entry, Pershing Rd. - P.O. Box 307, Columbus, NM 88029. Phones: (505)531-2694, -2695, -2696.
- Deming Border Patrol, P.O. Box 230, Deming, NM 88031. Phone: (505)546-9036.
- Las Cruces Border Patrol, 3120 N. Main, Las Cruces, NM 88001. Phone: (505)527-6895.
- Las Cruces Patrol Training Center, 2320 Temple St., Las Cruces, NM 88001. Phone: (505)524-4730.
- Lordsburg Border Patrol, 441 Duncan Hwy., P.O. Box 459, Lordsburg, NM 88045. Phone: (505)542-3221.
- Truth or Consequences Border Patrol, P.O. Box 3310, Truth or Consequences, NM 87901. Phone: (505)744-5235.

New York—Albany Sub-Office, U.S. Post Office and Customhouse - Rm.220, 445 Broadway, Albany, NY 12207. Phone: (518)431-0339.

- Thousand Island Bridge and Cape Vincent Ports of Entry, 46735 U.S. Interstate Rt. 81, Alexandria Bay, NY 13607-9796. Phones: (315)482-2681, -2065, 654-2781, ext.8.
- Buffalo District Office, 130 Delaware Ave., Buffalo, NY 14202. Phone: (716)846-4741.
- Burke Border Patrol, Burke, NY 12917-0125. Phone: (518)483-5941.
- Champlain Port of Entry, Border Inspection Station, 234 W. Service Rd., Champlain, NY 12919. Phones: (518)298-3221, -8433, -2526.
- Champlain Border Patrol, P.O. Box 1228, Ridge Rd., Champlain, NY 12919. Phone: (518)298-2531.
- Chateaugay Port of Entry, Border Inspection Station, Star Rt. 374, Chateaugay, NY 12920. Phone: (518)497-6772.
- Trout River Port of Entry, Trout River, State Rt. 30, Via Constable, NY 12926. Phone: (518)483-5021.
- Ft. Covington Port of Entry, Border Inspection Station, Water St., Ft. Covington, NY 12937. Phone: (518)358-2231.
- Fulton Border Patrol Station, 215 S. 1st St. - Rm.228, Fulton, NY 13069-0070. Phone: (315)598-8510.
- Office of Inspector General, JFK Airport Station, P.O. Box 999, Jamaica, NY 11430. Phone: (718)553-7520.
- JFK International Airport, Bldg. 50 - International Arrivals, Jamaica, NY 11430. Phones: (718)553-1688, -1689.
- Lewiston Port of Entry, 1 Lewiston Queenston Bridge, Lewiston, NY 14092-1980. Phone: (716)285-1676.
- Mooers Port of Entry, Border Inspection Station, State Rt. 22, Mooers, NY 12958. Phone: (518)236-7116.
- New York District Office, 26 Federal Plaza, New York, NY 10278. Phone: (212)264-3911.

Field Office Contacts 863

- Service Processing Center, 201 Varrick St. - 4th fl., New York, NY 10014. Phone: (212)620-3441.
- Niagara Falls Port of Entry, Rainbow Bridge, Niagara Falls, NY 14303. Phone: (716)282-3141.
- Niagara Falls Border Patrol, 1708 Lafayette Ave., Niagara Falls, NY 14305-0281. Phone: (716)285-6444.
- Ogdensburg Border Patrol, 127 N. Water St., Ogdensburg, NY 13669. Phones: (315)393-1150, -0100.
- Massena Port of Entry, P.O. Box 195, Roosevelt, NY 13683. Phones: (315)764-0310, -0677.
- Rouse Point Port of Entry, U.S. Rt. 9B, Rouse Point, NY 12979. Phone: (518)297-7521.
- Buffalo Border Patrol Sector Hdqtrs., 231 Grand Island Blvd., Tonawanda, NY 14150-6502. Phone: (716)551-4101.
- Watertown Border Patrol, Post Office Bldg., 153 Arsenal St., Watertown, NY 13601-0280. Phone: (315)482-7556.

North Carolina—Charlotte Sub-Office, 6 Woodlawn Green - Rm.138, Charlotte, NC 28217. Phone: (704)344-6313.

- Raleigh-Durham International Port of Entry, P.O. Box 80216, Raleigh, NC 27623. Phone: (919)840-5577.
- Wilmington Port of Entry, Lennon Federal Bldg. - Rm.105, 2 Princess St., Wilmington, NC 28401. Phone: (910)343-4876.

North Dakota—Ambrose Port of Entry, State Hwy 42, Rt. HC-1 - Box 202, Ambrose, ND 58833. Phone: (701)982-3211.

- Antler Port of Entry, Rural Rt. 1 - Box 7, Antler, ND 58711. Phone: (701)267-3321.
- Bottineau Border Patrol, P.O. Box 6, Bottineau, ND 58318. Phone: (701)228-3179.
- Carbury Port of Entry, Rural Rt. 1 - Souris, ND, Carbury, ND 58783. Phone: (701)228-2540.
- Dunseith Port of Entry, Rural Rt. 1 - Box 117, Dunseith, ND 58329. Phones: (701)263-4513, -4460.
- Northgate Port of Entry, Flaxton, ND 58737. Phone: (701)596-3805.
- Fortuna Port of Entry, Hwy. 85N - P.O. Box 37, Fortuna, ND 58844. Phone: (701)834-2493.
- Grand Forks Border Patrol Sector Hdqtrs., 2320 S. Washington St., Grand Forks, ND 52801. Phone: (701)775-6259. *For mail:* P.O. Box 12669, Grand Forks, ND 58208-2669.
- Grand Forks International Airport, Rural Rt. 2 - Box 72, 2787 Airport Dr., Hwy. 2 W., Grand Forks, ND 58203. Phone: (701)772-3301.
- Hannah Port of Entry, Hannah, ND 58239. Phone: (701)283-5271.
- Hansboro Port of Entry, Box 237, Hansboro, ND 58339. Phone: (701)266-5633.
- Maida Port of Entry, Hwy. 1, Maida, ND 58255. Phone: (701)256-5087.
- Neche Port of Entry, Hwy. 18, Neche, ND 58265. Phone: (701)886-7744.
- Noonan Port of Entry, Noonan, ND 58765. Phone: (701)926-5615.
- Pembina Port Of Entry, Rural Rt. 1 - P.O. Box 110, Noyes, Pembina, ND 58271. Phone: (701)825-6722.
- Portal Border Patrol, P.O. Box 298, Portal, ND 58772. Phone: (701)926-4111.
- Portal Port of Entry, P.O. Box 8, Portal, ND 58772. Phone: (701)926-4221.
- Sherwood Port of Entry, Rural Rt. 2 - Box 1D, Sherwood, ND 58782. Phone: (701)459-2250.
- St. John Port of Entry, Box 15 - Rt. 1, St. John, ND 58369. Phone: (701)447-3140.
- Sarles Port of Entry, P.O. Box 67 - Rt. 1, 6 miles from Village of Sarles, ND 58372. Phone: (701)697-5177.

97.010
(cont.)

- Walhalla Port of Entry, Rural Rt. 2 - Box 145, Walhalla, ND 58282-9459. Phone: (701)549-3233.

Ohio—Cleveland District Office, Celebreeze Federal Bldg. - Rm.1917, 1240 E. 9th St., Cleveland, OH 44199. Phone: (216)522-4766.

- Toledo Port of Entry, Federal Office Bldg. - Rm.713, 234 Summit St., Toledo, OH 43604-1536. Phone: (419)259-6474.

Oklahoma—Oklahoma Sub-Office, 4149 Highline Blvd. - Ste.300, Oklahoma City, OK 73108. Phone: (405)231-5928.

Oregon—Astoria Port of Entry, P.O. Box 236, Astoria, OR 97103. Phone: (503)325-3054.

- Coos Bay Port of Entry, P.O. Box 209, Coos Bay, OR 97420. Phone: (503)242-4785.
- Portland District Office, 511 NW Broadway, Portland, OR 97209. Phone: (503)326-3962.
- Portland International Airport, P.O. Box 55067, Portland, OR 97238-5067. Phone: (503)326-3409.
- Roseburg Border Patrol, 1036 SE Douglas, P.O. Box 1728, Roseburg, OR 97470. Phone: (503)440-4518.

Pennsylvania—Philadelphia District Office, 1600 Callowhill St., Philadelphia, PA 19130. Phone: (215)656-7150.

- Pittsburg Sub-Office, 2130 Federal Bldg., 1000 Liberty Ave., Pittsburgh, PA 15222. Phone; (412)385-4457.

Puerto Rico—Aquadilla Service Processing Center, P.O. Box 250480, Aquadilla, PR 00604-0408. Phones: (787)882-3565, -3567, -3568.

- Deferred Inspections, U.S. Federal Bldg. - Rm.380, Chardon St., Hato Rey, PR 00918. Phone: (809)766-5000.
- District Director's Office, New Federal Bldg. - 3rd fl., Carlos Chardon St., Hato Rey, PR 00918. Phone: (no number provided).
- San Juan International Airport, P.O. Box 37900, Isle Verde, PR 00937-0900. Phone: (809)253-4525.
- Mayaguez Port of Entry, Marina Station, Mayaguez, PR 00709-2990. Phone: (809) 831-3440.
- Ponce Port of Entry, Playa Station, P.O. Box 173, Ponce, PR 00734-3173. Phone: (809)843-3220.
- San Juan District Office, P.O. Box 365068, San Juan, PR 00936. Phone: (787)766-5514.

Rhode Island—Providence Sub-Office, 200 Dyer St., Providence, RI 02903-3993. Phones: (401)528-5528, -5323.

South Carolina—Charleston Port of Entry, Federal Bldg. - Rm.110, 334 Meeting St., Charleston, SC 29403. Phone: (803)727-4421.

Tennessee—Memphis Sub-Office, 245 Wagner Place - Ste.250, Memphis, TN 38103-3815. Phone: (901)544-4108.

Texas—Abilene Border Patrol, 555 Walnut St., Abilene, TX 79604-3076. Phone: (915)673-3010.

- Alpine Border Patrol, P.O. Box 958, Alpine, TX 79831. Phone: (915)837-3550.
- Amarillo Border Patrol, P.O. Box 2287, Amarillo, TX 79105. Phone: (806)324-2278.
- Austin Sub-Office, 3708 S. 2nd St., P.O. Box 6496, Austin, TX 78704. Phones: (512)482-7901, -7904.
- Big Bend Park Border Patrol, P.O. Box 67, Big Bend, TX 79834. Phone: (915)477-2287.
- Brackettville Border Patrol, 802 W. Spring St., P.O. Box 216, Brackettville, TX 78832. Phone: (830)563-2477.
- Brownsville Port of Entry, 1500 E. Elizabeth St. - Rm.203, Brownsville, TX 78520. Phone: (210)546-1675.

FIELD OFFICE CONTACTS 865

- Brownsville International Airport, Brownsville, TX 78520. Phone: (210)542-8296.
- Brownsville Border Patrol, P.O. Box 5076, Brownsville, TX 78520. Phone: (956)542-3585.
- Carrizo Springs Border Patrol, Hwy. 85 E., P.O. Box 194, Carrizo Springs, TX 78834. Phone: (830)876-3557.
- Corpus Christi Border Patrol, 6809 Leopard St., P.O. Box 10344, Corpus Christi, TX 78460-0344. Phone: (512)289-0552.
- Comstock Border Patrol, Hwy. 85 E. - P.O. Box 700, Comstock, TX 78837. Phones: (915)292-4450, -4680.
- Cotulla Border Patrol, 692 N. Main, Cotulla, TX 78014. Phone: (830)879-3051.
- Dallas District Office, 8101 N. Stemmons Freeway, Dallas, TX 75247. Phone: (214)655-3011.
- Dallas/Ft. Worth Port of Entry, P.O. Box 610365, Dallas-Ft. Worth, TX 75261. Phone: (214)574-2141.
- Del Rio Border Patrol Sector Hdqtrs. and Border Station, Qualia Dr., Del Rio, TX 78841-2020. Phone: (210)703-2100.
- Amistad Dam Port of Entry, Del Rio, TX 78841-4060. Phone: (210)775-7213.
- Eagle Pass Port of Entry, International Bridge, P.O. Box 4280, Eagle Pass, TX 78852. Phones: (210)773-9205, -9206.
- El Paso District Office, 1545 Hawkins - Ste.167, El Paso, TX 79925. Phones: (915)540-1700, -1701.
- Processing Center, 8915 Montana Ave., El Paso, TX 79925. Phone: (915)225-1941.
- Office of Inspector General, 3 Butterfield Trail Blvd. - Ste.120, El Paso, TX 79906. Phone: (915)534-7370.
- El Paso Border Patrol Sector Hdqtrs., 8901 Montana Ave., P.O. Box 9578, El Paso, TX 79986. Phone: (915)834-8350.
- Intelligence Center, 11339 SSG Sims St., El Paso, TX 79908-8098. Phone: (915)760-2031.
- El Paso Port of Entry, Paso Del Norte Bridge, El Paso, TX 79901. Phone: (915)534-6767.
- Dallas Border Patrol, 2800 S. Pipeline Rd., Euless, TX 76040. Phone: (817)540-0150.
- Fabens Border Patrol and Port of Entry, 802 E. Main, P.O. Box 908, Fabens, TX 79838. Phones: (915)764-2417, -2419.
- Falfurrias Border Patrol, P.O. Box 479, Falfurrias, TX 78355. Phone: (512)325-5616.
- Ft. Hancock Border Patrol, P.O. Box 218, Ft. Hancock, TX 79839. Phone: (915)769-3978.
- Ft. Hancock Port of Entry, P.O. Box 235, Ft. Hancock, TX 79839. Phone: (915)769-3810.
- Ft. Stockton Border Patrol, P.O. Box 607, Ft. Stockton, TX 79735. Phone: (915)336-2468.
- Freer Border Patrol, P.O. Box "W", Freer, TX 78357. Phone: (512)394-7613.
- Galveston Port of Entry, P.O. Box 388, Galveston, TX 77550. Phone: (409)766-3581.
- Harlingen District Office, 2102 Teege Rd., Harlingen, TX 78550. Phone: (210)427-8691.
- Harlingen Border Patrol, 901 Rangerville Rd., P.O. Box 642, Harlingen, TX 78551. Phone: (956)427-8511.
- Hebbronville Border Patrol, 802 N. Sigrid St., Hebbronville, TX 78361. Phone: (512)527-3256.
- Pharr Port of Entry, 99105 Cage Blvd. - Ste.C, Pharr, TX 78557-9723. Phones: (956)783-4739, -4758.
- Hidalgo Port of Entry, International Bridge, Hidalgo, TX 78557-3019. Phones: (210)843-2201, -2202.

97.010
(cont.)

- Houston Intercontinental Airport, P.O. Box 60457, Houston, TX 77205. Phone: (713)233-3700.
- Kingsville Border Patrol, Navel Air Station - Bldg.3731, Kingsville, TX 78363. Phone: (512)592-3284.
- Laredo Border Patrol Sector Hdqtrs., 207 W. Del Mar Blvd., Laredo, TX 78041. Phone: (956)723-4367.
- Laredo South Border Patrol Station, Rural Rt. 3 - P.O. Box USBP-SLS/L, Laredo, TX 78043. Phone: (210)727-0644.
- Administrative Offices - Bldg. 2, 700 Zaragoza St., P.O. Box 179, Laredo, TX 78042-0179. Phone: (210)722-3283.
- Juarez-Lincoln International Bridge 2, Bldg. 3 - 700 Zaragoza St., Laredo, TX 78042. Phone: (512)722-5440.
- Gateway to the Americas International Bridge 1, 100 Convent St., Laredo, TX 78040. Phone: (210)722-2484.
- Llano Border Patrol, 211 E. Tarrant, P.O. Box 134, Llano, TX 78643. Phone: (915)247-4912.
- Los Ebanos Port of Entry, International Ferry, P.O. Box 399, Los Ebanos, TX 78565. Phone: (512)485-2721.
- Port Isabel Service Processing Center, Rt. 3 - Box 341, Los Fresnos, TX 78566. Phone: (210)548-2530.
- Port Isabel Border Patrol, Rt. 3 - Box 340, Los Fresnos, TX 78566. Phone: (956)233-9554.
- Port Isabel Port of Entry, Alien Processing Center (PIC), Rt. 3 - Box 341, Buena Vista Rd., Los Fresnos, TX 78566. Phone: (210)233-4431.
- Lubbock Border Patrol, 1205 Texas Ave., P.O. Box 1632, Lubbock, TX 79408. Phone: (806)742-7355.
- Marfa Border Patrol Sector Hdqtrs., 300 Madrid St., P.O. Box 1, Marfa, TX 79843. Phone: (915)729-4353.
- McAllen Border Patrol Sector Hdqtrs., 2301 S. Main St., McAllen, TX 78503. Phone: (210)686-5496. *For mail:* P.O. Box 1179, McAllen, TX 78502.
- McAllen Border Patrol, 4201 W. Military Hwy., McAllen, TX 78503. Phone: (210) 618-8163.
- Mercedes Border Patrol, 623 International Blvd., P.O. Box 125, Mercedes, TX 78570. Phone: (956)968-0602.
- Midland Border Patrol Station, P.O. Box 60405, Midland, TX 79711. Phone: (915) 561-8911.
- Presidio Border Patrol, P.O. Box 929, Presidio, TX 79845. Phone: (915)229-3330.
- Presidio Port of Entry, International Bridge, P.O. Box 937, Presidio, TX 79845. Phones: (915)229-3265, -3663.
- Port Arthur Port of Entry, 4550 Jimmy Johnson Blvd. - Ste.3, Port Arthur, TX 77642. Phone: (409)727-3375.
- Port Arthur Port of Entry, 2875 75th St. - Rm.106, Port Arthur, TX 77640. Phone: (409)727-3375.
- Rio Grande City Border Patrol, 2230 E. Highway, P.O. Box 481, Rio Grande City, TX 78582. Phone: (956)487-2700.
- Rocksprings Border Patrol, 404 W. Austin, P.O. Box 576, Rocksprings, TX 78880. Phone: (830)683-2255.
- Falcon Heights Port of Entry, International Dam, P.O. Box 278, Roma, TX 78584. Phone: (210)848-5221.
- Rio Grande City Port of Entry, International Bridge, P.O. Box 278, Roma, TX 78584. Phones: (210)487-2200, 849-1676.
- San Angelo Border Patrol, P.O. Box 61106, San Angelo, TX 76906. Phone: (915)949-0139.

FIELD OFFICE CONTACTS   867

- San Antonio District Office, 8940 Four Winds Dr., San Antonio, TX 78239. Phone: (210)967-7109.
- San Antonio Border Patrol, 5000 N. Industrial Dr., San Antonio, TX 78268. Phone: (210)521-7926.
- San Antonio International Airport, 9800 Airport Blvd., Terminal 1, San Antonio, TX 78216. Phone: (210)826-6261.
- Sanderson Border Patrol, P.O. Box 628, Sanderson, TX 78268. Phone: (915)345-2972.
- Uvalde Border Patrol, Industrial Park #30, Uvalde, TX 78801. Phone: (830)278-7133.
- Van Horn Border Patrol, 700 NW Access Rd., P.O. Box 368, Van Horn, TX 79854. Phone: (915)283-2795.
- Progreso Port of Entry, International Bridge Rt. 2, Box 600, Westlaco, TX 78596. Phone: (210)565-6304.
- Zapata Border Patrol, Lot C-2015, U.S. Hwy. 83 S., Zapata, TX 78076-0685. Phone: (210)765-6395

Utah—5272 S. College Dr. - Ste.100, Salt Lake City, UT 84123. Phone: (801)265-8807.

Vermont—Alburg Springs Port of Entry, Rural Rt. 2, Alburg, VT 05440. Phone: (802)796-3704.

- Alburg Port of Entry, U.S. Border Station, State Rt. 225, Alburg, VT 05440. Phone: (802)796-3703.
- Beebe Plain Port of Entry, Beebe Plain, VT 05823. Phone: (802)873-3151.
- Beecher Falls Border Patrol, P.O. Box 215, Beecher Falls, VT 05902. Phones: (802)266-3035 (24 hours).
- Beecher Falls Port of Entry, Border Inspection, Route 102, Beecher Falls VT 05902. Phone: (802)266-3320.
- Canaan Port of Entry, Border Inspection Station, State Rt. 114, P.O. Box 129, Canaan, VT 05903. Phone: (802)266-8994.
- Derby Line Port of Entry, Rt. 91 - P.O. Box 367, Derby Line, VT 05830. Phone: (802)873-3316.
- East Richford Port of Entry, RFD 1 - P.O. Box 1690, East Richford, VT 05476. Phone: (802)848-3001.
- West Berkshire Port of Entry, RFD 1 - Box 1110, Enosburg Falls, VT 05450. Phone: (802)933-2301.
- Morses Line Port of Entry, RFD 1, Morses Line, VT 05457. Phone: (802)285-2214.
- Newport Border Patrol, P.O. Box 815, Newport, VT 05855. Phone: (802)334-6722.
- North Troy Port of Entry, State Rt. 105, North Troy, VT 05859. Phone: (802)988-2633.
- Norton Port of Entry, Border Inspection Station, State Rt. 114, P.O. Box 117, Norton, VT 05907. Phone: (802)822-5222.
- Richford Border Patrol, Main St., P.O. Box 67, Richford, VT 05476. Phone: (802)848-7713.
- Pinnacle Port of Entry, R.D. 1 - Box 300, Richford, VT 05476. Phone: (802)848-3319.
- Richford Port of Entry, Border Inspection Station, RFD 1 - Box 40, Richford, VT 05476. Phone: (802)848-7766.
- Eastern Region Operations and Administrative Center, 70 Kimball Ave., South Burlington, VT 05403-6813. Phones: (802)660-5000, 660-1111.
- St. Albans Sub-Office, Federal Bldg., P.O. Box 328, St. Albans, VT 05478. Phone: (802)527-3191.
- Eastern Service Center, 75 Lower Welden St., St. Albans, VT 05479-0001. Phone: (802)527-3100.
- Swanton Border Patrol Sector Hdqtrs., Grand Ave., P.O. Box 705, Swanton, VT 05488. Phone: (802)868-3361.

97.010
(cont.)

- Highgate Springs Port of Entry, Border Inspection Station, U.S. Rt. 7, RFD Swanton, VT 05488. Phone: (802)868-3349.
- Swanton Border Patrol Station, Rt. 78 - P.O. Box 209, Swanton, VT 05488. Phones: (802)868-3229, -3320 (24 hours).
- Eastern Form Center, Williston, VT 05495-0567. Phone: (802)951-6225.

Virgin Islands—Charlotte Amalie, St. Thomas, VI Sub-Office, Nisky Center - 1st fl.(Ste.1A), Charlotte Amalie, St. Thomas, VI 00801. Phone: (809)774-1390.

- Christiansted St. Croix Port of Entry, P.O. Box 1270 Kingshill, Christiansted, St. Croix, VI 00851. Phones: (809)778-6559, -6300.
- Cruz Bay Port of Entry, P.O. Box 450, Cruz Bay, St. John, VI 00831. Phone: (340)776-6390.

Virginia—Washington District Office, 4420 N. Fairfax Dr., Arlington, VA 22203. Phone: (202)307-1504.

- Norfolk Sub-Office, Norfolk Federal Bldg. - Rm.439, 200 Granby Mall, Norfolk, VA 23510-1882. Phone: (804)441-3095.

Washington—Bellingham Border Patrol, 2745 McLeod Rd., Bellingham, WA 98225. Phone: (360)733-8420. *For mail:*P.O. Box 31428, Bellingham, WA 98228-3428.

- Bellingham Border Port of Entry, 104 W. Magnolia and Cornall St. - Rm.207, P.O. Box 2055, Bellingham, WA 98227. Phones: (360)676-8411 (downtown), 734-3520 (airport).
- Blaine Border Patrol Sector Hdqtrs., 1590 H St., P.O. Box 3529, Blaine, WA 98231. Phones: (360)332-7707, -7919.
- Blaine Border Patrol, 1580 H St., P.O. Box 3529, Blaine, WA 98231. Phone: (360)332-4205.
- Pacific Hwy. Port of Entry, 9950 Pacific Hwy., Blaine, WA 98230. Phones: (360)332-6091, -7237.
- Blaine Port of Entry, Peace Arch POE, 100 Peace Portal Dr., Blaine, WA 98230. Phone: (360)332-8511.
- Colville Border Patrol, 209 E. Juniper Ave., P.O. Box 146, Colville, WA 99114. Phone: (509)684-6272.
- Boundary Port of Entry, 5338 N. Port Juanita Rd., Colville, WA 99114. Phone: (509)732-4470.
- Ferry Port of Entry, 3559 Toroda Customs Bridge Rd., Curlew, WA 99118-9715. Phone: (509)779-4655 (Customs).
- Danville Port of Entry, 19130 N. Highway 21, Danville, WA 99121-9704. Phone: (509)779-4860.
- Friday Harbor Port of Entry, Staffed by Customs, 202 Front St. N., P.O. Box 1907, Friday Harbor, WA 98250. Phone: (206)378-2080.
- Laurier Port of Entry, Hwy. 395 - P.O. Box 40, Laurier, WA 99146. Phone: (509)684-2100.
- Longview Port of Entry, P.O. Box 1027, Longview, WA 98632. Phone: (206)423-5550.
- Nighthawk Port of Entry, Star Rt., Loomis, WA 98827. Phone: (509)476-2125.
- Lynden Border Patrol, 8334 Guide Meridian Rd., P.O. Box 708, Lynden, WA 98264. Phone: (360)354-4118.
- Lynden Port of Entry, 9949 Guide Meridian Rd., Lynden, WA 98264. Phone: (206) 354-6661.
- Metaline Falls Port of Entry, P.O. Box 631, Metaline Falls, WA 99153. Phone: (509)446-2572.
- Frontier Port of Entry, 4939 Hwy. 25 N., Northport, WA 99157. Phone: (509)732-4418.
- Oroville Port of Entry, Rt. 1 - Box 130, Oroville, WA 98844. Phones: (509)476-2454, -3132.

FIELD OFFICE CONTACTS   869

- Oroville Border Patrol, 1105 Main St., P.O. Box 99, Oroville, WA 98844-9726. Phone: (509)476-3622.
- Vancouver-BC Canada, Point Roberts, WA 98281-0450. Phones: (604)278-3360, -3986, -2520.
- Port Angeles Border Patrol, 138 W. 1st St., Port Angeles, WA 98362. Phone: (360)452-5970.
- Port Townsend Port of Entry, Staffed by Customs, 1322 Washington, P.O. Box 951, Port Townsend, WA 98368-0004. Phone: (360)385-3777.
- Seattle District Office and Sea Inspections, 815 Airport Way S., Seattle, WA 98134. Phones: (206)553-1246, -0070.
- Seattle-Tacoma International Airport, S. 178 and Pacific Hwy., Seattle, WA 98158. Phones: (206)553-0466, -2299.
- Spokane Airport and Sub-Office, 691 U.S. Courthouse Bldg., Spokane, WA 99201. Phones: (509)353-2761, -4699.
- Spokane Border Patrol, N. 10710 Newport Hwy., Spokane, WA 99218. Phone: (no number provided).
- Sumas Port of Entry, 109 Cherry St., P.O. Box 99, Sumas, WA 98295. Phone: (360)988-4781.
- Tacoma Port of Entry, 3600 Port Tacoma Rd. - Ste.303, P.O. Box 1296, Tacoma, WA 98401. Phone: (206)922-0848.
- Wenatchee Border Patrol, McQuaig Bldg., 93 Eastmont, P.O. Box 1825, Wenatchee, WA 98807. Phone: (509)884-8893.
- Yakima Port of Entry, 417 E. Chestnut, P.O. Box 49, Yakima, WA 98907. Phone: (509)575-5944.

Wisconsin—Federal Bldg. - Rm.186, 517 E. Wisconsin Ave., Milwaukee, WI 53202. Phone: (414)297-3161.

U.S. COAST GUARD

97.011   DISTRICT OFFICES

ATLANTIC *(Alabama, Arkansas, Colorado, Connecticut, Delaware, District of Columbia, Florida, Georgia, Illinois, Indiana, Iowa, Kansas, Kentucky, Louisiana, Maine, Maryland, Massachusetts, Michigan, Minnesota, Mississippi, Missouri, Nebraska, New Hampshire, New Jersey, New Mexico, New York, North Carolina, North Dakota, Ohio, Oklahoma, Panama Canal Zone, Pennsylvania, Puerto Rico, Rhode Island, South Carolina, South Dakota, Tennessee, Texas, Vermont, Virgin Islands, Virginia, West Virginia, Wisconsin, Wyoming)*—Commander (md), Maintenance and Logistics Command (Atlantic), 300 E. Main St. - Ste.800, Norfolk, VA 23510. Phone: (757)628-4280.

PACIFIC *(Alaska, Arizona, California, Hawaii, Idaho, Montana, Nevada, Oregon, U.S. Pacific Island Possessions, Utah, Washington)*—Commander (md), Maintenance and Logistics Command (Pacific), Coast Guard Island, Bldg. 52, Alameda, CA 94501-5100. Phone: (510)437-3474.

97.014   District Bridge Administrator:

First Coast Guard District (obr), 408 Atlantic Ave., Boston, MA 02210-2209. Phones: (617)223-8364; FAX (617)223-8026.

- Battery Park Bldg. (obr), New York, NY 10004-5073. Phones: (212)668-7165; FAX (212)668-7967.

Western River Directorate (obr), 1222 Spruce St., St. Louis, MO 63103-2398. Phones: (314)539-3900; FAX (314)539-3755.

Fifth Coast Guard District (Aowb), Federal Bldg., 431 Crawford St., Portsmouth, VA 23704-5004. Phones: (757)398-6557; FAX (757)398-6334.

97.014 Seventh Coast District (oan), Brickell Plaza, 909 SE 1st Ave., Miami, FL 33130-3050.
(cont.) Phones: (305)415-6743; FAX (305)415-6757.

Eighth Coast Guard District (obc), Boggs Federal Bldg., 501 Magazine St., New Orleans, LA 70130-3396. Phones: (504)589-2965; FAX (504)589-3063.

Ninth Coast Guard District (obr), 1240 E. 9th St., Cleveland, OH 44199-2060. Phones: (216)902-6085; FAX (216)902-6088.

Eleventh Coast Guard District (oan-2), Bldg. 10 - Rm.50-6, Alameda, CA 94501-5100. Phones: (510)437-3514: FAX (510)437-5836.

Thirteenth Coast Guard District (ob), Federal Bldg., 915 2nd Ave., Seattle, WA 98174-1067. Phones: (206)220-7270; FAX (206)220-7285.

Fourteenth Coast Guard District (oan), Federal Bldg. - Rm.9139, 300 Ala Moana Blvd., Honolulu, HI 96850-4982. Phones: (808)541-2315; FAX (808)541-2318.

Seventeenth Coast Guard District (oan), Juneau, AK 99802-5517. Phones: (907)463-2268; FAX (907)463-2273.

UNITED STATES SECRET SERVICE

97.015 *Regional or local field offices are located in most state capitals and in some other cities. Consult local phone directory for addresses and phone numbers, or contact headquarters office directly (see main entry).*

FEDERAL EMERGENCY MANAGEMENT AGENCY

97.017 **REGIONAL OFFICES**
thru
97.070 **REGION I**—99 High St. - 6th fl., Boston, MA 02110. Phone: (617)223-9540.

REGION II—26 Federal Plaza - Rm.1307, New York, NY 10278-0002. Phone: (212)680-3600.

REGION III—615 Chestnut St., Philadelphia, PA 19106. Phone: (215)931-5608.

REGION IV—3003 Chamblee-Tucker Rd., Atlanta, GA 30341. Phone: (770)220-5200.

REGION V—536 S. Clark St., Chicago, IL 60605. Phone: (312)408-5500.

REGION VI—Federal Regional Center, 800 N. Loop 288, Denton, TX 76201-3698. Phone: (940)898-5399.

REGION VII—2323 Grand Blvd. - Ste.900, Kansas City, MO 64108-2670. Phone: (816)283-7061.

REGION VIII—Federal Center - Bldg. 710, Denver, CO 80225-0267. Phone: (303)235-4800.

REGION IX—1111 Broadway - Ste.1200, Oakland, CA 94607. Phone: (510)627-7100.

REGION X—Federal Regional Center, 130 - 228th St. SW, Bothell, WA 98021-9796. Phone: (425)487-4600.

AGENCY INDEX

NOTE: Entries cover administrative units and sub-units, referring to program numbers used in Parts II, III, and IV (explained in Part I under "Organization of the Federal Programs").

APPALACHIAN REGIONAL COMMISSION, 23.001-23.011

ARCHITECTURAL AND TRANSPORTATION BARRIERS COMPLIANCE BOARD, 88.001

COMMISSION ON CIVIL RIGHTS, 29.001

COMMODITY FUTURES TRADING COMMISSION, 78.004

CORPORATION FOR NATIONAL AND COMMUNITY SERVICE, 94.002-94.016

DEPARTMENT OF AGRICULTURE, 10.001-10.995
  Agricultural Marketing Service, 10.153-10.167
  Agricultural Research Service, 10.001, 10.700
  Animal and Plant Health Inspection Service, 10.025-10.029
  Cooperative State Research, Education, and Extension Service, 10.200-10.228, 10.303-10.308, 10.500
  Economic Research Service, 10.250
  Farm Service Agency, 10.051-10.056, 10.066, 10.069, 10.073-10.085, 10.404, 10.406, 10.407, 10.421, 10.435, 10.437, 10.449, 10.451, 10.452, 10.994, 10.995
  Food and Nutrition Service, 10.550-10.582
  Food Safety and Inspection Service, 10.475, 10.477
  Foreign Agricultural Service, 10.600-10.609, 10.960-10.962
  Forest Service, 10.652-10.680
  Local Television Loan Guarantee Board, 10.853
  National Agricultural Statistics Service, 10.950
  National Sheep Industry Improvement Center, 10.774
  Natural Resources Conservation Service, 10.062, 10.064, 10.070, 10.072, 10.900-10.921
  Office of Community Development, 10.772
  Office of Outreach (Assistant Secretary/Administration), 10.443
  Risk Management Agency, 10.450, 10.454-10.459
  Rural Business-Cooperative Service, 10.350-10.352, 10.767-10.769, 10.771, 10.773, 10.775, 10.854, 10.856, 10.860

Rural Housing Service, 10.405, 10.410-10.420, 10.427, 10.433, 10.438, 10.441, 10.442, 10.444-10.446, 10.766
Rural Utilities Service, 10.760-10.763, 10.770, 10.850-10.853, 10.855, 10.856-10.886

DEPARTMENT OF COMMERCE, 11.001-11.900
Bureau of the Census, 11.001-11.006
Bureau of Industry and Security (*formerly, Bureau of Export Administration*), 11.150
Economic Development Administration, 11.300-11.313
Economics and Statistics Administration, 11.025-11.027
International Trade Administration, 11.106-11.114
Minority Business Development Agency, 11.800-11.803
National Institute of Standards and Technology, 11.601-11.617
National Oceanic and Atmospheric Administration, 11.400-11.481
National Technical Information Service, 11.650
National Telecommunications and Information Administration, 11.550, 11.552
Office of the Secretary, 11.702
Patent and Trademark Office, 11.900

DEPARTMENT OF DEFENSE, 12.002-12.910
Defense Advanced Research Projects Agency, 12.910
Defense Logistics Agency, 12.002
Department of the Air Force, Material Command, 12.800
Department of the Army, National Guard Bureau, 12.400-12.404
Department of the Army, Office of the Chief of Engineers, 12.100-12.116
Department of the Navy, Office of Naval Research, 12.300
National Security Agency, 12.900-12.902
Office of Assistant Secretary/Strategy and Requirements, 12.550-12.551
Office of Economic Adjustment, 12.600-12.614
Office of the Secretary, 12.630
Secretaries of Military Departments, 12.700
U.S. Army Materiel Command, 12.431
U.S. Army Medical Command, 12.420

DEPARTMENT OF EDUCATION, 84.002-84.370
Institute of Education Sciences, 84.305
National Institute for Literacy, 84.257

Office of Educational Research and Improvement, 84.215
Office of Elementary and Secondary Education, 84.004,
    84.010-84.013, 84.040, 84.041, 84.060, 84.083, 84.141,
    84.144, 84.149, 84.196, 84.206, 84.209-84.214, 84.256,
    84.258, 84.281, 84.283, 84.287, 84.290, 84.302, 84.310,
    84.318, 84.319, 84.332, 84.349, 84.351, 84.356-84.359,
    84.362, 84.364-84.370
Office of Human Resources and Administration, 84.145
Office of Innovation and Improvement, 84.083, 84.165, 84.203,
    84.282, 84.286, 84.295, 84.310, 84.330, 84.350, 84.351,
    84.354, 84.361, 84.363, 84.370
Office of Federal Student Aid, 84.007, 84.032-84.038, 84.063,
    84.069, 84.268, 84.355
Office of Postsecondary Education, 84.015-84.022, 84.031,
    84.042-84.047, 84.066, 84.103-84.120, 84.153, 84.170,
    84.185, 84.200, 84.217, 84.220, 84.229, 84.269, 84.274,
    84.316, 84.333-84.345
Office of Safe and Drug-Free Schools, 84.184, 84.186, 84.255,
    84.304, 84.331
Office of Special Education and Rehabilitative Services, 84.027,
    84.126-84.133, 84.160, 84.161, 84.169, 84.173-84.181,
    84.187, 84.224, 84.234-84.240, 84.246, 84.250, 84.263-
    84.265, 84.275, 84.315, 84.323-84.329, 84.343
Office of Vocational and Adult Education, 84.002, 84.048,
    84.051, 84.101, 84.191, 84.243, 84.245, 84.259, 84.341,
    84.346, 84.353, 84.360

DEPARTMENT OF ENERGY, 81.003-81.123
    Energy Information Administration, 81.039
    National Nuclear Security Administration, 81,112, 81.113, 81.123
    Office of Civilian Radioactive Waste Management, 81.065
    Office of Electricity Delivery and Energy Reliability, 81.122
    Office of Energy Efficiency and Renewable Energy, 81.036,
        81.041, 81.042, 81.079, 81.086, 81.087, 81.105, 81.117,
        84.119
    Office of Energy Research, 81.064
    Office of Environment, Safety and Health, 81.108
    Office of Environmental Management, 81.104, 81.106
    Office of Fossil Energy, 81.057, 81.089
    Office of General Counsel, 81.003

Office of Nuclear Energy, Science and Technology, 81.114, 81.121
Office of Science, 81.022. 81.049, 81.064

DEPARTMENT OF HEALTH AND HUMAN SERVICES,
93.001-93.996
Administration for Children and Families, 93.009, 93.010, 93.235, 93.254, 93.550-93.676
Administration on Aging, 93.041-93.053
Agency for Health Care Research and Quality, 93.225, 93.226
Agency for Toxic Substances and Disease Registry, 93.161, 93.202-93.208, 93.240
Centers for Disease Control and Prevention, 93.061-93.068, 93.116, 93.118, 93.135, 93.136, 93.184, 93.185, 93.197, 93.262, 93.268, 93.283, 93.919, 93.938-93.947, 93.977, 93.978, 93.988, 93.991, 93.993
Centers for Medicare and Medicaid Services, 93.767-93.774, 93.777-93.786
Food and Drug Administration, 93.103, 93.447-93.449
Health Resources and Services Administration, 93.107, 93.110, 93.117, 93.124-93.134, 93.145, 93.153-93.157, 93.162, 93.165, 93.178, 93.181, 93.186, 93.189-93.192, 93.211, 93.212, 93.223, 93.224, 93.234-93.236, 93.241, 93.247-93.253, 93.255-93.259, 93.264-93.267, 93.288, 93.300, 93.301, 93.342-93.359, 93.364, 93.822, 93.824, 93.884, 93.887-93.890, 93.908, 93.912-93.918, 93.923- 93.928, 93.932, 93.952, 93.953, 93.962-93.970, 93.994, 93.996
Indian Health Service, 93.123, 93.164, 93.193, 93.210, 93.219, 93.228, 93.231, 93.237, 93.284, 93.441, 93.442, 93.933, 93.954, 93.971, 93.972
National Institutes of Health, 93.113-93.115, 93.121, 93.140-93.143, 93.172-93.173, 93.187, 93.209, 93.213, 93.220, 93.232, 93.233, 93.242, 93.271-93.273, 93.279-93.282, 93.285, 93.286, 93.307, 93.308, 93.361, 93.385-93.399, 93.837-93.879, 93.891, 93.894, 93.936, 93.989
Office for Civil Rights, 93.001
Office of Disease Prevention and Health Promotion, 93.990
Office of Inspector General, 93.775
Office of Minority Health, 93.004-93.006, 93.100, 93.105, 93.137, 93.910

Office of Population Affairs, 93.007, 93.111, 93.217, 93.260, 93.974, 93.995
Office of the Secretary, 93.003, 93.239
Office of the Surgeon-General, 93.008
Office on Women's Health, 93.012. 93.290
President's Committee for People with Intellectual Disabilities, 93.613
President's Council on Physical Fitness and Sports, 93.289
Program Support Center, 93.291
Substance Abuse and Mental Health Services Administration, 93.104, 93.138, 93.150, 93.229, 93.230, 93.238, 93.243, 93.244, 93.275, *93.276*, 93.958, 93.959, 93.982

DEPARTMENT OF HOMELAND SECURITY, 97.001-97.089

Advanced Research Projects Agency, 97.065
Federal Emergency Management Agency, 97.016-97.041, 97.043, 97.045-97.050, 97.055, 97.063, 97.064, 97.070, 97.082, 97.084, 97.085, 97.088
National Center for State and Local Law Enforcement Training, 97.081
Office of Defense Preparedness, 97.066
Office of Grant Policy and Oversight, 97.001, 97.002
Office of Procurement Operations, 97.086
Office of State and Local Government Coordination and Preparedness, 97.004, 97.008, 97.042, 97.044, 97.053, 97.056-97.059, 97.067-97.068, 97.071, 97.073, 97.075, 97.078, 97.083
Preparedness Directorate, 97.089
Protective Security Division, 97.080
Science and Technology Directorate, 97.077
Transportation Security Administration, 97.060, 97.069, 97.072
U.S. Coast Guard, 97.011-97.014
U.S. Immigration and Customs Enforcement, 97.009, 97.010
U.S. Secret Service, 97.015, 97.076
University Programs, 97.061-97.062

DEPARTMENT OF HOUSING AND URBAN DEVELOPMENT, 14.103-14.906

Office of Community Planning and Development, 14.218-14.250
Office of Fair Housing and Equal Opportunity, 14.400-14.415

Office of Healthy Homes and Lead Hazard Control, 14.900-14.906
Office of Housing-Federal Housing Commissioner, 14.103-14.199, 14.310-14.314
Office of Policy Development and Research, 14.506-14.521
Office of Public and Indian Housing, 14.850-14.875

DEPARTMENT OF THE INTERIOR, 15.020-15.978
Bureau of Indian Affairs, 15.020-15.147
Bureau of Land Management, 15.214-15.242
Bureau of Reclamation, 15.504, 15.508
Geological Survey, 15.805-15.812, 15.978
Indian Arts and Crafts Board, 15.850
National Park Service, 15.904-15.929
Office of Insular Affairs, 15.875
Office of Surface Mining Reclamation and Enforcement, 15.250-15.254
U.S. Fish and Wildlife Service, 15.602-15.647

DEPARTMENT OF JUSTICE, 16.001-16.743
Bureau of Alcohol, Tobacco and Firearms, 16.012
Bureau of Justice Assistance, 16.203, 16.571, 16.577-16.580, 16.592, 16.597, 16.606-16.616, 16.735, 16.737, 16.738, 16.740
Bureau of Justice Statistics, 16.550, 16.554, 16.734, 16.739
Civil Rights Division, 16.100-16.110
Community Capacity Development Office, 16.575
Community Relations Service, 16.200
Corrections Program Office, 16.202, 16.203, 16.586, 16.593, 16.596
Drug Court Program Office, 16.585
Drug Enforcement Administration, 16.001-16.005
Executive Office for Weed and Seed, *16.595*
Immigration and Naturalization Service, 16.201, 16.400
National Institute of Corrections, 16.601-16.603
National Institute of Justice, 16.560-16.566, 16.741-16.743
Office for Victims of Crime, 16.320, 16.321, 16.575, 16.576, 16.582, 16.583
Office of Community Oriented Policing Services, 16.710
Office of Juvenile Justice and Delinquency Prevention, 16.523, 16.540-16.549, 16.726, 16.727, 16.728, 16.730-16.732

Office of the Police Corps and Law Enforcement Education, 16.712

Office on Violence Against Women, 16.524-16.529, 16.587-16.590, 16.736

DEPARTMENT OF LABOR, 17.002-17.807

    Bureau of Labor Statistics, 17.002-17.005

    Employee Benefits Security Administration, 17.150

    Employment and Training Administration, 17.201-17.267

    Employment Standards Administration, 17.301-17.309

    Mine Safety and Health Administration, 17.600-17.602

    Occupational Safety and Health Administration, 17.502-17.505

    Office of Assistant Secretary for Veterans' Employment and Training, 17.801-17.807

    Office of Disability Employment Policy, 17.720

    Office of Labor-Management Standards, 17.309

    Office of the Secretary, Women's Bureau, 17.700

DEPARTMENT OF STATE, 19.204-19.522

    Bureau of Educational and Cultural Affairs, 19.400-19.432

    Bureau of Intelligence and Research, 19.300

    Bureau of Oceans and International Environmental and Scientific Affairs, 19.204

    Bureau of Near Eastern Affairs, 19.500

    Bureau of Population, Refugees, and Migration, 19.510-19.522

DEPARTMENT OF TRANSPORTATION, 20.001-20.930

    Federal Aviation Administration, 20.100-20.109

    Federal Highway Administration, 20.205, 20.215, 20.219

    Federal Motor Carrier Safety Administration, 20.217, 20.218, 20.230-20.232

    Federal Railroad Administration, 20.303-20.313

    Federal Transit Administration, 20.500-20.518

    Maritime Administration, 20.801-20.813

    National Highway Traffic Safety Administration, 20.600-20.608

    Office of Aviation Analysis, 20.930

    Office of the Secretary, 20.900-20.907

    Pipelines and Hazardous Materials Safety Administration, 20.700, 20.703

DEPARTMENT OF THE TREASURY, 21.003-21.021
 Internal Revenue Service, 21.003-21.008
 Under Secretary/Domestic Finance, 21.020, 21.021

DEPARTMENT OF VETERANS AFFAIRS, 64.005-64.203
 National Cemetery System, 64.201-64.203
 Veterans Benefits Administration, 64.100-64.128
 Veterans Health Administration, 64.005-64.026

ENVIRONMENTAL PROTECTION AGENCY, 66.001-66.952
 American Indian Environmental Office, 66.926
 Office of Administration and Resources Management, 66.508, 66.518, 66.600, 66.609-66.611
 Office of Administrator, 66.940
 Office of Air and Radiation, 66.001-66.036
 Office of Enforcement and Compliance Assurance, 66.305, 66.310, 66.700, 66.701, 66.709
 Office of Environmental Education, 66.950-66.952
 Office of Environmental Information, 66.606, 66.608
 Office of Environmental Justice, 66.306-66.309, 66.604
 Office of International Affairs, 66.931
 Office of Prevention, Pesticides, and Toxic Substances, 66.707, 66.708, 66.714-66.717
 Office of Research and Development, 66.509-66.516
 Office of Solid Waste and Emergency Response, 66.801-66.818
 Office of Water, 66.418-66.481
 Region 1, 66.110
 Region 2 and 9, 66.600
 Region 7, 66.111

EQUAL EMPLOYMENT OPPORTUNITY COMMISSION, 30.001-30.011

FEDERAL COMMUNICATIONS COMMISSION, 32.001

FEDERAL MARITIME COMMISSION, 33.001

FEDERAL MEDIATION AND CONCILIATION SERVICE, 34.001-34.002

FEDERAL TRADE COMMISSION, 36.001

Agency Index

GENERAL SERVICES ADMINISTRATION, 39.002-39.009

GOVERNMENT PRINTING OFFICE, 40.001-40.002

INDEPENDENT BOARDS AND COMMISSIONS 90.100-90.400
    DELTA REGIONAL AUTHORITY 90.200-90.202
    DENALI COMMISSION, 90.100
    JAPAN-U.S. FRIENDSHIP COMMISSION, 90.300
    U.S. ELECTIONS ASSISTANCE COMMISSION, 90.400-90.401

LIBRARY OF CONGRESS, 42.001-42.009

NATIONAL AERONAUTICS AND SPACE ADMINISTRATION, 43.001-43.002

NATIONAL ARCHIVES AND RECORDS ADMINISTRATION, 89.001-89.003

NATIONAL CREDIT UNION ADMINISTRATION, 44.001-44.002

NATIONAL FOUNDATION ON THE ARTS AND THE HUMANITIES, 45.024-45.313
    Federal Council on the Arts and the Humanities, 45.201
    Institute of Museum and Library Services, 45.301-45.313
    National Endowment for the Arts, 45.024, 45.025
    National Endowment for the Humanities, 45.129-45.168

NATIONAL GALLERY OF ART, 68.001

NATIONAL LABOR RELATIONS BOARD, 46.001

NATIONAL SCIENCE FOUNDATION, 47.041-47.079

OFFICE OF PERSONNEL MANAGEMENT, 27.001-27.013

OVERSEAS PRIVATE INVESTMENT CORPORATION, 70.002-70.003

PENSION BENEFIT GUARANTY CORPORATION, 86.001

RAILROAD RETIREMENT BOARD, 57.001

SCHOLARSHIP AND FELLOWSHIP FOUNDATIONS, 85.001-85.500
- BARRY M. GOLDWATER SCHOLARSHIP AND EXCELLENCE IN EDUCATION FOUNDATION, 85.200
- CHRISTOPHER COLUMBUS FELLOWSHIP FOUNDATION, 85.100
- HARRY S TRUMAN SCHOLARSHIP FOUNDATION, 85.001
- JAMES MADISON MEMORIAL FELLOWSHIP FOUNDATION, 85.500
- MORRIS K. UDALL SCHOLARSHIP AND EXCELLENCE IN NATIONAL ENVIRONMENTAL POLICY FOUNDATION, 85.400-85.402
- SMITHSONIAN INSTITUTION, 85.601
- WOODROW WILSON INTERNATIONAL CENTER FOR SCHOLARS, 85.300

SECURITIES AND EXCHANGE COMMISSION, 58.001

SMALL BUSINESS ADMINISTRATION, 59.002-59.054

SOCIAL SECURITY ADMINISTRATION, 96.001-96.020

U.S. AGENCY FOR INTERNATIONAL DEVELOPMENT, 98.001-98.012

U.S. INSTITUTE OF PEACE, 91.001-91.002

MASTER INDEX

NOTES

Index entries refer to program numbers used in Part II. The program numbering system is explained on page 12.

- Italicized program *numbers* indicate programs that provide financial assistance. (Assistance classifications are explained on page 4.) Examples:

    ABANDONED MINE LAND RECLAMATION (AMLR) PROGRAM, *15.252*
    Women, Infants, and Children (WIC) Program, *10.557*

- Subject headings are in bold-face type. Examples:

    Adult education
    Wildlife, waterfowl

- Program titles are in capital letters. Bracketed agency identifiers are inserted when the title inadequately describes program focus. Examples:

    BUSINESS AND INDUSTRY LOANS [USDA], *10.768*
    GENERAL RESEARCH AND TECHNOLOGY ACTIVITY [HUD], *14.506*

- Also provided are (1) popular and abbreviated program titles, (2) government departments and independent agencies, (3) names of Acts, (4) section and title numbers of Acts when in general usage, and (5) entries with general references and cross-references to program activities and governmental sub-entities. Examples:

    (1) Age Search, 11.006
    VBOP (Veterans Business Outreach Centers), SBA, *59.044*

    (2) Department of Defense (DOD), 12.002 through 12.910
    Environmental Protection Agency (EPA), 66.001 through 66.952

    (3) AIDS Housing Opportunity Act, *14.241*

    (4) Section 22, Water Resources Development Act, 12.110
    Title I, ESEA, migrants, *84.011*

    (5) Acid precipitation research, NOAA, 11.432, 11.459
    Brownfield projects, *see* Urban renewal
    National Institute on Drug Abuse (NIDA), NIH, 93.279

Remarks on using the index are offered in Part I in the section on "Obtaining Federal Assistance," under "STEP ONE: USE THE MASTER INDEX."

ABANDONED INFANTS, 93.551
ABANDONED MINE LAND RECLAMATION (AMLR) PROGRAM, 15.252
ABSTINENCE EDUCATION PROGRAM, 93.235
Academic facilities, *see* Education facilities
ACADEMIC RESEARCH ENHANCEMENT AWARD [HHS], 93.390
Access Board (Architectural and Transportation Barriers Compliance Board), 88.001
Access to Emergency Devices (AEDs), rural, HRSA, 93.259
Access to Recovery (ATR), SAMSHA, 93.275
Accident prevention, *see* Occupational health, safety; Public safety
ACF (Administration for Children and Families), HHS, *see* Agency Index
Acid Mine Drainage (AMD), DOI, 15.253
Acid precipitation research, NOAA, 11.432, 11.459
Acquired immune deficiency syndrome (AIDS), *see* AIDS (Acquired Immune Deficiency Syndrome)
ACQUIRED IMMUNODEFICIENCY SYNDROME (AIDS) ACTIVITY, 93.118
ACTION, *see* Corporation for National and Community Service
ACYPL (American Council of Young Political Leaders), BECA, 19.403
ADA (Americans with Disabilities Act), *see* Disabled, handicapped
ADA (Americans with Disabilities Act) technical assistance, 16.108
ADAA, (Anti-Drug Abuse Act of 1988), *see* Drug abuse
Adarand vs. Pena, SBA loans, 59.049
ADDI (American Dream Downpayment Initiative), 14.239
Addiction, *see* Alcohol abuse, alcoholism; Drug abuse; Tobacco
ADJUSTABLE RATE MORTGAGES, 14.175
Adjustment assistance, *see* Trade adjustment assistance
Administration for Children and Families (ACF), HHS, *see* Agency Index
Administration on Aging (AOA), HHS, *see* Agency Index
ADMINISTRATIVE COST GRANTS FOR INDIAN SCHOOLS, 15.046
Administrative Enforcement Initiative (AEI), fair housing, 14.408
ADOLESCENT FAMILY LIFE—DEMONSTRATION PROJECTS, 93.995
ADOLESCENT FAMILY LIFE RESEARCH GRANTS, 93.111
Adolescents, *see* Juvenile delinquency; Maternal, child health, welfare; Youth *entries*
Adoption, *see* Maternal, child health, welfare; Parenting
ADOPTION ASSISTANCE, 93.659
ADOPTION INCENTIVE PAYMENTS, 93.603
ADOPTION OPPORTUNITIES, 93.652
Adult education
Adult Education and Family Literacy Act (AEFLA), 84.002, 84.191
citizenship, naturalization, 97.010
Community Technology Centers, DOED, 84.341
consumer, homemaker, 10.500

Education Technology State Grants, 84.318
Educational Opportunity Centers, postsecondary tutoring, counseling, 84.066
Even Start, Indians, 84.258
Even Start, migrants, 84.214
Even Start, state, 84.213
food, nutrition, 10.500
Head Start, parent programs, 93.600
homemaking, 10.500
incarcerated youth, 84.331
Indian parents, 15.043
Indians, 15.026
institutionalized adults, 84.002
migrants, high school equivalence, 84.141
National Institute for Literacy, fellowships, 84.257
native American language preservation, 93.587
Occupational and Employment Information, DOED, 84.346
prisoners, 84.255
research, demonstrations, 84.191
state grants, 84.002
tax preparation, 21.003
telecommunications, instructional programming, Star Schools, 84.203
vocational, basic grants, 84.048
Women's Educational Equity Act Program, 84.083
see also Bilingual education, services; Education *entries*; Employment *entries*; Higher education; Home economics; Home management; Illiteracy; Indian education, training; Libraries; Maternal, child health, welfare; Parenting; Technical training; Tutoring; Veterans education, training; Vocational *entries*; Volunteers
ADULT EDUCATION—NATIONAL LEADERSHIP ACTIVITIES, 84.191
ADULT EDUCATION—STATE GRANT PROGRAM, 84.002
Adult Programs in the Territories, ACF, 93.560
ADVANCED EDUCATION NURSING GRANT PROGRAM, 93.247
ADVANCED EDUCATION NURSING TRAINEESHIPS, 93.358
ADVANCED PLACEMENT PROGRAM [DOED], 84.330
Advanced Research Projects Agency, DOD, *see* Agency Index (DOD, Defense Advanced Research Projects Agency)
ADVANCED TECHNOLOGY PROGRAM [USDC], 11.612
Advertising, false, misleading, 36.001
AEAP (Anti-Terrorism and Emergency Assistance Program), DOJ, 16.321
AEDs (Access to Emergency Devices), rural, HRSA, 93.259
AEI (Administrative Enforcement Initiative), fair housing, 14.408
Aeronautics, space
Air Force Defense Research Sciences Program, 12.800
commercial space transportation research, 20.108
environmental systems research, NOAA, 11.432
NASA K1-12 education services, 43.001
NASA Technology Transfer, 43.002
National Aeronautics and Space Act of 1958, 43.001, 43.002

MASTER INDEX 883

National Environmental Satellite, Data, and Information Service (NESDIS), NOAA, *11.428*
NESDIS environmental sciences education, research, *11.440*
NOAA Coastal Services Center, *11.473*
Spacemobile, 43.001
see also Astronomy; Engineering *entries*; Physical sciences; Scientific research
AEROSPACE EDUCATION SERVICES PROGRAM, 43.001
AFDC, *see* Aid to Families with Dependent Children
Affirmative action, *see* Civil rights
AFL (Adolescent Family Life) projects, *93.995*
AFRICAN ELEPHANT CONSERVATION, *15.620*
Age discrimination, *see* Civil rights
Age Search, 11.006
Agency for Health Care Research and Quality, HHS, *see* Agency Index
Agency for Toxic Substances and Disease Registry, HHS, *see* Agency Index

Aging and the aged
abuse, neglect, exploitation, staff training, *93.041*, *93.042*
abuse, sexual assault prevention training, OJP, *16.528*
age search, Census Bureau, 11.006
Aging Research, National Institute on Aging, *93.866*
Allied Health Projects, training, *93.191*
Alzheimer's disease, related disorders, *16.543*, *93.051*, *93.853*, *93.866*, *94.016*
assault victim protection arrest orders, *16.590*
blind, independent living services, *84.177*
care, demonstration projects, personnel training, *93.048*
caregiver support program, respite care, *93.052*
commodity foods, *10.565*
Community Services Block Grants, *93.569*
Compassion Capital Fund, ACF, *93.009*
discrimination, housing, HUD programs, 14.402
elder abuse prevention, *16.528*, *93.041*, *93.671*
employment, community service, *17.235*
employment discrimination, *30.002*, 30.005, 30.008
employment, environmental programs, *66.508*, *66.518*
employment, Foster Grandparent Program, *94.011*
U.S. Employment Service, *17.207*
EPA health protection activities, *66.609*
facilities, assisted living, care, nursing home, *14.129*
family violence victims services, *93.671*
food assistance, 10.550, *10.558*
Food Stamps, *10.551*
Foster Grandparent Program, *94.011*
Geriatric Academic Career Awards, *93.250*
geriatric education program, *93.265*
geriatrics education centers, *93.969*
geriatrics faculty, *93.156*
geriatrics research, *93.866*
geriatrics research NRSA, *93.225*
geriatrics residencies, *93.884*
health services, preventive, screening, counseling, *93.043*
home health services, Medicare, *93.773*, *93.774*
home weatherization, *81.042*
housing, Multifamily Housing Service Coordinators, *14.191*
housing, supportive, *14.157*, *14.314*
Indians, Social Services, *15.025*
Indians, supportive services, *93.047*
institutionalized, discrimination, 16.105
long-term care ombudsman services, *93.042*
meals, nutrition services, *93.045*
Medicaid, *93.778*
Medicare hospital insurance, *93.773*
Medicare Part B supplementary insurance, *93.774*
Medicare Part D prescription drug insurance, *93.770*
multipurpose centers, *93.044*
multipurpose centers construction, improvement, CDBG, *14.218*, *14.219*, *14.228*
multipurpose centers construction, improvement, CDBG, Indians, *14.862*
multipurpose centers construction, improvement, CDBG, insular areas, *14.225*
National Agenda for the Environment and the Aging, EPA, *66.609*
National Senior Service Corps, *94.002*
nutrition discretionary grants, *10.579*
Nutrition Services Incentive Program, AOA, *93.053*
Older Americans Act (OAA), 10.550, *17.235*, 39.003, *66.508*, *93.041*, *93.042*, *93.043*, *93.044*, *93.045*, *93.047*, *93.048*, *93.052*, *93.612*
part-time employment, *17.235*
pension plan insurance, *86.001*
program research, demonstrations, *93.048*
Retired and Senior Volunteer Program (RSVP), *94.002*
retired volunteers, SCORE business advisors, *59.026*
reverse mortgage loans, *14.183*
Scams Targeting the Elderly, telemarketing, DOJ, *16.613*
Senior Community Service Employment Program, *17.235*
Senior Companion Program, *94.016*
Senior Environmental Employment Program, *66.508*
Senior Farmers Market Nutrition Program, FNS, *10.576*
Social Security retirement benefits, *96.002*
Social Security Special Benefits, *96.003*
Social Services Block Grants, *93.667*
Supplemental Security Income, *96.006*
supportive, nutrition services, *93.044*
Survivors Insurance, SSA, *96.004*
tax counseling, *21.006*
transportation services, specialized vehicle purchases, *20.513*
veterans, disabled, pension, *64.104*
World War II veterans, SSI expatriate beneficiaries, *96.020*
see also Civil rights; Employee benefits; Food, nutrition; Group homes; Health, medical *entries*; Housing, congregate; Housing, elderly; Nursing homes; Social Security Act; Social services; Veterans *entries*; Victim assistance; Volunteers
AGING RESEARCH, *93.866*

Agreement on Coordination of Tax Administration, IRS, 21.004
AGRICULTURAL AND RURAL ECONOMIC RESEARCH, 10.250
Agricultural commodities, stabilization
Agricultural Act of 1949, *10.607*
Agricultural Act of 1970, *10.053, 10.452*
Agricultural Act of 1980, *10.079*
Agricultural Adjustment Act of 1938, *10.051, 10.167, 10.450*
Agricultural Assistance Act of 2002, *10.995*
Agricultural Assistance Act of 2003, *10.077*
Agricultural Credit Acts, *10.054, 10.435*
Agricultural Estimates, 10.950
Agricultural Market Transition Act, *10.454, 10.456*
Agricultural Risk Protection Act, *10.051, 10.075, 10.076, 10.450, 10.454, 10.917*
Agriculture and Consumer Protection Act of 1973, *10.565*
Agriculture and Food Act of 1981, 10.155
Avian Influenza Indemnity Program, *10.029*
Bioenergy Program), FSA, *10.078*
Boll Weevil Eradication Loan Program, *10.449*
Child and Adult Care Food Program, *10.558*
Commodity Partnerships for Risk Management Education, *10.457, 10.459*
Conservation Reserve Program, *10.069*
Crop Disaster Program, *10.073*
Crop Insurance, *10.450*
Crop Insurance in Targeted States, *10.458*
dairy indemnity, *10.053*
Dairy Options Pilot Program, *10.454*
developing countries, *10.606*
Direct and Counter-Cyclical Payments Program, *10.055*
disaster assistance, noninsured crops, *10.451*
donation, Indian reservations, *10.567*
emergency conservation, *10.054*
Emergency Food Assistance Program, *10.568*
Emerging Markets Program, *10.603*
Emerson Humanitarian Trust, FSA, *10.079*
Farm Storage Facility Loans, *10.056*
farmland rehabilitation, *10.054*
Federal Agriculture Improvement and Reform Act of 1996 (FAIRA), *10.051, 10.069, 10.072, 10.224, 10.225, 10.226, 10.450, 10.451, 10.454, 10.500, 10.603, 10.771, 10.773, 10.774, 10.855, 10.912, 10.913, 10.914, 10.919*
Federal Crop Insurance Act, *10.450, 10.455, 10.456, 10.457, 10.458*
food commodities donation, 10.550, *10.560, 10.565, 10.569*
Food For Peace programs, USAID, *98.007, 98.008*
Food for Progress, *10.606*
Food for Progress Act of 1985, *10.606*
Food Security Wheat Reserve (Emerson Humanitarian Trust), FSA, *10.079*
foreign market development, *10.600*
futures trading information, customer complaints, 78.004
Hard White Wheat Incentive Program, FSA, *10.995*
Homeland Security—Agricultural, *10.304*
inspection, grading 10.162

international humanitarian relief goods transport, USAID, *98.010*
international, Institutional Capacity Building, USAID, *98.005*
international, USAID Farmer-to-Farmer Program, *98.009*
Lamb Meat Adjustment Program, FSA, *10.081*
Livestock Assistance Program, *10.066*
Market Access Program, exports, *10.601*
Market News, 10.153
market protection, promotion, 10.163
marketing agreements, orders, 10.155
marketing improvement, *10.156*
Milk Income Loss Contract Program, *10.080*
noninsurance risk management research partnerships, *10.456*
Ocean Freight Reimbursement, USAID, *98.003*
Peanut Quota Buyout Program, FSA, *10.994*
Perishable Agricultural Commodities Act of 1930, 10.165
price supports, deficiency payments, *10.051*
Produce Agency Act, 10.165
Quality Samples Program, FAS, *10.605*
research, experiment stations *10.203*
risk management outreach, RMA, *10.455*
seed producers emergency loans, *10.076*
sheep, goat industry improvement center, *10.774*
soil, water conservation direct payments, *10.069*
Special Apple Program, *10.075*
storage, *10.567, 10.568*
Technical Assistance for Specialty Crops, FAS, *10.604*
Tobacco Loss Assistance Program, FSA, *10.083*
Tobacco Transition Payment Program, FSA, *10.085*
Trade Adjustment Assistance, FAS, *10.609*
transportation services, AMS, 10.167
Tree Assistance Program, FSA, *10.082*
unfair marketing practices, perishables, 10.165
Value-Added Producer Grants, RBCS, *10.352*
Wholesale Farmers and Alternative Market Development, 10.164
see also Agricultural *entries*; Commodity futures market; Dairy industry; Feed grains; Fisheries industry; Food inspection, grading; Food, nutrition; International commerce, investment; Livestock industry; Tobacco
Agricultural conservation
Agricultural Management Assistance, NRCS, *10.917*
Colorado River basin, *10.070*
Conservation Reserve Program, *10.069*
Conservation Security Program, NRCS, *10.921*
Direct and Counter-Cyclical Payments Program, *10.055*
DOE, waste reduction, NICE3 Program, *81.105*
emergency farmland rehabilitation, *10.054*
Environmental Quality Incentives Program-Klamath Basin, NRCS, *10.919*
Environmental Quality Incentives Program, NRCS, *10.912*
EPA Nonpoint Source Implementation Grants, *66.460*
Farm and Ranch Lands Protection Program, NRCS, *10.913*
farm ownership loans, *10.407*

Grassland Reserve Program, NRCS, *10.920*
Great Plains Conservation, *10.900*
ground, surface water quality incentives program, NRCS, *10.918*
Indian lands, *15.034*
organic agriculture, CSREES, *10.307*
Pesticide Environmental Stewardship, *66.714*
plant materials, 10.905
rural resource conservation, *10.901*
soil surveys, 10.903
soil, water, technical assistance, NRCS, 10.902
sustainable agriculture research, *10.215*
Water Bank Act, *10.062*
Water Bank Program, waterfowl, wetlands, *10.062*
water reclamation, reuse, *15.504*
Water 2025 Challenge Grants, western states, DOI, *15.507*
Wetlands Reserve Program, *10.072*
watershed, river basin projects, 10.906
see also Environmental management; Fertilizer; Flood prevention, control; Natural resources; Pesticides; Soil conservation; Water conservation; Water pollution abatement, prevention; Wetlands; Woodlands
Agricultural Cooperative Service, *see* Agency Index (USDA, Rural Business-Cooperative Service)

Agricultural cooperatives
Cooperative Marketing Act of 1926, 10.350
disaster recovery loans, SBA, *59.002*
emergency loans, *10.404*
farm operating loans, *10.406*
farm ownership loans, *10.407*
Food For Peace programs, USAID, *98.007, 98.008*
Interest Assistance Program, *10.437*
international, Cooperative Development Program, USAID, *98.002*
international, Institutional Capacity Building, USAID, *98.005*
livestock, Disaster Reserve Assistance, *10.452*
Market Access Program, exports, *10.601*
risk management outreach, RMA, *10.455*
Rural Business Investment Companies, RBCS, *10.860*
Rural Cooperative Development Grants, *10.771*
sheep, goat industry improvement center, *10.774*
Technical Assistance for Specialty Crops, FAS, *10.604*
technical assistance, training, 10.350
Value-Added Producer Grants, RBCS, *10.352*
see also Cooperatives; Farm, nonfarm enterprises; Housing cooperatives

Agricultural education
Alaska, Hawaii natives institutions, *10.228*
challenge grants, *10.217*
Commodity Partnerships for Risk Management Education, *10.457, 10.459*
cooperatives, 10.350
Crop Insurance in Targeted States, *10.458*
CSREES Integrated Programs, *10.303*
DHS Competitive Training Grants, *97.068*
1890 institutions entrepreneurial outreach, RBCS, *10.856*
1890 institutions support, *10.216*
EPA environmental sustainability design competition, *66.516*
Extension Service, *10.500*
forestry research training, *10.202*
Fund for Rural America, *10.224*
graduate fellowships, *10.210*
Hispanic-serving institutions, *10.223*
insular areas, *10.308*
international, CSREES, *10.305*
international research, training, *10.962*
international, USAID Farmer-to-Farmer Program, *98.009*
Minority Scholars Program, *10.220*
National Agricultural Research, Extension, and Teaching Policy Act of 1977 (NARETPA), *10.205, 10.207, 10.210, 10.215, 10.216, 10.217, 10.220, 10.223, 10.304, 10.305, 10.960, 10.961, 10.962*
1994 Institutions, *10.227*
secondary, postsecondary, *10.226*
sustainable agriculture, *10.215*
Television Demonstration Grants, *10.769*
tribal colleges, *10.221, 10.222*
see also Agricultural research, sciences; Education *entries*; Food, nutrition *entries*; Higher education *entries*; Land grant colleges, universities
Agricultural enterprises, *see* Farm, nonfarm enterprises
Agricultural Estimates, 10.950

Agricultural experiment stations
animal disease research, *10.207*
CSREES Integrated Programs, *10.303*
forestry research, *10.652*
Hatch Act of 1887, *10.203*
organic agriculture research, extension, CSREES, *10.307*
plant materials research, 10.905
research, *10.200, 10.203, 10.206*
sustainable agriculture research, *10.215*
see also Agricultural research, sciences; Land grant colleges, universities

Agricultural loans
agri-businesses, *10.768*
Boll Weevil Eradication Loan Program, *10.449*
commodities, *10.051*
emergency loans, *10.404*
farm operating expenses, *10.406*
farm ownership, *10.407*
Farm Storage Facility Loans, *10.056*
Interest Assistance Program, *10.437*
mediation services, *10.435*
seed producers emergency loans, *10.076*
see also Agricultural commodities, stabilization; Family farms; Farm, nonfarm enterprises
AGRICULTURAL MANAGEMENT ASSISTANCE, *10.917*

Agricultural marketing
Agricultural Estimates, 10.950
Agricultural Marketing Act of 1946, 10.153, *10.156*, 10.162, 10.163, 10.164, 10.167, 10.350, 11.413
Agricultural Marketing Agreement Act of 1937, 10.155
Agriculture and Consumer Protection Act of 1973, *10.053*
biodiesel fuel use, CSREES, *10.306*
business internships, Eurasian executives, scientists, *11.114*

Agricultural marketing *(continued)*
  CSREES international science, education, *10.305*
  commodities inspection, grading, 10.162
  commodity reports, bulletins, 10.153
  economic research information, 10.250
  Emerson Humanitarian Trust, FSA, *10.079*
  Emerging Markets Program, *10.603*
  Extension Service, *10.500*
  Food, Agriculture, Conservation, and Trade Act of 1990 (FACTA), *10.051, 10.053, 10.069, 10.072, 10.215, 10.307, 10.435, 10.443, 10.500, 10.603, 10.664, 10.673, 10.676, 10.680, 10.763, 10.678, 10.770, 10.771*
  Food Security Wheat Reserve (Emerson Humanitarian Trust), FSA, *10.079*
  foreign market development, *10.600*
  Fund for Rural America, *10.224*
  Hard White Wheat Incentive Program, FSA, *10.995*
  international research training, *10.962*
  international standards, commodities, 10.162
  international trade improvement, *10.156*
  Market Access Program, exports, *10.601*
  market promotion, protection, research, 10.163
  marketing agreements, orders, 10.155
  marketing services improvement, *10.156*
  meat, poultry inspection, *10.475, 10.477*
  organic agriculture, CSREES, *10.307*
  perishables, unfair practices, 10.165
  Quality Samples Program, FAS, *10.605*
  research, experiment stations, *10.203*
  sheep, goat industry improvement center, *10.774*
  small wood species, USFS Technology Marketing Unit, *10.674*
  Technical Assistance for Specialty Crops, FAS, *10.604*
  Trade Adjustment Assistance, FAS, *10.609*
  transportation services, AMS, 10.167
  Value-Added Producer Grants, RBCS, *10.352*
  Wholesale Farmers and Alternative Market Development, 10.164
  see also Agricultural commodities, stabilization; Commodity futures market; International commerce, investment
Agricultural Marketing Agreements, 10.155
Agricultural Marketing Service (AMS), USDA, *see* Agency Index
Agricultural patents, *see* Patents, trademarks, inventions
Agricultural price supports, *see* Agricultural commodities, stabilization
AGRICULTURAL RESEARCH—BASIC AND APPLIED RESEARCH, *10.001*
Agricultural research, sciences
  Agricultural Research, Extension, and Education Reform Act of 1998 (AREERA), *10.450, 10.500*
  animal disease, health, *10.207*
  basic, applied, *10.001*
  biomass energy, DOE, *81.087*
  biotechnology risk assessment, *10.219*
  Colorado River basin, *10.070*
  competitive research grants, *10.206*
  CSREES Integrated Programs, *10.303*
  DOE biomass energy programs, *81.079*
  DOE waste reduction, NICE3 Program, *81.105*
  economic research information, 10.250
  1890 institutions support, *10.216*
  experiment stations, *10.203*
  food safety, security monitoring, FDA, *93.448*
  food stamp program access, *10.580*
  forestry, rangeland management, *10.202*
  Fund for Rural America, *10.224*
  graduate fellowships, *10.210*
  international assistance, *10.960*
  international, CSREES, *10.305*
  international, exchanges, *10.961*
  international, training, *10.962*
  land grant institutions, *10.205*
  National Agricultural Library, 10.700
  1994 Institutions, *10.227*
  noninsurance risk management partnerships, *10.456*
  organic agriculture, CSREES, *10.307*
  plant materials for conservation, 10.905
  rural communities information, 10.250
  SBIR grants, *10.212*
  Small Business Innovation Development Act of 1982, *10.212*
  Special Research Grants, *10.200*
  sustainable agriculture, *10.215*
  Water 2025 Challenge Grants, western states, DOI, *15.507*
  watershed, river basin projects, 10.906
  see also Agricultural education; Agricultural experiment stations; Agricultural statistics; Energy research; Food, nutrition research, sciences; Land grant colleges, universities; Scientific research
Agricultural Research Service (ARS), USDA, *see* Agency Index
Agricultural stabilization, *see* Agricultural commodities, stabilization; Agricultural loans; Agricultural marketing; Dairy industry
Agricultural Stabilization and Conservation Service (ASCS), *see* Agency Index (USDA, Farm Service Agency)
Agricultural standards, *see* Complaint investigation; Dairy industry; Food inspection, grading; Livestock industry; Poultry, egg products
Agricultural statistics
  commodity market news, 10.153
  crop, livestock estimates, employment, rural communities, 10.950
  dairy market, 10.153
  economic research, 10.250
  Technical Assistance for Specialty Crops, FAS, *10.604*
  see also Agricultural research; Economics, research, statistics; Statistics
AGRICULTURAL STATISTICS REPORTS, 10.950
Agricultural storage, *see* Agricultural commodities, stabilization
Agricultural workers, *see* Farm workers
AGRICULTURE ON INDIAN LANDS, *15.034*
AHEC (Area Health Education Centers), *93.824*
AHEC (Area Health Education Centers) Model State-Supported Programs, *93.107*
Aid to Families with Dependent Children (AFDC), *93.583, 93.659*
AID TO TRIBAL GOVERNMENTS, *15.020*
AIDS (Acquired Immune Deficiency Syndrome)
  abandoned infants, *93.551*
  adolescents counseling, *93.995*

MASTER INDEX 887

AIDS/HIV dental services reimbursements, *93.924*
care providers education, training centers, *93.145*
children, women, families, *93.153*
dental, oral manifestations, research, *93.121*
emergency food, shelter, FEMA, *97.024*
epidemiologic research, *93.943*
FDA research, information, *93.103*
Global AIDS, CDCP, *93.067*
Global AIDS, HRSA, *93.266*
HIV/AIDS Surveillance, *93.944*
HIV care, *93.914, 93.917*
HIV outpatient early intervention, *93.918*
HIV, personnel training projects, *93.928*
HIV prevention, *93.939, 93.940*
HIV prevention efficacy research, dissemination, *93.941*
homeless, Shelter Plus Care, *14.238*
housing, HOPWA, *14.241*
immunology research, *93.855*
mental health research, *93.242*
mental health research training, *93.281*
mental health specialists training, *93.244*
microbiology, infectious diseases research, *93.856*
minorities, HHS prevention, education demonstrations, *93.006*
minority community health coalitions, *93.137*
neuro-AIDS research, *93.853*
NIH research education loan repayments, *93.936*
overseas refugee assistance, global priorities, BPRM, *19.522*
prevention, public education, *93.118*
prevention, school health projects, *93.938*
Ryan White Comprehensive AIDS Resources Emergency (CARE) Act Amendments of 2000, *93.145, 93.153, 93.914, 93.917, 93.918, 93.924, 93.928*
Substance Abuse Prevention and Treatment Block Grant, *93.959*
see also Communicable diseases; Community health services; Health, medical *entries*; Social services; Volunteers
AIDS EDUCATION AND TRAINING CENTERS, *93.145*
AIDS Housing Opportunity Act, *14.241*
AIDS-LRP (AIDS-Loan Repayment Program), NIH, *93.936*
AIP (Airport Improvement Program), *20.106*
AIR FORCE DEFENSE RESEARCH SCIENCES PROGRAM, *12.800*
Air Force Material Command, DOD, *see* Agency Index
Air pollution
biometry, risk estimation, NIEHS, *93.115*
Clean Air Act (CAA), *11.459, 20.106, 66.001, 66.033, 66.034, 66.035, 66.110, 66.111, 66.307, 66.308, 66.310, 66.307, 66.509, 66.510, 66.511, 66.513, 66.514, 66.515, 66.516, 66.600, 66.604, 66.606, 66.609, 66.610, 66.611, 66.709, 66.717, 66.810, 66.931, 66.940, 66.952*
Clean School Bus USA, EPA, *66.036*
climate research, services, *11.459*
community stakeholder projects, *66.035*
Compliance Assistance Centers, EPA, *66.305*
control, prevention, training, *66.001*
control surveys, studies, EPA R&D, *66.510*

Environmental Information Exchange Network Grants, *66.608*
EPA compliance capacity building, *66.709*
EPA Consolidated Program Support Grants, *66.600*
EPA consolidated research, *66.511*
EPA environmental sustainability design competition, *66.516*
EPA Performance Partnership Grants, *66.605*
EPA studies, special purpose assistance, *66.610*
Indoor Radon Abatement Act, *66.032*
mass transit, *20.507*
Ozone Transport, *66.033*
prevention, effects studies, demonstrations, *66.034*
prevention information projects, *66.708*
radon mitigation, information, training, *66.032*
surveys, studies, special grants, EPA, *66.606*
see also Environmental *entries*; Pollution abatement
AIR POLLUTION CONTROL PROGRAM SUPPORT, *66.001*
Air quality, *see* Air pollution
Air transportation
aerial bird hazing, *10.028*
Airport and Airway Planning Development Act of 1970, *20.100*
airport improvement, *20.106*
aviation research, *20.108, 20.109*
Aviation and Transportation Security Act, *97.072*
Aviation Security Act of 2001, *97.069*
Aviation Security Improvement Act of 1990, *20.108*
carrier subsidies, *20.901*
civil aviation public education, *20.100*
consumer affairs, complaints, *20.900*
DHS Aviation Research Grants, *97.069*
explosives detection canine teams, TSA, *97.072*
Federal Aviation Act, *11.431, 11.459, 20.900*
Federal Aviation Administration Research, Engineering and Development Authorization Act of 1990, *20.108, 20.109*
federal surplus airplanes, *39.003, 39.007*
federal surplus real property, airports, *39.002*
flight training, veterans, *64.124*
Indian airstrip maintenance, *15.033*
National Guard operations, maintenance, *12.401*
National Plan of Integrated Airport Systems, *20.106*
Small Community Air Service Development, *20.930*
Vision 100-Century in Aviation Reauthorization Act, *20.930*
Wendell H. Ford Aviation Investment and Reform Act for the 21st Century, *20.930*
see also Aeronautics, space; Transportation
AIR TRANSPORTATION CENTERS OF EXCELLENCE, *20.109*
Airlines, *see* Air transportation
AIRPORT IMPROVEMENT PROGRAM, *20.106*
Airports, *see* Air transportation
Alaska, Alaska natives
agriculture, food sciences education, *10.228*
Alaska Migratory Bird Co-Management Council, FWS, *15.643*
Alaska National Interest Lands Conservation Act (ANILCA), *15.055, 15.636*

Alaska, Alaska natives *(continued)*
Alaska Native Educational Program, *84.356*
arts, crafts development, 15.850
bilingual, bicultural health demonstrations, *93.105*
community development grants, *14.862*
community health coalitions, *93.137*
Cultural Resource Management, BLM, *15.224*
Denali Commission Grants and Loans, energy facilities, *10.858*
Denali Commission Program, *90.100*
diabetes program, *93.237*
economic, social self-sufficiency development, *93.612*
English Language Acquisition Grants, *84.365*
environmental impact mitigation, DOD activities, *93.582*
environmental quality regulation, *93.581*
farmer outreach, *10.443*
fish, wildlife subsistence management, *15.636*
health care research, demonstration, *93.933*
health careers, preprofessional scholarship program, *93.971*
health management program, *93.228*
health professions pregraduate scholarships, *93.123*
health professions recruitment, *93.970*
health professions scholarship program, *93.972*
health services disparities projects, *93.100*
IHE community assistance, *14.515*
injury prevention programs, CDCP, *93.284*
land acquisition loans, *10.421*
land allotments, *15.055*
language preservation, *93.587*
museum services, *45.308*
SBA Native American Economic Development Assistance, *59.052*
native American graves protection, repatriation, *15.922*
Native American Library Services, *45.311*
Southeast Alaska Economic Disaster Fund, USFS, *10.671*
supportive services, older persons, *93.047*
Tribal Work Grants, *93.594*
Udall doctoral fellowships, *85.401*
Udall undergraduate scholarships, *85.400*
WIA Native American Employment and Training, *17.265*
see also Indian *entries*
ALASKA MIGRATORY BIRD CO-MANAGEMENT COUNCIL, *15.643*
ALASKA NATIVE EDUCATIONAL PROGRAM, *84.356*
ALASKA NATIVE/NATIVE HAWAIIAN INSTITUTIONS ASSISTING COMMUNITIES, [HUD], *14.515*
ALASKA NATIVE SERVING AND NATIVE HAWAIIAN SERVING INSTITUTIONS EDUCATION GRANTS [USDA], *10.228*
ALASKA SUBSISTENCE MANAGEMENT [DOI], *15.636*
ALASKAN INDIAN ALLOTMENTS AND SUBSISTENCE PREFERENCE—ALASKA NATIONAL INTEREST LANDS CONSERVATION ACT, *15.055*
Alcohol, *see* Alcohol abuse, alcoholism; Crime; Energy research

Alcohol fuel, *see* Energy research
ALCOHOL NATIONAL RESEARCH SERVICE AWARDS FOR RESEARCH TRAINING, *93.272*
ALCOHOL RESEARCH CAREER DEVELOPMENT AWARDS FOR SCIENTISTS AND CLINICIANS, *93.271*
ALCOHOL RESEARCH CENTER GRANTS, *93.891*
ALCOHOL RESEARCH PROGRAMS, *93.273*
ALCOHOL, TOBACCO, AND FIREARMS— TRAINING ASSISTANCE, 16.012
ALCOHOL TRAFFIC SAFETY AND DRUNK DRIVING PREVENTION INCENTIVE GRANTS, *20.601*
Alcohol abuse, alcoholism
AIDS-afflicted persons, housing, services, *14.241*
Alcohol Open Container Requirements, DOT, *20.607*
biomedical, behavioral sciences research, *93.273*, *93.891*
crime-related, research, cause, prevention, DOJ, *16.560*
Driving While Intoxicated, repeat offender laws, DOT, *20.608*
Drug-Free Schools and Communities, national programs, *84.184*
Drug-Free Schools and Communities, states, *84.186*
drunk driving control programs, *20.600*, *20.601*, *20.605*
Food Stamps, *10.551*
health, mental health care services information, *93.230*
HIV care, *93.917*
HIV emergency relief projects, *93.914*
HIV prevention, *93.939*
homeless, mental health, social services, *93.150*
Indian Country Alcohol and Drug Prevention, DOJ, *16.616*
juveniles, prevention, *16.542*
mental health services, PRNS, *93.243*
minority community health coalitions, *93.137*
Offender Reentry Program, *16.202*
offenders, justice, health, social services networks, *93.229*
prevention, rehabilitation, treatment research training, *93.271*, *93.272*
research centers, *93.891*
Social Services Block Grant, *93.667*
Substance Abuse Pilot Treatment Block Grant monitoring, evaluation, *93.238*
Substance Abuse Prevention and Treatment Block Grant, *93.959*
Tribal Youth Program, OJJDP, *16.731*
underage drinking law enforcement, *16.727*
uninsured patients, Healthy Community Access Program, *93.252*
urban Indian program, *93.193*
veterans program, 64.019
see also Behavioral sciences, education, services; Drug abuse; Family therapy; Mental health; Social services; Volunteers
ALCOHOL OPEN CONTAINER REQUIREMENTS, *20.607*
ALCP (Assisted Living Conversion Program), HUD, *14.314*

Aleuts, see Alaska, Alaska natives; Indian *entries*
Aliens, immigrants, refugees
African refugees, BPRM, *19.517*
bilingual health demonstrations, *93.105*
citizenship education, training, 97.010
citizenship verification, 11.006
Cuban, Haitian resettlement, *97.009*
discretionary grants, *93.576*
East Asian refugees, BPRM, *19.511*
employment, civil rights education, enforcement, *16.110*
English Language Acquisition Grants, *84.365*
European, Central Asian refugees, BPRM, *19.520*
food stamps eligibility, *10.551*
Immigration and Nationality Acts, *16.110*, *16.606*, 17.202, 17.203, 17.252, 17.301, 17.303, *19.510*, *93.584*, 97.010
job, social services, *93.583*
labor certification, 17.202, 17.203
Migration and Refugee Assistance Act (MRA), *19.510*, *19.511*, *19.517*, *19.518*, *19.519*, *19.520*, *19.522*
Near Eastern refugees, BPRM, *19.519*
Office of Refugee Resettlement programs, *93.566*, *93.567*, *93.576*, *93.579*, *93.583*, *93.584*, *93.598*
overseas refugee assistance, global priorities, BPRM, *19.520*
Real ID Program, DHS, *97.089*
Refugee Act of 1980, *93.566*, *93.567*, *93.576*, *93.583*
Refugee Education Assistance Act of 1980, *93.566*, *93.576*, *93.583*, *93.584*, *97.009*
repatriation program, *93.579*
resettlement agencies, services, *93.567*
Services for Trafficking Victims, *16.320*
Social Security benefits, *96.001*, *96.002*
specialty occupations, employer attestations, 17.252
state-administered resettlement program, *93.566*
State Criminal Alien Assistance Program, DOJ, *16.606*
targeted assistance, jobs, *93.584*
temporary work, 17.202, 17.203
torture victims assistance, *93.604*
trafficking victims assistance, ACF, *93.584*, *93.598*
Unaccompanied Alien Children Program, *93.676*
undocumented, emergency health services reimbursement, *93.784*
U.S. Refugee Admissions Program, BPRM, *19.510*
victim assistance program personnel training, *16.582*
Western Hemisphere refugees, BPRM, *19.518*
Wilson/Fish programs, *93.583*
see also Bilingual education, services; English as a second language; Farm workers; International programs, studies; Public assistance; Social services; Volunteers
ALL-VOLUNTEER FORCE EDUCATIONAL ASSISTANCE [DVA], *64.124*
ALLERGY, IMMUNOLOGY AND TRANSPLANTATION RESEARCH, *93.855*
Allied health professions, see Health professions
ALLIED HEALTH SPECIAL PROJECTS, *93.191*
Alternative, complementary medicine, *93.213*
ALTERNATIVE OR INNOVATIVE TREATMENT TECHNOLOGY RESEARCH, DEMONSTRATION, TRAINING, AND HAZARDOUS SUBSTANCE RESEARCH GRANTS, *66.813*
ALZHEIMER'S DISEASE DEMONSTRATION GRANTS TO STATES, *93.051*
Alzheimer's disease, related disorders, see Aging and the aged
AMBCC (Alaska Migratory Bird Co-Management Council), FWS, *15.643*
Amblyopia research, *93.867*
Ambulance service, see Rescue services
AMD (Acid Mine Drainage), DOI, *15.253*
AMERICAN BATTLEFIELD PROTECTION, *15.926*
American Battlefield Protection Act, see Historic monuments, historic preservation
AMERICAN COUNCIL OF YOUNG POLITICAL LEADERS [BECA], *19.403*
American Dream Downpayment Initiative (ADDI), *14.239*
American Homeownership and Economic Opportunity Act of 2000, see National housing acts
American Indians, see Indian *entries*
American natives, see Alaska, Alaska natives; Hawaii, Hawaii natives; Indian *entries*; U.S. possessions, territories
AMERICAN OVERSEAS RESEARCH CENTERS, *84.274*
American Samoa, see U.S. possessions, territories
American Technology Preeminence Act, see Technology transfer, utilization
Americans with Disabilities Act (ADA), see Disabled, handicapped
AMERICANS WITH DISABILITIES ACT TECHNICAL ASSISTANCE PROGRAM, *16.108*
AmeriCorps
community service projects, *94.006*
higher education institutions, community programs, *94.005*
National and Community Service Act of 1990, *94.003*, *94.004*, *94.005*, *94.006*, *94.007*
National and Community Service Trust Act of 1993, *94.002*, *94.009*, *94.011*, *94.016*
planning, development, demonstration projects, *94.007*
school, community programs, *94.004*
State Commissions, *94.003*
training, technical assistance, *94.009*
VISTA program, 94.013
see also Volunteers
AMERICORPS, *94.006*
AMLR (Abandoned Mine Land Reclamation), *15.252*
AMS (Agricultural Marketing Service), USDA, see Agency Index
Anadromous Fish Conservation Act, see Fish
ANADROMOUS FISH CONSERVATION ACT PROGRAM, *11.405*
ANE (Alaska Native Education), DOED, *84.356*
Anesthesiology, see Pharmacology, pharmacy
Anesthetists, see Health professions
ANILCA (Alaska National Interest Lands Conservation Act), *15.055*

Animal and Plant Health Inspection Service, USDA,
    see Agency Index
Animal Damage Control, *10.028*
Animal disease control, health, welfare
    Animal Damage Control Act of 1931, *10.028*
    Animal Welfare Act, *10.025*
    Avian Influenza Indemnity Program, *10.029*
    competitive research grants, *10.206*
    endangered species conservation, *15.615*
    FEMA, disaster home study courses, 97.027
    Homeland Security—Agricultural, *10.304*
    international assistance, *10.960*
    international, great apes conservation, *15.629*
    international, elephant conservation, *15.620, 15.621*
    international research exchanges, *10.961*
    international, rhinoceros, tiger conservation, *15.619*
    interstate control, technical assistance, training, *10.025*
    Lyme Disease, *93.942*
    marine mammal data, *11.439*
    pest management research, *10.200*
    research, *10.207*
    research, SBIR, *10.212*
    rodent control, preventive health services block grant, *93.991*
    Ruminant Feed Ban Support Project, FDA, *93.449*
    Wild Horse and Burro Management, BLM, *15.229*
    wildlife-borne diseases, *10.028*
    see also Environmental management; Laboratory animals; Livestock industry; Poultry, egg products; Veterinary medicine; Wildlife, waterfowl
Animal drugs, *see* Animal disease control, health, welfare; Veterinary medicine
ANIMAL HEALTH AND DISEASE RESEARCH, *10.207*
Animal welfare, *see* Animal disease control, health, welfare
Anorexia research, *93.848*
Antarctic, Arctic research, *47.078*
Anthropology, *see* History; Humanities *entries*; Social sciences
Anti-discrimination, *see* Civil rights; Complaint investigation
Anti-Drug Abuse Act (ADAA), *see* Drug abuse
Anti-dumping duties, *see* International commerce, investment; Trade adjustment assistance
Anti-Terrorism and Effective Death Penalty Act of 1996 (ATEDPA), *see* Civil defense
ANTITERRORISM EMERGENCY RESERVE, *16.321*
Anti-terrorism, terrorism, *see* Civil defense
AOA (Administration on Aging), HHS, *see* Agency Index
AORC (American Overseas Research Centers), *84.274*
APPALACHIAN AREA DEVELOPMENT, *23.002*
Appalachian Corridors, *23.003*
APPALACHIAN DEVELOPMENT HIGHWAY SYSTEM, *23.003*
APPALACHIAN LOCAL DEVELOPMENT DISTRICT ASSISTANCE, *23.009*
Appalachian Program, *23.001*

Appalachian region
    Appalachian Corridors, *23.003*
    Appalachian Program, *23.001*
    Appalachian Regional Development Act, *23.001* through *23.011*
    economic, social development technical assistance, *23.011*
    flood warning systems, *11.450*
    highway system development, *23.003*
    Local Development Districts (LDD), planning assistance, *23.009*
    State Research, *23.011*
    Supplemental and Direct Grants, *23.002*
    Appalachian Regional Commission, 23.001 through 23.011
APPALACHIAN REGIONAL DEVELOPMENT, *23.001*
APPALACHIAN RESEARCH, TECHNICAL ASSISTANCE, AND DEMONSTRATION PROJECTS, *23.011*
APPLIED METEOROLOGICAL RESEARCH, *11.468*
APPLIED TOXICOLOGICAL RESEARCH AND TESTING, *93.114*
Apprenticeship training
    coastal ecosystem management, NOAA, *11.473*
    Community Food Projects, USDA, *10.225*
    disabled veterans, *17.801*
    HUD Youthbuild Program, *14.243*
    ironworkers, native Americans, *15.146*
    National Apprenticeship Act of 1937, 17.201
    native American language preservation, *93.587*
    program development, registration, 17.201
    Tech-Prep Education, *84.243*
    Tech-Prep Demonstration Grants, *84.353*
    work study programs, *84.033*
    see also Disadvantaged, employment and training; Employment development, training; Fellowships, scholarships, traineeships; Technical training; Veterans education, training; Vocational education
Apprenticeship Training, Employer and Labor Service (ATELS), DOL, 17.201
Aquaculture
    business financing, *11.415*
    Crop Disaster Program, *10.073*
    Crop Insurance, *10.450*
    damage, disease control, USDA, *10.028*
    disaster assistance, noninsured crops, *10.451*
    emergency loans, *10.404*
    farm operating loans, *10.406*
    fisheries development, utilization research, *11.427*
    Hawaii Sustainable Fisheries Development, *11.444*
    international research exchanges, *10.961*
    Livestock Compensation Program, *10.077*
    loans, farm enterprises *10.407*
    research, SBIR, *10.212*
    research, Sea Grant Support, *11.417*
    sport fish research, development, *15.605*
    see also Agricultural marketing; Agricultural research, sciences; Farm, nonfarm enterprises; Fish; Fisheries industry; Food inspection, grading
Aquaria, *see* Museums, galleries
AQUATIC PLANT CONTROL, 12.100
Aquatic plants, *see* Marine sciences; Plants

Arboreta, *see* Museums, galleries
Archaeology
American Battlefield Protection, NPS, *15.926*
Archaeological Resources Protection Act, *15.041, 15.224*
Cultural Resource Management, BLM, *15.224*
historic preservation, *15.904, 15.923*
Indian Programs, *15.041*
National Register of Historic Places, 15.914
native American graves protection, repatriation, *15.922*
Save America's Treasures, NPS, *15.929*
watershed, river basin projects, 10.906
see also Historic monuments, historic preservation; History; Humanities *entries*; Social sciences
ARCHITECTURAL AND TRANSPORTATION BARRIERS COMPLIANCE BOARD, 88.001
Architectural and Transportation Barriers Compliance Board (ATBCB), 88.001
ARCHITECTURAL BARRIERS ACT ENFORCEMENT, 14.407
Architecture
ADA technical assistance, *16.108*
Architectural Barriers Act, 88.001
Architectural Barriers Act Enforcement, HUD programs, 14.407
earthquake hazards mitigation, *15.807*
energy conservation, renewable energy outreach, training, *81.117*
EPA environmental sustainability design competition, *66.516*
handicapped, architectural barriers standards, training, 88.001
Hazard Mitigation Grant, FEMA, *97.039*
historic preservation, *15.904, 15.923*
historic properties preservation, technical services, 15.915
National Register of Historic Places, 15.914
Universities Rebuilding America Program, Hurricanes Katrina, Rita, HUD, *14.521*
Vessel Hull Design Protection Service, 42.009
see also Arts, arts education; Buildings; Construction; Historic monuments, historic preservation; Housing research; Urban planning
Arctic, Antarctic research, *47.078*
AREA (Academic Research Enhancement Award), NIH, *93.390*
Area studies, *see* Foreign languages; International programs, studies
AREERA (Agricultural Research, Extension, and Education Reform Act of 1998), *see* Agriculture research, sciences
Armed forces, *see* Military; Veterans *entries*
ARMS (Adjustable Rate Mortgages), *14.175*
Army Corps of Engineers, DOD, *see* Agency Index (DOD, Department of the Army, Office of the Chief of Engineers)
Army Materiel Command, DOD, *see* Agency Index
Army Medical Command, DOD, *see* Agency Index
ARS (Agricultural Research Service), USDA, *see* Agency Index
Arson, *see* Crime; Firefighting, fire prevention, control
Art, *see* Arts, arts education
Art galleries, *see* Museums, galleries

ARTHRITIS, MUSCULOSKELETAL AND SKIN DISEASES RESEARCH, *93.846*
Arthritis research, *see* Health, medical research
Arthritis State-Based Programs, CDCP, *93.945*
Artifacts indemnity, *45.201*
ARTS AND ARTIFACTS INDEMNITY, *45.201*
Arts, arts education
art works, artifacts indemnity, *45.201*
Arts in Education, OESE, *84.351*
BECA arts exchanges, *19.409*
employees, grant-assisted productions, wage standards, 17.303
federal real property transfer, 15.918
graduate fellowships, *84.170*
historical collections, preservation, *89.003*
IMLS assistance, *45.301*
Indian Arts and Crafts Acts, 15.850
Indian arts, crafts, 15.850
Japan-U.S. Friendship Commission Grants, *90.300*
Junior Duck Stamp Contest, FWS, *15.644*
National Foundation on the Arts and the Humanities Act of 1965 (NFAHA), *45.024* through *45.313*
National Gallery exhibits, 68.001
NEA grants, organizations, individuals, *45.024*
NEA Partnership Agreements, state plans, presenting, *45.025*
Save America's Treasures, NPS, *15.929*
Smithsonian fellowships, *85.601*
see also Audiovisual aids, film, video; Copyright services; Education *entries*; Foreign languages; Historic monuments, historic preservation; Humanities *entries*; Literature; Museums, galleries; Music; Teacher education, training
ARTS EXCHANGES ON INTERNATIONAL ISSUES [BECA], *19.409*
ARTS IN EDUCATION, *84.351*
ASCS (Agricultural Stabilization and Conservation Service), *see* Agency Index (USDA, Farm Service Agency)
ASHA (Assistance to Schools and Hospitals Abroad), USAID, *98.006*
ASIAN ELEPHANT CONSERVATION, *15.621*
ASSESSMENT AND WATERSHED PROTECTION PROGRAM GRANTS, *66.480*
ASSETS FOR INDEPENDENCE DEMONSTRATION PROGRAM [HHS], *93.602*
ASSISTANCE FOR INDIAN CHILDREN WITH SEVERE DISABILITIES, *15.045*
ASSISTANCE PROGRAMS FOR CHRONIC DISEASE PREVENTION AND CONTROL, *93.945*
ASSISTANCE FOR TORTURE VICTIMS, *93.604*
ASSISTANCE TO FIREFIGHTERS GRANT, *97.044*
ASSISTANCE TO HIGH ENERGY COST RURAL COMMUNITIES, *10.859*
Assistance to Schools and Hospitals Abroad (ASHA), USAID, *98.006*
ASSISTANCE TO STATE WATER RESOURCES RESEARCH INSTITUTES, *15.805*
ASSISTANCE TO TRIBALLY CONTROLLED COMMUNITY COLLEGES AND UNIVERSITIES, *15.027*
Assisted housing, *see* Housing, subsidized

Assisted Living Conversion Program (ALCP), HUD, 14.314
ASSISTIVE TECHNOLOGY, 84.224
Assistive Technology Act, see Disabled, handicapped
ASSISTIVE TECHNOLOGY—STATE GRANTS FOR PROTECTION AND ADVOCACY [DOED], 84.343
Asthma research, 93.855

Astronomy
Applied Meteorology Research, 11.468
basic research, 47.049
environmental systems research, NOAA, 11.432
meteorologic, hydrologic modernization development, 11.467
see also Aeronautics, space; Physical sciences; Scientific research

ATBCB (Architectural and Transportation Barriers Compliance Board), 88.001
ATEDPA (Anti-Terrorism and Effective Death Penalty Act of 1996), see Civil defense
ATELS (Apprenticeship Training, Employer and Labor Service), DOL, 17.201
ATF (Bureau of Alcohol, Tobacco and Firearms), Department of Justice, see Agency Index
ATLANTIC COAST FISHERIES COOPERATIVE MANAGEMENT ACT, 11.474
Atmospheric science, see Aeronautics, space; Astronomy; Climate; Geology; Physical sciences; Scientific research
Atomic energy, see Nuclear sciences, technology; Public safety; Radiation
Atomic Energy Act, see Nuclear sciences, technology
ATP (Advanced Technology Program), 11.612
ATR (Access to Recovery), SAMSHA, 93.275
ATTESTATIONS BY EMPLOYERS USING NON-IMMIGRANT ALIENS IN SPECIALTY OCCUPATIONS, 17.252
ATTORNEY FEES—INDIAN RIGHTS, 15.053
Attorneys, see Legal services
Audiology, see Audiovisual aids, film, video; Deafness and the deaf; Speech pathology

Audiovisual aids, film, video
ADA technical assistance, 16.108
aerospace, 43.001
AIDS prevention, school health projects, 93.938
BECA arts exchanges, 19.409
blind, handicapped persons, braille, cassette, talking books, instructional, library services, 42.001
chemical emergency planning, EPA, 66.810
child abuse, closed-circuit TV, DOJ, 16.611
Copyright Service, 42.002
humanities collections preservation, 45.149
mine safety, 17.602
National Audiovisual Center, NTIS, 11.650
National Gallery exhibits, 68.001
Ready to Teach, OERI, 84.286
Rural Business-Cooperative Service, 10.350
Rural Community Development Initiative, RHS, 10.446
special education services, 84.327
see also Arts, arts education; Educational resources; Libraries; Museums, galleries; Radio, television

Auditory defects, see Deafness and the deaf
Autistic children, see Disabled, handicapped children
AUTOMATED FLOOD WARNING SYSTEM, 11.450
Automatic data processing, see Computer products, sciences, services; Technology transfer, utilization
Automobiles, see Highways, roads, bridges; Motor vehicles; Transportation
AUTOMOBILES AND ADAPTIVE EQUIPMENT FOR CERTAIN DISABLED VETERANS AND MEMBERS OF THE ARMED FORCES, 64.100
AVIAN INFLUENZA INDEMNITY PROGRAM, 10.029
Aviation, see Aeronautics, space; Air transportation
AVIATION EDUCATION, 20.100
AVIATION RESEARCH GRANTS [DHS], 97.069
AVIATION RESEARCH GRANTS [DOT], 20.108
AWFS (Automated Flood Warning System), NOAA, 11.400

BANK ENTERPRISE AWARDS PROGRAM, 21.021

Banks, banking
agricultural loan mediation services, 10.435
Bank Enterprise Awards Program, 21.021
counterfeit currency control training, Secret Service, 97.015
debt collection practices complaints, 36.001
Equal Credit Opportunity Act of 1976, 16.103
guaranteed student loans, 84.032
Interest Assistance Program, farms, 10.437
low-income, Individual Development Accounts, 93.602
SBA Section 7(j) projects, 59.007
SEC activities, 58.001
see also Agricultural loans; Business development; Civil rights; Credit unions; Housing mortgage, loan insurance; Insurance; International commerce, investment; Small business

Barley, see Agricultural commodities, stabilization; Feed grains
Barry M. Goldwater Scholarship and Excellence in Education Foundation, see Agency Index (Scholarship and Fellowship Foundations)
BARRY M. GOLDWATER SCHOLARSHIP PROGRAM, 85.200
BASIC AND APPLIED SCIENTIFIC RESEARCH [DOD], 12.300
BASIC, APPLIED, AND ADVANCED RESEARCH IN SCIENCE AND ENGINEERING [DOD], 12.630
BASIC CENTER GRANTS [HHS], 93.623
Basic Center Program, runaway, homeless youth, 93.623
BASIC/CORE AREA HEALTH EDUCATION CENTERS, 93.824
Basic research, see subject of research—e.g., Agricultural research; Health, medical research; Scientific research
BASIC SCIENTIFIC RESEARCH [DOD], 12.431
BAT (Bureau of Apprenticeship and Training), see Apprenticeship Training, Employer and Labor Service (ATELS), DOL

MASTER INDEX 893

BATF (Bureau of Alcohol, Tobacco and Firearms), Department of Justice, *see* Agency Index
BCP (Basic Center Program), ACF, *93.623*
BEA (Bank Enterprise Awards), *21.021*
BEACH EROSION CONTROL PROJECTS, *12.101*
BEACH MONITORING AND NOTIFICATION PROGRAM IMPLEMENTATION GRANTS, *66.472*
BECA (Bureau of Educational and Cultural Affairs), Department of State, *see* Agency Index
BEDI (Brownfields Economic Development Initiative), HUD, *14.246*
Beef, *see* Livestock industry
Bees, *see* Agricultural commodities, stabilization; Farm, nonfarm enterprises
Behavioral sciences, education, services
  Academic Research Enhancement Award, health sciences, *93.390*
  AIDS studies, *93.943*
  aging research, biomedical, behavioral, social sciences, geriatrics, *93.866*
  Air Force Defense Research Sciences Program, *12.800*
  alcohol research centers, *93.891*
  alcoholism research, *93.273*
  alcoholism research training, *93.271*, *93.272*
  alternative, complementary medicine research, *93.213*
  Anti-Terrorism and Emergency Assistance Program, DOJ, *16.321*
  aviation research, *20.108*, *20.109*
  clinical psychology scholarships, disadvantaged, *93.925*
  Community Mental Health Services block grant, *93.958*
  corrections, law enforcement personnel, family support, *16.563*
  deafness, communicative disorders research, *93.173*
  DHS Scholars and Fellows, *97.062*
  digestive diseases, research, anorexia, bulimia, obesity, *93.848*
  disabilities prevention, *93.184*
  disasters, Crisis Counseling, *97.032*
  drug abuse, addiction behavioral research, *93.279*
  drug abuse, professionals training, DEA, *16.004*
  education assistance, disadvantaged, *93.822*
  education loan repayments, states, *93.165*
  environmental health hazards research, *93.113*
  faculty education loan repayments, disadvantaged, *93.923*
  FBI Academy training, *16.300*
  geriatrics education centers, *93.969*
  geriatrics faculty fellowships, *93.156*
  Great Lakes fish consumption effects, *93.208*
  injury prevention research, *93.136*
  international research awards, *93.989*
  mental health disciplines, training, *93.244*
  mental health research, *93.242*
  mental health research training, *93.281*, *93.282*
  minority health coalitions, *93.137*
  minority health, disparities research, researchers education loan repayment, *93.307*
  mothers, children, human development research, *93.865*
  NHSC education loan repayments, *93.162*
  NIH Clinical Research Loan Repayment Program (CR-LRP), *93.280*
  NIH intramural research training, *93.140*
  NIH Pediatric Research Loan Repayment Program, *93.285*, *93.385*
  NIH Undergraduate Scholarship Program, disadvantaged, *93.187*
  NSF research, *47.075*
  Nursing Research, *93.361*
  Public Health Research Accreditation Project, *93.993*
  rehabilitation personnel training, *84.246*
  repatriation program, *93.579*
  research, research infrastructure resources, training, NIH, *93.389*
  sleep disorders research, *93.233*
  substance abuse, dependency counseling, veterans, *64.019*
  substance abuse treatment, prisoners, DOJ, *16.593*
  torture victims assistance, *93.604*
  University-Based Homeland Security Centers, DHS, *97.061*
  veterans, service personnel, education, vocational counseling, *64.125*
  vocational rehabilitation personnel training, *84.275*
  see also Biological sciences; Community health services; Family therapy; Health, medical education, training; Health, medical research; Health professions; Mental health; Mental retardation; National Research Service Awards; Social sciences; Social services; Veterans *entries*; Victim assistance; Vocational rehabilitation
BENJAMIN GILMAN INTERNATIONAL SCHOLARSHIP, *19.425*
BIA (Bureau of Indian Affairs), DOI, *see* Agency Index
Bicycle paths, *see* Recreation
BILINGUAL/BICULTURAL SERVICE DEMONSTRATION GRANTS [HHS], *93.105*
Bilingual education, services
  bilingual, bicultural health demonstrations, *93.105*
  migrant children, *84.011*
  project technical assistance, training, *84.283*
  see also Adult education; Disadvantaged, education; Elementary and Secondary Education acts; English as a second language; Foreign languages; Teacher education, training; Tutoring
BILL EMERSON HUMANITARIAN TRUST [USDA], *10.079*
BIO (Bioenergy Program), FSA, *10.078*
Bioassay of Chemicals and Test Development, *93.114*
BIODIESEL, *10.306*
BIOENERGY PROGRAM, *10.078*
BIOLOGICAL RESPONSE TO ENVIRONMENTAL HEALTH HAZARDS, *93.113*
Biological sciences
  Academic Research Enhancement Award, health sciences, *93.390*
  aging, research, *93.866*
  agricultural, biotechnology risk assessment, *10.219*

Biological sciences *(continued)*
agricultural, graduate fellowships, *10.210*
agricultural research, *10.206, 10.224*
Air Force Defense Research Sciences Program, *12.800*
alcoholism, biomedical research, *93.273*
alcoholism, biomedical research training, *93.271, 93.272*
alcoholism, multidisciplinary research, *93.891*
allergy, immunology research, *93.855*
alternative, complementary medicine research, *93.213*
Army Research Office, *12.431*
biomedical imaging research, *93.286*
biomedical research traineeships, international program, *93.989*
biostatistics NRSA, *93.225*
biostatistics, public health graduate traineeships, *93.964*
cancer research, *93.396*
cancer research manpower development, NRSA, *93.398*
carcinogens research, *93.393*
deafness, communicative disorders research, *93.173*
DOD sciences research, fellowships, *12.630*
drug abuse, addiction research, *93.279*
energy-related basic research, *81.049*
environmental health, biometry, risk estimation, *93.115*
environmental health hazards research, *93.113*
Environmental Health Sciences Centers, *93.894*
EPA environmental sustainability design competition, *66.516*
FDA research, *93.103*
fish, wildlife water, land management, 15.608
fossil energy research, *81.089*
geosciences research, *47.050*
human development research, *93.865*
human genomes research, *93.172*
measurement, engineering research, standards, *11.609*
mental health research training, *93.282*
microbiology, infectious diseases research, *93.856*
military, biological-medical research, *12.420*
minority health, disparities research, researchers education loan repayment, *93.307*
Navy research, education support, *12.300*
neurosciences research, *93.853*
NIEHS Superfund research, hazardous materials, *93.143*
NIH Clinical Research Loan Repayment Program (CR-LRP), *93.280*
NIH intramural research training, *93.140*
NIH Pediatric Research Loan Repayment Program, *93.285, 93.385*
NIH Undergraduate Scholarship Program, disadvantaged, *93.187*
NOAA unallied projects, *11.452, 11.472*
NSF biomedical engineering education, research, *47.041*
NSF research, *47.074*
pharmacology, physiology, biorelated chemistry research, training, *93.859*
Polar Programs, *47.078*
research, research infrastructure resources, training, *93.389*
Sea Grant Support, *11.417*
sleep disorders research, *93.233*
stem cell research, *93.839*
transplantation biology research, *93.839, 93.855*
watershed, river basin projects, 10.906
WMD, domestic preparedness, *97.004, 97.005, 97.006, 97.007*
see also Behavioral sciences, education, services; Cancer control, prevention, research; Chemicals, chemistry; Civil defense; Drug abuse; Drugs, drug research; Environmental sciences; Genetics; Health, medical research; Minority education; National Research Service Awards; Pharmacology, pharmacy; Physical sciences; Science education; Scientific research
BIOLOGICAL SCIENCES, *47.074*
Biomass energy, *see* Energy *entries*
BIOMEDICAL RESEARCH AND RESEARCH TRAINING, *93.859*
BIOMETRY AND RISK ESTIMATION—HEALTH RISKS FROM ENVIRONMENTAL EXPOSURES, *93.115*
BIOTECHNOLOGY RISK ASSESSMENT RESEARCH, *10.219*
Bioterrorism, *see* Civil defense
BIOTERRORISM TRAINING AND CURRICULUM DEVELOPMENT [HHS], *93.996*
Birds, *see* Animal disease control, health, welfare; Poultry, egg products; Recreation*entries*; Wildlife, waterfowl
Birth control, *see* Family planning
Black lung, *see* Coal mining; Respiratory diseases
Black Lung Clinics, *93.965*
BLIND REHABILITATION CENTERS, 64.007
Blindness and the blind
braille, cassettes, talking books, instructional, library services, 42.001
elderly, independent living services, *84.177*
federal employment, 27.005
Food Stamps, *10.551*
home health services, Medicaid, *93.778*
income support, Guam, Puerto Rico, Virgin Islands, *93.560*
income support, Social Security, *96.006*
independent living services, *84.169*
interpreter, sign language training, *84.160*
National Eye Institute research, *93.867*
preschool education, *84.173*
rehabilitation personnel training, *84.264*
veterans, optical aids, 64.013
veterans rehabilitation centers, 64.007
vocational rehabilitation personnel training, *84.129, 84.275*
vocational rehabilitation services, *84.126, 84.128*
see also Audiovisual aids, film, video; Community health services; Disabled, handicapped *entries*; Health, medical *entries*; Veterans, disabled; Vocational rehabilitation; Volunteers
BLM (Bureau of Land Management), DOI, *see* Agency Index
Block grant programs
CDBG Economic Development Initiative, Section 108, *14.246*
Child Care and Development Block Grant Act of 1990, *93.575, 93.596*

MASTER INDEX 895

child care and development, CCDF, *93.575,*
  93.596
child care/social services, TANF, *93.558*
community development, entitlement, *14.218*
community development, Indians, *14.862*
community development, insular areas, *14.225*
community development, small cities, *14.219,*
  14.228
community development, states, *14.228*
community food, nutrition, CSBG, *93.571*
Community Mental Health Services, *93.958*
community services, CSBG, *93.569*
community services, discretionary, *93.570*
Empowerment Zones Program, *10.772, 14.244*
energy assistance, low-income, LIHEAP, *93.568*
Indian housing, *14.867*
Juvenile Accountability Incentives, *16.523*
law enforcement, local, *16.592*
Maternal and Child Health Services, *93.994*
Native Hawaiian housing, *14.873*
Preventive Health and Health Services, *93.991*
Residential Energy Assistance Challenge Program
  (REACH), ACF, *93.568*
social services, SSBG, *93.667*
Substance Abuse Pilot Treatment, monitoring,
  evaluation, *93.238*
Substance Abuse Prevention and Treatment,
  93.959
transit planning research, FTA, *20.515*
BLOCK GRANTS FOR COMMUNITY MENTAL
  HEALTH SERVICES, *93.958*
BLOCK GRANTS FOR PREVENTION AND
  TREATMENT OF SUBSTANCE ABUSE,
  93.959
BLOOD DISEASES AND RESOURCES
  RESEARCH, *93.839*
BLS (Bureau of Labor Statistics), DOL, *see* Agency
  Index
Boating, *see* Recreation, water; Water navigation
Boating Infrastructure Grant Program, *15.622*
BOATING SAFETY, 97.011
BOATING SAFETY FINANCIAL ASSISTANCE,
  97.012
BOLL WEEVIL ERADICATION LOAN
  PROGRAM, *10.449*
BOND GUARANTEES FOR SURETY
  COMPANIES, *59.016*
Bonds, *see* Insurance
BOOKS FOR THE BLIND AND PHYSICALLY
  HANDICAPPED, 42.001
BORDER ENFORCEMENT GRANTS [DOT],
  20.233
Botanical gardens, *45.301*
Botany, *see* Biological sciences; Plants
Braille, *see* Blindness and the blind
Brain tumors research, *93.853*
Breast cancer, *see* Cancer control, prevention,
  research
BRIDGE ALTERATION, 97.014
Bridges, *see* Highways, roads, bridges
Broadcasting, *see* Communications,
  telecommunications; Radio, television
BROWNFIELD JOB TRAINING COOPERATIVE
  AGREEMENTS [EPA], *66.815*
Brownfield projects, *see* Urban renewal
BROWNFIELDS ASSESSMENT AND CLEANUP
  COOPERATIVE AGREEMENTS [EPA],
  66.818
BROWNFIELDS TRAINING, RESEARCH, AND
  TECHNICAL ASSISTANCE GRANTS AND
  COOPERATIVE AGREEMENTS [EPA],
  66.814
Brucellosis, *see* Animal disease control, health,
  welfare
BUFFER ZONE PROTECTION PLAN [DHS],
  97.078
Buildings
  Architectural Barriers Act Enforcement, HUD
    programs, 14.407
  code enforcement, CDBG programs, *14.218,*
    14.219, 14.228
  code enforcement, CDBG programs, Indians,
    14.862
  code enforcement, CDBG programs, insular areas,
    14.225
  codes, standards, DOE special state initiatives,
    81.119
  demolition, CDBG programs, *14.218, 14.219,*
    14.228
  demolition, CDBG programs, Indians, *14.862*
  demolition, CDBG programs, insular areas, *14.225*
  earthquake hazards mitigation, *15.807*
  energy conservation, renewable energy outreach,
    training, *81.117*
  energy conservation, solar research, *81.087*
  energy conservation technology research, *81.086*
  EPA building decontamination research, *66.511*
  EPA environmental sustainability design
    competition, *66.516*
  handicapped, accessibility standards, design,
    research, training, 88.001
  Hazard Mitigation Grant, FEMA, *97.039*
  historic preservation, *15.904*
  historic preservation, technical assistance, 15.915
  HUD technology research, *14.506*
  industrial, "recycling," EDA projects, *11.300*
  lead-based paint hazard control, *14.900*
  manufactured home standards, 14.171
  National Register of Historic Places, 15.914
  nonresidential structure construction loans,
    14.142
  Pre-Disaster Mitigation, FEMA, *97.017, 97.047*
  property improvement loans, *14.142*
  rehabilitation, CDBG programs, *14.218, 14.219,*
    14.228
  rehabilitation, CDBG programs, Indians, *14.862*
  rehabilitation, CDBG programs, insular areas,
    14.225
  standards, research, *11.609*
  see also Architecture; Construction; Education
    facilities; Energy conservation; Health facilities
    entries; Historic monuments, historic
    preservation; Housing, *entries*
Bulimia research, *93.848*
BULLETPROOF VEST PARTNERSHIP
  PROGRAM, *16.607*
Burdick rural health training, *93.192*
Bureau of Alcohol, Tobacco and Firearms (ATF),
  Department of Justice, *see* Agency Index
Bureau of Apprenticeship and Training (BAT), *see*
  Apprenticeship Training, Employer and Labor
  Service (ATELS), DOL

Bureau of Economic Analysis, *see* Agency Index (USDC, Economics and Statistics Administration)
Bureau of Educational and Cultural Affairs (BECA), Department of State, *see* Agency Index
Bureau of Export Administration, USDC, *see* Agency Index (*now,* Bureau of Industry and Security)
Bureau of Indian Affairs (BIA), DOI, *see* Agency Index
BUREAU OF INDIAN AFFAIRS FACILITIES— OPERATIONS AND MAINTENANCE, *15.048*
Bureau of Industry and Security, USDC, *see* Agency Index
Bureau of Intelligence and Research, Department of State, *see* Agency Index
Bureau of Justice Assistance, DOJ, *see* Agency Index (DOJ, Office of Justice Programs)
Bureau of Justice Statistics, DOJ, *see* Agency Index
Bureau of Labor Statistics (BLS), DOL, *see* Agency Index
Bureau of Land Management (BLM), DOI, *see* Agency Index
Bureau of Near Eastern Affairs, Department of State, *see* Agency Index
Bureau of Oceans and International Environmental and Scientific Affairs, Department of State, *see* Agency Index
Bureau of Personnel, Department of State, *see* Agency Index
Bureau of Population, Refugees, and Migration, Department of State, *see* Agency Index
Bureau of Prisons, DOJ, *see* Agency Index (DOJ, National Institute of Corrections)
Bureau of Reclamation, DOI, *see* Agency Index
Bureau of the Census, USDC, *see* Agency Index
BURIAL EXPENSES ALLOWANCE FOR VETERANS, *64.101*
Burial sites, *see* Historic monuments, historic preservation; Veterans death benefits
BUSINESS AND INDUSTRY LOANS [USDA], *10.768*
BUSINESS AND INTERNATIONAL EDUCATION PROJECTS [DOED], *84.153*

Business development
Appalachian region, *23.002*
Bank Enterprise Awards Program, *21.021*
business, industrial facilities, EDA projects, *11.300*
Business and Industry Data Centers, 11.004
business internships, Eurasian executives, scientists, *11.114*
business internships, secondary students, *84.353*
CDBG programs, *14.218, 14.219, 14.228*
CDBG programs, Indians, *14.862*
CDBG programs, insular areas, *14.225*
Certified Development Company Loans, *59.041*
Community Development Financial Institutions Program, *21.020*
Delta region, *90.200, 90.201, 90.202*
disadvantaged, government procurement assistance, 59.006
DOD procurement assistance, *12.002*
DOE patent licensing, 81.003
economic data, analysis, national, 11.025
economic development technical assistance, *11.303*
energy-related inventions, *81.036*
export counseling, information, 11.108
export information, training, 11.150
Export Loans, SBA, *59.054*
Export Promotion Market Development Cooperation, *11.112*
foreign investments, OPIC, *70.002, 70.003*
foreign trade assistance, 11.110
foreign trade zones (U.S.), 11.111
Global Business Opportunities, ESA-USDC, 11.026
FTC services, 36.001
Indians, Alaska natives, *14.862*
Indians, tribal revolving loan funds, loan guarantees, *15.032*
ITA Special Projects, *11.113*
management, SBDC technical assistance, *59.026, 59.037*
Manufacturing Extension Partnership, NIST, *11.611*
manufacturing technology commercialization, *11.612*
microenterprise development training, technical assistance, *59.050*
Microloan Demonstration Program, *59.046*
Minority Business Opportunity Committee, *11.803*
minority, management, technical assistance, *11.800*
National Trade Data Bank, 11.026
Native American Program, *11.801*
New Markets Venture Capital, *59.051*
revolving loan funds, *11.307*
revolving loan funds, CDBG, *14.218, 14.219*
revolving loan funds, CDBG, Indians, *14.862*
revolving loan funds, CDBG, insular areas, *14.225*
Rural Business-Cooperative Service, 10.350
Rural Business Enterprise Grants, *10.769*
rural business, industry financing, *10.768*
Rural Business Investment Companies, RBCS, *10.860*
rural economic development, RBCS, *10.854*
rural, loans, *10.767*
rural public facilities, *10.766*
SEC activities, 58.001
small business, agriculture regulatory ombudsman, *59.053*
small business on-line counseling, 59.005
small business investment companies, *59.011*
State of the Nation, ESA, 11.027
trade agreement negotiation, enforcement, 11.110
U.S. Export-Import Bank, 11.108
women-owned, technical assistance, training, *59.043*
see also Community development; Disadvantaged, business development; Economic development; Farm, nonfarm enterprises; Fisheries industry; Indian economic, business development; Insurance; International commerce, investment; Minority business enterprise; Patents, trademarks, inventions; Private sector; Small business; Small Business Innovation Research (SBIR); Statistics; Technology transfer, utilization
Business statistics, *see* Economics, research, statistics; Statistics

BYRD HONORS SCHOLARSHIPS, *84.185*
BYRNE FORMULA GRANT PROGRAM [DOJ], *16.579*
BZPP (Buffer Zone Protection Plan), DHS, *97.078*

CAA (Clean Air Act), *see* Air pollution
CAA (Clean Air Act) Section 112, *66.810*
Cable systems licensing, 42.002
CALIBRATION PROGRAM, 11.601
CAMP (College Assistance Migrant Program), *84.149*
Campgrounds, public, *15.916*
Campus crime grants, *16.525*
CANCER BIOLOGY RESEARCH, *93.396*
CANCER CAUSE AND PREVENTION RESEARCH, *93.393*
CANCER CENTERS SUPPORT, *93.397*
CANCER CONSTRUCTION, *93.392*
CANCER CONTROL, *93.399*
Cancer control, prevention, research
　alternative, complementary medicine research, *93.213*
　biology, immunology, nutrition, tumor research, *93.396*
　biomedical research manpower development, NRSA, *93.398*
　biometry, risk estimation, environmental risks, *93.115*
　Breast and Cervical Cancer Mortality Prevention Act of 1990, *93.919*
　breast, cervical, *93.919*
　cause, prevention research, *93.393*
　centers support, *93.397*
　control, *93.399*
　detection, diagnosis research, *93.394*
　environmental health hazards research, *93.113*
　facilities construction, development, *93.392*
　hazardous waste sites health studies, *93.206*
　minority community health coalitions, *93.137*
　Radiogenetic Exposure Screening and Education Program, *93.257*
　Sea Grant Support, *11.417*
　therapy research, *93.395*
　see also Biological sciences; Chemicals, chemistry; Health, medical *entries*; Nuclear sciences, technology; Radiation; Tobacco
CANCER DETECTION AND DIAGNOSIS RESEARCH, *93.394*
CANCER RESEARCH MANPOWER, *93.398*
CANCER TREATMENT RESEARCH, *93.395*
CAP (Client Assistance Program), disabled, *84.161*
CAP (Conservation Assessment Program), IMLS, *45.304*
CAP-SSSE (Community Assistance Program-State Support Services Element), FEMA, *97.023*
CAPACITY BUILDING AMONG INDIAN TRIBES, *93.202*
CAPACITY BUILDING FOR TRADITIONALLY UNDERSERVED POPULATIONS [DOED], *84.315*
CAPACITY BUILDING GRANTS AND COOPERATIVE AGREEMENTS FOR COMPLIANCE ASSURANCE ACTIVITIES IN INDIAN COUNTRY AND OTHER TRIBAL AREAS [EPA], *66.310*
CAPITAL AND TRAINING ASSISTANCE PROGRAM FOR OVER-THE-ROAD BUS ACCESSIBILITY, *20.518*
CAPITAL ASSISTANCE PROGRAM FOR ELDERLY PERSONS AND PERSONS WITH DISABILITIES [DOT], *20.513*
CAPITAL CONSTRUCTION FUND [DOT], *20.808*
Capital Fund Program (CFP), public housing, *14.872*
CAPITALIZATION GRANTS FOR CLEAN WATER STATE REVOLVING FUND, *66.458*
CAPITALIZATION GRANTS FOR DRINKING WATER STATE REVOLVING FUND, *66.468*
Cardiovascular Health Programs, CDCP, *93.945*
Cardiovascular system research, *see* Health, medical research
CARE (Community Action for a Renewed Environment) Program, EPA, *66.035*
Carl D. Perkins Vocational and Applied Technology Education Act (CDPVATEA), *see* Vocational Education
Cartography, *see* Maps, charts
CASA (Court Appointed Special Advocates), child abuse, *16.547*
Cataract research, *93.867*
CBAE (Community-Based Abstinence Education), *93.010*
CCC, *see* Commodity Credit Corporation
CCDF (Child Care and Development Fund), ACF, *93.575, 93.596*
CCF (Capital Construction Fund), ships, *20.808*
CCF (Compassion Capital Fund), ACF, *93.009, 93.647*
CCOE (Community Centers of Excellence), women's health, *93.290*
CCSG (Cancer Center Support Grant), *93.397*
CCTV (Closed-Circuit Televising), child abuse, *16.611*
CDAPCA (Comprehensive Drug Abuse Prevention and Control Act of 1970), *see* Drug abuse
CDBG (Community Development Block Grants), *see* Block grant programs
CDCU (Community Development Credit Union), 44.002
CDFI (Community Development Financial Institutions) Program, *21.020*
CDP (Cooperative Development Program), USAID, *98.002*
CDP (Crop Disaster Program), *10.073*
CDPVATEA (Carl D. Perkins Vocational and Applied Technology Education Act), *see* Vocational Education
Cemeteries, *see* Historic monuments, historic preservation; Veterans death benefits
Census Bureau, *see* Agency Index (USDC, Bureau of the Census)
CENSUS BUREAU DATA PRODUCTS, 11.001
CENSUS CUSTOMER SERVICES, 11.002
CENSUS GEOGRAPHY, 11.003
CENSUS INTERGOVERNMENTAL SERVICES, 11.004
Census Mapping and Statistical Areas, 11.003
Census services
　Act of August 31, 1954, 11.001, 11.002, 11.003, 11.004, 11.005, 11.006
　age search, Census Bureau, 11.006
　Census Bureau user services, guides, training courses, 11.002

Census services (continued)
census geography, 11.003
citizenship verification, 11.006
customized tabulations, surveys, 11.005
data products, computer tapes, microfiche, publications, 11.001
Intergovernmental Services Program, training, 11.004
Personal Census Search, 11.006
TIGER (Topologically Integrated Geographic Encoding and Referencing) system, 11.003
see also Maps, charts; Statistics
CENSUS SPECIAL TABULATIONS AND SERVICES, 11.005
CENTER FOR SPONSORED COASTAL OCEAN RESEARCH—COASTAL OCEAN PROGRAM, *11.478*
Centers for Disease Control and Prevention (CDCP), HHS, *see* Agency Index
CENTERS FOR DISEASE CONTROL AND PREVENTION—INVESTIGATIONS AND TECHNICAL ASSISTANCE, *93.283*
CENTERS FOR GENOMICS AND PUBLIC HEALTH, *93.063*
CENTERS FOR HOMELAND SECURITY, *97.061*
CENTERS FOR INDEPENDENT LIVING, *84.132*
CENTERS FOR INTERNATIONAL BUSINESS EDUCATION, *84.220*
Centers for Medicare and Medicaid Services (CMS), HHS, *see* Agency Index
CENTERS FOR MEDICARE AND MEDICAID (CMS) RESEARCH, DEMONSTRATIONS AND EVALUATIONS, *93.779*
CENTERS FOR RESEARCH AND DEMONSTRATION FOR HEALTH PROMOTION AND DISEASE PREVENTION, *93.135*
CENTERS OF EXCELLENCE [HHS], *93.157*
CEPP (Chemical Emergency Preparedness and Prevention), EPA, *66.810*
CERCLA (Comprehensive Environmental Response, Compensation, and Liability Act), *see* Hazardous Materials, waste
CERCLA Implementation, FEMA, *97.021*
CERP (Cooperative Education and Research Program), NMFS, *11.455*
CERTIFICATION OF FOREIGN WORKERS FOR TEMPORARY AGRICULTURAL EMPLOYMENT, 17.202
CERTIFIED DEVELOPMENT COMPANY LOANS (504 LOANS), *59.041*
Cervical cancer, *see* Cancer control, prevention, research
CFCIP (Chafee Foster Care Independent Living Program), ACF, *93.674*
CFP (Capital Fund Program), public housing, *14.872*
CFRDA, (Consolidated Farm and Rural Development Act), *see* Rural areas
CGEP (Comprehensive Geriatric Education Program), *93.265*
CHAFEE EDUCATION AND TRAINING VOUCHERS PROGRAM, *93.599*
CHAFEE FOSTER CARE INDEPENDENCE PROGRAM, *93.674*
CHALLENGE COST SHARE [DOI], *15.642*

Challenge Grants, OJJDP, *16.549*
Chapter 30, DVA, education, *64.124*
Chapter 36 Counseling, DVA, 64.125
CHARTER SCHOOL FACILITIES FINANCING DEMONSTRATION, *84.354*
CHARTER SCHOOLS, *84.282*
CHEMICAL EMERGENCY PREPAREDNESS AND PREVENTION (CEPP) TECHNICAL ASSISTANCE GRANTS PROGRAM, *66.810*
CHEMICAL STOCKPILE EMERGENCY PREPAREDNESS PROGRAM [DHS], *97.040*
Chemicals, chemistry
Air Force Defense Research Sciences Program, *12.800*
animal health, diseases research, *10.207*
allergy, immunology, transplantation research, *93.855*
carcinogens research, *93.393*
chemical emergency planning, *66.810*
coal research, *81.057*
deafness, communicative disorders research, *93.173*
energy-related basic research, *81.049*
environmental health hazards research, *93.113*
environmental health research, resources, manpower development, *93.894*
EPA building decontamination research, *66.511*
EPA Compliance Assistance Centers, *66.305*
EPA environmental sustainability design competition, *66.516*
EPA pollution prevention studies, training, outreach, *66.716*
FEMA chemical emergency planning, DOD stockpiles, *97.040*
FEMA Hazardous Materials Assistance Program, training, *97.021*
fish, wildlife resource management, 15.608
fossil energy, *81.089*
industrial, agricultural waste reduction, DOE, *81.105*
infectious diseases research, *93.856*
measurement, engineering research, standards, *11.609*
mental health research training, *93.282*
National Standard Reference Data System, 11.603
NSF engineering education, research, *47.041*
NSF geosciences research, *47.050*
Pesticide Environmental Stewardship, *66.714*
pesticides compliance, *66.700*
pharmacology, biorelated chemistry research, training, *93.859*
research support, NSF, *47.049*
toxic substance compliance programs, *66.701*
toxicological research, testing, *93.114*
WMD, domestic preparedness, *97.004, 97.005, 97.006, 97.007*
see also Behavioral sciences, education, services; Biological sciences; Cancer control, prevention, research; Civil defense; Drugs, drug research; Emergency assistance; Environmental *entries*; Forensic sciences; Genetics; Hazardous materials, waste; Health, medical research; Minority education; National Research Service Awards; Pesticides; Pharmacology, pharmacy; Physical sciences; Scientific research; Toxic substances, toxicology

MASTER INDEX 899

Chemotherapy, *see* Cancer control, prevention, research
CHESAPEAKE BAY PROGRAM, *66.466*
CHESAPEAKE BAY STUDIES, *11.457*
CHGME (Children's Hospitals Graduate Medical Education) Payment, HRSA, *93.255*
CHILD ABUSE AND NEGLECT DISCRETIONARY ACTIVITIES, *93.670*
CHILD ABUSE AND NEGLECT STATE GRANTS, *93.669*
Child abuse, neglect, *see* Maternal, child health, welfare; Victim assistance
CHILD AND ADULT CARE FOOD PROGRAM, *10.558*
CHILD CARE ACCESS MEANS PARENTS IN SCHOOL, *84.335*
CHILD CARE AND DEVELOPMENT BLOCK GRANT, *93.575*
Child Care and Development Fund (CCDF), ACF, *93.596*
CHILD CARE MANDATORY AND MATCHING FUNDS OF THE CHILD CARE AND DEVELOPMENT FUND, *93.596*

Child care services
  abandoned infants services, care training, *93.551*
  adolescents counseling, *93.995*
  Child Care and Development Fund (CCDF), services, standards, licensing, *93.596*
  child care/social services, TANF, *93.558*
  Child Nutrition Discretionary Grants, *10.579*
  child protective services, training, *93.669*
  child welfare personnel training, *93.648*
  community-based child abuse prevention, *93.590*
  Community Services Block Grant, *93.569*
  day care facilities, CDBG, *14.218, 14.219, 14.228*
  day care facilities, CDBG, Indians, *14.862*
  day care facilities, CDBG, insular areas, *14.225*
  domestic violence victim transitional housing, *16.736*
  early childhood educator professional development, *84.349*
  Early Learning Fund, services, training, ACF, *93.577*
  employer-sponsored, planning assistance, 17.700
  facilities, HUD Dollar Home Sales, 14.313
  family support services, *93.556*
  family violence victim shelters, *93.671*
  farm laborers facilities development, *10.405*
  federal surplus personal property, 39.003
  food assistance, 10.550, *10.558*
  foster care, *93.658*
  Foster Grandparent Program, *94.011*
  homeless older youth, transitional, *93.550*
  Indian programs, *15.144*
  infant safe havens, *93.556*
  institutionalized neglected, education, *84.013*
  licensing, standard setting, *93.645*
  low-income working families, CCDF, *93.575*
  milk program, *10.556*
  National Center for Missing and Exploited Children, *97.076*
  nutrition program administration, states, *10.560*
  postsecondary low-income student-parents, *84.335*
  protective services, *93.645*
  Rural Community Development Initiative, RHS, *10.446*
  rural facilities, *10.766*
  School Breakfast Program, *10.553*
  School Lunch Program, *10.555*
  SED, mental health services, *93.104*
  Social Services Block Grant, *93.667*
  social service research, demonstration, *93.647*
  spina bifida, veterans dependents, *64.127*
  summer food program, *10.559*
  Unaccompanied Alien Children Program, *93.676*
  WIA Adult Program, *17.258*
  see also Behavioral sciences, education, services; Employment services; Maternal, child health, welfare; Parenting; Pediatrics; Social services; Victim assistance; Volunteers

Child development, *see* Disabled, handicapped children; Early childhood education; Indian children; Maternal, child health, welfare; Parenting; Pediatrics
Child health, *see* Community health services; Disabled, handicapped children; Indian children; Maternal, child health, welfare; Pediatrics
CHILD HEALTH AND HUMAN DEVELOPMENT EXTRAMURAL RESEARCH, *93.865*
CHILD NUTRITION DISCRETIONARY GRANTS LIMITED AVAILABILITY, *10.579*
CHILD SUPPORT DEMONSTRATION AND SPECIAL PROJECTS, *93.601*
CHILD SUPPORT ENFORCEMENT, *93.563*
CHILD SUPPORT ENFORCEMENT RESEARCH, *93.564*
Child welfare, *see* Maternal, child health, welfare
CHILD WELFARE SERVICES—STATE GRANTS, *93.645*
CHILD WELFARE SERVICES TRAINING GRANTS, *93.648*
CHILDHOOD BLOOD-LEAD SCREENING AND LEAD AWARENESS (EDUCATIONAL) OUTREACH FOR INDIAN TRIBES, *66.715*
CHILDHOOD LEAD POISONING PREVENTION PROJECTS—STATE AND LOCAL CHILDHOOD LEAD POISONING PREVENTION AND SURVEILLANCE OF BLOOD LEVELS IN CHILDREN, *93.197*
Children, *see* Child care services; Disabled, handicapped children; Indian children; Maternal, child health, welfare; Social services; Youth *entries*
Children, education, *see* Disabled, handicapped education; Disadvantaged, education; Early childhood education; Elementary and secondary education
Children, handicapped, *see* Disabled, handicapped children
Children's Advocacy Centers, *16.547*
Children's Health Protection, EPA, *66.609*
CHILDREN'S HOSPITALS GRADUATE MEDICAL EDUCATION PAYMENT, *93.255*
Children's Insurance Program (CHIP), CMS, *93.767*
CHILDREN'S JUSTICE ACT PARTNERSHIPS FOR INDIAN COMMUNITIES, *16.583*
Children's Justice and Assistance Act of 1986, *see* Maternal, child health, welfare
CHILDREN'S JUSTICE GRANTS TO STATES, *93.643*

Children's museums, 45.301
CHIP (Children's Insurance Program), CMS, 93.767
Chiropractic
  alternative, complementary medicine research, 93.213
  education assistance, disadvantaged, 93.822
  spinal, lower-back conditions, medical demonstrations, research, 93.212
  see also Health, medical education, training; Health professions
CHIROPRACTIC DEMONSTRATION PROJECT GRANTS, 93.212
Christopher Columbus Fellowship Foundation, see Agency Index (Scholarship and Fellowship Foundations)
CHRISTOPHER COLUMBUS FELLOWSHIP PROGRAM, 85.100
CHRONIC DISEASES: RESEARCH, CONTROL AND PREVENTION, 93.068
CIA (Cooperative Institute Agreement), NMFS, 11.455
CIFO (Cooperative Institute of Fishery Oceanography), NMFS, 11.455
CIMAS (Cooperative Institute for Marine and Atmospheric Studies), NMFS, 11.455
CIMRS (Cooperative Institute for Marine Resources Studies), NMFS, 11.455
CIR-LRP (Contraception and Infertility Research Loan Repayment Program), HHS, 93.209
CISE (Computer and Information Science and Engineering), NSF, 47.070
CITIZEN CORPS [DHS], 97.053
Citizen Councils, USA Freedom Corps, HHS, 93.008
Citizen Information Center, GSA, 39.009
Citizenship education, see Adult education; Aliens, immigrants, refugees
CITIZENSHIP EDUCATION AND TRAINING, 97.010
City planning, see Community development; Urban planning
CIVIC EDUCATION—COOPERATIVE EDUCATION EXCHANGE PROGRAM, 84.304
Civics, see Government
Civil aviation, see Air transportation
Civil defense
  agricultural, homeland security, 10.304
  agricultural security research, 10.206
  Anti-Terrorism and Effective Death Penalty Act of 1996 (ATEDPA), 16.321, 16.565, 16.575, 16.576, 16.582, 16.583, 16.614
  Anti-Terrorism and Emergency Assistance Program, DOJ, 16.321
  Anti-Terrorism Emergency Reserve, DOJ, 16.321
  anti-terrorism training, 16.614
  Aviation Research Grants, DHS, 97.069
  bioterrorism preparedness education, training, HRSA, 93.996
  Buffer Zone Protection Plan, DHS, 97.078
  Citizen Corps, DHS, 97.053, 97.067
  Citizen Corps, HHS, 93.008
  counter-terrorism technology development, DOJ, 16.565
  cyber security activities, DHS, 97.067
  Department of Homeland Security Act, 97.080
  DHS Competitive Training Grants, 97.068
  DHS Earmarked Research Projects, 97.002
  DHS Pilot Demonstration Projects, 97.001
  DHS Scholars and Fellows, 97.062
  Disaster Assistance Projects, specified projects, FEMA, 97.088
  DOE WMD nonproliferation research, 81.113
  drinking water security system training, 66.478
  electricity delivery, energy reliability, DOE, 81.122
  Emergency Federal Law Enforcement Assistance, 16.577
  Emergency Management Performance Grants, 97.042
  EMI training, 97.028
  explosives detection canine teams, TSA, 97.072
  federal surplus personal property, 39.003
  FEMA home study courses, 97.027
  food safety, security monitoring, FDA, 93.448
  Homeland Security Act of 2002, 93.676, 97.001, 97.002, 97.055, 97.060, 97.061, 97.062, 97.065, 97.072, 97.077, 97.084, 97.086, 97.088, 97.089
  homeland security advanced research projects, DHS, 97.065
  Homeland Security Grant Program, 97.067
  homeland security public awareness outreach, DHS, 97.086
  homeland security technology development, DHS, 97.077
  DHS Information Technology and Evaluation Program, 97.066
  hospital bioterrorism preparedness, HRSA, 93.889
  Information Analysis Infrastructure Protection, DHS, 97.080
  Intercity Bus Security Grants, DHS, 97.057
  International Terrorism Victim Assistance Expense Reimbursement Program, DOJ, 16.321
  Law Enforcement Terrorism Prevention Program (LETPP), DHS, 97.067, 97.074
  maritime transportation planning, 20.801
  Medical Reserve Corps, emergency response, HHS, 93.008
  Metropolitan Medical Response System, FEMA, 97.071
  National Guard facilities, 12.400
  National Guard operations, maintenance, 12.401
  NTIS Homeland Security Information Center, 11.650
  officers disability, death benefits, 16.571
  Operation Safe Commerce, DHS, 97.058
  port security grants, DHS, 97.056
  port security research, development, DHS, 97.060
  public health bioterrorism preparedness, 93.003
  Public Health Security and Bioterrorism Preparedness and Response Act of 2002, 66.478, 93.996, 97.088
  rail, transit security, ODP, 97.075
  Real ID Program, DHS, 97.089
  Ruminant Feed Ban Support Project, FDA, 93.449
  State Homeland Security Program (SHSP), 97.067, 97.073
  terrorism victims assistance, 16.575, 16.576
  transit planning, FTA, 20.514
  Truck Security Program, DHS, 97.059
  University-Based Homeland Security Centers, DHS, 97.061

Urban Areas Security Initiative, equipment, training, planning, DHS, *97.008*
U.S.A. Patriot Act of 2001, *16.321*, *16.575*, *16.576*, *16.582*, *97.001*, *97.002*, *97.004*, *97.005*, *97.006*, *97.007*, *97.008*, *97.067*, *97.073*, *97.074*, *97.075*
water protection coordination, planning, *66.474*
WMD, domestic preparedness, *97.004*, *97.005*, *97.006*, *97.007*
see also Crime; Disaster assistance; Emergency assistance; Firefighting, fire prevention, control; Maritime industry; Military; Police; Public health; Public safety; Radiation; Rescue services

Civil rights
Age Discrimination Act, 14.402, 93.001
Age Discrimination in Employment Act of 1967, *30.002*, 30.005, 30.008
age discrimination, housing, HUD programs, 14.402
aliens, employment, *16.110*
CDBG program discrimination, 14.406
children, *16.549*
Civil Rights Act of 1964, Title VI, 14.405
Civil Rights Acts, 16.100, 16.101, 16.103, 16.105, 16.200, 30.001, *30.002*, 30.005, 30.008, *30.009*, *84.004*, 93.001
Civil Rights Commission Reauthorization Act of 1991, 29.001
Civil Rights Prosecution, 16.109
Clinic Entrances Act, 16.105
Community Relations Service, 16.200
credit transactions, 16.103
developmentally disabled, *93.630*
disabled, advocacy, *84.132*
disabled, Client Assistance Program, *84.161*
disabled, employment discrimination, ADA, 30.011
disabled, handicapped, assistive technology services, *84.343*
disabled, housing-related discrimination, 14.414
disabled, Protection and Advocacy, *84.240*
Education Amendments Act of 1972, HUD programs discrimination, 14.415
Election Assistance for Individuals with Disabilities, ACF, *93.617*, *93.618*
employment, 16.101, 30.001
employment, attorney referral, 30.005
employment, federal contracts compliance, 17.301
employment, state, local enforcement assistance, *30.002*
Equal Credit Opportunity Act of 1976, 16.103
Equal Educational Opportunities Act of 1974, 16.100
Equal Enjoyment of Rights in Public Facilities, 16.105
Equal Pay Act, 30.005, 30.010
Fair Housing Act, 14.400, *14.401*, *14.408*, 16.103
Fair Housing Assistance Program, *14.401*
Fair Housing Initiatives Program, *14.408*
handicapped, housing, HUD programs, 14.404
Help America Vote Act, *93.617*, *90.400*, *93.618*
HHS programs compliance, training, HHS, 93.001
housing, 16.103
housing, HUD programs, 14.405
housing, technical assistance, 14.400, *14.401*
Indians, employment, *30.009*
information clearinghouse, 29.001
institutionalized persons, 16.105
mentally ill persons, *93.138*
mentally retarded, President's Committee, 93.613
Privacy Rule, 93.001
Religious Land Use and Institutionalized Persons Act of 2000 (RLUIPA), 16.103
school desegregation enforcement, 16.100
school desegregation, Magnet Schools, *84.165*
schools, compliance, technical assistance, training, *84.004*
state voting equipment payments, *90.401*
Underground Railroad Program, DOED, *84.345*
voting rights, 16.104
women, 17.700
Women's Educational Equity Act Program, *84.083*
see also Complaint investigation; Consumers, consumer sciences; Disabled *entries*; Legal services; Mental retardation
CIVIL RIGHTS AND PRIVACY RULE COMPLIANCE ACTIVITIES, 93.001
Civil Rights Division, DOJ, *see* Agency Index
CIVIL RIGHTS OF INSTITUTIONALIZED PERSONS, 16.105
CIVIL RIGHTS PROSECUTION, 16.109
CIVIL RIGHTS TRAINING AND ADVISORY SERVICES [DOED], *84.004*
Civil Service employment, *see* Federal employment
CIVIL WAR BATTLEFIELD LAND ACQUISITION GRANTS, *15.928*
Claims, *see* Complaint investigation; Insurance; Legal services
Clean Air Act, *see* Air pollution
CLEAN SCHOOL BUS USA [EPA], *66.036*
CLEAN VESSEL ACT, *15.616*
Clean Vessel Act Pumpout Grant Program, *15.616*
Clean Water Act, *see* Water pollution abatement, prevention
Clean Water State Revolving Fund, wastewater treatment, *66.458*
CLEARINGHOUSE SERVICES, CIVIL RIGHTS DISCRIMINATION COMPLAINTS, 29.001
Clearinghouses, *see* Information general, clearinghouses

Climate
air pollution effects studies, demonstrations, *66.034*
air quality research, services, *11.459*
airport weather reporting equipment, *20.106*
Applied Meteorology Research, *11.468*
atmospheric research, *47.050*
aviation research, *20.108*
education, research, facilities, NOAA, *11.469*
emergency snowmelt preparations, 12.111
environmental systems research, NOAA, *11.432*
flood warning systems, NOAA, *11.450*
Hydrologic Research, *11.462*
Hydrometeorological Development, education, training, NOAA, *11.467*
National Climate Program Act, *11.428*, *11.431*, *11.459*
National Environmental Satellite, Data, and Information Service (NESDIS), NOAA, *11.428*
NESDIS environmental sciences education, research, *11.440*

Climate *(continued)*
National Weather Service and Related Agencies Authorization Act of 1999, *11.460*
NMFS marine education, science projects, *11.455*
NOAA Educational Partnerships Program, minority, *11.481*
NOAA special projects, *11.460*
Polar Programs, *47.078*
regional centers, *11.428*
remote sensing research, *11.440*
research, *11.431*
research, Coastal Ocean Program, *11.478*
short-term fluctuation studies, *11.443*
snowmelt surveys, *10.907*
Weather Service Organic Act, *11.431, 11.459, 11.462, 11.467*
wind energy research, *81.087*
see also Earth sciences; Flood prevention, control; Hurricanes
CLIMATE AND ATMOSPHERIC RESEARCH, *11.431*
Clinic Entrances Act, *16.105*
CLINICAL RESEARCH LOAN REPAYMENT PROGRAM FOR INDIVIDUALS FROM DISADVANTAGED BACKGROUNDS, *93.220*
CLOSED-CIRCUIT TELEVISING OF CHILD VICTIMS OF ABUSE, *16.611*
Clothing, *see* Home economics
CLPPP (Childhood Lead Poisoning Prevention Program), *93.197*
CMEA/MESA (Colorado Minority Engineering Achievement Association/Mathematics, Engineering, Science Achievement), NOAA, *11.449*
CMER (Cooperative Marine Education and Research Programs), NMFS, *11.455*
CMHS (Community Mental Health Services) Block Grant, *93.958*
CMHS (Community Mental Health Services) Child Mental Health Service Initiative, *93.104*
CMS (Centers for Medicare and Medicaid Services), HHS, *see* Agency Index
CMS (Centers for Medicare and Medicaid Services) Research, *93.779*
CNCS (Corporation for National and Community Service), *94.002* through *94.016*
COAL MINE WORKERS' COMPENSATION, *17.307*
COAL MINERS RESPIRATORY IMPAIRMENT TREATMENT CLINICS AND SERVICES, *93.965*
Coal mining
abandoned mine land reclamation, *10.910, 15.252*
Abandoned Mine Reclamation Act of 1990, *10.910*
Acid Mine Drainage (AMD), *15.253*
Black Lung Clinics, *93.965*
disabled miners compensation, *17.307*
energy production research, *81.089*
Federal Mine Safety and Health Amendments Act of 1977, *17.307*
mine subsidence, CDBG, *14.219, 14.225, 14.228*
permits, regulation, inspection, *15.250*
research, *81.057*
subsidence insurance, *15.252*
see also Energy research; Mineral resources; Mining, mining industries; Occupational health, safety
Coast and Geodetic Survey Act, *see* Maps, charts
Coast Guard, *see* Agency Index (DOT, U.S. Coast Guard)
Coast Guard Auxiliary, *97.011*
COASTAL PROGRAM [DOI], *15.630*
COASTAL SERVICES CENTER, *11.473*
COASTAL WETLANDS PLANNING, PROTECTION AND RESTORATION ACT, *15.614*
Coastal zone
Atlantic, fisheries management, *11.474*
Beach Monitoring and Notification Program, EPA, *66.472*
Beaches Environmental Assessment and Coastal Health Act of 2000, *66.472*
boundary demarcation, NOAA, *11.400*
Clean Vessel Act, pumpout/dump stations, *15.616*
Clean Water Act studies, training, *66.436*
Coastal Program, FWS, *15.630*
Coastal Wetlands Planning, Protection and Restoration Act, *15.614*
Coastal Zone Management Act of 1972, *11.419, 11.420*
Coral Reef Conservation Act, *11.463*
ecological research, NOAA, *11.426*
ecosystem management, NOAA, *11.473*
emergency rehabilitation, *12.102*
environmental systems research, NOAA, *11.432*
erosion control, *12.101*
estuarine research reserves, *11.420*
FEMA Flood Mitigation Assistance, *97.029*
flood fighting, rescue, *12.103*
flood insurance, *97.022*
flood plain data, services, *12.104*
Gulf of Mexico Program, EPA, *66.475*
Long Island Sound Program, *66.437*
Marine Fisheries Initiative, *11.433*
Marine Sanctuary Program, *11.429*
Marine Turtle Conservation Fund, FWS, *15.645*
National Estuary Program, *66.456*
NOAA Educational Partnerships Program, minority, *11.481*
North American Wetlands Conservation Fund, FWS, *15.623*
NOS intern program, *11.480*
Pacific Salmon Treaty Program, *11.438*
program administration, *11.419*
research, Coastal Ocean Program, *11.478*
research, Sea Grant Support, *11.417*
southeast marine area monitoring, *11.435*
wetlands protection, *15.614*
see also Estuaries; Fisheries industry; Flood prevention, control; Great Lakes; Hurricanes; Maps, charts; Marine sciences; Maritime industry; Recreation, water; Water navigation; Wetlands
COASTAL ZONE MANAGEMENT ADMINISTRATION AWARDS, *11.419*
COASTAL ZONE MANAGEMENT ESTUARINE RESEARCH RESERVES, *11.420*
COATES (Community Opportunities, Accountability, and Training and Educational Services Act of 1998), *see* Community development

MASTER INDEX 903

Code enforcement, CDBG programs, *14.218, 14.219, 14.225, 14.228, 14.862*
CODIS (Combined DNA Index System), *16.307*
COEs (Centers of Excellence), HRSA, *93.157*
COLLABORATIVE FOREST RESTORATION, *10.679*
COLLABORATIVE RESEARCH AND DEVELOPMENT [DOD], *12.114*
Collaborative Science, Technology, and Applied Research (CSTAR), NWS, *11.468*
Collective bargaining, *see* Labor-management relations
College and university facilities, *see* Education facilities
College Assistance Migrant Program (CAMP), *84.149*
College Work-Study Program (CWS), *84.033*
Colleges and universities, *see* Higher education institutions; Land grant colleges, universities
Colorado Minority Engineering Achievement Association/Mathematics, Engineering, Science Achievement (CMEA/MESA), NOAA, *11.449*
COLORADO RIVER BASIN SALINITY CONTROL PROGRAM, *10.070*
COLUMBIA RIVER FISHERIES DEVELOPMENT PROGRAM, *11.436*
Columbus foundation fellowships, *85.100*
COMBINED DNA INDEX SYSTEM, *16.307*
COMET (Cooperative Program for Operational Meteorology, Education and Training), *11.467*
COMMERCIAL DRIVER LICENSE STATE PROGRAMS, *20.232*
COMMERCIAL SERVICE [USDC], 11.108
Commission on Civil Rights, 29.001
COMMODITY PARTNERSHIPS FOR RISK MANAGEMENT EDUCATION, *10.457*
COMMODITY PARTNERSHIPS FOR SMALL AGRICULTURAL RISK MANAGEMENT EDUCATION SESSIONS, *10.459*
Commodity Credit Corporation (CCC), *10.051, 10.053, 10.056, 10.085, 10.600, 10.601, 10.603, 10.604, 10.605, 10.606, 10.607, 10.912, 10.918, 10.919, 10.921*
Commodity futures market
Commodity Credit Corporation Charter Act, *10.051, 10.055, 10.605*
Commodity Exchange Act, 78.004
Dairy Options Pilot Program, *10.454*
Futures Trading Acts, 78.004
information, customer complaints, 78.004
market reports, agricultural, 10.153
risk management education, *10.450*
see also Agricultural commodities, stabilization; Agricultural marketing
COMMODITY FUTURES REPARATIONS CLAIMS, 78.004
Commodity Futures Trading Commission, 78.004
COMMODITY LOANS AND LOAN DEFICIENCY PAYMENTS, *10.051*
COMMODITY SUPPLEMENTAL FOOD PROGRAM, *10.565*
Commonwealth of the Pacific Trust Territory, *see* U.S. possessions, territories
Communicable diseases
CDCP assistance, *93.283*
childhood immunization, *93.283*
epidemic assistance, *93.283*
Immunization Grants, *93.268*
immunization research, information, *93.185*
infectious disease research, *93.856*
laboratory training, infrastructure development, *93.065*
oral, research, *93.121*
sexually transmitted, control, prevention, *93.283, 93.977*
sexually transmitted, research, information, training, *93.978*
tuberculosis control, *93.116*
see also AIDS (Acquired Immune Deficiency Syndrome); Community health services; Disease control; Epidemiology; Health, medical *entries*; Immunization, immunology; Preventive health services; Public health; Respiratory diseases
COMMUNICATIONS INFORMATION AND ASSISTANCE AND INVESTIGATION OF COMPLAINTS [FCC], 32.001
Communications, telecommunications
broadband access loans, rural areas, RUS, *10.886*
business internships, Eurasian executives, scientists, *11.114*
cable system licenses, 42.002
Communications Act of 1934, *11.550*, 32.001
Community Connect Grants, RUS, *10.863*
consumer services, FCC, 32.001
DHS Information Technology and Evaluation Program, *97.066*
early childhood education, Ready-to-Learn TV, *84.295*
Education Technology State Grants, *84.318*
FCC information, education services, 32.001
Information Analysis Infrastructure Protection, DHS, *97.080*
instructional programming, Star Schools, *84.203*
Interoperable Communications Equipment, DHS, *97.055*
Law Enforcement Terrorism Prevention Program (LETPP), DHS, *97.067, 97.074*
library information services, *45.310*
measurement, engineering research, standards, *11.609*
medical information science research, training, *93.879*
National Guard operations, maintenance, *12.401*
Native American Library Services, *45.311*
Public Housing Neighborhood Network Grants, *14.875*
Public Telecommunication Facilities Program, *11.550*
Ready to Teach, OERI, *84.286*
rural educational, medical computer networks, RUS, *10.855*
Rural EMS/Trauma Care, *93.952*
rural public television station digital transition grants, *10.861*
Scams Targeting the Elderly, telemarketing, DOJ, *16.613*
telecommunications infrastructure, *11.552*
Telehealth Network Grants, *93.211*
telephone service loans, rural, RUS, *10.851, 10.852*
Television Demonstration Grants, rural, *10.769*

Communications, telecommunications *(continued)*
see also Audiovisual aids, film, video; Civil defense; Computer products, sciences, services; Public utilities; Radio, television; Technology transfer, utilization
Communicative disorders, deafness, research, *93.173*
COMMUNITY ACTION FOR A RENEWED ENVIRONMENT (CARE) PROGRAM [EPA], *66.035*
COMMUNITY ASSISTANCE PROGRAM—STATE SUPPORT SERVICES ELEMENT [DHS], *97.023*
COMMUNITY BASE REUSE PLANS, *12.612*
COMMUNITY-BASED ABSTINENCE EDUCATION, *93.010*
COMMUNITY-BASED CHILD ABUSE PREVENTION GRANTS, *93.590*
COMMUNITY CAPACITY DEVELOPMENT [DOJ], *16.595*
Community Centers of Excellence (CCOE), women's health, *93.290*
Community colleges, *see* Higher education *entries*; Vocational education
COMMUNITY CONNECT GRANT PROGRAM [USDA], *10.863*
Community development
air carrier service subsidies, *20.901*
Alaska, Denali Commission Program, *90.100*
Alaska, Hawaii native IHE community assistance, *14.515*
AmeriCorps, *94.003, 94.006, 94.007, 94.009*
Bank Enterprise Awards Program, *21.021*
brownfield projects, *14.246, 66.814*
CDBG Economic Development Initiative, Section 108, *14.246*
code enforcement, CDBG, *14.218, 14.219, 14.228*
Community Connect Grants, RUS, *10.863*
Community Development Credit Union (CDCU), *44.002*
Community Development Financial Institutions Program, *21.020*
Community Food Projects, USDA, *10.225*
Community Opportunities, Accountability, and Training and Educational Services Act of 1998 (COATES), *93.568, 93.569, 93.570, 93.571, 93.600, 93.602*
Community Prosecution Program, *16.609*
Community Services Block Grant, *93.569, 93.570*
conflicts mediation, 16.200
Cops Grants, *16.710*
defense program changes impact, 12.600, *12.611, 12.612, 12.613, 12.614*
Demonstration Cities and Metropolitan Development Act, *66.804*
discrimination, CDBG program, 14.406
district heating/cooling, CDBG, *14.218, 14.219, 14.228*
Drug-Free Community Grants, *93.276*
Drug-Free Schools and Communities, states, *84.186*
EDA economic adjustment assistance, *11.307*
EPA New England Regional Office projects, *66.110*
1890 institutions entrepreneurial outreach, RBCS, *10.856*
Empowerment Zones, Enterprise Communities programs, *10.772, 14.244, 17.261, 17.263, 21.020, 84.213, 93.012, 93.570, 93.667*
energy conservation, CDBG, *14.218, 14.219, 14.228*
environmental justice projects, *66.032, 66.306, 66.604, 66.606*
Environmental Justice Research Assistance, EPA, *66.308*
Environmental Justice Surveys and Studies, EPA, *66.309*
Environmental Justice Training and Fellowships, EPA, *66.307*
evaluation, research, HUD, *14.506*
Extension Service, *10.500*
FEMA flood assistance program, *97.023*
fisheries investments, *11.415*
flood plain data, services, 12.104
HBCU Program, HUD, *14.520*
Hispanic serving institutions assistance, HUD, *14.514*
historic places, 15.914
homeland security public awareness outreach, DHS, *97.086*
housing mortgage insurance, *14.122*
HUD block grants, *14.218, 14.219, 14.228*
HUD projects, employment, business opportunities, 14.412
HUD Single Family Property Disposition, 14.311
HUD Youthbuild Program, *14.243*
IHE outreach, HUD, *14.511*
Indian communities block grants, *14.862*
insular areas, HUD block grants, *14.225*
Job Opportunities for Low-Income Individuals, TANF, *93.593*
Lead Outreach Grants, HUD, *14.904*
Learn and Serve America programs, *94.004, 94.005*
Magnet Schools Assistance, *84.165*
microenterprise development training, technical assistance, *59.050*
military base impact, 12.600, *12.607*
military/community joint land use plans, *12.610*
neighborhood revitalization, CDBG, *14.218, 14.219, 14.228*
NRC local public document rooms, *77.005*
Officer Next Door Sales Program, 14.198
Operation Lead Elimination Action Program, HUD, *14.903*
Project Safe Neighborhoods, *16.609*
public facilities, services, CDBG, *14.218, 14.219, 14.228*
relocation, demolition, clearance, CDBG, *14.218, 14.219, 14.228*
revolving loan funds, CDBG, *14.218, 14.219, 14.228, 14.246*
revolving loan funds, credit unions, *44.002*
Riegle Community Development and Regulatory Improvement Act of 1994, *59.050*
rural communities research, SBIR, *10.212*
Rural Community Development Initiative, RHS, *10.446*
rural public facilities, *10.766*
Safeguarding Communities, inmate reentry, OJP, *16.735*
Section 108 Loan Guarantees, *14.248*
senior volunteers in community service (RSVP), *94.002*

MASTER INDEX 905

slum elimination, CDBG, *14.218*, *14.219*, *14.228*
soil surveys, 10.903
streets, public services, CDBG, *14.218*, *14.219*, *14.228*
Superfund technical assistance to citizens groups, *66.806*
Teacher Next Door Initiative, 14.310
technical assistance, training program, CDBG, *14.227*
telecommunications infrastructure, *11.552*
Urban Community Forestry, *10.675*
urban forestry, *10.664*
urban parks, recreation, CDBG, *14.218*, *14.219*, *14.228*
VISTA program, 94.013
Weed and Seed Program, *16.595*
work-study, HUD, *14.512*
Youth Opportunity Grants, DOL, *17.263*
see also AmeriCorps; Appalachian region; Community health services; Crime; Depressed areas; Economic development; Highways, roads, bridges; Historic monuments, historic preservation; Homeless persons; Housing *entries*; Mass transportation; Public safety; Rural areas; Social services; Subdivisions; Transportation; Urban parks, playgrounds; Urban planning; Urban renewal; Volunteers; Water *entries*
Community development acts, *see* National housing acts
COMMUNITY DEVELOPMENT BLOCK GRANTS/BROWNFIELDS ECONOMIC DEVELOPMENT INITIATIVE, *14.246*
COMMUNITY DEVELOPMENT BLOCK GRANTS/ENTITLEMENT GRANTS, *14.218*
COMMUNITY DEVELOPMENT BLOCK GRANTS—SECTION 108 LOAN GUARANTEES, *14.248*
COMMUNITY DEVELOPMENT BLOCK GRANTS/SMALL CITIES PROGRAM, *14.219*
COMMUNITY DEVELOPMENT BLOCK GRANTS/SPECIAL PURPOSE GRANTS/INSULAR AREAS, *14.225*
COMMUNITY DEVELOPMENT BLOCK GRANTS/TECHNICAL ASSISTANCE PROGRAM, *14.227*
COMMUNITY DEVELOPMENT BLOCK GRANTS/STATE'S PROGRAM, *14.228*
Community Development Credit Union (CDCU), *44.002*
Community Development Financial Institutions (CDFI), *21.020*
Community Development Financial Institutions Fund, Department of the Treasury, *see* Agency Index
COMMUNITY DEVELOPMENT FINANCIAL INSTITUTIONS PROGRAM, *21.020*
COMMUNITY DEVELOPMENT REVOLVING LOAN FUND PROGRAM FOR CREDIT UNIONS, *44.002*
COMMUNITY DEVELOPMENT WORK-STUDY PROGRAM, *14.512*
COMMUNITY DISASTER LOANS, *97.030*
COMMUNITY ECONOMIC ADJUSTMENT [DOD], 12.600

COMMUNITY ECONOMIC ADJUSTMENT ASSISTANCE [DOD], 12.614
COMMUNITY ECONOMIC ADJUSTMENT PLANNING ASSISTANCE [DOD], *12.607*
COMMUNITY ECONOMIC ADJUSTMENT PLANNING ASSISTANCE FOR JOINT LAND USE STUDIES [DOD], *12.610*
COMMUNITY ECONOMIC ADJUSTMENT PLANNING ASSISTANCE FOR REDUCTIONS IN DEFENSE INDUSTRY EMPLOYMENT, *12.611*
Community Economic Development, CSBG, *93.570*
COMMUNITY FACILITIES LOANS AND GRANTS, *10.766*
Community Fire Protection, BIA, *15.031*
COMMUNITY FOOD PROJECTS, *10.225*
Community Gun Violence Prosecution, OJP, *16.609*
Community health services
AIDS-afflicted persons, housing, services, *14.241*
Appalachian region, *23.002*
Area Health Education Centers Model Programs, *93.107*
bilingual, bicultural health demonstrations, *93.105*
block grants, preventive health, health services, *93.991*
cancer early detection, breast, cervical screening, training, *93.919*
caregiver support program, respite care, *93.052*
chronic disease prevention, control, *93.945*
clinical researchers education loan repayment, disadvantaged, *93.308*
Consolidated Health Centers program, homeless, migrants, public housing residents, school-based, HRSA, *93.224*
Community Services Block Grant, *93.569*
Disadvantaged Minority Health Improvement Act of 1990, *93.100*
DVA specialized medical resource sharing, 64.018
environmental justice collaborative projects, *66.306*
EPA aging, children's health protection, *66.609*
EPA Performance Partnership Grants, *66.605*
EPA pollution prevention studies, training, outreach, *66.716*
facilities development, CDBG programs, *14.218*, *14.219*, *14.225*, *14.228*, *14.862*
federal surplus property assistance, 93.291
Hawaii natives, *93.932*
Health Centers Consolidation Act of 1996, *93.224*
Health Education and Training Centers, *93.189*
Health Services and Centers Amendments of 1978, *93.268*
health services disparities projects, *93.100*
Healthy Homes Demonstration Grants, HUD, *14.901*
HIV/AIDS, minorities, HHS prevention, education demonstrations, *93.006*
HIV care, *93.917*
HIV emergency relief projects, *93.914*
HIV outpatient early intervention, *93.918*
HIV prevention, *93.939*, *93.940*
HIV prevention efficacy research, dissemination, *93.941*
HIV projects, *93.928*
Home Health Care and Alzheimer's Disease Amendments Act of 1990, *93.051*

Community health services *(continued)*
IHE outreach, HUD, *14.511*
lead-based paint hazard control, *14.900*
lead-based paint removal training, certification, *66.707*
Lead Hazard Reduction Demonstration Grants, HUD, *14.905*
Lead Outreach Grants, HUD, *14.904*
lead poisoning prevention, *66.606, 93.197*
lead technical studies, HUD, *14.902, 14.906*
Medicaid, *93.778*
minority community health coalitions, *93.137*
minority health status improvement, *93.004*
nursing education loan repayments, *93.908*
Operation Lead Elimination Action Program, HUD, *14.903*
perinatal/maternal initiative, *93.926*
pollution source reduction information dissemination, outreach, EPA, *66.717*
primary care planning, coordination, *93.130*
promotional activities, national, *93.990*
rural areas, *93.223, 93.912, 93.913*
rural, computer linkages, *10.855*
Senior Companion Program, *94.016*
Social Services Block Grant, *93.667*
Specially Selected Health Projects, HRSA, *93.888*
technical assistance, training, *93.129*
telecommunications infrastructure, *11.552*
Telehealth Network Grants, *93.211*
toxic substances regulation, *66.701*
trafficking victims, *16.320*
Tribal Lead Grants, *66.715*
uninsured patients, Healthy Community Access Program, *93.252*
urban Indians, *93.193*
veterans, dependents services, 64.009
veterans, 64.022
women's health, Community Centers of Excellence, *93.290*
see also Aging and the aged; AIDS (Acquired Immune Deficiency Syndrome); Alcohol abuse, alcoholism; Aliens, immigrants, refugees; Behavioral sciences, education, services; Communicable diseases; Community development; Disease control; Drug abuse; Environmental health, research, services; Family *entries*; Farm workers; Health facilities *entries*; Health, medical services; Homeless persons; Immunization, immunology; Maternal, child health, welfare; Mental health; Preventive health services; Public health; Rural areas; Social services; Victim assistance; Veterans health, medical services; Volunteers
Community Mental Health Services (CMHS) Block Grant, *93.958*
Community Mental Health Services (CMHS) Child Mental Health Service Initiative, *93.104*
Community Opportunities, Accountability, and Training and Educational Services Act of 1998 (COATS), *see* Community development
COMMUNITY OUTREACH PARTNERSHIP CENTER PROGRAM [HUD], *14.511*
Community planning, *see* Community development; Economic development; Highways, roads, bridges; Historic monuments, historic preservation; Rural areas; Transportation; Urban planning
Community Planning and Development (CPD), HUD, *see* Agency Index
Community Planning Assistance, DOD, *12.607, 12.612, 12.613*
COMMUNITY PROGRAMS TO IMPROVE MINORITY HEALTH GRANT PROGRAM, *93.137*
COMMUNITY PROSECUTION AND PROJECT SAFE NEIGHBORHOODS, *16.609*
COMMUNITY RELATIONS SERVICE, 16.200
Community Relations Service (CRS), DOJ, *see* Agency Index
Community services, *see* Community development; Community health services; Social services; Volunteers
COMMUNITY SERVICES BLOCK GRANT, *93.569*
COMMUNITY SERVICES BLOCK GRANT—DISCRETIONARY AWARDS, *93.570*
COMMUNITY SERVICES BLOCK GRANT DISCRETIONARY AWARDS—COMMUNITY TECHNOLOGY CENTERS [DOED], *84.341*
COMMUNITY SERVICES BLOCK GRANT FORMULA AND DISCRETIONARY AWARDS FOR COMMUNITY FOOD AND NUTRITION PROGRAMS, *93.571*
Community water supply, *see* Rural areas; Water *entries*
Compassion Capital Fund (CCF), ACF, *93.009, 93.647*
COMPASSION CAPITAL FUND [HHS], *93.009*
Compensation, *see* Employee benefits; Insurance; Unemployment; Victim assistance
COMPENSATION AND WORKING CONDITIONS, *17.005*
Compensation, DVA, *64.109*
COMPENSATION FOR SERVICE-CONNECTED DEATHS FOR VETERANS' DEPENDENTS, *64.102*
COMPETITIVE TRAINING GRANTS [DHS], *97.068*
Complaint investigation
ADA technical assistance, *16.108*
advertising, deceptive, misleading, 36.001
age discrimination, housing, HUD programs, 14.402
air transportation, 20.900
aliens, employment discrimination, *16.110*
architectural barriers, HUD programs, 14.407
architectural, transportation barriers, accessibility standards enforcement, design, research, training, 88.001
Atlantic coast fisheries, *11.474*
Border Enforcement Grants, FMCSA, *20.233*
boycotts, 36.001
broadcast signal interference, 32.001
CDBG program, discrimination, 14.406
child abuse, *93.643*
child, spousal support, *93.563, 93.597, 93.601*
Child Support Enforcement Research, *93.564*
children's rights violations, *16.549*
civil rights, HHS programs, 93.001
civil rights, information clearinghouse, 29.001

clinic entrances act, 16.105
commodity futures trading, 78.004
communications, FCC, 32.001
community conflicts, 16.200
credit reporting, debt collection, 36.001
credit transactions, discrimination, 16.103
Criminal Section, DOJ, 16.109
disabled, ADA employment discrimination, 30.011
disabled, housing-related discrimination, 14.414
education discrimination, 16.100
elders abuse, 93.041, 93.042
employment discrimination, 16.101, 30.001
employment discrimination, age, 30.008
employment discrimination, attorney referral, 30.005
employment discrimination, Indians, 30.009
employment discrimination, state, local enforcement assistance, 30.002
EPA compliance capacity building, 66.709
Equal Pay Act, 30.005, 30.010
Fair Housing Initiatives Program, 14.408
fair housing training, technical assistance, 14.401
farm labor standards, 17.308
federal contract compliance, 17.301
Federal Wage Hour Laws, 17.303
food stamp program violations, 10.561
handicap discrimination, housing, HUD programs, 14.404
hazardous materials transport, 20.217
health fraud task forces, FDA, 93.447
housing discrimination, 14.400, 16.103
housing, HUD programs discrimination, 14.405
HUD projects, employment, business opportunities, 14.412
import competition, 11.106, 11.313
Indian arts and crafts, misrepresentation, 15.850
institutionalized persons, discrimination, 16.105
international trade agreement negotiation, enforcement, 11.110
Internet Fraud Complaint Center, 16.612
interstate land sales, 14.168
investors, 58.001
labor-management practices, relations, 46.001
labor organization practices, 17.309
long-term care employee background checks, 93.785
manufactured homes safety, construction, 14.171
marine sanctuaries violations, 11.429
maritime shipping rates, services, 33.001
Medicaid fraud control, 93.775
Medicaid, Medicare standards compliance, 93.777
mentally ill persons, abuse, neglect, 93.138
mergers, acquisitions, illegal, 36.001
migrant worker bondage, 16.109
monopolistic, unfair trade, 36.001
motor carrier safety, 20.217, 20.218
occupational safety, health, 17.503
packaging, 36.001
perishable foods, 10.165
pesticides regulation compliance, 66.700
political candidates, equal time, 32.001
price-fixing conspiracies, 36.001
Privacy Rule, 93.001
public facilities, institutions, discrimination, 16.105
racial violence, 16.109
railroad safety, 20.303
securities market, 58.001
small business, agriculture regulatory ombudsman, 59.053
telephone, telegraph service, rates, 32.001
travel agents, tour operators, air, 20.900
veterans employment, reemployment, 17.803
voting rights, 16.104
wage garnishment, 17.306
see also Air pollution; Civil rights; Community development; Consumers, consumer services; Crime; Food inspection, grading; Hazardous materials, waste; Hotlines; Information, general, clearinghouses; Labor standards; Legal services; Occupational health, safety; Pesticides; Pollution abatement; Toxic substances, toxicology; Water pollution abatement, prevention
Complaints and Inquiries, SEC, 58.001
Complementary medicine research, NIH, 93.213
COMPLIANCE ASSISTANCE SUPPORT FOR SERVICES TO THE REGULATED COMMUNITY AND OTHER ASSISTANCE PROVIDERS [EPA], 66.305
COMPREHENSIVE CENTERS [DOED], 84.283
COMPREHENSIVE COMMUNITY MENTAL HEALTH SERVICES FOR CHILDREN WITH SERIOUS EMOTIONAL DISTURBANCES (SED), 93.104
Comprehensive Drug Abuse Prevention and Control Act of 1970 (CDAPCA), *see* Drug abuse
Comprehensive Environmental Response, Compensation, and Liability Act (CERCLA), *see* Hazardous materials, waste
COMPREHENSIVE GERIATRIC EDUCATION PROGRAM, 93.265
COMPREHENSIVE SCHOOL REFORM DEMONSTRATION, 84.332
COMPUTER AND INFORMATION SCIENCE AND ENGINEERING, 47.070
Computer products, sciences, services
Advanced Technology Program, NIST, 11.612
agricultural commodity reports, 10.153
Air Force Defense Research Sciences Program, 12.800
aviation education, 20.100,
bioinformatics, computational biology research, training, 93.859
biomedical imaging research, 93.286
broadband access loans, rural areas, RUS, 10.886
census data, 11.001
census data, programs, training, 11.002
census geography, 11.003
census special tabulations, 11.005
coastal ecosystem management, NOAA, 11.473
Combined DNA Index System (CODIS), FBI, 16.307
Community Connect Grants, RUS, 10.863
Community Technology Centers, DOED, 84.341
computer fraud, FBI training, 16.300, 16.302
counter-terrorism technology development, DOJ, 16.565
criminal history improvement program, 16.554
cyber security activities, DHS, 97.067, 97.073
DHS Competitive Training Grants, 97.068
DHS Scholars and Fellows, 97.062

Computer products, sciences, services *(continued)*
  DNA laboratory improvement, training, DOJ, *16.564*
  DOD research projects, *12.910*
  DOE Advanced Simulation and Computing Academic Strategic Alliances Program, *81.112*
  domestic violence arrest policies, protection orders enforcement, *16.590*
  economic data, analysis, national, 11.025
  education project technical assistance, *84.283*
  Education Technology State Grants, *84.318*
  energy data, 81.039
  energy information data base, 81.064
  energy-related basic research, *81.049*
  Environmental Information Exchange Network Grants, *66.608*
  EPA environmental sustainability design competition, *66.516*
  fair housing programs, *14.401*
  federal computer products, services, 11.650
  food stamp program administration, *10.561*
  food stamp program access research, *10.580*
  foreign information access, education technology, *84.337*
  geologic map database, *15.810*
  geospatial data clearinghouse, *15.809*
  government publications, GPO, 40.001
  HIV/AIDS Surveillance, *93.944*
  information security research, NSA, *12.902*
  Internet Crimes Against Children Task Force Program, *16.543*
  Internet Fraud Complaint Center, *16.612*
  Interoperable Communications Equipment, DHS, *97.055*
  job listings, U.S. Employment Service, *17.207*
  library information services, *45.310*
  Literacy through School Libraries, *84.364*
  medical information science research, training, *93.879*
  mental health research models, *93.242*
  missing persons index, 16.304
  Motor Vehicle Theft Protection Act Program, *16.597*
  NASA Technology Transfer, 43.002
  National Crime Information Center, 16.304
  National Standard Reference Data System, 11.603
  National Trade Data Bank, 11.026
  Native American Library Services, *45.311*
  NSA language grants, *12.900*
  NSF computer, information science, engineering, *47.070*
  NSF engineering education, research, *47.041*
  Public Housing Neighborhood Network Grants, *14.875*
  rural cooperatives, systems, 10.350
  rural educational, medical networks, RUS, *10.855*
  Semiconductor Chip Protection Service, 42.008
  sex offender registry, *16.554*
  small business on-line counseling, 59.005
  small business, Procurement Marketing and Access Network (PRO- Net), 59.009
  State of the Nation, ESA, 11.027
  STAT-USA, ESA, 11.026
  TIGER (Topologically Integrated Geographic Encoding and Referencing) system, 11.003
  Uniform Crime Reports, 16.305
  University-Based Homeland Security Centers, DHS, *97.061*
  WIC Grants to States, FNS, *10.578*
  Women's Business Center, SBA, *59.043*
  Women's Educational Equity Act Program, *84.083*
  see also Communications, telecommunications; Education equipment; Engineering *entries*; Information *entries*; Mathematics; Publications; Science education; Scientific research; Statistics; Technology transfer, utilization
Condominium housing, *see* Housing, condominiums
Congregate housing, *see* Group housing; Housing, congregate
Congress-Bundestag Youth Exchange (CBYX), BECA, *19.410*
CONGRESSIONALLY IDENTIFIED AWARDS AND PROJECTS [NOAA], *11.469*
CONGRESSIONALLY IDENTIFIED PROJECTS [USDC], *11.617*
Conservation, agricultural, *see* Agricultural conservation
CONSERVATION ASSESSMENT PROGRAM [IMLS], *45.304*
Conservation, energy, *see* Community development; Energy conservation; Weatherization
CONSERVATION GRANTS PRIVATE STEWARDSHIP FOR IMPERILED SPECIES, *15.632*
CONSERVATION LAW ENFORCEMENT TRAINING ASSISTANCE, 15.602
CONSERVATION PROJECT SUPPORT [IMLS], *45.303*
CONSERVATION RESEARCH AND DEVELOPMENT, *81.086*
CONSERVATION RESERVE PROGRAM [USDA], *10.069*
CONSERVATION SECURITY PROGRAM [USDA], *10.921*
Conservation, soil, *see* Soil conservation
Conservation, water, *see* Water conservation
Conservation, wetlands, *see* Water conservation; Wetlands
Conservation, wildlife, *see* Wildlife, waterfowl
Consolidated Farm and Rural Development Act (CFRDA), *see* Rural areas
CONSOLIDATED HEALTH CENTERS, *93.224*
CONSOLIDATED KNOWLEDGE DEVELOPMENT AND APPLICATION (KD&A) PROGRAM [HHS], *93.230*
CONSOLIDATED PESTICIDE ENFORCEMENT COOPERATIVE AGREEMENTS, *66.700*
Consolidated Program Support Grants, EPA, *66.600*
CONSOLIDATED TRIBAL GRANT PROGRAM, *15.021*
Consolidation Loans, students, *84.032*
Constitutional rights, *see* Civil rights
Construction
  ADA technical assistance, *16.108*
  armories, *12.400*
  Census Bureau data, 11.001
  Davis-Bacon Act, 17.201, 17.303
  energy conservation, renewable energy outreach, training, *81.117*
  federal contracts, wage-hour laws, 17.303
  federally assisted contractors, 17.301

flood plain data, services, 12.104
handicapped, accessibility standards, design, research, training, 88.001
industrial, EDA projects, *11.300*
marine, atmospheric sciences projects, *11.469*
National Guard facilities, *12.400*
research, advanced technology, Corps of Engineers, *12.114*
soil surveys, 10.903
standards, research, *11.609*
Universities Rebuilding America Program, Hurricanes Katrina, Rita, HUD, *14.521*
see also Architecture; Buildings; Community development; Disabled, handicapped *entries*; Education facilities; Energy conservation; Health facilities *entries*; Highways, roads, bridges; Housing *entries*; Public works
CONSTRUCTION GRANTS FOR WASTEWATER TREATMENT WORKS, *66.418*
Construction Productivity Advanced Research (CPAR) Program, Corps of Engineers, *12.114*
CONSTRUCTION RESERVE FUND [DOT], *20.812*
CONSULTATION AGREEMENTS [DOL], *17.504*
CONSUMER CREDIT PROTECTION, 17.306
Consumer Expenditure Survey (CES), 17.003
Consumer Price Index (CPI), 17.003
Consumer protection, see Complaint investigation; Consumers, consumer services

Consumers, consumer services
advertising complaints, 36.001
agricultural marketing, 10.163
agricultural products inspection, 10.162
air travel problems, 20.900
broadcasting, communications complaints, 32.001
Citizen Information Center, 39.009
consumer credit reporting, debt collection, 36.001
Consumer Expenditure Survey, 17.003
Consumer Credit Protection Act, 16.103, 17.306
Consumer Price Index, 17.003
credit protection, public assistance recipients, 16.103
credit unions, *44.001*
Federal Trade Commission Act of 1914, 36.001
fisheries products inspection, 11.413
fraud information center, *16.613*
health fraud task forces, FDA, *93.447*
housing counseling, *14.169*
information, publications, 39.009
interstate land sales protection, 14.168
investment, securities market protection, 58.001
manufactured homes safety standards, 14.171
meat, poultry, eggs inspection, 10.477
meat, poultry inspection, *10.475*
MMA participants, State Pharmaceutical Assistance Programs, CMS, *93.786*
packaging complaints, 36.001
perishable foods complaints, 10.165
pollution source reduction information dissemination, outreach, EPA, *66.717*
Scams Targeting the Elderly, telemarketing, DOJ, *16.613*
wage garnishment protection, 17.306
Weights and Measures Service, NIST, 11.606
white-collar crime center, *16.612*
see also Complaint investigation; Food inspection, grading; Home management; Hotlines; Information, general; Legal services; Volunteers
Contagious diseases, see Communicable diseases
Continuing education, see Adult education; Higher education
Contraception, see Family planning
CONTRACEPTION AND INFERTILITY RESEARCH LOAN REPAYMENT PROGRAM, *93.209*
Contract Commodity Direct Payments, *10.055*
Contract Support, BIA, *15.024*
Contracts, see Government contracts
Controlled substances, see Drugs
COOPERATING TECHNICAL PARTNERS [DHS], *97.045*
COOPERATIVE AGREEMENTS FOR STATE-BASED COMPREHENSIVE BREAST AND CERVICAL CANCER EARLY DETECTION PROGRAMS, *93.919*
COOPERATIVE AGREEMENTS FOR STATE-BASED DIABETES CONTROL PROGRAMS AND EVALUATION OF SURVEILLANCE SYSTEMS, *93.988*
COOPERATIVE AGREEMENTS FOR STATE TREATMENT OUTCOMES AND PERFORMANCE PILOT STUDIES ENHANCEMENT, *93.238*
COOPERATIVE AGREEMENTS TO IMPROVE THE HEALTH STATUS OF MINORITY POPULATIONS, *93.004*
COOPERATIVE AGREEMENTS TO SUPPORT COMPREHENSIVE SCHOOL HEALTH PROGRAMS TO PREVENT THE SPREAD OF HIV AND OTHER IMPORTANT HEALTH PROBLEMS, *93.938*
COOPERATIVE AGREEMENTS TO SUPPORT STATE-BASED SAFE MOTHERHOOD AND INFANT HEALTH INITIATIVE PROGRAMS, *93.946*
COOPERATIVE AGREEMENTS WITH STATES FOR INTRASTATE MEAT AND POULTRY INSPECTION, *10.475*
COOPERATIVE DEVELOPMENT PROGRAM [USAID], *98.002*
Cooperative Education and Research Program (CERP), NMFS, *11.455*
COOPERATIVE ENDANGERED SPECIES CONSERVATION FUND, *15.615*
COOPERATIVE EXTENSION SERVICE, *10.500*
COOPERATIVE FISHERY STATISTICS, *11.434*
COOPERATIVE FORESTRY ASSISTANCE, *10.664*
COOPERATIVE FORESTRY RESEARCH, *10.202*
Cooperative housing, see Housing cooperatives
COOPERATIVE INSPECTION AGREEMENTS WITH STATES AND TRIBES [DOI], *15.222*
Cooperative Institute Agreement (CIA), NMFS, *11.455*
Cooperative Institute for Marine and Atmospheric Studies (CIMAS), NMFS, *11.455*
Cooperative Institute for Marine Resources Studies (CIMRS), NMFS, *11.455*
Cooperative Institute of Fishery Oceanography (CIFO), NMFS, *11.455*
Cooperative Institutes, NOAA, *11.432*
Cooperative Marine Education and Research Programs (CMER), NMFS, *11.455*

Cooperative Program for Operational Meteorology, Education and Training (COMET), *11.467*
COOPERATIVE RESEARCH UNITS PROGRAM [DOI], *15.812*
COOPERATIVE SCIENCE AND EDUCATION PROGRAMS [USDC], *11.455*
Cooperative State Research, Education and Extension Service (CSREES), USDA, *see* Agency Index
Cooperative State Research Service, USDA, *see* Agency Index (USDA, Cooperative State Research, Education and Extension Service)
Cooperatives
  Intermediary Relending Program, *10.767*
  international, Cooperative Development Program, USAID, *98.002*
  international, Food For Peace, USAID, *98.007, 98.008*
  international, Institutional Capacity Building, USAID, *98.005*
  Rural Business-Cooperative Service, 10.350
  rural business development, *10.768*
  Rural Business Investment Companies, RBCS, *10.860*
  Rural Cooperative Development Grants, *10.771*
  rural water, waste disposal systems, *10.760*
  RUS community assistance, high energy cost, *10.859*
  RUS electrification loans, *10.850*
  RUS telephone service loans, *10.851, 10.852*
  waste, water disposal systems, *10.770*
  waste, water systems, technical assistance, *10.761*
  water, wastewater projects revolving loan funds, *10.864*
  see also Agricultural cooperatives; Credit unions; Housing cooperatives
Cooperator Program, USDA, *10.600*
COORDINATED SERVICES AND ACCESS TO RESEARCH FOR WOMEN, INFANTS, CHILDREN, AND YOUTH, *93.153*
COP (Coastal Ocean Program), NOAA, *11.478*
Cops Grants, *16.710*
COPYRIGHT SERVICE, 42.002
Copyright services
  cable system licenses, 42.002
  Copyright Arbitration Royalty Panels, 42.002
  information, NCSCI, 11.610
  information, registration, 42.002
  Semiconductor Chip Protection Service, 42.008
  see also Patents, trademarks, inventions
CORA BROWN FUND [DHS], *97.031*
Core Centers and Research Training Program, NIEHS, *93.894*
Corn, *see* Agricultural commodities, stabilization; Feed grains
Corneal diseases research, *93.867*
Corporation for National and Community Service (CNCS), 94.002 through 94.016
Corporations, *see* Business development; Private sector; Small business
Corps of Engineers, DOD, *see* Agency Index (DOD, Department of the Army, Office of the Chief of Engineers)
CORRECTIONAL GRANT PROGRAM FOR INDIAN TRIBES, *16.596*

Corrections
  adult education, offenders, *84.002, 84.191*
  civil rights, inmates, 16.105
  DNA casework backlog reduction, *16.743*
  Drug Court Program, *16.585*
  education, institutionalized neglected, delinquent youth, *84.013*
  facilities, Byrne Formula Grant Program, *16.579*
  facilities, federal surplus property transfer, 16.578, 39.002
  Indian detention facilities improvement, repair, *15.063*
  Indian tribes, jail construction, *16.596*
  inmate education, federal surplus real property transfer, 84.145
  justice personnel, equipment, training, planning grants, *16.738*
  juvenile facilities improvements, personnel training, *16.523*
  juvenile gangs program, *16.544*
  juvenile justice, delinquency program improvement, training, *16.540*
  juvenile offenders, alternative programs, *16.541, 16.549*
  juveniles, personnel training, research, *16.542*
  Literacy Program for Prisoners, *84.255*
  mentally ill offenders, abuse, neglect, *93.138*
  Mentoring Children of Prisoners, ACF, *93.616*
  Offender Reentry Program, *16.202*
  offenders, justice, health, social services networks, *93.229*
  officers disability, death benefits, *16.571*
  personnel families support projects, research, *16.563*
  personnel, student loan cancellations, *84.037*
  Prison Grants, violent offenders, *16.586*
  Prison Rape Elimination Act of 2003, *16.735, 16.739*
  prison rape elimination, personnel training, victim services, *16.735*
  prison rape statistics program, *16.739*
  research, program evaluation, *16.602*
  Residential Substance Abuse Treatment, DOJ, *16.593*
  staff, ex-offenders development, training, *16.601*
  State Criminal Alien Assistance Program, DOJ, *16.606*
  tribal detention facilities, *15.030*
  upgrading facilities operation, clearinghouse, *16.603*
  vocational education, offenders, *84.048*
  youth, offenders, education, employment services, *84.331*
  see also Crime; Criminal justice system; Education counseling; Juvenile delinquency; Law enforcement education, training; Police
CORRECTIONS AND LAW ENFORCEMENT FAMILY SUPPORT, *16.563*
CORRECTIONS—RESEARCH AND EVALUATION AND POLICY FORMULATION, *16.602*
CORRECTIONS—TECHNICAL ASSISTANCE/ CLEARINGHOUSE, *16.603*
CORRECTIONS—TRAINING AND STAFF DEVELOPMENT, *16.601*
Counter-terrorism Technology Development, DOJ, *16.565*

Master Index 911

Cotton, *see* Agricultural commodities, stabilization
Counseling, *see* Behavioral sciences, education, services; Education counseling; Home management; Mental health; Social services
Court Appointed Special Advocates (CASA), child abuse, *16.547*
Courts, *see* Criminal justice system; Indian affairs; Legal services
CPAR (Construction Productivity Advanced Research), Corps of Engineers, *12.114*
CPS (Conservation Project Support), IMLS, *45.303*
Cranston-Gonzalez National Affordable Housing Act, *see* National housing acts (National Affordable Housing Act)
CRASH DATA IMPROVEMENT PROGRAM [DOT], *20.230*
CRBSCP (Colorado River Basin Salinity Control Program), *10.070*
CREDIT UNION CHARTER, EXAMINATION, SUPERVISION AND INSURANCE, *44.001*
Credit unions
 Community Development Credit Union, *44.002*
 establishment, operation, *44.001*
 Federal Credit Union Act, *44.001*
 financial counseling, *44.002*
 guaranteed student loans, *84.032*
 housing counseling assistance, *14.169*
 insurance, *44.001*
 revolving loan fund, *44.002*
 see also Banks, banking
Crew Leader, farm labor, 17.308
CRF (Construction Reserve Fund), ships, *20.812*
Crime
 arrest records, criminal history, 16.304
 ATF crime control training, 16.012
 Bulletproof Vest Partnership Program, *16.607*
 campus crime grants, *16.525*
 Civil Rights Prosecution, 16.109
 Combined DNA Index System (CODIS), *16.307*
 Comprehensive Crime Control Act of 1984, 16.578
 computer fraud detection, training, 16.302
 Cops Grants, *16.710*
 Crime Control Acts, 16.300, 16.302, *16.575, 16.576, 16.580, 16.609*
 criminal conspiracy, organized crime regional information sharing, *16.610*
 criminal history record systems, *16.554*
 domestic violence arrest policies, protection orders enforcement, *16.590*
 domestic violence, stalking victim transitional housing, *16.736*
 drug control improvement, *16.579, 16.580*
 Drug-Free Schools and Communities, national programs, *84.184*
 Emergency Federal Law Enforcement Assistance, *16.577*
 FBI Crime Laboratory, 16.301
 FBI fingerprint identification, 16.303
 Food Stamp fraud, *10.561*
 gang-related, reduction programs, *16.544*
 Gun Control Act, 16.012, 16.309
 Gun Violence Prosecution, OJP, *16.609*
 health fraud task forces, FDA, *93.447*
 Indian Country Alcohol and Drug Prevention, DOJ, *16.616*
 Internet Fraud Complaint Center, *16.612*
 Medicaid, Medicare fraud, *93.775*
 Motor Vehicle Theft Protection Act Program, *16.597*
 National Crime Information Center, 16.304
 National Firearms Act, 16.309
 National Fraud Information Center, *16.613*
 National Instant Criminal Background Check System, 16.309
 Omnibus Crime Control and Safe Streets Act (OCCSSA), 16.012, 16.105, 16.300, 16.301, 16.302, *16.550, 16.554, 16.560, 16.561, 16.562, 16.564, 16.565, 16.566, 16.571, 16.579, 16.580, 16.585, 16.587, 16.588, 16.593, 16.609, 16.610, 16.612, 16.710, 16.734, 16.739, 97.081*
 Operation Weed and Seed, *16.595*
 Organized Crime Control Act of 1970, 16.012
 prevention, Hawaiian housing, HUD, *14.873*
 prevention, Indian housing, *14.867*
 prison rape statistics program, *16.739*
 Project Safe Neighborhoods, OJP, *16.609*
 research, cause, prevention, *16.560*
 research fellowships, graduate, *16.561, 16.562*
 rural domestic violence, *16.589*
 Safe Schools/Healthy Students National Evaluation, DOJ, *16.732*
 Safeguarding Communities, inmate reentry, OJP, *16.735*
 Scams Targeting the Elderly, telemarketing, DOJ, *16.613*
 schools, reduction, *16.542*
 Sex Offender Management, *16.203*
 sex offender registry, *16.554*
 statistics, states, *16.550*
 statistics, trends, 16.305
 trafficking victims assistance, ACF, *93.598*
 Tribal Youth Program, OJJDP, *16.731*
 underage drinking law enforcement, *16.727*
 Uniform Crime Reports, 16.305
 victim assistance, *16.575*
 victim assistance personnel training, *16.582*
 victim compensation, *16.576*
 victim notification systems, *16.740*
 violence against women, *16.587, 16.588*
 violence, children's exposure, prevention initiative, Safe Start, *16.730*
 Violent Crime Control and Law Enforcement Act (VCCLEA), 16.105, *16.203*, 16.300, 16.302, 16.308, *16.563, 16.575, 16.576, 16.582, 16.583, 16.586, 16.587, 16.588, 16.589, 16.590, 16.596, 16.597, 16.606, 16.613, 16.710, 16.712, 93.557, 93.591, 93.592, 93.671*
 white collar, detection training, 16.300, 16.302
 white-collar, national center, *16.612*
 see also Civil defense; Civil rights; Complaint investigation; Corrections; Criminal justice system; Drug *entries*; FBI; Forensic sciences; Indian affairs; Juvenile delinquency; Law enforcement education, training; Legal services; Police; Public safety; Victim assistance; Women
CRIME LABORATORY IMPROVEMENT PROGRAM—COMBINED DNA INDEX SYSTEM BACKLOG REDUCTION, *16.564*
Crime statistics, *see* Crime; Statistics

CRIME VICTIM ASSISTANCE, *16.575*
CRIME VICTIM ASSISTANCE/
  DISCRETIONARY GRANTS, *16.582*
CRIME VICTIM COMPENSATION, *16.576*
CRIMINAL JUSTICE RESEARCH AND
  DEVELOPMENT—GRADUATE
  RESEARCH FELLOWSHIPS, *16.562*
Criminal justice system
  Alcohol Open Container Requirements, DOT, *20.607*
  anti-terrorism prosecution training, *16.614*
  child abuse, closed-circuit TV, DOJ, *16.611*
  child abuse investigation, prosecution, *93.643, 93.669*
  child abuse technical assistance, training, *16.547*
  civil rights, inmates, 16.105
  Civil Rights Prosecution, 16.109
  Community Prosecution Program, *16.609*
  corrections facilities operations, clearinghouse, *16.603*
  corrections research, policy, *16.602*
  corrections staff training programs, *16.601*
  crime laboratories, controlled substances, *16.579*
  crime victim assistance program, *16.575*
  crime victim compensation, *16.576*
  criminal conspiracy, regional information sharing, *16.610*
  Delinquency Prevention Program, *16.548, 16.549*
  DNA casework backlog reduction, *16.743*
  disabled, elder abuse, sexual assault prevention training, OJP, *16.528*
  Driving While Intoxicated, repeat offender laws, DOT, *20.608*
  DOJ Special Data Collections and Statistical Studies, *16.734*
  domestic violence arrest policies, protection orders enforcement, *16.590*
  domestic violence victim legal assistance, training, *16.524*
  drug control improvement, *16.580*
  drug control staff training, *16.579*
  Drug Court Program, *16.585*
  Drug-Free Schools and Communities, education partnerships, *84.186*
  family violence prevention, *93.591, 93.592*
  forensic DNA capacity enhancement, *16.741*
  forensic sciences improvement, *16.742*
  Gun Violence Prosecution, OJP, *16.609*
  Justice Assistance Act of 1984, *16.577*
  justice personnel, equipment, training, planning grants, *16.738*
  juvenile delinquency prevention, *16.540, 16.541*
  juvenile gangs program, *16.544*
  juvenile justice, delinquency research, training, *16.542*
  juvenile justice, improvement, drug courts, gun courts, *16.523*
  local law enforcement block grants, *16.592*
  missing children program, *16.543*
  National Crime Information Center, 16.304
  Offender Reentry Program, *16.202*
  offenders, justice, health, social services networks, *93.229*
  officers disability, death benefits, *16.571*
  personnel training, Federal Law Enforcement Training Center, DHS, *97.081*

  Prison Grants, violent offenders, *16.586*
  prison rape elimination, personnel training, victim services, *16.735*
  program evaluation, research, development, *16.560*
  Prosecutorial Remedies and Other Tools to End the Exploitation of Children Today Act of 2003 (PROTECT), *16.736*
  research fellowships, *16.561, 16.562, 16.566*
  rural domestic violence programs, *16.589*
  State Court Improvement Program, ACF, *93.586*
  state statistical systems, *16.550*
  Supervised Visitation, Safe Havens for Children, OJP, *16.527*
  trafficking victims assistance, ACF, *93.598*
  tribal courts, *15.029, 16.608*
  victim notification systems, *16.740*
  violence against women programs, *16.526, 16.587, 16.588*
  white-collar crime center, *16.612*
  see also Corrections; Crime; Drug *entries*; FBI; Forensic sciences; Indian affairs; Juvenile delinquency; Law enforcement education, training; Legal services; Maternal, child health, welfare; Police; Social sciences; Victim assistance
Criminal Section, DOJ, 16.109
Criminology, *see* Behavioral sciences, education, services; Corrections; Criminal justice system; Forensic sciences; Juvenile delinquency; Social sciences
CRIPA (Civil Rights of Institutionalized Persons Act), 16.105
Crippled children, *see* Disabled, handicapped children
CRISIS COUNSELING [DHS], *97.032*
CR-LRP (Clinical Research-Loan Repayment Program), NIH, *93.220*
CROP DISASTER PROGRAM, *10.073*
Crop insurance, *see* Agricultural commodities, stabilization; Insurance
CROP INSURANCE, *10.450*
CROP INSURANCE IN TARGETED STATES, *10.458*
Crops, *see* Agricultural *entries*; Feed grains; Fruit; Plants; Vegetables
CRP (Conservation Reserve Program), USDA, *10.069*
CRS (Community Relations Service), DOJ, *see* Agency Index
CRS (Community Relations Service), DOJ, 16.200
CRUP (Cooperative Research Units Program), USGS, *15.812*
CSBG (Community Services Block Grant), *93.569, 93.570*
CSBUSA (Clean School Bus USA), EPA, *66.036*
CSC (Coastal Services Center), NOAA, *11.473*
CSCOR/COP (Center for Sponsored Coastal Ocean Research—Coastal Ocean Program), NOAA, *11.478*
CSP (Conservation Security Program), NRCS, *10.921*
CSRD (Comprehensive School Reform Demonstration), *84.332*
CSREES (Cooperative State Research, Education and Extension Service), USDA, *see* Agency Index

CSSEPP (Chemical Stockpile Emergency Planning Program), FEMA, *97.040*
CSTAR (Collaborative Science, Technology, and Applied Research), NWS, *11.468*
CTP (Cooperating Technical Partners), FEMA, *97.045*
CUBAN/HAITIAN ENTRANT PROGRAM, *97.009*
Cubans, *see* Aliens, immigrants, refugees
Cultural affairs, *see* Arts, arts education; Foreign languages; History; Humanities *entries*; International programs, studies; Museums, galleries; Social sciences
CULTURAL EXCHANGE (PERFORMING ARTS) [BECA], *19.413*
CULTURAL RESOURCE MANAGEMENT [DOI], *15.224*
CW (Clean Water) State Revolving Fund, *66.458*
CWS (College Work-Study Program), *84.033*

DAIRY INDEMNITY PROGRAM, *10.053*
Dairy industry
  contamination indemnity payments, *10.053*
  Crop Insurance, *10.450*
  Dairy Market Loss Assistance Program, FSA, *10.084*
  Dairy Options Pilot Program, *10.454*
  international research training, *10.962*
  Market News, 10.153
  market promotion, protection, 10.163
  marketing agreements, orders, 10.155
  Milk Income Loss Contract Program, *10.080*
  milk program, children, *10.556*
  product inspection, grading, 10.162
  see also Agricultural commodities, stabilization; Food inspection, grading; Livestock industry; School breakfast, lunch
DAIRY MARKET LOSS ASSISTANCE PROGRAM, *10.084*
DAIRY OPTIONS PILOT PROGRAM, *10.454*
Dam Safety State Assistance Program, FEMA, *97.041*
Dams, levees, *see* Flood prevention, control
Dance, *see* Arts, arts education; Music
DAP (Development Assistance Program), USAID, *98.007*
Data processing, *see* Computer products, sciences, services
Davis-Bacon Act, 17.201, 17.303
Day care, *see* Aging and the Aged; Child care services; Employment services
DC SCHOOL CHOICE INCENTIVE PROGRAM, *84.370*
DCP (Direct and Counter-Cyclical Payments), FSA-USDA, *10.055*
DCPs (Diabetes Control Programs), *93.988*
DEA (Drug Enforcement Administration), DOJ, *see* Agency Index
Deafness and the deaf
  audiology, speech pathology, vocational rehabilitation personnel training, *84.129*
  biomedical research, *93.173*
  federal employment, 27.005
  independent living services, *84.169*
  interpreter, sign language training, *84.160*
  newborn hearing screening, *93.251*
  preschool education, *84.173*
  rehabilitation personnel training, *84.264*
  veterans, hearing aids, 64.013
  vocational rehabilitation services, *84.126*, *84.128*
  see also Audiovisual aids, film, video; Disabled, handicapped *entries*; Health, medical research; Speech pathology; Vocational rehabilitation; Volunteers
Death Compensation, DVA, *64.102*
Death Pension, DVA, *64.105*
DEBRIS REMOVAL INSURANCE [DHS], *97.064*
Defense, *see* Civil defense; Military
Defense Advanced Research Projects Agency, DOD, *see* Agency Index
Defense Logistics Agency, DOD, *see* Agency Index
DEFENSE NUCLEAR NONPROLIFERATION RESEARCH, *81.113*
Deficiency payments, agricultural, *see* Agricultural commodities, stabilization
Deleading, lead poisoning, *see* Community health services; Housing rehabilitation; Toxic substances, toxicology
Delinquency Prevention Program, Part E, *16.549*
Delinquency Prevention Program, Title V, *16.548*
DELTA ECONOMIC DEVELOPMENT, *90.201*
DELTA LOCAL DEVELOPMENT DISTRICT ASSISTANCE, *90.202*
Delta Regional Authority, 90.200 through 90.202
DELTA REGIONAL DEVELOPMENT, *90.200*
Demolition, *see* Community development; Construction
DEMOLITION AND REVITALIZATION OF SEVERELY DISTRESSED PUBLIC HOUSING, *14.866*
DEMONSTRATION COOPERATIVE AGREEMENTS FOR DEVELOPMENT AND IMPLEMENTATION OF CRIMINAL JUSTICE NETWORKS, *93.229*
DEMONSTRATION PROJECTS FOR INDIAN HEALTH, *93.933*
DEMONSTRATION PROJECTS TO ENSURE STUDENTS WITH DISABILITIES RECEIVE A HIGHER EDUCATION, *84.333*
DEMONSTRATION TO MAINTAIN INDEPENDENCE AND EMPLOYMENT [HHS], *93.769*
Denali Commission, 90.100
DENALI COMMISSION PROGRAM, *90.100*
Dental education, training
  AIDS/HIV dental services reimbursements, *93.924*
  dental residency, *93.236*, *93.884*
  disadvantaged, scholarships, *93.925*
  disadvantaged student loans, *93.342*
  education assistance, disadvantaged, *93.822*
  education loan repayments, states, *93.165*
  faculty education loan repayments, disadvantaged, *93.923*
  geriatric dentistry faculty fellowships, *93.156*
  Indians, health professions scholarships, *93.972*
  Indians, pregraduate scholarships, *93.123*
  NHSC loan repayments, *93.162*
  NHSC scholarships, *93.288*
  research fellowships, *93.121*
  see also Dental health, dental research; Health, medical education, training; Health professions

Dental health services, research
fluoridation program, block grant, 93.991
NIH Clinical Research Loan Repayment Program (CR-LRP), 93.280
NIH Pediatric Research Loan Repayment Program, 93.285, 93.385
NIH research training, 93.140
oral diseases, disorders, 93.121
research, research infrastructure resources, training, 93.389
veterans benefits information, assistance, 64.115
veterans, dependents services, 64.009
veterans services, 64.011
see also Community health services; Dental education, training; Health, medical *entries*; Veterans health, medical services

Dental Residency Training Grants, 93.236
Dentistry, *see* Dental *entries*; Health professions
DENTON PROGRAM [USAID], 98.010
Department of Agriculture (USDA), 10.001 through 10.962
Department of Commerce (USDC), 11.001 through 11.900
Department of Defense (DOD), 12.002 through 12.910
DEPARTMENT OF DEFENSE APPROPRIATION ACT OF 2003, 12.116
Department of Education (DOED), 84.002 through 84.370
Department of Energy (DOE), 81.003 through 81.123
Department of Energy Organization Act of 1977 (DOEOA), *see* Energy
Department of Health and Human Services (HHS), 93.001 through 93.996
Department of Homeland Security (DHS), 97.001 through 97.089
Department of Housing and Urban Development (HUD), 14.103 through 14.906
Department of Justice (DOJ), 16.001 through 16.743
Department of Labor (DOL), 17.002 through 17.807
Department of State, 19.204 through 19.510
Department of the Air Force, Material Command, DOD, *see* Agency Index
Department of the Army, National Guard Bureau, DOD, *see* Agency Index
Department of the Army, Office of the Chief of Engineers, DOD, *see* Agency Index
Department of the Army, U.S. Army Medical Command, DOD, *see* Agency Index
Department of the Interior (DOI), 15.020 through 15.978
Department of the Navy, Naval Surface Warfare Center, DOD, *see* Agency Index
Department of the Navy, Office of Naval Research, DOD, *see* Agency Index
Department of the Treasury, 21.003 through 21.021
Department of Transportation (DOT), 20.100 through 20.930
Department of Veterans Affairs (DVA), 64.005 through 64.203
Dependency and Indemnity Compensation (DIC), veterans, 64.110
DEPOSITORY LIBRARIES FOR GOVERNMENT PUBLICATIONS, 40.001
Depressed areas
Alaska, Denali Commission Program, 90.100
Bank Enterprise Awards Program, 21.021
Delta region, 90.200, 90.201, 90.202
Economic Recovery, forest-dependent communities, 10.670
EDA economic adjustment assistance, 11.307
Empowerment Zones Program, 10.772, 14.244
ETA pilots, demonstrations, research, 17.261
housing mortgage insurance, 14.123
public facilities construction, EDA projects, 11.300
Rural Business Opportunity Grants, 10.773
small business training, technical assistance, 59.007
technical assistance, 11.303
VISTA program, 94.013
see also Appalachian region; Business development; Community development; Economic development; Rural areas; Rural poor; Unemployment; Urban planning; Urban renewal; Volunteers

Desal R&D Program (Desalination Research & Development), DOI, 15.506
Desegregation, *see* Civil rights; Schools
DESEGREGATION OF PUBLIC EDUCATION, 16.100
Desert Terminal Lakes, DOI, 15.508
DEVELOPING, TESTING AND DEMONSTRATING PROMISING PROGRAMS [DOJ], 16.541
DEVELOPMENT AND COORDINATION OF RURAL HEALTH SERVICES, 93.223
DEVELOPMENT AND PROMOTION OF PORTS AND INTERMODAL TRANSPORTATION, 20.801
Development Assistance Program (DAP), USAID, 98.007
DEVELOPMENTAL DISABILITIES BASIC SUPPORT AND ADVOCACY GRANTS, 93.630
DEVELOPMENTAL DISABILITIES PROJECTS OF NATIONAL SIGNIFICANCE, 93.631
DHS (Department of Homeland Security), 97.001 through 97.089
DHS Earmarked Research Projects, 97.002
DHS Scholars and Fellows, 97.062
DIABETES, ENDOCRINOLOGY AND METABOLISM RESEARCH, 93.847
Diabetes programs, 93.237, 93.442, 93.847, 93.867, 93.988
DIC (Dependency and Indemnity Compensation), veterans, 64.110
Digestive disease research, *see* Health, medical research
DIGESTIVE DISEASES AND NUTRITION RESEARCH, 93.848
Dingell-Johnson (D-J) Program, DOI, 15.605
Dining facilities, *see* Education facilities; Food, nutrition; Group homes; Housing, congregate
DIRECT AND COUNTER-CYCLICAL PAYMENTS PROGRAM [USDA], 10.055
DIRECT IMPLEMENTATION TRIBAL COOPERATIVE AGREEMENTS [EPA], 66.473
DIRECT HOUSING—NATURAL DISASTER [USDA], 10.445
DIRECT HOUSING—NATURAL DISASTER LOANS AND GRANTS [USDA], 10.444

DISABILITIES PREVENTION, *93.184*
Disability and Health, CDCP, *93.184*
DISABILITY EMPLOYMENT POLICY
 DEVELOPMENT, *17.720*
Disability Insurance, SSA, *96.001*
Disabled, handicapped
 abuse, sexual assault prevention training, OJP,
  16.528
 ADA client assistance, *84.161*
 ADA employment discrimination, 30.011
 ADA technical assistance, *16.108*
 Americans with Disabilities Act (ADA), 14.404,
  14.414, *16.108*, 17.301, *17.720, 20.106,
  20.507, 30.002*, 30.005, 30.011, 88.001, 93.001
 AmeriCorps members, *94.007*
 Architectural Barriers Act Enforcement, HUD
  programs, 14.407
 architectural, transportation barriers, facilities
  accessibility standards enforcement, design,
  research, training, 88.001
 assault victim protection arrest orders, *16.590*
 assistive technology, *84.224*
 Assistive Technology Act, *84.224, 84.343*
 assistive technology protection, advocacy, *84.343*
 Client Assistance Program, benefits, services
  information, *84.161*
 coal miners, dependents benefits, *17.307*
 developmental disabilities, national projects,
  93.631
 developmental disabilities programs, university
  centers, research, personnel training, *93.632*
 developmentally disabled, advocacy, support,
  93.630
 disabilities prevention, epidemiology, research,
  93.184
 discrimination, housing related, 14.414
 Election Assistance for Individuals with
  Disabilities, ACF, *93.617, 93.618*
 employment promotion, *17.720*
 food, meals assistance, *10.558*
 Food Stamps, *10.551*
 health care systems research, *93.239*
 home health services, Medicaid, *93.778*
 homeless, Shelter Plus Care, *14.238*
 homeless, supportive housing, *14.235*
 housing discrimination, HUD programs, 14.404
 housing, Multifamily Housing Service
  Coordinators, *14.191*
 independent living centers, *84.132, 84.169*
 Indians, vocational rehabilitation, *84.250*
 instructional services, 42.001
 library services, 42.001
 longshore, harbor workers benefits, *17.302*
 maintenance assistance, Guam, Puerto Rico,
  Virgin Islands, *93.560*
 meals, nutrition services, *93.045*
 Medicare, *93.773*
 Medicare Part B supplementary insurance, *93.774*
 mentally retarded, President's Committee, 93.613
 National Limb Loss Information Center, *93.184*
 Protection and Advocacy, *84.240*
 rehabilitation personnel recruitment, training,
  minority students, *84.315*
 rehabilitation personnel training, *84.129, 84.246,
  84.263, 84.264, 84.265, 84.275*
 rehabilitation research, fellowships, *84.133*

 scientists, biomedical research training,
  alcoholism, *93.272*
 scientists, NIH intramural research training,
  93.140
 scientists, NSF research opportunities, *47.049,
  47.050, 47.075, 47.078*
 Senior Companion Program, *94.016*
 Social Security disability insurance, *96.001*
 Social Security, disabled dependents of retirees,
  96.002
 Social Security Survivors Insurance, *96.004*
 Social Services Block Grant, *93.667*
 Supplemental Security Income, *96.006*
 supportive housing, *14.181*
 transportation, over-the-road buses, capital,
  training, *20.518*
 transportation services, specialized vehicle
  purchases, *20.513*
 veterans, adaptive equipment, automobiles,
  64.100
 veterans benefits information, assistance, 64.115
 veterans pension, *64.104*
 vocational rehabilitation services, *84.126, 84.128*
 women, abuse, violence prevention, education,
  training, OJP, *16.529*
 see also Behavioral sciences, education, services;
  Blindness and the blind; Deafness and the deaf;
  Civil rights; Disabled, handicapped *entries*;
  Employee benefits; Mental health; Mental
  retardation; Social services; Veterans, disabled;
  Victim assistance; Vocational rehabilitation;
  Volunteers
Disabled, handicapped children
 Adoption Assistance, *93.659*
 developmental disabilities research, *93.865*
 developmentally disabled, advocacy, support,
  93.630
 early intervention, special education, *84.181,
  84.323, 84.324, 84.325, 84.326, 84.327,
  84.328, 84.329*
 food, meals assistance, *10.558*
 Foster Grandparent Program, *94.011*
 Head Start Program, *93.600*
 milk program, *10.556*
 Parent Information Centers, *84.328*
 preschool special education, *84.173*
 School Breakfast Program, *10.553*
 School Lunch Program, *10.555*
 see also Disabled, handicapped, education;
  Maternal, child health, welfare, Volunteers
Disabled, handicapped, education
 AmeriCorps members, *94.007*
 early intervention, special education, *84.027,
  84.181, 84.323, 84.324, 84.325, 84.326,
  84.327, 84.328, 84.329*
 Head Start Program, *93.600*
 higher education faculty training, *84.333*
 impact assistance, *84.041*
 independent living training, *84.132*
 Indian children, institutionalized handicapped,
  15.045
 Individuals with Disabilities Education Act
  (IDEA), *15.045, 84.027, 84.173, 84.181,
  84.323, 84.324, 84.325, 84.326, 84.327,
  84.328, 84.329*
 library services, 42.001

Disabled, handicapped, education *(continued)*
  NSF international science, engineering opportunities, *47.079*
  Parent Information Centers, *84.328*
  postsecondary counseling, tutoring, *84.042*
  preschool, *84.173*
  teachers, student loan cancellations, *84.037*
  see also Vocational rehabilitation; Volunteers

Disabled, handicapped, employment
  discrimination, ADA investigations, *30.002*, 30.005, 30.011
  DOL, special services, *17.207*
  employment promotion, *17.720*
  federal contract compliance, *17.301*
  federal employment, 27.001, 27.005
  Medicaid Ticket-to-Work Infrastructure Grants, *93.768*
  NSF international science, engineering opportunities, *47.079*
  Projects with Industry, *84.234*
  special vocational rehabilitation services, *84.235*
  SSA beneficiaries outreach, services, *96.008*, *96.009*
  supported employment, severely handicapped, *84.187*
  vocational rehabilitation service projects, *84.128*
  Work Incentives Grants, *17.266*
  see also Veterans, disabled; Vocational rehabilitation

Disabled, handicapped, housing
  cooperative, rental, *14.135*
  discrimination complaints, 14.404, 14.414, 16.103
  homeless, group homes, supportive services, *14.235*
  homeless, Shelter Plus Care, *14.238*
  independent living, *84.132*, *84.169*
  institutional, civil rights, 16.105
  Multifamily Housing Service Coordinators, *14.191*
  rental, *14.138*
  rural rental, *10.415*, *10.427*, *10.438*
  Section 236 Interest Reduction Payments, *14.103*
  supportive housing, *14.181*
  veterans, adapted housing, *64.106*
  veterans, purchase, *64.118*
  weatherization assistance, *81.042*
  see also Group homes; Housing, congregate; Housing, elderly

Disabled veterans, *see* Veterans, disabled
DISABLED VETERANS' OUTREACH PROGRAM (DVOP), *17.801*
Disadvantaged, *see* AmeriCorps; Depressed areas; Disadvantaged *entries*; Homeless persons; Indian *entries*; Minority *entries*; Public assistance; Rural poor; Social services; Volunteers; Women;

Disadvantaged, business development
  DOT contracts, Short Term Lending Program, *20.905*
  EPA studies, special purpose assistance, *66.610*
  equity capital, loans, *59.011*
  farmer outreach, *10.443*
  government contracts, 59.006, *59.049*
  HUD project contracts complaints, 14.412
  management, technical assistance, *59.007*
  microenterprise development training, technical assistance, *59.050*
  Microloan Demonstration Program, *59.046*
  New Markets Venture Capital, *59.051*
  New Assets for Independence Demonstration, *93.602*
  small wood species, USFS Technology Marketing Unit, *10.674*
  transportation, DOT contracts, *20.903*, *20.907*
  see also Business development; Economic development; Government contracts; Indian economic, business development; Minority business enterprise; Small business; Small Business Innovation Research (SBIR); Women

DISADVANTAGED BUSINESS ENTERPRISES— SHORT TERM LENDING PROGRAM [DOT], *20.905*

Disadvantaged, education
  adult education, basic skills, *84.002*
  adults, Educational Opportunity Centers, *84.066*
  advanced placement test fee payment, DOED, *84.330*
  clinical researchers education loan repayment, disadvantaged, *93.308*
  community development work-study, HUD, *14.512*
  Community Learning Centers, *84.287*
  Community Services Block Grant, *93.569*
  compensatory, *84.010*
  Comprehensive School Reform Demonstration, *84.332*
  Dropout Prevention Programs, *84.360*
  early childhood educator professional development, *84.349*
  elementary, secondary, innovative programs, *84.298*
  Even Start, *84.213*
  Extension Service, *10.500*
  foster children, Chafee vouchers, *93.599*
  Foster Grandparent Program, *94.011*
  graduate study, *84.217*
  Head Start, *93.600*
  health, allied health, *93.822*
  health professions faculty loan repayments, *93.923*
  health professions scholarships, *93.925*
  health professions student loans, *93.342*
  institutionalized neglected, delinquent children, *84.013*
  Leveraging Educational Assistance Partnership (LEAP), *84.069*
  Low-Income Taxpayer Clinics, *21.008*
  Magnet Schools Assistance, *84.165*
  New Assets for Independence Demonstration, *93.602*
  NIH Clinical Research Loan Repayment Program, *93.220*
  NIH Undergraduate Scholarship Program, *93.187*
  nursing, *93.178*
  Parental Assistance Centers, *84.310*
  postsecondary academic preparation, *84.042*, *84.047*
  postsecondary academic preparation, TRIO dissemination, *84.344*
  postsecondary low-income student-parents, child care, *84.335*
  postsecondary, staff training, *84.103*
  Reading First State Grants, *84.357*

MASTER INDEX 917

secondary students, supportive services, scholarships, *84.334*
teacher quality enhancement, recruitment, partnership, *84.336*
telecommunications, instructional programming, Star Schools, *84.203*
undergraduate, international, BECA, *19.425*
undergraduate, SEOG, *84.007*
Upward Bound, academic stipends, *84.047*
VISTA volunteers, 94.013
vocational, *84.048*
youth, secondary, postsecondary, dropout prevention, Talent Search, *84.044*
see also Agricultural education; Education counseling; Illiteracy; Indian education, training; Minority education; Student financial aid; Tutoring; Volunteers; Women; Youth *entries*

Disadvantaged, employment and training
community development work-study, HUD, *14.512*
Community Services Block Grant, discretionary, *93.570*
elderly, community services, *17.235*
Empowerment Zones Program, *14.244*
federal employment, 27.001
HUD projects employment complaints, 14.412
HUD Youthbuild Program, *14.243*
Job Access—Reverse Commute, DOT, *20.516*
Job Opportunities for Low-Income Individuals, TANF, *93.593*
Medicaid Ticket-to-Work Demonstrations, *93.769*
U.S. Employment Service, *17.207*
WIA Adult Program, *17.258*
WIA Dislocated Workers, *17.260*
WIA Youth Activities, *17.259*
see also Employment *entries*; Indian employment; Women; Youth employment

DISADVANTAGED HEALTH PROFESSIONS FACULTY LOAN REPAYMENT (FLRP) AND FELLOWSHIP PROGRAM (MFFP), *93.923*

Disaster assistance
atmospheric, climate research, *11.431*
climate monitoring, assessment, *11.428*
Community Disaster Loans, FEMA, *97.030*
Crisis Counseling, FEMA, *97.032*
Crop Disaster Program, *10.073*
Crop Insurance, *10.450*
crops, noninsured, *10.451*
Dairy Market Loss Assistance Program, FSA, *10.084*
Disaster Assistance Projects, specified projects, FEMA, *97.088*
Disaster Mitigation Act of 2000, *97.047*
Disaster Relief Act of 1970, *59.002*, *59.008*, *97.017*
EDA economic adjustment assistance, *11.307*
Emergency Management Performance Grants, *97.042*
EMI training, *97.026*, 97.028
engineering, earthquake hazard mitigation research, *47.041*
farm emergency loans, *10.404*
farmlands, Emergency Conservation Program (ECP), USDA, *10.054*

FEMA Public Assistance Grants, governments, *97.036*
Fisheries Disaster Relief, *11.477*
fisheries restoration, *11.407*
flood fighting, rescue, 12.103
flood, hurricane damage, 12.102
flood insurance, *97.022*
Flood Mitigation Assistance, FEMA, *97.029*
flood threat assistance, 12.111
highway, public works protection, 12.105
highway repairs, *20.205*
housing, remote, insular area residents, FEMA, *97.048*
housing rental assistance, FEMA, *97.049*
housing purchase, reconstruction, *14.119*
Hurricane Katrina Case Management Initiative, *97.084*
Hurricanes Katrina, Rita, Universities Rebuilding America Program, HUD, *14.521*
individuals, households, FEMA, *97.050*
legal services, *97.033*
library, archival humanities collections, planning, *45.149*
Livestock Assistance Program, *10.066*
Livestock Compensation Program, *10.077*
livestock, Disaster Reserve Assistance, *10.452*
Medical Reserve Corps, emergency response, HHS, *93.008*
mental health counseling, training, *93.982*
National Guard operations, maintenance, *12.401*
New York City, Debris Removal Insurance, *97.064*
Pre-Disaster Mitigation, FEMA, *97.017*, *97.047*
property repair, replacement, businesses, homeowners, nonprofits, renters *59.008*
Public Alert Radios for Schools, DHS, *97.079*
public health, social services, *93.003*
rental housing, *14.139*
Robert T. Stafford Disaster Relief and Emergency Assistance Act (Stafford Act), *17.225*, *93.982*, *97.025*,, *97.026*, *97.017*, 97.027, 97.028, *97.030*, *97.031*, *97.032*, *97.033*, *97.034*, *97.036*, *97.039*, *97.042*, *97.046*, *97.047*, *97.048*, *97.049*, *97.050*, *97.053*, *97.084*, *97.088*
rural housing, *10.444*, *10.445*
search, rescue system, *97.025*
small business loans, *59.002*
taxes, special IRS procedures, 21.003
training, EMI home study courses, 97.027
Tree Assistance Program, FSA, *10.082*
unemployment assistance, *97.034*
Unemployment Insurance, *17.225*
Universities Rebuilding America Program, Hurricanes Katrina, Rita, HUD, *14.521*
victim assistance, Cora Brown Fund, *97.031*
victim identification, FBI, 16.303
WIA Dislocated Workers, *17.260*
see also Agricultural commodities, stabilization; Civil defense; Climate; Earthquakes; Emergency assistance; Firefighting, fire prevention, control; Flood prevention, control; Health, medical services; Hurricanes; Missing persons; Rescue services; Small business; Victim assistance

DISASTER ASSISTANCE PROJECTS, *97.088*
DISASTER LEGAL SERVICES, *97.033*

DISASTER RESERVE ASSISTANCE [USDA], *10.452*
DISASTER UNEMPLOYMENT ASSISTANCE, *97.034*
DISCOVERY AND APPLIED RESEARCH FOR TECHNOLOGICAL INNOVATION TO IMPROVE HUMAN HEALTH, *93.286*
Discretionary Drug and Criminal Justice Assistance Program, *16.580*
Discrimination, *see* Civil rights; Complaint investigation
Disease control
　adolescents counseling, *93.995*
　animal disease, pest control, *10.025*
　cancer early detection, breast, cervical screening, training, *93.919*
　CDCP assistance, *93.283*
　chronic, *93.068*, *93.945*
　diabetes, *93.988*
　disease prevention research, *93.135*
　Global AIDS, *93.067*, *93.266*
　Immunization Grants, *93.268*
　immunization research, information, *93.185*
　Indians, epidemiology centers, *93.231*
　Infant Health Initiative, *93.946*
　Lyme Disease, *93.942*
　public education, promotion, *93.990*
　Radiogenetic Exposure Screening and Education Program, *93.257*
　sexually transmitted, *93.283*, *93.977*
　sexually transmitted, research, information, training, *93.978*
　zoonotic diseases, *10.028*
　see also Agricultural research, sciences; AIDS (Acquired Immune Deficiency Syndrome); Animal disease control, health, welfare; Cancer control, prevention, research; Communicable diseases; Epidemiology; Health, medical *entries*; Health planning; Immunization, immunology; Preventive health services; Public health; Respiratory diseases
DISPOSAL OF FEDERAL SURPLUS REAL PROPERTY, 39.002
DISPOSAL OF FEDERAL SURPLUS REAL PROPERTY FOR PARKS, RECREATION, AND HISTORIC MONUMENTS, 15.918
DISTANCE LEARNING AND TELEMEDICINE LOANS AND GRANTS, *10.855*
Distressed areas, *see* Depressed areas
DISTRIBUTION OF RECEIPTS TO STATE AND LOCAL GOVERNMENTS [DOI], *15.227*
District heating/cooling, *see* Energy *entries*
District of Columbia School Choice Incentive Program, *84.370*
DITCA (Direct Implementation Tribal Cooperative Agreements [EPA], *66.473*
Diversion payments, *see* Agricultural commodities, stabilization
Diving, *see* Recreation, water
D-J Program (Dingell-Johnson Program), DOI, *15.605*
DL (Disaster Loans), *59.008*
DMLA III (Dairy Market Loss Assistance), FSA, *10.084*
DNA Identification Act, *16.307*, *16.564*
Doctoral Dissertation Research Abroad, *84.022*

DOCTORAL DISSERTATION RESEARCH GRANTS [HUD], *14.516*
DOD (Department of Defense), 12.002 through 12.910
DOD Environmental Restoration Program, *12.113*
DOE (Department of Energy), 81.003 through 81.123
DOE Patents Available for Licensing, 81.003
DOED (Department of Education), 84.002 through 84.370
DOEOA (Department of Energy Organization Act of 1977), *see* Energy
DOI (Department of the Interior), 15.020 through 15.978
DOJ (Department of Justice), 16.001 through 16.743
DOL (Department of Labor), 17.002 through 17.807
DOLLAR HOME SALES, 14.313
Domestic terrorism preparedness, *see* Civil defense
Domestic Volunteer Service Act of 1973, *see* Volunteers
Domiciliary care, *see* Community health services; Health facilities *entries*; Health, medical services; Nursing homes; Veterans health, medical services
DONATION OF FEDERAL SURPLUS PERSONAL PROPERTY, 39.003
DONATIONS/LOANS OF OBSOLETE DOD PROPERTY, 12.700
DOPP (Dairy Options Pilot Program), *10.454*
DOT (Department of Transportation), 20.100 through 20.930
DRAP (Disaster Reserve Assistance Program), FSA, *10.452*
Drinking water, *see* Water *entries*
Drinking Water State Revolving Fund (DWSRF), *66.468*
DROPOUT PREVENTION PROGRAMS, *84.360*
Drought assistance, *see* Agricultural *entries*; Disaster assistance; Emergency assistance; Insurance; Water *entries*
Drug abuse
　abandoned infants care, *93.551*
　Access to Recovery, SAMSHA, *93.275*
　AIDS-afflicted persons, housing, services, *14.241*
　AIDS/HIV epidemiologic studies, *93.943*
　Anti-Drug Abuse Act of 1988 (ADAA), *16.560*, *16.561*, *16.562*, *16.564*, *16.565*, *16.566*, *16.575*, *16.576*, *16.582*, *16.583*
　biomedical, behavioral research, *93.279*
　community prevention coalitions, 16.005
　Comprehensive Drug Abuse Prevention and Control Act of 1970 (CDAPCA), 16.001, 16.003, 16.004, 16.005
　control, law enforcement demonstrations, *16.580*
　corrections facilities, Residential Substance Abuse Treatment, DOJ, *16.593*
　crime research, *16.560*
　DEA training, law enforcement, professional personnel, 16.004
　drug courts, *16.523*, *16.585*, *16.592*
　Drug-Free Communities Act of 1997, *93.276*
　Drug-Free Community Grants, *93.276*
　Drug-Free Schools and Communities, national programs, *84.184*
　Drug-Free Schools and Communities, states, *84.186*

Drug Prevention Program, *16.728*
Food Stamps, *10.551*
health, mental health care services information, *93.230*
highway safety programs, *20.600, 20.601*
HIV care, *93.917*
HIV emergency relief projects, *93.914*
HIV prevention, *93.939, 93.940*
homeless, mental health, social services, *93.150*
homeless, Shelter Plus Care, *14.238*
Indian Country Alcohol and Drug Prevention, DOJ, *16.616*
Indians, Social Services, *15.025*
justice personnel, equipment, training, planning grants, *16.738*
juvenile gangs program, *16.544*
juvenile justice system improvement, *16.523*
juveniles, prevention, *16.542*
mental health services, PRNS, *93.243*
minority community health coalitions, *93.137*
Offender Reentry Program, *16.202*
offenders, justice, health, social services networks, *93.229*
offenders, testing, *16.585, 16.586*
Operation Weed and Seed, *16.595*
prevention, information, publications, DEA, 16.005
Social Services Block Grant, *93.667*
Substance Abuse Pilot Treatment Block Grant monitoring, evaluation, *93.238*
Substance Abuse Prevention and Treatment Block Grant, *93.959*
Tribal Youth Program, OJJDP, *16.731*
uninsured patients, Healthy Community Access Program, *93.252*
urban Indian program, *93.193*
veterans treatment, rehabilitation, prevention, 64.019
Voucher Program, SAMSHA, *93.275*
see also Alcohol abuse, alcoholism; Behavioral sciences, education, services; Community health services; Drugs, drug research; Family therapy; Juvenile delinquency; Mental health; Social sciences; Social services; Volunteers
DRUG ABUSE AND ADDICTION RESEARCH PROGRAMS, *93.279*
DRUG COURT DISCRETIONARY GRANT PROGRAM, *16.585*
Drug Enforcement Administration (DEA), DOJ, *see* Agency Index
DRUG-FREE COMMUNITIES SUPPORT PROGRAM GRANTS, *93.276*
DRUG PREVENTION PROGRAM, *16.728*
Drugs, drug research
abuse, narcotics addiction research, *93.279*
alternative, complementary medicine research, *93.213*
control assistance, *16.579, 16.580*
DEA Microgram, 16.003
distribution, security personnel training, DEA, 16.004
FDA research, *93.103*
forensic sciences, DEA laboratory analysis, 16.001
interdiction, motor carriers, *20.218*
marine resources, *11.417*
Medicare Prescription Drug, Improvements and Modernization Act 2003 (MMA), *93.773*

neurological disorders, *93.853*
pharmacology, biorelated chemistry research, training, *93.859*
see also Biological sciences; Chemicals, chemistry; Crime; Drug abuse; Food, nutrition research, sciences; Forensic sciences; Health insurance; Health, medical research; Pharmacology, pharmacy; Scientific research; Veterinary medicine
DSMOA (DOD/State Memorandum of Agreement), CERCLA, *12.113*
DUA (Disaster Unemployment Assistance), FEMA, *97.034*
Dubois fellowships, DOJ, *16.566*
DVA (Department of Veterans Affairs), 64.005 through 64.203
DVOP (Disabled Veterans' Outreach Program), *17.801*
DWSRF (Drinking Water State Revolving Fund), *66.468*

EAID (Election Assistance for Individuals with Disabilities), ACF, *93.617, 93.618*
Earmarked Projects, DHS, *97.001*
Earmarked Research Projects, DHS, *97.002*
Early childhood education
Community Services Block Grant, *93.569*
Early Learning Fund, ACF, *93.577*
Early Learning Opportunities Act of 2001, *93.577*
Early Reading First, *84.359*
educator professional development, *84.349*
Even Start, *84.213, 84.214, 84.258*
Foster Grandparent Program, *94.011*
handicapped, special education, *84.173, 84.181, 84.323, 84.324, 84.325, 84.326, 84.327, 84.328, 84.329*
Hawaii, family-based centers, *84.362*
Head Start, *93.600*
Indians, *15.043*
low-income working families, CCDF, *93.575*
migrant children, *84.011*
Parental Assistance Centers, *84.310*
Ready-to-Learn TV, *84.295*
violence, children's exposure, prevention initiative, Safe Start, *16.730*
see also Child care services; Disabled, handicapped children; Disabled, handicapped education; Elementary and secondary education; Head Start Program; Maternal, child health, welfare; Parenting; Volunteers
EARLY CHILDHOOD EDUCATOR PROFESSIONAL DEVELOPMENT, *84.349*
EARLY DOCTORAL STUDENT RESEARCH GRANTS [HUD], *14.517*
EARLY LEARNING FUND [HHS], *93.577*
Early Learning Opportunities Act of 2001 (ELOA), ACF, *93.577*
EARLY READING FIRST, *84.359*
Earth sciences
atmospheric, climate research, *11.428, 11.431*
climate, short-term fluctuation studies, *11.443*
earthquake research, *15.807*
energy-related basic research, *81.049*
EPA environmental sustainability design competition, *66.516*
geospatial data clearinghouse, *15.809*

Earth sciences *(continued)*
NIEHS Superfund research, *93.143*
NSF research, *47.041, 47.050*
Polar Programs, *47.078*
research, *15.808*
water resources research, *15.805*
see also Climate; Environmental *entries*;
 Geology; Maps, charts; Marine sciences;
 Physical sciences; Scientific research
EARTHQUAKE CONSORTIUM, *97.082*
EARTHQUAKE HAZARDS REDUCTION
 PROGRAM, *15.807*
Earthquakes
Earthquake Hazards Reduction Act of 1977,
 97.025, 97.026, 97.027, 97.028, *97.082*
Emergency Management Performance Grants,
 97.042
EMI home study training courses, 97.027
engineering research, *47.041*
FEMA Community Disaster Loans, *97.030*
FEMA Earthquake Consortium, *97.082*
Hazard Mitigation Grant, FEMA, *97.039*
hazards mitigation, *15.807*
Pre-disaster Mitigation, FEMA, *97.017, 97.047*
search, rescue system, *97.025*
see also Disaster assistance; Emergency
 assistance; Geology
EBB (Economic Bulletin Board), *see* State of the
 Nation, EBSA (Employee Benefits Security
 Administration), DOL, *see* Agency Index
ECOA (Equal Credit Opportunity Act), 16.103
Ecology, *see* Earth sciences; Environmental *entries*;
 Marine sciences; Pollution abatement; Wildlife,
 waterfowl
ECONOMIC ADJUSTMENT ASSISTANCE,
 11.307
Economic Bulletin Board, *see* State of the Nation,
 ESA, 11.027
Economic development
Alaska, Denali Commission Program, *90.100*
Alaska, Hawaii native IHE community assistance,
 14.515
BIA Loan Guaranty Program, *15.124*
block grants, CDBG program, *14.218, 14.219,
 14.862, 14.225, 14.228*
Business and Industry Data Centers, 11.004
CDBG Economic Development Initiative, Section
 108, *14.246*
Community Development Credit Union (CDCU)
 financial counseling, *44.002*
Community Development Financial Institutions
 Program, *21.020*
community development work-study, *14.512*
Community Economic Development Act of 1981,
 10.767
Community Economic Development, CSBG,
 93.570
defense program changes impact, *11.307, 12.611,
 12.612, 12.613, 12.614*
Delta region, *90.200, 90.201, 90.202*
developing countries, *70.002, 70.003*
Economic Recovery, forest-dependent
 communities, *10.670*
EDA economic adjustment assistance, *11.307*
1890 institutions entrepreneurial outreach, RBCS,
 10.856

evaluation, research, HUD, *14.506*
foreign trade zones (U.S.), 11.111
Fund for Rural America, *10.224*
HBCU Program, HUD, *14.520*
Hispanic serving institutions assistance, HUD,
 14.514
IHE outreach, HUD, *14.511*
Indians, Alaska natives, *14.862*
insular areas, *14.225*
military base impact, 12.600, *12.607*
Native American Programs, *93.612*
Native American Economic Development
 Assistance, SBA, *59.052*
New Markets Venture Capital, *59.051*
planning assistance, *11.302*
public facilities construction, EDA projects, *11.300*
public housing residents opportunities, *14.870*
Public Works and Economic Development Act of
 1965 (PWEDA), *11.300* through *11.313*
revolving loan funds, *11.307*
revolving loan funds, credit unions, *44.002*
Rural Business Enterprise Grants, *10.769*
rural business, industry financing, *10.768*
Rural Business Investment Program, RBCS,
 10.860
Rural Business Opportunity Grants, *10.773*
Rural Community Development Initiative, RHS,
 10.446
Rural Housing and Economic Development,
 HUD, *14.250*
rural, Intermediary Relending Program, *10.767*
rural loans, grants, RBCS, *10.854*
rural public facilities, *10.766*
rural resource development, *10.901*
Section 108 Loan Guarantees, *14.248*
Small Business Investment Companies, *59.011*
Small Community Air Service Development,
 20.930
Southeast Alaska Economic Disaster Fund, USFS,
 10.671
technical assistance, *11.303, 14.227*
Trade Adjustment Assistance, *11.313*
U.S. insular areas, *15.875*
see also Appalachian region; Business
 development; Community development;
 Depressed areas; Economics, research,
 statistics; Employment *entries*; Indian
 economic, business development; Job creation;
 Private sector; Rural areas; Small business;
 Trade adjustment assistance; Urban planning
Economic Development Administration (EDA),
 USDC, *see* Agency Index
Economic Development Initiative (EDI), HUD,
 14.246
ECONOMIC DEVELOPMENT—SUPPORT FOR
 PLANNING ORGANIZATIONS, *11.302*
ECONOMIC DEVELOPMENT—TECHNICAL
 ASSISTANCE, *11.303*
Economic injury, *see* Community development;
 Complaint investigation; Consumers, consumer
 services; Disaster assistance; Fisheries
 industry; Insurance; Legal services; Small
 business; Trade adjustment assistance
ECONOMIC INJURY DISASTER LOANS,
 59.002
Economic Recovery, USFS, *10.670*

Economic Research Service, USDA, *see* Agency Index
ECONOMIC, SOCIAL, AND POLITICAL DEVELOPMENT OF THE TERRITORIES, *15.875*
Economics and Statistics Administration, USDC, *see* Agency Index
Economics, research, statistics
  Agricultural Estimates, 10.950
  agricultural, rural, 10.250
  biomedical, traineeships, international, *93.989*
  Census Bureau data, 11.001
  community economic depression research, training, *11.312*
  Consumer Price Index, 17.003
  economic data, analysis, national, 11.025
  environmental policy, programs innovation, stewardship, studies, analyses, 66.611
  EPA studies, special purpose assistance, *66.610*
  export, import price index, 17.003
  foreign trade, industry studies, 11.110
  forestry production, *10.652*
  health care financing research, CMS, *93.779*
  international, education exchange, *84.304*
  labor force, *17.002*
  National Trade Data Bank, 11.026
  NOAA unallied projects, *11.452*, *11.454*
  NSF research, *47.075*
  Producer Price Index, 17.003
  productivity studies, 17.004
  Social Security program research, demonstrations, *96.007*
  STAR (Science to Achieve Results) Research Program, EPA, *66.509*
  State of the Nation, ESA, 11.027
  Welfare Reform Research, *93.595*
  Woodrow Wilson Center fellowships, *85.300*
  see also Agricultural statistics; Census services; Economic development; Housing research; Information *entries*; Social sciences; Statistics
Economy Act of 1930, *97.009*
ECP (Emergency Conservation Program), USDA, *10.054*
EDA (Economic Development Administration), USDC, *see* Agency Index
EDMAP, USGS, *15.810*
Education
  AIDS prevention, school-age populations, *93.938*
  Charter Schools, *84.282*
  desegregation, legal services, 16.100
  elementary, secondary, innovative programs, *84.298*
  environmental education professionals training, *66.950*
  environmental education projects, *66.951*
  Gifted and Talented, *84.206*
  Global Development Alliance, USAID, *98.011*
  highway transportation, *20.215*
  international exchange, *84.304*
  library-museum partnerships, *45.312*
  Magnet Schools Assistance, *84.165*
  Mathematics and Science Partnerships, OESE, *84.366*
  model projects, *84.215*
  National Health Promotion, *93.990*
  native American language preservation, *93.587*
  NSF engineering, mathematics, science improvement, *47.076*
  pollution source reduction information dissemination, outreach, EPA, *66.717*
  postsecondary program improvement, access, FIPSE, *84.116*
  project technical assistance, training, *84.283*
  rural, Television Demonstration Grants, *10.769*
  teacher quality enhancement, recruitment, partnership, *84.336*
  telecommunications, instructional programming, Star Schools, *84.203*
  see also Adult education; Agricultural education; Aliens, immigrants, refugees; Arts, arts education; Behavioral sciences, education, services; Bilingual education, services; Civil rights; Dental education, training; Disabled, handicapped, education; Disadvantaged, education; Early childhood education; Education *entries*; Elementary and secondary education; English as a second language; Environmental education; Fellowships, scholarships, traineeships; Foreign languages; Health, medical education, training; Higher education; Humanities education, research; Illiteracy; Indian education, training; International programs, studies; Land-grant colleges, universities; Law enforcement education, training; Mathematics; Minority education; School, Schools *entries*; Science education; Teacher education, training; Technical training; Tutoring; Veterans education, training; Vocational *entries*
EDUCATION AND ENFORCEMENT OF THE ANTIDISCRIMINATION PROVISION OF THE IMMIGRATION AND NATIONALITY ACT, *16.110*
EDUCATION AND HUMAN RESOURCES [NSF], *47.076*
EDUCATION AND PREVENTION TO REDUCE SEXUAL ABUSE OF RUNAWAY, HOMELESS AND STREET YOUTH, *93.557*
EDUCATION AND TRAINING TO END VIOLENCE AGAINST AND ABUSE OF WOMEN WITH DISABILITIES, *16.529*
Education and Training Vouchers, ACF, *93.599*
Education counseling
  advanced placement test fee payment, DOED, *84.330*
  disabled, higher education assistance, *84.333*
  disadvantaged, graduate opportunities, *84.217*
  disadvantaged, postsecondary academic preparation, TRIO dissemination, *84.344*
  disadvantaged, postsecondary, personal, academic, career guidance, *84.042*
  disadvantaged, postsecondary, staff training, *84.103*
  disadvantaged youth, higher education preparation, Upward Bound, *84.047*
  disadvantaged youth, secondary, postsecondary, Talent Search, *84.044*
  Dropout Prevention Programs, *84.360*
  Educational Opportunity Centers, adults, *84.066*
  Extension Service, *10.500*
  Gifted and Talented, *84.206*
  health careers programs, *93.107*

Education counseling *(continued)*
  HUD Youthbuild Program, *14.243*
  Indians, *84.060*
  institutionalized neglected, delinquent children, *84.013*
  Juvenile Mentoring Program, *16.726*
  Learn and Serve America programs, *94.004, 94.005*
  low-income secondary students, TRIO supportive services, scholarships, *84.334*
  Mentoring Children of Prisoners, ACF, *93.616*
  migrant children, *84.011*
  migrants, college program, *84.149*
  migrants, guidance, *84.141*
  Occupational and Employment Information, DOED, *84.346*
  Services for Trafficking Victims, *16.320*
  veterans, service personnel, 64.125
  violence prevention, *93.910*
  Voluntary Public School Choice, *84.361*
  WIA Youth Activities, *17.259*
  see also Aliens, immigrants, refugees; Bilingual education, services; Corrections; Disadvantaged, education; Drug abuse; Illiteracy; Juvenile delinquency; Social services; Tutoring; Vocational education; Youth programs
Education, elementary, *see* Elementary and secondary education
Education equipment
  Army Research Office, sciences research, *12.431*
  Assistance to Schools and Hospitals Abroad, USAID, *98.006*
  biological sciences research, *47.074*
  agriculture, challenge grants, *10.217*
  Community Connect Grants, RUS, *10.863*
  DOD engineering, mathematics, sciences research, *12.630*
  DOD science, technology projects, *12.910*
  Education Technology State Grants, *84.318*
  1890 institutions, *10.216*
  elementary, secondary, innovative programs, *84.298*
  energy-related, used equipment, 81.022
  engineering science, higher education, *47.041*
  federal surplus personal property donations, 39.003
  geosciences research, *47.050*
  health research, research infrastructure resources, NIH, impact assistance, DOED-owned schools, *84.040*
  library information services, *45.310*
  mathematics, science research, NSF program, *47.049*
  minority higher education strengthening, *84.031*
  minority institutions, engineering, science programs, *84.120*
  Native American Library Services, *45.311*
  Navy research, *12.300*
  NSF engineering, mathematics, science improvement, *47.076*
  public radio, television, *11.550, 93.389*
  rural computer networks, RUS, *10.855*
  telecommunications infrastructure, *11.552*
  telecommunications, instructional programming, Star Schools, *84.203*
  undersea research, *11.430*

  vessels, State Marine Schools, *20.806*
  see also Agricultural education; Audiovisual aids, film, video; Computer products, sciences, services; Education resources; Technology transfer, utilization
Education exchange programs, *see* International programs, studies
Education facilities
  Assistance to Schools and Hospitals Abroad, USAID, *98.006*
  atmospheric, marine sciences research, NOAA, *11.469*
  campus crime grants, *16.525*
  charter schools, financing, *84.354*
  1890 institutions, *10.500*
  federal surplus real property, 39.002, 84.145
  Impact Aid, federally affected areas, *84.040, 84.041*
  Indian schools repair, replacement, *15.062*
  minority higher education strengthening, *84.031*
  physical disaster loans, *59.008*
  rural schools, *10.766*
  telecommunications, instructional programming, Star Schools, *84.203*
  tribal IHEs, HUD, *14.519*
  tribally-controlled IHEs, *15.027*
  vocational school construction, EDA projects, *11.300*
  see also Agricultural education; Health facilities *entries*; Higher education institutions; Schools *entries*
EDUCATION FOR HOMELESS CHILDREN AND YOUTH, *84.196*
Education, higher, *see* Higher education
Education personnel development, *see* Education *entries*; Elementary and secondary education; Minority education; Health *entries*; Teacher education, training
Education, postsecondary, *see* Adult education; Agricultural education; Higher education *entries*; Vocational education
Education research
  adult, *84.191*
  Charter Schools, *84.282*
  college faculty research abroad, *84.019*
  curriculum reform, OERI, *84.305*
  foreign language, area studies, *84.017*
  Gifted and Talented, *84.206*
  graduate academic fellowships, *84.200*
  international exchange, *84.304*
  international peace, conflict resolution, *91.001, 91.002*
  model projects, *84.215*
  National Institute for Literacy, fellowships, *84.257*
  overseas research centers, *84.274*
  postsecondary program improvement, access, FIPSE, *84.116*
  special education, *84.324, 84.327, 84.329*
  vocational education, *84.051*
  Women's Educational Equity Act Program, *84.083*
  see also Agricultural education; Higher education; International programs, studies; Libraries
EDUCATION RESEARCH, DEVELOPMENT AND DISSEMINATION, *84.305*

Education resources
 academic assessments, state activities, *84.369*
 aeronautics, aerospace, NASA, 43.001,
 BLM projects, Cultural Resource Management, *15.224*
 civil aviation materials, 20.100
 elementary, secondary innovative programs, *84.298*
 Eisenhower regional mathematics, science education consortia, *84.319*
 foreign language, area studies, *84.017*
 foreign language centers, *84.229*
 foreign language, international studies programs, *84.015, 84.016*
 international peace, conflict resolution, *91.001, 91.002*
 IRS materials, state, federal taxes, 21.003
 library information services, *45.310*
 model projects, *84.215*
 National Gallery exhibits, 68.001
 National Institute for Literacy, *84.257*
 Native American Library Services, *45.311*
 NOAA Educational Partnerships Program, minority, *11.481*
 Parental Assistance Centers, *84.310*
 project technical assistance, training, *84.283*
 Ready to Teach, *84.286*
 special education, media, technology, *84.327*
 special education, technical assistance, *84.326*
 vocational, national center, *84.051*
 see also Arts, arts education; Audiovisual aids, film, video; Computer products, sciences, services; Education equipment; Education facilities; Humanities education, research; Libraries; Science education
Education Sciences Reform Act of 2002, *see* Elementary and Secondary Education acts
Education, secondary, *see* Elementary and secondary education; Vocational education
EDUCATION TECHNOLOGY STATE GRANTS [DOED], *84.318*
Education, tutoring, *see* Tutoring
EDUCATIONAL EXCHANGE—CONGRESS-BUNDESTAG YOUTH EXCHANGE, *19.410*
EDUCATIONAL EXCHANGE—FULBRIGHT AMERICAN STUDIES INSTITUTES, *19.418*
EDUCATIONAL EXCHANGE—GRADUATE STUDENTS, *19.400*
EDUCATIONAL EXCHANGE—SCHOLAR-IN-RESIDENCE (U.S. INSTITUTIONS OF HIGHER EDUCATION HOST LECTURING FACULTY FROM ABROAD), *19.431*
EDUCATIONAL EXCHANGE—TEACHERS FROM SECONDARY AND POSTSECONDARY LEVELS AND SCHOOL ADMINISTRATORS, *19.408*
EDUCATIONAL EXCHANGE—UNIVERSITY LECTURERS (PROFESSORS) AND RESEARCH SCHOLARS, *19.401*
Educational Opportunity Centers, *84.066*
EDUCATIONAL PARTNERSHIP PROGRAM [USDC], *11.481*
Educational Technical Assistance Act of 2002, *see* Elementary and Secondary Education acts
EDWARD BYRNE MEMORIAL JUSTICE ASSISTANCE GRANT PROGRAM, *16.738*

EDWARD BYRNE MEMORIAL STATE AND LOCAL LAW ENFORCEMENT DISCRETIONARY GRANTS PROGRAM, *16.580*
EEG (Environmental Education Grants), EPA, *66.951*
EEOC (Equal Employment Opportunity Commission), 30.001 through 30.011
EETP (Environmental Education and Training Program), EPA, *66.950*
Eggs, *see* Agricultural marketing; Food inspection, grading; Poultry, egg products
EHR (Education and Human Resources), NSF, *47.076*
EHS (Environmental Health Sciences) Centers, *93.894*
EHT (Emerson Humanitarian Trust), FSA, *10.079*
EIA (Energy Information Administration), DOE, *see* Agency Index
EIDL (Economic Injury Disaster Loans), SBA, *59.002*
8A BUSINESS DEVELOPMENT, 59.006
1890 INSTITUTION CAPACITY BUILDING GRANTS [USDA], *10.216*
1890 LAND GRANT INSTITUTIONS RURAL ENTREPRENEURIAL OUTREACH PROGRAM [USDA], *10.856*
1890 Outreach, RBCS, *10.856*
EISENHOWER REGIONAL MATH AND SCIENCE CONSORTIA, *84.319*
Eisenhower Transportation Fellowship Program, *20.215*
EJCPS (Environmental Justice Collaborative Problem-Solving), *66.306*
EJRA (Environmental Justice Research Assistance), EPA, *66.308*
EJSS (Environmental Justice Surveys and Studies), EPA, *66.309*
EJSGP (Environmental Justice Small Grants Program), EPA, *66.604*
EJTF (Environmental Justice Training and Fellowships), EPA, *66.307*
Elder Abuse Prevention, *93.041*
Elderly, *see* Aging and the aged; Housing, elderly
Election Assistance for Individuals with Disabilities (EAID), ACF, *93.617, 93.618*
Elections, *see* Civil rights; Government
Elections Assistance Commission, 90.400
Electric power, *see* Energy; Public utilities; Rural areas
ELECTRICITY DELIVERY AND ENERGY RELIABILITY, RESEARCH, DEVELOPMENT AND ANALYSIS, *81.122*
Electronic data processing, *see* Computer products, sciences, services
Elementary and secondary education
 academic assessments, state activities, *84.369*
 agricultural, food sciences careers, Hispanics, *10.223*
 AIDS prevention, school-age populations, *93.938*
 Alaska natives, *84.356*
 Arts in Education, OESE, *84.351*
 Charter Schools, *84.282*
 charter schools facilities financing, *84.354*
 civil aviation, 20.100
 civil rights compliance assistance, training, *84.004*

Elementary and secondary education *(continued)*
Community Learning Centers, *84.287*
compensatory, *84.010*
Comprehensive School Reform Demonstration, *84.332*
Congress-Bundestag Youth Exchange, BECA, *19.410*
curriculum reform, OERI, *84.305*
DC School Choice Incentive Program, *84.370*
Delinquency Prevention Program, *16.548, 16.549*
DOD science, technology projects, *12.910*
Dropout Prevention Programs, *84.360*
Drug-Free Schools and Communities, national programs, *84.184*
Drug-Free Schools and Communities, states, *84.186*
Education Technology State Grants, *84.318*
English Language Acquisition Grants, *84.365*
environmental health information, careers, *93.113, 93.115*
EPA water quality internships, *66.463*
Even Start, Indians, *84.258*
Even Start, migrants, *84.214*
Even Start, state, *84.213*
federal surplus real property transfer, 84.145
foreign languages model programs, *84.293*
Freely Associated States, *84.256*
Gifted and Talented, *84.206*
handicapped children, youth, *84.027*
Hawaii, community-, family-based education centers, *84.362*
health careers programs, *93.107*
health sciences, minority institutions, *93.389*
homeless children, youth, *84.196*
humanities, NEH curriculum, materials development, *45.162*
impact aid, DOED-owned schools, construction, maintenance, *84.040*
impact aid, federally affected areas, maintenance, operation, *84.041*
Indian, supplementary, *84.060*
innovative programs, *84.298*
institutionalized, neglected, delinquent children, *84.013*
IRS materials, state, federal taxes, 21.003
Junior Duck Stamp Contest, FWS, *15.644*
Learn and Serve America programs, *94.004*
Literacy through School Libraries, *84.364*
low-income secondary students, TRIO supportive services, scholarships, *84.334*
Magnet Schools Assistance, *84.165*   marine environment projects, *11.429*
math telecommunications demonstrations, *84.286*
Mathematics and Science Partnerships, OESE, *84.366*
mathematics, sciences, Army support, *12.431*
mathematics, sciences regional consortia, *84.319*
mathematics, sciences, Navy support, *12.300*
migrant children, *84.011*
migrant education, interstate, intrastate coordination, *84.144*
migrant youth, high school equivalence, *84.141*
model projects, *84.215*
NASA education services, 43.001
NEH We the People program, *45.168*
NIH intramural research training, secondary students, *93.140*
NOAA Colorado areas math, engineering, science, *11.449*
NSF engineering, mathematics, science improvement, *47.076*
Parental Assistance Centers, *84.310*
project technical assistance, training, *84.283*
Reading First State Grants, *84.357*
Rural Education Achievement Program, *84.358*
School Leadership, principals incentive stipends, *84.363*
secondary, postsecondary agriculture education, *10.226*
social studies, secondary teachers, Madison fellowships, *85.500*
Talent Search, potential postsecondary, *84.044*
teacher quality enhancement, recruitment, partnership, *84.336*
teacher quality improvement, *84.367*
teachers, administrators, Fulbright exchange, *19.408*
teachers homeownership opportunities, 14.310
teachers, student loan cancellations, *84.037*
Tech-Prep Demonstration Grants, *84.353*
Tech-Prep Education, *84.243*
telecommunications, instructional programming, Star Schools, *84.203*
Transition to Teaching, *84.350*
Upward Bound, *84.047*
Voluntary Public School Choice, *84.361*
see also Adult education; Arts, arts education; Disabled, handicapped, education; Disadvantaged, education; Early childhood education; Education *entries*; Environmental education; Humanities *entries*; Indian education, training; Minority education; School, Schools *entries*; Teacher education, training; Tutoring; Vocational education; Volunteers; Youth programs
Elementary and Secondary Education acts
DC School Choice Incentive Act of 2003, *84.370*
Education Sciences Reform Act of 2002, *84.283, 84.305, 84.324*
Educational Technical Assistance Act of 2002, *84.318, 84.319*
Title I, Basic, Concentration, and Targeted Grants, *84.010*
Title I, Dropout Prevention Programs, *84.360*
Title I, Early Reading First, *84.359*
Title I, Even Start, *84.213, 84.214, 84.258*
Title I, Freely Associated States, *84.256*
Title I, Literacy through School Libraries, *84.364*
Title I, migrant, *84.011, 84.144*
Title I, neglected, delinquent, *84.013*
Title I, Reading First, *84.357*
Title I, School Reform, *84.332*
Title II, cooperative education exchange, *84.304*
Title II, early childhood educators, *84.349*
Title II, Teacher Quality Improvement State Grants, *84.367*
Title II, Mathematics and Science Partnerships, OESE, *84.366*
Title II, Ready-to-Learn Television, *84.295*
Title II, School Leadership, *84.363*
Title II, Transition to Teaching, *84.350*
Title III, English Language Acquisition Grants, *84.365*

MASTER INDEX 925

Title III, technology, *84.318*
Title IV, Community Learning Centers, *84.287*
Title IV, safe, drug-free schools, *84.184, 84.186*
Title V, Arts in Education, *84.351*
Title V, Charter Schools, *84.282*
Title V, Community Technology Centers, *84.341*
Title V, FIE, *84.215*
Title V, foreign languages, *84.293*
Title V, gifted and talented, *84.206*
Title V, innovative programs, *84.298*
Title V, magnet schools, *84.165*
Title V, Parental Assistance Centers, *84.310*
Title V, Ready to Teach, *84.286*
Title V, Star Schools, *84.203*
Title V, Voluntary Public School Choice, *84.361*
Title V, women's equity, *84.083*
Title VI, Rural Education Achievement Program, *84.358*
Title VI, state academic assessments, activities, *84.369*
Title VII, Alaska natives, *84.356*
Title VII, Hawaii natives, *84.362*
Title VII, Indian education, *84.060*
Title VIII, Impact Aid, *84.040, 84.041*
see also Education research
ELOA (Early Learning Opportunities Act of 2001), ACF, *93.577*
Embryo adoption, *93.007*
EMERGENCY ADVANCE MEASURES FOR FLOOD PREVENTION, 12.111

Emergency assistance
Anti-Terrorism and Emergency Assistance Program, DOJ, *16.321*
CERCLA response planning, training, *66.809*
channel dredging, 12.109
chemical emergency planning, *66.810*
children, medical services, *93.127*
Community Relations Service (CRS), 16.200
Crisis Counseling, FEMA, *97.032*
disaster victims, Cora Brown Fund, *97.031*
disaster victims housing, remote, insular area residents, FEMA, *97.048*
disaster victims housing rental assistance, FEMA, *97.049*
disasters, individuals, households, FEMA, *97.050*
earthquake hazards mitigation, *15.807*
Emerson Humanitarian Trust, FSA, *10.079*
Emergency Food Assistance Act of 1983, *10.568, 10.569*
emergency health services reimbursement, undocumented aliens, *93.784*
Emergency Management Performance Grants, *97.042*
EMI training, *97.026,* 97.028
farm disaster loans, *10.404*
farmland rehabilitation, *10.054*
FEMA chemical emergency planning, DOD stockpiles, *97.040*
FEMA Earthquake Consortium, response planning, *97.082*
FEMA Hazardous Materials Assistance Program, training, *97.021*
FEMA Public Assistance Grants, governments, *97.036*
Fire Management Assistance, FEMA, *97.046*
flood fighting, rescue, 12.103

flood, hurricane damage, 12.102
flood threat assistance, 12.111
food assistance, *10.558*
Food Donation Program, USDA, 10.550
Food Security Wheat Reserve (Emerson Humanitarian Trust), FSA, *10.079*
food, shelter program, FEMA, *97.024*
hazardous materials handling, planning, training, DOT, *20.703*
hazardous substances, state surveillance systems, *93.204*
health services planning, block grant, *93.991*
highway accidents, training, *20.600*
highways, bridge, river bank protection, 12.105
HIV emergency relief projects, *93.914*
home study training courses, 97.027
homeless persons shelter, *14.231*
imminent threat projects, CDBG programs, *14.218, 14.219, 14.225, 14.228*
Indian projects, *15.025*
law enforcement assistance, federal, *16.577*
levee construction, 12.111
livestock, Disaster Reserve Assistance, *10.452*
low-income, Community Services Block Grant, *93.569*
low-income, home energy, *93.568*
marine rescue, 97.011
Medical Reserve Corps, emergency response, HHS, *93.008*
mental health counseling, training, *93.982*
milk contamination, *10.053*
National Guard operations, maintenance, *12.401*
property repair, replacement, *59.008*
Public Alert Radios for Schools, DHS, *97.079*
public health, *93.283*
public health bioterrorism preparedness, *93.003*
public health, social services, *93.003*
public safety officers disability, death benefits, *16.571*
racial conflicts mediation, technical assistance, 16.200
repatriation program, *93.579*
rural, Access to Emergency Devices, training, HRSA, *93.259*
rural health networks, *93.912*
rural hospitals integrated care networks, *93.241*
rural water systems, *10.763*
search, rescue system, *97.025*
seed producers loans, *10.076*
toxic substances, public health response, *93.161*
transit planning, FTA, *20.514*
transuranic waste transport planning, *81.106*
tribal hazardous materials handling, planning, training, FEMA, *97.020*
water terrorism protection coordination, planning, *66.474*
WMD, domestic preparedness, *97.004, 97.005, 97.006, 97.007*
see also Civil defense; Climate; Disaster assistance; Earthquakes; Firefighting, fire prevention, control; Flood prevention, control; Hazardous materials, waste; Health, medical services; Homeless persons; Hotlines; Hurricanes; Police; Public safety; Rescue services; Victim assistance
Emergency Bank Protection, flood control, 12.105

Emergency broadcasting, *see* Civil defense; Radio, television
EMERGENCY COMMUNITY WATER ASSISTANCE GRANTS, *10.763*
EMERGENCY CONSERVATION PROGRAM, *10.054*
Emergency Dredging Projects, 12.109
EMERGENCY FEDERAL LAW ENFORCEMENT ASSISTANCE, *16.577*
EMERGENCY FOOD AND SHELTER NATIONAL BOARD PROGRAM, *97.024*
EMERGENCY FOOD ASSISTANCE PROGRAM (ADMINISTRATIVE COSTS), *10.568*
EMERGENCY FOOD ASSISTANCE PROGRAM (FOOD COMMODITIES), *10.569*
EMERGENCY LOAN FOR SEED PRODUCERS, *10.076*
EMERGENCY LOANS [USDA], *10.404*
EMERGENCY MANAGEMENT INSTITUTE (EMI) —INDEPENDENT STUDY PROGRAM, 97.027
EMERGENCY MANAGEMENT INSTITUTE (EMI) —RESIDENT EDUCATIONAL PROGRAM, 97.028
EMERGENCY MANAGEMENT INSTITUTE— TRAINING ASSISTANCE, *97.026*
EMERGENCY MANAGEMENT PERFORMANCE GRANTS, *97.042*
Emergency medical services, *see* Emergency assistance; Health, medical services; Rescue services
EMERGENCY MEDICAL SERVICES FOR CHILDREN, *93.127*
Emergency Medical Treatment and Active Labor Act (EMTALA), *93.784*
EMERGENCY OPERATIONS FLOOD RESPONSE AND POST FLOOD RESPONSE, 12.103
Emergency Planning and Community Right-to-Know Act (EPCRA), *20.703*
Emergency preparedness, *see* Civil defense; Disaster assistance; Emergency assistance
EMERGENCY REHABILITATION OF FLOOD CONTROL WORKS OR FEDERALLY AUTHORIZED COASTAL PROTECTION WORKS, 12.102
EMERGENCY SHELTER GRANTS PROGRAM, *14.231*
EMERGING MARKETS PROGRAM [USDA], *10.603*
Emerson Humanitarian Trust, FSA, *10.079*
EMP (Emerging Markets Program), USDA, *10.603*
EMPG (Emergency Management Performance Grants), FEMA, *97.042*

Employee benefits
coal miners, dependents, disability, death compensation, *17.307*
credit unions, *44.001*
data, compensation, working conditions, *17.005*
domestic violence, stalking victims, *16.736*
Employee Retirement Protection Act, *86.001*
Equal Pay Act, 30.005, 30.010
Family and Medical Leave Act of 1993, 17.303
farm employment, 10.950
Federal Wage Hour Laws, 17.303
longshore, harbor workers, *17.302*
merchant marine, information, 64.115
NHSC, NOAA, PHS, information, 64.115
pension, benefit plans information, standards, 17.150
Pension Funding Equity Act of 2004, *86.001*
pension plan insurance, *86.001*
Pension Protection Acts, *86.001*
President's Council on Physical Fitness and Sports, 93.289
public safety officers disability, death benefits, *16.571*
railroad workers, *57.001*
retirees, unearned Social Security benefits, *96.003*
Social Security program research, demonstrations, *96.007*
see also Health insurance; Insurance; Labor *entries*; Occupational health, safety; Social Security Act; Statistics; Unemployment; Veterans *entries*
EMPLOYEE BENEFITS SECURITY ADMINISTRATION, 17.150
Employee Benefits Security Administration (EBSA), DOL, *see* Agency Index
Employee-management relations, *see* Labor-management relations
Employee Retirement Income Security Act (ERISA), 17.150, *86.001*

Employment
aliens, specialty occupations, employer attestations, 17.252
college work-study program, *84.033*
disabled, ADA technical assistance, *16.108*
discrimination, legal services, 16.101
ETA pilots, demonstrations, research, *17.261*
farm statistics, 10.950
federal employment, 27.001
HUD projects, employment opportunities, 14.412
Job Opportunities for Low-Income Individuals, TANF, *93.593*
long-term care employee background checks, *93.785*
minimum wage-hour standards, 17.303
Occupational and Employment Information, DOED, *84.346*
pension, benefit plans information, standards, 17.150
productivity data, 17.004
Senior Community Service Employment Program (SCSEP), *17.235*
senior environmental employment programs, *66.508, 66.518*
statistics, *17.002*
Welfare Reform Research, *93.595*
WIA Incentive Grants, *17.267*
youth, temporary federal employment, 27.003
see also Aging and the aged; Apprenticeship training; Civil rights; Complaint investigation; Disabled, handicapped, employment; Disadvantaged, employment and training; Economic development; Employee benefits; Employment *entries*; Farm workers; Federal employment; Indian education, training; Indian employment; Job creation; Labor *entries*; Statistics; Technical training; Unemployment; Veterans employment; Vocational education; Women; Youth employment

MASTER INDEX 927

Employment and Training Administration, DOL, see Agency Index
EMPLOYMENT AND TRAINING ADMINISTRATION EVALUATIONS, *17.262*
EMPLOYMENT AND TRAINING ADMINISTRATION PILOTS, DEMONSTRATIONS, AND RESEARCH PROJECTS, *17.261*

Employment development, training
disabled, Job Accommodations Network (JAN), *17.720*
Delta region, *90.200, 90.201, 90.202*
Education Amendments Act of 1972, HUD programs discrimination, 14.415
ETA pilots, demonstrations, research, *17.261*
facilities, HUD Dollar Home Sales, 14.313
food stamp program-related, *10.561*
HUD Youthbuild Program, *14.243*
import-caused unemployment, *17.245*
Job Access—Reverse Commute, DOT, *20.516*
Job Opportunities for Low-Income Individuals, TANF, *93.593*
Job Training Partnership Act (JTPA), *14.243*
Jobs Training Bill, *93.667*
low-income elderly, *17.235*
National Guard Challenge Program, youth, *12.404*
Native American Employment and Training, *17.265*
Operation Weed and Seed, *16.595*
Presidential management interns, 27.013
Public Housing Neighborhood Network Grants, *14.875*
refugee training programs, *93.567, 93.584*
research and development, *11.312*
Services for Trafficking Victims, *16.320*
Tribal Work Grants, *93.594*
veterans, DOL projects, *17.802*
WIA Adult Program, *17.258*
WIA Dislocated Workers, *17.260*
WIA Incentive Grants, *17.267*
WIA program evaluations, *17.262*
WIA Youth Activities, *17.259*
Workforce Investment Act of 1998 (WIA), *17.207, 17.258, 17.259, 17.260, 17.261, 17.262, 17.263, 17.264, 17.265, 17.266, 17.267, 17.720, 17.802, 84.002, 96.008, 96.009*
Youth Opportunity Grants, DOL, *17.263*
see also Apprenticeship training; Disabled, handicapped, employment; Disadvantaged, employment and training; Economic development; Employment *entries*; Federal employment; Indian education, training; Indian employment; Job creation; Public assistance; Technical training; Unemployment; Veterans education, training; Veterans employment; Vocational *entries*
Employment, disadvantaged, *see* Disadvantaged, employment and training
Employment discrimination, *see* Civil rights
EMPLOYMENT DISCRIMINATION—AGE DISCRIMINATION IN EMPLOYMENT, 30.008
EMPLOYMENT DISCRIMINATION EQUAL PAY ACT, 30.010
EMPLOYMENT DISCRIMINATION—PRIVATE BAR PROGRAM, 30.005

EMPLOYMENT DISCRIMINATION PROJECT CONTRACTS—INDIAN TRIBES, *30.009*
EMPLOYMENT DISCRIMINATION—STATE AND LOCAL FAIR EMPLOYMENT PRACTICES AGENCY CONTRACTS, *30.002*
EMPLOYMENT DISCRIMINATION—TITLE I OF THE AMERICANS WITH DISABILITIES ACT, 30.011
EMPLOYMENT DISCRIMINATION—TITLE VII OF THE CIVIL RIGHTS ACT OF 1964, 30.001
Employment, elderly, *see* Aging and the aged
Employment, governmental, *see* Federal employment
Employment, handicapped, *see* Disabled, handicapped, employment
Employment, Indians, *see* Indian employment
EMPLOYMENT OPPORTUNITIES FOR LOWER INCOME PERSONS AND BUSINESSES, 14.412
EMPLOYMENT SERVICE, *17.207*

Employment services
age discrimination, 30.008
aliens, discrimination, *16.110*
aliens, specialty occupations, employer attestations, 17.252
apprenticeship registration, 17.201
Child Care and Development Fund, *93.596*
child care, low-income working families, CCDF, *93.575*
child care/social services, TANF, *93.558*
Community Services Block Grant, *93.569*
computerized job listings, *17.207*
counseling, testing, *17.207*
Cuban, Haitian entrants, *93.566, 97.009*
disabled, handicapped, *17.266, 17.720*
disabled, handicapped, mentally retarded, restored, federal, 27.005
disabled, Medicaid Ticket-to-Work Infrastructure Grants, *93.768*
disabled, special vocational rehabilitation services, *84.235*
discrimination, CDBG program, 14.406
discrimination, legal services, 16.101
employment discrimination, 30.001
employment discrimination, state, local enforcement assistance, *30.002*
Empowerment Zones Program, *10.772, 14.244*
ETA pilots, demonstrations, research, *17.261*
farm workers, ETA, *17.264*
foreign workers certification, 17.202, 17.203
homeless, mentally ill persons, *93.150*
homeless veterans, *17.805*
import-affected workers, *17.245*
incarcerated youth, *84.331*
Indians, *15.108*
Job Access—Reverse Commute, DOT, *20.516*
long-term care employee background checks, *93.785*
Medicaid Ticket-to-Work Demonstrations, *93.769*
military, Transition Assistance Program, DOL, *17.807*
Native American Employment and Training, *17.265*
Occupational and Employment Information, DOED, *84.346*

Employment services *(continued)*
Offender Reentry Program, DOJ, *16.202*
offenders, justice, health, social services networks, *93.229*
One-Stop job services, *17.207*
Personal Census Search, age, citizenship, 11.006
refugees, *93.566, 93.567, 93.576, 93.583, 93.584*
SSA beneficiaries outreach, services, *96.008*
SSA disabled beneficiaries outreach, services, *96.009*
students, summer federal employment, 27.006
supported employment, severely handicapped, *84.187*
Trade Adjustment Assistance, *11.313*
trafficking victims, *16.320*
Transition to Teaching, *84.350*
U.S. Employment Service, *17.207*
U.S. Refugee Admissions Program, *19.510*
veterans employment, reemployment rights, 17.803
veterans employment representative program, *17.804*
veterans, service personnel, 64.125
veterans, veterans dependents, federal jobs, 27.002
wage garnishment protection, 17.306
Wagner-Peyser Act, *17.207, 17.265*
WIA Adult Program, *17.258*
WIA Dislocated Workers, *17.260*
WIA Incentive Grants, *17.267*
WIA Youth Activities, *17.259*
women, 17.700
see also Adult education; Apprenticeship training; Census services; Child care services; Civil rights; Disabled, handicapped, employment; Disadvantaged, employment and training; Employment *entries*; Farm workers; Federal employment; Indian employment; Job creation; Trade adjustment assistance; Unemployment; Veterans employment; Vocational *entries*; Youth employment
Employment standards, *see* Labor standards
Employment Standards Administration, DOL, *see* Agency Index
Employment, veterans, *see* Veterans employment
Employment, women, *see* Women
Employment, youth, *see* Youth employment
Empowerment zones, *see* Community development
Empowerment Zones and Enterprise Communities, *14.244*
EMPOWERMENT ZONES PROGRAM [HUD], *14.244*
EMPOWERMENT ZONES PROGRAM [USDA], *10.772*
EMS (Emergency Medical Services) for Children, *93.127*
EMS/TRAUMA CARE SYSTEMS PLANNING AND DEVELOPMENT, *93.952*
EMTALA (Emergency Medical Treatment and Active Labor Act), *93.784*
Endangered species, *see* Animal disease control, health, welfare; Environmental management; Fish; Plants; Wildlife, waterfowl
Endangered Species Act of 1973, *see* Environmental management
ENDANGERED SPECIES ON INDIAN LANDS, *15.051*

Endocrinology research, *93.847*
Energy
biodiesel fuel use, CSREES, *10.306*
Bioenergy Program, FSA, *10.078*
biomass, small wood species, USFS Technology Marketing Unit, *10.674*
biomass technology, research, *81.079*
business internships, Eurasian executives, scientists, *11.114*
coastal facilities management, *11.419*
community development block grants, *14.218, 14.219, 14.225, 14.228, 14.862*
conservation, renewable, outreach, training, *81.117*
Denali Commission Grants and Loans, Alaska energy facilities, *10.858*
Department of Energy Organization Act of 1977 (DOEOA), 81.003, 81.022, *81.036*, 81.039, *81.041, 81.042, 81.049, 81.079, 81.086, 81.087, 81.089, 81.104, 81.105, 81.112, 81.113, 81.114, 81.117, 81.119, 81.121, 81.122, 81.123*
district heating/cooling, CDBG, *14.218, 14.219, 14.228*
DOE environmental cleanup, technology development, *81.104*
DOE patent licensing, 81.003
DOE workers, epidemiology, health studies, *81.108*
electricity delivery, energy reliability, DOE, *81.122*
Energy Policy Act of 1992, *10.910, 81.105, 81.117, 81.122*
Energy Reorganization Act of 1974, *81.049, 81.057, 81.089, 81.108, 81.112, 81.113, 81.114, 81.117, 81.121, 81.123*
Energy Security Act of 1980, *81.042, 81.122*
Energy Tax Act of 1978, *81.122*
EPA environmental sustainability design competition, *66.516*
exploration, OPIC, *70.003*
Federal Energy Administration Act, 81.039
Federal Oil and Gas Royalty Act of 1982, *15.222*
Federal Power Act, 15.921, 15.927
Fisherman's Contingency Fund, oil, gas activities, *11.408*
gas pipelines safety, states, *20.700*
geological resource appraisal, *15.808*
hydroelectric power projects, payments to states, *12.112*
Indian lands, resources, *15.038, 15.040*
industrial, agricultural waste reduction, DOE, *81.105*
inventions development assistance, *81.036*
low-income home energy assistance, *93.558, 93.568, 93.667*
municipal solid waste conversion technology, *81.079*
National Energy Information Center (NEIC), 81.039
National Gas Pipeline Safety Acts, *20.700*
nuclear waste disposal siting, *81.065*
ocean thermal energy conversion, ships financing, *20.802*
oil, gas lease inspection, federal, Indian lands, *15.222*
OSTI, 81.064

Renewable Energy Systems and Energy
 Efficiency Improvements, RBCS, *10.775*
research, development, renewable resources,
 81.087
RUS Bulk Fuel Revolving Fund Grants, *10.857*
RUS community assistance, high energy cost,
 10.859
scientific, technical information, 81.064
state conservation planning, *81.041*
statistics, data, 81.039
Superconductivity and Competitiveness Act of
 1988, *81.122*
transuranic waste transport, *81.106*
wood fuel, *10.664*
see also Energy *entries*; Mineral resources;
 Nuclear sciences, technology; Public utilities;
 Solar energy

Energy conservation
biodiesel fuel use, CSREES, *10.306*
community development block grants, *14.218,
 14.219, 14.225, 14.228, 14.862*
DOE special state initiatives, *81.119*
Energy Conservation and Production Act, *81.042*
EPA environmental sustainability design
 competition, *66.516*
HOME Program, *14.239*
improvements, health facilities, multifamily
 housing, *14.151*
industrial, agricultural waste reduction, DOE,
 81.105
Inventions and Innovations Program, DOE, *81.036*
low-income, assistance, *81.042, 93.568*
National Energy Policy and Conservation Act of
 1978, *81.041, 81.089, 81.119*
outreach, training, *81.117*
renewable resources, research, development,
 81.087
Residential Energy Assistance Challenge Program
 (REACH), ACF, *93.568*
State Energy Efficiency Programs Improvement
 Act of 1990, *81.042*
state plans, *81.041*
sustainable agriculture research, *10.215*
technology research, development, *81.086*
weatherization, *81.042*
see also Housing rehabilitation; Weatherization
ENERGY EFFICIENCY AND RENEWABLE
 ENERGY INFORMATION,
 DISSEMINATION, OUTREACH, TRAINING
 AND TECHNICAL ANALYSIS/
 ASSISTANCE, *81.117*
Energy Information Administration (EIA), DOE, *see*
 Agency Index

Energy research
aviation, *20.108*
basic research, science, technology, *81.049*
biomass technology, *81.079*
coal, *81.057*
conservation technology development, *81.086*
DOE nuclear, education, fellowships, *81.114*
DOE workers, epidemiology, health studies,
 81.108
electricity delivery, energy reliability, DOE,
 81.122
EPA environmental sustainability design
 competition, *66.516*
Federal Nonnuclear Energy Research and
 Development Act of 1974, *81.036, 81.049,
 81.057, 81.086, 81.089, 81.108, 81.112, 81.113*
fossil, *81.089*
gas pipeline safety, *20.700*
HBCU program, nuclear, DOE, *81.123*
industrial, agricultural waste reduction, DOE,
 81.105
Inertial Confinement Fusion, stockpile
 stewardship, *81.112*
inventions development assistance, *81.036*
municipal solid waste conversion technology,
 81.079
Nuclear Energy Research Initiative, *81.121*
renewable resources, research, development,
 81.087
Used Equipment Grants, 81.022
see also Engineering *entries*; Nuclear sciences,
 technology; Scientific research; Solar energy
ENFORCING UNDERAGE DRINKING LAWS
 PROGRAM, *16.727*
ENG (Engineering Grants), NSF, *47.041*

Engineering
agricultural, graduate fellowships, *10.210*
Barry M. Goldwater Scholarship Program, *85.200*
calibration, testing, 11.601
DHS Scholars and Fellows, *97.062*
DOD science, technology projects, *12.910*
earthquakes hazards mitigation, *15.807*
energy information, 81.064
energy-related inventions development, *81.036*
EPA environmental sustainability design
 competition, *66.516*
EPA STAR graduate fellowships, *66.514*
Hazard Mitigation Grant, FEMA, *97.039*
health-related, preprofessional scholarships,
 Indians, *93.971*
highway, bridge construction, *20.215*
historic properties preservation, *15.904*
historic register, 15.914
hydrometeorology development, education,
 training, NOAA, *11.467*
Mathematics and Science Partnerships, OESE,
 84.366
manufacturing technology commercialization,
 11.612
mass transit, *20.505*
minority institutions, program improvements,
 84.120
National Standard Reference Data System, 11.603
National Technical Information Service, 11.650
NIST Congressionally-Identified Projects, *11.617*
NOAA Colorado areas math, engineering, science
 education, *11.449*
NOS intern program, *11.480*
NSF education, *47.041, 47.076*
pollution control, environmental research, EPA,
 66.511
soil survey data, 10.903
Standard Reference Materials, 11.604
standards, *11.609*
standards and certification information center,
 NCSCI, 11.610
Tech-Prep Education, secondary, postsecondary,
 84.243
transportation, *20.515*

Engineering *(continued)*
Universities Rebuilding America Program, Hurricanes Katrina, Rita, HUD, *14.521*
vocational rehabilitation engineering scholarships, *84.129*
watershed, river basin projects, 10.906
Weights and Measures Service, NIST, 11.606
see also Computer products, sciences, services; Energy *entries*; Engineering research; Highways, roads, bridges; Mass transportation; Mathematics; Measurement; Physical sciences; Public works; Science education; Scientific research; Technology transfer, utilization; Transportation
ENGINEERING GRANTS, *47.041*
Engineering research
Air Force Defense Research Sciences Program, *12.800*
Army Research Office, *12.431*
biomedical, hazardous materials, *93.143*
biomedical imaging research, *93.286*
Christopher Columbus Fellowship Program, *85.100*
Construction Productivity Advanced Research, Corps of Engineers, *12.114*
deafness, communicative disorders, *93.173*
DOD science, technology projects, *12.910*
DOD sciences research, fellowships, *12.630*
DOE WMD nonproliferation, *81.113*
energy-related, basic sciences, technology, *81.049*
energy-related, conservation technology development, *81.086*
energy-related, used equipment, 81.022
environmental systems, NOAA, *11.432*
EPA environmental sustainability design competition, *66.516*
EPA IHE research support, *66.515*
EPA research fellowships, graduate, undergraduate, *66.513*
forest engineering, *10.652*
high-speed passenger rail systems, *20.312*
homeland security technology development, DHS, *97.077*
Hydrologic Research, *11.462*
injury prevention research, *93.136*
Manufacturing Extension Partnership, NIST, *11.611*
NASA Technology Transfer, 43.002
Navy, education support, *12.300*
NIST Congressionally-Identified Projects, *11.617*
NSF computer engineering, *47.070*
NSF education, *47.075*
NSF grants, *47.041*
NSF international, *47.079*
Nuclear Energy Research Initiative, *81.121*
pollution control, environmental research, EPA, *66.511*
standards, projects, *11.609*
STAR (Science to Achieve Results) Program Research, EPA, *66.509*
University-Based Homeland Security Centers, DHS, *97.061*
water desalination development, *15.506*
see also Biological sciences; Computer products, sciences, services; Energy *entries*; Engineering; Mathematics; Measurement; Nuclear sciences, technology; Physical sciences; Scientific research; Technology transfer, utilization

English as a second language
adult education demonstrations, *84.191*
BECA English Language Fellow Program, *19.421*
BECA English Language Specialist/Speaker Program, *19.423*
citizenship education, 97.010
language acquisition grants, *84.365*
Low-Income Taxpayer Clinics, *21.008*
Ready-to-Learn TV, early childhood education, *84.295*
refugees, *93.566, 93.567, 93.584*
school civil rights compliance, *84.004*
see also Aliens, immigrants, refugees; Bilingual education, services; Disadvantaged, education
English language, *see* Adult education; Bilingual education, services; English as a second language; Illiteracy; Literature
ENGLISH LANGUAGE ACQUISITION GRANTS, *84.365*
English Language Program, BECA, *19.421*
Enterprise Communities, *see* Community development
Enterprise Communities, *10.772, 14.244*
Entrepreneurial Training and Technical Assistance Program (ETTAP), DOT, *20.907*
Environmental education
BLM projects, Cultural Resource Management, *15.224*
brownfield projects job training, *66.815*
Chesapeake Bay Studies, education, training, *11.457*
coastal ecosystem management, NOAA, *11.420, 11.473*
Community Food Projects, USDA, *10.225*
Environmental Education and Training Program, *66.950*
Environmental Education Grants, *66.951*
environmental justice projects, *66.604*
Environmental Justice Training and Fellowships, EPA, *66.307*
environmental management studies fellowships, EPA, *66.952*
EPA environmental sustainability design competition, *66.516*
EPA New England Regional Office projects, *66.110*
EPA pollution prevention studies, training, outreach, *66.716*
EPA research fellowships, graduate, undergraduate, *66.513*
EPA STAR graduate fellowships, *66.514*
EPA studies, special purpose assistance, *66.610*
Global Development Alliance, USAID, *98.011*
Junior Duck Stamp Contest, FWS, *15.644*
Multi-State Conservation Grants, FWS, *15.628*
National Environmental Education Act, *66.110, 66.950, 66.951*
NESDIS environmental sciences education, research, *11.440*
NMFS marine education, science projects, *11.455*
NOS intern program, *11.480*
pollution source reduction information dissemination, outreach, EPA, *66.717*
Summer Watershed Intern, *15.254*

Superfund technical assistance to citizens groups, 66.806
Udall doctoral fellowships, 85.401
Udall undergraduate scholarships, 85.400
Woodrow Wilson Center fellowships, 85.300
see also Community development; Environmental entries; Science education; Teacher education, training
ENVIRONMENTAL EDUCATION AND TRAINING PROGRAM, 66.950
ENVIRONMENTAL EDUCATION GRANTS, 66.951

Environmental health, research, services
Academic Research Enhancement Award, 93.390
disabilities prevention, 93.184
energy-related, 81.049
environmental hazards, biological response, 93.113
environmental justice collaborative projects, 66.306
Environmental Justice Research Assistance, EPA, 66.308
Environmental Justice Surveys and Studies, EPA, 66.309
Environmental Justice Training and Fellowships, EPA, 66.307
EPA aging, children's health protection, 66.609
EPA compliance capacity building, 66.709
EPA IHE research support, 66.515
EPA consolidated research, 66.511
EPA Performance Partnership Grants, 66.605
EPA pollution prevention studies, training, outreach, 66.716
EPA studies, special purpose assistance, 66.610
Federal Insecticide, Fungicide, and Rodenticide Act (FIFRA), 66.035, 66.110, 66.111, 66.306, 66.307, 66.308, 66.309, 66.310, 66.509, 66.510, 66.511, 66.513, 66.514, 66.515, 66.516, 66.600, 66.604, 66.606, 66.609, 66.610, 66.611, 66.700, 66.709, 66.714, 66.716, 66.717, 66.931, 66.940, 66.952
Great Lakes fish consumption effects, 93.208
Hanford site, tribal public health capacity, 93.202
hazardous substances, biomedical research, graduate education, 93.143
hazardous substances emergencies, state surveillance systems, 93.204
hazardous waste sites health studies, 93.206
Healthy Homes Demonstration Grants, HUD, 14.901
Indians, preprofessional scholarships, 93.971
lead-based paint hazard control, HUD, 14.900
Lead Hazard Reduction Demonstration Grants, HUD, 14.905
Lead Outreach Grants, HUD, 14.904
lead poisoning prevention, 93.197
lead technical studies, HUD, 14.902, 14.906
multi-disciplinary, training, 93.894
Operation Lead Elimination Action Program, HUD, 14.903
Pesticide Environmental Stewardship, 66.714
pollution, air, water, lead poisoning, biometry, risk estimation, 93.115
pollution control surveys, studies, EPA R&D, 66.510
pollution source reduction information dissemination, outreach, EPA, 66.717
public health, graduate traineeships, 93.964
research, manpower development, 93.894
STAR (Science to Achieve Results) Research Program, EPA, 66.509
surveys, studies, special grants, EPA, 66.606
toxic substances compliance programs, 66.701
toxicology, 93.114
see also Air pollution; Behavioral sciences, education, services; Community health services; Environmental entries; Hazardous materials, waste; Health, medical research; Pesticides; Pollution abatement; Public health; Radiation; Toxic substances, toxicology; Waste treatment, disposal; Water entries
Environmental Health Sciences Centers (EHS Centers), 93.894
ENVIRONMENTAL INFORMATION EXCHANGE NETWORK GRANT PROGRAM, 66.608
Environmental justice, see Community development
ENVIRONMENTAL JUSTICE COLLABORATIVE PROBLEM-SOLVING COOPERATIVE AGREEMENTS PROGRAM, 66.306
ENVIRONMENTAL JUSTICE RESEARCH ASSISTANCE, 66.308
ENVIRONMENTAL JUSTICE SMALL GRANTS PROGRAM, 66.604
Environmental Justice Surveys and Studies, EPA, 66.309
ENVIRONMENTAL JUSTICE TRAINING AND FELLOWSHIP ASSISTANCE, 66.307

Environmental management
abandoned mine land reclamation, 15.252
BLM projects, Cultural Resource Management, 15.224
brownfield sites redevelopment, training, EPA, 66.814
Chesapeake Bay Program, 66.466
Clean Water Act studies, training, 66.436
coastal ecosystem, NOAA, 11.473
Coastal Ocean Program, research, 11.478
community stakeholder projects, 66.035
conservation law enforcement training, 15.602
DOD Environmental Restoration Program, 12.113
DOD program changes, 12.612
DOE cleanup, technology development, 81.104
Endangered Species Act of 1973, 15.051, 15.231, 15.615, 15.632, 15.640, 15.641, 15.811
endangered species conservation, 15.615, 15.632, 15.638
Environmental Information Exchange Network Grants, 66.608
environmental justice projects, 66.032, 66.306, 66.604
Environmental Justice Research Assistance, EPA, 66.308
Environmental Justice Surveys and Studies, EPA, 66.309
Environmental Justice Training and Fellowships, EPA, 66.307
Environmental Quality Incentives Program-Klamath Basin, NRCS, 10.919
Environmental Quality Incentives Program, NRCS, 10.912
environmental management studies fellowships, EPA, 66.952

Environmental management *(continued)*
environmental policy, programs innovation, stewardship, studies, analyses, *66.611*
Environmental Programs Assistance Act of 1984, *66.508, 66.518*
EPA Compliance Assistance Centers, *66.305*
EPA compliance capacity building, *66.709*
EPA consolidated research, *66.511*
EPA environmental sustainability design competition, *66.516*
EPA IHE research support, *66.515*
EPA international financial assistance projects, *66.931*
EPA Performance Partnership Grants, *66.605*
EPA pollution prevention studies, training, outreach, *66.716*
EPA projects, One Stop Reporting, *66.608*
EPA Region 7 projects, *66.111*
EPA studies, special purpose assistance, *66.610*
estuary protection, *66.456*
Fish, Wildlife and Plant Conservation Resource Management, BLM, *15.231*
fish, wildlife resources management, FWS, 15.608
FWS State Wildlife Grants, *15.634*
Great Lakes Program, *66.469*
ground, surface water quality incentives program, NRCS, *10.918*
Gulf of Mexico Program, EPA, *66.475*
Habitat Conservation, NOAA, *11.463*
hazardous waste clean-up, *66.802*
Indian Environmental General Assistance Program Act of 1992, *66.926*
Indian lands, 12.116, *93.581, 93.582*
Indian Programs, *15.041*
industrial, agricultural waste reduction, DOE, *81.105*
Land and Water Conservation Act of 1965, *15.633, 15.638, 15.639*
Marine Turtle Conservation Fund, FWS, *15.645*
mine land reclamation, *10.910*
National Agricultural Library, 10.700
National Environmental Policy Act, *15.041, 66.310, 66.606, 66.609, 66.610, 66.931*
National Guard assistance, *12.401*
NOAA Educational Partnerships Program, minority, *11.481*
North American Wetlands Conservation Fund, FWS, *15.623*
NOS intern program, *11.480*
nuclear waste disposal siting, *81.065*
oil spill trust fund, USCG, 97.013
pesticides control, *66.700*
petroleum underground storage tank program, *66.805*
plant use in conservation, 10.905
pollution control, EPA consolidated program support, *66.600*
pollution source reduction information dissemination, outreach, EPA, *66.717*
regional monitoring, assessment projects, EPA, *66.512*
Resource Conservation and Recovery Act (RCRA), *15.041, 66.305, 66.510, 66.511, 66.515, 66.600, 66.611, 66.717, 66.801, 66.804, 66.805, 66.808, 66.816, 66.931, 93.161, 93.240*
Rivers, Trails, and Conservation Assistance, 15.921
rural, *10.224*
rural resource conservation, development, *10.901*
senior environmental employment programs, *66.508, 66.518*
soils data, 10.903
solid waste management systems, *66.808*
STAR (Science to Achieve Results) Research Program, EPA, *66.509*
state policy studies, innovation grants, *66.940*
Superfund, hazardous waste, materials clean-up, *66.802*
tribal direct implementation agreements, EPA, *66.473*
Tribal Landowner Incentive Program, *15.638*
Tribal Wildlife Grants, FWS, *15.639*
underground storage tank program, *66.804, 66.816*
Upper Mississippi River ecosystem monitoring, *15.978*
USGS Cooperative Research Units Program, *15.812*
USGS Gap Analysis Program, *15.811*
Water Quality Cooperative Agreements, *66.463*
wetlands protection, restoration programs, *66.461*
wildlife damage, disease control, *10.028*
see also Agricultural conservation; Air pollution; Animal disease control, health, welfare; Coastal zone; Community development; Earth sciences; Energy *entries*; Environmental *entries*; Estuaries; Fish; Forestry; Hazardous materials, waste; Marine sciences; Natural resources; Pesticides; Physical sciences; Public lands; Pollution abatement; Radiation; Soil conservation; Toxic substances, toxicology; Urban renewal; Waste treatment, disposal; Water *entries*; Wetlands; Wildlife, waterfowl
ENVIRONMENTAL MANAGEMENT—INDIAN PROGRAMS, *15.041*
ENVIRONMENTAL POLICY AND INNOVATION GRANTS, *66.611*
ENVIRONMENTAL POLICY AND STATE INNOVATION GRANTS, *66.940*
Environmental pollution, *see* Air pollution; Energy *entries*; Environmental *entries*; Hazardous materials, waste; Mineral resources; Pesticides; Pollution abatement; Radiation; Waste treatment, disposal; Water pollution abatement, prevention
Environmental protection, *see* Environmental *entries*
Environmental Protection Agency (EPA), 66.001 through 66.952
ENVIRONMENTAL PROTECTION CONSOLIDATED GRANTS—PROGRAM SUPPORT, *66.600*
ENVIRONMENTAL QUALITY INCENTIVES PROGRAM [USDA], *10.912*
Environmental sciences
agricultural, biotechnology risk assessment, *10.219*
Air Force Defense Research Sciences Program, *12.800*
air quality research, services, *11.459*
aviation research, *20.108*
business internships, Eurasian executives, scientists, *11.114*

MASTER INDEX 933

climate, *11.431*
Coastal Ocean Program, *11.478*
DOD sciences research, fellowships, *12.630*
energy-related research, *81.049*
energy-related, used equipment, 81.022
environmental biology, *47.074*
environmental health, biometry, risk estimation, *93.115*
Environmental Health Sciences Centers, *93.894*
Environmental Justice Research Assistance, EPA, *66.308*
Environmental Justice Surveys and Studies, EPA, *66.309*
Environmental Justice Training and Fellowships, EPA, *66.307*
environmental management studies fellowships, EPA, *66.952*
regional monitoring, assessment projects, EPA, *66.512*
environmental policy, programs innovation, stewardship, studies, analyses, *66.611*
EPA consolidated research, training, *66.511*
EPA environmental sustainability design competition, *66.516*
EPA IHE research support, *66.515*
EPA research fellowships, graduate, undergraduate, *66.513*
EPA STAR graduate fellowships, *66.514*
hazardous substances, biomedical research, graduate education, *93.143*
industrial waste reduction, DOE, *81.105*
marine research, *11.417*
National Agricultural Library, 10.700
Navy research, education support, *12.300*
NIEHS education programs, *93.113*, *93.115*
NMFS marine education, science projects, *11.455*
NOAA Educational Partnerships Program, minority, *11.481*
NOAA research, *11.432*
NSF engineering education, research, *47.041*
NSF Geosciences, *47.050*
Polar Programs, *47.078*
Smithsonian fellowships, *85.601*
STAR (Science to Achieve Results) Research Program, EPA, *66.509*
toxicological research, testing, development, *93.114*
USGS Cooperative Research Units Program, *15.812*
see also Air pollution; Climate; Earth sciences; Energy *entries*; Environmental *entries*; Geology; Marine sciences; Pesticides; Physical sciences; Pollution abatement; Toxic substances, toxicology; Water *entries*
ENVIRONMENTAL SCIENCES APPLICATIONS, DATA, AND EDUCATION, *11.440*
EP (Emergency Program), USAID, *98.008*
EPA (Environmental Protection Agency), 66.001 through 66.952
EPA STAR (Science to Achieve Results) Fellowship Program, *66.514*
EPA STAR (Science to Achieve Results) Research Program, *66.509*
EPCRA (Emergency Planning and Community Right-to-Know Act), *20.703*
EPIDEMIOLOGIC RESEARCH STUDIES OF ACQUIRED IMMUNODEFICIENCY SYNDROME (AIDS) AND HUMAN IMMUNODEFICIENCY VIRUS (HIV) INFECTION IN SELECTED POPULATION GROUPS, *93.943*
Epidemiology
AIDS Activity, *93.118*
AIDS studies, *93.943*
alcoholism research, *93.273*
alcoholism research training, *93.271*, *93.272*
arthritis, musculoskeletal, skin diseases research, *93.846*
cancer, *93.393*, *93.397*, *93.399*
clinical researchers education loan repayment, disadvantaged, *93.308*
CDCP assistance, *93.283*
deafness, communicative disorders research, *93.173*
diabetes control, *93.988*
disabilities prevention, *93.184*
DOE workers, studies, *81.108*
drug abuse, addiction research, *93.279*
environmental health, biometry, risk estimation, *93.115*
environmental health sciences, *93.894*
hazardous substances emergencies, state surveillance systems, *93.204*
HIV/AIDS Surveillance, *93.944*
HIV projects, *93.928*
Indians, centers, *93.231*
Infant Health Initiatives, *93.946*
infectious diseases research, *93.856*
injury prevention research, *93.136*
Lyme Disease, *93.942*
mental health research, *93.242*
mental health research training, *93.282*
neurological diseases research, *93.853*
NIH Clinical Research Loan Repayment Program (CR-LRP), *93.220*, *93.280*
NIH Pediatric Research Loan Repayment Program, *93.285*, *93.385*
oral diseases, disorders, *93.121*
public health graduate traineeships, *93.964*
Public Health Research Accreditation Project, *93.993*
research NRSA, *93.225*
sexually transmitted diseases, *93.977*
Vital Statistics Reengineering Program, CDCP, *93.066*
see also Communicable diseases; Disease control; Health planning; Health, medical research; Immunization, immunology; Population research; Preventive health services; Public health
EPIDEMIOLOGY AND OTHER HEALTH STUDIES FINANCIAL ASSISTANCE PROGRAM [DOE], *81.108*
EPIDEMIOLOGY COOPERATIVE AGREEMENTS, *93.231*
Epilepsy research, *93.853*
EQIP (Environmental Quality Incentives Program), NRCS, *10.912*
EQIP-G&SW (Environmental Quality Incentives Program-Ground and Surface Water), NRCS, *10.918*
EQIP-KB (Environmental Quality Incentives Program-Klamath Basin), NRCS, *10.919*

Equal credit opportunity, *see* Consumers, consumer services
Equal Credit Opportunity Act (ECOA), 16.103
Equal Educational Opportunities Act, 16.100
Equal educational opportunity, *see* Civil rights
Equal employment opportunity, *see* Civil rights
EQUAL EMPLOYMENT OPPORTUNITY, 16.101
Equal Employment Opportunity Commission (EEOC), 30.001 through 30.011
Equal Enjoyment of Rights in Public Facilities, 16.105
EQUAL OPPORTUNITY IN HOUSING, 14.400
Equal Pay Act, *see* Employee benefits
Equal rights, *see* Civil rights; Women
ERDDIA (Educational Research, Development, Dissemination and Improvement Act of 1994), *see* Education research
ERISA (Employee Retirement Income Security Act), 17.150, *86.001*
Erosion, *see* Agricultural conservation; Flood prevention, control; Soil conservation
ESEA, *see* Elementary and Secondary Education acts
ESG (Emergency Shelter Grants), *14.231*
ESL, *see* English as a second language
Estuaries
  Atlantic coastal, fisheries management, *11.474*
  Chesapeake Bay Program, *66.466*
  Chesapeake Bay Studies, education, training, *11.457*
  Clean Water Act studies, training, *66.436*
  development, research, *11.420*
  EPA Nonpoint Source Implementation Grants, *66.460*
  Habitat Conservation, NOAA, *11.463*
  Marine Sanctuary Program, *11.429*
  NMFS marine education, science projects, *11.455*
  NOAA unallied projects, *11.452, 11.454, 11.472*
  protection, *66.456, 66.458*
  see also Coastal zone; Environmental management; Natural resources; Water resources, supply, management; Wetlands
Ethics, *see* Humanities *entries*
ETTAP (Entrepreneurial Training and Technical Assistance Program), DOT, *20.907*
EVEN START—INDIAN TRIBES AND TRIBAL ORGANIZATIONS, *84.258*
EVEN START—MIGRANT EDUCATION, *84.214*
EVEN START—STATE EDUCATIONAL AGENCIES, *84.213*
EXCHANGE—ENGLISH LANGUAGE FELLOW PROGRAM [BECA], *19.421*
EXCHANGE—ENGLISH LANGUAGE SPECIALIST/SPEAKER PROGRAM [BECA], *19.423*
EXCHANGE OF FEDERAL TAX INFORMATION WITH STATE TAX AGENCIES, 21.004
Executive Office for Weed and Seed, DOJ, *see* Agency Index
Experiment stations, *see* Agricultural experiment stations
Experimental housing, *see* Housing research
Explosives, *see* Civil defense; Crime; Forensic sciences; Firefighting, fire prevention, control
Export Assistance Centers, 11.108

Export Control, 11.150
Export-Import, *see* International commerce, investment
EXPORT LICENSING SERVICE AND INFORMATION, 11.150
Export Loans, SBA, *59.054*
Export Price Index, 17.003
EXPORT PROMOTION MARKET DEVELOPMENT COOPERATION, *11.112*
Exporter Assistance Program, 11.150
Extension Service, USDA, *see* Agency Index (USDA, Cooperative State Research, Education and Extension Service)
EXTRAMURAL LOAN REPAYMENT FOR INDIVIDUALS FROM DISADVANTAGED BACKGROUNDS CONDUCTING CLINICAL RESEARCH, *93.308*
EXTRAMURAL RESEARCH PROGRAMS IN THE NEUROSCIENCES AND NEUROLOGICAL DISORDERS, *93.853*
Extramural Research, USDA, *10.001*
Eye, vision research, *see* Blindness and the blind; Health, medical research

FAA Centers of Excellence, *20.109*
FAA (Federal Aviation Administration), DOT, *see* Agency Index
FACE (Family and Child Education), BIA, *15.043*
FACE (Freedom of Access to Clinic Entrances) Act, 16.105
FACTA (Food, Agriculture, Conservation, and Trade Act of 1990), *see* International commerce, investment
Factory housing, *see* Homes, manufactured, mobile
Faculty Loan Repayment Program (FLRP), HRSA, *93.923*
Faculty Research Abroad, *84.019*
Faculty training, *see* Teacher education, training
FAIR COMPETITION COUNSELING AND INVESTIGATION OF COMPLAINTS [FTC], 36.001
Fair Employment Practices Agencies, *30.002*
Fair housing, Fair Housing Act, *see* Civil rights
FAIR HOUSING AND EQUAL CREDIT OPPORTUNITY, 16.103
Fair Housing and Equal Opportunity, HUD, *see* Agency Index (HUD, Office of Fair Housing and Equal Opportunity)
FAIR HOUSING ASSISTANCE PROGRAM—STATE AND LOCAL, *14.401*
FAIR HOUSING INITIATIVES PROGRAM, *14.408*
FAIRA (Federal Agriculture Improvement and Reform Act of 1996), *see* Agricultural commodities, stabilization
Family and Child Education (FACE), BIA, *15.043*
FAMILY AND COMMUNITY VIOLENCE PREVENTION PROGRAM, *93.910*
Family farms
  Agricultural Management Assistance, NRCS, *10.917*
  Crop Insurance in Targeted States, *10.458*
  disabled veterans, purchase, *64.118*
  emergency loans, *10.404*
  Environmental Quality Incentives Program-Klamath Basin, NRCS, *10.919*

Environmental Quality Incentives Program, NRCS, *10.912*
Fund for Rural America, *10.224*
loans, interest subsidies, *10.437*
operating loans, *10.406*
organic agriculture extension, CSREES, *10.307*
outreach, socially disadvantaged, *10.443*
ownership loans, *10.407*
risk management outreach, RMA, *10.455*
Trade Adjustment Assistance, FAS, *10.609*
see also Agricultural *entries*; Farm, nonfarm enterprises; Farm workers; Housing, rural; Indian lands; Rural areas
Family Life Centers, HHS, *93.910*

Family medicine
geriatrics faculty fellowships, *93.156*
Medicaid, *93.778*
NHSC scholarships, *93.288*
primary care research training, *93.186*
residency training, *93.884*
see also Community health services; Genetics; Health, medical education, training; Health professions; Maternal, child health, welfare; Osteopathy; Pediatrics; Veterans health, medical services

Family planning
abstinence education, *93.010, 93.235*
adolescent family life research, information, *93.111*
adolescents, *93.217, 93.995*
comprehensive services program, *93.217*
contraception, infertility research, education loan repayments, *93.209*
counseling, *93.995*
embryo adoption public awareness, *93.007*
FACE Act violations prosecution, *16.109*
Family Planning Services and Population Research Acts, *93.217, 93.260, 93.974*
Freedom of Access to Clinic Entrances Act, *16.105*
HIV outpatient services, *93.918*
Medicaid, *93.778*
paramedical, paraprofessional training, *93.260*
perinatal/maternal initiative, *93.926*
research, services delivery improvement, *93.974*
youth services, *93.111*
see also Community health services; Health professions; Maternal, child health, welfare; Parenting; Population research; Social services
FAMILY PLANNING—PERSONNEL TRAINING, *93.260*
FAMILY PLANNING—SERVICE DELIVERY IMPROVEMENT RESEARCH GRANTS, *93.974*
FAMILY PLANNING—SERVICES, *93.217*
FAMILY SUPPORT PAYMENTS TO STATES—ASSISTANCE PAYMENTS, *93.560*

Family therapy
AIDS/HIV care, children, women, families, *93.153*
child abuse, *93.669*
child welfare services, *93.645*
community-based child abuse prevention, *93.590*
education loan repayments, states, *93.165*
family support services, *93.556*
family violence prevention, *93.591, 93.592, 93.671, 93.910*

Family Violence Prevention and Services Act, *93.591, 93.592, 93.671*
corrections, law enforcement personnel family support projects, research, *16.563*
mental health personnel, social worker training, *93.244*
rural domestic violence, *16.589*
veterans, substance abuse rehabilitation, *64.019*
violence, children's exposure, prevention initiative, Safe Start, *16.730*
violence prevention programs, *16.582*
see also Behavioral sciences, education, services; Crime; Health professions; Juvenile delinquency; Maternal, child health, welfare; Mental Health; Parenting; Social services; Victim assistance
FAMILY VIOLENCE PREVENTION AND SERVICES/GRANTS FOR BATTERED WOMEN'S SHELTERS—DISCRETIONARY GRANTS, *93.592*
FAMILY VIOLENCE PREVENTION AND SERVICES/GRANTS FOR BATTERED WOMEN'S SHELTERS—GRANTS TO STATE DOMESTIC VIOLENCE COALITIONS, *93.591*
FAMILY VIOLENCE PREVENTION AND SERVICES/GRANTS FOR BATTERED WOMEN'S SHELTERS—GRANTS TO STATES AND INDIAN TRIBES, *93.671*
FARM AND RANCH LANDS PROTECTION PROGRAM, *10.913*
Farm home loans, *see* Family farms; Housing, rural
Farm labor, *see* Farm workers
FARM LABOR CONTRACTOR REGISTRATION, *17.308*
FARM LABOR HOUSING LOANS AND GRANTS, *10.405*
Farm loans, *see* Agricultural loans; Farm, nonfarm enterprises

Farm, nonfarm enterprises
Bioenergy Program, FSA, *10.078*
biomass energy conversion technology, research, *81.079*
business, industrial development, *10.768*
Commodity Partnerships for Risk Management Education, *10.457, 10.459*
Community Food Projects, USDA, *10.225*
Crop Disaster Program, *10.073*
Crop Insurance, *10.450*
Crop Insurance in Targeted States, *10.458*
emergency loans, *10.404*
Farm Storage Facility Loans, *10.056*
farmer outreach, socially disadvantaged, *10.443*
Forestry Incentives Program, *10.064*
Fund for Rural America, *10.224*
Intermediary Relending Program, *10.767*
international, USAID Farmer-to-Farmer Program, *98.009*
BIA Loan Guaranty Program, *15.124*
loan mediation services, *10.435*
noninsurance risk management research partnerships, *10.456*
operating loans, *10.406*
organic agriculture extension, CSREES, *10.307*
ownership loans, *10.407*
risk management outreach, RMA, *10.455*

Farm, nonfarm enterprises *(continued)*
  Rural Business-Cooperative Service, 10.350
  Rural Business Enterprise Grants, *10.769*
  Rural Business Investment Program, RBCS, *10.860*
  Rural Cooperative Development Grants, *10.771*
  seed producers emergency loans, *10.076*
  small business, agriculture regulatory ombudsman, *59.053*
  small wood species, USFS Technology Marketing Unit, *10.674*
  Special Apple Program, *10.075*
  sustainable agriculture research, *10.215*
  Tree Assistance Program, FSA, *10.082*
  Wholesale Farmers and Alternative Market Development, 10.164
  see also Agricultural *entries*; Aliens, immigrants, refugees; Aquaculture; Business development; Family farms; Farm workers; Forestry; Rural areas; Small business; Woodlands
FARM OPERATING LOANS, *10.406*
FARM OWNERSHIP LOANS, *10.407*
Farm Security and Rural Investment Act of 2002 (FSRIA), *see* Rural areas
Farm Service Agency (FSA), USDA, *see* Agency Index
FARM STORAGE FACILITY LOANS, *10.056*
Farm workers
  aliens certification, 17.202
  bondage, Civil Rights Prosecution, 16.109
  children, state migrant education program, *84.011*
  College Assistance Migrant Program (CAMP), *84.149*
  contractor registration, Crew Leader, 17.308
  disabled, handicapped migrants, rehabilitation services, projects, *84.128*
  Even Start, migrant education, *84.214*
  Head Start, *93.600*
  health centers, *93.224*
  health, housing standards, 17.308
  health services outreach, *93.912*
  housing loans, grants, *10.405*
  Migrant and Seasonal Agricultural Worker Protection Act, 17.308
  migrant elementary, secondary education coordination, *84.144*
  migrant, seasonal, CSBG projects, *93.570*
  migrants, high school equivalence, postsecondary education financial assistance, *84.141*
  National Farmworker Jobs Program, ETA, *17.264*
  rental assistance, *10.427*
  seasonal workers certification, 17.202
  U.S. Employment Service, *17.207*
  see also Aliens, immigrants, refugees; Community health services; Farm, nonfarm enterprises; Rural poor
Farmer-to-Farmer Program, USAID, *98.009*
Farmers Home Administration (FmHA), *see* Agency Index (USDA, Farm Service Agency *and* Rural Housing Service)
Farmers' Market Nutrition Program (FMNP), *10.572*
Farmland rehabilitation, *see* Agricultural conservation; Disaster assistance; Soil conservation
FAS (Foreign Agricultural Service), USDA, *see* Agency Index

FBI
  Combined DNA Index System (CODIS), *16.307*
  FBI Academy Advanced Specialized Courses, 16.300
  field police training, 16.302
  fingerprint identification, 16.303
  Indian Country Investigations, training, 16.308
  laboratory services, training, 16.301
  National Crime Information Center, 16.304
  National Instant Criminal Background Check System, 16.309
  Uniform Crime Reports, 16.305
  victim identification, 16.303
  see also Forensic sciences; Law enforcement education, training; Legal services
FBI Criminal Justice Information Services Division, 16.303
FBI (Federal Bureau of Investigation), DOJ, *see* Agency Index
FBI Laboratory, 16.301
FCC (Federal Communications Commission), 32.001
FDA (Food and Drug Administration), HHS, *see* Agency Index
FDSLP (Federal Direct Student Loan Program), *84.268*
Federal Agriculture Improvement and Reform Act of 1996 (FAIRA), *see* Agricultural commodities, stabilization
Federal-Aid Highway Program, *20.205*
FEDERAL ASSISTANCE TO INDIVIDUALS AND HOUSEHOLDS—DISASTER HOUSING OPERATIONS, *97.049*
FEDERAL ASSISTANCE TO INDIVIDUALS AND HOUSEHOLDS—HOUSING [DHS], *97.048*
FEDERAL ASSISTANCE TO INDIVIDUALS AND HOUSEHOLDS—OTHER NEEDS [DHS], *97.050*
Federal Aviation Administration (FAA), DOT, *see* Agency Index
Federal Bureau of Investigation (FBI), DOJ, *see* Agency Index
FEDERAL CITIZEN INFORMATION CENTER, 39.009
FEDERAL CIVIL SERVICE EMPLOYMENT, 27.001
Federal Communications Commission (FCC), 32.001
Federal Consolidation Loans, students, *84.032*
Federal Council on the Arts and the Humanities, National Foundation on the Arts and the Humanities *see* Agency Index
Federal Credit Union Act, *44.001*
Federal Crop Insurance Corporation, *see* Agency Index (USDA, Farm Service Agency)
FEDERAL DIRECT STUDENT LOANS, *84.268*
Federal Emergency Management Agency (FEMA), Department of Homeland Security (DHS), *see* Agency Index
Federal employment
  benefits information, NHSC, NOAA, PHS, veterans, 64.115
  civil service jobs, 27.001
  Civil Service Reform Act of 1978, 27.001, 27.006
  collective bargaining, conciliation, mediation, FMCS, 34.001

MASTER INDEX 937

disabled, handicapped, mentally retarded, restored, 27.005
DOE workers, epidemiology, health studies, 81.108
employees, Anti-Terrorism and Emergency Assistance Program, DOJ, 16.321
Federal Employees and Ex-Service Members Act, 17.225
high school, college students, summer jobs, 27.006
intergovernmental mobility, federal, state, local personnel, 27.011
Intergovernmental Personnel Act of 1970, 27.011
Presidential management interns, 27.013
Selective Placement Program, 27.005
Unemployment Insurance, 17.225
USDC postsecondary student internships, 11.702
Veterans preference, 17.806
veterans, veterans dependents, 27.002
youth, temporary, 27.003
see also Employment services; Government; Technical training; Veterans entries
FEDERAL EMPLOYMENT ASSISTANCE FOR VETERANS, 27.002
FEDERAL EMPLOYMENT FOR INDIVIDUALS WITH DISABILITIES, 27.005
FEDERAL FAMILY EDUCATION LOANS, 84.032
Federal government, see Federal employment; Government
Federal Highway Administration (FHA), DOT, see Agency Index
FEDERAL HIGHWAY SAFETY DATA IMPROVEMENTS INCENTIVE GRANTS, 20.603
Federal Housing Commissioner (HUD), see Agency Index (HUD, Housing-Federal Housing Commissioner)
Federal Insecticide, Fungicide, and Rodenticide Act (FIFRA), see Environmental health, research, services
Federal Insurance Administration, FEMA, see Agency Index
FEDERAL JUNIOR DUCK STAMP CONSERVATION AND DESIGN, 15.644
Federal Land Policy and Management Act, see Public lands
Federal Land-to-Parks Program, 15.918
Federal Maritime Commission, 33.001
Federal Mediation and Conciliation Service, 34.001 through 34.002
Federal Motor Carrier Safety Administration, 20.217, 20.218
FEDERAL PELL GRANT PROGRAM, 84.063
FEDERAL PERKINS LOAN PROGRAM—FEDERAL CAPITAL CONTRIBUTIONS, 84.038
Federal PLUS Loans, DOED, 84.032
Federal property
aviation research, 20.108
BIA facilities operations, maintenance, 15.048
compensation to states, Corps of Engineers projects, 12.112
DOD donations, loans, 12.700
DOE patents, 81.003
education programs, 84.145
energy-related equipment, 81.022

Federal Property and Administrative Services Acts, 15.915, 15.918, 39.002, 39.003, 39.007, 84.145, 93.291
firefighting, FEMA reimbursement, 97.016
Good Neighbor Initiative, HUD, 14.311
HUD Dollar Home Sales, 14.313
HUD, Multifamily Property Disposition, 14.199
HUD, Officer Next Door Sales Program, 14.198
HUD, Single Family Property Disposition, 14.311
HUD, Teacher Next Door Initiative, 14.310
military/community joint land use plans, 12.610
minerals, BLM, 15.214
school impact aid, federally affected areas, 84.040, 84.041
vessels, marine schools, 20.806
see also Federal surplus property; Public lands
Federal Property Assistance Program, HHS, 93.291
Federal Railroad Administration, DOT, see Agency Index
FEDERAL REAL PROPERTY ASSISTANCE PROGRAM [DOED], 84.145
Federal Records Centers, 89.001
FEDERAL REIMBURSEMENT OF EMERGENCY HEALTH SERVICES FURNISHED TO UNDOCUMENTED ALIENS, 93.784
Federal Seed Program, 10.163
FEDERAL SHIP FINANCING GUARANTEES, 20.802
FEDERAL-STATE MARKETING IMPROVEMENT PROGRAM [USDA], 10.156
FEDERAL STUDENT TEMPORARY EMPLOYMENT PROGRAM, 27.003
FEDERAL SUMMER EMPLOYMENT, 27.006
FEDERAL SUPPLEMENTAL EDUCATIONAL OPPORTUNITY GRANTS, 84.007
Federal Supplemental Loans for Students (SLS), 84.032
Federal surplus property
correctional programs, 16.578
DOD donations, loans, 12.700
Federal Land for Parks and Recreation Act of 1949, 15.918
health, related facilities, 93.291
historic monument use, 15.918
parks, recreational use, 15.918
personal property donation, 39.003
personal property sales, 39.007
real property disposal, 39.002
Surplus Property Act of 1944, 39.002, 39.003
Surplus Property Amendments of 1984, 16.578
wildlife conservation, nature study use, 15.918
see also Federal property; Public lands
FEDERAL SURPLUS PROPERTY TRANSFER PROGRAM [DOJ], 16.578
Federal Trade Commission (FTC), 36.001
Federal Transit Administration (FTA), DOT, see Agency Index
FEDERAL TRANSIT—CAPITAL INVESTMENT GRANTS, 20.500
FEDERAL TRANSIT—FORMULA GRANTS, 20.507
FEDERAL TRANSIT—METROPOLITAN PLANNING GRANTS, 20.505
Federal Wage Garnishment Law, 17.306

Federal Wage-Hour Laws, 17.303
FEDERAL WORK-STUDY PROGRAM, *84.033*
Federated States of Micronesia, *see* U.S. possessions, territories

Feed grains
Bioenergy Program, FSA, *10.078*
conversion to biomass energy, research, *81.079*
Crop Insurance, *10.450*
Direct and Counter-Cyclical Payments Program, *10.055*
disaster assistance, noninsured crops, *10.451*
DOE industrial (NICE3), *81.105*
Emerson Humanitarian Trust, FSA, *10.079*
Farm Storage Facility Loans, *10.056*
Food Security Wheat Reserve (Emerson Humanitarian Trust), FSA, *10.079*
livestock, Disaster Reserve Assistance, *10.452*
Market News, 10.153
price supports, *10.051*
Ruminant Feed Ban Support Project, FDA, *93.449*
State Mediation Grants, *10.435*
United States Grain Standards Act of 2000, *10.435*
see also Agricultural commodities, stabilization; Livestock industry
Fellowship Foundations, *see* Scholarship and Fellowship Foundations

Fellowships, scholarships, traineeships
aging research, behavioral, biomedical, social sciences, *93.866*
agricultural, food sciences, Hispanics, *10.223*
agricultural, graduate, *10.210*
agricultural sciences, Minority Scholars Program, *10.220*
alcoholism researchers, *93.271, 93.272*
allergy, immunology, transplantation research, *93.855*
alternative, complementary medicine research, *93.213*
AmeriCorps, *94.006*
anesthetists, nurse, *93.124*
arthritis, musculoskeletal, skin diseases research, *93.846*
arts, graduate, *84.170*
arts, NEA, *45.024*
Barry M. Goldwater Scholarship Program, *85.200*
biological sciences, doctoral, postdoctoral, *47.074*
biomedical, behavioral research, international, *93.989*
blood diseases research, *93.839*
business, international, Eastern European, *11.114*
business internships, secondary students, *84.353*
Byrd honors, *84.185*
cancer research, *93.398*
child welfare personnel, *93.648*
Christopher Columbus Quincentenary Coins and Fellowship Foundation Act, *85.100*
coal research, *81.057*
coastal ecosystem management, NOAA, *11.473*
Columbus Fellowship Program, *85.100*
contraception, infertility research, *93.209*
criminal justice research, *16.561, 16.562, 16.566*
deafness, communicative disorders research, *93.173*
dental, oral health research, *93.121*
dentistry residencies, *93.236*
DHS Scholars and Fellows, *97.062*
diabetes, endocrinology, metabolism research, *93.847*
digestive diseases, nutrition research, *93.848*
disadvantaged, graduate opportunities, *84.217*
disadvantaged, handicapped, first-generation students, *84.042*
disadvantaged student program personnel, *84.103*
DOD engineering, mathematics, sciences research, *12.630*
DOI Summer Watershed Intern, *15.254*
Eastern, Southeast Europe, NIS research, training, *19.300*
emergency management, *97.026*
energy-related research, *81.049*
engineering, mathematics, sciences, *85.200*
engineering, sciences, computing, technology, *85.100*
English Language Program, BECA, *19.421*
environment-related, Udall, *85.400, 85.401*
environmental health, biometry, *93.115*
environmental health hazards research, *93.113*
environmental health sciences, *93.894*
Environmental justice, EPA, *66.307*
environmental management studies, EPA, *66.952*
EPA New England Regional Office projects, *66.110*
EPA research, graduate, undergraduate, *66.513*
EPA STAR graduate fellowships, *66.514*
EPA studies, special purpose assistance, *66.610*
EPA training, fellowships, *66.709*
EPA high school water quality internships, *66.463*
food sciences, graduate, *10.210*
food sciences, Minority Scholars Program, *10.220*
foreign language, area studies, doctoral research abroad, *84.022*
foreign language, area studies, faculty research abroad, *84.019*
foreign language, area studies, group projects abroad, *84.021*
foreign language, area studies, NSEP, *12.551*
foreign languages, graduate, *84.015*
Fulbright-Hays Program, lecturers, professors, scholars studies abroad, *19.401*
Fulbright Program, graduate studies abroad, *19.400*
genetics research, *93.172*
geologic mapping, graduate research, *15.810*
geriatrics faculty, *93.156, 93.250*
graduate academic, *84.200*
Harry S Truman Memorial Scholarship Act, *85.001*
health administration, planning, graduate, *93.962*
health careers, disadvantaged, *93.822*
health careers, preprofessional, Indians, *93.971*
health, minority disparities research, *93.307*
health professions, disadvantaged, *93.925*
health professions faculty loan repayments, disadvantaged, *93.923*
health professions, Indians, *93.219, 93.972*
health professions, minority faculty, students, *93.157*
health professions, pregradate Indians, *93.123*
health professions, rural specialists, *93.192*
health research infrastructure resources, *93.389*
health research, rural, *93.155*
health services NRSA, *93.225*

heart, vascular disease research, 93.837
higher education, Indians, 15.114
higher education, minority faculty, 84.031
history, government, social studies teachers, 85.500
honors scholarships, 84.185
hospital administration graduate, 93.962
HUD housing, urban development doctoral research, 14.516, 14.517
human development, clinical, biomedical, behavioral research, 93.865
humanities, 45.160, 45.161, 84.170, 85.300
Indian Employment Assistance, 15.108
Indians, graduate, 15.059
Indians, Haskell and SIPI, 15.058
Indians, tribal grants, 15.022
information security research, NSA, 12.902
international, area studies, graduate, 84.015
international public policy, minority students, 84.269
international, undergraduates, BECA, 19.425
James Madison Memorial Fellowship Act, 85.500
Junior Duck Stamp Contest, FWS, 15.644
kidney diseases, hematology, urology research, 93.849
Leveraging Educational Assistance Partnership (LEAP), 84.069
librarians, medical, 93.879
low-income secondary students, TRIO supportive services, 84.334
lung diseases research, 93.838
Madison fellowships, secondary school teachers, 85.500
marine, maritime studies, graduate, 11.429
mathematical sciences, NSA, 12.901
mathematics, science teachers, OESE, 84.366
mental health personnel, 93.244
mental health research, 93.281, 93.282
merchant marine, 20.806, 20.807
microbiology, infectious diseases research, 93.856
migrants, 84.141
Morris K. Udall Scholarship and Excellence in National Environmental and Native American Public Policy Act of 1992, 85.400, 85.401, 85.402
National Health Service Corps, 93.288
National Institute for Literacy, 84.257
native Americans, Udall congressional, 85.402
Navy research, 12.300
neurological disorders research, 93.853
NIH General Research Loan Repayment Program, 93.232
NIH intramural research, 93.140
NIH undergraduate, disadvantaged, 93.187
NOAA Educational Partnerships Program, minority, 11.481
NSF behavioral, social, economic sciences, 47.075
NSF engineering, mathematics, science education, 47.076
NSF graduate, undergraduate, 47.041
NSF international science, engineering, 47.079
nuclear sciences, 81.114
nurse anesthetist, 93.124
nursing, 93.359
nursing, disadvantaged students, 93.178
nursing professionals, graduate, 93.358

Nursing Research, 93.361
ocean service intern program, 11.480
overseas research, 84.274
Pell grants, undergraduate, 84.063
pharmacology, physiology, biorelated chemistry research, 93.859
podiatry residency, 93.181
Police Corps, officers, dependents, 16.712
Presidential management interns, 27.013
preventive medicine, 93.117
primary medical care research, 93.186
public health, graduate, 93.964
public safety officers' dependents, 16.615
public service, 85.001
rehabilitation research, 84.133
school principals, 84.363
scientific research, Army Research Office, 12.431
sleep disorders research, 93.233, 93.853
Smithsonian Institution, graduate, predoctoral, postdoctoral, 85.601
social sciences, graduate, 84.170, 85.300
social work, 93.244
teacher training seminars abroad, 84.018
toxicological research, 93.114
transportation, 20.215, 20.907
Truman Scholarship Program, public service, 85.001
undergraduate, international, BECA, 19.425
undergraduate, SEOG, 84.007
USDC postsecondary student internships, 11.702
vision research, National Eye Institute, 93.867
vocational rehabilitation personnel, 84.129
Wilson Center fellowships, 85.300
Woodrow Wilson Memorial Act of 1968, 85.300
youth, disadvantaged, Upward Bound, 84.047
see also Apprenticeship training; Disadvantaged, education; Health, medical education, training; Indian education, training; Law enforcement education, training; Minority education; National Research Service Awards; Student financial aid; Teacher education, training; Technical training; Veterans education, training
FEMA (Federal Emergency Management Agency), Department of Homeland Security (DHS), *see* Agency Index
Fertilizer
EPA Nonpoint Source Implementation Grants, 66.460
rural resource conservation, development, 10.901
sustainable agriculture research, 10.215
see also Agricultural experiment stations; Agricultural research; Pesticides
Festivals, *see* Arts, arts education; Music
FFE (Food for Education), FAS, 10.608
FFELP (Federal Family Education Loan Program), 84.032
FFVP (Fresh Fruit and Vegetable Program), FNS, 10.582
FGP (Foster Grandparent Program), 94.011
FHA (Federal Highway Administration), DOT, *see* Agency Index
FHA (Federal Housing Administration), *see* Agency Index (HUD, Housing-Federal Housing Commissioner)
FHAP (Fair Housing Assistance Program), 14.401
FHIP (Fair Housing Initiatives Program), 14.408

FHP (Forest Health Protection), USFS, *10.680*
FHWA (Federal Highway Administration), DOT, *see* Agency Index
FIE (Fund for the Improvement of Education), *84.215*
FIFRA (Federal Insecticide, Fungicide, and Rodenticide Act), *see* Environmental health, research, services
Film, slides, film strips, *see* Audiovisual aids, film, video
FINANCIAL ASSISTANCE FOR NATIONAL CENTERS FOR COASTAL OCEAN SCIENCE, *11.426*
FINANCIAL ASSISTANCE FOR NRC LOCAL PUBLIC DOCUMENT ROOMS (LPDR), *77.005*
Fingerprints, *see* Forensic sciences; Law enforcement education, training
FIP (Forestry Incentives Program), *10.064*
FIPSE (Fund for the Improvement of Postsecondary Education), *84.116*
Fire Academy, *97.018*, 97.019, *97.043*
Fire Administration, *see* Agency Index (FEMA, U.S. Fire Administration)
Fire Grants, FEMA, *97.044*
FIRE MANAGEMENT ASSISTANCE, *97.046*
Fire Protection, BIA Facilities, *15.064*
Firearms, *see* Crime; Forensic sciences
Firefighting, fire prevention, control
  airport improvement, *20.106*
  anti-terrorism training, *16.614*
  arson, explosives analysis training, 16.012, 16.300
  BIA facilities protection, training, *15.064*
  BLM assistance, *15.228, 15.242*
  Citizen Corps, DHS, *97.053*
  Federal Fire Prevention and Control Act, *97.016, 97.018*, 97.019, *97.044, 97.055*
  federal property, fire service reimbursement, *97.016*
  FEMA Fire Grants, equipment, training, *97.044*
  FEMA Earthquake Consortium, *97.082*
  fire, emergency response staffing, FEMA, *97.083*
  Fire Management Assistance, FEMA, *97.046*
  fire standards research, *11.609*
  Forest Land Enhancement Program, *10.677*
  forest fire research, *10.202, 10.652*
  hazardous materials transport, training, 20.217
  Indian Community Fire Protection, *15.031*
  Interoperable Communications Equipment, DHS, *97.055*
  National Fire Academy, training, *97.018*, 97.019
  National Fire Plan, BLM, *15.228, 15.242*
  National Guard assistance, *12.401*
  officers' dependents educational assistance, *16.615*
  officers disability, death benefits, *16.571*
  personnel training, Federal Law Enforcement Training Center, DHS, *97.081*
  rural, financial, technical assistance, *10.664*
  rural fire and rescue services, *10.766*
  search, rescue system, *97.025*
  shipboard safety training, 20.810
  State Fire Training System Grants, *97.043*
  WMD, domestic preparedness, *97.004, 97.005, 97.006, 97.007*
  see also Civil defense; Disaster assistance;

Emergency assistance; Hazardous materials, waste; Public safety; Rescue services
Fish
  Alaska Subsistence Management, *15.636*
  anadromous, conservation, management, research, *11.405*
  Anadromous Fish Conservation Act, *11.405*
  BLM Recreation Resource Management, *15.225*
  Boating Infrastructure Grant Program, *15.622*
  Chesapeake Bay Program, *66.466*
  Chesapeake Bay Studies, education, training, *11.457*
  Clean Water Act studies, training, *66.436*
  Coast Program, FWS, *15.630*
  coastal wetlands protection, *15.614*
  Columbia River basin, *11.436*
  conservation law enforcement training, 15.602
  conservation stewardships, *15.632*
  Dingell-Johnson (D-J) Program, *15.605*
  endangered species, Indian lands, *15.051*
  endangered species, pesticides control, *66.700*
  endangered, threatened species, *15.615*
  EPA pesticides, toxic chemicals pollution prevention studies, training, outreach, *66.716*
  Fish and wildlife acts, 11.413, *11.433, 11.434, 11.435, 11.452, 11.454, 11.455, 11.457, 11.463, 11.472, 15.231*, 15.602, *15.605*, 15.608, *15.611, 15.619, 15.620, 15.621, 15.622, 15.623, 15.626, 15.628, 15.629, 15.630, 15.631, 15.636, 15.637, 15.643, 15.647, 15.811, 15.812*
  Fish, Wildlife and Plant Conservation Resource Management, BLM, *15.231*
  fishery research, *11.427*
  Forest Land Enhancement Program, *10.677*
  forestry assistance, *10.664*
  FWS Challenge Cost Share, *15.642*
  Great Lakes, consumption health effects research, *93.208*
  Great Plains Conservation, *10.900*
  Habitat Conservation, NOAA, *11.463*
  habitat incentive program, *10.914*
  Hawaii program, *11.444, 11.445*
  Indian fishing rights, *15.050*
  Indian lands, *15.039*
  Indian Rights Protection, *15.036*
  Marine Fisheries Initiative, *11.433*
  Marine Turtle Conservation Fund, FWS, *15.645*
  Multi-State Conservation Grants, *15.628*
  NOAA unallied projects, *11.452, 11.454, 11.472*
  North American Wetlands Conservation Fund, FWS, *15.623*
  Pacific Coast Salmon Treaty Act, *11.438*
  Partners for Fish and Wildlife, FWS, *15.631*
  resource management, stocking, 15.608
  rural resource conservation, development, *10.901*
  sport fish restoration, *15.605*
  undersea research, *11.430*
  USGS Cooperative Research Units Program, *15.812*
  USGS Gap Analysis Program, *15.811*
  watershed projects, *10.904*
  wildlife without borders programs, education, research, training, FWS, *15.640, 15.641*
  see also Aquaculture; Environmental management; Fisheries industry; Food

inspection, grading; Marine sciences; Public lands; Wildlife, waterfowl
FISH AND WILDLIFE MANAGEMENT ASSISTANCE, 15.608
Fish and wildlife acts, DOI, *see* Fish
Fish and Wildlife Service, DOI, *see* Agency Index (DOI, U.S. Fish and Wildlife Service)
FISH, WILDLIFE, AND PARKS PROGRAMS ON INDIAN LANDS, *15.039*
FISH, WILDLIFE AND PLANT CONSERVATION RESOURCE MANAGEMENT, *15.231*
Fish-Wilson Program, ACF, *93.583*
FISHERIES DEVELOPMENT AND UTILIZATION RESEARCH AND DEVELOPMENT GRANTS AND COOPERATIVE AGREEMENTS PROGRAM, *11.427*
FISHERIES DISASTER RELIEF, *11.477*
FISHERIES FINANCE PROGRAM, *11.415*
Fisheries industry
Alaska Subsistence Management, *15.636*
Atlantic Coast Fisheries Cooperative Management Act, *11.474*
Atlantic coast fisheries management, *11.474*
Chesapeake Bay Program, *66.466*
Chesapeake Bay Studies, education, training, *11.457*
Columbia River basin, *11.436*
commercial, sport fishing statistics, southeast area, *11.434*
Community Development Quota groups, *11.415*
disaster assistance, *11.407*
economic loss payments, *11.408*, *19.204*
education, migrant children, *84.011*
elementary, secondary education coordination, migrant children, *84.144*
environmental systems research, NOAA, *11.432*
Even Start, migrant education, *84.214*
Fisheries Disaster Relief, *11.477*
Fishermen's Protective Act, *19.204*
fishery management councils, *11.441*
Hawaii program, *11.445*, *11.444*
Indian fishing rights, *15.050*
Indian lands, *15.039*, *15.052*
Indian Rights Protection, *15.036*
Individual Fishing Quota financing, *11.415*
Interjurisdictional Fisheries Act of 1986, *11.407*
Magnuson Fishery Conservation Act, *11.433*
Magnuson-Stevens Fishery Conservation and Management Act, *11.434*, *11.437*, *11.441*, *11.445*, *11.454*, *11.477*
Marine Fisheries Initiative, *11.433*
marine mammal data, *11.439*
Mitchell Act, NOAA, *11.436*
NMFS marine education, science projects, *11.455*
NOAA unallied projects, *11.452*, *11.454*, *11.472*
Outer Continental Shelf Lands Act Amendments of 1978, *11.408*
Pacific fisheries data, *11.437*
Pacific Salmon Treaty Program, *11.438*
product inspection, certification, 11.413
research, development, *11.427*
resources research, management, *11.407*
Saltonstall-Kennedy Act, *11.427*, *11.433*, *11.452*
Section 7, Guaranty Fund, *19.204*
ship construction, reconstruction tax deferments, *20.812*

shipping, ship construction, reconstruction subsidies, *20.808*
shoreside facilities financing, *11.415*
southeast marine area monitoring, *11.435*
Title IV, Contingency Fund, *11.408*
vessel financing, *11.415*
vessel seizure, damage, *19.204*
wildlife without borders programs, education, research, training, FWS, *15.640*, *15.641*
see also Aquaculture; Coastal zone; Farm workers; Fish; Food inspection, grading; Maritime industry; Water navigation
FISHERMEN'S CONTINGENCY FUND, *11.408*
FISHERMEN'S GUARANTY FUND, *19.204*
Fishermen's Protective Act, *see* Fisheries industry
FISHERY PRODUCTS INSPECTION AND CERTIFICATION, 11.413
FLRP (Faculty Loan Repayment Program), HRSA, *93.923*
FLAS (Foreign Language and Area Studies), fellowships, *84.015*
FLEP (Forest Land Enhancement Program), *10.677*
FLP (Forest Legacy Program), *10.676*
Flexible Subsidy Fund, housing, *14.164*
FLOOD CONTROL PROJECTS, 12.106
FLOOD INSURANCE, *97.022*
FLOOD MITIGATION ASSISTANCE, *97.029*
FLOOD PLAIN MANAGEMENT SERVICES, 12.104
Flood prevention, control
Automated Flood Warning System, NOAA, *11.400*
beach erosion control, 12.101
coastal protection works rehabilitation, 12.102
coastal zones management, *11.419*
compensation to states, Corps of Engineers projects, *12.112*
dam safety program, FEMA, *97.041*
emergency dredging, 12.109
emergency flood fighting, 12.103
farmland rehabilitation, *10.054*
FEMA community assistance program, *97.023*
FEMA Community Disaster Loans, *97.030*
Flood Control Acts, 12.102, 12.103, 12.104, 12.105, 12.106, 12.108, 12.111, *12.112*
flood-damaged facilities, 12.102
Flood Disaster Protection Act, *97.023*, *97.045*, *97.070*
flood hazard mapping, FEMA, *97.045*
flood insurance, *97.022*
Flood Mitigation Assistance, FEMA, *97.029*
flood plain data, services, 12.104
flood plain management, 10.906, *97.022*
flood prevention assistance, 12.111
Hazard Mitigation Grant, *97.039*
Hydrologic Research, *11.462*
Indian lands, dam safety, *15.049*, *15.065*
levee construction, 12.111
Map Modernization Management Support, FEMA, *97.070*
National Flood Insurance Act, *59.008*, *97.022*, *97.023*, *97.029*, *97.045*, *97.070*
Pre-Disaster Mitigation, FEMA, *97.017*, *97.047*
Public Law 84-99 Program, 12.102
river bank protection, 12.105
search, rescue system, *97.025*

Flood prevention, control *(continued)*
Small Flood Control Projects, 12.106
snagging, clearing waterways, 12.108
snowmelt preparations, 12.111
snowmelt surveys, 10.907
training, EMI home study courses, 97.027
watershed projects, *10.904*
Watershed Protection and Flood Prevention Act, *10.916*
Watershed Rehabilitation Program, *10.916*
watershed, river basin projects, 10.906
see also Agricultural conservation; Climate; Coastal zone; Disaster assistance; Emergency assistance; Environmental management; Hurricanes; Irrigation; Soil conservation; Water *entries*; Wetlands
Fluoridation programs, *see* Dental health, dental research; Preventive health services
FMA (Flood Mitigation Assistance), *97.029*
FMCS (Federal Mediation and Conciliation Service), 34.001 through 34.002
FmHA (Farmers Home Administration), *see* Agency Index (USDA, Farm Service Agency *and* Rural Housing Service)
FMNP (Farmers' Market Nutrition Program), *10.572*
FNS (Food and Nutrition Service), USDA, *see* Agency Index (USDA, Food and Consumer Service)
Folk arts, *see* Arts, arts education
Food, Agriculture, Conservation, and Trade Act of 1990 (FACTA), *see* International commerce, investment
FOOD AND AGRICULTURAL SCIENCES NATIONAL NEEDS GRADUATE FELLOWSHIP GRANTS, *10.210*
Food and Drug Administration (FDA), HHS, *see* Agency Index
FOOD AND DRUG ADMINISTRATION—RESEARCH, *93.103*
Food and Nutrition Service (FNS), USDA, *see* Agency Index (USDA, Food and Consumer Service)
Food banks, *see* Agricultural commodities, stabilization; Food, nutrition
Food distribution, *see* Food inspection, grading; Food, nutrition; Homeless persons; Public assistance
FOOD DISTRIBUTION PROGRAM ON INDIAN RESERVATIONS, *10.567*
FOOD DONATION, 10.550
FOOD FOR EDUCATION, *10.608*
FOOD FOR PEACE DEVELOPMENT ASSISTANCE PROGRAM, *98.007*
FOOD FOR PEACE EMERGENCY PROGRAM, *98.008*
FOOD FOR PROGRESS, *10.606*
Food inspection, grading
Agricultural Fair Practices Act, 10.162, 10.163
agricultural product grading, 10.162
Avian Influenza Indemnity Program, *10.029*
dairy indemnity, *10.053*
Federal Meat Inspection Act, *10.475*, 10.477
fishery products inspection, grading, 11.413
food safety, security monitoring, FDA, *93.448*
international training, *10.962*
interstate plant, animal disease, pest control, *10.025*
meat, poultry, *10.475*, 10.477
NOAA Unallied Industry Projects, *11.452*
perishable agricultural commodities, 10.165
seafood research, *11.417*
see also Agricultural marketing; Aquaculture; Complaint investigation; Consumers, consumer services; Fisheries industry; Food, nutrition research, sciences; Livestock industry; Poultry, egg products
Food, nutrition
advertising, deceptive, misleading, complaints, 36.001
AIDS-afflicted persons, HOPWA, *14.241*
Child and Adult Care Food Program, *10.558*
children, state administrative expenses, *10.560*
children, summer food program, *10.559*
Community Food Projects, USDA, *10.225*
commodity foods, supplemental, *10.565*
community food service agencies, *10.568*
Community Services Block Grant, *93.569*, *93.571*
elderly, home services, education, *93.045*
elderly Indians, *93.047*
elders, counseling, *93.043*
Emerson Humanitarian Trust, FSA, *10.079*
emergency assistance, FEMA, *97.024*
Emergency Food Assistance, *10.569*
Extension Service, *10.500*
Farmers' Market Nutrition Program (FMNP), *10.572*
Food and agriculture acts, *10.220*, 10.550, *10.565*, *10.567*
food donation program, 10.550, *10.560*
Food for Education, FAS, *10.608*
Food for Peace Title II Partners, *98.005*
Food for Progress, FAS, *10.606*, *10.607*
Food Security Act of 1985, *10.069*, *10.072*, 10.153, 10.162, *10.767*, *10.912*, *10.913*, *10.918*, *10.919*, *10.921*, *10.960*, *10.961*, *10.962*
Food Security Wheat Reserve (Emerson Humanitarian Trust), FSA, *10.079*
Food Stamp Act of 1977, *10.225*, *10.303*, *10.551*, *10.561*, *10.567*, *10.580*
food stamp program access research, *10.580*
Food Stamps, *10.551*, *10.561*
Fresh Fruit and Vegetable Program, FNS, *10.582*
Head Start, *93.600*
Homeland Security—Agricultural, *10.304*
Hunger Prevention Act of 1988, *10.569*
Indian reservations, *10.567*
international, Food For Peace, USAID, *98.005*, *98.007*, *98.008*
international humanitarian relief goods transport, USAID, *98.010*
international, Ocean Freight Reimbursement, USAID, *98.003*
milk program, children, *10.556*
nutrition education, 10.163
Nutrition Services Incentive Program, AOA, *93.053*
Puerto Rico, *10.566*
rural facilities, *10.766*
School Breakfast Program, *10.553*
School Lunch Program, *10.555*
schools, Team Nutrition Grants, FNS, *10.574*

senior centers, *93.044, 93.045*
Senior Farmers Market Nutrition Program, FNS, *10.576*
WIC Farmers' Market Nutrition Program (FMNP), *10.572*
women, infants, children (WIC), *10.557, 10.565, 10.578*
see also Emergency assistance; Food *entries*; Home economics; Home management; School breakfast, lunch; Volunteers

Food, nutrition research, sciences
agricultural, *10.203, 10.206*
alternative, complementary medicine research, training, *93.213*
cancer, *93.393, 93.395, 93.396, 93.399*
challenge grants, *10.217*
CSREES Integrated Programs, *10.303*
1890 institutions support, *10.216*
food, drug interaction, FDA, *93.103*
food pollutants, fish, *11.427*
food stamp program access, *10.580*
graduate fellowships, *10.210*
Indians, health professions scholarships, *93.972*
Minority Scholars Program, scholarships, *10.220*
National Agricultural Library, 10.700
NIH, digestive diseases, *93.848*
NOAA Unallied Industry Projects, *11.452*
organic agriculture, CSREES, *10.307*
public health graduate traineeships, *93.964*
research, SBIR, *10.212*
secondary, postsecondary agriculture education, *10.226*
tribal colleges, *10.221, 10.222*
USDA special research grants, *10.200*
see also Agricultural research, sciences; Food inspection, grading; Health, medical research; Health professions; Minority education; Pesticides; Science education

Food Safety and Inspection Service, USDA, *see* Agency Index
FOOD SAFETY AND SECURITY MONITORING PROJECT, *93.448*
Food stamps, *see* Food, nutrition; Public assistance
FOOD STAMP PROGRAM OUTREACH GRANTS, *10.580*
FOOD STAMPS, *10.551*
Foreign Agricultural Service (FAS), USDA, *see* Agency Index
Foreign aid, *see* International programs, studies; International commerce, investment
Foreign area studies, *see* International programs, studies
Foreign Assistance acts, *see* International commerce, investment
FOREIGN ASSISTANCE TO AMERICAN SCHOOLS AND HOSPITALS ABROAD, *98.006*
Foreign claims, *see* Complaint investigation; Insurance; International commerce, investment; Trade adjustment assistance
Foreign commerce, investment, *see* International commerce, investment
FOREIGN INVESTMENT FINANCING, *70.002*
FOREIGN INVESTMENT INSURANCE, *70.003*
Foreign Language and Area Studies (FLAS), DOED, *84.015*

FOREIGN LANGUAGE ASSISTANCE, *84.293*
Foreign languages
BECA English Language Fellow Program, *19.421*
bilingual, bicultural health demonstrations, *93.105*
doctoral research abroad, *84.022*
Eastern, Southeast Europe, NIS, *19.300*
faculty fellowships, research abroad, *84.019*
Fulbright program, educational exchange, *19.401*
foreign information access, education technology, *84.337*
group projects abroad, training, *84.021*
instruction research, *84.017*
international business education centers, *84.220*
international public policy programs, minority student fellowships, *84.269*
Language Resource Centers, *84.229*
model elementary, secondary study programs, *84.293*
National Security Education Program, DOD, *12.550*
native American language preservation, *93.587*
NSA language grants, *12.900*
NSEP training, *12.551*
resource centers, graduate fellowships, *84.015*
Star Schools Program, *84.203*
teacher training seminars abroad, *84.018*
translations, NEA, *45.024*
undergraduate programs, *84.016*
see also Bilingual education, services; English as a second language; Humanities *entries*; International programs, studies

FOREIGN MARKET DEVELOPMENT COOPERATOR PROGRAM [USDA], *10.600*
Foreign persons, *see* Aliens, immigrants, refugees; Farm workers
Foreign trade, *see* Agricultural marketing; International commerce, investment; Trade adjustment assistance
FOREIGN-TRADE ZONES IN THE UNITED STATES, 11.111
Foreigners, *see* Aliens, immigrants, refugees; Farm workers
FORENSIC CASEWORK DNA BACKLOG REDUCTION PROGRAM, *16.743*
FORENSIC DNA CAPACITY ENHANCEMENT PROGRAM, *16.741*
Forensic sciences
ATF training, 16.012
Combined DNA Index System (CODIS), *16.307*
controlled substances programs, facilities, training, *16.579*
DEA Microgram, 16.003
DNA casework backlog reduction, *16.743*
DNA capacity enhancement, *16.741*
DNA laboratory improvement, training, *16.564*
document analysis, Secret Service, 97.015
FBI Field Police Training, 16.302
FBI training, 16.300, 16.301
forensic sciences improvement, *16.742*
laboratory services, 16.301
narcotics, drug programs, personnel training, 16.004
narcotics, drugs, DEA laboratory assistance, 16.001
National Center for Missing and Exploited Children, *97.076*

Forensic sciences *(continued)*
  Paul Coverdell National Forensic Sciences
    Improvement Act of 2002, *16.742*
  research, *16.560*
  see also Chemicals, chemistry; FBI; Law
    enforcement education, training; Legal services
FOREST HEALTH PROTECTION, *10.680*
FOREST LAND ENHANCEMENT PROGRAM,
  10.677
FOREST LEGACY PROGRAM, *10.676*
FOREST PRODUCTS LAB: TECHNOLOGY
  MARKETING UNIT, *10.674*
Forest Service, USDA, *see* Agency Index
FOREST STEWARDSHIP PROGRAM, *10.678*
Forestry
  animal damage control, *10.028*
  BLM firefighting assistance, *15.228*, *15.242*
  cooperative assistance, states, *10.664*
  Cooperative Forestry Assistance Act of 1978,
    10.064, *10.664*, *10.675*, *10.678*, *10.680*
  Cooperative Forestry Research Act of 1962, *10.202*
  Economic Recovery, forest-dependent
    communities, *10.670*
  farm-forest enterprise loans, *10.406*
  Fire Management Assistance, FEMA, *97.046*
  Forest and Rangeland Renewable Resources
    Research Act of 1978, *10.652*
  Forest Health Protection, USFS, *10.680*
  Forest Land Enhancement Program, *10.677*
  Forest Legacy Program, *10.676*
  Forest Stewardship Program, *10.678*
  Forestry Incentives Program, NRCS, *10.064*
  Indian lands, *15.035*
  international research exchanges, *10.961*
  international research training, *10.962*
  McIntire-Stennis Act, *10.202*
  Minority Scholars Program, scholarships, *10.220*
  National Forest Dependent Rural Communities
    Economic Diversification Act of 1990, 10670
  national forests, USDA payments for schools,
    roads, *10.665*
  national grasslands, USDA payments to counties,
    10.666
  natural landmarks registry, 15.910
  New Mexico, forest restoration, *10.679*
  research, *10.202*, *10.652*
  Rural Development, *10.672*
  SBIR program, *10.212*
  small wood species, USFS Technology Marketing
    Unit, *10.674*
  Tongass National Forest, disaster fund, *10.671*
  Tree Assistance Program, FSA, *10.082*
  Urban Community Forestry, *10.675*
  urban forestry, *10.664*
  watershed, river basin projects, 10.906
  see also Agricultural experiment stations;
    Agricultural marketing; Plants; Public lands;
    Recreation; Timber industry; Woodlands
FORESTRY INCENTIVES PROGRAM, *10.064*
FORESTRY ON INDIAN LANDS, *15.035*
FORESTRY RESEARCH, *10.652*
FORMULA GRANTS FOR OTHER THAN
  URBANIZED AREAS [DOT], *20.509*
Fossil energy, *see* Coal mining; Energy *entries*
FOSSIL ENERGY RESEARCH AND
  DEVELOPMENT, *81.089*

Foster care, *see* Child care services; Maternal, child
  health, welfare; Parenting
FOSTER CARE—TITLE IV-E, *93.658*
FOSTER GRANDPARENT PROGRAM, *94.011*
Four-H projects, *10.500*
FPMS (Flood Plain Management Services), 12.104
Free Use of Mineral Material, 15.214
Freedom of Access to Clinic Entrances (FACE) Act,
  16.105
FREELY ASSOCIATED STATES—EDUCATION
  GRANT PROGRAM, *84.256*
FRESH FRUIT AND VEGETABLE PROGRAM,
  10.582
Fruit
  Crop Insurance, *10.450*
  disaster assistance, noninsured crops, *10.451*
  Fresh Fruit and Vegetable Program, FNS, *10.582*
  inspection, grading, 10.162
  Market News, 10.153
  market promotion, protection, 10.163
  marketing agreements, orders, 10.155
  plant disease control, *10.025*
  Special Apple Program, *10.075*
  Special Research Grants, *10.200*
  unfair marketing practices, 10.165
  see also Agricultural *entries*; Food inspection,
    grading; Plants
FSEOG (Federal Supplemental Educational
  Opportunity Grants), *84.007*
FSP (Forest Stewardship Program), *10.678*
FTA (Federal Transit Administration), DOT, *see*
  Agency Index
FTC (Federal Trade Commission), 36.001
Fuels, *see* Coal mining; Energy *entries*; Mining,
  mining industries; Nuclear sciences,
  technology; Solar energy
Fulbright-Hays Act, *see* International programs,
  studies (Mutual Educational and Cultural
  Exchange Act)
Fulbright-Hays Program, *19.401*, *19.402*
Fulbright Program, *19.400*, *19.408*
FUND FOR RURAL AMERICA—RESEARCH,
  EDUCATION, AND EXTENSION
  ACTIVITIES, *10.224*
FUND FOR THE IMPROVEMENT OF
  EDUCATION, *84.215*
FUND FOR THE IMPROVEMENT OF
  POSTSECONDARY EDUCATION, *84.116*
Fund for U.S. Artists at International Festivals and
  Exhibitions, BECA, *19.413*
Futures market, *see* Commodity futures market
FWS (Federal Work-Study), *84.033*

GAANN (Graduate Assistance in Areas of National
  Need), DOED, *84.200*
GAINING EARLY AWARENESS AND
  READINESS FOR UNDERGRADUATE
  PROGRAMS, *84.334*
Galleries, *see* Arts, arts education; Museums,
  galleries
GANG-FREE SCHOOLS AND COMMUNITIES—
  COMMUNITY-BASED GANG
  INTERVENTION, *16.544*
GANG RESISTANCE EDUCATION AND
  TRAINING, *16.737*
GAP ANALYSIS PROGRAM [USGS], *15.811*

GAP (General Assistance Program) for Tribes, EPA, 66.926
Gas, *see* Energy *entries*
GDA (Global Development Alliance), USAID, 98.011
GEAR-UP (Gaining Early Awareness and Readiness for Undergraduate Programs), DOED, 84.334
GECs (Geriatrics Education Centers), 93.969
GEMs (Growing Equity Mortgages), 14.172
General Assistance Program for Tribes (GAP), EPA, 66.926
GENERAL RESEARCH AND TECHNOLOGY ACTIVITY [HUD], 14.506
General Research Loan Repayment Program (GR-LRP), NIH, 93.232
General Services Administration (GSA), 39.002 through 39.009
Genetics
aging, research, 93.866
agricultural, biotechnology risk assessment, 10.219
alcoholism, biomedical research, 93.273
allergy, immunology, transplantation research, 93.855
arthritis, musculoskeletal, skin diseases research, 93.846
cancer research, 93.393, 93.396
Centers for Genomics and Public Health, 93.063
Combined DNA Index System (CODIS), FBI, 16.307
deafness, communicative disorders research, 93.173
diabetes, endocrinology, metabolism research, 93.847
disease testing, maternal, child, information, research, training, 93.110
DNA laboratory improvement, training, DOJ, 16.564
environmental health hazards research, 93.113
human genomes research, 93.172
mental health research, 93.242
neurological diseases research, 93.853
NOAA Unallied Industry Projects, 11.452
plant genome research, NSF, 47.074
pharmacology, physiology, biorelated chemistry research, training, 93.859
research, research infrastructure resources, training, NIH, 93.389
see also Forensic sciences; Health, medical research; Maternal, child health, welfare
Genomes, *see* Genetics
GEO (Geosciences), NSF, 47.050
GEODETIC SURVEYS AND SERVICES (GEODESY AND APPLICATIONS OF THE NATIONAL GEODETIC REFERENCE SYSTEM), 11.400
Geography, *see* Census services; Earth sciences; Geology; Maps, charts; Social sciences
Geological Survey, DOI, *see* Agency Index
Geology
earthquake research, 15.807
energy-related basic research, 81.049
energy-related research, geothermal, 81.087
FEMA Earthquake Consortium, 97.082
geologic mapping, 15.810
geosciences research, 47.050

geospatial data clearinghouse, 15.809
hydrologic, geologic data, coal mining, 15.250
National Geologic Mapping Reauthorization Act of 1997, 15.810
natural landmarks registry, 15.910
Organic Act of 1879, 15.808, 15.809
research, resource surveys, mapping, 15.808
water resources research, 15.805
see also Earth sciences; Earthquakes; Mineral resources; Physical sciences; Scientific research
GEOSCIENCES, 47.050
Geothermal energy, *see* Energy *entries*
GERIATRIC ACADEMIC CAREER AWARDS, 93.250
GERIATRIC EDUCATION CENTERS, 93.969
Geriatric Fellowships, 93.156
GERIATRIC TRAINING FOR PHYSICIANS, DENTISTS AND BEHAVIORAL/MENTAL HEALTH PROFESSIONALS, 93.156
Geriatrics, *see* Aging and the aged; Health *entries*
Geriatrics Education Centers (GECs), 93.969
Gerontology, *see* Aging and the aged; Health, medical research
GI Insurance, 64.103
Gifted and talented students, *see* Education counseling
Gilman International Scholarships, BECA, 19.425
Glaucoma research, 93.867
GLOBAL AIDS, 93.067
Global AIDS, HRSA, 93.266
GLOBAL DEVELOPMENT ALLIANCE [USAID], 98.011
GLOBUS (Global Business Opportunities), ESA-USDC, 11.026
Goats, *see* Agricultural marketing; Livestock industry
Goldwater scholarship program, 85.200
Gonzalez-Cranston National Affordable Housing Act, *see* National housing acts (National Affordable Housing Act)
Good Neighbor Initiative, HUD, 14.311
Government
BECA English Language Fellow Program, legislators, 19.421
Census Bureau data, 11.001
Census Intergovernmental Services, 11.004
census special tabulations, 11.005
College Pollworker Program, 90.400
community development work-study, HUD, 14.512
compensation to states for federally-acquired lands, flood control, navigation, hydropower projects, 12.112
disasters, Public Assistance Grants, FEMA, 97.036
Election Assistance for Individuals with Disabilities, ACF, 93.617, 93.618
employees, Anti-Terrorism and Emergency Assistance Program, DOJ, 16.321
environmental management studies fellowships, EPA, 66.952
Federal Citizen Information Center, 39.009
Federal Records Centers, 89.001
federal-state tax information exchange, 21.004
FEMA Community Disaster Loans, 97.030
Fulbright American Studies Institutes, BECA, 19.418

Government *(continued)*
geodetic surveys, *11.400*
Global Development Alliance, USAID, *98.011*
Help America Vote Act of 2002, *90.400, 90.401*
historical documents collection, preservation, training, *89.003*
intergovernmental exchange of personnel, 27.011
intergovernmental exchange, Presidential Management Interns, 27.013
international, education exchange, *84.304*
international peace, conflict resolution, *91.001, 91.002*
international public policy, minority student fellowships, *84.269*
international, USAID programs, *98.001*
International Visitors Program, BECA, *19.402*
Middle Eastern Partnership Initiative, 19.500
National Archives and Records Administration Act of 1984, 89.001, *89.003*
National Archives Reference Services, 89.001
native Americans, Udall congressional internships, *85.402*
officials misconduct, prosecution, 16.109
Professional Exchanges, BECA, *19.415*
public service career scholarships, *85.001*
publications, depository libraries, 40.001
publications sales, 40.002
small business, agriculture regulatory ombudsman, *59.053*
state voting equipment payments, *90.401*
statistical area boundaries, census, 11.003
teaching, Madison fellowships, *85.500*
telecommunications infrastructure, *11.552*
U.S. insular areas, *15.875*
USDC postsecondary student internships, *11.702*
voting rights, 16.104
Woodrow Wilson Center fellowships, *85.300*
young political leaders, international exchange, *19.403*
see also Aliens, immigrants, refugees; Civil rights; Complaint investigation; Federal employment; Government contracts; History; Indian affairs; Information *entries*; International programs, studies; Legislation; Publications; Social sciences; U.S. possessions, territories
Government Bookstore, 40.002
Government contracts
Davis-Bacon Act, 17.201, 17.303
DOD procurement assistance, *12.002*
Economic Opportunity Act of 1964, 59.009
employment discrimination, 16.101, 17.301
federal contract compliance, 17.301
minority business development, *11.803*
SBA procurement assistance, disadvantaged, 59.006, *59.049*
small business procurement technical assistance, 59.009
wage, hour standards, 17.303
Walsh-Healy Public Contracts Act, 17.303
see also Business development; Civil rights; Disadvantaged, business development; Indian economic, business development; Minority business enterprise; Small business; Small Business Innovation Research (SBIR)
Government employment, *see* Federal employment
Government Information Locator Service, 11.650
Government Printing Office (GPO), 40.001 through 40.002
GOVERNMENT PUBLICATIONS SALES AND DISTRIBUTION, 40.002
Governmental statistics, *see* Agricultural statistics; Census services; Computer products, sciences, services; Economics, research, statistics; Information *entries*; Publications; Statistics
GPO (Government Printing Office), 40.001 through 40.002
GR-LRP (General Research Loan Repayment Program), NIH, *93.232*
GRADUATE ASSISTANCE IN AREAS OF NATIONAL NEED [DOED], *84.200*
Graduate fellowships, *see* Fellowships, scholarships, traineeships
Graduate Research Fellowship Program, DOJ, *16.562*
Graduated Payment Mortgage Program, *14.159*
Grain, *see* Feed grains
GRANT PROGRAM TO ESTABLISH A FUND FOR FINANCING WATER AND WASTEWATER PROJECTS [USDA], *10.864*
GRANTING OF PATENT LICENSES, 81.003
GRANTS FOR AGRICULTURAL RESEARCH—COMPETITIVE RESEARCH GRANTS, *10.206*
GRANTS FOR AGRICULTURAL RESEARCH, SPECIAL RESEARCH GRANTS, *10.200*
GRANTS FOR DENTAL PUBLIC HEALTH RESIDENCY TRAINING, *93.236*
GRANTS FOR EDUCATION, PREVENTION, AND EARLY DETECTION OF RADIOGENETIC CANCERS AND DISEASES, *93.257*
GRANTS FOR PREVENTIVE MEDICINE, *93.117*
GRANTS FOR PUBLIC WORKS AND ECONOMIC DEVELOPMENT FACILITIES, *11.300*
GRANTS FOR STATE ASSESSMENTS AND RELATED ACTIVITIES [DOED], *84.369*
GRANTS FOR STATE LOAN REPAYMENT PROGRAM [HHS], *93.165*
GRANTS FOR TRAINING IN PRIMARY CARE MEDICINE AND DENTISTRY, *93.884*
GRANTS-IN-AID FOR RAILROAD SAFETY—STATE PARTICIPATION, *20.303*
GRANTS TO ENCOURAGE ARREST POLICIES AND ENFORCEMENT OF PROTECTION ORDERS, *16.590*
GRANTS TO INCREASE ORGAN DONATIONS, *93.134*
GRANTS TO PROVIDE OUTPATIENT EARLY INTERVENTION SERVICES WITH RESPECT TO HIV DISEASE, *93.918*
GRANTS TO REDUCE VIOLENT CRIMES AGAINST WOMEN ON CAMPUS, *16.525*
GRANTS TO STATES FOR ACCESS AND VISITATION PROGRAMS [ACF], *93.597*
GRANTS TO STATES FOR CONSTRUCTION OF STATE HOME FACILITIES, *64.005*
GRANTS TO STATES FOR INCARCERATED YOUTH OFFENDERS, *84.331*
GRANTS TO STATES FOR OPERATION OF OFFICES OF RURAL HEALTH, *93.913*

GRANTS TO STATES FOR OPERATION OF QUALIFIED HIGH-RISK POOLS [HHS], *93.780*
Graphic arts, *see* Arts, arts education; Audiovisual aids, film, video
GRASSLAND RESERVE PROGRAM, *10.920*
GREAT APES CONVERSATION [DOI], *15.629*
GREAT (Gang Resistance Education and Training), BJA, *16.737*
Great Lakes
  anadromous fish resources management, *11.405*
  Beach Monitoring and Notification Program, EPA, *66.472*
  Clean Vessel Act, pumpout/dump stations, *15.616*
  coastal wetlands protection, *15.614*
  coastal zone management, *11.419*
  ecosystem restoration, *66.469*
  EPA international financial assistance projects, *66.931*
  estuary research reserves, *11.420*
  fish consumption health effects research, *93.208*
  Great Lakes Critical Programs Act of 1990, *93.208*
  Great Lakes Legacy Act, *66.469*
  port security grants, DHS, *97.056*
  research, Coastal Ocean Program, *11.478*
  shipping, ship construction, reconstruction financing, *20.802*
  shipping, ship construction, reconstruction subsidies, *20.808*
  see also Coastal zone; Water navigation
GREAT LAKES HUMAN HEALTH EFFECTS RESEARCH, *93.208*
GREAT LAKES PROGRAM, *66.469*
GREAT PLAINS CONSERVATION, *10.900*
GREATER OPPORTUNITIES RESEARCH PROGRAM [EPA], *66.515*
GREATER RESEARCH OPPORTUNITIES FELLOWSHIP PROGRAM [EPA], *66.513*
GROUND AND SURFACE WATER CONSERVATION—ENVIRONMENTAL QUALITY INCENTIVES PROGRAM, *10.918*
Group homes
  AIDS-afflicted persons, *14.241*
  disabled, supportive housing, *14.181*
  emergency housing, homeless, *14.231*
  facilities, assisted living, care, nursing home, *14.129*
  food donations, commodities, *10.569*
  handicapped, independent living, *84.132, 84.169*
  juveniles, half-way houses, *16.540*
  meals services, elderly, handicapped, *93.045*
  rehabilitation personnel training, *84.263, 84.264*
  rural facilities, *10.766*
  SED, children, adolescents, mental health services, *93.104*
  Senior Companion Program, *94.016*
  Transitional Housing, homeless *14.235*
  veterans, homeless, DVA provider grants, *64.024*
  vocational rehabilitation personnel training, *84.129, 84.275*
  see also Disabled, handicapped, housing; Homeless persons; Housing, congregate; Maternal, child health, welfare
Group practice, *see* Health facilities *entries*
Group Projects Abroad, DOED, *84.021*
Growing Equity Mortgages (GEMs), *14.172*

GROWTH MANAGEMENT PLANNING ASSISTANCE [DOD], *12.613*
GRP (Grassland Reserve Program), NRCS, *10.920*
GSA (General Services Administration), 39.002 through 39.009
Guam, *see* U.S. possessions, territories
Guaranteed Student Loans, *84.032*
Guidance counseling, testing, *see* Education counseling; Employment services; Veterans education, training; Veterans employment; Vocational education
GULF OF MEXICO PROGRAM [EPA], *66.475*
Gun control, *see* Crime
Gun Control Act, 16.309

HABITAT CONSERVATION, *11.463*
Haitians, *see* Aliens, immigrants, refugees
Halfway houses, *see* Group homes
Handicapped, *see* Disabled, handicapped *entries*
HAP (Housing Assistance Plan), CDBG, *14.218*
Harbors, *see* Coastal zone; Water navigation
HARD WHITE WHEAT INCENTIVE PROGRAM, *10.995*
Harry S Truman Scholarship Foundation, *see* Agency Index (Scholarship and Fellowship Foundations)
HARRY S TRUMAN SCHOLARSHIP PROGRAM, *85.001*
Haskell Indians Nations University, *15.058*
Hatch Act, agriculture, *10.203*
Hatcheries, *see* Aquaculture; Fish; Fisheries industry
Hawaii, Hawaii natives
  agriculture, food sciences education, *10.228*
  bilingual, bicultural health demonstrations, *93.105*
  CDBG, small cities, *14.219*
  community-based learning centers, *84.362*
  English Language Acquisition Grants, *84.365*
  fish stock enhancement, *11.445*
  Hawaii Sustainable Fisheries Development, *11.444*
  Hawaiian Homelands Homeownership Act of 2000, *14.873, 14.874*
  health promotion, disease prevention, *93.932*
  health services disparities projects, *93.100*
  housing block grants, *14.873*
  housing loan guarantees, *14.874*
  IHE community assistance, *14.515*
  language preservation, *93.587*
  minority community health coalitions, *93.137*
  museum services, *45.308*
  native American graves protection, repatriation, *15.922*
  Native American Library Services, *45.311*
  Native Hawaiian Health Care Improvement Act, *93.932*
  nursing education loan repayments, *93.908*
  SBA Native American Economic Development Assistance, *59.052*
  social, economic, self-sufficiency development, *93.612*
  supportive services, older persons, *93.047*
  vocational education, *84.259*
  WIA Native American Employment and Training, *17.265*
  see also Indian *entries*
HAWAII STOCK MANAGEMENT PROGRAM, *11.445*

HAWAII SUSTAINABLE FISHERIES
DEVELOPMENT, *11.444*
HAZARD MITIGATION GRANT [DHS], *97.039*
HAZARDOUS MATERIALS ASSISTANCE
PROGRAM, *97.021*
Hazardous Materials Emergency Preparedness
(HMEP) Training and Planning Grants, *20.703*
HAZARDOUS MATERIALS TRAINING
PROGRAM FOR IMPLEMENTATION OF
THE SUPERFUND AMENDMENT AND
REAUTHORIZATION ACT (SARA) OF
1986, *97.020*

Hazardous materials, waste
  alternative, innovative treatment research,
    training, EPA, *66.813*
  CDCP Site Specific Activities, *93.240*
  CERCLA, *12.113, 15.041, 66.110, 66.307,
    66.308, 66.309, 66.511, 66.600, 66.604,
    66.606, 66.608, 66.609, 66.802, 66.806,
    66.809, 66.813, 66.814, 66.815, 66.817,
    66.818, 66.940, 66.952, 93.142, 93.143,
    93.161, 93.202, 93.204, 93.206, 93.208,
    93.240, 97.020, 97.021*
  CERCLA response planning, training, *66.809*
  chemical emergency planning, *66.810*
  control, management, state support, *66.801*
  DOD sites, *12.113*
  DOE cleanup, technology development, *81.104*
  emergencies, state surveillance systems, *93.204*
  emergencies, tribal education, planning, training,
    97.020
  emergency management training, *97.026*
  EMI home study training courses, *97.027*
  environmental justice projects, *66.604*
  EPA consolidated research, *66.511*
  EPA Performance Partnership Grants, *66.605*
  EPA projects, One Stop Reporting, *66.608*
  EPA studies, special purpose assistance, *66.610*
  Federal Hazardous Materials Transportation Act,
    20.703
  FEMA chemical emergency planning, DOD
    stockpiles, *97.040*
  FEMA Hazardous Materials Assistance Program,
    training, *97.021*
  Hazardous and Solid Waste Amendments of 1984,
    66.812
  Hazardous Materials Transportation Act, *20.217*
  Hazardous Materials Transportation Uniform
    Safety Act of 1990, *20.303, 81.104*
  Indian lands, BIA environmental management,
    15.041
  Indian tribal public health capacity, Hanford site,
    93.202
  Inertial Confinement Fusion, stockpile
    stewardship, *81.112*
  motor carrier transport, enforcement, training, *20.217*
  multidisciplinary basic research, *93.143*
  Nuclear Energy Research Initiative, *81.121*
  nuclear, siting, *81.065*
  oil spill trust fund, USCG, *97.013*
  petroleum underground storage tanks, *66.805*
  pipelines safety, states, *20.700*
  pollution control, EPA consolidated program
    support, *66.600*
  pollution control surveys, studies, EPA R&D,
    66.510
  radon mitigation, information, training, *66.032*
  railroad transport safety, training, *20.303*
  Small Business Liability Relief and Brownfields
    Revitalization Act, *66.817*
  Superfund Amendments and Reauthorization Act
    of 1986 (SARA), *66.816*
  Superfund clean-up, *66.802*
  Superfund research, *93.143*
  Superfund technical assistance to citizens groups,
    66.806
  Superfund Worker Training Program, *93.142*
  surveys, studies, special grants, EPA, *66.606*
  toxic substances and disease registry, *93.161*
  transportation planning, training, *20.703*
  transuranic waste transport, *81.106*
  tribes, EPA management grants, *66.812*
  underground storage tanks, *66.804, 66.816*
  Waste Isolation Pilot Land Withdrawal Act,
    81.106
  waste sites health studies, *93.206*
  WMD, domestic preparedness, *97.004, 97.005,
    97.006, 97.007*
  see also Chemicals, chemistry; Environmental
    entries; Firefighting, fire prevention, control;
    Pollution abatement; Public safety; Radiation;
    Toxic substances, toxicology; Transportation;
    Urban renewal; Waste treatment, disposal
HAZARDOUS WASTE MANAGEMENT GRANT
  PROGRAM FOR TRIBES, *66.812*
HAZARDOUS WASTE MANAGEMENT STATE
  PROGRAM SUPPORT, *66.801*
HCAP (Healthy Communities Access Program),
  HRSA, *93.890*
HCFA (Health Care Financing Administration),
  HHS, *see* Agency Index (HHS, Centers for
  Medicare and Medicaid Services)
HCOP (Health Careers Opportunity Program),
  93.822
HEA *see* Higher Education Act
HEAD START, *93.600*

Head Start Program
  early childhood educator professional
    development, *84.349*
  Early Reading First, *84.359*
  food, meals assistance, *10.557, 10.558*
  grants, *93.600*
  teachers, student loan cancellations, *84.037*
  see also Disadvantaged, education; Early
    childhood education; Maternal, child health,
    welfare
HEADQUARTERS AND REGIONAL
  UNDERGROUND STORAGE TANKS
  PROGRAM, *66.816*
Headstones and markers, *see* Veterans death benefits
HEALTH ADMINISTRATION TRAINEESHIPS,
  93.962
Health and Human Services Act of 1986, USDA,
  10.767
Health care, *see* Community health services; Health,
  medical services; Preventive health services;
  Veterans health, medical services
HEALTH CARE AND OTHER FACILITIES,
  93.887
Health Care Financing Administration (HCFA),
  HHS, *see* Agency Index (HHS, Centers for
  Medicare and Medicaid Services)

HEALTH CAREERS OPPORTUNITY
PROGRAM, *93.822*
HEALTH DISPARITIES IN MINORITY
HEALTH, *93.100*
HEALTH EDUCATION AND TRAINING
CENTERS, *93.189*
Health, environmental, see Environmental *entries*
Health facilities
Assistance to Schools and Hospitals Abroad,
USAID, *98.006*
Black Lung Clinics, *93.965*
clinic entrances act enforcement, 16.105
DVA specialized resource sharing, 64.018
employee background checks, long-term care,
93.785
federal surplus personal property donations,
39.003
federal surplus property, 93.291
federal surplus real property, 39.002
health, hospital administration traineeships, *93.962*
health services research, *93.226*
hospital bioterrorism preparedness, HRSA, *93.889*
Medicaid, Medicare providers standards
compliance, *93.777*
Medicare hospital insurance, *93.773*
Metropolitan Medical Response System, FEMA,
97.071
rural computer networks, RUS, *10.855*
rural hospitals emergency services, integrated care
networks, *93.241*
Senior Companion Program, *94.016*
Small Rural Hospital Improvement, *93.301*
Specially Selected Health Projects, HRSA, *93.888*
see also Community health services; Group
homes; Health facilities construction,
rehabilitation; Health, medical services; Indian
health, medical services; Nursing homes;
Veterans health, medical services
Health facilities construction, rehabilitation
additions, improvements, energy conservation,
14.151
Assistance to Schools and Hospitals Abroad,
USAID, *98.006*
bioterrorism preparedness, HRSA, *93.996*
cancer research, centers, *93.392, 93.393, 93.394,
93.395, 93.396, 93.399*
Critical Access Hospitals mortgage insurance,
14.128
hospital bioterrorism preparedness, HRSA, *93.889*
hospitals, mortgage insurance, *14.128*
medical libraries, *93.879*
nursing, board and care, assisted living, *14.129*
Renovation or Construction Projects, *93.887*
research infrastructure, minority institutions,
93.389
rural facilities, *10.766, 93.301*
Specially Selected Health Projects, HRSA, *93.888*
U.S. insular areas, *15.875*
veterans, state home facilities, *64.005*
vocational rehabilitation, *84.126*
see also Community health services; Education
facilities; Nursing homes
Health insurance
Children's Insurance Program, CMS, *93.767*
Emergency Medical Treatment and Active Labor
Act (EMTALA), *93.784*

health care financing research, CMS, *93.779*
health care systems research, *93.226, 93.239*
Health Insurance Portability and Accountability
Act of 1996, 93.001
Healthy Community Access Program, uninsured
patients, *93.252*
HIV coverage, *93.917*
Medicaid, *93.778*
Medicaid and Medicare Patient and Program Act
of 1987, *93.667*
Medicaid fraud control, *93.775*
Medicaid, Medicare providers standards
compliance, *93.777*
Medicaid Ticket-to-Work Demonstrations, *93.769*
Medicaid Ticket-to-Work Infrastructure Grants,
disabled, *93.768*
Medicare hospital insurance, *93.773*
Medicare, Medicaid and SCHIP Benefits
Improvements Act of 2000, *93.767, 93.773,
93.774*
Medicare Part B supplementary insurance, *93.774*
Medicare Part D prescription drug insurance,
93.770
Medicare Prescription Drug, Improvements and
Modernization Act 2003 (MMA), *93.770,
93.773, 93.782, 93.783, 93.784, 93.785, 93.786*
Medicare transitional drug assistance program,
93.783, 93.782
Privacy Rule, 93.001
railroad workers, *57.001*
Social Security, disability, *96.001*
Social Security program research, demonstrations,
96.007
Specially Selected Health Projects, HRSA, *93.888*
State Pharmaceutical Assistance Programs for
MMA participants, CMS, *93.786*
state high-risk pools, *93.780, 93.781*
uninsured, state planning grants, *93.256*
see also Employee benefits; Insurance; Social
Security Act; Veterans health, medical services
Health, maternal and child, *see* Maternal, child
health, welfare
Health, medical education, training
aging care personnel, *93.048*
AIDS, NIH research education loan repayments,
93.936
AIDS-related, *93.145, 93.938*
alcoholism research, *93.271, 93.272*
allied professions, *93.191*
anesthetists, nurse, *93.124*
Area Health Education Centers Model Programs,
93.107
bilingual, bicultural demonstrations, *93.105*
bioterrorism preparedness, *93.996*
cancer-related, *93.398, 93.919*
caregiver support program, respite care, *93.052*
Children's Hospitals Graduate Medical Education
Payment, HRSA, *93.255*
clinical researchers education loan repayment,
disadvantaged, *93.308*
communicable, chronic diseases control, *93.283*
contraception, infertility research, education loan
repayments, *93.209*
developmentally disabled programs, university
centers personnel, *93.632*
disabilities prevention, *93.184*

Health, medical education, training *(continued)*
  disadvantaged, assistance, 93.342, 93.822, 93.925
  disadvantaged, NIH Clinical Research Loan Repayment Program, 93.220
  disparities researchers education loan repayment, 93.307
  DOT, emergency medical services, disasters, highway safety, 20.600
  education loan repayments, states, 93.165
  Elder Abuse Prevention, 93.041
  EMS/trauma care, rural, 93.952
  faculty education loan repayments, disadvantaged, 93.923
  family planning paramedical, paraprofessional personnel, 93.260
  Geriatric Academic Career Awards, 93.250
  geriatric education program, 93.265
  geriatrics-related, 93.156, 93.969
  Global Development Alliance, USAID, 98.011
  health center technical assistance, 93.129
  health education centers, 93.189, 93.824
  health fraud task forces, FDA, 93.447
  health planning, policy, graduate traineeships, 93.962
  health services research NRSA, 93.225
  health workforce analysis, 93.300
  Healthy Communities Access Program, HRSA, 93.890
  highway accidents, DOT, 20.600
  HIV projects, 93.928
  hospital administration, graduate, 93.962
  IHS education loan repayments, 93.164
  independent living center personnel, 84.132
  Indians, 93.123, 93.970, 93.972
  Indians, preprofessional, 93.971
  Infant Adoption Awareness Training, 93.254
  injury prevention, control, 93.136
  internal medicine, 93.884
  laboratory medicine, pathology, 93.064
  lead poisoning prevention, 93.197
  librarians, medical, 93.879
  maternal, child health, 93.110
  mental health-related, 93.244
  mental health-related, emergency assistance, 93.982
  minority Centers of Excellence, 93.157
  minority health status improvement, 93.004
  native Americans, Udall fellowships, 85.400, 85.401
  neurological disorders research, minority faculty, 93.853
  NHSC education loan repayments, 93.162
  NHSC education scholarships, 93.288
  NIH General Research Loan Repayment Program, 93.232
  NIH Undergraduate Scholarship Program, 93.187
  Nurse Education, Practice and Retention Program, 93.359
  nursing-related, 93.247
  occupational medicine, 93.262
  pediatrics, 93.884
  podiatry residency programs, 93.181
  pollution source reduction information dissemination, outreach, EPA, 66.717
  preventive medicine residency, 93.117
  public education, promotion, 93.990
  public health, 93.249, 93.964
  public health laboratory technicians, 93.065
  radiation control, NRC training, 77.001
  rehabilitation medicine, 84.129
  rehabilitation personnel, 84.246 84.263, 84.264, 84.265, 84.275
  rural, Access to Emergency Devices, training, HRSA, 93.259
  rural computer networks, RUS, 10.855
  rural specialists, 93.192
  search, rescue, 97.025
  sexually transmitted diseases, 93.977
  Specially Selected Health Projects, HRSA, 93.888
  substance abuse, mental health services, PRNS, 93.243
  Superfund Worker Training Program, 93.142
  tuberculosis prevention, control, 93.947
  vocational rehabilitation personnel, 84.129
  women's health, Community Centers of Excellence, 93.290
  see also Behavioral sciences, education, services; Chiropractic; Dental education, training; Family medicine; Fellowships, scholarships, traineeships; Health, medical research; Health professions; Libraries; National Research Service Awards; Nursing; Optometry; Osteopathy; Pediatrics; Pharmacology, pharmacy; Podiatry; Social sciences; Speech pathology; Technical training; Veterinary medicine; Vocational rehabilitation

Health, medical research
  Academic Research Enhancement Award, 93.390
  aging, behavioral, biomedical, social sciences, 93.866
  AIDS/HIV epidemiologic studies, 93.943
  AIDS, NIH research education loan repayments, 93.936
  Air Force Defense Research Sciences Program, 12.800
  alcohol research centers, 93.891
  alcoholism, 93.271, 93.272, 93.273
  allergy, 93.855
  alternative, complementary medicine, 93.213
  Alzheimer's disease, 93.853
  anesthesia, biorelated chemistry, training, 93.859
  animal health, zoonotic diseases, 10.207
  applied public health, 93.061
  arthritis, 93.846
  asthma, 93.855
  aviation medicine, 20.108
  biomedical engineering, NSF, 47.041
  biosciences, NSF, 47.074
  blood diseases, resources, 93.839
  cancer, 93.393, 93.394, 93.395, 93.396, 93.397, 93.398
  cancer research facilities, 93.392
  Centers for Genomics and Public Health, 93.063
  chiropractic-medical demonstrations, spinal, lower-back conditions, 93.212
  clinical researchers education loan repayment, disadvantaged, 93.308
  chronic diseases control, prevention, 93.068
  communicative disorders, 93.173
  contraception, infertility research, education loan repayments, 93.209
  convulsive, infectious, immune disorders, 93.853

deafness, 93.173
developmental disabilities programs, university centers, 93.632
diabetes, 93.847
digestive diseases, nutrition, anorexia, bulimia, obesity, 93.848
disabilities prevention, 93.184
Discovery and Applied Research, biomedical imaging, bioengineering, NIH, 93.286
disease prevention, 93.135
disparities research, researchers education loan repayment, 93.307
DOE workers, epidemiology, health studies, 81.108
drug abuse, addiction, 93.279
DVA specialized medical resource sharing, 64.018
EMS/trauma care, rural, 93.952
endocrinology, 93.847
energy-related, used equipment, 81.022
environmental health, biometry, risk estimation, 93.115
environmental health hazards, 93.113
environmental health sciences, 93.894
FDA, 93.103
Great Lakes fish consumption health effects, 93.208
hazardous substances, Superfund, 93.143
hazardous waste sites health studies, 93.206
health care financing research, CMS, 93.779
health care policy issues, 93.239
health care systems, 93.226
health services NRSA, 93.225
health workforce analysis, 93.300
Healthcare Research and Quality Act of 1999, 93.255
Healthy Communities Access Program, HRSA, 93.890
heart diseases, 93.837
hematology, 93.849
HIV prevention efficacy, 93.941
human development, mothers, children, 93.865
human genomes, 93.172
immunology, 93.855
Indian health care, 93.933
infectious diseases, 93.856
injury prevention, 93.136
international, NIH-sponsored, 93.989
kidney diseases, 93.849
lung diseases, 93.838
marine resources, Sea Grant Support, 11.417
maternal, child health, 93.110
mental health, 93.242
mental health, training, 93.281, 93.282
metabolism, 93.847
microbiology, 93.856
military, biological-medical, 12.420
multiple, lateral sclerosis, 93.853
musculoskeletal diseases, 93.846
National Institutes of Health Revitalization Act, 93.186, 93.389
National Library of Medicine, 93.879
Navy, 12.300
neurological disorders, 93.853
NIH Clinical Research Loan Repayment Program, 93.220, 93.280
NIH General Research Loan Repayment Program, 93.232

NIH intramural training, 93.140
NIH Pediatric Research Loan Repayment Program, 93.285, 93.385
NIH Undergraduate Scholarship Program, 93.187
nuclear medicine, 81.049
nursing care, 93.361
occupational safety and health, 93.262
Parkinson's disease, 93.853
pharmacology, physiology, training, 93.859
primary medical care, training, 93.186
Public Health Research Accreditation Project, 93.993
rehabilitation, 84.133
research infrastructure resources, training, 93.389
rural centers, 93.155
rural services coordination, 93.223
rural specialists training, 93.192
Safe Schools/Healthy Students National Evaluation, DOJ, 16.732
sexually transmitted disease, 93.978
skin diseases, 93.846
sleep disorders, 93.233, 93.853
Specially Selected Health Projects, HRSA, 93.888
stroke, nervous system trauma, 93.853
Substance Abuse Pilot Treatment Block Grant monitoring, evaluation, 93.238
transplantation biology, 93.839, 93.855
tuberculosis prevention, control, 93.947
urology, 93.849
vascular diseases, 93.837
vision, National Eye Institute, 93.867
see also Alcohol abuse, alcoholism; AIDS (Acquired Immune Deficiency Syndrome); Behavioral sciences, education, services; Biological sciences; Cancer control, prevention, research; Chemicals, chemistry; Dental health, dental research; Drug *entries*; Environmental health, research, services; Environmental sciences; Epidemiology; Food, nutrition research, sciences; Genetics; Health *entries*; Immunization, immunology; Libraries; Mental health; National Research Service Awards; Nuclear sciences, technology; Pharmacology, pharmacy; Scientific research; Small Business Innovation Research (SBIR); Toxic substances, toxicology; Veterinary medicine

Health, medical services
AIDS-afflicted persons, housing, services, 14.241
AIDS/HIV, children, women, families, 93.153
Alzheimer's, related disorders demonstrations, 93.051
Appalachian region, 23.002
Black Lung Clinics, 93.965
block grants, 93.991
blood diseases patients, research, 93.839
cancer early detection, breast, cervical, training, 93.919
cancer, research-related, 93.393, 93.394, 93.395, 93.396, 93.399
caregiver support program, respite care, 93.052
Children's Insurance Program, CMS, 93.767
chiropractic-medical demonstrations, spinal, lower-back conditions, 93.212
Citizen Corps, DHS, 97.053

Health, medical services *(continued)*
clinical researchers education loan repayment, disadvantaged, *93.308*
communicable, chronic diseases control, *93.283*
Community Connect Grants, RUS, *10.863*
community health centers, *93.224*
crime victim assistance, *16.575, 16.576*
Crisis Counseling, FEMA, *97.032*
diabetes program, Indians, *93.237, 93.442*
disabled, handicapped, basic support, *84.126*
disabled, Medicaid Ticket-to-Work Infrastructure Grants, *93.768*
disasters, assistance to individuals, households, FEMA, *97.050*
DVA specialized medical resource sharing, 64.018
emergency health services reimbursement, undocumented aliens, *93.784*
emergency medical, children, *93.127*
emergency medical, equipment, highway safety, *20.600*
epilepsy control, *93.283*
Family Life Centers, violence prevention, HHS, *93.910*
Global AIDS, *93.067, 93.266*
Hawaii natives, *93.932*
health care financing research, CMS, *93.779*
health care systems research, *93.226, 93.239*
Health Services and Centers Amendments Act of 1978, *93.988*
Healthy Community Access Program, uninsured patients, *93.252*
heart health care programs, women, *93.012*
heart, vascular diseases patients, research, *93.837*
HIV care, *93.917*
HIV emergency relief projects, *93.914*
HIV outpatient early intervention, *93.918*
HIV projects, *93.928*
home health, block grant, *93.991*
home health, Medicaid, *93.778*
Immunization Grants, *93.268*
Indian, Alaska natives health management, *93.228*
Indian Self-Determination, *93.441*
international humanitarian relief goods transport, USAID, *98.010*
international, Ocean Freight Reimbursement, USAID, *98.003*
Interoperable Communications Equipment, DHS, *97.055*
lung diseases patients, research, *93.838*
Lyme Disease, *93.942*
maternal, child health, *93.110*
maternal, child health care block grants, *93.994*
Medicaid, *93.778*
Medicaid fraud control, *93.775*
Medicaid, Medicare providers standards compliance, *93.777*
Medicaid Ticket-to-Work Demonstrations, *93.769*
Medicare hospital insurance, *93.773*
Medicare Part B supplementary insurance, *93.774*
Medicare Part D prescription drug insurance, *93.770*
Metropolitan Medical Response System, FEMA, *97.071*
migrant children, *84.011*
minorities, health services disparities projects, *93.100*

MMA participants, State Pharmaceutical Assistance Programs, CMS, *93.786*
NIH Clinical Research Loan Repayment Program (CR-LRP), *93.280*
nurse midwife services, Medicaid, *93.778*
offenders, justice, health, social services networks, *93.229*
organ procurement assistance, *93.134*
perinatal/maternal initiative, *93.926*
Poison Control Centers, *93.253*
primary care research, NRSA, *93.186*
Radiogenetic Exposure Screening and Education Program, *93.257*
refugees, *93.566, 93.567*
repatriation program, *93.579*
rural areas, *93.223, 93.301, 93.912*
rural computer networks, RUS, *10.855*
sexually transmitted diseases control, *93.977*
Specially Selected Health Projects, HRSA, *93.888*
spina bifida, veterans dependents, *64.127*
substance abuse care, information, *93.230*
Substance Abuse Prevention and Treatment Block Grant, *93.959*
substance abuse treatment, prisoners, DOJ, *16.593*
telecommunications infrastructure, *11.552*
Telehealth Network Grants, *93.211*
trafficking victims assistance, ACF, *93.598*
traumatic brain injury, *93.234, 93.267*
uninsured, state planning grants, *93.256*
United States Leadership Against HIV/AIDS and Malaria Act of 2003, *93.266*
urban Indians, *93.193*
WIC program, referrals, *10.557*
WMD, domestic preparedness, *97.004, 97.005, 97.006, 97.007*
see also Aging and the aged; AIDS (Acquired Immune Deficiency Syndrome); Alcohol abuse, alcoholism; Behavioral sciences, education, services; Communicable diseases; Community health services; Disabled, handicapped *entries*; Drug abuse; Emergency assistance; Farm workers; Food, nutrition *entries*; Health *entries*; Homeless persons; Indian health, social services; Maternal, child health, welfare; Mental health; Mental retardation; Nursing *entries*; Occupational health, safety; Preventive health services; Public health; Respiratory diseases; Veterinary medicine; Veterans health, medical services; Victim assistance; Vocational rehabilitation

Health planning
Area Health Education Centers, *93.107, 93.824*
brucellosis, tuberculosis control, agricultural, *10.025*
cancer early detection, breast, cervical, training, *93.919*
chronic disease prevention, control, *93.945*
diabetes control, *93.988*
disparities research, researchers education loan repayment, *93.307*
health care financing research, CMS, *93.779*
health care systems research, *93.226, 93.239*
health fraud task forces, FDA, *93.447*
health services NRSA, *93.225*
health workforce analysis, *93.300*
HIV care, *93.917*

HIV prevention, *93.939*
HIV projects, *93.928*
hospital bioterrorism preparedness, HRSA, *93.889*
Indian Self-Determination, *93.441*
Indian tribal self-governance, *93.210*
Indians, health management, *93.228*
maternal, child health services, block grants, *93.994*
Metropolitan Medical Response System, FEMA, *97.071*
minority health coalitions, *93.137*
minority health status improvement, *93.004*
organ procurement organizations, *93.134*
policy, planning, graduate traineeships, *93.962*
preventive health block grants, *93.991*
public education, promotion, *93.990*
rehabilitation personnel training, state, *84.265*
rural areas, *93.223, 93.912, 93.913*
rural health research centers, *93.155*
rural hospitals emergency services, integrated care networks, *93.241*
Safe Schools/Healthy Students National Evaluation, DOJ, *16.732*
Small Rural Hospital Improvement, *93.301*
Social Security program research, demonstrations, *96.007*
Specially Selected Health Projects, HRSA, *93.888*
uninsured, state planning grants, *93.256*
Vital Statistics Reengineering Program, CDCP, *93.066*
WMD, domestic preparedness, *97.004, 97.005, 97.006, 97.007*
see also Community health services; Disaster assistance; Emergency assistance; Health facilities *entries*; Health professions; Public health; Public safety; Urban planning

Health professions
aging, care personnel training, *93.048*
allied professions, training improvement, *93.191*
alternative, complementary medicine research, *93.213*
anesthetists, *93.124, 93.358, 93.970*
Area Health Education Centers, *93.107, 93.824*
bioterrorism preparedness education, training, HRSA, *93.996*
cancer research personnel, *93.398*
community health center management, *93.129*
contraception, infertility research, education loan repayments, *93.209*
disadvantaged, clinical researchers education loan repayment, *93.308*
disadvantaged, faculty education loan repayments, *93.923*
disadvantaged, Health Careers Opportunity Program, *93.822*
disadvantaged, scholarships, *93.925*
disadvantaged student loans, *93.342*
disparities research, researchers education loan repayment, *93.307*
education loan repayments, states, *93.165*
EMS/trauma care, rural, *93.952*
environmental health sciences, *93.894*
family planning paramedical, paraprofessional training, *93.260*
geriatric education program, *93.265*
geriatrics education centers, *93.969*
Health Education and Training Centers, *93.189*
health program, hospital administration, graduate education, *93.962*
health services research, *93.226*
health services research NRSA, *93.225*
health workforce analysis, *93.300*
IHS education loan repayments, *93.164*
IHS recruitment, *93.954*
independent living center personnel, *84.132*
Indians, health management training, *93.228*
Indians, health professions recruitment, *93.970*
Indians, scholarship programs, *93.219, 93.971, 93.972*
laboratory medicine, pathology training, *93.064*
librarians, medical, training, *93.879*
long-term care employee background checks, *93.785*
maternal, child health care personnel training, *93.110*
mental health specialists training, *93.244*
minority education, Centers of Excellence, *93.157*
NHSC education loan repayments, *93.162*
NHSC scholarships, *93.288*
NIH Clinical Research Loan Repayment Program (CR-LRP), *93.220, 93.280*
occupational medicine, *93.262*
physician assistants, *93.822, 93.884, 93.925, 93.969*
public health graduate traineeships, *93.964*
Public Health Training Centers, *93.249*
rural specialists training, *93.192*
sexually transmitted disease control training, *93.977*
Specially Selected Health Projects, HRSA, *93.888*
tuberculosis prevention, control, *93.947*
vocational rehabilitation personnel training, *84.129*
see also Behavioral sciences, education, services; Chiropractic; Dental education, training; Family medicine; Fellowships, scholarships, traineeships; Food, nutrition *entries*; Health, medical education, training; Health planning; Indian health, social services; Mental health; Mental retardation; Minority education; National Research Service Awards; Nursing; Occupational health, safety; Optometry; Osteopathy; Pediatrics; Pharmacology, pharmacy; Podiatry; Preventive health services; Public health; Social sciences; Speech pathology; Technical training; Veterinary medicine; Vocational rehabilitation
HEALTH PROFESSIONS PREGRADUATE SCHOLARSHIP PROGRAM FOR INDIANS, *93.123*
HEALTH PROFESSIONS PREPARATORY SCHOLARSHIP PROGRAM FOR INDIANS, *93.971*
HEALTH PROFESSIONS RECRUITMENT PROGRAM FOR INDIANS, *93.970*
HEALTH PROFESSIONS SCHOLARSHIP PROGRAM, *93.972*
Health Professions Scholarships, Indian tribes, *93.219*
HEALTH PROFESSIONS STUDENT LOANS, INCLUDING PRIMARY CARE LOANS/LOANS FOR DISADVANTAGED STUDENTS, *93.342*

HEALTH PROGRAM FOR TOXIC SUBSTANCES AND DISEASE REGISTRY, 93.161
Health Resources and Services Administration (HRSA), HHS, see Agency Index
Health services, see Health, medical services
Health services, preventive, see Preventive health services
Health statistics, see Health planning; Information, general, clearinghouses; Statistics
HEALTHY COMMUNITIES ACCESS PROGRAM, 93.252
HEALTHY COMMUNITIES ACCESS PROGRAM (HCAP) DEMONSTRATION AUTHORITY, 93.890
HEALTHY COMMUNITIES GRANT PROGRAM [EPA], 66.110
HEALTHY HOMES DEMONSTRATION GRANTS [HUD], 14.901
HEALTHY HOMES TECHNICAL STUDIES GRANTS [HUD], 14.906
HEALTHY START INITIATIVE, 93.926
Hearing, see Deafness and the deaf
HEART AND VASCULAR DISEASES RESEARCH, 93.837
Heart diseases, see Health, medical research; Health, medical services
Help America Vote Act, see Civil rights; Government
HELP AMERICA VOTE ACT REQUIREMENT PAYMENTS, 90.401
HELP AMERICA VOTE COLLEGE POLLWORKER PROGRAM, 90.400
Hematology research, 93.849
Hemophilia, see Genetics; Health, medical research
HEP (High School Equivalency Program), migrants, 84.141
Herbicides, see Pesticides; Plants; Toxic substances, toxicology
Heritage conservation, see Historic monuments, historic preservation
HEROES STAMP PROGRAM [DHS], 97.085
HETC (Health Education and Training Centers), 93.189
HFA (Housing Finance Agency) Risk Sharing Program, 14.188
HHS (Department of Health and Human Services), 93.001 through 93.996
High School Equivalency Program (HEP), migrants, 84.141
High schools, see Elementary and secondary education; Schools entries
HIGH SPEED GROUND TRANSPORTATION—NEXT GENERATION HIGH SPEED RAIL PROGRAM, 20.312
Higher education
adults, Educational Opportunity Centers, 84.066
Army Research Office, 12.431
Byrd honors scholarships, 84.185
civil aviation, 20.100
disabled, faculty training, 84.333
disadvantaged, career counseling staff training, 84.103
disadvantaged, handicapped, first-generation student services, 84.042
disadvantaged, graduate opportunities, 84.217
disadvantaged youth, postsecondary preparation, Upward Bound, 84.047
disadvantaged youth, secondary, postsecondary, Talent Search, 84.044
Education Amendments Act of 1972, HUD programs discrimination, 14.415
Environmental Education Grants, 66.951
EPA environmental sustainability design competition, 66.516
Federal Direct Student Loans, 84.268
foster children, Chafee vouchers, 93.599
Fulbright program, educational exchange, 19.401
graduate academic fellowships, 84.200
HUD housing, urban development doctoral research, 14.516, 14.517
international business-education curricula linkage, 84.153
international agricultural science, education, 10.305
international education training, research, BECA, 19.430
Mathematics and Science Partnerships, OESE, 84.366
merchant marine, 20.806, 20.807
migrants, 84.149
Navy research, education support, 12.300
NSF engineering, mathematics, science improvement, 47.076
Overseas Educational Advising, BECA, 19.432
overseas research centers, 84.274
Pell grants, undergraduate study, 84.063
postsecondary program improvement, access, FIPSE, 84.116
Talent Search, 84.044
Tech-Prep Education, secondary, postsecondary, 84.243
Upward Bound, 84.047
work-study programs, 84.033
see also Agricultural education; Arts, arts education; Behavioral sciences, education, services; Dental education, training; Disabled, handicapped, education; Disadvantaged, education; Education entries; Engineering entries; Fellowships, scholarships, traineeships; Foreign languages; Health, medical education, training; Health professions; Higher education institutions; Humanities education, research; Indian education, training; International programs, studies; Land grant colleges, universities; Law enforcement education, training; Mathematics; Minority education; Nursing; Osteopathy; Pharmacology, pharmacy; Science education; Scientific research; Social sciences; Student financial aid; Teacher education, training; Veterans education, training; Veterinary medicine; Vocational education
Higher Education Act
Title II, Teacher Quality Enhancement, 84.336
Title III, Institutional Aid, 84.031
Title III, MSEIP, 84.120
Title IV, Byrd Honors, 84.185
Title IV, FSEOG, 84.007
Title IV, LEAP, 84.069
Title IV, loans, 84.268
Title IV, McNair Achievement, 84.217

Title IV, migrant education, *84.141*, *84.149*
Title IV, Pell Grants, *84.063*
Title IV-A, child care, *84.335*
Title IV-A, GEAR-UP, *84.334*
Title IV-A, TRIO, *84.042*, *84.044*, *84.047*, *84.066*, *84.103*, *84.344*
Title IV-B, education loans, *84.032*
Title IV-C, work study, *84.033*
Title IV-E, loan cancellations, *84.037*
Title IV-E, Perkins loans, *84.038*
Title VI, FLAS, *84.015*, *84.016*, *84.017*, *84.229*, *84.269*, *84.274*, *84.337*
Title VI, international business, *84.153*, *84.220*
Title VII, disabled, *84.333*
Title VII, FIPSE, *84.116*
Title VII, GAANN, *84.200*
Title VII, Javits Fellowships, *84.170*
Title VIII, Advanced Placement Incentive, *84.330*
Title VIII, Higher Education Amendments, campus crime, DOJ, *16.525*
Title VIII, Incarcerated Youth, *84.331*
Title VIII, Underground Railroad Program, *84.345*
Higher Education, BIA, *15.114*
HIGHER EDUCATION CHALLENGE GRANTS [USDA], *10.217*
HIGHER EDUCATION—INSTITUTIONAL AID, *84.031*
Higher education institutions
 agriculture, challenge grants, *10.217*
 AIDS prevention, school-age populations, *93.938*
 Alaska, Hawaii native, community assistance, *14.515*
 campus crime grants, *16.525*
 campus law enforcement personnel training, DHS, *97.081*
 child care programs, *84.335*
 College Pollworker Program, *90.400*
 community outreach, HUD, *14.511*
 Community Outreach Partnership Act of 1992, *14.511*
 desegregation, legal services, 16.100
 Drug-Free Schools and Communities, national programs, *84.184*
 economic development planning assistance, EDA, *11.303*
 Environmental Education and Training Program, *66.950*
 EPA IHE research support, *66.515*
 Family Life Centers, HHS violence prevention, *93.910*
 federal intergovernmental personnel, temporary assignments, 27.011
 federal surplus real property transfer, 84.145
 food program, National Youth Sports Program, *10.559*
 foreign language resource centers, *84.229*
 foreign scholars-in-residence, undergraduate, BECA, *19.431*
 Hispanic serving institutions community assistance, HUD, *14.514*
 Indian Post Secondary Schools, *15.058*
 international business education centers, *84.220*
 Japan-U.S. Friendship Commission Grants, *90.300*
 Learn and Serve America programs, *94.005*
 minority entrepreneurial training, DOT contracts, *20.907*
 Minority Science Improvement, *84.120*
 reimbursement for canceled student loans, *84.037*
 Small Business Development Centers, *59.037*
 Strengthening Institutions Program, *84.031*
 Tech-Prep Demonstration Grants, secondary students, *84.353*
 tribal, facilities, *14.519*
 tribally-controlled, *15.027*, *15.028*
 University-Based Homeland Security Centers, DHS, *97.061*
 U.S. Merchant Marine Academy, *20.807*
 USAID programs, *98.001*, *98.012*
 work-study programs, community development, *14.512*
 see also Agricultural education; Education *entries*; Higher education; International programs, studies; Land grant colleges, universities; Minority education; Vocational education
HIGHER EDUCATION MULTICULTURAL SCHOLARS PROGRAM [USDA], *10.220*
HIGHER EDUCATION—TRIO STAFF TRAINING, *84.103*
HIGHWAY PLANNING AND CONSTRUCTION, *20.205*
HIGHWAY TRAINING AND EDUCATION, *20.215*
Highway Trust Fund, *20.205*
Highways, roads, bridges
 Alcohol Open Container Requirements, DOT, *20.607*
 Appalachian highway construction, *23.003*
 bicycle paths, *20.205*
 Bridge Act of 1906, 97.014
 Bridge Alteration, USCG, 97.014
 bridge rehabilitation, replacement, *20.205*
 Driving While Intoxicated, repeat offender laws, DOT, *20.608*
 Federal-Aid Highway Program, *20.205*
 flood damage, erosion, 12.105
 forest highways, planning, construction, *20.205*
 highway beautification, *20.205*
 highway personnel training, education, *20.215*
 Highway Safety Acts, *20.600*, *20.601*, *20.602*, *20.603*, *20.604*, *20.605*, *20.607*, *20.608*
 highway safety data improvement, *20.603*
 Indian reservations, maintenance, *15.033*
 interstate highway construction, rehabilitation, *20.205*
 motor carrier safety enforcement, training, 20.217
 national forests, USDA payments to states, *10.665*
 national grasslands, USDA payments to counties, *10.666*
 parking facilities, *20.205*
 pedestrian walkways, *20.205*
 planning, research, *20.205*
 railroad grade crossings, *20.205*
 relocation assistance, *20.205*
 rest areas, *20.205*
 road, street improvement, *20.205*
 state, community highway safety, equipment, public education, training, *20.600*
 Truck Security Program, DHS, *97.059*
 Truman-Hobbs Act, 97.014
 U.S. insular areas, *15.875*
 Wood in Transportation, USFS, *10.673*

Highways, roads, bridges *(continued)*
see also Community development; Interstate commerce; Hazardous materials, waste; Mass transportation; Motor vehicles; Public safety; Public works; Transportation
HIP (Housing Improvement Program), BIA, *15.141*
HIPAA (Health Insurance Portability and Accountability Act of 1996), *see* Health insurance
HISPANIC SERVING INSTITUTIONS ASSISTING COMMUNITIES [HUD], *14.514*
HISPANIC SERVING INSTITUTIONS EDUCATION GRANTS [USDA], *10.223*
Historic monuments, historic preservation
advisory services, counseling, 15.912, 15.914, 15.915
American Battlefield Protection, *15.926*
American Battlefield Protection Act of 1996, *15.926, 15.928*
BLM projects, Cultural Resource Management, *15.224*
Civil War Battlefield Land Acquisition Grants, *15.928*
community development grants, *14.218, 14.219, 14.225, 14.228, 14.862*
DOD donations, loans, 12.700
federal surplus property, 15.918, 39.003
federal surplus real property, 39.002
grants-in-aid, *15.904*
highways, FHWA, *20.205*
historic landmarks registry, 15.912
Historic Sites Act of 1935, 15.910, 15.912
humanities research materials preservation, *45.149*
Indian Programs, *15.041*
maritime heritage grants, *15.925*
National Center for Preservation Technology and Training, *15.923*
National Historic Preservation Act of 1966, *15.041, 15.224, 15.904,* 15.912, 15.914, 15.915, *15.922, 15.923*
National Register of Historic Places, *15.904,* 15.912, 15.914, *15.926*
National Registry of Natural Landmarks, 15.910
native American graves protection, repatriation, *15.922*
NEH We the People program, *45.168*
Omnibus Parks and Public Lands Management Act of 1996, *15.926, 15.929*
planning, repair, *15.904*
rural resource development, *10.901*
Save America's Treasures, NPS, *15.929*
tax incentives, *15.904,* 15.912, 15.914
technical information, 15.915
see also Archaeology; Buildings; Community development; History; Museums, galleries
HISTORIC PRESERVATION FUND GRANTS-IN-AID, *15.904*
Historic Surplus Property Program, DOI, 15.918
HISTORICALLY BLACK COLLEGES AND UNIVERSITIES PROGRAM [HUD], *14.520*
History
Civil War Battlefield Land Acquisition Grants, *15.928*
collections preservation, arrangement, training, *89.003*

historical organizations, NEH challenge grants, *45.130*
humanities, NEH Public Programs, *45.164*
Indian history, tribal heritage, elementary, secondary education, *84.060*
international peace and conflict resolution, *91.001, 91.002*
Learning Opportunities Grants, IMLS, *45.301*
National Archives Reference Services, federal records, Presidential Libraries, 89.001
National Historical Publications and Records Commission, *89.003*
native American language preservation, *93.587*
NEH We the People program, *45.168*
NEH workshops, *45.163*
research materials preservation, *45.149*
Save America's Treasures, NPS, *15.929*
teaching, Madison fellowships, *85.500*
Underground Railroad Program, DOED, *84.345*
Woodrow Wilson Center fellowships, *85.300*
see also Government; Historic monuments, historic preservation; Humanities *entries*; International programs, studies; Museums, galleries; Social sciences
HIV (human immunodeficiency virus), *see* AIDS (Acquired Immunodeficiency Syndrome)
HIV/AIDS Dental Reimbursements, *93.924*
HIV CARE FORMULA GRANTS, *93.917*
HIV DEMONSTRATION, RESEARCH, PUBLIC AND PROFESSIONAL EDUCATION PROJECTS, *93.941*
HIV EMERGENCY RELIEF PROJECT GRANTS, *93.914*
HIV PREVENTION ACTIVITIES—HEALTH DEPARTMENT BASED, *93.940*
HIV PREVENTION ACTIVITIES—NON-GOVERNMENTAL ORGANIZATION BASED, *93.939*
HMEP (Hazardous Materials Emergency Preparedness) Training and Planning Grants, *20.703*
HMGP (Hazard Mitigation Grant Program), FEMA, *97.039*
Home economics
child welfare services, *93.645*
Community Food Projects, USDA, *10.225*
Extension Service, *10.500*
Minority Scholars Program, scholarships, *10.220*
New Assets for Independence Demonstration, *93.602*
vocational education program, *84.048*
see also Adult education; Consumers, consumer services; Food, nutrition; Home management; Volunteers
HOME EQUITY CONVERSION MORTGAGES, *14.183*
Home health services, *see* Aging and the aged; Blindness and the blind; Community health services; Disabled, handicapped; Food, nutrition; Health, medical services; Social Security Act; Social services; Veterans, disabled; Volunteers
Home improvement, *see* Housing rehabilitation; Indian housing; Veterans housing; Weatherization

HOME INVESTMENT PARTNERSHIPS
    PROGRAM, *14.239*
Home management
  AIDS-afflicted persons, housing, services, *14.241*
  American Dream Downpayment Initiative
    (ADDI), *14.239*
  blind elderly, independent living services,
    training, *84.177*
  counseling assistance, *14.169*
  counseling program, rural, *10.441*
  disabled, elderly, Multifamily Housing Service
    Coordinators, *14.191*
  Extension Service, *10.500*
  farmer outreach, socially disadvantaged, *10.443*
  Hawaii, housing block grants, *14.873*
  HBCU Program, HUD, *14.520*
  Healthy Homes Demonstration Grants, HUD,
    14.901
  HOME Program, *14.239*
  homeless persons supportive services, *14.235*
  homemaker vocational education, *84.048*
  Indian Housing Block Grants, *14.867*
  Lead Outreach Grants, HUD, *14.904*
  public housing residents, supportive services,
    14.870
  Rural Community Development Initiative, RHS,
    10.446
  Senior Companion Program, *94.016*
  see also Adult education; Community health
    services; Consumers, consumer services; Home
    economics; Homeownership, homebuying;
    Housing, subsidized; Social services;
    Volunteers
HOME Program, *14.239*
Homeland security, *see* Civil defense; Military
HOMELAND SECURITY ADVANCED
    RESEARCH PROJECTS AGENCY, *97.065*
HOMELAND SECURITY—AGRICULTURAL,
    10.304
HOMELAND SECURITY GRANT PROGRAM,
    97.067
Homeland Security Information Center, NTIS, 11.650
HOMELAND SECURITY INFORMATION
    TECHNOLOGY AND EVALUATION
    PROGRAM, *97.066*
HOMELAND SECURITY OUTREACH,
    EDUCATION, AND TECHNICAL
    ASSISTANCE, *97.086*
HOMELAND SECURITY PREPAREDNESS
    TECHNICAL ASSISTANCE, *97.007*
HOMELAND SECURITY TESTING,
    EVALUATION, AND DEMONSTRATION
    OF TECHNOLOGIES, *97.077*
Homeless persons
  AIDS-afflicted persons, housing, services, *14.241*
  children, educational programs, *84.196*
  community health center assistance, *93.129*
  Compassion Capital Fund, ACF, *93.009*
  emergency food, shelter, FEMA, *97.024*
  emergency shelter program, *14.231*
  facilities, federal surplus real property, 39.002,
    39.003
  food assistance, *10.558*, *10.559*
  food assistance, summer, *10.559*
  food assistance, WIC, *10.557*
  Food Donation Program, USDA, 10.550
  Food Stamps, *10.551*
  health center services, *93.224*
  health facilities, federal surplus property, 93.291
  Homeless Veterans Comprehensive Service
    Programs Act of 1992, *64.024*
  HUD Youthbuild Program, *14.243*
  mental health, transitional services, *93.150*
  Section 8 Moderate Rehabilitation SRO, *14.249*
  Shelter Plus Care, *14.238*
  Supportive Housing Program, *14.235*
  veterans, disabled, outreach, *17.801*
  veterans, DVA provider grants, *64.024*
  veterans employment, reintegration, *17.805*
  youth, sexual abuse, Street Outreach Program,
    93.557
  youth shelters, counseling, services, *93.623*
  youth, transitional services, *93.550*
  see also Disaster assistance; Emergency
    assistance; Housing, subsidized; Missing
    persons; Public assistance; Social services;
    Victim assistance; Volunteers
HOMELESS VETERANS REINTEGRATION
    PROJECT, *17.805*
Homeownership, homebuying
  acquisition, rehabilitation, *14.108*
  adjustable rate mortgages, *14.175*
  counseling program, rural, *10.441*
  disaster victims, *14.119*
  discrimination complaints, 16.103
  Dollar Home Sales, 14.313
  farmer outreach, socially disadvantaged, *10.443*
  farms, *10.407*
  Good Neighbor Initiative, HUD, 14.311
  graduated payment mortgage, *14.159*
  growing equity mortgages, *14.172*
  native Hawaiians, *14.873*, *14.874*
  HOME Program, *14.239*
  HOPE VI activities, *14.866*
  housing counseling, *14.169*
  Loan Guarantees for Indian Housing, *14.865*
  military impacted areas, *14.165*
  mortgage default counseling, *14.169*
  native Americans, DVA, *64.126*
  New Assets for Independence Demonstration,
    93.602
  Officer Next Door Sales Program, 14.198
  purchase, refinancing, *14.117*
  Rural Community Development Initiative, RHS,
    10.446
  rural housing loans, *10.410*
  rural, packaging grants, *10.442*
  Self-Help Homeownership Opportunity Program,
    14.247
  self-help, rural, *10.420*
  Single Family Property Disposition, HUD, 14.311
  Teacher Next Door Initiative, 14.310
  urban declining areas, *14.123*
  urban renewal areas, *14.122*
  veterans, dependents loans, *64.114*
  see also Family farms; Home management;
    Homes, manufactured, mobile; Housing,
    condominiums; Housing construction; Housing
    cooperatives; Housing, low to moderate
    income; Housing mortgage, loan insurance;
    Housing, rural; Housing research; Indian
    housing; Veterans housing

Homes, manufactured, mobile
construction, safety standards, 14.171
insured loans, *14.110*
lot and home loans, *14.162*
manufactured home parks, *14.127*
rural, *10.410*
rural rental projects, *10.415*
Title I, *14.110*
veterans, dependents loans, *64.114, 64.119*
see also Homeownership, homebuying; Housing mortgage, loan insurance; Housing, rural; Veterans housing

Honey, *see* Agricultural commodities, stabilization

HOPE VI (Housing Opportunities for People Everywhere), HUD, *14.866*

HOPWA (Housing Opportunities for Persons with AIDS), *14.241*

Horses, *see* Animal disease control, health, welfare; Livestock industry

Hospices, *see* Health facilities *entries*; Nursing homes

Hospital administration, *see* Health professions

Hospitalization and Medical Services, DVA, 64.009

Hospitals, *see* Health facilities *entries*; Health, medical services; Health professions; Veterans health, medical services

Hotlines
Employee Benefits Security Administration (EBSA), 17.150
Environmental Justice, *66.306, 66.604*
family violence, *93.592*
HHS civil rights compliance, 93.001
manufactured homes safety standards, 14.171
missing children, *16.543*
National Center for Missing and Exploited Children, *97.076*
radon, *66.032*
runaway, homeless youth, *93.623*
see also Consumers, consumer services; Emergency assistance; Information, general, clearinghouses; Victim assistance

HOUSEHOLD WATER WELL SYSTEM GRANT PROGRAM, *10.862*

Housing Act, National, *see* National housing acts

Housing acts, *see* National housing acts

HOUSING APPLICATION PACKAGING GRANTS, *10.442*

Housing Assistance Plan (HAP), CDBG, *14.218*

Housing, condominiums
construction, rehabilitation, *14.112*
conversion from rental, *14.133*
graduated payment mortgage, *14.159*
growing equity mortgages, *14.172*
purchase, *14.133*
veterans home loans, *64.114*
see also Housing *entries*; Veterans housing

Housing, congregate
AIDS-afflicted persons, services, *14.241*
commodity food donations, *10.569*
elderly, supportive, *14.157, 14.314*
farm workers, *10.405*
meal programs, *93.045*
see also Disabled, handicapped, housing; Farm workers; Group homes; Housing, elderly

Housing construction
AIDS-afflicted persons, services, *14.241*
condominiums, *14.112*
cooperative, *14.126, 14.135*
disabled, supportive housing, *14.181*
disabled veterans, *64.118*
disaster victims, *14.119*
elderly, handicapped, *14.135, 14.138*
elderly, supportive, *14.157, 14.314*
farm housing, *10.407*
farm laborers, *10.405*
HOME Program, *14.239*
housing finance agency risk sharing, *14.188*
manufactured homes standards, 14.171
native Hawaiian housing loan guarantees, *14.874*
rental, code enforcement, disaster, urban renewal areas, *14.139*
rental, middle income, *14.134*
rental, moderate income, *14.135*
rural, loans, *10.410*
rural site loans, *10.411*
Self-Help Homeownership Opportunity Program, *14.247*
single room occupancy project mortgages, *14.184*
soil surveys, 10.903
urban declining areas, *14.123*
urban renewal areas, owner-occupied, *14.122*
see also Buildings; Construction; Disabled, handicapped, housing; Family farms; Group homes; Housing *entries*; Indian housing; Veterans housing

Housing cooperatives
community development credit union loans, *44.002*
corporate certificate purchase, *14.163*
elderly, supportive, *14.157, 14.314*
mortgage insurance, *14.126, 14.132, 14.135*
rural, preservation grants, *10.433*
rural, rental, *10.415, 10.427*
rural site loans, *10.411*
Section 236 Interest Reduction Payments, *14.103*
see also Cooperatives

Housing counseling, *see* Home management; Homeownership, homebuying; Social services

HOUSING COUNSELING ASSISTANCE PROGRAM, *14.169*

Housing discrimination, *see* Civil rights

Housing, elderly
assisted living, care, nursing home facilities, *14.129*
cooperative, rental, *14.135*
institutional, civil rights, 16.105
Multifamily Housing Service Coordinators, *14.191*
public, *14.850*
rental, *14.138*
reverse mortgage loans, *14.183*
rural, loans, *10.415*
rural rental, *10.438*
rural rental assistance, *10.427*
rural, repair loans, grants, *10.417*
Section 236 Interest Reduction Payments, *14.103*
supportive, Section 202, *14.157, 14.314*
weatherization assistance, *81.042*
see also Aging and the aged; Group homes; Home management; Housing, congregate; Housing, low to moderate income; Nursing homes; Veterans *entries*; Volunteers

MASTER INDEX 959

Housing-Federal Housing Commissioner, HUD, *see* Agency Index
HOUSING FINANCE AGENCIES (HFA) RISK SHARING, *14.188*
Housing, handicapped, *see* Disabled, handicapped, housing
Housing Improvement Program (HIP), BIA, *15.141*
Housing, Indians, *see* Indian housing
Housing, land acquisition, *see* Family farms; Homeownership, homebuying; Housing, *entries*; Land acquisition; Subdivisions
Housing loan insurance, *see* Housing mortgage, loan insurance

Housing, low to moderate income
AIDS-afflicted persons, services, *14.241*
Alaska, Hawaii native IHE community assistance, *14.515*
Bank Enterprise Awards Program, *21.021*
CDBG technical assistance, *14.227*
Community Development Financial Institutions Program, *21.020*
community development grants, *14.218, 14.219, 14.228*
Community Services Block Grant, *93.569*
cooperative, rental, construction, rehabilitation, *14.135*
credit unions loans (CDCU), *44.002*
disabled, supportive housing, *14.181*
Dollar Home Sales, 14.313
energy subsidies, heating, cooling, *93.558, 93.568*
federal surplus real property, 39.002
HBCU Program, HUD, *14.520*
HOME Program, *14.239*
HOPE VI, public housing revitalization, *14.866*
Household Water Well System Program, RUS, *10.862*
housing counseling, *14.169*
housing finance agency risk sharing, *14.188*
HUD Youthbuild Program, *14.243*
insular areas, community development grants, *14.225*
operating loss subsidies, *14.164*
Project-based Section 8, *14.195*
public, *14.850*
Qualified Participating Entities (QPE) risk sharing, *14.189*
rehabilitation, *14.228*
Rent Supplement Program, *14.149*
rural, disaster assistance, *10.444, 10.445*
rural, loans, *10.410*
rural, packaging grants, *10.442*
rural, preservation grants, *10.433*
rural, repair grants, loans, *10.417*
rural, rental, *10.415, 10.427, 10.438*
rural, self-help grants, *10.420*
rural site loans, *10.411*
Section 8 Housing Choice Vouchers, *14.871*
Section 8 Moderate Rehabilitation, *14.856*
Section 8 Moderate Rehabilitation SRO, *14.249*
Section 108 Loan Guarantees, *14.248*
Section 236 Interest Reduction Payments, *14.103*
self-help, co-op homeownership, *44.002*
Self-Help Homeownership Opportunity Program, *14.247*
single room occupancy (SRO) housing, *14.135, 14.184, 14.188, 14.238, 14.241, 14.249*

weatherization, DOE, *81.042*
weatherization, HHS, *93.568*
see also Community development; Disabled, handicapped, housing; Home management; Homeless persons; Homeownership, homebuying; Housing rehabilitation; Housing, rental; Housing, rural; Housing, subsidized; Indian housing; Veterans housing

Housing mortgage, loan insurance
adjustable rate, *14.175*
condominiums, *14.112, 14.133*
cooperative, corporate certificate purchase, *14.163*
cooperatives, *14.126, 14.132, 14.135*
disaster victims, *14.119*
discrimination complaints, 16.103
elderly, handicapped, rental, *14.135, 14.138*
flood insurance, *97.022*
graduated payment, *14.159*
Growing Equity Mortgages (GEMs), *14.172*
homeownership, *14.117*
housing finance agency risk sharing, *14.188*
Loan Guarantees for Indian Housing, *14.865*
manufactured home parks, *14.127*
manufactured homes, *14.110, 14.162*
military impacted areas, *14.165*
mortgage default counseling, *14.169*
multifamily, existing, *14.155*
multifamily, supplemental loans, *14.151*
native Hawaiian housing loan guarantees, *14.874*
operating loss loans, multifamily projects, *14.167*
property improvement, residential, nonresidential, *14.142*
Qualified Participating Entities (QPE) risk sharing, *14.189*
rehabilitation, *14.108*
rental, code enforcement, disaster, urban renewal areas, *14.139*
rental, middle income, *14.134*
rental, moderate income, *14.135*
reverse mortgage loans, *14.183*
rural rental, *10.438*
section 8 reform, Market-to-Market, *14.197*
Section 108 Loan Guarantees, *14.248*
Single Family Property Disposition, 14.311
single room occupancy projects, *14.184*
Title I, existing, nonresidential, *14.142*
tribal housing activities, *14.869*
urban declining areas, *14.123*
urban renewal areas, owner-occupied, *14.122*
veterans, *64.114*
veterans mortgage protection life insurance, *64.103*
see also Disabled, handicapped, housing; Homeownership, homebuying; Homes, manufactured, mobile; Housing *entries*; Indian housing; Insurance; Veterans housing
Housing, multifamily, *see* Disabled, handicapped, housing; Group homes; Homeless persons; Housing, condominiums; Housing, congregate; Housing cooperatives; Housing, rental; Housing, rural; Housing, subsidized; Indian housing
Housing Opportunities for People Everywhere (HOPE VI), *14.866*
HOUSING OPPORTUNITIES FOR PERSONS WITH AIDS, *14.241*

Housing Opportunity Extension Act, *see* National housing acts
Housing Preservation Grants (HPG), rural, *10.433*
Housing rehabilitation
  AIDS-afflicted persons, services, *14.241*
  Assisted Living Conversion Program, HUD, *14.314*
  community development grants, *14.218*, *14.219*, *14.228*
  community development grants, Indians, *14.862*
  community development grants, Insular Areas, *14.225*
  condominiums, *14.112*
  cooperative, *14.126*, *14.135*
  deleading, CDBG funding, *14.218*, *14.219*, *14.228*
  disabled, supportive housing, *14.181*
  disaster housing, remote, insular area residents, FEMA, *97.048*
  disaster victims, *14.119*
  disaster victims, Cora Brown Fund, *97.031*
  DVA, native Americans, *64.126*
  elderly, handicapped, rental, *14.138*
  elderly, supportive, *14.157*, *14.314*
  farm laborers, *10.405*
  farm ownership loans, *10.407*
  farm properties, emergency, *10.404*
  Hazard Mitigation Grant, FEMA, *97.039*
  historic places, *15.904*
  historic properties preservation, technical services, 15.915
  HOME Program, *14.239*
  homeless, emergency shelters, *14.231*
  homeless, transitional, supportive services, *14.235*
  homeless veterans, DVA provider grants, *64.024*
  housing finance agency risk sharing, *14.188*
  HUD Youthbuild Program, *14.243*
  lead-based paint hazard control, *14.900*
  lead-based paint removal training, certification, *66.707*
  Lead Hazard Reduction Demonstration Grants, HUD, *14.905*
  Lead Outreach Grants, HUD, *14.904*
  lead technical studies, HUD, *14.902*, *14.906*
  low-, moderate-income, *14.228*
  manufactured home parks, *14.127*
  mortgage insurance, *14.108*
  multifamily, supplemental loans, *14.151*
  native Hawaiian housing loan guarantees, *14.874*
  physical disaster loans, *59.008*
  property improvement loans, residential, nonresidential, *14.142*
  public, *14.872*
  radon mitigation technical assistance, *66.032*
  rental, code enforcement, disaster, urban renewal areas, *14.139*
  rental, middle income, *14.134*
  rental, moderate income, *14.135*
  revolving loan funds, CDBG, *14.218*, *14.219*, *14.228*
  rural, *10.410*, *10.417*
  rural, disasters, *10.445*
  rural, preservation grants, *10.433*
  rural rental, *10.415*
  Section 8 Moderate Rehabilitation, *14.856*
  Section 8 Moderate Rehabilitation SRO, *14.249*
  Section 108 Loan Guarantees, *14.248*
  single room occupancy projects, *14.184*, *14.249*
  troubled projects, flexible subsidy, *14.164*
  urban declining areas, *14.123*
  urban renewal areas, owner-occupied, *14.122*
  water, waste disposal systems, rural, *10.770*
  Water Well System Program, RUS, *10.862*
  weatherization, low-income, *81.042*
  see also Buildings; Community development; Energy conservation; Historic monuments, historic preservation; Housing mortgage, loan insurance; Housing, rural; Indian housing; Urban renewal; Veterans housing; Weatherization
Housing, rental
  AIDS-afflicted persons, services, *14.241*
  code enforcement, disaster, urban renewal areas, *14.139*
  conversion to condominiums, *14.133*
  counseling program, rural, *10.441*
  disabled, supportive housing, *14.181*
  disaster victims assistance, FEMA, *97.049*
  discrimination complaints, 16.103
  domestic violence victim transitional housing, *16.736*
  elderly, handicapped, *14.138*
  elderly, supportive, *14.157*, *14.314*
  existing, purchase, refinancing, *14.155*
  HOME Program, *14.239*
  homeless, Shelter Plus Care, *14.238*
  housing finance agency risk sharing, *14.188*
  improvements insurance, *14.151*
  middle-income, construction, rehabilitation, *14.134*
  moderate-income, construction, rehabilitation, *14.135*
  Multifamily Housing Service Coordinators, *14.191*
  operating loss loans, *14.167*
  Project-based Section 8, *14.195*
  public, *14.850*
  Qualified Participating Entities (QPE) risk sharing, *14.189*
  Rent Supplement Program, *14.149*
  rental delinquency counseling, *14.169*
  rural, assistance payments, *10.427*
  rural, loans, *10.415*, *10.438*
  rural, packaging grants, *10.442*
  rural, preservation grants, *10.433*
  Section 8 Housing Choice Vouchers, *14.871*
  Section 8 Moderate Rehabilitation, *14.856*
  Section 8 Moderate Rehabilitation SRO, *14.249*
  section 8 reform, Market-to-Market, *14.197*
  Section 236 Interest Reduction Payments, *14.103*
  single room occupancy project mortgages, *14.184*
  supplemental loans, *14.151*
  troubled projects, management assistance, *14.164*
  urban declining areas, *14.123*
  urban renewal areas, owner-occupied, *14.122*
  see also Disabled, handicapped, housing; Group housing; Housing, elderly; Housing, low to moderate income; Housing, rural; Housing, subsidized; Indian housing
Housing repairs, *see* Housing rehabilitation
Housing research
  building standards, *11.609*
  Census Bureau data, 11.001

Education Amendments Act of 1972, HUD
 programs discrimination, 14.415
HUD housing, urban development doctoral
 research, *14.516, 14.517*
HUD grants, *14.506*
IHE outreach, HUD, *14.511*
lead technical studies, HUD, *14.902, 14.906*
Universities Rebuilding America Program,
 Hurricanes Katrina, Rita, HUD, *14.521*
see also Buildings; Census services; Economics,
 research, statistics; Social sciences

Housing, rural
cooperative, rental, *10.415*
counseling program, *10.441*
disabled veterans, purchase, *64.118*
disaster, *10.444, 10.445*
farm laborers, *10.405*
farm loans, *10.407*
farm loans, interest subsidies, *10.437*
farmer outreach, socially disadvantaged, *10.443*
homeownership loans, section 502, *10.410*
HUD, Rural Housing and Economic
 Development, *14.250*
Multifamily Housing Service Coordinators, *14.191*
packaging grants, *10.442*
preservation grants, *10.433*
rental assistance, *10.427*
section 504, repair loans, grants, *10.417*
section 514, 516, labor housing, *10.405*
section 515, 521, *10.415*
section 523 and 524 site loans, *10.411*
section 523, technical assistance, *10.420*
section 538, rental, loans, *10.438*
self-help, training, *10.420*
site loans, *10.411*
Water Well System Program, RUS, *10.862*
water, waste disposal systems, *10.770*
water, wastewater treatment systems, CSBG
 discretionary, *93.570*
see also Community development; Family farms;
 Farm workers; Indian housing; Rural *entries*;
 Veterans housing
Housing site preparation, *see* Housing *entries*;
 Indian housing; Land acquisition;
 Subdivisions; Veterans housing
Housing statistics, *see* Census services; Economics,
 research, statistics; Housing research; Statistics

Housing, subsidized
AIDS-afflicted persons, services, *14.241*
community health centers, *93.224*
counseling, *14.169*
disabled, supportive housing, *14.181*
disaster housing, remote, insular area residents,
 FEMA, *97.048*
disaster victims housing rental assistance, FEMA,
 97.049
elderly, supportive, *14.157, 14.314*
ETA pilots, demonstrations, research, *17.261*
evaluation, research programs, *14.506*
farm loans, *10.437*
Flexible Subsidy Fund, Troubled Projects, *14.164*
HBCU Program, HUD, *14.520*
HOME Program, *14.239*
homeless, Shelter Plus Care, *14.238*
homeless, transitional, supportive services, *14.235*
homeless veterans, DVA provider grants, *64.024*

HOPE VI, public housing revitalization, *14.866*
housing finance agency risk sharing, *14.188*
Multifamily Property Disposition, 14.199
Lead Outreach Grants, HUD, *14.904*
Officer Next Door Sales Program, 14.198
Project-based Section 8, *14.195*
Public Housing Neighborhood Network Grants,
 14.875
public housing residents, supportive services,
 14.870
public, modernization, rehabilitation, *14.872*
public, Operation Weed and Seed, *16.595*
public, projects, *14.850*
public, residents, health services, *93.224*
public, residents, literacy programs, *84.002*
Rent Supplement Program, *14.149*
rural, disasters, *10.445*
rural, rental, *10.427*
schools, Impact Aid, *84.041*
Section 8 Housing Choice Vouchers, *14.871*
Section 8 Moderate Rehabilitation, *14.856*
Section 8 Moderate Rehabilitation SRO, *14.249*
section 8 reform, Market-to-Market, *14.197*
Section 236 Interest Reduction Payments, *14.103*
Single Family Property Disposition, 14.311
Teacher Next Door Initiative, 14.310
Troubled Projects, flexible subsidy, *14.164*
see also Disabled, handicapped, housing; Group
 homes; Home management; Homeless persons;
 Housing, elderly; Housing, low to moderate
 income; Housing mortgage, loan insurance;
 Housing, rural; Indian housing
Housing, veterans, *see* Veterans housing
HPG (Housing Preservation Grants), rural, *10.433*
HPSL (Health Professions Student Loans), *93.342*
HSARPA (Homeland Security Advanced Research
 Projects Agency), *97.065*
HRSA (Health Resources and Services
 Administration), HHS, *see* Agency Index
HSTG (High Speed Ground Transportation), *20.312*
HUD (Department of Housing and Urban
 Development), 14.103 through 14.906
HUMAN GENOME RESEARCH, *93.172*
HUMAN HEALTH STUDIES—APPLIED
 RESEARCH AND DEVELOPMENT, *93.206*
Human immunodeficiency virus (HIV), *see* AIDS
 (Acquired Immunodeficiency Syndrome)
HUMAN IMMUNODEFICIENCY VIRUS
 (HIV)/ACQUIRED IMMUNODEFICIENCY
 SYNDROME (AIDS) SURVEILLANCE,
 93.944

Humanities
arts, artifacts indemnity, *45.201*
BECA arts exchanges, *19.409*
challenge grants, *45.130*
DHS Scholars and Fellows, *97.062*
Fulbright program, educational exchange, *19.400*
historical collections, preservation, *89.003*
Japan-U.S. Friendship Commission Grants, *90.300*
libraries, collections preservation training, *45.149*
local, state, regional projects, *45.129*
National Gallery of Art exhibits, 68.001
native American language preservation, *93.587*
NEH Public Programs, *45.164*
NEH We the People program, *45.168*
Save America's Treasures, NPS, *15.929*

Humanities *(continued)*
  Underground Railroad Program, DOED, *84.345*
  see also Arts, arts education; Historic monuments, historic preservation; History; Humanities education, research; International programs, studies; Social sciences
Humanities education, research
  BLM projects, Cultural Resource Management, *15.224*
  challenge grants, *45.130*
  graduate fellowships, *84.170*
  Indian history, tribal heritage, elementary, secondary education, *84.060*
  international exchange, *19.418*
  international peace, conflict resolution, *91.001, 91.002*
  Japan-U.S. Friendship Commission Grants, *90.300*
  Learning Opportunities Grants, IMLS, *45.301*
  NEH centers support, *45.161*
  NEH curriculum, materials development, *45.162*
  NEH fellowships, *45.160, 45.161*
  NEH Public Programs, *45.164*
  NEH Professional Development, *45.163*
  NEH We the People program, *45.168*
  NSF, cultural anthropology, *47.075*
  Smithsonian fellowships, *85.601*
  teacher training seminars abroad, *84.018*
  Underground Railroad Program, DOED, *84.345*
  Woodrow Wilson Center fellowships, *85.300*
  see also Arts, arts education; Foreign languages; History; Humanities; International programs, studies; Libraries; Museums, galleries; Social sciences; Teacher education, training
HUNTER EDUCATION AND SAFETY PROGRAM, *15.626*
Hunter safety programs, *15.611*
Hunting, see Public safety; Wildlife, waterfowl
HURRICANE KATRINA CASE MANAGEMENT INITIATIVE, *97.084*
Hurricanes
  coastal zone management, *11.419*
  coastal zone rehabilitation, 12.102
  Dairy Market Loss Assistance Program, FSA, *10.084*
  Emergency Management Performance Grants, *97.042*
  emergency rescue, 12.103
  farmland rehabilitation, *10.054*
  FEMA Community Disaster Loans, *97.030*
  Hurricane Katrina Case Management Initiative, *97.084*
  Hazard Mitigation Grant, FEMA, *97.039*
  Pre-disaster Mitigation, FEMA, *97.047*
  search, rescue system, *97.025*
  Universities Rebuilding America Program, Hurricanes Katrina, Rita, HUD, *14.521*
  see also Climate; Coastal zone; Disaster assistance; Emergency assistance; Flood prevention, control
HWW (Hard White Wheat) program, FSA, *10.995*
HWWS (Household Water Well System) Program, RUS, *10.862*
Hydrographic Center, NOAA, *11.400*
HYDROLOGIC RESEARCH, *11.462*
Hydrometeorological Development, NOAA, *11.467*
Hydropower, see Energy *entries*; Public utilities

HYDROPOWER RECREATION ASSISTANCE [DOI], 15.927
Hypertension, see Health, medical *entries*; Preventive health services

I&I (Inventions and Innovations Program), DOE, *81.036*
IAATP (Infant Adoption Awareness Training Program), *93.254*
IAIP (Information Analysis Infrastructure Protection), DHS, *97.080*
ICB (Institutional Capacity Building), USAID, *98.005*
ICF (Inertial Confinement Fusion), DOE, *81.112*
IDA (Individual Development Accounts) Demonstration Program, ACF, *93.602*
IDEA (Individuals with Disabilities Education Act), see Disabled, handicapped education
IFCC (Internet Fraud Complaint Center), *16.612*
IFLOWS (Integrated Flood Observing and Warning System), *11.450*
IHE (institution of higher education), see Higher education institutions
IHI (Infant Health Initiatives), *93.946*
IHS (Indian Health Service), HHS, see Agency Index
IHS (Indian Health Service) Loan Repayment Program, *93.164*
IIPP (Institute for International Public Policy), *84.269*
Illiteracy
  adult education programs, *84.002*
  Community Learning Centers, *84.287*
  Early Reading First, *84.359*
  Even Start, Indians, *84.258*
  Even Start, state, *84.213*
  Literacy Program for Prisoners, *84.255*
  Literacy through School Libraries, *84.364*
  National Institute for Literacy, fellowships, *84.257*
  National Literacy Act of 1991, *84.255*
  Ready-to-Learn TV, early childhood education, *84.295*
  see also Adult education; Bilingual education, services; Education counseling; Libraries; Tutoring; Volunteers
IMLS (Institute of Museum and Library Services), National Foundation on the Arts and the Humanities, see Agency Index
Immigration and Nationality Act, see Aliens, immigrants, refugees
Immigration and Naturalization Service (INS), DOJ, see Agency Index
Immigration, citizenship, see Adult education; Aliens, immigrants, refugees
Immigrants, see Aliens, immigrants, refugees
IMMUNIZATION GRANTS, *93.268*
Immunization, immunology
  cancer research, *93.393, 93.395, 93.396*
  childhood immunization, state, local programs, *93.283*
  deafness, communicative disorders research, *93.173*
  FDA research, *93.103*
  hazardous waste sites health studies, *93.206*
  health services block grant activities, *93.991*
  Immunization Grants, *93.268*

immunology, immunological diseases research, *93.855*
neurological disorders research, *93.853*
research, information, *93.185*
Urban Indian Health Services, *93.193*
see also Communicable diseases; Disease control; Epidemiology; Health, medical *entries*; Preventive health services
IMMUNIZATION RESEARCH, DEMONSTRATION, PUBLIC INFORMATION AND EDUCATION—TRAINING AND CLINICAL SKILLS IMPROVEMENT PROJECTS, *93.185*
IMPACT AID [DOED], *84.041*
IMPACT AID—FACILITIES MAINTENANCE [DOED], *84.040*
Import Price Index, 17.003
Imports, *see* International commerce, investment
IMPROVEMENT AND REPAIR OF INDIAN DETENTION FACILITIES, *15.063*
IMPROVING, ENHANCING, AND EVALUATING OUTCOMES OF COMPREHENSIVE HEART HEALTH CARE PROGRAMS FOR HIGH-RISK WOMEN, *93.012*
IMPROVING TEACHER QUALITY STATE GRANTS, *84.367*
IMPROVING THE CAPABILITY OF INDIAN TRIBAL GOVERNMENTS TO REGULATE ENVIRONMENTAL QUALITY, *93.581*
Income tax, *see* Taxes, tax incentives
Independent Boards and Commissions, 90.100 through 90.400
INDEPENDENT EDUCATION AND SCIENCE PROJECTS AND PROGRAMS [NOAA], *11.449*
Independent living, *see* Aging and the aged; Disabled, handicapped, housing; Group homes; Housing, congregate; Housing, elderly; Vocational rehabilitation
INDEPENDENT LIVING—STATE GRANTS, *84.169*
INDIAN ADULT EDUCATION, *15.026*
Indian affairs
American Indian Agriculture Resource Management Act, *15.034*, *15.049*
American Indian Trust Fund Management Reform Act of 1994, *15.147*
BIA facilities operations, maintenance, *15.048*
Children's Justice Act, *16.583*
Community Fire Protection, *15.031*
Consolidated Tribal Grant Program, *15.021*
detention facilities improvement, repair, *15.063*
DOD activities mitigation, 12.116
environmental quality regulation, *93.581*
EPA capacity building, *66.709*
EPA Direct Implementation Tribal Cooperative Agreements, *66.473*
EPA General Assistance Program, *66.926*
EPA Office of Enforcement and Compliance Assurance Tribal Resources, EPA, *66.310*
Fire Protection, BIA facilities, training, *15.064*
Hanford site, tribal public health capacity, *93.202*
hazardous materials handling, planning, training, *97.020*
health programs, tribal self-governance, *93.210*

hunting, fishing rights, *15.050*
Indian Claims Limitation Act of 1982, *15.052*, *15.053*, *15.055*
Indian Country Alcohol and Drug Prevention, DOJ, *16.616*
Indian Country Investigations, FBI training, 16.308
Indian Dams Safety Act of 1994, *15.049*
Indian Environmental General Assistance Program Act, *66.110*, *66.310*, *66.606*, *66.709*
Indian Environmental Regulatory Enhancement Act, *93.581*
Indian Law Enforcement Reform Act, *15.030*
Indian Rights Protection, *15.036*
Indian Self-Determination and Education Assistance Act (ISDEAA), *15.020*, *15.021*, *15.022*, *15.024*, *15.025*, *15.026*, *15.029*, *15.030*, *15.031*, *15.032*, *15.033*, *15.034*, *15.035*, *15.036*, *15.037*, *15.038*, *15.039*, *15.040*, *15.041*, *15.042*, *15.044*, *15.045*, *15.046*, *15.047*, *15.048*, *15.049*, *15.050*, *15.051*, *15.052*, *15.055*, *15.057*, *15.060*, *15.061*, *15.062*, *15.063*, *15.064*, *15.065*, *15.108*, *15.114*, *15.124*, *15.141*, *15.147*, *27.011*, *93.210*, *93.228*, *93.441*
Indian Self-Determination 638 Contracts, *93.441*
intergovernmental exchange of personnel, 27.011
language preservation, *93.587*
Law Enforcement, *15.030*
Loans to Indian Tribes and Tribal Corporations Act, *10.421*
local law enforcement block grants, *16.592*
museum operation, 15.850, *45.308*
Native American Graves Protection and Repatriation Act of 1990, *15.922*
Native American Programs Act of 1974, *93.581*, *93.587*, *93.612*
Navajo-Hopi Settlement Act, *15.057*
personnel training, Federal Law Enforcement Training Center, DHS, *97.081*
Real Estate Programs, *15.040*
self-determination contracts, *15.024*
Snyder Act of 1921, *15.025*, *15.026*, *15.032*, *15.035*, *15.037*, *15.038*, *15.039*, *15.050*, *15.051*, *15.058*, *15.059*, *15.060*, *15.061*, *15.065*, *15.108*, *15.113*, *15.114*, *15.124*, *15.146*
treaty rights, attorney fees, *15.053*
treaty rights, litigation support, *15.052*
Tribal Court Assistance Program, *16.608*
Tribal Courts, *15.029*
Tribal Courts Trust Reform Initiative, *15.147*
Tribal Employment Rights Offices, *30.009*
tribal government, *15.020*
tribal jail construction, *16.596*
Tribal Self-Governance Act of 1994, *15.063*, *15.064*
tribal self-government, *15.022*, *93.612*
Tribal Wildlife Grants, FWS, *15.639*
Tribal Youth Program, OJJDP, *16.731*
Udall congressional internships, *85.402*
Udall doctoral fellowships, *85.401*
Udall undergraduate scholarships, *85.400*
violence against women, programs, training, *16.587*
see also Alaska, Alaska natives; Hawaii, Hawaii natives; Indian *entries*; Legal services

Indian Arts and Crafts Board, DOI, *see* Agency Index
INDIAN ARTS AND CRAFTS DEVELOPMENT, 15.850
INDIAN CHILD AND FAMILY EDUCATION, 15.043
INDIAN CHILD WELFARE ACT—TITLE II GRANTS, 15.144
Indian children
 abuse, justice act grants, 16.583
 child and family services, day care, foster care, recreation, welfare, 15.144
 family violence prevention services, 93.671
 food assistance, women, infants, children, 10.565
 Head Start, 93.600
 Indian Child Welfare Act, 15.144
 Social Services program, 15.025
 Tribal Courts Trust Reform Initiative, 15.147
 Tribal Youth Program, OJJDP, 16.731
 see also Alaska, Alaska natives; Hawaii, Hawaii natives; Maternal, child health, welfare
INDIAN COMMUNITY DEVELOPMENT BLOCK GRANT PROGRAM, 14.862
INDIAN COMMUNITY FIRE PROTECTION, 15.031
INDIAN COUNTRY ALCOHOL AND DRUG PREVENTION, 16.616
INDIAN COUNTRY INVESTIGATIONS, 16.308
Indian Dams Safety Maintenance Program, 15.049
Indian economic, business development
 arts and crafts marketing, 15.850
 CDBG, 14.862
 CDBG planning assistance, 14.227
 government contracts, 59.006
 HUD, Rural Housing and Economic Development, 14.250
 Loan Guaranty Program, 15.124
 management, technical assistance, 11.800
 microenterprise development training, technical assistance, 59.050
 Native American Program, technical assistance, 11.801
 Rural Business Enterprise Grants, 10.769
 rural business, industrial loans, 10.768
 SBA Native American Economic Development Assistance, 59.052
 social, economic self-sufficiency development, 93.612
 tribal revolving loan funds, loan guarantees, administration, 15.032
 tribal self-government, 15.022
 see also Alaska, Alaska natives; Business development; Disadvantaged, business development; Economic development; Hawaii, Hawaii natives; Indian affairs; Indian lands; Small business
INDIAN ECONOMIC DEVELOPMENT, 15.032
INDIAN EDUCATION—ASSISTANCE TO SCHOOLS, 15.130
INDIAN EDUCATION FACILITIES, OPERATIONS, AND MAINTENANCE, 15.047
INDIAN EDUCATION—GRANTS TO LOCAL EDUCATIONAL AGENCIES, 84.060
INDIAN EDUCATION—HIGHER EDUCATION GRANT PROGRAM, 15.114

Indian education, training
 adult education, 15.026
 agricultural, 1994 Institutions, 10.227
 agriculture, food sciences, tribal colleges, 10.221, 10.222
 children, institutionalized handicapped, 15.045
 college scholarships, 15.022
 compensatory, 84.010
 Consolidated Tribal Grant Program, 15.021
 English Language Acquisition Grants, 84.365
 EPA research fellowships, graduate, undergraduate, 66.513
 EPA STAR graduate fellowships, 66.514
 Even Start, 84.258
 Family and Child Education, 15.043
 Haskell and SIPI, 15.058
 Head Start parent programs, 93.600
 health, allied professions recruitment, 93.970
 health professions scholarships, 93.123, 93.219, 93.971, 93.972
 higher education grants, 15.114
 higher education strengthening, 84.031
 IHS education loan repayments, 93.164
 Indian Adult Vocational Training Act of 1956, 15.060, 15.061, 15.108, 15.146
 Indian Education Amendments of 1978, 15.042, 15.043, 15.044, 15.045, 15.046, 15.047
 Indian School Equalization Program, 15.042
 Ironworker Training Program, 15.146
 Johnson-O'Malley Act, BIA, 15.130
 language preservation, 93.587
 museum services, 45.308
 Native American Languages Act of 1992, 93.587
 Native American Library Services, 45.311
 NEH curriculum, materials development, 45.162
 NEH fellowships, 45.160
 nurses, education loan repayments, 93.908
 personnel training, Federal Law Enforcement Training Center, DHS, 97.081
 school administrative costs, 15.046
 school operations costs, 15.047
 school repair, replacement, 15.062
 Special Higher Education Scholarships, 15.059
 student transportation, 15.044
 supplementary education programs, 15.130, 84.060
 Tech-Prep Education, 84.243
 tribal IHE facilities, HUD, 14.519
 tribally-controlled IHEs, 15.027, 15.028
 Tribally Controlled Community College Assistance Act, 15.027, 15.028
 Tribally Controlled Schools Act, 15.042, 15.044, 15.046, 15.047, 15.062, 15.064
 Udall congressional internships, 85.402
 Udall doctoral fellowships, 85.401
 Udall undergraduate scholarships, 85.400
 vocational, 84.101
 vocational, employment assistance, 15.108
 vocational rehabilitation, 84.250
 vocational, technical, tribally controlled, 84.245
 vocational, United Tribes Technical College, 15.060
 see also Adult education; Alaska, Alaska natives; Education *entries*; Hawaii, Hawaii natives; Indian affairs; Technical training; Vocational education

MASTER INDEX   965

Indian employment
adult education, *15.026*
community development block grants, *14.862*
Consolidated Tribal Grant Program, *15.021*
employment rights, *30.009*
Ironworker Training Program, *15.146*
Tribal Work Grants, *93.594*
United Sioux Tribes Development Corporation, *15.061*
vocational rehabilitation, *84.250*
vocational training, employment assistance, *15.108*
WIA Native American Employment and Training, *17.265*
see also Alaska, Alaska natives; Employment *entries*; Hawaii, Hawaii natives; Vocational education
INDIAN EMPLOYMENT ASSISTANCE, *15.108*
INDIAN ENVIRONMENTAL GENERAL ASSISTANCE PROGRAM (GAP), *66.926*
INDIAN GRADUATE STUDENT SCHOLARSHIPS, *15.059*
Indian Health Service (IHS), HHS, *see* Agency Index
INDIAN HEALTH SERVICE EDUCATIONAL LOAN REPAYMENT, *93.164*
INDIAN HEALTH SERVICE—HEALTH MANAGEMENT DEVELOPMENT PROGRAM, *93.228*
Indian health, social services
bilingual, bicultural health demonstrations, *93.105*
block grants, community development, *14.862*
child welfare, day care, foster care, counseling, family assistance, *15.144*
children's justice act, *16.583*
community health coalitions, *93.137*
crime victim assistance, *16.582*
diabetes program, *93.237*, *93.442*
elderly, special programs, *93.047*
epidemiology centers, *93.231*
family violence prevention services, *93.671*
food assistance, *10.550*, *10.565*, *10.567*
food assistance, WIC, *10.557*
Great Lakes fish consumption effects, *93.208*
Hanford site, tribal public health capacity, *93.202*
health care research, demonstration, *93.933*
health management development, *93.228*
health professionals recruitment, *93.954*, *93.970*
health professions scholarships, *93.219*, *93.971*, *93.972*
health programs, tribal self-governance, *93.210*
IHS education loan repayments, *93.164*
Indian Health Care Improvement Act, amendments, *93.123*, *93.164*, *93.193*, *93.219*, *93.231*, *93.954*, *93.970*, *93.971*, *93.972*
Indian Self-Determination, *93.441*
injury prevention, *93.228*, *93.284*
nurses, education loan repayments, *93.908*
social, economic self-sufficiency development, *93.612*
Social Services program, *15.025*
Tribal Courts Trust Reform Initiative, *15.147*
Tribal Lead Grants, *66.715*
tribal self-government, *15.022*
Udall doctoral fellowships, *85.401*
Udall undergraduate scholarships, *85.400*
urban Indians, *93.193*
violence against women, victim services, *16.587*
vocational rehabilitation, *84.250*
welfare assistance, *15.113*
see also Alaska, Alaska natives; Community health services; Hawaii, Hawaii natives; Health, medical services; Social services; Volunteers
Indian housing
block grants, *14.867*
construction, rehabilitation, *14.862*
counseling program, *10.441*
farm laborers, *10.405*
federal housing guarantees, *14.869*
Housing Improvement Program (HIP), *15.141*
HUD, Rural Housing and Economic Development, *14.250*
loan guarantees, *14.865*
Native American Housing Assistance and Self-Determination Act of 1996 (NAHASDA), *14.867*, *14.869*
outreach, socially disadvantaged, *10.443*
rehabilitation, *10.433*
Tribal Lead Grants, *66.715*
tribal self-government, *15.022*
veterans, *64.126*
see also Housing *entries*
INDIAN HOUSING ASSISTANCE, *15.141*
INDIAN HOUSING BLOCK GRANTS, *14.867*
Indian Housing Improvement Program (HIP), *15.141*
INDIAN JOB PLACEMENT—UNITED SIOUX TRIBES DEVELOPMENT CORPORATION, *15.061*
Indian lands
abandoned mine land reclamation, *15.252*
agriculture programs, *15.034*
Alaska native allotments, *15.055*
dam safety, *15.049*, *15.065*
DOD activities mitigation, 12.116
endangered species, *15.051*
environmental impact mitigation, DOD activities, *93.582*
environmental management, *66.926*, *93.581*
environmental management, historic, archaeological preservation, *15.041*
EPA Office of Enforcement and Compliance Assurance Tribal Resources, *66.310*
firefighting, FEMA reimbursement, *97.016*
forestry, *15.035*
hazardous materials handling, planning, training, *20.703*
hazardous waste management, *66.812*
Indian Land Consolidation Act, *15.040*
Indian Rights Protection, *15.036*
irrigation operations, dam safety, *15.049*
land acquisition loans, *10.421*
Loan Guarantees for Indian Housing, *14.865*
minerals, mining, energy resources, *15.038*
Navajo-Hopi settlement, *15.057*
oil, gas lease inspection, *15.222*
Real Estate Programs, *15.040*
road maintenance, *15.033*
schools, Impact Aid, *84.041*
transuranic waste transport, *81.106*
treaty rights, attorney fees, *15.053*
treaty rights, litigation support, *15.052*
Tribal Landowner Incentive Program, *15.638*

Indian lands *(continued)*
Tribal Wildlife Grants, FWS, *15.639*
water resources, *15.037*
watershed protection, *10.904*
Wildlife and Parks, *15.039*
see also Indian affairs; Public lands
INDIAN LAW ENFORCEMENT, *15.030*
INDIAN LOANS—ECONOMIC DEVELOPMENT, *15.124*
INDIAN POST SECONDARY SCHOOLS, *15.058*
Indian Program, WIA, *17.265*
INDIAN RIGHTS PROTECTION, *15.036*
INDIAN SCHOOL EQUALIZATION PROGRAM, *15.042*
INDIAN SCHOOLS—STUDENT TRANSPORTATION, *15.044*
INDIAN SELF-DETERMINATION [HHS], *93.441*
Indian Self-Determination and Education Assistance Act (ISDEAA), *see* Indian Affairs
INDIAN SELF-DETERMINATION CONTRACT SUPPORT, *15.024*
Indian social services, *see* Indian health, social services
INDIAN SOCIAL SERVICES—WELFARE ASSISTANCE, *15.113*
INDIAN TRIBES AND TRIBAL CORPORATION LOANS, *10.421*
INDIAN VOCATIONAL TRAINING—UNITED TRIBES TECHNICAL COLLEGE, *15.060*
Individual and Household Housing, FEMA, *97.048*
Individual and Household Housing Operations, FEMA, *97.049*
Individual and Household Other Needs, FEMA, *97.050*
Individual Development Accounts (IDA) Demonstration Program, *93.602*
Individuals with Disabilities Education Act (IDEA), *see* Disabled, handicapped, education
Industrial arts, *see* Vocational education
Industrial hygiene, *see* Occupational health, safety
Industrial safety, *see* Occupational health, safety
Industrial wastes, *see* Hazardous materials, waste; Toxic substances, toxicology; Waste treatment, disposal
Industry, *see* Business development; Economic development; Private sector
Inertial Confinement Fusion (ICF), DOE, *81.112*
Infant Health Initiatives, *93.946*
Infants, children, *see* Child care services; Disabled, handicapped children; Early childhood education; Indian children; Maternal, child health, welfare
Infectious diseases research, *93.856*
INFANT ADOPTION AWARENESS TRAINING, *93.254*
INFORMATION ANALYSIS INFRASTRUCTURE PROTECTION (IAIP) PILOT PROJECTS [DHS], *97.080*
Information, general, clearinghouses
ADA technical assistance, *16.108*
adoption services, *93.652*
agricultural commodity market news, 10.153
agricultural, rural economic research, 10.250
agriculture, National Agricultural Library, 10.700
AIDS/HIV prevention, public education, *93.118*
air transportation consumer affairs, 20.900

aviation, civil, 20.100
business management, minority, Indian, *11.800*
Census Bureau data, 11.001
census geography, 11.003
Census Intergovernmental Services, 11.004
census search, personal, 11.006
census tabulations, 11.005
civil rights clearinghouse, 29.001
commodity futures, 78.004
communications, FCC, 32.001
consumer protection, FTC, 36.001
copyright services, 42.002
corrections clearinghouse, *16.603*
crime information center, 16.304
crime statistics, *16.550*
criminal conspiracy, regional information sharing, *16.610*
criminal history record systems, *16.554*
disabilities, National Limb Loss Information Center, *93.184*
disabled, handicapped persons, employment, *17.720*
disabled, rehabilitation, benefits, services, *84.161*
disadvantaged adults, education, financial assistance, *84.066*
DOJ Special Data Collections and Statistical Studies, *16.734*
drug abuse prevention, DEA, 16.005
endangered species, plants, wildlife, *15.615*
energy information center, 81.039
energy, OSTI, 81.064
environmental affairs, National Agricultural Library, 10.700
families, youth clearinghouse, *93.550*
FBI crime statistics, 16.305
Federal Citizen Information Center, 39.009
Federal Records Centers, 89.001
food, nutrition, National Agricultural Library, 10.700
foreign markets, 11.108
foreign trade standards and regulations, NCSCI, 11.610
fraud information center, *16.613*
gifted and talented students, national center, *84.206*
Government Bookstore, government publications, 40.002
government publications, depository libraries, 40.001
health promotion, national, *93.990*
historic landmarks, 15.912
historic places, 15.914
Immigration and Nationality Act, *16.110*
international industry, markets, 11.110
Internet Fraud Complaint Center, *16.612*
interstate land sales, 14.168
juvenile delinquency clearinghouse, *16.542*
manufactured home standards, 14.171
maps, charts, census, 11.003
mental retardation, 93.613
National Archives, 89.001
National Center for Missing and Exploited Children, *16.543, 97.076*
National Register of Historic Places, 15.914
National Technical Information Service, 11.650
National Trade Data Bank, 11.026

natural landmarks registry, 15.910
NRC local public document rooms, *77.005*
Occupational and Employment Information, DOED, *84.346*
patents, trademarks, 11.900
physical fitness promotion, 93.289
pollution source reduction information dissemination, outreach, EPA, *66.717*
Presidential Libraries, 89.001
rehabilitation training materials clearinghouse, *84.275*
runaway youth, *93.623*
rural health care, *93.913*
securities market, 58.001
sexually transmitted disease research, *93.978*
small business, agriculture regulatory ombudsman, *59.053*
small business on-line counseling, 59.005
special education, *84.326*
SSA beneficiaries outreach, services, *96.008*
SSA disabled beneficiaries outreach, services, *96.009*
standards and certification information center, NCSCI, 11.610
State of the Nation, ESA, 11.027
statistical areas, census, 11.003
tax information, federal, 21.003
TIGER (Topologically Integrated Geographic Encoding and Referencing) system, 11.003
veterans benefits, 64.115
white-collar crime center, *16.612*
vocational education, *84.051*
women's educational equity, *84.083*
women's employment, 17.700
see also Agricultural statistics; Census services; Complaint investigation; Computer products, sciences, services; Consumers, consumer services; Economics, research, statistics; Hotlines; Information, scientific and technical; Libraries; Publications; Statistics
Information processing, *see* Computer products, sciences, services
Information science, *see* Computer products, sciences, services; Libraries
Information, scientific and technical
aerospace, 43.001, 43.002
agricultural research, National Agricultural Library, 10.700
agricultural, rural economic research, 10.950
animal, pest damage, disease control, *10.028*
calibration, testing, 11.601
census services, 11.001
chemical, physical properties of materials, 11.603
climate, *11.428*
computer products, services, federal, 11.650
crop estimates, 10.950
drugs, narcotics, DEA, 16.003
economic statistics, analysis, national, 11.025
endangered species, plants, wildlife, *15.615*
energy information center, 81.039
energy, OSTI, 81.064
engineering research, *11.609*
environmental affairs, National Agricultural Library, 10.700
Environmental Information Exchange Network Grants, *66.608*
farm employment, 10.950
FDA, *93.103*
fire research, *11.609*
flood plain data, services, 12.104
food, nutrition, National Agricultural Library, 10.700
foreign trade standards and regulation, NCSCI, 11.610
geodetic surveys, *11.400*
geologic mapping, *15.810*
geospatial data clearinghouse, *15.809*
handicapped, facilities accessibility standards, design, research, training, 88.001
hazardous materials, Superfund technical assistance to citizens groups, *66.806*
historical properties preservation, 15.915
livestock data estimates, 10.950
marine mammal data, *11.439*
National Standard Reference Data System, 11.603
National Technical Information Service, 11.650
NIST Congressionally-Identified Projects, *11.617*
NRC local public document rooms, *77.005*
patents, trademarks, 11.900
pollution source reduction information dissemination, outreach, EPA, *66.717*
snowmelt surveys, 10.907
soil survey data, 10.903
soil, water conservation practices, NRCS, 10.902
solid waste management, *66.808*
Standard Reference Materials, 11.604
standards and certification information center, NCSCI, 11.610
technology reports, data, 11.650
TIGER (Topologically Integrated Geographic Encoding and Referencing) system, 11.003
watershed, river basin surveys, NRCS, 10.906
weights, measures, 11.606
see also Agricultural statistics; Census services; Computer products, sciences, services; Economics, research, statistics; Information, general, clearinghouses; Libraries; Publications; Scientific research; Statistics; Technology transfer, utilization
INFORMATION SECURITY GRANT PROGRAM, *12.902*
Information Security University Research Program (URP), NSA, *12.902*
Injuries, *see* Occupational health, safety; Public safety
INJURY PREVENTION AND CONTROL RESEARCH AND STATE AND COMMUNITY-BASED PROGRAMS, *93.136*
INJURY PREVENTION PROGRAM FOR AMERICAN INDIANS AND ALASKAN NATIVES—COOPERATIVE PROGRAMS, *93.284*
Inmates, *see* Corrections
INNOVATIONS IN APPLIED HEALTH RESEARCH, *93.061*
Innovative Supportive Housing, HUD, *14.235*
INS (Immigration and Naturalization Service), DOJ, *see* Agency Index
Inspection and Grading of Fishery Products, 11.413
INSPECTION GRADING AND STANDARDIZATION [USDA], 10.162

Inspection services, *see* Agricultural marketing; Complaint investigation; Consumers, consumer services; Dairy industry; Fisheries industry; Food inspection, grading; Livestock industry; Poultry, egg products
INSTITUTE FOR INTERNATIONAL PUBLIC POLICY [DOED], *84.269*
Institute of Education Sciences, DOED, *84.305*
Institute of Museum and Library Services (IMLS), National Foundation on the Arts and the Humanities, *see* Agency Index
Institute of Peace, 91.001 through 91.002
INSTITUTIONAL CAPACITY BUILDING [USAID], *98.005*
Institutionalized Handicapped, BIA, *15.045*
Institutions of higher education, *see* Higher education institutions
Insular areas, *see* U.S. possessions, territories
Insular areas community development block grants, *14.225*
Insurance
 art works, artifacts, books, manuscripts, motion pictures, photographs, videotapes, *45.201*
 brownfields clean-up, *66.817*
 Certified Development Company Loans, *59.041*
 Commodity Partnerships for Risk Management Education, RMA- USDA, *10.457, 10.459*
 credit union deposits, *44.001*
 Crop Insurance in Targeted States, *10.458*
 crops, noninsured, disaster assistance, *10.451*
 data, Census Bureau, 11.001
 DOT contracts, bonds, *20.903*
 Employee Retirement Income Security Act (ERISA), *86.001*
 farm crops, *10.450*
 farm loans, subsidies, *10.437*
 farm premium payment loans, *10.406*
 farming risk management outreach, RMA, *10.455*
 FEMA community flood assistance program, *97.023*
 fishing vessels, seizure, *19.204*
 Flood Mitigation Assistance, *97.029*
 flood, mudflow, erosion, NFIP, *97.022*
 foreign investments, OPIC, *70.002, 70.003*
 GI insurance, *64.103*
 Inspector General Act of 1978, *59.016*
 international political risk, *70.003*
 law enforcement officers indemnification, *16.592*
 longshore, harbor workers compensation, *17.302*
 maritime war risk, *20.803*
 mine subsidence, *15.252*
 National Service Life Insurance Act, *64.103*
 New York City, Debris Removal Insurance, *97.064*
 pension, welfare benefits information, 17.150
 pension plans, *86.001*
 railroad workers, death, health, unemployment, *57.001*
 relationship verification, Census Bureau, 11.006
 Servicemen's Indemnity and Insurance Act, *64.103*
 Social Security program research, demonstrations, *96.007*
 Social Security, retirement, *96.002*
 Social Security survivors, *96.004*
 student loans, *84.032*
 surety bonds, *59.016*
 unemployment, *17.225*
 U.S. flagships, *20.803*
 veterans life, home mortgage protection, *64.103*
 War Risk Insurance Act, DVA, *64.103*
 World War Veterans Act, *64.103*
 see also Agricultural commodities, stabilization; Agricultural loans; Employee benefits; Flood prevention, control; Health insurance; Housing *entries*; Maritime industry; Small business; Social Security Act; Veterans *entries*
INTEGRATED PROGRAMS [USDA], *10.303*
INTERAGENCY HAZARDOUS MATERIALS PUBLIC SECTOR TRAINING AND PLANNING GRANTS, *20.703*
INTERCITY BUS SECURITY GRANTS [DHS], *97.057*
Interdisciplinary Training for Health Care for Rural Areas, *93.192*
INTEREST ASSISTANCE PROGRAM [USDA], *10.437*
INTEREST REDUCTION PAYMENTS—RENTAL AND COOPERATIVE HOUSING FOR LOWER INCOME FAMILIES, *14.103*
INTERGOVERNMENTAL CLIMATE—PROGRAM (NESDIS), *11.428*
Intergovernmental personnel, *see* Federal employment; Government
INTERGOVERNMENTAL PERSONNEL ACT (IPA) MOBILITY PROGRAM, 27.011
Intergovernmental Services Program, Census Bureau, 11.004
Interior design, *see* Architecture; Arts, arts education; Buildings; Disabled, handicapped; Disabled, handicapped, housing; Veterans housing
Interjurisdictional Fisheries Act, *see* Fisheries industry
INTERJURISDICTIONAL FISHERIES ACT OF 1986, *11.407*
INTERMEDIARY RELENDING PROGRAM [USDA], *10.767*
Intermediate care facilities, *see* Health facilities *entries*; Nursing homes
Internal medicine, *see* Family medicine; Health, medical education, training; Health, medical services; Osteopathy; Pediatrics
Internal Revenue Service (IRS), Department of the Treasury, *see* Agency Index
International Collaborative Research and Scientific Exchanges, USDA, *10.961*
International commerce, investment
 agricultural, Market Access Program, *10.601*
 agricultural marketing, states, *10.156*
 agricultural, rural economic research, 10.250
 agricultural standards, 10.162
 Agricultural Trade Act of 1978, *10.600, 10.601*
 agricultural transportation services, AMS, 10.167
 agriculture, export market development, *10.600*
 Agriculture, Trade and Development Assistance Act of 1954, *98.007, 98.009*
 antidumping duties, 11.106
 BECA English Language Fellow Program, *19.421*
 business education centers, *84.220*
 business-education linkage, *84.153*

MASTER INDEX 969

business internships, Eurasian executives, scientists, *11.114*
Census Bureau data, 11.001
commodity distribution, developing countries, *10.606*
countervailing duties, 11.106
CSREES international agricultural science, education, *10.305*
economic data, analysis, 11.025
Emerging Markets Program, USDA, *10.603*
Emerson Humanitarian Trust, FSA, *10.079*
Export Administration Act of 1979, 11.150
export control, information, licensing, regulations, 11.150
export counseling, information, 11.108
export, import price index, 17.003
Export Loans, SBA, *59.054*
Export Promotion Market Development Cooperation, *11.112*
Food for Education, FAS, *10.608*
Food for Progress, *10.606*
Food Security Wheat Reserve (Emerson Humanitarian Trust), FSA, *10.079*
Foreign Assistance acts, *11.114, 70.002, 70.003, 98.001, 98.002, 98.003, 98.004, 98.005, 98.006, 98.011*
foreign standards and regulations, NCSCI, 11.610
Foreign Trade Zones Act of 1934, 11.111
foreign trade zones, U.S., 11.111
Global Business Opportunities, ESA-USDC, 11.026
industrial data, 11.110
International Emergency Economic Powers Act, 11.150
investment financing, OPIC, *70.002, 70.003*
ITA Special Projects, *11.113*
Middle Eastern Partnership Initiative, 19.500
National Trade Data Bank, 11.026
North American Free Trade Agreement Implementation Act, *17.245*
Omnibus Trade and Competitiveness Act of 1988, 11.026, 11.027, 11.108, *11.112, 11.611, 11.612,* 11.650, *17.245*
Operation Safe Commerce, DHS, *97.058*
organic agriculture, CSREES, *10.307*
port security grants, DHS, *97.056*
productivity data, 17.004
Quality Samples Program, FAS, *10.605*
State of the Nation, ESA, 11.027
Technical Assistance for Specialty Crops, FAS, *10.604*
Trade Act of 1974, *10.609, 11.313, 17.225, 17.245*
Trade Act of 2002, *10.609, 93.780, 93.781*
trade adjustment allowances, *11.313, 17.245*
Trade Adjustment Assistance, FAS, *10.609*
trade agreement negotiation, enforcement, 11.110
Trade Agreements Act of 1979, 11.106, 11.610
trade development assistance, 11.110
Unemployment Insurance, *17.225*
unfair agricultural marketing practices, perishables, 10.165
Uruguay Round Agreements Act, 11.106
U.S. Export-Import Bank, 11.108
U.S. flagship subsidies, *20.813*
USAID programs, *98.001*
waterborne commerce, ship subsidies, *20.813*

see also Agricultural marketing; Business development; Insurance; International programs, studies; Maritime industry; Trade adjustment assistance
INTERNATIONAL EDUCATION—TECHNOLOGICAL INNOVATION AND COOPERATION FOR FOREIGN INFORMATION ACCESS, *84.337*
INTERNATIONAL EDUCATION TRAINING AND RESEARCH, *19.430*
INTERNATIONAL EDUCATION—U.S. COLLEGES AND UNIVERSITIES [DOD], *12.550*
INTERNATIONAL FINANCIAL ASSISTANCE PROJECTS SPONSORED BY THE OFFICE OF INTERNATIONAL AFFAIRS [EPA], *66.931*

International programs, studies
agriculture, *10.217, 10.960, 10.961, 10.962*
alcoholism, biomedical research, *93.273*
alternative, complementary medicine research, *93.213*
Assistance to Schools and Hospitals Abroad, USAID, *98.006*
atmospheric, climate, environmental systems, NOAA, *11.432*
BECA arts exchanges, *19.409*
BECA education training, research, *19.430*
BECA English Language Fellow Program, *19.421*
BECA English Language Specialist/Speaker Program, *19.423*
BECA Overseas Educational Advising, *19.432*
biomedical, behavioral research traineeships, *93.989*
business education centers, *84.220*
business-education linkage, *84.153*
business internships, Eurasian executives, scientists, *11.114*
college faculty research abroad, *84.019*
Colorado River basin salinity control, *10.070*
commodity distribution in developing countries, *10.606, 10.607*
Congress-Bundestag Youth Exchange, BECA, *19.410*
Cooperative Development Program, USAID, *98.002*
CSREES agricultural science, education, *10.305*
doctoral research abroad, *84.022*
Eastern, Southeast Europe, NIS, training, *19.300*
education research, methods, instructional materials development, *84.017*
educators exchange, *19.408, 84.304*
elephant conservation, *15.620, 15.621*
environmental education exchanges, *66.950, 66.951*
EPA aging, children's health protection, *66.609*
EPA air pollution effects studies, demonstrations, *66.034*
EPA international financial assistance projects, *66.931*
Farmer-to-Farmer Program, *98.009*
Food for Education, FAS, *10.608*
Food For Peace, USAID, *98.007, 98.008*
Food for Progress, *10.606*
foreign information access, education technology, *84.337*

International programs, studies *(continued)*
foreign language, area studies, *84.015, 84.016*
foreign scholars-in-residence, undergraduate, BECA, *19.431*
Fulbright American Studies Institutes, *19.418*
Fulbright program, *19.400, 19.401, 19.408, 19.418, 84.018, 84.019, 84.021, 84.022*
Global AIDS, *93.067, 93.266*
Global Development Alliance, USAID, *98.011*
graduate fellowships, *84.015*
Great Apes Conservation, *15.629*
group projects abroad, *84.021*
Habitat Conservation, NOAA, *11.463*
historic properties preservation technology, training, *15.923*
humanitarian relief goods transport, USAID, *98.010*
Institutional Capacity Building, USAID, *98.005*
International Visitors Program, BECA, *19.402*
Japan-U.S. Friendship Commission Grants, *90.300*
Middle Eastern Partnership Initiative, 19.500
Migratory Bird Joint Ventures, research, training, *15.637*
Mutual Educational and Cultural Exchange Act (MECEA), *19.400* through *19.432, 84.018, 84.019, 84.021, 84.022*
National Security Education Programs, DOD, *12.550, 12.551*
NEA arts exchanges, *45.024*
NEH collaborative research, *45.161*
Neotropical Migratory Bird Conservation, *15.635*
Non-Governmental Organization Strengthening, USAID, *98.004*
NSF behavioral, social, economic sciences, *47.075*
NSF science, engineering, *47.079*
Ocean Freight Reimbursement, USAID, *98.003*
organic agriculture research, CSREES, *10.307*
overseas refugee assistance, global priorities, BPRM, *19.522*
overseas research centers, *84.274*
peace, conflict resolution, *91.001, 91.002*
Professional Exchanges, BECA, *19.415*
public policy programs, minority student fellowships, *84.269*
Research and Training for Eastern Europe and the Independent States of the Former Soviet Union Act of 1983, *19.300*
Rhinoceros and Tiger Conservation, *15.619*
teacher seminars abroad, *84.018*
Technical Assistance for Specialty Crops, FAS, *10.604*
tuberculosis control, prevention research, education, *93.947*
undergraduate, BECA, *19.425*
undergraduate, SEOG, *84.007*
United States Leadership Against HIV/AIDS and Malaria Act of 2003, *93.266*
USAID foreign assistance programs, *98.001*
USAID university development partnerships, *98.012*
wildlife without borders programs, education, research, training, FWS, *15.640, 15.641*
Woodrow Wilson Center fellowships, *85.300*
young political leaders, international exchange, *19.403*
see also Aliens, immigrants, refugees; Foreign languages; Humanities *entries*; International commerce, investment; Social sciences
INTERNATIONAL RESEARCH AND RESEARCH TRAINING [HHS], *93.989*
INTERNATIONAL RESEARCH AND STUDIES [DOED], *84.017*
INTERNATIONAL SCIENCE AND EDUCATION GRANT PROGRAM [USDA], *10.305*
INTERNATIONAL SCIENCE AND ENGINEERING (OISE) [NSF], *47.079*
International trade, *see* International commerce, investment
International Trade Administration (ITA), USDC, *see* Agency Index
International Trade Administration Special Projects, *11.113*
INTERNATIONAL TRAINING—FOREIGN PARTICIPANT [USDA], *10.962*
INTERNATIONAL VISITORS PROGRAM, *19.402*
INTERNET-BASED TECHNICAL ASSISTANCE [SBA], 59.005
INTERNSHIP PROGRAM FOR POSTSECONDARY STUDENTS [USDC], *11.702*
INTEROPERABLE COMMUNICATIONS EQUIPMENT [DHS], *97.055*
Interstate commerce
agriculture, animal, plant disease control, *10.025*
agricultural transportation services, AMS, 10.167
Border Enforcement Grants, FMCSA, *20.233*
Federal Mediation and Conciliation Service, 34.001
labor-management relations assistance, complaint investigations, 46.001
land sales, 14.168
meat, poultry inspection, *10.475*, 10.477
motor carrier transport regulations, *20.218*
Perishable Agricultural Commodities Act, 10.165
railroad safety standards, *20.303*
see also Motor vehicles; Railroads; Small business; Transportation; Water navigation
Interstate Land Sales Registration Program, 14.168
INTRAMURAL RESEARCH TRAINING AWARD [HHS], *93.140*
Inventions, *see* Patents, trademarks, inventions
INVENTIONS AND INNOVATIONS [DOE], *81.036*
Investigation and Prosecution of Child Abuse Through the Criminal Justice System, *16.547*
Investigation of complaints, *see* Complaint investigation
IPA (Intergovernmental Personnel Act) program, 27.011
IRONWORKER TRAINING PROGRAM, *15.146*
Irrigation
Colorado River basin, *10.070*
farm loans, interest subsidies, *10.437*
Indian lands, *15.049*
snowmelt surveys, 10.907
water re-use program, *15.504*
watershed projects, *10.904*
see also Flood prevention, control; Soil conservation; Water *entries*
IRRIGATION OPERATIONS AND MAINTENANCE ON INDIAN LANDS, *15.049*

IRS (Internal Revenue Service), Department of the Treasury, *see* Agency Index
IRTA (Intramural Research Training Award), NIH, *93.140*
ISA (Institutional Support Assistance), USAID, *98.005*
ISDEAA (Indian Self-Determination and Education Assistance Act), *see* Indian affairs
ISEP (Indian School Equalization Program), BIA, *15.042*
ITA (International Trade Administration), USDC, *see* Agency Index
ITA SPECIAL PROJECTS [USDC], *11.113*
ITEP (Information Technology and Evaluation Program), DHS, *97.066*
ITVERP (International Terrorism Victim Assistance Expense Reimbursement Program), DOJ, *16.321*

JAIBG (Juvenile Accountability Incentive Block Grants), *16.523*
Jails, *see* Corrections; Criminal justice system
James Madison Memorial Fellowship Foundation, *see* Agency Index (Scholarship and Fellowship Foundations)
JAMES MADISON MEMORIAL FELLOWSHIP PROGRAM, *85.500*
JAN (Job Accommodations Network), disabled, *17.720*
Japan-U.S. Friendship Commission, 90.300
JAPAN-U.S. FRIENDSHIP COMMISSION GRANTS, *90.300*
JAVITS FELLOWSHIPS, *84.170*
JAVITS GIFTED AND TALENTED STUDENTS EDUCATION GRANT PROGRAM, *84.206*
JIMO (Joint Institute for Marine Observation), NMFS, *11.455*
JJDPA (Juvenile Justice and Delinquency Prevention Act), *see* Juvenile delinquency
JOB ACCESS—REVERSE COMMUTE, *20.516*
Job Accommodations Network (JAN), disabled, *17.720*

Job creation
Appalachian region, *23.002, 23.011*
CDBG Economic Development Initiative, Section 108, *14.246*
community development block grants, *14.218, 14.219, 14.228*
Community Services Block Grant, discretionary, *93.570*
Delta region, *90.200, 90.201, 90.202*
economic deterioration causes, research, *11.312*
Empowerment Zones Program, *10.772, 14.244*
HBCU Program, HUD, *14.520*
IHE outreach, HUD, *14.511*
Indian community development block grants, *14.862*
insular areas community development block grants, *14.225*
Job Creation and Worker Assistance Act of 2002, *86.001*
Job Opportunities for Low-Income Individuals, TANF, *93.593*
planning organizations support, *11.302*
public works projects, EDA, *11.300*
rural business, industrial development, *10.768*

Rural Business Investment Program, RBCS, *10.860*
rural, economic development loans, RBCS, *10.854*
technical assistance, *11.303*
see also Appalachian region; Business development; Community development; Depressed areas; Economic development; Employment *entries*; Unemployment
JOB OPPORTUNITIES FOR LOW-INCOME INDIVIDUALS, *93.593*
Job training, *see* Apprenticeship training; Disabled, handicapped, employment; Disadvantaged, employment and training; Employment *entries*; Fellowships, scholarships, traineeships; Indian education, training; Indian employment; Teacher education, training; Technical training; Unemployment; Veterans education, training; Vocational *entries*; Women
Job Training Partnership Act (JTPA), *see* Employment development, training
JOHN OGONOWSKI FARMER-TO-FARMER PROGRAM [USAID, *98.009*
Johnson-O'Malley Act, BIA, *15.130*
Joint Hydrographic Center, NOAA, *11.400*
Joint Institute for Marine Observation (JIMO), NMFS, *11.455*
JOLI (Job Opportunities for Low-Income Individuals) Program, *93.593*
JTPA (Job Training Partnership Act), *see* Employment development, training
Judicial Child Abuse Training, *16.547*
JUMP (Juvenile Mentoring Program), DOJ, *16.726*
Junior Duck Stamp Contest, FWS, *15.644*
Justice, *see* Criminal justice system; Legal services
JUVENILE ACCOUNTABILITY INCENTIVE BLOCK GRANTS, *16.523*

Juvenile delinquency
civil rights, inmates, 16.105
clearinghouse, information, *16.542*
corrections research, *16.602*
corrections staff, ex-offenders training programs, *16.601*
criminal justice research, graduate fellowships, *16.561*
Delinquency Prevention Program, *16.548, 16.549*
Dropout Prevention Programs, ESEA, *84.360*
Drug Court Program, *16.585*
Drug-Free Schools and Communities, national programs, *84.184*
education of institutionalized children, *84.013*
Foster Grandparent Program, *94.011*
Gang Resistance Education and Training, BJA, *16.737*
gangs, drug abuse, trafficking, *16.544*
halfway houses, group homes, *16.540*
Incentive Grants for Local Delinquency Prevention Program Act, *16.548*
Juvenile Justice and Delinquency Prevention Act (JJDPA), *16.540, 16.541, 16.542, 16.543, 16.544, 16.549, 16.601, 16.602, 16.603, 16.726, 93.669*
juvenile justice system improvement, *16.523*
Juvenile Mentoring Program, *16.726*
local law enforcement block grants, *16.592*
Offender Reentry Program, *16.202*

Juvenile delinquency *(continued)*
offenders, justice, health, social services networks, *93.229*
personnel training, *16.542*
prevention, control demonstrations, *16.541*
prevention, control research, *16.542*
prevention programs, *16.540*
Prison Grants, violent offenders, *16.586*
prison rape elimination, personnel training, victim services, *16.735*
research fellowships, *16.566*
Safe Schools/Healthy Students National Evaluation, DOJ, *16.732*
Sex Offender Management, *16.203*
State Court Improvement Program, ACF, *93.586*
State Formula Grants, *16.540*
Tribal Youth Program, OJJDP, *16.731*
see also Alcohol abuse, alcoholism; Corrections; Criminal justice system; Drug abuse; Volunteers; Youth *entries*
Juvenile Justice and Delinquency Prevention Act (JJDPA), *see* Juvenile delinquency
JUVENILE JUSTICE AND DELINQUENCY PREVENTION—ALLOCATION TO STATES, *16.540*
JUVENILE MENTORING PROGRAM, *16.726*

K Awards, alcoholism, *93.271*
K Series Awards, mental health, *93.281*
KD&A (Knowledge Development and Application), SAMHSA, *93.230*
Keeping Children and Families Safe Act of 2003, *see* Maternal, child health, welfare
Kidney disease research, *see* Health, medical research
KIDNEY DISEASES, UROLOGY AND HEMATOLOGY RESEARCH, *93.849*
Kings Point, *20.807*
KLAMATH BASIN—ENVIRONMENTAL QUALITY INCENTIVES PROGRAM, *10.919*
Knowledge Development and Application (KD&A), SAMHSA, *93.230*

LABOR CERTIFICATION FOR ALIEN WORKERS, 17.203
LABOR FORCE STATISTICS, *17.002*
Labor Housing, USDA, *10.405*
LABOR-MANAGEMENT COOPERATION, 34.002
Labor-management relations
BLS data, *17.005*
collective bargaining, conciliation, mediation, FMCS, 34.001
labor-management committees, FMCS, *34.002*
Labor-Management Cooperation Act of 1978, *34.002*
Labor-Management Relations Act of 1947, 34.001, 46.001
Labor-Management Reporting and Disclosure Act of 1959, 17.309
labor organization practices, reports, 17.309
Landrum-Griffin Act, 17.309
unfair labor practices, 46.001
union representation elections, 46.001
see also Labor *entries*
LABOR-MANAGEMENT RELATIONS, 46.001

LABOR MEDIATION AND CONCILIATION, 34.001
LABOR ORGANIZATION REPORTS, 17.309
Labor standards
child labor standards, 17.303
Equal Pay Act, 30.005, 30.010
Fair Labor Standards Act, 17.303, 30.010
farm labor contractor registration, 17.308
Federal Wage Garnishment Law, 17.306
Federal Wage-Hour Laws, 17.303
federally assisted construction, 17.301, 17.303
labor-management committees, FMCS, *34.002*
OSHA Data Initiative, *17.505*
performing arts employees, 17.303
prevailing wage determinations, 17.303
productivity data, 17.004
safety, health, *17.503, 17.504*
sex-based wage differentials, 30.010
union practices, 17.309
wage-hour standards, 17.303
whistle-blowers, 17.303
working conditions data, *17.005*
see also Employee benefits; Farm workers; Labor *entries*; Occupational health, safety
Labor statistics, *see* Economics, research, statistics; Statistics
Labor unions
collective bargaining data, *17.005*
collective bargaining, mediation assistance, FMCS, 34.001
disabled, employment, Projects with Industry, *84.234*
disclosure, reporting, 17.309
employment discrimination, 16.101, 30.001, 30.010
labor-management committees, FMCS, *34.002*
representation elections, 46.001
unfair practices, regulation, 46.001
union members rights, election standards, 17.309
see also Labor *entries*
Laboratory animals
alternative, complementary medicine research, *93.213*
cancer research, *93.393, 93.394, 93.395, 93.396, 93.399*
cancer research facilities, *93.392*
environmental risk research, *93.115*
Lyme Disease, *93.942*
mental health research, *93.242*
microbiology, infectious diseases research, *93.856*
research, research infrastructure resources, training, *93.389*
see also Animal disease control, health, welfare; Veterinary medicine
LABORATORY LEADERSHIP, WORKFORCE TRAINING AND MANAGEMENT DEVELOPMENT, IMPROVING PUBLIC HEALTH LABORATORY INFRASTRUCTURE, *93.065*
LABORATORY TRAINING, EVALUATION, AND QUALITY ASSURANCE PROGRAMS, *93.064*
LAKE CHAMPLAIN BASIN PROGRAM [EPA], *66.481*
Lake Champlain fish resources management, *11.405*

Lakes, *see* Great Lakes; Recreation, water; Water resources, supply, management; Wetlands
LAMB MEAT ADJUSTMENT PROGRAM, *10.081*
Land acquisition
  airport improvement, *20.106*
  business, industrial loans, rural, *10.768*
  CDBG, *14.218*, *14.219*, *14.225*, *14.228*, *14.862*
  Coastal Program, FWS, *15.630*
  coastal wetlands protection, *15.614*
  endangered species conservation, *15.615*
  estuaries, *11.420*
  flood plain data, services, 12.104
  health, related facilities, federal surplus property, 93.291
  historic sites, *15.904*
  Indian lands, Real Estate Programs, *15.040*
  Indian reservation land, *10.421*
  interstate land sales registration, 14.168
  outdoor recreation, *15.916*
  public land sale, donation, 39.002
  Recreational Trails Program, *20.219*
  rural housing site loans, *10.411*
  Self-Help Homeownership Opportunity Program, *14.247*
  subdivided land, interstate sales registration, 14.168
  Wildlife Restoration, *15.611*
  see also Community development; Education facilities; Family farms; Federal property; Federal surplus property; Health facilities *entries*; Homeownership, homebuying; Housing *entries*; Landowners; Mass transportation; Public lands; Subdivisions; Transportation; Urban planning
Land and Water Conservation Fund, *15.638*, *15.639*, *15.916*
Land grant colleges, universities
  basic support, *10.205*
  competitive research grants, *10.206*
  1890 institutions entrepreneurial outreach, RBCS, *10.856*
  1890 institutions support, *10.216*
  Equity in Educational Land-Grant Status Act of 1994, *10.221*, *10.222*, *10.227*
  Extension Service, *10.500*
  farmer outreach, socially disadvantaged, *10.443*
  1994 Institutions, *10.227*
  Small Business Development Centers, *59.037*
  sustainable agriculture research, *10.215*
  tribal, agriculture, food sciences, *10.221*, *10.222*
  see also Agricultural education; Agricultural experiment stations; Higher education institutions
Land, public, *see* Public lands
LAND SALES—CERTAIN SUBDIVIDED LAND [HUD], 14.168
LANDOWNER INCENTIVE [DOI], *15.633*
Landowners
  dam safety program, FEMA, *97.041*
  Environmental Quality Incentives Program-Klamath Basin, NRCS, *10.919*
  Environmental Quality Incentives Program, NRCS, *10.912*
  Farm and Ranch Lands Protection Program, NRCS, *10.913*
  Fire Management Assistance, FEMA, *97.046*
  Forest Legacy Program, *10.676*
  flood plain data, services, 12.104
  forestry assistance, *10.064*, *10.664*
  FWS Landowner Incentives, *15.633*
  Great Plains Conservation, *10.900*
  Indian lands, Real Estate Programs, *15.040*
  military/community joint land use planning, *12.610*
  mine land reclamation, *10.910*
  New Mexico, forest restoration, *10.679*
  Religious Land Use and Institutionalized Persons Act of 2000 (RLUIPA), 16.103
  soil surveys, 10.903
  Tribal Landowner Incentive Program, *15.638*
  Wetlands Reserve Program, *10.072*
  wetlands, waterfowl, Water Bank Program, *10.062*
  Wildlife Habitat Incentive Program, *10.914*
  see also Agricultural *entries*; Family farms; Homeownership, homebuying; Indian lands; Land acquisition; Subdivisions
Landrum-Griffin Act, *see* Labor-Management Relations
Landscape architecture, *see* Architecture
LANGUAGE GRANT PROGRAM [DOD], *12.900*
LANGUAGE RESOURCE CENTERS [DOED], *84.229*
Languages, foreign area studies, *see* Bilingual education, services; English as a second language; Foreign languages; Illiteracy; International programs, studies
LAP (Livestock Assistance Program), *10.066*
Law, *see* Civil rights; Complaint investigation; Crime; Criminal justice system; FBI; Law enforcement education, training; Legal services; Legislation; Police; Public safety
LAW ENFORCEMENT ASSISTANCE—FBI ADVANCED POLICE TRAINING, 16.300
LAW ENFORCEMENT ASSISTANCE—FBI CRIME LABORATORY SUPPORT, 16.301
LAW ENFORCEMENT ASSISTANCE—FBI FIELD POLICE TRAINING, 16.302
LAW ENFORCEMENT ASSISTANCE—FBI FINGERPRINT IDENTIFICATION, 16.303
LAW ENFORCEMENT ASSISTANCE—NARCOTICS AND DANGEROUS DRUGS—LABORATORY ANALYSIS, 16.001
LAW ENFORCEMENT ASSISTANCE—NARCOTICS AND DANGEROUS DRUGS TECHNICAL LABORATORY PUBLICATIONS, 16.003
LAW ENFORCEMENT ASSISTANCE—NARCOTICS AND DANGEROUS DRUGS TRAINING, 16.004
LAW ENFORCEMENT ASSISTANCE—NATIONAL CRIME INFORMATION CENTER, 16.304
LAW ENFORCEMENT ASSISTANCE—NATIONAL INSTANT CRIMINAL BACKGROUND CHECK SYSTEM, 16.309
LAW ENFORCEMENT ASSISTANCE—UNIFORM CRIME REPORTS, 16.305
Law enforcement education, training
  alcohol, arson, explosives, firearms, tobacco control, ATF, 16.012
  anti-terrorism training, *16.614*
  block grants, *16.592*

Law enforcement education, training *(continued)*
child abuse program personnel, *16.547*
Combined DNA Index System (CODIS), FBI, *16.307*
Community Prosecution Program, *16.609*
conservation officers, 15.602
controlled substances, personnel, 16.004
Cops Grants, *16.710*
corrections, law enforcement personnel family support projects, research, *16.563*
corrections staff, *16.601*
counter-terrorism technology development, DOJ, *16.565*
criminal conspiracy, regional information sharing, *16.610*
Delinquency Prevention Program, *16.548, 16.549*
DHS Competitive Training Grants, *97.068*
disabled, elder abuse, sexual assault prevention training, OJP, *16.528*
DNA capacity enhancement, *16.741*
DNA laboratory improvement, training, *16.564*
domestic violence arrest policies, protection orders enforcement, *16.590*
domestic violence victim legal assistance, *16.524*
drug abuse prevention, public education, 16.005
drug control, Byrne Formula Grant Program, *16.579*
drug control, demonstrations, *16.580*
drunk driving control programs, *20.605*
environmental regulation, Indian self-government, *93.581*
ex-offenders, *16.601*
family violence prevention, *93.591, 93.592*
FBI Academy, Advanced Specialized Courses, 16.300
FBI crime laboratory, 16.301
FBI Field Police Training, 16.302
Federal Law Enforcement Training Center, DHS, *97.081*
forensic sciences improvement, *16.742*
Gang Resistance Education and Training, BJA, *16.737*
Indian Country Investigations, FBI, 16.308
Indians, violence against women, *16.587*
justice personnel, equipment, training, planning grants, *16.738*
juvenile delinquency, justice personnel, *16.540, 16.542*
juvenile gangs program, *16.544*
juvenile justice system improvement, *16.523*
Law Enforcement Terrorism Prevention Program (LETPP), DHS, *97.067, 97.074*
Motor Vehicle Theft Protection Act Program, *16.597*
National Instant Criminal Background Check System, *16.554*
Police Corps, scholarships, officers, dependents, *16.712*
prison rape elimination, *16.735*
research fellowships, graduate, *16.561, 16.562*
Scams Targeting the Elderly, telemarketing, DOJ, *16.613*
Secret Service training, 97.015
sex offender registry, *16.554*
student loan cancellations, *84.037*
traffic safety control, alcohol, drugs, *20.601*
victim assistance, *16.582*
violence against women, *16.588*
WMD, domestic preparedness, *97.004, 97.005, 97.006, 97.007*
see also Civil defense; Civil rights; Corrections; Crime; Criminal justice system; Drugs, drug research; Family therapy; FBI; Forensic sciences; Indian affairs; Legal services; Police; Public safety; Social sciences
LAW ENFORCEMENT TERRORISM PREVENTION PROGRAM, *97.074*
Law Enforcement Terrorism Prevention Program, DHS, *97.067, 97.074*
LAW ENFORCEMENT TRAINING AND TECHNICAL ASSISTANCE, *97.081*
Law schools, *see* Higher education institutions
LC (Library of Congress), 42.001 through 42.009
LCP (Livestock Compensation Program), *10.077*
LDD (Local Development Districts), Appalachian region, *23.009*
LDD (Local Development Districts), Delta region, *90.202*
LDS (Loans for Disadvantaged Students), HRSA, *93.342*
LEAD-BASED PAINT HAZARD CONTROL IN PRIVATELY-OWNED HOUSING, *14.900*
LEAD HAZARD REDUCTION DEMONSTRATION GRANT PROGRAM [HUD], *14.905*
LEAD OUTREACH GRANTS [HUD], *14.904*
Lead poisoning, deleading, *see* Community health services; Environmental health, research, services; Housing rehabilitation; Toxic substances, toxicology
LEAD TECHNICAL STUDIES GRANTS [HUD], *14.902*
LEAKING UNDERGROUND STORAGE TANK TRUST FUND PROGRAM, *66.805*
LEAP (Lead Elimination Action Program), HUD, *14.903*
LEAP (Leveraging Educational Assistance Partnership), *84.069*
LEARN AND SERVE AMERICA—HIGHER EDUCATION, *94.005*
LEARN AND SERVE AMERICA—SCHOOL AND COMMUNITY-BASED PROGRAM, *94.004*
LEGAL ASSISTANCE FOR VICTIMS, *16.524*
Legal services
ADA technical assistance, *16.108*
age discrimination, housing, 14.402
aliens employment, *16.110*
Architectural Barriers Act Enforcement, HUD programs, 14.407
CDBG programs discrimination complaints, 14.406
census services, proof of age, citizenship, relationship, 11.006
child abuse investigation, prosecution, *93.643, 93.669*
child abuse, closed-circuit TV, DOJ, *16.611*
child support enforcement, *93.563, 93.601*
Child Support Enforcement Research, *93.564*
children's rights violations, *16.549*
Civil Rights Prosecution, 16.109
clinic entrances act, 16.105

Community Prosecution Program, *16.609*
Community Relations Service, 16.200
credit transactions discrimination, 16.103
crime victims assistance, *16.575*
developmentally disabled, *93.630*
disabled, Client Assistance Program, *84.161*
disabled, Protection and Advocacy, *84.240*
Disaster Legal Services, *97.033*
domestic violence, *16.524*, *16.590*
Education Amendments Act of 1972, HUD programs discrimination, 14.415
education discrimination, 16.100
employment discrimination, 16.101
employment discrimination, attorney referral, 30.005
employment discrimination, federal contracts, 17.301
fair housing, *14.401*, *14.408*
family violence, *93.591*, *93.592*
health fraud task forces, FDA, *93.447*
housing, HUD programs, discrimination complaints, 14.400, 14.404, 14.405, 14.406, 16.103
institutionalized persons, 16.105
labor union members, 17.309
mentally ill persons, *93.138*
missing children, youth, technical assistance, *16.543*
parent access, visitation programs, ACF, *93.597*
torture victims assistance, *93.604*
veterans employment, reemployment rights, 17.803
trafficking victims, *16.320*, *93.598*
traumatic brain injury protection, advocacy, *93.267*
violence against Indian women, *16.587*
violence against women, *16.588*
voting discrimination, 16.104
see also Civil rights; Complaint investigation; Consumers, consumer services; Crime; Criminal justice system; FBI; Forensic sciences; Indian affairs; Law enforcement education, training; Victim assistance

Legislation
agricultural transportation services, AMS, 10.167
Alcohol Open Container Requirements, DOT, *20.607*
CERCLA response planning, *66.809*
child abuse, *16.547*, *93.643*
coal mining regulation development, *15.250*
dam safety standards, enforcement, FEMA, *97.041*
Driving While Intoxicated, repeat offender laws, DOT, *20.608*
FEMA community flood assistance program, *97.023*
FEMA Emergency Management Performance Grants, *97.042*
mine workers health, safety, *17.600*
missing children laws, *16.543*
motor carrier safety, *20.218*
toxic substances regulation, *66.701*
underground storage tank regulation, *66.804*
weights, measures, model laws, 11.606
young political leaders, international exchange, *19.403*
see also Civil rights; Elementary and Secondary Education acts; Higher Education Act; Government; Indian affairs; National housing acts; Taxes, tax incentives
LETPP (Law Enforcement Terrorism Prevention Program), DHS, *97.067*, *97.074*
LEVERAGING EDUCATIONAL ASSISTANCE PARTNERSHIP, *84.069*
LIBRARIANS FOR THE 21ST CENTURY, *45.313*

Libraries
agriculture, 10.700
Books for the Blind, handicapped, 42.001
Community Connect Grants, RUS, *10.863*
Conservation Assessment Program, training, *45.304*
depository, government publications, 40.001
DOD property donations, loans, 12.700
education sciences centers, OESE, *84.283*
elementary, secondary school innovative programs, *84.298*
environmental education, *66.950*
federal surplus personal property donations, 39.003
federal surplus real property transfer, 84.145
foreign information access, education technology, *84.337*
foreign language, international studies resources, *84.015*, *84.016*
government publications, 40.001
Hispanic-serving institutions, agricultural, food sciences, *10.223*
historical collections, preservation, training, *89.003*
humanities, archival, collections preservation, *45.149*
humanities development, challenge grants, *45.130*
humanities, NEH Public Programs, *45.164*
IMLS librarians recruitment, education, faculty development, research, *45.313*
IMLS National Leadership Grants, *45.312*
international peace, conflict resolution information technology, *91.002*
Learning Opportunities Grants, IMLS, *45.301*
library-museum partnerships, research, model programs, *45.312*
Library Services and Technology Act, *45.311*
Literacy through School Libraries, *84.364*
medical information sciences NRSA, *93.225*
minority college, university strengthening, *84.031*
minority health professions Centers of Excellence, *93.157*
Museum and Library Services Act of 1996 (MSLA), *45.301* through *45.313*
National Agricultural Library, 10.700
National Archives, 89.001
National Gallery of Art exhibits, 68.001
National Library of Medicine, *93.879*
Native American Library Services, *45.311*
NEH We the People program, *45.168*
NIH medical libraries resource development, librarians training, *93.879*
NIH medical library research training, *93.140*
NRC local public document rooms, *77.005*
nutrition education resources, schools, FNS, *10.574*
postsecondary education access projects, FIPSE, *84.116*

Libraries *(continued)*
  preservation practices, training, *45.149*
  Presidential Libraries, 89.001
  rural computer networks, RUS, *10.855*
  Senior Community Service Employment Program, *17.235*
  State Library Program, *45.310*
  see also Adult education; Arts, arts education; Computer products, sciences, services; Humanities; Information *entries*
Library of Congress (LC), 42.001 through 42.009
Life insurance, *see* Insurance
LIFE INSURANCE FOR VETERANS, *64.103*
LIHEAP (Low-Income Home Energy Assistance Program), HHS, *93.568*
Literacy, *see* Illiteracy
LITERACY PROGRAM FOR PRISONERS, *84.255*
LITERACY THROUGH SCHOOL LIBRARIES, *84.364*
Literature
  BECA arts exchanges, *19.409*
  creative writing, NEA, *45.024*
  Save America's Treasures, NPS, *15.929*
  Woodrow Wilson Center fellowships, *85.300*
  see also Arts, arts education; Copyright services; Foreign languages; Humanities *entries*; Publications
LITIGATION SUPPORT FOR INDIAN RIGHTS, *15.052*
LIVESTOCK ASSISTANCE PROGRAM, *10.066*
LIVESTOCK COMPENSATION PROGRAM, *10.077*
Livestock industry
  animal health research, *10.207*
  Avian Influenza Indemnity Program, *10.029*
  Conservation Security Program, NRCS, *10.921*
  dairy products indemnification, *10.053*
  Disaster Reserve Assistance, *10.452*
  Environmental Quality Incentives Program-Klamath Basin, NRCS, *10.919*
  Environmental Quality Incentives Program, NRCS, *10.912*
  farm operating loans, *10.406*
  forage research, *10.202*
  Grassland Reserve Program, NRCS, *10.920*
  Homeland Security—Agricultural, *10.304*
  Indian lands, *10.421*, *15.034*
  inspection, grading, 10.162, *10.475*, 10.477
  international assistance, *10.960*
  international research training, *10.962*
  Lamb Meat Adjustment Program, FSA, *10.081*
  Livestock Assistance Program, *10.066*
  Livestock Compensation Program, *10.077*
  Navajo-Hopi Joint Use Area, *15.057*
  noninsurance risk management research partnerships, *10.456*
  production data, statistics, 10.950
  research, *10.200*
  Ruminant Feed Ban Support Project, FDA, *93.449*
  sheep, goat industry improvement center, *10.774*
  subsidized loans, *10.437*
  sustainable agriculture research, *10.215*
  Wetlands Reserve Program, *10.072*
  Wild Horse and Burro Management, BLM, *15.229*
  wildlife disease control, *10.028*
  see also Agricultural *entries*; Animal disease control, health, welfare; Dairy industry; Poultry, egg products; Veterinary medicine
LMA (Lamb Meat Adjustment), FSA, *10.081*
Loan Cancellations, DOED, *84.037*
Loan Guarantees for Indian Housing, *14.865*
LOAN GUARANTEES FOR NATIVE HAWAIIAN HOUSING, *14.874*
Loan Guaranty Program, BIA, *15.124*
LOAN REPAYMENT PROGRAM FOR GENERAL RESEARCH [HHS], *93.232*
Loans, *see* Agricultural loans; Banks, banking; Business development; Credit unions; Disadvantaged, business development; Housing *entries*; Minority business enterprise; Small business; Student financial assistance
Loans for Disadvantaged Students (LDS), HRSA, *93.342*
Local Development Districts (LDD), Appalachian region, *23.009*
Local government, *see* Community development; Government; Indian affairs; Urban planning
Local Law Enforcement Block Grants Act of 1996, *16.592*
LOCAL LAW ENFORCEMENT BLOCK GRANTS PROGRAM, *16.592*
Local Television Loan Guarantee Board, USDA, *10.853*
LOCAL TELEVISION LOAN GUARANTEE PROGRAM [USDA], *10.853*
LOCAL VETERANS' EMPLOYMENT REPRESENTATIVE PROGRAM, *17.804*
Logging, *see* Farm, nonfarm enterprises; Farm workers; Forestry; Timber industry; Woodlands
LONG ISLAND SOUND PROGRAM, *66.437*
Long Term Resource Monitoring Program (LTRMP), DOI, *15.978*
LONGSHORE AND HARBOR WORKERS' COMPENSATION, *17.302*
Low income, *see* Depressed areas; Disadvantaged *entries*; Housing, low to moderate income; Public assistance; Rural poor; Social services; Volunteers
LOW-INCOME HOME ENERGY ASSISTANCE, *93.568*
LOW-INCOME TAXPAYER CLINICS, *21.008*
LOWER INCOME HOUSING ASSISTANCE PROGRAM—SECTION 8 MODERATE REHABILITATION, *14.856*
LPDRs (Local Public Document Rooms), NRC, *77.005*
LTRMP (Long Term Resource Monitoring Program), DOI, *15.978*
LUNG DISEASES RESEARCH, *93.838*
LUST (Leaking Underground Storage Tanks), EPA, *66.805*
LVER (Local Veterans' Employment Representative) Program, *17.804*
Lyme Disease, *93.942*

MAGNET SCHOOLS ASSISTANCE, *84.165*
Magnuson-Stevens Fishery Conservation and Management Act, *see* Fisheries industry
Management, *see* Business development; Disadvantaged, business development; Employment *entries*; Federal employment; Fellowships, scholarships, traineeships;

Government; Higher education; Home management; Indian education, training; Labor-management relations; Minority business enterprise; Private sector; Small business; Social sciences; Technical training; Volunteers
Management-labor relations, *see* Labor-management relations
MANUFACTURED HOME CONSTRUCTION AND SAFETY STANDARDS, 14.171
MANUFACTURED HOME LOAN INSURANCE—FINANCING PURCHASE OF MANUFACTURED HOMES AS PRINCIPAL RESIDENCES OF BORROWERS, *14.110*
Manufactured Home Parks, Section 207, *14.127*
Manufactured housing, *see* Homes, manufactured, mobile
MANUFACTURING AND SERVICES [USDC], 11.110
MANUFACTURING EXTENSION PARTNERSHIP, *11.611*
MAP (Market Access Program), USDA, *10.601*
MAP (Museum Assessment Program), *45.302*
MAP MODERNIZATION MANAGEMENT SUPPORT [DHS], *97.070*
Maps, charts
 census geography, 11.003
 census products, services, 11.001
 Coast and Geodetic Survey Act, *11.400*, *11.430*
 coastal ecosystem, NOAA, *11.473*
 flood hazard mapping, FEMA, *97.045*
 flood plain data, services, 12.104
 geodetic surveys, *11.400*
 geologic mapping, *15.810*
 geospatial data clearinghouse, *15.809*
 metropolitan statistical areas, 11.003
 Map Modernization Management Support, FEMA, *97.070*
 see also Census services; Engineering; Measurement
MARFIN (Marine Fisheries Initiative), NOAA, *11.433*
Marine and Freshwater Biomedical (MFB) Centers, NIEHS, *93.894*
MARINE FISHERIES INITIATIVE, *11.433*
MARINE MAMMAL DATA PROGRAM, *11.439*
Marine Protection, Research, and Sanctuaries Act of 1972 (MPRSA), *see* Marine Sciences
MARINE SANCTUARY PROGRAM, *11.429*
Marine sciences
 atmospheric, climate research, *11.431*
 coastal ecosystem management, NOAA, *11.473*
 Coastal Ocean Program, *11.478*
 coastal zone management program, *11.419*
 Coral Reef Conservation Act, *11.463*
 ecological research, *11.426*
 education, research, facilities, NOAA, *11.469*
 energy-related, renewable resources research, *81.087*
 environmental health sciences centers, *93.894*
 environmental systems research, NOAA, *11.432*
 estuaries research reserves, *11.420*
 fisheries research, *11.427*
 Habitat Conservation, NOAA, *11.463*
 Hawaii, marine fish enhancement, *11.445*
 Hydrometeorological Development, NOAA, *11.467*
 Marine Fisheries Initiative, *11.433*
 Marine Mammal Acts, *11.439*
 marine mammal data, *11.439*
 Marine Protection, Research, and Sanctuaries Act of 1972 (MPRSA), *11.426*, *11.429*, *66.035*, *66.110*, *66.306*, *66.308*, *66.309*, *66.310*, *66.510*, *66.511*, *66.515*, *66.600*, *66.604*, *66.606*, *66.609*, *66.610*, *66.611*, *66.709*, *66.931*
 Marine Turtle Conservation Fund, FWS, *15.645*
 National Sea Grant College Program Act, *11.417*
 NMFS marine education, science projects, *11.455*
 NOAA Educational Partnerships Program, minority, *11.481*
 NOAA special projects, *11.460*
 NOAA unallied projects, *11.452*, *11.472*
 NOS intern program, *11.480*
 ocean research, *47.050*
 Oceans Act of 1992, *15.231*
 Outer Continental Shelf Lands, *11.430*
 Polar Programs, *47.078*
 remote sensing research, *11.440*
 research ships financing, *20.802*
 sanctuaries research, education, *11.429*
 scholarships, graduate, *11.429*
 Sea Grant College Program Improvement Act of 1976, *11.417*
 sea grants, *11.417*
 undersea research, *11.430*
 see also Biological sciences; Coastal zone; Earth sciences; Environmental sciences; Estuaries; Fish; Fisheries industry; Maritime industry; Scientific research
MARINE TURTLE CONSERVATION FUND, *15.645*
Maritime Administration, USDC, *see* Agency Index
Maritime industry
 Capital Construction Fund (CCF), *20.808*
 Construction Reserve Fund (CRF), *20.812*
 explosives detection canine teams, TSA, *97.072*
 fishing vessel loan guarantees, *11.415*
 insurance, U.S. flagships, war risk, *20.803*
 Kings Point, *20.807*
 Longshore and Harbor Workers' Compensation Act, *17.302*
 Maritime Security Act of 2003, *20.813*
 Maritime Security Fleet Program, *20.813*
 Maritime Transportation Security Act of 2002, *97.060*
 Merchant Marine Academy, *20.807*
 Merchant Marine Act (MMA), 20.801, *20.802*, *20.803*, *20.808*, 20.810, *20.812*, *20.813*
 merchant marine employee benefits, 64.115
 merchant marine training, *20.806*
 National Maritime Heritage Act of 1994, *15.925*
 National Maritime Heritage Grants, *15.925*
 Ocean Freight Reimbursement, USAID, *98.003*
 oil spill trust fund, USCG, 97.013
 Operation Safe Commerce, DHS, *97.058*
 port security grants, DHS, *97.056*
 port security research, development, DHS, *97.060*
 ports, intermodal development information, planning, 20.801
 ship construction, reconstruction financing, tax deferments, *20.802*, *20.808*, *20.812*

Maritime industry *(continued)*
  ship operation safety training, 20.810
  Shipping Act of 1984, 33.001
  shipping, shipping rates complaints, 33.001
  tax deferral, *20.808, 20.812*
  Title XI, *20.802*
  Vessel Hull Design Protection Service, 42.009
  Vessel Hull Design Protection Service Act of 1998, 42.009
  see also Coastal zone; Fisheries industry; Great Lakes; International commerce, investment; Marine sciences; Water navigation
MARITIME SECURITY FLEET PROGRAM, *20.813*
MARITIME WAR RISK INSURANCE, *20.803*
Mark-to-Market Extension Act, *see* National housing acts
MARKET ACCESS PROGRAM [USDA], *10.601*
Market Development Cooperation Program (MDCP), ITA, *11.112*
MARKET NEWS [USDA], 10.153
MARKET PROTECTION AND PROMOTION [USDA], 10.163
Market-to-Market, section 8, HUD, *14.197*
Marketing, *see* Agricultural marketing; Business development; International commerce, investment
MARKETING AGREEMENTS AND ORDERS [USDA], 10.155
Markets, *see* Banks, banking; Commodity futures market; Information *entries*; International commerce, investment; Statistics
Marshall Islands, *see* U.S. possessions, territories
Mass transportation
  acquisition, construction, improvement, *20.500*
  biodiesel fuel use, CSREES, *10.306*
  Capital Investment Grants, *20.500*
  capital, operating assistance, *20.507*
  DHS Urban Areas Security Initiative, *97.008*
  disabled, over-the-road buses, capital, training, *20.518*
  explosives detection canine teams, TSA, *97.072*
  Federal-Aid Highway Program, *20.205*
  Formula Grant Program, *20.507*
  High Speed Ground Transportation, *20.312*
  Intercity Bus Security Grants, DHS, *97.057*
  multi-modal, improvement planning, *20.515*
  nonurbanized areas, *20.509*
  planning, design, technical studies, *20.505*
  rail, transit security, ODP, *97.075*
  Transit Planning and Research, *20.514*
  Truck Security Program, DHS, *97.059*
  see also Railroads; Transportation; Urban planning
MATCHING GRANTS FOR HEALTH PROFESSIONS SCHOLARSHIPS TO INDIAN TRIBES, *93.219*
Maternal and Child Health Epidemiology Program (MCHEP), *93.946*
MATERNAL AND CHILD HEALTH FEDERAL CONSOLIDATED PROGRAMS, *93.110*
MATERNAL AND CHILD HEALTH SERVICES BLOCK GRANT TO THE STATES, *93.994*
Maternal, child health, welfare
  Abandoned Infants Assistance Act of 1988, *93.551*
  abandoned infants services, care training, *93.551*
  abstinence education, *93.010, 93.235*
  adolescent family life demonstrations, *93.995*
  adolescent pregnancy research, *93.111*
  Adoption Awareness Training, *93.254*
  adoption, foster care placement discrimination, 93.001
  Adoption Incentive Payments, *93.603*
  adoption payments, special needs children, *93.659*
  AIDS/HIV care, *93.153, 93.914*
  Appalachian region, *23.002*
  Chafee Foster Care Independence Act of 1999, *93.599, 93.674*
  child abuse, closed-circuit TV, DOJ, *16.611*
  child abuse, neglect investigation, prosecution, family services, *93.643*
  child abuse, neglect prevention, *16.547, 93.669*
  child abuse, neglect, victim assistance, *16.575, 16.576*
  Child Abuse Prevention, Adoption and Family Services Acts, *93.652, 93.669, 93.670, 93.671*
  Child Abuse Prevention and Treatment Act, *93.590, 93.591, 93.592, 93.643, 93.652, 93.669, 93.670, 93.671*
  child abuse, services, research, technical assistance, *93.670*
  child care/social services, TANF, *93.558*
  Child Nutrition Act of 1966, 10.550, *10.553, 10.556, 10.557, 10.560, 10.572, 10.578, 10.579*
  Child Nutrition Discretionary Grants, *10.579*
  Child Support Enforcement Research, *93.564*
  child support payments enforcement, *93.563, 93.601*
  Children's Health Act of 2000, *93.197, 93.243, 93.254, 93.255*
  Children's Insurance Program, CMS, *93.767*
  Children's Justice and Assistance Act of 1986 (CJAA), *16.575, 16.576, 16.582, 16.583*
  Community Mental Health Services Block Grant, *93.958*
  Community Services Block Grant, *93.569*
  Compassion Capital Fund, ACF, *93.009*
  contraception, infertility research, education loan repayments, *93.209*
  Cuban, Haitian refugees services, *97.009*
  domestic violence arrest policies, protection orders enforcement, *16.590*
  domestic violence, stalking victim transitional housing, *16.736*
  domestic violence victim legal assistance, training, *16.524*
  Early Learning Fund, services, training, ACF, *93.577*
  embryo adoption public awareness, *93.007*
  emergency medical services, *93.127*
  environmental health hazards research, *93.113*
  EPA Children's Health Protection, *66.609*
  EPA studies, special purpose assistance, *66.610*
  Extension Service, *10.500*
  family support services, *93.556*
  family violence prevention services, *93.671*
  Farmers' Market Nutrition Program (FMNP), *10.572*
  food assistance, 10.550, *10.565*
  Food Stamps, *10.551*
  food, supplemental, WIC, *10.557*
  foster care, *93.658*

MASTER INDEX 979

foster care, transition to independent living, training, *93.674*
foster children, Chafee vouchers, *93.599*
Foster Grandparent Program, *94.011*
Four-H program, *10.500*
genetic disease, hemophilia testing, counseling, treatment, *93.110*
hazardous waste sites health studies, *93.206*
Head Start, *93.600*
health care policy research, *93.239*
Healthy Homes Demonstration Grants, HUD, *14.901*
heart health care programs, women, *93.012*
homeless children, educational programs, *84.196*
human development research, mothers, children, *93.865*
immunization research, information, education, *93.185*
Indian Family and Child Education, *15.043*
Indian, Social Services, *15.025*
Infant Health Initiatives, *93.946*
Keeping Children and Families Safe Act of 2003, *93.591, 93.592, 93.669, 93.670, 93.671*
labor standards, 17.303
lead-based paint hazard control, HUD, *14.900*
Lead Outreach Grants, HUD, *14.904*
lead poisoning prevention, *93.197*
Maternal Health Research, *93.946*
Medicaid, *93.778*
Mentoring Children of Prisoners, ACF, *93.616*
minority community health coalitions, *93.137*
missing children programs, public education, research, *16.543*
newborn hearing screening, *93.251*
NIH international research awards, *93.989*
Operation Lead Elimination Action Program, HUD, *14.903*
parent access, visitation programs, *93.597*
Parental Assistance Centers, DOED, *84.310*
perinatal/maternal initiative, *93.926*
personnel training, *93.648*
Poison Control Centers, *93.253*
primary care coordination, *93.130*
Promoting Safe and Stable Families Amendments of 2001, *93.556, 93.599, 93.674*
public health graduate traineeships, *93.964*
research, training, *93.110*
runaway children, *93.645*
rural domestic violence, *16.589*
rural health services, *93.912*
Safe Motherhood Initiative, *93.946*
Safe Schools/Healthy Students National Evaluation, DOJ, *16.732*
SED, children, adolescents, mental health services, *93.104*
services, block grants, *93.994*
Social Security benefits, children of disabled parents, *96.001, 96.002*
Social Security survivors, *96.004*
Social Services Block Grant, *93.667*
social services research, demonstration, *93.647*
spina bifida, veterans dependents, *64.127*
state assistance programs, *93.645*
State Court Improvement Program, ACF, *93.586*
substance abuse, mental health services, PRNS, *93.243*
Substance Abuse Prevention and Treatment Block Grant, *93.959*
Supervised Visitation, Safe Havens for Children, OJP, *16.527*
traumatic brain injury, *93.234, 93.267*
Unaccompanied Alien Children Program, *93.676*
Vaccines for Children Program, *93.268*
Victims of Child Abuse Act, *16.611*
violence, children's exposure, prevention initiative, Safe Start, *16.730*
Welfare Reform Research, *93.595*
WIC Farmers' Market Nutrition Program (FMNP), *10.572*
WIC Grants to States, FNS, *10.578*
women's health, Community Centers of Excellence, *93.290*
youth, independent living education, training, *93.674*
see also Child care services; Community health services; Disabled, handicapped children; Early childhood education; Family planning; Family therapy; Head Start Program; Health, medical *entries*; Indian children; Indian health, social services; Juvenile delinquency; Parenting; Public assistance; Social Security Act; Social services; Victim assistance; Volunteers; Women; Youth *entries*
Maternal Health Research, *93.946*
MATHEMATICAL AND PHYSICAL SCIENCES, *47.049*
MATHEMATICAL SCIENCES GRANTS PROGRAM [DOD], *12.901*
Mathematics
Air Force Defense Research Sciences Program, *12.800*
Army Research Office, *12.431*
Barry M. Goldwater Scholarship Program, *85.200*
DHS Scholars and Fellows, *97.062*
DOD sciences research, fellowships, *12.630*
Eisenhower regional education consortia, *84.319*
energy sciences research, *81.049*
mathematical sciences research, *47.049*
mathematical sciences research, education, NSA, *12.901*
Mathematics and Science Partnerships, OESE, *84.366*
measurement, engineering research, standards, *11.609*
mental health research models, *93.242*
NASA education services, 43.001
Navy research, education support, *12.300*
NOAA Colorado areas math, engineering, science education, *11.449*
NSF education improvement, research, *47.075, 47.076*
Ready to Teach, OERI, *84.286*
Star Schools Program, *84.203*
Tech-Prep Education, secondary, postsecondary, *84.243*
Upward Bound, *84.047*
Women's Educational Equity Act Program, *84.083*
see also Adult education; Computer products, sciences, services; Education *entries*; Engineering *entries*; Physical sciences; Science education; Scientific research; Teacher education, training

MATHEMATICS AND SCIENCE PARTNERSHIPS [DOED], *84.366*
MBDA (Minority Business Development Agency), USDC, *see* Agency Index
MBDC (Minority Business Development Centers), *11.800*
MBOC (Minority Business Opportunity Committee), *11.803*
MCH (Maternal and Child Health) Block Grant, *93.994*
MCHEP (Maternal and Child Health Epidemiology Program), *93.946*
McIntire-Stennis Act, forestry, *10.202*
McKinney homeless assistance act, *see* National housing acts (McKinney-Vento Homeless Assistance Act, Stewart B. McKinney Homeless Assistance Act)
MCSAP (Motor Carrier Safety Assistance Program), *20.218*
MDCP (Market Development Cooperation Program), ITA, *11.112*
Measurement
business internships, Eurasian executives, scientists, *11.114*
calibration, testing, 11.601
geodetic surveys, *11.400*
National Bureau of Standards Organic Act (NBSOA), 11.601, 11.603, 11.604, 11.606, *11.609*, 11.610
National Standard Reference Data System, 11.603
research, *11.609*
Standard Reference Materials, 11.604
standards and certification information center, NCSCI, 11.610
weights, measures service, 11.606
see also Engineering *entries*; Maps, charts; Physical sciences; Scientific research
MEASUREMENT AND ENGINEERING RESEARCH AND STANDARDS, *11.609*
MEASURES AND ANALYSES OF THE U.S. ECONOMY, 11.025
Meat, *see* Food inspection, grading; Livestock industry; Poultry, egg products
Meat and Poultry Inspection State Programs, *10.475*
MEAT, POULTRY, AND EGG PRODUCTS INSPECTION, 10.477
MECEA (Mutual Educational and Cultural Exchange Act), *see* International programs, studies
Media, *see* Arts, arts education; Audiovisual aids, film, video; Communications, telecommunications; Radio, television
Medicaid, *see* Social Security Act
MEDICAID INFRASTRUCTURE GRANTS TO SUPPORT THE COMPETITIVE EMPLOYMENT OF PEOPLE WITH DISABILITIES, *93.768*
Medicaid, Title XIX, *93.778*
MEDICAL ASSISTANCE PROGRAM, *93.778*
Medical education, *see* Health, medical education, training
Medical facilities, *see* Health facilities *entries*
Medical libraries, *see* Libraries
MEDICAL LIBRARY ASSISTANCE, *93.879*
Medical research, *see* Health, medical research

MEDICAL RESERVE CORPS SMALL GRANT PROGRAM, *93.008*
Medical schools, *see* Health facilities; Health, medical education, training; Health professions
Medical services, *see* Community health services; Health, medical services; Indian health, social services; Maternal, child health, welfare; Preventive health services; Public health; Veterans health, medical services
Medical training, *see* Health, medical education, training
Medicare, *see* Social Security
MEDICARE—HOSPITAL INSURANCE, *93.773*
Medicare Part D, *93.770*
MEDICARE—PRESCRIPTION DRUG COVERAGE, *93.770*
Medicare Prescription Drug, Improvement and Modernization Act 2003 (MMA), *see* Health insurance; Social Security
MEDICARE—SUPPLEMENTARY MEDICAL INSURANCE, *93.774*
MEDICARE TRANSITIONAL DRUG ASSISTANCE PROGRAM FOR STATES, *93.783*
MEDICARE TRANSITIONAL DRUG ASSISTANCE PROGRAM FOR TERRITORIES, *93.782*
Medicine for Veterans, 64.012
Mental health
Access to Recovery, SAMSHA, *93.275*
advocacy and protection of mentally ill, staff training, *93.138*
AIDS-afflicted persons, housing, services, *14.241*
AIDS/HIV homeless patients housing, *14.238*
alcoholism research, *93.273*
alcoholism research training, *93.271*, *93.272*
Anti-Terrorism and Emergency Assistance Program, DOJ, *16.321*
civil rights, institutionalized persons, 16.105
Community Mental Health Services Block Grant, *93.958*
Crisis Counseling, disaster victims, *97.032*
Delinquency Prevention Program, *16.549*
elderly, *93.043*
emergency counseling, disaster areas, training, *93.982*
HIV care, *93.917*
HIV emergency relief projects, *93.914*
homeless, *93.150*
homeless, supportive housing, *14.235*
human development research, mothers, children, NRSA, *93.865*
Medicaid Ticket-to-Work Demonstrations, *93.769*
nutrition discretionary grants, *10.579*
Offender Reentry Program, *16.202*
offenders, justice, health, social services networks, *93.229*
personnel training, *93.244*
prevention, treatment, methods research, *93.242*
Protection and Advocacy for Individuals with Mental Illness Act of 1986, *93.138*
Religious Land Use and Institutionalized Persons Act of 2000 (RLUIPA), 16.103
repatriation program, *93.579*
research training, *93.281*, *93.282*
rural areas, *93.912*

MASTER INDEX 981

SED, children, adolescents, comprehensive services, 93.104
Senior Companion Program, 94.016
Services for Trafficking Victims, 16.320
Social Services Block Grant, 93.667
substance abuse services information, 93.230
substance abuse services, PRNS, 93.243
supportive housing, 14.181
torture victims assistance, providers training, 93.604
trafficking victims assistance, ACF, 93.598
uninsured patients, Healthy Community Access Program, 93.252
urban Indians, 93.193
veterans, dependents services, 64.009, 64.019
victim assistance program personnel training, 16.582
violence, children's exposure, prevention initiative, Safe Start, 16.730
Voucher Program, SAMSHA, 93.275
see also Behavioral sciences, education, services; Community health services; Disabled, handicapped entries; Health, medical entries; Health professions; Indian health, social services; Mental retardation; Social sciences; Veterans health, medical services

Mental Health and Behavioral Sciences Service, Substance Abuse Treatment Program, DVA, 64.019
MENTAL HEALTH CLINICAL AND AIDS SERVICE-RELATED TRAINING GRANTS, 93.244
MENTAL HEALTH DISASTER ASSISTANCE AND EMERGENCY MENTAL HEALTH, 93.982
MENTAL HEALTH NATIONAL RESEARCH SERVICE AWARDS FOR RESEARCH TRAINING, 93.282
MENTAL HEALTH RESEARCH CAREER/SCIENTIST DEVELOPMENT AWARDS, 93.281
MENTAL HEALTH RESEARCH GRANTS, 93.242
Mental illness, see Mental health; Mental retardation

Mental retardation
children, early intervention, special education, 84.027, 84.181, 84.323, 84.324, 84.325, 84.326, 84.327, 84.328, 84.329
civil rights, institutionalized persons, 16.105
Client Assistance Program, benefits, services information, 84.161
Developmental Disabilities Assistance and Bill of Rights Act, 93.138, 93.630, 93.631, 93.632
developmental disabilities, basic support, protection, rights advocacy, 93.630
developmental disabilities, national projects, 93.631
developmental disabilities programs, university centers personnel training, 93.632
disabilities prevention, 93.184
disabled, Protection and Advocacy, 84.240
employment, Projects with Industry, 84.234
employment promotion, 17.720
federal employment, 27.001, 27.005
human development research, mothers, children, NRSA, 93.865
independent living services, 84.169

Medicaid Ticket-to-Work Demonstrations, 93.769
mental health research, 93.242
Mental Retardation Facilities and Construction Act of 1963, 93.630, 93.631, 93.632
Parent Information Centers, 84.328
preschool special education, 84.173
President's Committee for People with Intellectual Disabilities, 93.613
rehabilitation research, fellowships, 84.133
Religious Land Use and Institutionalized Persons Act of 2000 (RLUIPA), 16.103
special vocational rehabilitation services, 84.235
vocational rehabilitation, basic support, 84.126
vocational rehabilitation personnel training, 84.129
vocational rehabilitation service projects, 84.128
see also Disabled, handicapped entries; Education entries; Group homes; Mental health; Vocational rehabilitation; Volunteers
MENTORING CHILDREN OF PRISONERS, 93.616
Mentoring programs, see Education counseling; Social services; Tutoring
MEPI (Middle Eastern Partnership Initiative), 19.500
Merchant Marine, see Maritime industry; U.S. Merchant Marine
Metabolism research, 93.847
METEOROLOGIC AND HYDROLOGIC MODERNIZATION DEVELOPMENT, 11.467
METROPOLITAN MEDICAL RESPONSE SYSTEM [DHS], 97.071
Metropolitan Planning, mass transit, 20.505
MFB (Marine and Freshwater Biomedical) Centers, 93.894
MFFP (Minority Faculty Fellowship Program), HRSA, 93.923
MGIB (Montgomery GI Bill), 64.124
MICROBIOLOGY AND INFECTIOUS DISEASES RESEARCH, 93.856
Microgram, DOJ, 16.003
MICROENTERPRISE DEVELOPMENT GRANTS, 59.050
MICROLOAN PROGRAM, 59.046
Micronesia, see U.S. possessions, territories
MIDDLE EASTERN PARTNERSHIP INITIATIVE, 19.500
Midwife training, see Health professions; Nursing
MIGRANT AND SEASONAL FARMWORKERS [DOL], 17.264
MIGRANT EDUCATION—COLLEGE ASSISTANCE MIGRANT PROGRAM, 84.149
MIGRANT EDUCATION—COORDINATION PROGRAM, 84.144
MIGRANT EDUCATION—HIGH SCHOOL EQUIVALENCY PROGRAM, 84.141
MIGRANT EDUCATION—STATE GRANT PROGRAM, 84.011
Migrant Health Centers, HRSA, 93.224
Migrant labor, see Farm workers
Migration and Refugee Assistance Act (MRA), see Aliens, immigrants, refugees
MIGRATORY BIRD CONSERVATION, 15.647
MIGRATORY BIRD JOINT VENTURES, 15.637
Military
Air Force Defense Research Sciences Program, 12.800

Military *(continued)*
American Battlefield Protection, NPS, *15.926*
Army Research Office, *12.431*
base reuse studies, *12.607*
biological-medical research, *12.420*
community economic impact, 12.600, *12.607*, *12.614*
community land use planning, *12.610*
Defense authorization acts, *12.610, 12.612, 12.613, 17.807, 81.113, 91.001, 91.002, 97.044, 97.071*
Defense Economic Adjustment, Diversification, Conversion, and Stabilization Act of 1990, *12.611*
Defense Production Act of 1950, 20.801, *97.026*, 97.027, 97.028
Department of Defense and Emergency Supplemental Appropriations for Recovery from and Response to Terrorist Acts on the United States Act of 2002, *66.474, 66.478, 97.056, 97.058*
Department of Defense Authorization Act of 1986, *97.040*
defense program changes impact, *11.307, 12.611, 12.612, 12.613*
disabled service-persons, adaptive equipment, *64.100*
DOD property donations, loans, 12.700
DOE WMD nonproliferation research, *81.113*
education assistance, post-Vietnam personnel, *64.120*
employment counseling, 64.125
FEMA chemical emergency planning, DOD stockpiles, *97.040*
foreign language, area studies, NSEP, *12.551*
home loans, improvement, repair, *64.114*
Homeland Security Information Center, NTIS, 11.650
humanitarian relief goods transport, USAID, *98.010*
impact assistance, schools, *84.040, 84.041*
impacted areas, home mortgage insurance, *14.165*
Indian lands environmental impact mitigation, 12.116, *93.582*
Inertial Confinement Fusion, stockpile stewardship, *81.112*
interment in national cemeteries, 64.201
Maritime Security Fleet Program, *20.813*
maritime vessels defense training, DOT, 20.810
Montgomery GI Bill education benefits, *64.124*
National Defense Authorization Act of 2000, *81.2000*
National Guard Challenge Program, youth, *12.404*
National Guard facilities, *12.400*
National Guard operations, maintenance, *12.401*
National Maritime Heritage Grants, NPS, *15.925*
National Security Acts, *12.901, 97.026*, 97.027, 97.028
National Security Education Program, DOD, *12.550*
NSA language grants, *12.900*
scientific research, Navy, *12.300*
Servicemen's Readjustment Act, *17.804*
service-persons, Transition Assistance Program, DOL, *17.807*
student loan cancellations, *84.037*
United States Institute of Peace Act, *91.001, 91.002*
University-Based Homeland Security Centers, DHS, *97.061*
veterans employment, reemployment rights, 17.803
vocational rehabilitation, disabled, hospitalized service personnel, *64.116*
WIA Dislocated Workers, *17.260*
WMD, domestic preparedness, *97.004, 97.005, 97.006, 97.040*
see also Business development; Civil defense; Government contracts; Historic monuments, historic preservation; History; Maritime industry; Small business; Veterans *entries*
MILITARY CONSTRUCTION, NATIONAL GUARD, *12.400*
MILITARY MEDICAL RESEARCH AND DEVELOPMENT, *12.420*
Milk, *see* Dairy industry
MILK INCOME LOSS CONTRACT PROGRAM, *10.080*
Milk Orders, 10.155
MINE HEALTH AND SAFETY COUNSELING AND TECHNICAL ASSISTANCE, 17.601
MINE HEALTH AND SAFETY EDUCATION AND TRAINING, 17.602
MINE HEALTH AND SAFETY GRANTS, *17.600*
Mine safety, *see* Coal Mining; Mining, mining industries; Occupational health, safety
Mine Safety and Health Administration, DOL, *see* Agency Index
Mineral resources
Census Bureau data, 11.001
geologic research, *15.808*
Indian lands, *15.038, 15.040*
Materials Act of 1947, 15.214
Mineral Revenue Payments Clarification Act of 2000, *15.227*
minerals disposal, BLM lands, 15.214
see also Coal mining; Energy *entries*; Geology; Mining, mining industries; Natural resources; Nuclear sciences, technology; Physical sciences; Public lands; Statistics
MINERALS AND MINING ON INDIAN LANDS, *15.038*
MINIMUM PENALTIES FOR REPEAT OFFENDERS FOR DRIVING WHILE INTOXICATED, *20.608*
Minimum wage, *see* Labor standards
Mining, mining industries
abandoned mine land reclamation, *15.252*
Federal Mine Safety and Health Acts, *17.307*, *17.600*, 17.601, 17.602, *93.283, 93.965*
futures trading information, customer complaints, 78.004
Indian lands, resources, *15.038*
Indian treaty rights, *15.052*
industrial waste reduction, DOE, *81.105*
land reclamation, plant materials, 10.905
mine land reclamation, *10.910*
Mining in National Parks Act of 1976, 15.910, 15.915
safety, advisory services, 17.601
safety, education, training, 17.602
safety standards enforcement, training, *17.600*

Summer Watershed Intern, *15.254*
Surface Mining Control and Reclamation Act of 1977, *10.910, 15.250, 15.252, 15.253, 15.254*
 see also Coal mining; Commodity futures market; Energy *entries*; Environmental management; Geology; Mineral resources; Nuclear sciences, technology; Occupational health, safety; Statistics
Minority Business Development Agency (MBDA), USDC, *see* Agency Index
MINORITY BUSINESS DEVELOPMENT CENTERS, *11.800*
Minority business enterprise
 agriculture, SBIR, *10.212*
 DOT Minority Resource Center, *20.903*
 DOT contracts, Short Term Lending Program, *20.905*
 1890 institutions entrepreneurial outreach, RBCS, *10.856*
 EPA studies, special purpose assistance, *66.610*
 farmer outreach, socially disadvantaged, *10.443*
 farming risk management outreach, RMA, *10.455*
 government contracts, 59.006, *59.049*
 HUD project contracts complaints, 14.412
 management, technical assistance, *11.800, 59.007*
 Microloan Demonstration Program, *59.046*
 Minority Business Opportunity Committee, *11.803*
 Native American Program, technical assistance, *11.801*
 public telecommunications facilities, *11.550*
 Rural Community Development Initiative, RHS, *10.446*
 SBIC loans, technical assistance, *59.011*
 transportation, DOT contracts, *20.903, 20.907*
 see also Business development; Disadvantaged, business development; Indian economic, business development; Small business; Small Business Innovation Research (SBIR); Women
MINORITY BUSINESS OPPORTUNITY COMMITTEE, *11.803*
Minority discrimination, *see* Civil rights
Minority education
 agricultural, food sciences, Hispanics, *10.223*
 agriculture-related, *10.220*
 Army Research Office, *12.431*
 biomedical research training, alcoholism, *93.272*
 community development work-study, HUD, *14.512*
 DOD science, technology projects, *12.910*
 DOE nuclear research program, *81.123*
 1890 institutions entrepreneurial outreach, RBCS, *10.856*
 1890 institutions support, *10.216*
 Eisenhower Transportation Fellowship Program, *20.215*
 EPA IHE research support, *66.515*
 EPA research fellowships, graduate, undergraduate, *66.513*
 EPA STAR graduate fellowships, *66.514*
 engineering, science programs improvement, *84.120*
 Family Life Centers, HHS violence prevention, *93.910*
 foreign scholars-in-residence, undergraduate. BECA, *19.431*
 geosciences research, *47.050*

HBCU Program, HUD, *14.520*
health professions, Centers of Excellence, *93.157*
health professions faculty fellowships, loan repayments, *93.923*
health professions scholarships, *93.925*
health services research, *93.226*
Healthy Communities Access Program, HRSA, *93.890*
international public policy programs, fellowships, *84.269*
Magnet Schools Assistance, *84.165*
marine, maritime studies, graduate, *11.429*
mathematics, science research, NSF program, *47.049*
Medicaid, Medicare research, *93.779*
mental health research scientists, *93.281, 93.282*
mental health specialists training, *93.244*
minority health, disparities research, researchers education loan repayment, *93.307*
Navy support, *12.300*
NEH curriculum, materials development, *45.162*
NEH fellowships, *45.160*
neurological disorders research, faculty, *93.853*
NIH intramural research training, *93.140*
NOAA Educational Partnerships Program, *11.481*
NOAA Colorado areas math, engineering, science, *11.449*
NSF biological sciences research, postdoctoral, *47.074*
NSF international science, engineering, *47.079*
payments, 1890 land grant colleges, Tuskegee, *10.205*
pharmacology, physiology, biorelated chemistry research, training, *93.859*
postsecondary, Institutional Aid, *84.031*
research, research infrastructure resources, training, NIH, *93.389*
transportation, DOT contracts, *20.907*
tribal IHE facilities, HUD, *14.519*
vision research, National Eye Institute, *93.867*
vocational rehabilitation personnel recruitment, training, *84.315*
 see also Alaska, Alaska natives; Aliens, immigrants, refugees; Bilingual education, services; Civil rights; Disadvantaged *entries*; Education *entries*; Farm workers; Hawaii, Hawaii natives; Indian education, training; Student financial aid; Women
Minority employment, *see* Disadvantaged, employment and training; Employment *entries*; Women
Minority Faculty Fellowship Program (MFFP), HRSA, *93.923*
MINORITY HEALTH AND HEALTH DISPARITIES RESEARCH, *93.307*
MINORITY INSTITUTIONS [DOT], *20.907*
Minority Resource Center, DOT, *20.903*
Minority Scholars Program, USDA, *10.220*
MINORITY SCIENCE AND ENGINEERING IMPROVEMENT, *84.120*
MISSING CHILDREN'S ASSISTANCE, *16.543*
Missing persons
 absent parent child support enforcement, *93.563, 93.601*
 Alzheimer's, related disorders, patients, *16.543*
 Child Support Enforcement Research, *93.564*

Missing persons *(continued)*
children, youth, *16.542, 16.543*
Combined DNA Index System (CODIS), FBI, *16.307*
computerized index, missing, unidentified persons, 16.304
Cuban, Haitian entrants, *97.009*
educational assistance, missing-in-action veterans dependents, *64.117*
fingerprint identification, FBI, 16.303
National Center for Missing and Exploited Children, *97.076*
Runaway, Homeless, and Missing Children Protection Act of 2003, *93.550, 93.557, 93.623*
runaway youth, *93.623, 93.645*
see also Census services; Homeless persons; Veterans *entries*; Volunteers; Youth *entries*
Mitchell Act, NOAA, *11.436*
MITIGATION OF ENVIRONMENTAL IMPACTS TO INDIAN LANDS DUE TO DEPARTMENT OF DEFENSE ACTIVITIES, *93.582*
MLS (Milk Income Loss), FSA, *10.080*
MMA (Medicare Prescription Drug, Improvement and Modernization Act 2003), *see* Health insurance; Social Security
MMA (Merchant Marine Act), *see* Maritime industry
MMMS (Map Modernization Management Support), FEMA, *97.070*
MMRS (Metropolitan Medical Response System), FEMA, *97.071*
Mobile homes, *see* Homes, manufactured
Mobility, intergovernmental, *see* Federal employment; Government
Model AHEC (Area Health Education Centers), HRSA, *93.107*
MODEL STATE-SUPPORTED AREA HEALTH EDUCATION CENTERS, *93.107*
Moderate income, *see* Disadvantaged *entries*; Housing, low to moderate income; Housing, subsidized; Rural poor
Moderate Rehabilitation, Section 8, HUD, *14.856*
Mohair, *see* Agricultural commodities, stabilization; Livestock industry
Monopolistic practices, 36.001
Montgomery GI Bill Act Active Duty, *64.124*
MONTHLY ALLOWANCE FOR CHILDREN OF VIETNAM VETERANS BORN WITH SPINA BIFIDA, *64.127*
Monthly Labor Review, *17.002*
MORRIS K. UDALL FELLOWSHIP PROGRAM, *85.401*
MORRIS K. UDALL NATIVE AMERICAN CONGRESSIONAL INTERNSHIP PROGRAM, *85.402*
Morris K. Udall Scholarship and Excellence in National Environmental Policy Foundation, *see* Agency Index (Scholarship and Fellowship Foundations)
MORRIS K. UDALL SCHOLARSHIP PROGRAM, *85.400*
Mortgage and loan insurance, *see* Housing mortgage, loan insurance; Insurance
MORTGAGE INSURANCE—COMBINATION AND MANUFACTURED HOME LOT LOANS, *14.162*

MORTGAGE INSURANCE—COOPERATIVE PROJECTS, *14.126*
MORTGAGE INSURANCE FOR CONSTRUCTION OR SUBSTANTIAL REHABILITATION OF CONDOMINIUM PROJECTS, *14.112*
MORTGAGE INSURANCE FOR SINGLE ROOM OCCUPANCY (SRO) PROJECTS, *14.184*
MORTGAGE INSURANCE FOR THE PURCHASE OR REFINANCING OF EXISTING MULTIFAMILY HOUSING PROJECTS, *14.155*
MORTGAGE INSURANCE—GROWING EQUITY MORTGAGES, *14.172*
MORTGAGE INSURANCE—HOMES, *14.117*
MORTGAGE INSURANCE—HOMES FOR DISASTER VICTIMS, *14.119*
MORTGAGE INSURANCE—HOMES IN URBAN RENEWAL AREAS, *14.122*
MORTGAGE INSURANCE—HOMES—MILITARY IMPACTED AREAS, *14.165*
MORTGAGE INSURANCE—HOSPITALS, *14.128*
MORTGAGE INSURANCE—HOUSING IN OLDER, DECLINING AREAS, *14.123*
MORTGAGE INSURANCE—MANUFACTURED HOME PARKS, *14.127*
MORTGAGE INSURANCE—NURSING HOMES, INTERMEDIATE CARE FACILITIES, BOARD AND CARE HOMES AND ASSISTED LIVING FACILITIES, *14.129*
MORTGAGE INSURANCE—PURCHASE OF SALES-TYPE COOPERATIVE HOUSING UNITS, *14.132*
MORTGAGE INSURANCE—PURCHASE OF UNITS IN CONDOMINIUMS, *14.133*
MORTGAGE INSURANCE—RENTAL AND COOPERATIVE HOUSING FOR MODERATE INCOME FAMILIES AND ELDERLY, MARKET INTEREST RATE, *14.135*
MORTGAGE INSURANCE—RENTAL HOUSING, *14.134*
MORTGAGE INSURANCE—RENTAL HOUSING FOR THE ELDERLY, *14.138*
MORTGAGE INSURANCE—RENTAL HOUSING IN URBAN RENEWAL AREAS, *14.139*
MORTGAGE INSURANCE—SINGLE-FAMILY COOPERATIVE HOUSING, *14.163*
MORTGAGE INSURANCE—TWO YEAR OPERATING LOSS LOANS, SECTION 223(D), *14.167*
Mothers, *see* Child care services; Family planning; Maternal, child health, welfare; Parenting; Women
MOTOR CARRIER SAFETY, 20.217
MOTOR VEHICLE THEFT PROTECTION ACT PROGRAM, *16.597*
Motor vehicles
automobiles, disabled veterans, *64.100*
biodiesel fuel use, CSREES, *10.306*
Commercial Driver License State Programs, *20.232*
Crash Data Improvement Program, FMCSA, *20.230*

drunk driving control programs, *20.600, 20.601, 20.605*
elderly, disabled, transportation services, *20.513*
energy conservation, renewable energy outreach, training, *81.117*
energy conservation technology development, *81.086*
federal surplus property, 39.003, 39.007
Motor Carrier Acts, 20.217, *20.218, 20.230*
motor carrier safety enforcement, training, 20.217
motor carrier safety regulation, *20.218*
Motor Vehicle Theft Protection Act Program, *16.597*
Occupant Protection, DOT, *20.602*
public safety education, *20.600*
Recreational Trails Program, *20.219*
Real ID Program, DHS, *97.089*
seatbelt use incentives, *20.604*
traffic safety control, alcohol, drugs, *20.601*
Truck Security Program, DHS, *97.059*
see also Hazardous materials, waste; Highways, roads, bridges; Public safety; Transportation
MPLIS/GIS (Multipurpose Land Information Systems/Geographic Information Systems), *11.400*
MPRSA (Marine Protection, Research, and Sanctuaries Act of 1972), see Marine Sciences
MPS (Mathematics and Physical Sciences), NSF, *47.049*
MRA (Migration and Refugee Assistance Act), see Aliens, immigrants, refugees
MRC (Medical Reserve Corps), HHS, *93.008*
MSEIP (Minority Science and Engineering Improvement Program), *84.120*
MULTIFAMILY ASSISTED HOUSING REFORM AND AFFORDABILITY ACT, *14.197*
Multifamily housing, see Housing *entries*
MULTIFAMILY HOUSING SERVICE COORDINATORS, *14.191*
MULTIFAMILY PROPERTY DISPOSITION, 14.199
MULTI-MEDIA CAPACITY BUILDING GRANTS FOR STATES AND TRIBES [EPA], *66.709*
Multiple, lateral sclerosis research, *93.853*
Multipurpose Land Information Systems/Geographic Information Systems (MPLIS/GIS), *11.400*
MULTI-STATE CONSERVATION GRANTS [DOI], *15.628*
Musculoskeletal diseases research, *93.846*
Museum and Library Services Act of 1996 (MSLA), see Libraries
MUSEUM ASSESSMENT PROGRAM, *45.302*
MUSEUM FOR AMERICA GRANTS, *45.301*
Museums, galleries
aeronautics, space information, 43.001
aquaria, Marine Mammal Data Program, *11.439*
art works, artifacts indemnity, *45.201*
Arts in Education, OESE, *84.351*
BECA arts exchanges, *19.409*
Conservation Assessment Program, training, *45.304*
conservation projects, research, training, *45.303*
DOD property donations, loans, 12.700
DOE used equipment, 81.022

federal surplus personal property donations, 39.003
historic properties preservation, 15.915, *15.923*
historical collections, preservation, training, *89.003*
humanities conservation, preservation, archival resources, *45.149*
humanities development, challenge grants, *45.130*
humanities, NEH Public Programs, *45.164*
IMLS National Leadership Grants, *45.312*
Indian arts, crafts, 15.850
insurance on exhibits, *45.201*
Learning Opportunities Grants, *45.301*
library-museum partnerships, research, model programs, *45.312*
Museum Assessment Program, *45.302*
National Gallery of Art local exhibits, 68.001
native American graves protection, repatriation, *15.922*
native American, Hawaiian services, *45.308*
NSF engineering, mathematics, science improvement, *47.076*
postsecondary education access projects, FIPSE, *84.116*
professionals training, *45.307*
research, research infrastructure resources, training, NIH, *93.389*
Save America's Treasures, NPS, *15.929*
Spacemobile, 43.001
traveling exhibits insurance, *45.201*
see also Arts, arts education; Audiovisual aids, film, video; History; Humanities; Libraries
Music
BECA arts exchanges, *19.409*
cable systems licenses, 42.002
LC Books for the Blind program, 42.001
music therapy, alternative medicine research, *93.213*
NEA grants, *45.024*
Performing Arts, BECA, *19.413*
royalty collection, 42.002
Save America's Treasures, NPS, *15.929*
see also Arts, arts education; Copyright services
Mutual Educational and Cultural Exchange Act (MECEA), see International programs, studies

NABDC (Native American Business Development Centers), *11.801*
NAGPRA (Native American Graves Protection and Repatriation Act), *15.922*
NAHASDA (Native American Housing Assistance and Self- Determination Act of 1996), see Indian housing
NAP (Native American Program), MBDA, *11.801*
NAP (Noninsured Assistance Program), USDA, *10.451*
NAP (Nutrition Assistance for Puerto Rico), USDA, *10.566*
Narcotics, see Crime; Drug abuse; Drugs, drug research; Forensic sciences
NARETPA (National Agricultural Research, Extension, and Teaching Policy Act of 1977), see Agricultural education
NASA (National Aeronautics and Space Administration), 43.001 through 43.002
NASA Tech Briefs, 43.002

NASA Technology Transfer, 43.002
National Aeronautics and Space Administration (NASA), 43.001 through 43.002
National Affordable Housing Act, *see* National housing acts
NATIONAL AGRICULTURAL LIBRARY, 10.700
National Agricultural Research, Extension, and Teaching Policy Act of 1977 (NARETPA), *see* Agricultural education
National Agricultural Statistics Service, USDA, *see* Agency Index
National and Community Service Trust Act of 1993, *see* AmeriCorps
National Archives and Records Administration, 89.001 through 89.003
NATIONAL ARCHIVES REFERENCE SERVICES—HISTORICAL RESEARCH, 89.001
National Biological Service, DOI, *see* Agency Index
NATIONAL BIOTERRORISM HOSPITAL PREPAREDNESS PROGRAM, *93.889*
National Bureau of Standards, *see* Agency Index (USDC, National Institute for Standards and Technology)
National Bureau of Standards Organic Act, *see* Measurement
National cemeteries, *see* Veterans death benefits
NATIONAL CEMETERIES, 64.201
National Cemetery System, DVA, *see* Agency Index
National Center for Complementary and Alternative Medicine, *93.213*
NATIONAL CENTER FOR HEALTH WORKFORCE ANALYSIS, *93.300*
NATIONAL CENTER FOR MISSING AND EXPLOITED CHILDREN, 97.076
NATIONAL CENTER FOR PRESERVATION TECHNOLOGY AND TRAINING [DOI], *15.923*
NATIONAL CENTER FOR RESEARCH RESOURCES [HHS], *93.389*
National Center for Research, vocational education, DOED, *84.051*
NATIONAL CENTER FOR STANDARDS AND CERTIFICATION INFORMATION [USDC], 11.610
NATIONAL CENTER ON SLEEP DISORDERS, *93.233*
National Coastal Wetlands Conservation Grants, *15.614*
NATIONAL COMMUNITY CENTERS OF EXCELLENCE IN WOMEN'S HEALTH, *93.290*
NATIONAL COOPERATIVE GEOLOGIC MAPPING PROGRAM, *15.810*
National Credit Union Administration (NCUA), 44.001 through 44.002
National Crime Information Center (NCIC), DOJ, 16.304
NATIONAL CRIMINAL HISTORY IMPROVEMENT PROGRAM, *16.554*
NATIONAL DAM SAFETY PROGRAM [DHS], *97.041*
National defense, *see* Civil defense; Military
National Direct Student Loan (NDSL) cancellation, *84.037*
National Endowment for the Arts (NEA), National Foundation on the Arts and the Humanities, *see* Agency Index
National Endowment for the Humanities (NEH), National Foundation on the Arts and the Humanities, *see* Agency Index
NATIONAL ENERGY INFORMATION CENTER, 81.039
National Environmental Information Exchange Network, EPA, *66.608*
National Environmental Satellite, Data, and Information Service (NESDIS), NOAA, *11.428, 11.440*
NATIONAL ESTUARY PROGRAM, *66.456*
NATIONAL EVALUATION OF THE SAFE SCHOOLS—HEALTHY STUDENTS INITIATIVE, *16.732*
NATIONAL EXPLOSIVES DETECTION CANINE TEAM PROGRAM, *97.072*
National Eye Institute, NIH, 93.867
National Fair Housing Training Academy, *14.401*
NATIONAL FAMILY CAREGIVER SUPPORT, *93.052*
National Farmworker Jobs Program, ETA, *17.264*
NATIONAL FIRE ACADEMY EDUCATIONAL PROGRAM, 97.019
NATIONAL FIRE ACADEMY TRAINING ASSISTANCE, *97.018*
National Fire Academy Training Grants, *97.043*
National Fire Plan, BLM, *15.228, 15.242*
NATIONAL FIRE PLAN—RURAL FIRE ASSISTANCE, *15.242*
NATIONAL FIRE PLAN—WILDLAND URBAN INTERFACE COMMUNITY FIRE ASSISTANCE, *15.228*
National Flood Insurance Program (NFIP), *see* Flood prevention, control
NATIONAL FOREST-DEPENDENT RURAL COMMUNITIES, *10.670*
National Foundation on the Arts and the Humanities, 45.024 through 45.313
National Foundation on the Arts and the Humanities Act of 1965 (NFAHA), *see* Arts, arts education
National Fraud Information Center, *16.613*
NATIONAL GALLERY OF ART EXTENSION SERVICE, 68.001
National Geodetic Reference System, *11.400*
National Guard Bureau, *see* Agency Index (DOD, Department of the Army, National Guard Bureau)
NATIONAL GUARD CIVILIAN YOUTH OPPORTUNITIES, *12.404*
NATIONAL GUARD MILITARY OPERATIONS AND MAINTENANCE (O&M) PROJECTS, *12.401*
NATIONAL HEALTH PROMOTION, *93.990*
National Health Service Corps, 93.129, 93.130, 93.162, 93.165, 93.288
National Health Service Corps, death benefits, 64.201, *64.202*
NATIONAL HEALTH SERVICE CORPS LOAN REPAYMENT PROGRAM, *93.162*
National Health Service Corps personnel benefits, 64.115
NATIONAL HEALTH SERVICE CORPS SCHOLARSHIP PROGRAM, *93.288*
National Highway Institute, DOT, *20.215*

National Highway Traffic Safety Administration, *93.127*
National Highway Traffic Safety Administration, DOT, *see* Agency Index
NATIONAL HISTORIC LANDMARK, 15.912
NATIONAL HISTORICAL PUBLICATIONS AND RECORDS GRANTS, *89.003*

National housing acts
AIDS Housing Opportunity Act, *14.241*
American Homeownership and Economic Opportunity Act of 2000, *14.157, 14.181*
Demonstration Cities and Metropolitan Development Act, EPA programs, *66.804, 66.816*
Department of Housing and Urban Development Reform Act of 1996, *14.856*
Emergency Home Purchase Assistance Act of 1974, *14.163*
Hope VI Program Reauthorization and Small Community Mainstreet Rejuvenation Housing Act of 2003, *14.866*
Housing Act of 1949, *10.405, 10.410, 10.411, 10.415, 10.417, 10.420, 10.427, 10.433, 10.438, 10.441, 10.442, 10.444, 10.445*
Housing Act of 1950, *14.126, 14.132*
Housing Act of 1954, *14.122*
Housing Act of 1956, *14.126*
Housing Act of 1959, *14.157, 14.314*
Housing Act of 1964, *14.112*
Housing and Community Development Act of 1974, *14.155, 14.159, 14.218, 14.219, 14.225, 14.227, 14.228, 14.246, 14.248,* 14.406, *14.512, 14.514, 14.515, 14.520, 14.521, 14.862*
Housing and Community Development Act of 1987, *14.183, 14.408, 14.512, 14.871*
Housing and Community Development Act of 1992, *14.157, 14.188, 14.189, 14.191, 14.243, 14.408, 14.511, 14.865, 14.871, 14.874, 14.900, 14.902, 14.903, 14.904, 14.905*
Housing and Community Development Amendments of 1979, *14.159*
Housing and Urban Development Act of 1965, *14.149*
Housing and Urban Development Act of 1968, *14.169,* 14.412
Housing and Urban Development Act of 1969, *14.129, 97.070*
Housing and Urban Development Act of 1970, *14.506, 14.516, 14.517, 14.901, 14.902, 14.906*
Housing and Urban-Rural Recovery Act of 1983, *14.175, 14.856*
Housing Opportunity Extension Act of 1996, *14.247, 14.856, 14.871*
HUD Reform Act of 1989, *14.314*
Interstate Land Sales Full Disclosure Act, 14.168
Mark-to-Market Extension Act of 2001, *14.197*
McKinney-Vento Homeless Assistance Act (MVHAA), *84.196, 93.150,*
Multifamily Assisted Housing Reform and Affordability Act of 1997, *14.197, 14.856*
National Affordable Housing Act (Cranston-Gonzalez act), *14.181, 14.191, 14.239, 14.243, 14.871*
National Manufactured Housing Construction and Safety Standards Act, 14.171
Native American Housing Assistance and Self-Determination Act of 1996 (NAHASDA), *14.867, 14.869*
Quality Housing and Work Responsibility Act of 1998, *14.871, 14.872*
section 8, *14.195, 14.871*
section 202, supportive housing, *14.157, 14.314*
section 203(b), home mortgage insurance, *14.117*
section 203(b), 203(k), 204, single-family property disposition, 14.311
section 203(h), disaster victims mortgage insurance, *14.119*
section 203(k), rehabilitation, *14.108*
section 203(n), cooperative housing, *14.163*
section 207, manufactured home parks, *14.127*
section 207, rental housing, *14.134*
section 207(k), (l), Multifamily Property Disposition, 14.199
section 213, cooperatives, *14.126, 14.132*
section 220, urban renewal homes, *14.122, 14.139*
section 221(d), single room occupancy projects, *14.184*
section 221(d)(3) and (4), rental, cooperative housing, *14.135*
section 223(d), operating loss loans, *14.167*
section 223(e), declining areas, *14.123*
section 223(f) and 207, existing multifamily housing, *14.155*
section 231, elderly, handicapped, *14.138*
section 232, nursing homes, *14.129*
section 234(c), condominiums, *14.133*
section 234(d), condominium construction, rehabilitation, *14.112*
Section 236 Interest Reduction Payments, *14.103*
section 238(c), military impacted areas, *14.165*
section 241(a), supplemental loans, *14.151*
section 242, hospitals, *14.128*
Section 245 Graduated Payment Mortgage Program, *14.159*
section 245(a), growing equity mortgages, *14.172*
section 251, adjustable rate mortgages, *14.175*
section 255, home equity conversion mortgages, *14.183*
section 502, rural housing loans, *10.410, 10.445*
section 504, rural housing repair, *10.417, 10.444*
section 509, RHS grants, *10.442*
section 514 and 516, labor housing, *10.405*
section 515 and 521, rural, *10.415*
section 521, rural rental assistance, *10.427*
section 523, rural self-help housing technical assistance, *10.420*
section 523, 524 rural site loans, *10.411*
section 525(a), rural counseling program, *10.441*
section 533, rural housing, *10.433*
section 538, rural rental housing, *10.438*
Stewart B. McKinney Homeless Assistance Act (SBMHAA), *14.231, 14.235, 14.238, 14.249, 17.805,* 39.002, 93.291, *97.024*
Title I, manufactured homes, lots, *14.162*
Title I, Section 2, manufactured homes, *14.110*
Title I, Section 2, property improvement, residential, nonresidential, *14.142*
U.S. Housing Act of 1937, *14.195, 14.850, 14.856, 14.866, 14.871, 14.872*
see also Civil rights; Community development; Homeless persons; Housing *entries*; Indian housing

NATIONAL INDUSTRIAL COMPETITIVENESS THROUGH ENERGY, ENVIRONMENT, AND ECONOMICS, *81.105*
National Instant Criminal Background Check System (NICS), 16.309, *16.554*
NATIONAL INSTITUTE FOR LITERACY, *84.257*
National Institute for Literacy, DOED, *see* Agency Index
National Institute of Child Health and Human Development, NIH, 93.209, 93.865
National Institute of Corrections, DOJ, *see* Agency Index
National Institute of Environmental Health Sciences (NIEHS), NIH, 93.113, 93.114, 93.115, 93.142, 93.143, 93.894
National Institute of Justice, DOJ, *see* Agency Index
NATIONAL INSTITUTE OF JUSTICE DOMESTIC ANTI-TERRORISM TECHNOLOGY DEVELOPMENT PROGRAM (COUNTER-TERRORISM RESEARCH AND DEVELOPMENT), *16.565*
NATIONAL INSTITUTE OF JUSTICE RESEARCH, EVALUATION, AND DEVELOPMENT PROJECT GRANTS, *16.560*
NATIONAL INSTITUTE OF JUSTICE VISITING FELLOWSHIPS, *16.561*
NATIONAL INSTITUTE OF JUSTICE W.E.B. DUBOIS FELLOWSHIP PROGRAM, *16.566*
National Institute of Mental Health (NIMH), NIH, 93.242, 93.281, 93.282
National Institute of Neurological Disorders and Stroke (NINDS), NIH, 93.853
National Institute of Standards and Technology Authorization Act, 11.650
National Institute of Standards and Technology (NIST), USDC, *see* Agency Index
National Institute on Aging, NIH, 93.866
National Institute on Alcohol Abuse and Alcoholism (NIAAA), NIH, 93.271, 93.272, 93.273, 93.891
NATIONAL INSTITUTE ON DISABILITY AND REHABILITATION RESEARCH, *84.133*
National Institute on Drug Abuse (NIDA), NIH, 93.279
National Institutes of Health (NIH), HHS, *see* Agency Index
NATIONAL INSTITUTES OF HEALTH ACQUIRED IMMUNODEFICIENCY SYNDROME RESEARCH LOAN REPAYMENT PROGRAM, *93.936*
NATIONAL INSTITUTES OF HEALTH LOAN REPAYMENT PROGRAM FOR CLINICAL RESEARCHERS, *93.280*
NATIONAL INSTITUTES OF HEALTH PEDIATRIC RESEARCH LOAN REPAYMENT PROGRAM, *93.285*
NATIONAL INSTITUTES OF HEALTH PEDIATRIC RESEARCH LOAN REPAYMENT PROGRAM, *93.385*
National Labor Relations Board (NLRB), 46.001
NATIONAL LEADERSHIP GRANTS [IMLS], *45.312*
National Library of Medicine, NIH, 93.879
National Limb Loss Information Center, 93.184
National Marine Fisheries Service (NMFS), NOAA, 11.405 through 11.415, 11.427, 11.433 through 11.439, 11.441, 11.444, 11.445, 11.452, 11.454, 11.455, 11.457, 11.463, 11.472, 11.474
NATIONAL MARITIME HERITAGE GRANTS, *15.925*
NATIONAL MOTOR CARRIER SAFETY, *20.218*
NATIONAL NATURAL LANDMARKS PROGRAM, 15.910
NATIONAL NETWORK FOR ENVIRONMENTAL MANAGEMENT STUDIES FELLOWSHIP PROGRAM, *66.952*
National Nuclear Security Administration, DOE, *see* Agency Index
NATIONAL NUCLEAR SECURITY ADMINISTRATION (NNSA) HISTORICALLY BLACK COLLEGES AND UNIVERSITIES (HBCU) PROGRAM, *81.123*
National Ocean Service (NOS), NOAA, 11.400, 11.419, 11.420, 11.426, 11.429, 11.473, 11.478, 11.480
NATIONAL OCEAN SERVICE INTERN PROGRAM, *11.480*
National Oceanic and Atmospheric Administration (NOAA), personnel, survivor benefits, 64.115, 64.201, *64.202*
National Ocean Pollution Planning Act, *see* Pollution abatement
National Oceanic and Atmospheric Administration (NOAA), USDC, *see* Agency Index
National Oil and Hazardous Substance Contingency Plan, *66.802*
National Park Service (NPS), DOI, *see* Agency Index
National Plan of Integrated Airport Systems (NPIAS), *20.106*
National Planning and Research Programs, FTA, *20.514*
National Poison Control Stabilization and Enhancement, *93.253*
NATIONAL PRISON RAPE STATISTICS PROGRAM, *16.739*
National Register, 15.914
National Register of Historic Places, *see* Historic monuments, historic preservation
NATIONAL REGISTER OF HISTORIC PLACES, 15.914
National Registry of Natural Landmarks, 15.910
National Research Initiative Competitive Grants Program, CSREES, *10.206*
NATIONAL RESEARCH SERVICE AWARD IN PRIMARY CARE MEDICINE, *93.186*
National Research Service Awards
aging, *93.866*
alcoholism, *93.272*
allergy, immunology, transplantation biology, SBIR, *93.855*
arthritis, musculoskeletal and skin diseases, *93.846*
blood diseases, resources, *93.839*
cancer, *93.398*
deafness, communicative disorders, *93.173*
diabetes, endocrinology, metabolism, *93.847*
Discovery and Applied Research, biomedical imaging, bioengineering, NIH, *93.286*
digestive diseases, nutrition, *93.848*
environmental health sciences, *93.894*
health services, *93.225*
heart, vascular diseases, *93.837*
human genomes, *93.172*

National Research Service Awards *(continued)*
  kidney diseases, urology, hematology, *93.849*
  lung diseases, *93.838*
  mental health, *93.282*
  microbiology, infectious diseases, *93.856*
  mothers and children, human development, *93.865*
  neurological disorders, neurosciences, *93.853*
  National Center for Research Resources, NIH, *93.389*
  nursing, *93.361*
  oral diseases, disorders, *93.121*
  primary medical care, *93.186*
  sleep disorders, *93.233*
  vision, National Eye Institute, *93.867*
  see also Fellowships, scholarships, traineeships; Health, medical education, training; Health, medical research; Scientific research
NATIONAL RESEARCH SERVICE AWARDS—HEALTH SERVICES RESEARCH TRAINING, *93.225*
NATIONAL RESOURCE CENTERS AND FELLOWSHIPS PROGRAM FOR LANGUAGE AND AREA OR LANGUAGE AND INTERNATIONAL STUDIES, *84.015*
National School Lunch Act, *see* School breakfast, lunch
NATIONAL SCHOOL LUNCH PROGRAM, *10.555*
National Science Foundation (NSF), 47.041 through 47.079
National Science Foundation Act of 1950, *see* Scientific research
National Sea Grant College Program Act, *see* Marine sciences
National security, *see* Civil defense; Military
National Security Agency (NSA), DOD, *see* Agency Index
National Security Education Program (NSEP), DOD, *12.550*
NATIONAL SECURITY EDUCATION—SCHOLARSHIPS, *12.551*
National Senior Service Corps, *94.011*
National Sex Offender Registry (NSOR), *16.554*
NATIONAL SHEEP INDUSTRY IMPROVEMENT CENTER, *10.774*
NATIONAL SPATIAL DATA INFRASTRUCTURE COOPERATIVE AGREEMENTS PROGRAM [DOI], *15.809*
NATIONAL STANDARD REFERENCE DATA SYSTEM, 11.603
National Technical Information Act of 1988, 11.650
National Technical Information Service (NTIS), USDC, *see* Agency Index
NATIONAL TECHNICAL INFORMATION SERVICE, 11.650
National Telecommunications and Information Administration (NTIA), USDC, *see* Agency Index
NATIONAL TRADE DATA BANK, 11.026
National, University Center and Local Technical Assistance, EDA, *11.303*
NATIONAL URBAN SEARCH AND RESCUE (US&R) RESPONSE SYSTEM, *97.025*
National Weather Service, NOAA, 11.428, 11.443, 11.450, 11.462, 11.467, 11.468
NATIONAL WETLAND PROGRAM DEVELOPMENT GRANTS, *66.462*

NATIONAL WHITE COLLAR CRIME CENTER, *16.612*
NATIVE AMERICAN AND NATIVE HAWAIIAN LIBRARY SERVICES, *45.311*
NATIVE AMERICAN BUSINESS DEVELOPMENT CENTERS, *11.801*
NATIVE AMERICAN ECONOMIC DEVELOPMENT ASSISTANCE, *59.052*
NATIVE AMERICAN EMPLOYMENT AND TRAINING [DOL], *17.265*
NATIVE AMERICAN GRAVES PROTECTION AND REPATRIATION ACT, *15.922*
Native American Housing Assistance and Self-Determination Act of 1996 (NAHASDA), *see* Indian housing
NATIVE AMERICAN/NATIVE HAWAIIAN MUSEUM SERVICES PROGRAM, *45.308*
NATIVE AMERICAN PROGRAMS [HHS], *93.612*
NATIVE AMERICAN VETERAN DIRECT LOAN PROGRAM, *64.126*
Native Americans, *see* Alaska, Alaska natives; Hawaii, Hawaii natives; Indian *entries*
Native Employment Works (NEW), ACF, *93.594*
NATIVE HAWAIIAN EDUCATION, *84.362*
NATIVE HAWAIIAN HEALTH SYSTEMS, *93.932*
NATIVE HAWAIIAN HOUSING BLOCK GRANTS, *14.873*
NATIVE HAWAIIAN VOCATIONAL EDUCATION, *84.259*
Natural disasters, *see* Disaster assistance; Earthquakes; Emergency assistance; Flood prevention, control; Hurricanes
Natural landmarks, *see* Historic monuments, historic preservation; Natural resources
Natural Landmarks Program, 15.910
Natural resources
  agricultural, protection research, *10.206*
  BLM Cultural Resource Management, *15.224*
  BLM Recreation Resource Management, *15.225*
  estuary research, *11.420*
  Farm and Ranch Lands Protection Program, NRCS, *10.913*
  historic properties preservation technology, training, *15.923*
  marine sanctuaries enforcement, research, *11.429*
  Minority Scholars Program, USDA, *10.220*
  natural landmarks registry, 15.910
  Omnibus Parks and Public Lands Management Act of 1996, *15.926*
  Rivers, Trails, and Conservation Assistance, 15.921
  Rural Development, Forestry, and Communities, *10.672*
  USGS Cooperative Research Units Program, *15.812*
  USGS Gap Analysis Program, *15.811*
  Water Bank Program, USDA, *10.062*
  wildlife damage, disease control, *10.028*
  Wildlife Habitat Incentive Program, *10.914*
  see also Agricultural conservation; Archaeology; Coastal zone; Earth sciences; Energy; Environmental management; Estuaries; Forestry; Geology; Indian lands; Mineral resources; Public lands; Water resources, supply, management; Wetlands
Natural Resources Conservation Service (NRCS), USDA, *see* Agency Index

Nature centers, *see* Museums, galleries
NAVAJO-HOPI INDIAN SETTLEMENT PROGRAM, *15.057*
Naval Surface Warfare Center, *see* Agency Index, DOD, Department of the Navy
Navigation, *see* Maritime industry; Water navigation
NAWCF (North American Wetlands Conservation Fund), FWS, *15.623*
NAVIGATION PROJECTS, 12.107
NCHIP (National Criminal History Improvement Program), *16.554*
NCHWA (National Center for Health Workforce Analysis), *93.300*
NCIC (National Crime Information Center), 16.304
NCMEC (National Center for Missing and Exploited Children), *97.076*
NCSCI (National Center for Standards and Certification Information), 11.610
NCUA (National Credit Union Administration), 44.001 through 44.002
NDSL (National Direct Student Loan) cancellation, *84.037*
NE RD&R (Nuclear Energy Research, Development and Demonstration), DOE, *81.121*
NEA (National Endowment for the Arts), National Foundation on the Arts and the Humanities, *see* Agency Index
NEH (National Endowment for the Humanities), National Foundation on the Arts and the Humanities, *see* Agency Index
NEIC (National Energy Information Center), 81.039
Neighborhoods, *see* Community development; Community health services; Historic monuments, historic preservation; Housing *entries*; Urban planning; Volunteers
NEMS (National Network for Environmental Studies) Fellowship Program, EPA, *66.952*
NEOTROPICAL MIGRATORY BIRD CONSERVATION, *15.635*
NEP (National Estuary Program), *66.456*
NEPR (Nurse Education, Practice and Retention), *93.359*
NESDIS (National Environmental Satellite, Data, and Information Service), NOAA, *11.428*, *11.440*
Neurological disorders research, *93.853*
NEW (Native Employment Works), ACF, *93.594*
New communities, *see* Community development; Subdivisions
NEW MARKETS VENTURE CAPITAL PROGRAM, OPERATIONAL ASSISTANCE (OA) GRANTS [SBA], *59.051*
NFAHA, (National Foundation on the Arts and the Humanities Act of 1965), *see* Arts, arts education
NFIP (National Flood Insurance Program), *see* Flood prevention, control
NFLP (Nursing Faculty Loan Program), *93.264*
NGO (Non-Governmental Organizations), USAID, *98.004*
NHSC, *see* National Health Service Corps
NHSC (National Health Service Corps) Loan Repayment Program, *93.162*
NHSC (National Health Service Corps) Scholarship Program, *93.288*
NIAAA, *see* National Institute on Alcohol Abuse and Alcoholism

NICE3 (National Industrial Competitiveness through Energy, Environment, and Economics), DOE, *81.105*
NICS (National Instant Criminal Background Check System), 16.309, *16.554*
NIDA, *see* National Institute on Drug Abuse
NIEHS, *see* National Institute of Environmental Health Sciences
NIEHS HAZARDOUS WASTE WORKER HEALTH AND SAFETY TRAINING, *93.142*
NIEHS SUPERFUND HAZARDOUS SUBSTANCES—BASIC RESEARCH AND EDUCATION, *93.143*
NIH AIDS Research Loan Repayment Program, *93.936*
NIH Clinical Research Loan Repayment Program (CR-LRP), *93.220*, *93.280*
NIH General Research Loan Repayment Program (GR-LRP), *93.232*
NIH Pediatric Research Loan Repayment Program (PR-LRP), *93.285*, *93.385*
NIH (National Institutes of Health), HHS, *see* Agency Index
NIH Undergraduate Scholarship Program (UGSP), *93.187*
NIL (National Institute for Literacy), *84.257*
NIMH, *see* National Institute of Mental Health
NINDS, *see* National Institute of Neurological Disorders and Stroke
9/11 Stamp Act of 2001, *97.085*
1994 INSTITUTIONS RESEARCH PROGRAM [USDA], *10.227*
NIST (National Institute for Standards and Technology), USDC, *see* Agency Index
NLRB (National Labor Relations Board), 46.001
NMFS, *see* National Marine Fisheries Service
NNSA-HBCU (National Nuclear Security Administration Historically Black Colleges and Universities) Program, *81.123*
No Child Left Behind Act of 2001, *see* Elementary and Secondary Education acts
NOAA (National Oceanic and Atmospheric Administration), USDC, *see* Agency Index
Noise pollution, *see* Air transportation; Pollution abatement
NON-DISCRIMINATION AND AFFIRMATIVE ACTION BY FEDERAL CONTRACTORS AND FEDERALLY ASSISTED CONSTRUCTION CONTRACTORS, 17.301
NON-DISCRIMINATION IN FEDERALLY ASSISTED AND CONDUCTED PROGRAMS (ON THE BASIS OF DISABILITY), 14.404
NON-DISCRIMINATION IN FEDERALLY ASSISTED PROGRAMS (ON THE BASIS OF AGE), 14.402
NON-DISCRIMINATION IN FEDERALLY ASSISTED PROGRAMS (ON THE BASIS OF RACE, COLOR OR NATIONAL ORIGIN), 14.405
NON-DISCRIMINATION IN THE COMMUNITY DEVELOPMENT BLOCK GRANT PROGRAM (ON THE BASIS OF RACE, COLOR, NATIONAL ORIGIN, RELIGION, OR SEX), 14.406
NON-DISCRIMINATION ON THE BASIS OF DISABILITY BY PUBLIC ENTITIES, 14.414

MASTER INDEX 991

NON-DISCRIMINATION ON THE BASIS OF SEX IN EDUCATION PROGRAMS AND ACTIVITIES RECEIVING FEDERAL FINANCIAL ASSISTANCE, 14.415
Nonfarm enterprises, *see* Farm, nonfarm enterprises
NONGOVERNMENTAL ORGANIZATION STRENGTHENING (NGO) [USAID], *98.004*
NONINSURED ASSISTANCE [USDA], *10.451*
NONPOINT SOURCE IMPLEMENTATION GRANTS, *66.460*
NON-SALE DISPOSALS OF MINERAL MATERIAL, 15.214
Nonurbanized Area Formula Program, FTA, *20.509*
NORTH AMERICAN WETLANDS CONSERVATION FUND, *15.623*
Northern Marianas Islands, *see* U.S. possessions, territories
NOS, *see* National Ocean Service
NOS (National Ocean Service) Intern Program, *11.480*
NOT FOR PROFIT AMD RECLAMATION [DOI], *15.253*
NPIAS (National Plan of Integrated Airport Systems), *20.106*
NPS (National Park Service), DOI, *see* Agency Index
NRC Local Public Document Rooms (LPDRs), *77.005*
NRC (Nuclear Regulatory Commission), 77.001 through 77.005
NRCS (Natural Resources Conservation Service), USDA, *see* Agency Index
NRSA, *see* National Research Service Awards
NSA (National Security Agency), DOD, *see* Agency Index
NSDI (National Spatial Data Infrastructure), USGS, *15.809*
NSEP (National Security Education Program), DOD, *12.550*, *12.551*
NSF (National Science Foundation), 47.041 through 47.079
NSIIC (National Sheep Industry Improvement Center), *10.774*
NSIP (Nutrition Services Incentive Program), AOA, *93.053*
NSL (Nursing Student Loans), *93.364*
NSOR (National Sex Offender Registry), *16.554*
NSRDS (National Standard Reference Data System), 11.603
NTDB (National Trade Data Bank), 11.026
NTIA (National Telecommunications and Information Administration), USDC, *see* Agency Index
NTIS (National Technical Information Service), USDC, *see* Agency Index
NTIS (National Technical Information Service), USDC, 11.650
Nuclear attack, *see* Civil defense; Radiation
NUCLEAR ENERGY RESEARCH, DEVELOPMENT AND DEMONSTRATION, *81.121*
Nuclear medicine, *see* Nuclear sciences, technology
Nuclear Regulatory Commission (NRC), 77.001 through 77.005
Nuclear sciences, technology
  Atomic Energy Act, 77.001, *77.005*, 81.003, 81.022, *81.049*, *81.057*, *81.104*, *81.108*, *81.112*, *81.113*, *81.114*, *81.121*, *81.123*

basic sciences, fusion energy, high-energy, nuclear physics research, *81.049*
DOE research, education, fellowships, *81.114*
DOE patents, licensing, 81.003
DOE used equipment, 81.022
DOE WMD nonproliferation research, *81.113*
environmental restoration, waste management technology development, *81.104*
HBCU program, DOE, *81.123*
Inertial Confinement Fusion, stockpile stewardship, *81.112*
information, OSTI, 81.064
National Energy Information Center, 81.039
National Security and Military Application of Nuclear Energy Authorization Act, *81.106*
NRC local public document rooms, *77.005*
Nuclear Energy Research Initiative, *81.121*
Nuclear Waste Policy Act, *81.065*
radiation control training, 77.001
Radiogenetic Exposure Screening and Education Program, *93.257*
radioactive waste disposal, *81.065*
transuranic waste transport, *81.106*
see also Civil defense; Disaster assistance; Emergency assistance; Energy *entries*; Hazardous materials, waste; Health, medical research; Physical sciences; Radiation; Technology transfer, utilization
Nuclear waste, *see* Hazardous materials, waste; Radiation
NUCLEAR WASTE DISPOSAL SITING, *81.065*
NURSE ANESTHETIST TRAINING, *93.124*
NURSE EDUCATION, PRACTICE AND RETENTION GRANTS, *93.359*
NURSE FACULTY LOAN PROGRAM, *93.264*
Nursing
  AIDS, NIH research education loan repayments, *93.936*
  anesthetist traineeships, *93.124*
  Area Health Education Centers, *93.824*
  disadvantaged, scholarships, *93.925*
  disadvantaged students assistance, *93.178*
  education loan repayments, *93.165*, *93.908*
  education programs, advanced, *93.247*
  faculty education loan repayments, disadvantaged, *93.923*
  faculty loan program, *93.264*
  geriatrics education centers, *93.969*
  graduate traineeships, *93.358*
  health workforce analysis, *93.300*
  Indians, recruitment, *93.970*
  Indians, scholarships, *93.972*
  Indians, scholarships, preprofessional, *93.971*
  Indians, training assistance, *15.108*
  mental health disciplines, training, *93.244*
  NHSC education loan repayments, *93.162*
  NHSC scholarships, *93.288*
  NIH Clinical Research Loan Repayment Program (CR-LRP), *93.280*
  NIH Pediatric Research Loan Repayment Program, *93.385*
  Nurse Education, Practice and Retention Program, *93.359*
  Nursing Reinvestment Act of 2002, *93.264*, *93.265*, *93.359*, *93.908*
  Pell grants, *84.063*

Nursing *(continued)*
  research, research fellowships, *93.361*
  Specially Selected Health Projects, HRSA, *93.888*
  student loan cancellations, *84.037*
  student loans, *93.364*
  veterans home-based care, 64.022
  see also Community health services; Fellowships, scholarships, traineeships; Health, medical education, training; Health professions; Nursing homes; Technical training
NURSING EDUCATION LOAN REPAYMENT PROGRAM, *93.908*
Nursing homes
  construction, rehabilitation, *14.129*
  employee background checks, long-term care, *93.785*
  expansion, improvements, *14.151*
  geriatrics education centers, *93.969*
  long-term care ombudsman services, *93.042*
  Medicaid payments, *93.778*
  Medicare payments, *93.773*, *93.774*
  patients rights, 16.105
  Senior Companion Program, *94.016*
  Specially Selected Health Projects, HRSA, *93.888*
  veterans, 64.010, *64.015*
  veterans domiciliary care, 64.008, *64.014*
  veterans, state, construction, alteration, expansion, *64.005*
  see also Group homes; Health facilities *entries*; Veterans health, medical services
NURSING RESEARCH, *93.361*
NURSING STUDENT LOANS, *93.364*
NURSING WORKFORCE DIVERSITY, *93.178*
Nutrition, *see* Food, nutrition *entries*
NUTRITION ASSISTANCE FOR PUERTO RICO, *10.566*
NUTRITION SERVICES INCENTIVE PROGRAM, *93.053*
NWCCC (National White Collar Crime Center), *16.612*

OAA (Older Americans Act), *see* Aging and the aged
OAR (Office of Oceanic and Atmospheric Research)
  Cooperative Institutes, *11.432*
OATELS (Office of Apprenticeship Training, Employer and Labor Service), DOL, 17.201
Oats, *see* Agricultural commodities, stabilization; Feed grains
Obesity research, *93.848*
OCCSSA (Omnibus Crime Control and Safe Streets Act), *see* Crime
OCCUPANT PROTECTION [DOT], *20.602*
Occupational health, safety
  advisory services, counseling, *17.504*
  cancer exposure, *93.399*
  CDCP assistance, *93.283*
  compliance, farms, Interest Assistance Program, *10.437*
  DOE workers, epidemiology, health studies, *81.108*
  education, training projects, *17.502*
  farm labor contractor registration, 17.308
  hazardous substances research, education, *93.143*
  health promotion, national, *93.990*
  IHS injury prevention, *93.228*
  Indians, injury prevention programs, CDCP, *93.284*
  Indians, scholarships, preprofessional, *93.971*
  injury prevention research, training, *93.136*
  mining, *17.600*, 17.601, 17.602
  Occupational Safety and Health Act, *17.502*, *17.503*, *17.504*, *93.262*, *93.283*
  OSHA Data Initiative, *17.505*
  pesticides application, *66.700*
  physical therapies, alternative, complementary medicine research, *93.213*
  pipeline safety, *20.700*
  radiation control, NRC training, 77.001
  research, disabilities, injuries prevention, epidemiology, *93.184*
  research, training, *93.262*
  seafarers, 20.810
  state program administration, *17.503*, *17.504*
  statistics, injury and illness, *17.005*
  Superfund Worker Training Program, *93.142*
  see also Environmental health, research, services; Farm workers; Hazardous materials, waste; Health, medical education, training; Health professions; Labor standards; Mining, mining industries; Preventive health services; Public safety
Occupational Safety and Health Administration Data Initiative, *17.505*
Occupational Safety and Health Administration (OSHA), DOL, *see* Agency Index
OCCUPATIONAL SAFETY AND HEALTH PROGRAM, *93.262*
OCCUPATIONAL SAFETY AND HEALTH—STATE PROGRAM, *17.503*
OCCUPATIONAL SAFETY AND HEALTH—SUSAN HARWOOD TRAINING GRANTS, *17.502*
Occupational therapy, *see* Health professions; Occupational health, safety; Vocational rehabilitation
Occupational training, *see* Apprenticeship training; Employment development, training; Health professions; Technical training; Veterans education, training; Vocational *entries*
OCEAN FREIGHT REIMBURSEMENT PROGRAM [USAID], *98.003*
Ocean sciences, oceanography, *see* Environmental sciences; Marine sciences; Physical sciences; Scientific research
OERI (Office of Educational Research and Improvement), DOED, *see* Agency Index
OFCCP (Office of Federal Contract Compliance Programs), 17.301
OFFENDER REENTRY PROGRAM, *16.202*
Offenders, *see* Corrections; Criminal justice system
Office for Civil Rights, HHS, 93.001
Office of Academic Exchange Programs, Study of the U.S. Program, BECA, *19.418*
Office of Administration, EPA, *see* Agency Index
Office of Advocacy and Enterprise (OAE), USDA, *see* Agency Index (USDA, Office of Civil Rights Enforcement)
Office of Air and Radiation, EPA, *see* Agency Index
Office of Apprenticeship Training, Employer and Labor Service, DOL, (OATELS),17.201
Office of Assistant Secretary (Economic Security), DOD, *see* Agency Index
Office of Assistant Secretary/Elementary and Secondary Education, DOED, *see* Agency Index

MASTER INDEX 993

Office of Assistant Secretary/Postsecondary Education, DOED, see Agency Index
Office of Assistant Secretary/Strategy and Requirements, DOD, see Agency Index
Office of Assistant Secretary/Veterans' Employment and Training, DOL, see Agency Index
Office of Assistant Secretary/Vocational and Adult Education, DOED, see Agency Index
Office of Aviation Analysis, DOT, see Agency Index
Office of Bilingual Education and Minority Languages Affairs, DOED, see Agency Index
Office of Citizen Exchanges, BECA, 19.415
Office of Civil Rights Enforcement (OCRE), USDA, see Agency Index
Office of Civilian Radioactive Waste Management, DOE, see Agency Index
Office of Community Development, USDA, see Agency Index
Office of Community Oriented Policing Services, DOJ, see Agency Index
Office of Defense Programs, DOE, see Agency Index
Office of Deputy Under Secretary/Human Resources and Administration, DOED, see Agency Index
Office of Disability Employment Policy, DOL, see Agency Index
Office of Disease Prevention and Health Promotion, HHS, see Agency Index
Office of Economic Adjustment, DOD, see Agency Index
Office of Educational Research and Improvement (OERI), DOED, see Agency Index
Office of Elementary and Secondary Education, DOED, see Agency Index
Office of Energy Efficiency and Renewable Energy, DOE, see Agency Index
Office of Energy Research, DOE, see Agency Index
Office of Enforcement and Compliance Assurance, EPA, see Agency Index
Office of Enforcement and Compliance Assurance Tribal Resources, EPA, 66.310
Office of Environment, Safety, and Health, DOE, see Agency Index
Office of Environmental Education, EPA, see Agency Index
Office of Environmental Justice, EPA, see Agency Index
Office of Environmental Management, DOE, see Agency Index
Office of Fair Housing and Equal Opportunity (OFHEO), HUD, see Agency Index
Office of Federal Activities, EPA, see Agency Index
Office of Federal Contract Compliance Programs (OFCCP), DOL, 17.301
Office of Fossil Energy, DOE, see Agency Index
Office of General Counsel, DOE, see Agency Index
Office of Human Resources and Administration, DOED, see Agency Index
Office of Insular Affairs, DOI, see Agency Index
Office of International Activities, EPA, see Agency Index (EPA, Office of Federal Activities)
Office of International Cooperation and Development, USDA, see Agency Index (USDA, Foreign Agricultural Service)
Office of Justice Programs, DOJ, see Agency Index

Office of Juvenile Justice and Delinquency Prevention (OJJDP), DOJ, see Agency Index
Office of Labor-Management Standards, DOL, see Agency Index
Office of Lead-Based Paint Abatement and Poisoning Prevention, HUD, see Agency Index
Office of Minority Economic Impact (OMEI), DOE, see Agency Index (DOE, Office of Economic Impact and Diversity)
Office of Minority Health, HHS, see Agency Index
Office of Naval Research, DOD, see Agency Index
OFFICE OF OCEANIC AND ATMOSPHERIC RESEARCH (OAR) JOINT AND COOPERATIVE INSTITUTES, 11.432
Office of Personnel Management (OPM), 27.001 through 27.013
Office of Polar Programs (OPP), NSF, 47.078
Office of Policy Development and Research (PD&R), HUD, see Agency Index
Office of Policy, DOE, see Agency Index
Office of Population Affairs, HHS, see Agency Index
Office of Postsecondary Education, DOED, see Agency Index
Office of Public Health and Science, HHS, see Agency Index
Office of Refugee Resettlement, ACF-HHS, see Aliens, immigrants, refugees
Office of Research and Development, EPA, see Agency Index
OFFICE OF RESEARCH AND DEVELOPMENT CONSOLIDATED RESEARCH/TRAINING [EPA], 66.511
OFFICE OF SCIENCE FINANCIAL ASSISTANCE PROGRAM [DOE], 81.049
OFFICE OF SCIENTIFIC AND TECHNICAL INFORMATION [DOE], 81.064
OFFICE OF SMALL DISADVANTAGED BUSINESS CERTIFICATION AND ELIGIBILITY [SBA], 59.049
Office of Solid Waste and Emergency Response (OSWER), EPA, see Agency Index
Office of Special Education and Rehabilitative Services (OSERS), DOED, see Agency Index
Office of Surface Mining Reclamation and Enforcement, DOI, see Agency Index
OFFICE OF ENVIRONMENTAL CLEANUP AND ACCELERATION [DOE], 81.104
Office of Territorial and International Affairs, DOI, see Agency Index (DOI, Office of Insular Affairs)
Office of the Chief of Engineers, DOD, see Agency Index (DOD, Department of the Army, Office of the Chief of Engineers)
Office of the Legal Adviser, Department of State, see Agency Index
Office of the Secretary, DOD, see Agency Index
Office of the Secretary, DOT, see Agency Index
Office of the Secretary, HHS, see Agency Index
Office of the Secretary, USDC, see Agency Index
Office of the Secretary, Women's Bureau, DOL, see Agency Index
Office of Vocational and Adult Education, DOED, see Agency Index
Office of Water, EPA, see Agency Index
OFFICER NEXT DOOR SALES PROGRAM [HUD], 14.198

OFHEO (Office of Fair Housing and Equal Opportunity), HUD, see Agency Index
OFR (Ocean Freight Reimbursement), USAID, 98.003
Oil and Hazardous Substance Contingency Plan, 66.802
Oil Spill Liability Trust Fund, USCG, 97.013
OJJDP (Office of Juvenile Justice and Delinquency Prevention), DOJ, see Agency Index
Older Americans Act (OAA), see Aging and the aged
Older persons, see Aging and the aged; Housing, elderly
Older Worker Program, 17.235
Ombudsman services, aging, 93.042
OMEI (Office of Minority Economic Impact), DOE, see Agency Index (DOE, Office of Economic Impact and Diversity)
Omnibus Crime Control and Safe Streets Act (OCCSSA), see Crime
Omnibus Trade and Competitiveness Act of 1988, see International commerce, investment
One-Time Funded Research Projects, DHS, 97.002
OPDR (Office of Policy Development and Research), HUD, see Agency Index
OPERATING ASSISTANCE FOR TROUBLED MULTIFAMILY HOUSING PROJECTS, 14.164
Operating Loss Loans, Section 223(d), HUD, 14.167
OPERATION LEAD ELIMINATION ACTION PROGRAM [HUD], 14.903
OPERATION SAFE COMMERCE COOPERATIVE (OCS) AGREEMENT PROGRAM [DHS], 97.058
Operation Weed and Seed, DOJ, 16.595
Operator Certification Expense Reimbursement Grants, EPA, 66.471
OPIC (Overseas Private Investment Corporation), 70.002 through 70.003
OPM (Office of Personnel Management), 27.001 through 27.013
OPP (Office of Polar Programs), NSF, 47.078
OPPORTUNITIES FOR YOUTH—YOUTHBUILD PROGRAM [HUD], 14.243
Optometry
education assistance, disadvantaged, 93.342, 93.822, 93.925
faculty education loan repayments, disadvantaged, 93.923
Indians, scholarships, 93.972
veterans, dependents services, 64.009
see also Health, medical education, training; Health professions
ORGANIC AGRICULTURE RESEARCH AND EXTENSION INITIATIVE, 10.307
ORAL DISEASES AND DISORDERS RESEARCH, 93.121
Organ procurement, HRSA, 93.134
Organized crime, see Crime
OSBDC&E (Office of Small Disadvantaged Business Certification and Eligibility), SBA, 59.049
OSC (Operation Safe Commerce), DHS, 97.058
OSERS (Office of Special Education and Rehabilitative Services), DOED, see Agency Index
OSHA DATA INITIATIVE [DOL], 17.505

OSHA (Occupational Safety and Health Administration), DOL, see Agency Index
Osteopathy
AIDS, NIH research education loan repayments, 93.936
Area Health Education Centers Model Programs, 93.107
disease prevention research, 93.135
education assistance, disadvantaged, 93.342, 93.822, 93.925
education loan repayments, states, 93.165
faculty education loan repayments, disadvantaged, 93.923
Geriatric Academic Career Awards, 93.250
geriatrics faculty fellowships, 93.156
health education centers, 93.824
health education, training centers, 93.189
Indians, health professions scholarships, 93.123, 93.972
NHSC education loan repayments, 93.162
NHSC scholarships, 93.288
NIH Clinical Research Loan Repayment Program (CR-LRP), 93.280
NIH Pediatric Research Loan Repayment Program, 93.285, 93.385
preventive medicine residency, 93.117
residency training, 93.884
see also Family medicine; Health, medical education, training; Health professions; Pediatrics
OSTI (Office of Scientific and Technical Information), DOE, see Agency Index
OSTI (Office of Scientific and Technical Information), DOE, 81.064
OSWER (Office of Solid Waste and Emergency Response), EPA, see Agency Index
OUTDOOR RECREATION—ACQUISITION, DEVELOPMENT AND PLANNING, 15.916
Outer Continental Shelf Lands Act, see Fisheries industry
OUTREACH AND ASSISTANCE FOR SOCIALLY DISADVANTAGED FARMERS AND RANCHERS, 10.443
OVERSEAS—DOCTORAL DISSERTATION, 84.022
OVERSEAS EDUCATIONAL ADVISING, 19.432
OVERSEAS—FACULTY RESEARCH ABROAD, 84.019
OVERSEAS—GROUP PROJECTS ABROAD, 84.021
OVERSEAS REFUGEE ASSISTANCE PROGRAMS FOR AFRICA, 19.517
OVERSEAS REFUGEE ASSISTANCE PROGRAMS FOR EAST ASIA, 19.511
OVERSEAS REFUGEE ASSISTANCE PROGRAMS FOR EUROPE, 19.520
OVERSEAS REFUGEE ASSISTANCE PROGRAMS FOR NEAR EAST, 19.519
OVERSEAS REFUGEE ASSISTANCE PROGRAMS FOR STRATEGIC GLOBAL PRIORITIES, 19.522
OVERSEAS REFUGEE ASSISTANCE PROGRAMS FOR WESTERN HEMISPHERE, 19.518
Overseas investment, see Business development; International commerce, investment

Overseas Private Investment Corporation (OPIC), 70.002 through 70.003
OVERSEAS PROGRAMS—SPECIAL BILATERAL PROJECTS, *84.018*
Ozone research, NOAA, *11.432*
OZONE TRANSPORT, *66.033*

P2 Grant Program, EPA pollution prevention, *66.708*
P3 AWARD: NATIONAL STUDENT DESIGN COMPETITION FOR SUSTAINABILITY [EPA], *66.516*
PACA (Perishable Agricultural Commodities Act), 10.165
PACIFIC COAST SALMON RECOVERY—PACIFIC SALMON TREATY PROGRAM, *11.438*
PACIFIC FISHERIES DATA PROGRAM, *11.437*
Pacific Trust Territory, *see* U.S. possessions, territories
Packaging, *see* Complaint investigation; Consumers, consumer services; Food inspection, grading; Measurement
Packers and Stockyards Administration, USDA, *see* Agency Index (USDA, Grain Inspection, Packers and Stockyard Administration)
PAIMA (Protection and Advocacy for Individuals with Mental Illness), CMHS, *93.138*
Pain disorders research, *93.853*
Painters, paintings, *see* Arts, arts education; Museums, galleries
PAIR (Protection and Advocacy of Individual Rights), disabled, *84.240*
Palau, *see* U.S. possessions, territories
Paraplegic Housing, veterans, *64.106*
PARENTAL ASSISTANCE CENTERS [DOED], *84.310*
Parenting
abandoned infants, foster care services, training, *93.551*
abstinence education, *93.010*, *93.235*
access and visitation programs, *93.597*
adolescent family life research, *93.111*
adolescent parents, demonstration projects, *93.995*
Adoption and Safe Families Act of 1997, *93.556*, *93.603*
Adoption Awareness Training, *93.254*
adoption, foster care placement discrimination, 93.001
Adoption Incentive Payments, *93.603*
adoption payments, special needs children, *93.659*
adoption services, *93.652*
AIDS prevention, school-age populations, *93.938*
Charter Schools, *84.282*
child abuse, neglect research, technical assistance, *93.670*
child abuse technical assistance, training, *16.547*
Child Care and Development Fund, *93.596*
child care, low-income working families, CCDF, *93.575*
child care, postsecondary low-income student-parents, *84.335*
child care/social services, TANF, *93.558*
Child Support Enforcement Research, *93.564*
child support payments enforcement, *93.563*, *93.601*
community-based child abuse prevention, *93.590*

Community Learning Centers, *84.287*
Comprehensive School Reform Demonstration, *84.332*
domestic violence, stalking victim transitional housing, *16.736*
Drug-Free Schools and Communities, national programs, *84.184*
Drug Prevention Program, *16.728*
Early Learning Fund, services, training, ACF, *93.577*
education project technical assistance, *84.283*
education reform, *84.298*, *84.305*
educational resource centers, *84.310*
embryo adoption public awareness, *93.007*
EPA Children's Health Protection, *66.609*
Even Start, Indians, *84.258*
Even Start, migrants, *84.214*
Even Start, state, *84.213*
Family and Medical Leave Act of 1993, 17.303
Family Life Centers, HHS violence prevention, *93.910*
family support services, adoption, foster care, *93.556*
foster care, *93.603*, *93.658*
Foster Care Independence Act of 1999, *96.020*
Foster Grandparent Program, *94.011*
Gang Resistance Education and Training, BJA, *16.737*
handicapped children, intervention, special education, *84.027*, *84.173*, *84.181*, *84.323*, *84.324*, *84.325*, *84.326*, *84.327*, *84.328*, *84.329*
Head Start, *93.600*
high-risk youth programs, *16.542*
Indian programs, *15.043*, *15.144*, *84.060*
juvenile delinquency prevention, *16.541*, *16.542*
juvenile gang members, *16.544*
Juvenile Mentoring Program, *16.726*
maternal, child health care, block grants, *93.994*
Mentoring Children of Prisoners, ACF, *93.616*
missing children program, *16.543*
Parent Information Centers, special education, *84.328*
Parental Assistance Centers, DOED, *84.310*
pregnant homeless youth, transitional living, *93.550*
Ready-to-Learn TV, early childhood education, *84.295*
runaway centers, communications systems, *93.623*
Safe Motherhood Initiative, *93.946*
single-parent vocational training, *84.048*
Safe and Stable Families Act of 2001, *93.616*
social services research, demonstration, *93.647*
Supervised Visitation, Safe Havens for Children, OJP, *16.527*
telecommunications, instructional programming, Star Schools, *84.203*
underage drinking law enforcement, *16.727*
violence, children's exposure, prevention initiative, Safe Start, *16.730*
Voluntary Public School Choice, *84.361*
WIA Youth Activities, *17.259*
working mothers, special employment assistance, 17.700
see also Child care services; Family planning; Family therapy; Maternal, child health, welfare; Volunteers; Youth

Parkinson's disease research, 93.853
Parks, playgrounds, see Public lands; Recreation; Urban parks, playgrounds
PART D—RESEARCH, EVALUATION, TECHNICAL ASSISTANCE AND TRAINING [DOJ], 16.542
PART E—STATE CHALLENGE ACTIVITIES [DOJ], 16.549
PARTNERS FOR FISH AND WILDLIFE, 15.631
PARTNERSHIP AGREEMENTS TO DEVELOP NON-INSURANCE RISK MANAGEMENT TOOLS FOR PRODUCERS (FARMERS), 10.456
Patent and Trademark Office, USDC, see Agency Index
PATENT AND TRADEMARK TECHNICAL INFORMATION DISSEMINATION, 11.900
Patents, trademarks, inventions
   aerospace technology, 43.002
   Christopher Columbus Fellowship Program, 85.100
   DOE patents, licensing, 81.003
   energy-related inventions, 81.036
   Inventions and Innovations Program, DOE, 81.036
   manufacturing technology commercialization, 11.612
   patent, trademark information, search, 11.900
   plant variety protection, 10.163
   Semiconductor Chip Protection Service, 42.008
   see also Business development; Copyright services; Technology transfer, utilization
PATH (Projects for Assistance in Transition from Homelessness), CMHS, 93.150
Patriot Act of 2001, see Civil defense (U.S.A. Patriot Act of 2001)
PAUL COVERDELL FORENSIC SCIENCES IMPROVEMENT GRANT PROGRAM, 16.742
PAYMENTS FOR ESSENTIAL AIR SERVICES, 20.901
PAYMENTS FOR SMALL COMMUNITY AIR SERVICE DEVELOPMENT, 20.930
PAYMENTS IN LIEU OF TAXES [DOI], 15.226
PAYMENTS TO AGRICULTURAL EXPERIMENT STATIONS UNDER THE HATCH ACT, 10.203
Payments to Counties, USFS, 10.666
PAYMENTS TO 1890 LAND-GRANT COLLEGES AND TUSKEGEE UNIVERSITY, 10.205
PAYMENTS TO STATES IN LIEU OF REAL ESTATE TAXES [DOD], 12.112
PCL (Primary Care Loans), HRSA, 93.342
PCPID (President's Committee for People with Intellectual Disabilities), 93.613
PD&R (Office of Policy Development and Research), HUD, see Agency Index
PDM (Pre-Disaster Mitigation), FEMA, 97.017, 97.047
Peace Institute, 91.001 through 91.002
Peace research, studies, see International programs, studies; Military; Social sciences
PEANUT QUOTA BUYOUT PROGRAM, 10.994
Peanuts, see Agricultural commodities, stabilization
PEDFAR (President's Emergency Plan for AIDS Relief), 93.266

Pediatrics
   Children's Hospitals Graduate Medical Education Payment, HRSA, 93.255
   emergency medical services, 93.127
   Infant Health Initiative, 93.946
   Medicaid payments, 93.778
   NHSC scholarships, 93.288
   NIH research loan repayment program, 93.285, 93.385
   perinatal/maternal initiative, 93.926
   residency training, 93.884
   see also Health, medical education, training; Health professions; Maternal, child health, welfare; Osteopathy; Public health
Pell Grants, DOED, 84.063
Pension and Welfare Benefits Administration, DOL, see Agency Index (DOL, Employee Benefits Security Administration)
Pension Benefit Guaranty Corporation, 86.001
PENSION FOR NON-SERVICE-CONNECTED DISABILITY FOR VETERANS, 64.104
PENSION PLAN TERMINATION INSURANCE, 86.001
PENSION TO VETERANS SURVIVING SPOUSES, AND CHILDREN, 64.105
PERFORMANCE PARTNERSHIP GRANTS [EPA], 66.605
Performing Arts, BECA, 19.413
PERISHABLE AGRICULTURAL COMMODITIES ACT, 10.165
PERKINS LOAN CANCELLATIONS [DOED], 84.037
Permanent Housing for Homeless Persons with Disabilities, 14.235
PERSONAL CENSUS SEARCH, 11.006
Personal Responsibility and Work Opportunity Reconciliation Act of 1996 (PRWORA), see Public assistance
Personnel exchange, see Federal employment; Government
PESP (Pesticide Environmental Stewardship Program) Regional Grants, 66.714
Pesticide Data Program, 10.163
PESTICIDE ENVIRONMENTAL STEWARDSHIP REGIONAL GRANTS, 66.714
Pesticides
   agricultural, data program, 10.163
   Agricultural Management Assistance, NRCS, 10.917
   Boll Weevil Eradication Loan Program, 10.449
   dairy products indemnity payments, 10.053
   enforcement program, 66.700
   environmental health hazards research, 93.113
   EPA Nonpoint Source Implementation Grants, 66.460
   EPA Performance Partnership Grants, 66.605
   EPA studies, special purpose assistance, 66.610
   forest pest control, 10.652, 10.664
   Pesticide Environmental Stewardship, 66.714
   pollution control, EPA consolidated program support, 66.600
   pollution control surveys, studies, EPA R&D, 66.510
   pollution prevention studies, training, outreach, 66.716
   Special Research Grants, USDA, 10.200

surveys, studies, special grants, EPA, *66.606*
sustainable agriculture research, *10.215*
Technical Assistance for Specialty Crops, FAS, *10.604*
see also Environmental health, research, services; Fertilizer; Pollution abatement; Toxic substances, toxicology

Pharmacology, pharmacy
alternative, complementary medicine research, *93.213*
antibiotics research, infectious diseases, *93.856*
cancer treatment research, *93.395*
deafness, communicative disorders research, *93.173*
DVA prescription service, 64.012
education assistance, disadvantaged, *93.342, 93.822, 93.925*
faculty education loan repayments, disadvantaged, *93.923*
Indians, health professions scholarships, *93.972*
Indians, scholarships, preprofessional, *93.971*
Medicare Prescription Drug, Improvements and Modernization Act 2003 (MMA), *93.773*
Medicare transitional drug assistance program, *93.783, 93.782*
Metropolitan Medical Response System, FEMA, *97.071*
narcotics, dangerous drugs, personnel training, DEA, 16.004
NIH Clinical Research Loan Repayment Program (CR-LRP), *93.280*
pharmacological sciences research, fellowships, *93.859*
State Pharmaceutical Assistance Programs for MMA participants, CMS, *93.786*
see also Biological sciences; Chemicals, chemistry; Drugs, drug research; Health insurance; Health, medical education, training; Health, medical research; Health professions
PHASE (Practical Hands-on Application to Science Education, NOAA, *11.449*
PHHS (Preventive Health and Health Services) Block Grants, *93.991*
Photography, *see* Arts, arts education; Audiovisual aids, film, video
PHS (Public Health Service), HHS, *see* Public health
PHYSICAL DISASTER LOANS, *59.008*
Physical disasters, *see* Disaster assistance; Earthquakes; Flood prevention, control; Hurricanes
Physical fitness, *see* Health, medical services; Occupational health, safety; Recreation
Physical Fitness and Sports, 93.289
Physical sciences
Air Force Defense Research Sciences Program, *12.800*
Army Research Office, *12.431*
atmospheric, marine sciences education, research, facilities, NOAA, *11.469*
Barry M. Goldwater Scholarship Program, *85.200*
calibration, testing, NIST, 11.601
climate, air quality research, services, *11.459*
climate monitoring, assessment, *11.428*
climate, short-term fluctuation studies, *11.443*
coal research, *81.057*
coastal ecosystem management, NOAA, *11.473*

DHS Scholars and Fellows, *97.062*
DOD research, fellowships, *12.630*
DOD science, technology projects, *12.910*
DOE used equipment, 81.022
energy-related, renewable resources research, *81.087*
energy sciences research, *81.049*
EPA consolidated research, *66.511*
EPA environmental sustainability design competition, *66.516*
forestry research, *10.652*
geosciences research, *47.050*
hazardous substances, multi-disciplinary research, education, *93.143*
Hydrometeorological Development, NOAA, *11.467*
measurement, engineering research, standards, *11.609*
National Standard Reference Data System, 11.603
Navy research, education support, *12.300*
NESDIS environmental sciences education, research, *11.440*
NIST Congressionally-Identified Projects, *11.617*
NMFS marine education, science projects, *11.455*
NOAA special projects, *11.460*
NOAA unallied program, *11.472*
Nuclear Energy Research Initiative, *81.121*
Polar Programs, *47.078*
research support, *47.049*
rural, research, education, *10.224*
Smithsonian fellowships, *85.601*
Standard Reference Materials, 11.604
see also Aeronautics, space; Astronomy; Agricultural research, sciences; Biological sciences; Chemicals, chemistry; Climate; Earth sciences; Energy *entries*; Engineering *entries*; Environmental sciences; Forensic sciences; Geology; Marine sciences; Mathematics; Minority education; Nuclear sciences, technology; Science education; Scientific research
Physical therapy, *see* Occupational health, safety; Vocational rehabilitation
Physically handicapped, *see* Disabled, handicapped *entries*; Veterans, disabled
Physicians, *see* Family medicine; Health, medical education, training; Health professions; Osteopathy; Pediatrics
Physics, *see* Engineering *entries*; Nuclear sciences, technology; Physical sciences; Scientific research
Physiology research, *93.859*
PILOT PROGRAM FOR NATIONAL AND STATE BACKGROUND CHECKS—DIRECT PATIENT ACCESS FOR LONG-TERM CARE, *93.785*
PILOT DEMONSTRATION OR EARMARKED PROJECTS [DHS], *97.001*
PILT (Payments in Lieu of Taxes), BLM, *15.226*
PIPELINE SAFETY, *20.700*
Pittman-Robertson (P-R) Program, FWS, *15.611*
Planetariums, *see* Museums, galleries
PLANNING AND PROGRAM DEVELOPMENT GRANTS [CNCS], *94.007*
PLANNING ASSISTANCE TO STATES [DOD], 12.110

PLANT AND ANIMAL DISEASE, PEST CONTROL, AND ANIMAL CARE, *10.025*
PLANT MATERIALS FOR CONSERVATION, 10.905
Plant Variety Protection Program, 10.163
Plants
agricultural, inspection 10.162
alternative, complementary medicine research, *93.213*
aquatic plant control, rivers, harbors, 12.100
competitive research grants, *10.206*
conservation stewardship, *15.632*
conservation use, *10.069*, 10.905
Crop Insurance, *10.450*
disaster assistance, noninsured crops, *10.451*
disease, pest control, *10.025*
endangered species conservation, *10.914*, *15.615*
endangered species, Indian lands, *15.051*
endangered species, pesticides enforcement, *66.700*
Environmental Quality Incentives Program-Klamath Basin, NRCS, *10.919*
Environmental Quality Incentives Program, NRCS, *10.912*
EPA pesticides, toxic chemicals pollution prevention studies, training, outreach, *66.716*
Fish, Wildlife and Plant Conservation Resource Management, BLM, *15.231*
Food Stamp purchases, *10.551*
Forest Health Protection, USFS, *10.680*
FWS Challenge Cost Share, *15.642*
FWS Landowner Incentives, *15.633*
Indian lands, noxious weed eradication, *15.034*
international research exchanges, *10.961*
market promotion, protection, 10.163
mine land reclamation, *10.910*
natural landmarks registry, 15.910
nurseries, disaster recovery loans, SBA, *59.002*
plant biology research, *47.074*
Plant Protection Act, *10.025*
research, SBIR, *10.212*
sustainable agriculture research, *10.215*
USGS Gap Analysis Program, *15.811*
vegetation use, Hazard Mitigation Grant, FEMA, *97.039*
wildlife without borders programs, education, research, training, FWS, *15.640*, *15.641*
see also Agricultural *entries*; Biological sciences; Environmental management; Fruit; Pesticides; Seedlings, seeds; Vegetables
Playgrounds, see Community development; Recreation; Urban parks, playgrounds
PLUS Loans, DOED, *84.032*, *84.268*
PODIATRIC RESIDENCY TRAINING IN PRIMARY CARE, *93.181*
Podiatry
education assistance, disadvantaged, *93.342*, *93.822*, *93.925*
faculty education loan repayments, disadvantaged, *93.923*
residency programs, *93.181*
veterans, dependents services, 64.009
see also Health, medical education, training; Health professions
Poison, see Chemicals, chemistry; Pesticides; Toxic substances, toxicology

Poison Control Centers, *93.253*
POISON CONTROL STABILIZATION AND ENHANCEMENT, *93.253*
POLAR PROGRAMS, *47.078*
Police
Bulletproof Vest Partnership Program, *16.607*
campus crime grants, *16.525*
Citizen Corps, DHS, *97.053*
Community Prosecution Program, *16.609*
Cops Grants, *16.710*
corrections, law enforcement personnel family support projects, research, *16.563*
criminal conspiracy, organized crime regional information sharing, *16.610*
domestic violence arrest policies, protection orders enforcement, *16.590*
drug control, *16.579*, *16.580*
drug interdiction, motor carriers, *20.218*
Emergency Federal Law Enforcement Assistance, *16.577*
FBI Field Police Training, 16.302
highway safety training, vehicles, equipment, *20.600*
housing, Officer Next Door Sales Program, 14.198
Indian Law Enforcement, *15.030*
Interoperable Communications Equipment, DHS, *97.055*
justice personnel, equipment, training, planning grants, *16.738*
local law enforcement block grants, *16.592*
misconduct, prosecution, 16.109
motor carrier safety regulation, training, 20.217
Motor Vehicle Theft Protection Act Program, training, *16.597*
officers' dependents educational assistance, *16.615*
officers, disability, death benefits, *16.571*
Police Corps, scholarships, officers, dependents, *16.712*
statistics, 16.305
traffic safety control, alcohol, drugs, *20.601*
Truck Security Program, DHS, *97.059*
underage drinking law enforcement, *16.727*
violence, children's exposure, prevention initiative, Safe Start, *16.730*
WMD, domestic preparedness, *97.004*, *97.005*, *97.006*, *97.007*
see also Crime; Criminal justice system; FBI; Law enforcement education, training; Public safety; Rescue services
POLICE CORPS, *16.712*
Political Risk Insurance, OPIC, *70.003*
POLICY RESEARCH AND EVALUATION GRANTS [HHS], *93.239*
Pollution, see Air pollution; Pollution abatement; Water pollution abatement, prevention
Pollution abatement
agriculture-related research, SBIR, *10.212*
air, prevention, effects studies, demonstrations, *66.034*
coal mining, *15.250*
coal research, *81.057*
coastal, estuarine areas research, *11.426*
community stakeholder projects, *66.035*
Compliance Assistance Centers, EPA, *66.305*
Conservation Security Program, NRCS, *10.921*

control techniques surveys, studies, EPA R&D, *66.510*
DOD sites, reimbursements, *12.113*
DOE industrial, agricultural, (NICE3), *81.105*
environmental health, biometry, risk estimation, *93.115*
environmental health research, resources, manpower development, *93.894*
Environmental Information Exchange Network Grants, *66.608*
environmental justice projects, *66.604*
Environmental Justice Research Assistance, EPA, *66.308*
Environmental Justice Surveys and Studies, EPA, *66.309*
Environmental Justice Training and Fellowships, EPA, *66.307*
environmental policy, programs innovation, stewardship, studies, analyses, *66.611*
EPA compliance capacity building, *66.709*
EPA consolidated program support, *66.600*
EPA consolidated research, *66.511*
EPA environmental sustainability design competition, *66.516*
EPA IHE research support, *66.515*
EPA Performance Partnership Grants, *66.605*
EPA Region 7 projects, *66.111*
EPA State Information Grants, *66.608*
EPA studies, special purpose assistance, *66.610*
estuary protection, *66.456*
Great Plains Conservation, *10.900*
hazardous wastes control, management, *66.801*
Indian lands, environmental management, *66.926*
mine land reclamation, *15.252*
National Ocean Pollution Planning Act of 1978, *11.426*
airports, air, noise, water, *20.106*
Oil Pollution Act of 1990, 97.013
Ozone Transport, *66.033*
Pesticide Environmental Stewardship, *66.714*
pesticides control, *66.700*
petroleum underground storage tank program, *66.805*
Pollution Prevention Act of 1990 (PPA), *66.110*, *66.708*
prevention information projects, *66.708*
regional monitoring, assessment projects, EPA, *66.512*
rural business, industrial loans, *10.768*
rural resource conservation, development, *10.901*
senior environmental employment programs, *66.508*, *66.518*
source reduction information dissemination, outreach, EPA, *66.717*
standards, testing, 11.604
STAR (Science to Achieve Results) Research Program, EPA, *66.509*
Superfund technical assistance to citizen groups, *66.806*
surveys, studies, special grants, EPA, *66.606*
tribal direct implementation agreements, EPA, *66.473*
underground storage tanks, *66.804*, *66.816*
watershed protection research, studies, training, *66.480*
watershed, river basin projects, 10.906

wetlands environmental outcome demonstrations, *66.479*
see also Agricultural conservation; Air pollution; Environmental *entries*; Hazardous materials, waste; Pesticides; Sewage facilities, treatment; Toxic substances, toxicology; Waste treatment, disposal; Water *entries*; Wetlands
POLLUTION PREVENTION GRANTS PROGRAM, *66.708*
Population research
adolescent family life, *93.111*, *93.995*
AIDS/HIV epidemiologic studies, *93.943*
Cancer Centers Support, *93.397*
Cancer Control, *93.399*
Census Bureau data, 11.001
Census Intergovernmental Services, 11.004
census services, 11.005
Centers for Genomics and Public Health, *93.063*
contraception, infertility research, education loan repayments, *93.209*
family planning services, *93.217*, *93.974*
Vital Statistics Reengineering Program, CDCP, *93.066*
see also Alaska, Alaska natives; Census services; Epidemiology; Family planning; Hawaii, Hawaii natives; Indian *entries*; Rural areas; Social sciences; Statistics
Pork, *see* Agricultural marketing; Food inspection, grading; Livestock industry
PORT SECURITY GRANT PROGRAM, *97.056*
PORT SECURITY RESEARCH AND DEVELOPMENT GRANT, *97.060*
Ports and Domestic Shipping and Intermodal Development, 20.801
Ports and harbors, *see* Maritime industry; Water navigation
Postsecondary education, *see* Fellowships, scholarships, traineeships; Higher education *entries*; Vocational education
POST-VIETNAM ERA VETERANS' EDUCATIONAL ASSISTANCE, *64.120*
Poultry, egg products
Avian Influenza Indemnity Program, *10.029*
farm operating loans, *10.406*
inspection, *10.475*, 10.477
inspection, grading, 10.162
Market News, 10.153
Poultry Products Inspection Act, *10.475*, 10.477
production data, statistics, 10.950
see also Agricultural marketing; Animal disease control, health, welfare; Food inspection, grading
Poverty, *see* Depressed areas; Disadvantaged *entries*; Public assistance; Rural poor; Social sciences; Social services
PPGs (Performance Partnership Grants), EPA, *66.605*
PQB (Peanut Quota Buyout Program), FSA, *10.994*
P-R (Pittman-Robertson) Program, FWS, *15.611*
Practical Hands-on Application to Science Education (PHASE), NOAA, *11.449*
PRAMS (Pregnancy Risk Assessment Monitoring System), *93.946*
PRE-DISASTER MITIGATION, *97.047*
PRE-DISASTER MITIGATION (PDM), COMPETITIVE GRANTS, *97.017*

Pregnancy, *see* Family planning; Maternal, child health, welfare; Parenting; Youth
Pregnancy Risk Assessment Monitoring System (PRAMS), *93.946*
Preparedness, Training and Exercises Directorate, FEMA, *see* Agency Index
Preschool, *see* Child care services; Early childhood education
Presidential Libraries, 89.001
PRESIDENTIAL MANAGEMENT INTERN PROGRAM, 27.013
PRESIDENT'S COMMITTEE FOR PEOPLE WITH INTELLECTUAL DISABILITIES, 93.613
President's Committee on Mental Retardation, *see* President's Committee for People with Intellectual Disabilities
PRESIDENT'S COUNCIL ON PHYSICAL FITNESS AND SPORTS, 93.289
President's Emergency Plan for AIDS Relief (PEDFAR), *93.266*
Prevention and Treatment Block Grant, substance abuse, *93.959*
Prevention Research Centers, CDCP, *93.135*
PREVENTIVE HEALTH AND HEALTH SERVICES BLOCK GRANT, *93.991*
Preventive health services
AIDS/HIV care, children, women, families, *93.153*
AIDS prevention, *93.118*
AIDS prevention, school health projects, *93.938*
block grants, *93.991*
brucellosis, tuberculosis control, USDA, *10.025*
CDCP assistance, *93.283*
chronic disease prevention, control, *93.068*, *93.945*
community health centers, *93.224*
diabetes control, *93.988*
disabilities, *93.184*
disease prevention research, *93.135*
elderly, *93.043*
EPA aging, children's health protection, *66.609*
Hawaii natives, *93.932*
health care systems research, *93.226*
HIV prevention, *93.939*, *93.940*
HIV prevention efficacy research, dissemination, *93.941*
immunization research, information, *93.185*
Indians, epidemiology centers, *93.231*
injury prevention research, training, *93.136*
maternal, child health care, block grants, *93.994*
National Health Promotion, *93.990*
Preventive Health Amendments of 1992, *93.197*
preventive medicine residency, *93.117*
Public Health Training Centers, *93.249*
rural areas, *93.912*
sexually transmitted diseases control, training, *93.977*
sexually transmitted diseases research, information, training, *93.978*
Social Services Block Grant, *93.667*
tuberculosis control, *93.116*
see also AIDS (Acquired Immune Deficiency Syndrome); Alcohol abuse, alcoholism; Communicable diseases; Community health services; Disease control; Drug abuse; Environmental health, research, services;
Epidemiology; Hazardous materials, waste; Health *entries*; Immunization, immunology; Occupational health, safety; Public health; Respiratory diseases; Toxic substances, toxicology
PREVENTIVE HEALTH SERVICES— SEXUALLY TRANSMITTED DISEASES CONTROL GRANTS, *93.977*
PREVENTIVE HEALTH SERVICES— SEXUALLY TRANSMITTED DISEASES RESEARCH, DEMONSTRATIONS, AND PUBLIC INFORMATION AND EDUCATION GRANTS, *93.978*
Preventive medicine, *see* Preventive health services
Preventive Medicine, *93.117*
Price-fixing conspiracies, 36.001
Price supports, *see* Agricultural commodities, stabilization
Price Supports, USDA, *10.051*
PRICES AND COST OF LIVING DATA, 17.003
Primary Care Loans (PCL), HRSA, *93.342*
PRIMARY CARE SERVICES—RESOURCE COORDINATION AND DEVELOPMENT, *93.130*
Primary Care Training, HRSA, *93.884*
PRIME, SBA microenterprise development, *59.050*
Printing, *see* Arts, arts education; Audiovisual aids, film, video; Publications
Prison Grants, *16.586*
Prison Rape Elimination Act of 2003, *16.735*
Prisoners, prisons, *see* Corrections; Criminal justice system
Private Bar Program, EEOC, 30.005
Private schools, *see* Schools, private
Private sector
Advanced Technology Program, *11.612*
Appalachian region, *23.002*
Apprenticeship training, 17.201
Business and Industry Data Centers, 11.004
Census Bureau data, 11.001
college work-study program, *84.033*
competition, unfair foreign, duties, 11.106
disabled, employment, Projects with Industry, *84.234*
energy conservation, renewable energy outreach, training, *81.117*
engineering, industry-university research centers, *47.041*
EPA Compliance Assistance Centers, *66.305*
ETA pilots, demonstrations, research, *17.261*
FTC activities, 36.001
Global Development Alliance, USAID, *98.011*
industrial energy conservation, *81.086*
industrial energy conservation, waste reduction, DOE, *81.105*
international business education, *84.153*
international, business internships, Eurasian executives, scientists, *11.114*
Manufacturing Extension Partnership, NIST, *11.611*
manufacturing technology commercialization, *11.612*
Operation Weed and Seed, *16.595*
plant closing statistics, *17.002*
pollution prevention information projects, *66.708*, *66.717*

postsecondary education, cooperative projects, FIPSE, *84.116*
President's Council on Physical Fitness and Sports, 93.289
productivity, technology data, 17.004
SEC activities, 58.001
Service Corps of Retired Executives (SCORE), *59.026*
Tech-Prep Demonstration Grants, secondary students, *84.353*
Tech-Prep Education, secondary, postsecondary, *84.243*
white-collar crime center, *16.612*
women's special employment programs, private industry councils, 17.700
see also Business development; Economic development; Economics, research, statistics; Employee benefits; Job creation; Labor-management relations; Occupational health, safety; Patents, trademarks, inventions; Small business; Technology transfer, utilization; Volunteers
Private Stewardship Grants Program, FWS, *15.632*
PRNS (Projects of Regional and National Significance), SAMHSA, *93.243*
PROCUREMENT ASSISTANCE TO SMALL BUSINESSES, 59.009
PROCUREMENT OF HEADSTONES AND MARKERS AND/OR PRESIDENTIAL MEMORIAL CERTIFICATES, *64.202*
PROCUREMENT TECHNICAL ASSISTANCE FOR BUSINESS FIRMS [DOD], *12.002*
Producer Price Index (PPI), 17.003
PRODUCTIVITY AND TECHNOLOGY DATA, 17.004
PROFESSIONAL EXCHANGE—ANNUAL OPEN GRANT [BECA], *19.415*
PROGRAM FOR STUDY OF EASTERN EUROPE AND THE INDEPENDENT STATES OF THE FORMER SOVIET UNION, *19.300*
PROGRAM OF PROTECTION AND ADVOCACY OF INDIVIDUAL RIGHTS, *84.240*
Project-based Section 8, HUD, *14.195*
PROJECT GRANTS AND COOPERATIVE AGREEMENTS FOR TUBERCULOSIS CONTROL PROGRAMS, *93.116*
Project Safe Neighborhoods, OJP, *16.609*
PROJECTS FOR ASSISTANCE IN TRANSITION FROM HOMELESSNESS, *93.150*
PROJECTS WITH INDUSTRY [DOED], *84.234*
PROMOTE THE SURVIVAL AND CONTINUING VITALITY OF NATIVE AMERICAN LANGUAGES, *93.587*
PROMOTING SAFE AND STABLE FAMILIES, *93.556*
Promoting Safe and Stable Families Amendments of 2001, *see* Maternal, child health, welfare
PROMOTION OF THE ARTS—GRANTS TO ORGANIZATIONS AND INDIVIDUALS, *45.024*
PROMOTION OF THE ARTS—PARTNERSHIP AGREEMENTS, *45.025*
PROMOTION OF THE HUMANITIES— CHALLENGE GRANTS, *45.130*
PROMOTION OF THE HUMANITIES— DIVISION OF PRESERVATION AND ACCESS, *45.149*
PROMOTION OF THE HUMANITIES— FEDERAL/STATE PARTNERSHIP, *45.129*
PROMOTION OF THE HUMANITIES— FELLOWSHIPS AND STIPENDS, *45.160*
PROMOTION OF THE HUMANITIES— PROFESSIONAL DEVELOPMENT, *45.163*
PROMOTION OF THE HUMANITIES—PUBLIC PROGRAMS, *45.164*
PROMOTION OF THE HUMANITIES— RESEARCH, *45.161*
PROMOTION OF THE HUMANITIES— TEACHING AND LEARNING RESOURCES AND CURRICULUM DEVELOPMENT, *45.162*
PROMOTION OF THE HUMANITIES— WE THE PEOPLE, *45.168*
Property, *see* Federal property; Federal surplus property
PROPERTY IMPROVEMENT LOAN INSURANCE FOR IMPROVING ALL EXISTING STRUCTURES AND BUILDING OF NEW NONRESIDENTIAL STRUCTURES, *14.142*
Property insurance, *see* Insurance
Property loss, *see* Disaster assistance; Insurance
Property rehabilitation, *see* Buildings; Community development; Construction; Disaster assistance; Historic monuments, historic preservation; Housing rehabilitation; Weatherization
Prosecution, *see* Criminal justice system; Legal services
Prosecutorial Remedies and Other Tools to End the Exploitation of Children Today Act of 2003 (PROTECT), *16.736*
Prosthetic devices, *see* Health, medical services; Veterans, disabled; Vocational rehabilitation
Prosthetics Services, DVA, 64.013
PROTECT (Prosecutorial Remedies and Other Tools to End the Exploitation of Children Today Act of 2003), *16.736*
PROTECTING INMATES AND SAFEGUARDING COMMUNITIES DISCRETIONARY GRANT PROGRAM, *16.735*
PROTECTION AND ADVOCACY FOR INDIVIDUALS WITH MENTAL ILLNESS, *93.138*
Protection and Advocacy of Individual Rights (PAIR), disabled, *84.240*
Protection and Advocacy Systems, disabled, *93.630*
PROTECTION, CLEARING AND STRAIGHTENING CHANNELS [DOD], 12.109
PROTECTION OF CHILDREN AND OLDER ADULTS (ELDERLY) FROM ENVIRONMENTAL HEALTH RISKS, *66.609*
PROTECTION OF ESSENTIAL HIGHWAYS, HIGHWAY BRIDGE APPROACHES, AND PUBLIC WORKS, 12.105
Protection of Rights to Reproductive Health Services, 16.105
PROTECTION OF VOTING RIGHTS, 16.104

PROVIDING WATER TO AT-RISK NATURAL DESERT TERMINAL LAKES, *15.508*
PRWORA (Personal Responsibility and Work Opportunity Reconciliation Act of 1996), *see* Public assistance
PSGP (Private Stewardship Grants Program), FWS, *15.632*
PSOEA (Public Safety Officers' Educational Assistance), DOJ, *16.615*
Psychiatry, *see* Behavioral sciences, education, services
Psychology, *see* Behavioral sciences, education, services
PTA (Procurement Technical Assistance) Cooperative Agreement Program, DOD, *12.002*
PTFP (Public Telecommunications Facilities Program), *11.550*
P2 Grant Program, pollution prevention, EPA, *66.708*
P3 AWARD: NATIONAL STUDENT DESIGN COMPETITION FOR SUSTAINABILITY [EPA], *66.516*
Public administration, *see* Federal employment; Government; Social sciences
PUBLIC ALERT RADIOS FOR SCHOOLS, *97.079*
PUBLIC AND INDIAN HOUSING, *14.850*
Public and Indian Housing, HUD, *see* Agency Index
PUBLIC AND INDIAN HOUSING—INDIAN LOAN GUARANTEE PROGRAM, *14.865*
Public assistance
 Assets for Independence Act, *93.602*
 Child Care and Development Fund, *93.596*
 Compassion Capital Fund, ACF, *93.009*
 credit discrimination, recipients, 16.103
 disabled, Guam, Puerto Rico, Virgin Islands, *93.560*
 emergency food, shelter, FEMA, *97.024*
 families, TANF, *93.558*
 Family Support Act, *93.593*, *93.667*
 food donation program, 10.550, *10.565*, *10.568*, *10.569*
 food, nutrition CSBG, *93.571*
 food stamp program access research, *10.580*
 Food Stamps, *10.551*
 food stamps program expenses, states, *10.561*
 health care policy research, *93.239*
 home energy subsidies, *93.558*, *93.568*
 homeless, shelter, *14.231*
 Indians, *15.113*
 Job Access—Reverse Commute, DOT, *20.516*
 Job Opportunities for Low-Income Individuals, TANF, *93.593*
 Medicaid, *93.778*
 Medicaid Ticket-to-Work Demonstrations, *93.769*
 New Assets for Independence Demonstration, *93.602*
 Personal Responsibility and Work Opportunity Reconciliation Act of 1996 (PRWORA), *93.558*, *93.575*, *93.595*, *93.596*, *93.601*
 Puerto Rico, food, *10.566*
 refugees, *19.510*, *93.566*
 retirees, unearned Social Security benefits, *96.003*
 social services research, demonstrations, *93.647*
 spina bifida, veterans dependents, *64.127*, *64.128*
 Supplemental Security Income, *96.006*
 TANF (Temporary Assistance for Needy Families) projects, *93.558*, *93.602*
 Ticket-to-Work and Work Incentives Improvement Act of 1999, *93.768*, *93.769*, *96.008*, *96.009*
 U.S. Refugee Admissions Program, *19.510*
 Welfare Reform Research, *93.595*
 Welfare-to-Work rental housing vouchers, *14.871*
 WIA Adult Program, *17.258*
 see also Aliens, immigrants, refugees; Disadvantaged *entries*; Employment development, training; Employment services; Homeless persons; Housing, subsidized; Indian *entries*; Maternal, child health, welfare; Social Security Act; Social services; Subsidies; Veterans *entries*
PUBLIC ASSISTANCE GRANTS [DHS], *97.036*
PUBLIC AWARENESS CAMPAIGNS ON EMBRYO ADOPTION, *93.007*
PUBLIC EDUCATION ON DRUG ABUSE— INFORMATION, 16.005
Public facilities, *see* Community development; Economic development; Federal surplus property; Public works; Recreation *entries*
Public health
 applied research, *93.061*
 bioterrorism preparedness, *93.003*
 cancer, research, prevention, treatment, *93.399*
 Centers for Genomics and Public Health, *93.063*
 chronic disease prevention, control, *93.068*, *93.945*
 Citizen Corps, DHS, *97.053*
 Dental Residency Training, *93.236*
 disease prevention research, *93.135*
 drinking water security system training, *66.478*
 education assistance, disadvantaged, *93.822*, *93.925*
 education loan repayments, states, *93.165*
 emergency services, disasters, *93.003*
 environmental justice collaborative projects, *66.306*
 Environmental Justice Research Assistance, EPA, *66.308*
 Environmental Justice Surveys and Studies, EPA, *66.309*
 Environmental Justice Training and Fellowships, EPA, *66.307*
 EPA environmental health research, *66.511*
 EPA New England Regional Office projects, *66.110*
 EPA pesticides, toxic chemicals pollution prevention studies, training, outreach, *66.716*
 EPA Region 7 projects, *66.111*
 EPA research fellowships, graduate, undergraduate, *66.513*
 EPA STAR graduate fellowships, *66.514*
 faculty education loan repayments, disadvantaged, *93.923*
 food safety, security monitoring, FDA, *93.448*
 Hanford site, tribal capacity building, *93.202*
 hazardous substances emergencies, state surveillance systems, *93.204*
 hazardous wastes, CDCP Site Specific Activities, *93.240*
 health services NRSA, *93.225*
 IHS education loan repayments, *93.164*

Indian Self-Determination, *93.441*
Indians, scholarship program, *93.972*
Infant Health Initiatives, *93.946*
injury prevention research, training, *93.136*
laboratory medicine, pathology training, *93.064*
laboratory training, infrastructure development, *93.065*
Lyme Disease, *93.942*
Medical Reserve Corps, emergency response, HHS, *93.008*
mental health research training, *93.282*
minority community health coalitions, *93.137*
minority health status improvement, *93.004*
National Health Promotion, *93.990*
NHSC education loan repayments, *93.162*
NHSC scholarships, *93.288*
nursing, advanced education, *93.247*
nursing, graduate traineeships, *93.358*
physical fitness promotion, 93.289
pollution source reduction information dissemination, outreach, EPA, *66.717*
preventive medicine residency, *93.117*
primary care coordination, *93.130*
Public Health Security and Bioterrorism Preparedness and Response Act of 2002, *93.448*, *93.449*, *93.889*
Public Health Service Act, *66.432*
Public Health Training Centers, *93.249*
research accreditation project, *93.993*
rural specialists training, *93.192*
STAR (Science to Achieve Results) Research Program, EPA, *66.509*
toxic substances and disease registry, *93.161*
traineeships, graduate, *93.964*
WMD, domestic preparedness, *97.005*
see also AIDS (Acquired Immune Deficiency Syndrome); Civil defense; Communicable diseases; Community health services; Disease control; Environmental health, research, services; Epidemiology; Health, medical *entries*; Health planning; Health professions; Nursing; Occupational health, safety; Preventive health services; Public safety
PUBLIC HEALTH AND SOCIAL SERVICES EMERGENCY FUND, *93.003*
PUBLIC HEALTH RESEARCH ACCREDITATION PROJECT, *93.993*
Public Health Service, death benefits, 64.201, *64.202*
PUBLIC HEALTH TRAINEESHIPS, *93.964*
PUBLIC HEALTH TRAINING CENTERS GRANT PROGRAM, *93.249*
Public housing, *see* Housing, low to moderate income; Housing, subsidized
PUBLIC HOUSING CAPITAL FUND, *14.872*
Public Housing Modernization, *14.872*
PUBLIC HOUSING NEIGHBORHOOD NETWORK GRANTS, *14.875*
Public lands
BLM Cultural Resource Management, *15.224*
BLM firefighting assistance, *15.228*
BLM, minerals disposal, 15.214
BLM Payments in Lieu of Taxes, *15.226*
BLM Recreation Resource Management, *15.225*
compensation to states for federally-acquired lands, flood control, *12.112*
disposal, public purposes, 39.002
education, surplus federal real property transfer, 84.145
Federal Land Policy and Management Act, *15.224*, *15.225*, *15.227*, *15.229*, *15.231*
federally impacted areas, school assistance, *84.040*, *84.041*
Fire Management Assistance, FEMA, *97.046*
firefighting, FEMA reimbursement, *97.016*
Fish, Wildlife and Plant Conservation Resource Management, BLM, *15.231*
highway planning, construction, *20.205*
historic monument use, 15.918
oil, gas lease inspection, Indian, federal, *15.222*
Omnibus Parks and Public Lands Management Act of 1936, *15.926*
Outer Continental Shelf Lands, *11.430*, *15.227*
park, recreation use, 15.918
Wild Horse and Burro Management, BLM, *15.229*
see also Federal property; Federal surplus property; Forestry; Indian lands; Mineral resources; Natural resources; Urban parks, playgrounds
Public Law 84-99 Code 200 Program, Corps of Engineers, 12.103
Public Law 84-99 Code 300 Program, Corps of Engineers, 12.102
Public Law 84-99 Code 500 Program, Corps of Engineers, 12.111
Public Law 104-134, Southeast Alaska, USDA, *10.671*
Public Law 566, NRCS, *10.904*, 10.906, *10.921*
Public libraries, *see* Libraries
Public media, *see* Communications, telecommunications; Radio, television
Public safety
airport improvement, *20.106*
Alcohol Open Container Requirements, DOT, *20.607*
Anti-Terrorism and Emergency Assistance Program, DOJ, *16.321*
automobile occupant protection, DOT, *20.602*
aviation research, *20.108*, *20.109*
boating, 97.011, 97.012
Border Enforcement Grants, FMCSA, *20.233*
campus crime grants, *16.525*
Community Prosecution Program, *16.609*
Community Connect Grants, RUS, *10.863*
Cops Grants, *16.710*
DHS Competitive Training Grants, *97.068*
DHS Information Technology and Evaluation Program, *97.066*
diving, deep-sea research, *11.430*
drinking water security system training, *66.478*
Driving While Intoxicated, repeat offender laws, DOT, *20.608*
drunk driving control programs, *20.605*
FEMA chemical emergency planning, DOD stockpiles, *97.040*
FEMA Fire Grants, public education, *97.044*
highway safety data improvement, *20.603*
highways, *20.205*
housing, Officer Next Door Sales Program, 14.198
hunter safety programs, *15.611*
injury prevention research, training, *93.136*
Interoperable Communications Equipment, DHS, *97.055*

1004　GOVERNMENT ASSISTANCE ALMANAC 2006–07

Public safety *(continued)*
  military/community joint land use planning, *12.610*
  motor carrier safety regulation, *20.218*
  motor carrier safety training, 20.217
  9/11 Heroes Stamp Program, DHS, *97.085*
  NRC local public document rooms, *77.005*
  officers' dependents educational assistance, *16.615*
  officers, disability, death benefits, *16.571*
  personnel training, Federal Law Enforcement Training Center, DHS, *97.081*
  pipelines inspection training, research, *20.700*
  Public Alert Radios for Schools, DHS, *97.079*
  Railroad Research and Development, *20.313*
  railroad safety standards, *20.303*
  Safeguarding Communities, inmate reentry, OJP, *16.735*
  seatbelt use incentives, *20.604*
  state, community highway safety, equipment, public education, training, *20.600*
  telecommunications infrastructure, *11.552*
  traffic safety control, alcohol, drugs, *20.601*
  transuranic waste transport, *81.106*
  Urban Areas Security Initiative, equipment, training, planning, DHS, *97.008*
  violence, children's exposure, prevention initiative, Safe Start, *16.730*
  WMD, domestic preparedness, *97.004*, *97.005*, *97.006*, *97.007*
  see also Civil defense; Crime; Disaster assistance; Emergency assistance; Firefighting, fire prevention, control; Hazardous materials, waste; Law enforcement education, training; Occupational health, safety; Police; Public health; Radiation; Rescue services
PUBLIC SAFETY OFFICERS' BENEFITS PROGRAM, *16.571*
PUBLIC SAFETY OFFICERS' EDUCATIONAL ASSISTANCE, *16.615*
PUBLIC SAFETY PARTNERSHIP AND COMMUNITY POLICING GRANTS, *16.710*
Public service, *see* Federal employment; Government; Social sciences
Public service scholarships, *85.001*
PUBLIC TELECOMMUNICATIONS FACILITIES PLANNING AND CONSTRUCTION, *11.550*
PUBLIC TELEVISION STATIONS DIGITAL TRANSITION GRANT PROGRAM, *10.861*
Public transportation, *see* Mass transportation; Transportation
Public utilities
  broadband access loans, rural areas, RUS, *10.886*
  Census Bureau data, 11.001
  compensation to states for federally-acquired lands, hydropower, *12.112*
  economic development loans, RBCS, *10.854*
  electricity delivery, energy reliability, DOE, *81.122*
  energy conservation technology research, *81.086*
  geodetic surveys, *11.400*
  Household Water Well System Program, RUS, *10.862*
  Hydrologic Research, *11.462*
  insular areas, *15.875*
  NRC local public document rooms, *77.005*
  Nuclear Energy Research Initiative, *81.121*

  Rural Business Enterprise Grants, *10.769*
  Rural Electrification Act of 1936 (REA), *10.850*, *10.851*, *10.852*, *10.854*, *10.857*, *10.858*, *10.859*, *10.886*
  rural telecommunications service, RUS loans, *10.852*
  rural telephone service, RUS loans, *10.851*
  rural facilities, *10.766*
  RUS Bulk Fuel Revolving Fund Grants, *10.857*
  RUS community assistance, high energy cost, *10.859*
  RUS electrification loans, *10.850*
  water supply forecasts, 10.907
  see also Communications, telecommunications; Energy; Nuclear sciences, technology; Public works; Rural areas
Public works
  Appalachian region, *23.002*
  Aquatic Plant Control, Corps of Engineers, 12.100
  Beach Erosion Control, Corps of Engineers, 12.101
  Bridge Alteration, USCG, 97.014
  Buffer Zone Protection Plan, DHS, *97.078*
  CDBG, *14.218*, *14.219*, *14.225*, *14.228*, *14.862*
  Community Disaster Loans, FEMA, *97.030*
  Construction Productivity Advanced Research, Corps of Engineers, *12.114*
  dam safety program, FEMA, *97.041*
  defense program changes impact, *12.613*
  Delta region, *90.200*, *90.201*, *90.202*
  Denali Commission Grants and Loans, Alaska energy facilities, *10.858*
  DHS Competitive Training Grants, *97.068*
  disasters, Public Assistance Grants, FEMA, *97.036*
  flood control projects, Corps of Engineers, 12.106
  flood control projects, snagging, clearing, Corps of Engineers, 12.108
  flood, erosion protection, 12.105
  highway personnel training, *20.215*
  Indian lands, dam safety, *15.049*, *15.065*
  navigation projects, Corps of Engineers, 12.107, 12.109
  Pre-Disaster Mitigation, FEMA, *97.017*, *97.047*
  public facilities construction, EDA projects, *11.300*
  Public Works and Economic Development Act of 1965 (PWEDA), *11.300* through *11.313*
  RUS community assistance, high energy cost, *10.859*
  U.S. insular areas, *15.875*
  water reclamation, reuse, *15.504*
  Watershed Rehabilitation Program, *10.916*
  WMD, domestic preparedness, *97.005*
  see also Civil defense; Coastal zone; Community development; Economic development; Flood prevention, control; Highways, roads, bridges; Public utilities; Sewage facilities, treatment; Transportation; Urban renewal; Waste treatment, disposal; Water *entries*
Public Works and Economic Development Act of 1965 (PWEDA), *see* Economic development
Publications
  ADA compliance, *16.108*
  aerospace technology, 43.002
  boating safety, 97.011
  books for the blind, handicapped, 42.001
  census studies, 11.001

citizenship, 97.010
civil aviation, 20.100
civil rights, 29.001
depository libraries, government publications, 40.001
drug abuse prevention, DEA, 16.005
energy-related, 81.039, 81.064
exporting, 11.108
Federal Citizen Information Center, 39.009
Government Bookstore, 40.002
historical documents collection, preservation, *89.003*
medical, health, National Library of Medicine, *93.879*
mental retardation, 93.613
Microgram, DEA, 16.003
National Archives and Records Administration, 89.001
National Center for Standards and Certification Information, 11.610
National Technical Information Service, 11.650
National Trade Data Bank, 11.026
newspaper cataloguing, preservation, *45.149*
small business on-line counseling, 59.005
Uniform Crime Reports, 16.305
Women's Bureau, DOL, 17.700
see also Agricultural statistics; Arts, arts education; Audiovisual aids, film, video; Census services; Computer products, sciences, services; Consumers, consumer services; Copyright services; Economics, research, statistics; Education resources; Humanities *entries*; Information *entries*; International programs, studies; Libraries; Literature; Statistics

Puerto Rico
aged, blind, disabled persons maintenance assistance, *93.560*
agriculture, food sciences education, CSREES, *10.308*
food assistance, *10.566*
see also U.S. possessions, territories
PWBA (Pension and Welfare Benefits Administration), *see* Agency Index (DOL, Employee Benefits Security Administration)
PWEDA (Public Works and Economic Development Act of 1965), *see* Economic Development
PWI (Projects with Industry), DOED, *84.234*

QSP (Quality Samples Program), FAS, *10.605*
QUALIFIED PARTICIPATING ENTITIES (QPE) RISK SHARING [HUD], *14.189*
Quality Assurance in Pathology and Laboratory Medicine, *93.064*
QUALITY SAMPLES PROGRAM [USDA], *10.605*
QUENTIN N. BURDICK PROGRAM FOR RURAL INTERDISCIPLINARY TRAINING [HHS], *93.192*

Racial and Ethnic Approaches to Community Health (REACH), CDCP, *93.945*
Racial discrimination, *see* Civil rights; Community development
Radiation
biohazard contaminant, cancer research facilities, *93.392*

cancer research, *93.395, 93.399*
control, EMI home study courses, 97.027
control, NRC health, safety training, 77.001
dairy products contamination, *10.053*
DOE environmental cleanup, technology development, *81.104*
DOE workers, epidemiology, health studies, *81.108*
Inertial Confinement Fusion, stockpile stewardship, *81.112*
nuclear waste disposal siting, *81.065*
Radiation Control and Health Safety Act of 1968, *93.103*
radiation emitting devices, FDA research, *93.103*
Radiation Exposure Compensation Act, *93.257*
radioactivity standards, testing, 11.604
Radiogenetic Exposure Screening and Education Program, *93.257*
radon mitigation, information, training, *66.032*
transuranic waste transport, *81.106*
WMD, domestic preparedness, *97.004, 97.005, 97.006, 97.007*
see also Cancer control, prevention, research; Civil defense; Disaster assistance; Emergency assistance; Hazardous materials, waste; Nuclear sciences, technology
RADIATION CONTROL—TRAINING ASSISTANCE AND ADVISORY COUNSELING, 77.001
Radio, television
aerospace education programs, 43.001
cable system licensing, Copyright Service, 42.002
child abuse, closed-circuit TV, DOJ, *16.611*
complaints, FCC, 32.001
educational, cultural, facilities, *11.550*
family violence prevention, *93.591*
Federal Citizen Information Center, scripts, 39.009
federal surplus personal property donations, 39.003
federal surplus real property transfer, 84.145
FEMA chemical emergency planning, DOD stockpiles, *97.040*
humanities challenge grants, *45.130*
humanities, NEH Public Programs, *45.164*
instructional programming, Star Schools, *84.203*
international peace and conflict resolution, *91.001*
licensing, regulation, FCC, 32.001
Local Television Loan Guarantee Program, USDA, *10.853*
National Gallery of Art exhibits, 68.001
NEA arts projects, *45.024*
physical fitness promotion, 93.289
Public Alert Radios for Schools, DHS, *97.079*
Ready-to-Learn TV, early childhood education, *84.295*
Ready to Teach, OERI, *84.286*
rural public television station digital transition grants, *10.861*
rural, Television Demonstration Grants, *10.769*
telecommunications infrastructure, *11.552*
see also Audiovisual aids, film, video; Communications, telecommunications
Radiogenetic Exposure Screening and Education Program, *93.257*
Radon, *66.032, 66.605, 66.606*

RAIL AND TRANSIT SECURITY GRANT
PROGRAM, 97.075
RAILROAD RESEARCH AND DEVELOPMENT,
20.313
Railroad Retirement Board, 57.001
Railroads
Bridge Alteration, USCG, 97.014
employee benefits, 57.001
explosives detection canine teams, TSA, 97.072
Federal Railroad Safety Act of 1970, 20.303
hazardous materials transport training, 20.303
High Speed Ground Transportation, 20.312
highway grade crossings, 20.205
operating practices inspection, training, 20.303
rail, transit security, ODP, 97.075
Railroad Research and Development, 20.313
Railroad Retirement Act of 1974, 57.001
Railroad Unemployment Insurance Act, 57.001
spur construction, EDA projects, 11.300
State Participation in Railroad Safety, 20.303
see also Mass transportation; Transportation
RAMP (Rural Abandoned Mine Program), 10.910
RAPID EXPANSION OF ANTIRETROVIRAL
THERAPY PROGRAMS FOR HIV-
INFECTED PERSONS IN SELECTED
COUNTRIES OF AFRICA AND THE
CARIBBEAN UNDER THE PRESIDENT'S
EMERGENCY PLAN FOR AIDS RELIEF,
93.266
RBCS (Rural Business-Cooperative Service),
USDA, see Agency Index
RC&D (Rural Conservation and Development),
NRCS, 10.901
REA (Rural Electrification Act of 1936), see Public
utilities
REA (Rural Electrification Administration), see
Agency Index (USDA, Rural Utilities Service)
RBEG (Rural Business Enterprise Grants), 10.769
RBICs (Rural Business Investment Companies),
RBCS, 10.860
RBIP (Rural Business Investment Program), RBCS,
10.860
RBOG (Rural Business Opportunity Grants),
10.773
RC&D (Resource Conservation and Development),
NRCS, 10.900
RCDG (Rural Cooperative Development Grants),
10.771
RCMI (Research Centers in Minority Institutions),
93.389
RCRA (Resource Conservation and Recovery Act),
see Environmental Management
RDA (Rural Development Administration), USDA,
see Agency Index (USDA, Rural Business-
Cooperative Service)
REA (Rural Electrification Act), see Public utilities
REA (Rural Electrification Administration), see
Agency Index (USDA, Rural Utilities Service)
REACH (Racial and Ethnic Approaches to
Community Health), CDCP, 93.945
REACH (Residential Energy Assistance Challenge)
Program, ACF, 93.568
Reading ability, see Adult education; Illiteracy;
Tutoring
Reading disabilities, see Disabled, handicapped,
education; Education counseling; Tutoring

READING FIRST STATE GRANTS, 84.357
READY-TO-LEARN TELEVISION, 84.295
READY-TO-TEACH, 84.286
Real estate, see Buildings; Construction; Housing
entries; Land acquisition; Landowners;
Subdivisions
REAL ESTATE PROGRAMS—INDIAN LANDS,
15.040
REAL ID PROGRAM [DHS], 97.089
REAP (Rural Education Achievement Program),
84.358
Reception and Placement Grant, refugees,
Department of State, 93.567
Recreation
Alaska Migratory Bird Co-Management Council,
FWS, 15.643
bicycle paths, 15.916, 20.205
BLM Recreation Resource Management, 15.225
campgrounds, 15.916
Community Connect Grants, RUS, 10.863
Delinquency Prevention Program, 16.548, 16.549
elderly, 93.043
Extension Service, 10.500
farm enterprise loans, 10.406
farm laborers facilities, 10.405
food program, National Youth Sports Program,
10.559
forest lands management research, 10.202
forests, research, 10.652
FWS Challenge Cost Share, 15.642
Great Plains Conservation, 10.900
Gun Control Act, 16.309
hunter safety education, 15.611, 15.626
Hydropower Recreation Assistance, 15.927
Indian lands, 15.039, 15.040
inner city parks, 15.916
Land and Water Conservation Fund Act of 1965,
15.916
National Trails System Act, 15.921
outdoor facilities, 15.916
Outdoor Recreation Act of 1963, 15.921, 15.927
park land acquisition, development, 15.916
Pittman-Robertson (P-R) Program, 15.611
planning, development, 15.916
President's Council on Physical Fitness and
Sports, 93.289
public facilities, 15.916
public land sale, donation, 39.002
recreation therapies, alternative, complementary
medicine research, 93.213
Recreational Trails Program, 20.219
Rivers, Trails, and Conservation Assistance,
15.921
rural housing facilities loans, 10.415
snowmelt surveys, water supply forecasts, 10.907
support facilities, roads, water supply, 15.916
Surplus Property Program, DOI, 15.918
swimming pools, 15.916
tennis courts, 15.916
tourism facilities, EDA projects, 11.300
Urban Community Forestry, 10.675
vocational rehabilitation service projects, 84.128
Wild and Scenic Rivers Act of 1968, 15.927
wildlife restoration, 15.611, 15.628
Wood in Transportation, USFS, 10.673
youth, CSBG projects, 93.570

see also Community development; Fish; Recreation, water; Social services; Urban parks, playgrounds; Wildlife, waterfowl; Youth *entries*

RECREATION RESOURCE MANAGEMENT [DOI], *15.225*

Recreation, water
beach erosion control, 12.101
Beaches Environmental Assessment and Coastal Health Act of 2000, *66.472*
Beach Monitoring and Notification Program, EPA, *66.472*
Boating Infrastructure Grant Program, *15.622*
BLM Recreation Resource Management, *15.225*
boat launching ramps, public, *15.916*
boating safety facilities, education, training, 97.012
boating safety, training, 97.011
Chesapeake Bay Program, *66.466*
Chesapeake Bay Stock Assessment, *11.457*
Clean Vessel Act, pumpout/dump stations, *15.616*
diving safety research, *11.430*
Great Lakes fish consumption health effects research, *93.208*
Indian lands, *15.039*
lake, stream rehabilitation, *15.605*
NOAA unallied projects, *11.452*
Multi-State Conservation Grants, *15.628*
resource conservation, development, *10.901*
Rivers, Trails, and Conservation Assistance, 15.921
small navigation projects, 12.107
sport fishing, *15.605*
sport fishing statistics, southeast area, *11.434*
swimming pools, public, *15.916*
Vessel Safety Checks, USCG, 97.011
watershed projects, *10.904*
Wild and Scenic Rivers Act of 1968, 15.921
see also Coastal zone; Fish; Recreation; Wildlife, waterfowl

RECREATIONAL TRAILS PROGRAM, *20.219*
Recycling, *see* Energy conservation; Environmental management; Waste treatment, disposal
Redevelopment, *see* Community development; Depressed areas; Economic development; Urban planning; Urban renewal
REDUCTION AND PREVENTION OF CHILDREN'S EXPOSURE TO VIOLENCE [DOJ], *16.730*
REFUGEE AND ENTRANT ASSISTANCE—DISCRETIONARY GRANTS, *93.576*
REFUGEE AND ENTRANT ASSISTANCE—STATE ADMINISTERED PROGRAMS, *93.566*
REFUGEE AND ENTRANT ASSISTANCE—TARGETED ASSISTANCE GRANTS, *93.584*
REFUGEE AND ENTRANT ASSISTANCE—VOLUNTARY AGENCY PROGRAMS, *93.567*
REFUGEE AND ENTRANT ASSISTANCE—WILSON/FISH PROGRAMS, *93.583*
Refugees, *see* Aliens, immigrants, refugees
REGIONAL BIOMASS ENERGY PROGRAMS, *81.079*
Regional Climate Centers, *11.428*

REGIONAL ENVIRONMENTAL MONITORING AND ASSESSMENT PROGRAM (REMAP) RESEARCH PROJECTS, *66.512*
REGIONAL ENVIRONMENTAL PRIORITY PROJECTS, *66.111*
REGIONAL FISHERY MANAGEMENT COUNCILS, *11.441*
REGIONAL INFORMATION SHARING SYSTEMS [DOJ], *16.610*
REGIONAL WETLAND PROGRAM DEVELOPMENT GRANTS, *66.461*
REGISTERED APPRENTICESHIP AND OTHER TRAINING, 17.201
Regular Business Loans—Section 7(a) Loans, *59.012*
REGULATION OF SURFACE COAL MINING AND SURFACE EFFECTS OF UNDERGROUND COAL MINING, *15.250*
Rehabilitation Act of 1973, *see* Vocational rehabilitation
Rehabilitation, health facilities, *see* Health facilities construction, rehabilitation
Rehabilitation, housing, *see* Housing rehabilitation
REHABILITATION LONG-TERM TRAINING, *84.129*
REHABILITATION MORTGAGE INSURANCE, *14.108*
REHABILITATION SERVICES—AMERICAN INDIANS WITH DISABILITIES, *84.250*
REHABILITATION SERVICES—CLIENT ASSISTANCE PROGRAM, *84.161*
REHABILITATION SERVICES DEMONSTRATION AND TRAINING PROGRAMS, *84.235*
REHABILITATION SERVICES—INDEPENDENT LIVING SERVICES FOR OLDER INDIVIDUALS WHO ARE BLIND, *84.177*
REHABILITATION SERVICES—SERVICE PROJECTS, *84.128*
REHABILITATION SERVICES—VOCATIONAL REHABILITATION GRANTS TO STATES, *84.126*
REHABILITATION SHORT-TERM TRAINING, *84.246*
REHABILITATION TRAINING—CONTINUING EDUCATION, *84.264*
REHABILITATION TRAINING—EXPERIMENTAL AND INNOVATIVE TRAINING, *84.263*
REHABILITATION TRAINING—GENERAL TRAINING, *84.275*
REHABILITATION TRAINING—STATE VOCATIONAL REHABILITATION UNIT IN-SERVICE TRAINING, *84.265*
Rehabilitation, vocational, *see* Vocational rehabilitation
REIMBURSEMENT FOR FIREFIGHTING ON FEDERAL PROPERTY, *97.016*
Religious Land Use and Institutionalized Persons Act of 2000 (RLUIPA), 16.103
Relocation, *see* Community development; Employment services; Trade adjustment assistance
REMAP (Regional Environmental Monitoring and Assessment Program) Research Projects, EPA, *66.512*

Remedial education, *see* Adult education; Education counseling; Elementary and secondary education; Illiteracy; Tutoring; Volunteers
REMEDIES FOR UNFAIR FOREIGN TRADE PRACTICES—ANTIDUMPING AND COUNTERVAILING DUTY INVESTIGATIONS, 11.106
Renal diseases research, *93.849*
Renewable energy, *see* Energy *entries*; Solar energy
RENEWABLE ENERGY RESEARCH AND DEVELOPMENT, *81.087*
RENEWABLE ENERGY SYSTEMS AND ENERGY EFFICIENCY IMPROVEMENTS PROGRAM, *10.775*
RENT SUPPLEMENTS—RENTAL HOUSING FOR LOWER INCOME FAMILIES, *14.149*
Rental Assistance, rural, *10.427*
Rental housing, *see* Housing, rental
REPLACEMENT AND REPAIR OF INDIAN SCHOOLS, *15.062*
Republic of the Marshall Islands, *see* U.S. possessions, territories
RES and EEI (Renewable Energy Systems and Energy Efficiency Improvements), RBCS, *10.775*
Rescue services
  Anti-Terrorism and Emergency Assistance Program, DOJ, *16.321*
  anti-terrorism training, *16.614*
  bioterrorism preparedness education, training, HRSA, *93.996*
  Citizen Corps, DHS, *97.053*
  disasters, Public Assistance Grants, FEMA, *97.036*
  Emergency Management Performance Grants, *97.042*
  EMI training, *97.026*, 97.027, 97.028
  EMS, children, *93.127*
  EMS/trauma care, rural, *93.952*
  FEMA Fire Grants, equipment, training, *97.044*
  flood response, 12.103
  highway safety training, 20.217
  highway safety training, vehicles, equipment, *20.600*
  Interoperable Communications Equipment, DHS, *97.055*
  officers' dependents educational assistance, *16.615*
  officers, disability, death benefits, *16.571*
  rural, Access to Emergency Devices, training, HRSA, *93.259*
  rural facilities, *10.766*
  search, rescue system, *97.025*
  WMD, domestic preparedness, *97.004*, *97.005*, *97.006*, *97.007*
  see also Civil defense; Disaster assistance; Emergency assistance; Firefighting, fire prevention, control; Flood prevention, control; Missing persons; Police; Public safety; Victim assistance
RESEARCH AND EVALUATION PROGRAM [USDC], *11.312*
Research and Special Programs Administration, DOT, *see* Agency Index
RESEARCH AND TECHNOLOGY DEVELOPMENT [DOD], *12.910*
RESEARCH AND TRAINING IN COMPLEMENTARY AND ALTERNATIVE MEDICINE, *93.213*
Research Career ("K") Awards, alcoholism, *93.271*
Research Career/Scientist Development ("K") Awards, mental health, *93.281*
Research Grants & Agreements, forestry, *10.652*
RESEARCH IN SPECIAL EDUCATION, *84.324*
Research libraries, *see* Higher education *entries*; Libraries
RESEARCH ON HEALTHCARE COSTS, QUALITY AND OUTCOMES, *93.226*
RESEARCH PROJECTS [DHS], *97.002*
RESEARCH RELATED TO DEAFNESS AND COMMUNICATION DISORDERS, *93.173*
RESEARCH, TREATMENT AND EDUCATION PROGRAMS ON LYME DISEASE IN THE UNITED STATES, *93.942*
RESIDENT INSTRUCTION GRANTS FOR INSULAR AREA ACTIVITIES [USDA], *10.308*
RESIDENT OPPORTUNITY AND SUPPORTIVE SERVICES [HUD], *14.870*
Residential Energy Assistance Challenge Program (REACH), ACF, *93.568*
Residential Lead-Based Paint Hazard Reduction Act, *see* Community health services
RESIDENTIAL SUBSTANCE ABUSE TREATMENT FOR STATE PRISONERS, *16.593*
RESOURCE AND MANPOWER DEVELOPMENT IN THE ENVIRONMENTAL HEALTH SCIENCES, *93.894*
RESOURCE CONSERVATION AND DEVELOPMENT [USDA], *10.901*
Resource Conservation and Development (RC&D), NRCS, *10.900*
Resource Conservation and Recovery Act (RCRA), *see* Environmental Management
Respiratory diseases
  allergy, immunology research, *93.855*
  biometry, risk estimation, environmental risks, *93.115*
  Black Lung Clinics, *93.965*
  Black Lung, disabled miners compensation, *17.307*
  environmental health hazards research, *93.113*
  hazardous waste sites health studies, *93.206*
  lung diseases research, research training, NRSA, *93.838*
  microbiology, infectious diseases research, *93.856*
  TB Prevention Amendments Act of 1990, *93.116*
  tuberculosis control, *93.116*, 93.283
  tuberculosis control, agricultural inspection service, *10.025*
  tuberculosis control demonstration, research, education, *93.947*
  tuberculosis prevention, treatment, substance abuse-related, *93.959*
  see also Coal mining; Communicable diseases; Environmental health, research, services; Health, medical research
Response and Recovery Directorate, FEMA, *see* Agency Index
Retinal diseases research, *93.867*

MASTER INDEX 1009

RETIRED AND SENIOR VOLUNTEER PROGRAM, *94.002*
Retirement Insurance, SSA, *96.002*
Retirement, pension, *see* Employee benefits; Insurance; Social Security Act; Veterans *entries*
Revenue Sharing, Public Lands and Resources, BLM, *15.227*
Reverse mortgage loans, *14.183*
RHINOCEROS AND TIGER CONSERVATION, *15.619*
RHS (Rural Housing Service), USDA, *see* Agency Index
Risk Sharing Program, HUD, *14.188*
RISS (Regional Information Sharing Systems), DOJ, *16.610*
River and Harbor Act, *see* Water navigation
River Basin Program, 10.906
Rivers and Trails, Hydropower Licensing, 15.927
RIVERS, TRAILS, AND CONSERVATION ASSISTANCE, 15.921
RLUIPA (Religious Land Use and Institutionalized Persons Act of 2000), 16.103
RMA COMMUNITY OUTREACH AND ASSISTANCE PARTNERSHIP PROGRAM [USDA], *10.455*
ROAD MAINTENANCE—INDIAN ROADS, *15.033*
Roads, *see* Highways, roads, bridges; Public works; Transportation
Robert C. Byrd Honors Scholarships, *84.185*
Robert T. Stafford Disaster Relief and Emergency Assistance (Stafford Act), *see* Disaster assistance
Rodent control, *see* Animal disease control, health, welfare; Community development; Preventive health services
Ronald E. McNair Post-Baccalaureate Achievement, *84.217*
ROSS (Resident Opportunity and Supportive Services), HUD, *14.870*
RSAT (Residential Substance Abuse Treatment), DOJ, *16.593*
RSVP (Retired and Senior Volunteer Program), *94.002*
RTB (Rural Telephone Bank) Loans, RUS, *10.852*
RTC, *see* Resolution Trust Corporation
RTCA (Rivers, Trails, and Conservation Assistance), 15.921
RUMINANT FEED BAN SUPPORT PROJECT, *93.449*
Runaway youth, *see* Homeless persons; Juvenile delinquency; Missing persons; Social services; Youth *entries*
RURAL ABANDONED MINE PROGRAM, *10.910*
RURAL ACCESS TO EMERGENCY DEVICES GRANT [HHS], *93.259*

Rural areas
Access to Emergency Devices, training, HRSA, *93.259*
air carrier subsidies, *20.901*
Appalachian regional development, *23.001*
BLM firefighting assistance, *15.228*
business, industrial development loans, *10.768*
Community Connect Grants, RUS, *10.863*
community development, Extension Service, *10.500*
community facilities, *10.766*
community health centers, *93.224*
Community Learning Centers, *84.287*
Community Technology Centers, DOED, *84.341*
Consolidated Farm and Rural Development Act of 1987 (CFRDA), *10.404, 10.406, 10.407, 10.410, 10.437, 10.445, 10.760, 10.761, 10.762, 10.763, 10.766, 10.768, 10.769, 10.770, 10.771, 10.860, 10.862, 10.864*
cooperatives development Grants, *10.771*
cooperatives research, technical assistance, training, 10.350
Delta region, *90.200, 90.201, 90.202*
DHS Competitive Training Grants, *97.068*
disaster housing, *10.444, 10.445*
domestic violence, *16.589*
economic development, Intermediary Relending Program, *10.767*
economic development, RBCS loans, *10.854*
Economic Recovery, USFS, *10.670*
economic research, 10.250
educational, medical computer networks, RUS, *10.855*
1890 institutions entrepreneurial outreach, RBCS, *10.856*
electrification loans, RUS, *10.850*
emergency water assistance, *10.763*
Empowerment Zones Program, *10.772*
EMS/trauma care, research, demonstrations, *93.952*
family planning paramedical, paraprofessional training, *93.260*
Farm and Ranch Lands Protection Program, NRCS, *10.913*
Farm Security and Rural Investment Act of 2002 (FSRIA), *10.025, 10.055, 10.078, 10.307, 10.308, 10.352, 10.500, 10.576, 10.604, 10.608, 10.677, 10.775, 10.912, 10.918, 10.921, 10.994, 15.508, 90.200, 90.201, 90.202, 98.009*
farmers, ranchers, outreach, *10.443*
firefighting assistance, *10.664*
flood plain data, services, 12.104
Forest Land Enhancement Program, *10.677*
Forest Service payments, counties, national grasslands, *10.666*
Forest Service payments, states, national forests, *10.665*
Fund for Rural America, research, education, *10.224*
Great Plains Conservation, *10.900*
health clinic services, Medicaid, *93.778*
health education, training, *93.189, 93.191*
health research centers, *93.155*
health services, *93.223, 93.913*
health services outreach, network development, *93.912*
health specialists training, *93.192*
heart health care programs, women, *93.012*
HIV projects, *93.928*
hospital emergency services, integrated care networks, *93.241*
Household Water Well System Program, RUS, *10.862*
housing construction, self-help, training, *10.420*
housing packaging grants, RHS, *10.442*

Rural areas *(continued)*
housing site development loans, *10.411*
HUD, Rural Housing and Economic Development, *14.250*
local law enforcement block grants, *16.592*
Local Television Loan Guarantee Program, USDA, *10.853*
mental health specialists training, *93.244*
National Forest Dependent Rural Communities Economic Diversification Act of 1990, *10.670*
New Mexico, forest restoration, *10.679*
nurses, education loan repayments, *93.908*
public television station digital transition grants, RUS, *10.861*
public transportation, *20.509*
Renewable Energy Systems and Energy Efficiency Improvements, RBCS, *10.775*
research competitive grants, *10.206*
research, land grant colleges, *10.205*
research, SBIR, *10.212*
resource conservation, development, *10.901*
Rural Business Enterprise Grants, *10.769*
Rural Business Investment Program, RBCS, *10.860*
Rural Business Opportunity Grants, *10.773*
Rural Development Act of 1972, 10.167, *10.446*
Rural Community Development Initiative, RHS, *10.446*
Rural Development, Forestry, and Communities, *10.672*
Rural Education Achievement Program, *84.358*
Rural Gang Initiative, OJP, *16.544*
RUS assistance, high energy cost, *10.859*
RUS Bulk Fuel Revolving Fund Grants, *10.857*
Secure Schools and Community Self-Determination Act of 2000, *10.679*
Small Community Air Service Development, *20.930*
Small Rural Hospital Improvement, *93.301*
soil surveys, 10.903
soil, water conservation, technical assistance, NRCS, 10.902
solid waste management, *10.762*
statistics, 10.950
telecommunications infrastructure, *11.552*
Telehealth Network Grants, *93.211*
telephone service, RUS loans, *10.851*, *10.852*
Television Demonstration Grants, *10.769*
Trade Adjustment Assistance, FAS, *10.609*
Urban-Rural Economic Development, CSBG, *93.570*
USFS Technology Marketing Unit, small wood species, *10.674*
victim assistance program personnel training, *16.582*
waste, water systems, technical assistance, *10.761*
water facilities, waste disposal systems, *10.760*
water, waste disposal systems, *10.770*
water, wastewater projects revolving loan funds, *10.864*
watershed protection, *10.904*
watershed, river basin projects, 10.906
see also Appalachian region; Community development; Economic development; Family farms; Farm *entries*; Housing, rural; Health professions; Public utilities; Rural poor

RURAL BROADBAND ACCESS LOANS AND LOAN GUARANTEES, *10.886*
Rural Business-Cooperative Service (RBCS), USDA, *see* Agency Index
RURAL BUSINESS ENTERPRISE GRANTS, *10.769*
RURAL BUSINESS INVESTMENT PROGRAM, *10.860*
RURAL BUSINESS OPPORTUNITY GRANTS, *10.773*
RURAL COMMUNITY DEVELOPMENT INITIATIVE, *10.446*
RURAL COOPERATIVE DEVELOPMENT GRANTS, *10.771*
Rural Development Administration (RDA), *see* Agency Index (USDA, Rural Business-Cooperative Service *and* Rural Utilities Service)
RURAL DEVELOPMENT, FORESTRY, AND COMMUNITIES, *10.672*
Rural Development Through Forestry, *10.672*
RURAL DOMESTIC VIOLENCE AND CHILD VICTIMIZATION ENFORCEMENT GRANT PROGRAM, *16.589*
RURAL ECONOMIC DEVELOPMENT LOANS AND GRANTS, *10.854*
RURAL EDUCATION, *84.358*
Rural Electrification Act of 1936 (REA), *see* Public utilities
Rural Electrification Administration (REA), *see* Agency Index (USDA, Rural Utilities Service)
RURAL ELECTRIFICATION LOANS AND LOAN GUARANTEES, *10.850*
Rural EMS/Trauma Care, HRSA, *93.952*
RURAL HEALTH CARE SERVICES OUTREACH AND RURAL HEALTH NETWORK DEVELOPMENT PROGRAM, *93.912*
RURAL HEALTH RESEARCH CENTERS, *93.155*
Rural housing, *see* Housing, rural
RURAL HOUSING AND ECONOMIC DEVELOPMENT, *14.250*
Rural Housing Loans and Grants (Section 504), *10.417*
Rural Housing Loans, Section 502, *10.410*
RURAL HOUSING PRESERVATION GRANTS, *10.433*
Rural Housing Service (RHS), USDA, *see* Agency Index
RURAL HOUSING SITE LOANS AND SELF-HELP HOUSING LAND DEVELOPMENT LOANS, *10.411*
Rural poor
housing loans, *10.410*
housing repair grants, loans, *10.417*, *10.433*
housing site loans, *10.411*
rental, cooperative housing, *10.415*
research, land grant colleges, *10.205*
Rural Education Achievement Program, *84.358*
self-help housing, *10.420*
VISTA program, 94.013
water, waste disposal systems, *10.770*
see also Appalachian region; Community development; Depressed areas; Disadvantaged; Farm workers; Housing, low to moderate income; Housing, rural; Rural areas; Volunteers

MASTER INDEX 1011

RURAL RENTAL ASSISTANCE PAYMENTS, *10.427*
RURAL RENTAL HOUSING LOANS, *10.415*
RURAL SELF-HELP HOUSING TECHNICAL ASSISTANCE, *10.420*
RURAL TELEPHONE BANK LOANS, *10.852*
RURAL TELEPHONE LOANS AND LOAN GUARANTEES, *10.851*
Rural Utilities Service (RUS), USDA, *see* Agency Index
RUS (Rural Utilities Service), USDA, *see* Agency Index
RUS DENALI COMMISSION GRANTS AND LOANS [USDA], *10.858*
Ryan White CARE Act, *see* AIDS (Acquired Immune Deficiency Syndrome)
Ryan White CARE Act Title IV Program, HRSA, *93.153*
RYAN WHITE HIV/AIDS DENTAL REIMBURSEMENTS/COMMUNITY-BASED DENTAL PARTNERSHIP, *93.924*
Rye, *see* Agricultural commodities, stabilization; Feed grains

SABIT (Special American Business Internship Training Program), ITA, *11.114*
SACs (Statistical Analysis Centers), DOJ, *16.550*
SAFE AND DRUG-FREE SCHOOLS AND COMMUNITIES—NATIONAL PROGRAMS, *84.184*
SAFE AND DRUG-FREE SCHOOLS AND COMMUNITIES—STATE GRANTS, *84.186*
Safe and Stable Families Act of 2001, *see* Parenting
Safe Drinking Water Act (SDWA), *see* Water pollution abatement, prevention
Safe Havens for Children, *16.527*
Safe Havens, homeless, *14.235*
Safe Neighborhoods, OJP, *16.609*
Safe Start, OJP, *16.730*
SAFER (Staffing for Adequate Fire and Emergency Response), FEMA, *97.083*
Safety, *see* Occupational health, safety; Public safety
Safeguarding Communities, inmate reentry, OJP, *16.735*
SAFETY INCENTIVE GRANTS FOR USE OF SEATBELTS, *20.604*
SAFETY INCENTIVES TO PREVENT OPERATION OF MOTOR VEHICLES BY INTOXICATED PERSONS, *20.605*
SAFETY OF DAMS ON INDIAN LANDS, *15.065*
SALE OF FEDERAL SURPLUS PERSONAL PROPERTY, 39.007
Salinity control, *see* Environmental management; Water *entries*
Saltonstall-Kennedy Act, *see* Fisheries industry
Samoa, *see* U.S. possessions, territories
Sanctuaries, *see* Coastal zone; Estuaries; Wildlife, waterfowl
SAPT (Substance Abuse Prevention and Treatment) Block Grant, *93.959*
SARA (Superfund Amendment and Reauthorization Act) Title III State Grants Program, EPA, *66.810*
SARA (Superfund Amendment and Reauthorization Act) Title III Training Program, *97.020*

SAVE AMERICA'S TREASURES [DOI], *15.929*
SAVIN (Statewide Automated Victim Information Notification), DOJ, *16.740*
Savings and loan institutions, *see* Banks, banking
SBA (Small Business Administration), 59.002 through 59.054
SBA Export Loans, *59.054*
SBDC (Small Business Development Center), *59.037*
SBE (Social, Behavioral, and Economic Sciences), NSF, *47.075*
SBIC (Small Business Investment Companies), *59.011*
SBIR, *see* Small Business Innovation Research (SBIR)
SBIR (Small Business Innovation Research) Program, USDA, *10.212*
SBMHAA (Stewart B. McKinney Homeless Assistance Act), *see* National housing acts
SCAAP (State Criminal Alien Assistance Program), DOJ, *16.606*
SCAMS TARGETING THE ELDERLY, *16.613*
SCHIP (State Children's Insurance Program), CMS, *93.767*
SCHOLARS AND FELLOWS [DHS], *97.062*
Scholarship and Fellowship Foundations, 85.001 through 85.601
Scholarships, *see* Fellowships, scholarships, traineeships
SCHOLARSHIPS FOR HEALTH PROFESSIONS STUDENTS FROM DISADVANTAGED BACKGROUNDS, *93.925*
School breakfast, lunch
 administrative expenses, states, *10.560*
 Child Nutrition Discretionary Grants, *10.579*
 food donation program, 10.550
 Fresh Fruit and Vegetable Program, FNS, *10.582*
 institutionalized children, *10.558*
 milk program, *10.556*
 National School Lunch Act, 10.550, *10.555, 10.558, 10.559, 10.574, 10.579, 10.582*
 School Breakfast Program, *10.553*
 School Lunch Program, *10.555*
 summer food program, *10.559*
 Team Nutrition Grants, FNS, *10.574*
 see also Food, nutrition; Schools *entries*
SCHOOL BREAKFAST PROGRAM, *10.553*
School construction, *see* Education facilities
School desegregation, *see* Civil rights
School Health Education to Prevent the Spread of AIDS (SHEPSA), *93.938*
SCHOOL LEADERSHIP, *84.363*
School lunch, *see* School breakfast, lunch
School Lunch Program, *10.555*
School Milk Program, *10.556*
Schools
 AIDS prevention, *93.938*
 Charter Schools, *84.282*
 charter schools facilities financing, *84.354*
 civil rights compliance, technical assistance, training, *84.004*
 Clean School Bus USA, EPA, *66.036*
 crime, alcohol, drug abuse prevention, *16.542*
 desegregation, legal services, 16.100
 Drug-Free Schools and Communities, national programs, *84.184*

Schools *(continued)*
  Drug-Free Schools and Communities, states, 84.186
  Drug Prevention Program, 16.728
  EPA New England Regional Office projects, 66.110
  Forest Service payments, counties, national grasslands, 10.666
  Forest Service payments, states, national forests, 10.665
  gifted, talented programs, 84.206
  health services, primary care, HRSA, 93.224
  impact aid, federally affected areas, 84.040, 84.041
  insular areas, 15.875
  juvenile gangs, drug abuse, trafficking prevention, 16.544
  Juvenile Mentoring Program, 16.726
  Learn and Serve America programs, 94.004
  Literacy through School Libraries, 84.364
  Magnet Schools Assistance, 84.165
  model projects, 84.215
  physical fitness promotion, 93.289
  Public Alert Radios for Schools, DHS, 97.079
  rural facilities, 10.766
  Safe Schools/Healthy Students National Evaluation, DOJ, 16.732
  security, local law enforcement block grants, 16.592
  telecommunications, instructional programming, Star Schools, 84.203
  Truck Security Program, DHS, 97.059
  underage drinking law enforcement, 16.727
  Vaccines for Children Program, 93.268
  violence prevention, 16.523
  Voluntary Public School Choice, 84.361
  see also Education *entries*; Elementary and secondary education; Indian education, training; School breakfast, lunch; Schools, private
SCHOOLS AND ROADS—GRANTS TO COUNTIES [USDA], 10.666
SCHOOLS AND ROADS—GRANTS TO STATES [USDA], 10.665
Schools, private
  Charter Schools, 84.282
  Drug-Free Schools and Communities, national programs, 84.184
  Drug-Free Schools and Communities, states, 84.186
  Early Reading First, 84.359
  Fresh Fruit and Vegetable Program, FNS, 10.582
  gifted, talented programs, 84.206
  Junior Duck Stamp Contest, FWS, 15.644
  milk program, 10.556
  model projects, 84.215
  School Breakfast Program, 10.553
  School Lunch Program, 10.555
  special education, 84.027
  summer food program, 10.559
  telecommunications, instructional programming, Star Schools, 84.203
  Vaccines for Children Program, 93.268
  see also Education facilities; Schools
Science, *see* Aeronautics, space; Agricultural research, sciences; Astronomy; Biological sciences; Chemicals, chemistry; Climate; Computer products, sciences, services; Earth sciences; Engineering *entries*; Environmental sciences; Forensic sciences; Food, nutrition research, sciences; Mathematics; Nuclear sciences, technology; Physical sciences; Science education; Scientific research; Social sciences; Technology transfer, utilization
Science education
  aeronautics, space information, 43.001
  aviation, civil, 20.100
  Barry M. Goldwater Scholarship Program, 85.200
  biomedical, health science partnerships, 93.389
  BLM projects, Cultural Resource Management, 15.224
  DOD science, technology projects, 12.910
  DOE used equipment, 81.022
  DOI Summer Watershed Intern, 15.254
  Eisenhower regional consortia, 84.319
  environmental education, 66.950, 66.951
  Hydrometeorological Development, NOAA, 11.467
  Marine Sanctuary Program, 11.429
  marine sciences, 11.417
  mathematical, physical sciences research, 47.049
  Mathematics and Science Partnerships, OESE, 84.366
  minority institution programs, 84.120
  Navy support, 12.300
  NIEHS programs, 93.113, 93.115
  NMFS marine education, science projects, 11.455
  NOAA Colorado areas math, engineering, science, 11.449
  NOAA Educational Partnerships Program, minority, 11.481
  NSF international, 47.079
  NSF research, improvement grants, 47.075, 47.076
  Star Schools Program, 84.203
  Upward Bound, 84.047
  Women's Educational Equity Act Program, 84.083
  see also Computer products, sciences, services; Earth sciences; Education *entries*; Engineering; Environmental *entries*; Health, medical *entries*; Higher education *entries*; Marine sciences; Mathematics; Physical sciences; Social sciences; Teacher education, training; Technical training
SCIENCE TO ACHIEVE RESULTS (STAR) FELLOWSHIP PROGRAM [EPA], 66.514
SCIENCE TO ACHIEVE RESULTS (STAR) RESEARCH PROGRAM [EPA], 66.509
Scientific and technical information, *see* Information, scientific and technical
SCIENTIFIC COOPERATION AND RESEARCH [USDA], 10.961
Scientific research
  Academic Research Enhancement Award, health sciences, 93.390
  agriculture, 10.001
  agriculture, CSREES Integrated Programs, 10.303
  Air Force Defense Research Sciences Program, 12.800
  Applied Meteorological Research, 11.468
  Army Research Office, 12.431
  atmospheric, climate, 11.428, 11.431
  aviation research, 20.108

MASTER INDEX 1013

Barry M. Goldwater Scholarship Program, *85.200*
biological sciences, NSF, *47.074*
calibration, testing, NIST, 11.601
Christopher Columbus Fellowship Program, *85.100*
climate, air quality research, services, *11.459*
coal chemistry, physics, *81.057*
Coastal Ocean Program, *11.478*
computer sciences, NSF, *47.070*
Discovery and Applied Research, biomedical imaging, bioengineering, NIH, *93.286*
DOD research, fellowships, *12.630*
DOD science, technology projects, *12.910*
DOE environmental cleanup, technology development, *81.104*
DOE nuclear, education, fellowships, *81.114*
DOE used equipment, 81.022
DOE WMD nonproliferation, *81.113*
energy information, OSTI, 81.064
energy sciences, *81.049*
environmental monitoring, assessment projects, EPA, *66.512*
EPA consolidated research, *66.511*
EPA IHE research support, *66.515*
EPA research fellowships, graduate, undergraduate, *66.513*
EPA STAR graduate fellowships, *66.514*
fossil energy, development, *81.089*
Geosciences, NSF, *47.050*
hazardous substances multi-disciplinary research, *93.143*
homeland security advanced research projects, DHS, *97.065*
homeland security technology development, DHS, *97.077*
Inertial Confinement Fusion, stockpile stewardship, *81.112*
marine sanctuaries, *11.429*
measurement, engineering projects, *11.609*
mental health research, *93.242*
National Science Foundation Act of 1950, *47.041* through *47.079*
National Standard Reference Data System, 11.603
Navy, education support, *12.300*
NESDIS environmental sciences education, research, *11.440*
NIH intramural research training, *93.140*
NIST Congressionally-Identified Projects, *11.617*
NMFS marine education, science projects, *11.455*
NOAA, *11.432*
NOAA Educational Partnerships Program, minority, *11.481*
NOAA special projects, *11.460*
NOAA unallied projects, *11.452*
NSF behavioral, economic, social sciences, *47.075*
NSF engineering education, research, *47.041*
NSF Mathematical and Physical Sciences, *47.049*
NSF international science, engineering, *47.079*
nuclear, DOE HBCU program, *81.123*
Nuclear Energy Research Initiative, *81.121*
Polar Programs, *47.078*
register of research in progress, 11.650
Research and Technical Services Act, 11.650
Sea Grant Support, *11.417*
Smithsonian fellowships, *85.601*
Standard Reference Materials, 11.604

STAR (Science to Achieve Results) Research Program, EPA, *66.509*
undersea, *11.430*
University-Based Homeland Security Centers, DHS, *97.061*
water resources, *15.805*
see also Aeronautics, space; Agricultural experiment stations; Agricultural research, sciences; Astronomy; Behavioral sciences, education, services; Biological sciences; Cancer control, prevention, research; Chemicals, chemistry; Climate; Computer products, sciences, services; Dental health, dental research; Earth sciences; Energy research; Engineering research; Environmental health, research, services; Environmental sciences; Food, nutrition research, science; Forensic sciences; Geology; Health, medical research; Immunization, immunology; Information, scientific and technical; Marine sciences; Mathematics; National Research Service Awards; Nuclear sciences, technology; Physical sciences; Social sciences; Technology transfer, utilization
SCORE (Service Corps of Retired Executives), 59.005, *59.026*
SCORPS (Statewide Comprehensive Outdoor Recreation Plans), *15.916*
SCP (Senior Companion Program), *94.016*
SCS (Soil Conservation Service), *see* Agency Index (USDA, Natural Resource Conservation Service)
SCSEP (Senior Community Service Employment Program), *17.235*
Sculptors, sculpture, *see* Arts, arts education; Fellowships, scholarships, traineeships; Museums, galleries
SDI (Services Delivery Improvement), family planning, *93.974*
SDPI (Special Diabetes Program for Indians), *93.442*
SDS (Scholarships for Disadvantaged Students), HHS, *93.925*
SDWA (Safe Drinking Water Act), *see* Water pollution abatement, prevention
Sea Grant College Program Improvement Act, *see* Marine sciences
SEA GRANT SUPPORT, *11.417*
SEAMAP (Southeast Area Monitoring and Assessment Program), *11.435*
Seamen, *see* Fisheries industry; Maritime industry; U.S. Merchant Marine; Water navigation
Seasonal workers, *see* Aliens, immigrants, refugees; Farm workers; Fisheries industry
SEC (Securities and Exchange Commission), 58.001
SECONDARY AND TWO-YEAR POSTSECONDARY AGRICULTURE EDUCATION CHALLENGE GRANTS, *10.226*
Secondary education, *see* Elementary and secondary education
SECRET SERVICE—TRAINING ACTIVITIES, 97.015
Secretaries of Military Departments, DOD, *see* Agency Index
Section 3 Emergency Dredging Projects, 12.109
Section 3, employment opportunities, HUD, 14.412

Section 7, Fishermen's Protective Act, *19.204*
Section 7(a) Loans, SBA, *59.012, 59.054*
Section 7(b) Loans, SBA, *59.008*
Section 7(J) Program, SBA, *59.007*
Section 8 Housing Assistance Payments Program for Very Low Income Families, Moderate Rehabilitation, *14.856*
SECTION 8 HOUSING ASSISTANCE PAYMENTS PROGRAM—SPECIAL ALLOCATIONS, *14.195*
SECTION 8 HOUSING CHOICE VOUCHERS, *14.871*
SECTION 8 MODERATE REHABILITATION SINGLE ROOM OCCUPANCY, *14.249*
Section 8(a) Business Development, SBA, 59.006
Section 22, Water Resources Development Act, 12.110
Section 104, Clean Air Act, monitoring, *66.512*
Section 104(b)(3), Clean Water Act, studies, *66.436*
Section 106 Grants, Clean Water Act, *66.419*
Section 106, 111, Clean Air Act, *66.033*
Section 108, CDBG Economic Development Initiative, *14.246*
Section 108 Loan Guarantees, HUD, *14.248*
Section 109, Title I, Housing and Community Development Act, nondiscrimination, 14.406
Section 112, Clean Air Act Program, *66.810*
Section 166, WIA Indian Program, *17.265*
Section 184A, native Hawaiian housing loan guarantees, *14.874*
Section 202 Agreements, BLM, *15.222*
SECTION 202 ASSISTED LIVING CONVERSION FOR ELIGIBLE MULTIFAMILY HOUSING PROJECTS, *14.314*
Section 202, supportive housing, *14.157, 14.314*
Section 203 Grants for Planning and Administrative Expenses, EDA, *11.302*
Section 203(b), NHA, home mortgage insurance, *14.117*
Section 203(b), 203(k), 204, HUD single-family property disposition, 14.311
Section 203(h), NHA, disaster victims mortgage insurance, *14.119*
Section 203(k), NHA, housing rehabilitation, *14.108*
Section 203(n), NHA, cooperative housing, *14.163*
Section 205(j)(2), Clean Water Act, *66.454*
Section 207 Manufactured Home Parks, NHA, *14.127*
Section 207, NHA, middle-income rental housing, *14.134*
Section 208, snagging, clearing waterways, 12.108
Section 213 Cooperatives, NHA, *14.126*
Section 213 Sales, NHA, cooperatives, *14.132*
Section 220 Multifamily, NHA, urban renewal areas, *14.139*
Section 220 Homes, urban renewal areas, *14.122*
Section 221(d) Single Room Occupancy, NHA, *14.184*
Section 221(d)(3) and (4) Multifamily-Market Rate Housing, NHA, *14.135*
Section 223(d) Two Year Operating Loss Loans, NHA, *14.167*
Section 223(e), NHA, declining areas, *14.123*
Section 223(f) and 207, NHA, existing multifamily housing, *14.155*

Section 231, NHA, rental housing, elderly, *14.138*
Section 232 Nursing Homes, NHA, *14.129*
Section 234(c), NHA, condominiums, *14.133*
Section 234(d) Condominiums, NHA, *14.112*
Section 236 Interest Reduction Payments, NHA, *14.103*
Section 238(c), NHA, military impacted areas, *14.165*
Section 241(a), NHA, multifamily housing, health care facilities, *14.151*
Section 242 Hospitals, NHA, *14.128*
SECTION 245 GRADUATED PAYMENT MORTGAGE PROGRAM, *14.159*
Section 245(a), NHA, Growing Equity Mortgages, *14.172*
Section 251 Adjustable Rate Mortgages, NHA, *14.175*
Section 255, NHA, home equity conversion mortgages, *14.183*
Section 301 and 317, PHSA, *93.268*
Section 306C, RUS, *10.770*
Section 319 Program, Clean Water Act, *66.460*
Section 410, traffic safety, *20.601*
SECTION 416(B) [USDA], *10.607*
Section 501(b)(2), work-study program, HUD, *14.512*
Section 502 Architectural Barriers Act, 14.407
Section 502 Rural Housing Loans, *10.410*
Section 502 Very Low and Low Income Loans, RHS, *10.445*
Section 503 Grants, WIA, *17.267*
Section 504 Loans, SBA, *59.041*
Section 504, Rehabilitation Act, discrimination, handicapped, 14.404
Section 504 Rural Housing Loans and Grants, *10.417, 10.444*
Section 509 Grants, RHS, *10.442*
Section 510(a-h), SSA, abstinence education, *93.010*
Section 514 and 516, labor housing, *10.405*
Section 515 and 521, rural rental housing, *10.415*
Section 521, Rural Rental Assistance Payments, *10.427*
Section 523 Technical Assistance, self-help housing, *10.420*
Section 523 and 524 Site Loans, RHS, *10.411*
Section 525(a), rural counseling program, *10.441*
Section 533, rural housing, *10.433*
SECTION 538 RURAL RENTAL HOUSING GUARANTEED LOANS, *10.438*
Section 542(b) Risk Sharing Program, HUD, *14.189*
Section 542(c) Risk Sharing Program, HUD, *14.188*
Section 638 ISDEAA, *93.441*
Section 811, supportive housing, disabled, *14.181*
Section 1110, 1115, SSA, child support enforcement, *93.563*
Section 1442, Safe Drinking Water Act, studies, *66.424*
Section 1928, SSA, immunization, *93.268*
Section 5303, Metropolitan Planning, FTA, *20.505*
Section 5307, Urbanized Area Formula Program, FTA, *20.507*
Section 5309, Capital Investment Grants, FTA, *20.500*
Section 5310, Elderly and Disabled, FTA, *20.513*
Section 5311, Nonurbanized Formula Grants, FTA, *20.509*

MASTER INDEX 1015

Section 5313(b) State Planning and Research, FTA, *20.515*
Section 5314(a), Transit Planning and Research Projects, FTA, *20.514*
Section 8044, Corps of Engineers, 12.116
Securities Act of 1933, 58.001
Securities and Exchange Commission (SEC), 58.001
SECURITIES—INVESTIGATION OF COMPLAINTS AND SEC INFORMATION, 58.001
SED (Serious Emotional Disturbances), HHS, *93.104*
SEE (Senior Environmental Employment Program), *66.508*
SEED GRANTS TO STATES FOR OPERATION OF QUALIFIED RISK POOLS [HHS], *93.781*
Seedlings, seeds
  Crop Disaster Program, *10.073*
  Crop Insurance, *10.450*
  disaster assistance, noninsured crops, *10.451*
  farm loans, interest subsidies, *10.437*
  field testing, conservation use, 10.905
  Grassland Reserve Program, NRCS, *10.920*
  market promotion, protection, 10.163
  mine land reclamation, *10.910*
  purchases, Food Stamps, *10.551*
  seed producers emergency loans, *10.076*
  Technical Assistance for Specialty Crops, FAS, *10.604*
  Tree Assistance Program, FSA, *10.082*
  tree seed improvement, production, distribution, *10.664*
  see also Agricultural *entries*; Forestry; Fruit; Plants; Soil conservation; Timber industry; Vegetables
Selective Placement Program, OPM, 27.005
SELF-HELP HOMEOWNERSHIP OPPORTUNITY PROGRAM, *14.247*
Self-help housing, *10.420*
Self-help housing site loans, *10.411*
SEMFISH (Stock Enhancement of Marine Fish in the State of Hawaii), *11.445*
SEMICONDUCTOR CHIP PROTECTION SERVICE, 42.008
Senior citizens, *see* Aging and the aged; Housing, elderly
SENIOR COMMUNITY SERVICE EMPLOYMENT PROGRAM, *17.235*
SENIOR COMPANION PROGRAM, *94.016*
SENIOR ENVIRONMENTAL EMPLOYMENT PROGRAM, *66.508*
SENIOR FARMERS MARKET NUTRITION PROGRAM, *10.576*
SEOG (Supplemental Educational Opportunity Grants), *84.007*
SEP (Student Expense Program), FEMA, *97.026*
Serious Emotional Disturbances (SED), HHS, *93.104*
SERVICE CORPS OF RETIRED EXECUTIVES, *59.026*
Servicemen's Readjustment Act, *17.804*
Services Delivery Improvement (SDI), family planning, *93.974*
SERVICES FOR TRAFFICKING VICTIMS, *16.320*
SERVICES TO INDIAN CHILDREN, ELDERLY AND FAMILIES, *15.025*

SERVICES TO VICTIMS OF A SEVERE FORM OF TRAFFICKING [HHS], *93.598*
7(A) LOANS (EXPORT LOANS) [SBA], *59.054*
7(J) TECHNICAL ASSISTANCE [SBA], *59.007*
Sewage facilities, treatment
  Appalachian region, *23.002*
  CDBG, *14.218, 14.219, 14.225, 14.228, 14.862*
  EPA consolidated program support, *66.600*
  EPA Performance Partnership Grants, *66.605*
  public works, EDA projects, *11.300*
  rural areas, *10.760*
  rural housing loans, *10.410*
  rural loans, *10.411*
  U.S. insular areas, *15.875*
  see also Hazardous materials, waste; Pollution abatement; Public works; Waste treatment, disposal; Water systems, treatment
Sex discrimination, *see* Civil rights; Women
SEX OFFENDER MANAGEMENT DISCRETIONARY GRANT [DOJ], *16.203*
Sexual abuse
  campus crime grants, *16.525*
  child, investigation, prosecution, family services, *93.643*
  Combined DNA Index System (CODIS), FBI, *16.307*
  disabled women, abuse, violence prevention, education, training, OJP, *16.529*
  domestic violence, stalking victim transitional housing, *16.736*
  homeless, runaway youth, Street Outreach Program, *93.557*
  Indian children, *16.583*
  investigations training, FBI Academy, 16.300
  offender registry, *16.554*
  prison rape elimination, personnel training, victim services, *16.735*
  prison rape statistics program, *16.739*
  Services for Trafficking Victims, *16.320*
  Sex Offender Management, *16.203*
  Supervised Visitation, Safe Havens for Children, OJP, *16.527*
  victim assistance, *16.524, 16.575*
  victim assistance, block grant, *93.991*
  see also Corrections; Crime; Family therapy; Maternal, child health, welfare; Parenting; Social services; Victim assistance
Sexual relations, *see* Family planning; Parenting; Sexual abuse; Youth
Sexually transmitted diseases, *see* AIDS (Acquired Immune Deficiency Syndrome); Communicable diseases
SFMNP (Senior Farmers Market Nutrition Program), FNS, *10.576*
SHARING SPECIALIZED MEDICAL RESOURCES [DVA], 64.018
Sheep, *see* Agricultural marketing; Livestock industry
SHELTER PLUS CARE, *14.238*
Shelters, *see* Civil defense; Emergency assistance; Homeless persons; Victim assistance
SHEPSA (School Health Education to Prevent the Spread of AIDS), *93.938*
Shipping, *see* Interstate commerce; Maritime industry; Railroads; Transportation
Shipping Act of 1984, 33.001

SHIPPING—INVESTIGATION OF COMPLAINTS, 33.001
Ships, *see* Fisheries industry; Maritime industry; Water navigation
SHOP (Self-Help Homeownership Opportunity Program), HUD, *14.247*
SHORT TERM CLIMATE FLUCTUATIONS, *11.443*
Short Term Lending Program, DOT, *20.905*
SHSP (State Homeland Security Program), *97.067, 97.073*
Sign language, *see* Deafness and the deaf
Sikes Act of 1974, *15.231, 15.608*
SINGLE-FAMILY PROPERTY DISPOSITION, 14.311
Single room occupancy (SRO) housing, *see* Housing, low to moderate income
SIPI (Southwestern Indian Polytechnic Institute), *15.058*
SIRG (State Indoor Radon Grants), *66.032*
Site Loans, Sections 523 and 524, *10.411*
Site Specific Cooperative Agreement Program, CDCP, *93.240*
Skin diseases research, *93.846*
SLATT (State and Local Anti-Terrorism Training), DOJ, *16.614*
Sleep disorders, *93.233, 93.853*
Slides, *see* Audiovisual aids, film, video
SLS (Supplemental Loans for Students), *84.032*
Slum elimination, *14.218, 14.219, 14.225, 14.228, 14.862*
Small Beach Erosion Control Projects, 12.101
Small business
  BIA Loan Guaranty Program, *15.124*
  bid, payment, performance bonds, *59.016*
  brownfields clean-up revolving loan funds, insurance, *66.817*
  business internships, secondary students, *84.353*
  CDBG, *14.218, 14.219, 14.225, 14.228, 14.862*
  Certified Development Company loans, *59.041*
  community development credit union loans, *44.002*
  Delta region, *90.200, 90.201, 90.202*
  disadvantaged, management, technical assistance, *59.007*
  disadvantaged, transportation, DOT contracts, *20.903, 20.907*
  disaster loans, *59.002, 59.008*
  DOD procurement assistance, *12.002*
  DOE patent licensing, 81.003
  DOT contracts, Short Term Lending Program, minority-, women- owned, *20.905*
  economic development, RBCS, *10.854*
  energy savings technology, invention assistance, *81.036*
  equity capital, SBIC loans, *59.011*
  fixed asset loans, *59.041*
  foreign investment financing, *70.002, 70.003*
  foreign trade zones (U.S.), 11.111
  forest products, USFS Technology Marketing Unit, small wood species, *10.674*
  FTC services, 36.001
  government procurement contracts, disadvantaged, 59.006, *59.049*
  government procurement contracts, technical assistance, 59.009
  Gramm-Leach-Bliley Act, *59.050*
  high-unemployment areas, *59.007*
  HUD project contracts complaints, 14.412
  Indians, tribal revolving loan funds, loan guarantees, *15.032*
  ITA Special Projects, *11.113*
  low-income, loans, *93.593*
  management, technical assistance, *59.037*
  management on-line training, counseling, 59.005, *59.026*
  Manufacturing Extension Partnership, NIST, *11.611*
  microenterprise development training, technical assistance, *59.050*
  Microloan Demonstration Program, *59.046*
  minority business development centers, *11.800*
  Minority Business Opportunity Committee, *11.803*
  Native American Economic Development Assistance, SBA, *59.052*
  Native American Program, technical assistance, *11.801*
  New Markets Venture Capital, *59.051*
  occupational safety, health, state consultation, *17.504*
  public transportation, nonurbanized areas, *20.509*
  refugees, entrants, micro-loans, *93.576*
  Regular Business Loans, *59.012*
  revolving loan funds, *14.218, 14.219, 14.228*
  Rural Business-Cooperative Service, 10.350
  rural business, industrial development, *10.768*
  Rural Business Investment Program, RBCS, *10.860*
  Rural Business Opportunity Grants, *10.773*
  Rural Cooperative Development Grants, *10.771*
  rural, revolving loan funds, *10.769*
  SBA national ombudsman services, *59.053*
  Section 7(a) Loans, *59.012*
  Section 7(J) Program, *59.007*
  Section 8(a) Program, 59.006
  Section 504 Loans, *59.041*
  Service Corps of Retired Executives (SCORE), *59.026*
  Small Business Acts, *59.002, 59.005,* 59.006, *59.007, 59.008,* 59.009, *59.012, 59.016, 59.026, 59.037, 59.041, 59.043, 59.044, 59.049, 59.052*
  small business, agriculture regulatory ombudsman, *59.053*
  Small Business Development Centers (SBDC), *59.037*
  Small Business Investment Act of 1958, *59.011, 59.051*
  Small Business Investment Companies, *14.218, 14.219, 14.228, 59.011*
  Small Business Liability Relief and Brownfields Revitalization Act, *66.817, 66.818*
  Small Business Regulatory Fairness Act of 1996, *59.053*
  Specialized Small Business Investment Companies (SSBIC), *59.011, 59.051*
  Surety Bond Guarantee, *59.016*
  tax workshops, 21.003
  transportation, elderly, handicapped, *20.513*
  veterans-owned business, training, *59.044*
  women-owned, technical assistance, training, *59.043*

see also Agricultural *entries*; Aquaculture; Business development; Disabled, handicapped, employment; Disadvantaged, business development; Economic development; Farm, nonfarm enterprises; Government contracts; Indian economic, business development; Minority business enterprise; Private sector; Small Business Innovation Research (SBIR)
Small Business Administration (SBA), 59.002 through 59.054
SMALL BUSINESS AND AGRICULTURE REGULATORY ENFORCEMENT OMBUDSMAN AND SMALL BUSINESS REGULATORY FAIRNESS BOARDS, *59.053*
SMALL BUSINESS DEVELOPMENT CENTER, *59.037*

Small Business Innovation Research (SBIR)
aging, *93.866*
agriculture-related, *10.212*
alcoholism, *93.273*
allergy, immunology, transplantation biology, *93.855*
arthritis, musculoskeletal and skin diseases, *93.846*
blood diseases, resources, *93.839*
cancer, *93.394, 93.395, 93.396, 93.393, 93.399*
deafness, communicative disorders, *93.173*
dental, oral diseases, *93.121*
diabetes, endocrinology, metabolism, *93.847*
digestive diseases, nutrition, *93.848*
Discovery and Applied Research, biomedical imaging, bioengineering, NIH, *93.286*
drug abuse, *93.279*
education, DOED international research, studies, *84.017*
environmental health, biometry, *93.115*
environmental health hazards, *93.113*
FDA, *93.103*
foreign languages, area studies, *84.017*
health care financing research, CMS, *93.779*
health, minority disparities research, *93.307*
heart, vascular disease, *93.837*
homeland security advanced research projects, DHS, *97.065*
human development, mothers, children, NRSA, *93.865*
human genomes, *93.172*
kidney diseases, urology, hematology, *93.849*
lung diseases, *93.838*
Medical Library Assistance, *93.879*
mental health, *93.242*
microbiology, infectious diseases, *93.856*
National Center for Research Resources, NIH, *93.389*
neurological disorders, neurosciences, *93.853*
NSF engineering, *47.041*
nursing, *93.361*
occupational safety and health, *93.262*
sleep disorders, *93.233*
Superfund Worker Training Program, *93.142*
toxicology, *93.114*
vision, National Eye Institute, *93.867*
see also Disadvantaged, business development; Minority business enterprise; Small business; Technology transfer, utilization
SMALL BUSINESS INNOVATION RESEARCH [USDA], *10.212*

Small Business Investment Companies, *see* Small business
SMALL BUSINESS INVESTMENT COMPANIES, *59.011*
SMALL BUSINESS LOANS, *59.012*
Small Business, Agriculture Regulatory Ombudsman, *59.053*
Small cities block grants, CDBG, *14.219, 14.228*
Small Flood Control Projects, 12.106
Small Navigation Projects, 12.107
SMALL RURAL HOSPITAL IMPROVEMENT GRANT PROGRAM, *93.301*
Small Watershed Program, *10.904*, 10.906
SMFCUs (State Medicaid Fraud Control Units), HHS, *93.775*
SMI (Supplementary Medical Insurance), *93.774*
Smith-Lever Act, *10.500*
SMITHSONIAN INSTITUTION FELLOWSHIP PROGRAM, *85.601*
Smoking, *see* Tobacco
SNAGGING AND CLEARING FOR FLOOD CONTROL, 12.108
SNOW SURVEY AND WATER SUPPLY FORECASTING, 10.907
Snyder Act of 1921, *see* Indian affairs
SOCIAL, BEHAVIORAL, AND ECONOMIC SCIENCES, *47.075*
SOCIAL INSURANCE FOR RAILROAD WORKERS, *57.001*

Social sciences
aging, biomedical, behavioral, geriatrics research, *93.866*
agriculture, rural areas research, information, 10.250
alcoholism research, *93.891*
Appalachian region, economic, social development research, *23.011*
biomedical, behavioral, traineeships, international, *93.989*
Child Support Enforcement Research, *93.564*
coastal, estuarine areas research, *11.426*
community development work-study, HUD, *14.512*
corrections, law enforcement personnel family support projects, research, *16.563*
corrections research, *16.602*
crime, criminal justice research, *16.560*
crime, criminal justice research fellowships, *16.561, 16.562, 16.566*
DHS Scholars and Fellows, *97.062*
DOJ Special Data Collections and Statistical Studies, *16.734*
Eastern, Southeast Europe, NIS research, training, *19.300*
economic development research, *11.312*
economic development technical assistance, *11.303*
EPA compliance capacity building, *66.709*
ETA pilots, demonstrations, research, *17.261*
FBI Academy training, 16.300
food stamp program access research, *10.580*
forestry research, *10.652*
Fulbright program, educational exchange, *19.400*
Fund for Rural America, research, education, *10.224*
Global Development Alliance, USAID, *98.011*

Social sciences *(continued)*
graduate fellowships, *84.170*
Habitat Conservation, NOAA, *11.463*
health care financing research, CMS, *93.779*
HUD housing, urban development doctoral research, *14.516, 14.517*
housing, community, economic development, HUD research, *14.506*
human development research, mothers, children, NRSA, *93.865*
Human Genome Research, *93.172*
international, education exchange, *19.418, 84.304*
international peace and conflict resolution, *91.001, 91.002*
International Visitors Program, BECA, *19.402*
juvenile delinquency causes, prevention research, *16.542*
juvenile justice system improvement, research, *16.523*
missing children research, *16.543*
native Americans, Udall congressional internships, *85.402*
NOAA unallied projects, *11.452, 11.454, 11.472*
NSF research, *47.075*
Polar Programs, *47.078*
Professional Exchanges, BECA, *19.415*
public service scholarships, *85.001*
Safe Schools/Healthy Students National Evaluation, DOJ, *16.732*
Social Security program research, demonstrations, *96.007*
STAR (Science to Achieve Results) Research Program, EPA, *66.509*
teacher seminars abroad, *84.018*
teaching, Madison fellowships, *85.500*
University-Based Homeland Security Centers, DHS, *97.061*
watershed, river basin surveys, *10.906*
Welfare Reform Research, *93.595*
white-collar crime center, *16.612*
WIA program evaluations, *17.262*
Woodrow Wilson Center fellowships, *85.300*
young political leaders, international exchange, *19.403*
see also Archaeology; Behavioral sciences, education, services; Census services; Crime; Criminal justice system; Economics, research, statistics; Forensic sciences; Government; History; Humanities *entries*; Information *entries*; International programs, studies; Law enforcement education, training

Social Security Act
abstinence education, *93.010, 93.235*
Adoption Assistance, *93.659*
Adoption Incentive Payments, *93.603*
child access and visitation programs, *93.597*
Child Care and Development Fund, *93.596*
child support enforcement, *93.563, 93.601*
Child Support Enforcement Research, *93.564*
child welfare services, *93.645, 93.648*
Children's Hospitals Graduate Medical Education Payment, HRSA, *93.255*
Compassion Capital Fund, ACF, *93.009*
Disability Insurance, *96.001*
Emergency Medical Treatment and Active Labor Act (EMTALA), *93.784*
family support services, *93.556*
Foster Care, *93.658*
foster children, Chafee vouchers, *93.599*
health care financing research, CMS, *93.779*
Immunization Grants, *93.268*
Independent Living, ACF, foster care, *93.674*
maternal, child health programs, *93.110, 93.994*
Medicaid, *93.778*
Medicaid fraud control, *93.775*
Medicaid, Medicare providers standards compliance, *93.777*
Medicare hospital insurance, *93.773*
Medicare Part B supplementary insurance, *93.774*
Medicare Part D prescription drug insurance, *93.770*
Medicare Prescription Drug, Improvements and Modernization Act 2003 (MMA), *93.770, 93.773, 93.782, 93.783*
Policy Research and Evaluation Grants, *93.239*
program research, demonstrations, *96.007*
railroad workers, *57.001*
repatriation program, *93.579*
Retirement Insurance, *96.002*
Small Rural Hospital Improvement, *93.301*
Social Services Block Grant, *93.667*
Social Services Research and Demonstration, *93.647*
special benefits, older persons, *96.003*
Special Veterans Benefits, SSI expatriate beneficiaries, *96.020*
SSA beneficiaries outreach, services, *96.008*
SSA disabled beneficiaries outreach, services, *96.009*
Supplemental Security Income, *96.006*
Survivors Insurance, SSA, *96.004*
Temporary Assistance for Needy Families, *93.558*
Tribal Work Grants, *93.594*
Unemployment Insurance, *17.225*
see also Employee benefits; Insurance; Public assistance; Unemployment
Social Security Administration (SSA), 96.001 through 96.020
SOCIAL SECURITY—BENEFITS PLANNING, ASSISTANCE, AND OUTREACH PROGRAM, *96.008*
SOCIAL SECURITY—DISABILITY INSURANCE, *96.001*
SOCIAL SECURITY—RESEARCH AND DEMONSTRATION, *96.007*
SOCIAL SECURITY—RETIREMENT INSURANCE, *96.002*
SOCIAL SECURITY—SPECIAL BENEFITS FOR PERSONS AGED 72 AND OVER, *96.003*
SOCIAL SECURITY STATE GRANTS FOR WORK INCENTIVES ASSISTANCE TO DISABLED BENEFICIARIES, *96.009*
SOCIAL SECURITY—SURVIVORS INSURANCE, *96.004*

Social services
abandoned infants, care training, *93.551*
Adoption Awareness Training, *93.254*
adoption services, *93.652*
aging, demonstration projects, personnel training, *93.048*
aging, long-term care ombudsman services, *93.042*
AIDS/HIV, children, women, families, *93.153*

Alzheimer's, related disorders demonstrations, 93.051
AmeriCorps, 94.003, 94.006, 94.007, 94.009
blind elderly, independent living, 84.177
caregiver support program, respite care, 93.052
child abuse prevention, treatment, research, technical assistance, 93.670
child care, social services, TANF, 93.558
child protective services, training, 93.669
child support special projects, 93.601
child welfare, 93.645
child welfare personnel training, 93.648
community-based child abuse prevention, 93.590
Community Learning Centers, 84.287
Community Services Block Grants, 93.569, 93.570
Compassion Capital Fund, ACF, 93.009, 93.647
conflicts mediation, 16.200
corrections, law enforcement personnel family support projects, research, 16.563
corrections staff, ex-offenders training programs, 16.601
crime victim assistance, 16.575, 16.576, 16.582
Cuban, Haitian entrants, 97.009
Delinquency Prevention Program, 16.548, 16.549
developmental disabilities, national projects, 93.631
developmentally disabled, basic support, advocacy projects, 93.630
disabled, elderly, Multifamily Housing Service Coordinators, 14.191
disabled, handicapped, basic support, 84.126
disaster emergency services, 93.003
disaster victims, Cora Brown Fund, 97.031
disasters, assistance to individuals, households, FEMA, 97.050
domestic violence, stalking victim transitional housing, 16.736
Drug Court Program, 16.585
Drug-Free Community Grants, 93.276
Drug Prevention Program, 16.728
Elder Abuse Prevention, 93.041
emergency food, shelter assistance, FEMA, 97.024
Empowerment Zones Program, 10.772, 14.244
Family Life Centers, HHS violence prevention, 93.910
family support services, 93.556
family violence prevention, 93.591, 93.592, 93.671
farm workers, ETA, 17.264
food donation, 10.565
food stamp program access research, 10.580
foster care, 93.658
Foster Grandparent Program, 94.011
Gang Resistance Education and Training, BJA, 16.737
geriatrics education centers, 93.969
handicapped, independent living, 84.169
Head Start parent programs, 93.600
health care systems research, 93.226, 93.239
HOME Program, 14.239
homeless, runaway youth, sexual abuse, 93.557
homeless, shelter, 14.231, 14.238
homeless, Supportive Housing Program, 14.235
homeless, transitional services, 93.150
homeless youth, transitional living, 93.550

housing counseling, 14.169
Hurricane Katrina Case Management Initiative, 97.084
Indians, 15.025, 15.113
Indians, social work scholarships, 93.972
international, Non-Governmental Organization Strengthening, USAID, 98.004
international, Ocean Freight Reimbursement, USAID, 98.003
international, USAID programs, 98.001
juvenile delinquency prevention, 16.540
juvenile gangs program personnel training, 16.544
juvenile justice system improvement, 16.523
Learn and Serve America programs, 94.004, 94.005
Low-Income Taxpayer Clinics, 21.008
Mentoring Children of Prisoners, ACF, 93.616
missing children program, education, research, training, 16.543
Native Americans Programs, 93.612
Offender Reentry Program, 16.202
older Indians, 93.047
Operation Weed and Seed, 16.595
parent access, visitation programs, 93.597
Public Health Research Accreditation Project, 93.993
public housing residents, supportive services, 14.870
refugees, entrants, 93.566, 93.567, 93.576, 93.583, 93.584
repatriation program, 93.579
research, demonstration, 93.647
rural domestic violence, 16.589
senior center programs, 93.044
Senior Community Service Employment Program, 17.235
Senior Companion Program, 94.016
senior volunteers, (RSVP), 94.002
Sex Offender Management, DOJ, 16.203
Social Services Block Grants, 93.667
social worker education loan repayments, states, 93.165
social worker student loan cancellations, 84.037
social worker training, clinical mental health, 93.244
social workers, NHSC education loan repayments, 93.162
SSA beneficiaries outreach, services, 96.008
SSA disabled beneficiaries outreach, services, 96.009
State Court Improvement Program, ACF, 93.586
substance abuse treatment, prisoners, DOJ, 16.593
Supervised Visitation, Safe Havens for Children, OJP, 16.527
telecommunications infrastructure, 11.552
torture victims assistance, providers training, 93.604
trafficking victims assistance, ACF, 93.598
transportation, elderly, handicapped, 20.513
Unaccompanied Alien Children Program, 93.676
underage drinking law enforcement, 16.727
veterans domiciliary, 64.008
veterans home care, 64.022
violence, children's exposure, prevention initiative, Safe Start, 16.730
VISTA program, 94.013

Social services *(continued)*
Welfare Reform Research, *93.595*
WIC Grants to States, FNS, *10.578*
women crime victims, technical assistance, training, OJP, *16.526*
see also Aging and the aged; Alcohol abuse, alcoholism; Aliens, immigrants, refugees; AmeriCorps; Early childhood education; Child care services; Community development; Community health services; Consumers, consumer services; Corrections; Disabled, handicapped *entries*; Disadvantaged *entries*; Drug abuse; Employment services; Family planning; Farm workers; Food, nutrition; Home management; Homeless persons; Housing, subsidized; Illiteracy; Indian health, social services; Juvenile delinquency; Maternal, child health, welfare; Mental health; Parenting; Public assistance; Recreation *entries*; Veterans *entries*; Victim assistance; Volunteers; Youth *entries*
SOCIAL SERVICES BLOCK GRANT, *93.667*
SOCIAL SERVICES RESEARCH AND DEMONSTRATION, *93.647*
Sociology, *see* Social sciences
SOIL AND WATER CONSERVATION, 10.902
Soil conservation
Agricultural Management Assistance, NRCS, *10.917*
Conservation Reserve Program, payments to farmers, *10.069*
development loans, farms, *10.407*
emergency farmland rehabilitation, *10.054*
Environmental Quality Incentives Program-Klamath Basin, NRCS, *10.919*
Environmental Quality Incentives Program, NRCS, *10.912*
Farm and Ranch Lands Protection Program, NRCS, *10.913*
Great Plains, *10.900*
international research exchanges, *10.961*
plant use, 10.905
research, forestry, *10.202*
resource conservation, development, *10.901*
river basin surveys, 10.906
Soil Conservation and Domestic Allotment Act of 1936, *10.900*, 10.902, 10.905, 10.907
soil surveys, 10.903
sustainable agriculture research, *10.215*
technical assistance, NRCS, 10.902
watershed projects, *10.904*
see also Agricultural conservation; Environmental management; Flood prevention, control; Forestry; Natural resources; Wetlands
Soil Conservation Service (SCS), *see* Agency Index (USDA, Natural Resources Conservation Service)
SOIL SURVEY, 10.903
Solar energy
DOE special state initiatives, *81.119*
EPA environmental sustainability design competition, *66.516*
NOAA research, *11.432*
research, development, *81.087*
see also Energy *entries*
SOLICITED GRANT PROGRAM [USIP], *91.002*

Solid waste, *see* Waste treatment, disposal
Solid Waste Disposal Act (SWDA), *see* Waste treatment, disposal
SOLID WASTE MANAGEMENT ASSISTANCE GRANTS, *66.808*
SOLID WASTE MANAGEMENT GRANTS, *10.762*
SOM (Sex Offender Management), DOJ, *16.203*
SOP (Street Outreach Program), ACF, *93.557*
Sorghum, *see* Agricultural commodities, stabilization; Agricultural marketing; Feed grains
SOTN (State of the Nation), ESA, 11.027
SOURCE REDUCTION ASSISTANCE [EPA], *66.717*
SOUTHEAST ALASKA ECONOMIC DISASTER FUND, *10.671*
SOUTHEAST AREA MONITORING AND ASSESSMENT PROGRAM [NOAA], *11.435*
Southwestern Indian Polytechnic Institute (SIPI), *15.058*
Soybeans, *see* Agricultural commodities, stabilization; Agricultural marketing; Feed grains
Space programs, *see* Aeronautics, space
Spacemobile, 43.001
SPAPs (State Pharmaceutical Assistance Programs), MMA, CMS, *93.786*
SPECIAL AMERICAN BUSINESS INTERNSHIP TRAINING PROGRAM, *11.114*
SPECIAL APPLE PROGRAM, *10.075*
SPECIAL BENEFITS FOR CERTAIN WORLD WAR II VETERANS [SSA], *96.020*
SPECIAL DATA COLLECTIONS AND STATISTICAL STUDIES [DOJ], *16.734*
SPECIAL DIABETES PROGRAM FOR INDIANS—DIABETES PREVENTION AND TREATMENT PROJECTS, *93.237*
SPECIAL DIABETES PROGRAM FOR INDIANS (SDPI)—COMPETITIVE GRANTS PROGRAM, *93.442*
SPECIAL EDUCATION—GRANTS FOR INFANTS AND FAMILIES WITH DISABILITIES, *84.181*
SPECIAL EDUCATION—GRANTS TO STATES, *84.027*
SPECIAL EDUCATION—PARENT INFORMATION CENTERS, *84.328*
SPECIAL EDUCATION—PERSONNEL PREPARATION TO IMPROVE SERVICES AND RESULTS FOR CHILDREN WITH DISABILITIES, *84.325*
SPECIAL EDUCATION—PRESCHOOL GRANTS, *84.173*
SPECIAL EDUCATION—STATE PERSONNEL DEVELOPMENT, *84.323*
SPECIAL EDUCATION—STUDIES AND EVALUATIONS, *84.329*
SPECIAL EDUCATION—TECHNICAL ASSISTANCE AND DISSEMINATION TO IMPROVE SERVICES AND RESULTS FOR CHILDREN WITH DISABILITIES, *84.326*
SPECIAL EDUCATION—TECHNOLOGY AND MEDIA SERVICES FOR INDIVIDUALS WITH DISABILITIES, *84.327*
Special Higher Education Scholarships, BIA, *15.059*
SPECIAL MILK PROGRAM FOR CHILDREN, *10.556*

SPECIAL OCEANIC AND ATMOSPHERIC PROJECTS, *11.460*
SPECIAL PROGRAMS FOR THE AGING—TITLE III, PART B—GRANTS FOR SUPPORTIVE SERVICES AND SENIOR CENTERS, *93.044*
SPECIAL PROGRAMS FOR THE AGING—TITLE III, PART C—NUTRITION SERVICES, *93.045*
SPECIAL PROGRAMS FOR THE AGING—TITLE III, PART D—DISEASE PREVENTION AND HEALTH PROMOTION SERVICES, *93.043*
SPECIAL PROGRAMS FOR THE AGING—TITLE IV—AND TITLE II—DISCRETIONARY PROJECTS, *93.048*
SPECIAL PROGRAMS FOR THE AGING—TITLE VI—PART A, INDIAN PROGRAMS—GRANTS TO INDIAN TRIBES—PART B, GRANTS TO NATIVE HAWAIIANS, *93.047*
SPECIAL PROGRAMS FOR THE AGING—TITLE VII, CHAPTER 2—LONG-TERM CARE OMBUDSMAN SERVICES FOR OLDER INDIVIDUALS, *93.042*
SPECIAL PROGRAMS FOR THE AGING—TITLE VII, CHAPTER 3—PROGRAMS FOR PREVENTION OF ELDER ABUSE, NEGLECT, AND EXPLOITATION, *93.041*
SPECIAL PROJECTS OF NATIONAL SIGNIFICANCE [HHS], *93.928*
Special Projects of Regional and National Significance (SPRANS), HHS, *93.110*
Special Research Grants, CSREES, *10.200*
SPECIAL SUPPLEMENTAL NUTRITION PROGRAM FOR WOMEN, INFANTS, AND CHILDREN, *10.557*
SPECIALLY ADAPTED HOUSING FOR DISABLED VETERANS, *64.106*
SPECIALLY SELECTED HEALTH PROJECTS, *93.888*
Specialty crops, *see* Agricultural commodities, stabilization; Agricultural marketing; Feed grains; Fruit; Vegetables
Speech pathology
 deafness, communicative disorders research, *93.173*
 Indian children, institutionalized handicapped, *15.045*
 Indians, health professions scholarships, *93.972*
 interpreters for deaf, deaf-blind, *84.160*
 speech disorders research, *93.853*
 vocational rehabilitation personnel training, *84.129, 84.264, 84.275*
 see also Audiovisual aids, film, video; Deafness and the deaf; Health, medical education, training; Health professions; Vocational rehabilitation
Spina bifida, *64.127, 64.128*
Spinal cord injury research, *93.853*
SPNS (Special Projects of National Significance), HIV, *93.928*
SPORT FISH RESTORATION, *15.605*
SPORTFISHING AND BOATING SAFETY ACT, *15.622*
Sports, *see* Recreation *entries*

SPRANS (Special Projects of Regional and National Significance), HRSA, *93.110*
SRM (Standard Reference Materials), 11.604
SRO (single room occupancy) housing, *see* Housing, low to moderate income
SSA (Social Security Act), *see* Social Security Act
SSA (Social Security Administration), 96.001 through 96.020
SSA (Social Security Administration) Research and Demonstration, *96.007*
SSBG (Social Services Block Grant), *93.667*
SSBIC (Specialized Small Business Investment Companies), *59.011*
SS/HS National Evaluation (Safe Schools/Health Students), DOJ, *16.732*
SSI (Supplemental Security Income), *96.006*
STAFFING FOR ADEQUATE FIRE AND EMERGENCY RESPONSE, *97.083*
Stafford Act, *see* Disaster assistance (Robert T. Stafford Disaster Relief and Emergency Assistance Act)
Stafford Student Loans, *84.032*
Standard Reference Data Act, 11.603
STANDARD REFERENCE MATERIALS [NIST], 11.604
STAR (Science to Achieve Results) Fellowship Program, EPA, *66.514*
STAR (Science to Achieve Results) Research Program, EPA, *66.509*
STAR SCHOOLS, *84.203*
STATE ACCESS TO THE OIL SPILL LIABILITY TRUST FUND, 97.013
STATE ADMINISTRATIVE EXPENSES FOR CHILD NUTRITION, *10.560*
STATE ADMINISTRATIVE MATCHING GRANTS FOR FOOD STAMP PROGRAM, *10.561*
STATE AND COMMUNITY HIGHWAY SAFETY, *20.600*
STATE AND LOCAL ANTI-TERRORISM TRAINING, *16.614*
STATE AND LOCAL HOMELAND SECURITY EXERCISE SUPPORT, *97.006*
STATE AND LOCAL HOMELAND SECURITY TRAINING PROGRAM, *97.005*
State and Regional Primary Care Associations, HRSA, *93.129*
STATE AND TERRITORIAL AND TECHNICAL ASSISTANCE CAPACITY DEVELOPMENT MINORITY HIV/AIDS DEMONSTRATION PROGRAM, *93.006*
STATE AND TRIBAL RESPONSE PROGRAM GRANTS [EPA], *66.817*
STATE AND TRIBAL UNDERGROUND STORAGE TANKS PROGRAM, *66.804*
STATE BULK FUEL REVOLVING FUND [USDA], *10.857*
STATE CAPACITY BUILDING [HHS], *93.240*
STATE CEMETERY GRANTS [DVA], *64.203*
STATE CHILDREN'S INSURANCE PROGRAM, *93.767*
STATE COMMISSIONS [CNCS], *94.003*
State Councils on Developmental Disabilities, *93.630*
STATE COURT IMPROVEMENT PROGRAM [HHS], *93.586*

STATE CRIMINAL ALIEN ASSISTANCE
PROGRAM, *16.606*
State Data Center Program, Census Bureau, 11.004
State Department, 19.204 through 19.510
STATE DOMESTIC PREPAREDNESS
EQUIPMENT SUPPORT PROGRAM, *97.004*
STATE ENERGY PROGRAM, *81.041*
STATE ENERGY PROGRAM SPECIAL
INITIATIVES, *81.119*
STATE FIRE TRAINING SYSTEMS GRANTS, *97.043*
State Formula Grants, OJJDP, *16.540*
State government, see Government; Legislation
STATE GRANTS FOR INNOVATIVE
PROGRAMS [DOED], *84.298*
State Grants for Long-Term Care Ombudsman
Services, HHS, *93.042*
STATE GRANTS FOR PROTECTION AND
ADVOCACY SERVICES, *93.267*
STATE GRANTS TO REIMBURSE OPERATORS
OF SMALL WATER SYSTEMS FOR
TRAINING AND CERTIFICATION COSTS, *66.471*
STATE HEALTH FRAUD TASK FORCE
GRANTS, *93.447*
State Home Construction, DVA, *64.005*
STATE HOMELAND SECURITY PROGRAM, *97.073*
State Homeland Security Program (SHSP), *97.067, 97.073*
STATE INDOOR RADON GRANTS, *66.032*
STATE JUSTICE STATISTICS PROGRAM FOR
STATISTICAL ANALYSIS CENTERS, *16.550*
State Lead Certification Grants, EPA, *66.707*
STATE LIBRARY PROGRAM, *45.310*
State Loan Repayment Program, HRSA, *93.165*
STATE MARINE SCHOOLS, *20.806*
STATE MEDIATION GRANTS [USDA], *10.435*
STATE MEDICAID FRAUD CONTROL UNITS, *93.775*
STATE MEMORANDUM OF AGREEMENT
PROGRAM FOR THE REIMBURSEMENT
OF TECHNICAL SERVICES [DOD], *12.113*
STATE OF THE NATION [USDC], 11.027
State Participation in Railroad Safety, 20.303
STATE PLANNING AND RESEARCH [DOT], *20.515*
STATE PLANNING GRANTS HEALTH CARE
ACCESS FOR THE UNINSURED, *93.256*
STATE PHARMACEUTICAL ASSISTANCE
PROGRAMS, *93.786*
State Primary Care Offices, HRSA, *93.130*
STATE PUBLIC WATER SYSTEM
SUPERVISION, *66.432*
STATE RURAL HOSPITAL FLEXIBILITY
PROGRAM, *93.241*
STATE SENIOR ENVIRONMENTAL
EMPLOYMENT PROGRAM [EPA], *66.518*
STATE SURVEY AND CERTIFICATION OF
HEALTH CARE PROVIDERS AND
SUPPLIERS, *93.777*
STATE UNDERGROUND WATER SOURCE
PROTECTION, *66.433*
STATE WILDLIFE GRANTS, *15.634*
STATEMAP, USGS, *15.810*
STATEWIDE AUTOMATED VICTIM
INFORMATION NOTIFICATION (SAVIN)
PROGRAM, *16.740*
Statewide Comprehensive Outdoor Recreation Plans
(SCORPS), *15.916*
States community development block grants, *14.228*
Statistical Analysis Centers (SACs), DOJ, *16.550*
Statistics
agricultural, rural, 10.950
biostatistics NRSA, *93.225*
biostatistics, public health graduate traineeships, *93.964*
business, 11.025
census data, 11.001, 11.002, 11.005
census geography, 11.003
Census Intergovernmental Services, 11.004
census use training, 11.002
Consumer Price Index, 17.003
crime, criminal justice, 16.304, 16.305, *16.550*
DOJ Special Data Collections and Statistical
Studies, *16.734*
DOT Crash Data Improvement Program, *20.230*
economic data, analysis, national, 11.025
energy, 81.039
environmental health, biometry, *93.115*
environmental monitoring, assessment projects,
EPA, *66.512*
environmental policy, programs innovation,
stewardship, studies, analyses, *66.611*
export, import price index, 17.003
fisheries, southeast area, *11.434*
highway safety data improvement, *20.603*
international industrial data, 11.110
juvenile delinquency, *16.542*
labor force, *17.002*
labor-management relations, *17.005*
mathematical sciences research, education, NSA, *12.901*
National Trade Data Bank, 11.026
occupational health, safety, *17.005*
OSHA Data Initiative, *17.505*
overseas trade markets, 11.108
Pacific fisheries, *11.437*
prison rape statistics program, *16.739*
Producer Price Index, 17.003
productivity, 17.004
State of the Nation, ESA, 11.027
TIGER (Topologically Integrated Geographic
Encoding and Referencing) system, 11.003
Vital Statistics Reengineering Program, CDCP, *93.066*
wages, benefits, *17.005*
see also Agricultural statistics; Census services;
Computer products, sciences, services;
Economics, research, statistics; Epidemiology;
Information *entries*; Publications
STEWARDSHIP SCIENCE GRANT PROGRAM
[DOE], *81.112*
Stewart B. McKinney Homeless Assistance Act, see
National housing acts
Stock Enhancement of Marine Fish in the State of
Hawaii (SEMFISH), *11.445*
Storage, agricultural, see Agricultural commodities,
stabilization
Strabismus research, *93.867*
Street Outreach Program (SOP), ACF, *93.557*

Streets, *see* Community development; Highways, roads, bridges; Public works
Stroke, nervous system trauma research, *93.853*
STRUCTURAL FIRE PROTECTION—BUREAU OF INDIAN AFFAIRS FACILITIES, *15.064*
Student financial aid
advanced placement test fee payment, DOED, *84.330*
AmeriCorps education awards, *94.006*
child care, postsecondary low-income student-parents, *84.335*
Children's Hospitals Graduate Medical Education Payment, HRSA, *93.255*
clinical researchers education loan repayment, disadvantaged, *93.308*
community development work-study, HUD, *14.512*
contraception, infertility research, education loan repayments, *93.209*
disadvantaged, graduate opportunities, *84.217*
disadvantaged, stipends, Upward Bound, *84.047*
disadvantaged, talented youth, information, Talent Search, *84.044*
disadvantaged, TRIO support, *84.042*
elementary, secondary, Social Security survivors benefits, *96.002*
emergency management personnel, FEMA stipends, *97.026*
Federal Direct Student Loans, graduate, undergraduate, *84.268*
Federal Family Education Loan Program (FFELP), *84.032*
foster children, Chafee vouchers, *93.599*
guaranteed loans, *84.032*
health, allied health information, disadvantaged, *93.822*
health disparities researchers education loan repayment, *93.307*
health education loan repayments, states, *93.165*
health education loans, *93.342*
health professions faculty loan repayments, disadvantaged, *93.923*
IHS education loan repayments, *93.164*
Indian Employment Assistance, *15.108*
information for adults, *84.066*
low-income, postsecondary, New Assets for Independence Demonstration, *93.602*
low-income secondary, TRIO supportive services, scholarships, *84.334*
merchant marine officers, *20.806, 20.807*
migrants, *84.141, 84.149*
NHSC education loan repayments, *93.162*
NIH AIDS research education loan repayments, *93.936*
NIH Clinical Research Loan Repayment Program, *93.220, 93.280*
NIH General Research Loan Repayment Program, *93.232*
NIH Pediatric Research Loan Repayment Program, *93.285, 93.385*
nursing education loan repayments, *93.908*
Nursing Faculty Loan Program, *93.264*
nursing, loans, *93.364*
Pell grants, *84.063*
post-Vietnam era veterans, *64.120*
public safety officers' dependents, *16.615*
student loan cancellations, *84.037*
Summer Jobs in Federal Agencies, 27.006
undergraduate, graduate, Perkins loans, *84.038*
undergraduate, SEOG, *84.007*
veterans, disabled, *64.116*
veterans, payments, *64.124*
veterans' spouses, children, *64.117*
work-study, *84.033*
see also Apprenticeship training; Disadvantaged, education; Fellowships, scholarships, traineeships; Indian education, training; Minority education; Technical training; Veterans education, training
Student Stipend Reimbursement Program, FEMA, *97.018*
Student Stipend Reimbursement Program (SEP), FEMA, *97.026*
Student Temporary Employment Program, 27.003
Study of the U.S. Program-Office of Academic Exchange Programs, BECA, *19.418*
Subdivisions
flood plain data, services, 12.104
interstate land sales registration, 14.168
see also Community development; Homeownership, homebuying; Homes, manufactured, mobile; Housing construction; Land acquisition
Subsidies
air transportation, *20.901*
farm loan interest, *10.437*
Food Stamps, *10.551*
ship construction, reconstruction, *20.808, 20.812*
ship operation, *20.813*
see also Agricultural commodities, stabilization; Housing, subsidized; Public assistance; Taxes, tax incentives
Subsidized housing, *see* Housing, subsidized
Substance abuse, *see* Alcohol abuse, alcoholism; Drug abuse; Tobacco
SUBSTANCE ABUSE AND MENTAL HEALTH SERVICES—ACCESS TO RECOVERY, *93.275*
SUBSTANCE ABUSE AND MENTAL HEALTH SERVICES—PROJECTS OF REGIONAL AND NATIONAL SIGNIFICANCE, *93.243*
Substance Abuse and Mental Health Services Administration (SAMHSA), HHS, *see* Agency Index
Substance Abuse Prevention and Treatment (SAPT) Block Grant, *93.959*
Substance Abuse Treatment Program, Mental Health and Behavioral Sciences Service, DVA, 64.019
Sugar, *see* Agricultural commodities; Agricultural commodities, stabilization
Summer employment, *see* Employment services; Federal employment; Youth employment
SUMMER FOOD SERVICE PROGRAM FOR CHILDREN, *10.559*
Summer Jobs in Federal Agencies, 27.006
SUMMER WATERSHED INTERN [DOI], *15.254*
Superconductivity and Competitiveness Act of 1988, *81.122*
Superfund, *see* Hazardous materials, waste
Superfund, *66.802*
Superfund TAGs (Technical Assistance Grants), *66.806* Superfund Amendments and Reauthorization Act of 1986 (SARA), *66.816*

Superfund Amendments and Reauthorization Act (SARA) Title III Training Program, *97.020*
Superfund NIEHS Research Program, *93.143*
SUPERFUND STATE AND INDIAN TRIBE CORE PROGRAM COOPERATIVE AGREEMENTS, *66.809*
SUPERFUND STATE, POLITICAL SUBDIVISION, AND INDIAN TRIBE SITE-SPECIFIC COOPERATIVE AGREEMENTS, *66.802*
SUPERFUND TECHNICAL ASSISTANCE GRANTS FOR CITIZEN GROUPS AT NATIONAL PRIORITY LIST (NPL) SITES, *66.806*
Superfund Worker Training Program, *93.142*
Superintendent of Documents, 40.001, 40.002
SUPERVISED VISITATION, SAFE HAVENS FOR CHILDREN [DOJ], *16.527*
Supplemental and Direct Grants, Appalachian region, *23.002*
Supplemental Educational Opportunity Grants (SEOG), *84.007*
SUPPLEMENTAL LOAN INSURANCE—MULTIFAMILY RENTAL HOUSING, *14.151*
Supplemental Loans for Students (SLS), *84.032*
SUPPLEMENTAL SECURITY INCOME, *96.006*
Supplementary Medical Insurance (SMI), *93.774*
SUPPLEMENTARY TRAINING [DOT], 20.810
SUPPORT MECHANISMS FOR DISADVANTAGED BUSINESS [DOT], *20.903*
SUPPORTED EMPLOYMENT SERVICES FOR INDIVIDUALS WITH SEVERE DISABILITIES, *84.187*
SUPPORTIVE HOUSING FOR PERSONS WITH DISABILITIES, *14.181*
SUPPORTIVE HOUSING FOR THE ELDERLY, *14.157*
SUPPORTIVE HOUSING PROGRAM, *14.235*
Surety Bond Guarantee, SBA, *59.016*
Surface mining, *see* Coal mining; Environmental management; Mining, mining industries
Surplus property, *see* Federal surplus property
Surplus Property Program, DOI, 15.918
SURPLUS PROPERTY UTILIZATION [HHS], 93.291
SURVEILLANCE OF HAZARDOUS SUBSTANCE EMERGENCY EVENTS, *93.204*
Survey of Current Business, 11.025
SURVEYS, STUDIES, INVESTIGATIONS AND SPECIAL PURPOSE ACTIVITIES RELATING TO ENVIRONMENTAL JUSTICE, *66.309*
SURVEYS, STUDIES, INVESTIGATIONS AND SPECIAL PURPOSE GRANTS [EPA], *66.606*
SURVEYS, STUDIES, INVESTIGATIONS AND SPECIAL PURPOSE GRANTS WITHIN THE OFFICE OF RESEARCH AND DEVELOPMENT [EPA], *66.510*
SURVEYS, STUDIES, INVESTIGATIONS AND SPECIAL PURPOSE GRANTS WITHIN THE OFFICE OF THE ADMINISTRATOR [EPA], *66.610*
SURVEYS, STUDIES, INVESTIGATIONS, DEMONSTRATIONS AND SPECIAL PURPOSE ACTIVITIES RELATING TO THE CLEAN AIR ACT, *66.034*
SURVEYS, STUDIES, INVESTIGATIONS, DEMONSTRATIONS AND SPECIAL PURPOSE GRANTS—SECTION 1442 OF THE SAFE DRINKING WATER ACT, *66.424*
SURVEYS, STUDIES, INVESTIGATIONS, DEMONSTRATIONS AND TRAINING GRANTS AND COOPERATIVE AGREEMENTS—SECTION 104(B)(3) OF THE CLEAN WATER ACT, *66.436*
SURVEYS, STUDIES, INVESTIGATIONS, TRAINING DEMONSTRATIONS AND EDUCATIONAL OUTREACH [EPA], *66.716*
SURVIVORS AND DEPENDENTS EDUCATIONAL ASSISTANCE [DVA], *64.117*
Survivors benefits, *see* Employee benefits; Insurance; Social Security Act; Veterans death benefits
Survivors Insurance, SSA, *96.004*
Susan Harwood Training Grants, OSHA, *17.502*
SUSTAINABLE AGRICULTURE RESEARCH AND EDUCATION, *10.215*
SVB (Special Veterans Benefits), SSA, *96.020*
SWDA (Solid Waste Disposal Act), *see* Waste treatment, disposal
SWG (State Wildlife Grants), FWS, *15.634*
Swimming pools, public, *15.916*

TAA (Trade Adjustment Assistance), EDA, *11.313*
TAA (Trade Adjustment Assistance), FAS, *10.609*
TAP (Targeted Assistance Grant), ACF, *93.584*
TAG (Technical Assistance Grant), Superfund, *66.806*
Talmadge-Aiken Act, *10.475*
TANF (Temporary Assistance for Needy Families), *93.558*
TANF (Temporary Assistance for Needy Families) projects, *see* Public assistance
TAP (Targeted Assistance Program), ACF, *93.584*
TAP (Transition Assistance Program), DOL, *17.807*
TAP (Tree Assistance Program), FSA, *10.082*
Tapes, recordings, *see* Audiovisual aids, film, video
Targeted Assistance Program (TAP), ACF, *93.584*
TARGETED WATERSHED GRANTS, *66.439*
Tariffs, *see* International commerce, investment; Trade adjustment assistance
TASC (Technical Assistance for Specialty Crops), FAS, *10.604*
TAX COUNSELING FOR THE ELDERLY, *21.006*
Taxes, tax incentives
BLM Payments in Lieu of Taxes, *15.226*
Community Renewal Tax Act of 2000, *14.244*
compensation to states, Corps of Engineers projects, *12.112*
counseling, elderly, *21.006*
credits, historic properties, *15.904*, 15.912, 15.914, 15.915
deferment, ship construction, reconstruction, *20.808*, *20.812*
Economic Recovery Tax Act of 1981, 15.914
Empowerment Zones Program, *10.772*, *14.244*
federal-state tax information exchange, 21.004
Forest Service payments, national forests, *10.665*
Forest Service payments, national grasslands, *10.666*

MASTER INDEX   1025

import duties, 11.106
IRS taxpayer services, 21.003
IRS training, volunteers, 21.003
Low-Income Taxpayer Clinics, 21.008
Revenue Act of 1978, 21.006
Revenue Sharing, Public Lands and Resources, BLM, 15.227
Tax Adjustment Act of 1966, 96.003
Tax Reform Act of 1986, 15.914, 15.915
Taxpayer Relief Act of 1997, 10.772, 14.244
TAXPAYER SERVICE, 21.003
TBI (Traumatic Brain Injury), 93.234
TDG (Television Demonstration Grants), rural, 10.769
Teacher and Administrator Program, BECA, 19.408

Teacher education, training
adult education, 84.002
aeronautics, space, 43.001
agriculture, food sciences, Hispanic-serving institutions, 10.223
agriculture, food sciences, tribal colleges, 10.221, 10.222
agriculture, international, 10.305, 10.962
agriculture, secondary, postsecondary, 10.226
AIDS prevention, 93.938
biomedical, health, minority, 93.389
civil aviation, 20.100
CNCS service-learning, 94.004
curriculum reform, OERI, 84.305
Dropout Prevention Programs, 84.360
early childhood, 84.349
Early Reading First, 84.359
Education Technology State Grants, 84.318
engineering, sciences, minority, 84.120
English Language Acquisition Grants, 84.365
English Language Fellow Program, BECA, 19.421
English Language Specialist/Speaker Program, BECA, 19.423
environmental, 66.950, 66.951
Even Start, 84.213, 84.214, 84.258
foreign languages, 84.229
foreign languages, area studies, 84.016
foreign languages, area studies abroad, 84.019, 84.022
Freely Associated States, 84.256
Fulbright-Hays international exchange, 19.401
Fulbright Program, elementary, secondary, postsecondary, 19.408
gifted and talented student instruction, 84.206
graduate academic fellowships, 84.200
group projects abroad, 84.021
Head Start, 93.600
homeless children, 84.196
humanities, 45.163
Indian children, institutionalized handicapped, 15.045
international exchange, 19.408, 84.304
international peace and conflict resolution, 91.001
interpreters for deaf, deaf-blind, 84.160
land grant institutions faculty, 10.216
language grants, NSA, 12.900
librarians, 45.313
mathematical sciences, NSA, 12.901
mathematics, sciences, 84.319
migrants, college program staff, 84.149
minority faculty development, higher education, 84.031
NEH We the People program, 45.168
NSF engineering, mathematics, sciences, 47.076
nutrition, 10.574
postsecondary education for disadvantaged, 84.103
projects, technical assistance, 84.283
Reading First, 84.357
Ready to Teach, OERI, 84.286
school civil rights compliance, 84.004
secondary, Madison fellowships, 85.500
seminars abroad, 84.018
sign language, interpreters, 84.160
special education, 84.323, 84.325, 84.326, 84.327
student loan cancellations, 84.037
teacher quality enhancement, recruitment, partnership, 84.336
teacher quality improvement, 84.367
Tech-Prep Education, 84.243
telecommunications, instructional programming, Star Schools, 84.203
Transition to Teaching, 84.350
USDA challenge grants, 10.217
vocational education, 84.051, 84.346
see also Agricultural education; Arts, arts education; Disadvantaged, education; Education *entries*; Elementary and secondary education; Environmental education; Fellowships, scholarships, traineeships; Health, medical education, training; Higher education *entries*; Humanities education, research; International programs, studies; Minority education; National Research Service Awards; Nursing; Schools *entries*; Science education; Technical training

TEACHER NEXT DOOR INITIATIVE [HUD], 14.310
TEACHER QUALITY ENHANCEMENT GRANTS, 84.336
Teacher training, *see* Teacher education, training
TEAM NUTRITION GRANTS, 10.574
TECH-PREP DEMONSTRATION GRANTS [DOED], 84.353
TECH-PREP EDUCATION, 84.243
TECHNICAL AGRICULTURAL ASSISTANCE, 10.960
TECHNICAL AND NON-FINANCIAL ASSISTANCE TO HEALTH CENTERS, 93.129
TECHNICAL AND SUPERVISORY ASSISTANCE GRANTS [USDA], 10.441
TECHNICAL ASSISTANCE AND TRAINING GRANTS [USDA], 10.761
TECHNICAL ASSISTANCE AND TRAINING INITIATIVE [DOJ], 16.526
TECHNICAL ASSISTANCE FOR SPECIALTY CROPS, 10.604
TECHNICAL ASSISTANCE TO COOPERATIVES, 10.350
Technical information, *see* Information, scientific and technical
TECHNICAL PRESERVATION SERVICES [DOI], 15.915

Technical training
agricultural products inspection, 10.163
agricultural, rural cooperatives, 10.350
air pollution control, 66.001
aviation personnel, 20.109
BLM Cultural Resource Management, 15.224
BLM firefighting assistance, 15.228
boating safety, 97.011, 97.012
business internships, Eurasian executives, scientists, 11.114
census use, 11.002, 11.004
chemical emergency planning, 66.810
College Pollworker Program, 90.400
drinking water security system training, 66.478
ecosystem management, NOAA, 11.473
elephant conservation, international, 15.620, 15.621
emergency management, home study courses, 97.027
Emergency Management Institute, 97.026, 97.028
ETA pilots, demonstrations, research, 17.261
export control, 11.150
fair housing, 14.401
flood warning systems, NOAA, 11.450
food service, school personnel, 10.574
hazardous materials handling, 20.217, 20.703, 93.142, 97.020, 97.021
highway personnel, 20.215
historic resources preservation, 15.923
historical records preservation, 89.003
home energy conservation, 93.568
homeland security activities, 97.067, 97.073
housing counselors, 10.441
housing, HUD Youthbuild Program, 14.243
housing, self-help, 10.420
independent living services personnel, 84.169
information security, NSA, 12.902
interpreters for deaf, deaf-blind, 84.160
lead-based paint hazard control, 14.900
lead-based paint removal, 66.707
mining health, safety, 17.600, 17.602
motor carrier safety, 20.217
National Center for Research, vocational education, 84.051
occupational health, safety, 17.502
pipelines inspection, 20.700
radon mitigation, 66.032
railroad safety, 20.303
rhinoceros, tiger conservation, international, 15.619
Secret Service activities, 97.015
shipboard firefighting, operations, safety, 20.810
solid waste management, 10.762, 66.808
tax counseling, 21.006
Tech-Prep Education, 84.243
toxic substances and disease registry, 93.161
transit planning, 20.514
transport security, DHS, 97.058, 97.059
transportation, public, 20.509
veterans, educational assistance, 64.120
wastewater operators, 66.467
water pollution control, 66.419
water research, 15.805
water storage, waste treatment, disposal, rural, 10.761
weights, measures, 11.606
wetlands protection, 66461

WIA Incentive Grants, 17.267
wildlife without borders programs, 15.640, 15.641
see also Apprenticeship training; Audiovisual aids, film, video; Computer products, sciences, services; Dental education, training; Disadvantaged, employment and training; Employment development, training; Environmental education; Firefighting, fire prevention, control; Health, medical education, training; Health professions; Home management; Indian education, training; Law enforcement education, training; Minority business enterprise; Police; Small business; Social services; Teacher education, training; Veterans education, training; Vocational *entries*; Women
Technological innovation, *see* Computer products, sciences, services; Small Business Innovation Research (SBIR); Technology transfer, utilization
Technology Assistance Program, disabled, OSERS, 84.224
TECHNOLOGY OPPORTUNITIES PROGRAM [USDC], 11.552
TECHNOLOGY TRANSFER [NASA], 43.002
Technology transfer, utilization
Advanced Technology Program, 11.612
agriculture, international, 10.960, 10.961
agriculture-related, SBIR, 10.212
Air Force Defense Research Sciences Program, 12.800
American Technology Preeminence Act of 1991, 11.611, 11.612, 11.650
biomass energy, 81.079
buildings research, HUD, 14.506
business internships, Eurasian executives, scientists, 11.114
coastal ecosystem management, NOAA, 11.473
Community Technology Centers, DOED, 84.341
computer sciences research, 47.070
Corps of Engineers Construction Productivity Advanced Research, 12.114
counter-terrorism technology development, DOJ, 16.565
data, trends, 17.004
disabled, assistive technology, 84.224
disabled, educational technology, 84.327
DHS Information Technology and Evaluation Program, 97.066
DOD science, technology projects, 12.910
DOE Advanced Simulation and Computing Academic Strategic Alliances Program, 81.112
DOE environmental cleanup, technology development, 81.104
education project technical assistance, 84.283
electricity delivery, energy reliability, DOE, 81.122
energy conservation, research, 81.086
energy-related, renewable resources, research, development, 81.087
energy sciences research, 81.049
foreign information access, education, 84.337
foreign language resource centers, 84.229
forestry assistance, 10.664
Fund for Rural America, 10.224
geosciences, research, 47.050

MASTER INDEX 1027

hazardous waste alternative, innovative treatment research, training, EPA, *66.813*
homeland security advanced research projects, DHS, *97.065*
homeland security technology development, DHS, *97.077*
Information Analysis Infrastructure Protection, DHS, *97.080*
Manufacturing Extension Partnership, NIST, *11.611*
manufacturing technology commercialization, *11.612*
measurement, engineering projects, *11.609*
NASA education services, 43.001
NASA Technology Transfer, 43.002
National Center for Preservation Technology and Training, *15.923*
National Technical Information Service, 11.650
NIST Congressionally-Identified Projects, *11.617*
NSF engineering, *47.041*
NSF research, *47.075*
NSF technology education reform, *47.076*
patent, trademark information, 11.900
Semiconductor Chip Protection Act of 1984, 42.008
Tech-Prep Education, *84.243*
Technology Administration Act of 1998, *11.611*
Technology Marketing Unit, small wood species, USFS, *10.674*
University-Based Homeland Security Centers, DHS, *97.061*
see also Business development; Computer products, sciences, services; Engineering *entries*; Information *entries*; Nuclear sciences, technology; Patents, trademarks, inventions; Private sector; Scientific research; Small Business Innovation Research (SBIR)
Teenagers, *see* Juvenile delinquency; Maternal, child health, welfare; Youth *entries*
TEFAP (Temporary Emergency Food Assistance Program), 10.550, *10.557*
Telecommunication, *see* Communications, telecommunications; Computer products, sciences, services
TELEHEALTH NETWORK GRANTS, *93.211*
Telephone service, *see* Communications, telecommunications; Hotlines; Public utilities
Television, *see* Radio, television
Television Demonstration Grants (TDG), rural, *10.769*
TEMPORARY ASSISTANCE FOR NEEDY FAMILIES, *93.558*
Temporary Emergency Food Assistance Program (TEFAP), 10.550, *10.557*
Tennis courts, public, *15.916*
TERO (Tribal Employment Rights Offices), *30.009*
Terrorism, anti-terrorism, *see* Civil defense
Theater, *see* Arts, arts education; Music
Thermal energy, *see* Energy *entries*
Ticket-to-Work Demonstrations, Medicaid, *93.769*
Ticket-to-Work Infrastructure Grants, Medicaid, *93.768*
TIGER (Topologically Integrated Geographic Encoding and Referencing) system, 11.003
Timber industry
  cooperative forestry assistance, *10.664*

Economic Recovery, forest-dependent communities, *10.670*
Fire Management Assistance, FEMA, *97.046*
foreign workers certification, 17.202
forest products utilization research, *10.202*
Forestry Incentives Program, nonindustrial lands, *10.064*
futures trading information, customer complaints, 78.004
Indian lands, *15.035*
disaster assistance, noninsured crops, *10.451*
research, forestry, *10.652*
resource conservation, development, *10.901*
Southeast Alaska Economic Disaster Fund, USFS, *10.671*
Wood in Transportation, USFS, *10.673*
see also Farm, nonfarm enterprises; Forestry; Woodlands
Title I, ADA, 30.011
Title I, ESEA, Basic, Concentration, and Targeted Grants, *84.010*
Title I, ESEA, Even Start, *84.213*, *84.214*, *84.258*
Title I, ESEA, migrants, *84.011*
Title I, ESEA, neglected, delinquent, *84.013*
TITLE I GRANTS TO LOCAL EDUCATIONAL AGENCIES, *84.010*
Title I, Section 2, NHA, manufactured homes, *14.110*, *14.162*
Title I, Section 2, NHA, nonresidential, residential improvement, *14.142*
Title I, Section 109, Housing and Community Development Act, 14.406
TITLE I PROGRAM FOR NEGLECTED AND DELINQUENT CHILDREN, *84.013*
Title II, ADA, 14.414
Title II, Civil Rights Act, public accommodations, 16.103
Title II Grants, Indian Child Welfare Act, *15.144*
Title II, IV, OAA, Discretionary Projects, *93.048*
Title III, HEA, Institutional Aid, *84.031*
Title III, Part B, OAA, supportive services, senior centers, *93.044*
Title III, Part C, OAA, Nutrition Services, *93.045*
Title III, Part F, OAA, preventive health services, *93.043*
Title III State Grants Program, SARA, *66.810*
Title III, Superfund training program, *97.020*
Title IV, Civil Rights Act, 16.100
Title IV, Fishermen's Contingency Fund, *11.408*
Title IV, Ryan White CARE Act Title IV, *93.153*
Title IV, TSCA, State Lead Certification Grants, *66.707*
Title IV-A, HEA, TRIO, *84.042*, *84.044*, *84.047*, *84.066*, *84.103*
Title IV-B, HEA, education loans, *84.032*
Title IV-C, HEA, work study, *84.033*
Title IV-D, SSA, child support, *93.563*
Title IV-E, SSA, Foster Care, *93.658*
TITLE V—DELINQUENCY PREVENTION PROGRAM, *16.548*
Title VI, Civil Rights Act of 1964, housing, HUD programs, 14.405
TITLE VI FEDERAL GUARANTEES FOR FINANCING TRIBAL HOUSING ACTIVITIES, *14.869*
Title VI, HEA, international studies, *84.017*

Title VI, Part A, OAA, Indian Programs, *93.047*
Title VI, Part B, OAA, Grants to Native Hawaiians, *93.047*
Title VII, Chapter 2, OAA, aging ombudsman, *93.042*
Title VII, Chapter 3, OAA, elders abuse, *93.041*
Title VII, Civil Rights Act, 16.101, 30.001, *30.002*, 30.005, *30.009*, 30.010
Title VII, ESEA, Indian education, *84.060*
Title VIII, Civil Rights Act, 16.103
Title VIII, Higher Education Amendments of 1998, *16.525*
Title VIII, Research and Training for Eastern Europe and the Independent States of the Former Soviet Union Act of 1983, *19.300*
Title IX, Education Amendments Act of 1972, HUD programs, 14.415
Title X, Civil Rights Act, Community Relations Service, 16.200
Title XI, Merchant Marine Act, *20.802*
Title XII, Merchant Marine Act, *20.803*
Title XIX, Social Security Act, Medicaid, *93.778*
TLAP (Tobacco Loss Assistance Program), FSA, *10.083*
TLIP (Tribal Landowner Incentive Program), FWS, *15.638*
TMU (Technology Marketing Unit) Biomass Grant/Assistance Program, USFS, *10.674*
TN (Team Nutrition) Training Grants, FNS, *10.574*
Tobacco
  abuse prevention, Drug-Free Schools and Communities, states, *84.186*
  cancer research, *93.393, 93.399*
  contraband cigarette control, ATF, 16.012
  Crop Insurance, *10.450*
  Fair and Equitable Tobacco Reform Act of 2004, *10.085*
  inspection, grading, 10.162
  Market News, 10.153
  market promotion, protection, 10.163
  price supports, *10.051*
  Substance Abuse Prevention and Treatment Block Grant, *93.959*
  Tobacco Loss Assistance Program, FSA, *10.083*
  Tobacco Transition Payment Program, *10.085*
  see also Agricultural commodities, stabilization; Cancer control, prevention, research; Food inspection, grading; Health, medical research; Preventive health services
TOBACCO LOSS ASSISTANCE PROGRAM, *10.083*
TOBACCO TRANSITION PAYMENT PROGRAM, *10.085*
Tongass National Forest, *10.671*
TOP (Technology Opportunities Program), NTIA, *11.552*
Topologically Integrated Geographic Encoding and Referencing System (TIGER) 11.003
Tornadoes, *see* Climate; Disaster assistance
Torture victims assistance, ACF, *93.604*
Tourism, *see* Recreation *entries*
TOXIC SUBSTANCES COMPLIANCE MONITORING COOPERATIVE AGREEMENTS, *66.701*
Toxic Substances Control Act (TSCA), *see* Toxic Substances, toxicology

Toxic Substances Control Act (TSCA) Title IV State Lead Grants, *66.707*
Toxic substances, toxicology
  alternative, innovative treatment research, training, EPA, *66.813*
  animal disease research, *10.207*
  chemical emergency planning, *66.810*
  chemicals research, training, *93.114*
  dairy products contamination, *10.053*
  enforcement, inspection, monitoring, *66.701*
  environmental health hazards research, *93.113*
  environmental health sciences research, resources, manpower development, *93.894*
  Environmental Information Exchange Network Grants, *66.608*
  environmental risks, statistical methods research, *93.115*
  EPA air pollution studies, *66.034*
  EPA building decontamination research, *66.511*
  EPA compliance capacity building, *66.709*
  EPA consolidated research, *66.511*
  EPA Performance Partnership Grants, *66.605*
  EPA State Information Grants, *66.608*
  EPA studies, special purpose assistance, *66.610*
  FDA poison control research, *93.103*
  FEMA chemical emergency planning, DOD stockpiles, *97.040*
  food safety, security monitoring, FDA, *93.448*
  Great Lakes fish consumption health effects research, *93.208*
  hazardous substances emergencies, state surveillance systems, *93.204*
  hazardous substances research, education, *93.143*
  hazardous waste sites health studies, *93.206*
  hazardous wastes, CDCP Site Specific Activities, *93.240*
  Healthy Homes Demonstration Grants, HUD, *14.901*
  lead-based paint hazard control, training, *14.900*
  lead-based paint removal training, certification, *66.707*
  Lead Outreach Grants, HUD, *14.904*
  lead poisoning prevention, *93.197*
  lead technical studies, HUD, *14.902, 14.906*
  Operation Lead Elimination Action Program, HUD, *14.903*
  pesticides enforcement program, *66.700*
  Poison Control Center Enhancement and Awareness Act, *93.253*
  Poison Control Centers, *93.253*
  pollution control surveys, studies, EPA R&D, *66.510*
  pollution prevention studies, training, outreach, *66.716*
  public health graduate traineeships, *93.964*
  radiation toxicity in cancer treatment research, *93.395*
  surveys, studies, special grants, EPA, *66.606*
  sustainable agriculture research, *10.215*
  toxic substances and disease registry, *93.161*
  Toxic Substances Control Act (TSCA), *66.032, 66.035, 66.111, 66.306, 66.308, 66.309, 66.310, 66.509, 66.510, 66.511, 66.513, 66.514, 66.515, 66.516, 66.604, 66.606, 66.609, 66.610, 66.611, 66.701, 66.707, 66.709, 66.715, 66.716, 66.717, 66.810, 66.931, 66.940*

MASTER INDEX 1029

see also Chemicals, chemistry; Environmental *entries*; Hazardous materials, waste; Pesticides; Pharmacology, pharmacy; Public safety
Toxicology, *see* Toxic substances, toxicology
Trade adjustment assistance
  antidumping duties, 11.106
  Tariff Act of 1930, 11.106
  technical assistance, *11.313*
  trade adjustment allowances, *11.313*, *17.245*
  Trade Adjustment Assistance, FAS, *10.609*
  Trade and Tariff Act of 1984, 11.106
  Unemployment Insurance, *17.225*
  Uruguay Round Agreements Act, 11.106
  worker assistance, *17.245*
  see also Employment services; International commerce, investment; Unemployment
TRADE ADJUSTMENT ASSISTANCE [USDA], *10.609*
TRADE ADJUSTMENT ASSISTANCE [USDC], *11.313*
TRADE ADJUSTMENT ASSISTANCE—WORKERS, *17.245*
Trade unions, *see* Labor unions
Trademarks, *see* Patents, trademarks, inventions
Traditional arts, *see* Arts, arts education
Traineeships, training, *see* Apprenticeship training; Employment development, training; Fellowships, scholarships, traineeships; Health, medical education, training; Health professions; Indian education, training; Law enforcement education, training; National Research Service Awards; Teacher education, training; Technical training; Veterans education, training
TRAINING AND TECHNICAL ASSISTANCE [CNCS], *94.009*
TRAINING GRANTS TO STOP ABUSE AND SEXUAL ASSAULT, *16.528*
TRAINING INTERPRETERS FOR INDIVIDUALS WHO ARE DEAF AND INDIVIDUALS WHO ARE DEAF-BLIND, *84.160*
Trains, *see* Mass transportation; Railroads
TRANSIT PLANNING AND RESEARCH, *20.514*
TRANSITION ASSISTANCE PROGRAM [DOL], *17.807*
TRANSITION TO TEACHING, *84.350*
TRANSITIONAL HOUSING ASSISTANCE FOR VICTIMS OF DOMESTIC VIOLENCE, STALKING, OR SEXUAL ASSAULT, *16.736*
Transitional Housing, homeless, *14.235*
TRANSITIONAL LIVING FOR HOMELESS YOUTH, *93.550*
Translating, translations, *see* Foreign languages; Humanities
Transplantation biology, *93.839*, *93.855*
TRANSPORT OF TRANSURANIC WASTE TO THE WASTE ISOLATION PLANT: STATES AND TRIBAL CONCERNS, PROPOSED SOLUTIONS, *81.106*
Transportation
  agricultural services, AMS, 10.167
  Alcohol Open Container Requirements, DOT, *20.607*
  biodiesel fuel use, CSREES, *10.306*
  Border Enforcement Grants, FMCSA, *20.233*
  Capital Investment Grants, FTA, *20.500*
  Census Bureau data, 11.001
  Clean School Bus USA, EPA, *66.036*
  Commercial Driver License State Programs, *20.232*
  Crash Data Improvement Program, FMCSA, *20.230*
  Delta region, *90.200*, *90.201*, *90.202*
  disabled, over-the-road buses, capital, training, *20.518*
  DOT contracts, disadvantaged, *20.903*, *20.907*
  DOT contracts, Short Term Lending Program, minority-, women- owned businesses, *20.905*
  Driving While Intoxicated, repeat offender laws, DOT, *20.608*
  EMS, children, *93.127*
  energy conservation, renewable energy outreach, training, *81.117*
  energy conservation technology research, *81.086*
  explosives detection canine teams, TSA, *97.072*
  EPA air pollution studies, *66.034*
  EPA Compliance Assistance Centers, *66.305*
  Federal-Aid Highway Program, *20.205*
  Federal Highway Act of 1921, *15.033*
  handicapped, facilities accessibility standards enforcement, design, research, training, 88.001
  hazardous wastes, *20.218*, *66.801*
  highway personnel training, fellowships, *20.215*
  highway safety data improvement, *20.603*
  Indian students, *15.044*
  Intercity Bus Security Grants, DHS, *97.057*
  Job Access—Reverse Commute, DOT, *20.516*
  motor carrier safety regulation, *20.218*
  Operation Safe Commerce, DHS, *97.058*
  port security research, development, DHS, *97.060*
  ports, intermodal information, planning, 20.801
  public, nonurbanized areas, *20.509*
  Railroad Research and Development, *20.313*
  railroad safety standards, *20.303*
  Recreational Trails Program, *20.219*
  rural facilities, *10.766*
  rural services, *10.769*
  Safe, Accountable, Feasible, and Efficient Equity Act, *20.233*
  specialized vehicle purchases, elderly, handicapped, *20.513*
  Surface Transportation Assistance Act of 1982, *20.218*
  transit planning, research, *20.514*
  Transportation Act, 20.217
  Transportation Equity Act for the 21st Century, *20.215*, *20.218*, *20.219*, *20.312*, *20.516*, *20.518*
  Truck Security Program, DHS, *97.059*
  Wood in Transportation, USFS, *10.673*
  see also Air transportation; Civil defense; Emergency assistance; Hazardous materials, waste; Highways, roads, bridges; Interstate commerce; Maritime industry; Mass transportation; Motor vehicles; Public safety; Public works; Railroads; Rescue services; Water navigation
TRANSPORTATION—CONSUMER AFFAIRS, 20.900
Transportation Security Administration (TSA), DHS, *see* Agency Index

TRANSPORTATION SERVICES [USDA], 10.167
Trauma research, 93.853, 93.859
TRAUMATIC BRAIN INJURY STATE DEMONSTRATION GRANT PROGRAM, 93.234
Treasury Department, 21.003 through 21.021
TREE ASSISTANCE PROGRAM, 10.082
Trees, see Forestry; Seedlings, seeds; Timber industry; Woodlands
TRIBAL COLLEGES AND UNIVERSITIES PROGRAM [HUD], 14.519
TRIBAL COLLEGES EDUCATION EQUITY GRANTS [USDA], 10.221
TRIBAL COLLEGES ENDOWMENT PROGRAM [USDA], 10.222
TRIBAL COURT ASSISTANCE PROGRAM, 16.608
TRIBAL COURTS, 15.029
TRIBAL COURTS—TRUST REFORM INITIATIVE, 15.147
Tribal Employment Rights Offices (TERO), 30.009
TRIBAL LANDOWNER INCENTIVE PROGRAM, 15.638
Tribal Lead Grants, EPA, 66.715
TRIBAL RECRUITMENT AND RETENTION OF HEALTH PROFESSIONALS INTO INDIAN HEALTH PROGRAMS, 93.954
TRIBAL SELF-GOVERNANCE, 15.022
TRIBAL SELF-GOVERNANCE PROGRAM: PLANNING AND NEGOTIATION COOPERATIVE AGREEMENTS AND IHS COMPACTS/FUNDING AGREEMENTS, 93.210
TRIBAL WILDLIFE GRANTS PROGRAM, 15.639
TRIBAL WORK GRANTS, 93.594
TRIBAL YOUTH PROGRAM, 16.731
TRIBALLY CONTROLLED COMMUNITY COLLEGE ENDOWMENTS, 15.028
TRIBALLY CONTROLLED POSTSECONDARY VOCATIONAL AND TECHNICAL INSTITUTIONS, 84.245
TRIO—DISSEMINATION PARTNERSHIP GRANTS [DOED], 84.344
TRIO—EDUCATIONAL OPPORTUNITY CENTERS [DOED], 84.066
TRIO—MCNAIR POST-BACCALAUREATE ACHIEVEMENT, 84.217
TRIO Staff Training, DOED, 84.103
TRIO—STUDENT SUPPORT SERVICES [DOED], 84.042
TRIO—TALENT SEARCH [DOED], 84.044
TRIO—UPWARD BOUND [DOED], 84.047
Troubled Projects, Flexible Subsidy Fund, housing, 14.164
TRUCK SECURITY PROGRAM [DHS], 97.059
Trucks, see Motor vehicles
Truman-Hobbs Act, 97.014
Truman scholarship program, 85.001
Trust Territory of the Pacific Islands, see U.S. possessions, territories
TSA (Transportation Security Administration), DHS, see Agency Index
TSCA TITLE IV STATE LEAD GRANTS CERTIFICATION OF LEAD-BASED PAINT PROFESSIONALS, 66.707

TSCA (Toxic Substances Control Act) Title IV, 66.707
TTPP (Tobacco Transition Payment Program), FSA, 10.085
Tuberculosis, see Respiratory diseases
TUBERCULOSIS DEMONSTRATION, RESEARCH, PUBLIC AND PROFESSIONAL EDUCATION, 93.947
Tuskegee University, see Land grant colleges, universities
Tutoring
 agriculture, food sciences, Hispanics, 10.223
 Delinquency Prevention Program, 16.548, 16.549
 disadvantaged college students, 84.042, 84.217
 disadvantaged youth, postsecondary preparation, 84.044, 84.047
 English Language Acquisition Grants, 84.365
 homeless children, 84.196
 Indian children, 15.130
 institutionalized neglected, delinquent children, 84.013
 Juvenile Mentoring Program, 16.726
 Learn and Serve America programs, 94.005
 Low-Income Taxpayer Clinics, 21.008
 math, engineering, science education, NOAA Colorado, 11.449
 migrant children, 84.011
 migrants, college program, 84.149
 postsecondary, adults, 84.066
 veterans, 64.120, 64.124
 see also Bilingual education, services; Disadvantaged, education; Education counseling; Illiteracy; Volunteers
TWENTY-FIRST CENTURY COMMUNITY LEARNING CENTERS, 84.287
21ST CENTURY MUSEUM PROFESSIONALS, 45.307
25 Percent Payments to States, USFS, 10.665
TWG (Tribal Wildlife Grants), FWS, 15.639
Two-Year Operating Loss Loans, Section 223(d), HUD, 14.167
TYP (Tribal Youth Program), OJJDP, 16.731

UCECD (University Centers for Excellence in Developmental Disabilities), ACF, 93.632
UCF (Urban Community Forestry), 10.675
Udall Foundation, 85.400, 85.401, 85.402
UGSP (Undergraduate Scholarship Program), NIH, 93.187
UMTA (Urban Mass Transportation Administration), see Agency Index (DOT, Federal Transit Administration)
UNACCOMPANIED ALIEN CHILDREN PROGRAM, 93.676
UNALLIED INDUSTRY PROJECTS [NOAA], 11.452
UNALLIED MANAGEMENT PROJECTS [NOAA], 11.454
UNALLIED SCIENCE PROGRAM [NOAA], 11.472
UNDERGRADUATE INTERNATIONAL STUDIES AND FOREIGN LANGUAGE PROGRAMS, 84.016
UNDERGRADUATE SCHOLARSHIP PROGRAM FOR INDIVIDUALS FROM DISADVANTAGED BACKGROUNDS [HHS], 93.187

UNDERGROUND RAILROAD EDUCATIONAL AND CULTURAL PROGRAM, *84.345*
Underground Storage Tanks (UST) Program, *66.804*
UNDERSEA RESEARCH, *11.430*
Under Secretary for Domestic Finance, Department of the Treasury, *see* Agency Index
Unemployment
 computerized job listing, *17.207*
 disasters, FEMA assistance, *97.034*
 Federal Unemployment Tax Act, *17.225*
 Food Stamps, *10.551*
 import-caused, payments, job placement, training, *17.245*
 international data, 17.004
 railroad workers, *57.001*
 research, *11.312*
 statistics, *17.002*
 Unemployment Insurance, *17.225*
 work disability insurance, *96.001*
 see also Depressed areas; Economic development; Employee benefits; Employment *entries*; Insurance; Job creation; Trade adjustment assistance
UNEMPLOYMENT INSURANCE, *17.225*
Uniform Crime Reports, 16.305
UNIFORMED SERVICES EMPLOYMENT AND REEMPLOYMENT RIGHTS, 17.803
Unions, *see* Labor unions
United Sioux Tribes Development Corporation, *15.061*
United States *listings, see* U.S. *listings*
United Tribes Technical College, *15.060*
Uniting and Strengthening America by Providing Appropriate Tools Required to Intercept and Obstruct Terrorism Act of 2001, *see* Civil defense (U.S.A. Patriot Act of 2001)
UNIVERSAL NEWBORN HEARING SCREENING, *93.251*
Universities, *see* Education *entries*; Higher education *entries*; Land grant colleges, universities
UNIVERSITIES REBUILDING AMERICAN PROGRAM—COMMUNITY DESIGN, *14.521*
University-Based Homeland Security Centers, DHS, *97.061*
UNIVERSITY CENTERS FOR EXCELLENCE IN DEVELOPMENTAL DISABILITIES EDUCATION, RESEARCH, AND SERVICE, *93.632*
UNIVERSITY COAL RESEARCH, *81.057*
UNIVERSITY REACTOR INFRASTRUCTURE AND EDUCATION SUPPORT, *81.114*
University Research Program (URP), NSA, *12.902*
UNRESOLVED INDIAN HUNTING AND FISHING RIGHTS, *15.050*
UNSOLICITED GRANT PROGRAM [USIP], *91.001*
UPPER MISSISSIPPI RIVER SYSTEM LONG TERM RESOURCE MONITORING PROGRAM, *15.978*
Upward Bound, DOED, *84.047*
URBAN AREAS SECURITY INITIATIVE, *97.008*
URBAN COMMUNITY FORESTRY PROGRAM, *10.675*

Urban counties, *see* Community development; Urban planning
Urban development, *see* Community development; Economic development; Urban planning; Urban renewal
URBAN INDIAN HEALTH SERVICES, *93.193*
Urban mass transit, transportation, *see* Mass transportation
Urban Mass Transportation Administration (UMTA), *see* Agency Index (DOT, Federal Transit Administration)
Urban parks, playgrounds
 federal surplus property, DOI, 15.918
 federal surplus real property, 39.002
 land acquisition, development, *15.916*
 Omnibus Parks and Public Lands Management Act of 1996, *15.926*
 planning, development, *15.916*
 Urban Community Forestry, *10.675*
 urban forestry, *10.652, 10.664*
 see also Community development; Public lands; Public works; Recreation; Urban planning; Urban renewal
Urban planning
 aviation research, *20.109*
 brownfield sites redevelopment, EPA, *66.814, 66.817, 66.818*
 Buffer Zone Protection Plan, DHS, *97.078*
 CDBG technical assistance program, *14.227*
 census geography, 11.003
 Census Intergovernmental Services, 11.004
 community development work-study, HUD, *14.512*
 community economic impact, military, 12.600
 defense program changes impact, *12.611, 12.612, 12.613, 12.614*
 earthquake hazards mitigation, *15.807*
 economic development, *11.302*
 flood plain data, services, 12.104
 geodetic surveys, *11.400*
 historic property preservation, 15.914, 15.915
 housing, community, economic development, research, HUD, *14.506*
 IHE outreach, HUD, *14.511*
 mass transit, *20.505, 20.507, 20.515*
 Metropolitan Medical Response System, FEMA, *97.071*
 military base re-use, *12.607*
 military/community joint land use planning, *12.610*
 neighborhood revitalization, CDBG, *14.218, 14.219, 14.228*
 parks, outdoor recreation, *15.916*
 rural resource development, *10.901*
 soil survey data, 10.903
 Universities Rebuilding America Program, Hurricanes Katrina, Rita, HUD, *14.521*
 Urban Areas Security Initiative, equipment, training, DHS, *97.008*
 Urban Community Forestry, *10.675*
 WMD, domestic preparedness, *97.004, 97.005, 97.006, 97.007*
 see also Civil defense; Community development; Disaster assistance; Economic development; Mass transportation; Military; Social sciences; Transportation; Urban renewal

Urban playgrounds, *see* Urban parks, playgrounds
Urban renewal
   brownfield projects, *14.246, 66.814, 66.817, 66.818*
   brownfield projects job training, *66.815*
   CDBG, *14.218, 14.219, 14.225, 14.228, 14.862*
   CDBG technical assistance, *14.227*
   Hispanic serving institutions assistance, HUD, *14.514*
   home purchase, rehabilitation, *14.122*
   Officer Next Door Sales Program, 14.198
   Renewal Communities, *14.244*
   rental housing construction, rehabilitation, *14.139*
   Section 108 Loan Guarantees, *14.248*
   Small Business Liability Relief and Brownfields Revitalization Act, *66.817*
   Universities Rebuilding America Program, Hurricanes Katrina, Rita, HUD, *14.521*
   see also Community development; Depressed areas; Economic development; Housing *entries*; Urban planning
Urban-Rural Economic Development, CSBG, *93.570*
Urban Search and Rescue Program (US&R), FEMA, *97.025*
Urbanized Area Formula Program, FTA, *20.507*
Urology research, *93.849*
URP (University Research Program), NSA, *12.902*
U.S. Agency for International Development (USAID), 98.001 through 98.012
U.S. Army Materiel Command, DOD, *see* Agency Index
U.S. Army Medical Command, DOD, *see* Agency Index
U.S. Coast Guard (USCG), Department of Homeland Security, *see* Agency Index
U.S. Department of Agriculture (USDA), 10.001 through 10.962
U.S. Department of Commerce (USDC), 11.001 through 11.900
U.S. Employment Service, 17.202, 17.203, *17.207, 17.225,* 17.252
U.S. Export-Import Bank, 11.108
U.S. Fire Administration, FEMA, *see* Agency Index
U.S. Fish and Wildlife Service, DOI, *see* Agency Index
U.S. Geological Survey, *see* Agency Index (DOI, Geological Survey)
U.S. GEOLOGICAL SURVEY—RESEARCH AND DATA ACQUISITION, *15.808*
U.S. Government Printing Office, *see* Government Printing Office
U.S. Housing Act of 1937, *see* National housing acts
U.S. Information Agency (USIA), *see* Agency Index (Department of State, Bureau of Educational and Cultural Affairs)
U.S. Institute of Peace (USIP), 91.001 through 91.002
U.S. Merchant Marine, *20.806, 20.807,* 20.810, 64.115, *64.202*
U.S. MERCHANT MARINE ACADEMY, *20.807*
U.S. possessions, territories
   Act of February 20, 1929, *15.875*
   agriculture, food sciences education, CSREES, *10.308*
   bilingual, bicultural health demonstrations, *93.105*
   community development grants, *14.225*
   disaster housing, remote, insular area residents, FEMA, *97.048*
   economic, political, social development, *15.875*
   education grants, Freely Associated States, *84.256*
   Federal-Aid Highway Program, *20.205*
   health services disparities projects, *93.100*
   HIV/AIDS, HHS demonstration program, *93.006*
   maintenance assistance, disabled, Guam, Puerto Rico, Virgin Islands, *93.560*
   Medicare transitional drug assistance program, *93.782*
   native American language preservation, *93.587*
   Pacific Fisheries Data Program, *11.437*
   social, economic self-sufficiency development, *93.612*
   see also Government; Puerto Rico
U.S. REFUGEE ADMISSIONS PROGRAM, *19.510*
U.S. REPATRIATION [HHS], *93.579*
U.S. Secret Service, Department of Homeland Security, *see* Agency Index
U.S. Virgin Islands, *see* U.S. possessions, territories
U.S.A. Freedom Corps, HHS, *93.008*
U.S.A. Patriot Act of 2001, *see* Civil defense
USAID (U.S. Agency for International Development), 98.001 through 98.012
USAID DEVELOPMENT PARTNERSHIPS FOR UNIVERSITY COOPERATION AND DEVELOPMENT, *98.012*
USAID FOREIGN ASSISTANCE FOR PROGRAMS OVERSEAS, *98.001*
USCG (U.S. Coast Guard), Department of Homeland Security, *see* Agency Index
USDA (U.S. Department of Agriculture), 10.001 through 10.962
USDC (U.S. Department of Commerce), 11.001 through 11.900
USED ENERGY-RELATED LABORATORY EQUIPMENT GRANTS, 81.022
USGS (U.S. Geological Survey), *see* Agency Index (DOI, Geological Survey)
USGS Cooperative Research Units Program, *15.812*
USGS Gap Analysis Program, *15.811*
USIA (U.S. Information Agency), *see* Agency Index (Department of State, Bureau of Educational and Cultural Affairs)
USIP (U.S. Institute of Peace), 91.001 through 91.002
US&R (Urban Search & Rescue) Program, FEMA, *97.025*
UST (Underground Storage Tanks) Program, *66.804*
Utilities, *see* Public utilities

VA Home Loans, *64.114*
VA HOMELESS PROVIDERS GRANT AND PER DIEM PROGRAM, *64.024*
VA Native American Veterans Housing Loan Program, *64.126*
VA (Veterans Administration), *see* Department of Veterans Affairs (DVA)
Vaccines for Children Program (VCF), *93.268*
VALUE-ADDED PRODUCER GRANTS [USDA], *10.352*
VAPG (Value-Added Producer Grants), RBCS-USDA, *10.352*
Vascular diseases research, *93.837*

MASTER INDEX 1033

VBOP (Veterans Business Outreach Centers), SBA, *59.044*
VCCLEA (Violent Crime Control and Law Enforcement Act), *see* Crime
VCF (Vaccines for Children), *93.268*

Vegetables
Crop Insurance, *10.450*
disaster assistance, noninsured crops, *10.451*
Extension Service, *10.500*
Fresh Fruit and Vegetable Program, FNS, *10.582*
inspection, grading, 10.162
Market News, 10.153
market promotion, protection, 10.163
marketing agreements, orders, 10.155
plant disease control, *10.025*
unfair marketing practices, 10.165
see also Agricultural commodities, stabilization; Agricultural experiment stations; Agricultural marketing; Agricultural research; Food inspection, grading; Plants; Seedlings, seeds

Venereal diseases, *see* AIDS (Acquired Immune Deficiency Syndrome); Communicable diseases; Disease control; Preventive health services
VERY LOW-INCOME HOUSING REPAIR LOANS AND GRANTS [USDA], *10.417*
VERY LOW TO MODERATE INCOME HOUSING LOANS [USDA], *10.410*
VESSEL HULL DESIGN PROTECTION SERVICE, 42.009
Veterans Administration, *see* Department of Veterans Affairs
Veterans Benefits Administration, DVA, *see* Agency Index
Veterans Business Outreach Program (VBOP), SBA, *59.044*
VETERANS COMPENSATION FOR SERVICE-CONNECTED DISABILITY, *64.109*

Veterans death benefits
burial allowance, *64.101*
Dependency and Indemnity Compensation (DIC), *64.110*
educational assistance, surviving spouse, dependents, *64.117*
headstones, grave markers, *64.202*
home loans, surviving spouse, *64.114*
housing loans, native American survivors, *64.126*
information, personal assistance, 64.115
life, mortgage protection insurance, *64.103*
National Cemeteries Act of 1973, 64.201, *64.202*
national cemeteries interment, veterans, dependents, 64.201
pensions for surviving spouses, children, *64.105*
state cemeteries, construction, expansion, *64.203*
surviving spouse, dependents, *64.102, 64.109, 64.110,* 64119
Veterans' Disability Compensation and Survivors' Benefits Act of 1978, *64.202*
Veterans' Housing Benefits Act of 1978, *64.203*
VETERANS DENTAL CARE, 64.011
VETERANS DEPENDENCY AND INDEMNITY COMPENSATION FOR SERVICE-CONNECTED DEATH, *64.110*

Veterans, disabled
apprenticeships, *17.801*
automobiles, adaptive equipment, 64.013, *64.100*
blind veterans rehabilitation, 64.007
compensation for service-connected disability, *64.109*
day health care, state, *64.026*
Disabled Veterans Outreach Program (DVOP), *17.801*
domiciliary care, 64.008, *64.014*
education assistance, spouse, children, *64.117*
employment counseling, training, *17.801, 17.802*
federal employment, 27.002, 27.005
housing, specially adapted, *64.106, 64.118*
information and assistance, 64.115
life, mortgage insurance, *64.103*
pension, *64.104*
prosthetic appliances, services, 64.013
Veterans Rehabilitation and Education Amendments of 1980, *17.801, 64.116*
vocational rehabilitation, counseling, training, loans, *64.116*
wheelchairs, adaptive equipment, 64.013
see also Disabled, handicapped *entries*; Veterans *entries*; Vocational rehabilitation; Volunteers
VETERANS DOMICILIARY CARE, 64.008

Veterans education, training
counseling, 64.125
Department of Defense Authorization Act of 1985, *64.124*
dependents, disabled, deceased, missing-in-action, *64.117*
disabled, vocational training, allowances, *64.116*
education assistance payments, *64.124*
Montgomery GI Bill, *64.124*
post-Vietnam era veterans, *64.120*
Upward Bound, *84.047*
Voluntary-Contributory Matching Program, *64.120*
see also Education *entries*; Higher education *entries*; Military; Technical training; Vocational *entries*

Veterans employment
counseling, 64.125
dependents employment preference, 27.002
disabled, adjustment allowance, *64.116*
disabled, outreach, state agencies, *17.801*
employment, reemployment rights, military examinees, rejectees, National Guard members, reservists, 17.803
federal contracts, 17.301
Federal Employees and Ex-Service Members Act, *17.225*
federal employment, 17.806, 27.001, 27.002
homeless veterans reintegration, *17.805*
information, personal assistance, 64.115
local employment representatives, *17.804*
LVER Program, *17.804*
Servicemen's Readjustment Act, *17.804*
training, employment services, *17.802, 64.116*
Transition Assistance Program, DOL, *17.807*
unemployed disabled veterans pension, *64.104,*
Unemployment Insurance, *17.225*
U.S. Employment Service, *17.207*
Veterans Education and Employment Programs Amendments, 64.125
Veterans Preference Act of 1944, 17.806, 27.002
Vietnam Era Veterans Readjustment Assistance Act of 1974, 17.301
see also Employment *entries*; Veterans education, training

VETERANS' EMPLOYMENT PROGRAM, *17.802*
VETERANS ENTREPRENEURIAL TRAINING AND COUNSELING, *59.044*
Veterans Health Administration, DVA, *see* Agency Index
Veterans health, medical services
day health care, state, *64.026*
dental services, 64.011
dependents, survivors, 64.009
domiciliary care, 64.008, *64.014*
domiciliary, nursing home, hospital construction, state, *64.005*
home care, 64.022
home health services, 64.009
homeless, mental health, social services, CMHS, *93.150*
hospital care, state, *64.016*
information, personal assistance, 64.115
medical, dental services, 64.009
mental health services, 64.009
nursing home care, 64.010
nursing home care, states, *64.015*
optometric services, 64.009
podiatric services, 64.009
prescription services, veterans, dependents, survivors, 64.012
prosthetic appliances, 64.009
Sharing Contracts (Exchange of Use or Mutual Use), 64.018
specialized medical resources sharing, 64.018
spina bifida, veterans dependents, *64.127*, *64.128*
substance abuse dependency, rehabilitation, 64.019
transportation for medical services, 64.009
see also Health, medical services; Veterans, disabled; Veterans specialized services
VETERANS HOME BASED PRIMARY CARE, 64.022
Veterans housing
condominium loans, *64.114*
construction, purchase, improvement, repair loans, *64.114*
disabled, specially adapted, *64.106*, *64.118*
information, personal assistance, 64.115
manufactured home loans, *64.114*, *64.119*
mortgage protection life insurance, *64.103*
native Americans, *64.126*
refinancing mortgages, liens, *64.114*
surviving spouse home loans, *64.114*
weatherization, *64.114*
see also Housing *entries*; Veterans specialized services
VETERANS HOUSING—DIRECT LOANS FOR CERTAIN DISABLED VETERANS, *64.118*
VETERANS HOUSING—GUARANTEED AND INSURED LOANS, *64.114*
VETERANS HOUSING—MANUFACTURED HOME LOANS, *64.119*
VETERANS INFORMATION AND ASSISTANCE, 64.115
Veterans interment, *see* Veterans death benefits
VETERANS MEDICAL CARE BENEFITS, 64.009
VETERANS NURSING HOME CARE, 64.010
Veterans Preference Act of 1944, 17.806
VETERANS' PREFERENCE IN FEDERAL EMPLOYMENT, 17.806

VETERANS PRESCRIPTION SERVICE, 64.012
VETERANS PROSTHETIC APPLIANCES, 64.013
VETERANS REHABILITATION—ALCOHOL AND DRUG DEPENDENCE, 64.019
Veterans Services, 64.115
Veterans specialized services
automobiles, adaptive equipment, *64.100*
blindness, rehabilitation, 64.007
day health care, state, *64.026*
disabled, rehabilitation, 64.008
disabled, vocational counseling, training, allowances, *64.116*
DOD property donations, loans, 12.700
domiciliary care, 64.008, *64.014*
entrepreneurial training, *59.044*
home care, 64.022
homeless, DVA provider grants, *64.024*
Homeless Veterans Comprehensive Service Programs Act of 1992, *64.024*
information, personal assistance, 64.115
prosthetics use training, 64.013
Special Veterans Benefits, SSI expatriate beneficiaries, *96.020*
spina bifida, veterans dependents, *64.127*, *64.128*
substance abuse, dependency, group, family therapy, 64.019
veterans organizations, DOD surplus property donations, 12.700
see also Social services; Veterans *entries*; Volunteers
VETERANS STATE ADULT DAY HEALTH CARE, *64.026*
VETERANS STATE DOMICILIARY CARE, *64.014*
VETERANS STATE HOSPITAL CARE, *64.016*
VETERANS STATE NURSING HOME CARE, *64.015*
Veterans' Workforce Investment Program (VWIP), DOL, *17.802*
Veterinary medicine
animal disease control, *10.025*
animal health research, *10.207*
education assistance, disadvantaged, *93.342*, *93.822*, *93.925*
faculty education loan repayments, disadvantaged, *93.923*
FDA drug research, *93.103*
international research, *10.960*
Minority Scholars Program, *10.220*
NIH research training, *93.140*
Ruminant Feed Ban Support Project, FDA, *93.449*
USDA research grants, competitive, *10.206*
see also Animal disease control, health, welfare; Health, medical research; Health professions; Laboratory animals
Victim assistance
asylees, *93.604*
Anti-Terrorism and Emergency Assistance Program, DOJ, *16.321*
campus crime grants, *16.525*
child abuse, *16.547*, *93.669*
child abuse, closed-circuit TV, DOJ, *16.611*
child abuse prevention, treatment services, research, technical assistance, *93.670*
child abuse, prosecution, family services, *93.643*
children, emergency medical services, *93.127*

children, missing, *16.543*
children's violence exposure prevention initiative, Safe Start, *16.730*
community-based child abuse prevention, *93.590*
compensation, *16.576*
crime victims, *16.575*
Crisis Counseling Assistance and Training Act, *97.032*
disabled, elder abuse, sexual assault prevention training, OJP, *16.528*
disaster housing, remote, insular area residents, FEMA, *97.048*
Disaster Legal Services, *97.033*
Disaster Unemployment Assistance, FEMA, *97.034*
disasters, assistance to individuals, households, FEMA, *97.050*
disasters, Cora Brown Fund, *97.031*
disasters, Crisis Counseling, *97.032*
disasters, housing rental assistance, FEMA, *97.049*
disasters, search, rescue system, *97.025*
discretionary grants, training, DOJ, *16.582*
domestic violence, *16.524*
domestic violence, stalking, transitional housing, *16.736*
Elder Abuse Prevention, *93.041*
emergency food, shelter, FEMA, *97.024*
Family Life Centers, violence prevention, *93.910*
family violence, *93.591, 93.592, 93.671*
Food Stamps, *10.551*
Hurricane Katrina Case Management Initiative, *97.084*
Indian children, *16.583*
Indian women, violence, *16.587*
International Terrorism Victim Assistance Expense Reimbursement Program, DOJ, *16.321*
9/11 Heroes Stamp Program, DHS, *97.085*
prison rape elimination, personnel training, victim services, *16.735*
public safety officers, disability, death benefits, *16.571*
refugees, trafficking, *93.566, 93.583*
rural domestic violence, *16.589*
Services for Trafficking Victims, *16.320*
sex offense victims, block grant, *93.991*
Social Services Block Grant, *93.667*
Supervised Visitation, Safe Havens for Children, OJP, *16.527*
terrorism, hospitals preparedness, *93.889*
Torture Victims Relief Act of 1998, *93.604*
trafficking victims assistance, ACF, *93.584, 93.598*
victim notification systems, *16.740*
Victims of Child Abuse Act of 1990, *16.547, 16.611*
Victims of Crime Act (VOCA), *16.321, 16.575, 16.576, 16.582, 16.583, 93.643*
Victims of Trafficking and Violence Prevention Act of 2000 (VTVPA), *16.320, 16.527, 16.528, 16.529, 16.575, 16.576, 16.582, 16.583, 93.584, 93.591, 93.592, 93.598, 93.671*
violence prevention research, *93.136*
women, violence services, prosecution, *16.588*
women violence victims advocacy, technical assistance, training, OJP, *16.526*
Women with Disabilities, OJP, *16.529*

youth, homeless, runaway, sexual abuse, *93.557*
see also Civil defense; Civil rights; Disabled, handicapped; Disaster assistance; Emergency assistance; Homeless persons; Legal services; Maternal, child health, welfare; Missing persons; Rescue services; Sexual abuse; Social services; Volunteers
Victims of a Severe Form of Trafficking, assistance, ACF, *93.598*
VICTIMS OF CHILD ABUSE, *16.547*
Victims of Crime Act (VOCA), *see* Victim assistance
Victims of Trafficking and Violence Prevention Act of 2000 (VTVPA), *see* Victim assistance
Video, *see* Audiovisual aids, film, video; Radio, television
Vietnam veterans, *see* Veterans *entries*
VIOLENCE AGAINST WOMEN DISCRETIONARY GRANTS FOR INDIAN TRIBAL GOVERNMENTS, *16.587*
VIOLENCE AGAINST WOMEN FORMULA GRANTS, *16.588*
Violent Crime Control and Law Enforcement Act (VCCLEA), *see* Crime
VIOLENT OFFENDER INCARCERATION AND TRUTH IN SENTENCING INCENTIVE GRANTS, *16.586*
Virgin Islands, *see* U.S. possessions, territories
VISION RESEARCH, *93.867*
VISTA (Volunteers in Service to America), *84.037,* 94.013
Visual disorders, *see* Blindness and the blind; Health, medical research
VITAL STATISTICS RE-ENGINEERING PROGRAM [HHS], *93.066*
VOCA (Victims of Crime Act), *see* Victim Assistance
VOCATIONAL AND EDUCATIONAL COUNSELING FOR SERVICEMEMBERS AND VETERANS, 64.125
Vocational education
Appalachian region, *23.002*
basic grants, *84.048*
Carl D. Perkins Vocational and Applied Technology Education Act (CDPVATEA), *17.267, 84.048, 84.051, 84.101, 84.243, 84.245, 84.259, 84.346, 84.353*
Community Technology Centers, DOED, *84.341*
Federal Direct Student Loans, *84.268*
federal surplus real property transfer, 84.145
Hawaii natives, *84.259*
incarcerated youth, *84.331*
Indian tribal, *84.101, 84.245*
Indians, *15.108*
Indians, United Tribes Technical College, *15.060*
ironworkers, native Americans, *15.146*
migrant youth, *84.011, 84.141*
National Center for Research, *84.051*
Occupational and Employment Information, DOED, *84.346*
Pell grants, *84.063*
Perkins loans, *84.038*
program improvement, planning, evaluation, research, training, *84.051*
refugees, entrants, *93.576, 93.584*
student loans, *84.032*

Vocational education *(continued)*
   substance abuse treatment, prisoners, DOJ, *16.593*
   Supplemental Educational Opportunity Grants (SEOG), *84.007*
   Tech-Prep Demonstration Grants, *84.353*
   Tech-Prep Education, *84.243*
   telecommunications, instructional programming, Star Schools, *84.203*
   veterans, counseling, 64.125
   veterans, educational assistance, *64.120*
   veterans, payments, *64.124*
   WIA Incentive Grants, *17.267*
   Women's Educational Equity Act Program, *84.083*
   work-study program, *84.033*
   see also Adult education; Apprenticeship training; Employment development, training; Education facilities *entries*; Employment *entries*; Indian education, training; Technical training; Tutoring; Veterans education, training; Vocational rehabilitation
VOCATIONAL EDUCATION—BASIC GRANTS TO STATES, *84.048*
VOCATIONAL EDUCATION—INDIANS SET-ASIDE, *84.101*
VOCATIONAL EDUCATION—NATIONAL PROGRAMS, *84.051*
VOCATIONAL EDUCATION— OCCUPATIONAL AND EMPLOYMENT INFORMATION STATE GRANTS, *84.346*
Vocational rehabilitation
   assistive technology, *84.224*
   assistive technology protection, advocacy, *84.343*
   basic support, facilities, services, *84.126*
   blind elderly, independent living, *84.177*
   Client Assistance Program, benefits, services information, *84.161*
   developmental disabilities, university centers personnel training, *93.632*
   disabilities prevention, *93.184*
   federal employment coordination, 27.005
   federal surplus real property transfer, 84.145, 93.291
   independent living centers, *84.132*
   independent living services personnel training, *84.169*
   Indian children, *15.045*
   Indians, *84.250*
   NIH Vision Research, *93.867*
   personnel recruitment, training, minority students, *84.315*
   personnel training, *84.246, 84.263, 84.264, 84.265, 84.275*
   personnel training scholarships, *84.129*
   Projects with Industry, *84.234*
   Rehabilitation Act of 1973, 14.404, 16.103, 17.301, 27.005, *84.126, 84.128, 84.129, 84.132, 84.133, 84.160, 84.161, 84.169, 84.177, 84.187, 84.234, 84.235, 84.240, 84.246, 84.250, 84.263, 84.264, 84.265, 84.275, 84.315*, 88.001
   research, personnel fellowships, *84.133*
   service projects, *84.128*
   severely handicapped, supported employment, *84.187*
   Social Security payments, *96.001*
   special services, *84.235*
   spina bifida cases, veterans' dependents, *64.128*
   SSA disabled beneficiaries outreach, services, *96.009*
   veterans benefits information, assistance, 64.115
   veterans, disabled, counseling, job placement, allowances, *64.116*
   veterans, substance abuse dependency, 64.019
   Work Incentives Grants, *17.266*
   see also Disabled, handicapped, employment; Health, medical research; Mental health; Mental retardation; Veterans, disabled; Vocational education; Volunteers
VOCATIONAL REHABILITATION FOR DISABLED VETERANS, *64.116*
VOCATIONAL TRAINING AND REHABILITATION FOR VIETNAM VETERANS' CHILDREN WITH SPINA BIFIDA AND OTHER COVERED BIRTH DEFECTS, *64.128*
Volcanoes, *see* Disaster assistance; Geology
Voluntary-Contributory Matching Program, DVA, *64.120*
VOLUNTARY PUBLIC SCHOOL CHOICE, *84.361*
Volunteers
   AmeriCorps, *94.006*
   AmeriCorps Education Awards, Martin Luther King Day of Service awards, *94.007*
   business management expertise, 59.005, *59.026*
   Citizen Corps, DHS, *97.053*
   Citizen Corps, HHS, *93.008*
   Coast Guard Auxiliary, 97.011
   Domestic Volunteer Service Act of 1973, *94.002, 94.011*, 94.013, *94.016*
   Foster Grandparent Program, *94.011*
   immunization programs, *93.268*
   juvenile delinquency programs, training, *16.542*
   Juvenile Mentoring Program, *16.726*
   Learn and Serve America programs, *94.004, 94.005*
   Retired and Senior Volunteer Program (RSVP), *94.002*
   Senior Companion Program (SCP), *94.016*
   Service Corps of Retired Executives (SCORE), 59.005, *59.026*
   tax counseling, 21.003, *21.006*
   VISTA program, 94.013
   VISTA, Peace Corps volunteers student loan cancellations, *84.037*
   see also AmeriCorps; Private sector; Social services
VOLUNTEERS IN SERVICE TO AMERICA (VISTA), 94.013
Voting, *see* Civil rights; Government
VOTING ACCESS FOR INDIVIDUALS WITH DISABILITIES—GRANTS FOR PROTECTION AND ADVOCACY SYSTEMS, *93.618*
VOTING ACCESS FOR INDIVIDUALS WITH DISABILITIES—GRANTS TO STATES AND LOCAL GOVERNMENTS, *93.617*
Voting Rights Act, 16.104
Voucher Program, housing, *14.871*
Voucher Program, substance abuse, *93.275*
VTVPA (Victims of Trafficking and Violence Prevention Act of 2000), *see* Victim assistance

MASTER INDEX 1037

VWIP (Veterans' Workforce Investment Program), DOL, *17.802*

W.E.B. Dubois fellowships, DOJ, *16.566*
WAGE AND HOUR STANDARDS, 17.303
Wages, salaries, *see* Employee benefits; Labor standards
Wagner-Peyser Act, *see* Employment services
Waste Isolation Pilot Plant (WIPP), DOE, *81.106*
Waste treatment, disposal
  Appalachian region, *23.001*
  Clean Vessel Act, pumpout/dump stations, *15.616*
  Compliance Assistance Centers, EPA, *66.305*
  construction, EDA projects, *11.300*
  construction, EPA projects, *66.418*
  Delta region, *90.200, 90.201, 90.202*
  Environmental Information Exchange Network Grants, *66.608*
  EPA consolidated program support, *66.600*
  EPA environmental sustainability design competition, *66.516*
  federal surplus property utilization, 93.291
  HUD community development grants, *14.218, 14.219*
  Indian housing, HIP, *15.141*
  industrial energy conservation, waste reduction, DOE, *81.105*
  industrial separation processes, DOE research, *81.086*
  integrated systems, municipal, *66.808*
  rural systems, *10.760, 10.770*
  rural systems, housing programs, *10.417*
  rural water, wastewater projects revolving loan funds, *10.864*
  Solid Waste Disposal Act (SWDA), *15.041, 66.035, 66.111, 66.305, 66.306, 66.307, 66.308, 66.309, 66.310, 66.509, 66.510, 66.511, 66.600, 66.604, 66.606, 66.608, 66.609, 66.610, 66.611, 66.709, 66.717, 66.801, 66.804, 66.805, 66.808, 66.816, 66.931, 66.940, 66.952*
  solid waste energy conversion, *81.079, 81.087*
  solid waste management, rural, *10.762*
  Superfund clean-up, *66.802*
  technical assistance, training, rural, *10.761*
  toxic substances and disease registry, *93.161*
  U.S. insular areas, *15.875*
  wastewater operator technical assistance, training, *66.467*
  wastewater, revolving fund, *66.458*
  watershed, river basin projects, 10.906
  see also Environmental management; Hazardous materials, waste; Public works; Sewage facilities, treatment; Toxic substances, toxicology; Water systems, treatment
WASTEWATER OPERATOR TRAINING GRANT PROGRAM (TECHNICAL ASSISTANCE), *66.467*
Watch Your Car program, *16.597*
WATER AND WASTE DISPOSAL LOANS AND GRANTS, *10.770*
WATER AND WASTE DISPOSAL SYSTEMS FOR RURAL COMMUNITIES, *10.760*
WATER BANK PROGRAM, *10.062*
Water conservation
  Agricultural Management Assistance, NRCS, *10.917*
  agricultural, reserve, *10.069*
  Conservation Security Program, NRCS, *10.921*
  emergency farmland rehabilitation, *10.054*
  Environmental Quality Incentives Program-Klamath Basin, NRCS, *10.919*
  Environmental Quality Incentives Program, NRCS, *10.912*
  EPA environmental sustainability design competition, *66.516*
  Farm and Ranch Lands Protection Program, NRCS, *10.913*
  Great Plains, *10.900*
  ground, surface water quality incentives program, NRCS, *10.918*
  plants, use in conservation, 10.905
  reclamation, reuse, *15.504*
  rural resource conservation, development, *10.901*
  state planning assistance, 12.110
  technical assistance, NRCS, 10.902
  Water 2025 Challenge Grants, western states, DOI, *15.507*
  watershed projects, *10.904*
  watershed, river basin projects, 10.906
  wetlands preservation, Water Bank Program, *10.062*
  see also Agricultural conservation; Environmental management; Estuaries; Irrigation; Soil conservation; Water *entries*; Wetlands; Wildlife, waterfowl
WATER DESALINATION RESEARCH AND DEVELOPMENT PROGRAM, *15.506*
Water management, *see* Water resources, supply, management
Water navigation
  aquatic plant control, 12.100
  Boating Infrastructure Grant Program, *15.622*
  boating safety, 97.011
  Bridge Alteration, USCG, 97.014
  channel clearance, 12.109
  Clean Vessel Act, pumpout/dump stations, *15.616*
  compensation to states, Corps of Engineers projects, *12.112*
  emergency dredging, 12.109
  flood control snagging, clearing, 12.108
  insurance, ships, war risk, *20.803*
  National Maritime Heritage Grants, NPS, *15.925*
  port facilities construction, EDA projects, *11.300*
  port, intermodal development information, planning, 20.801
  port security grants, DHS, *97.056*
  River and Harbor Acts, 12.100, 12.101, 12.107, 12.109, 97.014
  ship construction, reconstruction financing, *20.802*
  Small Navigation Projects, 12.107
  Upper Mississippi River Management Act of 1986, *15.978*
  see also Coastal zone; Fisheries industry; Maritime industry; Public works; Recreation, water
Water pollution abatement, prevention
  biometry, risk estimation, NIEHS, *93.115*
  Chesapeake Bay Program, *66.466*
  Clean Vessel Act, pumpout/dump stations, *15.616*
  Clean Water Act (CWA), *66.035, 66.110, 66.111, 66.306, 66.307, 66.308, 66.309, 66.310, 66.418, 66.419, 66.436, 66.437, 66.439,*

Water pollution abatement, prevention
(continued)
    66.454, 66.456, 66.458, 66.460, 66.461, 66.462, 66.463, 66.466, 66.469, 66.472, 66.475, 66.479, 66.480, 66.481, 66.509, 66.510, 66.511, 66.512, 66.513, 66.514, 66.515, 66.516, 66.600, 66.604, 66.606, 66.609, 66.610, 66.611, 66.709, 66.717, 66.931, 66.940, 66.952
Colorado River basin, *10.070*
control, enforcement, training, *66.419*
control surveys, studies, EPA R&D, *66.510*
emergency rural systems, *10.763*
EPA consolidated program support, *66.600*
EPA consolidated research, *66.511*
EPA environmental sustainability design competition, *66.516*
EPA Nonpoint Source Implementation Grants, *66.460*
EPA Performance Partnership Grants, *66.605*
EPA studies, special purpose assistance, *66.610*
estuary protection, *66.456*
Federal Water Pollution Control Act, *66.467*
Great Lakes, *66.469*
Gulf of Mexico Program, EPA, *66.475*
Lake Champlain Basin Program, EPA, *66.481*
Long Island Sound Program, *66.437*
management planning, *66.454*
mine land reclamation, *10.910*
oil spill trust fund, USCG, 97.013
Pesticide Environmental Stewardship, *66.714*
pollution prevention information projects, *66.708*
reclamation, reuse, *15.504*
Reclamation Wastewater and Groundwater Study and Facilities Act, *15.504*
research, *15.805*
Safe Drinking Water Act (SDWA), *10.763, 66.035, 66.036, 66.110, 66.111, 66.306, 66.307, 66.308, 66.309, 66.310, 66.424, 66.432, 66.433, 66.468, 66.471, 66.478, 66.509, 66.510, 66.511, 66.513, 66.514, 66.515, 66.516, 66.600, 66.604, 66.606, 66.609, 66.610, 66.611, 66.709, 66.717, 66.931, 66.952*
Salinity Control Act of 1974, *10.070*
solid waste management, rural, *10.762*
Section 106 Grants, *66.419*
source, drinking water studies, *66.424*
State Public Water System Supervision, *66.432*
state revolving funds, *66.468*
surveys, studies, special grants, EPA, *66.606*
Targeted Watershed Grants, *66.439*
technical assistance, training, rural personnel, *10.761*
underground injection control, *66.433*
wastewater operator technical assistance, training, *66.467*
wastewater treatment works construction, *66.418*
Water Desalination Act of 1996, *15.506*
Water Quality Act of 1987, *66.454, 66.458*
Water Quality Cooperative Agreements, *66.463*
watershed protection research, studies, training, *66.480*
watershed, river basin projects, 10.906
wetlands, *66.461, 66.462*
see also Agricultural conservation; Coastal zone; Environmental *entries*; Pollution abatement; Public works; Waste treatment, disposal; Water *entries*; Wetlands
WATER POLLUTION CONTROL STATE AND INTERSTATE PROGRAM SUPPORT, *66.419*
WATER PROTECTION GRANTS TO THE STATES, *66.474*
Water quality, *see* Water *entries*
WATER QUALITY COOPERATIVE AGREEMENTS, *66.463*
WATER QUALITY MANAGEMENT PLANNING, *66.454*
WATER RECLAMATION AND REUSE PROGRAM, *15.504*
Water Research Institute Program, *15.805*
WATER RESOURCES ON INDIAN LANDS, *15.037*

Water resources, supply, management
Acid Mine Drainage (AMD), *15.253*
Agricultural Management Assistance, NRCS, *10.917*
agricultural, research, *10.200*
agricultural sciences, graduate fellowships, *10.210*
Applied Meteorology Research, *11.468*
Clean Water Act studies, training, *66.436*
climate monitoring, *11.428*
Coastal Program, FWS, *15.630*
Colorado River basin salinity control, *10.070*
dam safety program, FEMA, *97.041*
Desert Terminal Lakes, supply, DOI, *15.508*
desalination research, development, *15.506*
DOI Summer Watershed Intern, *15.254*
drainage basins, state planning assistance, 12.110
Environmental Information Exchange Network Grants, *66.608*
EPA consolidated research, *66.511*
farms, *10.407*
farms, loan interest subsidies, *10.437*
Gulf of Mexico Program, EPA, *66.475*
Household Water Well System Program, RUS, *10.862*
hydrology, research, *11.462, 15.808*
Hydrometeorological Development, NOAA, *11.467*
Indian lands, *15.037*
international research exchanges, *10.961*
Lake Champlain Basin Program, EPA, *66.481*
PL-566 Program, *10.904,* 10.906
pollution control surveys, studies, EPA R&D, *66.510*
quality management planning, *66.454*
research, forestry, *10.202*
rural, emergency systems, *10.763*
rural housing, *10.410*
rural housing site loans, *10.411*
rural resource conservation, development, *10.901*
rural water, wastewater projects revolving loan funds, *10.864*
Safe Drinking Water Act enforcement, *66.432, 66.433*
Section 22, 12.110
small systems operators certification, *66.471*
snowmelt surveys, 10.907
source, drinking water studies, *66.424*
STAR (Science to Achieve Results) Research Program, EPA, *66.509*
state revolving funds, *66.468*

MASTER INDEX 1039

Targeted Watershed Grants, *66.439*
terrorism protection coordination, planning, *66.474*
wastewater, revolving fund, *66.458*
Water Research Institute Program, *15.805*
Water Resources Development Acts, 12.110, *12.114*, *97.041*
Water Resources Research Act of 1984, *15.805*
Water 2025 Challenge Grants, western states, DOI, *15.507*
watershed management research, *10.652*
watershed protection research, studies, training, *66.480*
watershed projects, *10.904*
Watershed Protection and Flood Prevention Act, *10.904*, 10.906, *10.916*
Watershed Rehabilitation Program, *10.916*
watershed, river basin projects, 10.906
see also Coastal zone; Environmental management; Estuaries; Fish; Flood prevention, control; Irrigation; Natural resources; Public works; Recreation, water; Water *entries*; Wetlands; Wildlife, waterfowl
WATER SECURITY TRAINING AND TECHNICAL ASSISTANCE, *66.478*

Water systems, treatment
Appalachian region, *23.002*
CDBG, *14.225*, *14.228*, *14.862*
construction, EDA projects, *11.300*
Delta region, *90.200*, *90.201*, *90.202*
desalination research, development, *15.506*
EPA consolidated program support, *66.600*
EPA Performance Partnership Grants, *66.605*
federal surplus property utilization, 93.291
Household Water Well System Program, RUS, *10.862*
Indian housing, HIP, *15.141*
rural communities, *10.760*, *10.770*
rural, Community Services Block Grants, discretionary, *93.570*
rural, emergency assistance, *10.763*
rural housing, *10.417*
rural water, wastewater projects revolving loan funds, *10.864*
technical assistance, training, rural, *10.761*
U.S. insular areas, *15.875*
wastewater operator technical assistance, training, *66.467*
wastewater treatment, revolving fund, *66.458*
see also Irrigation; Public works; Sewage facilities, treatment; Waste treatment, disposal; Water *entries*
WATER 2025, *15.507*
Water 2025 Challenge Grants, DOI, *15.507*
Waterfowl, *see* Wildlife, waterfowl
WATERSHED PROTECTION AND FLOOD PREVENTION, *10.904*
WATERSHED REHABILITATION PROGRAM, *10.916*
WATERSHED SURVEYS AND PLANNING, 10.906
Watersheds, *see* Natural resources; Water resources, supply, management; Wetlands
Weapons of Mass Destruction (WMD), *see* Biological sciences; Chemicals, chemistry; Civil defense; Fire fighting, prevention, control; Health, medical services; Health planning; Law enforcement education, training; Nuclear sciences, technology; Police; Public safety; Radiation; Rescue services; Urban planning
Weather, *see* Climate
WEATHER AND AIR QUALITY RESEARCH, *11.459*

Weatherization
CDBG projects, business, residential, *14.218*, *14.219*
HOME Program, *14.239*
Inventions and Innovations Program, DOE, *81.036*
low-income, assistance, *81.042*, *93.568*
Renewable Energy Systems and Energy Efficiency Improvements, RBCS, *10.775*
rural low-income housing loans, *10.410*
very low-income rural housing grants, loans, *10.417*
veterans housing loans, *64.114*
see also Energy conservation; Housing rehabilitation
WEATHERIZATION ASSISTANCE FOR LOW-INCOME PERSONS, *81.042*
Weed and Seed Program, *16.595*
WEIGHTS AND MEASURES SERVICE, 11.606
Weights, measures, *see* Measurement
Welfare payments, *see* Public assistance; Social Security Act; Subsidies
WELFARE REFORM RESEARCH, EVALUATIONS AND NATIONAL STUDIES, *93.595*
Welfare services, *see* Homeless persons; Indian health, social services; Maternal, child health, welfare; Public assistance; Social Security Act; Social services
Welfare-to-Work and Child Support Amendments of 1999, *see* Maternal, child health, welfare
WETLAND PROGRAM GRANTS—STATE/TRIBAL ENVIRONMENTAL OUTCOME WETLAND DEMONSTRATION PROGRAM, *66.479*

Wetlands
Clean Water Act studies, training, *66.436*
Coastal Program, FWS, *15.630*
coastal, protection, *11.419*, *15.614*
conservation, Direct and Counter-Cyclical Payments Program, *10.055*
environmental outcome demonstrations, *66.479*
EPA national research, training, studies, *66.462*
EPA Nonpoint Source Implementation Grants, *66.460*
EPA Performance Partnership Grants, *66.605*
Federal-Aid Highway Program, mitigation, *20.205*
flood plain data, services, 12.104
flood plain management, *97.022*
North American Wetlands Conservation Fund, FWS, *15.623*
protection, restoration, *66.461*
research, forestry, *10.202*
restoration program, NRCS, *10.072*
Targeted Watershed Grants, *66.439*
Water Bank Program, *10.062*
watershed protection, *10.904*
watershed, river basin projects, 10.906
watersheds, forestry research, *10.652*

Wetlands *(continued)*
Wildlife Habitat Incentive Program, *10.914*
see also Coastal zone; Estuaries; Environmental management; Forestry; Water conservation; Water resources, supply, management
WETLANDS RESERVE PROGRAM, *10.072*
WGS (WIC Grants to States), FNS, *10.578*
Wheat, *see* Agricultural commodities, stabilization; Agricultural marketing
Wheat incentive program, FSA, *10.995*
WHIP (Wildlife Habitat Incentive Program), *10.914*
Whistle-blowers, *see* Complaint investigation
White collar crime, *see* Crime
WHOLESALE FARMERS AND ALTERNATIVE MARKET DEVELOPMENT, 10.164
WIA ADULT PROGRAM [DOL], *17.258*
WIA DISLOCATED WORKERS [DOL], *17.260*
WIA INCENTIVE GRANTS—SECTION 503 GRANTS TO STATES [DOL], *17.267*
WIA YOUTH ACTIVITIES [DOL], *17.259*
WIA (Workforce Investment Act) programs, *see* Employment development and training
WIC FARMERS' MARKET NUTRITION PROGRAM (FMNP), *10.572*
WIC GRANTS TO STATES, *10.578*
WIC Program (Women, Infants, and Children), FNS, *10.557*, *10.565*, *10.572*
WILD HORSE AND BURRO MANAGEMENT, *15.229*
Wildlife acts, *see* Fish (Fish and wildlife acts)
Wildlife and Parks, BIA, *15.039*
WILDLIFE HABITAT INCENTIVE PROGRAM, *10.914*
WILDLIFE RESTORATION, *15.611*
WILDLIFE SERVICES, *10.028*
Wildlife, waterfowl
Alaska Migratory Bird Co-Management Council, FWS, *15.643*
Alaska Subsistence Management, *15.636*
animal, pest damage, disease control, *10.028*
BLM Recreation Resource Management, *15.225*
Coastal Program, FWS, *15.630*
coastal wetlands protection, *15.614*
conservation law enforcement training, 15.602
conservation stewardship, *15.632*
cooperative forestry assistance, *10.664*
damage, disease control, *10.028*
disease research, *10.207*
endangered species, Indian lands, *15.051*
endangered species, pesticides enforcement, *66.700*
endangered, threatened species, *15.615*, *15.638*
EPA pesticides, toxic chemicals pollution prevention studies, training, outreach, *66.716*
federal surplus real property transfer, 15.918, 39.002
Fish, Wildlife and Plant Conservation Resource Management, BLM, *15.231*
Forest Land Enhancement Program, *10.677*
FWS Challenge Cost Share, *15.642*
FWS Landowner Incentives, *15.633*
FWS State Wildlife Grants, *15.634*
Great Plains Conservation, *10.900*
Gun Control Act, 16.309
habitat improvement, agricultural conservation, *10.069*
habitat management research, *10.652*
hunter safety education, *15.611*, *15.626*
Indian hunting rights, *15.050*, *15.052*
Indian lands, *15.039*
Indian Rights Protection, *15.036*
international, elephant conservation, *15.620*, *15.621*
international, great apes conservation, *15.629*
international, rhinoceros, tiger conservation, *15.619*
Junior Duck Stamp Conservation and Design Program Act of 1994, *15.644*
Junior Duck Stamp Contest, FWS, *15.644*
Lyme Disease, *93.942*
Marine Turtle Conservation Fund, FWS, *15.645*
Migratory Bird Conservation, upper Midwest research, surveys, *15.647*
Migratory Bird Joint Ventures, research, training, *15.637*
Migratory Bird Treaty Act, *15.637*, *15.643*, *15.647*
Multi-State Conservation Grants, *15.628*
natural landmarks registry, 15.910
Neotropical Migratory Bird Conservation, *15.635*
Neotropical Migratory Bird Conservation Act of 2000, *15.635*
North American Wetlands Conservation Fund, FWS, *15.623*
Partners for Fish and Wildlife, FWS, *15.631*
Pittman-Robertson (P-R) Program, *15.611*
plant materials for conservation, 10.905
research, DOI, *15.611*
research, forestry, *10.202*
resource management, 15.608
restoration, management, *15.611*, *15.628*
rural resource conservation, development, *10.901*
Tribal Landowner Incentive Program, *15.638*
Tribal Wildlife Grants, FWS, *15.639*
USGS Cooperative Research Units Program, *15.812*
USGS Gap Analysis Program, *15.811*
waterfowl, Water Bank Program, *10.062*
watershed projects, *10.904*
Wild Free-Roaming Horse and Burros Act, *15.229*
Wildlife Habitat Incentive Program, *10.914*
wildlife without borders programs, education, research, training, FWS, *15.640*, *15.641*
see also Animal disease control, health, welfare; Environmental management; Estuaries; Fish; Forestry; Marine sciences; Natural resources; Recreation
WILDLIFE WITHOUT BORDERS—LATIN AMERICA AND THE CARIBBEAN, *15.640*
WILDLIFE WITHOUT BORDERS—MEXICO, *15.641*
Wilson Center fellowships, *85.300*
Wilson-Fish programs, refugees, entrants, *93.583*
WIPP (Waste Isolation Pilot Plant), DOE, *81.106*
WIT (Wood in Transportation), USFS, *10.673*
WMD, *see* Weapons of Mass Destruction
Women
agricultural research, SBIR, *10.212*
battered women's shelter programs, *93.591*, *93.592*, *93.671*
business owners, DOT contracts, *20.903*, *20.905*, *20.907*

MASTER INDEX   1041

business owners, SBA technical assistance, training, *59.043*
campus crime grants, *16.525*
cancer early detection, breast, cervical screening, training, *93.919*
disabled, abuse, violence prevention, education, training, OJP, *16.529*
domestic violence, stalking victim transitional housing, *16.736*
domestic violence victim legal assistance, training, *16.524*
educational equity program, *84.083*
employment assistance, DOL, 17.700
Equal Pay Act, 30.005, 30.010
Farmers' Market Nutrition Program (FMNP), *10.572*
food assistance, pregnant, postpartum, *10.557, 10.565*
health, Community Centers of Excellence, *93.290*
Healthy Start Initiative, perinatal/maternal, *93.926*
heart health care programs, *93.012*
HUD Youthbuild Program, *14.243*
Microloan Demonstration Program, *59.046*
NSF research opportunities, behavioral, economic, social sciences, *47.075*
NSF international science, engineering opportunities, *47.079*
overseas refugee assistance, global priorities, BPRM, *19.522*
prison rape elimination, personnel training, victim services, *16.735*
public telecommunications facilities, *11.550*
scientists, NIH intramural research training, *93.140*
scientists, NSF research opportunities, *47.049, 47.050, 47.078*
sex equity, vocational education, *84.048*
stalking victim legal assistance, training, *16.524*
Violence Against Women Act of 2000, *16.524, 16.525, 16.526, 16.587, 16.588, 16.589, 16.590*
violence prevention research, *93.136*
violence victim services, *16.587, 16.588*
violence victims advocacy, technical assistance, training, OJP, *16.526*
WIC Farmers' Market Nutrition Program (FMNP), *10.572*
WIC Grants to States, FNS, *10.578*
Women's Business Center Sustainability Act of 1999, *59.043*
Women's Business Ownership Act of 1988, *59.043*
see also Civil rights; Disadvantaged *entries*; Employee benefits; Home management; Insurance; Maternal, child health, welfare; Minority *entries*; Parenting; Small Business Innovation Research (SBIR); Sexual abuse; Social Security Act; Veterans death benefits; Victim assistance; Volunteers
Women, Infants, and Children (WIC) Program, *10.557*
Women with Disabilities, *16.529*
WOMEN'S BUREAU [DOL], 17.700
Women's Bureau Clearinghouse, 17.700
Women's Bureau, DOL, *see* Agency Index (DOL, Office of the Secretary, Women's Bureau)
WOMEN'S BUSINESS OWNERSHIP ASSISTANCE, *59.043*

WOMEN'S EDUCATIONAL EQUITY ACT PROGRAM, *84.083*
WOOD IN TRANSPORTATION PROGRAM [USDA], *10.673*
Wood products, *see* Forestry; Timber industry; Woodlands
Woodlands
Agricultural Management Assistance, NRCS, *10.917*
Bioenergy Program, FSA, *10.078*
Conservation Security Program, NRCS, *10.921*
cooperative forestry assistance, *10.664*
Forest Land Enhancement Program, *10.677*
Forest Stewardship Program, *10.678*
Forestry Incentives Program, nonindustrial lands, *10.064*
Rivers, Trails, and Conservation Assistance, 15.921
small wood species, USFS Technology Marketing Unit, *10.674*
Tree Assistance Program, FSA, *10.082*
see also Farm, nonfarm enterprises; Forestry; Timber industry
WOODROW WILSON CENTER FELLOWSHIPS IN THE HUMANITIES AND SOCIAL SCIENCES, *85.300*
Woodrow Wilson International Center for Scholars, *see* Agency Index (Scholarship and Fellowship Foundations)
Wool, *see* Agricultural commodities, stabilization; Agricultural marketing; Livestock industry
WORK INCENTIVES GRANTS, *17.266*
Worker compensation, *see* Employee benefits; Labor standards; Statistics
Worker safety, *see* Mining, mining industries; Occupational health, safety
Workforce Investment Act (WIA), *see* Employment development and training
Workforce Investment Act (WIA) Adult Program, *17.258*
Workforce Investment Act (WIA) Dislocated Workers, *17.260*
Workforce Investment Act (WIA) Youth Activities, *17.259*
WRP (Wetlands Reserve Program), *10.072*

YOG (Youth Opportunity Grants), DOL, *17.263*
Youth
abstinence education, *93.010, 93.235*
adolescent family life, demonstrations, *93.995*
adolescent pregnancy, child rearing, sexual relations research, *93.111*
AIDS prevention, school health projects, *93.938*
child abuse victims, *16.547*
delinquency prevention programs, *16.540*
disadvantaged, secondary, postsecondary education support, *84.042*
Dropout Prevention Programs, *84.360*
Drug-Free Community Grants, *93.276*
Drug Prevention Program, *16.728*
Extension Service, *10.500*
family planning services, *93.217*
family support services, *93.556*
foster care-independent living, transitional services, *93.674*
foster children, Chafee vouchers, *93.599*

Youth *(continued)*
Foster Grandparent Program, *94.011*
Four-H, *10.500*
gangs, delinquency prevention, *16.541*, *16.544*
Gifted and Talented, *84.206*
homeless, education, *84.196*
homeless, transitional living, *93.550*
human development research, *93.865*
incarcerated, education, employment services, *84.331*
institutionalized, neglected, education, *84.013*
juvenile delinquency prevention programs, *16.542*
juvenile justice system improvement, *16.523*
Mentoring Children of Prisoners, ACF, *93.616*
runaway children, *93.645*
Safe Schools/Healthy Students National Evaluation, DOJ, *16.732*
runaways, emergency food, shelter, FEMA, *97.024*
SED, mental health services, *93.104*
Social Security benefits, *96.001*, *96.002*, *96.004*
Social Services Block Grant, *93.667*
Street Outreach Program, homeless, runaway, sexual abuse, *93.557*
underage drinking law enforcement, *16.727*
violence prevention research, *93.136*
see also Adult education; AmeriCorps; Disabled, handicapped children; Indian children; Juvenile delinquency; Maternal, child health, welfare; Parenting; Social services; Volunteers; Youth *entries*

Youth employment
apprenticeship training information, 17.201
community development work-study, HUD, *14.512*
federal, temporary, 27.003
HUD Youthbuild Program, *14.243*
Operation Weed and Seed, *16.595*
Summer Jobs in Federal Agencies, 27.006
U.S. Employment Service, *17.207*
WIA Incentive Grants, *17.267*
WIA Youth Activities, *17.259*
Youth Opportunity Grants, DOL, *17.263*
see also AmeriCorps; Apprenticeship training; Employment *entries*; Indian education, training; Technical training; Tutoring; Vocational education; Youth *entries*

YOUTH OPPORTUNITY GRANTS [DOL], *17.263*
Youth programs
AmeriCorps, *94.006*
Community Food Projects, USDA, *10.225*
Congress-Bundestag Youth Exchange, BECA, *19.410*
Delinquency Prevention Program, *16.548*, *16.549*
disadvantaged, Talent Search, postsecondary education, *84.044*
Drug-Free Schools and Communities, national, *84.184*
ETA pilots, demonstrations, research, *17.261*
Extension Service, *10.500*
farm youth project loans, *10.406*
food donation program, 10.550
food, summer program, *10.559*
Four-H projects, *10.500*
Gang Resistance Education and Training, BJA, *16.737*
gangs, delinquency prevention, *16.544*
homeless, shelters, counseling, services, *93.623*
HUD Youthbuild Program, *14.243*
Juvenile Mentoring Program, *16.726*
Learn and Serve America, school, community programs, *94.004*
low-income, higher education stipends, *84.047*
milk program, *10.556*
National Guard Challenge Program, youth, *12.404*
NOAA Colorado areas math, engineering, science education, *11.449*
Operation Weed and Seed, *16.595*
President's Council on Physical Fitness and Sports, 93.289
runaway youth centers, *93.623*
rural, Community Services Block Grant, discretionary, *93.570*
School Breakfast Program, *10.553*
School Lunch Program, *10.555*
Tribal Youth Program, OJJDP, *16.731*
Upward Bound, *84.047*
see also AmeriCorps; Juvenile delinquency; Parenting; Social services; Volunteers; Youth *entries*
Youthbuild Program, HUD, *14.243*

Zoological parks, *see* Museums, galleries
Zoonotic disease control, *10.028*, *10.207*

WYNNEFIELD BRANCH LIBRARY

OCT 2006

Reference

WITHDRAWN from The Free Library of Philadelphia
Book contains theft-detection device that may set